Regulating Competition in the EU

Regulating Competition in the EU
Second Edition

Pernille Wegener Jessen
Bent Ole Gram Mortensen
Michael Steinicke
Karsten Engsig Sørensen

Published by:
Kluwer Law International B.V.
PO Box 316
2400 AH Alphen aan den Rijn
The Netherlands
E-mail: lrs-sales@wolterskluwer.com
Website: www.wolterskluwer.com/en/solutions/kluwerlawinternational

Sold and distributed by:
Wolters Kluwer Legal & Regulatory U.S.
920 Links Avenue
Landisville, PA 17538
United States of America
E-mail: customer.service@wolterskluwer.com

ISBN 978-94-035-4636-0

e-Book: ISBN 978-94-035-0688-3
web-PDF: ISBN 978-94-035-0698-2

© 2024 Kluwer Law International BV, The Netherlands

All rights reserved. No part of this publication may be reproduced, stored in a retrieval system, or transmitted in any form or by any means, electronic, mechanical, photocopying, recording, or otherwise, without written permission from the publisher.

Permission to use this content must be obtained from the copyright owner. More information can be found at: www.wolterskluwer.com/en/solutions/legal-regulatory/permissions-reprints-and-licensing

Printed in the Netherlands.

Table of Contents

Preface	xix

CHAPTER 1
Competition and Union Law		1
1	Laws Regulating Markets and Competition Law	1
2	The Structure of the Treaty	2
	2.1 Rules Directed at the Member States	2
	2.2 Rules Directed at Undertakings	3
	2.3 Grey Areas	4
3	The Regulation of Competition in the Internal Market	5
	3.1 Secondary Regulation	5
	3.2 Other Sources than Regulation	6
4	Sources of Information	7
5	Tendencies in Competition Law	8
Bibliography		9

CHAPTER 2
Introduction to Article 101		11
1	Introduction	11
2	Agreements, Decisions and Concerted Practices	12
	2.1 Agreements	12
	2.2 Decisions by Associations	17
	2.3 Concerted Practice	18
3	Between Undertakings	20
	3.1 The Definition of an 'Undertaking'	20
	3.2 The Exercise of Public Authority and Public Undertakings	24
4	The Effect on Trade in the EU	27
	4.1 The Requirement for an Effect on Trade Between Member States	27
	4.2 The International Extent of Article 101	28
5	Restriction on Competition	30

Table of Contents

	5.1	Workable Competition	30
	5.2	'Which Have as Their Object or Effect …'	31
	5.3	The Commission's *De Minimis* Notice	33
	5.4	Rule of Reason	35
	5.5	Ancillary Restraints	36
6	Possible Exemptions under Article 101(3)		38
	6.1	Change to the Notification Procedure	39
	6.2	Individual Exemptions: The Four Conditions	39
	6.3	Block Exemptions	43
7	The Consequences of Infringement		44
	7.1	Invalidity	44
	7.2	Remedies and Commitments	45
	7.3	Fines and Compensation	46
Bibliography			47

CHAPTER 3
Vertical Agreements 49
1 Introduction 49
2 The Competition Law Approach to Vertical Restraints: Article 101(1) TFEU and the Block Exemption Regulations 51
  2.1 Article 101(1) TFEU 52
    2.1.1 Territorial Protection: Dividing Up Markets 53
    2.1.2 Prohibition of Re-export with Sales to Third Countries 59
    2.1.3 Fixed Prices: Article 101(1)(a) TFEU 61
    2.1.4 Economic Analysis? 64
    2.1.5 Further Easing of Restrictions? 67
  2.2 Block Exemptions 69
3 The Concept of Restriction of Competition 72
4 Special Agreements That Only Exceptionally Fall Within the Scope of Article 101(1) TFEU 74
  4.1 Agency Agreements 74
  4.2 Franchising 79
  4.3 Selective Distribution 82
    4.3.1 Qualitative or Quantitative Selective Distribution Systems 83
    4.3.2 Particular Aspects of Quantitative Restrictions 88
  4.4 Commercial/Economic Considerations? 91
5 Development of the Block Exemption Regulations 92
  5.1 Green Paper on Vertical Restraints in EC Competition Policy 93
  5.2 Commission Regulation (EU) No 720/2022 93
  5.3 Agreements for Specifically Stated Purposes: The Regulation's Hardcore Restrictions 97
    5.3.1 Article 4(a): Price Discrimination and Selective Prices 99
    5.3.2 Article 4(b): Exclusive Distribution Systems 100
      5.3.2.1 Modifications 100

			5.3.2.2	Article 4(c) Selective Distribution	101
			5.3.2.3	Article 4(f) Components	102
			5.3.2.4	Free Distribution Systems	102
			5.3.2.5	Effective Use of the Internet	102
	5.4	Restrictions That Fall Outside the Scope of the Exemption			103
	5.5	Withdrawal of an Exemption			105
		5.5.1	Article 29.1 of Regulation No 1/2003: The Commission's Withdrawal of Exemption		106
		5.5.2	Withdrawal of Exemption Within the Territory of an Individual Member State		106
6	Conclusion				106
Bibliography					107

CHAPTER 4
Horizontal Agreements — 109

1	Introduction		109
2	The Assessment of Horizontal Agreements		110
	2.1	Actual and Potential Competitors	110
	2.2	The Basic Principles for Evaluation under Article 101(1)	111
	2.3	Exemptions under Article 101(3)	113
3	Price-Fixing Agreements and Agreements on Other Trading Conditions		113
	3.1	Agreements on Purchasing or Selling Prices	113
	3.2	Agreements on Other Trading Conditions	117
4	Agreements on the Exchange of Information		118
5	Agreements on Production		120
	5.1	Specialisation Agreements	121
	5.2	Agreements for the Restructuring of a Trade Sector	123
	5.3	Agreements on Common Norms and Technical Standards	124
6	Cooperation on Research and Development		126
7	Cooperation in Sales and Marketing		127
	7.1	Agreements on Market Sharing	127
	7.2	Commercialisation Agreements	129
	7.3	Procurements and Auctions	130
	7.4	Agreement to Refrain from or Restrict Marketing	130
8	Sustainability Agreements		132
9	Joint Ventures		134
	9.1	The Special Nature of Joint Ventures	134
	9.2	Restrictions on Competition Between the Joint Venture and the Joint Venture Partners	136
	9.3	Restrictions on Competition Between Joint Venture Partners	139
		9.3.1 Restriction on Competition by the Establishment of a Joint Venture	139
		9.3.2 'Spillover' Effects on the Market Where the Joint Venture Operates	141
		9.3.3 'Spillover' Effects on Other Markets	142

vii

	9.4	The Effects on Third-Party Undertakings	143
	9.5	Networks of Joint Ventures	145
	9.6	Special Provisions	146
	9.7	Exemptions	148
10	Cooperatives		150
11	Acquisition of Minority Shareholdings		153
Bibliography			155

CHAPTER 5
Technology Transfer Agreements: Commission Regulation (EU) No 316/2014   157

1   The Treaty and Intellectual Property Rights   157
2   Licence Agreements and EU Competition Law   163
    2.1   The Relationship to Article 101 TFEU   163
    2.2   The Relationship to Article 102 TFEU   164
3   Licence Agreement in General   166
4   Block Exemptions: The Development of the Legal Basis   169
5   Regulation (EU) No 316/2014: Block Exemptions for Technology Transfer Agreements   171
    5.1   Agreements   171
       5.1.1   'Entered into Between Two Undertakings'   172
       5.1.2   The Concept of an 'Undertaking'   173
       5.1.3   'Transfer' of Technology   173
       5.1.4   The Transferred Technology   174
       5.1.5   Definition of the Relevant Market   176
       5.1.6   Competing and Non-competing Undertakings   178
       5.1.7   Reciprocal Contra Non-reciprocal Agreements   179
       5.1.8   The Duration of the Block Exemption   179
6   Hardcore Restrictions   180
    6.1   Agreements Between Competitors   180
       6.1.1   Agreements on the Pricing of the Contract Products   181
       6.1.2   Production Restrictions   182
       6.1.3   The Allocation of Markets or Customers (Sales Restrictions)   182
             6.1.3.1   The Allocation of Markets   182
             6.1.3.2   Sales Restrictions (Allocation of Customers)   183
             6.1.3.3   Permitted Restrictions Pursuant to Article 4(1)(c)   183
             6.1.3.4   Exploitation of Own Technology, Etc.   185
    6.2   Agreements Between Non-competing Undertakings   185
       6.2.1   Agreements on the Pricing of Contract Products: Article 4(2)(a)   185
       6.2.2   Sales Restrictions Article 4(2)(b)   186
       6.2.3   Permitted Restrictions Pursuant to Article 4(2)(b)   190

7		Restrictions Which Fall Outside the Scope of the Block Exemption	191
	7.1	Article 5 of Regulation (EU) No 316/2014	191
	7.2	Article 5(1)	191
	7.3	Article 5(2)	193
	7.4	Other Block Exemption Regulations	193
8		Withdrawal of the Block Exemption in Individual Cases	193
	8.1	Article 6 of Regulation (EU) No 316/2014	193
	8.2	Article 6.2	194
	8.3	Article 7	195
Bibliography			195

CHAPTER 6
Abuse of Dominant Position 197

1	Introduction			197
2	The Meaning of an *Undertaking*			200
3	Dominant Position			201
	3.1	One or More Undertakings: Collective Dominance		202
		3.1.1	Oligopolistic Market Structure	204
	3.2	Relevant Factors for Assessing Market Dominance		205
		3.2.1	Market Share	205
		3.2.2	Other Factors	207
	3.3	The Relevant Market		209
		3.3.1	The Relevant Product Market	211
		3.3.2	The Relevant Geographic Market	212
		3.3.3	The Relevant Temporal Market	213
	3.4	A Substantial Part of the Internal Market		213
4	Abuse			214
	4.1	Examples of Abuse		217
		4.1.1	Article 102, Second Paragraph, Sub-paragraph (a)	217
		4.1.2	Predatory Pricing	220
		4.1.3	Article 102, Second Paragraph, Sub-paragraph (b)	222
		4.1.4	Article 102, Second Paragraph, Sub-paragraph (c)	226
		4.1.5	Article 102, Second Paragraph, Sub-paragraph (d)	230
5	The Effect on Trade			231
Bibliography				233

CHAPTER 7
Procedure and Enforcement Regulation (EC) No 1/2003 235

1	Introduction		235
	1.1	Regulation (EC) No 1/2003: Structure	237
	1.2	2001: The Modernisation of the Enforcement of Articles 101 and 102	237
2	The Relationship Between Union Competition Law and National Competition Law		239

Table of Contents

	2.1	Direct Applicability	239
	2.2	The Framing and Application of National Competition Law in Relation to Articles 101 and 102 of the Treaty	239
3	Allocation of Competence, Powers and Uniformity		240
	3.1	The Commission's Competences	242
	3.2	The Competences of the National Competition Authorities and Courts	243
	3.3	Self-Evaluation and Decisions on Inapplicability	245
4	Powers of Investigation		245
	4.1	The Commission's Powers of Investigation	245
	4.2	The Commission's Inspections	247
		4.2.1 The Commission's Inspections of Undertakings	247
		4.2.2 Inspections in Private Homes	249
	4.3	The Powers of the Member States to Carry Out Investigations	250
5	The Consequences of Infringement		250
	5.1	Fines	251
	5.2	Damages	253
		5.2.1 Directive on Obtaining Damages under National Law for Infringements of the Competition Rules	254
Bibliography			255

CHAPTER 8
Merger Control 257

1	Introduction		257
	1.1	Introduction to the Topic	257
	1.2	The Sources of Law	258
	1.3	Foreign Direct Investment Screening	260
2	Concentrations with an Obligation to Notify		260
	2.1	The Concept of a Concentration	261
	2.2	The Definition of Control	263
		2.2.1 Sole Control	264
		2.2.2 Joint Control	267
	2.3	Full-Function Joint Ventures	270
	2.4	Community Dimension	275
		2.4.1 Undertakings Concerned	276
		2.4.2 Calculation of Turnover	278
	2.5	Concentrations Without a Community Dimension	280
	2.6	The Territorial Scope of Application of the MCR	281
3	The Relevant Market		283
	3.1	The Relevant Product Market	284
	3.2	The Geographic Market	286
4	The Substantial Appraisal of Concentrations		289
	4.1	From the Dominance Test to Appraisal of Whether Effective Competition Would Be Significantly Impeded	289
	4.2	Non-coordinated Effects	293

x

		4.2.1	The Creation or Strengthening of a Dominant Position	293
			4.2.1.1 Market Share	294
			4.2.1.2 Other Indications of Market Strength	297
			4.2.1.3 Actual and Potential Competitors	297
			4.2.1.4 The Position on the Demand Side	301
		4.2.2	Non-coordinated Oligopolies	303
	4.3	Coordinated Effects (Collective Dominance)		305
	4.4	The Positive Effects of Mergers		311
	4.5	Failing Firm Defence		313
5	Conditional Approval			314
6	Ancillary Restraints			320
7	Assessment of Coordinated Practice in Joint Ventures			324
8	Merger Control Procedure			328
	8.1	The Duty to Notify		328
		8.1.1	When to Notify	328
		8.1.2	Early Implementation	330
	8.2	The First Phase of the Merger Control Procedure		334
	8.3	The Second Phase of the Merger Control Procedure		335
	8.4	The Simplified Procedure		337
Bibliography				337

CHAPTER 9
State Aid   339

1	Introduction		339
2	State Aid Procedure		342
	2.1	Existing State Aid Measures	342
	2.2	New Aid Measures	343
		2.2.1 Notifiable Measures	344
	2.3	Unlawful Aid Measures	345
	2.4	The Procedure for Existing Aid	345
	2.5	The Procedure for Notified Aid	346
	2.6	The Procedure for Unlawful Aid	347
		2.6.1 Interim Legal Measures	348
	2.7	Recovery of Unlawful Aid	348
		2.7.1 The Commission's Powers to Require Recovery	348
		2.7.2 The Conditions for Requiring Recovery	349
		2.7.3 Implementation of the Recovery Decision	350
		2.7.4 Possible Exceptions to the Obligation to Repay	352
	2.8	Interested Parties	354
		2.8.1 The Rights of Interested Parties	355
		2.8.2 Rights Before the CJ and the GC	355
		2.8.3 Rights Before the National Courts	356
3	The Prohibition of State Aid in Article 107(1) TFEU		358
	3.1	The Concept of *Aid*	359
		3.1.1 The Effect of Aid	359

Table of Contents

		3.1.2	The Form of the Aid	360
		3.1.3	The Purpose of the Aid	361
		3.1.4	The Intentions of the Parties	361
		3.1.5	Economic Advantages	362
		3.1.6	Variance from Normal Market Conditions	363
		3.1.7	Measures That Do Not Normally Constitute Aid	364
			3.1.7.1 Repayment of Unduly Levied Charges	364
			3.1.7.2 Damages	365
			3.1.7.3 Compensation	366
	3.2	Aid Granted by a Member State or Through State Resources		368
		3.2.1	The State and State Resources	368
			3.2.1.1 The Central Organs of the State and Other Public Authorities	368
			3.2.1.2 Public and Private Bodies Established or Appointed by the State to Administer Aid	369
			3.2.1.3 Private and Public Bodies Subject to State Control	369
		3.2.2	European Union Resources	371
		3.2.3	Private Resources	372
		3.2.4	Aid Provided on the Basis of the Legislation of a Member State	373
			3.2.4.1 Taxes	373
			3.2.4.2 Social Regulation	374
			3.2.4.3 Protection of Employees	375
			3.2.4.4 Minimum Price Harmonisation	375
	3.3	Selectivity		377
		3.3.1	Undertakings and Productions of Goods	377
			3.3.1.1 The Concept of Undertakings	377
			3.3.1.2 Production of Certain Goods	379
			3.3.1.3 Private Households	379
		3.3.2	General and Selective Measures	380
			3.3.2.1 General Measures	380
			3.3.2.2 Selective Measures	381
			3.3.2.3 The Assessment of Selectivity	383
	3.4	Aid Which Distorts or Threatens to Distort Competition and Which Affects Trade Between Member States		386
		3.4.1	Aid Which Distorts or Threatens to Distort Competition	387
			3.4.1.1 Competitive Effect	387
			3.4.1.2 Evidence of Distortions of Competition	388
		3.4.2	Aid That Affects Trade Between Member States	391
		3.4.3	The *De Minimis* Rule	393
4	Approval of State Aid			394
	4.1	Aid for Exports		397
	4.2	Operating Aid		398
	4.3	Investment Aid		398

	4.4	Possibilities for Approval	399
		4.4.1 Article 107(2)	399
		4.4.2 Article 107(3)	399
		4.4.3 Article 108(2), Third Paragraph	400
Bibliography			400

CHAPTER 10
Public Undertakings 403

1	Introduction		403
2	Presentation of the Provisions		404
	2.1	Terminology	405
3	The Aims and Structure of the Provisions		405
	3.1	The Application of Article 106 and Article 37	405
	3.2	Those to Whom the Provisions Are Addressed	406
	3.3	The Application of Article 106	407
4	Article 106(1)		407
	4.1	Concepts	407
		4.1.1 Special or Exclusive Rights	407
		4.1.2 The Grant of a Right	409
		4.1.3 Undertaking	410
		4.1.4 Public Undertaking	411
	4.2	The Application of Article 106	411
		4.2.1 The Demand Doctrine	411
		4.2.2 Cross-Subsidising	412
		4.2.3 Expansion of the Exclusive Right	413
		4.2.4 Essential Facilities	414
		4.2.5 Other Infringements	415
5	Article 106(2)		416
	5.1	Services of General Economic Interest	416
	5.2	Entrusted with the Operation of Services	417
	5.3	The Exception in Article 106(2)	418
		5.3.1 Conditions for Exceptions	418
		5.3.2 Special Financial Circumstances	418
6	Article 106(3)		420
	6.1	The Adoption of Directives and Decisions	421
	6.2	The Directive on the Transparency of Relations Between Member States and Public Undertakings	422
7	Other Regulation		423
	7.1	International Regulation	423
Bibliography			424

CHAPTER 11
The Liberalised Sectors 425

1	General Cross-Sectoral Considerations		425
	1.1	Which Sectors Are Dealt With?	429

Table of Contents

1.2	Facilities of Special Significance	431
1.3	The Regulatory Background	434
1.4	Regulating the Liberalised Sectors	437
	1.4.1	Exclusivity	438
	1.4.2	Cross-Subsidisation	440
		1.4.2.1	From Monopoly to Market	441
		1.4.2.2	Joint Production	443
	1.4.3	Division Between Undertakings Subject to Competition and Monopoly Undertakings, Etc.	446
	1.4.4	Access to Networks	449
		1.4.4.1	Direct Lines	453
		1.4.4.2	Transit	453
		1.4.4.3	Expansion of Capacity	454
	1.4.5	Management of Networks	455
		1.4.5.1	Unbundling	455
		1.4.5.2	Authorities	456
	1.4.6	Public Obligations	456
		1.4.6.1	Obligations to Supply	458
		1.4.6.2	Exclusivity and the Obligation to Supply	461
		1.4.6.3	Financial Compensation	461
		1.4.6.4	Price Regulation	464
	1.4.7	Authorisations	464
	1.4.8	Transparency	466
	1.4.9	The Cross-Border Provision of Services	468
	1.4.10	Public Authorities	469
	1.4.11	Authority at the EU Level	471
	1.4.12	Reciprocity	472
	1.4.13	A Sustainable Future	472
2 Energy		473
	2.1	Electricity Supply	477
		2.1.1	EU Regulation	478
			2.1.1.1	The Electricity Directive and the Regulation on the Internal Market of Electricity	479
			2.1.1.2	The Application of the General Competition Rules	480
		2.1.2	Authorisation Procedures	484
			2.1.2.1	Electricity Generation	485
			2.1.2.2	Network Supervisor	486
		2.1.3	Access to Networks	487
			2.1.3.1	Procedures for System Access	488
			2.1.3.2	Direct Lines	489
			2.1.3.3	Cross-Border Connections	489
		2.1.4	Public Service Obligations	490
		2.1.5	Transparency	490
		2.1.6	Public Authorities	491

		2.1.7	'Income Ceiling'	493
		2.1.8	'Prosumers and communities'	495
	2.2	Natural Gas	496
		2.2.1	Regulation under EU Law	497
			2.2.1.1 The Natural Gas Directive	497
			2.2.1.2 Application of the General Competition Rules	498
		2.2.2	Authorisation Procedures	499
			2.2.2.1 Network Management	499
			2.2.2.2 Unbundling	500
		2.2.3	Access to Networks	500
			2.2.3.1 Network Access Procedures	501
			2.2.3.2 Direct Lines	503
			2.2.3.3 Transit	504
		2.2.4	Public Service Obligations	504
		2.2.5	Technical Harmonisation	505
		2.2.6	Transparency	506
		2.2.7	Public Authorities	506
		2.2.8	Price Cap	507
3	Transport	508
	3.1	Air Transport	509
		3.1.1	EU Regulation	510
			3.1.1.1 The Application of the General Competition Rules	513
			3.1.1.2 Bilateral Agreements	516
			3.1.1.3 Pricing Regulation	517
		3.1.2	Authorisation Procedures	517
		3.1.3	Network Access	518
		3.1.4	Public Obligations	521
		3.1.5	Technical Standards	521
		3.1.6	Safety	522
		3.1.7	Transparency	524
		3.1.8	Public Authorities	524
	3.2	Railways	524
		3.2.1	EU Regulation	525
			3.2.1.1 The Application of the General Competition Rules	527
			3.2.1.2 Pricing	528
		3.2.2	Authorisation Procedures	528
			3.2.2.1 Unbundling	529
			3.2.2.2 Independence Between the State and Railway Undertakings	529
		3.2.3	Access to Networks	530
			3.2.3.1 Access to Other than the Track	532
			3.2.3.2 Pricing	533
			3.2.3.3 Transit	533

Table of Contents

		3.2.4	Public Service Obligations	534
		3.2.5	Technical Harmonisation	534
		3.2.6	Transparency	536
		3.2.7	Public Authorities	536
4	Communication			537
	4.1	Telecommunications		537
		4.1.1	EU Regulation	539
			4.1.1.1 The Application of the General Competition Rules	539
		4.1.2	Authorisation Procedures	540
			4.1.2.1 Telephone Numbers and Radio Frequencies	541
			4.1.2.2 Unbundling	542
		4.1.3	Access to Networks	543
			4.1.3.1 Access and Interconnection	543
			4.1.3.2 The General Competition Rules	544
			4.1.3.3 Price Controls	545
		4.1.4	Public Service Obligations	545
		4.1.5	Technical Harmonisation	546
		4.1.6	Public Authorities	547
	4.2	Postal Services		548
		4.2.1	Regulation under EU Law	549
			4.2.1.1 The Application of the General Competition Rules	550
			4.2.1.2 Unbundling	552
		4.2.2	Authorisation Procedures	553
		4.2.3	Access to Networks	553
		4.2.4	Public Service Obligations	554
			4.2.4.1 Pricing Regulations	554
			4.2.4.2 Exclusive Rights	556
			4.2.4.3 Financial Compensation	557
		4.2.5	Public Authorities	557
Bibliography				558

CHAPTER 12
Public Procurement 559

1	Introduction		559
	1.1	History and Background	559
	1.2	The Aim	561
	1.3	Description of the Tendering Procedure	562
	1.4	The Other Procurement Directives	563
		1.4.1 Particular Features of the Utilities Directive	563
		1.4.2 Particular Features of the Defence Procurement Directive	563
		1.4.3 Particular Features of the Concession Contracts Directive	564
2	The Obligation to Invite Offers		565

	2.1	Ex-house Contracting			565
	2.2	Threshold Values			566
3	Contracting Authorities			567
4	Preparation of the Contract Notice			568
	4.1	General			568
	4.2	Specification of the Object of the Contract			569
	4.3	Publication			571
		4.3.1	Requirements for Publication			571
	4.4	Determination of the Type of Task			571
	4.5	Documentation for Contract Notices			573
	4.6	Electronic Contract Notices			574
	4.7	Deadlines			574
5	Types of Contract			575
	5.1	Framework Agreements			575
6	Forms of Public Procurement Procedures			576
7	Selection and Award			578
	7.1	Selection of Candidates: Procedures and Criteria			579
	7.2	Award of the Contract: Procedures and Criteria			582
		7.2.1	Abnormally Low Tenders			584
	7.3	Selection or Award			584
	7.4	Non-financial Criteria			586
8	Exceptions			588
	8.1	General			588
	8.2	The Defence Exception			588
	8.3	Special Provisions on the Provision of Services			589
		8.3.1	Social and Other Specific Services			589
		8.3.2	Other Exceptions for Services			589
9	General Principles			590
	9.1	The Principle of Equal Treatment			590
		9.1.1	The Prohibition of Negotiation			590
			9.1.1.1	Fundamental Aspects		591
			9.1.1.2	Price		592
			9.1.1.3	Clarification or Negotiation		592
			9.1.1.4	Permitted Negotiations		593
			9.1.1.5	The Scope for Making Corrections		593
		9.1.2	Reservations			593
			9.1.2.1	Variant Tenders		595
		9.1.3	Technical Dialogue			597
		9.1.4	Cancellation			598
	9.2	The Transparency Principle			599
	9.3	Other Principles			599
10	Procurement and the Competition Rules			600
	10.1	Procurement and the Competition Rules			601
	10.2	Procurement and the State Aid Rules			603

11	Enforcement		604
	11.1	General	604
	11.2	Damages	605
12	Other Rules on Public Procurement		605
	12.1	General	605
	12.2	WTO Rules: The Government Procurement Agreement	606
Bibliography			606

Table of Cases — 607

Table of Commission Decisions — 623

Index — 633

Preface

Our aim in writing this book has been both to explain the traditional areas of competition law – such as the prohibition of agreements which restrict competition, the prohibition of abuse of dominant position, and the rules on merger control – as well as to describe other aspects of competition law which today play an essential role in regulating the conduct of undertakings and public authorities in the market. As in the previous editions, we have sought to give a more thematically comprehensive presentation of the subject, covering most of the areas which competition lawyers may be confronted with. On this basis the most important elements of competition law which affect public bodies have been included – elements such as State aid, the liberalised sectors and public procurement.

Since this book has a broader perspective than more traditional works on competition law, we have considered it important that it should be possible to read each chapter independently. For this reason, there will inevitably be some overlaps between chapters, though we have tried to keep these to a minimum. This text is primarily intended for use as a university textbook, but it is our hope that, given its comprehensive scope, it will also be of use to practitioners. References to Treaty articles are made using the numbering of the Treaty on the Functioning of the European Union. This also applies to the numbering of articles when referring, for example, to decisions which antedate the current numbering, except in the case of direct quotations. Only limited changes to the law since June 2023 are included.

Pernille Wegener Jessen has written Chapters 6 and 9, Bent Ole Gam Mortensen Chapters 5 and 11, Michael Steinicke Chapters 1, 3, 7, 10 and 12 and Karsten Engsig Sørensen Chapters 2, 4 and 8. The responsibility for each chapter belongs solely to the author of each chapter.

The Authors

CHAPTER 1
Competition and Union Law

1 LAWS REGULATING MARKETS AND COMPETITION LAW

The basis for the creation of the European Community was a desire to establish trade cooperation so that trade between the Member States could be strengthened. This aim still plays a major role in the cooperation, even though other aims have been added to the cooperation with the formation of the European Union. Article 3(2) of the Treaty on European Union (TEU) states that among its aims, 'The Union shall establish an internal market. It shall work for the sustainable development of Europe based on balanced economic growth and price stability, a highly competitive social market economy.'

The aims of the Union are to be achieved by implementing a number of policies that are laid down in Treaty provisions, the aims of which are to ensure freedom of trade between the Member States and to promote an environment that is favourable to trade in general.

The Treaty on the Functioning of the European Union (TFEU) contains a number of rules dealing with the establishment of the internal market, which has been the primary goal of the cooperation from the start. Thus, in its original form (the Treaty of Rome), the TFEU primarily contained provisions for the establishment of a European market. The most important of these provisions were those on freedom of movement and those on competition. The aim of these core provisions has been to establish protection for the actors on the market so that hindrances, whether imposed by the Member States, by their public bodies or by undertakings in the European market, should be prevented or eliminated.

The primary basis for competition law in the EU is to be found in Articles 101–109 TFEU, with the main focus being on Article 101 (prohibition of agreements in restraint of trade), Article 102 (abuse of a dominant position), Article 106 (the grant to public undertakings or undertakings of special or exclusive rights) and Article 107 (prohibition of State aid). In addition to these rules there are a number of other provisions which contain aspects of competition law, in particular secondary regulation.[1] Thus, competition law in the EU includes considerably more than the issues which are traditionally dealt with under the heading of competition law (i.e., Articles 101 and 102).[2]

2 THE STRUCTURE OF THE TREATY

The basic structure of the Treaty is that the provisions on freedom of movement are directed at the Member States and their public bodies,[3] while the provisions on competition are directed at undertakings. There are certain exceptions to this division; *see* section 2.3 below. The background to this structure is that the prohibitions in the rules of freedom of movement, on the one hand, and the prohibitions in the competition rules, on the other hand, are framed in different ways. The rules on freedom of movement are framed on the basis that the prohibition laid down shall be addressed to the administrative authority and the regulatory activity and the characteristics of such kinds of activities. In contrast the prohibitions in the competition rules take account of the special characteristics of carrying on commercial activities. Thus, the structure of the Treaty's system is based on the fundamental view that public bodies exercise administrative authority and carry out regulatory activities and that private bodies are engaged in commercial activities. In some cases, this assumption is not followed, and thus, the system in the Treaty is not followed (*see* further in section 2.3 below).

2.1 Rules Directed at the Member States

The provisions on freedom of movement cover rules to ensure the free movement of goods, persons, services and capital. The rules on freedom of movement are thus structured so that they contain both prohibitions on the establishment of obstacles to the freedom of movement and possibilities for exemptions to the prohibition, should the prohibition be infringed. The prohibition is based on the general ban on discrimination on the grounds of nationality in Article 18 TFEU and can, as such, be seen as a special expression of this prohibition. In addition to prohibiting discrimination, the rules on freedom of movement also prohibit certain hindrances that are not discriminatory, in other words, which do not affect citizens, services or goods from other

---

1. For example, *see* the regulation of mergers, the regulation of the liberalised sectors and the directives on public procurement.
2. Articles 101 and 102 are inspired by American antitrust legislation in Arts 1 and 2 of the Sherman Act. These provisions found their way into the Treaty via German law, which in the immediately post-war years was clearly influenced by the regulation of the occupying powers in this area. These similarities between the Sherman Act and Arts 101 and 102 TFEU have given rise to comparisons of the practice on the two sets of rules.
3. The Court of Justice (CJ) has several times pointed out that these provisions are not addressed to undertakings; *see* for example Case 311/85, *van Vlaamse*. However, the CJ has also expressed the view that private undertakings cannot ignore these provisions; *see* for example Case 58/80, *Dansk Supermarked*. On the horizontal obligations of the rules on free movement, *see* s. 2.3 below. The provisions on freedom of movement are not the primary topic of this book. For a general presentation of freedom of movement *see* Weatherill & Beaumont: EU Law; and *Damien Chalmers, Gareth Davies & Giorgio Monti*: European Union Law.

Member States differently from those of the host Member State. There have been a considerable number of cases on these kinds of hindrances, and the decisions vary from one kind of freedom of movement to another.

For every prohibition, there is one or more possible exception. These possibilities include a list of the circumstances which the Community considers to be acceptable potential exceptions to the prohibitions. In general, these legitimate considerations are characterised by being general societal considerations.[4] The exceptions in the TFEU include an exhaustive list of the considerations which the Member States can rely on to justify an infringement of the prohibitions. The Court of Justice (CJ) has also established a practice whereby certain infringements of the prohibitions (only infringements of a *non-discriminatory* character) can also be justified by a non-exhaustive number of considerations. However, these considerations are also characterised by being general societal considerations.

Also, in addition to the rules on freedom of movement, the Treaty's provisions on State aid are directed at public authorities. According to these rules, public authorities are prohibited from giving financial support to private undertakings (for more on this, *see* the chapter on State aid).

In addition to the Treaty provisions, there are also a number of secondary legal acts which are discussed in this book and which are directed at the Member States despite their competition-like character. This applies to the rules on public procurement and, to some extent, the rules on the liberalised sectors. The rules on public procurement are concerned with purchases made by public bodies, and their authority is based on the rules on freedom of movement. The liberalisation rules are typically addressed to state-owned monopolies, which have traditionally been responsible for a number of areas of service provision which are of key importance to society (such as energy supply, transport, postal services, telecommunications, etc.).

In addition to the provisions on the infringement of substantive competition rules, the Member States also have a duty to ensure that the rules are effectively enforced in their courts and by their competition authorities. In this connection, there is a clear tendency for these bodies to be given increased importance in the enforcement of European competition rules, most recently with the adoption of Council Regulation (EC) No 1/2003.[5]

2.2 Rules Directed at Undertakings

The rules which have been laid down with a view to removing hindrances to trade between Member States would not be so effective if private undertakings were free to put in place measures which would instead create hindrances to trade and to the

---

4. For example, infringements of the prohibitions can be justified by reference to the fact that the national legislation protects the interests of public policy or public security.
5. Moreover, this development has meant that most Member States have introduced competition rules which are inspired by the European provisions. In the present context, this development means that national provisions have to a certain extent been superseded, where these are identical with or substantially the same as the Community provisions.

functioning of the internal market. The TFEU provisions for preventing private (and public) undertakings from restricting the effective functioning of the market are set out in Part Three, Title VII, Chapter 1 TFEU (*see also* section 1 above).

In Case C-205/03 P, *Federación Española de Empresas de Tecnología Sanitaria (FENIN)*, the CJ stated that the activities of a public body on the market, which are not part of a commercial activity, fall outside the scope of application of the competition rules in Articles 101 and 102 TFEU, as such a body does not constitute an 'undertaking'. Thus, the purchase of goods and services by a public body for the purposes of carrying out its duties or exercising its authority will not be considered an economic activity, even though there is, in fact, a purchase agreement entered into under private law rules on the free market.[6]

2.3   Grey Areas

The basis for the division of regulations into those directed to public bodies and those directed to private undertakings is the simple and usually correct assumption that private undertakings carry out economic activities in the form of business undertakings and that public bodies carry out administrative activities and the exercise of authority. Even though this assumption is broadly correct, nevertheless, there are sometimes situations in which either a public body or a private undertaking does not fit this picture. Thus, in certain situations, a private undertaking will carry out activities which can be characterised as regulatory or the exercise of authority, and conversely, a public body will sometimes carry on commercial activities.

Where this normal pattern breaks down, it is the *activity* which will often be decisive for which regulation will apply rather than the formal classification of the organisation in question (i.e., whether the entity is public or private).

One example of these grey areas is the rules on public undertakings in Article 106 TFEU. The Article does not itself contain a prohibition but rather refers to the other provisions in the Treaty which are relevant to such undertakings. There is thus scope for applying the Treaty provisions, which regulate the circumstances in question (restrictions on competition or restrictive regulation). As the reference is to public *undertakings*, the competition rules will usually be used, but the provisions on free movement can also be relevant due to the influence of public authorities on such undertakings.

Another example of where the structure is departed from can be seen in relation to establishing who is subject to the rules on free movement. In principle, all public bodies are covered by these rules.[7] However, in several cases the CJ has held that certain private bodies can be covered by the rules if they have characteristics which are

---

6. On this case, *see Ronit Kreisberger:* FENIN: Immunity From Competition Law Attack for Public Buyers?, Public Procurement Law Review 2006 NA 214; *Catriona Munro:* Competition Law and Public Procurement: Two Sides of the Same Coin, Public Procurement Law Review 2006 p. 352; and *Albert Sanchez Graells:* Public Procurement and EU Competition Law 2015 pp. 150 ff. The CJ has subsequently arrived at the same conclusion in Case C-113/07 P, *Selex*.
7. The provisions refer to the Member States, and according to well-established practice this is interpreted as covering all public entities in the Member States.

normally seen in public authorities. The primary characteristic, in this context, is that the body in question has the power to lay down rules which affect others. This regulatory competence has been decisive in Case 36/74, *Walrave*, Case 13/76, *Donà*, Case C-415/93, *Bosman*,[8] and to some extent in Joined Cases 266 and 267/87, *Royal Pharmaceutical Society*,[9] and Case C-292/92, *Hünermund*.[10]

An example of the reverse situation, where a public authority is subject to competition rules, is found in the practice which is referred to in American law as the 'state-action doctrine'.[11] This refers to the circumstances where the CJ applies the competition rules (primarily Article 101) to situations where public authorities adopt regulations which have the aim or consequence of prescribing or promoting agreements which are contrary to Article 101 or which reinforce the effect of such agreements, including when such an agreement is elevated to the status of law. It is characteristic of such infringements that a public authority adopts a measure which leads to an infringement. Since the competition rules are not directed at public authorities, the CJ found it necessary to supplement Article 101 (formerly Article 81) with the provisions in Article 3(1)(g) and Article 10 of the Treaty establishing the European Community. Article 3(1)(g) provided for the adoption of a system ensuring that competition in the internal market is not distorted. Article 10 contained the 'loyalty principle' whereby the Member States were required to 'abstain from any measure which could jeopardise the attainment of the objectives of this Treaty'. Even though Article 3(1)(g) has not been carried forward in the new Treaties, the case law of the CJ is still applicable; *see* Protocol No. 27 of the TEU and TFEU on the internal market and competition. The application of Article 101 to the acts of public bodies is dealt with in further detail in Chapter 2.

3 THE REGULATION OF COMPETITION IN THE INTERNAL MARKET

3.1 Secondary Regulation

In addition to the Treaty rules on the establishment of the internal market, the measures of undertakings and public bodies which have implications for competition law are regulated by secondary regulation. This 'secondary regulation' covers rules primarily laid down in directives and regulations.

---

8. These cases concerned sports organisations which laid down employment conditions for players and others in connection with taking part in professional sports.
9. The *Royal Pharmaceutical Society and Hünermund* cases concerned trade organisations in the pharmacy sector.
10. This also played a role in the first case in which the CJ laid down a true horizontal obligation relating to the rules on the free movement of workers, Case C-281/98, *Angonese*, even though it appeared to be only one of several decisive elements. However, the facts in the *Angonese* case are not characterised by concerning a trade organisation or similar, as in the other cases, but rather an 'ordinary' undertaking, in this case a bank, which did not have any regulatory powers over others.
11. On this, *see Ulla Bøegh Neergaard:* Competition & Competences.

As established by different sets of rules, the Commission has the primary responsibility for and overall competencies in competition law. These competencies allow it to take decisions in respect of concrete infringements of the competition rules and give it the power to adopt directives and regulations with the aim of carrying out general regulation of certain competition law issues.

Secondary legislative acts are defined in more detail in Article 288 TFEU. Here, directives are defined as binding on each Member State to which it is addressed, as to the result to be achieved, but it leaves to the national authorities the choice of form and methods. This means that it is necessary for the Member States to implement a directive in order for it to have an effect on the national legal system. In the same provision, a regulation is defined as having general application. Thus, they are binding in their entirety and directly applicable in all Member States.

The question of direct applicability arises in connection with the Treaty's provisions and non-implemented (or incorrectly implemented) directives and decisions. Where a directive is correctly implemented, there is no need to consider direct applicability, as the directive will have been given its intended effect in the national legal system. For regulations, under Article 288 TFEU, they are directly applicable, so they have direct effect on the persons to whom they are addressed. Regulations neither can nor may be implemented in national law; *see* the definition in Article 288.

Direct applicability refers to the circumstances where a provision entails rights for private persons (rights which naturally give rise to corresponding obligations on others), and these rights can be relied upon before the national courts.

For the Treaty provisions, direct applicability is achieved if: (1) the provision contains clear and precise obligations; (2) there are no conditions or exceptions attached to the provision; and (3) the implementation of the provision is not dependent on implementing measures by the Member States or the institutions; *see* Case 26/62, *van Gend en Loos*. The same conditions apply to the provisions of directives but with the addition of a further condition that the directive provision in question does not require horizontal effects, in other words, effects between undertakings or private persons within the EU. This is particularly relevant in relation to the competition rules, as these are usually directed at undertakings in particular and are, therefore, intended to establish obligations for them.[12]

However, there is no reservation to allowing public bodies to be bound in connection with the direct applicability of directive provisions. This can be relevant to the competition rules directed at public authorities and undertakings, for example, rules on State aid, public undertakings and public procurement.

3.2 Other Sources than Regulation

Some of the most important sources of European competition law are the decisions of the Commission, the General Court and the CJ. The Commission has built up a

---

12. Where the imposition of obligations on private undertakings will constitute a hindrance to a provision having direct applicability, a private undertaking's loss of rights will prevent allowing the provision having direct applicability; *see* for example Case 194/94, *CIA Securities*.

comprehensive body of decisions in relation to several of the provisions where the Commission is (was) given exclusive powers. These decisions naturally have considerable weight as sources of law, subject to the reservation that the General Court and CJ can review the Commission's decisions. The decisions of the General Court on competition law questions also have major importance as a source of law. However, the greatest importance is attached to the decisions of the CJ, as this is the ultimate authority on the interpretation of the provisions of the TFEU and of secondary legislation, naturally including competition law issues.

In addition to the provisions laid down in the Treaty and in secondary legislation, there are also a number of non-binding sources of law in the EU, referred to as 'soft law'. Even though they may be non-binding, these acts are not entirely without legal effect, and in several contexts, the CJ has stated that these acts have a significant contribution, in particular in connection with the interpretation of secondary law. Thus, in Case 322/88, *Grimaldi*, in paragraph 18, the CJ stated that soft law (in this case recommendations) 'cannot therefore be regarded as having no legal effect. The national courts are bound to take recommendations into consideration in order to decide disputes submitted to them, in particular where they cast light on the interpretation of national measures adopted in order to implement them or where they are designed to supplement binding Community provisions'.

Examples of the significance of soft law in the field of competition law include the many notices on the application of Articles 101 and 102 TFEU, guidelines on the different elements of aid in the area of State aid, notices on the prohibition of negotiations in the area of public procurement, as well as notices on the central concepts in the area of merger control. For more information on these sources, *see* the respective chapters in this book.

4   SOURCES OF INFORMATION

Information about the various rules of competition law can be found on the EU's website (europa.eu). Among other things, this website contains a comprehensive database of all the legal acts which can be relevant to the different topics of competition law which are covered in this book. This gives access to the Official Journal and to the various legal acts both at Treaty level and secondary legislation, as well as the documentation which is prepared with a view to the adoption of new legislative initiatives in this rapidly developing area.

There is also useful material on the Commission's website (ec.europa.eu) primarily under the heading of the Directorate General for Competition, but also the Directorate General GROW (concerning public procurement), as well as the several Directorates General covering energy, transport, etc. (concerning the liberalised sectors). The Commission's powers to make decisions are of decisive importance in several areas of competition law.[13] These decisions can be found on the Commission's

---

13. *See* the amended enforcement procedure for Arts 101 and 102 TFEU in Council Regulation (EC) No 1/2003, discussed in Ch. 7.

website under the heading of the Directorate General for Competition, as well as under the classification for the area of competition which each decision concerns. Judgments on the topics covered in this book from the CJ and the General Court can be found on the CJ's website (curia.eu) under the headings of competition policy, rules for undertakings (tendering), and energy, the internal market, commercial policy and transport (the liberalised sectors), as well as State aid.

5   TENDENCIES IN COMPETITION LAW

In addition to the traditional themes that characterise the treatment of competition law, different challenges to the application of the rules in various respects are continuously seen. At a structural level, it appears that the changes that have taken place in the technologies over the past decades, to a certain extent, challenge the traditional application of the competition rules. For example, it may be more difficult to determine the relevant market in relation to different network solutions that procure different products or services. This can be seen in several of the major cases that the Commission has dealt with in recent years, see, e.g., the *Commission's decision v. Google* of 18 July 2018 (fine of approximately EUR 4.34 billion.[14] Furthermore, the tendency can be seen in the adoption of regulation of 14 September 2022 on the open and fair markets in the digital sector and on the amendment of directives (EU) 2019/1937 and (EU) 2020/1828 (the regulation on digital markets – Digital Market Act). The regulation regulates the behaviour of providers of core platform services (online intermediation services, online search engines, etc.), so-called gatekeepers. The regulation supplements the general competition rules, and the need is described in the preamble of the regulation, where it is pointed out that 'the market processes are often incapable of ensuring fair economic outcomes with regard to core platform services. Although Articles 101 and 102 of the Treaty on the Functioning of the European Union (TFEU) apply to the conduct of gatekeepers, the scope of those provisions is limited to certain instances of market power, for example dominance on specific markets and of anticompetitive behaviour, and enforcement occurs ex post and requires an extensive investigation of often very complex facts on a case by case basis. Moreover, existing Union law does not address, or does not address effectively, the challenges to the effective functioning of the internal market posed by the conduct of gatekeepers that are not necessarily dominant in competition-law terms'.

Another issue that has emerged over the recent years is the need for an adjusting mechanism for major disaster scenarios. The competition rules have, to varying extents, inserted rules that allow exemptions from the general prohibitions or procedures in very special cases where global disasters occur. Recent years have shown that such disasters or crisis situations may necessitate the occasional need for different and more flexible rules to apply. This was most clearly seen during the COVID-19 pandemic, where, among other things, there was a need for urgent procurement of, for

---

14. The infringement consisted of imposition of illegal restraints on the producers of Android-based equipment. *See* furthermore judgment of 14 Sep. 2022 in Case T-604/18 where the Court in outline maintained the result of the Commission.

example, face masks (which challenged the procurement rules) and a need for urgent approval of state aid measures to ensure the possibility of public insurance for the many undertakings that failed as a result of, e.g., shutdowns of many sectors during the pandemic. Where the procurement rules do not allow for the establishment of new emergency procedures (but do include general provisions, which, depending on the circumstances, may be suitable to meet the need in a crisis situation), the state aid rules allow the Commission to initiate adapted approval procedures.[15] As a natural consequence of disaster scenarios, security of supply can also play a decisive role. Practical examples from recent years are, for example, security of supply in relation to vaccines and energy (natural gas).

Another tendency, which to varying extents affects the application and/or the effectiveness of the competition rules in a wide sense, is the increasing focus on climate and environmental conditions. To a certain extent, this tendency means that there may be a need to exempt from the prohibitions in the competition law in order to safeguard environmental considerations in a way that does not fit the expected market behaviour, just as there may be a basis for adjustments to existing rules in order to meet the climate challenges.[16]

As appears from above, these tendencies entail certain challenges in relation to the individual parts of the competition law in a wide sense. The tendencies affect different areas, and we will discuss the relevant issues in relation to the specific competition rules below.

Bibliography

Catherine Barnard: *The Substantive Law of the EU*, 2013.
Damien Chalmers, Gareth Davies & Giorgio Monti: *European Union Law*, 2014.
Josephine Steiner & Lorna Woods: *EU Law*, 2014.
Paul Craig & Grainne de Burca: *EU Law*, 2015.

---

15. *See* thus information from the Commission: Temporary Framework for State aid measures to support the economy in the current COVID-19 outbreak (2020/C 91 I/01).
16. An example of such regulation is seen in the introduction of Art. 18(2) in directive 2014/24. The provision requires compliance with a number of national, EU legal and international rules mainly regarding environmental and climate conditions in connection with public procurement.

CHAPTER 2
Introduction to Article 101

1   INTRODUCTION

Article 101(1) of the Treaty on the Functioning of the European Union (TFEU or 'Treaty') states:

> The following shall be prohibited as incompatible with the internal market: all agreements between undertakings, decisions by associations of undertakings and concerted practices which may affect trade between Member States and which have as their object or effect the prevention, restriction or distortion of competition within the internal market.

This is often referred to as a prohibition on agreements in restraint of trade. In order for there to be a breach of Article 81(1), a number of conditions must be fulfilled:

(1) There must be an agreement, decision by an association of undertakings or a concerted practice.
(2) The agreement, etc., must be entered into between undertakings.
(3) The agreement must be capable of affecting trade between Member States.
(4) There must be a restraint of competition (prevention, restriction or distortion of competition).

Each of these conditions will be discussed in detail in sections 2–5 below. If there is an infringement of Article 101(1), it is possible that the agreement may nevertheless be exempted. The agreement may contain a number of advantages for consumers or for technological or economic development, which outweigh its negative effects on competition. The conditions for the exemption of agreements, etc., are discussed in section 6, and in section 7, there is a discussion of the sanctions which are associated with an infringement of the provision.

The aim of the present chapter is to give a general introduction to Article 101. There is a more detailed consideration of different kinds of agreements in the following

Chapters 3–5 on vertical agreements, horizontal agreements and technology transfer agreements, respectively. The details of the procedures for the enforcement of Articles 101 and 102 are dealt with in Chapter 7.

2 AGREEMENTS, DECISIONS AND CONCERTED PRACTICES

As stated, Article 101(1) refers to agreements, decisions by associations of undertakings and concerted practices. There follows a discussion of each of these three kinds of arrangements. However, it is important to emphasise that this distinction is of more theoretical than practical legal significance.[1] By including these different arrangements, Article 101 sends out a signal that it is of broad application, as, in principle, it covers all forms of coordination of the conduct of commercial undertakings. The problem can, therefore, be to determine where the lower limit lies for agreements, etc., to be covered by the provision.

There are no special legal consequences linked to whether an issue concerns an agreement, decision or coordinated practice since they are all equally illegal if they lead to a restraint on competition. However, as will be seen in the following, there will often be different evidential problems associated with whether there is an agreement, decision or coordinated practice, as the last named in particular gives rise to problems of proof.

In addition to this, a distinction is often made between 'horizontal' and 'vertical' agreements, even though these concepts are not found in Article 101. While horizontal agreements are entered into between undertakings at the same level of trade, i.e., between actual or potential competitors (e.g., between two manufacturers), vertical agreements are entered into between two undertakings at different levels of trade, i.e., between undertakings that cannot be expected to compete with each other (e.g., and agreement between a manufacturer and a sole distributor). This distinction is quite important in practice, as competition law assessments of horizontal and vertical agreements differ because the two types of agreement lead to different risks of restriction of competition.[2] Therefore, this distinction will also be used in the following two chapters. The distinction is less relevant in the present chapter, which concentrates on a number of more general issues.[3]

2.1 Agreements

The definition of an 'agreement' covers both oral and written agreements. They do not have to satisfy any formal requirements which may be required under national law, for

---

1. Thus, the Court of Justice (CJ) has accepted that an arrangement can be characterised either as an agreement or as a concerted practice, without it being necessary to decide which it is, *see* Case C-238/05, *Asnef-Equifax*, para. 32.
2. Horizontal agreements will normally have greater potential for restricting competition than vertical agreements. In Joined Cases 56 and 58/64, *Consten and Grundig*, the Italian government tried to argue that Art. 101 only prohibited horizontal agreements, but this was rejected by the CJ.
3. However, as will be seen in s. 5.3, the distinction is key in relation to the Commission's *de minimis* notices.

example, notarisation, consideration or similar. There is no requirement that the agreement should be legally binding. A so-called gentlemen's agreement is enough.[4] Consequently, there is no requirement that the agreement can be enforced, for example, by reference to the courts or to arbitration, nor is it required that sanctions should be agreed.[5] Finally, the character or designation of an agreement is not important, so, for example, a settlement in court or a protocol will be covered by the definition.[6] The fact that an agreement is entered into as part of the formation of a company (articles of association, promoters' agreements, and shareholders' agreements) does not alter the fact that the agreement may be covered by Article 101. The reader is referred to sections 9 and 10 in Chapter 4 for a review of the restrictions on competition that can arise in connection with joint ventures and cooperative companies.

If an agreement is terminated, the infringement of Article 101 will also normally be terminated. However, if the parties appear to continue their conduct unaltered, the fact that the agreement has not been legally renewed is not relevant. What is decisive is the economic effect of the agreement, while its legal form is, as stated, of subordinate importance.[7]

An agreement will, therefore, exist where undertakings have expressed their joint intention to conduct themselves on the market in a specific way.[8] If one is to determine where the lower limit lies for when an agreement exists, there must be the following conditions: (1) there must be a plan or an understanding; (2) entered into by at least two undertakings; and (3) voluntarily.

The first condition requires there to be an agreement entered into by the undertakings involved. It is not necessary that the agreement should have been entered into by a director of the company or some other person with authority to sign on behalf of the undertaking since it is unlikely that written authority will have been given to enter into an unlawful agreement. Thus, it is sufficient that the agreement has been entered into by a person who must be assumed to be acting on behalf of the undertaking.[9]

The requirement that there must be at least two undertakings means that the unilateral conduct of an individual undertaking cannot be condemned under Article 101. Instead, it must be assessed under Article 102 if the undertaking has a dominant position. However, the practice of the Court of Justice (CJ) shows that conduct which, on the face of it, appears to be unilateral can, in fact, be an expression of an agreement. For example, in one case, the CJ has held that if an undertaking adds to its invoices a

---

4. Case 41/69, *ACF Chemiefarma*, paras 106 et seq.
5. Commission Decision 94/599/EC PVC (OJ 1994 L 239/14), para. 30.
6. *See* Case 65/86, *Bayer AG*, para. 15, which concerned a settlement in court entered into in connection with a case on the validity of a registered utility design, and the 'pay for delay'-cases where the patent holders entered into a settlement in court with the producers of generic medical products according to which the latter against payments recognised the validity of the patent and thus refrained from competing for a period of time, *see, inter alia*, Case C-307/18, *Generics*.
7. On this, *see* Case 243/83, *SA Binon*, para. 17.
8. *See* Case C-450/19, *Kilpailu- ja kuluttajavirasto*, para. 21.
9. Case C-68/12, *Slovenská sporiteľna a.s.*, paras 25–26.

prohibition on its customers exporting the goods sold, this can constitute an agreement. Even if, from the point of view of contract law, the terms printed on an invoice did not constitute part of the contract, the CJ was of the view that this was the case when the customers must be regarded as having given their tacit acceptance of the terms. The CJ found that this tacit acceptance was, among other things, evidenced by the fact that the customers subsequently placed new orders on the same terms.[10] It follows that relatively little will be required for unilateral measures in trade between undertakings which have well-established and longstanding contractual dealings to be considered to be an agreement. The question of how little has been referred to the CJ in a number of cases concerning the conduct of a manufacturer towards its distributors.

In Case 107/83, *AEG*, AEG had refused to authorise a number of dealers. The Commission believed that this was because the dealers in question could not be assumed to follow AEG's pricing policies. AEG argued that it was a unilateral action which was, therefore, not covered by Article 101. The CJ rejected this argument, as it was of the view that the refusals were a part of a contractual relationship which AEG maintained with its existing dealers. The existing dealers had agreed to AEG's pricing policy, and it was part of the agreements with them that AEG refused to authorise dealers who breached this pricing policy.[11]

There was a similar example in Joined Cases 25 and 26/84, *Ford*, where Ford of Europe decided that it would no longer supply right-hand drive cars to its German dealers. Ford of Europe itself sold cars on the British market through a subsidiary company, and it had found that there was considerable parallel importation of right-hand drive cars from the German dealers because the cars were cheaper in Germany. The refusal to supply was thus based on the fact that Ford wanted to support its subsidiary so that in future, British customers should either buy their cars direct from the subsidiary or from one of the British dealers. The CJ considered that this refusal to supply was covered by Article 101 because the decision to refuse to supply was part of the contractual relations between Ford and its dealers.

In the extreme, this practice would mean that nearly all the decisions of an undertaking about marketing and distribution can be considered part of the undertaking's agreement with its dealers. However, in Case T-41/96, *Bayer AG*, the General Court (GC) made it clear that the concept of an agreement cannot be stretched that far. In this case, Bayer AG restricted the sale of a particular medicine to its distributors in France and Spain. The background to this was that the prices in the UK were considerably higher

---

10. On this, *see* Case C-277/87, *Sandoz*. For a comparison, *see also* Case 25/76, *Segoura*, where in its interpretation of the Convention on Jurisdiction and the Enforcement of Judgments in Civil and Commercial matters, the CJ also held that a clause concerning the choice of forum could be valid when one of the parties in a continuing relationship sent unilateral confirmation of the agreement and the other party did not object to it.
11. Case 107/82, *AEG*, paras 38–39.

than in these two countries, so there had been widespread parallel importation from France and Spain to the UK. In its decision, the Commission had been of the view that this was an expression of the existence of an agreement, but the GC rejected this. The GC emphasised that an agreement assumes that the two parties have a concurrence of wills. For unilateral action to be considered an agreement, the Commission had to prove that there was an express or tacit agreement from the counterparties, in other words, the distributors. The GC did not believe that such evidence existed. In particular, the GC rejected the argument that the fact that the distributors subsequently continued to trade with Bayer AG was an expression of their agreement with Bayer's policy.[12]

With exchanges of information, the Commission takes the view that if an individual undertaking gives strategic information to its competitors, this can be a breach of Article 101. Thus, there is not a requirement for a mutual exchange of information, nor is it necessary to prove that there is an underlying agreement that competitors should order their market activities according to the information. At the same time, if an undertaking unilaterally publishes information, for example, by posting it on a webpage, it will not necessarily be assumed that there is a breach of Article 101.[13]

Even though there must be at least two undertakings involved in an agreement, there is not a requirement that both must adopt some specific commercial conduct, as it is sufficient for one of the parties to do so. There was an example of such a one-sided obligation in a decision where a Japanese producer of ball bearings had promised a number of French producers that it would raise its prices on the French market. Even though it was the only party which had accepted such an obligation, the aim of the agreement was to ensure that the prices of the Japanese ball bearings approximated the price of the French-produced ball bearings and thereby sought to end price competition.[14]

In order for there to be a concurrence of wills, it is a requirement that the undertakings must enter into an agreement voluntarily. The fact that an undertaking feels itself forced into an agreement because it would otherwise meet with various sanctions from other undertakings (refusal to supply, etc.) is not sufficient for Article 101 not to apply. On the contrary, if the law in a Member State requires undertakings

---

12. Case T-41/96, *Bayer AG*, in particular paras 173–174. The judgment has since been upheld by the CJ in Joined Cases C-2/01 P and C-3/01 P, *Bundesverband der Arzneimittel-Importeure, eV*. See also Case T-208/01, *Volkswagen AG*, and Case C-74/04 P, *Volkswagen AG*, where the GC and the CJ likewise held that the Commission had not shown evidence that a unilateral action was an expression of an agreement.
13. Commission Communication – Guidelines on the applicability of Article 101 of the Treaty on the Functioning of the European Union to horizontal co-operation agreements, OJ 2023 C 259/1, paras 396–398. In the following these are referred to as Commission Guidelines on horizontal cooperation agreements. *See* further on this issue *Bern Meyring*: Signalling – When Should We Worry?, Journal of European Competition Law & Practice 2020 pp. 335–345 DOI: 10.1093/jeclap/lpaa021.
14. Commission Decision 74/634/EEC, *Franco-Japanese ball-bearings agreement* (OJ 1974 L 343/19).

to adopt a certain conduct, Article 101 is not applicable.[15] For example, this will be the case, if there are pricing regulations which lay down minimum prices which all must apply.[16] If, however, the pricing regulations allow for competition to a certain extent, the undertakings have no excuse for not making use of the scope for competition.[17] The fact that the law makes it easier to enter into agreements to restrict competition, or perhaps makes it easier to enforce such agreements, does not mean that such agreements fall outside the scope of Article 101. This would require that the law gives undertakings no choice.[18]

In the above, it is assumed that the Member State has issued regulations that are binding on the undertakings. However, in some cases, it is difficult to determine whether a 'law' has been laid down by a legislator or by the undertakings themselves. This is the case where trading terms, in particular prices, are set by a body or an organisation in which the industry is represented. In order to determine whether undertakings infringe Article 101 by complying with such 'laws', it is necessary to determine whether the organisation is acting as a legislator or as an association of undertakings. In order to determine this, it is normally necessary to assess the composition and authority of the body or organisation concerned.

> This is illustrated by the judgment in Case T-513/93, *Consiglio Nazionale degli Spedizionieri Doganali (CNSD)*, where CNSD was a regional council that set tariffs for the payment of customs clearance in Italy. The council consisted of nine members, selected by ballot from among persons who carried on business as customs clearers. The council was empowered by law to set the tariffs, and the same law provided that these had to be applied. The Commission believed that, in issuing rules on minimum tariffs, the council had infringed Article 101, as its rules were considered to be a decision by an association of undertakings. CNSD disputed this, arguing that it had the character of a public body, and thus, neither the council nor the customs clearers could be found to have contravened Article 101.
>
> The GC held that CNSD was not a public body and that, therefore, its decisions did not have the character of a decision of the state. The members of the CNSD were thus not required to take account of general interest when they set their tariffs, and the Italian Finance Minister could not intervene as to who might be appointed to the council and had no supervisory powers. Next, the GC considered whether the fact that the council was empowered by law to set the tariffs meant that the members had not voluntarily set minimum tariffs. However, the GC found that the law did not require a specific price level or price ceiling. It was, therefore, the council's own decision to provide for minimum prices, which in some cases involved a

---

15. Commission Guidelines on horizontal cooperation agreements, para. 19.
16. Case C-221/15, *Establissements Fr. Colrupt*, para. 45.
17. Case 246/86, *Balasco*; and Commission Decision in Case COMP/C.38.281, *Raw Tobacco Italy* (OJ 2006 L 353/45), paras 315–324.
18. Joined Cases C-359/95 P and C-379/95 P, *Ladbroke Racing Ltd*, paras 33–34.

price increase of 400%. The members, therefore, had room for manoeuvre, and this room for manoeuvre had been used to restrict competition.

In those cases where a law requires or promotes conduct which restricts competition, the question then arises as to whether the Member State itself is in contravention of Article 101; see the discussion on this in section 3.2 below.

2.2 Decisions by Associations

Instead of entering into an agreement, undertakings can coordinate their conduct by means of an association. Under Article 101(1), decisions by associations of undertakings are also prohibited. Not only will the undertakings which take part in the association be in breach of Article 101, but also the association itself will be in breach of the provision.

The definition of 'decision' should be interpreted broadly. It can be a decision or a recommendation to the member undertakings about some specific conduct (pricing policy, uniform trading terms, etc.), or it can be terms which are included in the articles of association of the association. On this basis, obligations to supply in the articles of association of a cooperative society can be contrary to Article 101; see the discussion in section 10 of Chapter 4. However, it is clear that an association will only incur liability for a breach of Article 101, where it has played a role in the adoption of the decision. It may be that it has taken the initiative to arrange meetings between undertakings or that it has contributed to putting into practice what the undertakings have agreed.[19]

An association can itself be an undertaking. For instance, a stock exchange listed company, for example, MasterCard Inc., could be an association by providing the framework for a number of banks to participate in decisions on the fees for using credit cards.[20] Normally, it will be the members of the association that coordinate their activities, but in principle, it is also possible for them to restrict competition in an area in which they are not themselves active but where the association is active.[21] It is not a requirement that the association should itself be an undertaking with economic activities.[22] It can, therefore be a trade organisation which coordinates the members' activities. However, it is a condition that it is not a body which is, in fact, a public authority. If this is the case, and if its articles of association have the character of legislation, Article 101 will not apply; see Case T-513/93, *CNSD* discussed in the preceding section.[23] What is decisive is not the legal status of the body but whether its

---

19. Joined Cases T-25/95 and others, *Cimenteries CBR*, para. 1326.
20. Case C-382/12 P, *Mastercard Inc.*
21. Case C-1/12, *OTOC*, where an association of accountants laid down rules for obligatory continuing professional training of accountants. The accountants were not themselves active in this market, but the CJ was of the view that it was sufficient that the association offered the courses.
22. Joined Cases T-25/95 and others, *Cimenteries CBR*, para. 1320; and Case T-193/02, *Piau*, para. 71.
23. *See* further Case C-309/99, *Wouters*, which concerned the question of whether the Dutch Bar Association was an association of undertakings or a public authority, and Case C-1/12, *OTOC*, on an association of accountants. In Case C-519/04 P, *Meca-Medina*, the CJ held that the

tasks are of an economic character or whether they are in the nature of the exercise of public authority. The fact that an organisation has public authority in certain areas does not mean that its decisions in other areas fall outside the scope of Article 101.

2.3 Concerted Practice

The CJ has defined a concerted practice as a form of coordination between undertakings, which, without having been taken to the stage where an agreement properly so-called has been concluded, knowingly substitutes for the risks of competition, practical cooperation between them.[24] The aim of introducing the concept of concerted practice was to prevent undertakings from getting around the competition rules by, instead of entering into an agreement, implementing less formal cooperation which restricts competition by, for example, informing each other in advance of the policy they intend to follow, well-knowing that the competitor will act in the same way.[25]

A concerted practice requires that the undertakings involved have the intention of coordinating their commercial conduct. This subjective requirement means that it is not enough that it can be shown that a number of undertakings have parallel conduct, for example, by implementing similar price increases at the same time. Parallel conduct can have many other explanations, for example, that one undertaking acts as the price leader or that there is an oligopolistic market where it is natural that the undertakings should follow the same commercial policy. On this basis, the CJ has annulled decisions where the Commission has not proved that a concerted practice was the only probable explanation for parallel conduct.[26] Parallel conduct can thus raise an assumption that there is a concerted practice, but the Commission must support this assumption, for example, by showing evidence that the parties have met and that they have exchanged competitively sensitive information, etc.[27] If the Commission succeeds in finding evidence which indicates that there is a concerted practice, it is then up to the undertakings to show that there is not a concerted practice. Thus, cases on concerted practices are often highly complex and extensive from a purely evidential point of view.

> Case 172/80, *Züchner*, illustrates the problem of evidence. The CJ laid down some guidelines for how national courts should assess whether there is a concerted practice. The background to the case was that a bank's customer had refused to pay a fee in connection with a transfer of money from a German bank to a bank in Italy. The fee was 0.15% of the amount transferred. The customer claimed that this fee was set on the basis of a

---

anti-doping rules issued by the International Olympic Committee fell outside the scope of Art. 101. Even though the IOC is arguably an undertaking, the CJ found that the rules fell outside the scope of Art. 101(1), to the extent that the rules were limited to what was necessary to ensure the proper conduct of competitive sport; *see* para. 47.
24. Joined Cases 40/73 and others, *Suiker Unie*, para. 26.
25. Commission Decision 1999/60/EC, *Pre-Insulated Pipe Cartel* (OJ 1999 L 24/1), para. 130.
26. Joined Cases C-89/85 and others, *Ahlström (Cellulose II)*, para. 126.
27. However, it should be emphasised that not all forms of exchange of information are contrary to Art. 101, *see* in more detail in Ch. 4, s. 4.

concerted practice between banks, contrary to Article 101, and could, therefore, not be demanded. The banks did not deny that the same fee was charged but denied that there was an agreement or concerted practice. The CJ found that if the uniform fee was due to a concerted practice, it was a restraint on competition because it hindered price competition for that type of service. It was up to the referring court to decide whether there was a concerted practice, and in doing so, it had to consider: (1) whether there were contacts between the banks conducting themselves in a like manner or, at least, exchanges of information on, for example, the rate of the charges actually imposed for comparable transfers or charges planned in the future; (2) whether, with regard to the conditions of the market in question, the rate of charge uniformly imposed was no different from that which would have resulted from free competition; (3) that consideration must also be given to the number and importance in the market of the banks participating in such a practice; and (4) the volume of transfers on which the charge in question is imposed compared with the total volume of cross-border transfers made by the banks.[28]

Apart from showing that the undertakings intended to coordinate their conduct, it must also be proved that the concerted practice has resulted in a given conduct on the market. It is necessary to show that there is a causal link between the concerted practice and the conduct.[29] Previously, the GC had adopted an interpretation according to which it was not necessary to prove that the concerted practice had led to specific conduct, as it was sufficient for there to be an infringement of Article 101 that there was an intention to restrict competition, see the words 'as their object' and the discussion in section 5.2 below. However, the CJ was of the view that the definition of 'concerted practice' requires that it is possible to point to conduct. This conduct need not necessarily have restrictive effects on competition so that an 'unsuccessful' concerted practice will also contravene Article 101.[30] Where undertakings that have been concerted together remain active in the market, there is, according to the CJ, a presumption that these will adjust their conduct on the market according to what they have learned.[31]

In order to find that an undertaking has contravened Article 101, evidence must be given to show that the individual undertaking has taken part in a concerted practice. While in the case of an agreement, there will seldom be doubt about who is a party, in some cases, it can be difficult to prove which undertakings have been sufficiently involved so as to be found to have taken part in a concerted practice. If the Commission is successful in showing that an undertaking has participated in the meetings and other activities that have led to the concerted practice, the burden of proof shifts to the

---

28. Case 172/80, *Züchner*, para. 21.
29. Case C-49/92 P, *Anic*, para. 118.
30. Case C-49/92 P, *Anic*, paras 122 and 124.
31. Case C-199/92 P, *Hüls*, para. 162; Case C-8/08, *T-Mobile Netherlands*, para. 51; and Case C-286/13 P, *Dole Food Company Inc.*, para. 127.

undertaking to prove that it is not part of a concerted practice.[32] This means that it is not necessary to prove that the undertaking's conduct shows that it has joined a concerted practice since passive participation in meetings, etc., will be sufficient. If it is proved that an undertaking is part of a concerted practice, it is assumed that it participates in the whole of the concerted practice.[33] This means that it is not necessary to prove that an undertaking has been present at all meetings and thereby supported all the aspects of the concerted practice. In many cases, it will be established that there is a single and continuous infringement, which implies that all participants are liable for all effects of the infringement as long as the undertakings are part of the concerted practice. For there to be a single and continuous infringement, the following conditions must be fulfilled: (1) there must be an overall plan pursuing a common objective, (2) the undertaking must have the intention to contribute to that plan, and (3) the undertaking must be aware (proved or presumed) of the offending conduct of the other participants.[34]

A concerted practice will often have the characteristics of horizontal cooperation, in other words, cooperation between competitors. Many of the cases are concerned with situations where competitors coordinate their prices or agree on market sharing. However, there is nothing to prevent a concerted practice from being established between undertakings at different levels of trade, for example, between a manufacturer and its distributors.[35]

3   BETWEEN UNDERTAKINGS

The requirement that an agreement shall have been entered into 'between undertakings' ensures that the scope of application of Article 101 differs from provisions that are directed at single undertakings. In addition, it means that the exercise of authority is not, in principle, covered by the provision.

3.1   The Definition of an 'Undertaking'

The CJ has defined an undertaking as encompassing every entity engaged in an economic activity, regardless of the legal status of the entity and the way in which it is

---

32. Joined Cases T-25/95 and others, *Cimenteries CBR*, paras 1353 and 1389, and Case C-49/92 P, *Anic*, para. 96. According to the CJ's statements in the succeeding paragraphs in the latter case, the Commission must also prove that the concerted practice has resulted in some specific conduct by the individual undertaking; *see* the condition discussed in the preceding paragraph.
33. The Commission has thus developed a practice where it holds the individual undertaking liable for the cartel as a whole, and the courts have accepted that an undertaking can be held liable for the whole, even if it has only taken part in certain aspects of the cartel; *see*, for instance, Joined Cases T-305/94 and others, *Limburgse Vinyl Maatschappij*, paras 773–774 and Case C-700/19 P, *Toshiba Samsung Storage Technology Corp.*, para. 73.
34. Joint Cases T-204/08 and T-212/08, *Team Relocations*, para. 37. The three conditions were confirmed by the CJ on appeal, *see* Case C-444/11 P, *Team Relocations*, para. 52.
35. Commission Decision 80/256/EEC, *Pioneer* (OJ 1980 L 60/21), paras 79–80.

financed.³⁶ Consequently, both undertakings carried on by natural persons and undertakings carried on by legal persons are covered by the definition. This applies regardless of the form of company chosen. Furthermore, foundations or organisations which do not, in principle, have the purpose of carrying on an undertaking will be covered, provided that they do in fact carry on an undertaking.³⁷ Likewise, public undertakings and authorities will be covered by Article 101, if they carry on an economic undertaking; *see* the next section.

The CJ has defined an undertaking as 'economic units which consist of a unitary organization of personal, tangible and intangible elements which pursues a specific economic aim on a long-term basis'.³⁸ This makes it clear that there must be certain resources present for there to be an undertaking, but the requirement is clearly not very great.

In principle it does not matter what kind of commercial activity is carried on. Article 101 covers undertakings that produce or sell goods and undertakings that provide services.³⁹ The liberal professions are also covered by Article 101, and the fact that some professions are regulated and possibly subject to authorisation does not mean that they fall outside the scope of the provision. However, there are some sectors of the economy that are only covered by the competition rules to a certain extent, including agriculture and military equipment.⁴⁰

Since undertakings carried on by sole entrepreneurs are covered by Article 101, it is necessary to define when a person is an independent self-employed person and when they are an employee. An employee is characterised by the fact that they are subject to the directions of an employer, and they do not normally share in the commercial risk involved in the economic activity.⁴¹ Therefore, to the extent that it represents workers, a trade union will not be an undertaking, and collective labour market agreements should, therefore, not, in principle, be evaluated under Article

---

36. Case C-41/90, *Höfner*, para. 21. It appears from this paragraph that the CJ uses the same definition for both Arts 101 and 102.
37. Thus the international football association, FIFA, was found to be covered by Art. 101, to the extent that it sold package tours in connection with the World Cup in 1990; *see* Commission Decision 92/521/EEC, *Distribution of package tours during the 1990 World Cup* (OJ 1992 L 326/31)
38. Case T-11/89, *Shell International Chemical Company*, para. 311.
39. If an organisation buys goods, it is the economic or non-economic nature of their subsequent use which determines whether the organisation is to be considered an undertaking. The CJ has held that the Spanish public health authorities are not an undertaking, even though they naturally buy many products which are used in the hospital sector; *see* C-205/03 P, *Federación Española de Empresas de Tecnología Sanitaria (FENIN)*, para. 26.
40. Richard Whish & David Bailey: Competition Law, 10. Ed., 2021 pp. 1019–1055. Other sectors have undergone a harmonisation to open up for competition, *see* Ch. 1.
41. *See* Case C-22/98, *Bécu*, para. 26; and Case C-413/13, *FNV Kunsten Informatie en Media*, paras 34-37; as well as the discussion in *Victoria Louri*: 'Undertaking' as a Jurisdictional Element for the Application of EC Competition Rules, Legal Issues of Economic Integration, 2002 pp. 143–176 (especially pp. 149-151) and *Mary Catherine Lucey*: Should Professionals in Employment Constitute 'Undertakings'? Identifying 'False-Employed', Journal of European Competition Law & Practice, 2015 pp. 702–708. The CJ thereby also referred to the definition of 'workers' which it has developed in relation to Art. 45 TFEU.

101.[42] If, however, an organisation is entering into agreements on behalf of self-employed persons without any employees, Article 101 may be applicable, but the Commission has indicated a certain restraint in using Article 101 in these cases.[43]

As stated above, the legal form of an undertaking is not decisive. The CJ has stressed this by establishing that several persons and companies can constitute one undertaking. The concept of an undertaking in competition law focuses on whether there is a single economic entity. Among other things, this means that a person who controls two companies can constitute an undertaking together with their companies.[44] In addition to this, in many cases, a parent company and its subsidiaries can constitute one undertaking. This is important in practice as it means that agreements which are entered into between companies in the same corporate group are typically not covered by Article 101.

> This was established in, among others, Case C-73/95 P, *Viho Europe*. A parent company, Parker Pen UK, had required its subsidiaries only to sell the company's products in the territories allocated to them. Viho complained to the Commission that this practice prevented it from buying from the subsidiary company that offered the best prices. The Commission rejected the complaint, as it believed that such agreements between parent companies and their subsidiaries fell outside the scope of Article 101, and it was this decision that Viho brought before the GC and subsequently before the CJ. The CJ found that Parker's subsidiaries in Europe were wholly owned subsidiaries, and their sales and marketing activities were led by an area team that was appointed by the parent company and which controlled the sales targets, gross margins, sales costs, cash flows and stocks. On this basis, the CJ found that the companies constituted 'a single economic unit within which the subsidiaries do not enjoy real autonomy in determining their course of action in the market, but carry out the instructions issued to them by the parent company controlling them'.[45] Therefore, the conclusion was that the situation was not covered by Article 101.

---

42. Case C-67/96, *Albany International*; Case C-115–117/97, *Brentjens*; and Case C-219/97, *Maatschappij Drijvende Bokken BV*, on supplementary pensions agreed in connection with collective agreements in the Netherlands. However, as Case C-413/13, *FNV Kunsten Informatie en Media* shows, this exception requires the agreement to be between labour market parties, and not just between a group of undertakings. The question of the status of trade unions has resulted in some debate, *see Shaun Bradshaw*: Is a trade union an undertaking under EU competition law?, European Competition Law Journal 2016 pp. 320–340 og *Giorgio Monti*: Collective labour agreements and EU competition law: five reconfigurations, European Competition Journal 2021 pp. 714–744.
43. *See* Commissions Guidelines on the application of Union competition law to collective agreements regarding the working conditions of solo self-employed persons, C(2022) 6846 final.
44. Case 170/83, *Hydrotherm*, para. 11.
45. Case C-73/95 P, *Viho Europe BV*, para. 16. In line with this, *see* Case C-30/87, *Bodson*, para. 19, and Case 66/86, *Ahmed Saeed Flugreisen*, para. 35. Hitherto, it has been assumed that the joint control which is established over a joint venture will not normally be so extensive that joint ventures would be considered as part of the participating undertakings (joint venture partners); *see*, e.g., Commission Decision 91/335/EEC, *Gosme/Martell – DMP* (OJ 1991 L 185/23), para. 30. However, the case law has subsequently been changed, *see* the further discussion in Ch. 4, s. 9.2.

These arguments mean that where a parent company makes the most important decisions concerning a subsidiary, the parent and subsidiary will be considered one undertaking. Thus, every internal agreement, instruction, etc., will fall outside the scope of Article 101. An earlier judgment gave the impression that this exemption only applied where there was an internal division of tasks within the corporate group, but it must be assumed to be immaterial what kind of agreement is involved.[46] If, conversely, a parent company has allowed its subsidiaries a certain measure of independence, there is a risk that the parent and subsidiaries will be considered separate undertakings, so that Article 101 will apply. This is an unsatisfactory state of law for several reasons. First, it is not clear when a subsidiary attains a sufficient degree of independence for it to constitute a separate undertaking, and second, the competition rules may act as an incentive for parent companies to exercise control over their subsidiaries. A consistent application of this approach would also mean that where a division of a company is effectively managed by its own divisional management, it too ought to be considered a separate undertaking. This would seem very difficult to enforce in practice.

In the *Viho* case, it was an advantage for the companies to argue that they were part of the same undertaking, as the internal agreement thereby fell outside the scope of Article 101(1), but in other cases, it could be a disadvantage. In a large number of cases, parent companies seek to deny that they should be liable for the anti-competitive conduct of their subsidiaries. When the amount of a fine is set, it is a disadvantage to be part of a larger economic unit, as the fine is often set as a proportion of the turnover of the undertaking. But the effect of being one undertaking is also that the parent company is liable for the fine imposed on a subsidiary.

In these cases, the CJ has established a practice in which there is a presumption that a parent company has active control over a subsidiary which it owns 100% or almost 100%. This presumption can be rebutted, but in practice, it has been seen to be difficult to do so.[47] In particular, it must be evaluated whether minority shareholders (if there are any) may have rights which rebut the presumption.[48] As the CJ uses the same concept of a single economic entity, it must be assumed that where a parent company owns (almost) 100% of the capital of a subsidiary, there will be a presumption that internal agreement between the two companies falls outside Article 101.

For subsidiaries that are not almost 100% owned, intra-group agreements will only be outside Article 101 if it can be assumed that the parent company exercises control. Such exercise of control will often be indicated by the fact that the parent

---

46. In line with this, *see Jens Fejø & Grith S. Ølykke*: EU-konkurrenceret, 2014 pp. 87–88.
47. Case C-286/98 P, *Stora Kopparbergs Bergslags*, para. 29; GC Case T-314/01, *Avebe*, para. 136; and Case C-97/08 P, *Akzo Nobel v. Commission*, para. 63. *See also* Case C-521/09 P, *Elf Aquitaine*, paras 51–72; and Case C-501/11 P, *Schindler Holding*, para. 109. These cases have been much debated, *see Okeoghene Odudu & David Bailey*: The Single Economic Entity Doctrine in EU Competition Law, Common Market Law Review 2014 pp. 1721–1758 (in particular pp. 1751–1752); *Andriani Kalentin*: Revisiting Parental Liability in EU Competition Law, European Law Review, 2018, pp. 145–166 and *Mark Leddy & Athina Van Melkebeke*: Parental liability in EU competition law, European Competition Law Review, 2019, pp. 407–410 *Bettina Leupold*: Effective Enforcement of EU Competition Law Gone too Far? Recent Case.
48. Case T-130/21, *CCPL*, para. 59.

companies control enough shares (and voting rights) to be able to exercise control. If it only holds a minority shareholding, this will only indicate control if this minority shareholding has been allocated special rights that go beyond the rights normally attached to such shareholdings.[49] To assess whether control has been exercised, the CJ has stressed that regard must be had 'in particular to the economic, organisational and legal links between those two legal entities'.[50] Consequently, a number of different elements may be taken into account. For instance, the CJ has relied on the fact that the same persons are occupying positions in the management of both companies.[51] If the parent company has formulated a compliance programme for all companies in the group in an effort to prevent competition law infringement, the mere fact that such a programme exists may indicate that the parent company exercises control.[52]

The concept of a single economic unit will also mean that an agent will typically have a dependent relation to their principal and will be a part of the latter's undertaking.[53] The CJ has also, in one case, indicated that an independent service supplier in certain cases may be subject to such a degree of control by the undertaking to whom they deliver that the supplier and the undertaking form a single economic entity.[54]

3.2 The Exercise of Public Authority and Public Undertakings

The definition of an undertaking covers any economic entity, regardless of its legal status. On this basis it is not surprising that undertakings that are publicly owned or which are carried on in the public sector are covered by Article 101. This principle is also emphasised in Article 106 TFEU; *see* Chapter 10.

It is also clear that activities that are connected with the exercise of public authority are not covered by Article 101. However, it is not always easy to determine whether an activity is the exercise of authority or an undertaking. If there is an activity, such as an employment agency, which is also often carried out by private undertakings, it is not difficult to establish that there is an undertaking.[55] In other cases, it is difficult to decide, and here, according to the CJ, it is necessary to take an overall view of whether, according to their nature, purpose and the rules to which they are subject, the activities are associated with the exercise of such public authority.

---

49. Case T-132/07, *Fuji Electronic System*, para. 183.
50. Case C-97/08 P, *Akzo Nobel NV*, para. 58.
51. Case C-480/09 P, *Acea Electrabel Produzione SpA*, para. 51 and Case C-595/18 P, Goldman Sachs Group, paras 93–94 and para. 100.
52. Case C-501/11 P, *Schindler Holding*, paras 113–114.
53. On this, *see* Ch. 3, s. 4.1 below.
54. Case C-542/14, SIA »VM Remonts«.
55. Case C-42/90, *Höfner*, para. 22; and Case C-55/96, *Job Centre coop*, para. 22. Another area in which a similar problem arises is health services, *see also* Duncan Sinclair: 'Undertakings' in Competition Law at the Public-Private Interface – an Unhealthy Situation, European Competition Law Review 2014 pp. 167–171 and *Juan Jorge Piernas López*: When is a company not an undertaking under EU competition law? The contribution of the Dôvera judgment, Common Market Law Review 2021 pp. 529–548.

On this basis, the CJ has established that the activities of Eurocontrol in relation to civil aviation cannot be considered an undertaking. On behalf of a number of countries, Eurocontrol collects route fees that are imposed on users of air space over the countries in question. It is the individual country which sets the amount of the fees; Eurocontrol collects these on behalf of the individual country and receives a proportion of the revenue. Eurocontrol is financed by contributions from the countries which set it up, and the organisation carries out its activities on behalf of these countries. According to the CJ, Eurocontrol carries out these tasks in the public interest, with the aim of contributing to the maintenance and improvement of the safety of air transport. Taking an overall view of the nature, purpose and rules to which it was subject, the CJ found that the organisation's undertaking was associated with policing air space and that this is typically a task of the public authorities.[56]

In a number of cases, the CJ has also had to assess whether a social insurance arrangement was an undertaking. In these cases, the CJ has made a distinction between whether membership of an arrangement is voluntary or obligatory, as the fact that it is a voluntary scheme is an indication that there is an undertaking. In addition, the CJ has put emphasis on whether an arrangement is based on the solidarity principle or the capitalisation principle, as in the latter case, there is an indication that there is an undertaking. Finally, it depends on whether the overall purpose of a scheme is a social function and whether the arrangement is subject to state control.[57]

If it is found that an activity is an exercise of public authority, it is not covered by Article 101, even if private undertakings carry out the activity.[58] In some cases, it can be difficult to determine whether or not an undertaking has taken on a task of a public authority. For example, this will be the case where an association has been given authority to set the prices for a particular activity or product. It will only be the exercise of public authority if the task is carried out for the purposes of the general good and typically under public control and supervision.[59] Another area where there have been cases is where private undertakings issue certificates.[60]

---

56. Case C-364/92, *Eurocontrol*, paras 19–30. In Case T-155/04, *SELEX*, the General Court found that in one area (technical assistance for national administrations) Eurocontrol carried on economic activities which could be assessed pursuant to Art. 102 TFEU. However, the CJ overruled this conclusion on the grounds that the activities were closely linked to Eurocontrol's activity of technical standardisation; *see* Case C-113/07 P, *SELEX*. Also, *see* Case C-309/99, *Wouters*, where the CJ did not find that the Dutch Bar Association carried out activities which, on an overall assessment, could be said to be linked to the exercise of the powers of a public authority. In Case C-82/01 P, *Aéroports de Paris*, the CJ held that a public body that provides airport facilities for airlines, for the payment of fees which it set itself, was an undertaking.
57. *See* in more detail Joined Cases C-159–160/91, *Poucet*; Case C-244/94, *FFSA*; Joined Cases C-264/01 and others, *AOK Bundesverband*; and Case C-350/07, *Kattner Stahlbau*.
58. *See*, e.g., Case C-343/95, *Diego Cali*, which concerned a private undertaking which had a concession from the harbour authorities in Genoa to carry out environmental monitoring.
59. On this, *see* Case T-513/93, *CNSD* (summarised above in s. 2.1); and Case C-185/91, *Reiff*.
60. Case C-113/07 P, *SELEX*; and Case C-327/12, *SOA*.

The CJ has also established that it is contrary to a Member State's obligations under Article 4(3) and Article 101 TFEU for it to adopt rules which require or favour the adoption of agreements which are contrary to Article 101 or to reinforce the effects of such agreements.[61]

In Case C-2/91, *Meng*, the CJ had to decide whether a German law which prohibited an insurance intermediary from surrendering commission on health insurance was contrary to Articles 10 and 81 (now Article 4(3) and Article 101 TFEU). The facts of the case were that, in a number of instances, *Meng* had surrendered the commission which he had received from an insurance company in connection with the writing of health insurance policies. However, *Meng* could not be found to have infringed the law if it was contrary to Article 4(3) and Article 101. By way of introduction, the CJ found that it would be contrary to these provisions if a Member State adopted or maintained measures, including laws, which could annul the intended effects of the competition rules. This means that a Member State is prevented from either requiring or favouring agreements in contravention of Article 101 or reinforcing the effects of such agreements. However, in the case at hand, it was found that the German rules neither required nor favoured the entry into unlawful agreements by insurance intermediaries since the prohibition laid down was sufficient in itself (in other words, it was not necessary to enter into any agreement). Nor did the CJ find that the law reinforced any agreement in restraint of competition since there was no agreement prior to the provisions of the law. Rules can only be regarded as having a reinforcing effect on an existing agreement if 'they simply reproduce the elements of an agreement, decision or concerted practice between economic agents in that sector'.[62]

In addition to this, a Member State could contravene the provisions referred to if it has delegated legislative competence to a private undertaking without ensuring that, in exercising such competence, the undertaking promotes general interest and not its own interests. There are several examples where Member States have left it to associations of undertakings to set minimum prices, with the result that the Member States have been found to contravene Article 4(3) and Article 101 TFEU.[63]

If a Member State contravenes the Treaty in this way, it will incur a liability to pay compensation to the undertakings that have suffered loss as a result of agreements in

---

61. Case 267/86, *Van Eycke*, para. 16; Case C-250/03, *Mauri*, para. 30; and Joined Cases T-94/04 and T-202/04, *Cipolla*, para. 47. *See also Ulla B. Neergaard:* Competition & Competences, 1998. However, the CJ has rejected a more extensive interpretation which would use Art. 101 to challenge, e.g., rules on opening hours and prohibitions of marketing; *see* Case C-446/05 *Doulamis;* and Case C-393/08, *Sbarigia.*
62. Case C-2/91, *Meng*, para. 19.
63. Case T-513/93, *CNSD* (summarised above in s. 2.1); Case C-185/91, *Reiff;* and Joined Cases C-184/13 and others, *API*.

restraint of competition. This follows from the general liability of Member States to pay compensation for qualifying infringements of their obligations under the Treaty.[64]

4 THE EFFECT ON TRADE IN THE EU

4.1 The Requirement for an Effect on Trade Between Member States

As discussed in Chapter 1, the competition rules have the aim of ensuring the completion of the internal market. This aim can be seen, among other things, in the requirement in Article 101 that trade between Member States shall be affected since the aim of the internal market is to remove hindrances to cross-border activities. However, the standard set for this condition to be fulfilled is not particularly high.

In 2004, the Commission issued a Notice on the effect on trade concept expressed in Articles 101 and 102 of the Treaty.[65] In this Notice, the Commission points out that the conditions focus on three elements in particular.

First, trade between Member States must be affected. This means that cross-border activities between at least two Member States must be affected. The effect can be on trade in goods or in services, or it can be an effect of the right of establishment in other Member States. If undertakings from different Member States enter into an agreement, the condition will often be satisfied. Also, even if they are undertakings located in the same Member State, trade can be affected if the agreement has the effect of making it more difficult for undertakings from other Member States to gain access to the market.[66]

Second, there is a requirement that the agreement, etc., 'may affect' trade. The CJ has established that it is sufficient if it can be shown that it is probable that an agreement, directly or indirectly, actually or potentially, can have an influence on trade between Member States.[67] Thus, it is not necessary to prove that cross-border trade is actually affected, as it is sufficient to show that it is probable that an agreement has such an effect or could have it. Even if it is shown that trade has increased, it is possible that the CJ will find that trade is affected if trade could have increased even more without the agreement. Even an agreement that increases trade can affect trade, for example, by channelling it through specific undertakings.[68] Even where trade does not yet exist for certain products, an agreement could hinder trade if it prevents trade from taking place at a later date.[69] Finally, it is possible that products that are not traded are

---

64. On the liability to pay compensation for infringements of Arts 81 and 82, *see Malin Thunström, Johan Carle & Stefan Perván Lindeborg:* State Liability Under the EC Treaty Arising From Anti-Competitive State Measures, World Competition 2002 pp. 515–528.
65. Commission Notice – Guidelines on the effect on trade concept contained in Articles 81 and 82 of the Treaty (OJ 2004 C 101/81).
66. Case 246/86, *Belasco;* Joined Cases C-295/04 to C-298/04, *Manfredi,* para. 45; and Case C-172/14, *ING Pensii,* para. 49.
67. Case 56/65, *Société Technique Minière.* This formulation was later used again by the CJ in Case 8/74, *Dassonville,* in connection with the interpretation of the meaning of 'quantitative restrictions' in Art. 34 TFEU.
68. Joined Cases 56 and 58/64, *Consten and Grundig;* and Commission Notice – Guidelines on the effect on trade concept contained in Articles 81 and 82 of the Treaty (OJ 2004 C 101/81), para. 34.
69. Case 19/77, *Miller,* para. 14.

ingredients in products that are traded, so that a restriction on trade in the former will have an effect on trade in the latter.[70]

Finally, as the *third* element, there must be an assessment of whether the effect on trade is appreciable. In its Notice, the Commission states generally that Article 101 does not apply to agreements where the parties do not have a cumulative share of any market of over 5% and where the annual turnover of the products covered by the agreement does not exceed EUR 40 million.[71] This limit supplements the requirement for appreciability formulated in the Commission's *De Minimis* Notice; *see* section 5.3 below.

4.2 The International Extent of Article 101

The purpose of Article 101 is to ensure that competition within the EU is not restricted, and consequently, a restriction on competition that arises in a third country will not be covered by the provision. However, this is not to say that agreements that regulate trade with a third country and agreements between undertakings located in a third country cannot be covered by the provision.

First, an agreement which restricts the import of goods from a third country to the EU can clearly affect competition within the EU, as such import restrictions can have a direct effect on the goods offered in the EU.[72] It is less obvious that agreements on exports to third countries can affect trade within the EU. However, it is possible that if in connection with their exports to third countries, undertakings located in the EU include a requirement that the goods may not be re-exported back to the EU, this could have an effect on trade between Member States. This would probably require the export to the third country to be of a certain extent, and that the competition on the product market in question in the EU is not optimal.[73]

Article 101 will also be applicable where one or more of the parties to an agreement are located in a third country. If one or more of the undertakings located in a third country has subsidiaries or branches in the EU, it follows from the definition of an undertaking discussed in section 3.1 above that its branches or subsidiaries will be part of the same undertaking and will, therefore, have a presence in the EU so that it is clearly covered by Article 101.

Even if an agreement is entered into between undertakings that do not have a physical presence in the EU, it could still be covered by Article 101. This will be the case either if the agreement has an immediate and substantial effect within the EU (effect doctrine) or if the agreement is intended to have effect within the EU (implementation

---

70. Joined Cases C-89/85 and others, *Ahlström (Cellulose II)*, para. 142.
71. Commission Notice – Guidelines on the effect on trade concept contained in Articles 81 and 82 of the Treaty (OJ 2004 C 101/81), para. 52. For vertical agreements, the threshold is whether the supplier of the products covered by the agreement has a turnover in the EU of over EUR 40 million.
72. Case 51/75, *EMI*.
73. Case C-306/96, *Javico*; and Joined Cases 29/83 and 30/83, *CRAM*.

doctrine).⁷⁴ The effect doctrine was established by the CJ in Case C-413/14 P, *Intel*, in a case concerning Article 102 and was earlier established by the GC in Case T-102/96 *Gencor*, which concerned the Merger Control Regulation; *see* Chapter 8, section 2.6.⁷⁵ The implementation doctrine was established by the CJ in Joined Cases C-89/85 and others, *Ahlström*, which concerned a breach of Article 101.⁷⁶

> This case concerned a number of producers of cellulose, all located in third countries. They had coordinated their prices applicable to sales in the EU, and the Commission decided that they were thereby in breach of Article 101. The undertakings disputed the decision, as they argued that the Commission was wrong with regard to the territorial extent of Article 101 and that the Commission's application of Article 101 was contrary to public international law.
>
> The CJ stated that an infringement of Article 101 involved conduct with two elements, namely, the formation of a cartel and its implementation. If the application of Article 101 were dependent on the place where the cartel was formed, undertakings would easily be able to avoid the prohibition under Article 101, as they would merely have to enter into an agreement in a third country. What must, therefore, be decisive is where the cartel is put into practice.⁷⁷ In the case before the CJ, the undertakings had put their price cartel into practice in the EU, and it was therefore covered by Article 101. It was of subordinate importance that they had used subsidiaries, agents or branches established in the EU in order to put the cartel into practice. In other words, undertakings that do not have established representatives in the EU are covered by Article 101, provided that they are part of a cartel which is implemented in the EU. Finally, the CJ stated that such an application of the Union's competence must be regarded as being protected by the principle of territoriality, and there was, therefore, no conflict with public international law.

---

74. Case T-286/09, *Intel Corp.*, paras 231–237 and Case T-363/18, *Nippon Chemi-Con Corporation*, paras 74–77.
75. Subsequently, the effect doctrine has been used and explained in several cases, *see* for instance Case T-324/17, *SAS Cargo Group*, paras 160–237.
76. For more on the two doctrines *see* Luca Prete: On Implementation and Effects: The Recent Case-law on the Territorial (or Extraterritorial?) Application of EU Competition Law, Journal of European Competition Law & Practice 2018 pp. 587–495, *Bernadette Zelger*: EU Competition law and extraterritorial jurisdiction – a critical analysis of the ECJ's judgment in *Intel*, European Competition Journal 2020 pp. 613–627 and *Marek Martyniszyn* in N. Cunha Rodrigues (ed.): Extraterritoriality of EU Economic Law, 2021.
77. The judgment was later confirmed by the General Court in Case T-395/94 *Atlantic Container v. Commission* (TAA Agreement). The Commission has also applied it, for example, in Decision of 25 Jun. 2008 relating to a proceeding under Art. 81 of the EC Treaty and Art. 53 of the EEA Agreement (Case COMP/39.180 – Aluminium fluoride) (OJ 2011 C 40/22), para. 101. The effect doctrine has also been used as a basic choice of law rule in relation to claims for compensation for competition law infringements. *See* further Regulation (EC) No 864/2007 of the European Parliament and of the Council of 11 Jul. 2007 on the law applicable to non-contractual obligations (Rome II), Art. 6(3).

5 RESTRICTION ON COMPETITION

There will be a breach of Article 101 where an agreement has the object or effect of preventing, restricting or distorting competition within the Union. In the following chapters, there will be a discussion of when a restriction on competition will be found to exist in relation to different types of agreements. But generally, the assessment of whether a restriction on competition exists must be made on the basis of an evaluation of how competition would evolve if the agreement with its alleged restrictions on competition did not exist or if the terms in the agreement which restrict competition did not exist.[78] The evaluation must include consideration of the probable effects of the agreement on inter-brand competition (i.e., between suppliers of competing brands) and intra-brand competition (i.e., between distributors of the same brand).[79] In addition to this, the following more general considerations apply to when a restriction on competition may be found to exist.

5.1 Workable Competition

Competition law is one of the areas of law in which economics has achieved the greatest influence. Economic theory influences what conduct ought to be prohibited by competition rules at the overall level, and it is also acknowledged that economic theory is increasingly taken into account in the assessment of concrete competition cases.

In order to evaluate the effects of different agreements or different kinds of conduct on competition, economic theory starts from the basis of different market models. This means that, among other things, the existing market situation is compared with extreme market models: perfect competition and monopolies.[80] A monopoly describes a situation where one undertaking has the whole market and where there are thus no competitors. Perfect competition describes the situation where there are numerous smaller undertakings on the market and these undertakings trade in a number of products which do not significantly differ from one another with regard to price, quality, etc. Traditionally, perfect competition has been regarded as the optimal situation. However, it is clear that perfect competition is not a realistic goal on most markets, and the aim of legislation must, therefore, be based on some other ideal of competition than perfect competition. In this connection a competitive situation referred to as *workable competition* (a standard which is less strict than perfect competition and is sometimes referred to as 'effective competition') is preferred. The CJ has defined workable competition as the situation where there is 'the degree of

---

78. *See* Case T-328/03, *O2*, where the GC set aside the Commission's decision because it did not include consideration of what the competitive situation would have been if the agreement had not existed.
79. *See also* Commission Notice – Guidelines on the effect on trade concept contained in Article 81(3) of the Treaty (OJ 2004 C 101/97), para. 17.
80. *See* among others, *Cédric Argenton, Damien Geradin & Andreas Stephan*: EU Cartel Law and Economics 2020; *Simon Bishop & Mike Walker*: The Economics of EC Competition Law: Concepts, Application and Measurement, 4th ed., 2019; and *Roger J. Van den Bergh, Peter D. Camessasca & Andrea Giannaccari*: Comparative Competition Law and Economics, 2017.

competition necessary to ensure the observance of the basic requirements and the attainment of the objectives of the treaty, in particular the creation of a single market achieving conditions similar to those of a domestic market'.[81]

Normally, mainstream economists set a target for economic effectiveness, understood as an effective social economic use of resources. Certain parts of economic theory also point towards other goals, such as consumer welfare and the protection of the economic freedom of market participants. It is not entirely clear what economic theory is used in the EU. However, as will appear from the analysis of the practice of the Commission and the courts in the individual areas, consideration for consumers often plays a key role. In addition to this, a number of other considerations are normally taken into account in economic theories, including consideration for the internal market and the aims of the EU's industrial policy.[82]

5.2 'Which Have as Their Object or Effect ...'

An infringement of Article 101 can occur both in cases where an agreement has a direct aim of restricting competition and in cases where it is not the intention of the agreement but where this is nevertheless the effect of the agreement.[83]

The wording means that where an agreement (or decision or concerted practice) clearly aims (or objects) to prevent, restrict or distort competition, this will be prohibited without there being any need to make an examination of the effect of the agreement (or decision or concerted practice).[84] Such agreements are said to be 'by object' restrictions. As no additional examinations are needed for such infringements, the CJ has held that the concept of restriction of competition 'by object' must be interpreted restrictively. The concept can be applied only to certain types of coordination, which reveal a sufficient degree of harm to competition. To evaluate whether an agreement is likely to have such harmful effects, it should be considered whether the type of agreement in question in previous cases has had such effect. The CJ has, however, also deemed agreements that are not classical examples of agreements that harm competition to cause 'by object' restrictions, and in doing so, the CJ has indicated how to determine whether an agreement restricts 'by object'. It requires an examination of the content of the agreement, the objectives of the agreement and finally, the economic and legal context of the agreement. In the examination of the economic and legal context, the nature of the goods or services affected, as well as the real conditions of the functioning and structure of the market or markets in question, must be taken

---

81. Case 26/76, *Metro*, para. 20.
82. Commission Notice – Guidelines on the effect on trade concept contained in Article 81(3) of the Treaty (OJ 2004 C 101/97), para. 13.
83. Case C-219/95 P, *Ferriere Nord*, where the wording of the Italian translation was assessed by the CJ. In the Italian version 'or' was replaced by 'and'. The CJ stated that the provision applies either when the restriction on competition is the aim of an agreement or when it is the effect of an agreement.
84. *See*, for example, Case C-306/20, »*Visma Enterprise*« SIA, para. 57 and Case C-228/18, *Budapest Bank Nyrt.*, para. 54. In these two cases, the CJ summarises its case law. It will be reminded that a concerted practice needs to have some effect, but there may be a presumption that this is the case when undertakings have concerted.

into consideration.[85] The intention of the undertakings involved is not decisive, and therefore, agreements pursuing a legitimate objective may pose a 'by object' restriction if the agreement also has an illegitimate object.[86] However, the CJ has accepted that it may be relevant to take the intention of the undertakings into consideration.

All this seems to indicate that a somewhat extensive examination must be undertaken to conclude whether there is a 'by object' restriction of competition. But this seems counterproductive as the purpose for having the 'by object' concept was to avoid making such examinations. It also appears that, in fact, extensive examination will normally not be required. For many types of agreements, there will be solid experiences indicating that such agreements are harmful, thus eliminating the need for any additional examinations.[87] Other agreements must be examined further by focusing on the agreement itself (content and purpose) and its context. The examination of the context does not require a full examination of the agreement's implication for competition but needs only a less intense overall examination.[88] After having examined the most likely effect of the agreement, only an additional 'basic reality check' is needed to ensure that the agreement does not restrict competition.[89]

The CJ has, in several cases, had to decide whether there is a restriction of competition 'by object'. This is normally the case with classic cartel agreements such as agreements on price fixing,[90] market sharing[91] or agreements to control production.[92] But also less 'classic' agreements have been held to be restriction 'by object', for instance, agreements on exchange of commercially sensitive information[93] and agreements to keep competitors from entering the market.[94] All these examples are horizontal agreements, but the CJ has also stressed that vertical agreements may restrict competition 'by object'.[95] In the subsequent chapters, there will be more examples of cases concerning restrictions 'by object'.

---

85. *See* the two judgments mentioned in the previous note, para. 62 and para. 51.
86. As a consequence there may be a 'by object' restriction even where the undertakings did not intend any restriction, *see* Case C-209/07, *Competition Authority mod Beef Industry Development Society Ltd.*, para. 21.
87. According to the CJ for such agreements the analysis may 'be limited to what is strictly necessary in order to establish the existence of a restriction of competition by object', *see* Case C-373/14 P, *Toshiba Corp*, para. 29.
88. It has been pointed out that the examination of whether there is a 'by object' restriction is primarily a legal examination, whereas the examination of a 'by effect' restriction will often involve economic examinations, *see Csongor István Nagy*: EU Competition Law Devours Its Children, Cambridge Yearbook of European Legal Studies 2021 ss 290–310.
89. Thus, AG Bobek in his Opinion in Case C-228/18, *Budapest Bank Nyrt.*, para. 49.
90. Case C-228/18, *Budapest Bank Nyrt.*, para. 36, but as this judgment also illustrates, not all agreements on fees may restrict competition 'by object'.
91. Case C-373/14 P, *Toshiba Corp*, para. 28.
92. Case C-209/07, *Competition Authority mod Beef Industry Development Society Ltd.*, paras 33–39. In the Commissions Guidelines on horizontal cooperation agreements, para. 222, it is assumed that agreements on price-fixing, limiting output or sharing markets or customers restrict competition by object.
93. Case C-8/08, *T-Mobile*, para. 43.
94. *See* the 'pay for delay' cases where the holders of certain patents paid potential competitors not to enter the market, *see, inter alia*, Case C-307/18, *Generics* and Case C-591/16 P, *Lundbeck A/S*.
95. Case C-306/20, »*Visma Enterprise*« *SIA*, para. 61, Case C-345/14, *Maxima Latvija*, para. 21 and Case C-32/11, *Allianz Hungária Biztosító*, para. 43.

If an agreement does not clearly have an aim of restricting competition, there must be an investigation of whether it has the effect of restricting competition. For such restrictions 'by effect,' there is no assumption that an agreement has restrictive effects of competition, so it must be established with a reasonable degree of certainty that the agreement can be expected to have a negative effect on prices, production, innovation, variety of goods offered or product quality on the market in question.[96] It must be examined how the situation would be if the agreement (decision or concerted practice) did not exist. This counter-factual scenario requires an examination of: (1) the economic and legal context in which the undertakings concerned operate, (2) the nature of the goods or services affected, as well as (3) the real conditions of the functioning and the structure of the market or markets in question.[97] An assessment must be made of both actual and potential effects on competition,[98] just as it must be assessed whether the effects are sufficiently appreciable; *see also* section 5.3 below. In addition, the CJ has held that the potential market power of the undertakings concerned must be taken into account. Finally, it needs to be assessed whether the agreement is the only one or just one of many similar agreements.[99] As it will be apparent, an examination of whether there is a restriction of competition 'by effect' may require extensive examination, and the CJ has made it clear that the required examination will differ according to the type of agreement and its potential for affecting competition.

In sum, the CJ has developed a distinction between restrictions 'by object' and 'by effect' that may not be very clear cut but, nevertheless, is very important for the correct application of Article 101. If there is a restriction 'by object', it will normally require fewer examinations to establish an infringement of Article 101(1), and therefore, it is tempting for the competition authorities to expand the application of the concept of 'by object' restriction. Similarly, the undertaking which may be the target of an examination is likely to argue for a more narrow concept. There is also the risk that the authorities will focus their effort on investigating restrictions 'by object' as these are less complicated to prove, and as a result, more complicated cases that are restrictions 'by effect' will not be dealt with.[100]

5.3 The Commission's *De Minimis* Notice

Article 101(1) does not apply if the deleterious effects on competition are found to be insignificant. The requirement for there to be an appreciable restriction was first established in the *Völk* case.[101]

---

96. Commission Notice – Guidelines on the effect on trade concept contained in Article 81(3) of the Treaty (OJ 2004 C 101/97), para. 24.
97. Case C-307/18, *Generics*, para. 116.
98. If an agreement has entered into force, it will be most relevant to examine its actual effects instead of its potential effects, *see also* Case T-684/14, *Krka*, para. 361. The judgment is under appeal.
99. Case 31/80, *L'Oréal*, para. 19.
100. This point is made by *Anne C. Witt*: The Enforcement of Article 101 TFEU: What Has Happened to Effects Analysis?, Common Market Law Review 2018 ss 417–488.
101. Case 5/69, *Völk v. Vervaecke*.

Subsequently, the condition that there should be an appreciable restriction was followed up by several notices from the Commission which have all specified precisely when it can be assumed that there is such a significant effect that the prohibition in Article 101 could come into play. These notices have popularly been called the '*De minimis* notices' and are in the nature of soft law. The current *De Minimis* Notice is from 2014.[102] The Commission has an obligation not to depart from the guidelines in connection with its decisions. Thus it is expected that the Commission will not initiate proceedings against undertakings on the basis of agreements which lie below the *de minimis* thresholds. Furthermore, the Commission will not impose fines on the basis of agreements which are below the *de minimis* thresholds. However, it is quite clear that neither the GC nor the CJ are bound by the notices in their application of Article 101.[103]

The principle is that horizontal agreements between undertakings (at the same level of trade and thus are actual or potential competitors) which represent a combined market share of less than 10% will not be caught by Article 101(1).[104] For vertical agreements (between undertakings at different levels of trade), the critical threshold is a market share of 15%. Where an agreement cannot be classified as either horizontal or vertical, it will be assessed according to the guidelines for horizontal agreements and thus must not concern a market share of more than 10% of the relevant market.

There are specific modifications to these general guidelines as to when an agreement is considered as being covered by the prohibition in Article 101(1). *First*, the threshold values do not apply where several agreements have been entered into concerning the same issue between different suppliers or distributors (parallel networks of agreement). In these cases, the critical threshold is reduced to 5%. At the same time, it is assumed that if such a parallel network has a combined market share of less than 30%, the cumulative effects of these agreements will not result in a foreclosure effect on the market in question.[105] Second, the threshold values do not apply to agreements that are intended to prevent, restrict or distort competition. These restrictions are listed in paragraph 13. For horizontal agreements, these include agreements on fixing prices for sales to third parties or allocating markets or customers. The provisions will also cover the 'hardcore' restrictions referred to in various block exemption regulations.

---

102. Commission Notice on agreements of minor importance which do not appreciably restrict competition under Article 101(1) of the Treaty on the Functioning of the European Union (*De Minimis* Notice) (OJ 2014 C 291/1).
103. *See* para. 7 of the *De Minimis* Notice. It seems that in many cases, the courts draw on the Commission's notices in their interpretation of the competition rules. Furthermore, in certain circumstances, the principle of legitimate expectation will mean that it would be difficult to depart from a notice if it has given rise to an expectation by undertakings that their agreements would fall outside the scope of Art. 101(1).
104. The assessment of market share is based on a definition of the relevant product market and relevant geographic market. The general guidelines for this (which apply to both Arts 101-102 and the Merger Control Regulation) are to be found in Commission Notice on the definition of relevant market for the purposes of Union competition law (C/2024/1645). The establishment of the relevant market is dealt with in more detail in Ch. 6, s. 3.3 (on Art. 102) and Ch. 8, s. 3 (merger control).
105. Paragraph 8 of the *De Minimis* Notice.

5.4 Rule of Reason

In American antitrust practice, there is a prohibition against agreements in restraint of competition corresponding to the prohibition in Article 101(1). In applying this prohibition, the American courts have developed two different tests known as the per se test and the rule of reason test.[106] A per se application of the competition rules means that attention is paid solely to the character of the agreement in question, and on that basis, it is decided whether there is an infringement of the prohibition. This test is applied to agreements where there is an obvious risk that they restrict competition. By contrast, in the application of the rule of reason, an infringement test is not established before an evaluation has been made between the negative effects of competition of the agreement and any positive effects. If, in connection with a rule of reason assessment, the positive effects are shown to outweigh the negative effects, the agreement or conduct will not be covered by the prohibition.

In principle, the rule of reason assessments are not possible under Article 101 TFEU.[107] However, there have been some cases where the CJ appears to have applied a test which has certain similarities to the rule of reason test. Several of these cases are linked to the practice on ancillary restraints, which are discussed in the next section, but as will be seen there, this practice is not identical to a rule of reason assessment.[108]

The principal reason why the rule of reason test is rejected is the structure of the European rules. Article 101 is structured with the prohibition in paragraph 1 and with possible exemptions in paragraph 3. In connection with an examination of a case, the negative effect of an agreement is assessed under paragraph 1, and any positive effect of an agreement is assessed under paragraph 3. This splits up the two assessments (positive and negative), while, under the rule of reason test, they are assessed simultaneously. If the rule of reason test model were to be used in connection with Article 101(1), then Article 101(3) would lose part of its importance.[109]

In the American system, the corresponding prohibition on the formation of cartels is structured differently, so there are no exemptions linked to it. In such a situation, there is naturally a need to be able to ease the application of the prohibition

---

106. For a more detailed review of the American practice, the early Community law practice and the concepts in general, see Jens Fejø: Monopoly Law and Market, 1990 Chs IV and V.
107. The GC has stated this in Case T-112/99, Métropole Télévision (M6), para. 72; and Case T-328/03, O2, para. 69 and the CJ has confirmed this in Case C-883/19 P, HSBC Holdings plc, para. 140.
108. However, it has previously been argued that the practice on ancillary restraints effectively introduces a rule of reason assessment, see Richard Whish & Brenda Sufrin: Article 85 and the Rule of Reason, Yearbook of European Law 1987 pp. 1–38. The judgment of the GC in Case T-112/99, Métropole Télévision (M6), seems to disprove this, since the GC both clearly rejected a rule of reason assessment while simultaneously applying the practice on ancillary restraints.
109. In the literature on free movement, the CJ's judgment in Case 120/78, Cassis de Dijon, is referred to as an expression of 'rule of reason'. The Treaty system is that the existence of an import restriction is established under Art. 34 TFEU, and thereafter, there is consideration of whether it is justified under Art. 36 TFEU. However, in Cassis de Dijon, the CJ introduced a test for non-discriminatory import restrictions which means that, as part of deciding whether Art. 34 TFEU has been contravened, an assessment is made of whether the restrictions can be justified by mandatory requirements, and thus, there are many parallels with the rule of reason test which is used in American competition law.

in connection with those agreements that have clear advantages and which need not necessarily be prohibited.

Against the background of the reform introduced by Regulation (EC) No 1/2003, it could be argued that the application of Article 101 will have a high degree of similarity to the rule of reason model. Previously, the Commission had sole competence to grant exemptions from the prohibition in Article 101(1); *see* Regulation (EEC) No 17/62. Since it was not possible for others other than the Commission to grant an exemption, it was not possible to make an overall assessment, as required by the rule of reason assessment. Under the current rules, assessments of whether the conditions for an exemption under Article 101(3) are met are left to the undertakings themselves. Thus, undertakings must themselves evaluate both whether they are covered by the prohibition and whether the conditions for exemption are satisfied. This assessment will be made simultaneously, so there is effectively a rule of reason assessment.[110]

The way restrictions 'by object' are handled, *see* section 5.2 above, means that certain agreements that have as their object to restrict competition will be contrary to Article 101 without the need for (much) examination. These agreements are thus subject to a treatment very similar to the per se application used in US law.

5.5 Ancillary Restraints

The Commission and the courts have developed a practice whereby conditions which restrict competition but which are part of a transaction which is not restricting on competition are not assessed individually, provided they are part of an agreement that is otherwise lawful. This assessment is distinguished from an assessment under Article 101(3) by not including a weighing of the elements which promote competition against the elements which restrict competition.[111]

The background to the doctrine on ancillary restraints is found in American competition law, where the courts have developed a practice on ancillary restraints under which terms of agreements that are part of lawful cooperation are not assessed individually but as part of the cooperation.[112] From the mid-1970s, the Commission used similar arguments to limit the scope of application of Article 101.

> One of the earliest decisions was Commission Decision 76/743/EEC, *Reuter/BASF*, where the Commission had to consider the legality of a non-competition clause which had been agreed in a transfer agreement,

---

110. For a similar argument, *see James Venit:* Brave New World: The Modernization and Decentralization of Enforcement under Articles 81 and 82 of the EC Treaty, Common Market Law Review 2003, p. 577.
111. Commission Notice – Guidelines on the effect on trade concept contained in Article 81(3) of the Treaty (OJ 2004 C 101/97), para. 30.
112. The concept was introduced by Judge Taft in the decision in *United States v. Addyston Pipe & Steel Co.*, 85 F.271 (6th Cir. 1898) and 175 U.S. 211 (1899), where he stated, among other things, that 'no conventional restraint of trade can be enforced unless the covenant embodying it is merely ancillary to the main purpose of a lawful contract, and necessary to protect the covenantee in the full enjoyment of the legitimate fruits of the contract, or to protect him from the dangers of an unjust use of those fruits by the other party'; *see* 85 F p. 282.

whereby Gottfried Reuter had disposed of his undertaking. Reuter had committed himself not to carry on a competing undertaking for a period of eight years after signing the agreement. Reuter had himself drawn the attention of the Commission to the non-competition clause, as he hoped to be released from it. The Commission established that the transfer of the undertaking not only included the physical assets but also goodwill and know-how, and the latter constituted a significant part of the value of the transfer. The Commission did not believe that Article 101 was applicable if the non-competition clause was necessary in order to ensure the value of the transferred undertaking. In the actual case the Commission found that, in order to ensure that Reuter did not attract his old customer base to him immediately after the transfer, it was necessary to prevent him from competing. Since Reuter had comprehensive information about the undertaking sold, he would be an especially dangerous competitor, and this too favoured Reuter being prevented from competing. In this situation, Article 101 could not be applied to the non-competition clause 'in such cases, since it would make more difficult or even impossible transactions which are generally recognized as legitimate'.[113] However, the Commission emphasised that the prohibition on competition must not go further than necessary for protecting the value of the transferred undertaking, and the prohibition must be limited geographically and substantially to the markets where the undertaking operated prior to the transfer or where, on the basis of the evidence of significant investment, it must be considered a possible competitor. On this basis the Commission rejected the non-competition clause in the case in question, as being too extensive on a number of points.

Furthermore, in Commission Decision 90/410/EEC, *Elopak/Metal Box – Odin*, the Commission found that Article 85 [now Article 101 TFEU] did not apply to a number of terms restricting competition agreed in connection with the setting up of the joint venture Odin, as it noted that 'Since such provisions cannot be disassociated from the creation of Odin without undermining its existence and purpose, and since the creation of Odin does not fall within the scope of Article 85(1), these specific provisions also fall outside the scope of Article 85(1).'[114]

The CJ has since had to consider a number of cases on ancillary restraints. In Case 42/84, *Remia BV and others*, it confirmed that a non-competition clause which a vendor accepts in connection with the transfer of an undertaking can fall outside the scope of Article 101. The CJ emphasised that there should be an examination of how the competitive situation would be without such a clause. Since it could not be assumed that the transfer would be carried out if the vendor were free to compete, such a clause ensured that a transfer was possible and effective. As long as such clauses did

---

113. Commission Decision 76/743/EEC, *Reuter/BASF* (OJ L 254/40), Part II.3(a).
114. Commission Decision 90/410/EEC, *Elopak/Metal Box – Odin* (OJ 1990 L 209/15), para. 36.

not go further than was necessary for the transfer to take place, they fell outside the scope of Article 101(1).[115]

These cases confirm that ancillary restraints that are linked to the transfer of an undertaking or a joint venture will not infringe on Article 101. However, the case law suggests that the doctrine on ancillary restraints is not only relevant in connection with agreements which involve structural changes, such as mergers and joint ventures. The doctrine seems to have a more general application so that it includes terms which are a necessary part of an otherwise lawful agreement. Such a broader application of the doctrine on ancillary restraints can be seen confirmed in, among others, Case 161/84, *Pronuptia de Paris*, and Case 250/92, *Gøttrup-Klim v. Dansk Landbrugs Grovvareselskaber*, where the CJ accepted that certain terms which restricted competition were necessary in connection with a franchise agreement and a purchasing cooperative agreement respectively.[116] In Case C-309/99, *Wouters*, the CJ has to decide whether a decision that solicitors were not allowed to enter into a partnership with persons who were not solicitors could be justified in the need to protect the integrity of the profession. Furthermore, the CJ has, in several cases, been asked whether organisations organising sports events may restrict who may participate in these events to ensure, *inter alia*, that the competitions are conducted fairly,[117] just as it has had to address whether the exchange of information on prices could be necessary to ensure the functioning of a particular financial market.[118]

In order for the doctrine on ancillary restraints to apply, the restraint in question must be necessary for the achievement of the lawful aim with which it is connected, and it must be proportional. These conditions will be fulfilled if it is concluded, based on an assessment of objective factors, that it would be difficult or impossible to achieve the legitimate aims without the restraint in question.[119]

6 POSSIBLE EXEMPTIONS UNDER ARTICLE 101(3)

As seen in the preceding section, Article 101(1) contains a broad prohibition that catches many forms of agreements which restrict competition. There is, therefore also a need to exclude agreements which, even if in principle they restrict competition, have more positive than negative effects from an overall perspective. This can be done either by making an individual assessment of whether there is a basis for an exemption under Article 101(3) or by considering whether the agreement falls under one of the block exemption regulations which exclude certain kinds of agreement, given that they do not contain certain conditions, and given that they do not exceed some stated thresholds for market shares.

---

115. Case 42/84, *Remia BV and others*, paras 18–20.
116. Case 161/84, *Pronuptia de Paris GmbH*, paras 15–26; and Case C-250/92, *Gøttrup-Klim v. Dansk Landbrugs Grovvareselskab*, para. 35.
117. Case C-519/04 P, *Meca-Medina* and Case T-93/18, *International Skating Union*.
118. Case C-382/12 P, *MasterCard*, para. 94 and Case T-105/17, *HSBC Holdings*, para. 157.
119. Commission Notice – Guidelines on the effect on trade concept contained in Article 81(3) of the Treaty (OJ 2004 C 101/97), para. 31.

6.1 Change to the Notification Procedure

Previously, it was possible to have individual agreements exempted after notification to the Commission. Because of the comprehensive procedure which had to be initiated in connection with each exemption case, the Commission prepared some informal procedures so that undertakings could get a quicker response. These informal 'comfort letters' could inform an undertaking that the Commission did not regard a notified agreement to be contrary to Article 101(1).

Under Regulation (EC) No 1/2003, the notification system, which had previously been a cornerstone of Union competition law, was abandoned. The change meant that it was no longer possible for undertakings to notify agreements to achieve an individual exemption. Thereafter, undertakings must themselves assess whether they are covered by the prohibition under Article 101(1), and if so, they must then assess for themselves whether the conditions in Article 101(3) are fulfilled so the agreement is exempted from the prohibition. Thus, there is no requirement for a stamp of approval from the Commission before an agreement can be exempt.

The procedure for the enforcement of Article 101 is discussed in more detail in Chapter 7.

6.2 Individual Exemptions: The Four Conditions

According to Article 101(3), it is possible to obtain an individual exemption if four conditions are fulfilled. These take the form of two positive and two negative conditions. The two positive conditions (i.e., circumstances that *must* be present) are:

(1) The agreement must contribute to improving the production or distribution of goods or services, etc., or promoting technical or economic progress.
(2) The agreement must allow consumers a fair share of the resulting benefits.

The two negative conditions (i.e., circumstances which *must not* be present) are:

(3) The agreement must not impose on the undertakings concerned restrictions which are not indispensable to the attainment of these objectives.
(4) The agreements must not afford such undertakings the possibility of eliminating competition in respect of a substantial part of the products in question.

The requirements that must be fulfilled before an agreement can be exempted from the prohibition in Article 101(1) were not changed by the reform of the notification procedure by Regulation (EC) No 1/2003. The conditions in Article 101(3) are cumulative so that all must be satisfied before exemption can be obtained. It is clear that the assessment of whether the conditions have been fulfilled leaves a wide discretion. Where this discretion is exercised by the Commission or by the national competition authorities, it must be assumed that it can be subjected to a limited judicial review.[120]

In 2004, the Commission issued a more comprehensive Notice on the application of Article 101(3).[121] This Notice lays down a set of analytical frameworks for evaluating the four conditions, and it also contains a number of comments on each condition.

The *first condition* for obtaining an exemption is that the agreement should contribute to improving the effectiveness of the production or distribution of goods or services, etc., or promoting technical or economic progress. For example, this could be an agreement between undertakings whereby they allocate the production of goods between them so that each concentrates on one area in which they specialise. The Commission has also had a positive approach to joint ventures as, among other things, it has found that joint ventures can contribute to the fulfilment of a number of general economic goals, including the integration of the internal market, the promotion of risk-bearing investments and innovation, the opening of new markets, and the improvement of the competitiveness of industry, not least among small and medium-sized enterprises.

In its Notice, the Commission lays down some general principles for evaluating this condition. First, only objective advantages are taken into consideration, so there must be evidence of all improvements in effectiveness so they can be tested. It should not only be possible to test the nature of the improvements but also that there is a sufficient causal connection between the agreement and the improvements claimed.[122]

There can be different kinds of efficiency gains. For example, there can be cost savings, which can be achieved through the development of new technology and production methods. Cost savings can also be made by the effects of synergy or by two undertakings deciding to combine their production so as to gain economies of scale.

In addition to this, there can be efficiency gains in the form of improved quality. The obvious example of this is agreements on joint research and development (R&D), which can result in new or improved products which the undertakings involved would not been able to develop individually. Qualitative efficiency gains can also be achieved by introducing more effective means of distribution.

The *second condition* for obtaining an exemption under Article 101(3) is that consumers should obtain a fair share of the benefits from the efficiency gains achieved as a result of the first condition. The requirement that consumers should get a fair share

---

120. The judgments of the GC in Joined Cases T-185/00 and others, *Métropole Télévision (M6)*, and Case T-168/01, *GlaxoSmithKline Services*, show that the GC does not refrain from examining the Commission's assessment or from setting aside an exemption if the Commission's assessment is clearly wrong. The CJ has also emphasised that the GC should not refrain from examining the Commission's legal classification of financial information. Thus, the GC should not merely examine the substantive correctness of the evidence relied on and its trustworthiness and context but should also ensure that the information given constitutes all the relevant information that must be taken into account; *see*, among others, Case C-67/13 P, *Groupement des cartes bancaires (CB)*.
121. Commission Notice – Guidelines on the effect on trade concept contained in Article 81(3) of the Treaty (OJ 2004 C 101/97).
122. Commission Notice – Guidelines on the effect on trade concept contained in Article 81(3) of the Treaty (OJ 2004 C 101/97), paras 51–52.

of the benefits can be seen as a sign that the agreement gives certain benefits to society, whereby one of the aims of the competition rules can also be achieved – *see* section 5.1 in this chapter.

There seems to be a requirement that, for the parties to an agreement to allow a reasonable share of the improvements to go to consumers, there must be a certain measure of competition in the market. If there is no such competition, whereby consumers can switch to another product if their chosen product becomes more expensive, there will not be a motivation for the undertakings to reduce prices. Where there is no such competition, it is nevertheless possible that the parties will prefer to reduce prices in order to prevent the agreement from being found invalid.

The advantage that consumers are to obtain can be expressed in various ways, for example, by lower prices, better quality, greater choice, etc. The practice of the Commission suggests that there are not very high evidential requirements for showing that this condition is fulfilled, as the Commission seems to assume that the requirements will normally be satisfied where there is sufficient competition.[123]

The *third condition* means that it must be shown that the negative effects of an agreement on competition must not be unreasonable in relation to the contribution of the agreement to economic or technological progress.[124] However, in practice, it can be very difficult to make such an assessment, as there are no tools for deciding how the advantages and disadvantages should be weighed, both individually and especially in relation to each other. Therefore, this area is left to the wide discretion of the Commission and the other competition authorities, which will, in future, assess whether the conditions for an exemption are fulfilled. Commission Notice – Guidelines on the effect on trade concept contained in Article 81(3) [now Article 101(3)] of the Treaty (2004) does give certain guidelines for the exercise of this discretion, though without limiting it significantly.

The Notice states that it is not just the agreement as such which must achieve the effectivity gains; this also applies to the individual terms of the agreement.[125] This means that, first, there must be an assessment of whether there is an alternative to the agreement, and if it is not possible to point to such alternative, there must be an evaluation of whether the individual terms in the agreement go further than is necessary.

The CJ has confirmed that it can be relevant to assess whether a joint venture is strictly necessary to enable the companies which set it up to enter a market.[126] This will not be the case where some of the joint venture partners could have carried out the joint venture activity on their own. This means that the assessment of the third condition can result in a conclusion that an agreement or a joint venture is unnecessary since some other form of cooperation could lead to more or less the same effectivity gains. The consequence of this is that, when entering into their cooperation agreement,

---

123. Commission Decision 91/301/EEC, *Ansac* (OJ 1991 L 152/54), paras 29–30, is one of the rare examples of where the Commission did not find the condition was fulfilled.
124. Case T-17/93, *Matra Hachette v. Commission*, para. 135.
125. Commission Notice – Guidelines on the effect on trade concept contained in Article 81(3) of the Treaty (OJ 2004 C 101/97), para. 73.
126. Case T-17/93, *Matra Hachette v. Commission*, para. 138.

the undertakings involved must make a corresponding assessment of the alternatives to the proposed agreement or joint venture. It is clear that such an assessment can be difficult for the parties, but it must be even more difficult for the competition authorities to assess whether such an alternative is a realistic possibility. For this reason, one may expect a certain reticence on this point, and this is confirmed by a reading of the Notice on the application of Article 101(3). It is stated in paragraph 75 of the Commission Notice that undertakings invoking the benefit of Article 101(3) are not required to consider hypothetical or theoretical alternatives, as the Commission will not second-guess the business judgment of the parties. The Commission will only intervene where it is reasonably clear that there are realistic and attainable alternatives.

The *fourth condition* is that it does not give the undertakings the possibility of eliminating competition in respect of a substantial part of the products in question. This assessment is based on, among other things, the market structure, the number of competitors and their size, etc. This condition is closely linked to the question of abuse of dominant position. If there is no competition on the market, it will be difficult for the undertakings to show that it is probable that the advantages of the agreement in question will outweigh the disadvantages. In recent years, it has been debated how to allow undertakings to enter into agreements aiming to promote sustainability objectives, such as protecting the environment, the climate or human rights, without infringing Article 101.[127] This may be achieved either by adjusting the application of Article 101(1) to make sure that agreements promoting sustainability are less likely to be caught or by taking the sustainability objective into consideration when assessing whether the agreement should be exempted under Article 101(3). The solution chosen by the Commission uses both of these models. Instead of changing the 2004 notice on the application of Article 101(3), the Commission has incorporated some comments on sustainability in its new guidelines on vertical agreements and horizontal cooperation agreements. In both sets of guidelines, the Commission attests to its intent to promote sustainable development.[128] The starting point may be that such agreements should be evaluated as other agreements, but to some extent, the sustainability objective of the agreements may be taken into account.[129] This may both affect the assessment under Article 101(1), but may also make it easier to get an exemption under Article 101(3).[130] This is especially elaborated in relation to sustainability agreements between competitors; *see* further Chapter 4, section 8.

---

127. *See Eva vander Zee*: Quantifying Benefits of Sustainability Agreements Under Article 101 TFEU, World Competition 2020 pp. 189–208, *David Wouters*: Which Sustainability Agreements Are Not Caught by Article 101(1) TFEU, Journal of European Competition Law & Practice 2021 pp. 257–270 and Martin Gassler: Sustainability, the Green Deal and Art 101 TFEU, Journal of European Competition Law & Practice 2021 pp. 430–442.
128. *See* the Guideline on vertical restraints, OJ 2022 C 248/01, para. 8 and the Guidelines for horizontal cooperation agreements, para. 3 and paras 517–518.
129. *See* the Guideline on vertical restraints, OJ 2022 C 248/01, para. 8 and the Guidelines for horizontal cooperation agreements, para. 533.
130. *See* the Guideline on vertical restraints, OJ 2022 C 248/01, para. 9 (as these refer to the more elaborate accounts in the Guidelines for horizontal cooperation agreements) and the Guidelines for horizontal cooperation agreements, paras 556–596.

When assessing whether such agreements could be exempted under Article 101(3), the Guidelines point out that such agreements may provide for different efficiency gains such as producing cleaner production and distribution, less pollution, etc.[131] Such efficiency gains still need to be substantiated. The second condition that consumers should obtain a fair share of the benefits from the efficiency gains may, according to the Commission, be fulfilled in different ways. First, the agreement may ensure better or cheaper products, which evidently will benefit the consumers. However, the fact that the agreements ensure that the environment is spared or that human rights are protected may not, as such, provide the consumer with any benefits. The Commission, however, accepts that the consumer may have more indirect benefits resulting from the fact that the consumer appreciates the impact of their sustainable consumption on others. These benefits are termed 'individual non-use value benefits'. Finally, the Commission accepts that there may be collective benefits, where the benefits are not linked to the individual consumers' appreciation of the product but the collective benefits of consumers.[132] By expanding on what constitutes a benefit for consumers, the Commission has made it easier for agreements pursuing sustainability objectives to be exempted.

6.3 Block Exemptions

The block exemption system was established by Regulation No 19/65/EEC and was later developed by several other authorising regulations.[133] The reason why the block exemption system was introduced was that the Commission could already see in the early 1960s that Regulation (EEC) No 17/62 and the system introduced with that Regulation, with a requirement for notification to the Commission in order to obtain an exemption from Article 101(1), led to an impossibly large number of notifications, far exceeding the Commission's resources to deal with it.[134] At the same time, it was recognised that certain categories of agreements had so many advantageous effects and so few harmful ones that it was possible to set up an arrangement whereby all agreements within a certain category were exempted without having to be notified to the Commission. Today, block exemptions play an important role in the EU system of competition law.

The most important block exemptions are all dealt with in this book. On block exemptions for vertical agreements, *see* Chapter 3. On block exemptions that primarily concern horizontal agreements (agreements on specialisation, research and development), *see* Chapter 4. For technology transfer agreements, *see* Chapter 5.

---

131. Guidelines for horizontal cooperation agreements, paras 558–559.
132. Guidelines for horizontal cooperation agreements, paras 569–589.
133. *See*, among others, Regulation (EEC) No 2821/71 on research and development, and Regulation (EEC) No 1534/91 on the insurance sector.
134. *See* the White Paper of 5 December 1999 on modernisation of the rules implementing Articles 85 and 86 of the EC Treaty, para. 25.

7 THE CONSEQUENCES OF INFRINGEMENT

Chapter 7 contains a more detailed description of the procedure for enforcing Articles 101 and 102, as well as the consequences of infringing these provisions. For this reason, the following comments will only illustrate some of the special consequences of infringing Article 101.

The primary consequence of an infringement of Article 101 is the invalidity of the agreement, and a fine is also normally imposed. In addition, in connection with the finding of an infringement of Article 101(1), a number of conditions can be imposed on the parties to ensure that the infringement is brought to an end, and it is also possible that the parties to an agreement can be required to pay compensation.

7.1 Invalidity

The immediate consequence of an infringement of Article 101 is that the agreement is considered invalid; in other words, it has no legal effect, *see* Article 101(2). The effect of invalidity does not require it to be shown that Article 101(1) has been infringed, as the invalidity applies retrospectively *(ex tunc)*. In principle, it is only those parts of an agreement that contain restrictions on competition that are affected by the invalidity. However, if it is not possible to separate the invalid terms from the rest of the agreement, the whole agreement will be invalid.[135]

The parties to an agreement which was covered by Article 101(1) but which fulfilled the conditions for exemption under Article 101(3) could previously not claim that the agreement was valid before the Commission had exempted the agreement. Since the introduction of Regulation (EC) No 1/2003, the situation is such that an agreement which fulfils the conditions in Article 101(3) will be valid, without requiring authorisation from the competent authority; *see* Article 1 of the Regulation.

The effect of invalidity applies in full to the relationship between the undertakings that are party to the agreement. This means that they cannot rely on invalid agreements or conditions, and they cannot be enforced. The question of whether the effects of invalidity also affect third parties is decided under national law. For example, if a joint venture agreement is declared invalid, it is clear that this can have wide-ranging consequences for third parties, such as the customers and creditors of the joint venture. In principle, the formation of a company can be invalidated if the formation of the company is contrary to Article 101(1).[136]

Article 101(1) has direct effect, which means that the provision may be relied upon in proceedings against an undertaking before the national courts.[137] In relation to a cartel or a joint venture, a third party who believes that the cartel or joint venture

---

135. Case C-234/89, *De limitis*, para. 40.
136. In the case of a limited company, the effects of invalidity must be implemented in accordance with Art. 12 of the Consolidated Company Law Directive (Directive 2017/1132), which requires that companies which have been invalidly formed should be liquidated by means of compulsory winding up.
137. Case 127/73, *BRT*, para. 16.

contravenes Article 101, for example, because the third party undertaking is excluded from participation, can bring the question before the national courts. A case can also be brought by one of the undertakings, which is a party to the agreement if it believes that the agreement entered into is contrary to Article 101 so that it cannot be enforced between the parties. This means that in certain situations a party that wants to get out of a disadvantageous cooperation or wishes to be released from some disadvantageous terms in the agreement which forms the basis of the cooperation can do so by reference to Article 101. However, the question of whether an agreement infringes Article 101 can also be raised by the national courts themselves in a case before them which concerns such cooperation.[138]

In practice, in many agreements, there will be an arbitration clause, and the arbitration clause can provide that the arbitrator shall not observe the competition rules. This can be agreed between the parties to the agreement because they are aware that their agreement cannot stand up to a close examination under competition law or because they want to avoid the uncertainty associated with such an examination. If, on the basis of such a provision, an arbitrator chooses not to deal with the question of whether an agreement is contrary to Article 101, then according to the CJ, this question can be brought before the national courts, which will be able to try an arbitration decision on the grounds of public policy.[139] Thus, an arbitration agreement cannot always prevent one of the parties to an agreement relying on Article 101.

7.2   Remedies and Commitments

According to Article 7 of Regulation (EC) No 1/2003, in connection with bringing an infringement to an end, the Commission may impose behavioural or structural remedies on the undertakings involved. 'Behavioural remedies' refers to conditions which require an undertaking to conduct its business in a particular way. 'Structural remedies' means that an undertaking is required to change its structure, for example, by returning it to what it was prior to entering into the unlawful agreement.[140] It is stated that structural remedies can only be imposed where there is no equally effective behavioural remedy.

According to Article 9 of the Regulation, the Commission also has the possibility of making binding a commitment by an undertaking in connection with a finding that

---

138. It depends on national law whether there is an obligation to apply these provisions automatically, but to the extent that a national court does have a duty to enforce certain national rules automatically, the corresponding duty applies in relation to Arts 101 and 102; see Joined Cases C-430/93 and C-431/93, *Van Schijndel*, para. 18. Under Regulation (EC) No 1/2003, Art. 3, 'Where the competition authorities of the Member States or national courts apply national competition law to agreements ... they shall also apply Article 81 of the Treaty to such agreements.'
139. Case C-126/97, *Eco Swiss China Time v. Benetton International*, para. 37. In the following paragraph, the CJ stated that Art. 101 is a public policy provision, so it is not against the New York Convention of 10 Jun. 1958 on the Recognition and Enforcement of Foreign Arbitral Awards to refrain from recognising an arbitration award that has failed to apply Art. 101.
140. Recital 12 in Regulation (EC) No 1/2003.

Article 101(1) has been infringed. It is the undertaking itself that offers the commitment in connection with the Commission's evaluation of the case, and if the Commission finds that the commitment is sufficient to remove its concerns, it can make the commitment binding on the undertaking.[141]

7.3 Fines and Compensation

In Regulation (EC) No 1/2003, there are more detailed rules on the possibility of imposing fines for infringements of Articles 101 (and 102). The detailed rules on the calculation of fines and the possibility of exemptions or reductions are discussed in Chapter 7.

The question of compensation for breaches of Union competition law was not regulated in Union law. The questions of when compensation may be payable, what conditions must be fulfilled, and how it is calculated are thus questions which are determined under national law. However, this starting point is departed from in several circumstances. First, the CJ has ruled that while the rules on compensation are, in principle, governed by national law, national law must comply with the principles of equivalence and effectiveness. In Article 101 cases, the question of compensation will normally arise in relation to third parties who are injured by the effects of the agreement, which restricts competition, for example, because they have paid too much for their goods or perhaps have been excluded from the market. In principle, it is also possible that one party to an agreement could seek compensation from the other parties to the agreement. However, if the party seeking compensation has gone into the agreement with open eyes, it is hard to imagine that the conditions for obtaining compensation will exist. Nevertheless, the CJ has held that national law may not entirely exclude the possibility of compensation in cases where one party does not bear a significant responsibility for the distortion of competition. In assessing this, it is necessary to focus on the economic and legal contexts of the parties, as well as their respective negotiating positions. If, accordingly, a party is in a clearly subordinate position in relation to the other party or parties, it may be possible for the subordinate party to obtain compensation.[142] The CJ is also of the view that national law may not exclude the possibility of seeking compensation from a cartel in situations where an undertaking has suffered loss by buying goods at artificial prices from undertakings that are not part of the cartel. Where a cartel is effective, this can lead to undertakings that are not part of the cartel being able to raise their prices (umbrella pricing), so the customers of such undertakings can suffer losses even when buying from undertakings that are outside the cartel. Even where there is no direct link between the loss suffered

---

141. Earlier on the CJ had signalled that they were reluctant to test the validity of commitments, but in its judgment in Case C-132/19 P, *Groupe Canal +*, the CJ did for the first time set aside a commitment.
142. Case C-453/99, *Courage v. Crehan*, paras 31–33. See similarly Joined Cases C-295–298/04, *Manfredi*.

and the cartel, the CJ has found that the full effect of Article 101 would be put at risk if the payment of compensation were to be denied in such situations.[143]

Directive 2014/104/EU on antitrust damages actions regulates certain aspects of the Member States' rules on liability to pay compensation. The Directive codifies the principles of effectiveness and equivalence, and it contains rules on the presentation of evidence to make it easier for those who have suffered loss to prove their loss. The Directive also contains provisions on limitation periods, joint and several liability, the passing-on of losses and the quantifying of damage. The Directive is discussed in more detail in Chapter 7.

Bibliography

David Bailey & Laura Elizabeth John (eds): *Bellamy & Child, European Union Law of Competition*, 8th ed., 2018.
Roger J. Van den Bergh with Peter Camessasca & Andrea Giannaccari: *Comparative Competition Law and Economics*, 2017.
Jonathan Faull & Ali Nikpay (eds): *The EC Law of Competition*, 3rd ed., 2014.
Richard Whish & David Bailey: *Competition Law*, 10th ed., 2021.

---

143. *See* Case C-557/12, *Kone AG*. *See also* Case C-536/11, *Donau Chemie AG*, according to which the Member States cannot make the provision, to a third party who is considering seeking compensation, of documents relating to competition proceedings conditional on all the parties to the proceedings agreeing to this.

CHAPTER 3
Vertical Agreements

1   INTRODUCTION

In recent years, vertical agreements under EU competition law have been the focus of considerable attention, not just in connection with the regulatory work of the Commission, the Council and the European Parliament, but also in the practice of the courts and in legal academic writings. The legal literature has been based on a number of specific cases where the EU's legal authorities have had to decide on the validity of contractual arrangements of this kind under EU competition law.[1]

From the point of view of the smaller Member States, this interest in the subject is due to the fact vertical agreements will often be a practical method for use by small- and medium-sized enterprises which wish to extend their marketing activities to the wider European market, and this is an interest which is unlikely to decrease in intensity as the market grows with the accession of new Member States.

Vertical agreements are contractual arrangements between undertakings which, according to the content of the agreements, are at different levels of the production or distribution chain. For example, this would apply to an agreement between the producer of goods and a wholesaler who buys goods from the producer with a view to selling them onwards to retailers on a particular market.[2] If the wholesale level is cut out, a vertical agreement can exist between the producer and the retailer.

---

1. Even prior to the first block exemption regulation, Regulation No 67/67/EEC on the application of Art. 85(3) of the Treaty to certain categories of exclusive dealing agreements, the CJ had laid down some principles on the permissibility of and prohibition of certain key restrictive terms in these kinds of contracts. For example, *see* the discussion below of Case 56/65, *Société Technique Minière v. Maschinenbau Ulm*, and Joined cases 56 and 58/64, *Consten and Grundig v. Commission*.
2. Agreements between wholesalers and retailers are also vertical agreements. The same applies to agreements between two producers, A and B, of substitutable goods if, for example, under the agreement A appoints B as its agent in a market, without B correspondingly selling goods to A, in other words, without there being a market-sharing agreement between the parties.

In addition to this, there are *horizontal agreements*, which are agreements between undertakings on the same level of the production or distribution chain. Horizontal agreements are discussed in more detail in Chapter 4. Such agreements exist when they have a 'Community dimension', affecting trade between Member States, etc., see Article 101(1) of the Treaty on the Functioning of the European Union (TFEU), and are considered as being a potential hindrance to the achievement of the goal of market integration. In contrast to vertical agreements, horizontal agreements have an inherent tendency to lead to market sharing, as the parties to such agreements can clearly be considered to be actual or potential competitors and to be in a position to enforce 'naked restrictions'[3] on their part of the shared market.

Only a minority of the producers who supply the internal market undertake the distribution of their goods to the end users themselves.

Instead, producers use specialised agents who have their place of business in the chosen export market. The competition for customers will often be won by the producer who has chosen a distribution chain whose marketing is more effective and has a higher service level than that of other distributors. For example, the developments in information technology in recent years and the use of modern 'just in time' methods, which rely on good logistics for the stockholding of goods, have meant that it is the precise planning of the demand for goods, and not for the needs of production, which are decisive for the movement of goods in the distribution chain. This puts the emphasis on closer cooperation between producers and distributors with a view to planning and sales strategies which are less demanding on resources.[4]

Among other things, such developments could change the terms of an arrangement between the producer and the distribution channel and could directly or

---

3. This term was used in earlier American legal practice as an expression of unilateral price setting and the exclusion of competitors from the market. In contrast to this there are 'ancillary restraints', which are restrictions on competition which are accessory to a transaction which is otherwise competitive; compare with Art. 2(3) of Commission Regulation (EU) No 720/2022 on the application of Art. 101(3) of the TFEU to categories of vertical agreements and concerted practices, and the more detailed discussion in s. 3 below. Ancillary restraints is a special term in common law countries which has arisen as a necessary consequence of the fact that s. 1 of the Sherman Act does not allow for a dispensation corresponding to that in Art. 101(3) TFEU. Refer also to the comments below on the *rule of reason* doctrine and Case T-112/99, *Métropole Télévision (M6)*. See also Valentine Korah & Denis O'Sullivan: *Distribution Agreements under the EC Competition Rules*, 2002 pp. 83–84.
4. If a producer chooses to undertake its own distribution and sales, or if it undertakes this through companies in the same corporate group (vertical integration), the assumption will be that there will not be an infringement of Art. 101(1) TFEU, as there will not be any agreement between 'undertakings' within the meaning of competition law.

    In mixed agreements, for example a distribution agreement between two competitors, A and B, where A undertakes to sell B's products and B undertakes to sell A's products, the horizontal nature of the agreement between the parties will be looked at first. Only if these relations fall outside the scope of Art. 101(1) will it be necessary to assess whether the vertical aspects are acceptable, i.e., that they do not restrict competition.

    A distribution chain can sometimes consist of three links, for example in the way that a producer has a vertical relation to one or more wholesalers, who in turn have sales arrangements with a number of dealers who have vertical agreements with the end users of the products. Art. 101 applies to each of these separate agreements. Thus, depending on the circumstances, an independent assessment in relation to Art. 101 must be made for each of the three arrangements.

indirectly have a knock-on effect on the ability of less competitive producers and distributors to compete for customers.

This dynamic, which characterises the distribution chain, will, therefore, create new demands for competition rules which the actors on the market will have to operate under. At the same time this development will bring new challenges for the authorities, both at national and Community levels, which will have to consider complaints about restrictions on competition which will arise as activities develop in the distribution chain.

As far as the Community is concerned, both in legislation and in practice, the Council, the Commission and the Courts (both the Court of Justice of the European Union (CJ) and the General Court (GC)) are constantly aware of the possible restrictions on competition arising from parts of agreements or concerted practices between undertakings at different levels of the production and distribution chain. Competition between supply chains increases as the battle for the favour of end users is fought by an increasing number of producers and/or distributors.

2 THE COMPETITION LAW APPROACH TO VERTICAL RESTRAINTS: ARTICLE 101(1) TFEU AND THE BLOCK EXEMPTION REGULATIONS

Vertically restrictive agreements are a controversial element of Union competition law. This does not apply only to determining the definition of vertical agreements as distinct from horizontal agreements; *see* above in section 1. Critics have questioned whether there is any general need, on the grounds of competition, to intervene against vertical restraints.[5]

Among other things, because of the decisions in Case 56/65, *Société technique v. Maschinenbau Ulm*, Joined Cases 56 and 58/64, *Consten and Grundig v. Kommissionen*, and Case 32/65, *Italy v. Council and Commission et al.*, on the basis of the authorising Regulation No 65/65/EEC, the Commission adopted Regulation No 67/67/EEC, containing guidelines in abstract form regarding the circumstances under which contracting undertakings could be exempt from the provision of Article 85(3) of the EEC Treaty [now Article 101(3) TFEU]. Regulation No 67/67/EEC dealt with block exemptions for certain categories of exclusive dealing agreements. Regulation No 67/67/EEC and the subsequent block exemption Regulation (EC) No 2790/1999 on the application of Article 101(3) TFEU to categories of vertical agreements and concerted practices have later been replaced by Regulation (EU) No 330/2010 on the application of Article 101(3) TFEU to categories of vertical agreements and concerted practices. With effect from 1 June 2022, this Regulation has, however, been replaced by Commission Regulation 720/2022 of 10 May 2022 on the application of Article 101(3) of the TFEU to categories of vertical agreements and concerted practices.

---

5. As early as in Joined Cases 56 and 58/64, *Consten and Grundig v. Commission* (discussed below), it was ruled that Art. 101(1) could apply to both vertical and horizontal restrictions on competition.

When the Court of Justice, the GC or the Commission have had to decide on competition matters, their considerations in this respect have, for all practical purposes, been separated from the interpretation of the block exemptions, and the case law is thus still of essential importance. It is on this basis that the following review is made of the case law concerning a number of practical agreements as well as of the theoretical arguments linked to Article 101(1) TFEU and its predecessor provisions. Given the guidelines established by the courts, there is a sound basis for giving a more precise presentation of the conditions under which Regulation (EU) No 720/2022 and the exemption criteria in Article 101(3) create a 'safe harbour' for undertakings which want to keep their contractual arrangements free from intervention by the competition authorities. The development of the block exemption regulations up to the present Regulation (EU) No 720/2022 is described below in section 2.2.

2.1   Article 101(1) TFEU

Elements of vertical agreements that restrict competition have traditionally been treated more leniently by the competition authorities than has been the case for horizontal restrictions. This tendency can be explained to some extent by the fact that the parties in a cross-border vertical agreement operate at different levels of trade and so they will not typically be actual or potential competitors on the market. It is also relevant that it is widely recognised that vertical agreements will often have been beneficial for effectiveness and that the terms of agreements, which will, to a large extent, protect a producer from attack, can sometimes be a commercial necessity for the producer wanting to sell its products in as many markets as possible in the EU.

However, in general, the desire to adopt a stricter approach to restrictive agreements is supported by the fundamental reasoning behind the EU competition rules, namely that in creating a transparent and effective internal market, measures should be taken against agreements and concerted practices which restrict the potential activities of market participants. Among other things, this tendency is expressed in the Commission's guidelines on vertical restraints; see the Commission Communication 2022/C 248/01 of 30 June 2022, referred to here as the 'Vertical Restraints Guidelines'. Given its status as an 'information', the Vertical Restraints Guidelines do not alter the exiting practice of the Court of Justice or the GC. However, in their detailed form, they are an important indicator of the area in which vertical restraints can cause problems or advantages for the creation of an effectively functioning internal market. The Vertical Restraints Guidelines are closely linked to the purpose of Article 101, which is to ensure that market participants do not use agreements (in this context, vertical agreements) to the disadvantage of one of the parties in a cross-border arrangement, for the unreasonable advantage of the other party or of end users.

In general, these considerations lead to the recognition that the competition authorities ought to intervene against vertical agreements which contain certain forms of particularly serious restrictions on trade, including certain forms of absolute territorial protection, for example, where third-party undertakings are prevented from trading in larger or smaller parts of the market if the area in question has been allocated to another trader as their exclusive territory. Another main area has been decisions addressing agreements where the restrictions have consisted of maintaining fixed prices in subsequent links of the distribution chain (resale price maintenance).

2.1.1   Territorial Protection: Dividing Up Markets

Article 101(1)(c) TFEU expressly prohibits the 'share markets or sources of supply'. The case law of the Court of Justice has considered this part of Article 101(1).

In Case 56/65, *Société technique v. Maschinenbau Ulm*, the CJ established that an exclusive dealing arrangement is not automatically in breach of Article 81(1) (now Article 101(1)) if: (1) it does not prohibit the concessionaire from re-exporting to any other markets; (2) it does not include an undertaking by the grantor to prohibit concessionaires in other Member States from selling the products in the concessionaire's territory; and (3) it does not fetter the right of dealers and consumers in the concessionaire's territory to obtain supplies through parallel imports from other Member States (other than that the concessionaire may not, without the consent of the grantor, sell goods likely to compete with the goods with which the concession is concerned).

At the same time, the CJ stated that the decision of whether there is a restriction on competition must be based on the conditions of competition as within the actual context in which it would occur in the absence of the agreement in dispute.[6] In order to be able to judge whether an agreement may be found prohibited on the grounds of the restriction of competition, which is its purpose or effect, it is necessary to decide how the competition would have developed if the agreement did not exist. For this purpose, it is necessary to take into account: the nature of the products that are covered by the agreement and whether or not their quantity is restricted; the positions of the parties and the significance of the goods in question on the market; and whether the agreement is an isolated agreement or is part of a large or small network of agreements. In other words, depending on the circumstances, a commercial agreement may be found unlawful if it contains provisions that are capable of creating artificial profit-based obstacles that restrict the free flow of goods between Member States and ultimately hold up the completion of the internal market.

The *Maschinenbau Ulm* case and the *Grundig* case were important steps towards creating clarity about the extent to which territorial restrictions could be agreed upon without intervention by the competition authorities, and at the same time, the decisions give guidance on the content of two earlier block exemption agreements for exclusive dealing agreements: Regulation No 67/67/EEC, and its replacement Regulation (EEC) No 1983/83. Despite the fact that the *Grundig* case, in particular, has sometimes been over-interpreted, the decision still stands as a leading case on Union competition law:

---

6. This approach, which has been repeated in a number of subsequent decisions, is one of the most important elements in the distinction between lawful and unlawful agreements that turns upon Art. 101(1).

In 1957, the German company Grundig entered into a contract for an unlimited period with the French trading company Consten, Paris, whereby Consten was given exclusive distribution rights for radio and television sets etc., and accessories to these in an agreed territory consisting of France, the Saar district and Corsica.

Consten undertook to buy an agreed minimum quota, buy in stocks regularly in advance, maintain a repair workshop with a stock of spare parts, take on guarantee obligations and customer service, and refrain from selling similar competing products and from selling either directly or indirectly to markets in other countries. Consten's exclusive distributorship meant that Grundig was obliged to delegate to Consten retail sales within the agreed territory and to refrain from selling, directly or indirectly, to other persons in the territory. Already prior to the Grundig/Consten contract, Grundig had required its German wholesalers and distributors not to supply from their own agreed territories into other territories.

In October 1957, Consten had the trade mark GINT (Grundig International) registered in France in its own name. This trade mark was registered internationally as Grundig's trade mark and was used on all Grundig's apparatus produced in Germany. In this connection, in January 1959, Consten declared that the trade mark GINT would only be used on Grundig's apparatus and that the trade mark rights would be assigned to Grundig or be revoked when the exclusive distribution agreement with Grundig was terminated.

When Consten found out that since April 1961, another French trading company, UNEF, had been buying Grundig apparatus from German wholesalers (which had therefore acted contrary to the export prohibition imposed on them by Grundig) and imported them to France, Consten brought a case against UNEF for *unfair competition and infringement of trademark rights.*

The case was brought before the Court of Appeal, which adjourned its hearing until a decision was given by the Commission in a case which UNEF had brought in March 1962 claiming that the agreement between Consten and Grundig should be declared an infringement of the Treaty.

Consten also brought a case claiming unfair competition before the Tribunal de Grande Instance in Strasbourg against Leissner, a radio retailer resident there, who had also bought Grundig sets in Germany with a view to selling them in France, in breach of Consten's exclusive distribution rights. This case was also adjourned.

In accordance with the then-applicable rules in Regulation 17/62, Grundig notified the Commission of its agreements with Consten and with exclusive distributors in other EC countries. After hearing the involved undertakings and the national authorities, in September 1964, the Commission gave its decision on the agreement between Grundig and Consten.

In the Official Journal in the same year (p. 2545 – there is no English version) when the case was published, it was stated:

> that the exclusive distribution agreement of April 1957 and the agreement for the registration and use of the trade mark GINT was contrary to Article 85(1)[Article 101(1) TFEU] of the Treaty,
> that a request for an exemption in accordance with Article 85(3) [Article 101(3) TFEU] was denied, and
> that Grundig and Consten were required to refrain from any measures which could hinder third parties or make it more difficult for them to obtain the goods covered by the agreement from wholesalers or distributors within the Community with a view to reselling them within the agreed territory.

Both Grundig and Consten referred this decision to the CJ, demanding that the decision should be repealed in its entirety. The two cases were joined in proceedings before the Court. UNEF and Leissner participated in the case on the Commission's side, while the plaintiffs' argument, which was of a general legal character, was supported by the Italian and German governments.

The Court substantially found in favour of the Commission's decision, though it did say that the Commission should either have confined itself to the operative part of the decision to declare that an infringement only lay in those parts of the agreement which came within the prohibition, or it should have set out the reasons why those parts did not appear to be severable from the whole agreement in the preamble to the decision.[7]

In addition to this, the Court expressed the view that neither the wording of Article 81 [now Article 101] nor of Article 82 [now Article 102] gives any basis for distinguishing between these two Treaty provisions with regard to the position of undertakings in the distribution chain and it therefore denied that Article 101(1) should only apply to *horizontal* agreements and not equally to *vertical* agreements. In the view of the Court, distortion of competition, within the meaning of Article 101(1), could be caused not only by agreements which restrict competition between the parties to the agreement but also by agreements which hinder or restrict competition which would otherwise exist between a party to the agreement and a third party. In this respect too, it was not significant whether the parties were in the same economic position or functionally at the same level.

In stating its reasons for finding the agreement partially invalid, the Court laid decisive weight on the fact that even if it does not involve abuse of a dominant position, an exclusive distribution agreement can affect trade between the Member States, and it can have the object or effect of restricting or distorting competition contrary to Article 101(1). However, exclusive distribution agreements concluded between a producer and a sole representative do not necessarily fall foul of the prohibition in Article 101(1). However, an agreement between a producer and a distributor, which is aimed at re-establishing national barriers to trade between Member States, would be contrary to the fundamental aims of the Community. The Court hereby expressed the view, which was later expressed in general legislation [e.g., Article 3 of Regulation No 1983/83, Article 4 of Regulation No 2790/99, Article 4 of Regulation (EU) No 330/2010 and now Article 4 of Regulation (EU) 720/2022], that the Treaty, which according to its preamble and its enacting terms has the aim of removing obstacles to trade between Member States, and which has strict provisions to prevent the re-establishment of such obstacles, cannot allow undertakings to create new obstacles by means of agreements. In support of this, the Court stated – as has been repeated since – that what is decisive in relation to Article 101(1) is whether an agreement is actually or potentially calculated to affect freedom of trade and not whether such negative effects can, in fact, be shown to have occurred.

---

7. Compare with the comments below in s. 5.4 on the legal situation if invalidity under Art. 101(2) affects only *part* of an agreement.

In assessing whether the agreement between Grundig and Consten constituted a restriction on competition contrary to Article 101(1), the Court next had to decide whether the prohibition referred to competition in interchangeable products of different brands (*inter-brand* competition) or whether it was sufficient that the agreement involved a restriction of trade in Grundig's products (*intra-brand* competition).

> On this, the Court stated that the principle of free competition must apply to all levels of trade and all forms of competition. The possibility that competition between producers in general may be more openly expressed than competition between traders in the same brand does not necessarily mean that an agreement which restricts competition between such traders will escape prohibition under Article 101(1). In other words, when determining whether a restriction of competition existed contrary to Article 101(1), it was sufficient that the agreement was capable of restricting competition between traders in Grundig's products, in other words that there was *intra-brand* competition.[8] Therefore, in the view of the Court, the Commission was right to apply an overall assessment of the system which Grundig had constructed and on this basis determined that the infringement of Article 101(1) followed from the geographic isolation which Consten had obtained under French law by means of the agreement. Within the contract territory, Consten had wished to exclude all forms of competition in the contract goods in the wholesale sector and for this purpose had used two approaches:
>
>> First, Grundig had undertaken not to supply to third parties, either directly or indirectly, such goods as were intended for the contract territory. The effect of this obligation in restricting the territory was clearly apparent since Consten and all Grundig's exclusive agents, as well as all German wholesalers, had been prevented from exporting. Second, the trade mark GINT had been registered in France in Consten's name (a trade mark which Grundig applied to all its products) with the aim of strengthening protection against parallel imports to France of Grundig's products which were covered by the exclusive distribution agreement, by means of the protection given by the intellectual property (trade mark) right. Thus, no third party could sell imported Grundig products from other Member States with a view to reselling them without running considerable risk.

The Court summarised its objections to the agreement between Grundig and Consten as follows: the Commission properly took into account the whole distribution system set up by Grundig in order to obtain a true picture of the contractual position of the contract in the economic and legal context in which it was concluded by the parties. The picture obtained showed the isolation of the French market, making it possible to charge higher prices for the products in question, which were sheltered from effective

---

8. In his Opinion, *Advocate General Roemer* proposed that the Court should reverse the Commission's decision because the Commission had failed to take into account possible competition from other producers.

competition. The more producers succeed in their efforts to render their own brands distinct in the eyes of the consumer, the more the effectiveness of competition between producers tends to diminish. It is pointless to compare the situation, to which Article 101 applies, of a producer bound by a sole distributorship agreement with a distributor of their products with that of a producer who undertakes the distribution of their own products by some means, for example, by commercial representatives, to which Article 101 does not apply.

Under the doctrine of a per se prohibition, which has been developed in American antitrust law, certain specified forms of agreement, including agreements on prices, are declared to be automatically illegal. This means, for example, that it is not necessary to prove in each case that an agreement binding prices in subsequent levels of the distribution chain have restricted competition. And even if an agreement has certain positive effects, it is not subject to any rule of reason examination.[9]

The starting point for Article 101(1)(b) TFEU is that a distribution agreement is not covered by a block exemption if the distributor is subject to an obligation not to execute orders received from dealers situated outside the area covered by the agreement or received from a customer who is not part of the group of customers covered by the agreement.

A prohibition against fulfilling orders from customers outside the territory or group of customers which has been allocated to a dealer (passive sales) can be formulated as an express condition in the agreement (export prohibition) or as an obligation for the dealer to refer orders from 'foreigners' to other distributors.[10]

Indirectly, a sales prohibition can arise from special measures taken by the producer, for example, by the refusal or reduction of bonuses or discounts, reductions in supplies, or threats to terminate an agreement. A number of cases before the Court and Commission in connection with infringement of the prohibition have shown that various measures have been used by producers who have breached the prohibition; *see*, for example, 93/46/EEC: Commission Decision relating to a proceeding pursuant to Article 85 of the EEC Treaty (*Ford Agricultural*) (OJ 1993 L 20/1). It does not matter whether it is the seller or the buyer who takes the initiative to include the prohibition in the agreement. The illegality consists regardless of whether the prohibition is stated in the main agreement, whether it is hidden away in the seller's standard terms, or whether it has been enforced in trade between the seller and buyer. A finding of the existence of a concerted practice likewise fulfils the conditions for finding the existence of an agreement between the parties; *see* Case T-49/95, *Van Megen*, paragraph 35.

---

9. *See* the comments below in s. 2.1.4 on Case T-112/99, *Métropole Télévision (M6)*. *See also* Ch. 2, s. 5.4, above on the rule of reason.
10. *See* for example 2001/135/EC: Commission decision relating to a proceeding pursuant to Art. 81 of the EC Treaty (*Nathan-Bricolux*) (OJ 2001 L 54/1), where the Commission decided that a French undertaking, Editions Nathan, a publisher of educational books, by having exclusive distribution agreements which restricted its exclusive distributors from making passive sales outside their sales areas, and restricting the right of other dealers to make passive sales to customers within these areas, had infringed Art. 101(1) TFEU. Also, one of the distributors, the Belgian company Bricolux, was fined for having refrained from selling to customers outside its exclusive distribution area and for having encouraged Editions Nathan to restrict other dealers' sales in its own exclusive territory, contrary to Art. 101(1).

See also the decision of the Court in Case T-176/95, *Accinauto v. Commission*:

The Belgian company Accinauto (A) was BASF's exclusive distributor for Glasurit products in Belgium and Luxembourg. The exclusive distributorship agreement contained a provision under which A was required to refer all enquiries from customers outside the agreed sales territory to BASF. It was also clear from the agreement that A could neither advertise nor have supply depots outside the territory for the sale of the contract goods. A also undertook not to sell the goods to customers outside the agreed sales territory or to customers within the territory if A knew that they would sell the products on to customers outside the territory. In return, the producer bound itself to ensure that, as far as legally possible, other dealers respected A's sales territory.

The Court held that the agreement between the parties contained a covert prohibition against making passive sales outside the agreed sales territory. Furthermore, an investigation into how the agreement was carried out confirmed that the aim was to prevent imports of Glasurit products to the UK. The Commission had therefore correctly concluded that there was an infringement of Article 101(1).

The Commission had defined the relevant market as the British market for paint for car repairs. In 1991 BASF's share of this market was 16%, of which 12% was Glasurit products. In the view of the Court, such a market position, taken together with the fact that during the relevant period the prices for Glasurit products were higher in the UK than in other Member States, showed that the agreement could affect trade. Since, because of its purpose, the agreement already constituted a restriction on competition contrary to Article 101(1), the Court found that it was not necessary to investigate whether the agreement had appreciably affected the market; compare with the comments in section 5 below, according to which the hardcore provisions corresponding to Article 4(a) and (b) of the Regulation (EU) No 720/2022 would have effect, regardless of whether the market thresholds in Article 3 of the Regulation were exceeded.

The Court held that the infringement only came to an end when the parties revoked the provision in question. The fact that a provision which has the aim of restricting competition has not been enforced does not mean that the provision falls outside the scope of Article 101(1).

Agreed restrictions of the kind referred to can lead to the isolation of the market and hinder the integration of the market which is a fundamental aim of the EU's competition rules. In combination with other vertical restraints, for example, a prohibition on a dealer carrying competing products, inter-brand competition could be restricted. Intra-brand competition could also be hindered as permanent isolation of the market could be abused as part of a price differentiation strategy.

In Case C-306/20, 'Visma Enterprise' SIA, the Court ruled from another perspective of the distribution of agreements between distributors. In the above case, a decision should be made in connection with an agreement which a supplier and a distributor had entered into, according to which the distributor, who first registers a potential transaction with the end user, has 'priority in progressing the sale process' for a period of six months from the registration of the transaction unless the user objects. The Court stated that such an agreement could not be classified as an agreement which had as its 'object' to prevent, restrict or distort competition within the meaning of the provision unless the agreement, in view of its provisions, objectives and context, may be regarded as revealing such a sufficient degree of harm to competition as to be so classified. The Court furthermore pointed out that if such an agreement does not constitute a restriction of competition 'by object' within the meaning of Article 101(1) TFEU, the national court must examine whether, in the light of all the relevant circumstances of the case in the main proceedings, namely, *inter alia*, the economic and legal context in which the undertakings concerned operate, the nature of the goods or services affected, and the actual conditions of the functioning and structure of the market in question, that agreement may be regarded as restricting competition to a sufficiently appreciable degree due to its actual or potential effects.[11]

2.1.2 Prohibition of Re-export with Sales to Third Countries

In Case C-306/96, *Javico International v. Yves Saint Laurent Parfums*, the Court gave a preliminary ruling on whether a distributor based in a Member State, who had been entrusted with distributing agreed goods in agreed territories *outside the Community*, could be bound by the producer's prohibition on selling goods in territories other than those agreed. This includes whether the producer could validly prohibit the distributor from directly or indirectly re-exporting the goods to a territory within the Community:

> In 1992, the French undertaking Yves Saint Laurent Parfums (YSLP) entered into two distribution agreements with Javico International, which was based in Germany but which was not part of YSLP's selective distribution system in Europe, for the sales of the goods to Russia, the Ukraine and Slovenia.
>
> The distribution agreements contained conditions preventing Javico's own exports from these territories as well as obligations on Javico to impose such export prohibitions on its buyers. The referring French appeal court (Cour d'appel de Versailles) asked the Court to rule on the lawfulness of these prohibitions, in other words, on their compatibility with Article 101(1) TFEU.
>
> The Court took a step-by-step approach, as it began by stating that it was first necessary to consider whether, had they been in agreements that were only operative within the EU, the prohibitions on supply had the aim or effect of appreciably restricting competition within the Community, and whether this could affect trade between Member States. Next, the Court stated that it had itself previously established that an agreement which had the aim of preventing a distributor from freely choosing its customers by requiring the distributor only to sell to customers within an agreed territory constitutes a restriction within the meaning of Article 101(1).[12] Moreover, the Court added that it had previously established that an agreement which obliges a distributor not to sell the contract goods outside its sales territory has the aim of hindering parallel imports within the Community and thus restricts competition in the single market.[13] On this basis, the Court concluded that conditions of the kind referred to would in themselves constitute a restriction on competition in distribution agreements within the Community.[14] However, it is only possible to intervene against such measures which restrict competition if they can affect trade between Member States. The Court pointed out that a decision, agreement or concerted practice only has such an effect if, on the basis of a majority of objective, legal or actual circumstances, it

---

11. Case C-306/20, para. 82.
12. In this connection the Court referred to Case 86/82, *Hasselblad (GB) Limited v. Commission*, and Case C-70/93, *Bayerische Motorenwerke v. ALD Auto-Leasing*.
13. Case C-279/87, *Tipp-Ex v. Commission*.
14. Case 19/77, *Miller International Schallplatten v. Commission*.

can be predicted with a sufficient degree of certainty that it could have a direct or indirect, actual or potential influence on trade between Member States and in such a manner as to harm the realisation of the aims of the establishment of the single market. Furthermore, this influence must be significant.[15] Finally, the Court referred to the fact that, in deciding whether an agreement had such an influence, regard had to be had for the position and strength of the parties on the market for the goods in question.[16] For example, an exclusive distribution agreement with absolute territorial protection could fall outside the scope of the prohibition in Article 101(1) if it only has an insignificant effect on the market, given the weak position of the parties on the market for the goods traded.[17]

The Court then went on to consider the agreement's compatibility with Article 101(1), given that it was to apply to an area *outside the EU*.

On this, the Court started by stating that a provision prohibiting exports in an agreement of the kind in question should be interpreted as a provision that is not intended to prevent parallel imports and an offer for the sale of the goods on the single market. The provision should ensure that the supplier can penetrate a market outside the Community by selling a sufficient quantity of the goods covered by the agreement on the market. In the view of the Court, such an interpretation could be supported by the fact that the prohibition on sales outside the area covered by the agreement applied to all other third countries.

On the face of it, it does not seem justifiable to draw a distinction between the situation where goods are moved from one Member State to another – in which case the existence of an export prohibition would have been contrary to Article 101(1) – and the situation where a distributor is allocated a territory outside the Community. In both situations, the aim of exclusive distribution agreement seems to be that the distributor should concentrate its marketing efforts in the given area and not spread its efforts to other areas, whether these are within the Community or in a third country.

However, to a certain extent, the Court mitigated the effect of its main argument by adding that even if the provisions in the agreement in question were not considered as having the aim of restricting or distorting competition within the Community within the meaning of Article 101(1), it was up to the national court to decide whether they did in fact have this effect. In this connection, it could be relevant whether there was a significant price difference between goods sold outside the Community and goods sold inside the Community. Unlike a factor which could exclude the agreement from the scope of Article 101(1), it is noted that the Commission had previously exempted YSLP's selective distribution system from the prohibition in Article 101(1) in accordance with Article 101(3).[18]

In conclusion, it must be stated that the dismissive approach to agreements giving absolute territorial protection, which the CJ adopted already in the 1960s with,

---

15. Case 5/69, *Völk v. Vervaecke*.
16. Case 99/79, *Lancôme v. Etos*.
17. Joined Cases 100–103/80, *Pioneer v. Commission*.
18. *See* the Commission Decision on the *Yves Saint Laurent* distribution system (OJ 1992 L 12/24).

among others, the *Maschinenbau Ulm* and *Grundig* cases, has, in all essentials, been upheld by the CJ and the Commission in the succeeding decades. Undertakings must still expect that measures will be taken against such arrangements.

2.1.3 Fixed Prices: Article 101(1)(a) TFEU

The following discussion concerns the prohibition of the fixing of prices in subsequent links of the distribution chain.

The prohibition is found in Article 101(1)(a) and applies to agreements and/or concerted practices which consist of directly or indirectly fixed purchase or selling prices or any other trading conditions. The prohibition ranks as a serious (hardcore) restriction, which can thus only be derogated from under Article 101(3) under exceptional circumstances.

In principle, independent undertakings have an indisputable right to agree to the commercial terms of the agreements made between them. A competitive measure will only become relevant if the parties seek by their agreement to regulate trade with a third party. In other words, the prohibition affects third parties, such as a sole distributor, which, as part of its business, sells the goods that are subject to the agreement which it has bought from its counterparty, i.e., the producer or supplier of the products.

The prohibition affects *minimum sales prices*.[19] Maximum sales prices and recommended sales prices fall outside the scope of the prohibition unless they assume the character of fixed or minimum prices as a result of pressure exerted or incentives given by one of the parties. A maximum or recommended price may work as a focal point for resellers, leading to a more or less uniform application of that price level.[20]

See further the explanation in section 6.1.1. of the Vertical Restraints Guidelines, according to which the hardcore restriction referred to in Article 4(a) of the Block Exemption Regulation concerns the fixing of resale prices, i.e., agreements or concerted practices which are intended to directly or indirectly set a fixed or minimum resale price or a fixed or minimum price level which the buyer is required to comply with. With provisions in agreements or concerted practices that directly fix the resale price, the restriction is clear. However, prices can also be fixed indirectly. An example of this is an agreement setting trade margins or setting the maximum discount that a distributor may give in relation to a given price level. Direct or indirect means of fixing prices can be made more effective if they are combined with measures to identify traders who use lower prices, for example, by monitoring systems or by requiring retailers to report other members of the distribution network who do not use the fixed pricing level.

A producer's provision of a list with recommended or maximum prices is not *in itself* regarded as leading to price fixing. However, see 96/438/EC:

---

19. The corresponding provision in the Block Exemption Regulation (Regulation (EU) No 720/2022) is in Art. 4(a).
20. *See*, e.g., the judgments in Case C-279/06, *CEPSA*; and Case C-260/07, *Pedro IV Servicios*.

Commission Decision relating to a proceeding pursuant to Article 85 [Article 101 TFEU] of the EC Treaty (*Fenex*) (OJ 1996 L 181/28), according to which, by sending out recommended tariffs in the transport sector, an association of undertakings was regarded as having given expression to the association's wish to coordinate the members' pricing policies in the area concerned. This was found to constitute 'a decision by an association of undertakings' and was therefore contrary to Article 101(1) TFEU. At the same time, the Commission stated that such a result would not necessarily be linked to the sending out of information which could help undertakings calculate their own costs so that they could set their own prices. In the *Pronuptia* case (see below in section 4.2), the Court stated in paragraph 25 of the judgment that: 'Although provisions which impair the franchisee's freedom to determine his own prices are restrictive of competition, that is not the case where the franchisor simply provides franchisees with price guidelines, so long as there is no concerted practice between the franchisor and the franchisees or between the franchisees themselves for the actual application of such prices.'

See also 2001/711/EC: Commission Decision relating to a proceeding under Article 81 of the EC Treaty [Article 101 TFEU] (*Volkswagen*) (OJ 2001 L 262/14), where the Commission found that the aim of various of Volkswagen's circulars and notices to German dealers was to get them to comply with the recommended catalogue prices and submit to binding resale prices, in other words a restriction of intra-brand competition on price. The circumstances were similar in 97/123/EC: Commission Decision relating to a proceeding pursuant to Article 85 [Article 101 TFEU] of the EC Treaty and Article 53 of the EEA Agreement (*Novalliance/Systemform*) (OJ 1997 L 47/11), where all the agreements which a German company had entered into with its European distributors restricted their freedom to set their own sales prices, to a greater or lesser extent, and the distributors were required to inform the company of their policy on the granting of discounts.

The reason for the prohibition is that binding resale prices could lead to a restriction on competition between dealers who have bought goods under an agreement with the preceding link in the distribution chain. The producer's interference in the dealers' right to set their own resale prices is contrary to Article 101(1) TFEU, which states that parties may not 'directly or indirectly fix purchase or selling prices', which also applies to vertical agreements. Where there are binding or minimum resale prices, the dealer can no longer compete on price for the brand concerned, which can result in the complete elimination of intra-brand competition. A series of clauses or binding prices could have the same effect as a horizontal restriction on competition and lead to market sharing.[21] As long as binding prices cover goods which a dealer imports to the area from other dealers who are not subject to corresponding price restrictions, that

---

21. Valentine Korah & Warwick A. Rothnie: *Exclusive Distribution and the EEC Competition Rules*, 1992 p. 120 and p. 170.

dealer will be subject to competitive restraints which do not apply to other dealers who parallel import the goods to the area.[22] At the same time, the prohibition of minimum prices gives rise to the 'free-rider' problem; in other words, the maintenance of fixed prices in a territory can sometimes be necessary to ensure that dealers in another area can cover their investments (sunk costs) made in connection with the introduction of a specific product to the market.[23]

> A special approach to obtaining protection from parallel trade has been the establishment of differentiated pricing and discount systems, so that higher prices have been set for goods that have been exported than for goods destined for the home market, see for example 78/163/EEC: Commission Decision relating to proceedings under Article 85 [Article 101] of the EEC Treaty *(Distillers Company)* (OJ 1978 L 50/16), and 91/335/EEC: Commission Decision relating to a proceeding pursuant to Article 85 [Article 101] of the EEC Treaty *(Gosme/Martell – DMP)* (OJ 1991 L 185/23). See the decision of the Court in Case T-41/96, *Bayer v. Commission*, application for the annulment of Commission Decision 96/478/EC relating to a proceeding under Article 85 of the EC Treaty *(Adalat)* (OJ 1996 L 201/1), on a similar use of a dual pricing system.
>
> Sometimes distributors have been subject to controls and threats of cessation of supplies or the reduction or removal of trade discounts if the contract goods are exported.[24]

In paragraph 118 of Commission Decision of 8 May 2001 relating to a proceeding pursuant to Article 81 of the EC Treaty Cases *(Glaxo Wellcome* and others) (OJ 2001 L 302/1), concerning the sales conditions for medicines which were sold to Spanish wholesalers, and which on the one hand distinguished between prices for wholesalers who sold on the products to Spanish pharmacies with a view to their use in Spain, and on the other hand higher prices for wholesalers who exported the products, the Commission expressed its view of price differentiation as follows:

> 'A pricing policy which makes it economically uninteresting for wholesalers to indulge in parallel trade must be considered to be at least as effective as an outright contractual export ban.'

The Commission maintained its existing practice as it found that, in its agreements with the Spanish wholesalers, Glaxo Wellcome had infringed Article

---

22. *See* 73/322/EEC: Commission Decision relating to proceedings under Art. 85 of the EEC Treaty *(Deutsche Philips GmbH)* (OJ 1973 L 293/40), where a German dealer was obliged to sell at prices determined by Deutsche Philips in Germany and elsewhere in the Community, regardless of whether the goods had been supplied direct from the producer in or outside Germany. *See* correspondingly 77/66/EEC: Commission Decision relating to a proceeding under Art. 85 of the EEC Treaty *(GERO-fabriek)* (OJ 1977 L 16/8), where the distributorship agreement contained a prohibition against any departure from the fixed retail price and against any form of discount.
23. There will often be quite substantial investments and risks.
24. *See*, e.g., Commission Decision 88/172/EEC, *Konica* (OJ 1988 L 78/34) and Decision, *Ford Agricultural* (OJ 1993 L 20/1). *See also* the Vertical Restraints Guidelines, paras 187 ff, which contains a comprehensive list of motivational measures which have been aimed, directly or indirectly, at ensuring that distributors comply with minimum prices.

101(1), and the Commission rejected Glaxo Wellcome's application for an exemption under Article 101(3). The Commission then drew a parallel with the *Distillers* decision,[25] according to which 'The non-applicability of price allowances on spirits for export and the application to the same customers of different prices for spirits for export and for spirits for United Kingdom consumption are clearly an attempt to impede parallel imports from the United Kingdom into EEC countries other than the United Kingdom, with the same object as a formal export prohibition and can be regarded as a more efficient way to discourage export.'[26]

If different price levels are set in different geographic areas for the same product, as previously stated, such binding prices can only be maintained in high-price areas if it is possible to prevent parallel exports to these areas, as such exports will otherwise undermine the high prices. In these and in other cases, an attempt to maintain the higher prices will, therefore, be combined with territorial protection. The Commission has adopted a consistently critical attitude to such arrangements.[27] The basic idea behind price competition continues to be that prices should be at the lowest possible level. Only thereby will undertakings be stimulated to use their resources in such a way that consumers will have an optimal opportunity to choose products which are assessed to be the best, both as regards price and other characteristics.

The restrictions in Article 101(1) TFEU affect agreements concerning trade within the internal market.

2.1.4 *Economic Analysis?*

In assessing the distorting effect on competition of vertical restrictions the practice of the Commission, especially its earlier practice, has been criticised particularly in respect of sole distributorships (restrictions on inter-brand competition). Among other things, the Commission has often considered such restrictions to be contrary to the prohibition in Article 101(1) TFEU, even if an economic analysis of the market conditions would have shown that existing inter-brand competition did not make intervention necessary.

According to the critics, such an analysis would have removed vertical agreements from the scope of Article 101(1) so that there would not have been a need to undertake the sometimes more complex assessment of whether there was an exemption under Article 101(3) TFEU or one of the block exemptions then in force.[28]

> For a more detailed discussion of this criticism see, among others: *Korah & Rothnie:* Exclusive Distribution and the EEC Competition Rules, 1992 pp. 51–56, *Korah & O'Sullivan:* Distribution Agreements under the EC Competition Rules, 2002 pp. 73–76, *Richard Whish:* Regulation No 2790/99: The

---

25. Commission Decision relating to proceedings under Art. 85 of the EEC Treaty (*Distillers Company*) (OJ 1978 L 50/16), and Case 30/78, *Distillers v. Commission*.
26. The Commission's *Glaxo Wellcome* Decision was upheld by the Court in Joined Cases C-501/06 P, C-513/06 P, C-515/06 P, and C-519/06 P, *GlaxoSmithKline Services Unlimited v. Commission*.
27. *See* Valentine Korah & Denis O'Sullivan: *Distribution Agreements under the EC Competition Rules,* 2002 p. 108 and pp. 173–175.
28. *See Korah & Rothnie:* Exclusive Distribution and the EEC Competition Rules, 1992 p. 78.

Commission's 'New Style' Block Exemption for Vertical Agreements, Common Market Law Review 2000 pp. 887–924, and *Barry E. Hawk:* System Failure: Vertical Restraints and EC Competition Law Common Market Law Review 1995 pp. 973–989. The last named points out that the Commission has been all too ready to regard a restriction as being covered by Article 101(1), even though a simple economic analysis would have shown that it would be entirely wrong to apply Article 101(1). *Hawk* also refers to the Commission's historical and ongoing reluctance, both within and without distribution areas, to learn from the CJ's frequent encouragement to apply Article 101(1) only when justified by a more sophisticated economic approach. According to the criticism, the Commission has 'given up', and instead based its assessment of the competition aspects of a given agreement on an interpretation of whether the conditions for an exemption in accordance with Article 101(3) are present or not.[29] In particular, in the Commission's earlier practice, only in few cases was there a hint that the Commission was willing to listen to the views of the CJ.

However, in more recent years the Commission's decisions do seem to indicate that it has accepted the criticism to some extent.

While, in Commission Decision 93/406/EEC on *Langnese-Iglo* (OJ 1993 L 183/19), the Commission related an analysis of the market structure to Article 101(3) in connection with Commission Decision 1999/230/EC on *Whitbread* (OJ 1999 L 88/26), which concerned the validity of a competition term under Article 101(1), the Commission used a detailed economic analysis of the market conditions.[30]

Both the CJ and the GC have adopted a more flexible approach, and in a number of cases, when deciding whether an agreed restriction is affected by Article 101(1), they have given weight to the actual economic and legal circumstances in which the agreement in question has been entered into, as well as an analysis of the effects of the agreement on the relevant market.[31]

> *See also* Case C-32/11, *Allianz Hungária Biztosító Zrt. and others*; Case 56/65, *Société Technique Minière v. Maschinenbau Ulm*; Case 23/67, *Brasserie de Haecht v. Consorts Wilkin-Janssen* (No 1); and Case C-234/89, *Stergios Delimitis v. Henninger Bräu*. An overall assessment of the market, including an investigation of inter-brand competition, was used in, among others: Case 26/76, *Metro SB-Großmärkte v. Commission* (1); Case 161/84, *Pronuptia*; Case 31/ 80, *L'Oréal v. De Nieuwe AMCK*; Case 99/79, *Lancôme*

---

29. *See*, among others, Commission Decision 93/405/EEC on *Schöller Lebensmittel* (OJ 1993 L 138/1).
30. On these decisions *see* Valentine Korah & Denis O'Sullivan: *Distribution Agreements under the EC Competition Rules,* 2002 pp. 78–80.
31. The comments in this connection have particularly concerned cases which fall outside the area of 'serious' restrictions on competition, for example cases where the parties have tried to secure absolute protection of their areas of the market, enforce maximum sales prices on distributors, etc. In these areas where, except in particular borderline cases, the Commission has followed the line laid down by the courts, the criticism has been more muted.

v. *Etos*; Case 258/78, *Nungesser and Eisele v. Commission*; and Case 27/87, *Erauw-Jacquery v. La Hesbignonne*.

Part of the problem that can be connected with the application of Article 101 is that it is split between, on the one hand, Article 101(1), which contains a description of the circumstances which make an agreement or parts of an agreement a restriction on competition, and on the other hand, Article 101(3), which sets out the circumstances that can mean that an agreement, or parts of an agreement, will not after all be affected by the prohibition in Article 101(2).

> Instead, according to the critics, there should first be an economic analysis of the actual or potential market structure together with a simultaneous evaluation of the positive and negative aspects of the agreement. The positive aspects will include, for example, an increase in inter-brand competition or possible consumer-related efficiency benefits connected with the restriction of intra-brand competition. If such analysis leads to the conclusion that the negative aspects of the agreement outweigh its positive aspects, the application of Article 101(3) and block exemptions could be reserved for the presumably few cases where other considerations exist which ought to justify exemption of the agreement.[32] If, conversely, such an assessment leads to the conclusion that the positive aspects outweigh the negative aspects, then according to this approach the agreement should be allowed under Article 101(1).
>
> However, this interpretation, which is based on American antitrust practice which uses the *rule of reason* model, cannot be implemented because of the differences in structure between the American prohibition and Article 101 TFEU.[33] If an interpretation of the agreement finds that in its economic and legal context, it does, in fact, contain a restriction on competition, then under the European system, Article 101(1) has fulfilled its role. There is no further requirement to compare the effects of the agreement, which restrict competition, with the effects which promote competition. If the restriction is to be exempted, this must be on the basis that one of the elements expressly stated in Article 101(3) (e.g., that the cost savings and effectivity gains connected with the restriction are to the *benefit of consumers*) justifies this.[34]

---

32. Cf. Barry E. Hawk: *System Failure: Vertical Restraints and EC Competition Law*, Common Market Law Review, 1995 p. 986.
33. The American prohibitions do not have exemptions corresponding to those in Art. 101(3) TFEU. *See also* Ch. 2 above, in the section on the significance of the fact that in Council Regulation (EC) No 1/2003 on the implementation of the rules on competition laid down in Arts 81 and 82 of the Treaty, it is provided that undertakings themselves, and if appropriate the competition authority which hears the case, can assess whether there is a basis for applying the exemption rule in Art. 101(3). In accordance with the earlier rules in Council Regulation (EEC) No 17/1962 First Regulation implementing Arts 85 and 86 of the Treaty [now Arts 101 and 102 TFEU], in relation to Art. 101, the Commission had sole competence to grant an exemption under Art. 101(3).
34. In the *Grundig* case, which is still considered to be a leading case in European competition law, the CJ stated that the attempt of the parties to create absolute territorial limits was sufficient

The refusal to apply a rule of reason interpretation to Article 101(1) was apparently supported by the Court of First Instance (now the GC) in Case T-112/99, *Métropole Télévision (M6) and others v. Commission*, which concerned the establishment of a system for the digital broadcasting of television programmes via satellite to francophone viewers in Europe. On the basis referred to – the distinction between Article 101(1) and (3) – the Court expressly stated that even a number of previous decisions, in which the CJ had apparently applied a more flexible interpretation of the prohibition in Article 101(1), could not be interpreted as an expression of the application of the rule of reason.[35] Furthermore, the Court characterised Article 101(3) as a provision in accordance with which – as an extension to Article 101(1) – an evaluation must be made of the effects of an agreement which promote competition and not of its positive effects in general, for example from the point of view of industrial policy, job creation and similar effects.[36] In light of these comments which reject an interpretation of Article 101(1) based on rule of reason considerations, the criticism by *Hawk*, referred to above, is very much to the point in so far as it presumes that the overall economic analysis of the advantages and disadvantages is conducted within the framework of Article 101(1).

2.1.5 *Further Easing of Restrictions?*

It is clear from the preceding comments that the EU's competition authorities still take a sceptical view of undertakings' infringements of the prohibition of agreements whereby the parties, or one of them, establish absolute territorial protection; *see* section 2.1.1 above. The authorities take a correspondingly uncompromising approach

---

grounds for regarding the group of agreements as being covered by Art. 101(1), even if the enforcement of the agreement would promote inter-brand competition, in other words increase the supply of substitute products.

35. Among the decisions of interest in this context which the Court of First Instance [now the General Court] referred to were: Case 56/65, *Société Technique Minière v. Maschinenbau Ulm*; Case 161/84, *Pronuptia*; and Case 258/78, *Nungesser and Eisele v. Commission*.
    The Court's statement in Joined Cases T-374/94 and others, *European Night Services and others v. Commission*, that when an agreement does not have the aim of restricting competition within the terms of Art. 101(1), a thorough evaluation of the effects of the agreement both on promoting competition and restricting it, is presumably not in accordance with the judgment in Case T-112/99, *Métropole Télévision (M6) and others v. Commission*. The same applies in Case C-234/89, *Stergios Delimitis v. Henninger Bräu*, and Case 399/93, *H.G. Oude Luttikhuis*, which the Court itself referred to. In Case T-65/98, *Van den Bergh Foods v. Commission*, the Court repeated the view expressed in the *Métropole Télévision (M6)* case.
36. However, in Case C-309/99, *Wouters and others v. Algemene Raad van de Nederlandse Orde van Advocaten*, on integrated cooperation between lawyers and accountants in the Netherlands, the Court used an approach where, within the framework of Art. 101(1) TFEU, an overall evaluation was made as to whether there was a restriction on competition, and whether this restriction was necessary. However, the Court did not refer to the *Métropole Télévision (M6)* case and it is for this reason, among other things, that it is not safe to assume that the CJ has taken a different view from the Court of First Instance [now the General Court] in the case.

to agreements on binding resale prices in subsequent links of the distribution chain; *see* section 2.1.3.

Neither the latest decisions of the CJ and the Commission nor the latest Block Exemption Regulation (Regulation (EU) No 720/2022) on vertical agreements and concerted practices contain any explicit indication that the EU competition authorities have changed their standpoint on these hardcore provisions.[37]

Where there is genuine testing of a new product in a limited territory or with a limited customer group, the distributors appointed to sell the new product on the test market or to participate in the first round of a staggered introduction may be restricted in their active selling outside the test market without falling within the scope of Article 101(1) for the period necessary for the testing or introduction of the product; see paragraph 197 of the Vertical Restraints Guidelines.

Also, there has clearly been a slight change in the Commission's attitude to the prohibition of resale price maintenance. According to paragraph 197 of the Vertical Restraints Guidelines, depending on the circumstances, an agreement that included resale price maintenance can fall within the scope of Article 101(3) TFEU if it can be shown that the agreement will have a positive effect on competition.

In the same way, fixed, and not merely maximum, resale prices can be necessary within the scope of a franchising scheme or equivalent distribution system based on a uniform distribution format in order to provide for a coordinated, short-term promotional campaign that will also benefit consumers.[38]

'Dual pricing' has normally been covered by the prohibition in Article 101(1), but the Commission Regulation has resulted in a softened stance on this matter. In the Vertical Restraints Guidelines, it is established that a requirement involving the buyer pays a different wholesale price for products sold online than for products sold offline can benefit from the exemption provided by Article 2(1) of Regulation (EU) No 720/2022, as it may incentivise or reward an appropriate level of investments in online or offline sales channels, provided that it does not have the object of restricting sales to particular territories or customers, as provided for in Article 4, points (b), (c) and (d).[39]

> The Commission has clarified this starting point in paragraph 209 of the Vertical Constraints Guidelines by pointing out that where the difference in the wholesale price has the object of preventing the effective use of the internet by the buyer to sell the contract goods or services to particular territories or customers, it is a hardcore restriction within the meaning of Article 4, point (e) of Commission Regulation (EU) No 720/2022. This would, in particular, be the case where the difference in the wholesale price makes selling online unprofitable or financially unsustainable or where dual pricing is used to limit the quantity of products made available to the buyer for sale online. Conversely, dual pricing can benefit from the exemption provided by Article 2(1) of Commission Regulation (EU) No 720/2022,

---

37. *See*, among others, Case C-260/07, *Pedro IV Servicios*; and Case T-111/08, *MasterCard*.
38. *See* the Vertical Restraints Guidelines, para. 197, b).
39. The Vertical Restraints Guidelines, para. 209.

where the difference in the wholesale price is reasonably related to differences in the investments and costs incurred by the buyer to make sales in each channel. The Commission also clarifies that similarly, the supplier may charge a different wholesale price for products that are to be sold through a combination of offline and online channels, where the price difference takes into account investments or costs related to that type of distribution. The parties may agree on an appropriate method to implement dual pricing, including, for example, an *ex post* balancing of accounts on the basis of actual sales.

2.2 Block Exemptions

The frequent questions about competition law, in the wake of the steady increase in cross-border trade in the Community and the rapid increase in notifications to the Commission with a view to obtaining an exemption in accordance with Article 101(3) TFEU, led at an early stage in the Community's development to the adoption of Council Regulation No 19/65/EEC on application of Article 101(3) TFEU to certain categories of agreements and concerted practices, authorising the Commission to issue regulations under which certain kinds of agreements were in general exempted from the duty to notify in accordance with Article 101(3).

This authorisation was already put into effect in Commission Regulation No 67/67/EEC on the application of Article 85(3) of the Treaty [Article 101(3) TFEU] to certain categories of exclusive dealing agreements.

Council Regulation No 19/65 focused exclusively on the acute problems which were the result of there being countless agreements on reselling goods being notified to the Commission in accordance with Council Regulation (EEC) No 17/1962 First Regulation implementing Articles 85 and 86 of the Treaty [now Articles 101 and 102 TFEU].[40] Other categories of agreements, for example, agreements for the provision of services, which have subsequently come to play an ever greater role, were not covered by Regulation No 19/65. Some of these agreements were later covered by Commission Regulation (EEC) No 4087/88 on the application of Article 85(3) of the Treaty to categories of franchise agreements. At the same time, neither the provision of services outside the field of franchises nor selective distribution agreements (*see* sections 3 and 4 below) were covered by a block exemption. With the benefit of hindsight, it would probably have been better if the Commission had limited its considerations to major cases and instead clarified the nature of the ancillary restraints to which a party to an agreement may be subject without thereby coming into conflict with Article 101(1).

Regulation No 67/67 was later replaced by Commission Regulation (EEC) No 1983/83 on the application of Article 85(3) of the Treaty [Article 101(3) TFEU] to categories of exclusive dealing agreements, which could take account of the experience gained in this area and the practice which the Court had established in the meantime.

---

40. According to Art. 2 of Regulation No 17/62, after notification by the participating undertakings, the Commission could decide that, in the circumstances of which Commission had knowledge, there was no cause for the Commission to take measures under Art. 85(1) or 86 [now Arts 101(1) and 102 TFEU] against an agreement, decision or concerted practice (comfort letters).

In this connection, Commission Regulation (EEC) No 1984/83 on the Application of Article 85(3) of the Treaty [Article 101(3) TFEU] to categories of exclusive purchasing agreements introduced a block exemption for exclusive purchasing arrangements which had hitherto been regulated under the 1967 Regulation.[41] In Case 47/76, *de Norre v. NV Brouwerij Concordia*, the Court stated that an exclusive purchase obligation could be covered by Regulation No 67/67, even if the agreement did not include any exclusive territorial provisions.

In 1999, growing criticism of the scope of application of the block exemption regulations led to all the regulations in the area of distribution being repealed and, with effect from 2000, being replaced by Commission Regulation (EC) No 2790/1999 on block exemptions for vertical restraints; *see* in more detail section 5 below. Regulation (EC) No 2790/1999 was replaced by Regulation (EU) No 330/2010 on the application of Article 101(3) TFEU to categories of vertical agreements and concerted practices. In all essentials, the new Regulation carries forward the approach adopted in Regulation (EC) No 2790/1999. Commission Regulation (EU) No 330/2010 expired in May 2022 and was replaced by Commission Regulation (EU) No 720/2022 with effect from 1 June 2022. The most recent Regulation is structured in the same way as its predecessors but with more adjustments, including especially adjustments in regard to increased online distribution.[42]

A block exemption regulation contains a set of rules which either directly or indirectly establish the terms for agreements in a particular category of agreements, which the parties can adopt in the confidence that, even if they restrict competition, they will not be objected to. As the name suggests, the idea of the regulation is that when the conditions laid down in the regulation are met, the terms are given prior exemption from measures being taken against them, as there will be an assumption that the agreement is valid under competition law. In addition to this, the regulation sets out the terms which, if they are part of an agreement in restraint of competition, will mean that the agreement will be without legal effect in whole or in part.[43] *See also* the commentary on the concept of block exemptions in Chapter 2 above.

There can be wide-ranging consequences for undertakings if their agreement is considered to restrict competition without it being, in accordance with Article 101(3), either individually or falling within a category (under a block exemption) of exempted agreements which are covered by Article 101(1).

---

41. It is characteristic of agreements that fell within the scope of Regulation No 1983/83 that a dealer would be allocated an area within which the principal would not be permitted to appoint other dealers. In contrast to this, Regulation No 1984/83 applied to agreements under which a supplier was subject to an exclusive obligation to purchase, but without at the same time being allocated a specific sales area and without the supplier being prevented from selling to other purchasers.
42. *See*, for example, preamble considerations 2, 10, 11, 14, 15 and 16, in which especially the importance of online intermediation services is pointed out.
43. According to Art. 101(3), whether individual or group, exemption is conditional on the agreements contributing to improving the distribution of goods, while allowing consumers a fair share of the benefit, while not imposing on the undertakings concerned restrictions which are not indispensable for the attainment of these objectives. For a discussion of the four cumulative conditions for obtaining an exemption.

To start with, as stated in Article 101(2), agreements which restrict competition contrary to Article 101(1) are void, and cannot therefore be enforced via the national courts. Also, by virtue of the rules of private international law (choice of law rules), a corresponding result could be reached in relation to courts in third countries (meaning courts outside the EU or European Economic Area (EEA)).

Next, an agreement to restrict competition, for example, a market-sharing agreement, could lead to punishment by a fine on undertakings which are party to the agreement, and sometimes such parties may be required by national courts to pay compensation to third parties who stand outside the agreement if it is considered that they have suffered loss as a result of the agreement between the parties.

In the EU it has predominantly been the practice that the enforcement of competition rules is a matter for the competition authorities, and not for the national courts. The sanctions applied have been prohibitions and fines, and not private law enforcement such as claims for compensation on the grounds of infringement of the competition rules. Among other things, this is due to the way in which the sanctions system is built up, including the fact that under Regulation No 17/62, the Commission previously had sole competence to grant exemptions under Article 101(1) TFEU, and that under the applicable rule, undertakings had the possibility of notifying agreements which were in restraint of competition, whereby further proceedings before the national courts were excluded. The changes to Regulation No 17/62 discussed below have removed these restrictions to the benefit of undertakings which believe themselves to be injured by the market conduct of a counterparty or by others who restrict competition.

In Case C-453/99, *Courage v. Crehan*, the Court gave a clear signal that the full effect of the prohibition in Article 101(1) would be put at risk unless undertakings which have suffered loss as a result of conduct that has restricted or distorted competition can effectively enforce their rights. Since there are no provisions under Community law for the payment of compensation, it is up to the individual Member States to establish the procedural rules for cases to be brought for the protection of the rights which the direct effect Community law gives to Union citizens.[44] The Court pointed out that such rules may not be less favourable than those that apply to corresponding cases under national law (the principle of equivalence), nor may it be impossible or unduly difficult to exercise the rights which are granted to Union citizens under Community law (the principle of effectiveness).[45] The Court expressly concluded that Article 101 of the Treaty prevents national laws being adopted which *prohibit* a party from claiming compensation for loss suffered solely on the grounds that the party was a party to an

---

44. However, note the measures to improve the possibility of obtaining compensation for breaches of the Union's competition rules in Directive 2014/104/EU on certain rules governing actions for damages under national law for infringements of the competition law provisions of the Member States, which the Member States must implement by 27 Dec. 2016.
45. *See* Case C-261/95, *Palmisani v. INPS*, para. 27.

agreement in restraint of competition. This can be relevant, for example, in a case where a supplier establishes a network of standard agreements with a number of smaller traders, in other words, where there are vertical transactions. On the contrary, Community law does not prevent there being a national law under which a party cannot rely on its own unlawful conduct with a view to obtaining compensation when this party bears a significant share of the responsibility for the restriction of competition. This decision is important, not least in relation to defining the principle of effectiveness, which in future the national courts will contribute to establishing, under a system of expanded direct effect, see immediately below.

A close examination of the provision on block exemptions can give significant guidance to an undertaking in which, for example, the producer of goods is to be a party to an agreement with a trader who has undertaken to distribute the goods on a given market.

Both parties can thereby be aware of the pitfalls which can risk bringing them into the spotlight of the competition authorities, just as they can use the Regulation's statement of exempting conditions as a suitable checklist for terms which they might not have previously considered.

A block exemption regulation is built up so that the introduction – a preamble which contains a number of recitals – sets out the background to the exemption. These considerations constitute an important basis for interpretation of the operative part of the regulation, just as the recitals will often give clear indications of the Commission's policy in the area covered by the regulation.

Regulation No 2790/99 [now Regulation (EU) No 720/2022] contained a number of major differences from the previous block exemption regulations on exclusive distribution, exclusive purchasing and franchising.

The Regulation should be seen in conjunction with the arrangement which entered into force in 1999 whereby agreements which contain restrictions on vertical competition should no longer be notified in accordance with Article 101(3) of the TFEU in order to be valid, on this *see* section 5 below concerning Council Regulation (EC) No 1216/1999.

Regulation (EU) No 720/2022 concerns the category of 'vertical agreements' and is therefore freed from the straightjacket effect associated with the earlier block exemption regulations, which is why each of them only covered a single type of contract, for example, sole distribution agreements.

3   THE CONCEPT OF RESTRICTION OF COMPETITION

The restriction on free trade, which can be the result of an agreement or a concerted practice within the meaning of Article 101(1), can have an effect both on the dealings between the parties to the agreement and on third parties, whereby competitors' commercial freedom is restricted. However, a measure against free trade is not in itself a restriction on competition. The measure must also constitute a restriction either on *intra-brand* competition (competition between traders in the same product) or *inter-brand* competition (competition between traders in substitutable goods).[46]

The concept of restriction of competition, including the condition of a Community dimension, etc., and the *de minimis* rule are discussed in more detail above in Chapter 2.

In a number of cases on vertical arrangements involving specific contractual arrangements, the courts have taken their starting point in an assessment of whether the overall category of the agreement has been a legitimate business activity. If the result of such an analysis is in favour of the agreement in question, and it is found to be a legitimate and natural element of effective competition, the next question is whether the special conditions of the agreement are necessary for achieving its purpose. If the conditions are relevant in the given context, they could be judged to be *ancillary restraints* as long as they are directly related to the main transaction and are not in themselves disproportionate. Such conditions would not be considered to be restrictions on competition, even if this might appear natural if the conditions had arisen in some other context.[47] However, if the restriction has the direct aim of restricting competition, it has not been accepted; *see*, for example, Case T-176/95, *Accinauto v. Commission*, discussed above in section 2.

> Whether a condition in an agreement can be considered necessary, and therefore constitute an ancillary restraint within the definition set out, was one of the themes of the *Métropole Télévision (M6)* case referred to above, where the Court considered whether the three major French national television broadcasting companies, which were some of the participants in a joint venture to transmit satellite television to France, could undertake to refrain from providing programmes to other satellite channels. The case must be classified as concerning a horizontal agreement, but in the present context it can illustrate the condition of 'necessity' associated with ancillary restraints.
>
> Among other things, the Court referred to the fact that other undertakings had established satellite channels without adopting such exclusive conditions. Therefore, the condition could not be considered necessary, and

---

46. *See* Case T-7/93, *Langnese-Iglo v. Commission*, in which the Court, in addition to finding that an exclusive purchasing agreement and a prohibition on competition constituted an infringement of the trader's commercial freedom, stated that the two restrictions together could lead to a restriction on both intra-brand and inter-brand competition, *see* paras 94–113 of the judgment. In the *Grundig* case, the Court found that the attempt of the parties to create strict territorial limits was sufficient reason to regard the agreement as being covered by Art. 101(1), even though there was a possible side-effect that in the longer term this could have the benefit of stimulating inter-brand competition; in other words, it could increase the supply of substitutable products. As stated above in s. 1.1, in Case C-309/99, *Wouters and others v. Algemene Raad van de Nederlandse Orde van Advocaten*, on the integrated cooperation between lawyers and accountants (i.e., at a horizontal level), the Court seems to have come close to making a rule of reason assessment.
47. This distinction of certain ancillary restraints is a result of the general Community principle of proportionality, and the main area where this applies is under the Treaty provisions on trade restrictions, but it has also been expressed in connection with the competition rules in Art. 101(3).

furthermore it was found to be disproportionate, as it denied competitors access to programmes that were demanded by French viewers. The decision was based on the approach that, when deciding whether a restraint is necessary, a relatively abstract assessment must be made. If the application of a rule of reason assessment to the main transaction is excluded, see the comments above in section 2.1, it cannot be applied to an assessment of ancillary restraints, as this would involve an assessment of the commercial necessity of the restraint.[48]

Necessity, in the narrow sense that was established in the *Métropole Télévision (M6)* case, is an extension of the opinions that the Court has expressed in cases where the main transaction has been accompanied by an ancillary restraint *in order to be carried out at all*. In respect of vertical restraints on competition, such considerations have been applied, among others, in the important areas of franchising and selective distribution.

4 SPECIAL AGREEMENTS THAT ONLY EXCEPTIONALLY FALL WITHIN THE SCOPE OF ARTICLE 101(1) TFEU

In the practice of the Court and the Commission, it is possible to identify special types of agreements under different conditions and for various reasons, which have been found particularly acceptable from a competition law perspective. However, individual special conditions in these agreements have received less sympathy.

These types of agreements include, among others, agency agreements, franchising agreements, and selective distribution agreements.[49]

4.1 Agency Agreements

Agreements between traditionally operating commercial agents and their principals have previously been considered to be agreements which are not affected by Article 101(1) TFEU.

In Directive 86/653/EEC on the coordination of the laws of the Member States relating to self-employed commercial agents, which is directed at the law of obligations aspect of the relationship between commercial agents and principals, such agents are defined as follows:

---

48. *See* Valentine Korah & Denis O'Sullivan: *Distribution Agreements under the EC Competition Rules,* 2002 pp. 83–85. The burden of proof that the condition of necessity has been satisfied rests on the undertakings. Compare with the area of merger controls, Case T-17/93, *Matra Hachette v. Commission.*
49. The comments in this section concern agreements which would not, for some other reason, be considered a restriction on competition, for example because they fall under the *De minimis* notice (Commission Notice on agreements of minor importance which do not appreciably restrict competition under Art. 101(1) of the TFEU establishing the European Community (*de minimis*) (OJ C 291 of 30 August 2014, pp. 1–4) – discussed above in Ch. 2).

For the purposes of this Directive, 'commercial agent' shall mean a self-employed intermediary who has continuing authority to negotiate the sale or the purchase of goods on behalf of another person, hereinafter called the 'principal', or to negotiate and conclude such transactions on behalf of and in the name of that principal.

In a Notice of 24 December 1962, which has since lapsed and been replaced by paragraphs 29–46 (section 3.2) of the Vertical Restraints Guidelines, the Commission expressed the view that an agent who does not undertake financial obligations in relation to third parties, other than an agreed guarantee of the solvency of the third party (*del credere*), does not for the competition purposes play a role which is different from the principal's own direct employees.

Paragraph 29 of the Vertical Restraints Guidelines defines the agency relationship somewhat differently, as the new wording provides that an agent can negotiate and enter into contracts on behalf of the principal, either in the agent's own name or in the name of the principal, for the purchase of goods or services or the sales of goods or services that are provided by the principal. This creates the possibility that an agent can have a status corresponding to an intermediary or, as known in several European systems, a commission agent. In addition to this, the definition of an agent under competition law also now applies where the subject of the agent's activities covers services as well as goods.[50]

The difference between the two definitions is not merely formal. The difference will presumably mean that in many more cases than previously, an intermediary could be considered to have the status of an independent dealer ('non-genuine agent') even if the intermediary otherwise has characteristics associated with a genuine agent. For the distinction between genuine and non-genuine agents, *see* below.[51]

> The first real decision on the position of agents in competition law was given in Joined cases 40/73 and others, *Suiker Unie and others v. Commission*, in which the Court stated that Article 85 of the Treaty [now Article 101 TFEU] did not apply to a non-compete obligation in accordance with which a commercial agent had undertaken to sell the principal's goods and otherwise take care of the principal's interests in the market. On the other hand, the Court found reason to state that a commercial agent who undertakes obligations which, from a financial point of view, are the same as those of an independent dealer, including the obligation to fulfil contracts entered into with third parties, cannot be regarded in competition law as an auxiliary organ. This view was repeated in Case C-266/93, *Bundeskartellamt v. Volkswagen and VAG Leasing*, where the Court stated that it was

---

50. However, in other legal systems in the EU, services are also covered by the concept of agency as it appears on the basis of Council Directive 86/653/EEC on the coordination of the laws of the Member States relating to self-employed commercial agents. For example this applies in French law and in German law; *see* Agustin Jausàs: *Agency and Distribution Agreements – An International Survey*, 1994, which includes a discussion of the concept of an agent in a number of European legal systems.
51. This distinction shows the difference between the different types of agents. However, it should be stressed that the terms 'genuine' and 'non-genuine' are not used in the Vertical Restraints Guidelines.

decisive for whether the intermediary should be considered to be an agent or not, whether the intermediary took on a *financial risk* in relation to the third party. Among other things, the fact that the agent's obligations in relation to some leasing contracts expired, including at least the agent's obligation to buy back leased motor vehicles, was regarded as being sufficient to establish that the agent had taken on a financial risk.

Paragraph 30 of the Vertical Restraints Guidelines assumes that genuine agency agreements (agency agreements under which the agent merely acts in mediating agreements in which the principal carries the full financial risk) fall outside the scope of Article 101(1) of the Treaty. This is because, in these cases, even if he or she is self-employed, a genuine agent is regarded as being integrated into the principal's sales organisation. The actions of the agent in the market are therefore considered to reflect that the agent acts as the extended arm of the principal in relation to third parties (the integration criterion). *See also* the situation referred to in paragraph 31 of the Guidelines, which point in the direction of excluding the agent from Article 101(1).

The purpose of the integration criterion is that the application of Article 101(1) TFEU will not take effect if the agent merely acts as an auxiliary organ for the principal, who does not withdraw from competition but merely uses the agent to arrange for the sale of goods in the market. A natural and probable consequence of establishing these definitions is that a genuine agent cannot be considered an 'undertaking' within the meaning of Article 101(1). Consequently, the principal can require an agent not to enter into contracts with parties to parallel trade, not to execute orders addressed to the agent by traders outside the agent's allocated territory (passive sales), and the agent must respect the instructions of the principal, among other things, not to give discounts, share sales commission with customers etc.

In contrast, in the agreements of non-genuine agents, the agent takes on wider financial and commercial risks, and an assessment of the agreement in relation to Article 101(1) will often be relevant (the risk criterion).

Conceptually, the risk criterion has the function of restricting traditional agency agreements to agreements where the supplier's counterparty (the agent) acts *on his or her own account* in one or more commercially significant respects.[52] This includes taking on financial risks which are directly connected with the contracts which the agent enters into and/or negotiates on behalf of the principal, for example, the building up and financing of stocks, including losses on unsold goods and the lack of a right to return these goods, as well as the risks connected with market-specific investments which are necessary for the kind of undertaking which the agent is expected to make. Examples of this include investments in real property, specially trained personnel, means of transport, etc. In these cases, to which could be added agreements on product liability, liability for customers' failure to fulfil their contracts, etc., where the agent is more or less outside an integrated relation to the principal, the agent can be considered

---

52. In such a case it will be more appropriate to consider the intermediary as an (exclusive) distributor and reserve the term 'agent' for the party who is referred to as the 'genuine agent'. Apart from this, it is probably not right to draw too wide conclusions from either the integration criterion or the risk criterion.

an independent distributor (independent dealer), who is free to plan his own marketing strategy to cover his own contract and market-specific investments. Investments of this kind are normally irrecoverable (sunk costs) if they cannot be used in other commercial activities or can only be sold at a loss if the agency agreement is terminated. Under these circumstances, where there can be considerable commercial risks for the agent, the agent can be classified as an independent operator in relation to Article 101(1).

> In Case 311/85, *Vereniging van Vlaamse Reisbureaus v. Sociale Dienst*, a question arose from agreements between an association of travel companies and an association of travel agents and the Court had to consider the status of intermediaries, either as an auxiliary organ or as an independent operator on the market. Among other things, the agreements, which were based on legislative provisions and administrative orders, laid down that travel agents should not sell at below the prices which had been determined by the travel companies and that they should not provide discounts or share their sales commission with their travelling customers. As there were a large number of travel companies and a correspondingly large number of travel agencies, it was found that the travel agents were not 'agents' in the traditional sense, in other words they were not intermediaries with the status of auxiliary organs. In the view of the Court, this would have required the individual travel agent to have been engaged by a specific travel company, and not by a multiplicity of travel companies. This was not altered by the fact that, in relation to its customers, the individual travel agent acted in the name of the travel company and on its behalf.[53]
>
> See also the illustrative example of 2002/758/EC: Commission Decision relating to a proceeding under Article 81 of the EC Treaty (*Mercedes-Benz*) (OJ 2002 L 257/1), which considered a number of specific obligations which Mercedes-Benz had imposed on its German agents. The investigation had been initiated with a view to deciding whether the agents should be characterised as genuine agents or non-genuine dealers, because of some export restrictions which Mercedes-Benz had imposed on the agents. Among a number of other factors, the Commission emphasised that the agents had to pay considerable costs for sales promotion activities out of their own pockets, including obtaining a number of demonstration models at their own expense and risk, and subsequently selling them under certain conditions. On the basis of these other heavy financial obligations which Mercedes-Benz imposed on its agents, Mercedes was fined EUR 72 million.
>
> Another case in this area, Case C-217/05, *Confederación Española de Empresarios de Estaciones de Servicio v. Compañía Española de Petróleos SA (CEPSA)*, concerned agreements entered into by the CEPSA oil company and a number of petrol stations in Spain for the supply of petrol. According to paragraph 46 of the judgment, the decisive factor for the purposes of

---

53. On the practice of the Court, *see* Swanson & Brown: *European Community Law Review*, 1991 p. 86.

determining whether a service station operator is an independent economic operator is to be found in the agreement concluded with the principal and, in particular, in the express or implied terms of the agreement on the assumption of the financial and commercial risks linked to sales of goods to third parties. In the Court's view (paragraph 52), it is likely that the service station operator assumes the risks linked to the sale of the goods when he receives them from the supplier, that is to say, prior to selling them to a third party. According to paragraphs 53 and 54, a corresponding assumption applies when the service station operator assumes, directly or indirectly, the costs linked to the distribution of those goods, particularly the transport costs. Furthermore, the fact that the service station operator maintains stocks at his own expense could be an indication that the risks linked to the sale of the goods are transferred to him. Finally, in paragraphs 55 and 56, there is focus on who assumes responsibility for any damage caused to the goods and whether the service station operator should pay for the fuel if he does not find a purchaser.

The question of risk must be assessed on a case-by-case basis, and in the view of the Commission, the starting point will be the economic reality rather than the nomenclature which is attached more or less randomly to the intermediary stage. The terms of agreements which are usual in agency arrangements, including rights and duties to maintain stocks of goods at the expense of the principal, to provide customer service at no extra cost, to monitor the market, do not fulfil the risk criterion and therefore fall outside Article 101(1).

However, as stated, an intermediary can lose the status of an agent in the traditional sense (as an auxiliary organ (genuine agent) for the principal), if the intermediary is required to contribute to the costs of supplying/buying the agreed goods, to invest in sales promotion measures, denied the right to return unsold goods which have been carried in stock, to provide an after-sales service, repair or guarantee system without being fully recompensed by the principal, to undertake investments for the specific market, premises or specially trained personnel (*see* the comments above), to be responsible towards third parties for damage caused by the goods sold (product liability), and to accept general responsibility for the customers' failure to fulfil their contracts, with the exception of the agent's loss of commission.

In future, it will presumably be the exception for a single factor or several individual factors to be significant from a competition law point of view and call into use Article 101(1) TFEU in cases where an agent has not had property rights over the goods bought or sold. The condition or conditions which may perhaps fall outside the scope of a traditional agency agreement should have a significant influence on the agreement. The risks associated with the business itself, which consists of providing the normal service of an agent, including the risk of the agent's income being dependent on how well he or she carries out the work, etc., or which is associated with general investments in premises and personnel, are not circumstances which in themselves make the agent more akin to some other status than that of an auxiliary organ for the principal. However, if the circumstances of the actual case indicate that the commercial agent has a position which is independent of the principal, whether organisationally or otherwise, the principles which regulate the assessment of vertical agreements under competition law will determine whether the agent's conduct is acceptable or prohibited.

4.2 Franchising

Neither in law nor in practical commerce is there a precise definition of what is meant by *franchising*. The term is usually used as a general concept for a *vertical* distribution system based on an agreement between *independent* undertakings.[54]

However, this abstract definition also covers sole distributorships, licensing agreements, etc. It is therefore necessary to define further that franchising typically involves the franchisor providing know-how, manuals and licences to intellectual property or commercial rights, etc., to the franchisee, in return for which the franchisee accepts certain restrictions on the purchase of goods, sales of competing products, the get-up of sales premises, etc., and above all undertakes to pay the franchisor a regular royalty. While in *sole distributorship agreements,* it will typically be the distributor who provides the market knowledge to the supplier, in *franchise agreements*, it is the franchisor who is responsible for systems development, etc., and who has the necessary experience with regard to advertising, sales and other matters which are important for promoting awareness of the products.

Franchising is often associated with the sales of fast-food and fashion, but after franchising was introduced to Europe in the 1960s, this form of distribution has been used on a wide range of other categories of goods or, as expressed by *Joanna Goyder*: EU Distribution Law, 5th ed. 2011 p. 175: 'it has been used to sell everything from pet dogs to hot dogs, and continues to increase in popularity as a distribution method'.

Franchising can take different forms:

- With *product franchising* (sometimes called *trademark licensing*), a producer of branded goods gives some other undertaking a licence to produce certain goods and to market them using the producer's trade mark.[55]
- *Service franchising* is an agreement whereby the franchisee can offer a service under the franchisor's name or trade mark and otherwise in accordance with the franchisor's directions.[56]

---

54. These characteristics mean that in principle franchising is treated similarly to other distribution forms that are regulated by Regulation (EU) No 720/2022; *see* s. 5 below. *See also* s. 4.6.3 of the Vertical Restraints Guidelines.
55. *See*, among others, 78/253/EEC: Commission Decision relating to proceedings under Art. 85 of the EEC Treaty (*Campari* – on the sale of special herbs for the manufacture of wine) (OJ 1978 L 70/69); and 90/186/EEC: Commission Decision relating to a proceeding under Art. 85 of the EEC Treaty (*Moosehead/Whitbread* on an agreement between a Canadian brewery and a British brewery on the production and sale in the UK of a beer under the trade mark 'Moosehead') (OJ 1990 L 100/32).
56. *See*, for example 88/604/EEC: Commission Decision relating to a proceeding under Art. 85 of the EEC Treaty (*ServiceMaster*) (OJ 1988 L 332/38).

- *Distribution franchising*, as the name suggests, is an agreement to sell the franchisor's products under the franchisor's trade mark and other get-up.[57]
- The *Pronuptia* case[58] was important in pointing the way for the assessment of franchise agreements under competition law and also contributed to the general assessment of the restriction on competition of special conditions on territorial limits, parallel imports and exports, cross-supplies, non-compete obligations, etc.; see the comments below in section 5 on Articles 4 and 5 of Regulation (EU) No 720/2022.[59]

The background to the case was that the German *Bundesgerichtshof* had referred a question to the CJ for a preliminary ruling on the claimed breach of a franchise agreement which the French undertaking, *Pronuptia de Paris*, had entered into with a German franchisee through its representative in Germany, for the sale of bridal equipment etc. in three German towns on a franchise basis.

According to the agreement, the franchisee had the sole right to use the trade mark 'Pronuptia de Paris' within the agreed territory, and undertook to carry on the business of selling bridal equipment etc. within the territory under the name Pronuptia from premises which were approved by the franchisor and furnished and decorated in accordance with the franchisor's instructions, and using the franchisor's know-how and business methods. The franchisor undertook to help the franchisee with the furnishing and decoration of the premises, training of personnel, and in connection with the franchisee's sales promotion activities.

The franchisee had to buy the products which were the subject of the agreement exclusively from the franchisor or from suppliers approved by the franchisor. The franchisee was to have the sale of bridal equipment as its primary activity, the franchisee's status as the sole responsible proprietor of the business was emphasised, and under certain circumstances, the franchisee could buy products from other Pronuptia franchisees. However, 80% of the bridal equipment had to be bought directly from the franchisor. According to the agreement, the franchisor was entitled itself to sell directly

---

57. *See* the decision in Case 161/84, *Pronuptia*.
58. *See* Case 161/84, *Pronuptia*.
59. The judgment in the *Pronuptia* case led to the adoption of Commission Regulation (EEC) No 4087/88 on the application of Art. 101(1) of the Treaty to categories of franchise agreements. Prior to that, the *Pronuptia* judgment's detailed description of the competitive status of the franchise agreement had clearly influenced the decisions which the Commission took in the following years, and the granting of exemptions under Art. 85(3) [Art. 101(3) TFEU] for certain parts of notified franchise agreements, *see* 87/14/EEC: Commission Decision relating to a proceeding under Art. 85 of the EEC Treaty (*Yves Rocher*) (OJ 1987 L 8/49), 87/17/EEC: Commission Decision in proceedings under Art. 85 of the EEC Treaty (*Pronuptia* standard agreements) (OJ 1987 L 13/39), 87/407/ EEC: Commission Decision relating to a proceeding under Art. 85 of the EEC Treaty (*Computerland*) (OJ 1987 L 222/12), 88/604/EEC: Commission Decision relating to a proceeding under Art. 85 of the EEC Treaty (*ServiceMaster* – service franchising) (OJ 1988 L 332/38), and 89/94/EEC: Commission Decision relating to a proceeding under Art. 85 of the EEC Treaty (*Charles Jourdan*) (OJ 1989 L 35/31).

into the territory by mail-order sales, and to pay 10% of its turnover from this to the franchisee. The franchisee was to refrain from any form of competition with other Pronuptia traders, among other things by refraining from opening shops with a similar purpose in Germany or elsewhere.

In the view of the CJ, a franchise agreement such as this could only function optimally if the franchisor was able to pass on its know-how without the risk that this knowledge would be used by competitors on the market and if the agreement could lawfully contain certain restrictions with the aim was of protecting the reputation and identity of the franchise network. The same applied to those parts of the agreement which obliged the franchisee to use the business methods developed by the franchisor, the requirements for the location of the shops, the prohibition on the transfer of the rights and duties under the agreement to a third party without the consent of the franchisor, and conditions whose purpose was to secure the franchisor's control over the goods offered for sale by the franchisee.[60]

Against the background of these considerations, the CJ necessarily came to the conclusion that the agreement's ancillary restraints – in so far as assessed – did not contain any restriction on competition contrary to Article 101(1). Likewise, these considerations led to the conclusion that the franchisee could lawfully be made subject to a non-compete obligation, also for a short period after the termination of the agreement.[61]

The Court was less persuaded of the acceptability of some of the other terms in the agreement. This applied in particular to the terms which led to or could lead to the sharing of the market between the franchisor and the franchisee, or between franchisees, as well as the terms which directly or indirectly hindered their right to compete on price (improper franchise agreements).

In the view of the Court, regard for the reputation and identity of the products could not justify such terms which, in relation to a product *which was already widespread*, constituted a restriction on competition as referred to in Article 101(1) TFEU, and which *were capable of affecting trade between Member States – even though they were entered into between undertakings from the same Member State.*[62]

> The Court put special emphasis on the fact that such restrictions on competition could arise because the franchisor gave the franchisee exclusive rights within a given area, without intrusion by the franchisor or other franchisees, to use the specific know-how etc., and at the same time the

---

60. *See* the Vertical Guidelines, paras (85)–(87).
61. *See* Regulation (EU) No 720/2022, Art. 5, discussed below in s. 5.4.
62. On this point, the *Pronuptia* judgment can be seen as supporting the general view that, in judging whether there is a distortion of competition, the circumstances must be taken into consideration as to whether an agreement which contains a certain measure of territorial protection is necessary to enable an undertaking to penetrate a market where it has not previously been active. In support of this *see* Case 56/65, *Société Technique Minière v. Maschinenbau Ulm*. In the area of technology transfer, *see* Case 258/78, *Nungesser and Eisele v. Commission*, which among other things concerned the transfer of an 'open exclusive licence'; for more on this case *see* s. 4.5 below and Ch. 5.

franchisee (and other franchisees) were bound to carry on the activities covered by the agreement at the appointed premises and was prohibited from opening further shops.

The Court also pointed out that the national courts should be alert to whether, in spite of the statement in the agreement that the franchisor's retail prices were merely *recommended*, there was nevertheless a tacit understanding which must be seen as a concerted practice to the effect that the prices could, in reality, be considered as *binding*.

In its formulation of the conditions for the block exemption, the Commission followed the comments of the Court on the significance of binding retail prices; see most recently Regulation (EU) No 720/2022, Article 4(a). For more details on this, *see* section 5.3.1, in which terms of an agreement or other measures outside an agreement which restrict a franchisee's freedom to set its own sales prices for the goods or services covered by a franchise agreement are classified as serious (hardcore) restrictions which prevent the block exemption.

The Court was aware of the possibility that a potential franchisee could be interested in participating in a franchise network if they could secure a certain degree of protection from the franchisor and the other franchisees. In the view of the Court, such a situation could be taken into account in connection with the possible application of the exemption provisions in Article 81(3)[now Article 101(3)].[63]

4.3 Selective Distribution

It is the starting point in the Community law-based competition rules that a producer or supplier of goods is not subject to restrictions regarding whom or on what conditions they sell their goods. Only the provision in Article 102 TFEU on abuse of a dominant position could be applicable and lead to a different result.

In some respects, selective distribution differs from this starting point. The characteristics of this form of distribution are that a producer (supplier), who trades in branded goods through a main dealer (wholesaler), seeks not only to control the dealer but also subsequent links in the distribution chain (retailers) by requiring these to be approved dealers, in other words, they should satisfy certain predetermined requirements of the producer. The restriction on retail sales is not a restriction on active sales to a given territory but a restriction on sales to retailers. Sales must thus only be made to approved retailers and to the end user.[64]

---

63. The Court's overall assessment of the relationship of the franchise agreement in question to Art. 101(1) is made clear in para. 27 of the judgment.
64. According to Regulation (EU) No 720/2022, Art. 1(g): '"selective distribution system" means a distribution system where the supplier undertakes to sell the contract goods or services, either directly or indirectly, only to distributors selected on the basis of specified criteria and where these distributors undertake not to sell such goods or services to unauthorised distributors within the territory reserved by the supplier to operate that system.'

Principally, the risks of competition can lead to a reduction of intra-brand competition and the exclusion of certain kinds of dealers, as well as a restriction in the producer's customer base.

In assessing these *restrictions on competition* by selective distribution under Article 101(1), prior to Regulation (EU) No 720/2022, the practice was to distinguish between qualitative and quantitative selective distribution.

With qualitative selection, there is a selection of dealers purely on the basis of objective criteria which are regarded as necessary due to the characteristics of the products (luxury, prestige and image goods), the training of sales personnel, the capacity of the dealer to provide after-sales service (e.g., for technical products), as well as the presence of a certain product range in the shop which sells to the end user, etc.[65]

With quantitative selection, further selection criteria are added, which more directly limit the potential number of dealers, for example, conditions about minimum sales levels, stockholding, etc.

4.3.1 Qualitative or Quantitative Selective Distribution Systems

In the context of Community competition law, selective distribution systems were accepted with a degree of tolerance quite early on, *see* 70/488/EEC: Commission Decision relating to a proceeding under Article 85 of the EEC Treaty (*Omega*) (OJ 1970 L 242/22 – not officially published in English), which concerned the sale of hi-fi equipment for home entertainment systems.

In a number of subsequent cases, both the Commission and the CJ have confirmed that in special circumstances, a producer can practice such a form of distribution without the restrictions which are imposed on wholesalers and retailers being affected by the prohibition in Article 101(1) TFEU.

It has been accepted that producers of, for example, luxury goods and high technology products, can have a legitimate interest in their products being exclusively sold in specialist shops or in specially fitted out departments in department stores, etc.

The objective criteria for keeping a qualitative system from infringing Article 101(1) were expressed in paragraph 20 of Case 26/76, *Metro SB-Großmärkte v. Commission*:

> On this view, the Commission was justified in recognizing that selective distribution systems constituted, together with others, an aspect of competition which accords with Article 85(1) [Article 101(1)], provided that resellers are chosen on the basis of objective criteria of a qualitative nature relating to the technical

---

65. *See* the preliminary ruling in Case C-439/09, *Pierre Fabre*, where the referring national court had to rule on a selective distribution arrangement which stipulated that the distributors had to sell the cosmetics in question exclusively in a physical space which fulfilled certain requirements and in which a qualified pharmacist had to be present. This meant there was a total prohibition of sales via the internet. The prohibition was in violation of the rules. *See also* Case C-230/16, *Coty*, in which the Court reached the opposite conclusion: the Court held that in was not in violation of the then Commission Regulation (EU) 330/2010 that a prohibition was imposed on members of a selective distribution system of luxury goods, who operated as resellers on the market, against the use of third-party undertakings for internet sales in a way that was visible for the outside.

qualifications of the reseller and his staff and the suitability of his trading premises and that such conditions are laid down uniformly for all potential resellers and are not applied in a discriminatory fashion.

These criteria for the compatibility of a selective system with Article 101(1) – usually called the 'Metro doctrine' – have been consolidated in subsequent decisions.

In paragraph 112 of Case T-19/92, *Groupement d'achat Édouard Leclerc* (Yves Saint Laurent) *v. Commission*, the CJ laid down four conditions which must be met for the criteria to be regarded as satisfied. It required: *that* the characteristics of the product in question necessitate a selective distribution system (the necessity criterion); *that* resellers are chosen on the basis of objective qualitative criteria which are laid down uniformly for all potential resellers (the non-discrimination criterion); *that* the system in question seeks to achieve a result which enhances competition and thus counterbalances the restriction of competition inherent in selective distribution systems (the market structure criterion); and *that* the criteria laid down do not go beyond what is necessary, namely the maintenance of specialist shops which can ensure the best possible trade in the special goods (the proportionality principle.).

The Necessity Criterion (Products of a Special Nature)

To illustrate this, *see* 85/45/EEC: Commission Decision relating to a proceeding under Article 85 of the EEC Treaty (*Ideal-Standard* distribution system) (OJ 1985 L 20/38). This decision, which concerned the sale of fittings for plumbing systems, should be seen against the background of the statement in paragraph 16 in Case 31/80, *L'Oréal v. De Nieuwe AMCK*, according to which it is necessary to determine 'whether the characteristics of the product in question necessitate a selective distribution system in order to preserve its quality and ensure its proper use, and whether those objectives are not already satisfied by national rules governing admission to the re-sale trade or the conditions of sale of the product in question.'[66]

> The Commission found it questionable, at least in relation to wholesalers, whether the products in question had such characteristics that regard the preservation of their quality and their correct use made it necessary to use a selective distribution system. Also, the restriction on sales (only plumbing engineers could be approved as retailers) was found to be a significant restriction as it would exclude retailers who were not also craftsmen from dealing in the fittings. The disadvantages which such a restriction would lead to were found to be significantly greater than any improvement in the distribution of the goods which would be achieved by selling them through plumbing engineers.

---

66. Regulation (EU) No 720/2022, which as its starting point keeps selective distribution outside the scope of Art. 101(1), does not contain a necessity criterion in relation to the nature of the products.

Nor have selective systems for the sale of tobacco products or the sale of mass-produced watches been accepted, see Case 209/78, *Heintz van Landewyck and others v. Commission*, and Case 31/85, *ETA Fabriques d'Ébauches v. DK Investment and others*.

On the other hand, for cases where the necessity criterion has been found to be satisfied, *see*: Case C-376/92, *Metro SB-Großmärkte v. Cartier*, concerning more expensive watches; Case T-19/92, *Groupement d'achat Édouard Leclerc v. Commission* (Yves Saint Laurent), Case T-88/92, *Groupement d'achat Édouard Leclerc v. Commission* (Givenchy), both concerning high-end cosmetics; and 85/616/EEC: Commission Decision relating to a proceeding pursuant to Article 85 of the EEC Treaty (*Villeroy & Boch*) (OJ 1985 L 376/15) on a selective distribution system for the sale of ornamental and table porcelain. In this last-named Decision, the Commission accepted that a selective distribution system had been built up for these products because 'some products or services, which are not simple products or services, possess certain characteristics which prevent them from being sold properly to the public without the intervention of specialist distributors'.[67] However, 91/153/EEC: Commission Decision relating to a proceeding under Article 85 of the EEC Treaty (*Vichy*) (OJ 1991 L 75/57), which was accepted by the Court in Case T-19/91, *Société d'Hygiène Dermatologique de Vichy v. Commission*, shows that the Commission has apparently sometimes laid down stricter requirements for the special character of products for the approval of some dealers and the exclusion of others than was the case in *Villeroy & Boch*.[68]

The Non-discrimination Criterion

If dealers who satisfy the qualitative conditions for taking part in a selective distribution network are excluded from participating in the network, for example, on the (covert) grounds that the quota of dealers in a given area has been filled or because the customer base is considered too small, this will not normally be compatible with Article 101(1) TFEU, *see* paragraph 72 of Case 75/84, *Metro SB-Großmärkte v. Commission* (*Metro II*), which expressly states that the non-discrimination criterion means that a refusal to approve distributors who satisfy the qualitative criteria of the selective distribution system must be considered unlawful.

A unilateral measure by the producer or by the main dealer, for example a failure to authorise a specific dealer in an attempt to influence pricing, cannot be treated as an infringement of Article 101(1), which only covers *agreements*, *decisions* by associations of undertakings and *concerted practices*. If, on the other hand, such measures are part of a contractual arrangement which the producer or main dealer seeks to uphold with its dealers, then there will be discriminatory measures which fall within the

---

67. Paragraph 22 of the decision.
68. Perhaps the decision expresses the proportionality criterion discussed below.

scope of Article 101(1), *see* paragraph 38 in Case 107/82, *AEG-Telefunken v. Commission*:

Indeed, in the case of the admission of a distributor, approval is based on the acceptance, tacit or express, by the contracting parties of the policy pursued by AEG which requires inter alia the exclusion from the network of all distributors who are qualified for admission but are not prepared to adhere to that policy.

And in paragraph 39, the Court continued:

The view must therefore be taken that even refusals of approval are acts performed in the context of the contractual relations with authorized distributors inasmuch as their purpose is to guarantee observance of the agreements in restraint of competition which form the basis of contracts between manufacturers and approved distributors. Refusals to approve distributors who satisfy the qualitative criteria mentioned above therefore supply proof of an unlawful application of the system if their number is sufficient to preclude the possibility that they are isolated cases not forming part of systematic conduct.[69]

The Commission seems to have emphasised that there must be such an automatic acceptance procedure that the possibility of discrimination is limited. Thus, in several cases, the Commission has made the approval of a selective distribution system conditional on the originally notified acceptance procedure being amended.

See for example 92/428/EEC: Commission Decision relating to a proceeding under Article 85 of the EEC Treaty (*Parfums Givenchy* system of selective distribution) (OJ 1992 L 236/11), in which the finally approved acceptance procedure included a requirement for Givenchy to decide on every application made to the company by interested dealers within specific deadlines, so that every qualified applicant is accepted in the distribution network, or if not, a reason should be given for refusing an application. This eliminated the risk of arbitrariness which was the consequence of the originally envisaged arrangement which gave Givenchy the right to decide on the acceptance of new dealers, according to its own judgment. On the other hand, the change to the arrangement meant that only dealers who were able to or willing to fit out their sales premises in the way demanded could have access to the distribution network. They did not have permission to sell the contract goods before or after the expiry of a relatively long period of notice, which could discourage many potentially qualified dealers. The duration of the deadlines was therefore found to be liable to affect competition between dealers in Givenchy products. The restriction was however exempted in accordance with Article 101(3), since the acceptance procedure was nevertheless found to ensure a smooth integration of new dealers into Givenchy's distribution network. In fact, the deadlines were found to take account of

---

69. Corresponding opinions were expressed by the CJ in Joined Cases 25 and 26/84, *Ford-Werke and Ford of Europe v. Commission*.

Givenchy's need to be able to organise, among other things, the inspection of the sales premises, training of personnel, the scheduling of the company's production programme and production of advertising material. The procedure was found to give retailers reasonable time to fit out their sales premises rationally, and that it was probably necessary to enable the fulfilment of the acceptance procedure laid down.

The Market Structure

Though qualitative selective distribution systems are not, according to the CJ, covered by the prohibition in Article 101(1), even if a selective distribution system satisfies the qualitative requirements and does not contain any quantitative restrictions, there can be a restriction or elimination of competition where the existence of a number of systems of this kind exclude other forms of distribution which are based on other kinds of sales policies or which lead to a rigid price policy which is not balanced by other competitive parameters between products of the same brand (intra-brand competition) or by effective competition between different brands (inter-brand competition). These comments come from paragraph 40 of Case 75/84, *Metro SB-Großmärkte v. Commission (Metro II)*, where it was also emphasised that the existence of a large number of corresponding sales systems would not in itself lead to the assumption that Article 101(1) had been infringed. In this case the Court approved the decision of 1975 by which SABA's selective distribution system had originally been approved.

If qualitative distribution systems are the norm within a given industry sector, so a serious lack of competition arises in the area these systems cover, Article 101(1) will, extraordinarily, apply to these arrangements.[70]

The Proportionality Principle

The requirement for proportionality exists in various forms in several areas of EU law.

In the present context, the principle expresses that a selective distribution system which formally satisfies the qualitative conditions will nevertheless be regarded as incompatible with Article 101(1) if it goes beyond what is necessary for the appropriate sale of the products, *see* 91/153/EEC: Commission Decision relating to a proceeding under Article 85 of the EEC Treaty (*Vichy*) (OJ 1991 L 75/57).

> One of the requirements of the producer Vichy, that the company's cosmetics should be sold exclusively through pharmacies, was found to be disproportionate, as the sales of the products differed from that of medicines as there was no other requirement than that they should not be harmful, and control of this could not be carried out by pharmacies as they did not have precise knowledge of the composition of the products. The judgment took account of the fact that competing products were normally sold through other sales channels. While it was regarded as legitimate to require the presence of a certain level of specialist advice, for example, a requirement that a

---

70. *See* Vivien Rose & David Bailey (eds): Bellamy & Child: *European Union Law of Competition*, 7th ed. 2013 ss 7.099 and 7.105.

pharmacist should be linked to the sales premises, it was not necessary to exclude other forms of traders in order to ensure the products' quality and correct use.

The agreements were therefore contrary to Article 101(1) and the Commission also concluded that there were no grounds for granting an exemption under Article 101(3), as the conditions for granting an exemption under this provision (contributing to improving the production or distribution of goods or promoting technical or economic progress to the benefit of consumers) were not satisfied.[71]

The case was referred to the CJ which upheld the decision of the Commission in Case T-19/91, *Société d'Hygiène Dermatologique de Vichy v. Commission*.

A selective distribution system which excludes the application of Article 101(1) will be valid under competition law, even if there are no agreements for selective distribution in third countries, partially or fully. In other words, the selective distribution system in the EU must be recognised even if the goods covered by the system can be freely acquired from unauthorised dealers in third countries and can be lawfully put into circulation in the Community. A restriction of the producer's guarantee so as to cover only goods bought from authorised dealers is therefore valid. The aim is the same as that which lies behind the selective distribution system, which is to prevent dealers outside the system from trading in the goods covered by the system and fulfilling the guarantee obligations.[72]

4.3.2 *Particular Aspects of Quantitative Restrictions*

Selective distribution agreements have been assessed from a different point of view when they have contained obligations and approval criteria which go beyond the qualitative restrictions referred to in section 4.3.1.

However, it should be made clear that both qualitative and quantitative selective distribution are, in principle, covered by block exemptions granted in accordance with Regulation (EU) No 720/2022, see section 5.2 below, when a market share of 30% (Article 3) is not exceeded, and when the selective system avoids one or more of the serious restrictions on competition in Article 4 and the restrictions in Article 5.[73]

The exemption applies even if the selective system is combined with other non-serious vertical restrictions,[74] such as non-compete obligations or exclusive distribution, which do not involve restrictions on sales by the approved dealers to each other or to end users. If the product's characteristics do not require the implementation

---

71. For a more detailed discussion of these conditions, *see* Ch. 2.
72. *See* Case C-376/92, *Metro SB-Großmärkte v. Cartier*.
73. According to the above comments on the Commission's and the CJ's practice, a purely qualitative selective distribution system is not contrary to Art. 101(1), so that in such cases there will not be a need for an exemption in accordance with Art. 101(3) – and neither in accordance with the block exemption regulation.
74. *See* below in s. 5.4 on Regulation (EU) No 720/2022, Art. 5.

of a selective distribution system, such a system will not normally be sufficiently effective so as to outweigh a significant reduction of inter-brand competition. And if there are appreciable effects on competitiveness, where a large, widespread network of dealers in a market without significant inter-brand competition prevents a competitor's access to the market (cumulative effects), the block exemption will probably be put at risk.[75]

In a number of cases prior to the adoption of Regulation (EU) No 720/2022, both the Commission and the CJ found that special quantitative conditions in a selective distribution system were contrary to Article 81(1) [Article 101(1)]. In exceptional cases, such systems can lose the advantages of a block exemption, see Article 29(1) of Regulation No 1/2003.[76]

These conditions will also be relevant if the basic market threshold in Article 3 of Regulation (EU) No 720/2022 is exceeded, as in this case, an evaluation will be made of the distribution system's compatibility with Article 101(1), independently of the block exemption regulation.

Among other places, the attitude of the CJ to quantitative restrictions has been expressed in paragraph 29 of Case 243/83, *Binon v. Agence et messageries de la presse*:

> In addition, access to such a system should be based on objective criteria of a qualitative nature because the use of quantitative criteria is, by definition, to be regarded as a restriction on competition within the meaning of Article 85 [Article 101]; the permissibility of quantitative criteria may only be taken into account in the context of a request for exemption under Article 85(3) [Article 101(3)] in respect of which the Commission alone is competent.

It is not clear what should be understood as quantitative restrictions in such a case, and thus, their incompatibility with Article 101(1) has not been absolutely determined. The restrictions vary from case to case, and an overall view is first obtained by putting together the restricting elements from several decisions, in which the economic and actual positions in the market in the case in question are taken into consideration.

> The control obligations imposed on the approved dealers in connection with sales to or purchases from other members of the distribution network (controlling that the customer is part of the official network), should make it possible for the producer to control the sales system. Such obligations mean that, as long as they do not go beyond what is necessary for suitable control, supplementary obligations which help ensure the fulfilment of the primary obligation are treated in the same way as the primary obligation (paragraph 27 in Case 26/76, *Metro SB-Großmärkte v. Commission* (1)). Since a prohibition on approved dealers supplying non-approved traders

---

75. *See* Vivien Rose & David Bailey (eds): Bellamy & Child: *European Union Law of Competition*, 7th ed. 2013 s. 7.105.
76. *See* the Vertical Restraints Guidelines, paras 74–78, and the criteria discussed for the possible repeal of an exemption under Art. 29 of Regulation No 1/2003.

would normally be regarded as a restriction on competition, this is exempted according to the practice followed and now expressed under Article 4, no. 3 of Regulation (EU) No 720/2022, and the same is the case for control obligations which have the purpose of ensuring compliance with and supervision of this prohibition.

As for the obligation to participate actively in advertising and sales promotion, in the *Metro* (1) case the Court stated that it could not be the task of a wholesaler to promote the sales of a particular producer. An obligation of this kind is restrictive on competition as, on the one hand, it means that undertakings which satisfy the qualitative requirements but which are not able to take on further obligations are deprived of the possibility of trading in the goods concerned, and on the other hand it restricts the freedom of approved dealers to follow their own independent business policy.

However, in Commission Decision 85/404/EEC relating to a proceeding under Article 85 of the EEC Treaty (*Grundig* EEC distribution system) (OJ 1985 L 233/1) and in the *Parfums Givenchy* Decision, among others, the Commission exempted this provision in accordance with Article 101(3). The obligation was regarded as ensuring that the goods in question were only sold by dealers which could give customers professional advice and, in particular in relation to the sale of durable consumer goods, ensuring the necessary after-sales service in connection with the use and maintenance of the goods.

Conditions on stockholding, in other words, an obligation to invest in a stock of goods, are principally of a quantitative character, as they can mean that only those dealers who are able to take on such an obligation can be accepted in the distribution system. Such an obligation is a restriction on competition but, for example, in the *Grundig* distribution system Decision (OJ 1985 L 233/1), the *Yves Saint Laurent* distribution system Decision (OJ 1992 L 12/24), and the *Parfums Givenchy* Decision (OJ 1992 L 236/11) such a provision was nevertheless exempted out of regard for consumers in accordance with Article 101(3).

An obligation on a dealer to make a minimum purchase from the producer restricts both intra-brand and inter-brand competition, as on the one hand, it means that only those dealers who are able to satisfy the condition can be admitted to the distribution network, and on the other hand, it forces approved dealers to put a significant part of their sales efforts into the sale of the goods of the producer, and this, therefore, restricts freedom of supply.

However, in the *Parfums Givenchy* Decision and elsewhere the Commission has exempted this restriction on competition in accordance with Article 101(3). The obligation to buy a minimum quantity was found to help ensure regular supplies and make it possible to concentrate distribution in the sales outlets with the widest assortment. The obligation could thus ensure better allocation of the costs associated with the sale of the products and the help provided to sales outlets.

The restrictions which are independently laid down in Regulation (EU) No 720/2022, including the prohibition on exclusive territories, and restrictions on the right to determine prices in subsequent stages of the distribution chain (hardcore restrictions), etc., and which apply in general to all vertical agreements, are discussed below in section 5.

4.4 Commercial/Economic Considerations?

Other than in connection and selective distribution, in special cases, the Court has adopted a more commercially-based assessment of certain restrictions on competition, while the fixed attitude to other parts of an agreement has been maintained unaltered.

> In Case 56/65, *Société Technique Minière v. Maschinenbau Ulm*, which concerned an agreement for a sole distributorship in a market where the goods in question had not previously been marketed, the CJ emphasised that the starting point must be the competitive conditions as they would have been if the agreement in question had not existed. The agreement, which neither imposed an obligation on the distributor to refrain from re-exporting the goods, nor an obligation on the producer to prohibit dealers in other EU countries from selling goods into the agreed territory, was found not to infringe Article 101(1).[77]

The *Nungesser* case[78] concerned an instance where the absence of certain provisions restricting competition would have had the effect that *new technology would not have been introduced to the market.*

The decision shows that there can be a need to allow a licensee a certain area of protection without Article 101(1) being immediately brought to bear on the ground that unlawful market-sharing has been established. The decision is discussed below in Chapter 5, as is the latter case of *Louis Erauw-Jacquery v. La Hesbignonne.*[79] In this case, the CJ held that a clause in an agreement on the propagation and sale of seed, under which one of the parties was the holder of certain plant breeders' rights and which contained a prohibition on the propagating firm selling and exporting the basic seed, was compatible with Article 101(1), in so far as it was necessary to enable the plant breeder to choose authorised propagating firms, *see* paragraph 11:

> A provision of an agreement concerning the propagation and sale of seed, in respect of which one of the parties is the holder or the agent of the holder of certain plant breeders' rights, which prohibits the licensee from selling and exporting the basic seed is compatible with Article 85(1) [Article 101(1) TFEU] of the treaty in so far as it is necessary in order to enable the breeder to select the growers who are to be licensees.[80]

---

77. The case is discussed above in s. 2.1.
78. Case 258/78, *Nungesser and Eisele v. Commission.*
79. Case 27/87, *Erauw-Jacquery v. La Hesbignonne.*
80. In the *Nungesser* case the export prohibition was directed against both certified seed and basic seed, whereas the prohibition in the *Erauw-Jacquery* case only covered basic seed. The basis for

In the part of the judgment given here, the decision expressed a point of view that there can often be a need to adopt an *ex ante* approach when assessing whether an agreement is a restriction on competition. Once success has been achieved (the product is established on the market – *ex post*), it becomes less questionable, from a competition law point of view, to allow others to forage in a previously protected area.

5   DEVELOPMENT OF THE BLOCK EXEMPTION REGULATIONS

The development of the block exemption regulations in the area of vertical agreements was previously driven by dissatisfaction with block exemption regulations[81] and was particularly directed at the fact that the regulations, which individually contained guidelines for one particular type of contract, prevented the development of new and innovative forms of distribution adapted to the dynamic which characterises contractual relations in the area of distribution (the straightjacket effect).[82] A need for drawing on the guidelines of the Commission and the Courts to deal with *selective distribution* was identified. It has also been pointed out that it was unsatisfactory that the regulations only took account of contractual relations between two undertakings, that the rules (including the Regulation on exclusive distribution agreements) were only concerned with the resale of finished products, and not equally with semi-finished products for incorporation in products for onward sale, and that the Regulation, in general, did not regulate the provisions of services.[83]

A constantly repeated objection to the block exemption regulations was their inability to tackle a number of the more egregious cases of *vertical* restraints on competition. A system in which an agreement which formally satisfies the content of a number of specific whitelisted (i.e., approved) conditions is exempt from any objection will not catch those agreements where one or more of the parties has such a strong position in the market that, taken in isolation, the agreement can be considered to have the character of an abuse of dominant position.[84] Furthermore, until the new millennium, such a dominant actor in the distribution chain could take advantage of the benefits associated with a *notification* of the agreement. In principle, the parties could claim exemption even if the case involved a market share of up to 100%, which should not have been covered by the block exemption regulations. The amendment to Regulation No 17/62, First

---

the decision can therefore presumably be sought in the special nature of the exclusive right which gives the owner of that right the right to oppose the unauthorised use of the right by third parties. This decision is discussed below in Ch. 5.

81. Including Commission Regulation (EEC) No 1983/83 on the application of Art. 85(3) of the Treaty to categories of exclusive distribution agreements; Commission Regulation (EEC) No 1984/83 on the application of Art. 85(3) of the Treaty to categories of exclusive purchasing agreements; and Commission Regulation (EEC) No 4087/88 on the application of Art. 85(3) of the Treaty to categories of franchise agreements.
82. In Case 161/84, *Pronuptia*, the CJ held that a franchise agreement did not fall within the scope of any of the then existing block exemption regulations.
83. Special rules on selective distribution, *see* Regulation (EU) No 720/2022, Art. 4(c), as well as Art. 5(1)(c) depart from the point of view that all types of vertical contracts should be subject to uniform rules.
84. On this point of view compared with a more in depth economic analysis of the market conditions, *see* the comments above in s. 1.1.

Regulation implementing Articles 85 and 86 of the Treaty, by Regulation No 1216/99, under which the notification system for *vertical* agreements was scrapped and replaced by a system with exemptions determined by law together with subsequent controls of agreements which restrict competition, has taken some of the edge off the criticism. The new rules mean that an agreement which restricts competition and is caught by Article 101(1) but cannot satisfy the requirement for an exemption in Article 101(3) will be unlawful and, therefore, without legal effect from the time when the agreement comes into being.[85]

5.1 Green Paper on Vertical Restraints in EC Competition Policy

Because, among other reasons, new distribution methods can have an effect on future competition policy, in 1997, the Commission prepared a green paper which, in addition to containing a review of the legal and economic situation with regard to vertical restraints which had applied hitherto, contained a number of proposals for amending the conditions for block exemptions. During consultations, the green paper was laid before the European Parliament, the Member States and other interested parties, including producers, distributors, employees' and consumers' organisations, etc.[86] As could be expected, there was far from unanimity between the bodies consulted as to how competition policy should be shaped.

However, the Commission found that, on the basis of the responses received, it was possible to identify two main tendencies. First, there seemed to be a need, in principle, to depart from the formal use of whitelisted and blacklisted conditions. Second, market-share thresholds ought to be included in assessing the competitive effects of vertical restraint agreements so as to give significant weight to the actual market positions of the participating undertakings.

5.2 Commission Regulation (EU) No 720/2022

The Council's criteria for the new block exemption Regulation resulted in the adoption of Regulation No 2790/99, which entered into force in 2000. As stated, Regulation No 2790/99 has been replaced by Regulation (EU) No 330/2010 and now by Regulation (EU) No 720/2022, which, apart from a couple of amendments, in many ways corresponds to the content of Regulation No 2790/99.

The block exemption Regulation only applies to agreements which would otherwise be caught by Article 101(1) TFEU and, therefore, has no effect on the Commission's *De minimis* Notice or other explanatory notices which clarify the scope of Article 101(1).

---

85. Even though, later block exemption regulations, including the most recent, Regulation (EU) No 720/2022, in principle no longer make an express distinction between permitted (whitelisted) restrictions on competition and prohibited (blacklisted) restrictions, nevertheless the content of Art. 4 of the Regulation effectively continues the blacklisted restrictions which applied under the earlier Regulation.
86. Green Paper on Vertical Restraints in EC Competition Policy COM(96) 721 final, of 22 Jan. 1997.

The preamble to Regulation (EU) No 720/2022 contains twenty-one recitals and eleven enacting articles. In comparison to Regulation (EU) 330/2010, it appears that the most recent block exemption contains a more in-depth and detailed regulation. It appears from the preamble as well as, of course, from the provisions in the Regulation that the greatest innovation in regard to previous block exemptions is the increased focus on online sales. In Recital 2 of the preamble, it is pointed out that one of the developments that has been included is the growth of e-commerce. The use of online intermediation services plays a central role in the new set of rules, and in Recital 10 of the preamble, it is stressed that 'The online platform economy plays an increasingly important role in the distribution of goods and services. Undertakings active in the online platform economy make it possible to do business in new ways, some of which are not easy to categorise using concepts associated with vertical agreements in the traditional economy. In particular, online intermediation services allow undertakings to offer goods or services to other undertakings or to final consumers, with a view to facilitating the initiation of direct transactions between undertakings or between undertakings and final consumers. Agreements relating to the provision of online intermediation services are vertical agreements and should therefore be able to benefit from the block exemption established by this Regulation, subject to the conditions set out in this Regulation.' This focus has resulted in several provisions in the Regulation, including Article 1(1), point (e), according to which 'online intermediation services' means information society services within the meaning of Article 1(1), point (b), of Directive (EU) 2015/1535 of the European Parliament and of the Council which allows undertakings to offer goods or services: (i) to other undertakings, with a view to facilitating the initiating of direct transactions between those undertakings, or (ii) to final consumers, with a view to facilitating the initiating of direct transactions between those undertakings and final consumers, irrespective of whether and where the transactions are ultimately concluded.[87]

According to Article 2(1) of the Regulation (together with Article 1(1)(a)), the exemption applies to vertical restraints in agreements or concerted practices entered into between two or more undertakings which, in relation to the agreement or concerted practice, operate at different levels of the production or distribution chain, and relating to the conditions under which the parties may purchase, sell or resell certain goods or services.

In general, the 'restrictions' referred to in the provision can include the following negative effects which the EU's competition law seeks to prevent:

(1) the exclusion either of other producers or other purchasers (dealers);
(2) the reduction of competition either for goods of the same brand or between different brands;
(3) agreements between suppliers and dealers, which are promoted by the vertical restraints; and

---

87. In regard to the use of the prohibitions in the Regulation in connection with online intermediation services – *see*, for example, s. 4.3 of the Vertical Restraints Guidelines.

(4) the creation of hindrances to market integration, including restrictions on consumers' freedom to purchase goods or services in any Member State, according to their choice.

In relation to these restraints, in its Follow-up to the Green Paper on vertical restraints COM(98) 544 final (OJ 1998 C 365/3), the Commission made a number of general comments as follows:

> That a restraint which consists of the purchaser being induced to concentrate their orders for a particular type of good with one supplier generally has greater negative effects on competition than agreements on exclusive distribution, where the supplier only sells its products to one or a limited number of dealers. By excluding other brands the former obligations can prevent these brands being able to gain access to the market at all.
> That exclusive agreements (one dealer covering all or practically all its requirements with its counterparty, so that it is prevented from buying, selling-on or using competing goods or services) are generally more harmful to competition than non-exclusive agreements. In this situation a risk can arise that the market will be isolated from competing or potentially competing suppliers, to the disadvantage of inter-brand competition.
> That the possible negative consequences of vertical restraints are reinforced when not only one supplier practises certain vertical restraints with its dealers, but when other suppliers organise their trade correspondingly (cumulative effects).

It follows from Article 1(1)(a) of Regulation (EU) No 720/20122 that the exemption also applies to agreements between more than two undertakings, that the scope of exemption is extended to cover the purchase of semi-finished products and that the agreements etc. can concern *service provision*. However, vertical agreements with end consumers fall outside the scope of the Regulation. See the wording of Article 1(1)(a), which presumes that the parties to the agreement are undertakings which, for the purposes of the agreement, operate at a different level of the production or distribution chain.[88]

Agreements entered into between an association of undertakings and its members, or between such an association and its suppliers, are covered by the exemption subject to the conditions in Article 2(2), provided that no individual member of the association, together with its connected undertakings, has a total annual turnover exceeding EUR 50 million.

A vertical agreement which contains restraints imposed in connection with the licensing or use of *intellectual property rights*, including trademarks, patents, copyright and neighbouring rights (*see* Article 1(1)(i)), is only covered by the block exemption as long as these rights do not constitute the primary object of such agreements and are directly related to the use, sale or resale of goods or services, *see* Article 2(3). A pure sales

---

88. Distribution agreements in the motor vehicle industry are not covered by Regulation (EU) No 720/2022 as long as they are covered by a special block exemption agreement; *see* Commission Regulation (EU) No 461/2010 on the application of Art. 101(3) of the TFEU to categories of vertical agreements and concerted practices in the motor vehicle sector. This Regulation actually expired in 2023, but was extended until 31 May 2028 in Commission Regulation (EU) 822/2023.

licence, by which an intermediary obtains an exclusive right to sell a product on an export market, is comparable with a distribution agreement, and its effects are assessed in accordance with Regulation (EU) No 720/2022; *see also* the corresponding provision in Article 1(1)(c) of Regulation No 316/2014 on technology transfer agreements.

A vertical agreement between *competing undertakings* falls outside the block exemption; *see* Article 2(4).[89] However, the exemption under Article 2(1) does apply when the agreement is of a non-reciprocal nature (producer A is the distributor of producer B's products, without producer B being the distributor of producer A's products) and when the two conditions in Article 2(4)(a) or (b) are fulfilled. These situations include (a) the supplier is a producer or dealer of the goods, and the purchaser is a dealer who does not produce competing goods (parallel distribution); or (b) the supplier provides services at several business levels, and the purchaser does not provide competing services at the business level where it buys the services. These conditions were already included in Commission Regulation (EU) No 330/2010, but Commission Regulation (EU) No 720/2022 limits the possibilities of using the first two exemptions mentioned immediately above in certain situations. According to Article 2(5) of Commission Regulation (EU) No 720/2022, the exceptions shall not apply to the exchange of information between the supplier and the buyer that is either not directly related to the implementation of the vertical agreement or is not necessary to improve the production or distribution of the contract goods or services, or which fulfils neither of those two conditions. In Article 2(6) of the Regulation, it is established that the exceptions in the two situations described above do not apply to vertical agreements relating to the provision of online intermediation services where the provider of the online intermediation services is a competing undertaking on the relevant market for the sale of the intermediated goods or services.[90]

Pursuant to Article 3(1), the exemption applies provided the supplier's market share does not exceed 30% of the relevant market on which it sells the goods or services covered by the agreement, and the buyer's market share does not exceed 30% of the relevant market where it buts the goods or services covered by the agreement.

The Regulation thus assumes that with most vertical restraints, problems with competition will only arise if there is insufficient *inter-brand* competition, in other words, because of the market strength of the supplier or purchaser or both. This concept includes the ability to increase prices above the level that would apply in a competitive market. An undertaking can have *market strength* without having market dominance, which is the criterion for the application of Article 102 TFEU. If several undertakings compete in a non-concentrated market, there will be an assumption that non-serious vertical restraints will not have significant negative effects.

A calculation of the market share requires a definition to be made of 'the relevant market', in other words, both the relevant product market and the relevant geographic market; *see* Commission Notice on the definition of relevant market for the purposes of Community competition law (OJ 1997C 372/5). The relevant product market includes

---

89. Status on agreements between competing undertakings is dealt with in more detail in s. 4.4.3 of the Vertical Restraints Guidelines.
90. *See* more on this topic in s. 4.4.4 of the Vertical Restraints Guidelines.

products or services which are regarded as interchangeable or substitutable by the consumer by reason of the products' characteristics, prices and intended use, while the relevant geographic market covers the area in which the undertakings concerned are involved in the supply of products or services, in which the conditions of competition are sufficiently homogeneous, and which can be distinguished from neighbouring areas because the conditions of competition are appreciably different. The relevant market for assessing a problem under competition law is, therefore, defined by a combination of the product market and the geographic market.[91]

The assumption behind the simplified procedure in Article 3, in which there is a reference to the supplier's and buyer's market shares in the market between the two parties, is that the effects in *the subsequent links* in the distribution chain will be limited when the market share is below 30%.[92]

5.3 Agreements for Specifically Stated Purposes: The Regulation's Hardcore Restrictions

While the block exemption regulations that have hitherto applied in the area of distribution have been based on certain conditions in the relations between the producer and the distributor being to the advantage of consumers (whitelisted conditions), the opposite has been the case for restrictions that have given the parties the possibility of implementing price differentiation and isolating the market. Such restrictions are considered to work counter to market integration, which has been one of the core principles behind the establishment of the internal market, and they have consistently been blacklisted; in other words, they are the ultimate hindrances to the granting of block exemptions.[93]

The straightjacket effect previously referred to, which has been associated with the whitelisted conditions, necessarily requires giving up the distinction between white and black if the aim of replacing the previous block exemption regulations with one regulation for all vertical restraints is to become a reality for the benefit of the future distribution of goods and services in the internal market.

These considerations lie behind the provision in Article 4 of Regulation (EU) No 720/2022, with its prohibition of conditions which restrict the buyer's ability to determine its sale price and the prohibition on agreements on sales restrictions to subsequent distribution stages, which must be respected regardless of whether or not

---

91. For an illustrative case, *see* Case T-25/99, *Roberts & Roberts v. Commission* (the *Greene King* case), on restrictions on the sale of beer from pubs and restaurants.
92. Any negative variations from this position could be countered via Art. 29(1) of Regulation No 1/2003, under which the Commission can take measures if an agreement which is subject to an exemption nevertheless has effects which are incompatible with Art. 101 TFEU. This is particularly directed at situations in which competing suppliers or distributors have parallel networks of similar agreements which significantly restrict competition on the market concerned.
93. *See*, for example, Art. 3 of Regulation No 1983/83 (exclusive distribution) and Arts 4 and 5 of Regulation No 4087/88 (franchising).

the market threshold referred to in Article 3 is crossed; *see* Case T-176/95, *Accinauto v. Commission*, referred to in section 2 above.[94]

It is a consistent characteristic of monopolies legislation in Western countries that conditions which impose *fixed prices on subsequent stages* of the distribution chain (vertically bound prices) are considered to be harmful to competition and are, therefore, usually prohibited. The prohibition on fixing sales prices is maintained in Article 4(a) of Regulation (EU) No 720/2022 as a condition which will prevent the granting of an exemption. In addition to this, for the same reason, the EU's competition authorities have looked very closely and very seriously into arrangements which, directly or indirectly, have the aim of restricting dealers' sales into a specific *territory* or to a specific *customer group* (agreements on market sharing), *see* Article 4(b), Article 4(c)(i), and Article 4(d)[95]

Agreements which have been criticised by the courts have often contained both clauses on binding prices and provisions prohibiting the distributor from selling outside a defined territory (exclusive rights territory). If, for the same product, different price levels are set in different geographic areas, the prohibited binding prices can only be maintained in the high-price territories if it is possible to hinder parallel exports to these territories, as such exports would otherwise undermine the higher prices. In these cases and in other cases, an attempt to maintain the higher prices will often be combined with restrictions in the form of territorial protection or customer group protection.

The prohibitions in Article 4(a) and (b) have been the main theme of several decisions where undertakings have attempted to counteract *parallel imports* into a protected territory.

> The term 'parallel imports' is usually used to refer to imports of products which are made outside the producer's official distribution system by a third party who buys the products in area A and sells them to an unauthorised importer in area B who resells the products in area B in competition with the authorised importers. According to this definition, it is characteristic for parallel imports that there is no difference between the products which are sold to the authorised dealer and those that are sold by the unauthorised importer. The expression is sometimes used with a broader meaning to cover cases where an imported good has been produced under licence in a third country by an undertaking other than the authorised importer's supplier (the producer) so that the parallel importer's product is not of the same manufacture as that which is supplied through the authorised channels.[96]

On a more general level, the basis for allowing parallel imports is found in Article 34 TFEU, as the sole importer's ability to rely on intellectual property rights would constitute a measure having an equivalent effect to a quantitative restriction. In the

---

94. The serious restrictions in Art. 4 affect agreements on trade within the Community. As for exports from the Community or imports/re-imports from third countries, *see* Case C-306/96, *Javico International v. Yves Saint Laurent Parfums*.
95. The three provisions maintain the prohibition in regard to exclusive distribution systems, selective distribution systems and free distribution systems respectively.
96. The term 'pirate imports' is used to refer to imports of goods which are typically of poorer quality, for example counterfeit goods, which are sold as original goods.

area of competition, claims of patent rights or trade mark rights could be an expression of a restriction on competition contrary to Article 101(1).

From the point of view of the authorised importer, the general acceptance of parallel imports is not always reasonable. This importer will often incur considerable costs in generating consumer interest in the goods, and the parallel importer will be able to benefit from this goodwill without incurring costs. This is often reasonably enough considered a gross injustice by the authorised importer. However, the view of the Commission and the Court is clear: parallel importation is a legal form of business.

See 95/477/EC: Commission Decision relating to a proceeding pursuant to Article 85 of the EC Treaty (*BASF Lacke + Farben, and Accinauto*) (OJ 1995 L 272/16), which contains an instructive review of the Commission's approach to parallel imports and market sharing.

The concepts 'active sales' and 'passive sales' play a decisive role in connection with the use of Article 4 of Commission Regulation (EU) No 720/2022 on hardcore restrictions. The two concepts have to do with who initiates the sale: the seller or the customer. In active sales, the seller actively targets the customer, and in passive sales, it is thus the customer who actively targets the seller. Commission Regulation (EU) No 720/2022 has contributed to a considerable clarification of these concepts. In Article 1(1)(l) of the Regulation, active sales are described in this way: actively targeting customers by, for example, visits, letters, emails, calls or other means of direct communication or through targeted advertising and promotion, offline or online, for instance by means of print or digital media, including online media, price comparison services or advertising on search engines targeting customers in particular territories or customer groups, operating a website with a top-level domain corresponding to particular territories, or offering on a website languages that are commonly used in particular territories, where such languages are different from the ones commonly used in the territory in which the buyer is established. Article 1(1)(m) of the Regulation establishes similarly the concept of passive sales like this 'sales made in response to unsolicited requests from individual customers, including delivery of goods or services to the customer, without the sale having been initiated by actively targeting the particular customer, customer group or territory, and including sales resulting from participating in public procurement or responding to private invitations to tender.'[97]

5.3.1   Article 4(a): Price Discrimination and Selective Prices

The prohibition, in Article 4(a) of Regulation (EU) No 330/2010, of agreements that restrict the buyer's ability to determine its sales price and other trading terms for goods that are covered by the agreement has a parallel in Article 101(1)(a) TFEU. The attitude of the CJ and the Commission to such restrictive agreements is reflected in the case law, which is reviewed above in section 2.1.3.

---

97. *See also* s. 6.1.2.2 (item 211–215) of the European Commission's Guidelines on vertical constraints (2022/C 248/01), in which further examples of the difference between active and passive sales are available.

Article 4(a) fulfils the aim set out in Recital 15 of the Regulation, according to which the Regulation should not exempt vertical agreements containing restrictions which are likely to restrict competition and harm consumers or which are not indispensable to the attainment of the efficiency-enhancing effects, which is the purpose of the regulation of competition in the EU.

The provision expressly exempts agreements imposing a maximum sales price or recommending a sales price. This limit to the extent of the prohibition is not expressly referred to in Article 101(1)(a) TFEU, but it is fully reflected in the EU competition authorities' interpretation of the Treaty provision.

5.3.2 *Article 4(b): Exclusive Distribution Systems*

The hardcore restrictions in Article 4(b) of the Regulation are targeted at exclusive distribution systems. Such systems are defined as distribution systems where the supplier allocates a territory or group of customers exclusively to itself or to a maximum of five buyers and restricts all its other buyers from actively selling into the exclusive territory or to the exclusive customer group.[98]

The starting point in Article 4(b) of the Regulation is a prohibition of agreements restricting the territory into which or customers to whom a buyer party to the agreement may actively or passively sell the goods or services subject to the agreement.[99]

Five restrictions linked to Article 4(b) are discussed immediately below.

5.3.2.1 *Modifications*

- The restriction in Article 4(b) of Regulation (EU) No 330/2010 does not concern prohibitions against *active* sales into the exclusive territory or to an exclusive customer group reserved to the supplier or allocated by the supplier to up to five other buyers. The producer and any other dealers can therefore still be protected from another dealer who is bound by a prohibition attempting to take over their customer base, and if others of the supplier's dealers are subject to a corresponding restriction, that dealer can be protected against others trying to make inroads in their territory.
- Without reference to block exemptions, an agreement between a producer and a wholesaler may impose obligations on the wholesaler, which restrict sales to end users, meaning buyers who themselves use the goods, cf. Article 4(b)(iv).[100]
- A third modification of the starting position is that it is legitimate to set up restrictions in regard to active or passive sales by the exclusive distributor and its customers to unauthorised distributors located in a territory where the supplier operates a selective distribution system for the contract goods or

---

98. *See* Art. 1(1)(b) of Commission Regulation (EU) No 720/2022.
99. The provisions correspond with Recital 15 of the Regulation preamble.
100. In such a case the wholesaler could offer a lower price to end users than a retailer who acquires the products from a wholesaler with a view to offering them to end users.

services, cf. Article 4(b)(ii). By this, the considerations from the selective distribution system are also in connection with the supplier's use of an exclusive distribution system.[101]
- The exemption applies even if, while complying with the market threshold in Article 3(1), the selective distribution system is combined with other non-serious vertical restraints, such as non-compete obligations within the scope of Article 5 (*see* section 5.4 below), stockholding, minimum purchases etc., in other words, conditions which, in the practice of the Court and the Commission prior to Regulation (EU) No 720/2022, had been classified as quantitative restrictions contrary to Article 101(1). If the characteristics of the product to not require the establishment of a selective distribution system, even if this is not expressly stated in Regulation (EU) No 7202022, such a system will not normally have sufficient effectiveness benefits to outweigh the significant reduction of intra-brand competition. And if appreciable restrictions on competition arise, the block exemption will presumably be at risk. In extraordinary cases, particularly where competition is significantly restricted by the cumulative effect of parallel networks of similar vertical restraints implemented by competing suppliers or buyers, such agreements could lose the benefits associated with block exemptions; *see* Article 29(1) of Regulation No 1/2003.
- A fourth modification of the starting position in Article 4(b) allows a supplier of components for incorporation in other products to prohibit distributors from supplying such components to customers who would use them to manufacture the same type of goods as those produced by the supplier, cf. Article 4(b)(v).
- A fifth modification is seen in Article 4(b)(iii), according to which it is legitimate to restrict the exclusive distributor's place of establishment. In the Vertical Restraints Guidelines, it is specified that as regards mobile distribution outlets, the agreement may specify an area outside which the outlet cannot be operated. However, the establishment and use of an online store by the distributor is not equivalent to the opening of a physical outlet and thus cannot be restricted.[102]

5.3.2.2   Article 4(c) Selective Distribution

The starting point in relation to selective distribution systems is that where the supplier operates an exclusive distribution system, the restriction of the territory into which, or of the customers to whom, the exclusive distributor may actively or passively sell the contract goods or services, restrictions on the territory or the group of customers to whom members of the selective distribution system actively or passively are allowed to sell goods or services are prohibited cf. Article 4(c)(i). Article 4(c)(i) Nos 1-5,

---

101. *See also* para. 223 of the Vertical Constraints Guidelines.
102. Paragraph 224 of the Vertical Constraints Guidelines.

contains similar legitimate modifications which are seen in relation to Article 4(b) on exclusive distribution systems (*see* the section immediately above).[103]

A corresponding hardcore restriction applies to *cross-supplies* between authorised distributors, and if the block exemption applies, such authorised distributors must be free to execute orders received from other members of the selective distribution system, including orders from distributors operating at different levels of trade (Article 4(c)(ii)).

5.3.2.3 Article 4(f) Components

Article 4(f) is aimed at the situation where a buyer of components which are incorporated into its products seeks to impose an obligation on the supplier of the components not to supply corresponding components either to end users or to other undertakings which compete with the buyer with regard to repair work on the products in which the buyer incorporates the components. The buyer's motive is thus not just related to operations on the market for finished products but also to the subsequent repair and service market. The provision means that such an agreement between the buyer and supplier of components falls outside the exemption in Article 2 of the Regulation.[104]

5.3.2.4 Free Distribution Systems

Article 4(d) of the Regulation relates to distribution systems which are not exclusive distribution systems or selective distribution systems. These distribution systems are called free distribution systems.[105] The provision represents the same starting point as is seen in Article 4(b)(c) for exclusive distribution systems and selective distribution systems, respectively, and thus, it is prohibited for suppliers (who do not use an exclusive distribution system or a selective distribution system) to limit the territory or the group of customers to whom a buyer actively or passively is allowed to sell contract goods and services. This prohibition is subject to the same modifications that are included in Article 4(b)(i)-(v) and Article 4(c)(i) Nos 1-5 cf. the above.

5.3.2.5 Effective Use of the Internet

The greatest innovation in Commission Regulation (EU) No 720/2022 in relation to hardcore restrictions is the introduction of Article 4(e), which deals with restrictions on

---

103. *See also* case law from before Commission Regulation (EU) No 720/2022, Case C-230/16, *Coty*, where the CJ held that the fact that an agreement contained a restriction, which was placed on the members of a selective distribution system for luxury goods, which operated as distributors on the market, against the use of third-party undertakings in connection with internet sales in a way which was visible for the outside, is not a restriction of the group of customers dealt with in Art. 4(b) of Commission Regulation (EU) No 330/2010, or a restriction of passive sales to end users dealt with in Art. 4(c) of the Regulation.
104. *See* the Vertical Restraints Guidelines, para. 245.
105. *See* the Vertical Restraints Guidelines, para. 116, s. 4.6.

the buyer's possibility to use the Internet to sell contract goods. It is decided that the prevention of the effective use of the Internet by the buyer or its customers to sell the contract goods or services, as it restricts the territory into which or the customers to whom the contract goods or services may be sold, is prohibited. However, the supplier is allowed to impose on the buyer (i) other restrictions on online sales; or (ii) restrictions on online advertising that do not have the object of preventing the use of an entire advertising channel.

The restriction in Article 4, point (e) includes a vertical agreement containing one or more restrictions of online sales or online advertising which de facto prohibit the buyer from using the internet to sell the contract goods or services as such agreements, at the very least, have the object of restricting passive sales to end users wishing to purchase online and located outside the buyer's physical trading area.[106] The same applies to vertical agreements, which do not directly prohibit but have the object of preventing the effective use of the internet by a buyer or its customers to sell the contract goods or services to particular territories or customers. For instance, this is the case for vertical agreements which have the object of significantly diminishing the aggregate volume of online sales of the contract goods or services or the possibility for end users to buy the contract goods or services online. Similarly, this is the case for vertical agreements that have the object of preventing the use of one or more entire online advertising channels by the buyer, such as search engines or price comparison services, or of preventing the buyer from establishing or using its own online store. In the Vertical Restraints Guidelines, it is pointed out that the assessment of whether a restriction is hardcore within the meaning of Article 4, point (e) of the Regulation may take into account the content and context of the restriction, but it cannot depend on market-specific circumstances or the individual characteristics of the parties to the vertical agreement.[107]

5.4 Restrictions That Fall Outside the Scope of the Exemption

Article 5 of Regulation (EU) No 720/2022, on restrictions on competition, refers to restrictions that are non-exempt, even if the market-share threshold in Article 3 is not exceeded. As distinct from the serious restrictions in Article 4, the exemption still applies to the other parts of an agreement as long as they can be distinguished from the non-exempt parts of the agreement.

According to the definition in Article 1(1)(f) of Regulation (EU) No 720/2022, a 'non-compete obligation' means any direct or indirect obligation causing the buyer not to manufacture, purchase, sell or resell goods or services which compete with the contract goods or services, or any direct or indirect obligation on the buyer to purchase from the supplier or from another undertaking designated by the supplier more than 80% of the buyer's total purchases of the contract goods or services and their

---

106. The Vertical Restraints Guidelines, para. 116, s. 4.6.
107. The Vertical Restraints Guidelines, para. 203.

substitutes on the relevant market, calculated on the basis of the value of its purchases in the preceding calendar year, where such is standard industry practice.

The principal reason for Article 5 follows from Recital 16 of the Regulation, which talks about the need to ensure access to the market for competing undertakings and to prevent unlawful collusion. It is also necessary to ensure that contractual obligations which require members of a selective distribution system not to sell the brands of particular competing suppliers should be excluded from the benefit of the block exemption.

On this basis, Article 5(1)(b)[108] provides that a non-compete obligation which continues after the expiry of the agreement is not exempt if it is of indefinite duration or exceeds five years.

Non-compete obligations that are tacitly renewable beyond a period of five years are deemed to have been concluded for an indefinite duration; *see* Article 5(1)(c), last paragraph. However, there is nothing to prevent a non-compete obligation for five years from being *renewed* for a further five-year period if this is based on the parties' *express* agreement, and provided that there are no conditions which mean that the distributor is, in fact, prevented from ending the non-compete obligation at the end of the five year period.[109]

Under Article 5(1)(b) of the Regulation, non-compete obligations which continue after the termination of an agreement normally fall outside an exemption unless, among other things, they are indispensable to protect know-how[110] transferred by the supplier to the buyer and in this case, the distributor can be bound for up to one year after the termination of the agreement; *see* Article 5(3)(c) and (d). Article 5(1)(b) does not prevent the imposition of a restriction of unlimited duration on the use and disclosure of know-how which has not entered the public domain; *see* Article 5(3), last paragraph.

In agreements that are part of a selective distribution system, a non-compete obligation which requires the distributor not to resell competing products, in general, will be covered by a block exemption. However, if a producer directly or indirectly prevents authorised distributors from buying products for resale from particular competing producers, then an exemption will not be allowed, *see* Article 5(1)(c). The aim of excluding such an obligation from exemption is to prevent a number of producers from using the same selective sales channels and shutting out one or more

---

108. On the interpretation of the exemption provisions in Art. 5(2), *see* Case C-260/07, *Pedro IV Servicios*, on a petrol distribution contract in which certain terms applied for more than twenty years.
109. If, for example, an agreement includes a five year non-compete obligation and the producer extends a loan to the distributor, the repayment of this loan must not prevent the distributor from ending the obligation at the end of the five-year period; the repayment must be made in equal or diminishing instalments, but they may not increase over time, *see* the Vertical Restraints Guidelines, para. 58. In any case, the distributor must have the possibility of repaying the balance if there is any outstanding debt when the non-compete obligation expires.
110. 'Know-how' is defined in Art. 1(g). The exemption in Art. 5(3)(b) limiting non-compete clauses to the premises and land from which the buyer carried on business during the contractual period was interpreted narrowly in Case C-117/12, *La Retoucherie de Manuela*, so as only to cover the premises and land from which the contractual goods or services were offered for sale, and not the whole of the area in which goods or services can be sold on the basis of the franchise agreement; *see* para. 41.

specific competitors from distributing their products through the sales channels in question (protection of the market from a competing supplier), which would be a form of collective boycott.[111]

With Commission Regulation (EU) No 720/2022, a new part of Article 5 was introduced, according to which the exemption in Article 2 does not apply to the following obligation: any direct or indirect obligation causing a buyer of online intermediation services not to offer, sell or resell goods or services to end users under more favourable conditions via competing online intermediation services, see Article 5(1)(d). The provision deals with so-called parity obligations, and in the Vertical Restraints Guidelines, it is stated that such conditions can relate to prices, inventory, availability or any other terms or conditions of offer or sale. The retail parity obligation may result from a contractual clause or from other direct or indirect measures, including the use of differential pricing or incentives whose application depends on the conditions under which the buyer of the online intermediation services offers goods or services to end users via competing online intermediation services. For example, where the provider of online intermediation services makes the offering of better visibility for the buyer's goods or services on the provider's website or the application of a lower commission rate dependent on the buyer granting it parity of conditions relative to competing providers of such services, this amounts to an across-platform retail parity obligation.[112]

5.5   Withdrawal of an Exemption

If a vertical agreement keeps within the market-share threshold laid down in Article 3 of Regulation (EU) No 330/2010 and does not otherwise infringe either the hardcore restrictions in Article 4 or the restrictions in Article 5, there will be an assumption that the agreement is lawful, and this will normally mean that the agreement can be acted on without the risk of intervention by the competition authorities. However, in special cases, this assumption can be overturned with effect from the date of the decision, either by a decision of the Commission or the competent authorities of a Member State.

The authority to withdraw an exemption was originally given in Articles 6 and 7 of Regulation No 2790/99. After the implementation of Regulation No 1/2003, these provisions were moved to Article 29(1) and (2) of the new Regulation.

In relation to taking concrete steps against existing agreements, the authority for the Commission and the national competition authorities to take steps against parallel networks of vertical agreements is a continuation of corresponding precautionary measures in Article 6 of Regulation No 1983/83 on exclusive distribution agreements and Article 8 of Regulation No 4087/88 on franchising. This authority to intervene was not, in fact, directly used under the previous arrangement. The Commission's authority to deny an exemption by a special regulation is a new measure which did not exist in the earlier regulations.

---

111. There was an example of indirect measures with such protective effects in Commission Decision on the *Parfums Givenchy* case (OJ 1992 L 236/11). *See also* para. 252 of the Guidelines.
112. Paragraph 253 of the Vertical Restraints Guidelines.

5.5.1 Article 29.1 of Regulation No 1/2003: The Commission's Withdrawal of Exemption

The withdrawal of a block exemption under Article 29(1) of Regulation No 1/2003 will be relevant if competing suppliers or purchasers have parallel networks of similar vertical agreements, which together have the effect of significantly restricting access to the relevant market.[113]

The Commission has the burden of proof for showing that agreements fall within the terms of Article 101(1) TFEU and that the conditions do not exist for one or more of the four exemption criteria in Article 101(3). Full evidence will be relevant not only in those cases where several suppliers have arranged their distribution agreements with vertical restraints of the same kind but also when they have used different combinations of vertical restraints. Depending on the circumstances, the withdrawal of an exemption will only concern restraints which lead to a reduction in the number of distributors, and responsibility for the cumulative effect of restrictions on competition can only be ascribed to undertakings which have contributed appreciably to it.

5.5.2 Withdrawal of Exemption Within the Territory of an Individual Member State

Article 29(1) of Regulation No 1/2003 concerns the Commission's authority to act on its own initiative to withdraw exemptions for vertical agreements that restrict competition on a geographic market which is greater than the area of a single Member State.

According to Article 29(2), *the competition authorities of individual Member States* can withdraw exemptions for agreements whose cumulative effects affect all or part of the Member State's territory when this territory has all the characteristics of a distinct geographic market. The substantive conditions for the withdrawal are the same as those laid down in Article 29(1).

6 CONCLUSION

On the basis of the foregoing explanation of the Commission's preparatory legislative work, the statements that have accompanied the block exemption regulations, etc., and the competition law principles which form the basis of the decisions of the Commission and the Community Courts, the conclusion must be that on competitive markets the effects of restrictions on competition which are associated with vertical restraints will only have a modest negative effect. Apart from the serious restrictions on

---

113. *See* Recital 18 of Regulation (EU) No 720/2022 which is repeated in the Vertical Restraints Guidelines, paras 257–258. *See also* the comments in Case C-234/89, *Stergios Delimitis v. Henninger Bräu*, paras 24–26. Paragraph 261 of the Vertical Restraints Guidelines states that responsibility for an anti-competitive cumulative effect can only be attributed to those undertakings which make an appreciable contribution to it. Agreements entered into by undertakings whose contribution to the cumulative effect is insignificant are not subject to the withdrawal mechanism.

competition referred to in Article 4 and the restrictions referred to in Article 5 of Regulation (EU) No 720/2022, which the Commission and the Courts have consistently been alert to and will no doubt be so in future, individual terms or different kinds of vertical restraints have not in themselves had a negative effect on competition or integration.

It has been seen that an analysis of a specific situation surrounding an agreement must concentrate on the *effects* of the agreement on the relevant market rather than on the *form* of the agreement, and an important parameter of the analysis of the market will be whether the vertical agreement, in combination with their market position, gives the supplier or the distributor a possibility of imposing different prices for their products in different Member States.

The way in which the block exemption regulations are applied will show whether there are reasons to fear that there will be an increase in legal uncertainty as a result of the fact that in future, it will normally be up to the parties' own judgment whether a market share is higher or lower than the permitted threshold.

The Commission's legal acts or decisions did not previously give the highest priority to paying close attention to whether there can be significant economic risks to new and smaller undertakings' entry into new markets or the expansion of markets, in other words, the establishment of new trade flows which integrate the market. However, the Commission has not been entirely unaware that such spreading of new products can often only take place if there is a significant monetary or intellectual investment and that, as will be significant from a national perspective, such initiatives will seldom be undertaken unless they are given more favourable treatment, at least for a limited period.

The formulation of the special restrictions laid down in Article 5 of Regulation (EU) No 720/2022, which differ from those contained in the earlier block exemption regulations, expresses the Commission's recognition that vertical restraints can have positive as well as negative effects.

The positive effects can refer both to the undertakings that are parties to a distribution agreement and consumers and can, therefore, be factors which constitute the basis for an individual exemption in accordance with Article 101(3) TFEU. A combination of restrictions, for example, allowing territorial protection together with a non-compete obligation for a limited period (in accordance with Article 5(a) of the Regulation) could, in certain circumstances, satisfy both traders and consumers and at the same time, without being an absolute restriction on parallel trade, could help with some of the less fortunate effects (for the trader) of the free-rider problem.

At the same time, Article 5 of Regulation (EU) No 720/2022 has taken account of the negative effects of non-compete obligations for unlimited periods and of quantitative restrictions linked to membership of a selective distribution system.

Bibliography

D.G. Goyder: *EC Competition Law*, 2009.
Joanna Goyder: *EU Distribution Law*, 5th ed. 2011.

Mendelsohn & Rose: *Distribution Agreements under the EU Competition Rules*, 2002.
Richard Whish & David Bailey: *Competition Law*, 8th ed. 2015.
Valentine Korah & Denis O'Sullivan: *Distribution Agreements under the EC Competition Rules*, 2002.
Valentine Korah & Warwick A. Rothnie: *Exclusive Distribution and the EEC Competition Rules*, 1992.
Vivien Rose & David Bailey (eds): Bellamy & Child: *European Union Law of Competition*, 7th ed. 2013.

CHAPTER 4
Horizontal Agreements

1 INTRODUCTION

'Horizontal agreements' means agreements between undertakings on the same level in the market. In a competition law context, the most interesting agreements are those between undertakings which are actual or potential competitors. This will be the case, for example, with agreements between two producers of the same product or two distributors of the same product.

The list of prohibited agreements in Article 101(1)(a) to (e) of the Treaty on the Functioning of the European Union (TFEU or 'Treaty') contains several examples of horizontal agreements. Thus, an agreement to fix purchasing or selling prices or for the application of the same trading conditions will typically be entered into by competitors. Two competing producers can also have an interest in entering into an agreement to limit or control production so as to ensure that their products can be sold at a higher price. Finally, two competitors can have an interest in market sharing so they avoid having to compete against each other in future.

Such price-fixing agreements, agreements on production limits, and agreements on market sharing are classic cartel agreements, and they are often referred to as 'hardcore cartels'. In the case of such agreements, it is clear that they will lead to restrictions on competition. These will normally be 'by object' restrictions so that it is not necessary to undertake any further examination of how the agreements affect the competitive situation in practice.[1] The strict approach adopted towards these types of agreements is also clear from the fact that the *De minimis* Notice does not apply to

---

1. *See* Ch. 2, s. 5.2 and Communication from the Commission – Guidelines on the applicability of Art. 101 of the Treaty on the Functioning of the European Union to horizontal co-operation agreements, endorsed by the Commission 1 Jun. 2023 (OJ 2023 C 259/1), para. 222. Hereinafter these guidelines are referred to as Commission Guidelines on horizontal cooperation agreements.

price-fixing agreements, agreements to limit production or market-sharing agreements.[2]

Competitors can also enter into other kinds of agreements where it is not quite so obvious that the agreement has a negative effect on competition. Such agreements can include agreements on specialisation, joint research and development (R&D cooperation), cooperation on joint purchasing, etc. For these agreements, there is a need for a closer examination of the effect of the cooperation on competitive conditions before it is decided whether Article 101(1) is infringed.

The Commission has published a Notice giving guidelines on the application of Article 101 to horizontal agreements.[3] These guidelines contain both general comments on the assessment of horizontal agreements and a review of several of the most common types of agreements. The review does not include the classic cartel agreements on price-fixing and market sharing, which, as stated above, are seldom difficult to evaluate, but focuses instead on a number of commonly used agreements which are sometimes, but not always, contrary to Article 101.

By way of introduction, the following presentation will contain some general comments on the evaluation of horizontal agreements. In the following sections, there will be a review of several different kinds of agreements. In the first place, this review concentrates on different kinds of agreements classified according to their subject matter, in other words, whether they are price-fixing agreements or market sharing agreements, etc. However, certain forms of horizontal agreements go beyond simple traditional cooperation agreements, as they involve setting up new undertakings or changes to the ownership of the parties to the agreement. Such horizontal agreements, which affect the structure of undertakings, can be more difficult to assess, and they are, therefore, dealt with separately in the last sections.

2   THE ASSESSMENT OF HORIZONTAL AGREEMENTS

2.1   Actual and Potential Competitors

The Commission's guidelines on horizontal cooperation agreements apply to cooperation established between competitors. Competitors can either be actual or potential competitors.

An undertaking is an actual competitor if it operates in the same relevant market as the other party or parties to the agreement. An undertaking is also considered to be an actual competitor if it is active on the same product marked and geographical market.

In paragraph 16 of the Commission's guidelines on horizontal cooperation agreements, a potential competitor is defined as an undertaking which 'in the absence of the agreement it is likely that the former, within a short period of time, would undertake the necessary additional investments or other necessary switching costs to

---

2. On this, *see* Ch. 2, s. 5.3.
3. *See* note above for reference.

enter the relevant market ' The Commission does not say how long a 'short period of time' is but refers to the fact that the block exemption regulations on specialisation agreements and R&D both point to a maximum of three years, *see* sections 5.1 and 6 below. In addition to this, it is stated that the assessment has to be based on realistic grounds and that the mere theoretical possibility of entering a market is not sufficient. This means that when an assessment is made of whether an undertaking can be expected to be active on a particular market, there must be an evaluation of, among others, whether the undertaking has a firm intention and an inherent ability to enter the market within a short period of time, whether the undertaking has taken sufficient preparatory steps to do so, whether it has real and concrete possibilities to enter the market, an evaluation of the structure of the market and finally whether the undertakings established perceive the undertaking as a potential competitor.[4]

2.2 The Basic Principles for Evaluation under Article 101(1)

An infringement of Article 101(1) requires that the agreement is capable of effecting trade between Member States, has an anticompetitive object or actual or potential restrictive effects on competition. In its guidelines on horizontal cooperation agreements, the Commission accepts that such agreements can lead to substantial economic benefits, as they can be means to share risk, save costs, increase investments, pool know-how, may enhance product quality and variety.[5] But there is also the risk that such agreements may limit competition:

- *First*, horizontal cooperation agreements may result in the loss of competition between the parties to the agreements. The agreement may reduce the competitive pressures on the parties, allowing them to increase their prices.
- *Second*, horizontal cooperation agreements may raise the risk of collusion between the parties to the agreement. In this case, it is not the agreement as such that limits competition but the fact that the parties may use the agreement as an opportunity to make additional secret agreements aiming to limit competition. The fact that they are already cooperating may also make the secret collusion more robust.[6] Therefore, setting up a joint venture will often raise the risk of such collusion; *see* further section 9 below.
- *Third*, horizontal cooperation agreements may result in foreclosure, whereby competitors that are not part of the agreement could be impeded from competing effectively. This may be the case if the competitors are denied access to an important input or are blocked from an important route to the market. Also, if the parties exchange commercially sensitive information, this may place their competitors at a significant competitive disadvantage.[7]

---

4. *See* Commission Guidelines on horizontal cooperation agreements, para. 16.
5. Commission Guidelines on horizontal cooperation agreements, para. 20.
6. Commission Guidelines on horizontal cooperation agreements, para. 21.
7. Commission Guidelines on horizontal cooperation agreements, para. 21.

However, not all horizontal cooperation agreements are likely to limit competition in this way. As already mentioned in Chapter 2, section 5.2, a distinction should be made between agreements that restrict competition 'by object' and those that restrict it 'by effect', and only for the former, it can be said that a negative impact on competition is the most likely scenario. These are the classic cartel agreements, such as price-fixing agreements, agreements on production limits, and agreements on market sharing. For other horizontal cooperation agreements, it will normally be necessary to make a more detail evaluation to decide whether they involve the parties coordinating their competitive conduct. The Commission's Guidelines make it easier to analyse the following different forms of cooperation: agreements for information exchange, research and development, production agreements, purchasing agreements, commercialisation agreements, standardisation agreements, and sustainability agreements. Several of these forms of agreement are considered in more detail in the following sections.

The application of the Commission's Guidelines requires the placing of an agreement in one of the categories of agreement referred to. However, sometimes agreements will concern cooperation, which covers several areas. In this situation, the Guidelines' different parts should be used where relevant to the different parts of the agreement. However, when determining whether there is a restriction of competition by object or by effect it is the centre of gravity of the agreement which determines which part of the Guidelines should apply. The centre of gravity of the agreement is determined by two factors: first, the starting point of the cooperation, and second, the degree of integration of the different functions which are combined.[8]

As it will be clear from the above, the evaluation of agreements normally requires an analysis to be made of the *market power* of the undertakings and the *market structure* of the relevant market. It will, therefore, be necessary to define the relevant market, which will be done in accordance with the Commission Notice on the definition of relevant market for the purposes of Community competition law.[9] Once the relevant market has been determined, market power can be estimated by measuring, in particular, the market shares of the undertakings. A small market share will normally mean that it is unlikely that the cooperation will lead to a restriction on competition. This is also in line with the Commission's *De minimis* Notice, according to which a market share of less than 10% normally means that a horizontal agreement is not covered by Article 101(1).[10] In addition to this, it can be relevant to assess market concentration, the stability of the market shares, barriers to entry to the market, and the

---

8. Commission Guidelines on horizontal cooperation agreements, para. 7. These not specifically operational factors are exemplified in the same paragraph. If an R&D agreement involves joint research and thereafter joint production, the agreement will normally be classified as an R&D agreement, as the production will only take place if the R&D activity is successful. The R&D activity is thus the starting point of the cooperation. However, it will be otherwise if the agreement shows an intention to carry out joint production, regardless of the joint R&D. In this case, the joint production would be the centre of gravity of the agreement.
9. C/2024/1645. These guidelines are considered in more detail in Chs 6 and 8, in connection with the corresponding evaluation of the relevant market in the application of Art. 102 and the Merger Control Regulation.
10. OJ 2014 C 291/1, para. 8(a).

market power of buyers/suppliers in order to determine the market power of the parties to a cooperative agreement.

2.3 Exemptions under Article 101(3)

For horizontal cooperation agreements that are not classic cartel agreements (price-fixing agreements, etc.), it will be relevant to consider whether the agreement can be exempted under Article 101(3). In connection with the individual types of agreement discussed, the Commission's guidelines contain a more detailed review of what circumstances can influence assessments under Article 101(3).

For a more general review of the two positive and two negative conditions for allowing an exemption, *see* Chapter 2, section 6.

In order to ease the assessment of special agreements, the Commission has issued two block exemption regulations which exempt agreement on research and development (R&D agreements) and specialisation agreements. These kinds of agreements often involve effectivity gains, which outweigh their effects limiting competition, and they therefore fulfil the criteria in Article 101(3). Both regulations where issued under the authority of Regulation (EEC) No 2821/71 of the Council on the application of Article 101(3) of the Treaty (previously Article 85(3)). The exemption for R&D agreements is discussed in section 6, and the exemption for specialisation agreements is discussed in section 5.1.

3 PRICE-FIXING AGREEMENTS AND AGREEMENTS ON OTHER TRADING CONDITIONS

3.1 Agreements on Purchasing or Selling Prices

According to Article 101(1)(a) of the EC Treaty, agreements which directly or indirectly fix purchase or selling prices could restrict competition. If competitors agree on their prices, this eliminates the price competition, which both ensures that prices are held down and helps ensure that there can be parallel imports and, thereby, economic integration of markets in the EU. A price-fixing agreement prevents the undertaking which has the lowest costs from lowering its prices, and such an agreement, therefore, normally benefits those undertakings which have the poorest control of their production costs. In the long run, it thus becomes difficult to maintain cooperation on the application of common prices as there will normally be undertakings that will have an advantage from trying to reduce prices contrary to such an agreement. Such agreements will usually contain elements to ensure that the price-fixing cartel is not breached, including mechanisms to reveal breaches of the common pricing policy and sanctions for undertakings which do not follow the pricing policy. However, price-fixing agreements will be contrary to Article 101, regardless of whether there are such mechanisms. Agreements on price-fixing will normally be 'by object' restrictions, and therefore, there is no need to examine whether a price-fixing agreement has worked in practice.

The practice of the Commission shows that most agreements that are intended to influence the pricing policies of the participating undertakings are assumed to be contrary to Article 101. It is clear that agreements on fixed prices or minimum prices or that the same price increase should be implemented are contrary to the prohibition. A price-fixing agreement need not be framed so as to regulate the prices of the principal products of the undertakings, as it is sufficient that prices are agreed for certain products or services as long as these constitute a competitive parameter.[11] The prohibition also covers recommended prices, as these have the effect of enabling competing businesses to predict their competitors' pricing policies with a reasonable degree of certainty.[12] Furthermore, Article 101 covers agreements whereby the parties undertake not to sell their products at below cost price, usually referred to as 'dumping prices'. Apart from price-fixing agreements of this kind being contrary to Article 101(1), there will be a further breach of the provision if the undertakings attempt to implement their agreements by getting their distributors to use the agreed prices.

Discount arrangements and common discount policies are likewise covered by the prohibition, since this is merely another way of regulating the level of prices.[13] In markets where, because of strong competition and transparency, there are uniform prices, discount arrangements can be the only competitive parameter, so that an agreement on these will restrict competition. Also, agreements on fixed prices or minimum prices will usually, as a supplement, prevent the parties from giving rebates, which would prevent the application of their uniform pricing policy.[14]

---

11. Commission Decision 96/428/EC, *Fenex* (OJ 1996 L 181/28), where agreements were entered into on prices (here called tariffs) concerning a number of services which freight companies provided in addition to the provision of the transport itself. Even though the services about which agreement was entered into would normally only constitute a minor part of the overall price for the transport service, the Commission found that profit margins were generally very small and that any anticompetitive practice, even if restricted to part of the total price, affected competition; see para. 51 of the Decision. See also Case 123/83, *BNIC*, para. 29, under which an agreement on minimum prices for an intermediary product (spirits), which was not itself traded between the Member States, was a restriction on competition, because the intermediary product was a significant part of the final product (cognac) which was traded between Member States.
12. *See* Case 8/72, *Cementhandelaren*, para. 21, as well as Commission Decision 96/428/EC, *Fenex* (OJ 1996 L 181/28), paras 45–49. The Commission also assumed that 'target pricing' can be in breach of Art. 101 since this establishes goals for the prices which undertakings are to use. Even if the prices must still be negotiated with customers and even if it is not always possible to ensure that they are applied, they have the effect of restricting the negotiating scope of the parties; see Commission Decision of 11 Jun. 2008, in Case COMP/38695 – *Sodium Chlorate* (OJ 2009 C 137/6).
13. *See* Case C-74/14, '*Eturas*', where the provider of a web platform for online sale of travels had suggested that a ceiling for discounts was introduced for all travel agencies active on the platform, and even offered to implement a technical solution that ensured that all agencies complied.
14. However, it is by no means a condition that an agreement on minimum prices should be combined with an agreement to limit the use of discounts. Even if the use of discounts makes a price-fixing agreement less effective, it must still be assumed to have a certain effect – otherwise there would be no point in entering into it. This was the Commission's reasoning in Commission Decision 74/634/EEC concerning a *Franco-Japanese ball-bearings agreement* (OJ 1874 L 343/19), Part II, para. 3.

There was an example of an extensive price-fixing agreement in the *Belasco* case.[15] Belasco was a cooperative set up by a number of Belgian manufacturers of roofing felt. The members had an agreement which, among other things, included the implementation of price increases, and agreement about what discount margins the members could use, and a prohibition on giving gifts and selling at a loss. The Commission, and later the Court of Justice of the European Union (CJ), held that these agreements were contrary to Article 101. It was clear that the agreed prices and discounts directly affected competition, and that the prohibitions on giving gifts and selling at a loss were aimed at preventing parties from getting around the agreed prices. Before the Commission, the undertakings had argued that all the price increases were a consequence of the Belgian legislation on pricing, which allowed undertakings to seek collective approval of price increases. Even though the Belgian legislation required approval of price increases, it was possible for members to seek individual approval for price increases, so a certain measure of competition was possible under the Belgian legislation. Therefore, the Commission held that the legislation was not the cause of the price coordination.

Furthermore, it was held that it was irrelevant that they had not, in fact, succeeded in holding the members to the agreed price increases, as it was clear that the purpose of the agreement was to restrict competition on prices. The agreement was also notified to undertakings which were not party to it. The CJ found that the fact that notification of price increases had been given was intended to encourage these undertakings to bring their prices into line with the members' prices, and thereby to increase the effect of the price cartel beyond the cartel's members.

It appeared from this case that the Belgian legislation on pricing allowed undertakings to implement price increases at different times and by different amounts.[16] If, on the contrary, pricing legislation did, in fact, dictate prices, there would not be a price-fixing agreement, contrary to Article 101. This applies even if the undertakings themselves have proposed the prices which the legislation makes obligatory, provided that it is not, in fact, the undertakings which fix the prices which the legislation puts into effect.[17]

Agreements on maximum prices will not necessarily harm competition. However, it is possible to imagine that such an agreement could be aimed at forcing a

---

15. Commission Decision 86/399/EEC concerning *roofing felt* (OJ 1986 L 232/15), and the subsequent Case 246/86, *Belasco*.
16. *See also* Joined Cases 209 to 215 and 218/78, *van Landewyck*, and Case 260/82, *NSO*, where the CJ concluded that the Belgian and Dutch pricing rules for cigarettes still allowed competition on certain points, so that an agreement which excluded competition on these points was contrary to Art. 101.
17. Case C-35/99, *Manuele Arduino*, and Case C-38/97, *Autotrasporti Librandi Snc di Librandi F & C*. If one cannot blame the undertakings for the lack of competition, one may ask whether the Member States themselves can infringe on Art. 101 by implementing such pricing legislation; *see* the comments on this in Ch. 2, s. 3.2.

competitor out of the market (predatory pricing). If a number of undertakings agree on the maximum purchase prices they will pay their suppliers, this will be an agreement in restraint of competition.[18] The same will be the case if an agreement is made between undertakings that submit offers in connection with public or private procurement and which restricts competition by the fact that the offer of an individual undertaking is not based on its own cost calculations but on prior knowledge of the offers of others. This can be because the undertakings exchange information about costs in connection with the offer, agree on common margins, or maybe even agree on who should give the lowest offer.[19]

Instead of entering into a price-fixing agreement, undertakings can choose to set up a common sales company. Such a sales company will often be a commonly controlled joint venture company; section 9 below gives a review of the Commission's practice on joint ventures. However, there will seldom be economies of scale or other advantages associated with an activity that is only joint selling, and these will normally be judged on the same basis as pure price-fixing agreements and not exempted from Article 101(3). This is particularly clear when the participating undertakings are obliged to sell through the joint venture, so they are prevented from taking individual sales initiatives and thus from practising an alternative pricing policy.[20]

Even though price-fixing will normally be a 'by object' restriction and, therefore, likely to harm competition, there may be exceptions. Thus, the CJ has, in two instances, rejected that prices on fees for financial services were 'by object' restrictions.[21]

This was the case in Case C-228/18, *Budapest Bank*, where seven banks who had all joined the card payment systems set up by Visa and MasterCard agreed to use a uniform amount for interchange fees relating to payments made by means of cards issued by the banks. In evaluating whether there was a 'by object' restriction, the CJ first noted that the agreement was not focussed on purchase or selling prices, as it standardises the cost that the banks would have to meet when their customers use the cards. Even though it was still an agreement that indirectly fixed the purchase and selling prices, the CJ was not convinced that the agreement harmed competition in this case. It was clear that the fees had been decreased several times. Furthermore, the content of the agreement was not necessary to restrict competition, as its purpose was not to guarantee a minimum threshold for service charges but to establish a degree of

---

18. Commission Decision 84/405/EEC, concerning a *zinc producer group* (OJ 1984 L 220/27), para. 66 (the purchase price of zinc ore); and Commission Decision 85/206/EEC concerning *aluminium imports from Eastern Europe* (OJ 1985 L 92/1), para. 11.1. In both cases, the agreed purchase prices were part of a larger network of agreements which had the aim of restricting competition in various ways. Compare this with the comments on purchasing agreements in Commission Guidelines on horizontal cooperation agreements, paras 273–316, and *see* ss 7 and 10 below.
19. Case T-29/92, *Vereniging van Samenwerkende Prijsregelende Organisaties in de Bouwnijverheid*, Commission Decision 73/109/EEC concerning the *European sugar industry* (OJ 1973 L 140/17); Commission Decision 1999/60/EC concerning a *pre-insulated pipe cartel* (OJ 1999 L 24/1), para. 33, and Commission Decision of 28 Jan. 2009, COMP/39406 – *Marine Hoses* (OJ 2009 C 168/6).
20. Commission Decision 80/182/EEC, *Floral* (OJ 1980 L 39/51), and Commission Decision 91/301/EEC, *ANSAC* (OJ 1991 L 152/54).
21. *See also* C-67/13 P, Groupement des cartes bancaires (CB).

balance between the banks issuing the credit card and the banks accepting the payment. The purpose was thus to ensure that certain costs resulting from the use of cards in payment transactions are covered while protecting the system from the undesirable effects that would arise from an excessively high level of interchange fees.[22] According to the CJ, the agreement may even have had the result of intensifying competition. In conclusion, there was not a 'by object' restriction, and instead, it was necessary to undertake an examination as to whether there was a 'by effect' restriction.

Price-fixing agreements are subject to a very strict assessment and can only very exceptionally be exempted under Article 101(3). However, an exemption has been given for banks' uniform fees for Eurocheques, as it was found appropriate to have transparency about the payment fees for precisely this kind of payment method, which applied to the whole of the internal market.[23]

3.2 Agreements on Other Trading Conditions

Article 101(1)(a) also refers to agreements on 'other trading conditions' than purchasing or selling prices. If there is uniformity of trading conditions, which would otherwise act as a competitive parameter, such an agreement will mean that competition is restricted. This is obvious where an agreement on other trading conditions is a supplement to a price-fixing agreement,[24] but it can also be the case that where an agreement on uniform trading conditions stands alone, competition can be restricted. For example, a restriction on competition will likely exist where competitors agree on common guarantee conditions, common credit conditions, common after-sales service conditions, common delivery conditions and so on.[25] In the same way, common conditions for purchasing can infringe Article 101. However, if the use of common conditions has only limited influence on competition, Article 101 will not be infringed, and the Commission has thus accepted that banks can agree on opening hours and on uniform rules for clearing and direct debits.[26]

The result of this legal position is that attempts by undertakings to apply uniform sales or purchase terms by developing standard conditions within a specific trade sector can be contrary to Article 101.[27] However, not all standard conditions may harm competition, especially if they are drawn up by a trade organisation. The effect of such

---

22. *See* paras 73–74 of the judgment.
23. Commission Decision 85/77/EEC, *Uniform Eurocheques* (OJ 1985 L 35/43). *See also* Commission Decision 2002/914/EC, *Visa International* (OJ 2002 L 318/17), where the Commission likewise thought there was a basis for exempting inter-bank fees which were used by Visa.
24. *See*, e.g., Commission Decision of 28 Jan. 2009, COMP/39406 – *Marine Hoses* (OJ 2009 C 168/6).
25. Joined Cases 209 to 215 and 218/78, *van Landewyck*, paras 154–156, and Case 8/72, *Cementhandelaren*, paras 23–24.
26. Commission Decision 86/507/EEC, *Irish Banks' Standing Committee* (OJ 1986 L 295/28), paras 16–17.
27. Commission Decision 74/431/EEC concerning *Papiers peints de Belgique* (OJ 1974 L 237/3), where, in addition to an agreement on common pricing, a number of Belgian wallpaper manufacturers had agreed common terms for delivery, payment, refusal to exchange goods, the conditions for accepting complaints, and the length of rolls of wallpaper.

standard conditions used by many undertakings could be to create greater transparency for consumers. These can thus be assumed either to fall outside the scope of Article 101(1) or to be exempted under Article 101(3). This, however, requires that all undertakings may be part of the adoption of such standard conditions, that the conditions are not binding (and undertakings, therefore, need not use them), and that the conditions may be used for all undertakings which want to.[28]

4 AGREEMENTS ON THE EXCHANGE OF INFORMATION

If competitors exchange information on their activities, it may, in some cases, generate different types of efficiency gains. It may solve the problems caused by information asymmetries, making the market more efficient. Exchange of information may allow the undertakings to make more informed decisions, for instance, by using big data analytics or machine learning techniques.[29] But exchange of information may also result in restriction of competition. This is, for instance, the case if the exchange facilitates a coordination of the competitive behaviour of the undertakings involved. If commercially sensitive information is exchanged, this may affect the commercial behaviour of the undertaking even if there is no express agreement that this should happen. As mentioned above in Chapter 2, section 2.3, a concerted practice requires a conduct on the market, but if there has been an exchange of commercially sensitive information, there is a presumption that the undertakings will make use of this information in determining their conduct on the market. Therefore, in this case, there may be no need to prove any conduct.[30]

Also, exchanges of information can lead to foreclosure; the most obvious example of this is where commercially sensitive information is exchanged, and this leads to significant competitive disadvantages for competitors that are not part of the exchange arrangement.[31]

Consequently, agreements for the exchange of commercially sensitive information will often be contrary to Article 101. This is especially so in oligopolistic markets, where undertakings have particular incentives to adapt their conduct to each other,[32] and in markets where the information is exchanged between undertakings which have

---

28. *See* Commission Guidelines on horizontal cooperation agreements, para. 499. The Guidelines make reservations for two situations where such standard terms can nevertheless have the effect of restricting competition: where standard terms restrict product choice, and where standard terms are de facto binding; *see* paras 500–505.
29. Commission Guidelines on horizontal cooperation agreements, para. 373.
30. Commission Guidelines on horizontal cooperation agreements, para. 375.
31. *See* Commission Guidelines on horizontal cooperation agreements, paras. 381–383.
32. Commission Decision 92/157/EEC, *UK Agricultural Tractor Registration Exchange* (OJ 1992 L 68/19), where eight British manufacturers and importers of tractors had agreed to exchange information about sales volumes and market shares. This was contrary to Art. 101, given the market structure, which was highly concentrated with high entry barriers, and with regard to the degree of detail of the information exchanged. In particular, the Commission attached importance to the fact that it was difficult for new competitors to enter the market, so an exemption under Art. 101(3) was refused. This decision was later followed by the GC in Case T-35/92, *John Deere*, and by the CJ in Case C-7/95 P, *John Deere*.

a key role for the functioning of the market.³³ There is also a greater probability of there being concerted practices where the conditions of supply and demand are stable, and where there is a symmetrical market structure and the undertakings involved cover a major part of the relevant market.³⁴

Another relevant factor is, of course, the nature of the information exchanged, as distortions of competition are most likely when information is involved, which undertakings can use in framing their future strategy. This is particularly the case if the information exchanged can eliminate the uncertainty that normally exists about how competitors can be expected to act in the market in the future.³⁵ This would be the case if information about future prices is exchanged,³⁶ but also information about production capacity or business strategy. It is thus less likely that exchanges of historical information will be able to harm competition, and there is less likely to be a distortion of competition where information is aggregated for a larger group of undertakings so that it is not possible to identify the activities of individual competitors.³⁷

An exchange of information may be effected in different ways. The exchange may be the only activity going on between the undertakings involved, or the exchange of information may be a supplement to another cooperation agreement. If, for instance, undertakings are setting up a joint venture, they may be tempted to exchange information that is not strictly related to the running of the joint venture; *see* further sections 9.3.2 and 9.3.3 below. However, the exchange of information may also be part of a price-fixing agreement to ensure that all members of the cartel comply with the agreement.

The exchange of information may take place between the competitors directly, or the exchange may be facilitated through a third party, for instance, a trade organisation or the operator of an online platform. Especially the latter has been the focus of attention in recent years as operators of online platforms will normally have access to much commercially sensitive information and may, therefore, easily make this available for those using the platform. Such exchange of information is referred to as 'hub and spoke' agreements.³⁸ If the operator of an online platform (or another third party)

---

33. This could be the case where exchange is taking place between traders who have the status of 'market makers' in a particular market; *see*, for instance, Case T-105/17, *HSBC*, para. 145.
34. *See* Commission Guidelines on horizontal cooperation agreements, para. 412.
35. *See* Case C-286/13 P, *Dole Food Company Inc.*, para. 122. Where information is exchanged as part of a concerted practice, there is also a requirement that there should be conduct on the market. However, the CJ has accepted that there may be a presumption that undertakings will take information into account when competitors exchange information about their intended conduct on the market; *see* para. 127 of the Judgment.
36. It need not be information about consumer prices or purchase prices, but it may also include information about other price elements that allow them indirectly to fix purchase or selling prices, *see* Case T-105/17, *HSBC*, paras 63–64.
37. *See* Commission Guidelines on horizontal cooperation agreements, paras 390–392.
38. Such agreements that may be both vertical and horizontal agreements have been discussed extensively in the literature, *see* for instance Rodrigo Londoño van Rutten & Caroline Buts: *Hub and Spoke Cartels*, European Competition and Regulatory Law Review, 2019 pp. 4–16 DOI: 10.21552/core/2019/1/4, Antti Aine, Tom Björkroth & Aki Koponen: *Horizontal Information Exchange and Innovation in the Platform Economy – A Need to Rethink?*, European Competition Law 2019 pp. 347–371 DOI: 10.1080/17441056.2019.1687187, and Stefan Thomas: *Horizontal*

facilitates the exchange of information, they themselves may be liable for infringing Article 101, even if they are not operating on the market that has been affected by the exchange.[39] The exchange of information will often be a 'by object' restriction if the exchange involves commercially sensitive information and the exchange is capable of removing uncertainty between the participants as regards the others' future competitive conduct on the market. To assess whether this is the case, the Commission will focus its attention on the content of the information exchanged and the objective of the exchange. If there is no 'by object' restriction, a closer examination is required.[40]

If the information exchanged leads to greater transparency on the market, so consumers can gain access to the information and be better informed about the supplier who gives the best terms, this would favour allowing the exchange of information.[41] It is also possible that the exchange of information can contribute to making a market more effective, even if consumers do not have access to the information.[42]

5 AGREEMENTS ON PRODUCTION

If production is restricted and demand remains unchanged, undertakings will be able to demand higher prices, so a restriction on production will lead to a restriction on competition; *see* Article 101(1)(b). If an agreement means that the participating undertakings limit their production, there is, therefore, little doubt that it contravenes Article 101. An agreement might be framed so that each undertaking is given a quota which is has to comply with.[43] An agreement that no undertaking may increase its production without the agreement of the other undertakings will also infringe Article 101.[44] An agreement limiting production can be an alternative to a price-fixing agreement, as a limit on production can be easier to implement and monitor than a price-fixing agreement. However, an agreement limiting production will often be a supplement to a price-fixing agreement.[45]

An agreement which is merely aimed at limiting production cannot be expected to be exempted under Article 101(3). However, there are a number of other agreements on production which either do not infringe Article 101(1) or are exempted under Article 101(3), because they give certain technical or economic advantages which outweigh any negative effects which restrict competition. Three different categories of such

---

Restraints on Platforms: How Digital Ecosystems Nudge into Rethinking the Construal of the Cartel Prohibition, World Competition 2021 pp. 53–80 DOI: 10.54648/woco2021004.

39. *See* Commission Guidelines on horizontal cooperation agreements, paras 401–404.
40. Commission Guidelines on horizontal cooperation agreements, paras 422–424.
41. Commission Guidelines on horizontal cooperation agreements, para. 425.
42. Case C-238/05, *Asnef-Equifax*, where the CJ accepted that a system that provided for the exchange of information on customers' solvency improved the effective provision of credit, as it made it easier to identify bad payers. For further on when exchanges of information can be exempted under Art. 101(3), *see* Commission Guidelines on horizontal cooperation agreements, para. 425.
43. Commission Decision 86/596/EEC, *MELDOC* (OJ 1986 L 348/50), which concerned a quota arrangement entered into by the Dutch dairy industry, mainly to do with long-life milk.
44. Commission Decision 72/474/EEC, *Re Cimbel* (OJ 1972 L 303/24), para. 14.
45. Commission Decision 86/399/EEC concerning *roofing felt* (OJ 1986 L 232/15), para. 73, and Commission Decision 94/601/EC, *Cartonboard* (OJ 1994 L 243/1), para. 130.

agreements are referred to in the Commission Guidelines on horizontal cooperation agreements. The first concerns *joint production agreements*, which are normally carried out by the cooperating parties setting up a joint venture; these are discussed in section 9. The guidelines also refer to *specialisation agreements*, where each party agrees to cease production of a product and purchase it from the other party. The third category is *subcontracting agreements*, where the contractor entrusts the production of a product to the subcontractor.[46]

The Guidelines contain some general comments on the evaluation of these agreements under competition law.[47] It appears from this that production agreements may lead to a direct limitation of competition between the parties. This will be the case if they align output levels, quality or prices. Such alignment may take place even if the parties continue to sell their products independently as opposed to setting up a joint venture that conducts their joint sales. Next, production agreements may result in the coordination of the parties' competitive behaviour as suppliers. This effect is most likely if the parties have market power and if the agreements mean that the proportion of variable costs, which the parties have in common, increases. Production agreements that involve joint distribution or marketing carry a higher risk of restrictive effects in the form of joint setting of prices and sales, as this type of cooperation is much closer to the customers. Finally, production agreements may have foreclosing effects, for instance, where a product that is jointly produced is needed by an undertaking operating on a downstream market. This kind of foreclosure effect is only likely if at least one of the parties to the production agreement has a strong market power on the downstream market.

Paragraphs 228-237 of the Commission Guidelines on horizontal cooperation agreements state that production agreements are unlikely to have restrictive effects on competition if the parties to the agreement do not have market power in the market concerned. This normally requires that the parties have a combined market share of more than 20%. If the combined market share exceeds this, it will be necessary to make a more specific evaluation, as the market power will not necessarily be a problem if the market concerned is dynamic.

Categories of the agreements that have repeatedly been granted exemptions are agreements on specialisation, agreements to restructure a trade sector that is in crisis, and agreements on technical standards. These are discussed briefly below.

5.1   Specialisation Agreements

Specialisation agreements involve two or more undertakings agreeing that the production of a particular product will be carried on by one of the undertakings or by a jointly

---

46. Commission Guidelines on horizontal cooperation agreements, paras 172-272. If a subcontracting agreement is entered into between undertakings that do not compete against each other, the agreement should be assessed according to the rules for vertical agreements; *see* Ch. 3. Such agreement may also be covered by the Commission Notice of 18 Dec. 1978 concerning its assessment of certain subcontracting agreements in relation to Art. 85(1) (OJ 1979 C 1/2).
47. Commission Guidelines on horizontal cooperation agreements, paras 217-221.

owned undertaking. Such agreements normally contribute to the improvement of production or the allocation of goods since the undertakings can thereby concentrate on the manufacture of certain goods, work more rationally and offer the goods at a lower price. Specialisation agreements mean that some undertakings stop production or refrain from starting competing production, which is, on the face of it, contrary to Article 101(1). However, such agreements do not always restrict competition, especially when the parties are neither actual nor potential competitors. At the same time, if the agreement is between competitors, there is a clear risk of it having a restrictive effect on competition, but in this case, it may qualify for an exemption under the Commission's block exemption Regulation on specialisation agreements.[48]

According to Article 1 of the block exemption Regulation on specialisation agreements, the following agreements are exempt: *Unilateral specialisation agreements*, where one party or several parties which are active on the same product market agree to fully or partly cease the production of certain products (these may be goods or services), or alternatively to refrain from starting production, and instead commits to purchasing the products from one of the other participants in the agreement. This covers the situation where an undertaking outsources its production. The next exempted class is *reciprocal specialisation agreements*, where two or more parties which are active on the same product market agree reciprocally to cease or refrain from producing different products and to purchase these products from the other party or parties. The last form of exempted agreement is a *joint production agreement*, where two or more parties agree to produce certain products jointly.

According to Article 2 of the Regulation, the exemption also applies where the parties accept an exclusive purchase and/or exclusive supply obligation. This means that it is possible to agree that the party taking on a specialisation shall only sell to the other party or parties to the agreement, just as the other party or parties can be obliged to buy the product. It is also possible to agree that the sale of the products that are the subject of a specialisation agreement shall not be carried out via the participating undertakings but shall be carried out jointly. Finally, the assignment of or grant of a licence to intellectual property rights (IPR) is exempt as long as the assignment or licence is not the main purpose of the agreement but is necessary for implementing a specialisation agreement.

Article 3 of the Regulation provides that the exemption only applies if the combined market share of the participating undertakings does not exceed 20% of the relevant market to which the specialisation product belongs. Article 4 deals with the market share threshold in more detail and states, among other things, that if the market share is initially not more than 20% but subsequently rises above this level (without exceeding 25%), the exemption provided for in Article 1 can continue to apply for two consecutive calendar years following the year in which the 20% threshold was first exceeded.

Article 5 of the Regulation describes the specialisation agreements that are excluded from exemption, which includes agreements which have as their aim the

---

48. Regulation (EU) No 2023/1067 on the application of Art. 101(3) of the Treaty on the Functioning of the European Union to certain categories of specialisation agreements (OJ 2023 L 143/20).

fixing of prices for sales to third parties, the limitation of production or sales, and the allocation of markets. However, in all specialisation agreements, it is possible to agree on the quantity of the product in question that is to be produced. If there is a joint production agreement, normally that would be in the form of a joint venture, it is also possible to set capacity and production volumes.

5.2 Agreements for the Restructuring of a Trade Sector

In principle it must be left to market forces to solve the problems of a trade sector which may have overcapacity. This is normally resolved by the least profitable undertaking in the sector being squeezed out, so the sector is 'rationalised'. Nevertheless, a practice has developed whereby the Commission has exempted agreements for 'crisis cartels', whereby it is made possible for a trade sector which is hit by a structural chronic overcapacity to reduce its production capacity in accordance with a plan laid down.[49] It is a condition that the undertakings should have registered a significant fall in their capacity utilisation over a longer period and that there should be no prospect of improvement in the longer term. Such problems may be due, for example, to the fact that new technology has made it possible to produce more effectively, or it may be due to a fall in demand.

Capacity must be cut through the coordinated efforts of the undertakings so as to create a healthy and competitive sector in the longer term. It is a condition that the participants would not individually undertake the capacity reduction unless they had the security of knowing that their competitors would do the same and that new production capacity would not be created.[50] An agreement to reduce capacity can be either between two competing undertakings or can involve all the undertakings in the sector.[51] It is a condition that the agreement should contain a detailed and binding closure programme that ensures that the overcapacity is actually and irrevocably reduced. It must ensure that the closures do not go further than necessary, as consumers should have sufficient choice and security of supply.[52] In addition, the Commission will ensure that the conditions for an exemption under Article 101(3) are fulfilled so that the rationalised sector will be able to have better and more profitable production to the advantage of consumers. Typically, the least modern factories will be closed so the overheads are reduced.[53] It is a condition that the undertakings do not otherwise restrict competition, and the agreement must ensure that the undertakings set their prices individually and that they themselves control the production capacity

---

49. The Commission's Twelfth Annual Report on Competition Policy, paras 38–41.
50. Commission Decision 84/380/EEC, *Synthetic fibre* (OJ 1984 L 207/17), para. 32, and Commission Decision 94/296/EC, *Stichting Baksteen* (OJ 1994 L 131/15), para. 24.
51. *See* the mutual production agreement on PVC between two undertakings, which was approved because it reduced the industry's capacity by closing down certain production facilities, Commission Decision 84/387/EEC, *BPCL/ICI* (OJ 1984 L 212/1).
52. Commission Decision 94/296/EC, *Stichting Baksteen* (OJ 1994 L 131/15), para. 30.
53. Commission Decision 94/296/EC, *Stichting Baksteen* (OJ 1994 L 131/15), para. 26.

which remains. Finally, the Commission states that the plan must be carried out in such a way as to secure employment in the industry in question.[54]

5.3 Agreements on Common Norms and Technical Standards

The drawing up of technical standards which undertakings can choose to follow plays a key role in the technical harmonisation which ensures the free movement of goods in the EU. As a result of this, a large number of technical standards are drawn up, most of which are drawn up by recognised national or European standardisation bodies. These standards are voluntary and can be used by all. In principle, the Commission has a positive approach to standards adopted by such bodies.

However, standards may sometimes limit competition, in particular, if these are not agreed upon within the regime of a standardisation body. Such agreements will often be aimed at ensuring that the undertakings involved produce products of the same quality and can naturally reduce price competition on the market in question.[55] All things being equal, uniform products exclude the scope for competing on the characteristics of products.[56] In addition to this, standardisation agreements can have the effect of creating further barriers to entry into a market. This is particularly the case where the standards are drawn up by undertakings that are dominant in the market and where the standards are not accessible to third parties.[57]

The Commission accepts that standardisation agreements may not harm competition where participation in the development of the standard is unrestricted, the procedure for adopting the standard is transparent, there is no obligation to comply with the standard, and finally, all interested may access the standard on fair, reasonable and non-discriminatory terms (these are also called 'FRAND terms').[58]

---

54. The Commission's Twelfth Annual Report on Competition Policy, para. 41. The Commission expresses that this ought to be the case, so it cannot be assumed to be an absolute condition. In Commission Decision 94/296/EC, *Stichting Baksteen* (OJ 1994 L 131/15), para. 27, it was established that the agreement made it possible to carry out the restructuring of the sector on acceptable social terms and with better possibilities for the re-employment of the workers.
55. Commission Guidelines on horizontal cooperation agreements, paras 439–445, which set out in more detail the assessment of standardisation agreements. In para. 438 the Commission states that such agreements can lead to restrictions in three other markets: the technology market that may develop as part of the standard setting, the market for standard setting where different bodies or agreements exits, and the distinct market for testing and certification.
56. Case 246/86, *Belasco*, where the CJ found that the agreement which ensured that all the producers of roofing felt who were members of Belasco used the same product standards, had the purpose of preventing members from differentiating their products and thereby avoiding competition between them.
57. Joined Cases 96/82 and others, *IAZ International Belgium*, which involved an association of producers and distributors of washing machines and dishwashers which had agreed to use a conformity label which showed that a product fulfilled certain standards. The CJ disallowed the arrangement as, among other things, it emphasised that parallel importers did not have the possibility of being covered by the arrangement; see paras 24–25.
58. Commission Guidelines on horizontal cooperation agreements, para. 451. In Case T-432/05, *EMC Development*, the GC upheld the Commission's decision that the adoption of a European standard for cement had been transparent and non-discriminating. Also the GC rejected the argument by the complainant that the standard was de facto binding.

IPRs, in particular patents, may cause problems for standardisation agreements if the application of a standard requires that the user acquires a license for a particular IPR. To ensure that this may not make it difficult to access the standard, the patent holder (or other rights holders) must offer to license their IPR to all third parties on FRAND commitment.[59] In addition, the Commission stresses the need for an IPR policy that ensures that those participating in the development of a standard disclose information about their IPR that might be essential for the implementation of the standard.[60]

However, standards can have certain advantages which can justify them being exempted under Article 101(3).[61] Agreements that cover the EU can thus make it easier for the undertakings to market their products in several Member States. They may lower transaction costs for both sellers and buyers and may ensure lower prices for the final consumer. In addition to this, standardisation can make products more compatible, which promotes competition based on quality. However, the Commission will normally only exempt agreements if the standards are made accessible to all undertakings that wish to enter the market and if a major part of the industry transparently takes part in setting the standards. Moreover, the standards may not restrict innovation, and they should preferably be technology-neutral.

There is an example of a standardisation agreement in Commission Decision 78/156/EEC concerning *Video cassette recorders*.[62] Philips had developed the videocassette recorder (VCR system) which, at that time, competed with a system developed by Sony (the U-MATIC system). In order to promote the use of their systems, both Philips and Sony had allowed other undertakings to produce video recorders and video tapes using their systems. However, Philips had gone a step further and agreed with a number of major manufacturers (including Grundig and Blaupunktwerke) that they were only allowed to manufacture according to the technical standards that were appropriate for the Philips system. At the same time, Philips made its licence rights available without charge.

The Commission was of the view that the agreement infringed Article 101(1) (then Article 85), as the participating undertakings were obliged only to produce according to Philips's standards. In view of Philips's leading position on the market, there was a clearly appreciable restriction on competition. Moreover, the Commission did not believe the circumstances justified an exemption since the agreement prevented consumers acquiring video recorders which were produced according to other standards. Thus the agreement went further than was necessary, as it would have been sufficient

---

59. Commission Guidelines on horizontal cooperation agreements, paras 456–462. *See also* David Telyas: *The Interface Between Competition Law, Patents and Technical Standards*, Kluwer, 2014.
60. Commission Guidelines on horizontal cooperation agreements, para. 457.
61. Article 1(1)(a) of Regulation (EEC) No 2821/71 on application of Art. 85(3) of the Treaty to categories of agreements, decisions and concerted practices, authorises the Commission to issue block exemptions for these, but the Commission has not hitherto made use of this authorisation. Instead, there are now Commission Guidelines on horizontal cooperation agreements, paras 475–489.
62. OJ 1978 L 47/42.

to require the undertakings to comply with Philips's standards when they wanted to produce according to the VCR system, but instead the agreement bound the undertakings only to produce according to this system.

In comparison, the Commission allowed an exemption in Decision 87/69/EEC concerning *X/Open Group*.[63] In this case, a number of major European producers in the information technology sector had agreed on common use of an operating system for data handling (Unix). The aim was to overcome the problem that different machines used different operating systems, so the owner of a machine was prevented from using software that was adapted for use with another operating system, and the acquisition of a new machine could involve costs for rewriting existing programs, or even, in the worst case, the acquisition of new programs. Since the purpose of the agreement was to overcome these problems, the Commission felt that the agreement promoted technical progress and was to the advantage of consumers. The Commission emphasised that the aim of the cooperation was the establishment of an open industry standard, accessible to all. However, while not all undertakings could be members of X/Open, the organisation that administered the standards, the Commission accepted that there would be practical, logistical and administrative difficulties if all producers had a right to be members. It was therefore accepted that membership was reserved for major producers.

6   COOPERATION ON RESEARCH AND DEVELOPMENT

Cooperation in research and development (R&D) will generally contribute to the promotion of technical and economic progress. Such cooperation helps prevent duplication of research that can be economically inefficient, and it is often possible to spread the high costs associated with R&D and thus undertake research that individual undertakings would not be able to finance on their own. Also, R&D cooperation makes it possible to pool the know-how of several undertakings and thereby achieve results which either could not have been achieved by an individual undertaking or which could not have been achieved so quickly.

R&D cooperation can also have negative effects on competition. First, it can restrict innovation where it may be assumed that the undertakings which participate in R&D cooperation would have carried out the R&D on their own had they not been party to the agreement. Next, the cooperation can lead to a concerted practice on existing markets. This is particularly likely where there is cooperation for the improvement of existing technology, though less likely where the cooperation is aimed at developing a new product. Finally, R&D cooperation can lead to market protection.[64]

The forms of restriction on competition referred to will normally occur where the cooperating undertakings have significant strength on existing markets. On this basis,

---

63. OJ 1987 L 35/36.
64. Commission Guidelines on horizontal cooperation agreements, para. 54.

the Commission has exempted R&D agreements where the parties do not exceed a certain market share threshold, provided they fulfil a number of other conditions.[65]

The block exemption Regulation covers the situation where two or more undertakings carry out joint R&D of contract products or contract technologies; *see* Article 1(1). 'Research and development' is defined in Article 1(3) as activities aimed at acquiring know-how relating to products, technologies or processes, the carrying out of theoretical analysis, systematic study or experimentation, including experimental and demonstrator production, technical testing of products or processes, the establishment of the necessary facilities up to demonstrator scale and the obtaining of IPRs for the results. According to Article 1(10), joint research can be carried out by a joint team, organisation or undertaking. However, it can also be carried out by delegating the research to a third party or apportioning it between the parties according to their specialisations in research, development and exploitation. The exemption covers not only those parts of the agreement that concern joint research but also the joint exploitation of the results of the research. This means it is possible to produce and distribute the product that results from the investment in research or alternatively to grant a licence for the exploitation of the research results. However, it is a condition that the results that are exploited jointly are either protected by IPR or constitute know-how that is of decisive importance for the production.[66] If this condition did not exist, it would be easy to camouflage joint production as being the consequence of research cooperation.

There are a number of conditions and reservations linked to an exemption. Among other things, all parties must have access to the results of the joint research; *see* Article 3. Where R&D agreements include the joint exploitation of the results, the exemption lasts for at least seven years, but it can continue thereafter until the parties to the agreement have a market share of 25% of the relevant market for the products or technologies covered by the agreement; *see* Article 6(4). If an agreement is made by competing undertakings (according to Article 1(15), this includes actual or potential competitors), exemption will only be granted if the combined market shares of the parties do not exceed 25% of the product market in which the R&D cooperation is active. In addition, Article 8 lists the different kinds of agreements and conditions in agreements which will prevent an exemption from being granted under the Regulation.

7   COOPERATION IN SALES AND MARKETING

7.1   Agreements on Market Sharing

According to Article 101(1)(c), an agreement on market sharing could have the effect of restricting competition. Such market sharing can be made by undertakings agreeing to divide the market territorially or otherwise sharing customers. Even if the division of

---

65. Commission Regulation (EU) No 2023/1066 on the application of Art. 101(3) of the Treaty on the Functioning of the European Union to certain categories of research and development agreements (OJ 2023 L 143/9).
66. Article 5(1) of the Regulation.

customers is carried out on an objective basis, and maybe even with the consent of the customers, there will be an infringement of Article 101.[67] Also, it will include agreement on the division of customers in markets where the parties to the agreement are not yet active if the agreement has the effect of preventing potential competition in that market.[68] These forms of market sharing agreements will normally restrict competition 'by object'.[69]

> There was an example of a market-sharing agreement in Commission Decision 1999/60/EC concerning a *pre-insulated pipe cartel*, in which a number of European undertakings had entered into a network of agreements which restricted competition.[70] A number of Danish undertakings agreed on a number of basic principles for what the Commission Decision referred to as the 'Danish cartel'. First, they agreed on a number of price increases, and then they agreed on a quota arrangement laying down how large a percentage market share each should have. The market-sharing arrangement was based on the 'established customer' principle. Where each party was allowed to keep its existing customers, and it was not permitted to conduct an active policy to take over the customers of the other parties. The quota arrangement was supervised by the sales directors, who met regularly. One person acted as coordinator and allocated tenders between the cartel's members. Thus, it was decided, in advance, who should 'win' the order in question. The undertaking which had the honours informed the other parties what price it intended to offer, and the other parties thereupon put forward higher bids. At the end of each year, the parties exchanged auditor-certified information about the year's sales of pipes, and there was a compensation arrangement to back up the quota arrangement.
>
> Another example of a market-sharing agreement was the subject of Commission Decision 94/815/EC relating to cement.[71] The case concerned a number of agreements between European cement producers and industry associations, in which Cembureau, the European industry association, played a central role. The Commission established that there was an agreement to respect the home market principle. To the extent that there were cross-border sales, an exchange of price information ensured that the exporting undertaking could set its prices in relation to the local price leader so as to avoid the cross-border trade in cement upsetting prices in the market in question. There were a number of other agreements between producers in particular Member States containing further details on market

---

67. Joined Cases 209 to 215 and 218/78, *van Landewyck*, paras 134–141.
68. Case T-519/09, *Toshiba*, para. 230.
69. *See* as an example Case C-373/14 P, *Toshiba*, paras 28–29.
70. OJ 1999 L 24/1.
71. OJ 1994 L 343/1. The Decision was referred to the GC in Joined Cases T-25/95 and others, *Cimenteries*.

sharing. An agreement between producers in Spain and Portugal ensured that there should not be transport of cement between the two countries.

7.2 Commercialisation Agreements

Competitors can also cooperate on sales and marketing without this necessarily involving market sharing. This may take the form of cooperation on joint distribution, for example, through a joint venture sales company. As already referred to in section 3, such an arrangement would inevitably lead to the coordination of their pricing policies and could also lead to market sharing; therefore, the Commission has been very reluctant to accept such forms of cooperation.[72] However, it is not impossible that there could be certain effectivity gains which could justify the acceptance of such joint distribution.[73] Instead of joint distribution, two competitors may enter into a mutual agreement to distribute the products of the other party. In this case, there is also a risk that the agreement will result in the participation of the markets between parties or may lead to collusion.[74] Cooperation can also consist of joint marketing, which may involve joint advertising or even cooperation on after-sales services. Such cooperation can be contrary to Article 101 because it gives greater scope for the exchange of sensitive information, particularly on pricing. Also, joint marketing can in itself restrict competition where marketing costs constitute a major part of the total costs, as the cooperation will remove an important competitive parameter.[75] Just as agreements on joint distribution this type of cooperation may, however, risk leading to price-fixing, market sharing or reduced production.

The shared use of a trade mark can have the effect of restricting competition as products sold under the trade mark will appear to consumers to be the same, so there will no longer be competition between the products in question.[76] In the same way, agreements not to make comparative advertising can have an anticompetitive effect.[77]

In its Guidelines on horizontal cooperation agreements, the Commission has accepted that, provided that the commercialisation agreements between undertakings

---

72. Commission Guidelines on horizontal cooperation agreements, paras 322–327.
73. Commission Guidelines on horizontal cooperation agreements, paras 341–346; and e.g., Commission Decision 89/467/EEC, *UIP* (OJ 1989 L 226/35).
74. Commission Guidelines on horizontal cooperation agreements, para. 318.
75. Commission Decision 85/76/EEC, *Milchförderungsfonds* (OJ 1985 L 35/35), where it was not so much that the marketing costs were harmonised, but that they had been reduced for certain undertakings. The case concerned a fund which, by voluntary contributions made by German milk producers, among other things, paid for an advertising campaign for cheese in Italy. This distorted competition as these activities supported German cheese exporters without the sales price having to bear the direct costs (because, as stated, the fund was financed by voluntary contributions); *see* para. 30.
76. Case 246/86, *Belasco,* para. 30, where the common use of the designation 'Belsaco' and a collective advertising campaign was aimed at ensuring that all products had the same image, thereby removing competition between the parties to the agreement.
77. Commission Decision 1999/267/EC, *EPI* (OJ 1999 L 106/14).

that have less than 15% market share will not normally be covered by Article 101(1) or that an exemption can be granted under Article 101(3).[78]

7.3   Procurements and Auctions

A special kind of market sharing takes place where competing undertakings participating in a public or private procurement agree on who should make a bid or agree on what price they should ask.[79] Such coordination, called bid-rigging, is clearly anticompetitive.[80] Bid-rigging must be distinguished from situations where competitors agree to make a joint bidding.[81] Joint bidding will often require that the competitors set up a bidding consortium agreement. This kind of cooperation need not restrict competition if the undertakings that are part of the joint bidding would not have been able to make a bid on their own, in which case the undertakings in the consortium are not potential competitors. To be able to evaluate whether this is the case or not, a closer examination of the tender is necessary. If the tender rules allow for submission of bids on parts of the contract (lots), undertakings that have the capacity to bid for a lot are competitors, even if none of them had the capacity to bid for the whole tender. Where bids for lots are allowed, it is thus more likely that joint bidding will restrict competition.[82] Joint bidding may, however, also provide for efficiency gains in the form of lower prices, better quality or faster realization, and this may merit an exemption according to Article 101(3).[83]

If undertakings cooperate on developing joint auctions, exhibitions or trade fairs, there can be conditions which will restrict competition. This will especially be the case if the participating undertakings are prevented from taking part in other auctions, etc., or if third-party undertakings are, to an unreasonable extent, prevented from taking part or are only able to take part on unreasonable terms.[84]

7.4   Agreement to Refrain from or Restrict Marketing

If two competitors agree to refrain from marketing their products or to restrict their marketing, this is likely to limit (price) competition.[85] The same is the case if

---

78. Commission Guidelines on horizontal cooperation agreements, paras 338–340.
79. *See* Commission decision 92/204/EEC, *Building and contruction industry in the Netherlands* (OJ 1992 L 92/1), para. 80.
80. Commission Guidelines on horizontal cooperation agreements, para. 348.
81. As pointed out by the Commission, it is not always easy to distinguish between these two forms of coordination, in particular in cases of subcontracting, e.g., where two tenders cross-subcontract, *see* Guidelines on horizontal cooperation agreement, para. 349.
82. Commission Guidelines on horizontal cooperation agreements, paras 352–357. *See also* Albert Sanchez-Graells: *Competition and Public Procurement*, Journal of European Competition Law & Practice, 2018 pp. 551–559 DOI: 10.1093/jeclap/lpy060.
83. Commission Guidelines on horizontal cooperation agreements, paras 358–359.
84. Among others, Commission Decision 88/477/EEC, *British Dental Trade Association* (OJ 1988 L 233/1), and Commission Decision 88/491/EEC, *Bloemenveilingen Aalsmeer* (OJ 1988 L 262/27).
85. *See* Commission Decision of 13 Apr. 2011, COMP/39579 – *Consumer Detergents*. In this case, the agreement to restrict marketing was linked to pricing agreements.

undertakings agree not to enter a market for a given period. This was the case in the so-called pay-for-delay cases.[86]

Case C-591/16 P, *Lundbeck*, concerned the Danish Lundbeck group, which had obtained a patent for a medical product, citalopram. The patent expired in 2002, but Lundbeck still owned two patents for processes for producing the product, and it used these patents to keep manufacturers of generic medicines out of the market. This resulted in a number of cases against such manufacturers for infringement of the patents, but these cases were closed by entering into agreements with each of these. According to these agreements, the manufacturers of generic products accepted that entering the market was likely to infringe the patent rights of Lundbeck, and therefore, they would abstain from doing so and as compensation, Lundbeck agreed to pay the manufacturers certain agreed amounts. The agreements were termed 'pay for delay' since it seemed that Lundbeck paid the manufacturers to wait before entering the market. The Commission argued that these agreements infringed Article 101, and both the General Court (GC) and CJ agreed.

When the case reached the CJ, the Court first established that Lundbeck and the manufacturers of generic products were potential competitors. Lundbeck had argued that since it held patents that prevented the manufacturers from entering the market, they were not potential competitors. According to the CJ, in order to evaluate whether an undertaking is a potential competitor, it must be determined whether there are real and concrete possibilities of that undertaking joining that market and competing. In the case where a patent may be a barrier, it should be assessed whether the manufacturer of generic medicines has, in fact, a firm intention and an inherent ability to enter the market and does not meet barriers to entry that are insurmountable.[87] The fact that there is a process patent cannot as such amount to an insurmountable barrier as the manufacturer may be willing to take the risk upon entering the market of being subject to infringement proceedings brought by the patent holder. If they are deemed willing to take such a risk, the manufacturers are potential competitors, without it being necessary for the competition authority to carry out a review of the strength of the patent and evaluate the most likely outcome of such infringement proceedings.[88]

Lundbeck had also argued that there was no restriction of the competition 'by object', which is why the Commission needed to conduct a more thorough evaluation of the effect of the agreements. The CJ disagreed as it was plain that the agreement restricted competition when the transfer of value from Lundbeck to the manufacturers of generic products cannot have

---
86. Apart from the judgment referenced in the main text, this complex of cases include, *inter alia*, Case C-307/18, *Generics* and Case C-611/16 P, *Xellia Pharmaceuticals*.
87. *See* paras 54–56 of the judgment.
88. Paragraphs 58–61.

any explanation other than to prevent the manufacturers from entering the market, and thereby, the competitors deliberately substituted corporation with the risk of competition. Furthermore, in this case, the payments were sufficient to have the effect that the manufacturers keep out of the market, and therefore, there was a 'by object' restriction.[89]

8   SUSTAINABILITY AGREEMENTS

In the recent revision of the Commission Guidelines on horizontal cooperation agreements, a section has been added on sustainability agreements, that is, agreements between competitors that pursue one or more sustainability objectives. Sustainability objectives include addressing climate change, reducing pollution, limiting the use of natural resources, upholding human rights, reducing food waste and ensuring animal welfare.[90] This could, for instance, be a standardisation agreement that ensures more sustainable products or an agreement to phase out the marketing of energy-demanding products that may be legal to sell but not sustainable.

The Commission points out that such sustainability objectives will normally be addressed through public policies, e.g., regulation, but if there is no such public intervention, it may be necessary for undertakings to act by entering into agreements. Even though such agreements are pursuing sustainability objectives, it is still necessary to evaluate whether they infringe on Article 101, as they cannot escape the prohibition of that provision just because they have sustainability objectives.[91]

The Commission accepts that some agreements are not likely to restrict competition since they do not affect parameters of competition, such as price, quantity and quality. This would be the case with agreements that focus on the internal affairs of the undertaking, the creation of databases about sustainable suppliers or an agreement on a campaign raising customers' awareness of the environmental footprint of their consumption.[92]

Some sustainability agreements may, however, restrict competition. Some of the agreements may be of the same type as those discussed above and will, therefore, have to be assessed as such. This is, for instance, the case for an R&D agreement aiming to develop a new sustainable product or an agreement to use common product standards. The Commission is, however, willing to take a more positive view of such an agreement if it is proven that its aim is to promote sustainability objectives. How this more positive view will be exercised is not entirely clear, apart from the case of sustainability standardisation agreements where the Guidelines provide a more detailed account.[93]

Sustainability standardisation agreements are, for instance, agreements between competitors to phase out or replace non-sustainable products or processes with more

---

89. Paragraphs 114–119.
90. Commission Guidelines on horizontal cooperation agreements, para. 517.
91. Commission Guidelines on horizontal cooperation agreements, para. 521.
92. Commission Guidelines on horizontal cooperation agreements, para. 527–531.
93. A more detailed assessment of such standardisation agreements is outlined in paras 537–555.

sustainable ones. It could be agreements to harmonise packaging material to facilitate recycling, or competitors may agree only to buy production input if these are manufactured in a sustainable manner. Such agreements have some similarities with the agreements mentioned in section 5.3 but are likely to differ in some ways: first, sustainability standardisation agreements are often combined with the establishment of a green label, logo or brand that may only be used if the undertaking complies with the standard. Second, it will often be costly to comply with such a standard and third, the issue of interoperability and comparability between technologies is generally irrelevant to sustainability standards. Fourth, sustainability standards are often process, management or performance based, whereas 'normal' technical standards will often focus on the use of specific technologies or production methods.

Because of these differences, the Commission is prepared to assume that there is no restriction of competition if the following cumulative conditions are fulfilled (the Commission terms this a 'soft safe harbour'):

(1) The procedure for developing the sustainability standard is transparent, and all interested competitors can participate in the process.
(2) The agreement does not require the undertakings to comply with the standard.
(3) The agreement may set binding requirements, but the undertakings must remain free to adopt for themselves a higher sustainability standard than the one agreed.
(4) The undertakings should not exchange commercially sensitive information that is not necessary to develop or adopt the standard.
(5) Undertakings that have not participated in the standard development process should have effective and non-discriminatory access to use the standard.
(6) The use of the standard should not lead to a significant increase in price or a significant reduction in the choice of products available on the market. However, in this case, the safe harbour still applies if the combined market share of the participating undertakings does not exceed 20% on any relevant market affected by the standard.

If all of the above conditions are not fulfilled it will require an additional assessment to determine whether the agreement has anticompetitive effects. This may not be the case if, for instance, the market coverage of the agreement is not that extensive and, as a consequence, that way still be a substantial production of products that are either conventional or produced under an alternative sustainability label or standard.

Even if a sustainability standardisation agreement infringes Article 101(1), it may still benefit from Article 101(3). This requires that the four cumulative conditions are fulfilled, and as explained in Chapter 2, section 6.2, the Commission is ready to accept that there are different ways such agreements may benefit consumers.

9 JOINT VENTURES

9.1 The Special Nature of Joint Ventures

Many horizontal cooperation agreements are entered into in the form of a joint venture. This is clearly seen in the fact that even though the Commission's Guidelines on the applicability of Article 101 to horizontal cooperation agreements do not devote one or several sections to joint ventures, nevertheless, many of the examples given involve joint ventures.[94]

The Commission considers joint ventures to be a special institutionalised form of commercial cooperation.[95] Already in 1974, the Commission pointed out that a joint venture could involve a number of special problems in competition law, and in this connection, it defined a joint venture as an enterprise that is controlled by two or more independent undertakings.[96] Subsequently, the Commission has developed this definition by referring to the fact that the undertakings that control a joint venture shall be independent of each other,[97] that it is not material whether or not the joint venture is for a limited period, and that the corporate form by which the joint venture is carried on is immaterial.[98]

It is clear that joint ventures can involve agreements which restrict competition and, therefore, ought to be judged in accordance with Article 101 TFEU. For example, a joint venture can form the framework within which two producers can agree on uniform pricing. A form of price-fixing agreement can be ensured by the producers agreeing that their sales shall be made through their joint venture, so there will be an automatic alignment of prices.

A joint venture can also form the framework for more extensive cooperation, where two or more undertakings (joint venture partners) agree to combine resources and conduct joint activities, such as R&D or joint production. This form of joint venture is more difficult to evaluate under Article 101 for two particular reasons: first, the formation of such a joint venture can be regarded as a partial merger, and this merger element is subject to separate evaluation; and second, such extensive cooperation gives rise to the need to assess whether the cooperation between the joint venture partners is extended beyond the setting up of a jointly owned company and can result in the coordination of other activities.

---

94. In most cases, it is directly stated that cooperation agreements of a particular kind can be established in the form of a joint venture; *see* para. 52 on R&D agreements, paras 173–174 on production agreements, and indirectly para. 273 which refers to a company which the parties jointly control in relation to purchasing arrangements.
95. Commission Notice concerning the assessment of cooperative joint ventures pursuant to Art. 85 of the EEC Treaty (OJ 1993 C 43/2), para. 1, hereinafter the 'Joint Venture Notice'.
96. The Fourth Report on Competition Policy 1974, para. 37.
97. The Thirteenth Report on Competition Policy 1983, para. 53.
98. The Thirteenth Report on Competition Policy 1983, para. 54, and Commission Notice concerning the assessment of cooperative joint ventures pursuant to Art. 85 of the EEC Treaty (OJ 1993 C 43/2), para. 3.

On a number of points, joint ventures are subject to special evaluation under competition law. If a joint venture has a Community dimension and is fully functioning, it should be notified under the Merger Control Regulation. As well as evaluating such a joint venture under the special merger control test, *see* Chapter 8, such a joint venture may also involve some agreements which restrict competition, and in this case, it must be evaluated under Article 2(4) of the Merger Control Regulation. This provision states that a joint venture that has as its object or effects the coordination of the competitive behaviour of undertakings that remain independent shall be appraised in accordance with the criteria of Article 101(1) and (3). The appraisal to which joint ventures are subject under Article 2(4) of the Merger Control Regulation is discussed in more detail in Chapter 8, section 7.

If a joint venture is not covered by the Merger Control Regulation, for example, because it does not have a Community dimension,[99] there must be an evaluation in accordance with Article 101 of whether the joint venture contains any agreements which restrict competition. The Commission has developed a special practice for the investigation of different forms of restriction of competition, which can be seen in connection with joint ventures. This practice involves an investigation of the following circumstances:[100]

(a) There is an investigation of whether competition between the joint venture partners is restricted. This requires it to be established that the joint venture partners are either actual or potential competitors in one or more areas. If, for example, the joint venture partners combine their existing activities in a particular area, the joint venture can have the effect of restricting competition, as two undertakings are reduced to one. Also, a joint venture can have an influence on the joint venture partners' other activities – the 'spillover' effect'.[101]

(b) If a joint venture is an independent undertaking, there must be an investigation of whether there is any restriction on competition between the joint venture partners and the joint venture company.

(c) Next, the Commission investigates whether the setting up of a joint venture affects the position of any third parties. Depending on the circumstances, the

---

99. If a joint venture is fully functioning but does not have a Community dimension, the Commission has accepted a number of restrictions on the application of Art. 101 to such joint ventures. First, the Commission will not allow an exemption under Art. 101(3) to a joint venture which a national authority intends to prohibit under national merger control rules. Next, the Commission only finds it relevant to apply Art. 101 to restrictions on competition that occur through the joint venture partners' coordination of their commercial activities outside the joint venture, i.e., the 'spillover' effect; *see* ss 9.3.2 and 9.3.3. However, the Commission will to the greatest possible extent leave it to the Member States to assess such joint ventures. Even though the Commission has thus accepted a number of restrictions on its application of Art. 101, there is not a total exclusion of the Commission's application of Art. 101, and an Art. 101 case can be initiated by national authorities or may arise before the national courts.
100. An example of an early decision which reviewed these points is Commission Decision 90/410/EEC *Elopak/Metal Box – Odin* (OJ 1990 L 209/15), which marks the new practice after the introduction of the Merger Control Regulation.
101. Sometimes the term 'group effect' or 'indirect effect' is used instead.

setting up of a joint venture can have consequences for the suppliers or customers of the joint venture partners. Also, the establishment of a joint venture can mean that potential competitors are prevented from entering the market.
(d) The Commission evaluates whether a joint venture is part of a network of joint venture companies, whereby the effect of the individual joint venture is reinforced.
(e) Even if it is concluded that the establishment of a joint venture does not in itself lead to a restriction of competition, the Commission will also investigate whether the individual provisions of the joint venture partners' agreement to set up a joint venture company have the effect of restricting competition.

The following sections will review in more detail the individual elements of the Commission's analysis of joint ventures. The review will be based on the Commission's practice and the relatively few judgments there have been on the issue. In 1993, a Notice was issued on the assessment of cooperative joint ventures,[102] but this Notice was withdrawn in connection with the entry into force of the Commission's first Guidelines on horizontal cooperation agreements in 2001.[103] The 1993 Notice contains a number of more general comments on the assessment of joint ventures, which have not been included in the later Notice, so the older Notice can still be of interest.

This review focuses on the Commission's practice for when a restriction on competition will be found to exist. Joint ventures will often involve cooperation of the types that have been discussed in the previous sections, and as a consequence, there are some overlaps. But as it will also become clear, joint ventures raise a number of special problems that warrant that this type of cooperation is addressed separately.

9.2   Restrictions on Competition Between the Joint Venture and the Joint Venture Partners

If a joint venture is an independent undertaking, it will be relevant to assess whether, in the relationship between a joint venture and a joint venture partner, restrictions are agreed, which contravene Article 101. If one joint venture partner controls the joint venture company, it follows from the concept of an undertaking, which is analysed in Chapter 2, section 3.1, that they are considered to be one undertaking, and it is thus not relevant to apply Article 101 to the relationship between the two. The Commission initially decided that a joint venture and its joint venture partner did not constitute one undertaking. In Commission Decision 91/335/EEC, *Gosme/Martell – DMP*, which concerned a joint venture owned in equal shares by two joint venture partners, the Commission did not believe that the joint venture partners could control the joint venture's commercial activities. In this, it emphasised that both joint venture partners had 50% of the voting rights and appointed half the members of the board of directors

---

102. The Joint Venture Notice.
103. Commission Notice – Guidelines on the applicability of Art. 81 of the EC Treaty to horizontal cooperation agreements, OJ 2001 C 3/2, para. 8 together with para. 5.

of the joint venture company. The joint venture company also distributed products which did not belong to the joint venture partners, and the joint venture company had its own sales team. Since this joint venture was sufficiently independent in relation to the joint venture partners, the Commission was of the view that an agreement between the joint venture company and Martell was contrary to Article 101 since it was intended to restrict parallel imports.[104]

However, later, the GC and the CJ ruled that a joint venture and one or more of its joint venture partners could constitute an undertaking. The case law has addressed the question of whether joint venture partners were liable for fines imposed on their joint venture. But as pointed out in Chapter 2, section 3.1, the outcome of this question depends on the concept of an undertaking, and the same concept also determines whether an agreement is between two undertakings or not, and thus whether it is within the scope of Article 101 or not.

The first of these cases was Case T-314/01, *Avebe*, where the GC had to decide whether a joint venture partner could be made liable for the fact that the joint venture company was part of a cartel. The GC established that the joint venture was subject to the joint control of the joint venture partners. In this situation, the GC held that it could be assumed that the joint venture partners had, in fact, exercised control and were thus liable for the conduct of the joint venture company. The GC concluded that the joint venture and the two joint venture partners constituted an economic unit in relation to the concept of an undertaking.[105]

The GC and CJ have confirmed this finding in several subsequent cases.[106] In these cases, the courts did not use the assumption which was used in the *Avebe* judgment, which has made it easier for the joint ventures to reject that they exercise control over their joint venture (which makes it less likely that they will be liable for fines imposed on the joint venture). The CJ has also stressed that it is not necessary to prove that all joint venture partners exercise control, as it may be possible that some partners do and some do not.[107] At the same time, the Court has stressed that the fact that a joint venture partner has negative control is enough to establish control over the joint venture if they use that negative control to influence the joint venture. Thus, it is possible to control a joint venture by having extensive veto rights that allow a joint venture partner to dictate what the joint venture cannot do.[108] The CJ has gone as far as stating that the fact that a joint venture partner has extensive veto rights is an indication that there is an intention to exercise control.[109] The fact that these veto rights

---

104. Commission Decision 91/335/EEC, *Gosme/Martell – DMP* (OJ 1991 L 185/23), para. 30. In line with this; see Commission Decision 91/562/EC, *Eirpage* (OJ 1991 L 306/22), para. 9, and the Decision of 21 Dec. 2005 in Case COMP/F/38.443 – *Rubber chemicals* (OJ 2006 L 353/50), para. 263.
105. *See* para. 141 of the judgment.
106. *See* for instance Case T-132/07, *Fuji Electric Co Ltd*, C-480/09 P, *AccaElectrabel*, and Case C-179/12 P, *Dow Chemical*.
107. *See inter alia* Joint Cases C-293/13 P & C-294/13 P, *Del Montes*, para. 78, and Case C-623/15 P, *Toshiba Corp*, para. 48.
108. Case T-77/08, *Dow*, para. 92.
109. Joint Cases C-293/13 P og C-294/13 P, *Del Montes*, para. 79, Case C-623/15 P, *Toshiba Corp*, para. 51.

have never been used is not proof that control has not been exercised, as the veto rights may still ensure that a partner is consulted before important decisions and thus given a chance to influence these.[110] The fact that veto rights can only be used to control a joint venture if it proves possible to cooperate with the other joint venture partner who often has similar veto rights does also not prove that there is no exercise of control. According to the GC, the fact that the joint venture partners agreed to allow for these veto rights indicates that the partners are capable of cooperating and thus exercising control together.[111] Other indications of the joint venture partners exercising control may be the fact that the same persons are sitting in the management of the joint venture and its partners[112] or that the joint venture is dependent on supplies from a joint venture partner.[113]

As a consequence of this case law, it is likely that joint venture partners will be liable for the fines imposed on their joint ventures. But more importantly, in the present context, the consequence is that in many joint ventures, agreements between the joint venture and (some of) its joint venture partners will be outside the application of Article 101. The Commission has, in its recent Guidelines on horizontal cooperation agreements, confirmed that it will not apply Article 101 on agreements between the joint venture and its partners to the extent that these exercise decisive influence over the joint venture.[114]

But even so, it will still be relevant to apply Article 101 on agreements between a joint venture and its partners if the joint venture partner does not have sufficient rights to exercise control or if the agreement is outside the geographical scope of the joint ventures or concern other products than that in which the joint venture is engaged.

In these cases, there is a clear possibility that competition between a joint venture and one or more joint venture partners will be restricted if they are competitors. This is confirmed by the fact that the joint venture partners will often have agreed to a non-competition clause whereby they will not compete with their joint venture.

If one looks at the existing decisions, only a few of them include an evaluation of restrictions on competition between a joint venture and the joint venture partners. The decisions which do contain such an evaluation restrict themselves to evaluating the restrictions on competition, which are the direct consequence of the various contractual provisions concerning the joint venture company, such as non-competition clauses, supply clauses, etc. These are considered below in section 9.6. However, there are no examples of cases where the Commission has assessed whether there is a high risk of there being a concerted practice between a joint venture and the joint venture partners, contrary to Article 101. The fact that this is so can probably be explained by the Commission not having a real expectation that a joint venture partner will compete with its joint venture, so the Commission is content with looking into any contractual terms which seem to be unnecessarily restrictive.

---

110. Case C-623/15, P, *Toshiba Corp.*, para. 73.
111. Case T-104/13, *Toshiba Corp.*, para. 106.
112. Case T-104/13, *Toshiba Corp.*, para. 100, and Case C-623/15, P, *Toshiba Corp.*, para. 78.
113. Joint Cases C-293/13 P og C-294/13 P, *Del Montes*, para. 86.
114. *See* Commission Guidelines on horizontal cooperation agreements, para. 12.

9.3 Restrictions on Competition Between Joint Venture Partners

The key question in joint venture cases is often whether the establishment of the cooperation means that competition between the joint venture partners is restricted, either by the establishment of the joint venture or because it can be assumed that the cooperation will affect the joint venture partners' other activities. Both of these questions will be considered below.

The assessment of this question will, however, also be affected by the evolution of the concept of an undertaking discussed above. If several joint venture partners exercise decisive influence over their joint venture, these will also, to some degree, be part of the same undertaking, and to the extent this is the case, any agreement between these partners will not be relevant under Article 101. The CJ has held that even though joint venture partners may be part of the same undertaking in relation to some activities, they may be independent undertakings in relation to other activities or markets other than the one in which the joint venture is active.[115]

Based on this case law, the Commission has concluded that in the case where several joint ventures exercise decisive influence over their joint venture, they will typically not apply Article 101(1) to agreements between the joint venture partners, apart from the following agreements:[116]

- Agreements between the joint venture partners to create the joint venture.
- Agreements between the joint venture partners to modify the scope of their joint venture.
- Agreements between the joint venture partners and the joint venture outside the product and geographic scope of the activity of the joint venture.

These guidelines seem to be a consequence of the fact that the joint venture partners may form one undertaking with their joint venture. The Commission, however, also reserves the right to apply Article 101 to agreements between the joint venture partners that are within the scope of the activities of the joint venture but without the joint venture being a part of the agreement. It may be questioned whether the joint venture partners are not one undertaking in this area, even if the joint venture is not part of the agreement.

In the following, the focus is on the agreements between joint venture partners where it will normally still be relevant to consider the application of Article 101.

9.3.1 *Restriction on Competition by the Establishment of a Joint Venture*

The setting up of a joint venture can have a direct influence on competition between the joint venture partners. This will be so if two competing undertakings set up a joint venture which is active in an area where they have previously competed. If the joint venture partners transfer their own business activities in the area, in reality, two or

---

115. Case C-588/15 P og C-622/15 P, *LG Electronics*, para. 79.
116. Commission Guidelines on horizontal cooperation agreements, paras 12–13.

more competing undertakings will be replaced by one undertaking, and consequently, competition will be restricted. If the joint venture partners continue to be active in the area, competition may not be immediately restricted unless it can be assumed that setting up the joint venture will have a 'spillover' effect on the joint venture partners' conduct in connection with such activities; see below.

> An example of this is the *P&O Stena Line* case, where the two joint venture partners ran ferry routes between Dover and Calais, which they wanted in future to run through a jointly controlled joint venture. Since this was a joint venture between two actual competitors, its establishment was considered to be contrary to Article 101.[117] Another example was the case of *Asahi/Saint-Gobain*, where the Commission considered that the joint venture partners were competitors in respect of the research activity which the planned joint venture should undertake. The Commission found that both joint venture partners were undertaking existing research in similar areas, and that the effect of the joint venture would therefore be to make it impossible for the joint venture partners to take individual initiatives, which could give one of the partners an advantage over the other. Thereby, the joint venture meant that two competing research projects were reduced to one, and competition was diminished.[118]

Competition can also be restricted if joint venture partners are potential competitors in the area in which the joint venture is active. The setting up of a joint venture means that it cannot be expected that the joint venture partners will become as active in the market where the joint venture company is active. If several joint venture partners could be expected to be active in the area where the joint venture is to be active, the consequence of setting up the joint venture will be that competition will be restricted; there will only be one player where there could have been several. The same will be the case where one joint venture partner is an actual competitor and another is a potential competitor on the market where a joint venture is to be active.

In many cases, there does not seem to be any great doubt about whether the individual joint venture partners could carry out the production or research activity on their own. Many cases involve joint venture partners with considerable resources, and here, the Commission seems merely to state briefly that the necessary financial, technical and research capacity exists.[119]

The cases where the Commission concludes that the joint venture partners are not potential competitors are, among others, cases where it is established that the individual joint venture partners do not have the necessary technology to carry out the

---

117. Commission Decision 1999/421/EC, *P&O Stena Line* (OJ 1999 L 163/61), para. 61.
118. Commission Decision 94/896/EC, *Asahi/Saint-Gobain* (OJ 1994 L 354/87), in particular para. 21.
119. Commission Decision 94/986/EC, *Philips-Osram* (OJ 1994 L 378/37), para. 16, and Commission Decision 93/49/EEC, *Ford/Volkswagen* (OJ 1993 L 20/14), para. 19.

activity on their own.[120] Next, there are a number of cases where the Commission has rejected the idea that the joint venture partners were potential competitors because the joint venture either required such resources or was associated with such risk that it could not be expected that the individual joint venture partners would carry on the activity on their own.[121] Finally, it is possible that the individual joint venture partner does not have enough know-how to carry out the planned activity on its own.[122] In relation to this latter, it must be assessed whether a joint venture partner could acquire the necessary know-how by buying it.[123] As for consortiums set up for joint bidding it may be more difficult to evaluate whether the bidders are potential competitors, as this depends on how the tender is structured, *see* above section 7.3.

9.3.2 *'Spillover' Effects on the Market Where the Joint Venture Operates*

In many cases, the joint venture partners will refrain from competing with their joint venture after setting it up. It may be that the joint venture partners will transfer their existing assets to their joint venture or that they will allow their joint venture the exclusive right to a particular market. Typically, the joint venture partners will also be subject to a non-competition clause which will prevent them from subsequently initiating activity which will compete with their joint venture. In all these cases, there cannot be a 'spillover' effect on the joint venture company's own market. There will also be no risk of spillover effect in this market where the joint venture partners have agreed to terminate their operations, which compete with the joint venture company within a given number of years.[124]

However, if the joint venture partners remain active on the market in which the joint venture company operates, it is clear that there is a considerable risk that they will coordinate their conduct in the area. As mentioned above, it will, however, only be relevant to use Article 101 if not all joint venture partners exercise decisive influence,

---

120. Commission Decision 94/770/EC, *Pasteur Mérieux-Merck* (OJ 1994 L 309/1), in particular paras 65–68, where it was assessed that in the case of certain vaccines there was no certainty that any of the joint venture partners could have developed them on their own.
121. Among others Commission Decision 97/39/EC, *Iridium* (OJ 1997 L 16/87), para. 40, and Commission Decision 94/895/EC, *International Private Satellite Partners* (OJ 1994 L 354/75), para. 55(b). This assessment must also include the speed of technological development in the area, as the fact that development is very rapid is a further argument against making considerable investments; see Commission Decision 88/88/EEC, *Olivetti/Canon* (OJ 1988 L 52/51), para. 41.
122. Commission Decision 86/405/EEC, *Optical fibres* (OJ 1986 L 236/30), para. 46, where the special cooperation between an undertaking which manufactured glass and a number of undertakings which manufactured cables could not have been carried on by any of the joint venture partners individually, because they did not have sufficient insight into each other's areas of activity.
123. Commission Decision 87/100/EEC, *Mitchell Cotts/Sofiltra* (OJ 1987 L 41/31), para. 19, according to which one of the joint venture partners entirely lacked the necessary know-how and research and development facilities to develop a component which was of core importance to the planned activity. It could not be assumed that this joint venture partner could have bought or obtained a licence for the production of these products.
124. JV.44, *Hitachi/NEC – DRAM/JV*, Decision of 3 May 2000, para. 32, where the Commission dismissed the idea that the market was a candidate market for coordination since both parent companies would eventually withdraw from the market.

and – according to the Commission – where the joint venture is not a party to the coordination.

> In those situations where it is still relevant to assess any collaboration between the joint venture partners, there should be an evaluation of how important the joint venture is for the joint venture partners, since a very small joint venture would perhaps not give the joint venture parties the incentive to coordinate their conduct. Also, if the joint venture partners themselves have very large market shares, their general incentive for a concerted practice will be greater, so that even a joint venture with modest operations can form the framework for a concerted practice.[125]

9.3.3 'Spillover' Effects on Other Markets

The fact that joint venture partners cooperate in connection with a joint venture operation can mean that they may also coordinate their operations in other areas. As mentioned above, this type of coordination must be assessed under Article 101 regardless of whether the joint venture partners exercise decisive influence or not.

In principle, such coordination may take place in areas which have absolutely nothing to do with the joint venture activity, but in such a case, it seems difficult to see the establishment of a joint venture as being the true cause of the partners trying to coordinate their activities. For this reason, the evaluation of spillover effects will be concentrated on the markets which are more closely linked to the market in which the joint venture operates. This will typically be markets that are upstream or downstream in relation to the joint venture company's market, as well as in neighbouring markets.[126]

The decisions taken in accordance with Article 101 point to a number of special circumstances which indicate that a particular joint venture cooperation can have a 'spillover' effect. One of the circumstances which has been emphasised in a number of decisions is that the participation of the joint venture partners in the management of the joint venture company makes it possible for them to exchange confidential information.[127]

In addition to this, it will be significant to assess what connection there is between the operations of the joint venture and the operations of the joint venture partners:

> (1) If a joint venture operates downstream as a sales channel for the products of the joint venture partners, this will, by its very nature, automatically diminish competition between the joint venture partners on the market in question.

---

125. *See also* Jonathan Faull & Ali Nikpay (eds): *The EU Law of Competition*, 3rd ed., 2014 pp. 902–903.
126. Commission Guidelines on horizontal cooperation agreements, para. 183, which states that 'spillover' effects are more likely if the markets are interdependent and if the joint venture partners have a strong position on the 'spillover' market. The relevant 'spillover' markets are defined in the same way as in the Merger Control Regulation, Art. 2(5), and in the note to para. 183 in the Guidelines there is an express reference to this provision.
127. Commission Decision 93/49/EEC, *Ford/Volkswagen* (OJ 1993 L 20/14), para. 21.

Furthermore, such a joint venture can create entry barriers to new competitors.[128]

(2) If, in contrast, the joint venture operates upstream from the joint venture partners, it will depend on an evaluation of the importance of the input supplied by the joint venture. For example, if a joint venture produces certain components which are included in the products of the joint venture partners, this could reduce competition between the products of the joint venture partners, if the components are an important part of the finished product.[129] If the joint venture is demanding higher prices for these components, it will result in higher prices downstream, and as a result, the joint venture may increase its prices even more.[130] A similar effect can arise where a joint venture is responsible for the purchase of raw materials or components which are included in a product which several joint venture partners sell. The joint purchasing means that one of the factors which could contribute to price differentiation is no longer present.[131] A concerted practice is most probable if the joint venture is the only source for the joint venture partners of the product in question (e.g., because they have undertaken to buy only from their joint venture).

(3) If a joint venture is to operate in another territorial market than the ones where the joint venture partners compete, a concerted practice would be natural. By coordinating prices, the joint venture partners and the joint venture can help ensure that it is not attractive for parallel importers to operate, and this can contribute to maintaining divisions into several different territorial markets.[132]

9.4 The Effects on Third-Party Undertakings

A joint venture can also restrict competition by affecting the position of a third party. This will typically be the case where a joint venture achieves a certain economic strength which affects undertakings which compete with the joint venture company.

---

128. Commission Notice concerning the assessment of cooperative joint ventures pursuant to Art. 85 of the EEC Treaty (OJ 1993 C 43/2), para. 38, and Commission Decision 93/50/EEC, *Astra* (OJ 1993 L 20/23), para. 6.
129. Commission Decision 94/322/EC, *Exxon/Shell* (OJ 1994 L 144/21), para. 55. In Commission Decision 94/986/EC, *Philips-Osram* (OJ 1994 L 378/37), the Commission dismissed the idea that spillover effects would arise in the market for lamps, where both joint venture partners competed, as the components produced by the joint venture company only constituted 2%–3% of the costs of producing a lamp; see para. 18. The standardisation brought about by the use of common components was thus not sufficiently significant to be a restriction on competition.
130. Commission Guidelines on horizontal cooperation agreements, para. 238. According to para. 243 this effect is most likely where the joint venture partners have a high proportion of variable costs in common.
131. Commission Notice concerning the assessment of cooperative joint ventures pursuant to Art. 85 of the EEC Treaty (OJ 1993 C 43/2), para. 39 with reference to this practice. *See also* Commission Guidelines on horizontal cooperation agreements, para. 201.
132. *See* John Temple Lang in Barry E. Hawk (ed.): *Fordham Corporate Law Institute*, 2000 pp. 381–464 (in particular p. 405); and Joseph F. Brodley: *Joint Ventures and Antitrust Policy*, Harvard Law Review, 1982 p. 1523.

However, it is not enough to establish that a joint venture has economic strength; it must also be shown that one or more third-party undertakings are, as a result, put in a position where they cannot compete, typically because they are excluded from the market.

Even though there are a number of decisions that include an assessment of the effect of a joint venture on third-party undertakings, there are only a few where this is the decisive element. This will typically be one of many effects restricting competition that is found to exist in connection with a joint venture.

First of all, the effects restricting competition for third parties can be established in relation to the customers or suppliers of a joint venture. Where joint venture partners combine their sales in a joint venture, this can mean there are fewer choices and/or higher prices for customers.[133] Similarly, purchasing cooperation can mean that such a great purchasing strength is created that it has a serious negative effect on competition.[134] If a third-party undertaking cannot receive deliveries, for example, because the joint venture partners have the exclusive right to supply from the joint venture, this can constitute an infringement of Article 101(1) if there is market concentration.[135] In many cases, the joint venture will have bound itself to take deliveries of raw materials or components from the joint venture partners so that other suppliers are excluded from supplying in competition with the joint venture partners.[136]

Next, a restriction on competition can be found to exist in relation to undertakings that compete with the joint venture company or the joint venture partners. For example, a purchasing cooperation can obtain such economic strength that competitors are effectively unable to compete with the joint venture partners that are part of the cooperation.[137] A joint venture can also develop and produce a unique product which others than the joint venture partners must have access to in order to compete. For example, this can be because the joint venture has acquired the sole right to exploit some particular technology,[138] or because a joint venture has a production which can prevent third parties from supplying because there are not (enough) alternative supply channels.[139] In these cases, it is often decisive whether the third party can participate in the cooperation or can at least obtain supplies on non-discriminatory terms.[140]

---

133. Commission Guidelines on horizontal cooperation agreements, para. 329.
134. On the assessment of purchasing cooperation, *see* Commission Guidelines on horizontal cooperation agreements, paras 273–316.
135. Commission Decision 88/88/EEC, *Olivetti/Canon* (OJ 1988 L 52/51), para. 45.
136. Commission Decision 88/88/EEC, *Olivetti/Canon* (OJ 1988 L 52/51), para. 47, where it was found that the restriction on competition was not appreciable, as the situation was only that the joint venture partners had a preferential status in the supply of components to their joint venture, as long as the joint venture partners' components were competitive.
137. Commission Decision 93/403/EEC, *EBU/Eurovision* (OJ 1993 L 179/23), para. 51.
138. Commission Decision 94/770/EC, *Pasteur Mérieux-Merck* (OJ 1994 L 309/1), paras 70–71, where the joint venture partners had agreed they would only supply vaccines and grant licences via their joint venture. However, it was judged that even though this could affect other producers, as they were thereby prevented from acquiring the technology they needed from the joint venture partners, the restriction on competition was not significant, as there were other potential suppliers of this technology.
139. Commission Decision 94/986/EC, *Philips-Osram* (OJ 1994 L 378/37), para. 17, where the Commission assessed that the setting up of a joint venture could give the joint venture partners

In other cases, the essential question is whether a joint venture creates barriers to entry which potential competitors cannot be expected to be able to surmount. In these cases, the Commission appears to be satisfied with finding that very large economic strength is created, and if this means that there are barriers to entry to the market, the Commission will be disinclined to approve the joint venture.[141]

>An example of this is Commission Decision *Astra*, where the Commission emphasised that the customers who had signed contracts with the joint venture, which was to be responsible for running the new Astra satellite, were bound for a period of ten years, and that during this period others were excluded from access to this market.[142]

9.5 Networks of Joint Ventures

If a joint venture is part of a network of joint venture companies, this can reinforce the individual joint venture companies' effect on the joint venture partners' business policies and the position of third parties. For this reason, such joint ventures are assessed with regard to the overall effect of the network of joint ventures.[143]

The fact that many joint ventures are set up between the same joint venture partners is an indication that the joint venture partners work closely together and that it is, therefore, probable that they cooperate in other areas.[144] In addition to this, with a network of joint ventures, it is necessary to include the restrictions on competition that arise in the relationships between the different joint ventures. For example, if the joint venture partners set up several joint ventures which operate on the same product market, but in different territorial markets, it is often clear that competition between the joint ventures will be restricted. Competition will also be restricted where the joint venture partners set up a number of joint venture companies for complementary products, which the joint venture partners themselves prepare. A joint venture between joint venture partners who do not compete will not normally constitute a restriction on competition, but if a joint venture is part of a network of joint ventures, it is possible that a restriction on competition could arise if these joint ventures have been set up in the same product market.

---

the possibility of preventing independent manufacturers getting hold of lead glass. However, as it was shown that there was overcapacity, the Commission found this was not the case.
140. Commission Decision 2001/696/EC, *Identrus* (OJ 2001 L 249/12), para. 46, where the Commission found that other undertakings could become shareholders in the company, provided they fulfilled a number of objective criteria.
141. Commission Decision 91/130/EEC, *Screensport/EBU Members* (OJ 1991 L 63/32), para. 63, Commission Decision 91/562/EEC, *Eirpage* (OJ 1991 L 306/22), para. 12, and Commission Decision 96/546/EC, *ATLAS* (OJ 1996 L 239/23), para. 40.
142. Commission Decision 93/59/EEC, *Astra* (OJ 1993 L 20/23), para. 17.
143. Commission Notice concerning the assessment of cooperative joint ventures pursuant to Art. 85 of the EEC Treaty (OJ 1993 C 43/2), para. 27.
144. *See* John Temple Lang in Barry E. Hawk (ed.): *Fordham Corporate Law Institute*, 2000 p. 409.

This was the case in the Commission Decision on *Optical fibres*, where the American company Corning Glass Works had set up three joint ventures together with European undertakings located in different EU Member States. It was the intention that all three joint ventures should produce optical fibres, which was a newly developed product which could be used for communications technology. Since the new product was intended to replace more traditional cables, Corning had chosen to enter into joint venture agreements with companies that produced cables. Since Corning itself was primarily involved in the production of glass and ceramic products, the joint venture partners in the three joint ventures were not its competitors. For this reason, the Commission did not find that the individual joint ventures restricted competition. However, restrictions on competition arose between the three joint ventures since they were involved in the same production, and together they created an oligopolistic market. Because of Corning's financial involvement and the fact that Corning occupied the key technical and financial position in all three joint ventures, the Commission found that Corning was able to coordinate the conduct of the three joint venture companies. It could, therefore, be expected that the notified joint venture agreements would result in restrictions on competition.[145]

9.6 Special Provisions

Even where it is found that the setting up of a joint venture does not restrict competition and that there are no restrictions between the joint venture partners or in relation to third-party undertakings, in some cases, the Commission has undertaken an assessment of the agreements made in connection with the setting up of a joint venture company, with a view to seeing whether these contain contractual terms that restrict competition. This practice means that even if, in principle, the Commission has no objection to a joint venture, it retains the right to assess the terms agreed in the joint venture agreement, the articles of association of the joint venture company, and any other agreements associated with the cooperation.

The terms which the Commission eliminates in this way are often terms which restrict competition between the joint venture company and the joint venture partners. As mentioned in section 9.2 it will not in all cases be relevant to assess such agreements. But even in situations where an assessment is required under Article 101, the Commission has admitted that some terms are necessary for the establishment and operation of a joint venture. Such restraints are, therefore, ancillary to the setting up of a joint venture and cannot be challenged.[146]

---

145. Commission Decision 86/405/EEC, *Optical fibres* (OJ 1986 L 236/30), paras 47 and 56.
146. For more detail on the practice on ancillary restraints, *see* s. 5.5 in Ch. 2.

In 2005, the Commission issued a Notice on ancillary restraints in relation to the Merger Control Regulation.[147] According to its wording, this Notice is limited to cases under the Merger Control Regulation, and no corresponding notice has been issued in relation to the assessment of joint ventures under Article 101. For this reason, a review of what constitutes an ancillary restraint under Article 101 must be based on the Commission's decisions.[148]

In general, the Commission seems to accept that a non-competition clause, which prevents the joint venture partners and the joint venture company from competing with each other, is ancillary, even if it applies for the whole duration of the joint venture agreement. According to the Commission, the prohibition on competition is merely a concrete expression of the joint venture partners' enduring and mutual commitment to their joint venture.[149] The Commission has even allowed that the duration of a non-competition clause may be extended so that it binds a joint venture partner for a short period after it has sold its ownership interest in the joint venture company on the grounds that the exiting joint venture partner would otherwise have an unreasonable competitive advantage because of the know-how acquired through participation in the joint venture company.[150] However, it is obvious that the Commission cannot be expected to accept terms whereby the joint venture partners restrict competition between them in areas which are outside the area of activity of the joint venture company.[151] Nor will the Commission accept that a joint venture partner

---

147. Commission Notice on restrictions directly related and necessary to concentrations (OJ 2005 C 56/24). For more on this, see Ch. 8, s. 6.
148. However, there are certain general comments on the assessment of ancillary restraints in Communication from the Commission – Notice – Guidelines on the application of Art. 81(3) of the Treaty (OJ 2004 101/97), paras 28–31.
149. Commission Decision 94/986/EC, *Philips-Osram* (OJ 1994 L 378/37), para. 20, Commission Decision 96/546/EC, *ATLAS* (OJ 1996 L 239/23), para. 42, and Commission Decision 1999/242/EC, *TPS* (OJ 1999 L 90/6), para. 97. The Commission also accepted an open-ended non-competition clause in Commission Decision 94/579/EC, *BT-MCI* (OJ 1994 L 223/36), para. 46, and Commission Decision 96/547/EC, *PHOENIX/GlobalOne* (OJ 1996 L 239/57), para. 53, but here, the Commission seems to have required there to be special circumstances relating to the joint venture company's market in order for an open-ended non-competition clause to be acceptable. In particular, this can be the case where substantial investments and risks are associated with the joint venture. In Commission Decision 1999/242/EC, *TPS* (OJ 1999 L 90/6), para. 99, the Commission only accepted a non-competition clause in the start-up phase, specifically three years. Commission Decision 93/48/EEC, *Fiat/Hitachi* (OJ 1993 L 20/10), is difficult to reconcile with this practice, as para. 21 of the Decision seems to conclude generally that a non-competition clause is contrary to Art. 101, without determining whether it was ancillary or not. However, the agreements were exempted under Art. 101(3). The decision must be regarded as incorrect on this point.
150. Commission Decision 94/823/EC, *Fujitsu AMD Semiconductor* (OJ 1994 L 341/66), para. 35, in which the Commission accepted that the non-competition clause should be extended for two years following the sale, provided that this took place within ten years of setting up the joint venture company. *See also* Commission Decision 1999/781/EC, *British Interactive Broadcasting/Open* (OJ 1999 L 312/1), paras 125 and 148, where the Commission accepted that the prohibition on competition applied for twelve months after a joint venture partner had sold its controlling shareholding, provided that this took place within the first three years. *See also* Ruchi Bhandari: *Enforceability of Non-competition Clauses in Sale of Business in Joint Venture: Conundrum*, European Competition Law Review, 2014 pp. 445–452.
151. *See* Jonathan Faull & Ali Nikpay (eds): *The EU Law of Competition*, 3rd ed. 2014 p. 906.

which does not have a share in the control of the joint venture company can be bound by a non-competition clause.[152]

The Commission also seems to accept terms whereby a joint venture company or joint venture partner take on purchase and supply obligations. Thus, in several cases, the Commission has accepted an obligation, limited in time, for joint venture partners to buy the joint venture company's products since, among other things, this helps to ensure the effective and economic use of the joint venture company's production capacity, and can create a stable financial basis for the operations of the joint venture company.[153] In this connection, the Commission has accepted agreements whereby joint venture partners are given priority in receiving supplies,[154] and it has also accepted favouritism provisions which ensure that the joint venture partners obtain the best prices.[155] If joint venture partners not only have an obligation to fulfil their own needs for the product by buying it from the joint venture company but also have the status of sole distributors, the Commission will look more critically at whether this constitutes an ancillary restraint. The Commission seems to hold the view that a non-exclusive distributorship is sufficient to secure the interests of the joint venture company.[156]

In connection with the setting up of a joint venture, the sole right to exploit certain know-how will often be granted to the joint venture or the joint venture will be granted a licence to use some technology. This will not be contrary to Article 101, even if certain restrictions are imposed on the joint venture in connection with how the licence can be used, for example, by restricting it to sales to a certain territory or preventing the joint venture company from producing products that compete with the licensed products.[157] It is more questionable whether the Commission will accept an exclusive licence which excludes the joint venture partners themselves from using some specific technology. However, the Commission seems to accept such a restriction during the start-up period.[158]

9.7 Exemptions

The practice of the Commission shows many examples where a joint venture is assumed to be contrary to Article 101(1) but qualifies to be exempted under Article

---

152. Commission Decision 1999/781/EC, *British Interactive Broadcasting/Open* (OJ 1999 L 312/1), para. 125.
153. Commission Decision 96/546/EC, *ATLAS* (OJ 1996 L L239/23), para. 42.
154. Commission Decision 94/986/EC, *Philips-Osram* (OJ 1994 L 378/37), para. 20. See also Commission Decision 1999/573/EC, *Cégétel + 4* (OJ 1999 L 218/14), paras 52–55.
155. Commission Decision 94/895/EC, *International Private Satellite Partners* (OJ 1994 L 354/75), para. 61.
156. Commission Decision 96/547/EC, *PHOENIX* (OJ 1996 L 239/57), para. 53. However, the Commission accepted such an exclusive distribution right in Commission Decision 97/39/EC, *Iridium* (OJ 1997 L 16/87), para. 49.
157. Commission Decision 90/410/EEC, *Elopak/Metal Box – Odin* (OJ 1990 L 209/15), para. 30. See also Commission Notice concerning the assessment of cooperative joint ventures pursuant to Art. 85 of the EEC Treaty (OJ 1993 C 43/2), paras 72–73.
158. Commission Decision 87/100/EEC, *Mitchell Cotts/Sofiltra* (OJ 1987 L 41/31), para. 23.

101(3). However, in many cases, the Commission attaches terms and conditions to an exemption. An exemption can also be granted on the basis of a block exemption regulation, and here, reference is made to the review of the block exemption regulations on specialisation agreements and R&D agreements, given above in sections 4.1 and 5, respectively.

If one looks at the Commission's practice, it is characterised by the fact that the Commission accepts that joint ventures can contribute to the improvement of production and distribution in many different ways. This is the case with joint ventures, which it is assumed will bring forth a new or significantly improved product.[159] Therefore, the Commission is usually very positive about R&D joint ventures whose main purpose is the development of new products.[160] This applies even if the Commission finds that several joint venture partners could have developed a corresponding product on their own, provided that it is either considered less likely that the joint venture partners would have taken on the risks and costs associated therewith[161] or if it is assumed that the joint venture partners would be able to develop the product more effectively, economically and quickly than they would have been able to on their own.[162] In cases of R&D joint ventures, the Commission has also relied on the fact that the product which it is sought to develop has great economic significance[163] or can otherwise be considered as contributing to progress.[164]

Some of the same advantages can be associated with a production joint venture. These can lead to the introduction of new production methods,[165] and they can contribute to introducing new or increased production capacity.[166] There can also be cost savings associated with such joint ventures, but the Commission is normally reluctant to accept that such an advantage can outweigh the disadvantages associated with joint ventures.[167]

---

159. Commission Decision 93/48/EEC, *Fiat/Hitachi* (OJ 1993 L 20/10), para. 25, Commission Decision 94/322/EC, *Exxon/Shell* (OJ 1994 L 144/20), para. 67, Commission Decision 94/770/EC, *Pasteur Mérieux-Merck* (OJ 1994 L 309/1), para. 82, Commission Decision 96/6546/EC, *ATLAS* (OJ 1996 L 239/23), paras 48-50, and Commission Decision 97/781/EC, *Uniworld* (OJ 1997 L 318/24), paras 68-75.
160. The Commission's Twenty-fourth Report on Competition Policy 1983, para. 155.
161. Commission Decision 77/781/EEC, *GEC-Weir/Sodium Circulators* (OJ 1977 L 327/26), p. 33, and Commission Decision 2000/182/EC, *GEAE/P&W* (OJ 2000 L 58/16), para. 80. However, it is noted that, in more recent practice, the fact that there are major risks and investments associated with an activity will normally lead to the conclusion that the joint venture partners are not potential competitors, so the joint venture in question may not in fact infringe on Art. 101(1).
162. Commission Decision 91/562/EEC, *Eirpage* (OJ 1991 L 306/22), para. 14; Commission Decision 77/781/EEC, *GEC-Weir/Sodium Circulators* (OJ 1977 L 327/26), p. 33; and Commission Decision 2000/182/EC, *GEAE/P&W* (OJ 2000 L 58/16), para. 80.
163. Commission Decision 86/405/EEC, *Optical fibres* (OJ 1986 L 236/30), para. 59.
164. Commission Decision 94/770/EC, *Pasteur Mérieux-Merck* (OJ 1994 L 309/1), paras 83-84.
165. Commission Decision 93/49/EEC, *Ford/Volkswagen* (OJ 1993 L 20/14), para. 25.
166. Commission Decision 94/322/EC, *Exxon/Shell* (OJ 1994 L 144/20), para. 67, and Commission Decision 94/986/EC, *Philips-Osram* (OJ 1994 L 378/37), para. 25.
167. Thus, in Commission Guidelines on horizontal cooperation agreements, para. 253, the Commission rejects the idea that cost savings that are due to a reduction in production or to market sharing, can be allowed any influence.

In contrast, the Commission looks much more critically at joint ventures that are primarily concerned with sales. Even though, in certain circumstances, a sales joint venture can support market penetration, the Commission will normally judge them negatively unless the sales cooperation is part of a wider cooperation in which there are other elements which are persuasive that there are advantages.[168] A purchasing joint venture can also give a number of economic benefits, such as economies of scale in connection with transaction costs, transport, and warehousing, and these advantages can outweigh the reservations to which these kinds of joint ventures can give rise because they can give greater purchasing power to the joint venture in question.[169]

More generally, in its notices, the Commission states that most efficiency gains arise from a combination and integration of different forms of knowledge and resources.[170] Therefore, it is relevant to evaluate the know-how and resources which the individual joint venture partners otherwise contribute, and the extent to which the joint venture involves their integration.

The Commission has the possibility of attaching both structural and behavioural conditions when assessing whether a joint venture agreement can be exempted.[171] In contrast to the case with the Merger Control Regulation, the Commission has not issued a notice giving a more detailed explanation of its practice.[172]

10   COOPERATIVES

A cooperative company is characterised by the fact that its business is based on trade with its members. For example, a cooperative company buys the members' production (e.g., flowers, cereals, pigs, etc.) and sells these after having carried out a measure of processing. There can also be a purchasing cooperative, where the cooperative company buys goods and sells them to the members. In many of the EU Member States, cooperatives are a special form of company, characterised by the fact that the company's profits are distributed to the members in proportion to their share of the turnover.[173] However, it is clear that for the purposes of evaluation under competition law, the form of incorporation is largely irrelevant, and purchasing cooperation will, in principle, be evaluated in the same way, whether it takes the form of a limited company or a cooperative company.

---

168. Commission Notice concerning the assessment of cooperative joint ventures pursuant to Art. 85 of the EEC Treaty (OJ 1993 C 43/2), para. 60.
169. Commission Guidelines on horizontal cooperation agreements, para. 305.
170. Commission Communication from the Commission – Guidelines on the application of Art. 81(3) of the Treaty [now Art. 101(3) TFEU] (OJ 2004 101/97), para. 60.
171. Under Art. 9 of Regulation (EC) No 1/2003, the Commission has the possibility of imposing conditions when it assesses whether an agreement can be exempted.
172. Commission Notice on remedies acceptable under Regulation (EC) No 139/2004 on the control of concentrations between undertakings (the EC Merger Regulation) (OJ 2004 L 24/1) and Regulation (EC) Regulation (EC) No 802/2004 implementing Regulation (EC) No 139/2004 (OJ 2004 L 133/1), discussed in more detail in Ch. 8, s. 5. The Notice is clearly directed at solutions for dealing with dominant position.
173. In order to make it easier for cooperative companies to merge and to cooperate across borders in the EU, the Council adopted Regulation (EC) No 1435/2003 on the Statute for a European Cooperative Society (SCE) (OJ 2003 L 207/1).

Chapter 4

Many cooperatives are active in the area of agriculture. In principle, agriculture is excluded from the competition rules of the Treaty, *see* Article 42 TFEU, unless the Council decides otherwise. In Regulation No 26 of 1962, the Council decided that, to a large extent, the competition rules should apply in the area of agriculture, but in Article 2(1) of the Regulation, a reservation is made that 'Article 85 (1) of the Treaty [now Article 101] shall not apply to such of the agreements, decisions and practices referred to in the preceding Article as form an integral part of a national market organisation or are necessary for attainment of the objectives set out in Article 39 of the Treaty. In particular, it shall not apply to agreements, decisions and practices of farmers, farmers' associations, or associations of such associations belonging to a single Member State which concern the production or sale of agricultural products or the use of joint facilities for the storage, treatment or processing of agricultural products, and under which there is no obligation to charge identical prices unless the Commission finds that competition is thereby excluded'.[174] This provision, which has been carried forward unchanged in Regulation (EC) No 1184/2006, means that it is also possible to adopt restrictions on competition in cooperative companies established between farmers.[175]

A cooperative company can infringe the competition rules in various ways. First, the company's undertaking may have a dominant position on the market, so that its conduct may infringe on Article 102. But, because the company's activities are closely linked to the activities of its members, the company can also be assessed under Article 101. For example, in a purchasing cooperation, it can have a restrictive effect on the market for purchases if the company acquires considerable market strength on this market. In addition, purchasing activities can have a spillover effect on the members' competition on the market where they sell their products. For example, if there is purchasing cooperation for shops, the fact that they buy most of their goods from the same place will make it less likely that the shops will compete with each other.[176]

In principle, the evaluation of the activities of cooperative companies does not differ from the evaluation of other horizontal cooperation agreements for the same activities. However, cooperative companies do have a special position in that their existence is based on modest capital contributions from the members, but in return, the members are subject to a number of different obligations. These obligations will normally be laid down in the articles of association of the company, and they can include an obligation to supply, an obligation to purchase, a prohibition on membership of other cooperatives, a general prohibition on competition, special terms for leaving the cooperative, etc. As most of these conditions can have the effect of

---

174. EEC Council: Regulation No 26 applying certain rules of competition to production of and trade in agricultural products (OJ 30, 20.4.1962), p. 993, English special edition: Series I Chapter 1959-1962 p. 129.
175. For further details *see* Case C-399/93, *H.G. Oude Luttikhuis*, paras 27-31. For a more detailed review of the application of the competition rules to agriculture, *see* David Bailey & Laura Elizabeth John (eds): Bellamy & Child: *European Union Law of Competition*, 8th ed. 2018 pp. 1101-1106.
176. On purchasing agreements, *see* Commission Guidelines on horizontal cooperation agreements, paras 273-316. In para. 291 it is stated that if the parties to an agreement have a market share of less than 15%, it is unlikely that that there will be a significant restriction on competition.

restricting competition, it is relevant to consider whether they infringe on Article 101.[177]

In a number of cases, the CJ and GC have had an opportunity to assess various provisions and obligations in the articles of association of cooperative companies. In this, they have taken as their starting point that there is nothing in principle that makes the organisation of an undertaking in the form of a cooperative a restriction on competition, but that, nevertheless, such a cooperative can be capable of influencing the business conduct of the members of the cooperative and thereby restrict competition.[178] Some of these restrictions may be necessary to enable the cooperative to operate, and these can be compatible with Article 101, provided that the restrictions do not go further than is necessary to ensure the effective running of the cooperative.

On this basis, in Case T-61/89, *Dansk Pelsdyravlerforening*, the GC found that it was natural that members should be subject to an obligation to supply, so they had a duty to sell their production through the cooperative company. In principle, the obligation to supply can be justified by the fact that a cooperative company has only a small capital base, so it would be difficult for it to finance its activities unless there was certainty that the members would supply their products to the company. In the case in question, the members were subject to a non-competition clause, which in the opinion of the GC went further than could be considered reasonable because of its general and unlimited character.[179]

In Case C-250/92, *Gøttrup-Klim*, the CJ had to consider the articles of association of Dansk Landbrugs Grovvareselskab (DLG). The members were divided into different categories, and for B and D members it was provided that they could not be members of or otherwise participate in undertakings which competed with DLG in the distribution of fertiliser and plant protection. If the members did not comply with this obligation, they could be excluded from DLG. The CJ found that it could undermine the cooperatives' ability to achieve its aims if some members also participated in other cooperative purchasing associations. Such double membership could make it difficult to carry on the cooperative undertaking satisfactorily and diminish its bargaining power with producers. At the same time, the non-competition clause was a restriction on competition, so it was necessary to ensure that it did not go further than was necessary for ensuring the satisfactory running of the cooperative. The CJ did not find that this was so in the case in question, as the non-competition clause was first of all limited so as to cover fertilisers and plant protection preparations, which are the only bulk goods where there is a direct relationship between quantity and

---

177. The conditions for membership can also be contrary to Art. 102, e.g., where a cooperative company with a dominant position has unreasonable conditions for admitting new members or has an unreasonably long period of notice for leaving.
178. Case T-61/89, *Dansk Pelsdyravlerforening*, para. 51, and Case C-399/93, *H.G. Oude Luttikhuis*, para. 12.
179. Case T-61/89, *Dansk Pelsdyravlerforening*, in particular, paras 72–77.

price, and where it was thus clear that it would damage DLG if members bought part of their needs elsewhere. Next, it was possible for members to buy fertiliser and plant protection preparations other than through DLG, as long as it was not through some organised cooperative. In connection with this, the CJ noted that non-members could also buy from DLG at the same prices as members. Finally, the CJ did not find that the conditions for exclusion were unreasonably strict.[180]

In Case C-399/93, *H.G. Oude Luttikhuis*, the CJ had to assess a number of the terms of the articles of association of some Dutch dairy cooperative companies. The members were obliged to supply all their milk to the cooperative company (which was, in turn, obliged to buy all their milk). In addition, in the event of withdrawal or exclusion from the cooperative, a fee had to be paid amounting to 2% of the amount which the member had received for the milk he had supplied over the preceding five years. The CJ commented that the combination of a supply obligation and a very high fee upon withdrawal could cause the market to become very rigid, and it could give the cooperative market power, which made it very difficult for others to enter the market. The CJ refrained from passing judgment on the concrete case, as it was a referral for a preliminary ruling from a national court.[181]

11 ACQUISITION OF MINORITY SHAREHOLDINGS

If undertaking A acquires shares in undertaking B, this can result in A controlling B. This will be the case if a controlling shareholding is acquired, for example, where more than half of the voting rights are acquired. This is also possible if A's shareholding allows A to exercise joint control with another shareholder with whom A has an agreement. If control or joint control is acquired in this way, notification of it must be given in accordance with the Merger Control Regulation, provided that the other conditions of the Regulation are fulfilled; *see* Chapter 8.

If a minority shareholding is acquired, there will normally not be a merger, but instead, it can be considered whether the acquisition should be assessed in accordance with Article 101.[182] The acquisition of a minority shareholding in different ways restricts competition, most likely where it is a competitor that makes the acquisition.[183]

---

180. Case C-250/92, *Gøttrup-Klim*, in particular paras 32–42.
181. Case C-399/93, *H.G. Oude Luttikhuis*, in particular paras 12–20.
182. Depending on the circumstances, the acquisition of a minority shareholding can also constitute an infringement of Art. 102, *see* Commission Decision 93/252/EEC, *Warner-Lambert/Gilette* (OJ 1993 L 116/21).
183. *See, inter alia,* Einer Elhauge: *Horizontal Shareholding*, Harvard Law Review, 2016 pp. 1267–1317. Another problem that is linked to the one discussed in the text here is the fact that many institutional investors may hold smaller holdings in many companies, and this raises the question whether such holdings may have the effect of reducing competition between the latter. *See* the report prepared by the Commission by *Rosita and others*: Common Shareholding in Europe, 2020. Similar problems as those discussed here, occur when the same persons are sitting on the boards of competing companies. This phenomenon is regulated in the US, but not

First of all, the fact that a company now owns part of a competitor may make it less likely that it will compete with the latter company since any profit made by it will benefit its investment. Next, the minority holding may grant the shareholder some influence (although not control), and this may be used to influence the competitive behaviour of the investee company. Finally, the minority shareholding may give the shareholder access to information about the competitor which would otherwise not be made available to it. If two (or more) competitors hold minority shareholdings in each other (cross-holdings), the risk described goes both ways.

Even so, the acquisition of a minority shareholding will not in itself be an infringement of Article 101. Such an infringement will only occur if the acquisition leads to establishing an agreement or concerted practice whereby two undertakings align their business policies. In the *Philip Morris* case, the CJ confirmed that the acquisition of a minority shareholding can infringe Article 101.[184]

> Philip Morris had originally intended to enter into a joint venture with the Rembrandt Group to run Rothman Holdings, which had hitherto been 100% owned by Rembrandt. Philip Morris and Rothmans were competitors in the tobacco industry. The plan was that Philip Morris should own 50% of the holding company which controlled Rothmans. Philip Morris and Rembrandt should have the right to appoint equal numbers of Rothmans's management. However, as the Commission objected to this joint venture under both Articles 101 and 102, the agreement was changed so that Philip Morris should instead only acquire a minority shareholding, giving control of less than 25% of the voting rights in Rothmans, and an undertaking was given that Philip Morris would not be entitled to appoint members to Rothmans's board or otherwise have access to strategic information about Rothmans's business. The Commission thereafter decided not to object to the agreement, but this decision was referred to the CJ by some competing undertakings in the tobacco industry.
>
> The CJ confirmed the decision of the Commission, but on the basis of some ambiguous reasons.
>
> In paragraph 31 of the judgment, it is stated that since the acquisition of shares in Rothmans International was the subject matter of agreements between companies which remained independent after the entry into force of the agreements, the issue had to be examined under Article 101. In paragraph 37, it is stated that although the acquisition by one company of an equity interest in a competitor does not in itself constitute conduct-restricting competition, it may nevertheless serve as an instrument for influencing the commercial conduct of the companies in question so as to restrict or distort competition. Thereafter, paragraph 38 continues:

---

in the EU, *see* Florence Thépot, Florian Hugon & Mathieu Luinaud: *Interlocking Directorates and Anticompetitive risk: An Enforcement Gap in Europe*, Concurrence No 1. 2016.

184. Joined Cases 142 and 156/84, *British-American Tobacco & R.J. Reynolds v. Commission*.

That will be true in particular where, by the acquisition of a shareholding or through subsidiary clauses in the agreement, the investing company obtains legal or de facto control of the commercial conduct of the other company or where the agreement provides for commercial cooperation between the companies or creates a structure likely to be used for such cooperation.

This decision gave rise to a debate about whether Article 101 could be used for the control of mergers, especially where one undertaking acquired control over another. However, the actual case did not involve a merger. Even though paragraphs 37-38 suggest that Article 101 also applies where one undertaking acquires control of another, even if this is normally understood to mean that the undertakings are no longer independent, the CJ in paragraph 31 emphasises that the application of Article 101 requires that the undertakings remain independent of each other. It, therefore, seems that an acquisition of effective control will not be covered by Article 101. However, there is less doubt about whether acquisitions of minority shareholdings, which give the shareholder a certain measure of control, though without giving full control, can be an indication that an agreement exists that restricts competition. It will, however, not be enough to establish that there has been such an acquisition, as there must be additional elements indicating an agreement or concerted practice for Article 101 to have been infringed. Such indication could, for example, take the form of underlying agreements or overlapping personnel on the boards of directors.[185] There is, therefore, still considerable uncertainty in assessing when Article 101 is applicable to the acquisition of minority shareholdings. The Commission has itself come to the conclusion that Article 101 is not suitable for regulating minority shareholdings, and in 2014, it proposed the introduction of a special system for ensuring the transparency of minority shareholdings.[186]

Bibliography

David Bailey & Laura Elizabeth John (eds): Bellamy & Child: *European Union Law of Competition*, 8th ed. 2018.
Jonathan Faull & Ali Nikpay (eds): *The EU Law of Competition*, 3rd ed. 2014.
Alison Jones, Brenda Sufrin & Niamh Dunne: *Jones and Sufrin's EU Competition Law*, 7th ed. 2019.
Richard Whish & David Bailey: *Competition Law*, 10th ed. 2021.

---

185. Commission Decision 94/771/EC, *Olivetti-Digital* (OJ 1994 L 309/24), where the Commission assessed Digital's acquisition of a minority shareholding of 8% in Olivetti which was established in connection with technology cooperation, as well as a shareholders' agreement that secured Digital's right to representation on Olivetti's board. For a more detailed review of the assessment of the acquisition of minority shareholdings from a competition law point of view, see Mark Friend: *Regulating Shareholdings and Unintended Consequences*, European Competition Law Review, 2012 pp. 303-306, Riccardo Fadiga: *Horizontal Shareholding with European Competition Law Framework*, European Competition Law Review, 2019 pp. 157-165 and Einer Elhauge: *How Horizontal Shareholding Harms Our Economy – and Why Antitrust Law Can Fix It*, Harvard Business Law Review, 2020 pp. 207-285.
186. COM(2014) 449 final.

CHAPTER 5
Technology Transfer Agreements: Commission Regulation (EU) No 316/2014[*]

1   THE TREATY AND INTELLECTUAL PROPERTY RIGHTS

The following is a review of the competition law assessment of technology transfer agreements.[1] These are agreements under which a licensee obtains a right to exploit the technology of another (the licensor). The starting point for this review is the current Regulation on block exemptions in this area, Commission Regulation (EU) No 316/2014, on the application of Article 101(3) of the Treaty on the Functioning of the European Union (TFEU) to categories of technology transfer agreements (referred to in the following as Regulation (EU) No 316/2014).[2] Regulation (EU) No 316/2014 remains in force until 30 April 2026; *see* its Article 9. Regulation (EU) No 316/2014 replaced Regulation (EC) No 772/2004 when that expired on 30 April 2014.[3]

The purpose of this chapter is to cast some light on the conditions under which such licences may be compatible with the EU competition rules.

The subjects of the agreements referred to, i.e., patents, copyright, etc., are traditionally dealt with under the heading of *intellectual property law*, which, in respect

---

[*] This chapter builds on the work of deceased Professor Bent Iversen in previous editions.
1. A 'technology transfer agreement' is defined in Art. 1(1)(c) of Regulation (EU) No 316/2014; *see* further in s. 5.1.
2. Also referred to as the Technology Transfer Block Exemption – TTBE.
3. For a comment on the changes as from Regulation (EC) No 772/2004, *see* Suzanne Rab: *New EU Technology Transfer Block Exemption: A Note of Caution*, Journal of European Competition Law & Practice, pp. 439 ff., 2014 DOI: 10.1093/jeclap/lpu056. Regarding the development of the EU policy on technology transfer, *see* Stefano Barazza: *The Technology Transfer Block Exemption Regulation and Related Guidelines: Competition Law and IP Licensing in the EU*, Journal of Intellectual Property Law and Practice, pp. 189 ff., 2014 DOI: 10.1093/jiplp/jpt235.

of most of these rights, is based on laws which give intellectual or industrial property rights the character of legally protected *exclusive rights*.[4]

At the regional level (meaning the area of the European Union), the provisions in Articles 34 and 36 of TFEU are particularly relevant. These provisions state as follows:

Article 34

'Quantitative restrictions on imports and all measures having equivalent effect shall be prohibited between Member States.'

Article 36

'The provisions of Articles 34 and 35 shall not preclude prohibitions or restrictions on imports, exports or goods in transit justified on grounds of public morality, public policy or public security; the protection of health and life of humans, animals or plants; the protection of national treasures possessing artistic, historic or archaeological value; or the protection of industrial and commercial property. Such prohibitions or restrictions shall not, however, constitute a means of arbitrary discrimination or a disguised restriction on trade between Member States.'

These two provisions should be understood in light of the fact that the legal regulation of intellectual property is still primarily a matter of *national* law and is not based on Community legislation.[5]

Formally, national authorities still determine the content and exercise of intellectual property rights; *see* Article 345 TFEU, according to which systems of property ownership are not affected by the Treaties. However, there has been considerable EU harmonisation in this area. Thus, for example, the legal effects of intellectual property rights are, to a certain extent, laid down in binding directives.

Moreover, national rules on intellectual property must be framed in such a way that they may only prevent the free movement of goods if the prevention is justified by the protection of the rights that constitute the specific subject matter of the intellectual property right (the existence of the right rather than its exercise); *see* further below on this distinction.

The restriction on the content of national rules on intellectual property rights first arose in connection with Community competition law in Joined Cases 56 and 58/64,

---

4. The comments that follow will primarily concern patent licence agreements. Licence agreements concerning know-how and software copyright will be touched on when relevant in respect of Regulation (EU) No 316/2014, particularly when the rules differ because of the differences in the kinds of rights referred to.
5. However, there are certain important exceptions to this, e.g., *see* the implementation of the First Council Directive 89/104/EEC of 21 Dec. 1988 to approximate the laws of the Member States relating to trade marks (the Trade Marks Directive, now directive 2015/2436) (OJ 1989 L 40/7). However, this Directive was not aimed at implementing a complete harmonisation of the Member States' laws on trade marks, but was restricted to dealing with national provisions that were believed to have the most direct effect on the functioning of the internal market, including the exhaustion of rights referred to in Art. 7(1) of the Directive; *see* below on the content of this principle in relation to patent rights. Furthermore, there are a number of directives and a few regulations that harmonize various aspects of the copyright field.

Consten and Grundig v. Commission, and has since reappeared in different forms in a number of judgments of the Court of Justice of the European Union (CJ).[6]

The essence of these decisions relating to, for example, *patent law* is that the 'specific subject matter' of patent rights is to *secure for the patent owner the sole right to exploit an invention* by being the first to put a product on the market and thereby, depending on the circumstances, make it possible for the inventor to obtain a financial *reward for the inventor's creativity* and to *compensate for the costs* of developing the product to the stage where it can be traded. There are also other aspects of the specific subject matter, including the *right to issue licences* to third parties and the right to *oppose the sale of copies* of the product.

> *See* for example Case 15/74, *Centrafarm BV and Adriaan de Peijper v. Sterling Drug*, in particular paragraph 9: 'In relation to patents, the specific subject matter of the industrial property is the guarantee that the patentee, to reward the creative effort of the inventor, has the exclusive right to use an invention with a view to manufacturing industrial products and putting them into circulation for the first time, either directly or by the grant of licences to third parties, as well as the right to oppose infringements.'
>
> *See also* Case 187/80, *Merck v. Stephar*.

When there is no exploitation of an intellectual property right, particularly where there is an agreement or a 'concerted practice' between the owner of a right and an undertaking about the latter's taking a licence to exploit the right, the agreement will fall outside the scope of Article 101(1). The abuse provision in Article 102, which relates to an undertaking's 'abuse of a dominant position' and does not typically refer to an agreement between two or more undertakings, will not be widely applicable. However, *see* section 2.2 on, among other things, the *Volvo, Renault* and *Magill* cases.

Outside the area of agreements, the CJ's decisions have primarily considered the question in relation to national laws and other measures on whether national prohibitions of hindrances to trade and/or other measures are compatible with Articles 34 and 36 TFEU.

See, for example, Case 15/74, *Centrafarm and Adriaan de Peijper v. Sterling Drug*, and paragraph 22 in Case 19/84, *Pharmon BV v. Hoechst AG* (on the principle of exhaustion of rights, discussed below):

> It must be recalled that the Court has consistently held that Articles 30 and 36 of the EEC Treaty [now Articles 34 and 36] preclude the application of national provisions which enable a patent owner to prevent the importation and marketing of a product which has been lawfully marketed in another Member State by the patent proprietor himself, with his consent, or by a person economically or legally dependent on him.

---

6. The *Grundig* case, which is referred to above in s. 2 of Ch. 3, and which contained the Commission's and the CJ's criticisms of measures for achieving complete territorial protection, is illustrative in the present context, primarily because it found that a French sole distributors' use of Grundig's trade mark was contrary to Art. 101(1) TFEU, to the extent it under the applicable French law could hinder parallel imports to France.

See also Case 24/67, *Parke, Davis & Co. v. Centrafarm*, where the referring Dutch appeal court wanted the CJ's opinion on whether a patent owner would be acting contrary to, among other things, Article 101(1) TFEU by exercising the rights granted to a patent owner under Dutch law with regard to medicines, in order to prevent the import to the Netherlands of similar products which were manufactured in a country where, at that time, medicines could not be patented. The Dutch rules, which the CJ did not find to be contrary to the Treaty, gave the owner of a patent registered in the Netherlands the possibility of imposing an injunction against patent-protected products from another Member State where patent protection was not granted to these products or to the method for their production. *See* likewise the CJ's decision in Case C-23/99, *Commission v. France*, where it stated: 'by implementing, pursuant to the Code de la Propriété Intellectuelle, procedures for the detention by the customs authorities of goods lawfully manufactured in a Member State of the European Community which are intended, following their transit through French territory, to be placed on the market in another Member State where they may be lawfully marketed, the French Republic has failed to fulfil its obligations under Article 30 of the Treaty [now Article 36 TFEU]'. The French Republic tried to justify the detention of the products by reference to French law on design rights. But in the view of the Commission, which was accepted by the CJ, goods in transit are not covered by the specific subject matter of a design right, and the detention of the goods was not found to be justified by regard for the protection of intellectual property rights.

While the acknowledgement of the existence of intellectual property rights is an expression that competition law must accept these rights for what they are, the problem changes when it comes to the exercise of these rights.[7] The distinction between the existence of a right (the right's specific subject matter) and its exercise must not be given undue importance, as it would probably not stand up to jurisprudential analysis. Care should be taken in binding conclusions from whether something is characterised as being the content of a right or its exercise.

Regional competition law (EU competition law) is based on the goal of integration. Undertakings must not, by making agreements, be able to recreate barriers whose removal is the main aim of the single market; *see also* section 2.

There are two aspects of the interests of society. On the one hand, there is consideration for the owners of rights and their exploitation of their own productions, thereby the spread of useful knowledge and technology. On the other hand, there is consideration for the goal of market integration. These interests can conflict.

---

7. The distinction is found elsewhere, e.g., in German law (the Immanenz doctrine), cf. on this *Morten Rosenmeier, Clement Salung Petersen & by Jens Schovsbo*, and in US law (the Inherency doctrine). *See also* Valentine Korah: *Technology Transfer Agreements and the EC Competition Rules*, pp. 36–40, 1996. The distinction has been claimed as being a method for helping objectify the result of the CJ's balancing of different interests in concrete cases, between on the one hand consideration for maintaining respect for the arrangements of intellectual property law, and on the other hand the considerable weight which must be attached to the attempts to break down artificial barriers which are injurious to the establishment of the internal market. *See also* the comments of Claus Gulmann in his capacity as Advocate General in Joined Cases C-241/91 P and C-242/91 P, *Radio Telefis Eireann v. Commission* (generally referred to as the *Magill* case), which is discussed below in s. 2.2. On the development from the earlier practice up to the more refined presentation of the distinction in more recent cases on the existence of rights and their exercise, *see* Steven D. Anderman: *EC Competition Law and Intellectual Property Rights*, pp. 8–16, 2011.

However, intellectual property law has, to a certain extent, itself sought to make good some of its inherent restrictions to integration.

For example, a source of conflict, which would otherwise arise from the restrictions to integration that are inherent in intellectual property law, is that an owner of intellectual rights might refuse to grant a licence to another, is countered on a European basis by provisions in the intellectual property legislation itself. A patent owner's refusal to grant a licence is kept outside the realm of competition law, except that in extraordinary circumstances, it can be relevant to the application of the abuse of dominant position provisions in Article 102 TFEU (see section 2.2).

Another example of where the problem of the restrictions to integration, which are inherent in intellectual property law, has been suppressed before it could cause harm is the intellectual property doctrine of exhaustion of rights. Once products have been put on the market (by the patent owner or a licensee or by others who may lawfully market the products), neither the patent owner nor the licensee may restrict the further circulation of the products in the market.[8]

The EU's goal of market integration requires that the right of the owner of rights (the patent owner) and others to control the circulation of products in the market ceases once the product has been marketed in one of the Member States with their consent. For example, a purchaser may not be restricted from reselling products to a distributor who intends to export the products to another area within the internal market. In other words, the doctrine of exhaustion of rights supports the Commission's and the CJ's well-known principle of allowing parallel imports.

National exhaustion of rights would not satisfy this goal, and the CJ has previously interpreted TFEU Articles 34 and 36 so that putting a product on the market in one Member State results in regional (EU-wide) exhaustion of rights.[9]

Exhaustion of rights requires that the product is put on the market 'by the patent owner or with his consent'. The principle of exhaustion, therefore, does not apply when a product is put on the market by virtue of a compulsory licence or upon the import of counterfeit products or other copies (pirate imports).[10]

> See Case 19/84, *Pharmon BV v. Hoechst AG*, where an English company, which had been granted a compulsory licence to exploit the invention of a medicine in the UK, for which Hoechst had a patent in force in Germany and parallel patents in the Netherlands and the UK. In breach of an export prohibition, the English company sold a large batch of the medicine to the

---

8. *See also* the comments above on Art. 7(1) of the Trade Marks Directive.
9. *See* Case 15/74, *Centrafarm BV and Adriaan de Peijper v. Sterling Drug*, in which Sterling Drugs attempt to prevent the Dutch company Centrafarm importing the medicine NEGRAM to the Netherlands from Germany and England was found to be contrary to Arts 34 and 36. The medicine had been bought in Germany and England, where it had been marketed by Sterling Drugs local marketing companies. Concerning the exhaustion of rights in respect of trade marks, *see* Case C-355/96, *Silhouette*, according to which Art. 7(1) of the Trade Marks Directive must be interpreted as expressing regional (EU) exhaustion of rights, and not global exhaustion.
10. By contrast, the original product may compete against copied products that are manufactured in a Member State where they have not been granted patent protection, *see* Case 15/74, *Centrafarm BV and Adriaan de Peijper v. Sterling Drug*, para. 11.

Dutch medicine firm Pharmon, which intended to resell the goods in the Netherlands. The question which the referring Dutch Supreme Court laid before the CJ for a preliminary ruling was whether it would be contrary to the provisions of the Treaty (now Articles 34 and 36 TFEU) on the free movement of goods, if Hoechst used the authority of the applicable Dutch laws to prevent the marketing of the products in the Netherlands. The clear message from the CJ was that it must be regarded as necessary that a patent owner, who in the case of a compulsory licence would not normally have given consent, could still have the possibility of preventing the import and marketing of the products. Only in this way was it possible to secure for the patent owner the sole right to be the first to put a patented product on the market and thus to 'obtain the reward for his creative effort.'.

See also Case 35/87, *Thetford Corporation v. Fiamma SpA*, where the CJ found in favour of Thetford, which had a UK patent for the production of portable toilets, and wished to prevent Fiamma, which did not have any licence from Thetford, from selling toilets which Fiamma imported from Italy. The CJ found that a prohibition could be imposed without the English law on this, thereby coming into conflict with the Treaty rules on free movement of goods, and regardless of the fact that the British patent, under a special British recognition of the patent law principle of 'relative novelty', had been published more than fifty years before the current patent application.

The especially emphasised condition that the product should have been marketed by the patent owner or with the patent owner's consent will be fulfilled as long as either the owners of the rights in the exporting and importing countries are identical or they have such a close economic connection with each other that the product is put on the market by an undertaking in the same corporate group or by a licensee; *see* Case 15/74, *Centrafarm BV and Adriaan de Peijper v. Sterling Drug*.

There was a special situation in Case 187/80, *Merck v. Stephar*:

Merck, which was the owner of two Dutch patents for medicines, put a medicine on the market in Italy where it could not be patented, because of the then applicable prohibition under Italian law on the granting of patents for medicines or methods for producing medicines. The medicine was bought in Italy by Stephar and imported to the Netherlands, where it was put on the market in competition with Merck. The referring Dutch court wanted to know whether Merck would infringe Article 30 of the EC Treaty [now Article 36] if, with the support of the national Dutch rules which prohibited the import, Merck opposed the parallel import of the medicines to the Netherlands in the circumstances described. In its answer, the CJ stated that it is up to the patent owner whether it will market its product or not, and it must be assumed to have full knowledge of the conditions under which it can market the products, including when this is on a market where patent protection does not apply. If it decides to undertake such marketing, it must accept the consequences of its choice and accept that its control over the further circulation of the product is exhausted.

In Joined Cases C-267/95 and C-268/95, *Merck v. Primecrown*, the result was in line with the first Merck case, though the CJ added that, to the extent that under national or Community rules the patent owner had a legal obligation to market its goods in a Member State where its exclusive rights were not protected, it could lawfully oppose the import to and marketing of the products in a Member State where they were protected.[11]

2 LICENCE AGREEMENTS AND EU COMPETITION LAW

2.1 The Relationship to Article 101 TFEU

When individual intellectual property rights grant an 'exclusive right', it is obvious – especially if 'the exclusive right to the commercial exploitation of an intellectual property right' is rewritten as a 'monopoly' – that competition law should be brought into play to protect against abuse of the monopoly. This is particularly indicated at the regional (EU) level since exclusive rights are, by definition, calculated to hinder integration, which is the goal of the internal market.

Among other things, the EU-based competition rules are aimed at regulating agreements and concerted practices which may affect competition between undertakings within the Community when such agreements, etc., can affect trade between the Member States and hinder the integration of the markets (Article 101(1) TFEU).

In connection with the exploitation of an intellectual property right, for example, when entering into a licence agreement, both the licensor and the licensee can have an interest in laying down certain restrictions on the other party's exploitation of the licence.

From a competition law point of view, some of the restrictions will be neutral in relation to society's ideal of promoting the effective use of resources through effective competition.

Competition law will not normally be concerned with purely contractual issues between the parties, for example, the fees for a licensee to exploit the licensor's invention or know-how for a certain period. The same will apply to the territorial extent of a licence – whether the licensee has the right to use the licence in one or more countries or maybe only in a limited part of a single country – at least in so far as the conditions on territorial extent are not combined with other terms which restrict the licence out of consideration for third parties, including other licensees, or it the licensor itself that wishes to operate on the market and therefore has an interest in restricting the extent of the first licensees activities.

However, experience has shown that there will be a need for the competition authorities to intervene against more or less sophisticated terms which are aimed at

---

11. *See* **Valentine Korah:** *Technology Transfer Agreements and the EC Competition Rules*, pp. 42–43, 1996.

taking care of concerns other than the due recognition of the parties' rights to take part in the free competition on a given market, without seeking to impose restrictions on competition, whether unilaterally or by agreement.

One example could be a term whereby the licensor restricts the quantity of products which the licensee may produce under the licence since this may restrict the availability of products which a third party might buy and export to a territory where the licensor has agreed to help another licensee as part of a policy of pricing differentiation in order to maintain a higher price for the products.[12]

Examples of restrictions on competition of the kind described and other kinds are legion, and these will be discussed below. However, the comments so far have already shown that an undertaking will often need to know in advance, and with a reasonable degree of certainty, whether the terms which it wishes to include in a contract can be expected to be accepted by the competition authorities, which in this instance means the Commission, the CJ and the Court of First Instance (now the General Court), and the national competition authorities.[13]

In this context, Regulation (EU) No 316/2014 on the application of Article 101(3) TFEU to categories of technology transfer agreements (block exemptions for licence agreements)[14] will be an invaluable tool for undertakings which want to avoid the effects of Article 101(1) TFEU ('safe harbours').

2.2 The Relationship to Article 102 TFEU

Article 102 is the other key provision on competition rules laid down in the Treaty. Article 102, which is discussed in detail in Chapter 6, concerns the prohibition of the abuse by one or more undertakings of their dominant position in the internal market.

It is emphasised in section 1 above that the competition rules do not usually affect the exclusive right of, for example, a patent owner to decide for itself whether it will exploit its rights by granting a licence or not since this is part of the 'specific subject matter' of the patent, in respect of which the Treaty does not give authority to intervene. In other words, the competition rules do not usually provide for compulsory licensing, which would thereby highlight the fundamentally opposed aims previously referred to of the competition law principle of free access to the market and the exclusive rights provided for in intellectual property law.[15]

---

12. *See* the comments below in s. 6.1.2.
13. The practice which is built up by the national courts plays a special role after the implementation of the amendment to Council Regulation No 17/62. *See* now Council Regulation (EC) No 1/2003 on the implementation of the rules on competition laid down in Arts 81 and 82 of the Treaty (OJ 2003 L 1/1), according to which with effect from 1 May 2004 the Commission's sole authority to grant exemptions from Art. 101(1) TFEU is repealed, so that the whole of Art. 101, including the right to grant exemptions under Art. 101(3), can be applied by the national courts and other national authorities. *See* more on this above in Chs 2 and 3.
14. For more detailed discussion, *see* s. 5.
15. The right of an owner of a right to decide whether it will grant another party a licence to its exclusive right must not be confused with the situation where the owner of rights refuses to supply the products which are subject to the protection of intellectual property rights. If the owner of the exclusive right has first established itself on an open market, the reference to the

These basic considerations in principle on the balance to be struck between competition law and intellectual property law has also been the basis of the CJ's practice; see Case 238/87, *Volvo v. Veng*, and Case 53/87, *Maxicar v. Renault*, which both considered – and accepted – that the owner of a protected design for car bodywork had the right to object to others producing products which were covered by the design right, with a view to selling the products on the domestic market or on export markets (the 'specific subject matter of the exclusive right'). To prevent the application of national law in such circumstances would effectively be the same as putting the existence of such a right in doubt. Consequently, a refusal to give a third party a licence to produce the protected elements of the bodywork – even upon payment of a reasonable royalty – could not be considered an abuse of a dominant position.

However, the CJ held that in the three instances described (paragraph 9 in the *Volvo* case, and paragraph 16 in the *Renault* case), the refusal of the owner of the rights to grant a licence could be covered by the prohibition in Article 102 TFEU. This was, particularly the case where (1) the owner of the rights relatively refuses arbitrarily to supply spare parts to independent repair workshops; (2) sets unreasonably high prices for spare parts; or (3) stops production of spare parts for a model of the motor car of which a large number are still found on the roads.[16]

Thus, the two cases recognise that in very special circumstances, a compulsory licence can be imposed under competition law.

In Joined Cases C-241/91 P and C-242/91 P, *Radio Telefis Eireann v. Commission* (generally referred to as the *Magill* case), which is the result of three cases decided by the Court of First Instance (now the General Court), the CJ upheld the Commission's decision that for three television broadcasting companies to refuse to make previews of television programmes available to Magill, who was the publisher of a TV guide, was an infringement of Article 102.

In other words, the case concerned the extent to which the owner of copyright could be required to give a licence to exploit the work protected by copyright. The CJ upheld the view of the Commission and of the General Court that the three companies had been wrong in assuming that their conduct (laying down a prohibition) towards Magill, who had published programme previews in a weekly magazine, fell within the

---

specific subject matter of the exclusive right will not usually justify different treatment of potential purchasers of the products. Such refusal to supply is dealt with under the ordinary rules of competition, including Art. 102 TFEU.

16. Only the last named situation (termination of production of spare parts) concerns an intervention in the specific subject matter of the exclusive rights, since the car manufacturer must either meet demand by maintaining production itself, or by granting a licence to a third party to do so. However, according to the practice of the CJ on refusal of supply and Art. 102(a) TFEU, the first two situations constitute an abuse of dominant position, regardless of any sole right to produce the spare parts in question.

scope of the specific subject matter and was thus excluded from any assessment under Article 102.

The *Magill* case seems to have gone a step further than the previous practice (*Volvo* and *Renault*), as Magill had not previously had the right to print the whole of the week's preview and, therefore (in contrast to the dealers in the *Volvo* and *Renault* cases), had not based his business on this. In addition, the product which Magill wanted to produce was a 'new product' (a weekly guide to television programmes). Furthermore, in the *Magill* case, the CJ seems to have stated that the refusal to grant a licence could, in itself, constitute a restriction contrary to Article 102.

If the line in the *Magill* case[17] is followed in relation to intellectual property rights other than copyright, and if the case is not merely dependent on the concrete circumstances, then a considerable breach has been opened in the previously accepted view of the relationship between exclusive intellectual property rights and the abuse of dominant position provisions in Article 102.

3 LICENCE AGREEMENT IN GENERAL

In this context, a licence agreement is an agreement for the licensing of technology rights entered into between two undertakings[18] for the purpose of the production of contract products by the licensee or an assignment of technology rights between two undertakings for the purpose of the production of contract products where part of the risk associated with the exploitation of the technology remains with the assignor; *see* Regulation (EU) No 316/2014, Article 1(1)(c), which makes it possible for a licensee to exploit the intellectual property rights which can otherwise only be exploited by the owner of these rights.[19]

With a licence agreement, there is a partial transfer of an exclusive right by the owner of that right. The property right in the intellectual property remains with the owner of those rights, which means, among other things, that the licence agreement lapses at the end of the licence period.

There is no standard formula for licence agreements for the transfer of technology, and there are few places in legislation where such an agreement is explicitly affected.

There are no special forms provided for licence agreements, but in the nature of things, it is not advisable to rely on an oral contract.

The lack of direct legislative treatment might lead one to suppose that a licence agreement is subject to the principle of freedom of contract and that the parties to the agreement are, therefore, free to determine the content of their agreement without being bound by anything other than the terms they agree between them.

---

17. The judgment is discussed in Valentine Korah: *Technology Transfer Agreements and the EC Competition Rules*, pp. 18 and 51–54, 1996.
18. On Technology Transfer Models, *see* Dana Mietzer & Christian Schultz: *New Perspectives in Technology Transfer*, pp. 2–4, 2021.
19. Regulation (EU) No 316/2014 only covers agreements between two undertakings. If there are more than two parties, the situation will be governed by Art. 101(1) and (3) TFEU. *See* s. 5.1.1 below.

In the relationship between the licensor and the licensee, there are several factors under the principles of the law of obligations which affect the agreement and its legal effects.

> Among other things this applies to the terms on the amount of the royalty which the licensor is to receive – whether a royalty is to be paid according to the number of units produced, or as a proportion of the gross or net earnings or otherwise.[20] The same applies to a licence agreement's territorial and temporal extent, with the restriction that follows from the period of validity of the right and the rules on the effects of breach of the agreement by late payment of royalties, including the conditions for revoking the agreement, compensation and repayment of royalties paid, for example, if the licensor cannot grant the licensee the intended right etc. The same applies, i.e., terms are not contrary to Article 101(1) TFEU, if the terms concern confidentiality obligations concerning the transferred technology, obligations not to use the transferred technology after the expiry of the licence, provided that the transferred technology is still valid and in use, obligations to help the licensor enforce the intellectual property rights in respect of which the licence is granted, obligations to use the licensor's trade mark or to state the licensor's name on the product, etc.; *see* paragraph 155 of Commission Notice – Guidelines on the application of Article 81 of the EC Treaty (now Article 101 TFEU) to technology transfer agreements.
>
> It is also a natural consequence of the general principles of the law of obligations that, without a special agreement thereon, the licence rules will not give the licensee a legal claim to reward and competitiveness in connection with the use of the licence. Nor does the licensee have an automatic right to exploit any know-how related to a patent.

In principle, licensors and licensees – at least typically in their own view – are not competitors but two undertakings that have the same aim, namely to obtain as high a turnover as possible from the same product. In other words, they have a shared aim, which is, to a certain extent, in line with the interests of society in disseminating useful technology. Not surprisingly, many technology transfer agreements will not constitute an infringement of Regulation (EU) No 316/2014.[21] In fact, Recital 4 of Regulation (EU) No 316/2014 expresses a general positive view on technology transfer agreements:

> Technology transfer agreements concern the licensing of technology rights. Such agreements will usually improve economic efficiency and be pro-competitive as

---

20. However, it is a requirement that the obligation to pay a royalty should not be equivalent to price fixing, since this would be a hardcore restriction which would fall foul of Art. 4(1)(a) of the Regulation (*see* s. 6.1.1 below), e.g., if competitors pay each other ongoing royalties, even if there is no real licence arrangement. In this case the agreement will not normally serve the purpose of integrating complementary technologies or some other purpose which promotes competition; *see* para. 157 of Commission Notice – Guidelines on the application of Art. 81 of the EC Treaty [Now Art. 101 TFEU] to technology transfer agreements (OJ 2004 C 101/02). These Guidelines are discussed below in s. 4.
21. *See* Richard Whish & David Bailey: *Competition Law*, p. 825, 2015.

they can reduce duplication of research and development, strengthen the incentive for the initial research and development, spur incremental innovation, facilitate diffusion and generate product market competition.

However, consideration for the interests of society in disseminating useful technology will not always carry weight in relation to that aspect of competition law, which is concerned with licence agreements not being unduly restrictive of the commercial opportunities of the parties to the agreement or affected third parties.

The distinction between acceptable and unacceptable contractual terms, which follows from Articles 4 and 5 of Regulation (EU) No 316/2014 and which essentially reflect the view of the Commission and the European courts on restrictions on competition, shows that in a number of cases that freedom of contract must give way not only out to consideration for the parties to a contract but also to consideration for third parties, in other words, competing undertakings. The introductory comments on Articles 34 and 36 TFEU, as well as Article 101, give hints of this, just as the competition rules and their relation to intellectual property law are the main themes in the interpretation of Regulation (EU) No 316/2014.

Partly in accordance with American and German theory, at the European level it has also been suggested that certain restrictions on competition in patent licensing agreements should not be covered by prohibitions corresponding to those in Article 101(1) TFEU, as they are covered by the specific subject matter of the patent. On this basis a distinction has been proposed between the 'patent law effects' of licence restrictions, which are not affected by competition law, and the 'independent contract law' effects of licence restrictions which are subject to Article 101(1) TFEU.

These considerations are linked to the fact that the legislator has recognised intellectual property law rights, and that as a result only the owner of the right has a right to decide about the time and place of their exploitation.

It is also possible to see a connection between this theory and the related doctrine of implied powers (that a greater right implies the existence of a lesser right). When the owner of a right has an absolute right to decide that it does not want to exercise that right by granting a licence, then it ought also to have the 'lesser' right of exploiting the patent on special terms – without that right being affected by competition law. It is argued that there would be a conflict between regulatory systems if competition law included a general prohibition of such an effect of patent law, but this would not be the case with the contract law effects of restrictions, in other words restrictions that are not derived from the patent (exclusive rights).

The categorical view that certain licensing restrictions are per se immune from intervention under competition law does not accord with the practice of the Commission. Already in the predecessor to Regulation (EC) No 240/96 (Regulation (EEC) No 2349/84, on block exemptions for patent agreements) the distinction seems to have been pushed into the background. The distinction between restrictions under patent law and under contract law was only significant as a starting point, which did not prevent a relevance-based examination of whether the licence restrictions did in fact lead to a restriction which was harmful to competition within the terms of Article 101(1) TFEU. Such an examination ought naturally to take account of the fact that a patent is in itself an expression of a legitimate restriction on competition.

A more radical and perhaps more effective solution would be to give up the distinction between the two types of licence restrictions.[22]

4 BLOCK EXEMPTIONS: THE DEVELOPMENT OF THE LEGAL BASIS

As is the case with distribution agreements (*see* above in Chapter 3), over a number of years, a number of regulations have been drawn up on block exemptions for technology transfer agreements.[23] The latest of these is Commission Regulation (EU) No 316/2014 on the application of Article 101(3) of the TFEU to categories of technology transfer agreements. The Commission Guidelines on the application of Article 101 of the TFEU to technology transfer agreements (OJ 2014 C 89/3) (referred to in this chapter as the 'Guidelines') are associated with this Regulation. These Guidelines are indispensable for understanding the Regulation and will be referred to frequently in the following.

With effect from 1 May 2014, Regulation (EU) No 316/2014 replaced Regulation (EC) No 772/2004, which replaced Regulation (EC) No 240/96, which in its turn replaced Regulation (EEC) No 2349/84 and Regulation (EEC) No 556/89.

In relation to the earlier regulations, Regulation (EC) No 240/96 was an expression of considerable liberalisation of the assessment of licence agreements. This was evident, among other things, in the increased number of 'whitelisted' provisions (Article 2) and the decreased number of 'blacklisted' provisions (Article 3). Thereby, it was reflected that a less strict assessment of when an agreement would be considered to restrict competition would also apply in the area of licences. Article 4 of the Regulation introduced an opposition procedure, as an agreement containing one or more 'grey conditions' (meaning conditions which were not automatically covered by Article 2 or 3) was exempted if the agreement was notified to the Commission and the Commission did not oppose such exemption within a period of four months from the date of notification in accordance with the procedure described in the Regulation. Such an agreement was assumed to be valid until the Commission's decision was made known.

---

22. The contractual restrictions which, in German law, are considered as belonging to the specific subject matter of the patent, see §17 in the GWG *(Gesetz gegen Wettbewerbsbeschränkungen)*, are, in reality, arbitrarily chosen and unsuitable for supporting a dynamic competition law assessment aimed at achieving 'workable competition'.
23. The concept of a block exemption is discussed above in Chs 2 and 3.

Regulation (EEC) No 2349/84 applied to patent agreements and agreements, which were a combination of a patent licence and a know-how licence, where in the licence or the patents, this was necessary to achieve the goal of the transfer of technology. A condition for the application of the Regulation was that the licensed products should be protected by parallel patents in all Member States where the licence applied. This condition restricted the scope of the Regulation, as an agreement which granted a patent licence in one Member State could often contain provisions in relation to other Member States where the same technology had not received a patent but was only covered by the know-how agreement.

Regulation (EEC) No 556/89 applied to pure know-how licences as well as mixed know-how and patent licences that were not exempted under Regulation (EEC) No 2349/84.

Regulation (EU) No 316/2014 is structured in the same way as Regulation (EC) No 330/2010 on block exemptions for vertical distribution agreements and concerted practices.[24] This means that black, white and grey conditions are abandoned in favour of exemption criteria, which are based on the market strength of the parties to the agreement; see below in section 5.1.5 on Regulation (EU) No 316/2014, Article 3.

> In December 2001, in connection with drawing up the new block exemption Regulation, the Commission sent out an evaluation report, which was later followed up by a round of consultations. The responses from the trade organisations involved etc. indicated that a substantial part of the business sector believed there was a need for a change to the regulatory basis.
>
> According to Article 13 of Regulation (EC) No 240/96, the Regulation was intended to stay in force until 31 March 2006.
>
> Meanwhile, the consultation of the undertakings affected by the Regulation showed that there was already a significant need to change to a different 'safe harbour' than that hitherto provided under the Regulations distinction between black, white and grey-listed obligations.

There has not yet been any official decision which could help with the interpretation of the new Regulation. However, in describing the Regulation, see sections 5–8 below, a number of Commission decisions and decisions of the European courts are discussed, and it is assumed that they still express the applicable law. Naturally, this applies primarily to those parts of the new Regulation's operative provisions whose content is the same as the provisions which applied under the previous regulations.

The Regulation has the same substantive scope as Article 101(1) TFEU. This means that only those agreements which can affect trade between Member States under the conditions referred to in Article 101(1) (direct or indirect, actual or potential) are covered by the rule. If an agreement only has effects in a single Member State, it will be assessed under national law. Nor are agreements whose full effects take place in a

---

24. Kfo 330/2010 has now been superseded by Ko 2022/720, which is referred to in Ch. 5.

third country (i.e., outside the European Economic Area (EEA)) covered by the Regulation.[25]

As is the case with block exemption regulations in general, see Chapter 3 above on Regulation (EU) No 2022/720 on the application of Article 101(3) TFEU to categories of vertical agreements and concerted practices, Regulation (EU) No 316/2014 is only directed at restrictions on competition which, if they were not exempted by Regulation (EU) No 316/2014, would infringe Article 101(1) TFEU. Therefore, if, according to its content, an agreement or a condition in an agreement is not covered by Article 101(1) (because the agreement or condition in question is not found to be an expression of a restriction on competition), there is no need for an exemption under a block exemption regulation.

On the one hand, if the content of an agreement is contrary to Article 101(1) but is covered by one of the grounds for exemption in Regulation (EU) No 316/2014, the parties can normally confidently perform their agreement, as there will be an assumption in favour of the validity of the agreement under competition law.[26] The grounds for block exemptions constitute the safe harbour for the parties to the agreement. On the other hand, there is no assumption that agreements that restrict competition and that are not covered by one of the grounds for exemption in Regulation (EU) No 316/2014 will automatically fall within the scope of Article 101(1). Whether or not this will be the case will depend on whether an individual evaluation of the agreement finds that there is a basis for an exemption under Article 101(3), as discussed in Chapter 2.

Regulation (EU) No 316/2014 is *lex specialis* in relation to Regulation (EU) No 2022/720; thus, Regulation (EU) No 2022/270 does not apply to vertical agreements that are covered by Regulation (EU) No 316/2014 unless otherwise is specified herein.[27]

Regulation (EU) No 316/2014 has eleven articles and nineteen recitals in the preamble which forms part of the Regulation, and the Guidelines which are associated with the Regulation, contain important aids to the interpretation of the substantive rules. In the review of the individual provisions in Regulation (EU) No 316/2014 below in section 5, there will be extensive references to these aids to interpretation.

5 REGULATION (EU) NO 316/2014: BLOCK EXEMPTIONS FOR TECHNOLOGY TRANSFER AGREEMENTS

5.1 Agreements

According to Regulation (EU) No 316/2014, Article 2(1), cf. Article 1(1)(c), the agreements covered by the exemption for technology transfer agreements are:

---

25. Compare this with the comments on Case C-306/96, *Javico International v. Yves Saint Laurent Parfums*, in s. 2.1.2 of Ch. 3 above.
26. The Guidelines, para. 40.
27. See s. 4.5, item 112 in Guidelines on vertical restraints (2022/C 248/01).

(i) technology rights licensing agreements entered into between two undertakings for the purpose of the production of contract products by the licensee and/or its subcontractor(s); and
(ii) assignments of technology rights between two undertakings for the purpose of the production of contract products where part of the risk associated with the exploitation of the technology remains with the assignor.

The following are comments on the individual elements of this area.

5.1.1 'Entered into Between Two Undertakings'

This condition is satisfied even if the agreement lays down conditions for more than one level of trade; see Recital 6 in the preamble to the Regulation. For example, this situation will exist if the licence agreement requires the licensee to set up a special distribution system or sets out obligations which the licensee shall or may impose on distributors of the product[28] produced under licence. However, it will be a requirement that such obligations must be compatible with the rules of competition law relating to supply and distribution agreements. They may not, for example, contain any of the hardcore restrictions referred to in Article 4 of Regulation (EU) No 2022/270, see Chapter 3.

If the licensee exercises a right to grant sub-licences, then the block exemption regulation applies in its entirety to agreements between the licensee and the sub-licensee.[29]

If the licensor wishes to exercise control over any sub-licensees, this must be provided for in the agreement with the licensee. The licensor cannot be a party to an agreement between the licensee and a sub-licensee since Article 2(1) of the Regulation only allows for exemptions between two undertakings.

> Agreements between parent companies and their subsidiaries will not normally constitute an agreement between two undertakings within the meaning of the Regulation, as long as the two companies are integrated parts of an economic unit; see the statement of the CJ in Case 15/74, *Centrafarm and Adriaan de Peijper v. Sterling Drugs*, according to which a subsidiary company's organisational relationship to a parent company means that it does not have any real freedom to take decisions on its own, so that agreements with the parent company cannot restrict competition when an agreement concerns the internal allocation of tasks between the companies. This is in line with the aim of the EU competition rules, which is to ensure the existence of workable competition in the internal market by the regulation of agreements between independent undertakings.

---

28. Product and contract products are defined in Art. 1(1)(f).
29. A prohibition on the licensor giving a licence to another undertaking is not a restriction on competition and is therefore not contrary to Art. 101(1) TFEU; see the Guidelines, para. 183.

However, if a subsidiary company can operate independently on the market, or if the matter concerns something other and more than an internal allocation of tasks, the parent and subsidiary could be regarded as two independent undertakings.

5.1.2 The Concept of an 'Undertaking'

The concept of an 'undertaking' is not expressly defined in Regulation (EU) No 316/2014, but it may be assumed to correspond to the meaning of 'undertaking' as interpreted in relation to the use of this term in Articles 101 and 102 TFEU; on this *see* Chapter 2. In addition to this, Article 1(2) of Regulation (EU) No 316/2014 adds that the terms 'undertaking', 'licensor' and 'licensee' include their respective connected undertakings; *see* the full provisions in Article 1(2)(a)-(e).

5.1.3 'Transfer' of Technology

According to Recital 7 of Regulation (EU) No 316/2014, the term 'transfer', in the context of 'technology transfer agreements', should be understood as meaning that the technology flows from one undertaking to another in the form of a licence agreement whereby the licensor, upon payment of a licence fee, allows the licensee to use its technology.[30] The agreement must concern the production of the contract products, in other words, the goods or services produced with the licensed technology; *see* Article 1(1)(g) of the Regulation. Pure sales, in other words, a transfer in the form of a sale of the technology, are thus not covered by the block exemption Regulation. The same applies to pooling agreements, the purpose of which is cooperation between two or more undertakings to pool technologies, for example, with the aim of licensing the created package of intellectual property rights to third parties; *see* Recital 7. If the purpose of an agreement is that the licensor transfers technology to the licensee, who is then obliged to produce certain products for the licensor, then such a subcontracting agreement is also covered by the exemption.

A subcontracting agreement can also mean that the licensor provides *equipment* for the production of the goods or services which are covered by the agreement. However, it is the transferred technology and not the transferred equipment which must be the principal purpose of the agreement.

As already stated, if the licensee is entitled to grant sub-licences of the transferred technology, such an agreement is covered by the exemption, provided that in this case too, the production of the contract products is the principal purpose of the agreement. If this is not the case, the Commission will apply the principles of the Regulation by analogy to such 'master licensing agreements' between licensor and licensee; *see* paragraph 60 of the Guidelines.

---

30. *See* the Guidelines, para. 48.

5.1.4 *The Transferred Technology*

The transferred technology constitutes primarily the license for the rights referred to in section 5.1, in other words, the patents, know-how and software copyright or mixed agreements for the exploitation of these rights. 'Technology' is an input which is integrated either in a product or in a production process.

> A patent right is a right which is created by legislation and is protected for a number of years. This applies regardless of whether the patent owner has exploited the patent or not.
>
> The Regulation's definition of a 'patent' is based on patent legislation, according to which a patent is an *exclusive right* created by virtue of the registration of an invention which is novel in relation to what was known before the submission of the patent application, and which is sufficiently different from it (*novelty* and the *degree of invention*).
>
> The Regulation applies to the grant of licences for the national patents of the Member States and licences for European Patents.
>
> According to the definition in Article 1(1)(i), 'know-how' means a package of technical information resulting from experience and testing, which is:
>
> (i) secret, that is to say, not generally known or easily accessible;
> (ii) substantial, that is to say, significant and useful for the production of the contract products; and
> (iii) identified, that is to say, described in a sufficiently comprehensive manner so as to make it possible to verify that it fulfils the criteria of secrecy and substantiality.
>
> The connection between patents and know-how is operative in the sense that the confidentiality of special know-how can be a precursor to a later patent application, and even if such an application is later made, there will often be some additional knowledge about processes, etc.
>
> If the owner of some know-how, for example, the process for the production of a chemical compound, is doubtful about whether the method can be patented, they can sometimes keep their knowledge confidential until it may later be clarified whether the conditions for a patent application exist (novelty and the degree of invention). Or they can instead publish a so-called patent prophylaxis so that when the process is later made public, a patent cannot be granted either to a competitor or the owner of the right themselves. However, this means that the process is surrendered since anyone can now use it. If the patent holder decides to keep the process secret, the period of the patent can be extended, as long as the process is secret. The product may be put into the market, but the process can remain secret.
>
> A licensee can take on and exploit both the conceptual idea, which is expressed in the patent and the technical knowledge, which is expressed in the know-how. There

is, nevertheless a fundamental difference between the two types of rights, which is also reflected in competition law. Unlike patents, know-how is not protected by special laws, and its value ceases when the knowledge about the processes, etc., which constitute the substance of the know-how is no longer secret.

The term 'software' is not defined either in the Regulation or the Guidelines. According to the general view of the character of this intellectual property right it is natural to consider it as concerning computer programs, in other words instructions or information presented in whatever form or by whatever medium, which are intended, directly or indirectly, to enable a computer to carry out a particular function or achieve a particular result. It appears from point 62 of the Guidelines on technology transfers that the licensing of software copyrights solely for the purpose of reproduction and distribution of the protected work is not covered by Regulation (EU) but is instead covered by Regulation (EU) 2022/720 on the application of TEU Article 101, subsection 3, on categories of vertical agreements and concerted practice and the associated Guidelines on vertical restraints (2022/C 248/1).

As stated above, the Regulation primarily exempts licence agreements relating to patents, know-how, or software copyright, or a mixed licence for these rights. At the same time, agreements containing provisions for the grant of a licence or assignment of other intellectual property rights are only covered by the Regulation if these provisions are directly related to the production or sale of the contract products.[31] From this it follows that these other rights only qualify for a block exemption if they enable the licensee to better exploit the transferred technology. For example, a trade mark licence may enable the licensee to exploit the technology better as it may give consumers the impression that there is a direct connection between the goods offered and the characteristics they have been given via the transferred technology. Likewise, an obligation to use the licensors trade mark can serve to promote the dissemination of the technology, where the licensor is identified as the source of the underlying technology. On the contrary, if the transferred technology is of limited value to the licensees, because they already use identical or very similar technology, and if the core element of the agreement is the trade mark itself, then Regulation (EU) No 316/2014 does not apply.[32]

---

31. *See* Regulation (EU) No 316/2014, Art. 2(3); and the Guidelines, para. 50.
32. Compare with Commission Decision 90/186/EEC, *Moosehead/Whitbread* (OJ 1990 L 100/32), where the trade mark rather than the other parts of the agreement were found to constitute the commercial centre of gravity of the agreement. On this decision, *see* among others: Terence Prime & David Booton: *European Intellectual Property Law*, pp. 49 and 64, 1998; Valentine Korah: *Technology Transfer Agreements and the EC Competition Rules*, pp. 68–71 and 116–121, 1996; and the commentary on Art. 2(3) of Regulation (EU) No 330/2010 in Ch. 3, s. 5.2.

5.1.5 Definition of the Relevant Market

Where the undertakings party to the agreement are competing undertakings, the block exemption is conditional on the *combined market share* of the parties not exceeding 20% of the relevant market; see Article 3(1) relating to agreements between competing undertakings (horizontal agreements). Where the undertakings party to the agreement are not competing undertakings (vertical agreements), the *individual market shares* of each of the parties may not exceed 30% of the relevant market; see Article 3(2).

Article 3 includes both the technology market and the product market under the definition of the 'relevant market' as the technology market provides an input which is integrated either into the product or the production process; *see* paragraph 20 of the Guidelines. Technology transfers can thus affect competition on both the input and output markets. The *product market* is defined by the products which buyers consider are interchangeable with or substitutable for the contract products which incorporate the transferred technology, by reason of their characteristics, price or intended use.[33] Product markets also include the products which are produced by means of the transferred technology.

The *technology market* consists of the technology transferred to the licensee and alternatives to it; in other words, other technologies which are regarded by licensees as interchangeable with or substitutable for the licensed technology by reason of its characteristics, royalties and intended use. Starting from the technology which is marketed by the licensor, it is necessary to identify the other technologies to which licensees could switch in response to a small but permanent increase in relative prices, i.e., the royalty payments.[34]

When the relevant markets have been defined, the market shares can be allocated to the different sources of competition on the market and used as an indication of the relative strengths of the market participants, which Article 3 emphasises as being relevant to distinguish between competitors and non-competitors.

In connection with technology markets, the market shares can be calculated on the basis of each technology's share of the total licence revenue. However, this would be a purely theoretical and impractical method for calculating market shares since there would usually be a lack of clear information about royalty incomes, etc.[35] For this reason, among other things, in practice, it will be *the product market* that will be indicative of the different legal effects referred to in Article 3 of the Regulation and whether a technology transfer agreement will covered by the block exemption or not.

According to Article 8(b), the market share is calculated on the basis of information about the turnover on the market for the previous calendar year. The calculation is made according to the generally applicable competition law principles.[36] If initially, the market share referred to in Article 3(1) or (2) does not exceed 20% or

---

33. The Guidelines, para. 19.
34. The Guidelines, para. 21.
35. The Guidelines, para. 25.
36. Commission Notice on the definition of relevant market for the purposes of Community competition law (OJ 1997 C 372/5), *see* Ch. 3, s. 5.2 above.

30%, respectively, but subsequently crosses these thresholds, then the exemption referred to in Article 2 continues to apply for the two calendar years following the year in which the 20% or 30% threshold was first exceeded; *see* Article 8(e).

The abandonment of the system with whitelisted, blacklisted and grey-listed restrictions on competition in favour of a system which makes the application of the block exemption dependent on certain market share thresholds not being crossed (market strength) has meant that a number of restrictions on competition which were expressly stated to be black or grey now fall within the block exemption.

Among other things, the focus on market strength has meant that *tie-in sales* in agreements that do not exceed the market share thresholds referred to in Article 3 are covered by the block exemption.[37] Tie-in sales are not included in either Article 4 or 5 (*see* section 6 below) as restrictions which exclude the granting of exemptions, regardless of whether Article 3 is complied with or not.[38]

This may seem surprising, given that Article 101(1)(e) TFEU particularly exemplifies tie-in sales as the kind of agreement that can affect trade between Member States and which is incompatible with the aims of the internal market if the conditions in Article 101(1) are otherwise fulfilled.[39]

In relation to technology transfers, there will be a tie-in sale if the licensor makes the grant of a licence for a technology (the primary product) conditional on the licensee accepting a licence on some other technology or buying a particular product from the licensor or from an undertaking appointed the licensor (the tied product). The same exemption applies to 'bundling', where two technologies or technology and a product are only sold together as a pack. Both tie-ins and bundling are concerned with special technologies in the sense that, on the relevant market, there is a distinct demand for the individual products included in the tie-in sale or pack. There will not normally be such a tie-in if the technologies or products are necessarily bound together in such a way that the transferred technology cannot be used without the tied-in product or if neither of the products in the package can be used without the other.[40]

The market share thresholds apply to each relevant technology and product market affected by the licence agreement, including the market for a tied product.[41]

If the market thresholds in Article 3(1) or (2) of the Regulation are exceeded, the block exemption does not apply, and it will therefore be necessary to evaluate the restrictions on competition and the competition-promoting effects of the tie-in sale and

---

37. On tie-ins, *see* Valentine Korah: *Technology Transfer Agreements and the EC Competition Rules*, pp. 173–180, 1996.
38. However, Regulation (EC) No 240/96, which was the predecessor to Regulation (EC) No 772/2004 and Regulation (EU) No 316/2014, had already indicated that the Commission would adopt a milder stance towards such tie-ins, since the prohibition was included in Art. 4(2)(a) as part of the grey list, i.e., terms which were subject to an opposition procedure, *see* s. 4 above. Previous block exemption regulations had classified tie-in clauses as blacklisted; *see* the practice of the Commission in Commission Decision 79/86/EEC, *Vaessen/Morris* (OJ 1979 L 19/32), Valentine Korah: *Technology Transfer Agreements and the EC Competition Rules*, pp. 176–178, 1996; and Steven D. Anderman: *EC Competition Law and Intellectual Property Rights*, pp. 57–63, 1998.
39. *See also* Art. 102(2)(d) TFEU, which is discussed in Ch. 6.
40. The Guidelines, para. 221.
41. The Guidelines, para. 222.

bundling before it can be decided whether sales on these terms are contrary to Article 101(1).

5.1.6 Competing and Non-competing Undertakings

The idea behind many of the provisions in Regulation (EU) No 316/2014 is that agreements between competitors (horizontal agreements) constitute a greater threat to competition than agreements between non-competitors (vertical agreements);[42] *see* the comments above in section 5.1.5 on the market thresholds that are triggered at a lower level of market share for agreements between competitors than they are for agreements between non-competitors, and *see* further in section 6 on the hardcore restrictions; *see* Article 4 of the Regulation.

However, the intra-technology competition between licensees, i.e., competition between undertakings that use the same technology, will lead to lower prices for the products that incorporate the technology in question, which should not only be a direct and immediate advantage to the consumers who use these products but also intensify the competition between undertakings that use the competing products. In connection with licence agreements, it is also necessary to be aware that licensees sell their own products and do not, as in the case of distributors covered by Regulation (EU) No 330/2010 on vertical agreements, resell the products of another undertaking. There are thus better opportunities for product differentiation than there are in connection with vertical agreements for the re-sale of products; *see* paragraph 27 of the Guidelines.

In order to determine the competitive situation between a licensor and a licensee, it is first necessary to evaluate whether, *without the agreement*, the parties would have been actual or potential competitors; *see* the distinction below. If, without the agreement, the parties would not have been actual or potential competitors on the relevant market affected by the agreement, they are considered to be non-competitors.[43]

The parties are thus not competitors in relation to Regulation (EU) No 316/2014 if the licensor is neither an actual or potential supplier of products on the relevant market and the licensee, who must already be active on the product market, does not grant the licensor a licence on competing technology, even though it owns competing technology and produces on the basis thereof. However, the parties become competitors if the licensee subsequently begins to grant licences on its technology or if the licensor becomes an actual or potential supplier of products on the relevant market. In this case, the hardcore restrictions discussed in section 6 continue to apply to the agreement unless the agreement is materially amended on its important points, which do not correspond to the context in which it was entered into; *see* Article 4(3) of the Regulation.

According to Article 1(1)(j) of the Regulation (*see* paragraphs 30 and 35 of the Guidelines), the parties are *actual* competitors when they are both active on the same product market and the same territorial market on which the products are sold which

---

42. On the distinction between horizontal and vertical agreements, *see* the Guidelines, paras 27–39.
43. The Guidelines, paras 28 and 82.

incorporate the transferred technology.[44] They are also regarded as competitors (*potential* competitors) if, on the basis of realistic considerations, it is likely that they will be prepared to invest in the costs of organising their production with the aim of penetrating the relevant product and/or territorial markets within a reasonably short period, in response to a small and permanent increase in relative prices.

5.1.7   *Reciprocal Contra Non-reciprocal Agreements*

The distinction between reciprocal contra non-reciprocal agreements is relevant to several of the restrictions referred to in Article 4 of the block exemption Regulation. The difference is seen in the fact that non-reciprocal agreements are treated more advantageously in competition law than reciprocal agreements; *see* Article 4(1)(b) and (c) and the more detailed discussion in section 6. Reciprocal agreements and non-reciprocal agreements are defined in Article 1(1)(d) and (e).

According to the definition in Article 1(1)(d), a 'reciprocal agreement' is a technology transfer agreement where two undertakings grant each other, in the same or separate contracts, a technology rights licence and where these licences concern competing technologies or can be used for the production of competing products (cross-licences).[45]

According to the definition in Article 1(1)(e), a 'non-reciprocal agreement' is a technology transfer agreement where one undertaking grants another undertaking a technology rights licence or where two undertakings grant each other technology rights licences but where these licences do not concern competing technologies and cannot be used for the production of competing products.

5.1.8   *The Duration of the Block Exemption*

According to Regulation (EU) No 316/2014, a block exemption lasts as long as the intellectual property rights covered by the agreement have not lapsed, expired or been invalidated.[46] However, the period of validity of the Regulation expires on 30 April 2026; *see* Article 11.

In particular, with regard to know-how, the exemption lasts as long as the know-how covered by the licence remains confidential from the outside world unless it becomes generally known as a result of the actions of the licensee, in which case the exemption applies to the duration of the agreement; *see* paragraph 67 of the Guidelines. The block exemption applies for each of the intellectual property rights covered by the technology transfer agreement and expires on the date on which the last of the intellectual property rights which constitute the technology covered by the block exemption

---

44. Products are goods and services, including both intermediary goods and services and finished goods and services. On intermediary products, *see* Ch. 3, s. 5.
45. An agreement is not reciprocal merely because the agreement contains a grant-back obligation or because the licensee licenses back its own improvements of the licensed technology. Grant back is discussed in s. 7.2.
46. *See* Regulation (EU) No 316/2014, Art. 2(2) and the Guidelines, para. 67.

Regulation expires, is declared invalid or enters the public domain; see paragraph 68 of the Guidelines.[47] Even though the block exemption only applies as long as the technology is valid and in use, the parties can normally agree to extend the obligation to pay royalties for the intellectual property rights beyond the period of validity without infringing Article 101(1).

Once these rights expire, third parties can legally exploit the technology in question and compete with the parties to the agreement; see paragraph 187 of the Guidelines.

6 HARDCORE RESTRICTIONS

Article 4 of Regulation (EU) No 316/2014 contains certain 'hardcore restrictions' which, if one or more of them is agreed between a licensor and a licensee, will nearly always mean that the agreement in its entirety will not qualify for the exemption provided for in Article 2.[48] The intention is to balance consideration for competition against the right to exploit intellectual property rights.

The restriction can be expressed either in the purpose of the agreement itself, or in the specific circumstances of an individual case, without it being necessary to give evidence of concrete effects on the market for the purposes of the application of Article 101(1) TFEU.[49] Moreover, it is unlikely that an agreement containing one or more of these restrictions would be exempted under Article 101(3) TFEU.[50]

Article 4 distinguishes between competing undertakings and non-competing undertakings, and for a number of the restrictions, a distinction is made between reciprocal and non-reciprocal agreements; on the latter distinction, see section 5.1.7, with the emphasis on the fact that reciprocal agreements (cross-licences) are treated more strictly in competition law than non-reciprocal agreements.

6.1 Agreements Between Competitors[51]

When the parties to an agreement are undertakings which compete with each other, the exemption provided for in Article 2 of the Regulation does not apply to agreements

---

47. Compare with the comments on the individual rights in s. 5.1.4.
48. In other words, for the application of the block exemption Regulation, hardcore restrictions are not separated from the rest of the agreement so that the agreement can continue with the hardcore restriction excised. The doctrine of severance does not apply to hardcore restrictions; see the comments above in Ch. 3, s. 5.4, on distribution agreements, and s. 7 below on Art. 5 of the Regulation.
49. See Case C-49/92, Anic, para. 99, on hardcore cartels.
50. The Guidelines, para. 95.
51. In the following account of the hardcore restrictions in Art. 4, it is important to bear in mind that, as appears from its wording, the comments in s. 6.1 (concerning Art. 4.1) relate to agreements between competing undertakings, while s. 6.2 (Art. 4.2) relates to agreements between non-competing undertakings. When the undertakings to an agreement do not compete with each other at the time of entering into an agreement, but subsequently become competing undertakings, the rules relating to the relationship between non-competing undertakings (s. 6.2) apply to the agreement for the whole of the period, unless the agreement is subsequently materially amended; see Art. 4.3. However, the distinction between reciprocal and non-reciprocal agreements is operative in each of the two parts.

which, directly or indirectly, in isolation or in combination with other factors under the control of the parties, contain the restrictions set out in Article 4(1)(a)–(d) of the Regulation.

6.1.1 Agreements on the Pricing of the Contract Products

Article 4(1)(a) of the Regulation concerns the restriction on a party's right to determine its prices for the sale of its products to third parties, including sales prices for products which incorporate the transferred technology. It does not matter whether the restriction concerns fixed prices, minimum prices, maximum prices or recommended prices; see paragraph 99 of the Guidelines.[52]

Article 4(1)(a) concerns one of the key considerations of block exemption regulations in general: an undertaking (the licensee) that acts as an intermediary between the principal (the licensor) and a customer must be free to determine for itself the pricing policy it will apply in relation to third parties. A provision on binding prices which apply to downstream levels of trade has always been characterised as a restriction on trade in the legal practice on licence agreements; see, for example, Case 27/87, *Erauw-Jacquéry v. la Hesbignonne*, paragraph 15:

> In this connection, it must be pointed out that article 85(1) [now Article 101(1) TFEU] of the Treaty expressly mentions as being incompatible with the common market agreements which 'directly or indirectly fix purchase or selling prices or any other trading conditions'. According to the judgment of the national court the plaintiff in the main proceedings concluded with other growers agreements identical to the contested agreement, as a result of which those agreements have the same effects as a price system fixed by a horizontal agreement. In such circumstances the object and effect of such a provision is to restrict competition within the common market.[53]

A pricing agreement can, for example, take the form of a direct agreement on the exact price, or a price list with the maximum permitted discounts which the licensee can allow third parties. The pricing conditions can also be imposed indirectly via measures which are intended to warn the licensee from departing from the agreed pricing, for example, by stating that the royalty will be increased if the price for the products is reduced below a certain level.

Article 4(1)(a) also affects agreements in relation to which royalties are calculated on the basis of total sales of products, whether or not they use the transferred

---

52. On this point the wording of Regulation (EU) No 316/2014 is stricter than the corresponding provision in the vertical agreements regulation; see Ch. 3, s. 5.3.1 on Regulation (EU) No 330/2010, Art. 4(a), which only contains a prohibition on the setting of binding minimum prices, whereas in principle maximum sales prices and recommended prices fall outside the prohibition. On the other hand, see s. 6.2 below on Art. 4(2)(a), which concerns agreements between non-competing undertakings and which allows agreements on re-sale prices as long as these are not fixed prices or minimum sales prices.
53. For a commentary on this case, see Valentine Korah & Denis O'Sullivan: *Distribution Agreements under the EC Competition Rules*, pp. 81–83, 2002; and Valentine Korah: *Technology Transfer Agreements and the EC Competition Rules*, pp. 16–19 and 190–194, 1996.

technology.⁵⁴ Such agreements generally restrict competition as it could make it more expensive for the licensee to use its own technology and restrict the competition which existed prior to entering into the agreement.⁵⁵

6.1.2   Production Restrictions

The hardcore restriction referred to in Article 4(1)(b) concerns reciprocal production limitations and production limitations imposed on the licensor with regard to its own technology. However, production limitations imposed on a licensee in a non-reciprocal agreement or a limitation which is only imposed on one of the licensees in a reciprocal agreement are not covered by the provision. Such a restriction is, therefore, in this respect, covered by the block exemption; *see* paragraph 103 of the Guidelines.⁵⁶

A production limitation is a limitation on the quantity that an undertaking may produce and sell. When competing undertakings enter into an agreement under which both the licensor and the licensee accept obligations to limit production, this will often be an indication that they intend to restrict output on the market – and presumably succeed in doing so.

If a licensee in a non-reciprocal agreement is willing to accept a unilateral restriction of its production, the reason can be that it wishes to implement the integration of complementary technologies or the integration of the licensors' more advanced technology in the licensees' own production. In a reciprocal agreement, an output restriction on one of the licensees is likely to reflect the higher value of the technology licensed by one of the parties and may serve to promote pro-competitive licensing.⁵⁷

6.1.3   *The Allocation of Markets or Customers (Sales Restrictions)*

6.1.3.1   The Allocation of Markets

Both exclusive licences and sole licences refer to activities within the territory of the relevant market.

An *exclusive licence* means that the licensee is the only one who is permitted to produce on the basis of the licensed technology within a given territory. The licensor

---

54. Agreements of this kind are also affected by Art. 4(1)(d) (*see* s. 6.1.3.4 below), under which the licensor may not prevent the licensee using its own technology.
55. On one particular method of calculation, *see* Case 193/83, *Windsurfing International v. Commission*, para. 67, where the CJ found that it was contrary to Art. 101(1) TFEU to calculate the license fee based on the sales of a product which was not covered by the licensed technology, in the case in question sailboards without rigs. For a commentary on this case *see* Valentine Korah: *Technology Transfer Agreements and the EC Competition Rules*, pp. 145–148, 1996 and Terence Prime & David Booton: *European Intellectual Property Law*, pp. 53–54, 1998.
56. In all agreements between non-competing undertakings (including reciprocal agreements), all sales restrictions which otherwise fulfil the conditions of the Regulation, including that they are below the threshold in Art. 3(2), are covered by the block exemption; *see* the Guidelines, para. 201, and s. 6.2 below.
57. The Guidelines, para. 104.

thus undertakes not to produce itself, using the licensed technology, or license others to produce within the given territory.[58]

By granting a licensee a *sole licence*, the licensor undertakes not to licence third parties to produce within a given territory, but the licensor is not itself prevented from using the technology in question.[59]

Reciprocal exclusive licences between competing undertakings are categorised as a hardcore restriction in Article 4(1)(c), with the consequence that the whole agreement is invalid.

Sole licences between competing undertakings are covered by the block exemption up to the market share threshold of 20% (*see* the definition of the market in section 5.1.5 above). The exemption applies regardless of whether the agreement is reciprocal or non-reciprocal; *see* Article 4(1)(c)(iii) and Recital 10.[60]

6.1.3.2 *Sales Restrictions (Allocation of Customers)*

Restrictions on one or both of the parties' active and passive sales, as part of a reciprocal agreement between competing undertakings, constitute hardcore restrictions on competition and are prohibited in Article 4(1)(c).[61] Sales restrictions of this nature in a reciprocal agreement will normally be considered as evidence of market sharing, as the restriction will prevent the party concerned from either actively or passively selling into the territories and thus to customers whom the party already sells to or could realistically sell to if the agreement did not prevent it from doing so.

By contrast, the assessment of sales restrictions in non-reciprocal agreements is quite liberal, as will appear from several of the qualifications on the extent of Article 4(1)(c) discussed immediately below in section 6.1.3.3, with reference to Article 4(1)(c)(i)–(vii).[62]

6.1.3.3 *Permitted Restrictions Pursuant to Article 4(1)(c)*

The scope for market sharing has been restricted compared with Regulation (EC) No 772/2004. However, the following possibilities still remain:

Article 4(1)(c)(i)

The exception under sub-sub-paragraph (ii) concerns cases where, as part of a non-reciprocal agreement, the licensor grants the licensee an exclusive licence to produce products on the basis of the licensed technology within a specific territory, and thereby binds itself not to produce the contract products in the territory in

---

58. The Guidelines, para. 191.
59. The Guidelines, para. 191.
60. The Guidelines, para. 186.
61. The Guidelines, para. 198. For the meaning of active and passive sales, *see* the comments on Art. 4(b) in the Regulation (EU) No 330/2010 on vertical agreements in Ch. 3, s. 5, and in the Guidelines, para. 51 on vertical agreements referred to there, as well as s. 6.1.3.3 below on Art. 4(1)(c)(iv) and (v).
62. *See also* Art. 4(2)(b)(i) and (ii), on agreements between non-competing undertakings (s. 6.2 below).

question or to supply the contract products from this area. Such agreements are not considered as hardcore agreements, regardless of the size of the area concerned. The aim of such agreements may be to give the licensee an incentive to invest in and develop the licensed technology, and not necessarily to share markets.[63]

Article 4(1)(c)(ii)

The restriction which, according to Article 4(1)(c)(iv), is exempted under Article 2 is not considered as market sharing, as it would be if the restriction were reciprocal. The provision refers to a part of a non-reciprocal agreement which is a restriction on the licensee's and/or the licensor's active and/or passive sales into the exclusive territory or to the exclusive customer group reserved for the other party, i.e. the licensee or the licensor.

Article 4(1)(c)(iii)

According to Article 4(1)(c)(iii), a licensor can, without affecting the block exemption, restrict the licensee's production so as only to produce the contract products for its own use.[64] If the contact product is a component, the licensee can be required only to produce the component in question for incorporation in the products which it produces itself. However, the restriction will only apply as long as the licensee is not at the same time prevented from actively or passively selling the contract products as *spare parts* for the licensee's own products.

The permissibility of the restriction under sub-sub-paragraph (vi) is justified by, among other things, consideration for the dissemination of technology, particularly between competitors. The provision does not cover sales of the contract products with a view to their incorporation in other producer's products. These restrictions are covered by the block exemption up to the market share threshold of 20%.

Article 4(1)(c)(iv)

According to Article 4(1)(c)(iv), in a non-reciprocal agreement a licensee can be obliged to produce the contract products only for a particular customer, where the licence is granted in order to create an alternative source of supply for that customer.

The provision is aimed at situations where an undertaking is granted a licence to produce spare parts and other components. If this undertaking is a subcontractor to the producer of the principal product, for example motor cars, an interruption of supply, for example a strike, which affects the licensee's business could develop so that the producer of the principal product is unable to produce and may be required to halt production for a shorter or longer period, with corresponding financial consequences.[65] The basis for Article 4(1)(c)(iv), under which a (second) licensee can be obliged to supply only a limited quantity of the contract goods to a specific customer, is therefore not primarily to restrict the delivery quantities of the second (new) licensee, but to procure for the customer in question a further source of supply. The risk that such agreements will result in

---

63. The Guidelines, para. 111.
64. The Guidelines, para. 111.
65. According to Valentine Korah: *Know-How Licensing Agreements and the EC Competition Rules,* Regulation No 556/89, p. 170, 1989, the provision was originally included at the wish of the motor car industry.

market sharing is limited when a licence is granted with the aim of supplying one specific customer.⁶⁶

The provision also covers cases where more than one undertaking is granted a licence for the same specific customer.

6.1.3.4 Exploitation of Own Technology, Etc.⁶⁷

According to the hardcore restriction in Article 4(1)(d), the licensee must not be prevented from using its own competing technology, provided the licensee does not use the technology licensed by the licensor in connection with this. With regard to the use of its own technology, the licensee must be free to decide how and how much it will produce and sell and at what price. It must likewise be free to grant licences of its technology to third parties.

The restriction also applies to the right of one of the parties to the agreement to carry out research and development unless such a restriction is indispensable to prevent the disclosure of the licensed know-how to third parties.

The basis for the provision is clear: if a licensee is subject to restrictions on the use of its own technology or in the area of research and development, its technology will be less competitive on the existing product and technology markets, and it will reduce its incentive to invest in the further development of its technology.

6.2 Agreements Between Non-competing Undertakings

When the parties to an agreement are undertakings which do not compete with each other, the exemption provided for in Article 2 of the Regulation does not apply to agreements which, directly or indirectly, in isolation or in combination with other factors under the control of the parties, contain the restrictions which are set out in Article 4(2)(a)–(c) of the Regulation.

6.2.1 Agreements on the Pricing of Contract Products: Article 4(2)(a)

The hardcore restriction in Article 4(2)(a) concerns the fixing of sales prices when selling products produced using the licensed technology to third parties; for the reasons for this provision, see the comments in section 6.1.1 on the corresponding provision in Article 4(1)(a) relating to agreements between competing undertakings.

While Article 4(1)(a) covers all kinds of pricing (ability to determine its prices), Article 4(2)(a) expressly allows for the possibility of a block exemption of agreements both on maximum sales prices and recommended prices, provided they do not amount to a fixed or minimum sales price as a result of pressure from, or incentives offered by, any of the parties.

---

66. The Guidelines, para. 112.
67. The Guidelines, para. 116.

Paragraph 118 of the Guidelines refers to a number of examples of agreements which have as their direct or indirect object the establishment of a fixed or minimum selling price or a fixed or minimum price level to be observed by the licensor or the licensee when selling products to third parties.

In the case of agreements that directly establish the selling price, the restriction is clear-cut. However, the fixing of selling prices can also be achieved through indirect means which can be difficult to see through, whether this is the purpose of the agreement or it is due to special measures linked to the sales price. Examples of this are agreements that fix the seller margin, agreements that fix the maximum level of discounts in connection with setting the sales price, agreements linking the sales price to the sales prices of competitors, threats to restrict supplies, or measures outside the scope of the agreement such as threats, intimidation, warnings, penalties, or contract termination in relation to observance of a given price level. The direct or indirect means of achieving price fixing can be made more effective if, for example, they are combined with a hidden price monitoring system, or the obligation on licensees to report deviations of prices from the fixed price level, or are combined with a most-favoured-customer clause, i.e., an obligation to grant to a customer any more favourable terms granted to any other customer.[68]

However, the provision of a list of recommended prices to or the imposition of a maximum price on the licensee by the licensor is not *in itself* considered as leading to fixed or minimum selling prices.[69]

6.2.2 Sales Restrictions Article 4(2)(b)

The core of Article 4(2)(b) is the hardcore restriction, which restricts a licensee's passive sales to specific territories or to specific customer groups. The aim or consequence of an agreement or concerted practice with the licensor binding the licensee by such an obligation is a division of the market, which is contrary to Article 101(1)(c) TFEU.

The obligation can be in the form of a direct order not to sell to customers in a specific territory or to customers of a particular customer group or a requirement to pass on orders received from such customers to another licensee who has been given

---

68. On most-favoured-customer clauses, *see* Valentine Korah: *Technology Transfer Agreements and the EC Competition Rules*, pp. 199–200, 1996.
69. Compare with the provisions in the area of distribution agreements in para. 111 of the guidelines for vertical agreements referred to above in Ch. 3, s. 5.3.1, and Commission Decision 96/438/EC, *Fenex* (OJ 1996 L 181/28), Commission Decision 2001/711/EC, *Volkswagen* (OJ 2001 L 262/14), and Commission Decision 97/123/EC, *Novalliance/Systemform* (OJ 1997 L 47/11).

exclusive rights to the specified territory or customer group from which the order has been received.[70]

The obligation of licensees to refrain from making passive sales can also arise in the form of indirect measures which have the effect of countering the licensees' sales to such customers, for example, financial incentives and the establishment of a control system that can be used to verify where the products, in fact, end up. The same applies to quantitative restrictions, which can be used to restrict passive sales, for example, if there are quantitative adjustments over time with the aim of only covering the local demand if the quantitative restriction is combined with an obligation for the licensee to sell a certain minimum quantity to the allocated territory, or if the requirement for the payment of a certain minimum on royalties is linked to sales in the allocated territory, etc.; *see* paragraph 119 of the Guidelines.

Article 4(2)(b) does not affect agreed sales restrictions which a licensee imposes on a *licensor*, and all such restrictions agreed between the licensee and the licensor are therefore covered by the block exemption up to the market share threshold of 30%; *see* Article 3(2).[71] The block exemption likewise applies to all restrictions on the licensees' active sales, without regard for whether measures such as advertising campaigns in another licensee's territory originate from a licensee that has not been allocated an exclusive territory or an exclusive customer group.

The statement of intent on exclusions from the block exemption (in the introduction to Article 4(2)) and the introductory wording to Article 4(2)(b) are diluted by a number of exceptions; *see* Article 4(2)(b)(i)-(v). These exceptions are discussed in section 6.2.3 below.

In addition to this, there still seems to be a lack of clarity in the judicial practice about the importance that should be attached to the views on exclusive licences that were expressed in the *Nungesser* case, which is discussed immediately below.

It has always been the Commission's view that an exclusivity clause that protects a licensee against competition both from the licensor and from parallel imports from licensees in other territories is contrary to Article 101(1). The Commission has argued that even if a licensor could grant or refrain from granting a licensee the right, for example, to use a patent, this could not in itself justify the licensor undertaking not to grant *other licensees* the right to use their patents. In the view of the Commission, such a restriction would lead to full territorial protection, contrary to Article 101(1) TFEU.

However, a possibly decisive break with this practice occurred with the CJ's decision in Case 258/78, *Nungesser and Eiscle v. Commission*, which concerned a new technology for producing hybrid maize. The decision can be read as a recognition that there can be a legitimate need to allow a licensee a certain measure of territorial protection without Article 101(1) being immediately brought to bear under a claim of unlawful market sharing.

---

70. The view that a combination of agreements on territorial protection and intellectual property rights could artificially contribute to the maintenance of national markets was established as early as in Cases 56 and 58/64, *Grundig and Consten v. Commission,* which is referred to above in Ch. 3.
71. The Guidelines, para. 120.

The CJ had to consider a reference for a preliminary ruling on an agreement between a French research institute, INRA, and a German undertaking, Nungesser, for the use of seed for hybrid maize varieties which had been developed by INRA.

Nungesser had been given an exclusive licence for Germany, and INRA bound itself not to sell or produce in Germany either itself or through other licensees. In addition to this, INRA bound itself to prevent all direct or indirect exports to Germany. In one clause in the licence agreement it was stated that INRA bound themselves to do 'everything in their power to prevent the export' of the varieties of seeds in question to Germany, and for its part, Nungesser undertook not to export the products.

In its reasoning the CJ made a distinction between the two types of obligation, as the first restriction (Nungesser's exclusive right in relation to the licensor and the other licensees appointed by the licensor) was classified as an 'open exclusive licence', where the exclusivity only concerned the relations between the licensor and the licensee, and therefore, 'having regard to the specific nature of the products in question ... the grant of an open exclusive licence, that is to say a licence which does not affect the position of third parties such as parallel importers and licensees for other territories, is not in itself incompatible with article 85(1) [now Article 101(1) TFEU] of the Treaty'.

The CJ justified this on the grounds that when, as in the case before it, there was a licence for an invention that had been recently developed in a Member State, an undertaking located in another Member State might be reluctant to take on the financial risks of cultivating the product and putting it on the market unless it was granted such protection against other licensees or the licensor itself. In the view of the CJ, this would be injurious to the spread of new technology and thus also to competition between the new product and equivalent existing products in the EU.

As for the obligation to prevent exports to the licensees' territory – the CJ referred to this as an exclusive licence or a sole licence with absolute territorial protection – the CJ only expressed itself in relation to the case as presented, which only concerned the attempt of the parties to restrict parallel imports/exports of products which had already been put on the market by INRA, in other words a case where there had been *exhaustion of rights* (*see* section 1 above for a discussion of this concept).

Parallel importers and exporters that offered INRA's seed to German buyers had been subject to civil proceedings and other pressure from INRA and Nungesser to protect Nungesser's position as the exclusive producer and distributor on the German market. In addition, the CJ found that, according to well-established practice, full territorial protection with a view to controlling and restricting parallel imports was incompatible with Article 101(1) TFEU, and such measures would clearly lie outside the scope of what could be exempted under Article 101(3).

At the same time, the CJ did not directly address the question of whether Nungesser, as licensee, would be bound by a provision which prevented the undertaking from exporting to potential customers in other licensees' territories or whether licensees in other territories could be bound not to export to customers in Germany.

It is presumed that, following the CJ's reasoning, such a prohibition would be covered by Article 101(1) since the CJ apparently considered a restriction on parallel imports and an export prohibition on the licensee to be equivalent. In paragraph 58, the CJ stated that the grant of an open exclusive licence, which in the view of the CJ was not in itself incompatible with Article 101(1) TFEU, 'does not affect the position of third parties such as parallel importers and licensees for other territories'. *See also* the careful statement in recital 11 in Regulation (EC) No 240/96 (in other words, the technology transfer regulation prior to (now) Regulation (EU) No 316/2014), according to which the exemption of export bans on the licensor and on the licensees does not prejudice any developments in the case law of the CJ with respect to Articles 30–36 (now Articles 34 and 36 TFEU) and Article 85(1) (now Article 101(1) TFEU).

However, in the latter Case 27/87, *Erauw-Jacquéry v. la Hesbignonne*, the CJ found that a clause in an agreement on the propagation and sale of seed, under which one of the parties was the owner of certain breeding rights, which included a prohibition on the propagator selling or exporting basic seed, was compatible with Article 101(1), in so far as the agreement was necessary for the plant breeder to choose authorised propagators. As emphasised in paragraph 11 of the judgment: 'Therefore, the answer to the first part of the question referred by the national court must be that a provision of an agreement concerning the propagation and sale of seed, in respect of which one of the parties is the holder or the agent of the holder of certain plant breeders' rights, which prohibits the licensee from selling and exporting the basic seed is compatible with Article 85(1) [now Article 101(1) TFEU] of the Treaty in so far as it is necessary in order to enable the breeder to select the growers who are to be licensees.'[72]

However, it is doubtful, both after the *Nungesser* case and the *Erauw-Jacquéry* case, whether the courts would hold that an open exclusive licence is only exempted when it refers to *new* technology or whether the scope of the judgment could be stretched to *other* technology than the specific technology relating to seed. However, it is presumably reasonable to interpret the fact that the *Nungesser* case so strongly emphasised the importance of new technology being spread as an expression that, given the many other circumstances that could be linked to such heavy costs of implementing technology in a new area, it ought to be possible, at least in an

---

72. The case is discussed in, among others, Valentine Korah: *Technology Transfer Agreements and the EC Competition Rules*, pp. 16–18, 1996.

introductory period, to give a licensee some protection, whether the exclusivity in question relates to new or previously proven technology.[73]

6.2.3 Permitted Restrictions Pursuant to Article 4(2)(b)

Article 4(2)(b)(i)

According to Article 4(2)(b)(i), the restriction on passive sales into an exclusive territory or to an exclusive customer group that is reserved for *the licensor* is not a hardcore restriction on competition. Agreements of this nature are therefore covered by the block exemption, as long as the market share threshold laid down in Article 3(2) is not exceeded. In paragraph 121 of the Guidelines it is presumed that such restrictions, if they restrict competition, will contribute to the dissemination of technology which will promote competitiveness and the integration of such technology into the production of the licensee. It is not important whether the licensor does in fact produce by means of the licensed technology in the territory in question or for the customer group in question, as this territory or customer group could be reserved to the licensor for later exploitation.

Article 4(2)(b)(ii)

The content of Article 4(2)(b)(ii) corresponds to the provision in Article 4(1)(c)(iii) (*see* section 6.1.3.3 above) so that in this respect (restriction to producing the contract products only for own use) the same legal considerations apply to agreements between non-competing undertakings as to agreements between competing undertakings.

Article 4(2)(b)(iii)

This provision (for ensuring the existence of alternative sources of supply) corresponds to Article 4(1)(c)(iv) (*see* section 6.1.3.3 above). In paragraph 123 of the Guidelines it is added that in the case of agreements between non-competitors, such restrictions are unlikely to be caught by Article 101(1) TFEU.

Article 4(2)(b)(iv)

Article 4(2)(b)(iv) provides for a block exemption for an obligation on a licensee only to sell the contract products to retailers, and not to end users of the products. The provision makes it possible for the licensor to grant the licensee a distribution function at the wholesale level; *see* paragraph 124 of the Guidelines, and such a restriction will normally fall outside the scope of Article 101(1) TFEU.

Article 4(2)(b)(v)

Article 4(2)(b)(v), under which a licensee can be required not to sell to non-authorised distributors, has a counterpart in Article 4(b) in Regulation (EU) No 330/2010 on block exemptions for vertical distribution agreements. The block exemption for an obligation of this kind makes it possible for the licensor, while complying with the provisions of the Regulation on vertical distribution agreements, to bind a licensee to participate in a *selective distribution system* (*see* recital 6 in Regulation (EU) No 316/2014 referred to in section 5.1.1 above).

---

73. *See* Valentine Korah: *Technology Transfer Agreements and the EC Competition Rules*, p. 50, 1996.

7 RESTRICTIONS WHICH FALL OUTSIDE THE SCOPE OF THE BLOCK EXEMPTION

7.1 Article 5 of Regulation (EU) No 316/2014

Article 5 of Regulation (EU) No 316/2014 contains four restrictions which are excluded from the block exemption and which, therefore, require individual assessment of their effects on restricting and promoting competition before a decision can be taken about their effect; see paragraph 128 of the Guidelines.

Corresponding to the effect associated with Article 5 of Regulation (EU) No 330/2010 on block exemptions for vertical distribution agreements, it follows from the wording of Article 5 of Regulation (EU) No 316/2014 that even if a licence agreement contains one or more of the restrictions referred to therein, this does not automatically mean that the block exemption will not be applicable to the remaining part of the agreement. In accordance with, among other things, the doctrine of severance in English law, any invalidity of an agreement under competition law only affects the specific restriction but will not necessarily affect the whole agreement so as to be considered an infringement of the provisions on hardcore restrictions under Article 4.[74] Thus, if a restriction covered by Article 5 can be separated from the agreement, the rest of the agreement will continue to be valid.

7.2 Article 5(1)

Article 5(1) covers both agreements between competing undertakings and agreements between non-competing undertakings.

The restriction in Article 5(1)(a) on grant-back agreements is directed at obligations for the licensee to grant the licensor, or a third party appointed by the licensor, an exclusive licence to its own severable improvements to or its own new applications of the licensed technology.[75]

> As referred to in Article 5(1)(a) and (b) and in recital 15, such obligations could be a disincentive to innovation and the appropriate application of intellectual property rights, if, because of the restrictions, the licensee had no prospect of itself being able to exploit any improvements, including via a licence entered into between the licensee and a third party. This would be the case if there were a severable improvement that concerned the same application as the licensed technology or newly developed applications of this technology.

---

74. See Ch. 3, s. 5.4 and the references made there to the doctrine of severance.
75. See Commission Decision 88/143/EEC, *Rich Products* (OJ 1988 L 69/21), which pre-dated Regulation (EC) No 772/2004 and Regulation (EU) No 316/2014, on the assignment of the sole right to know-how about the production of yeast.

The block exemption will be excluded, regardless of whether the licensor gives the licensee payment or an exclusive licence for the improvements.[76] If payment of a fee is provided for in connection with a grant-back obligation, the amount of the fee could be a relevant factor for assessing whether an exemption could be granted outside the scope of application of the block exemption regulation, i.e., under Article 101(3) TFEU.

The general principles of interpretation seem to lead to the conclusion that the licensor has a right to use improvements that are not severable from the licensed technology without being required to allow the licensee to use the now-improved technology after the expiry of the licence agreement.[77]

According to Article 5(1)(b), neither direct nor indirect hindrances may be put in the way of the licensee's possibility of challenging the validity or the confidential or significant character of the licensor's intellectual property rights within the internal market (non-challenge clause).

The purpose of excluding non-challenge clauses from the block exemption is to avoid disputes arising about whether an intellectual property right is valid at all. It will normally be the licensee who will have the best qualification for assessing whether an intellectual property right is valid and if the licensee does not have the possibility of intervening, a non-challenge clause will contribute to creating a fluid and uncertain situation. The right in question could still serve outwardly as a means for blocking competition and unjustifiably give the licensor who claims that the rights should validly remain in force competitive advantages at the expense of others. The right to challenge intellectual property rights, which has been a topic of particular interest in patent law, reflects the ideal of a system based on well-defined and well-controlled property rights.[78]

> A condition that the licensor will have the right to terminate a contract if the licensee challenges the validity of one or more parts of the licensed technology is covered by the block exemption; *see* the reservation in Article 5(1)(b). The licensor is thus not forced to continue dealing with a licensee who challenges the very subject matter of the licence agreement; *see* paragraph 138 of the Guidelines. If, after termination of the licence, the licensee continues to use the challenged technology, this will be at its own risk. The significance of Article 5(1)(b) is thus primarily that it ensures that the block exemption does not cover contractual obligations that prevent the licensee from challenging the licensed technology. In this case, the licensor

---

76. *See* para. 130 of the Guidelines; and Commission Decision 85/410/EEC, *Velcro/Aplix* (OJ 1985 L 233/22), which pre-dates Regulation (EC) No 772/2004 and Regulation (EU) No 316/2014. *See also* Valentine Korah: *Technology Transfer Agreements and the EC Competition Rules*, pp. 160–161, 1996.
77. However, for a contrary view, *see* Valentine Korah: *Technology Transfer Agreements and the EC Competition Rules*, p. 171, 1996.
78. On the Commission's changing approach to non-challenge clauses, *see* Valentine Korah: *Technology Transfer Agreements and the EC Competition Rules*, pp. 180–186, 1996, and Case 65/86, *Bayer and Hennecke v. Süllhöfer*.

will have the possibility of suing the licensee for breach of contract and thus deter the licensee from further challenging the validity of the intellectual property rights. The provision thus ensures that the licensee's position is equivalent to that of any third party.

7.3 Article 5(2)

Article 5(2) provides that the exemption provided for in Article 2 does not apply to any direct or indirect obligation in technology transfer agreements between non-competing undertakings which limits the licensee's right to exploit its own technology rights or limits the ability of any of the parties to the agreement to carry out research and development. However, this restriction does not apply if it is necessary to prevent the disclosure of the licensed know-how to third parties.

> The restriction in Article 5(2) corresponds to the hardcore restriction referred to in Article 4(1)(d), relating to agreements between competing undertakings; *see* section 6.1.3.4 above. As regards agreements between non-competing undertakings, it is the Commission's view that it cannot be assumed that such restrictions generally have a negative effect on competition, or that the conditions in Article 101(3) TFEU are generally not fulfilled; *see* paragraph 141 of the Guidelines. Therefore, in these cases there is a need for an individual assessment.

7.4 Other Block Exemption Regulations

There are other licensing agreements that are governed by special block exemption regulations. Regulation (EU) No 316/2014 does not apply to areas which have their own block exemption regulations. This concerns specific licensing agreements in connection with two types of agreements; *see* Article 9 of the Regulation:

- Research and development agreements; *see* Regulation (EU) No 1217/2010 on the application of Article 101(3) of the TFEU to certain categories of research and development agreements.
- Specialization agreements; *see* Regulation (EU) No 1218/2010 on the application of Article 101(3) of the TFEU to certain categories of specialization agreements.

8 WITHDRAWAL OF THE BLOCK EXEMPTION IN INDIVIDUAL CASES

8.1 Article 6 of Regulation (EU) No 316/2014

Corresponding to the provisions in Articles 6 and 7 of Regulation (EU) No 316/2014 on the possibility for the Commission and the competition authorities in the individual

Member States to withdraw exemptions given under it, under Article 6(1) of Regulation (EC) No 772/2004, and in accordance with Article 29(1) of Council Regulation (EC) No 1/2003, the Commission can withdraw a block exemption if, in the individual case, it finds that a technology transfer agreement in fact gives rise to effects that are incompatible with the conditions in Article 101(3) TFEU, and in particular where:

(a) access of third parties technologies to the market is restricted, for instance, by the cumulative effect of parallel networks of similar restrictive agreements prohibiting licensees from using third parties' technologies;
(b) access of potential licensees to the market is restricted, for instance, by the cumulative effect of parallel networks of similar restrictive agreements prohibiting licensors from granting licenses to other licensees or because the only owner of relevant technology rights enters into an exclusive licensing agreement with a licensee who is already active on the product market on the basis of substitutable technology rights.

8.2 Article 6.2

According to Article 6(2), corresponding to the powers given to the Commission under Article 6(1), the competition authority of *a Member State* may withdraw a block exemption if a technology transfer agreement has unintended effects in the territory of the Member State, or a part thereof which has all the characteristics of a distinct territorial market.

According to paragraph 148 of the Guidelines, the reason for the rules in Article 6 is that Articles 4 and 5, on hardcore restrictions and provisions that are not covered by the block exemption, do not sufficiently take account of the effects of an agreement on third parties. Depending on the circumstances, a licence agreement could lead to the exclusion of third parties, both as licensors and as licensees.

The exclusion of other licensors from the market can stem from the cumulative effect of networks of licence agreements which oblige licensees not to use competing technologies. The exclusion of other licensees from the market can also be the result of the cumulative effect of licences, which obliges the licensor not to grant licences to other licensees so that other potential licensees are denied access to the necessary technology.

The aim of granting the block exemption that there will be efficiency-enhancing activities will thus not be realised, and in the case of licensing between competitors, the fact that the parties do not exploit the licensed technology may be an indication that the arrangement is a disguised cartel; *see* paragraph 59 of the Guidelines.

In paragraph 59 of the Guidelines, the Commission states that for these reasons, it will examine cases of non-exploitation very closely.

If a block exemption is withdrawn in accordance with Article 6, which will presumably be a seldom-used safety valve, the burden of proof is on the authority withdrawing the exemption to show that the agreement falls within the scope of Article

101(1) TFEU and does not fulfil the conditions of Article 101(3); *see* paragraph 146 of the Guidelines.[79]

8.3 Article 7

According to Article 7 of Regulation (EU) No 316/2014, the Commission may, by a regulation, declare that a block exemption does not apply where parallel networks of similar technology transfer agreements cover more than 50% of a relevant market. Such a measure is not directed against individual undertakings but concerns all undertakings whose agreements are defined in the regulation withdrawing the block exemption. A regulation withdrawing a block exemption adopted in accordance with Article 7 would merely annul the block exemption in relation to the restrictions and markets in question so that Article 101(1) and (3) TFEU would again apply in full; *see* paragraphs 149 and 150 of the Guidelines.

Bibliography

Richard Whish & David Bailey: *Competition Law*, 2015.
Stefano Barazza: *The Technology Transfer Block Exemption Regulation and Related Guidelines: Competition Law and IP licensing in the EU*, 2014.
Steven D. Anderman & Hedvig Schmidt: *EU Competition Law and Intellectual Property Rights*, 2nd ed. 2011.
Suzanne Rab: *New EU Technology Transfer Block Exemption: A Note of Caution*, 2014.
Valentine Korah: *Franchising and the EC Competition Rules*, 1989.
Valentine Korah: *Technology Transfer Agreements*, 1996.

---

[79]. As far as can be determined, the withdrawal of an exemption, or the threat of such, has only been practised by the Commission in Case T-51/89, *Tetra Pak Rausing v. Commission,* where the Commission persuaded Tetra Pak to surrender an exclusive licence which the undertaking had acquired from a competing undertaking, and would thereby have been in a position to make a number of users of Tetra Pak's products dependant on Tetra Pak. The decision thus raised the question of whether Art. 86 [now Art. 102 TFEU] of the Treaty could have been applied, even if the block exemption had not yet been withdrawn. The CJ answered this in the affirmative, as the block exemption would otherwise mean that Tetra Pak would be protected from sanctions under Art. 86 [now Art. 102 TFEU].

CHAPTER 6
Abuse of Dominant Position

1   INTRODUCTION

Article 102 of the Treaty on the Functioning of the European Union (TFEU), together with the other competition rules, is part of a system which is intended to ensure that competition in the internal market is not distorted. The competitive concerns which relate to dominant undertakings are that as such an undertaking's position in the market is strengthened, so the self-regulatory forces in the market are weakened. Such undertakings are, therefore, able to use a dominant position to restrict supplies to the market or obtain a supernormal profit and act in a way which is harmful to effective and non-distorted competition in the internal market. Article 102 of the Treaty, therefore, states that:

> Any abuse by one or more undertakings of a dominant position within the internal market or in a substantial part of it shall be prohibited as incompatible with the internal market in so far as it may affect trade between Member States.
>   Such abuse may, in particular, consist in:
>
> a. directly or indirectly imposing unfair purchase or selling prices or other unfair trading conditions;
> b. limiting production, markets or technical development to the prejudice of consumers;
> c. applying dissimilar conditions to equivalent transactions with other trading parties, thereby placing them at a competitive disadvantage;
> d. making the conclusion of contracts subject to acceptance by the other parties of supplementary obligations which, by their nature or according to commercial usage, have no connection with the subject of such contracts.

The specific conditions for the application of the prohibition in Article 102 to the unilateral conduct of an undertaking are thus: (1) that there is an undertaking; (2) that the undertaking has a dominant position in a substantial part of the internal market; (3)

that this dominant position is abused; and (4) that this abuse affects trade between the Member States.

While Article 101 is directed at multilateral conduct based on agreements between undertakings, Article 102 is directed at unilateral conduct, which has negative consequences for competition and trade within the internal market as a result of the market dominance of an undertaking.[1] Article 102 is thus only directed at cases where an undertaking abuses its dominant position. The prohibition of abuse of dominant position in TFEU is complemented by the Digital Markets Act (DMA), which regulates core digital platforms with considerable economic power – the so-called *gatekeepers*.[2] The Act imposes a number of obligations on gatekeeper platforms with the aim of preventing unfair behaviour and practices towards businesses and end users having a major negative impact on the access to the market.[3] There is no prohibition on an undertaking having or acquiring a dominant position, nor is the strengthening of a dominant position prohibited by Article 102, as long as it is not strengthened as a result of abuse of the dominant position. Thus, for example, a dominant undertaking will lawfully be able to have a pricing policy which increases its market share, as long as the prices cannot be characterised as abuse, for example, in the form of unlawful predatory pricing.[4]

However, if a dominant position is created or strengthened in relation to a merger, the merger may be declared incompatible with the internal market and, therefore, prohibited if the merger significantly impedes effective competition within the internal market or a substantial part of it.[5] Regardless of Article 21 of the Merger Regulation, the complementary application of the merger control rules and Article 102 does not exclude the application of Article 102 in relation to merger transactions which fall below the thresholds for notification, for example, if a dominant undertaking acquires innovative start-ups to prevent future competition (*killer acquisitions*).[6]

Article 102, second paragraph, lists forms of conduct which constitute an abuse covered by the prohibition. However, this list is not exhaustive, and is supplemented by other forms of abuse which appear from the practice of the Court of Justice of the European Union (CJ). In contrast to Article 101, Article 102 does not make provision for exemptions from the prohibition of certain kinds of conduct.[7] If an undertaking's

---

1. For a more detailed discussion of the distinction between unilateral and multilateral actions, *see* Ch. 2, s. 2.1.
2. EP&Rfo 2022/1937 of 14 September 2022 on contestable and fair markets in the digital sector (Digital Markets Act), (OJ 2022 L 265/1). Different forms of abusive behaviour previously addressed in practice under Art. 102 that may be conducted by digital platforms are addressed in the Act.
3. Forms of abuse that digital platforms risk to carry out, as for example *self-preferencing*, *see* Case T-612/17, *Google and Alphabet (Google shopping)*, have found their way into the Act as preventive obligations.
4. On the limits to predatory pricing, *see* s. 4.1.2.
5. *See* Art. 2, ss 2 and 3 of EC Merger Regulation 139/2004 (OJ 2004 L24/1). Also *see* Ch. VIII, s. 4.
6. *See* further in Case C-449/21, *Towercast*.
7. Joined Cases T-191/98 and T-212/98 to T-214/98, *Atlantic Container Line and others v. Commission*, para. 1455. However, *see also* Case C-377/20, *Servizio Elettrico Nazionale*, para. 103, in which the possibility to argue objective justifications or efficiency gains is characterised as an exemption (*see also* para. 84 in the judgment).

conduct can be characterised as abuse, it will not be possible to allow the abuse, and it will be prohibited in all circumstances.

Nevertheless, according to a number of decisions, it is possible that some disputed conduct may be objectively justifiable.[8] This means that a dominant undertaking can, for example, take measures to protect its trading interests when these are threatened, as long as it complies with the principle of proportionality.[9] Such objectively justified conduct is not characterised as abuse and, therefore, does not fall within the scope of application of Article 102.[10]

The fact that a dominant undertaking's conduct leads to efficiency advantages can also mean that such conduct will not be characterised as abuse.[11] When assessing the application of Article 102 of the Treaty to exclusionary abuses, the Commission will, therefore, include efficiency improvements in its analysis.[12]

Article 102 only prohibits the abuse of a dominant position to the extent that trade between the Member States is affected. This condition limits the scope of the provision in relation to national law.

Article 102 has direct effect in national law. Thus, it is possible for natural and legal persons to rely on the provision directly in national courts, and national courts have jurisdiction and an obligation to apply the provision in order to protect the rights which Article 102 gives to the parties involved.[13] In addition to this, national competition authorities have the power to apply Article 102 in individual cases.[14] This means that the authorities do not have the power to lay down general rules on the application of the Treaty provisions, such as the block exemption regulations laid down by the Commission in relation to Article 101 of the Treaty.

As will be shown below, the CJ interprets Article 102 in the light of its purpose, in other words to prevent dominant undertakings abusing their market position. This means that a broad interpretation of the scope and conditions of the provision is generally applied.

---

8. Case C-163/99, *Portugal v. Commission*, para. 53; Case T-83/91, *Tetra Pak II*, paras 115, 136 and 207; Case C-52/09, *TeliaSonera*, paras 31 and 75; Case C-209/10, *Post Danmark*, paras 40 and 41, Case C-307/18, *Generics*, para. 165, and Case C-377/20, *Servizio Elettrico Nazionale*, paras 84 and 103.
9. Case 27/76, *United Brands*, paras 189–190.
10. *See* the Opinion of Advocate General Jacobs in Case C-53/03, *Syfait*, point 72.
11. Case C-209/10, *Post Danmark*, paras 41 and 42.
12. Communication from the Commission – Guidance on the Commission's enforcement priorities in applying Art. 82 of the EC Treaty to abusive exclusionary conduct by dominant undertakings (OJ 2009 C 45/7), as amended in Amendments to the Communication from the Commission, (OJ 2023 C116/1). Along with the publication of the Amendments, the Commission on 27 March 2023 started a process with a view to adopt a revised Communication.
13. Case 123/73, *BRT II*; and Council Regulation (EC) No 1/2003 on the implementation of the rules on competition laid down in Arts 81 and 82 of the Treaty, Art. 6 (OJ 2003 L 1/1). (The Regulation is currently subject to an evaluation process aiming at adapting the Regulation to the demands posed by the increased digitalisation of the market economy. A working document with the results of the evaluation process is expected to be available in the second quarter of 2024.
14. Article 5 of Regulation (EC) No 1/2003. For a further discussion of the powers of national authorities and courts, *see* Ch. 7, s. 4.2.

2 THE MEANING OF AN *UNDERTAKING*

In relation to Article 102 and the other provisions on competition, the term *undertaking* is defined by the CJ as covering any entity which carries on economic activity, regardless of the legal status of the entity or the method by which it is financed.[15] In this context, any activity which consists of offering goods or services for sale on a market constitutes an economic activity.[16] It is not necessary to separate an activity which consists of purchasing goods from the subsequent use of the goods in order to assess whether an activity is an economic activity. It is the economic or non-economic nature of the subsequent use of a product which necessarily determines the nature of the activity.[17]

In order to fall within the scope of the concept of an undertaking, it will be sufficient if the undertaking, in fact, carries on economic activity. This means that the CJ does not require that the activities of the undertaking should be carried on for profit.[18] This means that non-profit organisations[19] are also covered by the term *undertaking*.

Both private and public undertakings can be an undertaking for the purposes of competition law.[20] This follows not only from the practice of the CJ but also from Article 106 TFEU and the Transparency Directive,[21] which states that public undertakings are subject to the Treaty's competition rules.[22]

The CJ does not make any special demands as to the legal form of undertakings. This means that public limited companies, private limited companies, trusts, mutual institutions, one-man businesses, etc., are all covered by the concept of an undertaking. For public bodies, for the purposes of the definition of an undertaking, it does not matter whether the body in question is a separate legal entity or whether it is part of the central government administration.[23] However, the concept of an undertaking does not cover the exercise of public authority, for example, the collection of air navigation fees from airlines[24] or carrying out tasks of a social character, such as the administration of

---

15. Case C-41/90, *Hofner & Elser*, para. 21; Case C-280/06, *ETI and others*, para. 38 and Case C-74/16, *Congregación de Escuelas Pías Provincia Betania*, para. 41. The concept of an undertaking in relation to Art. 102 does not differ from the concept of an undertaking in relation to Art. 101. For further discussion of the concept, *see* Ch. 2, s. 3.1.
16. Case T-155/04, *Eurocontrol*, para. 50; and Case T-81-83/07, *Jan Rudolf Maas*, para. 178.
17. Case C-113/07 P, *Selex*, para. 102; and Case C-205/03, *FENIN*, para. 26.
18. Case C-41/90, *Höfner & Elser*, paras 19–23.
19. Case C-437/09, *AG2R*, para. 65.
20. Case C-74/16, *Congregación de Escuelas Pías Provincia Betania*, para. 42.
21. Commission Directive 2006/111/EC on the transparency of financial relations between Member States and public undertakings as well as on financial transparency within certain undertakings (OJ 2006 L 318/17). Art. 106 is discussed in more detail in Ch. 9.
22. Subject to the reservation for undertakings covered by Art. 106(2). Moreover, under Art. 345 of the Treaty, public and private undertakings must be treated equally under the competition rules, as the Treaties do not affect systems of property law in the Member States.
23. Case 118/85, *Commission v. Italy*, para. 13; Case C-69/91, *Decoster*, para. 15; and Case C-92/91, *Taillandier*, para. 14.
24. Case C-364/92, *Eurocontrol*, para. 30.

health insurance and pension arrangements.[25] If a public entity exercises several different kinds of activity, each of the different activities must be examined to determine whether it should be classified as an economic activity.[26] If an economic activity cannot be separated from the exercise of a public entity's public power, the activity should, however, be regarded as part of the exercise of those public powers.[27]

3 DOMINANT POSITION

In order for conduct to be in breach of Article 102, an undertaking must have a dominant position in the internal market or in a substantial part of the internal market. The term *dominant position* is defined by the CJ as:

> a position of economic strength enjoyed by an undertaking which enables it to prevent effective competition being maintained on the relevant market by affording it the power to behave to an appreciable extent independently of its competitors, its customers and ultimately of the consumers.[28] An undertaking with sufficient buyer power will also be able to hold a dominant position.[29]

What is decisive is the ability of the undertaking concerned to behave to an appreciable extent independently of its competitors, its customers and ultimately of the consumers. The assessment of this is made on the basis of the economic circumstances that apply at the time of the alleged abuse.

The legal definition of when an undertaking can be considered to be dominant has been criticised as being unusable in practice. The reason for this is that the ability of a dominant undertaking to act independently of its competitors, customers and consumers does not differ significantly from the ability of a non-dominant undertaking to act independently.[30]

The ability to act independently in the terms described depends on the market strength of an undertaking in the relevant market. The undertaking should thus have a market strength which enables it 'if not to determine, at least to have an appreciable influence on the conditions under which that competition will develop, and in any case to act largely in disregard of it so long as such conduct does not operate to its detriment.'[31]

---

25. Joined Cases C-264, 306, and 354–355/01, *AOK*, paras 47 and 55; and Case T-319/99, *FENIN*, paras 38 39. See also Case T-155/04, *Eurocontrol*, where the Court held that Eurocontrol's activities concerning technical standardisation were not an economic activity, (para. 69), nor were the research and development activities which Eurocontrol financed (para. 82), while Eurocontrol's activities in the form of providing technical support for national authorities was an economic activity (para. 92). See also, in more detail, the distinction between the exercise of public authority and the concept of an undertaking in Ch. 2, s. 3.2.
26. Case 74/16, *Congregación de Escuelas Pias Provincia Betania*, para. 44.
27. Case C-138/11, *Compass-Datenbank*, paras 35–39.
28. Case 85/76, *Hoffmann-La Roche*, para. 38; Case T-193/02, *Laurent Piau*, para. 109; and Case C-52/09, *TeliaSonera*, para. 23.
29. Case T-219/99, *British Airways*.
30. See João Pearce Azevedo & Mike Walker: Dominance: Meaning and Measurement, European Competition Law Review 2002 pp. 363–367.
31. Case 85/76, *Hoffmann-La Roche*, para. 39.

Whether or not an undertaking has the necessary market strength depends on the undertaking's market share, as well as on a number of other factors, such as the barriers to entry to the market, the relative market shares of competitors, etc. The market strength of an undertaking will thus be the result of a combination of these different factors, though without these factors necessarily being decisive in themselves. However, where an undertaking has a comprehensive market share, this will be highly relevant to the assessment of dominance.[32] On the contrary, the smaller the market share of an undertaking, the more significant seems to be the role of the other factors, so there is a need to assess whether the other elements indicate the existence of a dominant position.

3.1 One or More Undertakings: Collective Dominance

According to Article 102, the provision is applicable to the abuse of a dominant position by *one or more undertakings*. In a narrow sense, this wording covers, first, an individual undertaking's abuse of a dominant position. Next, it covers abuse of a dominant position, which is the result of the collective conduct of several independent legal entities which belong to the same group of companies and which, therefore, constitute a *collective economic entity* which is considered to be a single entity for the purposes of competition law.[33]

It is also clear from the practice of the courts that the reference to more than one undertaking can be understood so that several entities which are financially and legally independent of each other and which are therefore not considered as one undertaking for the purposes of competition law, can together have a dominant position.[34] If such undertakings act collectively, there will not be genuine competition between the parties.[35]

In deciding whether Article 102 is applicable in this context, an assessment must first be made of whether the undertakings concerned constitute a collective entity. If this is the case, it is next necessary to examine whether the collective entity does, in fact, have a dominant position and, third, whether this dominant position is abused.[36]

---

32. Case 85/76, *Hoffmann-La Roche*, para. 39; and Case T-340/03, *France Télécom*, para. 100. *See also* Case C-23/14, *Post Danmark II*, para. 40: 'An undertaking which has a very large market share is by virtue of that share in a position of strength which makes it an unavoidable trading partner and which secures for it freedom of action.'
33. Case 6/72, *Continental Can*. The interpretation of the concept of an economic entity has in practice been developed determine the relationship between a parent company and its subsidiaries. However under certain circumstances, the conduct of a distributor may also be attributed the dominant company, *see* in this regard Case C-680/20, *Unilever*, para. 33: '...actions of distributors forming part of the distribution network for goods and services of a producer in a dominant position may be imputed to that producer if it is established that those actions were not adopted independently by those distributors, but form part of a policy that is decided unilaterally by that producer and implemented through those distributors'.
34. Joined Cases T-68, 77 and 78/89, *Italian Flat Glass*, para. 358.
35. Case C-96/94, *Centro Zervizi Spediporto*, para. 34.
36. Joined Cases C-395–396/96 P, *CMB*, para. 39.

Collective dominance can exist where, in economic terms, two or more economic entities which are legally independent of each other present themselves or act together on a particular market as a collective entity.[37]

In assessing this, an examination is made of the mutual economic cooperation and the mutual economic relations between the undertakings concerned, among other things, in order to determine whether such economic cooperation exists between the undertakings and whether they act independently of their competitors, customers and, ultimately, their consumers.[38]

The case law does not clearly define what forms of economic activity (and legal relationships) are decisive for this assessment, but in this connection, the CJ has emphasised that collective dominance cannot be established solely on the basis that there may be an agreement, decision or concerted practice between the parties involved, within the meaning of Article 101(1).[39] However, when such an agreement, etc., is implemented, this can mean that the undertakings involved are bound with regard to their conduct on a given market so as to act on the market as a collective entity.[40] Thus, depending on the nature or wording of an agreement, from the way in which it is implemented, and the consequent cooperation and relations between the undertakings, a collective dominant position can be found to exist.[41]

However, there need not be an agreement or other legal connection between the undertakings involved in order for a collective entity to be found to exist. Such a collective entity can be found to exist on the basis of other relations between the undertakings involved and requires an economic assessment to be made, as well as an assessment of the structure of the relevant market.[42]

In practice, collective dominance may be found to exist both on a contractual basis and on the basis of an economic connection between the undertakings involved. In the *Italian Flat Glass* case, the CJ gave the example that an economic connection can exist where, through agreements or licences, two or more independent undertakings jointly have a technological lead, affording them the power to act independently to an appreciable extent.[43] Other examples could be cross-shareholdings, common directorships, family links,[44] and the pursuit of a common marketing strategy or sales policy.[45]

Where several undertakings are found to constitute a collective entity, it is the collective entity as such which must fulfil the conditions for the existence of a dominant position in a substantial part of the internal market, as well as the conditions for the existence of abuse of that dominant position. Thus, there can be an infringement of

---

37. Joined Cases C-395–396/96 P, *CMB*, para. 36.
38. Joined Cases C-395–396/96 P, *CMB*, para. 41.
39. Joined Cases C-395–396/96 P, *CMB*, para. 43.
40. Joined Cases C-395–396/96 P, *CMB*, para. 44. *See also* Case T-193/02, *Laurent Piau*, discussed below in s. 3.1.1.
41. Joined Cases C-395–396/96 P, *CMB*, para. 45.
42. Joined Cases C-395–396/96 P, *CMB*, para. 45, and Case C-413/06, *Bertelsmann*, para. 119.
43. Joined Cases T-68, 77 and 78/89, *Italian Flat Glass*, para. 358. *See also* Case T-193/02, *Laurent Piau*, discussed below in s. 3.1.1.
44. *See* the Opinion of Advocate General Fennelly in Joined Cases C-395–396/96 P, *CMB*, point 28.
45. Case C-393/92, *Almelo*, para. 42; Case 30/87, *Bodson;* and Joined Cases 40/73 etc., *Suiker Unie*.

Article 102 even if the individual undertakings could not in themselves be considered dominant within the meaning of Article 102, and regardless of whether all the undertakings or only one of the undertakings engages in conduct which can be characterised as an abuse of the collective dominance.[46]

3.1.1 Oligopolistic Market Structure

The possibility of using Article 102 to sanction undertakings' abuse of a collective dominant position is particularly relevant where the market structure is characterised by having few large market participants (duopoly or oligopoly) and where the Commission is unable to prove that apparently coordinated conduct between the undertakings concerned is due to a concerted practice covered by Article 101, rather than by the oligopolistic market structure.[47]

On such oligopolistic markets, there will be assumed to be a collective dominant position as long as three cumulative conditions are fulfilled:

> First, each member of the dominant oligopoly must have the ability to know how the other members are behaving in order to monitor whether or not they are adopting the common policy; second, the situation of tacit coordination must be sustainable over time, that is to say, there must be an incentive not to depart from the common policy on the market; thirdly, the foreseeable reaction of current and future competitors, as well as of consumers, must not jeopardise the results expected from the common policy.[48]

On this basis, in Case T-193/02, *Laurent Piau*, the General Court held that FIFA had a collective dominant position:

> In the present case, the market affected by the rules in question is a market for the provision of services where the buyers are players and clubs and the sellers are agents. In this market FIFA can be regarded as acting on behalf of football clubs since, as has already been stated ... it constitutes an emanation of those clubs as a second-level association of undertakings formed by the clubs.
>
> A decision like the FIFA Players' Agents Regulations may, where it is implemented, result in the undertakings operating on the market in question, namely the clubs, being so linked as to their conduct on a particular market that they present themselves on that market as a collective entity vis-à-vis their competitors, their trading partners and consumers.
>
> Because the regulations are binding for national associations that are members of FIFA and the clubs forming them, these bodies appear to be linked in the long term as to their conduct by rules that they accept and that other actors (players and players' agents) cannot break on pain of sanctions that may lead to their exclusion from the market, in particular in the case of players' agents. ... such

---

46. Case T-228/97, *Irish Sugar*, para. 66, confirmed by the ruling of the CJ in Case C-497/99 P. See also Case C-393/92, *Almelo*, para. 51.
47. See also Ch. 8, s. 4.3, on collective dominance in relation to merger control.
48. Case T-193/02, *Laurent Piau*, para. 111. The judgment refers to the conditions which were laid down in connection with assessment of collective dominance for the purposes of the Merger Control Regulation in Case T-342/99, *Airtours*, para. 62, as confirmed in Case T-374/00, *Verband der freien Rohrwerke*, para. 121. On collective dominance in connection with the Merger Control Regulation, *see* Ch. 8, s. 4.3.

a situation therefore characterises a collective dominant position for clubs on the market for the provision of players' agents' services, since, through the rules to which they adhere, the clubs lay down the conditions under which the services in question are provided.[49]

However, the CFI did not find that it had been established that FIFA had abused its dominant position, as the rules did not lay down quantitative restrictions on the right to act as a players' agent, which were harmful to competition, but rather that the restrictions were qualitative and could be justified in the circumstances.[50]

3.2 Relevant Factors for Assessing Market Dominance

An undertaking's dominant position on the relevant market is generally due to a combination of a number of factors, which are not necessarily decisive in themselves.[51] If an undertaking has a large market share, this will be a strong indication that it has market dominance,[52] but both the market shares of competitors and barriers to market entry by actual or potential competitors could overturn an assumption of market dominance.[53] The same can apply if the undertaking's customers have negotiating strength such that the undertaking cannot act autonomously.[54]

3.2.1 Market Share

The structure of a market can mean that an undertaking is in possession of the whole market because of a monopoly in law or in fact.[55] Where such an undertaking is not exposed to actual or potential competition, it will be assumed that it has a dominant position within the terms of Article 102.[56]

In other cases too, the possession of a very large market share will also, in itself, be regarded as evidence that an undertaking has a dominant position, unless there are unusual circumstances.[57]

> In Case T-83/91, *Tetra Pak II*, the CFI found that the undertaking concerned with 90% market share had a dominant position. Likewise, in Case 85/76,

---

49. Case T-193/02, *Laurent Piau*, paras 112–114.
50. Case T-193/02, *Laurent Piau*, para. 118.
51. Case C-250/92, *Gøttrup-Klim*, para. 47.
52. Case C-250/92, *Gøttrup-Klim*, para. 48. *See also* Case C-23/14, *Post Danmark II*, para. 40.
53. Communication from the Commission – Guidance on the Commission's enforcement priorities in applying Art. 82 of the EC Treaty to abusive exclusionary conduct by dominant undertakings, point 7 (OJ 2009 C 45/7) (as amended).
54. Communication from the Commission – Guidance on the Commission's enforcement priorities in applying Art. 82 of the EC Treaty to abusive exclusionary conduct by dominant undertakings, points 12 and 18 (OJ 2009 C 45/7) (as amended).
55. *See* Commission Decision of 27.06.2017 in Case AT.39740, *Google Search (Shopping)*, where Google with a market share of more than 90% of the market for general search services in the vast majority of the EU and EEA countries is getting close to a de facto monopoly. *See* the Decision, s. 6.
56. Case 127/73, *BRT II*; and Case C-260/89, *ERT*.
57. Case 85/76, *Hoffmann-La Roche*, para. 41.

Hoffmann-La Roche, where the undertaking had a market share of 75%, it was found to have a dominant position in the relevant market for vitamins.[58]

In this context, a *very large market share* appears to include market shares of 50% or more of the relevant market so that a market share of this size can, in itself, be regarded as evidence of an undertaking's dominant position.[59] However, regardless of this, the CJ will often assess whether other factors, in particular the relative market shares of competitors, indicate that the undertaking has a dominant position,[60] so there only appears to be a strong presumption or indication of the existence of a dominant position that can actually be rebutted.

Depending on the circumstances, an undertaking that has a market share of less than 50% of the relevant market can also be considered to be dominant. However, this will often require other relevant factors to support the finding.[61]

However, the Commission regards it as unlikely that there will be a dominant position if an undertaking has a market share of less than 40% of the relevant market unless there are special circumstances.[62]

If an undertaking has a market share of less than 25%, it is unlikely it could be considered to have a dominant position.[63] As for market shares of less than 10%, these are clearly insufficient for the undertaking concerned to be considered dominant.[64]

Undertakings which, in accordance with the above, are not regarded in themselves as having a dominant position for the purposes of Article 102 are not excluded from the possibility of having a collective dominant position, together with other undertakings, as discussed in section 3.1.

However, it is not only an undertaking's absolute market share that is relevant to an assessment of dominance. In certain cases, it will also be relevant to examine the relative market share of an undertaking, in other words, an undertaking's market share compared with its competitors' market shares.[65] The structure of the market can thus be relevant to the size of a market share for assessing dominance.

For example, this will be the case where the market is characterised by having many participants, and where the undertaking concerned has a market share which is

---

58. Case 85/76, *Hoffmann-La Roche*, paras 41 and 56.
59. Case C-62/86, *AKZO*, para. 60; Case T-340/03, *France Télécom*, para. 100, and Case T-336/07, *Telefónica*, para. 150.
60. Case 322/81, *Michelin*, para. 52; Case T-30/89, *Hilti*, paras 92 and 93, and Case T-219/99, *British Airways*, para. 210.
61. In Case 27/76, *United Brands*, the CJ found that a market share of 40%–45% was not in itself sufficient for an undertaking to be regarded as dominant; see para. 48. See also Case 85/76, *Hoffmann-La Roche*, paras 57–58.
62. There can be special cases below this threshold where competitors are not sufficiently able to restrict the conduct of an undertaking and where there can therefore be dominance. Communication from the Commission – Guidance on the Commission's enforcement priorities in applying Art. 82 of the EC Treaty to abusive exclusionary conduct by dominant undertakings, point 14 (OJ 2009 C 45/7 (as amended).
63. In relation to mergers, this is indicated in Recital 32 of the Merger Control Regulation.
64. Case 75/84, *Metro SB-Großmärkte v. Commission (Metro II)*, paras 85 and 86.
65. See, e.g., Joined Cases T-24/93 and others, *CMB*, para. 78, and Case T-219/99, *British Airways*, para. 210.

relatively greater than its competitors. The smaller the competitors' market shares in relation to the share of the undertaking concerned, the greater the probability that the undertaking will be considered to have a dominant position.[66] In this context, the collective relative market share of several undertakings can form the basis for a finding of the existence of collective dominance.

Another factor that can be significant for deciding whether an undertaking is dominant is how the market share has developed over time.[67] If, over a longer period, an undertaking has had a very large market share, and undertakings with considerably smaller market shares are unable quickly to meet a demand which the undertaking in question no longer wishes to meet, this can mean that the undertaking is an indispensable business connection for its customers, and is therefore dominant.[68]

In Case 85/76, *Hoffmann-La Roche*, on the basis of an investigation into market shares over a period of three years, the CJ found that the undertaking had a dominant position.[69] However, the practice of the courts has not defined precisely what is meant by a *longer period* but seems to emphasise that it is relevant the undertaking has shown an ability to maintain a high market share for a sufficiently long time that it can have the kind of conduct that is characteristic of a dominant position.[70] In Case T-340/03, *France Telecom*, Wanadoo held a dominant position for a period of one year and eight months.[71]

3.2.2 Other Factors

In practice, when assessing whether an undertaking can be considered to have a dominant position on the relevant market, it is seldom sufficient to look only at the market share of the undertaking. Market share is thus calculated with regard to the effective and immediate competitive pressure to which the undertaking is subject. An assessment of an undertaking's market strength will often require other factors, which may express the potential competitive pressure, to be taken into consideration. While *effective and immediate* competition refers to competition from substitutable products

---

66. Thus, given that its closest competitors' market shares were 14.8% and 6.3%, in Case 85/76, *Hoffmann-La Roche*, the CJ found that the undertaking had a dominant position in the market for Vitamin C when it had a market share of 64.8%.
67. Communication from the Commission – Guidance on the Commission's enforcement priorities in applying Art. 82 of the EC Treaty to abusive exclusionary conduct by dominant undertakings, point 13 (OJ 2009 C 45/7) (as amended).
68. Case 85/76, *Hoffmann-La Roche*, para. 41; and Case T-83/91, *Tetra Pak II*, para. 109, and Case T-336/07, *Telefónica*, para. 149.
69. See also Joined cases T-191/90 and others, *Atlantic Container Line*, para. 920.
70. Case 85/76, *Hoffmann-La Roche*, para. 41, Case T-83/91, *Tetra Pak II*, para. 109, and Case T-336/07, *Telefónica*, para. 149. However, the maintenance of a market share over a longer period does not automatically mean that the undertaking is dominant; Case 85/76, *Hoffmann-La Roche*, para. 44. In Communication from the Commission – Guidance on the Commission's enforcement priorities in applying Art. 82 of the EC Treaty to abusive exclusionary conduct by dominant undertakings, note 6, (OJ 2009 C 45/7) (as amended), it is stated that a period of two years will normally be sufficient.
71. Case T-340/03, *France Telecom*, paras 102–103. Furthermore, it was emphasised in para. 104 that a decline in this marked share, which was still very high, could not in itself constitute proof of absence of a dominant position.

and services (demand substitution), and undertakings which already produce or can switch at short notice to produce the relevant (substitutable) products and market them (supply substitution), *potential competition* covers the competitive pressure from undertakings which only have the possibility, over the medium to long term, of switching to the production of relevant (substitutable) products, as well as new entrants to the market, requiring an assessment of the likelihood, timeframe and magnitude of any entry.[72]

Potential competitive pressure from potential competitors will be limited by barriers to entry into the market. The existence of such barriers is thus necessary for an undertaking to be able to maintain a dominant position, as the undertaking would not be able, in the longer term, to abuse its position in order to obtain a supernormal profit without potential competitors, thereby being attracted to a freely accessible market.[73]

When assessing whether an undertaking has a market share which makes it dominant within the meaning of Article 102, it is necessary to take into consideration whether there are any legal or actual barriers to entry to the market which make it difficult or impossible for potential competitors to enter the market in question in the longer term.

Such barriers to entry can be, for example, a monopoly based on law,[74] intellectual property rights,[75] or public regulation of the conduct of business in the market concerned.[76] The cost and competitive advantages of undertakings that are already established on a market will also be barriers to entry. For example, this can be the case with capital-intensive investments (high sunk costs),[77] economies of scale,[78] technological advances,[79] or priority access to natural resources, innovation, research and development,[80] vertical integration – including a well-developed distribution system,[81] and consumer preferences,[82] as well as brand image.[83] Furthermore, switching costs and

---

72. *See* further Commission Notice on the definition of relevant market for the purposes of Union competition law point 23 (OJ C/2024/1645, 22.2.2024).
73. Communication from the Commission – Guidance on the Commission's enforcement priorities in applying Art. 82 of the EC Treaty to abusive exclusionary conduct by dominant undertakings, point 11 (OJ 2009 C-45/7) (as amended).
74. Case 311/84, *CBEM*, para. 18; and Case C-260/89, *ERT*, para. 31.
75. Joined Cases C-241 and 242/91 P, *Magill*, para. 46. The possession of for example a patent does not necessarily imply that the holder of the patent has a dominant position, cf. Case C-170/13, *Huawei Technologies*, para. 57. *See also* Case C-307/18, *Generics*, para. 46.
76. Commission Decision *Decca Navigator System* (OJ 1989 L 43/27); and Commission Decision *British Midland/Aer Lingus* (OJ 1992 L 96/34).
77. Case 85/76, *Hoffmann-La Roche*, para. 33; and Case 27/76, *United Brands*, paras 122 and 123.
78. *See, e.g.*, Commission Decision of 04.05.2017 in Case AT.40153, *Amazon*, point 65(3).
79. Case T-83/91, *Tetra Pak II*, para. 110; and Case 27/76, *United Brands*, paras 52–54.
80. *See also* Case T-336/07, *Telefónica*, paras 151–167, (the wholesale broadband access market), and the considerations in Commission Decision of 18.07.2018 in Case AT.40099, *Google Android*, points 621–626, (confirmed by the Court in Case T-604/18).
81. Case 27/76, *United Brand*, Case 85/76, *Hoffmann-La Roche, para.* 48, *and* Case 322/81, *Michelin*, para. 58.
82. Commission Decision on interim measures in *BBI/Boosey & Hawkes*, point 18 (OJ 1987 L 286/36).
83. *See, e.g.*, Commission Decisions in Case AT.39711, *Qualcomm (predation)* of 18.07.2019, points 303–310, Case AT.40099, *Google Android*, of 18.07.2018, points 462–463, (confirmed by the

network effects could constitute market barriers,[84] just as an undertaking can create barriers to entry by its conduct on the market, for example, by entering into exclusive distribution arrangements, agreeing tied sales, giving loyalty discounts and by refusal of supply.[85]

3.3 The Relevant Market

The assessment of an undertaking's dominance of a market requires a definition to be made of the market in which, given its market share and the other relevant factors, the undertaking can have a dominant position. This market is referred to as the *relevant market*.

The relevant market is defined both by reference to the relevant product market and the relevant geographic market. In certain circumstances, it can also be necessary to define the relevant market from a time perspective. The purpose of defining the relevant market is to identify the undertaking's actual competitors, in other words, to define who, on the basis of effective and immediate competitive pressure, are able to restrict the conduct of the undertaking in question and thereby prevent it from acting independently. This determines whether there are, in fact, any competitors who can, at short notice, act as alternative sources of supply for the customers of the undertaking in question, both with regard to the relevant products and services and with regard to the geographic location of the suppliers.[86]

The competitive pressure which is taken into consideration when defining the relevant market is, in particular, demand substitution and, under certain circumstances, supply substitution.[87] In economic terms, demand substitution is considered to be the competitive pressure which has the greatest disciplinary influence on an undertaking's pricing.[88] If an undertaking's customers can find alternative suppliers or substitutable products without difficulty, then that undertaking will not be able to behave independently in its pricing.

Supply-side substitution is taken into consideration if it has the same effective and immediate effect as demand substitution. This implies among others that suppliers should be able to

---

Court in Case T-604/18), *Google*, and Case AT.39740, *Google Search (shopping)*, of 27.06.2017, points 286-291, (confirmed by the Court in Case T-612/17, *Google & Alphabet (Google shopping)*).

84. Commission Decisions in Case AT.40099, *Google Android*, of 18.07.2018, points 306-324, (confirmed by the Court in Case T-604/18), *Google*, and Case AT.39740, *Google Search (shopping)*, of 27.06.2017, points 292-296 (confirmed by the Court in Case T-612/17, *Google & Alphabet (Google shopping)*).
85. Case 27/76, *United Brands*, paras 67-68.
86. *See* further Commission Notice on the definition of relevant market for the purposes of Union competition law, points 22-24 (OJ C/2024/1645).
87. Potential competition, which constitutes the one of the three main sources of competitive restraints which an undertaking is subjected to, is not taken into consideration in the definition of the relevant market; *see* Commission Notice on the definition of relevant market for the purposes of Union competition law, point 23(c) (OJ C/2024/1645). On the other hand, it is relevant in assessing the market strength of an undertaking in the relevant market.
88. *See* further Commission Notice on the definition of relevant market for the purposes of Union competition law, points 32-37 (OJ C/2024/1645).

switch production to the relevant products and market them in the short term without incurring significant additional costs or risks in response to small and permanent changes in relative prices.[89] Conversely, it means that supply-side substitution is not taken into consideration when this would entail 'the need to significantly adjust existing tangible and intangible assets outside the core of business; to incur more than insignificant additional investments, sunk costs or risks; to take strategic decisions of a lasting nature, or to incur time delays'.[90]

In determining whether there are any easily available alternative sources of supply for the customers of the undertaking in question, a test is made – the SSNIP test – which examines whether a hypothetical small permanent increase of 5%–10% of the relative price of the products concerned in the area concerned would make the undertaking's customers switch to substitution products or to other suppliers.[91] If the level of substitution is enough to make the price increase unprofitable because of the resulting loss of sales, additional substitutes and areas are included in the relevant market. This is done until the set of products and geographical areas is such that small, permanent increases in relative prices would be profitable. If, on the contrary, the increase means that the undertaking's customers switch to competing alternative sources of supply, and the price increase is unprofitable in relation to the fall in sales, the substitutable products and the alternative suppliers are part of the relevant market.[92]

Once the relevant market has been defined, it is possible to calculate the market share of the undertaking concerned[93] and thereby get a significant indication of the undertaking's market strength with a view to deciding whether it can be regarded as having a dominant position. The definition of the relevant market is thus central to the assessment of whether an undertaking has a dominant position.[94] It is for this reason that the Commission's definition of the relevant market will often be disputed in cases brought before the court for the annulment of decisions.

---

89. *See* further Commission Notice on the definition of relevant market for the purposes of Union competition law, point 34 (OJ C/2024/1645).
90. Commission Notice on the definition of relevant market for the purposes of Union competition law, point 37 (OJ C/2024/1645).
91. Commission Notice on the definition of relevant market for the purposes of Union competition law, point 29 (OJ C/2024/1645). The test is usually called the SSNIP test – 'small but significant non-transitory increase in price'. The Commission can also use other tests for evaluating demand substitution, including, e.g., cross-price elasticities for the demand of a product, *see* point 31 in the Notice, and in case of zero monetary price product, the SSNDQ test – 'small but significant non-transitory decrease of quality', *see* footnote 54 in the Notice. In situations where the price has already been raised to a level above competitive levels, an increase in price may result in a significant change in consumer demand, and the SSNIP test will thus not provide a correct result in respect of determining the substitutability of products. Referring to case *United States v. E.I. du Pont de Nemours & Co*, 351 U.S. 377, 391-91, 1956, this is termed as the Cellophane Fallacy, *see* footnote 55 in the Notice.
92. *See* the explanation in the previous Commission Notice on the definition of relevant market for the purposes of Community competition law, point 17 (OJ 1997 C-372/5).
93. On the calculation of market shares, *see* Commission Notice on the definition of relevant market for the purposes of Union competition law, points 105-113 (OJ C/2024/1645).
94. Previous Commission findings where it has been established that an undertaking is to be regarded as dominant, cannot as such constitute the basis for a future evaluation under Art. 102. Thus, the delineation of the relevant market and an analysis of the conditions of competition must be made again based on the actual market situation at the time of the conduct under investigation, *see* further joined Cases T-125/97 & T-127/97, *Coca-Cola Co*, para. 82.

The established definition of the relevant market is especially challenged by the platform economy and the emergence of two- or more-sided platforms, where direct or indirect network effects may be of importance when determining the relevant market and, thus, the possible market dominance of the specific digital platform. This issue and the delineation of the relevant market in this context and under other special market circumstances have been addressed in the new Commission Notice on the definition of the relevant market.[95]

3.3.1   The Relevant Product Market

The purpose of defining the relevant product market is to define which products are suitable for competing with the products of the undertaking in question. The key word in determining the product market is, therefore, *substitution* – seen from the consumer's point of view.[96] The relevant product market is therefore determined on the basis of those products and/or services which are regarded as interchangeable or substitutable by the consumer, by reason of the products' 'characteristics, prices, functionalities, intended use, barriers to switching and switching costs'.[97]

When considering which products or services should be regarded as substitutes for the products or services of the undertaking concerned, importance is attached to the physical similarities, characteristics and qualities,[98] differences in price, previous substitutions between products, the views of customers and competitors, consumer preferences, the obstacles and costs of redirecting demand to potential substitutes, as well as differences in the end use of the products. Regardless of whether products can be regarded as substitutes on the basis of their characteristics and prices, they will only be considered part of the relevant market if there is such a degree of interchangeability for the same purposes that there is effective competition between the products.[99]

In determining whether two products can be substituted on the demand side, it is not always sufficient to concentrate exclusively on the characteristics and purposes of the products. Differences in competitive structure can thus result in the establishment

---

95. *See further* Commission Notice on the definition of relevant market for the purposes of Union competition law, points 84-104 (OJ C/2024/1645).
96. Commission Decision *British Sugar*, point 42 (OJ 1988 L 204/41), according to which liquid sugars and syrups were not substitutes for granulated sugar from the customer's point of view. *See also* Commission Notice on the definition of relevant market for the purposes of Union competition law, point 25 (OJ C/2024/1645).
97. Commission Notice on the definition of relevant market for the purposes of Union competition law, point 26 (OJ C/2024/1645). *See also* Case 322/81, *Michelin*, para. 37; and Case C-333/94 P, *Tetra Pak II*, para. 63.
98. Case 85/76, *Hoffmann-La Roche*, according to which the individual vitamin groups which the undertaking produced constituted separate product markets, as the vitamins had different effects on the metabolism, and could therefore not be substituted by other vitamin groups. However, differences in product characteristics are not in themselves sufficient to exclude demand substitution, as this depends to a large extent on consumer perceptions of the different characteristics.
99. Case 322/81, *Michelin*; and Case C-62/86, *AKZO*.

of two separate product markets – for example, this is the case with the markets for original components and spare parts for cars.[100]

3.3.2 The Relevant Geographic Market

The purpose of defining the relevant geographic market is to define which undertakings located in other geographic areas can be characterised as competitors to the undertaking concerned. The relevant geographic market is thus defined as 'the area in which the undertakings concerned are involved in the supply and demand of products or services, in which the conditions of competition are sufficiently homogeneous and which can be distinguished from neighbouring areas because the conditions of competition are appreciably different in those area'.[101]

The assessment of the extent of the relevant market for a product or service for the purposes of Article 102 will not necessarily be the same as an assessment for the purposes of the Merger Control Regulation. In examining a merger, the assessment of the relevant geographic market looks at future circumstances, in contrast to the assessment for the purposes of Article 102, where the assessment is based on the circumstances existing at the time when the disputed conduct arose.[102]

The relevant geographic market in relation to Article 102 will often cover the whole of the internal market. However, various factors can mean that the relevant market is narrowed to a limited part of the internal market, for example, to an individual Member State or regional[103] or local areas or facilities.[104] Nevertheless, in order to fall within the scope of Article 102, the relevant geographic market must at least constitute a significant part of the internal market.

A restriction of the relevant geographic market so as only to cover part of the internal market will be due to the fact that the special competitive conditions which apply in the respective areas effectively limit the area where the undertaking competes. This will be the case where there is an appreciable difference in the competitive conditions on the relevant market and the conditions in the surrounding geographic areas. Thus, disproportionate transport costs[105] and special import arrangements[106] will limit the geographic market to a greater or lesser part of the internal market, just as national or

---

100. Regarding market definition and after-markets, bundles and (digital) ecosystems, *see* Commission Notice on the definition of relevant market for the purposes of Union competition law, points 99-104 (OJ C/2024/1645).
101. Case 27/76, *United Brands*, paras 11 and 44.
102. *See further* Commission Notice on the definition of relevant market for the purposes of Union competition law, point 18(c) (OJ C/2024/1645); and *see* Ch. 8, s. 3.
103. Joined Cases 40/73 and others, *Suiker Unie*, concerning parts of Germany.
104. For example harbours, *see* Case C-179/90, *Porto di Genova;* and Case C-242/95, *GT-Link.*
105. The transport costs associated with a product set a natural limit to how far it can be profitable to transport it. *See* Commission Notice on the definition of relevant market for the purposes of Union competition law, point 39 (OJ C/2024/1645).
106. *See* Case 27/76, *United Brands,* where the Commission's definition of the relevant geographic market for bananas excluded the Member States which had special import arrangements for the benefit of selected banana-producing countries, because in these Member States the undertaking in question competed on different terms than in the Member States where there was an open market for bananas.

local preferences in customers' purchasing habits,[107] sole rights provided by law,[108] and limits inherent in the subject of the case[109] will justify such a limitation.[110]

3.3.3 The Relevant Temporal Market

In order to define which actual competitors are able to compete effectively with the undertaking in question, in some cases, it is not enough to define the relevant market in terms of the product market and the geographic market, as it can also be necessary to assess the relevant time during which the relevant market exists.

Competitive and market conditions on the relevant market can change over time and this can be relevant to how the market should be defined.[111] Seasonally determined variations in the demand for the relevant product can be relevant to whether other products can exert effective competitive pressure and be regarded as substitutes.

> There was such a situation in Case 27/76, *United Brands*, where the CJ examined the relevant market for bananas. This product was offered on the market throughout the year. The CJ, therefore, found that only other fresh fruits which competed throughout the year and did not provide only seasonal competition could be regarded as substitutes for bananas. However, the CJ found that neither of the other fruits which were on the market throughout the year – apples and oranges – could be regarded as substitutes for bananas.

3.4 A Substantial Part of the Internal Market

As previously stated, the relevant geographic market for the purposes of Article 102 can be defined as the whole of the internal market or a greater or lesser part of it. According to the provision, for the application of Article 102 there is a requirement that the area

---

107. Case T-504/93, *Tiercé Ladbroke*, paras 103–107, which concerned the definition of the geographic market for sound and picture transmission of horse races. In this connection the CJ held that the competitive conditions in this market were determined by the conditions in the main market for betting, which was in turn characterised by a close geographic link between gamblers and bookmakers, as the gamblers' mobility was regarded as limited and marginal. On this basis the geographic market could be restricted to the national market.
108. Where an undertaking acquires a sole right, granted by law, to carry on a specific undertaking in a given area, the assumption must be that the geographic market is coextensive with this area. See Case 26/75, *General Motors*; and Case 226/84, *British Leyland*.
109. Joined Cases C 241 and 242/91 P, *Magill*, where the relevant geographic market for TV programme listings was limited to the area where it was possible for viewers to see the programmes referred to.
110. Commission Notice on the definition of relevant market for the purposes of Union competition law, points 39 and 62–75 (OJ C/2024/1645).
111. Case 77/77, *BP*. Because of the shortage of supply during the oil crisis in 1973, it was not possible for BP's customers to get supplies from alternative sources. The Commission limited the duration of the relevant market so as to cover the period 1973–1974, and found that in this period BP had had a dominant position with regard to its customers. The CJ did not make a ruling on the definition of the market on this basis, but annulled the Commission's decision on the grounds that there had been no abuse. *See also* Commission Notice on the definition of relevant market for the purposes of Union competition law, point 13 (OJ C/2024/1645).

which is defined as the relevant market should at least be a *substantial part* of the internal market. This requirement means that Article 102 does not apply to an undertaking which has a dominant position in an insignificant part of the internal market, and it, therefore, seems to have the same effect as the appreciability requirement in relation to Article 101.

In assessing whether an area is big enough to constitute a substantial part of the internal market, the CJ takes into account the structure and extent of production and consumption of the product in question, as well as the customs and economic possibilities of buyers and sellers.[112] The assessment of substantiality is thus not based purely on the geographic extent of the area in relation to the European Union as a whole[113] but also on an assessment of the product market in the geographic area in question. Basically, this assessment involves a quantitative assessment of the market's economic importance in relation to the internal market as a whole.[114]

Where an undertaking is found to have a dominant position on the internal market as a whole, the substantiality requirement is naturally considered to be satisfied. This also seems to be the case where the market is defined as being the territory of a Member State,[115] regardless of the size of the Member State. The CJ has also accepted that a dominant position in part of a Member State can fulfil the substantiality requirement.[116] Furthermore, due to their importance for transport, local facilities such as harbours and airports have been regarded as a substantial part of the internal market.[117]

4   ABUSE

Under Article 102 of the Treaty, the conduct of an undertaking which is found to have a dominant position on the relevant market is restricted to the extent to which such conduct can be considered to be an abuse of its dominant position.

In Case 85/76, *Hoffmann-La Roche*, the CJ defined the concept of *abuse* as follows:

> The concept of abuse is an objective concept relating to the behaviour of an undertaking in a dominant position which is such as to influence the structure of a market where, as a result of the very presence of the undertaking in question, the degree of competition is weakened and which, through recourse to methods different from those which condition normal competition in products or services on the basis of the transactions of commercial operators, has the effect of hindering

---

112. Joined Cases 40/73 and others, *Suiker Unie*, para. 371.
113. *See Richard Whish*: Competition Law, 2021, p. 193.
114. *See* Joined Cases 40/73 and others, *Suiker Unie*, where the CJ found that the market for sugar in Belgium and Luxembourg constituted a substantial part of the internal market.
115. Case 322/81, *Michelin*, para. 28; Case C-7/97, *Bronner*, para. 36; and Case C-340/99, *TNT Traco*, para. 43.
116. *See, e.g.*, Joined Cases 40/73 and others, *Suiker Unie*, where the CJ found that the South German market constituted a substantial part of the internal market; and Case 22/78, *Hugin*, where the City of London was also considered to be a substantial part of the internal market.
117. With regard to harbours, *see* Case C-179/90, *Porto di Genova*; and Case C-242/95, *GT-Link. See also* Commission Decision 94/119 (OJ 1994 L 55/52), concerning Rødby harbour.

the maintenance of the degree of competition still existing in the market or the growth of that competition.[118]

It is clear from this that the definition of abuse is an objective definition.[119] Conduct which can be characterised as abuse is therefore covered by Article 102, regardless of whether the disputed conduct has, in fact, resulted in distortion of competition[120] and regardless of whether the undertaking concerned has intended the conduct whereby it abuses its dominant position.[121] In order to be characterised as abuse, the conduct should, however, be capable of producing effects restricting competition.[122]

As stated in the introduction, Article 102 does not prohibit an undertaking either from acquiring or having a dominant position, nor does it prohibit an undertaking from strengthening its market position, as long as this is not a result of the abuse of its dominant position.

The special obligations which Article 102 imposes on dominant undertakings not to conduct themselves in a way which harms effective and undistorted competition in the internal market,[123] meaning that conduct, such as entering into exclusive purchasing arrangements or the use of discriminatory discount schemes, which could be considered normal and legitimate if carried out by non-dominant undertakings, can constitute abuse if there is the same conduct on a market on which competition has already been weakened as a result of the existence of a dominant undertaking.[124] This means that a dominant undertaking cannot justify its conduct, for example, in the form of tied sales, by claiming that its conduct is in accordance with trade practice.[125]

An undertaking which, together with other undertakings, can be considered collectively dominant is likewise restricted by this special obligation, regardless of whether the undertaking can in itself be considered dominant within the terms of Article 102.[126]

However, a dominant undertaking has the possibility of establishing that its conduct is objectively necessary.[127] However, this special obligation does not mean that, in order to avoid infringing Article 102, dominant undertakings must remain

---

118. Case 85/76, *Hoffmann-La Roche*, para. 91; Case C-52/09, *TeliaSonera*, para. 27, and Case C-307/18, *Generics*, para. 148.
119. *See also* Case C-377/20, *ENEL*, para. 60.
120. *See* in that direction Case 377/20, *ENEL*, para. 53.
121. This means that the intentions of a dominant undertaking cannot excuse its conduct, but the intentions may be relevant in relation to determining the amount of a fine. *See* the guidelines for the Commission's calculation of fines in Art. 23(2)(a) in Council Regulation (EC) No 1/2003 (OJ 2006 C210/2) on the implementation of the rules on competition laid down in Arts 81 and 82 of the Treaty, according to which the Commission can impose a fine, whether an undertaking infringes Art. 102 intentionally or negligently. *See also* Ch. 7, s. 6.1.
122. *See* Case C-377/20, *ENEL*, para. 50 and paras 70–72. *See also* Case T-235/18, *Qualcomm*, where the Court disregarded the Commission's analysis of the anti-competitive effects of the conduct (exclusivity payments), *see* para. 151.
123. Case 322/81, *Michelin*, para. 57.
124. Case T-65/89, *BPB Industries*, paras 65–71 and 94.
125. Case T-83/91, *Tetra Pak II*, para. 137.
126. *See also* s. 3.1.
127. *See* Case 311/84, *CEBM*, para. 27; and Case C-209/10, *Post Danmark*, para. 41.

altogether passive in the face of aggressive marketing by their competitors. Thus, the CJ recognises that a dominant undertaking is entitled to protect its commercial interests – 'meet competition' – by taking measures which are proportionate and appropriate in the circumstances.[128]

In Case 27/76, *United Brands*, the CJ thus stated:

> Although it is true, as the applicant points out, that the fact that an undertaking is in a dominant position cannot disentitle it from protecting its own commercial interests if they are attacked and that such an undertaking must be conceded the right to take such reasonable steps as it deems appropriate to protect its said interests, such behaviour cannot be countenanced if its actual purpose is to strengthen this dominant position and abuse it.
>
> Even if the possibility of a counter-attack is acceptable, that attack must still be proportionate to the threat, taking into account the economic strength of the undertakings confronting each other.
>
> The sanction consisting of a refusal to supply by an undertaking in a dominant position was in excess of what might, if such a situation were to arise, reasonably be contemplated as a sanction for conduct similar to that for which UNC blamed Olesen.[129]

However, it is possible that a dominant undertaking may claim that efficiency gains are an objective justification for its conduct.[130] In Case C-209/10, *Post Danmark*, the CJ stated that the exclusionary effect of the conduct of a dominant undertaking 'may be counterbalanced, outweighed even, by advantages in terms of efficiency that also benefit consumers'.[131] In this context, the CJ emphasised that:

> it is for the dominant undertaking to show that the efficiency gains likely to result from the conduct under consideration counteract any likely negative effects on competition and consumer welfare in the affected markets, that those gains have been, or are likely to be, brought about as a result of that conduct, that such conduct is necessary for the achievement of those gains in efficiency and that it does not eliminate effective competition, by removing all or most existing sources of actual or potential competition.[132]

The forms of abuse that are covered by Article 102 include both structural abuse and exploitative or exclusionary abuse, or a combination of these. 'Exploitative abuse' means a behaviour which affects the dominant undertaking's immediate trading partners, such as unreasonable sales or purchasing prices or tied sales. In contrast, 'exclusionary abuse' affects the dominant undertaking's actual or potential competitors so that competition from these competitors is weakened or their access to the market is impeded. Such behaviour can include, for example, refusing to supply or predatory pricing. In the last resort, both exploitative and exclusionary conduct can be harmful for consumers, as it can lead to a limited offering of goods on the market or

---

128. Case 27/76, *United Brands*, paras 189–190; Joined Cases T-24 to 26 and 28/93, *CMB*, para. 148; and Case T-228/97, *Irish Sugar*, para. 189.
129. Case 27/76, *United Brands*, paras 189–191. *See also* Case T-340/03, *France Télécom*, para. 185.
130. Case C-95/04 P, *British Airways*, para. 86; Case C-52/09, *TeliaSonera*, para. 76; and Case C-209/10, *Post Danmark*, para. 41.
131. Case C-209/10, *Post Danmark*, para. 41.
132. Case C-209/10, *Post Danmark*, para. 42. *See also* Case C-23/14, *Post Danmark II*, para. 49.

abnormally high pricing. Finally, structural abuse can harm effective competition on the market. Structural abuse will exist where, for example, a dominant undertaking takes over competing undertakings and thus effectively eliminates the competition.[133]

When it is established that an undertaking has abused its dominant position, the Commission has the power to order the undertaking in question to bring the abuse to an end.[134] In this connection the Commission is empowered, while complying with the principle of proportionality, to impose on undertakings the necessary behavioural or structural remedies. However, structural remedies should only be imposed if there are no less burdensome behavioural remedies that are equally effective. Thus, changes to the structure of an undertaking, as it existed before the infringement of Article 102 was committed, will only be proportionate in relation to the infringement if there is a material risk of continual or repeated infringements which are caused by the undertaking's structure.

4.1 Examples of Abuse

The second paragraph of Article 102 of the Treaty contains a non-exhaustive list of examples of conduct that may constitute abuse covered by the provision.[135] There follows a presentation of the different kinds of abuse covered by the provision, and examples are also given of other forms of abuse which can likewise be covered by Article 102 according to the practice of the courts.

4.1.1 *Article 102, Second Paragraph, Sub-paragraph (a)*

According to Article 102, second paragraph, sub-paragraph (a), abuse may consist of the dominant undertaking directly or indirectly imposing unfair purchase or selling prices or other unfair trading conditions on trading partners.

Excessive prices

A dominant undertaking can be tempted to exploit its market position and impose unreasonably high selling prices on its customers for goods or services or, where a purchaser has a dominant position, to require unreasonably low prices from its suppliers. This typical form of abusive conduct, whereby the dominant undertaking takes an above-normal profit, falls under Article 102, second paragraph, sub-paragraph (a).

In judging whether the price of goods or services is excessive, in its practice, the CJ attaches importance to whether the sales price of goods and services of the dominant undertaking is proportionate to the economic value of the product or of the service performed[136] and whether the actual price thus reflects the price on a market

---

133. Case 6/72, *Continental Can*. Such mergers may be subject to an assessment under the Merger Control Regulation – *see* the discussion in Ch. 8. *See also* Case C-449/21, *Towercast* (regarding the so-called 'killer acquisitions').
134. Council Regulation (EC) No 1/2003 on the implementation of the rules on competition laid down in Arts 81 and 82 of the Treaty (OJ 2003 L 1/1), Art. 7(1).
135. Case C-52/09, *TeliaSonera*, para. 26.
136. Case C-242/95, *GT-Link,* para. 39; and Case C-385/07, *Der Grüne Punkt,* para. 142.

with sufficiently effective competition (the benchmark price).[137] In order to be able to assess excessive pricing, a two-step test is applied, on the basis of which the Court carries out an objective evaluation of: (1) whether the following can be identified: (a) a (substantial) *difference* between the actual price and the hypothetical market price assessed on the basis of appropriate benchmarks, and if a substantial difference is identified; (b) whether this difference/the price either in itself or in comparison with the price of competitive goods is *unfair*; and finally (2) whether the difference in price can be explained by *objective conditions*.[138] In the identification of whether a (substantial) *difference* between the actual price and the hypothetical benchmark price exists, appropriate and relevant methods/comparison benchmarks may be applied,[139] including the actual price charged (sales price) compared to the production costs,[140] the sales price compared to the sales prices of competitors/other undertakings (on the same geographic and other geographic markets),[141] the sales price over time,[142] and the sales price of the dominant undertaking's own sale in other geographic markets.[143]

As the use of these methods involves a certain degree of uncertainty is not always possible, for example, to calculate the production costs of a product with sufficient certainty in all cases. In such cases, the price of the product may thus be compared with the price of equivalent products from other undertakings or in other Member States in order to obtain an indication of whether the undertaking has abused its dominant position by setting an unreasonably high price for the product.[144]

If it can be established on the basis of one or more of the methods that a significant difference between the actual price and the benchmark price exists, then it is assessed whether the price in itself or compared to the price of competitive goods is *unfair* or not.[145]

There is no minimum level for when a price may be considered *excessive*, but a difference between the actual price and the benchmark price may be considered

---

137. *See* in this regard Case 27/76, *United Brands*, para. 249.
138. *See* in this regard Case 27/76, *United Brands*, paras 249 and 252, and Case C-177/16, *Autortiesību un komunicēšanās konsultāciju aģentūra/Latvijas Autoru apvienība*, paras 35f and 57.
139. *See* in more detail in draft decision of AG Wahl in Case C-177/16, *Autortiesību un komunicēšanās konsultāciju aģentūra/Latvijas Autoru apvienība*.
140. *See* Case 27/76, *United Brands*, paras 251 and 252.
141. *See*, *e.g.*, Case 24/67, *Parke, Davis & Co*, Case 53/87, *Maxicar v. Renault*, para 17, Case 78/70, *Deutsche Grammophon Gesellschaft*, Case 30/87, *Bodson*, Case 395/87, *Tournier*, para 38, Case 110/88, 241/88 and 242/88, *Lucazeau*, para. 25, and Case C-177/16, *Autortiesību un komunicēšanās konsultāciju aģentūra/Latvijas Autoru apvienība*, para. 38. *See also* para. 51 of the judgment from which it follows that when comparing with the prices applicable in other Member States, the reference Member States should be selected on the basis of objective, appropriate and verifiable criteria, and the comparisons must be made on a consistent basis.
142. *See* Case 26/75, *General Motors Continental*, and Case 226/84, *British Leyland*.
143. *See* Case 26/75, *General Motors Continental*, and Case 226/84, *British Leyland*.
144. Case 24/67, *Parke Davis;* Case 40/70, *Sirena;* and Case 78/70, *Deutsche Grammophon*. *See also* Joined Cases 110/88 and others, *Lucazeau;* and Case 395/87, *Tournier*.
145. Case 27/76, *United Brands*, paras 249–253. *See also* draft decision of AG Wahl in Case C-177/16, *Autortiesību un komunicēšanās konsultāciju aģentūra/Latvijas Autoru apvienība*, point 20.

substantial if the difference is significant and persistent, i.e., it must be of a certain size, must persist for a length of time and must not be temporary or episodic.[146]

As the above factors are merely indicative of the existence of an unfair price, the dominant undertaking can justify the price difference by relying on *objective reasons* for the difference.[147] Thus, it must be investigated whether the difference in price is merely the result of an abusive use of market power by the dominant undertaking or the consequence of other legitimate reasons.[148]

In relation to intellectual property rights, the assessment of whether the price for a protected product is unreasonably high must, for example, take into account the entitlement of the owner of the right to cover the production costs, to obtain a reasonable profit, and to cover the costs of research and development.[149] This entitlement may thus, to some extent, explain any price difference between the product and equivalent products in, for example, other Member States.

In practice, the provisions of Article 102, second paragraph, sub-paragraph (a) have only occasionally been applied in this context.[150] Among other things, this is because it is difficult to determine whether a price is unreasonable, and market forces will normally be sufficient in themselves to press unreasonably high prices down to a normal level.[151]

Other unfair trading conditions

Other unfair trading conditions can be imposed by a dominant undertaking, both in its capacity as a purchaser[152] and as a seller.[153] In assessing whether trading conditions are unfair, an overall assessment is made, where, among other things, there is a focus on the burdensome element in relation to the advantages which the trading partner obtains on the basis of the trading agreement, as well as the interest of the dominant undertaking in maintaining the trading conditions.[154]

For example, there can be unfair trading conditions where the trading partner binds itself to obtain permission from the dominant undertaking for the transfer of equipment bought from the dominant undertaking[155] or where the members of an

---

146. Case C-177/16, *Autortiesību un komunicēšanās konsultāciju aģentūra/Latvijas Autoru apvienība*, paras 55, 56 and 61.
147. *See also* Case C-177/16, *Autortiesību un komunicēšanās konsultāciju aģentūra/Latvijas Autoru apvienība*, para. 57, pointing out the possibility to make reference to objective dissimilarities between the situation in the Member State concerned and the situation prevailing in the reference Member States, including the difference in the citizens' purchasing power as expressed by the PPP index, cf. para. 46.
148. *See* opinion of AG Wahl in Case C 177/16, *Autortiesību un komunicēšanās konsultāciju aģentūra/Latvijas Autoru apvienība*, point 21.
149. Case 53/87, *Maxicar v. Renault*, para. 17. *See also* Case 24/67, *Parke Davis*.
150. However, especially at national level, in recent years, the rules on abuse of dominance have been invoked in an attempt to reduce the prices of medical products.
151. *See* in more detail in draft decision of AG Wahl in Case C-177/16, *Autortiesību un komunicēšanās konsultāciju aģentūra/Latvijas Autoru apvienība*, points 1-4.
152. Case 127/73, *BRT II*.
153. *See, e.g.,* the Commission Decision in *Tetra Pak II* (OJ 1992 L 72/1).
154. Case 127/73, *BRT II*.
155. Commission Decision in *Tetra Pak II* (OJ 1992 L 72/1).

association impose restrictions on the conduct of their business to a greater extent than is necessary for the association to achieve its aims.[156]

4.1.2 Predatory Pricing

A dominant undertaking can try to force competitors out of the market or prevent new competitors from entering the market by setting prices below the level of the undertaking's costs.[157] Once competitors have been excluded, the undertaking can then raise its prices to a level which lies above that which would apply in a competitive market, and recover the losses suffered by the price reduction.[158] According to the practice of the courts, such predatory pricing can constitute an abuse, which is covered by Article 102.[159] The CJ has stated in Case C-62/86, *AKZO*:

> 'Prices below average variable costs (that is to say, those which vary depending on the quantities produced) by means of which a dominant undertaking seeks to eliminate a competitor must be regarded as abusive. A dominant undertaking has no interest in applying such prices except that of eliminating competitors so as to enable it subsequently to raise its prices by taking advantage of its monopolistic position, since each sale generates a loss, namely the total amount of the fixed costs (that is to say, those which remain constant regardless of the quantities produced) and, at least, part of the variable costs relating to the unit produced.'[160]

> 'Moreover, prices below average total costs, that is to say, fixed costs plus variable costs, but above average variable costs, must be regarded as abusive if they are determined as part of a plan for eliminating a competitor. Such prices can drive from the market undertakings which are perhaps as efficient as the dominant undertaking but which, because of their smaller financial resources, are incapable of withstanding the competition waged against them.'[161]

Thus, if a dominant undertaking sets *prices that are lower than the average variable costs* (AVC), there will be an assumption that there is predatory pricing, which is contrary to Article 102.[162] However, this assumption can be overturned if it can be shown that the conduct is due to circumstances other than the wish to eliminate a competitor, for example, the wish to reduce stocks of perishable goods or to match a

---

156. Case 127/73, *BRT II*, where the CJ held that there could be abuse in cases where a copyright protection association required a new member to transfer all existing and future copyright to the association, and the right to exploit these rights would remain with the association for five years following the termination of membership. See also Case 247/86, *Alsatel*; and Case C-250/92, *Gøttrup-Klim*.
157. Communication from the Commission – Guidance on the Commission's enforcement priorities in applying Art. 82 of the EC Treaty to abusive exclusionary conduct by dominant undertakings, point 63 (OJ 2009 C 45/7) (as amended).
158. However, in order to establish the existence of predatory pricing it is not necessary to prove that the loss can be recovered. See Case T-340/03, *France Télécom*, para. 228; and Case T-83/91, *Tetra Pak II*, para. 150.
159. Case 298/83, *CICCE*.
160. Case C-62/86, *AKZO*, para. 71.
161. Case C-62/86, *AKZO*, para. 72.
162. Case T-83/91, *Tetra Pak II*, para. 150; and Case T-340/03, *France Télécom*, para. 130.

competitor's offer.[163] However, a dominant undertaking cannot claim a general or absolute right to match its competitors' prices as a justification for its conduct,[164] but in relation to specific customers, it will have the possibility of matching the prices at which another producer would be able to supply.[165]

If prices are *above the AVC* but *below the average total costs* (ATC) and thus not profitable in the longer term, the Commission must show that the undertaking has the intention of eliminating a competitor before Article 102 becomes applicable.[166] In cases where there is no evidence of such an intention to eliminate a competitor, according to the CJ in Case C-209/10, *Post Danmark*, there can nevertheless be an abuse of a dominant position if it can be shown that the dominant undertaking's pricing policy, without objective justification, produces an actual or likely exclusionary effect, to the detriment of competition and, thereby, of consumers' interests.[167]

In this connection, setting *prices that are higher than the ATC* will not be considered abuse under the terms of Article 102 but could be regarded as abuse in connection with a selective price reduction.

While in the *AKZO* case, the CJ used both AVC and ATC methods for calculating costs,[168] in its 2009 Communication, the Commission stated that it would use average avoidable cost (AAC) and long-run average incremental cost (LRAIC) as cost benchmarks.[169]

Among other things, the use of LRAIC as a benchmark leads, in some cases, to certain commercial sectors having cost structures, which means that the *AKZO* test is not suitable for determining the existence of predatory pricing. For example, in the telecommunications, oil and gas industries, the cost structures are characterised by having very high fixed costs and very low variable costs, so the AVC are so low that it is virtually impossible for there to be predatory pricing.[170]

The Commission applied this standard for covering costs in the *Deutsche Post* case and assessed as follows:

---

163. *See Jonathan Faull & Ali Nikpay* (eds): The EU Law of Competition, 3rd ed. 2014 ss 4.290–4.297.
164. Case T-340/03, *France Télécom*, para. 187.
165. Case T-340/03, *France Télécom*, para. 179, with reference to Commission Decision 83/462, *AKZO*.
166. Such an intention to eliminate a competitor was established in Case T-83/91, *Tetra Pak II; see* para. 151. The decision was confirmed by the CJ in Case C-333/94 P.
167. *See* Case C-209/10, *Post Danmark*, paras 37, 38 and 44. The use of *the as-efficient-competitor test* is only one out of several methods applicable to assess the conduct of a dominant undertaking. *See* more about the details of the test in Communication from the Commission — Guidance on the Commission's enforcement priorities in applying Art. 82 of the EC Treaty to abusive exclusionary conduct by dominant undertakings, point 23f (OJ 2009 C45/7) (with later amendments), and the judgments in Case C-23/14, *Post Danmark II*, Case C-413/14 P, *Intel*, Case C-680/20, *Unilever*, and Case T-604/18, *Google and Alphabet (Google Android)*.
168. *See also* Case T-340/03, *France Télécom*, para. 130, a decision upheld in Case C-202/07 P, *France Télécom*, and Commission Decision COMP/38.233, *Wanadoo Interactive*, where the Commission concluded that Wanadoo Interactive had abused its dominant position in the market for household access to high-speed internet access with predatory pricing of its services.
169. Communication from the Commission – Guidance on the Commission's enforcement priorities in applying Art. 82 of the EC Treaty to abusive exclusionary conduct by dominant undertakings, points 26 and 64 (OJ 2009 C 45/7).
170. *See Richard Whish:* Competition Law, 2021, pp. 785–786.

In the period 1990 to 1995 Deutsche Post AG's revenue from mail-order parcels was below the incremental costs of providing this specific service (*see* Table 3). This means that in the period 1990 to 1995 every sale by DPAG in the mail-order parcel services business represented a loss which comprises all the capacity-maintenance costs and at least part of the additional costs of providing the service. In such circumstances, every additional sale not only entailed the loss of at least part of these additional costs, but made no contribution towards covering the carrier's capacity-maintenance costs. In the medium term, such a pricing policy is not in the carrier's own economic interest. This being so, DPAG had no economic interest in offering such a service in the medium term. DPAG could increase its overall result by either raising prices to cover the additional costs of providing the service or – where there is no demand for this service at a higher price – to discontinue providing the service, because revenue gained from its provision is below the additional costs incurred in providing it. However, DPAG, by remaining in this market without any foreseeable improvement in revenue restricted the activities of competitors which are in a position to offer this service at a price that covers their costs.[171]

On this basis, the Commission concluded that in the period 1990–1995, Deutsche Post had infringed Article 102 by supplying parcel services at prices below the additional costs of providing those services.[172]

4.1.3 Article 102, Second Paragraph, Sub-paragraph (b)

According to Article 102, second paragraph, sub-paragraph (b), a dominant undertaking can be found to have abusive conduct if it limits production, marketing or technical development to the prejudice of consumers. Thus, depending on the circumstances, the provision can cover abuse in the form of refusal to supply,[173] margin squeeze,[174] restriction of production with a view to creating the possibility for increasing prices and profits,[175] imposing an obligation on a dealer to restrict its exports,[176] and by hindering technical development.[177]

Refusal to supply

In principle, undertakings are free to choose their trading partners. However, if a dominant undertaking refuses to supply a trading partner, with the result that competition is significantly restricted, this could constitute abuse within the meaning of Article 102 unless the refusal is objectively justified.[178] In such a case, with a view to promoting competition in the short term and depending on the circumstances, it may

---

171. Commission Decision COMP/35.141, *Deutsche Post*, para. 36 (OJ 2001 L 125/27).
172. Commission Decision COMP/35.141, *Deutsche Post*, para. 30 (OJ 2001 L 125/27).
173. Joined Cases C-241 and 242/91 P, *Magill;* and the Commission Decision in *Sabena* (OJ 1988 L 317/47).
174. *See, e.g.*, Case C -52/09, *TeliaSonera*.
175. *See, e.g.*, the Commission Decision in *British Sugar* (OJ 1988 L 284/41); the Commission Decision in *Sabena* (OJ 1988 L 317/47); and Commission Decision in *BPB Industries* (OJ 1989 L 10/50).
176. Case 40/73, *Suiker Unie*, paras 396–402.
177. Case T-51/89, *Tetra Pak;* and Case C-179/90, *Porto di Genova*.
178. Case T-201/04, *Microsoft*, para. 319.

be possible to order the dominant undertaking to supply the trading partner in question.

However, the breach of the principle of freedom to choose trading partners is not without problems. Thus, there is a risk that competition will be weakened in the longer term as, out of concern that trading partners can obtain their goods, undertakings will be deprived of the incentive to make investments in developing new production or distribution facilities or production methods, just as trading partners, who can gain access to the goods of other producers on the basis of Article 102, will lose the incentive to invest themselves in competitive facilities and methods.[179] The obligation to supply should thus be imposed with care, having regard to intervention in the freedom of contract of the dominant undertaking, and only after carefully weighing regard for competition in the short term against consideration for promoting competition in the longer term.

A refusal to supply can relate to products, services, information,[180] the issue of licences,[181] as well as denial of access to important facilities or infrastructure,[182] and it can be directed at both existing and new customers.[183]

Where a refusal to supply affects an existing customer, the refusal can constitute abuse if, for example, the refusal to supply involves a clear risk that competition from a customer in a downstream stage of distribution[184] or on a related market[185] will be eliminated or if the existing customer is prevented from establishing itself on the supplier's market.[186] However, there can also be abuse where a dominant undertaking refuses to supply an existing customer who does not compete directly with the dominant undertaking, for example, with a view to preventing the trading partner from starting trade with a competing product.[187]

If a refusal to supply affects new trading partners, with a view to preventing their entry into the market, Article 102 will also be applicable. This is so regardless of

---

179. Communication from the Commission – Guidance on the Commission's enforcement priorities in applying Art. 82 of the EC Treaty to abusive exclusionary conduct by dominant undertakings, point 75 (OJ 2009 C 45/7) (as amended).
180. Commission Decision, *Decca Navigator System* (OJ 1989 L 43/27); the XIVth Report on Competition Policy, 1984, points 94–95 concerning *IBM;* and the XXXth Report on Competition Policy, 2000 p. 164 concerning *Microsoft*.
181. *See, e.g.,* Case T-201/04, *Microsoft,* para. 331, concerning the refusal to supply information to competitors about interoperability, and the preliminary ruling of the CJ in Case C-418/01, *IMS Health/ NDC Health,* para. 38, on the refusal to grant a licence to use a copyright protected brick structure used to supply regional sales data for pharmaceutical products in a Member State.
182. Commission Decision 94/19/EC, *Sea Containers v. Stena Sealink* (OJ 1994 L 15/8); and Commission Decision 92/213/EEC, *British Midland* (OJ 1992 L 96/34). Also *see* Case C-42/21 P, *Lietuvos*.
183. Communication from the Commission – Guidance on the Commission's enforcement priorities in applying Art. 82 of the EC Treaty to abusive exclusionary conduct by dominant undertakings, point 83 (OJ 2009 C 45/7) (as amended).
184. Joined Cases 6 and 7/73, *Commercial Solvents,* para. 25.
185. Case 311/84, *CBEM;* and Case C-18/88, *RTT*.
186. Commission Decision in *BBI/Boosey & Hawkes* (OJ 1987 L 286/36); and Commission Decision in *British Sugar* (OJ 1988 L 284/41).
187. Case 27/76, *United Brands,* para. 182.

whether the new trading partner is an actual or potential competitor to the dominant undertaking.[188]

In determining whether there is a refusal of supply contrary to Article 102, the Commission will have regard for: (1) whether the refusal concerns a product or a service that is objectively necessary for enabling an undertaking to compete effectively in a downstream market; (2) whether the refusal is capable of preventing effective competition on the downstream market; and (3) whether the refusal will be to the disadvantage of consumers.[189]

The application of Article 102 presupposes that the refusal to supply cannot be objectively justified[190] or is otherwise justified by relevant effectivity gains.[191] In this context, a dominant undertaking's desire to remove existing customers from the market because it wishes to begin production of products corresponding to those of the customer is not an objective justification for refusing supply.[192] The same was the case in relation to refusal to supply because the repair of the products (cash machines) required special technical skills,[193] as well as the desire to avoid losing market share to a new competitor.[194] However, lack of capacity or the customer's payment problems will be objectively justified grounds for refusing to supply.

Essential facilities

An essential facility is defined by the Commission as being some facility or infrastructure to which it is necessary for competitors to have access in order to be able to provide services to their customers.[195]

Where the owner of such a facility – for example, a harbour or a telephone network – denies an actual or potential competitor access to the facility in question or gives the competitor access but on discriminatory terms, then under certain circumstances, this can constitute an abuse of a dominant position under Article 102, so that the owner can be required to give the trading partner access to the facilities on the same terms as those that are used for the dominant undertaking's own service provision.

As stated above, such an intervention in the freedom of contract of the owner of the facility should be made with care, and only after a careful assessment of whether

---

188. Joined Cases C-241 and 242/91 P, *Magill;* Commission Decision in *Sabena* (OJ 1988 L 317/47); and Commission Decision in *British Midland* (OJ 1992 L 96/34).
189. Communication from the Commission – Guidance on the Commission's enforcement priorities in applying Art. 82 of the EC Treaty to abusive exclusionary conduct by dominant undertakings, point 80, with further discussion in points 82–87, (OJ 2009 C 45/7), (as amended).
190. A dominant undertaking can take reasonable and proportionate measures necessary to protect its own trading interests; *see* Joined Cases C-468-478/06, *GlaxoSmithKline,* paras 69–71, on the refusal to supply medicinal products to wholesalers that were engaged in parallel exporting.
191. On the more detailed assessment of effectivity gains in connection with refusals of supply, *see* Communication from the Commission – Guidance on the Commission's enforcement priorities in applying Art. 82 of the EC Treaty to abusive exclusionary conduct by dominant undertakings, point 88–89 (OJ 2009 C 45/7) (as amended).
192. Joined Cases 6 and 7/73, *Commercial Solvents.*
193. Commission Decision in *Hugin* (OJ 1978 L 22/23).
194. Commission Decision in *British Midland* (OJ 1992 L 96/34).
195. Commission Decision on interim measures in *Sea Containers/Stena Link,* point 66 (OJ 1994 L 15/8).

consideration for promoting competition in the short term, by giving a trading partner access to the facility, outweighs the possible harmful effects on competition in the longer term, because of the reduced incentive to invest in the development and construction of such essential facilities.

The principle of essential facilities is closely connected with the question of refusal of supply, and the Commission assesses it on the basis of the same principles referred to above.[196] The application of the principle of essential facilities presupposes that the facilities in question are *essential*, in the sense that it is necessary for an undertaking's access to the market that it should have access to the facilities in question.[197] It must thus either be impossible or extraordinarily difficult due to physical, geographic or legal restrictions, or there must be an insurmountable financial burden for the competitor to create a corresponding facility.[198]

It is also a requirement for the application of the principle of essential facilities that there is no objective justification for denying a trading partner access to the facility in question. Security or technical reasons, as well as limited capacity, will presumably be legitimate grounds.

The application of the principle concerning essential facilities has been raised in several cases concerning the denial of access to transport facilities. This has especially concerned harbours, where the Commission has assessed denial of access in relation to Rødby Harbour,[199] Helsingør Harbour,[200] Roscoff Harbour,[201] as well as Holyhead Harbour.[202] Access to facilities in the air transport sector has also been assessed in several of the Commission's decisions; see, for example, access to the provision of ground handling services,[203] access to underground pipes for providing fuel to aircraft,[204] and access to a computerised reservation system.[205] The principle concerning essential facilities may also be relevant in the liberalised sectors and may be linked to the risk of margin squeeze.[206]

---

196. Communication from the Commission – Guidance on the Commission's enforcement priorities in applying Art. 82 of the EC Treaty to abusive exclusionary conduct by dominant undertakings, point 78 (OJ 2009 C 45/7) (as amended).
197. Case C-7/97, *Bronner*, where the CJ did not accept Bronner's claim that the facility was essential.
198. *See* the Opinion of Advocate General Jacobs in Case C-7/97, *Bronner*.
199. Commission Decision in *Rødby Havn* (OJ 1994 L 55/52).
200. XXVIth Report on Competition Policy, 1996 point 131.
201. XXVth Report on Competition Policy, 1995 pp. 120–121.
202. Commission Decision on interim measures in *Sea Containers/Stena Link* (OJ 1994 L 15/8).
203. Commission Decision in *Flughafen Frankfurt/Main* (OJ 1998 L 72/30).
204. *See* the *Disma* case in the XXIIIth Report on Competition Policy, 1993 points 223–224.
205. Commission Decision in *Sabena* (OJ 1988 L 317/47). *See*, conversely, in the rail transport sector, Joined Cases T-374 and 375, 384 and 388/94, *European Night Services*.
206. For example, the telecommunication sector is regulated in various ways to ensure access to electronic communications networks and services, among others by appointing undertakings with significant market power (SMPs), that – based on EU law - may be subject to price monitoring by national authorities. (*see, e.g.*, Directive 2002/21/EC, on a common regulatory framework for electronic communications networks and services (Framework Directive), OJ 2002 L 108/33, Art. 14(2), and Guidelines on market analysis and the assessment of significant market power under the EU regulatory framework for electronic communication network and services, OJ 2018 C-159/1).

Margin squeeze

Instead of refusal to supply, the dominant undertaking can limit the competition by means of a so-called margin squeeze, by which the dominant undertaking demands a price for the product on the upstream market, which, according to the price that the dominant undertaking demands on the downstream market, will not offer just as efficient a competitor the possibility to conduct profitable trade on the downstream market.[207] Such behaviour constitutes an independent kind of abuse, which is different from refusal to supply.[208]

4.1.4 Article 102, Second Paragraph, Sub-paragraph (c)

According to Article 102, second paragraph, sub-paragraph (c), a dominant undertaking can abuse its market dominance if it applies dissimilar conditions to equivalent transactions with different trading partners, thereby placing a trading partner at a competitive disadvantage. The provision covers discriminatory pricing as well as other forms of discrimination, for example in the form of refusal to supply or discriminatory business terms.

This means that a dominant undertaking's pricing policy can be an expression of abuse covered by Article 102. For example, if an undertaking practises discriminatory discount or bonus schemes, or if the undertaking sets unreasonably high or low prices, or even predatory prices, this can have both an exploitative and an exclusionary effect.

Discriminatory pricing can be directed against specific customers or groups of customers with the aim of increasing the undertaking's profits by making customers who value the product most pay a higher price than others. Discrimination can also be based on the nationality of trading partners[209] or involve geographic price discrimination by applying different prices in different Member States.[210]

Likewise, depending on the circumstances, a dominant undertaking's use of selective pricing can be covered by Article 102. Selective pricing can be seen, for example, in the form of price reductions, whereby the undertaking reduces its prices for certain trading partners with a view either to retaining an existing customer or to capturing a chosen customer from a competitor.[211]

Discount arrangements

Undertakings often offer their customers various forms of discounts or bonuses as part of ordinary customer care and price competition. Such discount and bonus arrangements can involve price discrimination, which is covered by Article 102, in the form of

---

207. Communication from the Commission – Guidance on the Commission's enforcement priorities in applying Art. 82 of the EC Treaty to abusive exclusionary conduct by dominant undertakings, point 90 (OJ 2009 C 45/7) (as amended).
208. Cf. Case C-52/19, *TeliaSonora*, para. 56.
209. Case T-83/91, *Tetra Pak II*.
210. Case 27/76, *United Brands*.
211. Case T-228/97, *Irish Sugar*; Case T-30/89, *Hilti*; Joined Cases C-395 and 396/96 P, *CMB*; and Case C-209/10, *Post Danmark*.

applying dissimilar conditions – in this case, dissimilar prices – to equivalent transactions with other trading partners. However, there will not only be price discrimination where a dominant undertaking uses *differing prices*. The application of the *same prices* in circumstances that are not comparable will also involve price discrimination. This can be the case where an undertaking uses the same price for goods delivered carriage-free, without regard for where the customer is located in relation to the producer so that a customer located closest to the producer does not have the opportunity of taking advantage of the low transport costs.[212]

It must nevertheless be assumed that a dominant undertaking can use the same prices for trading partners in comparable situations, as it can hardly be required that the dominant undertaking should take into account individual differences in each customer's cost profile.[213]

A discount or bonus scheme which, on the face of it, seems to involve different treatment for the customers of an undertaking will not be considered discriminatory as long as the differences in treatment are objectively justified by the market situation or can otherwise be justified on the grounds of effectivity gains.[214] Thus, it is not considered to be discriminatory if a discount reflects cost savings, which the dominant undertaking has in relation to the customer. Depending on the circumstances, a dominant undertaking can offer a discount which is based on lower transport costs, cash payment, quantity, differences in the costs of maintaining a distribution network in different areas, etc.

Quantity discounts, which are offered automatically according to the quantity which a customer buys from a dominant undertaking, will usually be an expression for a normal difference in prices which does not involve a discriminatory difference in treatment of the undertaking's customers. Where such discounts merely reflect the cost savings obtained by the dominant undertaking in selling the quantity in question, compared with selling smaller quantities, the scheme will not normally be objectionable under Article 102. However, quantity discounts could be covered by Article 102 where the quantity which a customer must buy in order to benefit from the discount amounts to the greater part of the customer's needs or where the discount scheme is so arranged that, for example, only certain larger trading partners can, in fact, benefit from the scheme.[215]

In addition to being discriminatory, discount and bonus schemes can also have the effect of tying-in the undertaking's customer base. Thus, it may be that loyalty discounts are only given on condition that the customer buys all or most of its purchases from the dominant undertaking.[216] In this way, the dominant undertaking

---

212. Commission Decision in *British Sugar* (OJ 1988 L 284/41).
213. See Katja Høegh: Hvor snævre grænser gælder for større virksomheder og dominerende virksomheders rabat og bonussystemer?, UfR 2002B.32, at p. 37.
214. Communication from the Commission – Guidance on the Commission's enforcement priorities in applying Art. 82 of the EC Treaty to abusive exclusionary conduct by dominant undertakings, point 46 (OJ 2009 C 45/7) (as amended).
215. *See, e.g.*, the case of *Brussels Airport,* in the Commission's XIXth Report on Competition Policy, 1989 para. 50.
216. *See, e.g.*, Case C-549/10 P, *Tomra*.

deprives its trading partners of any financial incentive to switch to a competing supplier, as this would only be beneficial to the customer if the competitor could offer discounts which would compensate for the discounts which the customer would lose by switching suppliers.[217] This form of discount thus has, de facto, the same effect as an exclusive purchasing agreement.[218] In this context, in order to establish the existence of abuse, it is not always required to show that there is an actual effect on the market.[219]

Loyalty discounts do not relate to cost savings and will, therefore, usually fall foul of the prohibition in Article 102.

The effect of loyalty discounts in tying-in customers can also be achieved by, among other things, 'top slice' discounts and discounts related to specific purchase targets, as such discounts give great incentives to customers to buy all their purchases from the dominant undertaking.

Top slice discounts are used when a trading partner has bought its core quantity from the dominant undertaking and, by offering a particularly large discount, the dominant undertaking seeks to give the trading partner the incentive to buy additional quantities from it – extra quantities which the trading partner might otherwise have bought from a competitor.[220]

Discount schemes which are tied to the customer reaching a specific purchase target do not necessarily require the trading partner to make all or a large part of its purchases from the dominant undertaking. Therefore, the compliance of such discount schemes with Article 102 will often depend on the length of the reference period against which the discount is calculated and on whether the conditions for obtaining the discount are objective and transparent. In this context, a reference period of one year will not be acceptable, while a reference period of three months seems to be acceptable.[221]

The significance of the 'efficient competitor test' to the assessment of the discount arrangements of a dominant undertaking was the subject of a preliminary ruling by the CJ in Case C-23/14, *Post Danmark II*. The test consists of 'examining whether the pricing practices of a dominant undertaking could drive an equally efficient competitor

---

217. Communication from the Commission – Guidance on the Commission's enforcement priorities in applying Art. 82 of the EC Treaty to abusive exclusionary conduct by dominant undertakings, point 40 (OJ 2009 C 45/7) (as amended).
218. Case 85/76, *Hoffmann-La Roche*, para. 89. *See also* Joined Cases 40/73 and others, *Suiker Unie*, paras 518-528. According to the Commission, an exclusive purchasing obligation is one which 'requires a customer on a particular market to purchase exclusively or to a large extent only from the dominant undertaking'; *see* Communication from the Commission – Guidance on the Commission's enforcement priorities in applying Art. 82 of the EC Treaty to abusive exclusionary conduct by dominant undertakings, point 33 (OJ 2009 C 45/7) (as amended). *See*, *e.g.*, Case 322/81, *Michelin*, para. 210; and Case T-65/89, *BPB Industries*, paras 65-77.
219. *See* Case T-286/09 RENV, *Intel*, para. 522, concerning the foreclosing capability of a rebate system. *See also* Case C-549/10 P, *Tomra*.
220. Commission Decision *Solvay* (OJ 1990 L 152/21).
221. Case 322/81, *Michelin*, concerning a reference period of one year; and Commission Decision, *Coca-Cola* (OJ 1997 L 218/15), where the reference period was voluntarily reduced to three months.

from the market', and it 'is based on a comparison of the prices charged by a dominant undertaking and certain costs incurred by that undertaking as well as its strategy'.[222]

This test has been used in particular in connection with the CJ's evaluation of low-pricing policies in the form of selective pricing,[223] predatory pricing[224] and margin squeezing.[225] However, the CJ's case law does not establish that there is an obligation always to apply the 'efficient competitor test' when assessing whether a dominant undertaking's discount system involves abuse.[226] In Case C-549/10 P, *Tomra*, the CJ found that the lack of a comparison between the prices used in connection with the discounts and the dominant undertaking's costs did not constitute an error of law.[227]

However, as stated by the CJ in Case C-23/14, *Post Danmark II*, this does not mean that the 'efficient competitor test' should not be used in principle when assessing a discount system, but:

> in a situation such as that in the main proceedings, characterised by the holding by the dominant undertaking of a very large market share and by structural advantages conferred, inter alia, by that undertaking's statutory monopoly, which applied to 70% of mail on the relevant market, applying the as-efficient-competitor test is of no relevance inasmuch as the structure of the market makes the emergence of an as-efficient competitor practically impossible.[228]
>
> Furthermore, in a market such as that at issue in the main proceedings, access to which is protected by high barriers, the presence of a less efficient competitor might contribute to intensifying the competitive pressure on that market and, therefore, to exerting a constraint on the conduct of the dominant undertaking.[229]

The application of the test was thus found not to be relevant in the *Post Danmark II* case.[230]

The question of dominant undertakings' use of marketing contributions does not seem to have been sanctioned as abuse in relation to EU law. Marketing grants have, however, been the subject of consideration by the Danish competition authorities in connection with the *Arla* dairy products company's use of such contributions. The Danish competition authorities found that such contributions should be assessed according to the same principles as those used in relation to the evaluation of discount schemes. Thus, the Danish Competition Council has stated that:

> Just as dominant undertakings can give their customers various discounts, when this is justified on cost grounds, in certain situations it must also be possible for

---

222. Case C-23/14, *Post Danmark II*, paras 53 and 54; and Case C-209/10, *Post Danmark*, para. 28. See also the clarifications in Communication from the Commission – Guidance on the Commission's enforcement priorities in applying Art. 82 of the EC Treaty to abusive exclusionary conduct by dominant undertakings, point 23ff. (OJ 2009 C 45/7) (as amended).
223. Case C-209/10, *Post Danmark*, paras 28–35.
224. Case C-62/86, *AKZO*, paras 70–73; and Case C-202/07 P, *France Télécom*, paras 107 and 108.
225. Case C-52/09, *TeliaSonera*, paras 40–46.
226. Case C-23/14, *Post Danmark II*, para. 57, and Case 680/20, *Unilever*, paras 57–58.
227. Case C-549/10, *Tomra*, para. 80.
228. Case C-23/14, *Post Danmark II*, para. 59.
229. Case C-23/14, *Post Danmark II*, para. 60.
230. Case C-23/14, *Post Danmark II*, para. 62.

dominant undertakings to give customers various forms of marketing contributions. On the basis of analogy, different marketing contributions can be given when it can be shown that the contribution primarily benefits the supplier – and not the retailer – and when it is neither the purpose nor the consequence of giving the contribution that other suppliers are excluded.[231]

4.1.5 Article 102, Second Paragraph, Sub-paragraph (d)

According to Article 102, second paragraph, sub-paragraph (d), there will also be abuse where a dominant undertaking makes the entering into a contract subject to acceptance by the other party of supplementary obligations which, by their nature or according to commercial usage, have no connection with the subject of such contracts.

Tied sales

Tied sales can take various forms. 'Tying' covers sales whereby, in order to obtain a right to buy the product or service required (the primary product), a trading partner must also agree to buy supplementary products or services (the secondary product). 'Bundling' refers to the usual way in which products are offered for sale and priced, including situations where products are only sold together in fixed ratios and where products can be bought individually, but the combination of individual prices is higher than the 'bundled' price.[232]

Tied sales may occur where an undertaking has a dominant position on the market for the tying product (the primary product) and can exploit this dominant position to reserve to itself a derived or associated market by forcing contracting parties to accept supplementary products or services (the secondary product). The undertaking will not necessarily have a dominant position on the market for the secondary product but can use tying-in arrangements to strengthen its position on the secondary market at the expense of consumers and competitors. Thus, in certain circumstances, the conduct of a dominant undertaking on markets other than the one in which it is dominant can constitute abuse contrary to Article 102.[233]

First, the supplementary transaction in a tied sale can consist of the contracting trading partner agreeing to buy other products from the dominant undertaking – the tied products. This kind of tied sale is referred to as a 'tie-in agreement'. The price of the tied-in products will often be above the market price, so that not only is the trading partner forced to buy the tied-in products, but it is also forced to buy them on less favourable terms than could be obtained elsewhere.

Second, the supplementary transaction can consist of the contracting trading partner agreeing not to buy the tied products from other specified suppliers. This

---

231. Decision of the Danish Competition Council of 30 March 2005, *Arla Foods rabatter og markedsføringstilskud*, Journal No: 3/1120-0289-0055, para. 66 (unofficial translation).
232. Communication from the Commission – Guidance on the Commission's enforcement priorities in applying Art. 82 of the EC Treaty to abusive exclusionary conduct by dominant undertakings, point 48 (OJ 2009 C 45/7) (as amended).
233. Case C-52/09, *TeliaSonera*, para. 85.

exclusionary conduct thus shuts out competitors from the derived or associated market. This type of tied sale is referred to as a 'tie-out agreement'.

Tied sales agreements can thus contain elements which are both exploitative and exclusionary.

For the prohibition in Article 102 to apply in connection with tied sales, the conditional supplementary transaction should not, by its nature or by commercial usage, be connected to the subject of the agreement.

In determining this, attention is paid to whether, from a consumer's point of view, the tying and the tied products are regarded as the same product or as separate products. According to the Commission, it will be assumed that there are separate products if, from the purchaser's point of view, 'in the absence of tying or bundling, a substantial number of customers would purchase or would have purchased the tying product without also buying the tied product from the same supplier, thereby allowing stand-alone production for both the tying and the tied product'.[234] For example, if a media player and an operating system are sold together, this will be a tied sale,[235] while it is natural to buy shoes and shoelaces together.[236] However, the result of this assessment can change over time, in line with product developments and changes to trade customs and consumer preferences. For example, while it was previously usual to buy surfboards and rigs as a composite product, this is no longer the case.

Regardless of whether it is found that, because of the nature of the products or because it is in line with commercial usage, the tied products are sold as a whole, the tied-in sale could be covered by Article 102 if the dominant undertaking cannot show that the tied-in sale is objectively justified and is in accordance with the principle of proportionality.[237] For example, the sale may be justified with regard to efficiency, whereby the dominant undertaking can reduce its costs or obtain technical or qualitative advantages.[238] However, it seems that this bears a high evidential burden.[239]

5 THE EFFECT ON TRADE

An undertaking's abuse of its dominant position is only prohibited to the extent that trade between the Member States is affected by the abuse; see Article 102. In this context, the effect on trade covers not only traditional cross-border trade in goods and

---

234. Communication from the Commission – Guidance on the Commission's enforcement priorities in applying Art. 82 of the EC Treaty to abusive exclusionary conduct by dominant undertakings, point 51 (OJ 2009 C 45/7) (as amended).
235. Case T-201/04, *Microsoft*, paras 917, 921 and 922. *See also* Case T-604-18, *Google and Alphabet (Google Android)*.
236. Case T-30/89, *Hilti*, on tied sales of cartridge magazines and nails for nail guns; and Case T-83/91, *Tetra Pak II*, concerning tied sales of filling machines and cartons for the packaging of liquid foods.
237. Case 333/94 P, *Tetra Pak II*, para. 37; and Case T-201/04, *Microsoft*, para. 942.
238. Communication from the Commission – Guidance on the Commission's enforcement priorities in applying Art. 82 of the EC Treaty to abusive exclusionary conduct by dominant undertakings, point 62 (OJ 2009 C 45/7).
239. Case 333/94 P, *Tetra Pak II*, para. 138.

services but any form of effect on cross-border economic activities between at least two Member States, including through a foreclosure of national markets or a change in the competitive structure of the internal market.[240] The application of the criterion is independent of how the relevant geographic area is defined – trade between Member States can thus be affected even though the relevant market is defined as national or sub-national.[241]

As previously stated, this condition limits the scope of application of Union law in relation to national law.[242] Thus, if a dominant undertaking's conduct is only relevant to the national market, then whether the conduct should be prohibited should be assessed according to national law.[243]

The requirement in Article 102 for there to be an effect on trade is interpreted broadly,[244] and it is, therefore, relatively easy to meet the requirement. Conduct which directly or indirectly, actually or potentially affects trade between Member States will thus fall within the scope of the provision.[245] If the conduct has an effect on trade flows and competition in the internal market, for example, where the abusive undertaking hinders competitors' access to the market, it is irrelevant for the application of Article 102 whether the conduct complained of exclusively takes place within the territory of a single Member State.[246]

Where the abusive conduct consists of several elements, in this context, it is not necessary to make a separate assessment of these individual elements, but rather, the conduct should be assessed as a whole. This means that if a dominant undertaking uses different kinds of abusive behaviour for the realisation of a strategy, for example, to

---

240. Case C-407/04 P, *Dalmine*, para. 89, and Case C-177/16, *Autortiesību un komunicēšanās konsultāciju aģentūra/Latvijas Autoru apvienība*, para. 26. Commission Notice – Guidelines on the effect on trade concept contained in Arts 81 and 82 of the Treaty, paras 19–21 (OJ 2004 C 101/81).
241. Commission Notice – Guidelines on the effect on trade concept contained in Arts 81 and 82 of the Treaty, para. 22 (OJ 2004 C 101/81).
242. The concept of effect on trade acts as a jurisdiction criterion which defines the scope of application of the EU's competition rules, *see* Joined Cases 56/64 and 58/64, *Consten & Grundig;* Joined Cases 6 and 7/73, *Commercial Solvents*, and Case C-177/16, *Autortiesību un komunicēšanās konsultāciju aģentūra/Latvijas Autoru apvienība*, para 26, as well as Commission Notice – Guidelines on the effect on trade concept contained in Arts 81 and 82 of the Treaty, para. 12 (OJ 2004 C 101/81).
243. There is an example of the lack of an effect on trade in Case 22/78, *Hugin*. Where trade is affected, national courts and competition authorities must apply the EU competition rules; *see* Council Regulation (EC) No 1/2003 on the implementation of the rules on competition laid down in Arts 81 and 82 of the Treaty, Art. 3(1), (OJ 2003 L 1/1). However, it is possible for national competition rules to be applied in parallel; *see* Ch. 7.
244. Joined Cases 6 and 7/73, *Commercial Solvents;* and Case 22/79, *SACEM*, para. 11. However, the need for a broad interpretation in order to ensure the implementation of the EU's competition policy has been gradually diminished as the competition laws of the Member States have increasingly been based on the Treaty's competition provisions.
245. Case C-407/04 P, *Dalmine*, para. 90, and Case C-177/16, *Autortiesību un komunicēšanās konsultāciju aģentūra/Latvijas Autoru apvienība*, para. 27.
246. Case 322/81, *Michelin*, para. 103.

eliminate its competitors, Article 102 applies to all these kinds of conduct if just one of them can affect trade between Member States.[247]

As is the case in relation to Article 101, the effect on trade must be appreciable/not insignificant.[248] The broad interpretation of the requirement for an effect on trade means that it is not necessary to give evidence of an actual appreciable effect on trade, but it is sufficient to show that the disputed conduct *could* affect trade appreciably.[249] Where a dominant undertaking practices conduct which can mean that a competitor is eliminated, it is not necessary to examine more closely whether the conduct directly affects the pattern of trade between Member States (imports and exports), but it is sufficient to establish that the structure of competition in the internal market will be changed if the competitor is eliminated.[250]

Bibliography

Beata Mäihaäniemi: *Competition Law and Big Data*, 2020.
Chiara Fumagalli, Massimo Mottta & Claudia Calcagno: *Exclusionary Practices*, 2018.
Christian Bergqvist (ed.): *Where Do We Stand on Discounts? – A Nordic Perspective*, 2017.
Christopher Bellamy & Graham Child (red.): *European Union Law of Competition*, 2018.
Fabiana Di Porto & Rupprecht Podszun (eds.): *Abusive Practices in Competition Law*, 2018.
Ivo Van Bael & Jean-Francois Bellis: *Competition Law of the European Community*, 2021.
Johan W. Van De Gronden & Catalin S. Rusu: *Competition Law in the EU*, 2021.
Jonathan Faull & Ali Nikpay (eds.): *The EU Law of Competition*, 2014
Miguel Sousa Ferro: *Market Definition in EU Competition Law*, 2019.
Pinar Akman, Or Brook & Konstantinos Stylianou (eds.): *Research Handbook on Abuse of Dominance and Monopolization*, 2023.
Richard Whish & David Bailey: *Competition Law*, 2021.

---

247. Commission Notice – Guidelines on the effect on trade concept contained in Arts 81 and 82 of the Treaty, para. 17 (OJ 2004 C 101/81). See Case 85/76, *Hoffmann-La Roche*, paras 126 and 127.
248. *See* Case C-407/04 P, *Dalmine*, para. 90, and Case C-177/16, *Autortiesību un komunicēšanās konsultāciju aģentūra/Latvijas Autoru apvienība*, para. 27, and Commission Notice – Guidelines on the effect on trade concept contained in Arts 81 and 82 of the Treaty, para. 13 (OJ 2004 C 101/81); *see* the CJ's judgment in Case 22/71, *Béguelin*, para. 16. *See also* paras 44–57 and 97–99 of the Commission Notice.
249. Joined Cases C-241 and 242/91 P, *Magill*, para. 69; and Case C-41/90, *Höfner & Elser*, para. 32.
250. Case 6 and 7/73, *Commercial Solvents*, para. 33; and Joined Cases T-24/93 and others, *CMB*, para. 203.

CHAPTER 7
Procedure and Enforcement Regulation (EC) No 1/2003

1 INTRODUCTION

In recent years, the procedural and enforcement system associated with Articles 101[1] and 102 is characterised by a high degree of decentralisation. Thus, enforcement takes place partly at the EU level, where it is taken care of by the Commission, subject to the judicial review of the Court of Justice of the European Union (CJ), and partly at the national level, where the national competition authorities and courts are involved.

Such a decentralised enforcement system requires close cooperation between all the authorities involved, both to ensure the uniform interpretation of Articles 101 and 102 and to ensure that the proper division of competence is complied with. The framework for the division and implementation of this competence and for cooperation to ensure the uniform application of the rules is laid down in Council Regulation (EC) No 1/2003 on the implementation of the rules on competition laid down in Articles 101 and 102 of the Treaty on the Functioning of the European Union (TFEU).[2] Among other things, the Regulation contains rules on the relevant authorities' powers of investigation and what types of sanctions can be imposed in connection with infringements of its provisions.

Regulation (EC) No 1/2003 constitutes the key legal framework for especially the Commission's enforcement of Articles 101 and 102. However, the Regulation does not stand alone; it is supplemented by a number of non-binding guidelines and notices issued by the Commission. Among other things, these guidelines and notices are aimed

---

1. Including the associated block exemption regulations discussed in more detail in Chs 2–5.
2. OJ 2003 L 1/1. Parts of the Regulation are implemented by Commission Regulation (EC) No 773/2004 relating to the conduct of proceedings by the Commission pursuant to Arts 81 and 82 of the EC Treaty (OJ 2004 L 123/18).

at clarifying and defining the key concepts, the frameworks for cooperation between the authorities involved, as well as the setting and imposition of fines and penalties.[3] At the national level, Directive 2019/1 of 11 December 2018 on reinforcement of the national competition authorities' power to enforce the competition rules effectively and to ensure a well-functioning internal market is the most important contribution to the enforcement of the European Competition rules. The Directive does, to a great extent, continue the enforcement framework which is laid down in Council Regulation 1/2003 so that the Commission's and the Member States' enforcement of Articles 101 and 102 is based very much on identical rules. The enforcement of Articles 101 and 102 is also based on a number of implementing provisions in the national legal systems in areas which do not fall under the heading of EU legal cooperation but where it remains a matter for the Member States to lay down the detailed rules.

Regulation (EC) No 1/2003 entered into force on 24 January 2003 and has applied since 1 May 2004[4] as the basis for dealing with cases on anticompetitive agreements and cases on abuse of a dominant position. From this date the Regulation has replaced the previous enforcement Regulation No 17/62,[5] which represented a central enforcement system under the authority of the Commission as the central and sole competent authority. The Member States should have complied with Directive 2019/1 by 4 February 2021.[6]

The aim of this chapter is to present the basic elements on which the enforcement system relating to Articles 101 and 102 is based. The enforcement system in Regulation (EC) No 1/2003 is specifically related to the application and implementation of Articles 101 and 102 of the Treaty, but the system is also based on the same legal principles as applied to the enforcement of the Treaty's other competition provisions. The focus of Directive 2019/1 is on ensuring that national enforcement is based on a system where

---

3. *See* Guidelines on the method of setting fines imposed pursuant to Art. 23(2)(a) of Regulation (EC) No 1/2003 (OJ 2006 C 210/2), Commission Notice on Immunity from fines and reduction of fines in cartel cases (OJ 2006 C 298/17), Commission Notice on cooperation within the Network of Competition Authorities (OJ 2004 C 101/43), Commission Notice on the cooperation between the Commission and the courts of the EU Member States in the application of Arts 81 and 82 EC (OJ 2004 C 101/54), Commission Notice on the handling of complaints by the Commission under Arts 81 and 82 of the EC Treaty (OJ 2004 C 101/65), Commission Notice on informal guidance relating to novel questions concerning Arts 81 and 82 of the EC Treaty that arise in individual cases (guidance letters) (OJ 2004 C 101/78), Commission Notice – Guidelines on the effect on trade concept contained in Arts 81 and 82 of the Treaty (OJ 2004 C 101/81), Communication from the Commission – Notice – Guidelines on the application of Art. 81(3) of the Treaty (OJ 2004 C 101/97), Commission Notice on the rules for access to the Commission file in cases pursuant to Arts 81 and 82 of the EC Treaty, Arts 53, 54 and 57 of the EEA Agreement and Council Regulation (EC) No 139/2004 (OJ 2005 C 325/7), Commission Notice on agreements of minor importance which do not appreciably restrict competition under Art. 81(1) of the Treaty establishing the European Community (*de minimis*) (OJ 2001 C 368/13), and Commission Notice on the definition of relevant market for the purposes of Community competition law (OJ 1997 C 372/5).
4. Regulation (EC) No 1/2003, Art. 45.
5. EEC Council: Regulation No 17: First Regulation implementing Arts 85 and 86 of the Treaty (OJ 1962 13/204) (English special edition: Series I Chapter 1959–1962 p. 87).
6. *See* Directive 2019/1, Art. 34.

independent enforcement takes place,[7] where the system has sufficient resources,[8] and where the fundamental guarantees are maintained.[9]

1.1 Regulation (EC) No 1/2003: Structure

Regulation (EC) No 1/2003 consists of forty-five articles divided into eleven chapters under the following headings:[10]

> Chapter I: Principles (Articles 1-3)
> Chapter II: Powers (Articles 4-6)
> Chapter III: Commission decisions (Articles 7-10)
> Chapter IV: Cooperation (Articles 11-16)
> Chapter V: Powers of investigation (Articles 17-22)
> Chapter VI: Penalties (Articles 23-24)
> Chapter VII: Limitation periods (Article 25-26)
> Chapter VIII: Hearings and Professional secrecy (Articles 27-28)
> Chapter IX: Exemption regulations (Article 29)
> Chapter X: General provisions (Articles 30-33)
> Chapter XI: Transitional, amending and final provisions (Articles 34-45)

1.2 2001: The Modernisation of the Enforcement of Articles 101 and 102

From the mid-1990s onwards, the system for the enforcement of the competition rules was subject to detailed consideration. This led to the publication, in 1999, of the Commission's White Paper on the modernisation of the rules implementing Articles 101 and 102 of the Treaty, which had the aim of presenting the main outlines of the changes which the Commission was considering for proposing as reforms of the enforcement system.[11] The background to the desire for reform was the existence of a number of unintended consequences and restrictions in connection with the application of the system that had been established under the-then applicable implementation Regulation No 17/62.[12]

Under the Regulation then in force, upon application by the undertakings concerned, the Commission could certify that, on the basis of the facts in its possession, there were no grounds for action on its part in respect of the conduct of the undertakings.[13] Similarly, on the basis of a notification to the Commission concerning

---

7. Directive 2019/1, Art. 4.
8. *See* Directive 2019/1, Art. 5.
9. It appears from Directive 2019/1, Art. 3(1) that in regard to enforcement, the general principles of Union law and the Charter of Fundamental Rights of the European Union must be observed.
10. Directive 2019/1 has a different structure, but the central themes are very much identical.
11. Commission White Paper of 5 Dec. 1999 on modernisation of the rules implementing Arts 85 and 86 of the EC Treaty, COM(1999) 101 final (OJ 1999 C 132/1).
12. EEC Council: Regulation No 17: First Regulation implementing Arts 85 and 86 of the Treaty (OJ 1962 13/204) (English special edition: Series I Chapter 1959-1962 p. 87).
13. EEC Council: Regulation No 17, Art. 2.

their agreements, decisions and practices, the undertakings concerned could seek individual exemption under Article 101(3).[14] Regulation No 17/62 required the Commission to concentrate its efforts on dealing with notifications received, rather than concentrating on more pro-active control functions, which was the role which the Commission preferred to play in relation to Articles 101 and 102. This was so even though the Commission had put in place several measures to reduce the number of notifications, such as introducing informal procedures which were less demanding on resources than the formal procedures (comfort letters), as well as establishing a fixed *de minimis* threshold which excluded certain agreements from the scope of Article 101, thus removing them from the notification process.

Another factor was that, even with the increase in the number of EU Member States, no amendment had been made to Regulation No 17/62. So it was the view of the Commission that there was a need to bring the Regulation up to date, as the accumulated effects of increased market integration, the accession of new Member States, the entry into agreements with third countries, and the globalisation of the economy since the 1960s had led to a significant expansion of the role of the Commission and the number of cases which the Commission was required to deal with.[15]

The conduct of undertakings was also relevant. The Commission noted that undertakings quickly discovered that they could benefit from the opportunity to make notifications because they knew that, due to their large number, the Commission's processing of notifications was long drawn out, while being aware that during the processing period, i.e., after notifications were made, they obtained immunity from fines.

At the same time, the developments in the EU and in relation to the competition rules meant that the need for an enforcement system had gone beyond the central enforcement system laid down by Regulation No 17/62. This was primarily because in the practice of the Commission, in notices and suchlike, as well as in the cases decided by the CJ and the General Court (GC), such a large body of information about the competition rules had been accumulated that, on the basis of this material, undertakings and their advisers would themselves be able to assess whether they were covered by the scope of the competition rules.[16]

These considerations formed the background to the drafting of Regulation (EC) No 1/2003. The Regulation retains certain aspects of the procedural rules which were previously found in Regulation No 17/62, while making a number of key changes.

The most obvious changes in Regulation (EC) No 1/2003 in relation to Regulation No 17/62 were: (1) the notification system was abandoned in favour of a system by which, in the first instance, undertakings must themselves assess whether there is an infringement; (2) the Commission was given increased scope for controls and increased powers for obtaining information; and (3) Member States' bodies (competition

---

14. EEC Council: Regulation No 17, Arts 4(1) and 5(1).
15. Paragraphs 19–23 of the White Paper.
16. Paragraph 51 of the White Paper.

authorities and courts) were given the possibility of applying the exemptions under Article 101(3) of the Treaty.[17]

2 THE RELATIONSHIP BETWEEN UNION COMPETITION LAW AND NATIONAL COMPETITION LAW

2.1 Direct Applicability

The CJ has previously established that both Article 101(1) and Article 102 are directly applicable.[18] Thus, both natural and legal persons can rely on these provisions directly before national courts, and the national courts have an obligation to apply the provisions in order to protect the rights that Article 101(1) and Article 102 ascribe to the parties involved.

The direct applicability of these rules is further emphasised and expanded by Regulation (EC) No 1/2003 since, according to Articles 5 and 6 of the Regulation, national courts and competition authorities are given powers to apply the provisions, including the right of an exemption under Article 101(3).

While under the previous Regulation, the Commission had sole powers to decide on the right to an exemption under Article 101(3), the direct applicability of the provisions means that an agreement which is covered by Article 101(1) and which satisfies the conditions for an exemption in accordance with Article 101(3), is considered lawful without it being necessary for a competition authority to make a decision on this.[19]

In contrast, abuse covered by Article 102, as well as agreements covered by Article 101(1) which do not fulfil the conditions for exemption under Article 101(3), are considered prohibited, though likewise without it being necessary for a competition authority to make a decision on this.[20]

2.2 The Framing and Application of National Competition Law in Relation to Articles 101 and 102 of the Treaty

The provisions of national competition law apply in cases where cartel agreements or an undertaking's abuse of a dominant position does not affect trade between Member States. However, regardless of whether trade between Member States is affected, under certain conditions, it is possible for the national competition authorities to apply national competition law to a situation.

---

17. For a further discussion of Regulation (EC) No 1/2003, see Jonathan Faull & Ali Nikpay: *The EC Law of Competition*, 2007, Ch. 2, and James Venit: *Brave New World: The Modernization and Decentralization of Enforcement under Articles 81 and 82 of the EC Treaty*, Common Market Law Review, 2003 pp. 545–580.
18. Case C-453/99, *Courage*, para. 23.
19. Regulation (EC) No 1/2003, Art. 1(2).
20. Regulation (EC) No 1/2003, Arts 1(1) and 3.

It appears from Article 1(1) of Directive 2019/1 that the Directive applies to the parallel use of Articles 101 and 102 and national competition law to the same case.

Where the competition authorities or courts of a Member State apply national competition law to an agreement, etc., as referred to in Article 101(1), or to the abuse of a dominant position under Article 102, which can affect trade between Member States, as referred to in the article concerned, they must also apply Article 101 or Article 102, as appropriate, to such agreement or abuse.[21]

However, under no circumstances may the application of national competition law lead to the ban of agreements, etc., which can affect trade between Member States, but which are not covered by the prohibition in Article 101.[22] National rules on prohibitions of agreements which can affect trade between Member States may thus not be more restrictive than the rules of Union law. There is no corresponding rule against there being stricter national regulation prohibiting or penalising unilateral conduct, and therefore, in this context, the Member States can adopt more restrictive national competition rules.[23]

The question of the effect on trade is thus central, not only in relation to which set of competition rules is applicable to given circumstances but also in relation to the obligations to which national courts, competition authorities and legislators are subject. As part of its reform package, the Commission has published a Notice giving guidelines on the effect on trade concept in Articles 101 and 102 of the Treaty.[24] Apart from giving an account of the principles which the courts have developed in relation to the interpretation of the concept of trade, the Notice sets out the 'non-appreciable affectation of trade rule' or 'NAAT-rule', which can be used by the courts and competition authorities of the Member States as guidance for establishing when agreements can, in general, be assumed to affect trade between Member States appreciably.[25]

3   ALLOCATION OF COMPETENCE, POWERS AND UNIFORMITY

As referred to above, the enforcement of Articles 101 and 102 of the Treaty is the task of both the Commission and the national competition authorities and courts. This enforcement is carried out through close cooperation between the authorities involved.

---

21. Regulation (EC) No 1/2003, Art. 3(1). *See,* e.g., the Decision of the Danish Competition Authority of 26 Oct. 2011, *Dansk Brand- og Sikringsteknisk Instituts retningslinie 001.*
22. This is so regardless of whether the reason why the situation is not covered by the prohibition in Art. 101(1) is due to the fact that competition is not restricted in accordance with Art. 101(1), that the conditions for exemption under Art. 101(3) are fulfilled, or that the agreement is covered by a block exemption.
23. Regulation (EC) No 1/2003, Art. 3(2). Article 3(1) and (2) do not in principle apply to the application of national rules on merger control by national authorities and courts, nor national rules which have some other primary purpose than that pursued by Arts 101 and 102 of the Treaty; *see* Art. 3(3).
24. Commission Notice – Guidelines on the effect on trade concept contained in Arts 81 and 82 of the Treaty (OJ 2004 C 101/81).
25. Commission Notice – Guidelines on the effect on trade concept contained in Arts 81 and 82 of the Treaty, point 3 (OJ 2004 C 101/81).

In addition to helping to ensure the uniform application of Articles 101 and 102, this cooperation also helps both to ensure that specific cases are dealt with by the authority which has the competence to do so and to prevent several authorities which have the competence to deal with the same case from initiating parallel proceedings.

For this purpose, the Commission and the competition authorities of the Member States are part of a competition network which constitutes a forum for discussion and cooperation on the implementation and enforcement of Articles 101 and 102, and within which the authorities can exchange information about, for example, investigations which they have initiated and cases they have concluded.[26]

Cooperation between the Commission and the national courts also involves exchange of information about, among other things, decided cases, and the national courts have the possibility of obtaining the opinion of the Commission on the application of Articles 101 and 102.[27]

It should also be noted that self-regulation by undertakings plays a role in the overall enforcement of Articles 101 and 102. This self-regulation is not explicitly referred to in Regulation (EC) No 1/2003, but it is a direct consequence of the ending of the notification system and the full direct applicability of the provisions. Thus, today many large undertakings have formulated compliance programmes which are directly focused on ensuring that they act in accordance with Articles 101 and 102.

In cases where there is a dispute about whether the competition rules have been infringed, according to the CJ's decision in Case C-185/95 P, *Baustahlgewebe v. Commission*, it is up to the Commission to show evidence of an infringement and that the circumstances which constitute such infringement do in fact exist.[28]

This rule on the burden of proof has now been codified in Regulation (EC) No 1/2003, Article 2, and has been extended so as to cover the other authorities which enforce the competition rules with a view to ensuring the effective enforcement of the competition rules, while respecting the fundamental right of a party to defend themselves.[29] Thus, the burden of proof to show that there is an infringement of Article 101(1) and Article 102 rests on the party or the authority which asserts the existence of such infringement.

In contrast, the burden of proof for satisfying the conditions of Article 101(3) rests on the undertakings or associations of undertakings which claim the benefit of the exemption in question.[30]

---

26. Regulation (EC) No 1/2003, Art. 11. *See also* Commission Notice on cooperation within the Network of Competition Authorities (OJ 2004 C 101/43).
27. Regulation (EC) No 1/2003, Art. 15. *See also* Commission Notice on the co-operation between the Commission and the courts of the EU Member States in the application of Arts 81 and 82 EC (OJ 2004 C 101/54).
28. Case C-185/95 P, *Baustahlgewebe v. Commission*, para. 58.
29. Regulation (EC) No 1/2003, Recital 5.
30. Regulation (EC) No 1/2003, Art. 2. The provision expresses the general principle on the allocation of the burden of proof; if any person makes a claim about some circumstances (e.g., that they infringe the competition rules), they have the burden of proof for showing that this is so. At the same time, the burden of proof relating to Art. 101(3), requires that, in accordance with the general rules on exemptions in Union law, an undertaking has the burden of proof for showing the existence of circumstances which justify the exemption claimed.

The requirements which, in a concrete case, are made as to the standard of proof or to the enforcing authority's obligation to ascertain the relevant facts of a case are not regulated in the Regulation but are governed by the rules which apply in the legal systems within which the respective authorities operate, whether this concerns the EU Commission or the national competition authorities or courts.[31]

The rules for the cooperation between the national competition authorities in the different Member States are laid down in Directive 2019/1. Chapter VII of the Directive deals with the duty to assist other national authorities in connection with competition law cases.

3.1 The Commission's Competences

The Commission's powers in relation to the application of Articles 101 and 102 are laid down in Regulation (EC) No 1/2003,[32] which defines the powers of the Commission in respect of, among other things, initiating proceedings, dealing with complaints, the form and content of decisions, and the right to carry out control inspections. In principle, the Commission's involvement with actual competition cases and the subsequent application of the competition rules arises either from a complaint or from taking up a case on its own initiative.

Thus, if, on the basis of a complaint[33] or on its own initiative, the Commission finds that there is an infringement of Article 101 or 102, it can make a decision requiring the undertakings or undertakings concerned to bring such infringement to an end.[34] In this connection, the Commission has the possibility of imposing *behavioural remedies* on undertakings, in other words, in practice to stop certain conduct and to refrain from it in future.

The Commission also has powers to impose *structural remedies* on the undertakings concerned under Article 7(1), second sentence of Regulation (EC) No 1/2003, for example, the disposal of a subsidiary or part of an undertaking. The imposition of such obligations is also a key power in relation to the Merger Control Regulation.[35]

However, in Article 7(1), it is stated that structural remedies can only be imposed either where there is no equally effective behavioural remedy or where any equally effective behavioural remedy would be more burdensome for the undertaking concerned than the structural remedy.

Prior to making a final decision about an infringement of Article 101 or 102, the Commission has the possibility of deciding on interim measures on the basis of a prima facie finding of infringement. However, this only applies if there is a risk of serious and irreparable damage to competition; *see* Article 8(1) of Regulation (EC) No 1/2003.[36]

---

31. Regulation (EC) No 1/2003, Recital 5.
32. Regulation (EC) No 1/2003, Art. 4.
33. According to Art. 7(2) of Regulation (EC) No 1/2003, a complaint can be lodged by a natural or legal person who can show a legitimate interest, or by a Member State.
34. Regulation (EC) No 1/2003, Art. 7.
35. *See* in more detail in Ch. 8.
36. A decision on interim measures will apply for a specified period but may be renewed if necessary and appropriate.

Where the Commission intends to adopt a decision to bring to an end an infringement of the competition rules, the undertakings concerned may offer commitments to meet the concerns of the Commission. Where undertakings give such commitments, the Commission may decide to make them binding on the undertakings. Such a decision may be adopted for a specified period, and it must be concluded in the decision that there are no longer grounds for action by the Commission; see Article 9(1), second sentence of Regulation (EC) No 1/2003. However, reasons may nevertheless arise for the Commission to reopen the proceedings either upon request or on its own initiative: (a) if there has been a material change in any of the facts on which the decision was based; (b) if the undertakings concerned act contrary to their commitments; or (c) if the decision was based on incomplete, incorrect or misleading information provided by the parties.[37]

Finally, where the 'Community public interest relating to the application of Articles 101 and 102 of the Treaty so requires', the Commission, acting on its own initiative, may decide that Article 101 or Article 102 is not applicable to an agreement in a specific case.[38]

3.2 The Competences of the National Competition Authorities and Courts

According to Article 5 of Regulation (EC) No 1/2003, the competition authorities of the Member States have the power to apply Articles 101 and 102 of the Treaty in individual cases. Conversely, this means that the authorities do not have the power to apply the provisions generally, for example, to grant a block exemption. In connection with the treatment of a specific case, national competition authorities can require infringements to be brought to an end and decide on interim measures, accept commitments, impose fines, periodic penalty payments or any other penalty provided for in the national law of the Member State concerned.

However, national authorities lose their powers to apply Articles 101 and 102 if the Commission itself initiates proceedings in relation to infringements of the competition rules. Where a national competition authority is already dealing with a case, the Commission will first initiate proceedings after having consulted the competition authority in question.[39]

Where several national competition authorities have jurisdiction to deal with a specific case, it will be sought to have the case dealt with by the most suitable authority.[40] But in certain cases, it may be most appropriate to have the case dealt with

---

37. Regulation (EC) No 1/2003, Art. 9(2). There is no obligation for the Commission to reopen a decision to make an commitment binding; see Case T-342/11 *CEEES II*.
38. Regulation (EC) No 1/2003, Art. 10. No more specific definition has been given of what is meant by the 'Community public interest'. However, it may be possible to draw on the term 'the interests of the Community', which is found in Art. 106(2), last sentence of the Treaty. Under this provision it is possible that the Community public interest means an interest which is in line with the purposes of the Community set out in Art. 3 of the Treaty on European Union.
39. Regulation (EC) No 1/2003, Art. 11(6).
40. Commission Notice on cooperation within the Network of Competition Authorities, points 7 and 8 (OJ 2004 C 101/43).

in parallel by more than one national competition authority.[41] Where a competition authority of a Member State receives a complaint about a case which is already being dealt with by another competition authority, it may reject it.[42] When a national competition authority or the Commission receives a complaint about a case, a decision made within an association of undertakings, or a practice which has already been dealt with by another competition authority, the same applies, and the case may be rejected.[43]

In relation to national courts, their jurisdiction is established by Article 6 of Regulation (EC) No 1/2003 to the effect that: 'National courts shall have the power to apply Articles 81 and 82 [now Articles 101 and 102] of the Treaty.'

In contrast to the earlier Regulation No 17/62, under Regulation (EC) No 1/2003, both the national competition authorities and the national courts have jurisdiction to apply Article 101(3) of the Treaty.[44] Before Directive 2019/1 was adopted, there was a risk that delegating jurisdiction for the enforcement of the competition rules to national competition authorities and courts would lead to the loss of the uniformity which was guaranteed by the sole jurisdiction of the Commission.[45] On this basis, Article 16 of Regulation (EC) No 1/2003 includes a provision to the effect that when national courts rule on agreements, decisions or practices under Article 101 or Article 102 of the Treaty which are already the subject of a Commission decision, they cannot make decisions which run counter to the decision adopted by the Commission. National courts must also 'avoid giving decisions which would conflict with a decision contemplated by the Commission in proceedings it has initiated'.[46] If the Commission has already made a decision in a case, the national competition authorities cannot make decisions which would run counter to the decision of the Commission in a case concerning the same facts.[47]

Where there is doubt about the interpretation of competition law, the national courts can make referrals to the CJ for preliminary rulings in accordance with Article 267 of the Treaty. Against the background of the *Syfait* case,[48] it is hardly likely that a national competition authority will be considered as being entitled to make a referral

---

41. Commission Notice on cooperation within the Network of Competition Authorities, point 12 (OJ 2004 C 101/43).
42. Regulation (EC) No 1/2003, Art. 13(1).
43. Regulation 1/2003, Art. 13(2). *See* Case T-355/13, *easyJet Airline Co. Ltd*.
44. However, in Case C-375/09, *Tele2 Polska*, the CJ pointed out that it is not within the competence of national competition authorities to decide that Art. 102 TFEU has not been breached. The CJ was of the view that allowing such national competence would prevent the Commission coming to a different conclusion.
45. This risk is eliminated through Directive 2019/1, which requires uniformity of certain issues related to the enforcement.
46. Since it can be difficult for the national courts to predict what decision the Commission will make, it is pointed out in Art. 16(1) of the Regulation that they may assess whether it is necessary to stay their proceedings. It is also made clear in Art. 16(1) that the obligation of the national courts under the Regulation is without prejudice to the rights and obligations of courts to make referrals for preliminary rulings under Art. 267 of the Treaty.
47. Regulation (EC) No 1/2003, Art. 16(2).
48. Case C-53/03, *Syfait*.

3.3 Self-Evaluation and Decisions on Inapplicability

Regulation (EC) No 1/2003 departed from the notification system, which was previously the cornerstone of Union competition law. This change meant that it was no longer possible for undertakings to give notifications to the Commission with a view to obtaining clarification on the assessment of an agreement under competition law. In relation to exemptions under Article 101(3) of the Treaty, the situation is thus that undertakings must themselves apply the whole of Article 101 and assess for themselves whether they are, on the one hand, covered by Article 101(1), and if so whether the conditions of Article 101(3) are satisfied so the undertaking is exempted from the prohibition. Thus, there is no requirement for a stamp of approval from the Commission in order to obtain an exemption.[49]

However, there is always a risk that an undertaking will make a wrong assessment of the compatibility of a given agreement with Article 101. Both the Commission and the national competition authorities may assess the situation differently so that a decision will be made that the undertaking has infringed Article 101. The undertaking's assessment is thus by no means binding on the enforcing authorities. However, it can be an element which is taken into account in connection with the assessment of the seriousness of an infringement and, thereby the size of a fine which may be imposed on the undertaking for the infringement.

However, Article 10 of Regulation (EC) No 1/2003 allows the possibility for the Commission to decide, on its own initiative, that Article 101(1) does not apply to an agreement etc. This scope for the Commission to make a 'Finding of inapplicability'[50] in relation to a specific agreement can be based either on the grounds that the conditions for applying Article 101(1) do not exist or that the conditions for granting an exemption under Article 101(3) do exist.

Undertakings cannot rely on the Commission making such a finding of inapplicability in relation to their agreements on its own initiative. There is thus not the same direct possibility of obtaining a formal declaration that the enforcement authorities do not regard the agreement in question to be contrary to Article 101, and undertakings must thus rely on their own assessments of the lawfulness of their agreements.

4 POWERS OF INVESTIGATION

4.1 The Commission's Powers of Investigation

In connection with the investigation of whether an undertaking's conduct is in accordance with Article 101 or Article 102 on the basis of Regulation (EC) No 1/2003,

---

49. Regulation (EC) No 1/2003, Art. 1(2).
50. The heading of the Article.

the Commission has powers to conduct general investigations of sectors of the economy and to make more specific investigations on the premises of undertakings and certain private premises, as well as obtaining relevant information and taking statements in order to throw light on a case. These powers can be used individually or together, depending on the actual case and on what is proportionate in the context in question.[51]

According to Article 17 of Regulation (EC) No 1/2003, the Commission can conduct inquiries into a particular sector of the economy or into a particular type of agreement across various sectors if, for example, the development of trade between Member States or the lack of price elasticity provokes the suspicion that competition is restricted or distorted.[52] In this connection, the Commission may request the undertakings or associations of undertakings concerned to supply the information necessary for the application of the competition rules.[53]

In addition to the cases where there is a suspicion of a restriction on competition, the Commission can, by a request or a decision, require undertakings to provide all necessary information, where this is required in order to carry out the duties assigned to it by the Regulation.[54]

The more detailed rules for the Commission's request for information are laid down in Article 18 of the Regulation. Regardless of whether the Commission uses a request or a decision to obtain the information, the document in question must state:[55] (1) the legal basis and the purpose of the request, (2) what information is required, (3) the time limit within which it is to be provided, (4) and the penalties for providing incorrect or misleading information.[56] Where information is sought on the basis of a decision, it must also be stated that the decision can be referred to the CJ.

Information can be required from owners of the undertakings or their representatives.[57] In the case of legal persons, companies, or associations, the persons authorised to represent them by law or by their constitution must supply the information requested.

Finally, lawyers duly authorised to act may supply the information on behalf of their clients. However, the clients remain fully responsible for the information supplied being complete, correct and not misleading.

---

51. *See* Case T-145/06, *Omya AG*, para. 34, and Case T-340/04, *France Télécom SAT,* para. 147.
52. For example, in this connection the Commission has examined the European electricity and gas sectors; *see* COM(2006) 851 final.
53. According to Art. 17(1) fourth sentence, the Commission may publish a report on the results of its inquiries and invite comments from interested parties.
54. Regulation (EC) No 1/2003, Art. 18(1).
55. Regulation (EC) No 1/2003, Art. 18(2) and (3).
56. According to Art. 23(1)(a), fines can be imposed for giving incorrect or misleading information in response to a request made pursuant to Art. 17 or Art. 18(2). Likewise, under Art. 18(1)(b), fines can be imposed for giving incorrect, incomplete or misleading information or failing to give information within the required time limit. Furthermore, where information is obtained from undertakings on the basis of decision, under Art. 24(1)(d) periodic penalty payments can be imposed with a view to getting undertaking to supply complete and correct information which has been requested.
57. Regulation (EC) No 1/2003, Art. 18(4).

If the Commission so requests, the governments and competition authorities of the Member States are obliged to provide the Commission with all the necessary information for carrying out the duties assigned to it by the Regulation.[58]

In addition to obtaining information, the Commission also has the power to take statements.[59] The Commission may interview any natural or legal person who consents to be interviewed.[60] The aim of such an interview is to obtain information about the circumstances in a particular case. Where an interview is conducted on the premises of an undertaking, the Commission must inform the competition authority of the Member State where the interview takes place, and, at its request, representatives of the competition authority of that Member State may assist the officials of the Commission at the interview.[61]

However, the principle that a person may not be obliged to incriminate themselves does limit the Commission's powers to obtain information to a certain extent. Thus, an undertaking is not obliged to confess to an infringement of Article 101 or 102,[62] but an undertaking is obliged to provide information and documents, even if this information may be used against it.[63]

4.2 The Commission's Inspections

4.2.1 *The Commission's Inspections of Undertakings*

The Commission is empowered to carry out all necessary inspections of undertakings and associations of undertakings in order to carry out the duties assigned to it by Regulation (EC) No 1/2003.[64]

These powers include the right:

(a) to enter any premises, land and means of transport of undertakings and associations of undertakings;
(b) to examine the books and other records related to the business, irrespective of the medium on which they are stored;
(c) to take or obtain in any form copies of or extracts from such books or records;
(d) to seal any business premises and books or records for the period of the investigation and to the extent necessary for the inspection;

---

58. Regulation (EC) No 1/2003, Art. 18(6).
59. Regulation (EC) No 1/2003, Art. 19.
60. However, there is no right to force people to take part in an interview.
61. Regulation (EC) No 1/2003, Art. 19(2).
62. Regulation (EC) No 1/2003, Recital 23; and Case 374/87, *Orkem*, para. 35.
63. Case 374/87, *Orkem*, paras 34–35; Joined Cases T-236/01, T-239/01, T-244 to 246/01, and T-251 and 252/01, *Tokai and others v. Commission*, paras 402–403; and Case C-301/04 P, *Commission v. SGL*, paras 41–42. *See also* Commission notice on best practices for the conduct of proceedings concerning Arts 101 and 102 TFEU (OJ 2011 C 308/60).
64. Regulation (EC) No 1/2003, Art. 20(1).

(e) to ask any representative or member of staff of the undertaking or association of undertakings for explanations on facts or documents relating to the subject matter and purpose of the inspection and to record the answers.

There are certain formal requirements for the documentation on which an inspection is based. Thus, the Commission's representatives and others who accompany them and who are authorised by the Commission to carry out an inspection must show written authority. This must specify the subject matter and purpose of the inspection and the penalties applicable if there is incomplete provision of the books required or other records related to the business or if the answers given to questions asked under Article 20(2) are incorrect or misleading.[65]

The Commission must give notice of the inspection to the competition authority of the Member State, where it is to be conducted in good time before the inspection is carried out.

Representatives of the competition authorities, as well as persons authorised or appointed by the competition authorities of the Member State where the inspection is to be carried out, must, at the request of the competition authority concerned or of the Commission, actively assist the Commission's representatives and others who accompany them and who are authorised by the Commission.

Undertakings have an obligation to submit to inspections to which the Commission has subjected them by a decision. The decision must state the subject matter and purpose of the inspection, the date for the commencement of the inspection, and give information about the penalties applicable,[66] as well as the right to refer the decision to the CJ. The Commission takes such decisions after consulting the competition authorities in the Member State where the inspection is to be carried out.

If the Commission's representatives and those accompanying them who are authorised by the Commission establish that an undertaking opposes an inspection ordered in accordance with the Regulation, the Member State concerned must give them the necessary assistance to enable them to conduct their inspection. This may include requesting the assistance of the police or of an equivalent enforcement authority.[67]

If, under national rules, such assistance requires authorisation from a judicial authority, such authorisation shall be applied for. Upon such an application being made, the national court can control that the Commission's decision is authentic and that the coercive measures envisaged are neither arbitrary nor excessive having regard to the subject matter of the inspection. In its control of this, the national court may ask the Commission, directly or through the Member State's competition authority, for detailed explanations of the grounds which the Commission has for suspecting infringement of Articles 101 and 102 of the Treaty, as well as of the seriousness of the suspected infringement and the nature of the involvement of the undertaking concerned. However, the national court may not call into question the necessity for the

---

65. Regulation (EC) No 1/2003, Art. 20(3).
66. Regulation (EC) No 1/2003, Arts 23 and 24.
67. Regulation (EC) No 1/2003, Art. 20(6).

inspection nor demand that it be provided with the information in the Commission's file. In this context, the CJ has sole jurisdiction to examine the lawfulness of the Commission's decisions.

4.2.2 Inspections in Private Homes

Regulation (EC) No 1/2003 gives the Commission powers to carry out inspections other than on the premises of an undertaking, including in private homes; *see* Article 21. Mostly, these inspections follow the same rules as normal inspections.

If the Commission believes that there is a reasonable suspicion that books or other records related to the business and to the subject matter of the inspection, which may be relevant for proving the existence of a serious violation of Article 101 or Article 102 of the Treaty, are being kept in any other premises, land or means of transport, including the homes of directors, managers and other members of staff, the Commission can, by a decision, order an inspection of such other premises to be carried out.

As is the case for normal inspections,[68] the Commission's decision must specify the subject matter and purpose of the inspection, appoint the date on which it is to begin and indicate the right to have the decision reviewed by the CJ.[69]

Also, and in particular, the Commission must state the reasons that have led it to conclude that books or other records related to the business are being kept in any other premises than those of the undertaking. The Commission must take any decision referred to in Article 21(2) of the Regulation after consulting the competition authority of the Member State where the inspection is to be conducted. A decision under Article 21(1) may not be carried out without the prior permission of a national court of the Member State in question; *see* Article 21(3).

As with a normal inspection,[70] in this connection, a national court may not call into question the necessity for the inspection nor demand that it be provided with the information in the Commission's file, as the CJ has sole jurisdiction to examine the lawfulness of the Commission's decisions.

However, the national court can control that the Commission's decision is authentic and that the coercive measures envisaged are neither arbitrary nor excessive having regard to the subject matter of the inspection. In its control of this, the national court may take account of the seriousness of the presumed infringement and the importance of the evidence sought, the involvement of the undertaking concerned, and the reasonable likelihood that business books and records relating to the subject matter of the inspection are kept on the premises for which the authorisation is requested. In this connection, the national court may ask the Commission for detailed explanations concerning those elements which are necessary to allow it to assess the proportionality of the measures envisaged.[71]

---

68. Regulation (EC) No 1/2003, Art. 20(4).
69. Regulation (EC) No 1/2003, Art. 21(2), first sentence.
70. Regulation (EC) No 1/2003, Art. 20(8).
71. Regulation (EC) No 1/2003, Art. 21(3).

4.3 The Powers of the Member States to Carry Out Investigations

One of the aims of Regulation (EC) No 1/2003 is to establish better possibilities for cooperation between the competition authorities of the different Member States, among other things, in relation to the investigation and clearing up of competition cases.[72] It was thus also necessary to lay down rules on the powers of national competition authorities to carry out investigations, as regards investigations carried out at the request of other Member States or the Commission. Against this background, Article 22 of the Regulation lays down that the competition authority of a Member State may, in its own territory, carry out any inspection or other fact-finding measure under its national law on behalf and for the account of the competition authority of another Member State, in order to establish whether there has been an infringement of Article 101 or Article 102 of the Treaty. Any exchange and use of the information collected must comply with Article 12 of the Regulation. This means that it is possible to exchange evidence on any matter of fact or of law, including confidential information.[73] The information exchanged may only be used in evidence for the purpose of applying Article 101 or Article 102 and only in respect of the subject matter for which it was collected; see Article 12(2) of the Regulation.

At the request of the Commission, the competition authorities of the Member States undertake such inspections as the Commission considers necessary or has ordered by a decision (for both situations, see Article 20 of the Regulation). Those who are responsible for carrying out these inspections exercise their powers in accordance with national law.[74] In connection with inspections carried out at the request of the Commission, the national competition authorities can be assisted by representatives of the Commission.

In addition to the rules in Regulation 1/2003, more detailed rules are laid down in Directive 2019/1, where greater demands are made on the national competition authorities' opportunity to carry out inspections. In Articles 6 and 7 of the Directive, the framework for inspections of business premises and other premises (including private homes) is established.

5 THE CONSEQUENCES OF INFRINGEMENT

Where there is an infringement of the prohibition in Article 101 of the Treaty, the consequence of this is the invalidity of the agreement.[75] However, in the context of agreements that restrict trade, invalidity is not a very effective sanction. This is because, in principle, none of the parties to the agreement will have an advantage from

---

72. Commission White Paper of 5 Dec. 1999 on modernisation of the rules implementing Arts 85 and 86 of the EC Treaty, paras 91–98.
73. Regulation (EC) No 1/2003, Art. 12(1).
74. Regulation (EC) No 1/2003, Art. 22(2).
75. For further discussion of invalidity, see Ch. 2, s. 7.1.

claiming invalidity. On the contrary, the parties to such an agreement are often more interested in maintaining the agreement, which is a true expression of the parties' wishes in relation to their conduct in the market. Thus, in addition to invalidity, other sanctions can be applied to infringements of Article 101. The most important sanction – also in relation to Article 102 – is a fine, but it is also possible to impose periodic penalty payments, as well as to award damages for losses suffered because of an agreement which restricts competition.

5.1 Fines

Regulation (EC) No 1/2003 lays down detailed rules on the possibility of imposing fines for infringements of Articles 101 and 102. Such fines are not of a criminal law nature; *see* Article 23(5).

The Commission's scope for imposing fines is set out in Article 23.[76] Fines can be imposed in two situations: first, in connection with the infringement of the formal rules which apply to enforcement, and second, in connection with substantive infringements of the competition rules in the Treaty.[77] For infringement of the rules which apply to enforcement, the Commission can impose on undertakings and associations of undertakings fines not exceeding 1% of the total turnover in the preceding business year. The culpability for applying such a fine is based on intention or negligence.[78] Fines can be imposed if an undertaking gives incorrect or misleading information in reply to a request made in accordance with Article 17 or Article 18(2) of Regulation (EC) No 1/2003; if in response to a request made by a decision adopted pursuant to Article 17 or Article 18(3), an undertaking gives incorrect, incomplete or misleading information or fails to supply information within the required time limit; if seals affixed in accordance with Article 20(2)(d) by officials or other accompanying persons authorised by the Commission have been broken.[79]

Furthermore, fines can be imposed where undertakings subject to investigation in accordance with Article 20 of the Regulation produce the required books or other records related to the business in incomplete form or refuse to submit to inspections ordered by a decision adopted pursuant to Article 20(4).

Finally, it is possible to impose fines where, in response to a question asked in accordance with Article 20(2)(e), an undertaking gives an incorrect or misleading answer; fails to rectify within a time limit set by the Commission an incorrect, incomplete or misleading answer given by a member of staff, or fails or refuses to provide a complete answer on facts relating to the subject matter and purpose of an inspection ordered by a decision adopted pursuant to Article 20(4).

---

76. The rules concerning the opportunity to impose fines with regard to the Member States are stated in Arts 13-15 of Directive 2019/1.
77. In regard to the Member States' competition authorities, *see* Art. 13(1) and (2) of Directive 2019/1.
78. The same applies to the Member States, *see also* Art. 13(1) and (2) of Directive 2019/1.
79. *See*, e.g., Case T-141/08 *E.ON Energie AG*.

In relation to substantive infringements of the competition rules, for each undertaking which participates in the infringement, a fine may not exceed 10% of its total turnover in the preceding business year.[80]

When calculating the amount of a fine, regard shall be had both to the gravity and to the duration of the infringement, *see* Article 23(3) of Regulation (EC) No 1/2003.[81] Moreover, there is a possibility of exemption from a fine or a reduction of a fine in accordance with the Commission's Guidelines.

The Commission's Notice on immunity from fines in cartel cases must be taken into account.[82]

Whereas Regulation (EC) No 1/2003 does not mean there is any harmonisation of fines for infringements of Articles 101 and 102, the rules stated in Articles 13-15 of Directive 2019/1 set a harmonised framework for the Member States. In principle, in a corporate group, the parent company of a wholly owned subsidiary that has breached the competition rules will be jointly and severally liable for a fine. Where there is not 100% ownership of a subsidiary, it will be necessary to make a case-by-case assessment of whether the parent and subsidiary companies constitute an economic entity, thus giving rise to joint and several liability.[83]

In addition to fines, it is also possible to impose periodic penalty payments to the extent that this can compel undertakings to:[84]

(a) put an end to an infringement of Article 101 or Article 102 of the Treaty in accordance with a decision taken pursuant to Article 7 of Regulation (EC) No 1/2003;
(b) comply with a decision ordering interim measures taken pursuant to Article 8 of the Regulation;
(c) comply with a commitment made binding by a decision pursuant to Article 9 of the Regulation;
(d) supply complete and correct information which it has requested by decision taken pursuant to Article 17 or Article 18(3) of the Regulation; and
(e) submit to an inspection which it has ordered by decision taken pursuant to Article 20(4) of the Regulation.

---

80. Regulation (EC) No 1/2003, Art. 23(2). Detailed guidelines for the calculation of fines are laid down in the Commission's Guidelines on the method of setting fines imposed pursuant to Art. 23(2)(a) of Regulation (EC) No 1/2003 (OJ 2006 C 210/2). In regard to the Member States, the rules establish that the maximum amount of a fine should not be less than 10% of the total turnover, *see* Art. 15 of Directive 2019/1. On how to estimate the total turnover in the preceding business year, *see* Case C-76/06 P, *Britannia Alloys & Chemicals v. Commission* and Case C-90/13 P, 1. *garantovaná a.s v. Commission*.
81. *See* the Commission's Guidelines on the method of setting fines imposed pursuant to Art. 23(2)(a) of Regulation (EC) No 1/2003 (OJ 2006 C 210/2). In regard to the Member States, *see* Art. 14(1) of Directive 2019(1).
82. Commission Notice on Immunity from fines and reduction of fines in cartel cases (OJ 2006 C 298/17) with later amendments, *see* the Official Journal 2015/C 256/01. For the Member States, the framework for leniency is established in Arts 17-23 (Ch. VI) of Directive 2019/01.
83. Case T-587/08, *Fresh Del Monte Produce*; and Case C-521/09 P, *Elf Aquitaine*.
84. Regulation (EC) No 1/2003, Art. 24. In regard to Member States, *see* Art. 16g Directive 2019/1, which has a certain overlap with the Regulation.

The CJ has unlimited jurisdiction to review decisions whereby the Commission has fixed a fine or periodic penalty payment; *see* Article 31 of Regulation (EC) No 1/2003. According to the practice of the CJ, the GC also has unlimited jurisdiction in this respect.[85]

While there are no formal deadlines within which the Commission can commence an investigation of conduct that restricts competition contrary to Articles 101 and 102, there are rules on limitation periods for the Commission's powers to impose fines and periodic penalty payments and to enforce decisions on this.

The power of the Commission to impose fines or periodic penalty payments ends three years after an infringement of provisions concerning requests for information or the conduct of inspections.[86] This period of limitation is, in principle, calculated from the date on which the infringement is committed, while the period in cases where there is a continuing or repeated infringement is calculated from the date when the infringement ends.[87] The period of limitation is interrupted each time the Commission, or the competition authorities of a Member State, takes steps to investigate or prosecute the infringement, and thereafter, the period starts afresh, just as the period of limitation will be suspended as long as a case on the Commission's decision is pending before the CJ.[88]

The Commission's powers to enforce decisions on fines and periodic penalty payments expire after five years.[89] This period is calculated from the date on which the decision is made final and will, in certain circumstances, be interrupted or suspended.[90]

5.2 Damages

The EU rules do not state what possibilities there are for obtaining damages in connection with infringements of the competition rules (however, *see* section 5.2.1 below). The Member States still have an obligation to ensure that there is accessible and effective scope for enforcement. However, since provisions for obtaining damages are still a matter of national law, when damages may be awarded, the conditions that must be fulfilled to obtain damages and how damages are to be assessed are all questions to be decided under national law.

---

85. Case C-219/95 P, *Ferriere Nord v. Commission*, para. 31.
86. Regulation (EC) No 1/2003, Art. 25(1).
87. Regulation (EC) No 1/2003, Art. 25(2). *See* Case C-450/19, *Kilpailu- ja kuluttajavirasto*, in which the Court opined that the end date of a cartel in connection with the conclusion of a public contract was the date at which the contract was entered into, as this is the time at which the content of the contract is determined.
88. Regulation (EC) No 1/2003, Art. 25(5) and (6). According to Art. 25(5), the period of limitation expires 'at the latest on the day on which a period equal to twice the limitation period has elapsed without the Commission having imposed a fine or a periodic penalty payment. That period shall be extended by the time during which limitation is suspended pursuant to paragraph 6'. Article 29 of Directive 2019/1 contains detailed rules on when suspension of limitation periods takes place due to the authorities' treatment of competition cases.
89. Regulation (EC) No 1/2003, Art. 26(1).
90. Regulation (EC) No 1/2003, Art. 26(2) to (5).

However, there are certain EU rules on the conditions which must be fulfilled in connection with obtaining damages on the grounds of infringements of EU competition rules. This is subject to the general principle of EU law that the Member States must ensure the effective sanctioning of infringements of EU law.[91]

Among other things, the CJ has stated that: 'As regards the possibility of seeking compensation for loss caused by a contract or by conduct liable to restrict or distort competition, it should be remembered from the outset that, in accordance with settled case-law, the national courts whose task it is to apply the provisions of Union law in areas within their jurisdiction must ensure that those rules take full effect and must protect the rights which they confer on individuals.' The CJ continued: 'The full effectiveness of Article 85 of the Treaty and, in particular, the practical effect of the prohibition laid down in Article 85(1) would be put at risk if it were not open to any individual to claim damages for loss caused to him by a contract or by conduct liable to restrict or distort competition.'[92] The more detailed requirements for damages are laid down by the CJ, which has stated that 'in the absence of Community rules governing the matter, it is for the domestic legal system of each Member State to designate the courts and tribunals having jurisdiction and to lay down the detailed procedural rules governing actions for safeguarding rights which individuals derive directly from Community law, provided that such rules are not less favourable than those governing similar domestic actions (principle of equivalence) and that they do not render practically impossible or excessively difficult the exercise of rights conferred by Community law'; see Case C-453/99, *Courage*, paragraph 29.

5.2.1 Directive on Obtaining Damages under National Law for Infringements of the Competition Rules

As stated above, the regulation of the possibility of obtaining damages for breaches of the competition rules has traditionally been a matter that falls under the laws of the Member States. First, in practice, claims for damages are heard by national courts and second, the legal framework for awarding damages has been based on national rules, with only a few overriding Union law rules. The unintended effect of this situation has been that the scope for obtaining damages has varied between Member States, and it has been difficult to ensure that the possibilities for obtaining damages have been effective.

The legislator has found it necessary to adopt a directive with a view to ensuring effective scope for obtaining damages: *see* Directive 2014/104/EU on certain rules governing actions for damages under national law for infringements of the competition law provisions of the Member States and of the European Union.

This Directive introduces a basic framework for dealing with claims for damages before the national courts of the Member States. The Directive makes it clear that Member States must ensure that any natural or legal person who has suffered harm

---

91. In relation to the competition rules, *see* Case C-453/99, *Courage*.
92. Case C-453/99, *Courage*, paras 25 and 26. On the duty to pay damages, *see also* Ch. 3, s. 1.2.

caused by an infringement of competition law can claim and obtain full compensation for that harm (Article 3(1)). 'Full compensation' means that a claimant who has suffered harm is placed in the position in which they would otherwise have been placed if the infringement of competition law had not occurred. Thus, 'full compensation' covers actual loss, loss of profit and the payment of interest. At the same time, the Directive makes it clear that there must not be over-compensation (Article 3(3)). The Directive also contains rules on the problem of the passing-on of loss, and in this connection, it provides that damages can be awarded to both direct and indirect purchasers. The Directive also contains provisions on limitation periods, joint and several liability and the assessment of loss.

The Member States must adopt the provisions of the Directive by the end of 2016.

Bibliography

D.G. Goyder: *EC Competition Law*, 2009.
Giorgi Monti: *EC Competition Law*, 2007.
Ioannis Lianos & Ioannis Kokkoris (eds): *The Reform of EC Competition Law*, 2010.
Jonathan Faull & Ali Nikpay (eds): *The EU Law of Competition*, 3rd ed. 2014.
Richard Whish & David Bailey: *Competition Law*, 8th ed. 2015.
Vivien Rose & David Bailey (eds): Bellamy & Child: *European Union Law of Competition*, 7th ed. 2013.

CHAPTER 8
Merger Control

1   INTRODUCTION

1.1   Introduction to the Topic

In the years leading up to the adoption of the first Merger Control Regulation in 1989, the Commission had, to a certain extent, attempted to control mergers by using what is today Articles 101 and 102 of the Treaty on the Functioning of the European Union (TFEU or the 'Treaty'). The application of these provisions was the subject of a comprehensive report prepared by the Commission in 1966.[1] In its report, the Commission concluded that Article 101 was not suitable for regulating concentrations, among other things, because it required the existence of two independent undertakings, and many concentrations resulted in only one undertaking remaining.[2] As for Article 102, it was stated in the report that this could be applicable to a concentration where one of the merger parties had previously had a dominant position, and the merger further eliminated competition. This view was later confirmed by the Court of Justice (CJ) in its judgment in Case 6/72, *Continental Can*. Article 102 can thus be used for *ex post* control of certain concentrations, but in practice, the provision has been shown to be of limited significance in this area.

In recognition of the fact that the two provisions were inadequate to ensure effective control of concentrations, already in 1973, the Commission put forward a

---

1. *See* the report, Das Problem der Unternehmenskonzentration im Gemeinsamen Markt, Kollektion Studien, Reihe Wettbewerb No 3, 1966.
2. The possibility of applying Art. 101 to mergers was also considered by the CJ in Joined Cases 142 and 156/84, *British American Tobacco (BAT) & R.J. Reynolds Industries v. Commission*. The CJ indicated that Art. 101 can be used where one undertaking acquires a certain level of control over another undertaking through the acquisition of a minority shareholding, but without the control being so extensive that the two undertakings should be treated as a single undertaking for the purposes of competition law. *See* the discussion in Ch. 4, s. 9.

proposal for a merger control regulation.[3] However, it was not before 1989 that an agreement was reached on Council Regulation (EEC) No 4064/89 on the control of concentrations between undertakings, commonly called the Merger Control Regulation (MCR).[4] A number of amendments were implemented in 1997, including changes to the threshold values which determine when a concentration is considered to have a Community dimension, as well as changes to the special rules on joint ventures.[5] In 2004, a completely new regulation was adopted (Regulation (EC) No 139/2004), which included amendments to the test to which mergers are subject.[6]

The MCR introduces an obligation to notify mergers and full-function joint ventures where these have a certain size (Community dimension). There is a more detailed definition of this in section 2 below. If a concentration is notified, it must be assessed whether it significantly impedes effective competition, in particular as a result of creating or strengthening a dominant position. In order to evaluate whether this is the case, it is first necessary to define the relevant market (*see* section 3), and next, there must be an investigation of the effect of the concentration on that relevant market (*see* section 4). A concentration will seldom be totally prohibited as the Commission often uses the possibility of laying down different terms and conditions for the approval of a concentration instead. This issue is dealt with in more detail in section 5. If a concentration is approved, this raises the question of which terms of the agreement should still be assessed according to Article 101 on the grounds that they are not an integrated part of the concentration (*see* section 6). In the case of joint ventures, there can also be a need to evaluate whether, in connection with the setting up of a joint venture company, there is cooperation on other activities, and if so, such cooperation has to be evaluated in accordance with Article 2(4) of the MCR (*see* section 7). Finally, section 8 contains a brief review of the procedure for the notification of concentration.

1.2   The Sources of Law

The following review will be based on the decisions adopted by the Commission in its decisions. Only the decisions of the Commission taken under Article 8 of the MCR in the second phase are published in the Official Journal of the European Union.[7] The decisions taken in the first phase, under Article 6, are only published on the Commission's website (http://ec.europa.eu/competition/index_en.html), where they are typically available in English and in some cases in French or in German. Since the first MCR entered into force, cases which have been notified have been given the prefix 'M' followed by a serial number. During the period 1998–2002, instead of 'M', the prefix 'JV' was used for joint ventures, which were notified, and they were independently numbered.

---

3. OJ 1973 C 92/1.
4. OJ 1990 L 257/13.
5. Regulation (EC) No 1310/97 (OJ 1997 L 180/1).
6. Council Regulation (EC) No 139/2004 on the control of concentrations between undertakings (OJ 2004 L 24/1). Since this Regulation codifies the regulation of merger controls, it is this legal act which is referred to when referring to the Merger Control Regulation (MCR) in the following.
7. For more details on the procedural rules, *see* s. 8 below.

In addition, references are made to several of the Commission's notices issued in connection with the MCR. Even though these are only claimed to be 'guidelines', they have a certain value as sources of law, in part because they have been drawn up on the basis of the practice of the Commission, as can be seen from the fact that they refer to the relevant decisions, and in part because the Commission refers to its notices in its decisions, which must be seen as an expression of the fact that the Commission itself feels bound to follow its own guidelines.[8] The most important notice is the Jurisdictional Notice from 2008, which deals with the question of which mergers and joint ventures must be notified.[9] In addition, the Commission has issued a Notice on restrictions directly related and necessary to concentrations (ancillary restraints), Guidelines on the assessment of horizontal mergers and Guidelines on the assessment of non-horizontal mergers, which are discussed below.[10]

In recent years, there has been a sharp increase in the number of cases referred to the CJ and the General Court (GC) concerning the MCR. Both courts have adopted the starting position that several of the provisions in the MCR allow the Commission discretion with regard to economic assessments, and the judicial review of the Commission's decisions shows respect for the fact that the Commission is allowed a certain margin for discretion.[11] However, it is mainly in the assessments made under Article 2 of the MCR that both courts have accepted that the Commission has such a margin for discretion; *see* sections 3 and 4. Even though the courts recognise that the Commission has a margin of discretion with regard to these economic matters, they will review whether the evidence relied on by the Commission is factually accurate, reliable and consistent, whether the evidence contains all the information which must be taken into account, and whether there has been a manifest error of assessment. This does not mean that the courts will refrain from reviewing the Commission's interpretation of concepts of EU law, even if this interpretation requires an economic analysis when implemented.[12]

The Commission often uses different econometrical models as part of its examination. This is accepted by the courts as long as these models do not result in outcomes that are not in conformity with the competition rules or the guidelines provided by the Commission.[13] Given the importance of these models, the CJ has held that it may be a

---

8. M.604, *Albacom*, decision of 15.9.1995, para. 13; and JV.12, *Ericsson/Nokia/Psion/Motorola*, decision of 22.12.1998, para. 13.
9. Commission Consolidated Jurisdictional Notice under Council Regulation (EC) No 139/2004 on the control of concentrations between undertakings (hereinafter referred to as the 'Jurisdictional Notice') (OJ 2008 C 95/1).
10. These are published in OJ 2005 C 56/24, OJ 2004 C 31/5 and OJ 2008 C 265/6 respectively. The Guidelines on non-horizontal mergers was prompted by the fact that in 2005 the Commission partially lost two cases on conglomerate mergers; *see* Case C-12/03 P, *Tetra Laval*, and Case T-210/01, *General Electric*.
11. Joined Cases C-68/94 and C-30/95, *France and others v. Commission (Kali & Salz)*, paras 223–224; Case T-22/97, *Kesko v. Commission*, para. 142; Case T-102/96, *Gencor v. Commission*, paras 164–165; and Case T-221/95, *Endemol Entertainment v. Commission*, para. 106.
12. *See*, for instance, Case T-162/10, *Niki Luftfahrt*, para. 86 and Case C-376/20 P, *Commission v. CK Telecoms UK Investment*, paras 84 and 125–126.
13. In Case T-162/10, *Niki Luftfahrt*, the GC accepted that the Commission used the O&D approach when defining the relevant market in a case concerning air transport.

breach of the right of defence if the Commission omits to inform the merging undertakings about any substantial changes it has made to such models.[14]

1.3 Foreign Direct Investment Screening

With the adoption of Regulation 2019/452, establishing a framework for the screening of foreign direct investments into the Union, the EU has encouraged the Member States to adopt rules whereby certain investments by non-EU investors in their territories are subject to review. It is not a requirement that the Member States introduce such a screening mechanism, but the Regulation suggests that any mechanisms that are in place or will emerge should comply with the rules set out.

The aim of such a screening mechanism is not to prevent competition from being restricted, as this is the role of the MCR, but to prevent certain risks to the security and public order in the Member States. More specifically, the assessment may include an evaluation of the potential effects on critical infrastructure, critical technologies, the supply of critical inputs, access to sensitive information and the freedom and pluralism of the media, *see* Article 4.

The screening mechanism will include transactions that are also covered by the MCR, as an investment is defined as establishing or maintaining a lasting and direct link between the foreign investor and the investee. According to Article 2(1) of the Regulation, this includes 'investments which enable effective participation in the management or control of a company carrying out an economic activity'. If an investor establishes sole control within the meaning of the MCR, this control is also likely to trigger a screening process if the investor is foreign and the target is operating in the sectors that a national screening mechanism covers. However, the Regulation leaves it to the Member States to define the investment covered, and many Member States have adopted thresholds that are much lower than the control threshold applied in the MCR, for instance, 10% of the voting rights.

2 CONCENTRATIONS WITH AN OBLIGATION TO NOTIFY

If the following conditions are fulfilled, there is an obligation to notify a concentration:

(1) There must be a concentration, as defined in the Regulation. This also covers the situation where one or more undertakings acquire control of another undertaking. The concept of concentration and the concept of control are reviewed in more detail in sections 2.1 and 2.2.
(2) If there is a joint venture, there is only an obligation to notify if it has full-function status (i.e., it operates independently); *see* section 2.3.

---

14. Case C-265/17 P, *United Parcel Service Inc*. Subsequently the GC held that the mistake made by the Commission was sufficient to make the Commission liable for any damages incurred by the parties, *see* Case T-834/17, *United Parcel Service Inc*. The latter case is appealed to the CJ.

(3) For a concentration to be notifiable, it must have a Community dimension; *see* section 2.4, as concentrations without a Community dimension are subject to different rules; *see* section 2.5.

(4) Finally, there is a requirement that the concentration shall have some geographic connection to the EU; *see* section 2.6.

2.1 The Concept of a Concentration

The MCR involves an obligation to notify concentrations, which is a very broad term and includes measures which can lead to a permanent change to the structure of an undertaking.[15] A concentration is defined in Article 3(1) of the MCR as either the merger of undertakings or the situation where one or more undertakings directly or indirectly acquire control over one or more other undertakings.[16]

A true merger occurs when there is a merger as understood in company law, whereby a company transfers all its assets and liabilities to another company, and the first company ceases to exist. It has long been possible to carry out such mergers between companies situated in the same Member State, and since October 2004, it has also been possible to carry out cross-border mergers of public limited companies.[17] It is also possible to create a concentration when two or more undertakings, without carrying out a company law merger, establish an economic entity with common management, where, in one way or another, there is a sharing of profits and losses between the different undertakings in the entity. In certain countries, such arrangements can be established by entering into wide-ranging cooperation agreements, by establishing cross-shareholdings, etc.[18]

A concentration can also occur when one undertaking acquires control of another, meaning the acquisition of sole control. Such acquisition can take many forms, but it will typically be through the acquisition of shares which carry a majority of the voting rights in the target company. An acquisition of shares in this way can take place following the making of a public takeover bid.

A joint venture can also constitute a concentration which is covered by the MCR, provided it meets a number of conditions. First, it must be under the joint control of the participating undertakings (the 'joint venture partners'); next, it must be an independently operating undertaking (full-function), and finally, it must be set up on a lasting basis. These conditions are discussed in more detail below.

---

15. Recital 23 in the preamble to the original Regulation.
16. There is a standstill obligation in Art. 7(1) MCR, and in order to be able to determine when it has been breached, it is necessary to determine precisely when a merger is implemented. This question is discussed below in s. 8.1.2.
17. Since October 2004 it has been possible to set up an SE company by means of a cross-border merger; *see* Regulation (EC) No 2157/2001 on the Statute for a European company (SE) (OJ 2001 L 294/1). From December 2007 it became possible for all companies to carry out cross-border mergers; *see* Directive 2005/56/EC on cross-border mergers of limited liability companies (OJ 2005 L 310/1). The latter rules are now consolidated in the Company Law Directive, 2017/1132, OJ 2017 L 169/46.
18. Jurisdictional Notice, para. 10.

It is not only the setting up of a new joint venture company that can constitute a concentration under the MCR. It can also be that an existing company comes under joint control[19] or that a joint venture that has hitherto been under joint control becomes subject to sole control.[20] This can have the practical consequence that the dissolution of a joint venture can involve an obligation to notify.

An arrangement whereby there is a change to the joint control, but without there being a move to sole control, can also amount to a concentration which must be notified. This will be the case if there is a change in the composition of the group of joint venture partners[21] or if there is an increase in the number of joint venture partners.[22] A change in the activity of a joint venture may constitute a concentration, for instance, where the joint venture partners decide to enlarge the joint venture by transferring additional assets, know-how, etc., if this results in an extension of the activities of the joint venture into new markets.[23]

There is a special form of joint venture formation where the aim of the acquisition of joint control is to make an immediate distribution of the assets of the joint venture. In this situation, the arrangement is considered as a whole, so that it is considered as two mergers, whereby the acquiring companies acquire sole control over their respective parts of the assets of the joint venture. Such an arrangement should still be notified (provided the other conditions of the MCR on turnover, etc., are fulfilled), but it is not notified and processed as a joint venture.

A concentration necessarily involves at least two undertakings. This is why the starting point in Article 3(1)(a) of the MCR is that a concentration involves two or more previously independent undertakings. According to subparagraph (b) in the same Article, there can also be a concentration where a person who already controls at least one undertaking acquires control of another undertaking.

The MCR does not provide a specific definition of an 'undertaking'. However, it must be assumed that this should be interpreted broadly so as to include any entity that carries on some commercial activity, regardless of its corporate form. It must also be assumed that the case law of the CJ and the GC on the definition of an undertaking in

---

19. M.2840, *Danapak/Teich/JV*, decision of 30.8.2002, para. 8.
20. M.23, *ICI/Tioxide*, decision of 28.11.1990, para. 2; M.2838, *P & O Stena Line (Holding) Limited*, decision of 7.8.2002, para. 4; and Jurisdictional Notice, para. 89.
21. M.376, *Synthomer/Yule Catto*, decision of 9.9.1993, where one of two joint venture partners was changed. A consistent application of the view that a change of joint venture partners constitutes a merger means that if the control of a joint venture partner changes hands, there is then indirectly a new joint venture partner and therefore a merger which must be notified. *Morten P. Broberg*: Broberg on the European Commission's Jurisdiction to Scrutinise Mergers, 4th ed. 2013 pp. 48–49 states that the Commission will not normally deal with such indirect changes in joint control, unless the purpose of the takeover is to obtain control of the joint venture.
22. M.902, *Warner Bros/Lusomundo/sogecable*, decision of 12.5.1997; and M.1014, *British Steel/Europipe*, decision of 26.2.1998, where in both cases the number of joint venture partners was increased from two to three.
23. Jurisdictional Notice, paras 106–109.

relation to Articles 101 and 102 TFEU applies to the interpretation of the concept of an undertaking under the MCR.[24] The Commission mentions that the transfer of a client base of a business or the transfer of intangible assets such as brands or patents may be considered a transfer of an undertaking if these assets constitute a business.[25]

In situations where public bodies participate in a concentration by taking over control of an undertaking or by participating as a joint venture partner, the public body will be treated as equivalent to a person who controls other undertakings.[26]

Finally, Article 3(5) of the MCR contains a list of special exceptions where the acquisition of control is not covered by the MCR. This applies to temporary (twelve months) acquisitions by financial institutions, office-holders' acquisitions in connection with liquidations, insolvencies and suchlike, as well as acquisitions by financial holding companies. The list of exceptions is exhaustive and will be interpreted very restrictively.[27]

2.2 The Definition of Control

In practice, the great majority of concentrations are carried out by one or more undertakings acquiring control over another undertaking, and for this reason, the definition of control is central to the MCR.

There is an overall definition of control in Article 3(2) of the MCR as the possibility of exercising decisive influence on another undertaking. Furthermore, the provision states that influence can be exercised in the following ways, among others:

- by the controlling undertaking obtaining ownership or the right to use all or part of the assets of an undertaking;
- by the controlling undertaking securing decisive influence on the composition, voting or decisions of the organs of an undertaking.

In its decisions, the Commission uses the terms de jure and de facto control. These terms show that control must be assessed from all factual and legal points of view. Several times, the Commission has stressed that the definition of control in the MCR is not identical to the definition of control used in other areas of legislation.[28]

While the concept of control is defined in Article 3(2), there is no corresponding definition of the terms 'sole control' or 'joint control'. In Article 3(1)(b), it is stated that a merger occurs when one or more persons acquire control of another undertaking, and

---

24. See Ch. 2, s. 3.1.
25. Jurisdictional Notice, para. 24.
26. M.157, *Air France/Sabena,* decision of 5.10.1992, para. 11c. As for the situation where a state-controlled undertaking takes part in a merger or in the setting up of a joint venture, it appears from Recital 22 to the MCR that the calculation of the turnover of an undertaking should take account of undertakings making up an economic unit with an independent power of decision.
27. See Jonathan Faull & Ali Nikpay (eds): The EU Law of Competition, 3rd ed. 2014, p. 566.
28. Jurisdictional Notice, para. 23. More specifically, in a decision the Commission has rejected the idea that the concept of control is the same as the threshold for the obligation to make a mandatory takeover bid under the British City Code on Takeovers and Mergers; see M.754, *Anglo American/Lonrho* (OJ 1998 L 149/21), para. 40.

this implies that the concept of control includes both kinds of control. The term 'joint control' is used in the MCR,[29] though without this being defined, and the term 'sole control' is not used. However, the terms have been defined in decisions and judgments, and the key elements are reviewed in the following.

2.2.1   Sole Control

Sole control means that one undertaking takes over control of the strategic commercial decisions of another undertaking. This can be either by the first undertaking acquiring assets which together constitute an undertaking or by the undertaking otherwise acquiring control of the target undertaking. Sole control often arises through the purchase of shares in another undertaking, whereby the acquirer either obtains control of a majority of the voting rights in the company or obtains control of an effective majority. An effective majority will exist where a shareholder does not, in fact, have a majority of the voting rights in the company but where there is a high probability that they will be able to secure a majority of the votes at a general meeting of the company. This is particularly relevant in companies with dispersed ownership, as, in this case, it is unlikely that all small shareholders will exercise their voting rights.[30] A minority shareholding can also give sole control where special rights are attached to the shares, which give the minority shareholding decisive influence, for example, by giving the right to appoint more than half the members of the board.[31]

> There was an example of de facto control in Decision M.1046, *Ameritech/ TeleDanmark*, decision of 5.12.1997, where, in the first instance, Ameritech acquired 34% of the voting rights in TeleDanmark. By acquiring the State's remaining shares, Ameritech could acquire control of 42% of the voting rights. This was sufficient to give Ameritech de facto control, particularly as: (i) the remaining shares in TeleDanmark had dispersed ownership, and no other shareholder owned more than 7.5% of the company's shares, and (ii) in the last three years, no more than 54% of the voting rights had been represented at the company's general meeting, so Ameritech could expect to have a de facto majority.

---

29. Article 4(2). In Art. 5 there are several references to the situation where undertakings together have certain rights and powers.
30. This form of effective majority existed in, among others, M.754, *Anglo American/Lonrho* (27.47% of the voting rights) (OJ 1998 L 149/21) and in M.5469, *Renova Industries/Sulzer*, (31.1% of the votes), decision of 17.6.2009, but it was rejected in M.197, *Laporte/Interox*, decision of 30.4.1992. In all three cases, the Commission investigated how votes had been cast in previous general meetings of the companies.
31. Jurisdictional Notice, para. 57. As discussed above in Ch. 4, s. 11, there has been a discussion about whether the acquisition of minority shareholdings ought to be covered by the MCR to a greater extent; *see* COM(12014) 449 final and *Porter Elliott & Joham Van Acker*, A Critical Review of the European Commission's Proposal to Subject Acquisitions of Non-controlling Minority Stakes to EU Merger Control, European Competition Law Review 2015, pp. 97–100 and *Martin Gassler*, Non-Controlling Minority Shareholdings and EU Merger Control, World Competition 2018, pp. 3–42.

There can also be de facto control where an undertaking has a purchase option, which enables it to acquire shares in another company so that de jure control can be acquired later. The Commission has adopted the view that an option to purchase shares or an option to convert securities to shares does not in itself give a basis for control unless the option will be exercised in the near future.[32] In Case T-2/93, *Air France v. Commission*, the GC accepted that the Commission did not take into account an option which had not yet been exercised and where, furthermore, it had not been substantiated that the owner of the option intended to exercise the option.[33] On the contrary, there have been several cases where the Commission has assessed that option/conversion possibilities of this kind can create or contribute to creating de facto control.

> In Decision M.397, *Ford/Hertz*, decision of 7.3.1994, a stock conversion right was in itself enough to demonstrate de facto control. Ford owned 49% of the voting rights in Hertz and had a right to appoint four out of the nine members of the board. Even though Ford had a veto right over certain decisions, the veto right did not include strategic commercial decisions, so Ford did not have de jure control. However, according to an agreement with the other investors in Hertz, Ford had a right to convert its C class shares into B class shares, which would mean that Ford would be entitled to appoint two further members of Hertz's board, and Ford would thereby have a majority on the board. The Commission was of the view that Ford had, therefore, acquired de facto control, as the conversion right could be exercised at very short notice and did not require Ford to make further investments or otherwise pay for the exercise of this right. The decision was thus unusual, as the conversion right enabled de jure control to be acquired at any time, but an option or conversion right would not typically be so effective for securing control. For this reason, in other cases, the Commission has merely stated that such rights are one of several elements which point towards the existence of de facto control.[34]

The undertaking gaining control will normally be able to determine the strategical commercial decisions of the other undertaking. However, the Commission also assumes that control may be gained by being the only shareholder that has the right to veto such strategical commercial decisions.[35] In this situation, negative control rights may suffice to establish control according to Article 3(2) of the MCR. This type of negative control differs from the situation in joint ventures where joint control is established; *see* below. In cases of joint control, several participants in the joint venture have negative control rights, whereas in the case discussed here, only one has.

Control does not necessarily mean that the controlling undertaking is a shareholder of the target company. An undertaking may have control or a

---

32. Jurisdictional Notice, para. 60.
33. Case T-3/93, *Air France v. Commission*.
34. M.967, *KLM/Air UK*, decision of 22.9.1997, para. 12.
35. Jurisdictional Notice, para. 54.

share in control if it has de facto control of a shareholding via a shareholder who is formally the holder of the rights but only acts as a vehicle.[36] It is also possible for an undertaking to acquire considerable influence on the running of another company via other legal means than ownership. For instance, a management agreement which can give the managing undertaking considerable influence and, depending on the circumstances, can also obtain a share of the joint control.[37] It is clear that what matters is not the category of an agreement but its effect.[38]

The Commission has adopted the view that a situation of economic dependence can result in de facto control. For example, this can be due to wide-ranging long-term supply agreements or credit provided by suppliers or customers combined with structural links.[39] So far, when the Commission has assessed whether there is de facto control on this basis, it has refrained from finding that control has existed.[40]

In certain cases, legislation can secure influence in a company for a public authority, employees or other stakeholders. Even though such public prerogatives can secure others than the shareholders' de jure control over a company, the Commission has adopted the view that this form of influence does not amount to control for the purposes of the MCR.[41]

If an undertaking has control, this is enough to establish that there is an obligation to notify under the MCR. The fact that the undertaking does not use its influence is irrelevant; what matters is that the undertaking has the possibility of exercising controlling influence.[42] However, there is a special exception for credit institutions and other financial undertakings that trade in securities as part of their usual business, as well as certain holding companies; *see* Article 3(5) of the MCR. Even though these undertakings acquire a controlling shareholding, there will not be a

---

36. Jurisdictional Notice, para. 13.
37. *See C.J. Cook & C.S. Kerse:* EC Merger Control, 5th ed., 2009 p. 50. In German law, a range of different types of contract has been developed which can all lead to an undertaking securing control of another company.
38. M.890, *Blokker/Toys 'R' Us* (OJ 1998 L 316/1), where the Commission stated that the fact that a franchise agreement existed between the parties did not exclude the possibility that, in the context of other agreements, the agreement could involve a merger; *see* para. 14 of the Decision.
39. Jurisdictional Notice, para. 20.
40. This was the case in M.258, *CCIE/GTE,* decision of 25.9.1992, where the Commission denied that the fact that Siemens had financed CCIE's takeover of the undertaking IL was sufficient for it to be said that Siemens had control over either CCIE or IL. In M.697, *Lockheed Martine/Loral Corporation,* decision of 27.3.1996, the Commission likewise denied that there was control in a situation where an undertaking (LMC) which owned non-voting shares in another company (LSCL) had provided guarantees for LSCL for up to USD 250 million, had granted LSCL a number of important licences, and where there was an overlap of personnel in several important positions in LMC and LSCL.
41. Jurisdictional Notice, para. 22.
42. M.330, *McCormick/CPC/Rabobank/Ostmann,* decision of 14.9.1993, where a bank was secured wide veto rights in a joint venture. Even though the bank stated that it would not become involved in important business decisions, the Commission held that the bank had a share in the joint control; *see C.J. Cook & C.S. Kerse:* EC Merger Control, 5th ed., 2009 p. 38.

merger, provided that the undertakings do not exercise their voting rights to determine the undertaking's competitive conduct, i.e., its business strategy.

2.2.2 Joint Control

Joint control means that two or more undertakings together have control over another undertaking. To exercise control, the joint venture partners need to agree on important matters so that joint control is, in fact, a (qualified) veto right.

When assessing a joint venture, it is first necessary to establish whether the joint venture partners together have the necessary control to exercise decisive influence on the running of the joint venture. This assessment corresponds largely to the assessment of the rights which give sole control over a company. In many cases, it will be obvious that there is the necessary control, for example, where the joint venture partners together own all the shares in the company. To establish the existence of joint control, it is next necessary to investigate whether there are veto rights so that control can only be exercised if all the joint venture partners agree.

In the case of a 50/50 joint venture, where two joint venture partners have the same voting rights, there will normally be joint control. In such a joint venture, either party can block any decision in the joint venture and thus have a negative decision-making influence on the running of the company.[43] In a joint venture where the joint venture partners do not have equal voting rights, it will often be laid down in agreements, etc., that the parties will have a veto right in relation to certain decisions, and in this situation, the question arises as to whether the veto rights are sufficiently extensive.

According to the Jurisdictional Notice, it is decisive whether veto rights concern strategic decisions on the joint venture company's business policies. The Commission's Notice paragraph 67 states that 'veto rights which confer joint control typically include decisions and issues such as the budget, the business plan, major investments or the appointment of senior management'. The Commission's view is that a veto right on the business plan or on the amendment of an already adopted business plan can in itself be enough for it to be found that joint control exists.[44] In Case T-2/93, *Air France v. Commission*, the GC accepted that the Commission had assessed that there was joint control, as it emphasised that important decisions required the support of at least one of the members of the board appointed by each of the two joint venture partners, just as it emphasised that a business plan containing the most important directions for the running of the joint venture company could only be amended with the agreement of both joint venture partners.[45] However, budgets and business plans are not the only

---

43. This presupposes that there are no special rules giving one of the joint venture partners a casting vote, or similar.
44. Jurisdictional Notice, para. 70.
45. Case T-3/93, *Air France v. Commission*, para. 65. In its practice hitherto, the GC had accepted the Commission's assessment of whether there is joint control or sole control. *See also* Case T-221/95, *Endemol Entertainment Holding*; and Case T-102/96, *Gencor*, where the GC agreed with the Commission that the case concerned sole control and not joint control, paras 167–194.

important strategic decisions. Depending on the actual circumstances, other decisions can be just as strategically significant.

> In Decision M.998, *OBS! Danmark*, decision of 10.11.1997, the Commission emphasised that even relatively small investments required unanimity. Since the joint venture in question had to make a decision about the modernisation of its shops and thus make a number of investments, the veto right was especially important.[46] However, this decision should be contrasted with Decision JV.46, *Blackstone/CDPQ/Kabel Nordrhein-Westfalen*, decision of 19.6.2000; and Decision JV.50, *Blackstone/CDPQ/Kabel Baden-Württemberg*, decision of 1.8.2000, where the Commission did not accept that a veto right which included investments and sales of a certain size was sufficient to establish the existence of joint control. The Commission referred to the fact that the veto right did not cover business plans and budgets and that there was nothing to prevent the joint venture partners from making investments alongside their joint venture. In several cases the Commission has found that the veto rights which ensure joint control go further than the veto rights that are normally allowed to minority shareholders.[47] Since the content of minority rights varies from country to country, it can be difficult to assess the extent of this statement.[48]

When joint venture partners wish to regulate their influence in their joint venture in more detail, they will typically make an agreement on the composition of the management or supervising body, including giving each joint venture partner a right to appoint a given number of board members. By combining this with a provision that all important strategic decisions shall be put before the board, it is possible to ensure that the individual joint venture partners acquire an indirect veto right. This will be the case if there is a requirement for unanimity or if a measure requires the support of at least one member appointed by the different joint venture partners. In these cases, the joint venture partners try to establish the veto right in the board rather than in the general meeting. However, the Commission has accepted that a veto right at this level corresponds to a veto right at a higher level in the decision-making hierarchy of the company.

> This last case is particularly interesting since the GC went into considerable detail in assessing the question of control, which suggests that the GC will not always uncritically accept the Commission's assessment.

46. *See also* Case T-102/96, *Gencor,* where the GC pointed out that marketing policy was a very important aspect of the competitive strategy of the joint venture in question; *see* para. 178.
47. M.10, *Conagra/Idea,* decision of 30.5.1991 para. 14; and M.308, *Kali + Salz/MdK/Treuhand* (OJ 1994 L 186/38).
48. *See C.J. Cook & C.S. Kerse:* EC Merger Control, 5th ed., 2005 p. 37. Minority rights are still not fully harmonised in the EU. However, certain minority rights in connection with company capital, mergers etc. have already been harmonised. In Case T-221/95, *Endemol Entertainment Holding BV,* the GC accepted the Commission's point of view that ordinary minority shareholders' rights are, in principle, not enough for establishing that there is joint control, but it did not otherwise contribute to establishing the content of the concept of 'normal' minority rights.

While such a composition of the management or supervising body is an important part of assessing the existence of joint control, it is less important how the day-to-day management is composed. In many companies, the day-to-day management will not be concerned with taking strategic decisions but will 'only' be concerned with implementing them. This means that the fact that one joint venture partner takes care of the day-to-day running of the company does not exclude the possibility of there being joint control as long as the strategic decisions require unanimity.[49]

In other cases, the joint venture partners bind themselves to exercise their voting rights in a specific way, thereby establishing a 'pooling' agreement. A pooling agreement means that several shareholders bind themselves to exercise their voting rights in cooperation with each other. In this way, two minority shareholders who cannot individually exercise control can acquire control jointly, so they both partake of the joint control.[50] Instead of entering into an agreement about the exercise of voting rights, joint venture partners can choose to set up a holding company to which they transfer their ownership rights in the joint venture company. By establishing the decision-making process in this way, the owners of the holding company can exercise a veto right in connection with the holding company's exercise of its voting rights in the joint venture and achieve the same result as in a pooling agreement.

> This is illustrated by Decision M.141, *UAP/Transatlantic/Sun Life*, decision of 11.11.1991, where the undertakings involved pooled their shares in Sun Life in a jointly-owned holding company whose only activity was to own a majority of the shares in Sun Life. Each of the two joint venture partners owned 50% of the holding company, and the Commission held that the holding company was merely a vehicle used by the joint venture partners to secure their joint control over Sun Life.

There will also be joint control where minority shareholders act collectively on a de facto basis – in other words, without having entered into a pooling or similar agreement. According to the Jurisdictional Notice, paragraph 76, it is only 'very exceptionally' that there will be such a de facto basis for collective action, as it requires there to be 'strong common interests' which prevent the minority shareholders from acting against each other. This can be indicated by previous connections between the shareholders, by the fact that they have acquired their shareholdings at the same time with a coordinated acquisition, that they have set up the joint venture in question

---

49. M.269, *Shell/Montecatini* (OJ 1994 L 332/48), paras 9–10. It is also clear from the Jurisdictional Notice, para. 81, that the fact that one joint venture partner has specialist knowledge about the activities of the joint venture company, and the other joint venture partner therefore plays no role in the day-to-day management, does not exclude there being joint control.
50. JV.2, *ENEL/FT/DT*, decision of 22.6.1998, where two shareholders who each had 24.5% of the voting rights in a joint venture ensured themselves a share in the joint control by entering into a pooling agreement; and JV.4, *VIAG/Orange UK*, decision of 11.8.1998, where two participants each had 35% of the voting rights in a joint venture likewise ensured that they jointly acquired control by entering into a pooling agreement.

together, or the fact that all the minority shareholders have invested essential assets in the joint venture, or have made some other vital contribution.[51]

There is an example of where the Commission has found there to be such a collective de facto control in Decision M.382, *Philips/Grundig*, decision of 3.12.1993, where Grundig was controlled through a company which was 40% owned by Philips, while the other 60% of the voting rights were divided between three banks. The Commission found that the three banks together had de facto control, even though none of the banks individually had a veto right. The Commission emphasised that according to the articles of association of the company, the banks appointed one of the two managing directors of the company. Since the banks did not have the expertise required to run a company like Grundig, the Commission found that the banks would most probably follow the advice of the managing director jointly appointed by them, and so it was probable that they would act collectively.

The establishment of joint control requires that the joint venture partners have the possibility of exercising control over a longer period. This means that if joint control only lasts for a limited period and is replaced by sole control, the Commission will consider that sole control was established from the start. There have been many examples of this in practice, where the partners have established a temporary joint venture but where the agreements provide for the joint venture to be controlled by one of the parties after a given number of years.[52]

Some joint venture agreements or articles of association include special provisions which are intended to deal with the deadlock problem which can lead to a joint venture being paralysed. These solutions necessarily mean that the veto right of one of the joint venture partners is restricted since consideration for the interest of the activities of the joint venture means that a joint venture partner cannot maintain its veto unconditionally. To a large extent, the Commission has accepted that such deadlock provisions do not alter the fact that there is joint control. It has readily accepted solutions whereby decisions on which agreement cannot be reached are referred to a group of experts or to an arbitrator.[53] This practice also seems to have been accepted by the GC.[54]

2.3 Full-Function Joint Ventures

According to Article 3(4) of the MCR, the Regulation only applies to 'a joint venture performing on a lasting basis all the functions of an autonomous economic entity'. According to the judgment in Case T-87/96, *Assicurazioni Generali and Unicredito*, the

---

51. Jurisdictional Notice, paras 77–80.
52. M.425, *BS/BT*, decision of 28.3.1993; and M.604, *Albacom*, decision of 15.9.1995, where it was only for the first three years that one of the parties had extensive veto rights, and this was not long enough for it to be considered that there was joint control.
53. M.683, *GTS-Hermes Inc./HIT Rail*, decision of 5.3.1996 para. 10; and M.662, *Leisure Plan*, decision of 21.12.1995, (para. not numbered).
54. Case T-221/95, *Endemol Entertainment v. Commission*, para. 162.

determination of the existence of a 'full-function joint venture' involves the putting together of assets and/or activities so that a new undertaking is created alongside the joint venture partners. The practice of the Commission shows that it takes account of a number of different elements when assessing whether a joint venture has full-function status. Even if the Commission has not made such clear distinctions, it seems that the conditions can be divided into the following four categories:

(1) According to the Jurisdictional Notice, in order to fulfil the requirement, a joint venture must have access to *sufficient resources*, including finance, staff, and assets (tangible and intangible).[55]

> In several cases the Commission has considered whether a joint venture has sufficient financial resources to be able to operate autonomously, in other words, without being dependent on credits and/or injections of cash from the joint venture partners. The financial resources will normally be secured in the form of investments by the joint venture partners, which are either already invested upon the formation of the company or which the joint venture partners have committed themselves to invest as the need arises.[56] However, financing can also be obtained indirectly, by the joint venture partners helping their joint venture to establish a bank loan; see Decision JV.36, *TXU Europe/EDF-London Investment*, decision of 3.2.2000, paragraph 17. On the other hand, it would be less appropriate if the joint venture's credit facilities essentially consisted of a loan from the joint venture partners; see Decision M.722, *Teneo/Merill Lynch/Bankers Trust*, decision of 15.4.1996, paragraph 14, where the Commission decided that the joint venture in question did not have full-function status. If a joint venture has sufficient financing, it will usually buy the assets it needs. Some assets, in particular registered intellectual property rights and know-how, can only be made available to the joint venture by one of the joint venture partners, and the Commission, therefore, investigates whether this is the case. If the rights and the necessary know-how are transferred to the joint venture, there will naturally be no problem.[57] However, in many cases, the joint venture partners do not want to transfer their rights, as they also want to exploit the rights for themselves. A common solution for this is to grant the joint venture a licence to use the technology. The Commission has accepted that a licence can be equivalent to an assignment of the rights.[58] However, this requires the licence to be irrevocable, though the licence can be for a predetermined period.[59] It is also a requirement that the licence should be given without conditions which would significantly restrict the joint venture's possibility of exploiting the rights. The Commission has also accepted that a major part of the personnel who work for the joint venture is made available

---

55. Jurisdictional Notice, para. 94.
56. M.222, *Mannesmann/Hoesch* (OJ 1993 L 114/34), para. 8, where the joint venture partners had committed themselves to make further investments if their joint venture did not have sufficient finances, provided it was not possible to obtain more advantageous financing from third parties.
57. See, e.g., M.310, *Harrisons & Crosfield/Akzo*, decision of 29.4.1993, para. 13. In this situation there seems to be nothing to prevent one or more of the joint venture partners receiving a licence from their joint venture to exploit the technology; *see*, e.g., M.527, *Thomson/Deutsche Aerospace*, decision of 2.12.1995, para. 10.
58. M.527, *Thomson/Deutsche Aerospace*, decision of 2.12.1995, para. 10, which seem to treat an assignment of rights and a licence which applies for the duration of the joint venture's existence as being equivalent.
59. M.1049, *AKZO/PLV-EPL*, decision of 4.12.1997, para. 7 (10 years); and JV.11, *Home Benelux B.V.*, decision of 15.9.1998, para. 9 (number of years not disclosed).

by the joint venture partners.[60] As for particularly important resources, the Commission sometimes makes an evaluation of the reasons why they are not transferred to the joint venture.

(2) In addition to resources, the Jurisdictional Notice requires a joint venture to have *management* dedicated to its day-to-day operations.[61] It is clear that the requirement does not require the joint venture to be independent of the joint venture partners, as what is decisive is whether there is sufficient autonomy from an organisational point of view. Thus, there is a requirement that the joint venture should have a management and that the management of the joint venture should not be left entirely to a joint venture partner.

In the decisions adopted by the Commission, it seems that the requirement for an autonomous management plays only a minor role. Sometimes, the Commission merely determines whether a joint venture has 'its own management dedicated to day-to-day operations'.[62] In most cases, the Commission does not make a more detailed analysis other than finding that there is such management. However, there have been individual decisions where it has been looked at in more detail.

An example of a case which addressed the question more explicitly is Decision M.3576, *ECT/PONL/EUROMAX*, decision of 22.12.2004. In this case, the joint venture partners argued that there was not a full-function joint venture, among other things, because the management of the joint venture had limited decision-making powers. The joint venture partners referred in particular to the fact that the management board of the joint venture had to obtain the consent of the supervisory board for a number of decisions. However, the Commission did not find that these decisions meant that the management did not have some autonomy. It is not clear from the Decision what kind of decisions of the joint venture required consent, but it is clear that the Commission attached importance to the fact that the supervisory board did not have direct influence on the joint venture's commercial relationships with its customers; *see* paragraph 12. Since the management of the joint venture was still responsible for that part of the day-to-day management, the Commission found there was sufficient autonomy.

---

60. M.994, *Dupont/Hitachi*, decision of 24.10.1997, where there had not been time to transfer the personnel. The Commission accepted this, but also found that the personnel were under the management of the joint venture. There was another example in M.1049, *AKZO/PLV-EPL*, decision of 4.12.1997, para. 10, where it appears from the decision that the personnel had not wanted to be transferred. But *see* in contrast, M.551, *ATR/BAe*, decision of 25.7.1995 para. 17, where the Commission apparently used the fact that the personnel were loaned out by one of the joint venture partners as one of several arguments for finding that there was not a full-function joint venture.
61. Jurisdictional Notice, para. 94.
62. JV.14, *Panagora/DG Bank*, decision of 26.11.1998 para. 12; JV.22, *Fujitsu/Siemens*, decision of 30.9.1999 para. 11; JV.23, *Telefonica/Portugal Telecom/MEDI Telecom*, decision of 17.12.1999 para. 13; JV.28, *Sydkraft/HEW/Hansa Energy Trading*, decision of 30.9.1999 para. 17; and JV.44, *Hitachi/NEC-Dram/JV*, decision of 3.5.2000, para. 11.

(3) In addition to this, there is a requirement that a joint venture must carry on *autonomous business activities*. This means that there must be an initial evaluation of whether the planned activities correspond to an activity which is normally carried on by an undertaking in the business sector in question.[63] If a joint venture only takes on one specific function for the joint venture partners, it will merely have an auxiliary function in relation to them, and it will thus not be operating autonomously. According to the Commission, this will be the case if a joint venture is only concerned with research and development or with production.[64] A joint venture which primarily undertakes the sales of the joint venture partners' products will often also not fulfil the requirement.[65]

There have been a number of cases on the question of whether a joint venture which does not itself have a distribution system can have full-function status. However, there is no strict requirement that a joint venture must have its own distribution system. It is presumably acceptable for part of its sales to be made by one or more of the joint venture partners acting as a distributor and buying the joint venture's products with a view to their resale.[66] However, if the joint venture partners act as distributors and buy the major part of the joint venture's production, and thereby also determine the pricing, it is less likely that the joint venture will be considered to have full-function status.[67]

In many cases, doubt has been raised about whether a joint venture has full-function status because the planned activity of the joint venture is based to a large extent on trade with the joint venture partners. The Commission accepts that a joint venture can be dependent on the joint venture partners either as suppliers or as customers during a start-up period, which is normally up to three years.[68] Next, the Commission normally requires the trade to be on arm's length terms. Finally, in some cases, the Commission has attached importance to whether the joint venture is contractually bound to the trade, i.e., whether it has the possibility of finding other suppliers or customers.[69]

In some situations, the Commission accepts that a joint venture acts as a sales agent for one or more of its joint venture partners. This is the case where the joint venture operates in a trade market where there are undertakings which specialise in sales

---

63. Case T-87/96, *Assicurazioni Generali and Unicredito*, para. 73.
64. Jurisdictional Notice, para. 95. Such an assessment appears to have been persuasive for the result in M.168, *Flachglas/Vegla*, decision of 13.4.1992; and M.904, *RSB/TENEX/Fuel Logistic*, decision of 2.4.1997, which both concluded that joint ventures had an auxiliary function; see expressly para. 13 of the former Decision (*Hilfsfunktion*) and para. 10 in the latter Decision
65. There was an example in M.58, *Baxter/Nestle/Salvia*, decision of 6.2.1991. See also M.551, *ATR/BAe*, decision of 25.7.1995, where the Commission did not believe that a joint venture would develop new products, so it was most probable that it would merely function as a sales agency for the joint venture partners.
66. M.441, *Daimler-Benz/RWE*, decision of 20.6.1994 para. 17, where the Commission emphasised whether the cooperation between the joint venture and the joint venture partners was on arm's length terms.
67. M.353, *British Telecom/MCI*, decision of 13.9.1993 para. 6. See also Adrian Brown: Distinguishing between Concentrative and Cooperative Joint Ventures: Is It Getting Any. Easier, European Competition Law Review 1996 pp. 240–249 (in particular pp. 244 et seq.)
68. Jurisdictional Notice, para. 97. See however M.168, *Flachglas/Vegla*, decision of 13.4.1992 para. 21, where the Commission seems to have accepted a start-up period of five years.
69. M.179, *Spar/Dansk Supermarked*, decision of 3.2.1992 para. 8.

and distribution without being vertically integrated with the undertakings which produce the goods and where different sources of supply are available.[70]

(4) Finally, there is a requirement that a joint venture must be set up on a *lasting basis*; in other words, it is not merely of a temporary character. This requirement is presumed to be satisfied if a joint venture is set up for an indeterminate period, e.g., without it being expressly provided that it will terminate at a given date. Naturally, in such joint ventures, it will often be possible for the joint venture to be wound up if disagreements arise or if the project fails. This does not alter the conclusion that a joint venture is established on an enduring basis.[71] The fact that a joint venture agreement can be terminated by one of the joint venture partners after a certain period also does not mean that it is not set up on a lasting basis. What is important is that, when setting it up, the partners intend that it should be lasting.

A joint venture can also be set up for a specific period, and the question here is how long the period must be in order for the joint venture to be considered enduring. The Commission's practice is not clear, but it can be assumed it must be for at least five years.[72]

The way in which a joint venture is set up is important for the way in which the Commission makes its assessment. Many joint ventures are set up by joint venture partners establishing joint control over an existing company. If, in this way, the joint venture has hitherto been an independent undertaking, typically owned by one of the joint venture partners, the Commission will assume, prima facie, that the joint venture will continue to have full-function status.[73] Where a joint venture is set up as a start-up, in other words, where it does not take over existing activities or a package of assets and resources, there is no assumption as to whether it is a full-function joint venture. As the joint venture partners will not yet have established such a joint venture (and may not establish it prior to notification), the Commission's assessment is based on the agreements and the information submitted by the joint venture partners.

In Case C-248/16, *Austria Asphalt GmbH & Co. OG*, two large construction groups operating, in particular in the field of road networks, established a joint venture which

---

70. Jurisdictional Notice, para. 102.
71. Jurisdictional Notice, para. 103.
72. The practice in the decisions of the Commission is ambiguous. It appears from M.722, *Teneo/Merill Lynch/Bankers Trust*, decision of 15.4.1996, and M.3858, *Lehman Brothers/SCG/Starwood/Le Meridien*, decision of 25.7.2005, that three years is too short. At the same time, 6½ years was sufficient in M.259, *British Airways/TAT*, decision of 27.11.1992 para. 10. In this decision, the Commission emphasised that the business sector in question was in a permanent state of change, and this fact favoured acceptance of a joint venture of a shorter duration. This means that when assessing whether the joint venture has a lasting character, one must consider the rate of change in the business sector in question.
73. See, e.g., M.58, *Baxter/Nestle/Saliva*, decision of 6.2.1991; M.222, *Mannesmann/Hoesch* (OJ 1993 L 114/34); M.249, *Northern Telecom/Matra Telecommunication*, decision of 10.8.1992; and more recently, JV.3, *BT/Airtel*, decision of 8.7.1998; JV.17, *Mannesmann/Bell Atlantic/OPI*, decision of 21.5.1999; JV.24, *Bertelsmann/Planeta/Bol Spain*, decision of 3.12.1999; and JV.37, *B SKY B/Kirch Pay TV*, decision of 21.3.2000.

was owned 50/50%. The joint venture took over control of an asphalt plant, which had previously been owned by one of the construction groups, where it supplied asphalt to that group. After transferring the plant to the joint venture, the intention was that it should supply asphalt to two groups. The CJ did not think that there was a duty to notify this transaction under MCR. Even though there was a change of control on a lasting basis (since the plant went from being under the sole control of one group to the joint control of two groups), the new joint venture was not a full-function joint venture since the plan was for the joint venture to deliver all of its production to the two joint venture partners.

It could be considered whether the form of incorporation chosen for the joint venture is significant for the assessment of whether a joint venture has full-function status. Unsurprisingly, the Commission does not rely on such formal factors in its practice. Conversely, a joint venture can be a full-function joint venture, even if it is not set up as a company, in other words, if it is a 'contractual joint venture'.[74]

2.4 Community Dimension

According to Article 1(1) of the MCR, the Regulation applies to all concentrations with a Community dimension. The Community dimension is defined by reference to certain threshold values which require that merging companies have a turnover of a certain size and a certain cross-border element. According to the original threshold values in Article 1(2) of the MCR, a concentration has a Community dimension where:

(a) the combined aggregate worldwide turnover of all the undertakings concerned is more than EUR 5,000 million; and
(b) the aggregate Community-wide turnover of each of at least two of the undertakings concerned is more than EUR 250 million;

unless each of the undertakings concerned achieves more than two-thirds of its aggregate Community-wide turnover within one and the same Member State.

This definition was the result of a compromise between those Member States that wanted merger control and those Member States that did not think it appropriate for the Commission to be given further powers in this area.[75] The 'one-stop-shop' principle means that mergers or concentrations that have a Community dimension can only be examined by the EU, thereby excluding the competence of the Member States.[76]

From the beginning, it was intended that the MCR's original turnover threshold should be revised after the start-up period. In 1996, the Commission published a Green Paper, setting out different possible solutions.[77] The result of this consultation was the

---

74. Such was the situation in JV.19, *KLM/Alitalia*, para. 11.
75. *See* Morten P. Broberg: Broberg on the European Commission's Jurisdiction to Scrutinise Mergers, 4th ed., 2013 pp. 3–5.
76. Under Art. 9 of the MCR the Commission can, in certain specified circumstances, refer a notified case to the competition authorities of the Member States.
77. COM(96) 19 final.

addition of new threshold values in Article 1(3), which were added in Regulation (EC) No 1310/97.[78] These thresholds were as follows:

(a) the combined aggregate worldwide turnover of all the undertakings concerned is more than EUR 2,500 million;
(b) in each of at least three Member States, the combined aggregate turnover of all the undertakings concerned is more than EUR 100 million;
(c) in each of at least three Member States included for the purpose of point (b), the aggregate turnover of each of at least two of the undertakings concerned is more than EUR 25 million; and
(d) the aggregate Community-wide turnover of each of at least two of the undertakings concerned is more than EUR 100 million;

unless each of the undertakings concerned achieves more than two-thirds of its aggregate Community-wide turnover within one and the same Member State.

This provision expands the scope of application of the MCR so as to include concentrations between smaller undertakings. The focus is directed towards concentrations where the participating undertakings have their sales across at least three Member States. The turnover threshold is applied by seeing first whether the threshold in paragraph (b) has been met, and if not, then by seeing whether the threshold in paragraph (c) is met.

The application of the above threshold requires it to be established which undertakings are the participating undertakings concerned with and how their turnover should be calculated.

2.4.1 *Undertakings Concerned*

To apply the turnover threshold, it is necessary to determine which undertakings are taking part in a concentration. Where one undertaking takes over another undertaking, it is, on the face of it, unproblematic to determine which are the undertakings concerned. However, in cases which involve joint ventures it can sometimes be difficult to decide this.

If two or more undertakings acquire control of a newly established company, the undertakings concerned are those which have a share of the control, i.e., the joint venture partners.[79] If a joint venture is set up by the acquisition of joint control of an existing undertaking, the undertakings concerned are the joint venture partners and the joint venture itself. However, the joint venture company itself is not an undertaking concerned where it is an existing undertaking subject to the sole control of one of the joint venture partners prior to the establishment of joint control. The reason for this difference is that, in this case, the joint venture company's turnover will be counted with that of the original owner, which, as one of the joint venture partners, is one of the

---

78. Regulation (EC) No 1310/97 on the control of concentrations between undertakings (OJ 1997 L 180/1).
79. Jurisdictional Notice, para. 139.

undertakings concerned. If there is an existing joint venture, a change from joint control to sole control will normally constitute a concentration, and in this case, the undertakings concerned will be the remaining (acquiring) joint venture partner together with the joint venture company. If in an existing joint venture, some of the partners are exchanged for others or new partners are added to the joint venture, the undertakings concerned will be the partner that continues as well as the new partners and the joint venture itself.

If a joint venture acquires control of another undertaking, the undertakings concerned are assumed to be the joint venture and the acquired undertaking. In certain situations, it may seem somewhat formalistic to adopt this view, as it is effectively the joint venture partners that are behind the acquisition and which, therefore, ought to be considered the participating undertakings. For example, this is the case where undertakings A and B set up a joint venture (C) with the sole aim of using C to acquire control over undertaking D. This transaction is equivalent to the situation where A and B take over control of D themselves, and therefore both A and B ought to be considered as undertakings concerned. The difficult question to decide is when a joint venture is considered to be an undertaking concerned and when the joint venture partners are the undertakings concerned. According to the Jurisdictional Notice, the Commission will normally consider the joint venture company to be the undertaking concerned where the joint venture is a full-function joint venture.[80] This refers back to the definition of a full-function joint venture developed in relation to Article 3(4) of the MCR. In addition to this, in its Notice, the Commission has listed a number of circumstances which indicate that a joint venture is merely being used by the joint venture partners as a vehicle for carrying out a takeover so that it is the joint venture partners that ought to be included as the participating undertakings. In paragraph 147, the Notice refers to the following circumstances:

- where the joint venture is set up, especially for the purpose of acquiring the target company;
- where the joint venture has not yet started to operate;
- where an existing joint venture has no full-function character.

The judgment in Case T-380/17, *HeidelbergCement AG*, illustrated that sometimes the joint venture partners in a full-function joint venture will be the undertakings concerned. The background to the case was that a joint venture had acquired control of two undertakings. The joint venture has a turnover of more than EUR 250 million, whereas the acquired undertaking had smaller turnovers. Therefore, the thresholds in Article 1(2) MCR were not exceeded. According to the Commission, the two joint venture partners were the undertakings concerned, and since both had turnovers over EUR 250 million, the thresholds were exceeded. The GC accepted that the joint ventures were the undertakings concerned not only when the joint venture is a mere vehicle set up to perform the acquisition but also in other cases where the joint venture

---

80. Jurisdictional Notice, para. 146.

partners are the real players behind the transaction.[81] The latter may also be the case when the joint venture is a full-function joint venture and even has its own strategic interest in the merger. The decisive element is whether the joint venture partners have a significant involvement in the initiation, organisation and financing of the transaction.[82]

2.4.2 Calculation of Turnover

According to Article 5(1) of the MCR, the basis for calculating turnover is the sale of products and the provision of services falling within the undertakings' ordinary activities in the preceding financial year, after the deduction of sales rebates and of value-added tax and other taxes directly related to turnover.[83] Article 5(3) of the MCR contains special rules for credit institutions and other financial institutions. By focusing on sales, it is clear that a merger in a business sector where there are large sales turnovers, but low margins will exceed the thresholds more easily than a merger in a business sector with low turnovers and high margins. Since the consequences for competition will not necessarily be different in the two kinds of sectors, the thresholds may be inappropriate in some respects. In the digital economic and the pharmaceutical industry, new undertakings have been established – undertakings that have not yet generated a large turnover but may be assumed to be able to develop into having a significant impact on competition in time. Such undertakings may be the target of what has been termed 'killer acquisitions', where they are acquired by an established undertaking in the market to ensure that they never develop to be a competitor to the acquiring undertaking. Since the target company in this situation may have a low turnover, the acquisition will not be within the thresholds in the MCR.

However, so far, the Commission has chosen to maintain the focus on turnover, as this is relatively easy to establish and also because turnover can be used as a measure of the financial resources and activities covered by a concentration.[84] Instead, the Commission has suggested using the referral mechanism in Article 22 MCR to ensure that it will be presented with mergers not exceeding the MCR thresholds but where these appear to cut off mergers that do have a Community interest.[85]

According to Article 5(1), the geographic allocation of turnover is determined by focusing on where the customer is located, regardless of where the customer receives the goods or services. This information will not always be apparent from the official

---

81. Paragraph 123 of the judgment.
82. Paragraph 125.
83. The definition closely follows the definition in Art. 2(2) of the Accounting Directive, Directive 2013/34/EU as amended. In practice, the calculation of turnover is based on the latest audited annual accounts unless more recent figures are available which can have a decisive influence; see *C.J. Cook & C.S. Kerse:* EC Merger Control, 5th ed., 2009, p. 90; and *Jonathan Faull & Ali Nikpay* (eds): The EU Law of Competition, 3rd ed., 2014, p. 584.
84. *See* the Commission Staff Working Document on evaluation of procedural and jurisdictional aspects of EU merger control, SWD (2021) 66.
85. Commission Guidance on the application of the referral mechanism set out in Art. 22 of the Merger Regulation to certain categories of cases, OJ 2021 C 113/1.

accounts. The Commission will usually be satisfied with the calculations made by the undertakings themselves.[86]

When the participating undertakings are part of a larger corporate group, it can sometimes be necessary to include the turnover of associated companies as part of the turnover of the undertaking concerned. This is regulated in more detail in Article 5(4) and (5) of the MCR.

Article 5(4)(b) of the MCR defines the subsidiary companies whose turnover should be included in the calculation of turnover. These are undertakings in which the undertaking concerned, directly or indirectly:

(i) owns more than half the capital or business assets;
(ii) has the power to exercise more than half the voting rights;
(iii) has the power to appoint more than half the members of the supervisory board, the administrative board or bodies legally representing the undertakings; or
(iv) has the right to manage the undertakings' affairs.

This definition is used in several places in competition law, and is found, among others, in the *De minimis* Notice from 2001, as well as in several of the block exemption regulations. In Article 5(4)(c) of the MCR it is stated that those undertakings which have the rights or powers listed in subparagraph (b) are also included. This means that the parent company of an undertaking concerned is included. The same can apply to sister companies; *see* subparagraph (d). To the extent that an undertaking concerned is part of a corporate group, as defined in Article 5(4), its turnover from transactions with other group companies is excluded.

If the undertaking concerned is a joint venture, for example, where a joint venture takes over another undertaking, the question then arises whether the joint venture partners' turnover should be added to the turnover of the joint venture company. Here, it is necessary to investigate whether the individual joint venture partner fulfils the criteria in subparagraph (b). There seems to be agreement that the different sub-subparagraphs in subparagraph (b) do not exclude each other. They are alternatives to the extent that it must be investigated whether each of the joint venture partners fulfils one of them.[87]

However, the Commission has adopted an even wider interpretation of subparagraph (c), according to which the joint venture partners who exercise joint control are included, regardless of whether each of the joint partners individually fulfils the criteria in the sub-subparagraphs to subparagraph (b).[88] The Commission's extended interpretation of subparagraph (c) in this way has been criticised.[89]

Article 5(4)(e) deals with the situation where a joint venture is set up by several companies in the same corporate group. The turnover of such a joint venture should also be included in the turnover of the participating undertaking.

According to its wording, Article 5(5) deals with the situation where a joint venture is jointly controlled by the undertakings concerned. This will be the case where two undertakings which merge or which wish to set up a joint venture already have a joint venture. Article 5(5) provides that the calculation of the turnover of such a joint venture does not include the turnover which is derived from sales between the joint venture and the joint venture partners (and with companies in the same corporate group as them). Finally, according to Article 5(5)(b), the turnover of the undertakings concerned is to be allocated in proportion to their

---

86. Jurisdictional Notice, para. 195.
87. *See C.J. Cook & C.S. Kerse:* EC Merger Control, 5th ed., 2009 p. 102.
88. Jurisdictional Notice, para. 182.
89. *See Morten P. Broberg:* Broberg on the European Commission's Jurisdiction to Scrutinise Mergers, 4th ed., 2013 pp. 112–114; and *C.J. Cook & C.S. Kerse:* EC Merger Control, 5th ed., 2009 p. 104.

participation. For example, if two joint venture partners already have a joint venture, half the turnover in the joint venture is to be allocated to each joint venture partner. The Commission has used the principle in Article 5(5)(b) in cases where an undertaking concerned controls a joint venture together with a third-party undertaking.

2.5 Concentrations Without a Community Dimension

If a concentration does not exceed the thresholds in Article 1(2)-(3), it does not have a Community dimension and therefore cannot, in principle, be assessed under the MCR. However, this does not mean that such concentrations are never subject to an assessment under competition law.

First, Article 22 of the MCR contains the so-called Dutch clause, whereby one or more Member States can request the Commission to deal with a concentration which does not have a Community dimension.[90] The Member State may request the Commission to evaluate a merger, even though the merger does not qualify for examination under national merger control regulation.[91] As a consequence, Member States may request the Commission to evaluate mergers that do neither merit evaluation under national nor EU merger control rules. Based on such a request, the Commission can intervene under Article 8 if a concentration creates or strengthens a dominant position with the effect that competition is actually significantly restricted in one or more Member States. There is also a requirement that the concentration should affect trade between Member States. This condition should be interpreted in the same way as the condition concerning the effect on trade between Member States in Articles 101 and 102 TFEU.[92]

Next, the undertakings concerned can request the Commission to consider a concentration, even if it does not have a Community dimension, *see* Article 4(5). There is a requirement that the concentration must be capable of being reviewed under the national competition laws of at least three Member States. A Member State that has the competence to deal with the concentration under its national competition law can object to the case being referred to the Commission, and if it does so, the reference will not be made.

In principle, the Commission and the Member States[93] have the possibility of applying Articles 101 and 102 TFEU to mergers without a Community dimension. According to Article 21(1) of the MCR, Council Regulation No 17 (EEC): First Regulation implementing Articles 85 and 86 of the EC Treaty and Regulation (EC) No 1/2003 does not apply, so that such enforcement would have to be under the provisions in Article 105 TFEU. In its commentary on Article 22 of the original MCR, the Commission stated that under no circumstances does it intend to intervene against a

---

90. The Commission has recently adopted some guidelines on how the Member States may use this mechanism, *see* Guidance on the application of the referral mechanism set out in Art. 22 of the Merger Regulation to certain categories of cases, OJ 2021 C 113/1.
91. Case T-227/21, *Illumina*.
92. Case T-22/97, *Kesko v. Commission*, paras 103–110.
93. Case C-449/21, *Towercast SASU*.

concentration which has a global turnover of less than EUR 2 billion or a minimum turnover at the EU level of less than EUR 100 million, since concentrations below this level will not normally have an appreciable influence on trade between Member States.[94] This limit can be especially relevant to the application of the Dutch clause, and it can also restrict the application of Articles 101 and 102 TFEU.

Several joint ventures are covered by the Regulation, including autonomously operating joint ventures with cooperative elements. As a consequence, Article 21(1) now states that Regulation No 17 (EEC) and Regulation (EC) No 1/2003 still apply to joint ventures without a Community dimension if their establishment has the aim or consequence of coordinating the competitive behaviour of undertakings which continue to be autonomous. In this way, the Commission has secured full access to apply Article 101 (and, in principle, Article 102, though this is normally less relevant) to joint ventures, where there is a concerted practice between the joint venture partners. However, in a declaration recorded in the minutes of a Council meeting, the Commission has stated that it is normally the job of the national competition authorities to control full-function joint ventures which do not have a Community dimension.[95]

It is also clear that the national competition authorities have the possibility to apply their own competition rules to concentrations which do not have a Community dimension.

2.6 The Territorial Scope of Application of the MCR

Apart from the turnover threshold laid down in its Article 1(2) and (3), the MCR does not have any requirements as to the link which a concentration must have to the EU in order to be covered by the Regulation. This raises the question of whether there are any limits to the territorial reach of the MCR.

In its practice, the Commission has applied the MCR to concentrations between undertakings outside the EU,[96] and it has also dealt with the establishment of joint ventures located outside the EU between joint venture partners who were not located in the EU.[97] It thus appears that the starting point is that if the turnover threshold laid down in Article 1 of the MCR is met, the concentration should be notified and assessed in accordance with the MCR.[98]

The application of the MCR has to respect the principles of public international law, which set a limit to the territorial extent of regulations of this nature. However,

---

94. *See* the commentary on Art. 22 of the MCR published in Bull. Suppl. 2/90.
95. *See* document 9296 of 20 June 1997.
96. *See*, e.g., M.877, *Boeing/McDonnell Douglas* (OJ 1997 L 336/16).
97. *See*, e.g., M.346, *JCSAT/SAJAC*, decision of 30.6.1993; and M.994, *Dupont/Hitachi*, decision of 24.10.1997.
98. For the sake of completeness, it should be mentioned that under Art. 57 of the EEA agreement, the EFTA Surveillance Authority has powers to deal with concentrations which have an EFTA dimension; *see* the more detailed review in *Morten P. Broberg:* Broberg on the European Commission's Jurisdiction to Scrutinise Mergers, 4th ed., 2013 pp. 205–223.

legal theorists do not agree on where the boundaries are according to public international law, but the GC has had an opportunity to judge the question in a single case.[99]

The problem came before the GC in Case T-102/96, *Gencor v. Commission*. The case concerned a South African company, Gencor, which owned another South African company, Impala, which was responsible for the group's activities concerning platinum. The intention was that Impala should be transferred so as to be controlled jointly by Gencor and the English company Lonrho. This concentration had been notified to and approved by the South African competition authorities, but upon its subsequent notification to the Commission, the Commission declared that the concentration was incompatible with the internal market in accordance with Article 8(3) of the MCR. Gencor challenged this decision under various headings, including that the concentration did not fall within the jurisdiction of the MCR. Gencor pointed out that the planned concentration concerned economic activities in the territory of a third country, and according to the international law principle of territoriality, the MCR was not applicable.

On the scope of application of the MCR, the GC stated that Article 1 of the MCR does not require the undertakings concerned to be established in the EU or that the production activities covered by the concentration be located in the EU; see paragraph 79 of the judgment. The GC refused to interpret the preamble to the MCR as requiring there to be some link to the EU, over and above that the undertakings should have sales, and thus turnover, in the EU.

Next, the GC stated that, under public international law, if a concentration would have a direct and significant effect in the EU, there was an entitlement to apply the MCR. The GC thereby stated that the so-called effects doctrine applies when deciding what limits public international law puts on the territorial application of the MCR. This principle has primarily been developed in American *law*.[100]

---

99. In particular, the question of the territorial application of the MCR has given rise to problems in relation to the USA, not least in the wake of the merger between Boeing and McDonnell Douglas. In 1991, the USA and the EU entered into a cooperation agreement (OJ 1995 L 95/47), which among other things means that the competition authorities must give each other notice of cases which are being dealt with by one of the parties, which affect important interests of the other party. In practice, it is mostly merger cases of which notification is given in this way; see COM(96) 479 final, Annex 1. In 1998 the cooperation was extended, but this did not apply to merger control; see Decision 98/386 (OJ 1998 L 173/26). For a review of these cooperative relations, see *Mads Andenas & Anestis Papadopoulos:* Antitrust Law and International Companies, European Business Law Review 2002 pp. 193–216 and *Marek Martyniszyn i N. Cunha Rodrigues* (ed.): Extraterritoriality of EU Economic Law, 2021, pp. 29–56.

    After Brexit, the collaboration with the UK competition authorities is being regulated by the EU-UK Trade and Cooperation Agreement, OJ 2021 L 149/10, Arts 358–360.

100. See *G. Porter Elliott:* The Gencor Judgment: Collective Dominance, Remedies and Extraterritoriality under the Merger Regulation, European Law Review 1999 pp. 638–652 (especially p.

In the *Gencor* decision, the GC next assessed whether the three international law criteria that the effect should be direct, significant and predictable were fulfilled in this case. The GC held that this was the case. The GC's application of these three criteria in the actual case shows that they are characterised by having a very wide margin for discretion. For this reason it is difficult to establish precisely the requirements under public international law which must be fulfilled in order for a concentration to have a sufficient link to the EU. The GC found that it was not a problem in this case, but it did not make it clear in what situations it would be contrary to public international law to apply the MCR.

3   THE RELEVANT MARKET

In order to measure the effects of a concentration on competition, the Commission starts by defining the relevant market. The definition of the market is necessary in order to calculate the market shares of the merging undertakings, but in addition, the definition of the market is also a prerequisite for enabling other aspects of the competition in a given area to be analysed; *see* further on this in section 4.[101]

In principle, the relevant market is the market where the merging undertakings are active, or in the case of a joint venture, the markets where the joint venture company is active.

The Commission has published a Notice on the definition of the relevant market.[102] This Notice applies equally to the definition for the purposes of Articles 101 and 102 TFEU and the MCR. While the market definition for Article 102 is aimed at judging whether an undertaking had a dominant position at the time when it has had certain conduct (abuse), the aim of the market definition under the MCR is to assess whether the merging undertakings can in future be assumed to acquire or to strengthen a dominant position. This difference can be the reason why market definitions can differ.[103]

Defining the relevant market means that the Commission must determine both the relevant product market and the relevant geographic market. Normally, the Commission will make a final determination of the market, but sometimes, the

---

641J; and C.J. Cook & C.S. Kerse. EC Merger Control, 5th ed., 2009 p. 14. The CJ has confirmed the application of the effect doctrine in Case C-413/14 P, *Intel*, a judgment addressing Art. 102.

101. The definition of the market was previously an obligatory part of the Commission's assessment under the MCR. This was also confirmed by the CJ in Joined Cases C-60/94 and C 30/95, *France and others v. Commission (Kali & Salz)*, para. 143; and by the GC in Case T-2/93, *Air France v. Commission*, para. 80. Following the reform of the MCR in 2004 it has been possible to prohibit certain concentrations, even if they do not create a dominant position (*see* more on this in s. 4), so it is no longer clear that it is necessary to make a definition of the market in all cases. However, it seems that since 2004 the Commission has retained the practice of always starting by defining the relevant market.
102. Commission Notice on the definition of relevant market for the purposes of Union competition law (C/2024/1645) (hereinafter 'Commission Notice on the definition of relevant market').
103. Commission Notice on the definition of relevant market, para. 21, and *see* the comments on this in s. 3.2 below.

Commission leaves the question partially open. This will be the case where the Commission can see that regardless of whether it chooses the narrowest possible product market or the narrowest possible geographic market, the concentration will under no circumstances create or strengthen a dominant position.

3.1 The Relevant Product Market

The 'relevant market' means all those products and/or services which are regarded as interchangeable or substitutable by the consumer by reason of the products' characteristics, prices and intended use.[104]

The definition of the relevant market is made by the Commission, taking into account such market analysis as exists, and the Commission itself undertakes an analysis of customers, competitors, etc. There is thus no fixed procedure for how the Commission tackles cases, as the Commission decides from case to case what investigations should be included.

The key issue in defining the relevant market is to investigate which products/services are considered substitutable on the demand side. This can be done on the basis of market analysis, which shows which products consumers typically regard as substitutable, or it can be deduced from how the goods are sold. The Commission has said that it uses a conceptual experiment where it evaluates what effect a price increase would have on consumption. The test involves evaluating whether a hypothetical price increase in the range of 5%–10% in the relative price of product A would make so many of A's consumers shift to product B as to make the price increase unprofitable for the suppliers of A.[105] If the price increase is unprofitable, this means that A and B are in the same market. Thereafter, a new hypothetical test is made to see whether a price increase of both A and B would be profitable or not. If, for example, it is judged that consumers would not shift to product C, then C is not considered part of the relevant product market, and this is so regardless of why consumers cannot be expected to shift. For example, this can be because of consumer preferences or because the products are not comparable in price or function.

However, in many cases, the Commission makes an assessment of which products are substitutable on the demand side on the basis of a number of less structured evaluations of the circumstances of the market in question.

> The market for beverages can be used to illustrate the Commission's practice. First, the Commission has rejected the idea that it is possible to adopt a narrow functional approach where it is argued that all beverages belong to the same product market because they all quench thirst.[106] Even though it is normally relevant to distinguish products that have the same

---

104. Commission Notice on the definition of relevant market, para. 12.
105. Commission Notice on the definition of relevant market, para. 27 and the attached footnote. This test is based on the 'SSNIP test' (Small but Significant Non-transitory Increase in Price); see David Bailey & Laura Elizabeth John (eds): Bellamy & Child: European Union Law of Competition, 8th ed., 2018, pp. 273–279.
106. M.190, *Nestlé/Perrier* (OJ 1992 L 356/1), para. 9.

function,[107] this cannot be a standalone criterion. The Commission has stated that carbonated and non-carbonated soft drinks cannot be assumed to belong to the same product market. There are differences in patterns of consumption which mean they cannot be said to belong to the same market. While mineral water and fruit juices in particular are used at breakfast, carbonated soft drinks are often used on other occasions, particularly in fast food restaurants and at social gatherings.[108] Another difference is that some beverages, such as milk and fruit juice, satisfy nutritional needs, while others, such as mineral water, have a consumer image as a natural product and are associated with good health and a healthy lifestyle.[109] Consumers do not associate any of these qualities with fizzy drinks. The fact that there are different product markets is also confirmed by statements of consumers and the fact that supermarkets do not put fizzy drinks on the same shelves as coffee, juice or milk, for example.[110] If one looks at pricing developments it is also possible to see that the prices of different beverages have developed independently of each other. On this basis the Commission has concluded that the market for bottled mineral water constitutes a separate product market.[111] Fizzy drinks with cola flavouring also constitute a market which is distinct from other beverages, including other fizzy drinks.[112] Finally, beers constitute a separate market, as they cannot be substituted with non-alcoholic soft drinks.[113]

The market for spirits is clearly different from markets for other beverages, but the Commission has gone further and denied that all forms of spirits are part of the same market.[114] Nor does the Commission accept that spirits should be divided between a market for 'white' spirits and a market for 'brown' spirits, as it is of the view that, on the basis of consumer demand and preferences, the product markets must be divided according to the type of spirit. As well as each type of spirit belonging to a separate product market, for some kinds of spirits a further division of product markets is made, as among other things the Commission has found that there are separate markets for whiskeys of different origins (Scotch, Irish, Canadian and American), and there are also whiskeys of differing prices and qualities which can hardly be assumed to belong to the same product markets.

---

107. *See also* M.580, *ABB/Daimler-Benz* (OJ 1997 L 11/1), para. 13.
108. M.794, *Coca-Cola/Amalgamated Beverages GB* (OJ 1997 L 218/15), para. 30.
109. M.190, *Nestlé/Perrier* (OJ 1992 L 356/1), para. 10.
110. M.833, *The Coca-Cola Company/Carlsberg* (OJ 1998 L 145/41), para. 36.
111. M.190, *Nestlé/Perrier* (OJ 1992 L 356/1), para. 19.
112. M.794, *Coca-Cola/Amalgamated Beverages GB* (OJ 1997 L 218/15), para. 26. *See also* M.289, *Pepsico/KAS*, decision of 21.12.1992, para. 5.1.2, where the Commission was inclined to say that the market for fizzy drinks should be divided up according to flavour, so that in addition to a market for cola flavour there was a market for lime/citrus, orange, tonic water, etc. However, the Commission refrained from making a final decision on this question.
113. M.582, *Orkla/Volvo* (OJ 1996 L 66/17), para. 28.
114. M.938, *Guinness/Grand Metropolitan* (OJ 1998 L 288/24).

In addition to distinguishing between product markets on the basis of product characteristics, there can also be a basis for distinguishing between different groups of consumers if the competitive conditions differ in relation to the different groups of consumers. Thus, in relation to the market for fizzy drinks with cola flavour, the Commission considered whether the product market could be divided into three different segments, depending on the consumers: one for sales of colas to multiple retailers for home consumption, one for sales of colas to pubs and restaurants for on-premises consumption, and one for sales to small independent grocers. etc.[115] The Commission chose not to decide on this question in the case in question, but in another case it has decided that sales of beer for retail sales and sales of beer to hotels and restaurants are two different markets.[116] The Commission has developed similar practices in other areas where it has found that a product is sold on different terms to different customer groups.[117]

In addition to assessing the substitution of demand, the Commission sometimes also considers the supply situation when defining the relevant product market. If, in reaction to small permanent changes to relative prices, a supplier can switch to production of the relevant products and market them in the short term without incurring significant extra costs, this can have a disciplinary effect on the behaviour of the undertakings involved. The Commission gives the example of a situation where there is production of a product with a range of different qualities, for example, paper. Even if the different paper qualities are not substitutable from the consumer's point of view, they can be considered as part of the same product market because the producers can switch production from one paper quality to another at short notice and without incurring major costs.[118]

3.2 The Geographic Market

The relevant geographic market is a defined geographic area where the product in question is marketed and where the competitive conditions are sufficiently uniform for all undertakings so that it is possible to make a reasonable assessment of the effect on competition of the notified concentration.[119] By determining the geographic area, one also physically limits the undertakings, which are actual or potential competitors to the merged undertaking. Undertakings which are located outside the area will thus

---

115. M.794, *Coca-Cola/Amalgamated Beverages GB* (OJ 1997 L 218/15), para. 26.
116. M.582, *Orkla/Volvo* (OJ 1996 L 66/17), para. 32.
117. The authors of *Barry E. Hawk & Henry L. Huser:* European Community Merger Control: A Practitioner's Guide, 1996 pp. 126–129, are critical of this, believing that the Commission's practice is wrong as it only focuses on whether there are different prices in relation to different groups of customers, without investigating whether the price differences are due to the different costs associated with the different groups of customers.
118. Commission Notice on the definition of relevant market, paras 32–37.
119. Joined Cases C-68/94 and C-30/95, *France and others v. Commission (Kali & Salz)*, para. 143, where the CJ refers to its decision in Case 27/76, *United Brands*, paras 11 and 44. In Case T-151/05, *NVV*, a competitor tried, unsuccessfully, to challenge the Commission's decision approving a merger, alleging that the Commission had made a number of mistakes in its definition of the geographical market.

normally be prevented from competing, since they will not be able to gain access to the market in the short term or without incurring major costs.

The geographic market will typically be either global or national. However, it can also be regional so that it either covers several Member States (or even the whole of the EU/EEA) or perhaps only a part of a Member State. There could typically be a global market for advanced technology products where there are relatively few suppliers. This is the case with the market for aircraft and for landing gear for aircraft.[120] Even simple products can have a global market, as in the case of platinum.[121]

In many cases the Commission will find circumstances which indicate that the geographic market is smaller.[122] This can be seen from an analysis of price differences, as major price differences in different areas suggest that these areas do not belong to the same geographic market.[123] Finally, an analysis of trade flows and developments in trade flows can be used to define the geographic market. If there is only a small quantity of exports/imports to or from an area, this suggests that it is a self-contained geographic market.[124]

However, the finding of pricing differences and the lack of trade between different geographic areas cannot stand on their own. It is also necessary to investigate the cause of the apparent division of the markets, and in particular, to assess whether such division is only short term. For example, there can be historical reasons for why markets are divided nationally with large national producers. Even though producers may still have large market shares in their home markets, barriers to trade may have since been removed, so the markets belong to the same geographic area.[125]

If the reason for the pricing differences and/or the lack of trade between areas is due to more substantial barriers to market access, this suggests that the geographic market cannot be extended beyond these barriers. Such barriers to market access can be due to a number of factors, including consumer preferences, culture, language, restricted access to the distribution network, and legislative barriers. Finally, they can

---

120. *See* respectively M.877, *Boeing/McDonnell Douglas* (OJ 1997 L 336/16), para. 20; and M.368, *Snecma/TI*, decision of 17.1.1994, para. 21.
121. M.754, *Anglo American Corporation/Lonrho* (OJ 1998 L 149/21), para. 94.
122. As pointed out by *Ulf Bernitz & Irina Gutu:* The Effect of EU Merger Policy on Large Multinationals Based in Sweden and Other Smaller EU Member States: Is the Policy Discriminatory?, European Competition Law Review 2003 pp. 19–29, the fact that the Commission often finds that a geographic market is limited to individual national markets prevents undertakings in smaller countries, such as Denmark, from consolidating. A Danish undertaking will have limited opportunities for growing by taking over its closest Danish competitors, as it would soon acquire a dominant position in Denmark. By comparison, a German undertaking has better opportunities for growing through consolidation before giving rise to problems of competition on the German market. This means that the German market is better suited than the Danish market for developing large undertakings which are able to compete on the global market.
123. The CJ seemed to accept this reasoning in Joined Cases C-68/94 and C-30/95, *France and others v. Commission (Kali & Salz)*, para. 148.
124. In this connection, the Commission has rejected the application of the *Elzinga-Hoharty* test which is used by the US competition authorities, *see* M.315, *Mannesmann/Vallourec/Ilva* (OJ 1994 L 102/15), para. 33.
125. *See*, e.g., M.308, *Kali + Salz/MdK/Treuhand* (OJ 1994 L 186/38), para. 44, where the producers' very large market shares on their home markets did not influence the definition of the geographic market.

be due to physical factors, such as very high transport costs.[126] The Commission's analyses of the retail sector often result in findings of very small geographic areas, as consumers cannot be expected to travel far to do their shopping.[127]

> As examples of the Commission's practice, the market for television broadcasts will often be national, since cultural, linguistic and legislative conditions mean that the broadcasts of programmes and advertisements in one country cannot be broadcast to other countries.[128] Similarly, the market for beverages will often be defined as being national. In addition to transport costs, this can be due to consumer preferences, problems with getting access to the distribution network, and legislative requirements (e.g., the Danish requirements for the use of returnable bottles, the special rules in Norway on the state monopoly on sales of alcohol, and the Norwegian taxation on disposable packaging).[129]

In many cases, legislation has resulted in a market being considered as national. Thus, differences in accounting rules and tax law mean that the market for accountancy and tax advice remains national.[130] Perhaps some products cannot be sold because technical harmonisation has still not been implemented or because the

---

126. Among other things, transport costs have played a role in the assessment of the geographic market in several of the cases concerning beverages. Since it is expensive to transport beer and soft drinks, this will restrict the geographic markets so that these are generally national markets; see M.582, *Orkla/Volvo* (OJ 1996 L 66/17), para. 43; and M.794, *Coca-Cola/Amalgamated Beverages GB* (OJ 1997 L 218/15), para. 97. According to M.358, *Pilkington-Techint/SIV* (OJ 1994 L 158/24), para. 16, even high transport costs do not always prevent there being trade between national markets. The case concerned float glass which is expensive to transport, and it was shown that 80%-90% of float glass was sold within a radius of 500 km from where it was produced. However, at the time when the case was decided, there were thirty-six production plants in the EU, and they therefore lay so close that their radii of activity overlapped. For this reason, the relevant market was considered to be the EU. Such considerations were also relevant in JV.29, *Lafarge/Readymix*, decision of 20.12.1999, which concerned the market for ready mixed cement. This can only be transported for about one hour, so the extent to which the radiuses of the producers overlapped was decisive. The Commission started from where the planned joint venture should be located, and concluded that the overlap could only be considered to exist in the Rhine-Ruhr area. The Commission left open the final decision of the definition of the geographic market; see para. 14 of the decision.
127. M.784, *Kesko/Tuko* (OJ 1997 L 110/53), para. 21, according to which the relevant geographic market for a supermarket is the distance that consumers can travel in twenty minutes. However, if a retail market consists of a chain of stores, these can be considered as a whole, so the geographic market will typically be nationwide; M.890, *Blokker/Toys 'R' Us* (OJ 1998 L 316/1), para. 38.
128. M.553, *RTL/Veronica/Endemol* (OJ 1996 L 134/32), para. 25.
129. See decisions M.582, *Orkla/Volvo* (OJ 1996 L 66/17), paras 42-55; M.794, *Coca-Cola/Amalgamated Beverages GB* (OJ 1997 L 218/15), paras 95-107; M.833, *The Coca-Cola Company/Carlsberg* (OJ 1998 L 145/41), paras 44-48; and M.938, *Guinness/Grand Metropolitan* (OJ 1998 L 288/24), paras 24-29.
130. M.1016, *Price Waterhouse/Coopers & Lybrand* (OJ 1999 L 50/27), para. 63. In this same decision, the Commission left open the question of whether the market for management consultancy was greater, which is naturally connected with the fact that this market is not so dependent on national laws.

necessary technical standards have still not been created at the European level.[131] However, in many cases, the Commission has found the beginnings of harmonisation that will liberalise the market in question. In these cases, the question is whether the liberalisation can be assumed to create uniform competitive conditions throughout the EU within a relatively short period (normally two to three years).[132] In order to assess the expected developments in the near future, the Commission will often focus on how far the harmonisation process has reached in a particular area. However, in many cases, it will be relevant to look at the influence of the directives on public procurement, as these directives often contribute towards opening national markets.[133] Finally, it is clear that a tariff which is imposed on the import of goods to the EU can have the effect of being a barrier to access which protects the EU from the rest of the world.[134]

4 THE SUBSTANTIAL APPRAISAL OF CONCENTRATIONS

4.1 From the Dominance Test to Appraisal of Whether Effective Competition Would Be Significantly Impeded

Under the previous wording of Article 2(2) and (3), a concentration should either be declared compatible or incompatible with the common market depending on whether or not the concentration creates or strengthens a dominant position so that effective competition would be significantly impeded within the common market or in a substantial part thereof. The wording indicated that there are two separate parts to the dominance test: first, whether a dominant position would be created or strengthened, and next, whether effective competition would be significantly impeded. A reading of the Commission's decisions gives the impression that the dominance test only consists

---

131. See, e.g., M.222, *Mannesmann/Hoesch* (OJ 1993 L 114/34), paras 79–85, where the Commission concluded that, despite Directive 89/106/EEC (the 'Construction Products Directive'), and despite the mandate given to the European Committee for Standardization (CEN), the market for steel tubes was still dominated by national standards, so that Germany was considered a separate geographic market.
132. M.580, *ABB/Daimler-Benz* (OJ 1997 L 11/1), para. 43, where the Commission seems to have stated that the evaluation of potential competition and the evaluation of the geographic market should, in principle, be based on what can be expected in the coming two to three years. In the case in question, however, the Commission accepted that the evaluation should look five years forward. See also the assessment in M.477, *Mercedes-Benz/Kässbohrer* (OJ 1995 L 211/1), para 41, on the market for buses, M.1845, *AOL/Time Warner*, OJ 2001 L 268/28, on the market for online music services, and M.7428, *Centrica/Bond Gais Energy*, on the energy market.
133. The public procurement directives have been assessed in the following decisions: M.221, *ABB/Brel*, decision of 26.5.1992, para. 11 (railway equipment); M.222, *Mannesmann/Hoesch* (OJ 1993 L 114/34), paras 85–86 (steel tubes); M.477, *Mercedes-Benz/Kässbohrer* (OJ 1995 L 211/1), paras 95–100 (buses); and M.580, *ABB/Daimler-Benz* (OJ 1997 L 11/1), para. 32 (railway equipment).
134. M.315, *Mannesmann/Vallourec/Ilva* (OJ 1994 L 102/15), para. 37, where the EU market for steel tubes was protected by a 10% tariff. See also M.269, *Shell/Montecatini* (OJ 1994 L 332/48), para. 46.

of a single step. However, the CJ has made it clear that there were two independent conditions.[135]

The Commission's practice and the practice of the CJ gave rise to another important element in the definition of the dominance test, as it was established that collective dominance was also covered. Collective dominance exists in a situation where the merged undertaking does not itself have a dominant position, but it would obtain a dominant position together with one or a few other undertakings. If it is assumed that, after a concentration, these undertakings will coordinate their competitive behaviour, the concentration can be said to create a dominant position for the group of undertakings. The problem of collective dominance (or coordinated effects) will be discussed in more detail in section 4.3.

In 2001, the Commission commenced work on a major reform of the MCR. The Commission considered whether it ought to change the dominance test and perhaps replace it with the SLC test (substantial lessening of competition), which is known from American and English competition law. However, the Commission concluded that there was no great difference between the two tests, so there would be no great benefit in giving up the dominance test.[136] Instead, the Commission proposed to create greater clarity about the dominance test in the Regulation by defining the dominance criterion in a new Article 2(2). However, not all the Member States agreed with the Commission's assessment. In particular, there was a discussion as to whether the existing test, in addition to covering the dominance of individual undertakings and collective dominance, could be used to regulate concentrations in oligopolistic markets where, after a concentration, there would not be a prospect of the remaining undertakings on the market coordinating their conduct (non-coordinated oligopolies). Such concentrations can be declared to be contrary to the US/English SLC test if it can be shown that there is a restriction on effective competition, even if it cannot necessarily be said to create a dominant position.[137] The Commission believed that the original dominance

---

135. Case T-3/93, *Air France v. Commission*, para. 79; and Case T-5/02, *Tetra Laval/Sidel*, para. 120.
136. COM(2001) 745. See also the discussion in *Ulf Böge & Edith Müller:* From the Market Dominance Test to the SLC Test: Are There Any Reasons for a Change, European Competition Law Review 2002 pp. 495-498.
137. In particular, the judgment of the GC in Case T-342/99, *Airtours,* discussed in more detail below in s. 4.3, has been seen by many as confirmation that there is such a lacuna in the dominance test. In the *Airtours* case the GC stated that collective dominance requires there to be shown that it is probable that, after the concentration, there will be coordination between the remaining undertakings, and that it is therefore natural to conclude that where it cannot be assumed that such a coordination will take place, the dominance test cannot apply. For a more detailed review of the debate which preceded the introduction of the new test *see*, among others: *Francisco Enrique González Diaz:* The Reform of European Merger Control: *Quid Novi Sub Sole?*, World Competition 2004, pp. 177-199; *Rhodri Thompson:* Goodbye to 'The Dominance Test'? Substantive Appraisal under the New UK and EC Merger Regimes, Competition Law 2003 pp. 332-346; *Ioannis Kokkoris:* The Reform of the European Control Merger Regulation in the Aftermath of the Airtours Case. The Eagerly Expected Debate: SLC v Dominance Test, European Competition Law Review 2005, pp. 37-47; *Vijay S.V. Selvam:* The EC Merger Control Impasse: Is There a Solution to This Predicament?, European Competition Law Review 2004, pp. 52-67; and *Kyriakos Fountoukakos & Stephen Ryan:* A New Substantive Test for EU Merger Control, European Competition Law Review 2004, pp. 277-296.

test could be used in cases where a concentration results in non-coordinated oligopolies, but the fact that several people pointed out that there could be an 'enforcement gap' made it necessary to consider making a change to the test.

This debate led to a change of the wording of Article 2(2) and (3) so that the test now is whether a concentration would 'significantly impede effective competition in the common market or in a substantial part of it, in particular as a result of the creation or strengthening of a dominant position'.[138] It is notable that the new test has many similarities with the old test, as the most significant change is that the two steps have been switched around. However, such reformulation means that it is no longer a necessary condition that a concentration will create dominance. The creation of dominance is merely an example of how effective competition can be impeded; see the use of the words 'in particular'. Since this is not merely a cosmetic change to the provision, it is necessary to consider what the consequences of the new test are.

The first question which must be considered is whether the new formulation of Article 2(2) and (3) affects the dominance test developed under the previous formulation of the same provision. The fact that it was decided to repeat the dominance test in the new Article 2(2) and (3) must mean that, in principle, it has not been changed. This is also confirmed by the fact that several of the decisions which the Commission has adopted under the new test are entirely in accordance with the practice which the Commission developed before the new Regulation entered into force on 1 May 2004.[139]

Even if, in principle, the finding and evaluation of the dominance of individual undertakings and collective dominance seem to be the same, it is natural that in future, it will be easier to argue that efficiency gains, which are a justification for allowing concentrations, create dominance. This is indicated by the fact that the dominance test is made subsidiary to an assessment of the concentration's effect on the market, and it is confirmed in the Commission's Guidelines on the assessment of horizontal mergers, which makes reference to 'efficiency gains'. This is discussed in more detail below in section 4.5.

The next question to be considered is what new forms of restrictions on competition are covered by the new formulation of Article 2(2) and (3). The wording suggests that the Commission has wide discretion to step in against concentrations that impede competition, even if they do not create dominance. Thus, a textual interpretation seems to indicate that the new Article 2(2) and (3) have not only been introduced to close the 'enforcement gap' in relation to non-coordinated oligopolies, which may have existed under the old dominance test. However, Recital 25 of the Regulation indicates that the new test should be used to catch all cases where non-coordinated oligopolies restrict competition. By way of introduction, this recital sets out why it can be necessary to take action to maintain effective competition on oligopolistic markets, 'even in the absence of a likelihood of coordination between the members of the

---

138. A 'significant impediment to effective competition' (SIEC).
139. *See* also the Commission's Guidelines on the assessment of horizontal mergers under the Council Regulation on the control of concentrations between undertakings (OJ 2004 C 31/5), para. 4, (hereinafter the 'Commission's Guidelines on the assessment of horizontal mergers') according to which the Commission has chosen to retain the guidance that can be drawn from past practice.

oligopoly'. According to the recital, the European courts have not to date expressly interpreted the MCR as covering such non-coordinated concentrations. In an effort to ensure legal certainty, the new Regulation makes it clear that these types of concentrations can also be prohibited where they significantly impede effective competition. The preamble has hereby made it clear that the test has been changed primarily in order to close the enforcement gap which may have existed in the dominance test. Recital 25 then continues:

> The notion of 'significant impediment to effective competition' in Article 2(2) and (3) should be interpreted as extending, beyond the concept of dominance, only to the anti-competitive effects of a concentration resulting from the non-coordinated behaviour of undertakings which would not have a dominant position on the market concerned.

This formulation, especially the use of the word 'only', indicates that, in addition to cases of dominance (individual or collective), the new test can only be used to prohibit concentrations that create restrictions on competition, which can arise as a result of the existence of non-coordinated oligopolies. Preambles are often used by the European courts for the interpretation of legal acts, so it seems natural to assume that the new test cannot be used other than in cases of non-coordinated oligopolies.[140] If one looks at the practice of the Commission following the introduction of the new test, there are no clear examples of cases where a concentration has been prohibited without either the presence of dominance or a non-coordinated oligopoly.[141] The Commission's Guidelines on the assessment of horizontal mergers also indicate that, apart from cases of dominance, the new test only covers non-coordinated oligopolies, as these are the only kind of restrictions referred to.[142]

The Commission has issued Guidelines both on the assessment of horizontal mergers and on the assessment of non-horizontal mergers. As the former constitute mergers between actual or potential competitors, it is clear that this form of merger is more likely to create problems. Normally, a merger between undertakings that are not

---

140. *See Jessica Schmidt:* The New ECMR: 'Significant Impediment' or 'Significant Improvement'?, Common Market Law Review 2004 pp. 1555-1582 (at p. 1469). However, for a contrary view, *see Francisco Enrique Gonzales Diaz:* The Reform of European Merger Control: Quid Novi Sub Sole?, World Competition 2004 pp. 177-199 (in particular at pp. 188-189).
141. A possible modification to this statement is that the Commission seems prepared to reject mergers that impede innovation in general, instead of examining whether the mergers are likely to have as the effect that product that are under development may not have the effect on competition that they would likely have if the merger was not taking place. *See* Commission decision M.7932, *Dow/DuPont*, decision of 27.3.2017 as well as *Jorge Padilla:* Revisiting the Horizontal Mergers and Innovation Policy Debate, Journal of European Competition & Practice 2019 pp. 463-471 and *Agustín Waisman & Martín Hevia:* Merger Control and Innovation: A Rights-Based Approach, Journal of European Competition Law & Practice 2021 pp. 419-429.
142. Even though the Commission has thus had the possibility of intervening against several mergers, it must be noted that the number of cases in which the Commission has intervened against mergers has fallen. This indicates greater reticence on the party of the Commission, presumably due to the strict requirements for evidence which the European courts have repeatedly demanded; *see Michael Rosenthal & Stefan Thomas:* European Merger Control, 2010 p. 87.

competitors[143] does not involve the creation or strengthening of a dominant position, though in some cases, it can create a barrier whereby competitors to the merged undertakings are denied access to supplies or to markets.

The following review will begin by looking at how a merger can harm competition, either by having coordinated or non-coordinated effects; *see* sections 4.2 and 4.3 below. In section 4.4, the focus is on what role efficiency gains play in cases assessed under the MCR.

4.2 Non-coordinated Effects

Until 2004, the MCR was only focused on whether a concentration created or strengthened a dominant position. Even after the amendment to the MCR in 2004, this has been the theme of most of the Commission's decisions. As stated above, the 2004 amendment does not mean that the assessment of a dominant position has been changed, and the practice from before 2004 is still good law.

At the same time, according to the latest changes, it is necessary to distinguish between non-coordinated effects, which arise when a single undertaking is dominant, and effects that arise when two or more undertakings are dominant. The first situation occurs when the merged undertaking creates or reinforces a dominant position. This will typically be the case where the merged undertaking is considerably bigger than its competitors, but other circumstances can also lead to dominance. This is the situation that occurs most frequently in practice, and it is thus this situation that is discussed in most detail. However, following the latest revision, it is also necessary to take account of the situation in which an oligopolistic market arises following a merger, where competition is reduced even if coordination between the undertakings remaining in the market is unlikely. This situation is discussed in section 4.2.2 below.

4.2.1 The Creation or Strengthening of a Dominant Position

In assessing whether a dominant position exists, it is necessary to take a number of factors into account. These factors are listed in Article 2(1) of the MCR:

a. the need to maintain and develop effective competition within the common market in view of, among other things, the structure of all the markets concerned and the actual or potential competition from undertakings located either within or out with the Community;
b. the market position of the undertakings concerned and their economic and financial power, the alternatives available to suppliers and users, their access to supplies or markets, any legal or other barriers to entry, supply and demand trends for the relevant goods and services, the interests of the intermediate and ultimate consumers, and the development of technical and economic progress

---

143. In its Guidelines on non-horizontal mergers, the Commission distinguishes between two types: vertical mergers, between companies operating at different levels of the supply chain; and conglomerate mergers, between firms that do not compete in the same market, but are active in closely related markets; *see* the Guidelines in OJ 2008 C 265/6, paras 4–5.

provided that it is to consumers' advantage and does not form an obstacle to competition.

As can be seen, there are many factors which can potentially be included in the assessment. In practice, the most important factors are the market shares of the merging undertakings, other signs of strength, the position of competitors and the position on the demand side. Each of these is commented on below.

4.2.1.1 Market Share

The Commission will start by calculating the market shares in the markets which are affected by the concentration. The first question this raises is which markets are affected by the concentration, and the next question is how market shares are calculated.

In a merger, the Commission will usually concentrate on the markets where most of the merging undertakings are active. In special cases, it can also be relevant to investigate markets where there is a vertical integration, which can strengthen the position of the undertakings; see the comments on this in section 4.2.1.2. The calculation of market share is done by simply adding together the market shares that the merging companies had before the merger.

With a joint venture, the Commission's investigations will normally focus on the activities which the joint venture partners put into their joint venture company. If, for example, two joint venture partners both transfer their production of a particular product to their joint venture, then the market shares of these two production units are added together in order to evaluate the market share of the new joint venture. If one or more of the joint venture partners has retained a production unit in the same sector, then the market share for which that production unit is accountable is also included in the calculation of the market share of the new joint venture.[144]

When adding together the market shares of the merging undertakings and the market shares of the joint venture and the joint venture partners, in some cases, it can be difficult to decide which companies should be allocated to which merging undertaking or joint venture partner. This problem has certain parallels with the question of which undertakings should be allocated to the undertakings concerned when calculating whether a merger has a Community dimension. As discussed in section 2.4.2, this is regulated by Article 6(4) and (5) of the MCR. However, the corresponding problem of calculating the collective market shares should be carried out independently of the rules referred to, as the Commission has more discretion when deciding on the effect of a concentration.[145] In these cases, the concept of an undertaking should be used, where

---

144. M.774, *Saint-Gobain/Wacker Chemie/NOM* (OJ 1997 L 247/1). One could question whether, in situations where there is no indication that the joint venture and the joint venture partners will coordinate their activities, they should be considered as a whole. However, there has not hitherto been much sign that such an argument would be accepted; see Karsten Engsig Sørensen: Joint ventures – struktur og regulering, 2006 pp. 307-311.
145. Case T-22/97, *Kesko v. Commission*, para. 139, where the GC held that the Commission, when assessing the effect of a merger on competition, was not obliged to apply the conditions for

the focus will be on what entities that form part of the joint venture partners or the merging undertakings either because these have a sufficient degree of influence over another entity or are themselves controlled by that entity.

The calculation of market shares will typically be based either on turnover or on the number of units sold. While the Commission normally uses turnover in its calculations, there can be cases where it is more correct to use the number of units sold. This depends on the concrete circumstances.[146] For the same reasons, in some cases, the Commission will focus on entirely different factors, such as the number of viewers.[147]

The market shares of the merging undertakings are probably the most important factor in assessing whether a dominant position is created or strengthened. If the market share is below 25%, there is a clear presumption against the existence of a dominant position.[148] This is also supported by Recital 15 of the original preamble to the MCR. The practice suggests that a market share must be up around 40%–45% before the existence of a dominant position is considered probable.[149]

Conversely, it is not possible to point to an upper limit, where a market share is so high that there is necessarily considered to be a dominant position. In Decision M.477, *Mercedes-Benz/Kässbohrer* (OJ 1995 L 211/1), paragraph 65, the Commission stated:

> High market shares do not in themselves justify the assumption of a dominant position. At any rate, they do not allow a dominant position to be assumed if other structural factors are detectable which, in the foreseeable future, may alter the conditions of competition and justify a more relative view of the significance of the market share of the merged companies ... Such structural factors could, for example, be the ability of actual competitors to constrain the action of the new entity, the expectation of a significant increase in potential competition from powerful competitors, the possibility of a quick market entry or the buying power of important customers. In the present case, the market shares of the merged companies are relativized by the fact that it may be expected that there will be

---

control in Art. 3 of the MCR. In the underlying M.794, *Coca-Cola/Amalgamated Beverages GB* (OJ 1997 L 218/15), para. 98, the Commission assessed that the market shares for a number of retailers which were part of a chain should be allocated to the merging parties, because they exercised significant influence on the retailers.
146. *See* the comments in M.190, *Nestlé/Perrier* (OJ 1992 L-356/1), para. 40; and M.430, *Procter & Gamble/VP Schickedanz* (OJ 1994 L 354/32), paras 113–117, where in both cases the Commission reached the conclusion that calculation according sales volumes was more correct.
147. M.553, *RTL/Veronica/Endemol* (OJ 1996 L 134/32).
148. M.289, *Pepsico/KAS*, decision of 21.12.1992, para. 6.3; and Commission Guidelines on the assessment of horizontal mergers under the Council Regulation on the control of concentrations between undertakings (OJ 2004 C 31/5), para. 18. However, for non-horizontal mergers, the minimum threshold is a market share of 30%; *see* the Guidelines at OJ 2008 C 265/6, para. 25.
149. *See* the Commission's Tenth Annual Report on Competition Policy, 1981 para. 150. *See also* M.315, *Mannesmann/Vallourec/Ilva* (OJ 1994 L 102/15), para. 51, where 36% market share did not indicate market dominance; and M.344, *Codan/Hafnia*, decision of 28.5.1993, where 33% market share did not indicate market dominance. Finally, the threshold of 40% may be seen confirmed in M.1016, *Price Waterhouse/Coopers & Lybrand* (OJ 1999 L 50/27), para. 85, where the Commission stated, by way of introduction, that the merger would not give a market share of over 40% in any Member State so that a dominant position would not be created.

substantial actual and in particular potential competition, as explained in the following sections.

As is clear from this quotation, the Commission cannot be expected to find that there is a dominant position solely on the basis of the calculated market share, as it will normally also assess the actual and potential competition as well as the situation on the demand side; *see* the following sections. Nevertheless, it must be assumed that a very high market share can give rise to an assumption that there is a dominant position.[150]

If a merger only leads to a very small increase in market share or even no increase at all, this is an indication that a dominant position is neither created nor strengthened.

Prior to 2004, the Commission was dismissive of the use of the *Herfindahl-Hirschman Index* (HHI) as an indicator of the extent to which a market is concentrated and thereby creates a dominant position. However, in its Guidelines on the assessment of horizontal mergers, the Commission suggested that it would use the HHI to a greater extent.[151] This index can be used to measure the extent of market concentration before and after a concentration is carried out. The HHI uses the sum of the squares of the market shares of all undertakings on the market in question. If the merger is carried out, the HHI predicts whether the merger will lead to a high concentration, which ought to undergo a closer examination,[152] or to a low concentration, which means that there is no risk of market strength or abuse thereof. Where the concentration is of a certain degree, it depends on how much the merger leads to increased concentration, according to the HHI. According to the Commission's Guidelines, an HHI of less than 1,000 is an indication that the merger does not create problems for competition. If the merger creates an HHI of between 1,000 and 2,000, and the increase in the index is below 250, it is unlikely that the merger will create problems for competition. If the HHI is above 2,000 and the increase is below 150, it is also assumed that there are no problems. However, in the last case the Commission makes the reservation that there can nevertheless be circumstances which make the merger problematic. The rules laid down by the Commission are thus only 'safe harbour rules' for mergers that result in an HHI of less than

---

150. The Commission also seems to assume this in some of its decisions. *See*, e.g., M.222, *Mannesmann/Hoesch* (OJ 1993 L 114/34), para. 91, where it stated: 'High market shares represent an important factor as evidence of a dominant position provided they not only reflect current conditions but are also a reliable indicator of future conditions'. *See also* M.890, *Blokker/Toys 'R' Us* (OJ 1998 L 316/1), where a retail chain obtained a market share of 55%-65%, on which the Commission commented (para. 59): 'This high market share in itself creates a presumption of dominance, especially when compared to the fragmented structure of the rest of the market.' *See also* M.1229, *American Home Products/Monsanto*, decision of 28.9.1998, para. 24. This also seems to have been assumed by the GC which, in Case T-102/96, *Gencor*, para. 205 stated: 'although the importance of the market shares may vary from one market to another, the view may legitimately be taken that very large market shares are in themselves, save in exceptional circumstances, evidence of the existence of a dominant position'. *See* the similar statement in Case T-342/07, *Ryanair*, para. 41.
151. The Commission's Guidelines on the assessment of horizontal mergers, para. 16 (OJ 2004 C 31/5).
152. According to the GC, the fact that the HHI exceeds the thresholds mentioned in the main text will not create a presumption that there is a significant impediment to effective competition, *see* Case T-240/18, *LOT S.A.*, para. 80.

1,000.[153] For mergers with an HHI of over 1,000, the Commission's guidelines create doubts and mean that the HHI is less suitable for guiding undertakings.

4.2.1.2 Other Indications of Market Strength

Apart from market shares, the Commission can also focus on other factors concerning the merging undertakings, which indicate whether they occupy a dominant position. For example, sometimes, the Commission refers to the fact that the merging undertakings have a far superior financial position than their competitors.[154] In the case of joint ventures it is not so much the financial strength of the joint venture as that of the joint venture partners which is assessed.[155] In addition, the Commission can attach weight to the fact that a new entity has a strong position because of the patents and know-how of the undertaking.[156] The fact that an undertaking is able itself to produce a complete or very broad product range can also indicate that it has a dominant position.[157]

Finally, sometimes, the Commission focuses on vertical integration as an indicator of a dominant position. In these cases, the Commission looks at whether the concentration can contribute to creating or strengthening vertical integration and whether this in itself contributes to creating or strengthening a dominant position.[158] In its practice, the Commission is particularly alert to situations where vertical integration, which results from a merger, leads to third parties being excluded from a market.[159]

4.2.1.3 Actual and Potential Competitors

Even though the assessment of the existence of a dominant position must necessarily take the planned merger as its starting point, it is clear that the assessment must also take into account the new undertaking's position relative to its competitors – both actual and potential.

---

153. However, for non-horizontal mergers, the threshold is 2000; *see* the Commission Guidelines at OJ 2008 C 265/6, para. 25.
154. M.12, *Varta/Bosch* (OJ 1991 L 320/26), para. 32; and M.580, *ABB/Daimler-Benz* (OJ 1997 L 11/1), para. 64.
155. M.469, *MSG Media Service* (OJ 1994 L 364/1), paras 60 et seq., where the Commission emphasised that all the joint venture partners had great prior market strength in a number of different areas.
156. *See*, e.g., M.877, *Boeing/McDonnell Douglas* (OJ 1997 L 336/16), para. 102.
157. M.222, *Mannesmann/Hoesch* (OJ 1993 L 114/34), para. 99; M.580, *ABB/Daimler-Benz* (OJ 1997 L 11/1), para. 65; and M.938, *Guinness/Grand Metropolitan* (OJ 1998 L 288/24), para. 86.
158. *See*, e.g., M.833, *Coca-Cola Company/Carlsberg* (OJ 1998 L 145/41), where the Commission held that the fact that Coca-Cola entered into a joint venture with Carlsberg on bottling, effectively strengthened Coca-Cola's dominant position. This joint venture meant that Coca-Cola went from being a licensor to also being the co-owner of a bottling plant, and this vertical integration increased Coca-Cola's market strength; *see* paras 50 and 83–90. *See also* M.469, *MSG Media Service* (OJ 1994 L 364/1), where in relation to several of the joint venture partners, the planned joint venture would strengthen their dominant position on markets which were related to the joint venture's own market.
159. *See* the Commission Guidelines on the assessment of non-horizontal mergers (OJ 2008 C 265/6).

If the nearest competitors only have very small market shares and do not otherwise have a strength, which makes it likely they will be able to offer the merged undertaking much competition, this indicates the existence of a dominant position. If, on the contrary, the nearest competitors are of a corresponding size to the merging undertaking, this indicates that there is not a dominant position. However, if it is possible that, after the merger, two or three undertakings will dominate the market in question, non-coordinated or coordinated effects may be found to exist; *see* sections 4.2.2 and 4.3.

When assessing the nearest competitors' possibilities for competing effectively, it is again relevant to focus on their market shares. Even if the competing undertakings have relatively modest market shares, they may nevertheless have a position, which means that they can be expected to compete effectively. When assessing this, the Commission takes into account, among other things, their financial strength, their technical know-how, their distribution systems and their production capacity. If, for example, the competitors have filled their production capacity, it cannot be expected that they will be able to compete effectively,[160] but if there is excess capacity, this can be an indicator against a finding of the existence of a dominant position.[161] If there is a competitor with a very strong financial position, this can be an argument against the existence of a dominant position, even if, for the time being, the competitor only has a modest market share.

> In Decision M.12, *Varta/Bosch* (OJ 1991 L 320/26), the Commission changed its assessment of a concentration which concerned the market for car batteries, as in the course of the proceedings, it became clear that Fiat had taken over the next largest competitor. Even though the merged undertaking would have a market share of 44% and the Fiat-controlled competitor only had 10% of the market, the Commission found that Fiat's entry into the market would ensure effective competition.

If, for a longer period, the nearest competitor has tried to compete but without gaining market share, this can indicate that it is not in a position to ensure that there will be effective competition.

---

160. *See*, e.g., M.1313, *Danish Crown/Vestjyske Slagterier*, decision of 9.3.1999, para. 122, where it was found that the other pig slaughterhouses in Denmark made full use of their capacity, so they could not compete effectively with the merged undertaking. *See also* M.358, *Pilkington-Techint/SIV* (OJ 1994 L 158/24), where the closest competitor had reached its full capacity, para. 43.
161. Even if the competitors have overcapacity, this does not automatically mean they can in fact use it to gain market share. This was the case in M.582, *Orkla/Volvo* (OJ 1996 L 66/17), where the two small breweries may have had reserve capacity, but the Commission nevertheless did not believe they could use it, as they could not overcome the distribution costs associated with this, and they would find it difficult to get access to the shelf space in the retail trade; *see* paras 64–67. There are other and more recent decisions where the Commission, in a similar way, assesses whether the competitor has an incentive to use its reserve capacity, *see* Thomas Buettner, Andrea Cilea & Massimiliano Kadar: Horizontal Mergers in Homogeneous Goods Industries: When Is Spare Capacity Sufficient to Offset Unilateral Effects?, World Competition 2016, pp. 57–66.

This was the case in M.877, *Boeing/McDonnell Douglas* (OJ 1997 L 336/16), where the Commission did not believe that Airbus, with a market share of 30%, would be able to ensure effective competition if the merger between the two American aircraft manufacturers were permitted, as it emphasised that throughout the 1990s, Airbus had been unable to increase its market share.

If there have been previous signs that competition does not function effectively, this can indicate that there is a dominant position.

If there are no current significant competitors, potential competitors may be able to prevent a merged undertaking from exploiting its market strength. Potential competitors can either exist among the undertakings that have the possibility of switching their production apparatus to serve the market concerned or among undertakings that are active in other geographic markets. The Commission assesses whether it is realistic (or meaningful)[162] in terms of competition that other undertakings will seek to enter the market and whether this will be of such an extent and at such a price level that it would rapidly and effectively put a stop to any attempt by the merging undertakings to exploit their market strength by, for example, maintaining a price level which is far above what would otherwise apply under conditions of effective competition.[163]

Potential competitors will often be found in the same geographic market as the merging undertakings. In many cases, the geographic market is defined by reference to whether there are barriers to market access (*see* section 3.2 above), so it seems logical that undertakings that are active in other markets cannot immediately be considered as potential competitors. Where there are special cultural or legal circumstances, which mean that a market is considered a separate geographic market, the same circumstances naturally make it less likely that a foreign producer will be able to penetrate the market in question.[164] However, the Commission's assessment of how a geographic market should be defined and its assessment of potential competition need not go hand in hand.

For example, this was not the case in Decision M.315, *Mannesmann/ Vallourec/Ilva* (OJ 1994 L 102/15), where the geographic market was defined as being Western Europe, but the Commission nevertheless assumed that there was no risk of there being a collective dominant position since both Japanese and Eastern European producers were considered potential competitors.

The assessment of potential competitors concentrates, in particular, on investigating whether there are barriers to market access and, if so, whether these can be surmounted within a reasonable period. This can be on the basis of an empirical assessment, as in a number of cases, the Commission has attached importance to whether there has previously been entry into the market or whether, on the contrary,

---

162. *See* the choice of words in M.430, *Procter & Gamble/VP Schickedanz* (OJ 1994 L 354/32), para. 175.
163. M.190, *Nestlé/Perrier* (OJ 1992 L-356/1), para. 91.
164. M.582, *Orkla/Volvo* (OJ 1996 L 66/17), paras 78-79, on the potential for Swedish brewers to gain access to the Norwegian market.

there have been many failed attempts to do so.¹⁶⁵ However, in most cases, the question is assessed on the basis of considering what barriers to entry exist and what is necessary in order to overcome them. Where the Commission can identify potential competitors, the Commission will also assess their concrete possibilities for gaining access to the market.¹⁶⁶

There can be various forms of barriers to entry. For example, a high level of customer loyalty can prevent potential competitors from gaining market access to a market, which will typically be the case in markets which are characterised by the existence of strong brand franchises.¹⁶⁷ There can also be a need for control of special technology or means of distribution in order to gain access to a market.¹⁶⁸ If the existing competitors operate with a special discount system, this can make it difficult for new competitors to gain access.¹⁶⁹ Finally, various kinds of exclusive agreements can make market access difficult, if not impossible.¹⁷⁰

Even if it is possible to gain entry to a market in principle, this can be associated with such major costs that there is almost an assumption that it will not happen. For example, this is the case where there would be a requirement for significant investment in research or in production capacity in order to start production.¹⁷¹ Where a market is characterised by having strong brand loyalties, there will be a requirement for substantial marketing investment in order to launch a new product.¹⁷² In particular, where these investments are in the nature of 'sunk costs' (investments which cannot be recovered if the attempt to enter the market is unsuccessful), the Commission will assume that it is less likely that new competitors will attempt to enter the market.¹⁷³

---

165. M.477, *Mercedes-Benz/Kässbohrer* (OJ 1995 L 211/1), para. 73 (repeated examples of foreign undertakings entering the German market); M.737, *Ciba-Geigy/Sandoz* (OJ 1997 L 201/1), para. 161 (several new competitors); and conversely M.430, *Procter & Gamble/VP Schickedanz* (OJ 1994 L 354/32), para. 178 (repeated examples of failure to enter the market).
166. M.774, *Saint-Gobain/Wacker Chemie/NOM* (OJ 1997 L247/1), where the Commission judged that there were potential competitors in China and Eastern Europe.
167. See, for example, the cola market, which is characterised by there being very few brands and where it would be very difficult to build up a new brand with an image and brand recognition corresponding to those of the established brands; M.833, *The Coca-Cola Company/Carlsberg* (OJ 1998 L 145/41), paras 72-74. The market for sanitary towels is also characterised by a high level of brand loyalty among consumers, so it is difficult for a new competitor to gain access; M.430, *Procter & Gamble/VP Schickedanz* (OJ 1994 L 354/32), para. 126.
168. M.833, *The Coca-Cola Company/Carlsberg* (OJ 1998 L 145/41), para. 74, according to which a new producer of fizzy drinks would either have to make considerable investment in its own distribution network, or negotiate with a competitor in order to gain access to their network.
169. M.190, *Nestlé/Perrier* (OJ 1992 L-356/1), para. 95.
170. M.1313, *Danish Crown/Vestjyske Slagterier*, decision of 9.3.1999, para. 125, where there was an obligation to supply which the Danish pig slaughterhouses imposed on their cooperative members and which made it difficult for foreign slaughterhouses to enter the market.
171. M.877, *Boeing/McDonnell Douglas* (OJ 1997 L 336/16), para. 49, where it would require investments in the order of USD 10 billion to develop an aircraft from the ground up; and M.358, *Pilkington-Techint/SIV* (OJ 1994 L 158/24), para. 44, where it would costs something in the order of EUR 100 million in order to build a new plant for the production of float glass.
172. M.430, *Procter & Gamble/VP Schickedanz* (OJ 1994 L 354/32), para. 145.
173. M.430, *Procter & Gamble/VP Schickedanz* (OJ 1994 L 354/32), para. 147 (advertising investment as 'sunk costs'); M.190, *Nestlé/Perrier* (OJ 1992 L-356/1), para. 97 (advertising investment as 'sunk costs'); and M.358, *Pilkington-Techint/SIV* (OJ 1994 L 158/24), para. 44 (costs of new production plant as 'sunk costs').

For the Commission to consider a potential competitor as a guarantee for effective competition, it requires that such barriers to entry can be overcome within a reasonable period, normally two years.[174] In order to assess whether this is the case, it is first necessary to evaluate how market conditions can be expected to develop and sometimes also to assess whether the potential competitors have the ability to overcome the barriers sufficiently quickly. For example, the Commission can decide that harmonisation is necessary in order to ensure the market access of potential competitors within this time horizon.[175] If entry to a market requires the development of know-how or patents, this can take so long that it is not realistic for there to be potential competition.[176] The same is the case if switching production[177] or the construction of a new production plant would take several years.[178]

In some situations, the barriers to access cannot be overcome, and in this case, potential competitors can be disregarded. For example, this can be the case if there are legal or actual monopolies.[179]

If a merger or a joint venture eliminates a potential competitor, this can in itself be an indication of the creation or strengthening of a dominant position. This will be the case, for example, if one or more of the joint venture partners are potential competitors to the newly established joint venture, and it is assessed that if the planned joint venture were not realised, then one or more of the joint venture partners could have carried through the project on their own.[180]

4.2.1.4 The Position on the Demand Side

If customers for the products on the market concerned have a strong negotiating position, this can help prevent the merged undertakings from abusing their market strength. In order for the customers to adopt such a position, there must either be a buying monopoly or at least a limited number of customers. While examples of buying

---

174. Commission Guidelines on the assessment of horizontal mergers, para. 74.
175. M.222, *Mannesmann/Hoesch* (OJ 1993 L 114/34), paras 107–114, where the Commission assessed that the public procurement directives as well as the implementation of technical harmonisation of the rules on gas pipes within a period of two to four years would ensure access for new competitors. Therefore, even if a merger immediately created a dominant position, it would only exist for a limited period, and therefore the merger would not create a dominant position.
176. M.269, *Shell/Montecatini* (OJ 1994 L 332/48), paras 85–91.
177. M.774, *Saint-Gobain/Wacker Chemie/NOM* (OJ 1997 L247/1), paras 217–219, where the producers in Eastern Europe could not be expected to raise their levels of production quality to Western European levels within a period of three years. Therefore, the Commission concluded that these producers could not be considered as potential competitors of the merged undertaking.
178. M.358, *Pilkington-Techint/SIV* (OJ 1994 L 158/24), para. 44, where it was emphasised that a new float glass production plant would take more than two years to construct, as merely getting planning permission was difficult because of the environmental problems involved.
179. M.754, *Anglo American Corporation/Lonrho* (OJ 1998 L 149/21), para. 118, where it was found that nobody had yet discovered a platinum mine which was not being worked and there could therefore not be expected to be any potential competitors.
180. M.469, *MSG Media Service* (OJ 1994 L 364/1), paras 56–59.

monopolies are rare, they do exist.[181] There will normally be several customers, and the question will be whether they have sufficient strength and a sufficient interest in pushing the merged undertaking to compete effectively. For example, there can be pricing regulations, which means that no one has any special interest in putting downward pressure on prices.[182] If there is no other supplier, then even the strongest customer group cannot be expected to exploit its market strength. For example, this can be the case with certain branded goods which retailers absolutely have to have on their shelves.[183]

> In M.1313, *Danish Crown/Vestjyske Slagterier*, the Commission did not believe that the fact that two Danish retail chains (FDB and Dansk Supermarked) took 50% of the merging undertakings' sales of pork was sufficient to find that a dominant position would not result from the planned merger of the slaughterhouses.[184] First, the Commission did not think that the fact that the two supermarket chains had a strong negotiating position, was in itself enough to ensure that there was not an abuse of the dominant position. The two supermarket chains would not have been able to prevent the slaughterhouses from exploiting their position in relation to other customers. Next, the Commission pointed out that while the supermarkets were virtually bound to buy their pork from the merged slaughterhouses, the slaughterhouses themselves could, without great difficulty, export the pork which the supermarkets did not buy. This meant that the negotiating position of the slaughterhouses was stronger than that of the supermarkets. *See also* M.190, *Nestlé/Perrier* (OJ 1992 L-356/1), where the Commission likewise assessed that the producers' position was stronger, even though four large retail chains took 50% of the mineral water production from the merging undertakings.[185]

The position of buyers can also be strong in markets where retailers market products under their own brands. For example, this is the case with packaged processed nuts, where the retailers' own brands are stronger than those of the producers. Since retailers can relatively easily switch suppliers, it would be difficult for a producer to acquire a dominant position, even if they had a high market share.[186]

---

181. M.580, *ABB/Daimler-Benz* (OJ 1997 L 11/1), where Deutsche Bahn was the only customer for railway equipment on the German market.
182. M.582, *Orkla/Volvo* (OJ 1996 L 66/17), para. 76, where the buyers of beer on the Norwegian market may have had a strong market position, but they nevertheless lacked the incentive to put pressure on the producers as the many restrictions on the sale of beer in Norway meant that they did not effectively profit from their sales of beer. Another reason why buyers can lack an incentive to put pressure on producers can be because they buy such small amounts that the effort is disproportionate to the return.
183. M.430, *Procter & Gamble/VP Schickedanz* (OJ 1994 L 354/32), para. 169 (sanitary towels); and M.833, *The Coca-Cola Company/Carlsberg* (OJ 1998 L 145/41), para. 79.
184. M.1313, *Danish Crown/Vestjyske Slagterier*, decision of 9.3.1999, paras 171-173.
185. M.190, *Nestlé/Perrier* (OJ 1992 L-356/1), paras 77-89.
186. JV.32, *Granaria/Ültje/Interschnack/May Holding*, decision of 28.2.2000, paras 41-48.

4.2.2 Non-coordinated Oligopolies

The concentrations at which the new test is particularly aimed are mergers in oligopolistic markets, which eliminate important competitive pressures which previously existed between the merging parties, so that competition is weakened even where coordination between the oligopolistic undertakings is not likely.[187] This will typically be in the situation where a market consists of three or four undertakings which produce similar but differentiated products. If two undertakings on such a market merge, and customers can easily switch to the remaining undertakings, the merged undertakings do not have the possibility of raising prices. However, if the customers of the two merged undertakings have the products of the two undertakings as their first and second choice, it is less likely that the customers will switch suppliers even if the merged undertaking raises prices. In this situation, there could, therefore, be a restriction of competition after the merger, even if the remaining undertakings do not coordinate their conduct.[188] Usually, such a restriction on competition arises when numbers two and three undertakings in the market merge so as to have a market share just below that of the biggest undertaking in the market.

There have been some decisions where the Commission has assessed the effect of non-coordinated conduct in an oligopolistic market. Sometimes, the Commission has assessed both the coordinated and the non-coordinated (unilateral) effects, so the decisions on collective dominance and on non-coordinated effects support each other.[189]

It was not until Case T-399/16, *CK Telecoms* and Case C-376/20 P, *Commission v. CK Telecoms UK Investment*, that the courts were asked to review the Commission's assessment of such cases.

The mergers whereby Hutchison 3G (Three) acquired control over O2 meant that the number of mobile network operators in the UK was reduced from four to three. The new entity would have a market share of 30–40% on the retail market for mobile communication. The two remaining competitors would have market shares that were 30–40% and 10–20%. In its decision from May 2016, the Commission declared the merger incompatible with the internal market based on an analysis of harm caused by

---

187. The Commission's Guidelines on the assessment of horizontal mergers (OJ 2004 C 31/5), para. 25.
188. For a more detailed review of the circumstances that can lead to such non-coordinated restrictions on competition, *see Ben Dubow, David Elliott & Eric Morrison:* Unilateral Effects and Merger Simulations Models, European Competition Law Review 2004 pp. 114–117; *Vincent Verouden, Claes Bengtsson & Svend Aalbaek:* The Draft EU Notice on Horizontal Mergers: A Further Step toward Convergence, Antitrust Bulletin 2004 pp. 243–285; *Sven B. Völcker:* Mind The Gap: Unilateral Effects Analysis Arrives In EC Merger Control, European Competition Law Review 2004 pp. 395–409; *Simon Baxter:* Unilateral Effects under the European Merger Regulation: How Big Is the Gap?, European Competition Law Review 2005 pp. 380–389; and *Simon Baxter:* Collective Dominance under EC Merger Control – After Airtours and the Introduction of Unilateral Effects Is There Still a Future for Collective Dominance?, European Competition Law Review 2006 pp. 148–160. This situation is often referred to as 'unilateral effects', which is the term used for the corresponding situation in US anti-trust law.
189. *See inter alia* M.3465, *Syngenta CP/Advanta*, decision of 17.8.2004.

non-coordinated effects in the market. The efficiencies alleged by the merging undertakings were either not verifiable, not specific to the concentration or were unlikely to benefit consumers.[190]

The decision was annulled by the GC. The GC criticised the Commission's decision on a number of accounts, but subsequently, this criticism was, in the main, rejected by the CJ. Here, only the most important points in the disagreement will be highlighted.

Initially, on the one hand, the GC insisted that the Commission is required to demonstrate with a 'strong probability the existence of significant impediments' to effective competition following the concentration in order to prohibit it. Thus, the GC indicated that the burden of proof for reaching such a conclusion is strict.[191] The CJ, on the other hand, did not accept that there were special requirements for the proof in the type of case at hand nor that the proof for prohibiting a concentration was stricter than that required for approving a concentration. The MCR did not formulate any general presumption that a concentration is compatible with or incompatible with the internal market, and consequently, the standard of proof for both these decisions should be the same.[192]

The GC interpreted Article 2(3) in light of Recital 25 of the Regulation to the effect that two cumulative conditions have to be met to prohibit a merger that creates non-coordinated effects in an oligopolistic market. First, competition between the merging parties must be restricted, and second, there must be a reduction of competitive pressure on the remaining competitors. The CJ disagreed with this interpretation, as it argued that MCR aimed to prevent all concentration that significantly impeded effective competition even if the case was that this was effected by only one of the two conditions. Therefore, there was no requirement that both anticompetitive effects needed to be present.[193]

The GC then examined the different theories of harm developed and used by the Commission and found that the Commission had failed to apply these correctly. *Inter alia*, the Court found that it was wrong that the Commission asserted that Three was an important competitive force. This would require that Three should have more influence on the competition than their competitors, which the GC did not find was the case.[194] The CJ disagreed that the Commission was required to demonstrate that Three competed particularly aggressively in order to establish that it was an 'important competitive force'. Given the nature of an oligopolistic market, a number of undertakings may be classified as an 'important competitive force'.[195] The GC had assumed that to prohibit the merger, the Commission needed to prove that the two merging undertakings were close competitors on the retail market. Since this was not proved, the GC rejected the decision.[196] The CJ found that the GC had erred in law since it was

---

190. M.7612, *Hutchison 3G UK/Telefónica UK*, decision of 11.5.2016.
191. Case T-399/16, *CK Telecoms*, para. 118.
192. Case C-376/20 P, *Commission v. CK Telecoms UK Investment*, paras 69–71.
193. Case C-376/20 P, *Commission v. CK Telecoms UK Investment*, para. 114.
194. Paragraphs 158 and 189.
195. Case C-376/20 P, *Commission v. CK Telecoms UK Investment*, para. 163 and 168.
196. Paragraph 247 of the judgment by the GC.

not necessary to prove that the merging parties were particularly close competitors to prohibit a merger in an oligopolistic market.[197] Finally, on the one hand, the GC criticised that the Commission had not made an overall assessment of the non-coordinated effects to establish where the effects were 'significant'.[198] The CJ, on the other hand, decided that the GC had erred in law by only addressing the findings contested by CK Telecom and not making an overall assessment of the findings of the Commission.[199]

4.3 Coordinated Effects (Collective Dominance)

As stated above, in assessing a dominant position, it will often be relevant to assess the status of the nearest competitor to the merging undertakings. If the nearest competitor or competitors are of almost the same size as the merged undertaking, this is an indication that there is not a dominant position. However, in this situation it is possible that the merged undertaking and its nearest competitors together have a dominant position. This will be the case if a small group of undertakings is able, to a large extent, to act independently of the existing or potential competitors, customers or, ultimately, the consumers.[200] Such a group may be able to coordinate their behaviour, including raising their prices, even without entering into an agreement or resorting to a concerted practice that is caught by Article 101. This was originally referred to as collective dominance. In the Commission's Guidelines on the assessment of horizontal mergers, this is referred to as 'coordinated effects'.

The Commission has assessed whether coordinated effects exist in a number of cases. However, it was first in a judgment in 1998 that the CJ had an opportunity to confirm that collective dominance can also be prohibited under Article 2(3) of the MCR. The CJ found that the interpretation of the provision according to its purpose leads to this conclusion since the opposite conclusion would lead to the provision losing a significant part of its effect.[201] However, in this judgment, it was emphasised that the Commission has a heavy burden of proof in such cases, and the CJ did not believe that the Commission had satisfied the burden of proof in the actual case. In 2002, the GC gave judgment in Case T-342/99, *Airtours plc*, where it had the opportunity to lay down in more detail the conditions which must be satisfied for coordinated effects to be found to exist. In particular, the GC emphasised that there

---

197. Case C-376/20 P, *Commission v. CK Telecoms UK Investment*, para. 192.
198. Case T-399/16, *CK Telecoms*, para. 289.
199. Case C-376/20 P, *Commission v. CK Telecoms UK Investment*, para. 270.
200. M.315, *Mannesmann/Vallourec/Ilva* (OJ 1994 L 102/15), para. 53. It can be debated whether it is more appropriate to counteract this risk by preventing such coordinated effects (i.e., by application of the MCR) or to prevent undertakings in oligopolistic markets coordinating their actions; see the discussion in Antoine Winckler & Marc Hansen: Collective Dominance under the EC Merger Control Regulation, Common Market Law Review 1993 pp. 787–828 (in particular at p. 791). The background to this discussion is that Art. 102 TFEU has also been used against cases of collective dominance.
201. Joined Cases C-68/94 and C-30/95, *France and others v. Commission (Kali & Salz)*, para. 171.

must be sufficient deterrents to ensure that each member of the oligopoly has no interest in departing from parallel conduct with the other members.

In its Guidelines on the assessment of horizontal mergers, the Commission has had an opportunity to summarise what elements indicate the existence of coordinated effects. *First*, it must be possible to establish that the market is conducive to coordination. Here, it is relevant to look at the structure of the market, as collective dominance will normally require there to be few actors in the market sector, a homogeneous product and relatively stable conditions of supply and demand. The *second* condition is that the coordination must be sustainable.

To assess whether, according to the first condition, the market structure makes it easy to establish coordinated conduct, the Commission starts from the basis of the economic theory on oligopolistic markets.[202] These are markets with few suppliers, which, because of the nature of the market, have an incentive not to compete. On the basis of economic theory, the Commission has sought to define what characterises oligopolistic markets. First, it is characteristic that there are few suppliers on the market. In most cases of coordinated effects, two undertakings dominate the market, but in one case, the Commission has concluded that there were coordinated effects between three undertakings.[203] Coordinated effects between more than three or four undertakings would be far too complex and unstable to be sustainable.[204] Next, the two or three dominant suppliers should have a large combined market share, and their individual market shares should be similar (i.e., the market should be symmetrical).[205]

---

202. See Erik Kloosterhuis: Joint Dominance and the Interaction between Firms, European Competition Law Review 2001 pp. 79–92; *Derek Ridyard:* Economic Analysis of Single Firm and Oligopolistic Dominance under the European Merger Regulation, European Competition Law Review 1994, pp. 255–262. *Ioannis Kokkoris:* The Development of the Concept of Collective Dominance in the European Community Merger Regulation. From Its Inception to Its Current Status, World Competition 2007 pp. 419–448; and *Antoine Winckler & Marc Hansen:* Collective Dominance under the EC Merger Control Regulation, Common Market Law Review 1993 pp. 787–828, also give accounts of the American practice that has been the model for the Commission's practice. There is a simplified but illustrative analogy given by *G. Porter Elliott:* The Gencor Judgment: Collective Dominance, Remedies and Extraterritoriality under the Merger Regulation, European Law Review 1999 pp. 638–652 (in particular at p. 645), which compares the situation to two sumo wrestlers living in a cupboard. Neither of them will be inclined to fight, as they both know this will merely result in them both suffering cuts and bruises, while ending up just where they started.
203. M.1524, *Airtours/First Choice,* decision of 22.9.1999. This decision was later reversed by the GC in Case T-342/99, *Airtours plc,* not so much because there were too many participants in the collective dominance, but because on a number of points the Commission had not produced enough evidence in support of its claims and because the Commission had made a number of wrong judgments.
204. M.1016, *Price Waterhouse/Coopers & Lybrand* (OJ 1999 L 50/27), para. 113. In the same decision the Commission decided that the merger between Coopers & Lybrand and Price Waterhouse would not create a situation of collective dominance since there would be five major undertakings on the market after the merger; *see* para. 119. However, in M.1383, *Exxon/Mobil,* decision of 29.9.1999, the Commission decided that seven undertakings together had collective dominance.
205. *See also* the Commission's Guidelines on the assessment of horizontal mergers (OJ 2004 C 31/5), para. 48. In M.358, *Pilkington-Techint/SIV* (OJ 1994 L 158/24), the fact that the market positions of the five remaining float glass producers were asymmetric was one of the main reasons why the Commission did not think that parallel conduct in restraint of competition would occur; *see* para. 63 of the decision.

Chapter 8

A large collective market share will be an indication of the existence of coordinated effects,[206] but this is not enough in itself. The factors which further support a finding of the existence of an oligopolistic market are as follows, on the demand side and on the supply side, respectively:[207]

> On the *demand side* there is only moderate growth, and demand is inelastic. If, on the contrary, there is significant concentration on the demand side, this can indicate that suppliers will compete with each other.[208]

The *supply side* is, as stated above, strongly concentrated. Next, the market must have a high degree of transparency, as transparency is a prerequisite for suppliers being able to see whether the others overstep tacit pricing agreements. If there is a commodity such as platinum, potash or mineral water, the condition will be fulfilled in principle, but it can be more difficult to evaluate this with more complex products.[209] Next, the Commission will have regard for whether the production technology is well developed, as the fact that further developments can be expected will make it less likely that the suppliers will have parallel competitive conduct.[210] Conduct that restricts competition will also be more likely if there are high barriers to entry to the market (with high sunk costs). The Commission will often investigate whether the undertakings have the same cost structures. If not, this can mean the parties will be less likely to accept a tacit coordination of their pricing policies.[211] If the remaining undertakings have different sales strategies, this may indicate that coordination is less likely.[212] On the supply side the Commission will also have regard for how competition on the market has previously developed. Thus, if there have previously been examples of

---

206. Case T-102/96, *Gencor v. Commission*, para. 206.
207. M.619, *Gencor/Lonrho* (OJ 1997 L 11/30), para. 141; M.1016, *Price Waterhouse/Coopers & Lybrand* (OJ 1999 L 50/27), para. 96; and M.1524, *Airtours/First Choice*, decision of 22.9.1999, para. 87, where the Commission summarised the most important factors it will investigate when assessing whether there is an oligopolistic market.
208. M.580, *ABB/Daimler-Benz* (OJ 1997 L 11/1), where Deutsche Bahn's market strength as a buyer meant that it was most probable that the planned joint venture and Siemens would compete with each other on a number of the market sectors for railway equipment; *see* para. 137.
209. For example, the Commission has assumed that the market for auditing work is transparent. It believes that there is a homogeneous service as each auditing task will require uniform control, analysis, reports and whatever else is required under national laws. It was therefore easy to compare services, and the Commission found that in practice the major auditing firms knew their competitors' fee rates; *see* M.1016, *Price Waterhouse/Coopers & Lybrand* (OJ 1999 L 50/27), para. 100.
210. Commission's Guidelines on the assessment of horizontal mergers (OJ 2004 C 31/5), para. 45.
211. M.190, *Nestlé/Perrier* (OJ 1992 L-356/1), para. 125. In M.315, *Mannesmann/Vallourec/Ilva* (OJ 1994 L 102/15), para. 68, the Commission emphasised that there must be large cost differences before it will be interesting for producers to break away from parallel conduct. Even though in the actual case there were differences in cost structures, especially as one of the two producers of steel pipes was vertically integrated, the Commission did not believe that the differences were in fact big enough to rebut the assumption that there was an oligopolistic market; *see* paras 68–79. In its Guidelines on the assessment of horizontal mergers, para. 48, the Commission emphasises that it can also be relevant whether undertakings are the same on other points, for example, with regard to their capacity levels and their degree of vertical integration.
212. M.8792, *T-Mobile NL/Tele2 NL*, decision of 27.11.2018, para. 867.

competition not functioning optimally, because cartels have been formed or because there have been high price levels, this can be taken as evidence that the market already has oligopolistic characteristics.[213]

The Commission will also investigate whether there are *structural links* between producers which will make it less likely they will compete. For example, such structural links can be the existence of joint ventures or cross-shareholdings between the companies.[214] There was previously some discussion as to whether there was a requirement for such structural links to exist, but the GC has established that this is not a requirement, but merely one of the factors which point towards the existence of collective dominance.[215]

> An example of the Commission's practice is Decision M.190, *Nestlé/Perrier* (OJ 1992 L-356/1), which was one of the first cases in which the Commission found there were coordinated effects. The decision concerned the merger of two undertakings which were both active on the French market for mineral water. After the merger, the new undertaking and BSN would jointly have considerable market shares on the French market for mineral water, e.g., 75% of the market by volume and over 82% of the market by value.[216] The Commission found that the merger meant that the number of suppliers would be reduced from three to two and thus rejected the argument that it would merely be a cosmetic change to the market structure.[217] Next, the Commission found that the following factors were indicative of the existence of an oligopolistic market: first, there was a market with great homogeneity and transparency, as the undertakings regularly exchanged price lists and information about turnover. The two remaining producers would have more or less the same capacity and market shares, so there would be a symmetrical duopoly, and this mutual dependence was a strong incentive to seek to maximise their profits by entering into a coordinated practice in restraint of competition. There was a relative lack of price elasticity on the demand side, as consumers usually had strong loyalty towards their normal brands. Finally, the two producers had more or less the same cost structures, so it was to be expected that they would have an interest in following the same pricing policy. In particular, in this area, there

---

213. This was the case with the market for platinum; see M.619, *Gencor/Lonrho* (OJ 1997 L 11/30), paras 165–172, where it was found that there was a very high price level and a poor competitive environment even before the merger. *See also* M.1524, *Airtours/First Choice*, decision of 22.9.1999, paras 128–138.
214. The existence of joint ventures between producers was emphasised in the following cases: M.308, *Kali + Salz/MdK/Treuhand* (OJ 1994 L 186/38), para. 58; M.619, *Gencor/Lonrho* (OJ 1997 L 11/30), para. 156; and M.942, *Veba/Degussa* (OJ 1998 L 201/102), para. 55. *See also* the Commission's Guidelines on the assessment of horizontal mergers (OJ 2004 C 31/5), para. 48.
215. Case T-102/96, *Gencor v. Commission*, paras 273–278. The question was previously debated, e.g., in M.1313, *Danish Crown/Vestjyske Slagterier*, decision of 9.3.1999, para. 179, where the merging undertakings argued that the Commission had to prove that there were structural links.
216. Paragraph 119.
217. Paragraph 120.

was no prospect that any of the producers would be able to establish a technological advantage, as the market used well-established technology. Furthermore, there were significant barriers to accessing the market, and the existing competitors were too small to be able to prevent the two major producers from exploiting their market strength. On this basis, the Commission was of the view that the merger would create a collective dominance, and the merging undertakings had to undertake to dispose of sources of water and brand names, as well as bottling capacity, to a competitor before the Commission accepted the merger.[218]

Next, there is an examination of whether the *coordination is sustainable*. There are three conditions which must be fulfilled for a coordination to be sustainable:[219]

(1) The first condition is that the coordinating undertakings must be able *to control* whether the terms of their coordination are complied with. To a large extent, this is a question of the degree of market transparency. Normally, the fewer the actors on the market, the more transparent the market will be. It can also depend on how transactions on the market are carried out. If it is fully open to the public, for example, by public auctions, it is easy to control, but it is more difficult if the transactions are made with customers in confidence. Where markets are less transparent, undertakings may have instituted exchanges of information, which makes control easier, just as having people from other undertakings as members of the board of directors can be used as a method of mutual monitoring.

(2) Next, it must be possible to apply *credible deterrents* if deviations are found to exist. If such measures cannot be applied with a degree of certainty, rapidity and force, it is unlikely that the coordination will be sustainable. The deterrent mechanisms can consist, for example, of the other undertakings instituting a price war or significantly increasing production, with a view to penalising the undertaking that has breached the coordination. The retaliation need not take place on the market where there is coordination, as it can also be applied on other markets. For example, it is possible that undertakings will dissolve joint ventures entered into with an undertaking which breaches the coordination, or they may refuse to enter into new joint ventures.[220]

---

218. *See* para. 136 of the Decision, and *see also* s. 5 on conditional approvals.
219. The conditions are set out in the Commission's Guidelines on the assessment of horizontal mergers (OJ 2004 C 31/5), paras 49–57.
220. A joint venture as retaliation was considered by the Commission in M.3333, *Sony/BMG*, decision of 19.7.2004. In this case, the Commission had to consider the consequences of the fact that Sony and Bertelsmann put their music activities together in a joint venture. This led to concentrations on several music-related product markets which were dominated by five to six major actors. The Commission investigated whether this gave rise to collective dominance on the market for recorded music. In assessing whether there was retaliation, the Commission found that it was possible to penalise undertakings which breached the coordinated conduct by refusing to allow undertakings to take part in compilation joint ventures, which are joint ventures put together by several music producers to produce CDs on a particular theme, or the hits of a certain period. For such CDs, several producers have to cooperate since an individual

(3) Finally, it is a requirement that *third-party* undertakings and customers cannot put the coordination at risk. This condition requires that neither actual nor potential competitors, nor customers are able to put at risk the expected results of the coordination. *See* the review in sections 4.2.1.3 and 4.2.1.4.[221]

These three conditions were formulated by the GC in Case T-342/99, *Airtours*, where the Court set aside the decision of the Commission because the Commission had not produced evidence to prove that there were sufficient deterrent mechanisms. This was a major blow for the Commission, and not surprisingly, it led to a change of practice so that in subsequent cases, the Commission investigated whether there were such deterrents. In Decision M.3333, *Sony/BMG*, decision of 19.7.2004, the Commission reached the conclusion that there was insufficient evidence to show that a reduction in the number of undertakings from five to four would result in collective dominance. This decision was set aside by the GC in Case T-464/04, *Impala*. Among other things, the GC found that the Commission was wrong to conclude that there had not already been collective dominance prior to the merger. The GC pointed out that the Commission's assessment of whether there was evidence of the existence of the three conditions formulated in the *Airtours* case could be 'established indirectly on the basis of what may be a very mixed series of indicia and items of evidence relating to the signs, manifestations and phenomena inherent in the present of a collective dominant position'.[222] The GC also found that the Commission's assessment of whether the conditions for sustainable coordination existed after the merger was highly inadequate.[223] However, this judgment was overturned by the CJ in Case C-413/06 P, *Bertelsmann & Sony*. The CJ confirmed that the GC was right to state that identifying the three conditions can be established indirectly but also found that the GC had not examined the matter correctly. According to the CJ, it is necessary to avoid a mechanical approach examining each criterion in isolation. Instead, the examination should be carried out using the mechanism of a hypothetical tacit coordination, which the GC had failed to do.[224] The CJ thus adopted a stricter assessment of whether there was collective dominance than that adopted by the GC.[225]

---

producer would not normally have control, on their own, of the necessary songs (hits, etc.). At the same time, since it is a very profitable form of issuing CDs the exclusion of a producer from participation in these joint ventures would be an effective sanction. However, the Commission could not establish that such exclusions had previously been practised; *see* paras 114–118.
221. In M.315, *Mannesmann/Vallourec/Ilva* (OJ 1994 L 102/15), the Commission believed that, in principle, the conditions for collective dominance were fulfilled, but as there were both actual and potential competitors of a certain strength, the Commission found that there was not dominance.
222. Paragraph 251.
223. *See* especially para. 528.
224. *See* paras 117–133.
225. The Commission has since attempted to follow the directions of the CJ, on the first occasion in M.4980, *ABF/GBI Business*, decision of 23.9.2008.

4.4 The Positive Effects of Mergers

In principle, there may be so many positive effects from mergers that they counteract the fact that a merger can lessen competition. This argument is often referred to as the 'efficiency defence' – a term borrowed from US anti-trust law. Even so, for many years, there was hardly any assessment of the positive effects of concentrations.

Following the amendment of the MCR in 2004, efficiency gains ought to play a more central role in the assessment of mergers. According to recital 29 of Regulation (EC) No 139/2004 on the control of concentrations between undertakings, in evaluating a merger, 'it is appropriate to take account of any substantiated and likely efficiencies put forward by the undertakings concerned'. The recital goes on to say that it is possible that the efficiencies brought about by the concentration will counteract the effects on competition, and the Commission is encouraged to issue guidelines on this.

There is no doubt that the rewording of the test in Article 2(2) and (3) of the provision gave efficiency gains a more central role.[226] This is also confirmed by the Commission in its Guidelines on the assessment of horizontal mergers, where the Commission lays down three conditions for taking into account efficiency claims.[227]

1. Benefit consumers

This condition presumably means that only certain forms of efficiency gains can be considered. The Commission's Guidelines particularly refer to cost savings, which lead to a reduction of the variable or marginal costs as these will most likely lead to lower prices and thereby benefit consumers; *see* paragraph 80.[228] Consumers can also benefit from new or better goods or services as a result of efficiency gains in research and development. Here the Commission refers to the fact that a joint venture which is set up to develop a new product can have such efficiency gains; *see* paragraph 81.

2. Be merger-specific

The condition that the efficiency gains must be merger-specific means that the Commission assesses whether there are alternatives to the merger which are less

---

226. *See Jessica Schmidt:* The New ECMR: 'Significant Impediment' or 'Significant Improvement'?, Common Market Law Review 2004 pp. 1555-1582 (in particular at p. 1572); and *Liam Colley:* From 'Defence' to 'Attack'? Quantifying Efficiency Arguments in Mergers, European Competition Law Review 2004 pp. 342-349.
227. The Commission's Guidelines on the assessment of horizontal mergers (OJ 2004 C 31/5), para. 78. The three conditions are set out in more detail in paras 79-88. On these three conditions, *see also Hanne Iversen:* The Efficiency Defence in EU Merger Control, European Competition Law Review 2010 pp. 370-376, *Pál Szilágyi,* How to Give a Meaningful Interpretation to the Efficiency Defence in European Competition Law, European Competition Law Review 2014, pp. 539-541 and *David Cardwell:* The Role of the Efficiency Defence in EU Merger Control Proceedings Following UPS/TNT, FedEx/TNT and UPS v Commission, Journal of European Competition Law & Practice 2017, pp. 551-560.
228. Given the large market share that Ryanair would obtain in certain markets through a merger with Aer Lingus, the Commission did not believe that there was a prospect of any efficiency gains benefitting consumers. The GC accepted this view in Case T-342/07, *Ryanair,* para. 441. Conversely, the Commission acknowledged the efficiency gains of the merger between UPS and TNT; *see* M.6570, *UPS/TNT Express,* decision of 30/1-2013.

harmful to competition. For example, the Commission refers to the fact that the setting up of a cooperative joint venture or a concentrative joint venture can be an alternative to a merger.[229] It thus seems that the Commission will make an assessment of whether a joint venture could be an alternative way to realise the efficiency gains, and if so, the Commission will disallow the merger and refer the parties to the alternative. The Commission emphasises that it only considers alternatives that are reasonably commercially practical in the situation of the merger parties.

3. Be verifiable

Finally, it is a condition that the efficiency gains should be verifiable.[230]

Apart from efficiency gains of various kinds, it is possible to imagine that some concentrations can have other positive effects, such as creating jobs or environmental benefits. The wording of Article 2 of the MCR does not suggest that the Commission will be able to take such considerations into account when evaluating concentrations. However, it does seem that the possibility of taking account of other considerations was opened up in the thirteenth recital of the original preamble to the MCR (Regulation (EEC) No 4064/89), according to which the Commission must place its appraisal within the general framework of the achievement of the fundamental objectives referred to in Article 3 TFEU, including the strengthening of the Union's economic and social cohesion, referred to in Article 174 TFEU. In particular, the reference to Article 174 supports the suggestion that the Commission should have regard for whether certain regions may be less developed in its appraisal of a merger.[231] The reference to Article 3 TFEU also means that a number of other goals (social, industrial policy and environmental) can be included.[232] This has been confirmed by the GC which has assumed that the thirteenth recital opens the way for the Commission to include consideration of the consequences of a merger for employees, including the effect on the level of employment or the terms of employment.[233] These years, EU competition law is undergoing a transition towards accepting that some restrictions on competition may be balanced by achieving sustainability objectives. However, in the area of merger

---

229. The Commission's Guidelines on the assessment of horizontal mergers (OJ 2004 C 31/5), para. 85. In M.4000, *Inco/Falconbridge*, decision of 4.7.2006, the Commission found that the synergies identified by the parties which would be realised by the merger could equally well be realised by the setting up of a joint venture that was limited to mining and processing, and this would be an alternative which would be less harmful to competition than the proposed full merger; *see* paras 538–542.
230. The GC has confirmed that it is the merging undertakings that must verify the gains, *see* Case T-175/12, *Deutsche Börse AG*, para. 275 and the same was emphasised by the CJ in Case C-376/20 P, *Commission v. CK Telecoms UK Investment*, para. 245.
231. It is this element which the Commission particularly reads from the thirteenth recital; *see* the Commission's comments on the MCR, Art. 2, published in Bull. Suppl. 2/90.
232. *See* the discussion in *David Banks*: Non-competition Factors and Their Future Relevance under European Merger Law, European Competition Law Review 1997 pp. 182–186.
233. Case T-96/92, *Comité Central D'entreprise de la Société générale des grandes sources and others v. Commission*, para. 28.

control the Commission has so far not formulated any policy on how this balancing will be achieved.[234]

4.5 Failing Firm Defence

Several cases have concerned the situation where an undertaking which is in difficulties can be saved by being acquired by another undertaking. Even though such a takeover can create or strengthen a dominant position, the question is whether there are other positive effects of such a concentration which can make up for this. If the alternative to the takeover is that the undertaking in difficulties has to be declared insolvent and close its business, the concentration can have positive effects by avoiding the dismissal of (some of) the employees and by preserving the resources and know-how which exist in the undertaking. On this basis, the Commission has accepted the 'failing firm defence' – sometimes called a 'rescue merger'.

In the first decision on the failing firm defence, the Commission laid down the following three conditions for this defence: (1) the acquired undertaking would be forced out of the market in the near future if not taken over by another undertaking; (2) the acquiring undertaking would take over the market share of the acquired undertaking if it were forced out of the market; and (3) there is no less anti-competitive alternative takeover option.[235] These conditions were subsequently accepted by the CJ in Joined Cases C-68/94 and C-30/95, *France and others v. Commission* (*Kali & Salz*). In the same case, the CJ stated that there is a requirement for there to be a causal link between the dominant position and the fact that effective competition is restricted, and if it can be assumed that the acquiring undertaking itself would have taken over the acquired undertaking's market share if it had not taken over the company, then the merger will not have been the cause of the creation or strengthening of dominance.[236] On this basis, the failing firm defence is not so much an expression of the Commission allowing a merger because it has positive benefits but because the merger is not in itself the true cause of the creation or strengthening of dominance.[237]

The second condition that the Commission laid down for accepting the failing firm defence sets very narrow limits to the scope of the defence. Unless there was a duopoly, where only the two merging undertakings were active in the market, it would be improbable that the acquiring undertaking would, in all circumstances, acquire the whole of the market share of the undertaking, which is in difficulties. The Commission has rephrased the condition in a later decision so that instead, it must be assessed

---

234. The Commission has, however, consulted on the topic, see the document Competition Policy supporting the Green Deal Call for contributions, dated 13 October 2020.
235. M.308, *Kali + Salz/MdK/Treuhand* (OJ 1994 L 186/38). As a further argument in favour of the merger, at the conclusion of the decision, the Commission stated that the closure of the acquired undertaking would have serious consequences for the eastern German regions, so the decision to allow the merger was in line with the thirteenth recital.
236. See paras 109–124 of the judgment.
237. For a more detailed review of the arguments, see Giorgio Monti & Ekaterina Rousseva: Failing Firms in the Framework of the E.C. Merger Control Regulation, European Law Review 1999 pp. 38–55; and Ioannis Kokkoris: Failing Firm Defence in the European Union. A Panacea for Mergers?, European Competition Law Review 2006 pp. 494–509.

whether the assets of the undertaking, in difficulties and thus its production capacity, would inevitably leave the market unless the merger was allowed.[238] In the case in question, the Commission assessed that if the merger were not allowed, the assets of the undertaking in difficulties would be lost, and this would result in a lack of production capacity in the market. Thus, the negative effects of not allowing the merger would outweigh the negative effects of allowing it.

In its Guidelines on the assessment of horizontal mergers, the Commission has confirmed that it will accept the failing firm defence if: (1) the failing firm would be forced out of the market in the near future because of financial difficulties if it were not taken over; (2) that there are no alternatives to the notified merger which would be less harmful to competition; and (3) if the failing firm's assets will inevitably leave the market if the merger is not carried through.[239] The Commission has also accepted a so-called failing division defence, whereby an undertaking that is otherwise sound is selling off a division that is failing. In this case, the Commission will focus on whether the division fulfils the condition outlined above.[240]

The failing firm defence is based on a contra-factual evaluation. Instead of comparing the effect of the merger with the situation before the merger, the effect of the merger is compared with the scenario which seems more likely to happen in the situation where the merger does not take place.

5 CONDITIONAL APPROVAL

If the Commission judges that a merger would significantly impede effective competition, it can declare that the concentration is incompatible with the common market so that the concentration may not take place. In practice, this only happens in a few cases,[241] as the Commission will instead allow the merger, subject to certain conditions.[242]

The possibility of attaching conditions or obligations has always existed in Article 8(2) of the MCR, which concerns the second phase of the merger process. Article 6(2) of the MCR was amended by Regulation (EC) No 1310/97, so it is now also possible to apply such conditions for the approval of a concentration in the first phase. Different deadlines apply for proposing conditions in the two phases, but apart from this, there is no clear distinction in the MCR as to when conditions are applicable in the two phases.

---

238. M.2314, *BASF/Eurodiol/Pantochim*, decision of 11.7.2001, paras 149–163.
239. Paragraph 90 of the Guidelines. This defence is not often used, but it was allowed in M.6796, *Aegean/Olympic* II, decision of 9.10.2013.
240. M.6360, *Nynas/Shell/Harburg Refinery*, decision of 2.9.2013, OJ 2014 C 368/5.
241. However, in recent years, there have been some examples of mergers that have not been accepted. A controversial one was M.8677, *Alstrom/Siemens*, decision of 6.2.2019, where the merger would have resulted in a huge train manufacturer – a merger that was supported by both the French and German government.
242. Since the introduction of Art. 2(4) of the MCR, it is also possible to lay down conditions to meet the concerns of the Commission on competitive aspects linked to a joint venture. This problem is dealt with in more detail in s. 7.

According to the wording of the MCR, it is the undertakings which propose commitments and the Commission which accepts them, either as conditions or as obligations. If the Commission makes its approval conditional on compliance with certain conditions or obligations, the failure to comply with these can make the undertaking subject to a fine under Article 14(2)(d). Failure to comply with a condition also means that the approval can lapse.[243] In practice, the Commission will normally make key commitments conditions and not merely obligations.[244]

Sometimes, the parties propose commitments which, for one reason or another, the Commission does not accept. This means that these become neither formal conditions nor obligations, but the Commission merely notes them. This raises doubts as to the legal status of such commitments. Unless there are good reasons to the contrary, such commitments must be regarded as non-binding, so the approval of the concentration is not conditional on compliance with them.[245]

Different kinds of commitments can be given; in particular, a commitment can be of a structural or behavioural character. It is clear that a *structural commitment* ensures that the structure of a given market is changed so a dominant position is neither created nor strengthened can be accepted. This applies in particular to measures by which a new competitor is created (typically by disposing of part of an undertaking – so-called divestment commitment) or where connections with competitors are severed:

(1) If the sale of part of an undertaking creates competition, the activity which is disposed of must consist of a viable business. The divestment commitment will include a more general description of what the undertaking is committed to dispose of. If several activities from different locations are gathered together, there must be a broad description of the activities included in the disposal, typically including the intellectual property rights and personnel involved. Other cases may involve a party disposing of its shares in an existing (subsidiary) company, and in this case, there is no need for any further description of the assets that are to be disposed of.[246]

---

243. The GC considers such conditions to be structural measures, without which the merger would not have been declared compatible with the internal market; see Case T-471/11, *Édition Odile Jacob SAS*, paras 79 80. In the case of an infringement of an obligation, according to Art. 8(6)(b) the Commission can revoke a decision.
244. However, the duty to report to the Commission is only an obligation and not a condition, just as the other implementation measures that are necessary to fulfil the conditions are normally only obligations; see Commission notice on remedies acceptable under Council Regulation (EC) No 139/2004 and under Commission Regulation (EC) No 802/2004 (OJ 2008 C 267/1), para. 19 (hereinafter 'Commission Notice on remedies acceptable under the MCR').
245. As such, commitments are non-binding, they can also not be the basis of a suit for annulment; see Joined Cases C-68/94 and C-30/95, *France and others v. Commission (Kali & Salz)*, paras 60–69; and Joined Cases T-125/97 and 127/97, *Coca-Cola Company v. Commission*, paras 96–106. In particular, according to the latter case the GC will make a more detailed investigation of the commitments before concluding that they have no binding effect.
246. M.833, *The Coca-Cola Company/Carlsberg* (OJ 1998 L 145/41), para. 110, where Carlsberg undertook to dispose of its shares in Dansk Coladrik (Jolly Cola) and Jyske Bryg, which it controlled.

For the disposal to have the desired effect, there may be a requirement for the assets to be transferred to a suitable buyer approved by the Commission. The buyer will normally be a viable actual or potential competitor, which is independent of the merging undertakings. There is a further requirement that the buyer should have the necessary financial means and professional know-how to carry on the business.[247]

The Commission has also developed a more detailed procedure for carrying out the divestment.[248] It must be agreed that the divestments will be made by a certain deadline. There is no agreement about the price at which the disposal is to be made, as the merging undertakings must naturally be allowed to sell at the best price they can get from an approved buyer. If the price is not acceptable, the condition for the merger cannot be fulfilled, and the approval for the merger will lapse.[249] During the period up to the sale, the Commission will also require a commitment that the activities to be divested of are kept separate from the merging undertakings' own activities. This means that such activities should be carried on independently and, in particular, that the merging undertakings refrain from acquiring know-how or commercially confidential information.[250] Next, the parties commit themselves to carry on the separate activities on ordinary terms, i.e., with responsible management, and sufficient capital and salary framework. In order to ensure that this happens, the Commission approves the appointment of a trustee to oversee the parties' compliance with such commitments (a so-called hold-separate trustee).[251]

The divestment itself can also be regulated by commitments. Apart from the criteria for approval of the buyer, there can be requirements for periodical reporting and conditions for the approval of prospectuses or advertising materials. As the Commission cannot be directly involved in overseeing compliance with such interim preservation measures on a daily basis, it approves the appointment of a divestiture trustee for this task, and this will often be an investment bank, a financial consultant or an accountancy firm. It is the parties who propose and pay the trustee, but the Commission must approve the appointment and approve the mandate given to the trustee. Normally, the trustee should only monitor the attempts of the merging undertakings to dispose of the part undertaking, but if these are not successful, the trustee will take on this task.[252]

In recent years, the Commission has often required that mergers may only be implemented once a buyer has been found and a binding agreement has been entered into. This type of commitment is termed 'up-front-buyer' and may

---

247. Commission Notice on remedies acceptable under the MCR (OJ 2008 C 267/1), para. 48. The Commission states in a footnote that it does not accept seller-financed disposals, as this would naturally make it less likely that competition would be generated.
248. See *Simon Holmes & Sarah Turnbull:* Remedies in Merger Cases: Recent Developments, European Competition Law Review 2002, pp. 499–511.
249. However, if the uncertainty surrounding the disposal is due to circumstances over which the merging parties have no control, e.g., prior purchase rights or uncertainty about the transfer of important contracts, the Commission accepts that the parties should propose an alternative to the disposal. However, such an alternative must be at least as appropriate for establishing effective competition, and will often mean that a 'crown jewel' must be disposed of; Commission Notice on remedies acceptable under the MCR (OJ 2008 C 267/1), para. 45.
250. M.190, *Nestlé/Perrier* (OJ 1992 L-356/1), para. 136 sub-para. b); and M.833, *The Coca-Cola Company/Carlsberg* (OJ 1998 L 145/41), para. 109 sub-para. 9.
251. Commission Notice on remedies acceptable under the MCR (OJ 2008 C 267/1), para. 112.
252. Commission Notice on remedies acceptable under the MCR (OJ 2008 C 267/1), paras 117–127.

make it more likely that the divestment has the desired effect. On the other hand, it may prevent the merger from taking place for some additional time.

(2) Another way to ensure increased competition is to remove all structural links which may exist between the merging undertakings and their competitors. In several cases, the Commission has accepted commitments whereby the parties bind themselves to sell or to wind up a joint venture which they have together with competitors,[253] commitments to sell minority shareholdings in competing undertakings[254] or commitments to terminate other kinds of cooperation.[255] In other cases, the Commission has accepted commitments whereby the merging undertakings agree to limit their scope for exercising influence on competing undertakings.[256] This can be by agreeing to reduce their shareholding in competing undertakings or by surrendering specific rights, for example, the right to appoint a member of the board of a competing company.[257] The effect of a *behavioural commitment* is more questionable. If an undertaking gives a commitment to refrain from some particular form of conduct, it is difficult to monitor that such a commitment is honoured, and for this reason alone, this type of commitment is less suitable for ensuring effective competition. In its previous practice, the Commission had established that it would not accept any commitments of a behavioural nature.[258] However, this practice was, to some extent, overruled by the GC in Case T-102/96, *Gencor v. Commission*. The GC did not find that a commitment could be accepted whereby the merging undertakings promised not to abuse their dominant position since Article 2 of the MCR requires the Commission to refuse mergers which create a dominant position.[259] However, in general, the GC did not exclude the possibility of commitments of a behavioural nature, which could contribute to preventing the creation or strengthening of a dominant position. It accepted that, in principle, commitments of a structural

---

253. M.269, *Shell/Montecatini* (OJ 1994 L 332/48), para. 117; M.942, *Veba/Degussa* (OJ 1998 L 201/102), paras 56–57; M.1467, *Rohm and Haas/Morton*, para. 41; M.1082, *Allianz/AGF*, decision of 8.5.1998, para. 72; JV.56, *Hutchinson/ECT*, decision of 29.11.2001, para. 47; and M.3436, *Continental/Phoenix*, decision of 26.10.2004, para. 220.
254. M.2416, *Tetra Laval/Sidel*, decision of 30.1.2002, para. 97.
255. *See* M.1229, *American Home Products Monsanto*, decision of 28.9.1998, paras 53–54, where the Commission accepted a commitment to terminate a distribution agreement which one of the merging undertakings had on the French market for a medicinal product which competed with a product which was produced by another undertaking which was included in the merger. By terminating the distribution agreement this opened the possibility that the distributorship would be given to an undertaking which would compete with the merged undertaking.
256. M.754, *Anglo American Corporation/Lonrho* (OJ 1998 L 149/21), para. 126, whereby the merging undertakings agreed to reduce their shareholdings in the closest competitor to a maximum of 9.99% of the share capital.
257. M.1082, *Allianz/AGF*, decision of 8.5.1998, para. 66; and M.1080, *Thyssen/Krupp*, decision of 2.6.1998, para. 35. However, a commitment of this kind was rejected by the Commission in M.3440 *ENI/EDP/GDP*, decision of 9.12.2004, paras 759 et seq.
258. M.619, *Gencor/Lonrho* (OJ 1997 L 11/30), para. 216.
259. Case T-102/96, *Gencor v. Commission*, para. 317.

nature are preferable because they change the structure of the market once and for all and, therefore, do not require controlling measures. The CJ has subsequently gone a step further and held that it was wrong of the Commission not to take account of commitments of a behavioural nature when these are proposed by the parties.[260]

There have been a number of Commission decisions in which an undertaking has been required to take certain steps to improve competitive conditions without these measures being of a purely structural character. For example, if a sector of business has exclusive agreements, the termination of these can often open up the market for competitors. This will typically come about if the merging undertakings release their suppliers from exclusive agreements,[261] but increased competition can also be created by freeing distributors and their customers from certain obligations.[262] Where a merging undertaking possesses some key technology, a commitment to allow others a licence to use the technology can be enough to ensure effective competition. In such cases, the merging undertaking will normally commit itself to giving licences to suitable undertakings on fair and reasonable terms, and the commitment often states that the licence fee will not exceed a certain percentage of the turnover obtained by using the licence.[263] Finally, the merging undertakings may have some essential facility at their disposal and they can give a commitment that they will allow competitors access to it.[264]

In some individual cases, the Commission has sought to improve competition by accepting commitments that part of an undertaking will be carried on independently from the merging undertakings or joint venture partners. In these cases, the separation is not just for a short period until a sale is carried out but is for a longer period.

---

260. Case C-12/03 P, *Tra Laval*, para. 89.
261. M.986, *Agfa-Gevaert/DuPont* (OJ 1998 L 211/22), para. 110(a); and M.1313, *Danish Crown/Vestjyske Slagterier*, decision of 9.3.1999, para. 200, where the two slaughterhouses accepted the partial release of their members from their obligations to supply, as they would be free to supply up to 15% of their weekly production to other slaughterhouses. In M.5046, *Friesland Foods/Campina*, decision of 17.12.2008, the merging cooperatives undertook to give financial support to members who agreed to supply milk to other companies. A looser commitment was given in M.877, *Boeing/McDonnell Douglas* (OJ 1997 L 336/16), para. 119, where Boeing committed itself not to put pressure on its suppliers to refrain from supplying competing undertakings. See also M.9730, *Fiat Chrysler/Peugeot*, decision of 21.12.2020, where the two car producers committed to amend the agreements, they had with their repairer networks in order to facilitate access for third-party.
262. M.1168, *DHL/Deutsche Post*, decision of 26.6.1998, para. 110(b) and (c), whereby distributors were made freer; and M.877, *Boeing/McDonnell Douglas* (OJ 1997 L 336/16), para. 116, where Boeing committed itself to allowing their customers more freedom.
263. M.986, *Agfa-Gevaert/DuPont* (OJ 1998 L 211/22), para. 110(a); M.737, *Ciba-Geigy/Sandoz* (OJ 1997 L 201/1), para. 275; and JV.37, *B Sky B/Kirch Pay TV*, decision of 21.3.2000, annex para. 8.
264. M.259, *British Airways/TAT*, decision of 27.11.1992, and M.5440 *Lufthansa/Austrian Airlines*, decision of 28.8.2009 (both concerning landing slots at airports) as well as M.8864, *Vodafone/Certain Liberty Global Cases*, decision of 18.7.2019 (on cable networks).

In M.1168, *DHL/Deutsche Post*, decision of 26.6.1998, Deutsche Post agreed to keep separate accounts for two divisions in order to ensure that there were no cross-subsidies.[265] There was a special situation in M.877, *Boeing/McDonnell Douglas* (OJ 1997 L 336/16), where the Commission accepted that it was not possible to find a buyer for McDonnell Douglas's aircraft division. In order to ensure a certain measure of competition, the Commission therefore accepted a commitment that this division should be kept separate, in a separate legal entity, for ten years. However the company was only given limited independence by this, as it was also stated that Boeing had management rights which it could exercise in its capacity as owner of all the shares in the new company. The aim was to ensure the continued separate legal existence of the division so it was stated how Boeing should give the division certain possibilities for carrying on its business.[266]

In some cases, the Commission has accepted commitments intended to ensure that information about competitors is not given to some of the undertakings involved in the concentration. For example, this is the case where an acquired undertaking possesses information about competitors and where, in order to ensure competition, it is necessary to restrict the acquiring undertaking's access to this information. In other decisions, the Commission has required that information belonging to an acquired undertaking cannot be used in part of the acquiring undertaking.[267] However, the Commission seems reluctant to accept this kind of commitment, which may be linked to the fact that it is very difficult to monitor whether such a condition is complied with.[268]

The Commission's practice with regard to such commitments has given rise to a number of cases in which claimants have either argued that the Commission has made a formal error or made an incorrect assessment of the facts. It seems clear that, especially in relation to the latter, the Commission has wide discretion to decide what commitment is sufficient to overcome the competitive concerns to which a merger gives rise.[269] For the same reason, it will be difficult to recover damages from the Commission on the basis of a claim that it is in error.[270]

---

265. M.1168, *DHL/Deutsche Post*, decision of 26.6.1998, para. 34 with annex.
266. M.877, *Boeing/McDonnell Douglas* (OJ 1997 L 336/16), para. 115.
267. M.9660, *Google/Fitbit*, decision of 17.12.2020.
268. In M.3440, *ENI/EDP/GDP*, decision of 9.12.2004, para. 799, the Commission rejected such measures as inadequate. However, the Commission did accept such measures in M.2268, *Pernod Ricard/Diageo/Seagram Spirits*, decision of 8.5.2001, para. 51.
269. See the decision of the GC in Case T-342/07, *Ryanair*, paras 447–526 and Case T-162/10, *Niki Luftfahrt*, paras 286–299.
270. See Case T-212/03, *MyTravel Group*.

6   ANCILLARY RESTRAINTS

If a concentration is approved as being compatible with the common market, then according to Article 6(1)(b) and Article 8(2) of the MCR, such a decision will also clear restrictions which are directly related and necessary to the implementation of the concentration. These are normally called 'ancillary restraints'.

The definition of what restraints are ancillary to a concentration is relevant to when Article 2(4) is applicable to the various terms of an agreement which is part of the setting up of a joint venture, and whether Article 101 TFEU is applicable to some of the terms agreed in relation to other mergers. If a condition is a necessary part of a concentration, it cannot be challenged even if it may restrict competition between undertakings. The corresponding problem arises with joint ventures, which are assessed in accordance with Article 101, and reference is made to the review of this in Chapter 4, section 9.6.

In 1990 the Commission published a Notice on restrictions directly related and necessary to concentrations, and the Commission's latest revised notice was published in 2005.[271] In 2001, the Commission stated that it would no longer make an appraisal of all the different restraints in its merger decisions.[272] In the previous decisions, the Commission had evaluated each of the actual terms of the agreement as they appeared from the notifications. The new practice means that the parties themselves have to determine whether various terms are ancillary or not, and this determination must be made on the basis of the Commission's previous practice, which is now summarised in the new Notice.

The conditions for accepting that a term is an ancillary restraint are that it must be a term which (1) constitutes a restraint, (2) is directly linked to the merger, and (3) is necessary for carrying out the merger.

The *first* of these conditions means that the freedom of action of one or more of the parties involved must be restricted. In the absence of this, there is no restrictive effect on competition.

The *second* condition means that the term must have a connection with the merger. Thus, a term which is wholly unrelated to the concentration is not covered.[273] The condition also means that the restraint must be agreed upon at the same time as the merger.[274] If the agreement is entered into prior to the merger or if it is entered into after the merger, then in principle, it is not ancillary.

---

271. OJ 1990 C 203/5 and OJ 2005 C 56/24 respectively.
272. This practice was criticised by the GC, as Art. 8 of the MCR provided that the Commission has an obligation to assess ancillary restraints; *see* Case T-251/00, *Legardére SCA and Canal+ SA v. Commission,* para. 90. As a consequence of this judgment, Arts 6 and 8 of the MCR were amended so as to make it clear that the Commission does not have an obligation to assess such restraints.
273. M.1298, *Kodak/Imation,* decision of 23.10.1998, para. 75, where the Commission noted that a clause that the merger parties should resolve some disputes concerning the ownership of some intellectual property rights was 'completely unrelated to the transaction at stake and therefore is not covered by the present decision'.
274. Commission Notice on restrictions directly related and necessary to concentrations (OJ 2005 C 56/24), para. 14.

The *third* condition means that either the concentration could not be implemented or could only be implemented under considerably more uncertain conditions, at substantially higher cost, over an appreciably longer period or with considerably less chance of a successful outcome.[275] This makes it clear that the Commission has a certain scope for discretion. However, the Commission tries to make the assessment as objective as possible, as it has stated that restrictions are not directly related and necessary to the implementation of a concentration simply because the parties regard them as such.[276]

In addition to assessing whether it is necessary to have a term with the restriction in question, there is also a requirement that the restriction should not go further than is reasonably necessary. The Commission's Notice states that in its subject matter and geographic field of application, a restriction may not go further than is necessary, thereby clearly aiming at non-competition clauses. It is also stated that where there are effective alternatives available for attaining the legitimate aim pursued, the undertakings must choose the one which is objectively the least restrictive of competition.[277] Thus, the proportionality principle has found its way into the regulation of ancillary restraints.

The Commission's Notice focuses on non-competition clauses, licensing agreements, and purchasing and supply obligations, as well as on certain terms related to the establishment of joint control:

(1) The Commission's Notice from 2005 contains detailed guidelines as to what *non-competition clauses* are ancillary, and it distinguishes between a condition that is imposed on the seller upon the sale of an undertaking and non-competition clauses that are imposed on joint venture partners upon the setting up of a joint venture. The Commission is more receptive to such clauses in joint ventures than upon the disposal of an undertaking.

With a transfer of an undertaking which includes both goodwill and know-how, the Commission normally accepts non-competition clauses which last for three years, but a period of two years is normally considered reasonable if only goodwill is involved.[278] For joint ventures, the Commission generally accepts non-competition clauses that apply for as long as the lifetime of the joint venture.

In the case of joint ventures, there is the further question of whether the non-competition clause can be extended to apply after the dissolution of the joint venture or after the date when a joint venture partner no longer participates in the joint venture. The Commission previously accepted that

---

275. Commission Notice on restrictions directly related and necessary to concentrations (OJ 2005 C 56/24), para. 13.
276. Commission Notice on restrictions directly related and necessary to concentrations (OJ 2005 C 56/24), para. 11.
277. Commission Notice on restrictions directly related and necessary to concentrations (OJ 2005 C 56/24), para. 13.
278. Commission Notice on restrictions directly related and necessary to concentrations (OJ 2005 C 56/24), para. 20.

such a clause could apply to a period after the dissolution of a joint venture.[279] However, subsequently the Commission has rejected such clauses.[280]

A non-competition clause will typically mean that the joint venture partners or the selling undertaking are prevented from competing with the joint venture or the transferred undertaking. In this respect, the Commission ensures that such clauses do not go further than necessary in the products or geographic areas they cover.

Non-competition clauses will often cover both the undertakings themselves and the companies they control.[281] According to the Commission's Notice, a non-competition clause can bind the undertaking's agents, but it cannot bind third parties, for example, distributors or customers. Clauses prohibiting undertakings from investing in competing undertakings may be accepted.

In addition to preventing competing business itself, the Commission also accepts joint venture partners binding themselves not to contact customers and employees of the joint venture, which can be particularly relevant where a joint venture partner has transferred part of its undertaking to the joint venture. Finally, the Commission accepts confidentiality clauses whereby the joint venture partners may not disclose confidential information which they have or acquire about the activities of the joint venture.[282]

(2) The Commission considers *licence agreements* between joint venture partners for the exploitation of intellectual property rights and know-how as ancillary, regardless of whether they are exclusive or not and regardless of whether they are for a limited period or not.[283] It is not unusual for joint venture partners to allow their joint venture to use all the intellectual property rights that are necessary for the joint venture's activities, and this is often without the payment of a licence fee.[284] The Commission has also accepted terms whereby a joint venture allows one or more of the joint venture partners a licence to the rights which it either has or expects to obtain.[285] However, the

---

279. M.523, *Akzo Nobel/Monsanto*, decision of 19.1.1995, para. 50, where a restriction was accepted during the lifetime of the joint venture and for two years thereafter.
280. M.1113, *Nortel/Norweb*, decision of 18.3.1998, para. 31; M.1132, *BT/ESB*, decision of 19.5.1998, para. 20; JV.2, *Enel/FT/Wind*, decision of 22.6.1998, para. 42; and JV.36, *TXU Europe/EDF-London Investments*, decision of 3.2.2000, para. 53.
281. Where a joint venture partner or a selling undertaking is itself controlled, it is sometimes accepted that the non-competition clause can be extended to the shareholders; see C.J. Cook & C.S. Kerse: EC Merger Control, 5th ed., 2009 p. 76.
282. Commission Notice on restrictions directly related and necessary to concentrations (OJ 2005 C 56/24), para. 41. However, a confidentiality clause can be limited so as only to cover sensitive information, such as know-how, while information of a more general nature is not accepted as ancillary; see M.1167, *ICI/Williams*, decision of 29.4.1998, para. 22.
283. Commission Notice on restrictions directly related and necessary to concentrations (OJ 2005 C 56/24), para. 42. See also M.1137, *Exxon/Shell*, decision of 8.7.1998, para. 27, where the Commission noted that licence agreements are a substitute for a transfer of rights.
284. M.310, *Harrisons & Crosfield/Akzo*, decision of 29.4.1993, para. 39.
285. M.310, *Harrisons & Crosfield/Akzo*, decision of 29.4.1993, para. 40.

Commission will normally not accept licence agreements between joint venture partners as ancillary restraints.[286]

With transfers of undertakings, the Commission accepts that licence agreements can be necessary where the seller will not transfer some of the rights or know-how, so the buyer must be allowed a licence to these in order to be able to make full use of the transferred assets. It is also possible that a seller will agree to transfer the rights but needs a licence itself in connection with activities other than the transferred activities. The Commission also accepts that such licence agreements can be entered into without a time limit, but it will not accept restrictions which are aimed more at protecting the licensor than the licensee.[287] Nor, in connection with the transfer of intellectual property rights, does the Commission accept the imposition of restrictions on the seller that are intended to protect the intellectual property rights where the buyer already has the necessary protection under intellectual property law.[288]

(3) *Buying and selling agreements* can be ancillary both in connection with the transfer of an undertaking and the setting up of a joint venture. The Commission's Notice lays down a number of conditions for accepting such agreements, and these conditions are the same in both situations. First, the buying and selling agreements must be necessary to ensure continuity of supply of the products. Therefore, if the products concerned can be easily acquired from other suppliers, this would be an argument against there being an ancillary restraint.[289]

In principle, the Commission only accepts such agreements if they are entered into for a limited period, as the aim of such agreements is to ensure continuity of supply during a transition period.[290] In its latest Notice, the Commission has stated that this transition period can be for up to five years; *see* paragraph 33 of the Notice. In its practice, the Commission has acknowledged that the assessment of what can be an acceptable period depends in part on an assessment of how long it would take to find or create alternative sources of supply and – in accordance with the principle of proportionality – the effect of the agreement on third parties.[291]

The Commission has an assumption that buying and selling obligations for unlimited quantities are not ancillary and the opposite assumption if the agreements are for specific amounts.[292] However, it is difficult to reconcile

---

286. Commission Notice on restrictions directly related and necessary to concentrations (OJ 2005 C 56/24), para. 43.
287. Commission Notice on restrictions directly related and necessary to concentrations (OJ 2005 C 56/24), para. 30.
288. M.1188, *Kingfisher/Wegert/Promarkt*, decision of 18.6.1998, para. 22.
289. JV.50, *Blackstone/CDPQ/Kabel Baden-Würtember*, decision of 1.8.2000, para. 52.
290. JV.15, *BT/AT&T*, decision of 30.3.1999, paras 209–212, where the Commission systematically restricted the duration of all the buying and selling agreements.
291. M.550, *Union Carbide/Enichem*, decision of 13.3.1995 para. 96.
292. Commission Notice on restrictions directly related and necessary to concentrations (OJ 2005 C 56/24), para. 34.

this with the practice, as it is seldom apparent from the decisions that quantitative restrictions are associated with such agreements.

Finally, the Commission will often set aside exclusive buying and selling agreements which it considers too extensive.[293] This does not mean that exclusive agreements are never accepted, merely that they must be justified by the circumstances of the case.[294] In many cases, it is agreed that one party will make its purchases from a particular source as far as possible, and these less binding terms seem to be accepted, even though they are presumably just as effective in the context of a cooperative joint venture.[295]

(4) The Commission's Notice contains a number of comments on the terms which are ancillary in connection with the situation where two or more undertakings agree together to acquire control of another undertaking, and where the aim is to share the assets between them. In this situation, the Commission accepts a number of restraints which are necessary for carrying out the joint acquisition of control, as well as restraints aimed at the sharing of the assets.[296]

7 ASSESSMENT OF COORDINATED PRACTICE IN JOINT VENTURES

As stated in the review given in Chapter 4, section 9, joint ventures can include a number of restrictions on competition, which can be contrary to Article 101 TFEU. The same applies to joint ventures which contain elements of concentration and which are notified under the MCR. Previously, there was an attempt to distinguish between those joint ventures where it could be assumed that the cooperation would cover activities outside the actual joint venture in question (these are also referred to as 'cooperative joint ventures', as distinct from 'concentrative joint ventures'). However, it was very difficult to distinguish these joint ventures, and so in 1997, the MCR was amended so that it became possible to make an assessment of joint ventures with cooperative aspects under Article 101 as part of the merger control procedure. This was done with the introduction of Article 2(4) and (5) which state as follows:

> 4. To the extent that the creation of a joint venture constituting a concentration pursuant to Article 3 has as its object or effect the coordination of the competitive behaviour of undertakings that remain independent, such coordination shall be appraised in accordance with the criteria of Article 81(1) and (3) of the

---

293. Commission Notice on restrictions directly related and necessary to concentrations (OJ 2005 C 56/24), para. 34.
294. M.102, *TNT/Canada Post and others*, decision of 13.12.1991, para. 61, where exclusivity was accepted; and M.1298, *Kodak/Imation*, decision of 23.10.1998, para. 74 and JV.22, *Fujitsu/Siemens*, decision of 30.9.1999, para. 83, where the Commission found that exclusivity was not justified.
295. M.951, *Cable and Wireless/Maersk Data – Nautec*, decision of 10.7.1997, para. 21 ('will use Nautec as their preferred channel for the supply of'); and M.409, *ABB/Renault Automation*, decision of 9.3.1993, para. 20 ('shall endeavour to satisfy its demand for').
296. Commission Notice on restrictions directly related and necessary to concentrations (OJ 2005 C 56/24), paras 15–16.

Treaty, with a view to establishing whether or not the operation is compatible with the common market.
5. In making this appraisal, the Commission shall take into account in particular:
   – whether two or more parent companies retain, to a significant extent, activities in the same market as the joint venture or in a market which is downstream or upstream from that of the joint venture or in a neighbouring market closely related to this market,
   – whether the coordination which is the direct consequence of the creation of the joint venture, affords the undertakings concerned with the possibility of eliminating competition in respect of a substantial part of the products or services in question.

It is immediately clear that not only is there a reference to the applicability of Article 101, but there seems to have been an adaptation or clarification of how the Commission should make its assessment. To a large extent, the wording reflects the practice that the Commission has developed under Article 101 (*see* Chapter 4, section 9). However, the provision assumes that it is not relevant to assess any coordination between the joint venture and some of the joint venture partners where these are active on the same market, as there is a requirement for two or more joint venture partners to be active on a market for it to be necessary to assess whether any restriction on competition exists. However, as mentioned in Chapter 4, the evolution of the concept of an undertaking may mean that a joint venture and its partners are not separate enterprises, and therefore, the application of Article 101 seems to move closer to the solution chosen in Article 2(5).

Very early on, the Commission established that it would first assess which markets are likely candidates for a concerted practice, candidate markets being those markets where the joint venture and at least two joint venture partners are active or a closely related market to the joint venture's market where at least two joint venture partners are active.[297] In assessing whether there is coordination on the candidate markets identified, 'it is necessary that the co-ordination of the parent companies' competitive behaviour is likely and appreciable and that it results from the creation of the joint venture, be it as its object or its effect'.[298] In this test, the Commission seems to have added a number of further conditions that it had not previously consistently taken account of in its assessments under Article 101. First, it must assess whether coordination is 'likely', which suggests that the assumption must have a secure basis. Then, the coordination must be 'appreciable'. Next, there is a requirement for a causal connection – i.e., the coordination must 'result' from the creation of the joint venture.

Some comments must be made on these three steps of the assessment:

(1) First, there is an assessment of whether it is the aim or the effect of the creation of a joint venture that there is coordination on the candidate markets. Since it is not normally the direct aim of a joint venture to ensure that there is such coordination, the decisions have concentrated on deciding whether it is

---

297. JV.1, *Telia/Telenor/Schibsted*, decision of 27.5.1998, decided immediately after the new provisions entered into force.
298. JV.1, *Telia/Telenor/Schibsted*, decision of 27.5.1998, para. 28.

the effect of a joint venture. In assessing whether such coordination is likely, the Commission takes account of the following circumstances: (1) the structure of the candidate markets; (2) the market shares of the parties on the candidate markets; and (3) the structural changes resulting from the creation of a joint venture.

The practice shows that in the assessment of market structure, a number of factors can be included as indicators of the existence of coordination. In Decision JV.22, *Fujitsu/Siemens*, the Commission listed no fewer than six reasons why the market for dynamic random access memory (DRAM) semiconductor chips was not suitable for coordination. First, pricing on the market was not transparent. Next, the buyers were all large undertakings with strong negotiating positions; and third, price developments were highly unpredictable. Fourth, the market was constantly swinging between undersupply and oversupply, and fifth, there was an ongoing adjustment of supply and demand. Finally, the DRAM market was a market in which there was rapid technological development, and consequently, there was strong competition with regard to innovation. By comparison, in the same decision, it was found that the market for financial workstations was suitable for coordination, among other things, because the market was highly concentrated and the technology was well-developed and mature.[299] It can also be relevant to assess whether the barriers to access to the market are high or low, as in the latter case, coordination would be less likely.[300] Finally, the fact that a market is characterised by rapid growth[301] and that buyers have a strong negotiating position[302] can be indicators that there is no coordination.

If the market shares of joint venture partners on the candidate market are very small, this can be an argument against the assumption of coordination.[303] Coordination is also unlikely if, for example, one of the joint venture partners is entirely new to the market and would, therefore, be assumed to work hard to achieve a certain market share.[304] If there are many competitors, this will also contraindicate coordination.[305] The Commission thus assumes that the parties to a coordination have a certain market strength on the candidate market.[306] If it is found that the joint venture partners have a position on the candidate market, which effectively gives them collective dominance, this clearly indicates that there will be coordination. This was the case in Decision JV.22, *Fujitsu/Siemens*, where the Commission found that one of the candidate markets was concentrated, and the two joint venture partners and their closest competitor had a market share of about 70%. In addition, the two joint venture partners and their closest competitor had nearly symmetrical market shares, and none of the other competitors had a market share of over 10%.[307] If only one joint venture partner has a significant market share, it will not be

---

299. JV.22, *Fujitsu/Siemens*, decision of 30.9.1999, para. 63.
300. JV.1, *Telia/Telenor/Schibsted*, decision of 27.5.1998, para. 43; and JV.35, *Beiselen/Bay WA/MG Chemag*, decision of 1.2.2000, para. 29.
301. JV.1, *Telia/Telenor/Schibsted*, decision of 27.5.1998, para. 43.
302. JV.11, *@ HOME Benelux*, decision of 15.9.1998, para. 38.
303. JV.7, *Telia/Sonera/Lithauanian/Telecommunications*, decision of 14.8.1998, para. 31, according to which a market share of less than 10% made coordination less likely.
304. M.1327, *NC/Canal+/CDPQ/Bank America*, decision of 3.12.1998, para. 32.
305. JV.22, *Fujitsu/Siemens*, decision of 30.9.1999, para. 61, according to which coordination was not considered likely where the joint venture partners had a market share of 15% and where there was a relatively large number of competitors.
306. *See* this expressly stated in JV.21, *Skandia/Storebrand/Pohjola*, decision of 17.8.1999, para. 37.
307. JV.22, *Fujitsu/Siemens*, decision of 30.9.1999, para. 63.

assumed that parties with very different market shares will coordinate their behaviour.[308]

Finally, in several cases, the Commission has attached weight to how extensive the joint venture activity is in relation to the other activities of the joint venture partners. If a joint venture is of relatively modest extent, it cannot be assumed that it will lead to coordinated conduct in the areas where the joint venture partners have significant activities.[309]

(2) Many cases have been decided on the basis of an assessment that, even though it is assumed that there will be restrictions on competition, these would not have an appreciable effect. If the collective market shares of the joint venture partners are less than 10%, the Commission will not normally make any more detailed examination of whether setting up the joint venture would lead to a concerted practice on the market in question.[310] In some cases, the Commission even seems to accept that there will be no appreciable effect even if the joint venture partners have more than 10% market share.[311]

(3) In some cases the Commission has had the opportunity to make a closer examination of the requirement for there to be a causal connection. Thus, there have been several cases where the Commission has found that the joint venture partners do not seem to have competed on a candidate market before the establishment of a joint venture, and in these cases, the Commission has rejected the creation of the planned joint venture should be the cause of the lack of competition.[312] It is thus clear that if the parties have previously set up some cooperation, the joint venture cannot be the cause. As stated above, in several cases, the Commission has pointed out that the fact that a joint venture is of a very modest extent compared to the joint venture partners' other activities makes it less likely that the joint venture partners will use the formation of the joint venture as an occasion to undertake coordination. In several decisions, the Commission has justified this conclusion by the lack of a causal connection between the formation of a joint venture and any concerted practice.[313]

However, the Commission does not seem to require proof that the actual cooperation is arranged in such a way as to make it probable that it will lead to a

---

308. JV.35, *Beiselen/Bay WA/MG Chemag*, decision of 1.2.2000, para. 28.
309. JV.6, *Ericsson/Nokia/PSION*, decision of 11.8.1998, para. 38; JV.7, *Telia/Sonera/Lithuanian/ Telecommunications*, decision of 14.8.1998, para. 30; and JV.29, *Lafarge/Readymix*, decision of 20.12.1999, para. 20.
310. JV.1, *Telia/Telenor/Schibsted*, decision of 27.5.1998, para. 41; and JV.5, *Cegetel/CANAL+/ AOL/Bertelsmann*, decision of 4.8.1998, paras 35-37.
311. JV.8, *Deutsche Telecom and others.*, decision of 28.9.1998, para. 30 (commercially confidential information, but less than 20%); JV.11, *@ HOME Benelux*, decision of 15.9.1998, para. 38 (11.8% and 11.6%); JV.17, *Mannesmann/Bell Atlantic/OPI*, decision of 21.5.1999, para. 20 (11%).
312. JV.35, *Beiselen/Bay WA/MG Chemag*, decision of 1.2.2000, para. 30; JV.23, *Telefonica/Portugal Telecom/Medi Telecom*, decision of 17.12.1999, para. 29; and JV.2 *ENEL/FT/DT/WIND*, decision of 22.6.1998, paras 37 and 39.
313. JV.23, *Telefonica/Portugal Telecom/Medi Telecom*, decision of 17.12.1999, para. 29.

concerted practice.[314] The Commission is normally satisfied by establishing that cooperation on the market can be expected to result in an effect on other markets. Thus, the assessment is often based on an evaluation of the market rather than on an evaluation of the individual elements of the cooperation.

The method for evaluation, which is followed in Article 2(4) cases, has generally been welcomed in the legal literature, where it has been seen as expressing a more realistic method for evaluating joint ventures under Article 101 TFEU.[315]

8   MERGER CONTROL PROCEDURE

The MCR contains a number of rules on the procedure to which notified mergers are subject. Besides the MCR, there are a number of supplementary rules in Regulation (EC) No 802/2004,[316] and the Commission has further issued a number of notices on certain procedural questions.[317] The following review is chronologically structured; the first section looks at the different steps in the normal procedure, and then there is a brief outline of the simplified procedure used for some mergers.

8.1   The Duty to Notify

If there is a concentration which has a Community dimension, as defined in detail in section 2 above, then according to Article 4(1) of the MCR, it must be notified. Before it can be implemented, it must have been notified and declared compatible with the common market. This raises the question of when a merger may be notified and what the consequences are of implementing the merger before the Commission has approved it.

8.1.1   *When to Notify*

Prior to 2004, according to the MCR, notification had to be made within one week of the entry into the merger or joint venture agreement, but this deadline has been removed. It is now up to the parties to determine when to notify, but as they may not implement

---

314. See the view on this in *John Temple Lang* in *Barry E. Hawk* (ed.): Fordham Corporate Law Institute, 2000 p. 428.
315. See *Jonathan Faull & Ali Nikpay* (eds): The EU Law of Competition, 3rd ed., 2014 p. 911; and *Francisco Enrique González-Diaz* in *Marianne Dony & d'Aline de Walsche* (eds.): Mélanges en hommage à Michel Waelbroeck, vol. II, 1999 pp. 1019-1069 (in particular at p. 1061).
316. Regulation (EC) No 802/2004 implementing Council Regulation (EC) No 139/2004 on the control of concentrations between undertakings (OJ 2004 L 133/1), most recently amended by Commission Implementing Regulation (EU) No 1269/2013. A proposal for a new regulation has been published in 2022, see C(2022) 2918 final.
317. See the Commission's 'Best Practices on the conduct of EC merger control proceedings' from January 2004, published on the Commission's website (DG Competition), and Commission Notice on a simplified procedure for treatment of certain concentrations under Council Regulation (EC) No 139/2004 (OJ 2005 C 56/32).

their merger before the concentration is approved, in practice, they will have an interest in giving notification in good time.

The parties will often be interested in having their merger assessed before they make a final agreement. For this reason, before 2004, it was not unusual for the parties to contact the Commission prior to official notification with a view to discussing how the notification should be carried out, as well as to get some idea of how the Commission would appraise the proposed merger.[318] The business community found this form of informal contact very practical, and the view was expressed that it ought to be possible to give notification prior to the point when there was a binding agreement. Thus, in the 2004 amendment, a provision was included making it possible to give notification 'where the undertakings concerned demonstrate to the Commission a good faith intention to conclude an agreement'; *see* Article 4(1). It is not absolutely clear how advanced the parties' negotiations should be for the condition to be satisfied. A certain help to interpretation is given in recital 34 to the new MCR, where it is stated that it is a condition that the intended merger 'is sufficiently concrete, for example, on the basis of an agreement in principle, a memorandum of understanding, or a letter of intent signed by all undertakings concerned'. It is thus clear that most agreements should be in place.

There is a further possibility for voluntary notification of concentrations without a Community dimension in Article 4(5); *see* the discussion on this in section 2.5 above.

The more detailed requirements for the content of the notification are set out in Regulation (EC) No 802/2004. According to Article 3(1) of this Regulation, notifications must contain the information and documentation prescribed by Form CO as set out in Annex I to the Regulation. In addition to information about the form of the concentration, including attaching the final documents on the merger, the parties have to give comprehensive information about the product markets affected by the concentration.[319] For joint ventures, there is also an obligation to give information about the effects on cooperation; *see* section 10 of Annex I. The parties' information is intended to give the Commission the information necessary to assess the concentration under Article 2(1)-(3) as well as – for joint ventures – to assess them under Article 2(4). The notification may be made in one of the official languages, but in practice, most notifications are made in English, and this is the language for the further processing of cases.

The Commission can give a dispensation from the obligation to give some of the information required in Form CO (*see* Regulation (EC) No 802/2004, Article 4(2)), and this is often the subject of discussion at meetings held with the Commission prior to notification.[320] In addition, the Commission has decided that certain smaller joint ventures can be notified in short form; *see* Article 3(1). This applies if they fulfil the following conditions: (1) the joint venture's turnover and/or the turnover of the allocated activities is less than EUR 100 million in the EEA; and (2) the assets transferred to the joint venture have a total value of less than EUR 100 million in the EEA. Form CO states in more detail what information must be given when notifying such joint ventures.

---

318. In its Best Practices on the conduct of EC merger control proceedings, the Commission has laid down some guidelines on how such a meeting is conducted and what is normally discussed at such meetings.
319. If the parties provide the Commission with misleading information, this may result in substantial fines; *see*, for instance, M.8228, *Facebook/WhatsApp*, decision of 17.5.2017 (EUR 110 million) and M.8436, *General Electric/LM Wind Power*, decision of 8.4.2019 (EUR 55 million).
320. *See* the Commission's Best Practices on the conduct of EC merger control proceedings.

8.1.2 Early Implementation

According to Article 7(1) of the MCR, the implementation of a concentration must be suspended until the Commission has declared the concentration compatible with the common market or its compatibility can be established on the basis of the presumption in Article 10(6) of the MCR. If the merger is implemented despite this standstill obligation, there will be a case of what is informally called 'gun jumping'. In principle, the duty not to implement may be infringed in two ways: either a merger may not be notified at all, or the merger may be notified but nevertheless implemented before it has been approved.

If the parties neglect to notify the merger and just implement it, two provisions in the MCR will be breached. There will be a violation of the duty to notify according to Article 4(1) and a violation of the duty not to implement a merger before it has been approved, see Article 7(1). The reason for not notifying may be that the parties have ignored the duty, but likely, the reason may be that they have overlooked the duty. Sometimes, it may be difficult to evaluate whether there is a merger at all, for instance, whether de facto control has been established or whether a joint venture is a full-function joint venture or not. It may also be difficult to decide whether the turnover threshold of the MCR has been met. There are several examples illustrating this.[321]

In 2013, Marine Harvest notified their intention to launch a voluntary bid to acquire shares in the company Morpol. After examining the case, the Commission approved the merger but, at the same time, fined Marine Harvest in the amount of EUR 20 million. The reason for the fine was that according to the Commission, Marine Harvest had already acquired de facto control over Morpol in 2012, when they had acquired 48.5% of the shares in Morpol. Since this merger had not been notified before the acquisition in 2012, there was an infringement of both Articles 4(1) and 7(1) of the MCR.[322]

The decision was brought before the GC, who upheld it, see Case T-704/14, *Marine Harvest ASA*. Marine Harvest had argued that the exception applicable to public bids (found in Article 7(2) MCR) was applicable, and as a consequence the standstill duty according to Article 7(1) did not apply. The GC disagreed since the fact that a public bid was launched in 2013 did not change the fact that control was acquired in 2012. It did not matter that Marine Harvest had not exercised the voting rights attached to the 48.5% shares acquired in 2012, as it had been able to exercise control.[323] This judgment was subsequently appealed to the CJ, who upheld the conclusions of the GC, see Case C-10/18 P, *Mowi ASA*.

If the merger has been duly notified, the standstill obligation in Article 7(1) means that the merger agreements or transfers may only be executed once the merger has been approved. In practice, it can be difficult to decide when the standstill

---

321. See also M.969, A.P. Møller, decision of 10.02.1999 and M.4994, *Electrabel/Compagnie Nationale du Rhône*, decision of 10.06.2009.
322. M.7184, *Marine Harvest/Morpol*, decision of 23.7.2014.
323. Paragraph 58 of the judgment.

obligation has been infringed, and in recent years, the issue has been addressed by the European courts in several judgments.

The first judgment to address the issues was Case C-633/16, *Ernst & Young P/S.*, KPMG DK, the Danish member of KPMG International Cooperative, entered into a merger agreement with Ernst & Young. According to the agreement, KPMG DK had to terminate their cooperation agreement with KPMG International Cooperative, which they did. After this, the merger agreement was notified to the Danish Competition Authorities. The Danish authorities decided that the termination of the cooperation agreement with KPMG International Cooperative was an infringement of the standstill obligation according to Danish law. This decision was brought before the Danish courts, which decided to ask the CJ for a preliminary ruling on how to interpret the Danish standstill obligation. Since Danish law at this point mirrors MCR, the CJ accepted that it was relevant to interpret how Article 7(1) was to be used in a situation like this.

In the judgment, the CJ started by establishing that since the wording of Article 7(1) did not permit its precise scope to be assessed, the provision must be interpreted by reference to its purpose and general scheme.[324] As the purpose of the standstill obligation is to prevent mergers that significantly impede competition, it is clear that only transactions which contribute to a concentration, as defined in Article 3, may infringe Article 7(1). Therefore, Article 7(1) only prevents that the merging parties 'implement operations contributing to a lasting change in the control of the target undertaking'.[325] This includes any partial implementation of a concentration, as otherwise, it would reduce the efficiency of Article 7(1) if it was possible for the merging parties to circumvent the standstill obligation by successive partial operations.[326] However, transactions carried out in the context of a concentration that are not necessary to achieve a change of control of the undertaking concerned do not fall within the scope of Article 7(1) as long as they do not present a direct functional link with the implementation of the merger.[327] Even though such transactions may have an effect on the market, this alone will not be sufficient for them to be caught by Article 7(1).

The CJ also made the point that this interpretation ensures that the MCR and Article 101 TFEU supplement each other. Article 101 may be used to prevent coordination of undertakings that are not merged, and therefore, the standstill provision in Article 7(1) should not be extended to apply to situations that are covered by Article 101.[328]

The CJ concludes that Article 7(1) is breached only if there is 'a transaction which, in whole or in part, in fact or in law, contributed to the change in control of the target undertaking'.[329] As for the case at hand, the CJ noted that the transaction (termination of the cooperation agreement) only involved one of the merging parties and a third party and, furthermore, did not make it possible for Ernst & Young P/S to

---

324. Paragraph 40.
325. Paragraph 46.
326. Paragraphs 47–48.
327. Paragraph 49.
328. Paragraphs 53–58.
329. Paragraph 59.

exercise any influence over KPMG DK. The merging parties were in the context of competition law independent both before and after the termination of the cooperation agreement. Therefore, there was no implementation of the merger in whole or in part, in fact or in law, contributing to the change of control.

The judgment means that preparation made by one of the merging parties will not infringe the standstill obligation. Thus, the merging parties may – on their own – take the steps they think prudent by changing their organisation, dismissing or employing personnel or cancelling agreements with third parties. However, the merging parties must be careful not to exchange commercially sensitive information or to coordinate their commercial behaviour as this is likely to infringe Article 101 TFEU, which will apply until the moment when the merger is implemented.[330]

According to the judgment, both a whole and a partial implementation will infringe Article 7(1). The first is not surprising as it cannot be allowed that the merging parties start acting as if the mergers have already taken place. In particular, when one undertaking is acquiring control over another, it will be tempting for the acquiring company in the period until the approval to try to control the target undertaking to ensure that it does not perform any acts that may make the merger less attractive. This was the problem in the judgment in Case T-425/18, *Altice Europe NV*:

> The Dutch company Altice agreed with the Brazilian company Oi S.A. to acquire a majority shareholding in the Portuguese company PT Portugal. The transfer of the shareholding was scheduled to take place once the Commission had finalised its examination of the merger, but in the period until the implementation of the merger it was agreed between Altice and Oi S.A. that Altice would be allowed to veto certain decisions in PT Portugal. The Commission decided that these veto rights were so extensive that there was an infringement of the standstill obligation. The Commission also noticed that Altice had been involved in business decisions in PT Portugal, even in questions that were not covered by the veto rights, and furthermore the influence used by Altice had allowed for an extensive exchange of confidential information from PT Portugal to Altice.[331]

The GC agreed with the Commission's assessment. Altice had argued that the veto rights were necessary to preserve the value of the investment it made in PT Portugal, and therefore it was ancillary restraints according to point 13 of the Notice on Ancillary Restraints, OJ 2005 C 56/24. However, the GC decided that the veto rights agreed upon went beyond what was necessary to preserve the value of the investment. The veto right included the right to veto any recruitment or dismissal of a director, any termination or modification of what was termed a material contract and any modification of the company's pricing policies. The veto rights were so extensive that Altice had control over PT Portugal, and the way the veto rights had been exercised also substantiated this.[332]

---

330. *See also Sergio Baches Opi & Adela Boitos*: Gun Jumping in the European Union: An Analysis in Light of Ernst & Young, Journal of European Competition Law & Practice 2019, pp. 269–280.
331. M.7993, *Altice/PT Portugal*, decision of 24.4.2018.
332. These operational parts of the judgement were endorsed by the CJ in Case C-746/21 P, *Altice Group Lux*.

It will be more difficult to decide when there is a partial implementation of the merger. Will it, for instance, be a partial implementation of a merger if a minority shareholding is acquired, and it is the intention to acquire more shares subsequently? Is it possible to allow an acquiring company to fill one seat on the board of directors of the target, or will this be a partial implementation since this is likely just to be the first of many seats to be filled by the acquiring company? So far, the GC has had the chance to decide on a partial implementation in Case T-609/19, *Canon Inc.*:

> Canon Inc. had agreed to acquire a subsidiary in the Toshiba group. While awaiting the approval of the Commission, the merging parties made use of what has been termed 'warehousing'. The arrangement was that Toshiba transferred the control of the subsidiary to a newly formed company that was separated from both of the merging companies. After the Commission had approved the merger, the plan was to transfer control of the subsidiary to Canon Inc. The Commission took the position that this was a partial implementation of the merger, and this decision was challenged before the GC.[333]
>
> The GC upheld the decision, and in doing so rejected a number of arguments presented by Canon Inc. First the GC rejected that an infringement of Article 7(1) requires that there has been a change of control. Referring to the CJ's judgment in *Ernst & Young P/S* the GC held that it was enough that there had been operations that 'contribute' to a change of control.[334] To decide whether there is a partial implementation, it is necessary to ascertain the economic reality underlying the transaction and the economic aim pursued by the parties. In particular it should be determined whether the parties would have been inclined to conclude each transaction in isolation or whether each transaction more likely is only an element of a more complex operation.[335]
>
> In the case at hand, the GC did not think the parties would have used the warehousing arrangement if it was not for the fact that it was part of a merger. The primary reason for using the arrangement was that Toshiba wanted that the sale of the subsidiary appeared as completed in its annual accounts, but according to the GC this did not change the fact that the arrangement was undertaken in the interest of both parties. The fact that Canon Inc. did not have any control over the subsidiary during the 'warehousing' arrangement was not important as a partial implementation does not require that any form of control has been transferred.[336]

If the parties ignore or forget the standstill obligation, this can, as mentioned, result in one or more fines. The civil law effects of such an infringement are only partly regulated by Article 7(4), where it is stated that the validity of any transaction carried out in contravention of the standstill obligation will dependent on a decision pursuant to Article 6(1)(b) or Article 8(1), (2) or (3). Next, it is stated that the provision does not have any effect on the validity of transactions in securities admitted to trading on a regulated market such as a stock exchange unless the buyer and seller knew or ought to have known that the transaction was carried out in contravention of Article 7(1). This means that mergers that are carried out by the transfer of securities listed on a stock exchange can only be declared invalid if both the buyer and the seller act in bad

---

333. M.8179, Canon/Toshiba Medical Systems Corporations, decision of 27.6.2019.
334. Paragraphs 68 and 70.
335. Paragraph 111.
336. Paragraph 222.

faith. Conversely it must be assumed that mergers which come into existence by other means must, in principle, be declared invalid, given that there is a decision by the Commission which declares the merger to be incompatible with the common market.

According to Article 7(3), the merging parties have the possibility of seeking a derogation from the standstill obligation. This may be possible if the parties have good commercial reasons for wishing the merger to be carried out quickly in order to avoid negative consequences for the parties or for third parties and if the concentration does likely not significantly affect competition. Article 7(3) is thus most relevant to concentrations that are notified under the simplified procedure; *see* section 8.4. However, the Commission has been reluctant to allow such derogations.[337]

Where a merger is carried out contrary to the standstill obligation under the new Article 8(5), the Commission may take appropriate interim measures to restore or maintain conditions of effective competition.[338]

8.2 The First Phase of the Merger Control Procedure

The first introductory phase of the merger control procedure must, in principle, be concluded within twenty-five working days after the Commission receives notification; *see* MCR Article 10(1).[339] If the Commission does not decide otherwise within the period provided, the concentration will be considered as approved; *see* Article 10(6).

In this phase, the Commission's investigations will be based on the information which the parties provide in their notification. The Commission can demand further information from the parties, and there will often be negotiations with the parties concerning various commitments; *see* Article 6(2). The first phase can result in a decision that the case should proceed to the second phase because the concentration is covered by the MCR, and there is serious doubt as to whether it is compatible with the common market; *see* Article 6(1)(c). Moreover, the Commission can take one of the following decisions, which means that the case is concluded in the first phase:

(1) According to Article 6(1)(a), the Commission can conclude that the concentration notified does not fall within the scope of the MCR. For example, this can be because the parties have estimated incorrectly when calculating that the turnover thresholds have been fulfilled. More typically, it will be due to a

---

337. See Van Bael & Bellis: Competition Law of the European Union, 6th ed., 2021 p. 770.
338. Such measures are seldom used but were applied in M.10493, *Illumina/GRAIL*, decision of 29.10.2021 in a merger that was referred to the Commission according to Art. 22 MCR, but the merging parties opposed the referral and declared their intension to implement the merger. The Commission adopted a number of interim measures, including a requirement that the target undertaking should be run by a Hold-Separate Manager, and that the merging parties should refrain from exchanging any commercial sensitive information and that any transaction conducted between them should be on arm's length terms.
339. However, according to the same provision this period can be extended to thirty-five working days, *i.a.*, in cases where following the notification the undertakings concerned offer commitments pursuant to Art. 6(2) with a view to rendering the concentration compatible with the common market.

decision that the parties have incorrectly assessed that the notified joint venture would be a full-function joint venture.

(2) According to Article 6(1)(b), the Commission can decide that the concentration notified does not raise serious doubts as to its compatibility with the common market. If there are found to be restrictions on competition which are not ancillary restraints, these will be assessed under Article 2(4). However, the assessment under Article 2(4) is made within the deadlines laid down in the MCR.[340]

8.3 The Second Phase of the Merger Control Procedure

The relatively few concentrations which pass on to the second phase of the merger control procedure are subject to a very thorough analysis, under which the effect of the concentration on competition is assessed. In this assessment, the Commission will often make use of its powers to obtain further information. This can be by requesting information under Article 11 of the MCR, either from the Member States or from undertakings, including the participating undertakings. It is also possible for the Commission to undertake inspection visits of the undertakings under Article 13.

The parties will be consulted at every stage of the second phase procedure. According to Article 18(1) of the MCR, before the Commission takes any decision under Article 8, the parties will have had the chance to make their views known on the objections concerning the effect of the concentration on competition. The Commission may not base its decision on objections to which the parties have not had an opportunity to submit their observations; *see* Article 18(3). Normally, the hearing of the parties will be in writing, but there can be an oral hearing if the parties so request.

Under Article 18(4), the Commission can also obtain the views of other natural or legal persons. Persons are also entitled to be heard if they so request and if they have a legitimate interest. The Commission often consults third parties on the commitments which the participating undertakings make in order to satisfy the Commission's concerns about the compatibility of the concentration with the common market.[341]

The second phase may last a maximum of ninety working days from the date when it has begun. In exceptional circumstances, this period can be suspended; *see* Article 10(4). Before a decision is made as a conclusion of the phase, the Advisory Committee on concentrations must be consulted. This is a committee which consists of representatives of the competent authorities of the Member States.[342] According to Article 8, the decisions which the Commission can take are as follows:

(1) A concentration can be approved as being compatible with the common market, as set out in Article 8(2), which is what happens in the great majority of cases which reach the second phase. Approval can be given on the basis of

---

340. *See Lennart Ritter & W. David Braun:* European Competition Law: A Practitioner's Guide, 3rd ed., 2004 p. 679.
341. *See C.J. Cook & C.S. Kerse:* EC Merger Control, 5th ed., 2009 pp. 165–166.
342. Article 19(3)-(7) of the MCR.

changes which the parties have made to their merger plan, or by reference to various kinds of commitments which the parties may have made. The various kinds of commitments and the conditions and obligations associated with these are discussed above in section 5. Where there is a cooperative joint venture, approval will be dependent on the notified concentration fulfilling the criterion for an exemption under Article 101(3) TFEU.

(2) A concentration can be declared incompatible with the common market under Article 8(3), and this can be because the concentration either significantly impedes effective competition or because a joint venture contains restrictions on competition which are not exempt under Article 101(3) TFEU. Such a decision means that the parties cannot carry out the concentration as it stands.

(3) If a concentration is declared incompatible with the common market under Article 8(3), and it has already been carried out, then under Article 8(4) of the MCR, the Commission can require the undertakings concerned to dissolve the concentration, including requiring the joint control to be terminated or requiring any other measure to be taken which can restore effective competition.[343]

In accordance with the general obligation in Article 296 TFEU, the Commission has an obligation to state the reasons for its decisions.[344] The decisions may be brought before the CJ by a Member State, or before the GC by the parties or by an individual third party who is affected.[345]

If the parties infringe on a decision made in accordance with Article 8(3) or (4) or fail to comply with an obligation imposed in a decision under Article 8(2), the Commission can impose a fine in accordance with Article 14(2) for up to 10% of the undertaking's total annual turnover. Next, in the event of an infringement of a condition imposed under Article 8(2), the Commission can take measures for dissolution, etc., under Article 8(4). Under Article 8(5), the Commission can now take interim measures, for example, by requiring joint venture partners not to exercise their joint control. Under Article 15(2), periodic penalty payments can be imposed on the parties until they comply with an order or comply with a decision for the restoration of effective competition under Article 8(4) or 8(5).

---

343. The GC has held that the logical consequence of a decision that a merger is incompatible with the common market is that the undertakings should be split again, in other words the restoration of the *status quo ante*; see Case T-80/02, *Tetra Laval*, para. 36. In the latest amendment to the MCR, it is stated in Art. 8(4) that such a measure is within the Commission's powers.
344. In Case T-290/94, *Keysersberg*, paras 141–152, the GC made clear the requirements for the Commission's statement of reasons in merger control cases.
345. If the validity of conditions imposed is challenged, the CJ or the GC can decide to nullify the conditions associated with the decision, provided the conditions are separable from the other parts of the decision; *see* Art. 10(5) of the MCR, and Joined Cases C-68/94 and C-30/95, *France and others v. Commission (Kali & Salz)*, para. 256. In the latter case the CJ annulled the decision in its entirety.

8.4 The Simplified Procedure

The Commission has issued a notice in which it set out its practice concerning a simplified procedure for dealing with certain kinds of concentrations.[346] The simplified procedure is reserved for those kinds of mergers and joint ventures which, in the experience of the Commission, only rarely give rise to problems of competition.[347] The simplified procedure means that the Commission does not make the investigations which it normally makes in the first phase of the merger procedure. Upon receipt of a notification, a short notice is published in the Official Journal, stating, among other things, that the case will be dealt with according to the simplified procedure. Unless special circumstances apply, the simplified procedure will be concluded by the Commission making a decision under Article 6(1)(b) within twenty-five working days or by refraining from taking a decision which, as stated above, indicates tacit approval.

Three different forms of concentrations are covered by the procedure. First, there are smaller joint ventures which fulfil the following conditions: (i) the joint venture company or the transferred activities have a turnover of less than EUR 100 million within the EEA; and (ii) the total value of the assets which are transferred to the joint venture company is less than EUR 100 million within the EEA. Next, there are mergers or joint ventures where none of the participating undertakings are active on the same market or markets which are in an upstream or downstream trading relation to each other. Finally, there are the mergers or joint ventures in which the participating undertakings are active on the same market (horizontal connections) but where they do not jointly have a market share of 15% or above and vertical connections where the parties do not have a market share of 25% or above.[348] The Notice states that there can be cases where there may nevertheless be problems of competition so that, in these cases, the Commission reserves the right to implement the usual first phase procedure.[349]

Bibliography

Morten P. Broberg: *Broberg on the European Commission's Jurisdiction to Scrutinise Mergers,* 4th ed. 2013.
John Cook & Christopher Kerse: *EC Merger Control,* 2009.
Jonathan Faull & Ali Nikpay (eds): *The EU Law of Competition,* 3rd ed. 2014.
Ioannis Kokkoris & Howard Shelanski: *EU Merger Control,* 2009.

---

346. Commission Notice on a simplified procedure for treatment of certain concentrations under Council Regulation (EC) No 139/2004 (OJ 2013 C 366/4), which extends the scope of mergers that can benefit from the simplified procedure compared with the previous notice from 2005.
347. *See* para. 5 of the Notice.
348. *See* para. 5 of the Notice. A vertical connection will exist where a party to a merger is active on a market which is upstream or downstream from a product market where one of the other participants in the merger is active.
349. *See* paras 7–12 of the Notice.

Lennart Ritter, W. David Braun & Francis Rawlinson: *EC Competition Law: A Practitioner's Guide*, 2004.
Michael Rosenthal & Stefan Thomas: *European Merger Control*, 2010.
Vivien Rose & David Bailey (eds): *Bellamy & Child: European Union Law of Competition*, 7th ed. 2013.
Ulrich Schwalbe & Daniel Zimmer: *Law and Economics in European Merger Control*, 2009.
Richard Whish & David Bailey: *Competition Law*, 8th ed. 2015.

CHAPTER 9
State Aid

1   INTRODUCTION

The provisions on State aid in Articles 107–109 in the Treaty on the Functioning of the European Union (TFEU) are part of the legal basis for ensuring the establishment of an internal market in which competition is not distorted. In this context the special role of the provisions on State aid is to establish a barrier against the disruptive effects which the provision of State aid by the Member States can have on the proper functioning of the internal market. Thus, in contrast to Articles 101 and 102, the provisions on State aid are directed at the conduct of the Member States and not at the conduct of undertakings.

The Member States can use State aid as an effective instrument of financial control to promote, for example, employment policies, social policies or environmental aims. Further, State aid can play an important role in the management of social crises, such as the financial/systemic crisis,[1] the COVID-19 pandemic,[2] and the energy crisis that emerged in relation to the Russian aggression against Ukraine.[3] Where such aid is directed towards specific undertakings or sectors rather than to the Member State's undertakings in general, the aid may distort competition in the relevant market. The undertakings or sectors which receive aid thus obtain an economic advantage which puts them in a better competitive position than their competitors both in the same Member State and in other Member States.[4]

---

1. *See also*: https://competition-policy.ec.europa.eu/sectors/financial-services/legislation_en.
2. *See also*: https://competition-policy.ec.europa.eu/state-aid/coronavirus_en.
3. *See also* the Temporary Crisis and Transition Framework for State Aid measures to support the economy following the aggression against Ukraine by Russia (OJ 2023 C 101/3): https://competition-policy.ec.europa.eu/state-aid/temporary-crisis-and-transition-framework_en.
4. 'In order to favour the aided enterprise, taxes must be levied on the rest of the economy. Thus not only are enterprises in other Member States put at a competitive disadvantage by the aid because the aided enterprises are favoured in a way outside the normal fiscal or social security systems that contribute to the equilibrium between the Member States, but also enterprises not receiving

Article 107(1) thus states that any aid granted by a Member State or through State resources, in any form whatsoever, which distorts or threatens to distort competition by favouring certain undertakings or the production of certain goods is incompatible with the internal market in so far as it affects trade between Member States. Accordingly, Article 107 does not cover all forms of aid granted by Member States, but only such measures that distort the conditions which normally apply to competition between undertakings and affect the trade of goods and services between Member States.

Article 107(1) is not framed as an absolute prohibition but merely states that State aid is in principle incompatible with the internal market. However, the Court of Justice of the European Union (CJ) seems to apply Article 107(1) as a prohibitory provision, so in this chapter, the Article is referred to as containing a prohibition.[5]

The application of Article 107(1) as a prohibitory provision is based on the fact that the consequences that follow from the fact that a State aid is in principle incompatible with the internal market largely correspond to the consequences that generally follow from a provision which is framed as a prohibition.[6] State aid measures that are found to be incompatible with the internal market are thus either repealed or amended and aid paid out under such measures must be repaid.

The prohibition of State aid is not absolute but is modified to a certain extent both by other parts of the provisions on State aid and by other Treaty provisions.[7] Thus, in certain circumstances, the Commission has powers to approve State aid measures subject to Article 107(1) TFEU. This power stems from Article 107(2), which lists certain forms of support which *are* compatible with the internal market, and Article 107(3), which lists certain forms of aid which *may be considered* to be compatible with the internal market. Furthermore, under Article 108(2), third paragraph, the Council has powers to decide that a specific aid measure is to be considered compatible with the internal market.

The scope of the prohibition of State aid depends on how the term *incompatible State aid* – in other words, State aid that is incompatible with the internal market according to Article 107(1) – is interpreted. The interpretation of this is decisive for whether a measure is covered by the Commission's exclusive competence to assess the compatibility of a State aid measure with the internal market. In such a case the Member States have an obligation to notify the measure to the Commission (notification requirement)

---

aid in the same Member State are disadvantaged and pay higher taxes directly or indirectly.' Second Survey on State aids in the European Community in the Manufacturing and Certain Other Sectors, at p. 7, SEC(90) 1165/3, 10 Jul. 1990.

5. *See, e.g.*, the CJ's application of the provision in Case 78/76, *Steinike & Weinlig;* and Case C-354/90, *FNCE.*
6. However, in contrast to what is normally the case with prohibition provisions, Art. 107(1) does not have direct effect; *see* Case 78/76, *Steinike & Weinlig,* para. 10. *See also* Case C-249/17, *Eesti Pagar,* para. 88, and Case C-75/18, *Vodafone,* para. 22.
7. 'Save as otherwise provided in the Treaties' – Art. 107(1). The provisions are modified by Arts 38–44 (agriculture), Art. 106(2) (services of a general economic interest), Art. 93 (transport), Art. 107(2) and (3), Art. 108(2), third paragraph, Arts 143–144 (difficulties as regards balance of payments), and Art. 346 (protection of essential security interests).

and await the Commission's approval before implementing it (standstill obligation), cf. Article 108(3).

The Commission thus has powers to use the rules on State aid to control parts of the Member States' financial support for business.[8] The more broadly the term is defined, the broader the scope of the Commission's powers at the expense of the powers of the Member States. For this reason, the definition of the term *incompatible State aid* will often be the cause of political tension, prompted on the one hand by the Member States' desire to retain the freedom to implement their chosen economic and social policies and on the other hand by the Commission's desire to secure an effective internal market against State aid which distorts competition, by being able to sanction any measure that has the least hint of State aid that could be incompatible with the internal market.

In order to ensure effective control of national State aid measures, the Member States must give notification of new State aid measures to the Commission, whereas the compatibility with the internal market of existing State aid measures is subject to constant evaluation by the Commission.[9] There are detailed provisions on the notification of State aid and the legal consequences in Article 108 TFEU and in the Procedure Regulation.[10] These lay down more detailed rules on the Commission's scope to control and react, as well as the procedure that applies in the event that a Member State does not comply with the obligation to notify or the standstill obligation.

The Procedure Regulation was adopted by the Council under Article 109 which gives the Council authority to make appropriate regulations for the application of Articles 107 and 108. Article 109 also gives the Council authority to determine the conditions in which Article 108(3) is to apply the categories of aid exempted from the obligation to notify and the procedure associated with this. In accordance with this, the Council has adopted Regulation (EU) No 2015/1588, which gives the Commission powers to adopt block exemption regulations in relation to certain identified forms of horizontal State aid.[11] Such regulations may also be adopted by the Commission on the basis of Article 108(4).

---

8. State aid decisions adopted by the Commission are subject to the legal review of the Court of Justice of the European Union, *see* Art. 263 TFEU. The General Court holds jurisdiction at first instance actions for annulment with the possibility of its decisions being subject to appeal before the Court of Justice, *see* Art. 256 TFEU and the Statute of the European Court of Justice of the European Union.
9. However, State aid covered by the *de minimis* regulation and the block exemption regulations are exempt from the duty to notify; *see* more on this in section 2.2.1.
10. Council Regulation (EU) No 2015/1589 laying down detailed rules for the application of Art. 108 of the Treaty on the Functioning of the European Union (OJ 2015 L 248/9) (hereinafter the 'Procedure Regulation').
11. Council Regulation (EU) No 2015/1588 on the application of Arts 107 and 108 of the Treaty on the Functioning of the European Union to certain categories of horizontal State aid (OJ 2015 L 248/1) (as amended by Council Regulation (EU) 2018/1911). With reference to this Regulation and to Art. 108(4) TFEU, the Commission has adopted Commission Regulation (EU) No 2023/2831 on the application of Arts 107 and 108 of the Treaty on the Functioning of the European Union to *de minimis* aid (OJ L, 2023/2831, 15.12.2023), and Commission Regulation (EU) No 651/2014 declaring certain categories of aid compatible with the internal market in application of Arts 107 and 108 of the Treaty (the 'General block exemption Regulation') (OJ 2014 L 187/1) (with later amendments). Besides those general rules, certain special *de minimis*

2 STATE AID PROCEDURE

In assessing the compatibility of a State aid measure with the internal market, the Commission has to follow the procedure provided for in Article 108 TFEU. In 1999, the practice and principles which had been developed over time and established by the CJ and the Commission were codified in the Procedure Regulation, which created a much-needed if not entirely comprehensive overview of the procedure in the area of State aid.[12]

The procedure which the Commission has to follow in relation to a specific State aid measure depends on whether the measure is classified as a new State aid measure or an existing State aid measure. Existing aid measures are governed by Article 108(1) and (2), while new aid measures are subject to the procedure in Article 108(2) and (3), supplemented by the codified rules in the Procedure Regulation.

2.1 Existing State Aid Measures

The term *existing aid* is defined in Article 1 of the Procedure Regulation. The term covers all forms of aid that existed before the Treaty's entry into force in the Member State concerned. This means that aid that is provided in accordance with individual aid measures[13] or general aid schemes[14] which a Member State has implemented prior to the Treaty's entry into force in the Member State, and which are still in force, are considered to be existing aid.

Next, existing aid includes existing aid schemes and individual aid which have been approved by the Commission or by the Council in accordance with Article 108(2), third paragraph. Third, aid is considered to be existing aid if it is approved in accordance with Article 4(6) of the Procedure Regulation, or considered to be approved under the corresponding procedure which applied before the Procedure Regulation entered into force,[15] as a result of the Commission exceeding the deadline for taking a

---

rules and block exemptions for agriculture, aquaculture and services of general economic interest exists. Art. 108(4) TFEU, which was inserted by the Lisbon Treaty, authorises the Commission to adopt regulations relating to the categories of State aid that the Council has determined may be exempted from the procedure provided for by Art. 108(3) TFEU.

12. Council Regulation (EC) No 659/1999 (OJ 1999 L 83/1). This Regulation and its amendments have now been codified by Council Regulation (EU) No 2015/1589 laying down detailed rules for the application of Art. 108 of the Treaty on the Functioning of the European Union (OJ 2015 L 248/9).
13. *Individual aid* is defined in the Procedure Regulation as 'aid that is not awarded on the basis of an aid scheme and notifiable awards of aid on the basis of an aid scheme'; Art. 1(e).
14. *Aid scheme* is defined in the Procedure Regulation as 'any act on the basis of which, without further implementing measures being required, individual aid awards may be made to undertakings defined within the act in a general and abstract manner and any act on the basis of which aid which is not linked to a specific project may be awarded to one or several undertakings for an indefinite period of time and/or for an indefinite amount'; Art. 1(d). In this connection, the term *act* not only includes the formal acts, but also may include the authorities' general administrative practices, *see* further in Case C-337/19 P, *Commission v. Belgium Magnetrol International*, para. 86.
15. The previous procedure meant that, after notifying the Commission, a Member State could implement measures after the expiry of a deadline of two months; *see, e.g.*, Case 120/73, *Lorenz*, para. 4; and Case C-312/90, *Spain v. Commission*, para. 18.

decision and failure to react to the Member State's subsequent notification that the measure will be implemented.

Fourth, aid which the Commission can no longer require to be repaid, because of the expiry of the ten-year period of limitation in Article 17 of the Procedure Regulation, is considered to be existing aid.[16]

Finally, aid is considered to be existing aid if it can be shown that, upon the introduction of the aid, it was not aid within the meaning of Article 107(1) and that the measure later came to be considered as aid because of the development of the internal market, without the Member State having made any changes to the measure. Such a change could be the result of the liberalisation of a market which has previously not been subject to competition, such as the electricity market (liberalised in 2003).[17] However, measures that acquire the character of State aid as a result of the EU's liberalisation of an activity are not considered to be existing aid after the date on which the liberalisation takes effect but are regarded as new aid.[18]

In accordance with Article 108(1), existing aid schemes are subject to continuing control carried out in cooperation between the Commission and the Member States. In principle, such aid is considered to be compatible with the internal market and can be implemented until the Commission states that it is incompatible with the internal market.

2.2 New Aid Measures

In the Procedure Regulation *new aid* is defined as all 'aid schemes and individual aid, which is not existing aid, including alterations to existing aid'.[19] The Regulation thus defines the term negatively in relation to existing aid.

New aid measures are subject to prior controls which are in part based on a duty to notify[20] and in part on a standstill obligation.[21] The obligation to notify means that the Member States must inform the Commission of any proposed introduction of or change to an aid measure so that the Commission has the opportunity to give its opinion on the aid measure before it is put into effect. The obligation is supplemented by a standstill obligation which means that a Member State may not put a proposed measure into effect before the Commission gives its final approval or can be regarded as having approved it. This prevents aid which is incompatible with the Treaty being instituted and has a

---

16. *See* in more detail in section 2.7.
17. *See, e.g.*, Case T-288/97, *Friuli Venezia v. Commission*, para. 89 (concerning the cabotage market), and Case C-387/17, *Fallimento Traghetti*, where the relevant market at the time of the provision of aid was not yet open to competition.
18. Procedure Regulation, Art. 1(b)(v).
19. Procedure Regulation, Art. 1(c). Changes to an existing arrangement thus mean that the scheme will be considered new, which gives rise to certain procedural consequences. Commission Regulation (EC) 794/2004 implementing Council Regulation (EC) No 659/1999 laying down rules for the application of Art. 93 of the EU Treaty, (Implementing Regulation), Art. 4, and, for example, Joined Cases C-915/19–917/19, *Eco Fox*, and Case C-470/20, *AS Veejaam and OÜ Espo*, paras 40ff.
20. Article 108(3), first paragraph, TFEU and the Procedure Regulation, Art. 2.
21. Article 108(3), third paragraph, TFEU and the Procedure Regulation, Art. 3.

damaging effect. In Case 120/73, *Lorenz*, the CJ established that, as the only such part of the State aid provisions, the standstill clause has a direct effect.[22]

In principle, new State aid measures are regarded as being incompatible with the internal market and are therefore considered unlawful if they are not notified or suspended in accordance with the above.[23] Subject to certain procedural modifications, such unlawful aid is dealt with in the same way as notified State aid measures.[24]

2.2.1 Notifiable Measures

According to Article 108(3) TFEU, Member States have a duty to notify the Commission of any plans to alter existing aid schemes and any proposal to introduce new aid schemes.[25] The aim of this is to give the Commission the possibility of controlling whether an aid scheme is compatible with the internal market before the measure is implemented.

However, the duty to notify is not without exceptions. On the basis of Council Regulation (EU) No 2015/1589, the Commission has the possibility of declaring that certain forms of aid either do not fulfil the criteria in Article 107(1) TFEU or are regarded as being compatible with the internal market in accordance with Article 107(3), and are therefore exempted from the notification obligation under Article 108(3).[26] On the basis of this authority, the Commission has adopted Regulation (EU) No 2023/2831 on *de minimis* aid and the General Block Exemption Regulation, which exempt certain forms of aid from the obligation to notify.[27]

Individual aid which is given in accordance with an approved aid scheme need not be notified to the Commission, unless a reservation to this effect is made in the Commission's decision giving approval.[28] In this case, the aid will be treated procedurally in the same way as existing aid. The reason why there is not a general duty to notify is that the circumstances which the Commission has taken into account in connection with

---

22. Case 120/73, *Lorenz*, para. 8, which refers to Case 6/64, *Costa/ENEL*. See also Case C-249/17, *Eesti Pagar*, para. 88, and Case C-75/18, *Vodafone*, para. 22.
23. See the definition of *unlawful aid* in the Procedure Regulation, Art. 1(f).
24. Procedure Regulation, Art. 15(2).
25. Procedure Regulation, Art. 2 (*see* Art. 1(c)). Only the Member States are under the obligation to notify, and the obligation cannot be satisfied by notification by the undertaking receiving the aid. Neither does the beneficiary of an unlawfully granted aid have the possibility to submit a complaint to the Commission with the view to having the aid found compatible with the internal market, but the recipient may bring proceedings before a national court to have a penalty imposed on the Member State on account of an express or implied refusal to comply with the obligation to notify, see further Case T-678/20, *Solar Electric v. Commission*, paras 18–40.
26. Articles 1 and 2 of Council Regulation (EU) No 2015/1589 laying down detailed rules for the application of Art. 108 of the Treaty on the Functioning of the European Union (OJ L, 2015 L 248/1) (as amended by Council Regulation (EU) 2018/1911). *See also* Art. 108(4) TFEU.
27. Article 3 of Commission Regulation (EU) No 2023/2831 on the application of Arts 107 and 108 of the Treaty on the Functioning of the European Union to *de minimis* aid (OJ L, 2023/2831, 15.12.2023); and Art. 3 of Commission Regulation (EU) No 651/2014 declaring certain categories of aid compatible with the internal market in application of Arts 107 and 108 of the Treaty (the 'General block exemption Regulation') (OJ 2014 L 187/1) (as amended by Commission Regulations 2017/1084, 2020/972 and 2021/1237).
28. Case C-47/91, *Italy v. Commission*, para. 21.

approving an aid measure will be the same as those the Commission would have to assess in relation to individual aid which is granted as part of the implementation of the general aid scheme. Where there is no requirement for notification as a condition for the approval of an aid measure which is associated with an existing aid scheme, the Member State nevertheless has a duty to send annual reports to the Commission with a view to controlling whether the aid scheme is used correctly.[29]

2.3 Unlawful Aid Measures

In Article 1(f) of the Procedure Regulation, *unlawful aid* is defined as new aid put into effect in contravention of Article 108(3) TFEU. As previously stated, Article 108(3) imposes on Member States both a notification obligation and a standstill obligation. New aid which has not been notified in accordance with Article 108(3), first paragraph, is thus considered unlawful aid. The same applies to new aid which has been correctly notified in accordance with Article 108(3), first paragraph, but which has been put into effect prior to notification, or subsequent to notification but prior to the Commission's final decision on approval, and aid has therefore been paid in breach of the standstill requirement in Article 108(3), third paragraph.[30] Aid that has been fully or partly paid at the time of notification without the approval of the Commission is dealt with in the same procedural context as non-notified aid, regardless of whether the aid has in fact been notified to the Commission[31] and it is considered unlawful in line with other non-notified aid.

2.4 The Procedure for Existing Aid

As stated above, aid schemes that are characterised under the Procedure Regulation as existing schemes are considered compatible with the internal market. However, the gradual growth and development of the internal market can mean that such an aid scheme will no longer be considered compatible with the internal market. For example, if overcapacity arises in a particular business sector, it would not serve the interests of the Union if aid continued to be given under an existing aid scheme for an expansion of production capacity in the sector in question. In order to prevent such situations from arising, the Member States and the Commission together undertake a constant review of the aid schemes in each of the Member States.[32] However, such reviews are not only undertaken with a view to identifying existing aid schemes which have become incompatible with the internal market, but also with a view to identifying existing aid schemes which were never compatible with the internal market. If such a

---

29. Procedure Regulation, Art. 26(1).
30. The expression *unlawful aid* thus refers to the fact that the aid has not been notified and/or has been paid without approval, and does not refer to the compatibility of the aid with the internal market under Art. 107(1).
31. See, e.g., the Commission Decision in Case C-23/2000, *Ojala-Yhtymä* (OJ 2000 C 278/2), where the case was treated as non-notified aid, as a part of the planned aid had already been allocated and paid to the undertakings in question at the date when the aid was notified.
32. Article 108(1) TFEU.

scheme is identified, the Commission will, after giving the Member State an opportunity to give its opinion,[33] propose suitable measures to change an aid scheme to make it compatible with the internal market by amending the content of the aid scheme, introducing procedural requirements or repealing the aid scheme.[34]

If the Member State concerned accepts the Commission's recommendation, the Member State is bound by its acceptance.[35] However, if the Member State does not accept the Commission's recommendation, the Commission can initiate a formal examination procedure.[36] Member States are not subject to a standstill obligation in relation to existing aid, and the aid may continue to be paid until the Commission decides that the aid is incompatible with the internal market.[37]

2.5 The Procedure for Notified Aid

According to the Treaty, notified aid is subject to a two-part procedure, namely the preliminary examination and the formal investigation procedure.

Under the *preliminary examination*, within two months,[38] the Commission must form a preliminary view of the compliance of the aid arrangement with the provisions on State aid and take a decision accordingly.

The Commission thus has the possibility of deciding that the measure in question does not involve State aid, or it can approve a measure which does involve State aid but which is considered compatible with the internal market.[39] A decision to approve an aid measure must be unconditional so that, unlike the case of the formal investigation procedure, the Commission does not have the possibility of making the approval subject to special terms or conditions.

If the two-month deadline for making a decision is exceeded, the aid scheme is considered having been approved by the Commission. However, the Member State in question must give the Commission notice before an aid measure is implemented, and the Commission then has fifteen working days from receiving such notice in which to take any decision in accordance with Article 4.[40] In order to prevent the implementation of aid schemes that are contrary to the provisions on State aid, the standstill obligation has effect throughout the whole of the preliminary examination procedure.[41]

---

33. Procedure Regulation, Art. 21(2). The Member State has a deadline of one month to give its views. This deadline can be extended by the Commission if there are good grounds for doing so.
34. Article 108(1) and the Procedure Regulation, Art. 22. The Commission's proposal of suitable measures under Art. 108(1), and the Member States acceptance thereof may also occur in conjunction with the Commission's guidelines and communications, *see, e.g.*, Communication from the Commission, Guidelines on State aid for climate, environmental protection and energy 2022, OJ 2022 C 80/1, point 468.
35. Procedure Regulation, Art. 23(1).
36. Procedure Regulation, Art. 23(2) (cf. Art. 4(4)).
37. *See* Case T-116/16, *Port autonome du Centre et de Lóuest SCRL v. Commission*, para. 20.
38. The deadline of two months begins on the day following the receipt of notification of an aid scheme or individual aid; *see* the Procedure Regulation, Art. 4(5), which also states that: 'The notification will be considered as complete if, within two months from its receipt, or from the receipt of any additional information requested, the Commission does not request any further information'.
39. Procedure Regulation, Art. 4(2) and (3).
40. Procedure Regulation, Art. 4(6).
41. Case 84/82, *Germany v. Commission*, para. 11.

The Commission can also decide to initiate the *formal investigation procedure*. This will occur where, after the preliminary examination, the Commission is in doubt about the compatibility of an aid measure with the internal market,[42] and there is, therefore, a need to gather full information as a basis for making a decision about the aid measure, as well as consulting the interested parties.[43]

As a conclusion to the formal investigation procedure, the Commission can decide that the measure does not constitute a State aid – possibly after the Member State in question has made some change to the measures. The Commission can also take a positive decision that the aid measure can be approved as being compatible with the internal market. Such a decision will contain a reference to the Treaty provision used as authority for exempting the measure from the prohibition of State aid. The Commission can make the approval conditional on compliance with certain specified requirements, as well as instituting control measures enabling the Commission to monitor compliance with the decision. Finally, the Commission can take a negative decision that the aid is incompatible with the internal market.[44]

As soon as the Commission is no longer in doubt about the compatibility of a measure with the internal market, it makes one of the decisions referred to above. As far as possible, this decision is taken within eighteen months of the initiation of the procedure.[45]

If the Commission does not decide within the eighteen months deadline, the Member State concerned can request the Commission to decide on the basis of the existing information within two months or, if the existing information is insufficient, to take a negative decision.[46] It is not clear from Article 9(7) of the Procedure Regulation whether the Commission's inaction means – as it does in relation to Article 4(6) of the Regulation – that after the expiry of the two months, the Member State has a right to implement the aid measure. However, there seems little purpose in a Member State triggering this deadline if the expiry of the deadline does not result in a right to implement the aid measure. However, the Procedure Regulation does not contain such an express authorisation, so it must be left to the CJ to decide whether such a meaning can be ascribed to Article 9(7).

2.6 The Procedure for Unlawful Aid

It is not all Member States that live up to the obligation to notify planned aid measures. Such non-notified aid measures can come to the attention of the Commission on the basis of information about them or of complaints received from other Member States or competitors. The Commission must then investigate the measures in question in more

---

42. Procedure Regulation, Art. 4(4), as well as Art. 108(2), second paragraph, TFEU. The procedure is also initiated where, in accordance with Art. 11 of the Regulation, the Commission intends to revoke a decision based on incorrect information which was a determining factor.
43. The Commission publishes its views on aid measures in the Official Journal, inviting the Member State in question and other interested parties to comment. Such comments must be made within a deadline laid down, which is normally not longer than one month; Procedure Regulation, Art. 6(1).
44. Procedure Regulation, Art. 9(2)–(5).
45. Procedure Regulation, Art. 9(6).
46. Procedure Regulation, Art. 9(7).

detail.[47] This investigation is concluded with a decision in accordance with Article 4(2), (3) or (4) of the Procedure Regulation or, in the event of a decision to initiate the formal investigation procedure, by a decision in accordance with Article 9 of the Regulation.[48]

The procedure for unlawful State aid thus corresponds generally to the procedure for notified aid. However, there is the important difference that in dealing with unlawful State aid, the Commission is not bound by any of the deadlines for processing the case.[49] In practice, the deadlines for non-notified measures will not vary much from those that apply to notified measures, among other things, out of regard for good administrative practice to complete the processing of cases within a reasonable time.

2.6.1   Interim Legal Measures

As a non-notified aid measure is characterised as unlawful, in special circumstances the Commission can apply interim measures. Thus, the Commission can order the Member State concerned to either suspend the aid measure, or recover aid already paid out, or both.[50] Since these measures are of an interim nature, they only have effect up to the point when the Commission makes its final decision on the compatibility of the aid measure with the internal market.

The power given in Article 13(2) of the Regulation to order recovery of non-notified aid can only be used in special circumstances. According to the established practice, first, there must be no doubt about the nature of the aid in question; second, it must be necessary to take immediate steps; and third, the measure must involve a serious risk of substantial and irreparable damage to a competitor.[51] These provisions can only be applied if all the conditions are fulfilled. This is assumed to apply in only very few cases, and thus, the provision is not of great practical importance.

2.7   Recovery of Unlawful Aid

2.7.1   The Commission's Powers to Require Recovery

Since 1973, the CJ has recognised that, under the authority of Article 108(2) TFEU, the Commission can require the recovery of unlawful aid. This was established in Case 70/72, *Kohlengesetz*, where the CJ concluded that the Commission's right to require a Member State to suspend or abolish an aid measure which is found incompatible with the internal market implies authority to require that payment made which is contrary

---

47. Procedure Regulation, Art. 12.
48. Procedure Regulation, Art. 15(1). On these provisions, for the preliminary examination *see* Art. 4, and for the formal investigation procedure *see* Art. 9.
49. Procedure Regulation, Art. 12(2).
50. Procedure Regulation, Art. 13(1) and (2), according to which the Commission may require the Member State to suspend and to recover any unlawful aid. If the Member State fails to comply with a suspension injunction or a recovery injunction, the Commission can refer the matter to the CJ directly and apply for a declaration that the failure to comply constitutes an infringement of the Treaty; the Procedure Regulation, Art. 14.
51. Procedure Regulation, Art. 13(2).

to the provisions on State aid should be recovered.[52] This is necessary in order to ensure that a decision of the Commission to abolish or alter an aid scheme can be effective in practice.

If a Member State does not comply with a Commission decision on the recovery of incompatible State aid, that Member State can be subject to an action for breach of the Treaty.[53]

The Commission's powers to recover State aid which is incompatible with the Treaty is now codified in Article 16 of the Procedure Regulation. According to this, where the Commission takes a negative decision in a case of unlawful aid, the Commission will decide that payments made must be recovered, provided that such a decision is not contrary to general principles of Union law.[54] If the conditions for requiring repayment of State aid are fulfilled, the Commission has a duty to seek recovery of the aid. In contrast to the situation under previous practice, the exercise of the Commission's power to require repayment is no longer a matter of the Commission's choice, it is an obligation.[55]

2.7.2 The Conditions for Requiring Recovery

The Commission can only require recovery under Article 16 of the Procedure Regulation in special circumstances. Thus, the recovery requires that the aid measures should be classified as new aid,[56] the aid must be unlawful,[57] the aid must be incompatible with the internal market, payments must have been made in accordance with the aid scheme, that the period of limitation in Article 17(1) of the Procedure Regulation must not have been exceeded, and the requirement for repayment must not be contrary to general principles of Union law.

In this context, the recovery of unlawfully paid aid in accordance with Article 16 of the Procedure Regulation also requires that the Commission has taken a negative decision in accordance with Article 107(1) TFEU and has thereby established that the aid measure is incompatible with the internal market.

The powers of the Commission to recover aid under Article 16 of the Procedure Regulation are subject to a limitation period of ten years.[58] The limitation period begins

---

52. Case 70/72, *Kohlengesetz*, para. 13.
53. Case 70/72, *Kohlengesetz*, para. 13. *See also* Case C-24/95, *Alcan*, para. 22.
54. For example, the principle of proportionality and the principle of legitimate expectations, which are discussed further below.
55. In the recovery notice, the Commission explains more about the rules and procedures that apply in connection with recovery of State aid, and at the same time describes how the Commission will cooperate with the Member States in order to ensure that they fulfil their EU legal obligations, *see Commission Notice on the recovery of unlawful and incompatible State aid*, (OJ 2019/C 247/01). Furthermore, it follows from Case C-349/17, *Eesti Pagar*, that a Member State which discovers that aid has been granted in violation of the General block exemption Regulation or the implementation ban in Art. 108(3) TFEU, is obliged to recover the grant on its own initiative, cf. para. 92. *See also* Joined Cases C-102/21 and C-103/21, *Autonome Provinz Bozen*, para. 48.
56. Procedure Regulation, Art. 1(c).
57. Procedure Regulation, Art. 1(f).
58. Procedure Regulation, Art. 17(1).

on the day on which the unlawful aid is awarded to the recipient.[59] In this context, the criterion for determining the time of granting the aid is that of the legally binding act by which the competent national authority undertakes to grant aid to the recipient by an unconditional and legally binding promise.[60] Thus, a decisive factor is the time at which the aid is in fact granted, regardless of whether the aid is awarded individually or as part of an aid scheme, implying that the time at which the aid scheme itself is adopted is not decisive.[61] On the same principle, the period of limitation for aid which is paid in instalments or on a periodic basis is calculated from the payment date for each instalment, i.e., where the aid was in fact received by the beneficiary.[62]

In certain circumstances, the period of limitation can be interrupted or suspended; see the Procedure Regulation, Article 17(2). The interruption occurs whenever a measure is taken in relation to unlawful aid by the Commission or by a Member State at the prompting of the Commission. For example, such a measure can take the form of the Commission's recommendation to the Member State concerning the support measure or the Member State's legal steps taken to recover the aid.[63] After each interruption, the ten-year limitation period starts again from the beginning. If the decision of the Commission is brought before the CJ, the period of limitation is suspended as long as the case is pending.[64]

Upon the expiry of the period of limitation, what was originally new unlawful aid changes its status to become existing aid.[65]

2.7.3 Implementation of the Recovery Decision

The Commission's decision on the recovery of unlawful aid is addressed to the Member State concerned, and as such, it is binding on it.[66] The Member State is responsible for taking all the measures necessary to recover the aid paid to the recipient.[67] According to Article 16(3) of the Procedure Regulation, the repayment must be made without delay and in accordance with the procedures of the national law of the Member State concerned.[68] For this purpose, 'the Member States concerned shall take all necessary

---

59. Procedure Regulation, Art. 17(2).
60. See Case T-818/14, *BSCA v. Commission*, para. 72.
61. See Case C-81/10 P, *France Télécom*, para. 80. For more details on the time of award of the aid, see Case T-818/14, *BSCA v. Commission*, para. 72, and Joined Cases C-702/20 and C-17/21, *DOBELES HES*, para. 110, of which the latter explicitly determines that the time from when the period within which the Commission may recover unlawfully paid aid starts to run, cannot be fixed as a date prior to the date on which the unlawful aid was paid.
62. See Case C-81/10 P, *France Télécom*, para. 82.
63. In Case C-233/16, *ANGED*, paras 84 and 85, it was recognised that a request by the Commission for information from a Member State is a measure which can interrupt the limitation period.
64. Procedure Regulation, Art. 17(2).
65. Procedure Regulation, Art. 17(3).
66. Article 288 TFEU.
67. Procedure Regulation, Art. 16(1).
68. However, in connection with an appeal against the Commission's decision, the CJ can order the postponement of the implementation of the legal act which is being challenged; *see* Art. 242 TFEU. In order to ensure the rapid execution of the repayment requirement, on the basis of Joined Cases T-244 and 486/93, *Deggendorf*, and Case C-355/95 P, *TWD*, the Commission can

steps which are available in their respective legal systems, including provisional measures, without prejudice to Community law'.[69]

The actual implementation of the recovery demand is thus subject to the relevant national law. However, the national law must not make it impossible to seek recovery of the unlawful aid in practice,[70] for example, because the Member State's provisions on payments made under beneficial legal acts prevent the implementation of the recovery decision. Where a Member State meets an unexpected or unpredictable problem in implementing the recovery decision, it cannot merely refrain from implementing the decision but must refer the matter to the Commission with a view to cooperating in order to overcome the problems.[71] In this context, administrative problems are not circumstances that can justify the failure to implement a recovery decision.[72]

If a Member State does not implement the recovery of incompatible aid in accordance with the Commission's decision, then either the Commission or another Member State can bring an action for breach of the Treaty directly before the CJ in accordance with Article 108(2), second paragraph, TFEU[73] and thereby move more rapidly than the longer procedure for cases of breach of the Treaty under its Articles 258 and 259. According to the practice of the CJ, the only objection the Member State can make in such a case is to produce concrete evidence that it is absolutely impossible to recover the aid paid out from the recipient[74] This is interpreted restrictively by the CJ; for example, the financial collapse of an undertaking as a result of the recovery of incompatible aid is not an argument that justifies a Member State refraining from requiring the aid in question to be repaid.[75]

It is the advantage that the recipient has procured by receiving the aid and not the possible economic profit that the recipient has enjoyed as a result of exploiting this advantage that must be recovered.[76]

The Member State addresses the order for repayment to the recipient of the aid concerned, who is normally identified in the Commission's decision,[77] and it will normally be possible to make the identification without any problems. On the contrary, in some cases, if an undertaking or part of an undertaking has been sold or transferred,

---

order the suspension of any payment of new aid to undertakings that have not repaid unlawful or incompatible State aid; *see* in this context Commission Notice on the recovery of unlawful and incompatible State aid, (OJ 2019/C 247/01), section 6.2.
69. Procedure Regulation, Art. 16(3).
70. Case C-24/95, *Alcan*, para. 24; and Case C-5/89, *Commission v. Germany*, para. 12.
71. Case C-507/08, *Commission v. Slovenia*, para. 44; and Case C-214/07, *Commission v. France*, paras 45 and 46.
72. Case C-280/95, *Commission v. Italy*, para. 23.
73. Case C-232/05, *Commission v. France*, commented on by *Antonis Metaxas*: Recovery Obligation and the Limits of National Procedural Autonomy, European State Aid Law Quarterly (2) 2007 pp. 407–415.
74. Case C-214/07, *Commission v. France*, para. 44; Case C-261/99, *Commission v. France*, para. 23; and Case C-404/97, *Commission v. Portugal*, para. 39. *See also* Case 280/95, *Commission v. Italy*, para. 13; and Joined Cases C-485 & 490/03, *Commission v. Spain*, paras 72 and 74.
75. Case C-261/99, *Commission v. France*, para. 15; and Case 52/84, *Commission v. Belgium*.
76. Cf. Joined Cases C-164/15 P and C-165/15 P, *Irish Travel Tax*, para. 92.
77. For more details on the limits to the Commission's powers to identify debtors in repayment cases, *see* Case C-277/00, *Germany v. Commission*,

it can be difficult to establish to whom the Member State should address its recovery order.[78] However, if an undertaking which has received unlawful State aid is sold at the market price, the aid element is assessed at the market price and is included in the sales price, and the purchaser, therefore, does not benefit from a competitive advantage associated with receipt of the aid.[79] This means that a claim for repayment cannot be made against the purchaser unless it is proved that the purchaser has in fact had a competitive advantage associated with the aid, for example, if the setting up of a hived-off company in order to carry on the business and to circumvent the obligation of the insolvent company to make a repayment.[80]

2.7.4 Possible Exceptions to the Obligation to Repay

As stated above, the Commission can demand that unlawful and incompatible State aid should be recovered as long as this is not contrary to general principles of Union law; see the Procedure Regulation, Article 16(1). In practice, this primarily involves an assessment of whether an order to recover unlawful or incompatible State aid is contrary to the proportionality principle or the principle of legitimate expectations.

In so far as it is a logical consequence of the incompatibility of the unlawful aid with the internal market that it is sought to be recovered, and the recovery of payment has the sole purpose of restoring the *status ante quo*, in several cases, the CJ has stated that the duty to repay should not, in principle, be a disproportionate burden in relation to the aims of the Treaty provisions on State aid.[81] In these circumstances, the Commission's order to repay will, therefore, comply with the proportionality principle.

The principle of legitimate expectations, meaning the principle that the expectation that a legal ruling is final is sufficiently justified as to be entitled to legal protection under the control of the courts, is a principle that is recognised by the CJ as part of Union law.[82]

The problems that have been of particular concern in the area of State aid are whether, in cases of breach of the Treaty, the Member States can use the principle of legitimate expectations in order to justify not complying with a Commission decision to seek recovery of unlawfully paid aid, and whether, in connection with a case of annulment of an aid scheme, the recipient of the aid can claim legitimate expectations as the basis for revocation of the Commission's decision on the recovery of unlawful State aid.[83]

---

78. *See* further Commission Notice on the recovery of unlawful and incompatible State aid (OJ 2019/C 247/01), section 4.3. and the practice stated herein.
79. Case T-291/06, *Operator ARP*, para. 67; and Case C-214/07, *Commission v. France*, para. 58.
80. Case C-277/00, *Germany v. Commission*, para. 86.
81. Joined Cases T-298/97 and others, *Alzetta*, para. 169. *See also*, e.g., Case C-142/87, *Tubemeuse*, para. 66; and Case C-169/95, *Spain v. Commission*, para. 47.
82. Joined Cases 205–215/82, *Deutsche Milchkontor*, para. 30; and Case 5/89, *Commission v. Germany*, para. 13.
83. *See* further in Commission Notice on the recovery of unlawful and incompatible State aid, (OJ 2019/C 247/01), section 2.4.1.2., and the practice mentioned herein.

The possibility of a Member State relying on a recipient's legitimate expectation as a basis for not implementing recovery of incompatible State aid is closely linked to the question of the extent to which the Member State's law may impede the implementation of the recovery decision. As previously stated, national law must be applied, subject to the reservation that recovery of payment must not be made impossible in practice.[84]

In connection with a prosecution for breach of the Treaty in Case C-5/89, *Commission v. Germany*, Germany claimed that it was absolutely impossible to implement recovery of the aid, as such recovery would mean setting aside the principle of the protection of legitimate expectations, which was expressed in the relevant administrative law. According to the administrative law in question, the revocation of an unlawful beneficial administrative act requires weighing up the various interests involved, including the interests of the undertaking which has received the aid and the public interest of the Union in having the aid recovered, and that recovery of the aid should take place within one year of the administrative authority becoming aware of the circumstances constituting grounds for revocation – this deadline was exceeded in the actual case. In reply to this, the CJ stated that a Member State which has granted aid contrary to the procedural rules laid down in Article 108 may not rely on the legitimate expectations of recipients in order to justify a failure to comply with the obligation to recover the aid. If the CJ allowed this possibility, it would deprive Articles 107 and 108 of their intended effect, as the national authorities would be able to rely on their own unlawful conduct in order to prevent the effective implementation of the Commission's decisions in the area of State aid.[85] This means that a Member State cannot rely on the provisions, practice or circumstances in its national legal system as a basis for failing to fulfil its obligations under Union law.[86] Therefore, if the national legal system lays down a provision stating a period of limitation for the revocation of a beneficial administrative act, this provision must be applied in such a way that the recovery of unlawfully paid State aid is not made impossible in practice, and so that the interests of the Union are fully taken into consideration.[87]

In Case C-5/89, *Commission v. Germany*, the CJ also ruled on the scope for the recipient to rely on legitimate expectations.[88] In this connection, the CJ held that a recipient of aid cannot have a legitimate expectation

---

84. Case C-24/95, *Alcan*, para. 24; Case 94/87, *Commission v. Germany*, para. 12; and Case C-5/89, *Commission v. Germany*, para. 12.
85. Case C-5/89, *Commission v. Germany*, para. 17.
86. Case C-5/89, *Commission v. Germany*, para. 18.
87. Case C-5/89, *Commission v. Germany*, para. 19.
88. *See also* Case 223/85, *RSV*; Case 310/85, *Deufil*; Case C-298/00 P, *Alzetta*; and Case T-55/99, *CETM*.

that the aid received is lawful unless the aid has been provided in compliance with the State aid procedure in Article 108 TFEU.[89] The CJ stated that a diligent businessman should normally be able to determine whether that procedure has been followed.[90] However, if the recipient of aid can point to extraordinary circumstances that would reasonably give rise to a legitimate expectation that the aid is lawful, the CJ would not exclude the possibility of the recipient being able to avoid having to make repayment. According to the practice of the CJ, if a long period elapses before the Commission takes a decision on the aid scheme, this can constitute such an extraordinary circumstance.[91] Thus, in Case 223/85, *RSV*, the CJ found that the two years and two months that had elapsed before the Commission took its decision meant that the plaintiff could have acquired legitimate expectations which prevented the Commission requiring the Dutch authorities seeking to recover the aid.[92] On the basis of the existing practice it seems that, in principle, it will only be possible to claim that there are legitimate expectations if it is the Union itself that has created the legitimate expectation of the recipient of aid.[93]

Where a recipient of aid receives compensation from the aid-granting authority for the loss suffered as a result of the repayment of the aid which the undertaking in question had relied on, this compensation ought to be considered State aid covered by Article 107 TFEU. Such compensation merely serves to compensate for the loss of the economic advantage which the undertaking received from the aid, and it therefore seems in itself to constitute State aid which is incompatible with Article 107 TFEU.[94] The alternative would mean that the Commission's scope for demanding the recovery of unlawful State aid would be nugatory, and the scope for getting round Article 107 would be strengthened.

2.8 Interested Parties

According to Article 1(h) of the Procedure Regulation, *interested party* means 'any Member State and any person, undertaking or association of undertakings whose interests might be affected by the granting of aid, in particular the beneficiary of the aid, competing undertakings and trade associations.'

---

89. Case C-24/95, *Alcan*, para. 25; and Case C-169/95, *Spain v. Commission*.
90. Case C-5/89, *Commission v. Germany*, para. 14. See also Joined Cases T-298/97 and others, *Alzetta*, para. 171.
91. Case 223/85, *RSV*, para. 17.
92. Case 223/85, *RSV*, para. 12.
93. *See, e.g.*, the Commission Decision C 45/07 of 28 Oct. 2009 on the tax amortisation of financial goodwill for foreign shareholding acquisitions, paras 164–167 (OJ 2011 L 7/48); Case C-297/01, *Sicilcassa*, paras 40–41, and Case C-630/11 P, *HGA*, para. 132.
94. Commission Decision 96/434/EC, para. 3.1 (OJ 1996 L 180/31). *See also* the Opinion of Advocate General Slynn in Joined Cases 106–120/87, *Asteris*.

2.8.1 The Rights of Interested Parties

The rights of interested parties in the Commission's investigation proceedings relating to aid measures are laid down in Article 20 of the Procedure Regulation. The precise extent of the rights depends partly on who the party is and partly on the point in the process at which the interested party intends to exercise their rights.

According to Article 24(2) of the Procedure Regulation, all interested parties may submit a complaint to the Commission about any alleged unlawful aid and any alleged misuse of aid.[95] Competitors, business organisations or one of the other Member States thus have the possibility of getting the Commission to assess whether an undertaking has received State aid in breach of the Treaty's State aid provisions.

The interested party must complete a standard form and provide the mandatory information requested therein. If the Commission considers that there are insufficient grounds for proceeding with the case, it must inform the interested party thereof and call on it to submit comments within a prescribed period, normally within one month. If the interested party fails to make known its views within this period, the complaint will be deemed to have been withdrawn.[96]

Interested parties do not have any opportunity to submit comments on a case during a preliminary examination.[97] The opposite applies in relation to the formal investigation procedure. Any interested party may submit comments pursuant to Article 6 following a Commission decision to initiate the formal investigation procedure; see Article 24(1) of the Procedure Regulation.[98] These comments are then forwarded to the Member State concerned with a view to obtaining its reactions. Interested parties are not entitled either to receive information about or to submit comments on any reaction by the Member State to their comments, nor are interested parties informed about the comments submitted by other interested parties.

Where an interested party submits comments in a case concerning State aid, that party is entitled to receive a copy of the Commission's decision on the State aid. The recipient of the State aid is entitled to receive such a copy, whether or not it exercises its right to submit comments.[99]

2.8.2 Rights Before the CJ and the GC

According to Article 263 TFEU, the positive and negative decisions which the Commission makes at the conclusion of a preliminary examination or a formal investigation procedure can be referred to the CJ or the General Court (GC) with a view to having the

---

95. On the legal protection of those who complain, see Case T-351/02, *Deutsche Bahn*.
96. Procedure Regulation, Art. 24(2).
97. However, see Case T-95/94, *Sytraval*, para. 78, where the GC found that, in certain circumstances, the Commission's duty to justify its decisions can require it to conduct an adversarial proceeding with a complainant.
98. In practice, a notice is published in the C series of the Official Journal, in which the State aid and the Commission's view on it is described, while interested parties are encouraged to submit comments on the case.
99. Procedure Regulation, Art. 24(1).

decision overturned. The rights of Member States to bring an action are set out in Article 263, second paragraph, and the rights of other interested parties are set out in Article 263, fourth paragraph. In the case of Member States, it is the CJ which has jurisdiction, and for natural and legal persons it is the GC that has jurisdiction.

Actions brought by natural and legal persons require either that the decision is addressed to the person in question or, if the decision is addressed to some other person or is made in the form of a regulation, that it directly and individually concerns that person,[100] and that the person in question has a legal interest in having the decision annulled.[101] In relation to the Commission's decisions on State aid, it will thus be of decisive importance that the interested party is able to show that they are directly and individually affected, as the direct addressee for the Commission's decision will be the Member State concerned. In this context, the recipient of State aid is considered to be directly and individually affected. Moreover, in the area of State aid, the CJ has identified persons, undertakings or associations as interested parties whose interests may be affected by the aid given, i.e., competing undertakings and trade organisations.[102]

Actions for annulment must be submitted within two months. This period runs from the date when the disputed legal act has been published in accordance with the formal requirements or the plaintiff has been informed or, in default of this, within two months after the plaintiff has become aware of the legal act.[103]

Actions for breach of the Treaty can be brought by the Commission or by the other Member States in cases where the Member State concerned does not fulfil its obligations under the Commission's decision; see Article 108(2), second paragraph. Other interested parties do not have this possibility but must try to get an action for breach of the Treaty brought via their national authorities.

2.8.3 *Rights Before the National Courts*

The Commission has sole competence to assess the compatibility of State aid with the internal market; in other words, only the Commission has jurisdiction to decide whether a State aid is covered by the prohibition in Article 107(1) TFEU and whether the exceptions in Article 107(2) and (3) apply.[104] Article 107(1) is, therefore, not directly applicable to national legal systems. However, the CJ has held that the provision can be relied upon in a national court to the extent that it has been put in concrete form by acts having general application provided for by Article 109 TFEU or

---

100. See Art. 263, fourth paragraph, TFEU, as interpreted in Case C-25/62, *Plaumann*. See also Case C-198/91, *Cook*, paras 23–26; Case C-225/91, *Matra*, paras 17–20; Case C-78/03 P, *ARE*, paras 35–37; and Case T-395/04, *Air One*, where the GC went so far as to recognise the right of a potential competitor to bring an action, and Joined Cases T-73/22 P and T-77/22 P, *Grupa Azoty*, para. 62.
101. See, e.g., Case T-212/00, *Nuove Industrie Molisane*.
102. Case C-367/95 P, *Sytraval*, para. 41; Case 323/82, *Intermills*, para. 16; and Case T-167/04, *Asklepios*, para. 49.
103. Article 263, fifth paragraph, TFEU.
104. Case C-119/05, *Lucchini*, para. 52; Joined Cases C-261/01 & 262/01, *van Calster*, para. 45, Case T-73/98, *Prayon-Rupel*, para. 40, and Case C-598/17, *A-Fonds*, para. 46.

by decisions, in particular cases under Article 108(2).[105] Under the authority of Article 109, the Council has adopted Regulation (EU) No 2015/1588 on the application of Articles 107 and 108 TFEU to certain categories of horizontal State aid.[106] On this basis, the Commission has adopted the General block exemption Regulation on the compatibility of certain forms of aid with the State aid rules, as well as Regulation (EU) No 2023/2831 on *de minimis* aid.[107] These have a direct effect on national law.

The CJ has also laid down that the standstill obligation in Article 108(3), third paragraph, has a direct effect so that the rights which the provision creates must be protected by the national courts of the Member States.[108] This direct effect of the standstill obligation covers both notified and non-notified aid.[109] A competing undertaking which fulfils national requirements for bringing an action thus has the possibility of getting a national court to assess whether State aid has been paid in breach of the standstill obligation. In this connection, national courts can decide whether a measure should be categorised as State aid within the meaning of Article 107(1) TFEU, and national courts thus have jurisdiction to interpret the concept of State aid.[110] However, the national courts cannot decide whether the State aid measure in question is compatible with the internal market, as the Commission has sole jurisdiction to decide this.[111] In the event of doubt about the categorisation of a measure, a national court can ask the Commission for further information on this or refer the question to the CJ with a request for a preliminary ruling.[112]

If a national court finds that State aid is paid out in breach of the standstill obligation, the court concerned must take all the necessary measures that follow from the disregard for the Treaty provision, including seeking recovery of the aid paid out.[113] A Member State that breaches the standstill obligation may also risk being required to seek recovery of the aid in accordance with the national procedural rules, regardless of whether the Commission may later find that the aid in question is compatible with the internal market. The Commission's decision that a non-notified aid is compatible with the internal market does not mean that implementation measures that are unlawful because they have been taken in breach of the standstill obligation subsequently become lawful.[114] However, a national court does not have a duty to recover all the

---

105. Case 77/72, *Capolongo*, para. 6.
106. Council Regulation (EU) No 2015/1588 on the application of Arts 107 and 108 of the Treaty on the Functioning of the European Union to certain categories of horizontal State aid (OJ 2015 L 248/1).
107. Commission Regulation (EU) No 651/2014 declaring certain categories of aid compatible with the internal market in application of Arts 107 and 108 of the Treaty (the 'General block exemption Regulation') (OJ 2014 L 187/1) (with later amendments); and Commission Regulation (EU) No 2023/2031 on the application of Arts 107 and 108 of the Treaty on the Functioning of the European Union to *de minimis* aid (OJ L, 2023/2831, 15.12.2023).
108. Case 120/73, *Lorenz*, para. 8; with reference to Case 6/64, *Costa/ENEL*.
109. Case 120/73, *Lorenz*, para. 8.
110. Case C-39/94, *SFEI v. La Poste*, para. 49; Case C-143/99, *Adria-Wien Pipeline*, para. 29; and Case C-368/04, *Transalpine Ölleitung*, para. 39. *See also* Commission notice on the enforcement of State aid law by national courts (OJ 2021 C 305/1).
111. *See* Case C-598/17, *A-Fonds*, para. 46.
112. Case C-39/94, *SFEI v. La Poste*, para. 50; and Art. 267 TFEU.
113. Case C-354/90, *FNCE*, para. 12; and Case C-39/94, *SFEI v. La Poste*, para. 40.
114. Case C-368/04, *Transalpine Ölleitung*, para. 59.

unlawful aid if the Commission has taken a final decision on the compatibility of the aid,[115] but it does have a duty to require the aid recipient to pay interest for the period in which there was unlawful aid.[116]

Apart from seeking to have the prohibition of implementation enforced by a national court, a competing undertaking also has the possibility of challenging the administrative act whereby the Member State has granted the disputed aid in accordance with the national administrative procedures. Finally, if a competitor suffers a loss as a result of the damaging effects of the aid on competition, the competitor has the possibility of seeking compensation for such loss.[117]

However, the recipient of aid can try to challenge the Member State's demand for the recovery of unlawful aid by, for example, claiming that it had a legitimate expectation that the aid was lawful or that the aid measures are covered by one of the Commission's block exemption regulations. The recipient of aid also has the possibility of seeking compensation from the Member State for the possible damage that the undertaking suffers from having to repay the aid. However, as mentioned above, in an EU context, compensation for the aid not received will also be considered State aid.[118]

3 THE PROHIBITION OF STATE AID IN ARTICLE 107(1) TFEU

Article 107(1) TFEU states as follows: 'Save as otherwise provided in the Treaties, any aid granted by a Member State or through State resources in any form whatsoever which distorts or threatens to distort competition by favouring certain undertakings or the production of certain goods shall, in so far as it affects trade between Member States, be incompatible with the internal market.'

It follows from this provision that the application of the prohibition of State aid requires a number of conditions to be fulfilled. First, there must be some form of *aid*. Second, this aid must be *granted by a Member State or through State resources* and – according to legal practice – be *imputable* to the State. Third, the aid must *favour certain undertakings or the production of certain goods*, i.e., be *selective* in regard to one or more undertakings. Fourth, the aid must *affect trade* between Member States. Fifth and finally, the aid must be able to *distort competition* within the internal market.

All these conditions must be fulfilled before an aid measure can be characterised as *incompatible State aid* within the terms of the Treaty.[119] The first two conditions are decisive for whether a specific aid measure can be characterised as *State aid*, while the latter two conditions are decisive for whether aid can be characterised as incompatible with the internal market within the context of State aid law. These conditions are intended to prevent the implementation of State aid which is contrary to the aims and principles of the Treaty. Once the incompatibility of State aid with the internal market

---

115. Case C-199/06, *CELF*, paras 45–46.
116. Case C-199/06, *CELF*, para. 52, and Case C-470/20, *AS Veejaam and OÜ Espo*, præmis 58–60.
117. *Michael Honoré & Nanna Eram Jensen:* Damages in State Aid Cases, European State Aid Law Quarterly (2) 2011 pp. 265–286.
118. *See* section 2.7.
119. Case C-345/02, *Pearle*, para. 32.

has been established in principle, it then becomes possible to apply the provisions on exceptions in Article 107(2) and (3) and Article 108(2), third paragraph, so as to approve aid measures which, because of the purposes which they are intended to pursue, are nevertheless found to be compatible with the internal market.

3.1 The Concept of *Aid*

In order to be covered by the prohibition of State aid in Article 107(1) TFEU, the measure of the Member State must involve *aid*. The meaning of this term has been defined several times by the CJ and by the Commission, but without this having led to the establishment of an exhaustive definition. For example, the CJ has defined aid as including measures whereby a Member State independently and unilaterally makes financial means available to undertakings or gives them advantages which are intended to contribute to the implementation and realisation of the economic and social goals of the Member State.[120] In other decisions, aid has been defined as an economic advantage to an undertaking which it would not have obtained under normal market conditions.[121] Even though it is not possible to give an exhaustive definition of the term, the decisions of the CJ and the Commission point to a number of characteristic elements of aid, which indicate whether a state measure involves aid within the meaning of Article 107.

3.1.1 The Effect of Aid

In establishing the scope of application of Article 107(1), the CJ starts from the position that the aim of the provisions on State aid is 'to prevent trade between Member States from being affected by benefits granted by the public authorities which, in various forms, distort or threaten to distort competition by favouring certain undertakings or the production of certain goods.'[122] The realisation of this aim requires the concept of aid to be interpreted sufficiently widely so that all the benefits that fulfil the relevant characteristics are covered by the definition of aid. The CJ has, therefore, stated that aid measures should be defined purely by their effects,[123] while the form in which the aid is given and the aim or intention of giving the aid in question is not important.[124] The decisive factor is thus the financial effect of the benefit on the recipient's competitive position, in other words, whether it gives the recipient an economic advantage which it would not be given under normal competitive conditions and which means that the

---

120. Case 61/79, *Denkavit*, para. 31.
121. Case C-39/94, *SFEI v. La Poste*, para. 60.
122. Case 173/73, *Italy v. Commission*, para. 26, and Case 387/92, *Banco Exterior*, para. 12.
123. However, this is modified in relation to compensation paid for the provision of services of general economic interest – *see* below.
124. Case 173/73, *Italy v. Commission*, para. 27. *See also* Case C-75/97, *Maribel bis/ter*, para. 25; and Case C-81/10 P, *France Télécom*, para. 17.

recipient undertaking's financial position is improved so its competitive position is likewise improved in relation to its competitors.[125]

3.1.2 The Form of the Aid

Regardless of its form, a state measure that gives an undertaking an economic advantage will be covered by the concept of aid.[126] The concept of aid is therefore not limited to aid in the form of normal direct grants but also covers more general forms of aid.[127] This means that all measures which, in one way or another, ease the burdens that are normally imposed on an undertaking's finances and which, without giving a subsidy as normally understood, are nevertheless of the same nature and have a corresponding effect[128] are covered by the aid concept. When assessing an aid measure, it is thus not necessary to distinguish whether, in principle, the aid is given in the form of a direct grant to the undertakings or whether the aid is provided in an indirect form, such as relief from taxes or duties, advantageous terms for loans, or investments in the company's capital, since all these forms of support are covered by the concept of State aid.[129]

For example, it is also not necessary to determine whether the economic advantage is granted to the undertaking by a reduction in investment or in operating costs.[130] However, when assessing whether a State aid can be approved, this distinction can be relevant, as investment support is more widely accepted than support for operation costs.

The broad definition of aid also means that it is not relevant to the assessment of aid, whether the undertaking concerned receives the aid directly or indirectly.[131] Thus the concept of aid first covers the economic advantage which is given to the direct addressee of the aid measure. Second, it covers the economic advantage which, because of the aid measure, is indirectly given to undertakings on the basis of their links with the direct recipient of the aid. For example, an exemption from a tax applied to bio fuels of agricultural origin will be a direct aid for the production of such fuels (to

---

125. When assessing whether an aid measure has a beneficial effect, the starting point is the competitive position that existed in the internal market before the disputed measure was adopted; see Case 173/73, *Italy v. Commission*, para. 36.
126. Joined Cases 106–120/87, *Asteris*, para. 22; and Case C-140/09, *Fallimento* Traghetti, para. 34.
127. Case 30/59, *Steenkolenmijnen*, p. 217, (on the interpretation of the ECSC Treaty); and Case C-387/92, *Banco Exterior*, para. 13.
128. Case C-387/92, *Banco Exterior*, para. 13; Joined Cases T-204 and 270/97, *EPAC*, para. 65, Case C-518/13, *Eventech Ltd*, paras 42ff, Case C-238/20, *Santinis*, and Case C-251/21, *Piltenes Mezi SA*.
129. Case 323/82, *Intermills*, para. 31. As explained immediately below, the terms *direct* and *indirect* aid are used both in respect of the form in which the aid is provided and the recipient of the aid.
130. Case 173/73, *Italy v. Commission*, which concerned the reduction of the textile industry's payments for social benefits.
131. *See, e.g.*, Commission Decision of 7 May 2016 in Case SA.42680, *France*, and Commission Decision of 19 Sep. 2019 in Case SA.53520, *Greece*. However, whether or not the aid is directly addressed to an undertaking can be relevant in determining whether unlawful aid will be sought to be recovered; *see, e.g.*, Commission Decision 97/542/EC, *Biofuels* (OJ 1997 L 222/26).

the producer), as well as an indirect aid for the production of the materials from which the bio fuels are produced (the suppliers).[132]

Finally, the particular legal basis for giving the aid is irrelevant. The prohibition of State aid in Article 107(1) TFEU covers, for example, aid provided on the basis of an administrative decision, aid provided on the basis of an agreement, and aid such as a tax advantage provided by legislation.

3.1.3   The Purpose of the Aid

The specific purpose for which a Member State provides aid is not a factor which can place a measure outside the scope of Article 107 TFEU. In Case 173/73, *Italy v. Commission*, the CJ stated that Article 107 does not distinguish between measures of state intervention by reference to their causes or aims but, as stated above, defines them in relation to their effects.[133] In this case, this meant that neither the possible fiscal nature of the disputed measure nor its social purposes were sufficient to put it outside the scope of the prohibition of State aid.[134]

However, the aim of an aid measure is relevant when assessing whether the exemptions in Article 107(2) and (3) can apply. When assessing whether an aid measure can be approved as being compatible with the internal market, an assessment is made of whether the negative effects of the measure can be counterbalanced by its furtherance of one of the other goals of the EU. In making an assessment under Article 107(1) of whether a measure involves aid, a clear distinction is made between, on the one hand, the measure's financial and competitive effects and, on the other hand, the purpose for which the aid is given.[135] The opposite approach would mean that the Member States could attempt to avoid the prohibition of State aid by claiming various praiseworthy purposes. In practice, the aim of an aid measure can, however, be included where the assessment of selectivity requires the establishment of a reference framework.[136]

3.1.4   The Intentions of the Parties

The assessment of the aid is made independently of whether, subjectively, the parties intend either to give or to receive State aid.

---

132. Commission Decision 97/542/EC, *Biofuels* (OJ 1997 L 222/26).
133. Case 173/73, *Italy v. Commission*, para. 26; and the similar Case 78/76, *Steinike & Weinlig*, para. 21; and Case C-81/10 P, *France Télécom*, para. 17.
134. Case 173/73, *Italy v. Commission*, para. 28. *See also* Case C-241/94, *France v. Commission*, para. 21.
135. However, payment for carrying out services of general economic interest is subject to a special test; *see* the discussion of the *Altmark* case below in the section on Compensation.
136. An assessment of whether an aid scheme is selective will thus often be based on whether the aid measure constitutes an exemption from the normal scheme by discriminating between the market actors, who in regard to the objective pursued by the normal scheme are in a comparable factual and legal situation. *See, e.g.,* Joined Cases C-885/19 P and C-898/19 P, *Fiat*, para. 67, and further in section 3.3.

In the Commission Decision 92/11/EC, Toyota, the Commission fully accepted that the United Kingdom Government did not intend aid to be given to Toyota in connection with the transfer of a site, and that there was no evidence to suggest that Toyota requested State aid or intended to benefit directly or indirectly from State aid through the terms of transfer of the site. However, the Commission did not attach importance to the subjective intentions of the parties, but considered it crucial whether the terms and condition for the transfer of the site were contrary to normal business practice to such an extent that the transfer could be assumed to be State aid for the benefit of Toyota.[137] In this connection the Commission considered that the difference of GBP 4.2 million between the sales price and the market price constituted incompatible State aid within the meaning of Article 107(1).

The existence of an advantage must be determined objectively and without regard to the reasons of the originator of the aid measures for giving the aid. Thus, the nature of the purpose of aid measures and their justification is not decisive for determining whether they constitute State aid, and such measures must only be defined according to their effects, without distinction as to their aims or reasons.[138]

3.1.5 *Economic Advantages*

As shown by the Commission's decision in the *Toyota* case[139] and confirmed by the CJ in, among others, Case C-39/94, *SFEI v. La Poste*, what is crucial for the assessment of an aid measure is whether or not the undertaking to which the aid measure is addressed obtains an economic advantage[140] which it would not have obtained under normal market conditions.[141] Aid measures are characterised by benefiting the recipient by giving a unilateral economic advantage. Such an economic advantage can be given, regardless of whether it corresponds to the actual cost to the state, and it is not relevant whether the recipient's position becomes better or worse or is unchanged in relation to the situation which existed before the implementation of the aid measure.[142] What matters is only whether the aid measure in question, taken in isolation, benefits

---

137. *See* Part V of Commission Decision 92/11/EC, *Toyota* (OJ 1992, L 6/36).
138. Case C-81/10 P, *France Télécom*, para. 17.
139. Commission Decision 92/11/EC, *Toyota* (OJ 1992, L 6/36).
140. Whether the recovery of an economic benefit should be calculated according to its nominal or actual value was considered in Joined Cases C-164/15 P and C-165/15, *Aer Lingus & Ryanair*, according to which the Commission at the time of recovery must ensure that the actual economic benefit is recovered. For further details *see* para. 92.
141. Case C-39/94, *SFEI v. La Poste*, para. 60; Joined Cases T-204 and 270/97, *EPAC*, para. 66; and Case C-140/09, *Fallimento Traghetti*, para. 34.
142. Case C-143/99, *Adria-Wien Pipeline*, para. 41; and Case 57/86, *Greece v. Commission*, para. 10. *See, e.g.*, the Commission's decision in the Danish CO2 case, XXIIth Report on competition policy, 1993, para. 451, and Commission Decision 92/411/ECSC (OJ 1992 L 223/28).

some undertakings rather than other undertakings which, with regard to the purpose of the measure in question, are in a corresponding factual or legal situation.[143]

If the recipient provides remuneration, this does not necessarily eliminate the beneficial element of the measure.[144] Where aid is given for remuneration which does not correspond to the value of the aid but is insufficient or merely symbolic, the aid measure will still be characterised as unilateral. The same is the case if the nature of the consideration differs from what is usually given in a business transaction on normal market terms. For example, if the aid is given on condition that the undertaking carries out some restructuring,[145] create jobs, or reduce production capacity with the aim of realising the Member State's social and economic goals,[146] such remuneration will not be typical in relation to what is normal under market conditions and will not, of itself, place the aid outside the scope of Article 107.

3.1.6 Variance from Normal Market Conditions

When assessing whether an undertaking receives a financial benefit which is covered by the definition of a State aid, it is decisive whether the benefit received is more than the undertaking could expect to receive under normal market conditions. In this connection, it is necessary to establish what the normal conditions would be for the service in question. The answer to this depends on an economic analysis 'taking into account all the factors which an undertaking acting under normal market conditions should have taken into consideration when fixing the remuneration for the services provided'.[147]

> In Case C-39/94, *SFEI v. La Poste*, the Commission considered that the cross-subsidies resulting from the provision of logistical and commercial assistance by a public undertaking to its subsidiaries, which are governed by private law and carry on an activity open to free competition, were capable of constituting State aid, provided that remuneration for the services was less than that which would have been demanded under normal market conditions.[148]

The assessment of whether an undertaking is given a unilateral advantage, and whether this advantage varies from normal market terms, is decided in accordance

---

143. Case C-143/99, *Adria-Wien Pipeline*, para. 41; Case C-88/03, *The Azores*, paras 54 and 56; Case C-106/09 P & 107/09 P, *Gibraltar*, para. 75, and Joined Cases C-885/19 P and C-898/19 P, *Fiat*, para. 67.
144. There is no requirement that the benefit should be given completely free or without the payment of a fee. *See, e.g.*, Case C-353/95 P, *Ladbroke SA*.
145. Case 323/82, *Intermills*, where in return the undertaking was obliged to switch to a specific type of production.
146. Case 61/79, *Denkavit*, para. 31.
147. Case C-39/94, *SFEI v. La Poste*, para. 61.
148. Case C-39/94, *SFEI v. La Poste*, para. 62. *See* Joined Cases C-83/01, P. C-93/01 P and C-94/01 P, *Chronopost*, paras 31ff., and the abovementioned Commission Decision 92/11/EC, *Toyota* (OJ 1992, L 6/36).

with the *market economy operator principle*.[149] According to this principle, a measure does not constitute aid as long as the terms on which the public authority provides resources to an undertaking would be acceptable to a private investor/actor under the conditions of the normal market economy.[150] This assessment is made with reference to a private operator who, from a strategic investment perspective, is as close as possible to that of the State.[151] The market economy operator principle is of particular importance in relation to financial transactions between the state and public undertakings (and between public undertakings themselves).[152] For example, such transactions may occur where a state participates in the financing of a public undertaking which provides financial support for a subsidiary which is in difficulties or otherwise deals with a public undertaking.

In this context, the market economy operator principle can be used to distinguish between aid measures and transactions that are carried out on the normal terms of the market economy, as well as to quantify the amount of aid given.[153]

3.1.7 Measures That Do Not Normally Constitute Aid

3.1.7.1 Repayment of Unduly Levied Charges

According to the practice of the CJ, a Member State's repayment of a charge to an undertaking will not constitute State aid in all cases. This applies if the Member State has been required to repay a charge which has been collected and found to be contrary to Union law and which the taxpayer was, therefore, not required to pay.[154]

Such unduly levied charges must be repaid in accordance with the national law of the Member State.[155] In this connection, there is no requirement for the Member States to take into account whether the taxpayer has suffered a loss as a result of the tax obligation. However, the CJ does not regard it as incompatible with the Treaty if, under national law, it is possible to take account of the fact that it has been possible for the charges unduly levied to be incorporated in the prices of the undertaking liable for the

---

149. *See* Joined Cases C-533/12 and C-536/12 P, *Corsica Ferries*. *See also* Case T-613/97, *Ufex*, both the judgment of 14 Dec. 2000 and the judgment of 7 Jun. 2006, which concerned logistical and commercial support given by a public undertaking which provides services of general economic interest within the postal sector to a subsidiary which did not carry on business in an area reserved to a monopoly but rather in an area where there was competition. *See also* Case C-305/89, *Alfa Romeo*; and Case C-303/88, *ENI-Lanerossi*, Case T-747/15, *EDF*, and Case C-579/16 P, *FIH Holding A7S and FIH Erhvervsbank*.
150. *See* Commission Notice on the notion of State aid (OJ 2016 C 262/1), point 4.2.
151. *See* further in Case C-244/18 P, *Larko*, para. 28.
152. In certain circumstances public undertakings are regarded as being part of the state, and can thereby risk giving aid which is covered by the prohibition of State aid in Art. 107(1) TFEU; *see* below in section 3.2. *See*, *e.g.*, Case C-39/94, *SFEI v. La Poste*.
153. For a further discussion of the market economy operator principle, *see* various articles in *European State aid law Quarterly*.
154. Case 61/79, *Denkavit*, para. 32.
155. Case 68/79, *Just*, paras 25 and 27.

charge and to be passed on to the purchasers.[156] Depending on the formulation of the national law, the taxpayer could demand that the charge paid in breach of the Treaty should be refunded, without regard for whether the taxpayer has suffered loss or has been able to pass on the burden to other undertakings or consumers, and thus without regard for whether the undertaking receives an economic advantage by the tax refund. Such an economic advantage is not covered by the prohibition on State aid which may seem inappropriate if, because of the framing of the tax provisions, some undertakings are favoured more than others.

3.1.7.2 Damages

The CJ has also considered whether a Member State's payment of compensation is permitted under the provisions on State aid. In its preliminary ruling in Joined Cases 106–120/87, *Asteris*, the CJ held that State aid is fundamentally different in its legal nature from damages which Member States may be ordered to pay to individuals in compensation for the damage they have caused to those individuals.[157] The aim of such compensation is in part to compensate the injured party for the losses caused, and in part to restore the injured party to the position it was in prior to the occurrence of the action which incurred liability. Thus, the injured party is not given any economic advantage, and the compensation is not covered by Article 107(1).[158]

However, in certain circumstances, compensation paid by a Member State can be covered by Article 107(1). This will be the case where the Member State gives an undertaking compensation for the loss of an economic advantage or right which in itself constitutes State aid.[159]

> This problem arose in Commission Decision 96/434/EC. The case concerned an Italian law which gave the state authority to provide financial help to undertakings whose insolvency had arisen from the obligation to repay aid which the Commission or the CJ had found to be in breach of Articles 107 and 108 TFEU. The provisions of the law did not necessarily lead to the transfer of new state resources to the recipients, but it did mean that undertakings that had an obligation to repay incompatible aid could retain the advantages from the aid and avoid the repayment of the benefits they had obtained, contrary to EU law.[160] The law thus had the effect that there was not full implementation of the decisions of the Commission and CJ on the recovery of incompatible aid, and the unlawful advantages which

---

156. Case 68/79, *Just*, para. 26. In regard to the recovery of State aid and the possibility of passing-on the advantage that follows from receiving State aid, *see* Joined cases C-164/15 P and C-165/15, *Aer Lingus & Ryanair*, and T-500/12, *Ryanair*.
157. Joined Cases 106–120/87, *Asteris*, para. 23.
158. Joined Cases 106–120/87, *Asteris*, para. 24. On compensation in connection with expropriation, *see* Case T-53/08 *Italy v. Commission*; and Case T-62/08, *Termi v. Commission*.
159. Commission Decision 96/434/EC (OJ 1996 L 180/31).
160. Commission Decision 96/434/EC, part VI (OJ 1996 L 180/31).

the decisions were intended to annul were perpetuated.[161] The Commission therefore found that the provisions of the law were contrary to the Treaty provisions on State aid.

In cases where an undertaking receives damages from a Member State on the grounds of a legitimate expectation of receiving State aid based on national law which the Commission has found to be incompatible with the internal market and which must therefore be repaid, the corresponding arguments apply. A Member State's payment of damages in this situation will constitute State aid.[162] This is the case regardless of whether the payment is made voluntarily or it is made on the basis of a judgment of a national court of the Member State concerned.

3.1.7.3 Compensation

To a certain extent, both private and public undertakings can provide services in the common interest. This is on the basis of agreements or obligations laid down in law to provide certain services, for example, in the fields of radio and television broadcasting, transport, telecommunications, postal services, pharmacies, energy supply, etc.[163]

In connection with the transfer of the provision of such services, Member States often grant undertakings which provide these services special or exclusive rights, and in certain cases these undertakings receive financial support to cover the additional costs incurred by carrying out the obligations.

In Case C-53/00, *Ferring SA*, the CJ laid down that compensation paid to undertakings for the provision of services of general economic interest does not constitute aid within the meaning of Article 107(1) TFEU.[164] Such compensation is in the nature of a charge paid to the undertaking for the provision of the service in question.

Nevertheless, this requires that the conditions laid down by the CJ in Case C-280/00, *Altmark*, are fulfilled.[165] The *Altmark* case thus establishes that compensation paid to undertakings for the provision of services of general economic interest does not constitute aid within the meaning of Article 107(1) if: (1) the recipient undertaking does actually have public service obligations to discharge, and the obligations are clearly defined; (2) the compensation is calculated on the basis of criteria which are

---

161. Commission Decision 96/434/EC, part IV (OJ 1996 L 180/31).
162. *See, e.g.*, the case of *Spar Nord*, Skat Udland, 1995 p. 68, which did not constitute incompatible State aid, however, because of the lack of effect on trade.
163. Several of these sectors are now liberalised in whole or in part, and these are discussed in Chapter 11.
164. Case C-53/00, *Ferring SA*, para. 27. However, the GC has considered such compensation to be State aid within the meaning of Art. 107(1) TFEU in among others, Case T-106/95, *FFSA*, paras 178 and 199; and Case T-46/97, *SIC*, para. 84.
165. Case C-280/00, *Altmark*, paras 89–93. For a discussion of this decision and its implications for the law of State aid, public procurement and economic advantage, *see* various articles in *European State aid Law Quarterly*; and, e.g., Erika Szyszczak & Johan Willem van de Gronden (eds): Financing Services of General Economic Interest, 2013.

established in advance in an objective and transparent manner; (3) the compensation does not exceed what is necessary to cover all or part of the costs incurred in the discharge of public service obligations;[166] and finally (4) when the selection of an undertaking for the provision of public services is not carried out pursuant to a public procurement procedure[167] – which allows for the selection of the tenderer capable of providing the services in question at the least cost to society – the level of compensation must be determined on the basis of an analysis of the costs which a typical undertaking would incur in discharging the obligations.

According to the decision of the CJ, a measure of a Member State which fails to comply with one or more of these conditions is considered to be State aid within the meaning of Article 107(1).[168] Thus, in relation to services of general economic interest, it is not the economic effect of the aid which is decisive to the assessment of the aid, but compliance with these four criteria. For example, aid will be considered to be present in cases where the compensation is not calculated on the basis of criteria that are established in advance in an objective and transparent manner, regardless of whether the undertaking in fact receives an economic advantage.

In cases where compensation for the performance of services of general economic interest is regarded as aid covered by Article 107(1), it may be possible for the aid to be exempted from the prohibition of State aid by the application of the special provision in Article 106(2) TFEU.[169] This provision allows for exemption from the application of the provisions prohibiting State aid in relation to undertakings entrusted with the operation of services of general economic interest. However, this only applies in so far as the application of such rules does not obstruct the performance, in law or in fact, of the particular tasks assigned to them, and the development of trade must not be affected to such an extent as would be contrary to the interests of the EU.[170]

---

166. Case T-106/95, *FFSA*, para. 178; Case C-174/97 P, *FFSA*, para. 6; and Case C-53/00, *Ferring SA*, para. 27.
167. Compliance with the public procurement rules does not in itself exclude State aid, *see, e.g.*, Joined Cases T-37/15 and T-38/15, *Abertis Telecom Terrestre and Telecom Castilla-La Mancha*, paras 73–76 and 139–141.
168. Case C-280/00, *Altmark*, para. 94. The Altmark-test is used in a number of judgments – *see, e.g.*, Joined Cases T-231/06 and T-237/06 *Netherlands and NOS*, Case C-660/15 P, *Visat Broadcasting Ltd*, and Case C-586/18 P, *Buonotourist SRL*.
169. For more on this provision *see* Chapter 10.
170. The approach of the Commission to the application of Art. 107 and Art. 106(2) in relation to the prohibition of State aid is set out in Communication from the Commission on the application of the European Union State aid rules to compensation granted for the provision of services of general economic interest (OJ 2012 C 8/4); Communication from the Commission – European Union framework for State aid in the form of public service compensation (2011) (OJ 2012 C 8/15); Commission Decision 2012/21/EU of 20 Dec. 2011 on the application of Art. 106(2) of the Treaty on the Functioning of the European Union to State aid in the form of public service compensation granted to certain undertakings entrusted with the operation of services of general economic interest (OJ 2012 L 7/3); and Commission Regulation (EU) No 2023/2832 on the application of Arts 107 and 108 of the Treaty on the Functioning of the European Union to *de minimis* aid granted to undertakings providing services of general economic interest (OJ L, 2023/2832, 15.12.2023).

3.2 Aid Granted by a Member State or Through State Resources

Article 107(1) only covers *aid granted by a Member State or through State resources*. According to the wording of the Article, these two criteria could appear to be alternative conditions. Nevertheless, according to the practice of the CJ, the application of Article 107(1) requires both criteria to be fulfilled. This means that aid must both be the consequence of the actions of a state and be financed from the state's resources.[171] Both of these conditions are interpreted broadly. As will be seen in the following, in certain circumstances, private bodies can be considered part of the state, and in certain circumstances, private resources will be covered by the concept of State aid.

In addition to what seems to be directly covered by the terms, *state* and *state resources*, it is also important for compliance with the rules that a public authority de jure or de facto hold *control* over a given *entity*, that the applied *aid* is constantly under the *control* of the public authorities and thus is available for the competent national authorities,[172] and that the aid is *imputable* to the relevant public authorities.[173]

3.2.1 The State and State Resources

3.2.1.1 The Central Organs of the State and Other Public Authorities

The prohibition of State aid in Article 107(1) covers both aid provided by the central organs of the state and aid provided by the regional or local authorities of the state. In Case 248/84, *Germany v. Commission*, the CJ thus rules that the prohibition covers aid which is granted by regional and local bodies of the Member States, whatever their status and description, and must be scrutinised to determine whether it complies with Article 107 TFEU.[174]

In this context, the concept of *state resources* should be understood in such a way that resources coming from the state treasury, as well as public resources in a broad sense, such as resources from regional or local authorities, can be used to finance incompatible aid.

The financing of State aid can be on the basis of a direct grant from the state, or in the form of an actual or potential reduction in the income of the authority which provides the aid. However, the applicability of Article 107(1) does not seem to be

---

171. Case C-379/98, *PreussenElektra*, para. 58.
172. *See, e.g.*, Case T-47/15, *Germany v. Commission*, and Case C-405/16 P, *Germany v. Commission*.
173. Cf. Case C-345/02, *Pearle*, para. 35, and Case C-482/99, *Stardust Marine*, paras 52–58. *See also* Case C-329/15, *ENEA*.
174. Case 248/84, *Germany v. Commission*, para. 17. See correspondingly Case T-358/94, *Air France*, para. 56. *See also* Case C-518/13, *Eventech* (London Black Cabs), where it was found that State resources were not used; *see* para. 41: 'the fact that Black Cabs are not obliged to pay fines because of their use of bus lanes does not involve additional burdens on the public authorities which might entail a commitment of State resources'. *See also* Joined Cases C-508/21 P and C-509/21 P, *Commission v. Dansk Erhverv*, regarding the question of whether the failure to impose fines on border shops for their non-charging of a deposit on certain drinks packaging may constitute State aid.

conditional on the aid imposing a financial burden on the state.[175] Thus, for example, a guarantee by the state will be a potential financial burden on the state, but it will only be an actual burden if the guarantee is called upon.[176] Nor is it decisive for the evaluation of State aid whether the state resources used come from the general state budget, from specially targeted taxes, or from contributions that are provided for by the act of an authority.[177]

3.2.1.2 Public and Private Bodies Established or Appointed by the State to Administer Aid

In Case 78/76, *Steinike & Weinlig*, the CJ stated that the prohibition in Article 107(1) covers 'all aid granted by a member state or through state resources without its being necessary to make a distinction whether the aid is granted directly by the state or by public or private bodies established or appointed by it to administer the aid.'[178] Such public or private bodies are thereby regarded as being a part of the state in the context of the law on State aid.

The resources of the public or private bodies concerned will be considered state resources within the meaning of Article 107(1). For example, specially targeted taxes which are collected at the request of the state and paid into a fund which is then used for financing aid will be considered State aid covered by Article 107(1).[179]

3.2.1.3 Private and Public Bodies Subject to State Control

The application of the provisions of Article 107(1) in cases where aid is provided by public or private bodies which have not been established or appointed by the state to administer the aid depends on whether the state has a de jure or de facto degree of control over or influence on the body concerned and the decision to provide aid, which is sufficient in order to regard the body as part of the state and the resources as state resources. In this context, it must be shown that an aid-giving body could not have taken its decision to provide aid without having regard for the public authorities. Consequently, the aid has to be regarded as imputable to the State.[180]

> There is an example of this in Joined Cases 67, 68 and 70/85, *van der Kooy v. Commission*, where the CJ stated that the undertaking Gasunie in no way enjoyed full autonomy in the fixing of gas tariffs, but acted under the control

---

175. Case 57/86, *Greece v. Commission*, para. 12. However, see Case 82/77, *van Tiggele*, para. 52.
176. For more on state guarantees and their compliance with the regulation of State aid, see Commission Notice on the application of Arts 87 and 88 of the EC Treaty to State aid in the form of guarantees (OJ 2008 C 155/10), and the Corrigendum to it (OJ 2008 C 244/32). (Please be aware that the guarantee notice is currently under revision).
177. Case 47/69, *France v. Commission;* and Case 1873/73, *Italy v. Commission*.
178. Case 78/76, *Steinike & Weinlig*, para. 21; Case C-305/89, *Alfa Romeo*, para. 13; and Case C-345/02, *Pearle*, para. 34.
179. Case 173/73, *Italy v. Commission;* and Case 259/85, *France v. Commission*.
180. Case C-126/01, *GEMO*, para. 24; Case C-345/02, *Pearle*, para. 35; and Case C-279/08 P, *NOx*, para. 103.

of and on the instructions of the public authorities, so it was clear that it could not fix the tariff without taking account of the requirements of the public authorities.[181] This finding was sufficient to conclude that the establishment of the disputed tariff was the result of the conduct of the Dutch state, and was thus covered by Article 107(1).[182]

An undertaking or a body is considered public and can thus be part of the state within the meaning of Article 107(1) if the state directly or indirectly exercises dominant influence over it as a result of legal or actual control.[183]

Where the state exercises either de jure or de facto control over a public or private body, it is not necessary to distinguish whether the aid given is financed by public resources or from the body's own private resources. In this context, the resources are regarded as being state resources for the purposes of Article 107(1) – regardless of their origin.[184]

In Case C-482/99, *Stardust Marine*, the CJ thus stated that Article 107(1):

> covers all the financial means by which the public authorities may actually support undertakings, irrespective of whether or not those means are permanent assets of the public sector. Therefore, even if the sums corresponding to the measure in question are not permanently held by the Treasury, the fact that they constantly remain under public control, and therefore available to the competent national authorities, is sufficient for them to be categorised as State resources.[185]

However, this does not mean that all financial transactions of public undertakings in principle may involve State aid subject to Article 107(1). The provision of aid by public undertakings will only be covered by Article 107(1) if the aid is considered imputable to the state. The state must, therefore, have exercised its control in fact, for example, by taking the initiative for the implementation of the aid measures or by otherwise being involved in its implementation.

The fact that a measure is decided by a public undertaking which is subject to public control is thus not in itself enough for the aid measure in question to be regarded as imputable to the state. In determining whether the aid is imputable to the state, it is necessary to make a more detailed examination of whether the public authorities can, by one means or another, be considered involved in the adoption of the measure in question.[186]

---

181. Joined Cases 67, 68 and 70/85, *van der Kooy v. Commission*, para. 37. *See also* Case C-44/93, *Namur*, para. 31; and Case C-345/02, *Pearle*, para. 35.
182. Joined Cases 67, 68 and 70/85, *van der Kooy v. Commission*, para. 38.
183. With regard to undertakings, the definition of scope in the Transparency Directive can serve as an inspiration for the definition of a public undertaking in the context of State aid; *see* Directive 2006/111/EC on the transparency of financial relations between Member States and public undertakings as well as on financial transparency within certain undertakings, Art. 2(b) (OJ 2006 L 318/17).
184. Joined Cases 67, 68 and 70/85, *van der Kooy v. Commission*, where Gasunie and the state each financed half of the aid resources. In spite of this, the whole amount was considered being covered by Art. 107(1).
185. Case C-482/99, *Stardust Marine*, para. 37.
186. Case C-482/99, *Stardust Marine*, paras 51 and 52. *See, e.g.,* the CJ's assessment in Case C-345/02, *Pearle*, paras 35–39.

The broad interpretation of the concept of State aid prevents Member States from getting round the application of Article 107(1) by channelling their aid through a state-controlled undertaking or fund, for example, by requiring the state undertaking to invest in an undertaking which a private investor/actor would not have invested in on the basis of normal commercial considerations.[187]

However, the problem of State aid not only arises when the State aid is channelled to other undertakings via a public undertaking[188] but also where resources are transferred internally in a public undertaking from an activity in an area which is not subject to competition to a competitive area. For example, there was such cross-subsidisation in Case C-39/94, *SFEI v. La Poste*, where part of the French state's payment to the French postal service for the conduct of the postal monopoly was used as a cross-subsidy to part of the undertaking's activities which lay outside the scope of the monopoly.[189]

3.2.2 European Union Resources

The European Union has established a number of structural funds and aid programmes which provide financial support to undertakings in the Member States with a view to promoting specially chosen aims.[190]

Where undertakings receive such aid directly from the EU, the aid is not covered by the prohibition of State aid in Articles 107–109 TFEU. The basis for this is that the EU institutions are not regarded as part of the state, and the EU's resources are not considered to be state resources within the meaning of Article 107(1).[191]

In certain cases, aid resources from the EU's aid programmes will be paid to the Member States with a view to the Member States being responsible for the administration and payment of EU aid. Such financial aid, which is wholly financed by the EU's aid programmes but which is in fact paid to the undertakings by the Member States themselves, will not, in principle, be covered by Article 107(1). However, such aid is likely to be regarded as Member State resources provided the payment of aid from the EU's aid programmes allows the Member States a certain measure of discretion with regard to the distribution of the aid.[192]

In other cases, there is an obligation for Member States to co-finance projects, etc., in order to be able to attract EU aid payments. The requirement for such

---

187. Case C-305/89, *Alfa Romeo*.
188. Case C-305/89, *Alfa Romeo*, where it could not be characterised as normal commercial conduct that a state owned public undertaking invested in a financially weakened subsidiary.
189. On cross-subsidies between a reserved (non-competitive area) and an area subject to free competition, *see also* Case T-613/97, *Ufex*, paras 68–76.
190. For example, undertakings can obtain support from the European Social Fund Plus, European Regional Development Fund, the European Agricultural Guidance and Guarantee Fund and the European Agricultural Fund for Rural Development, the European Maritime, Fisheries and Aquaculture Fund, or from the Just Transition Fund.
191. *See* Joined Cases 213–215/81, *BALM*, para. 22.
192. However, *see* the Opinion of Advocate General VerLoren van Themaat in Joined Cases 213–215/81, *BALM*, from which it was stated that in case where the Member States are given some discretion in relation to the allocation of EU resources, this can lead to favouring an undertaking within the meaning of Art. 107(1). *See also* Commission Decision of 22 Nov. 2006 in Case N 157/06, *UK Broadband*, points 21 and 29.

co-financing follows directly from Union legislation, and since the Member States have no choice but to provide the co-financing, the aid payments are in principle not imputable to the Member State and the aid is thus not covered by the Treaty provisions on State aid.[193]

If a Member State voluntarily combines means from the EU's aid programmes with its own means, the State aid rules must naturally be complied with.

3.2.3 Private Resources

The prohibition of State aid in Article 107(1) TFEU presumes that a given amount of aid is given by the state and is financed from state resources. This means that aid given by private bodies or by public bodies that is financed by a body's private resources and is provided without state intervention, for example, the award of scholarships by a private trust fund or a private parent company giving support to a financially weakened subsidiary, is not covered by Article 107(1).[194]

However, on the basis of the above, it may be presumed that aid financed out of private resources that is given by a private or public body will fall within the scope of the prohibition of State aid in the following situations: first, where the body in question has been established or appointed by the state to administer aid;[195] second, where it can be shown that the aid is imputable to the state;[196] and third, where the resources for the aid result from obligatory contributions required by law (as explained in the following section).

In these cases, it is considered that State aid is provided by the state through state resources within the meaning of Article 107(1), without it being necessary to determine whether the resources are derived from private or public means.

> Case 290/83, *CNCA*, concerned a public agricultural credit fund, *Caisse nationale de crédit agricole* (CNCA). CNCA had decided to give a 'solidarity grant' of FRF 1.5 billion to those French farmers who were worst off. This aid was to be financed from the operating profit which CNCA had accumulated in the previous years. In this connection, the CJ held that aid which, like the solidarity grant concerned, was agreed and financed by a public

---

193. See Case C-460/07, *Puffer*, paras 69 and 70.
194. For example, State resources were not involved in Case C-379/98, *PreussenElektra* (see section 3.2.4 below) or in Case T-674/11, *TV2*, concerning advertising revenues that were derived from private resources that were not subject to public control.
195. Case 78/76, *Steinike & Weinlig*, para. 21; it is not necessary to distinguish between aid given by such a body and aid given by the state.
196. Case C-482/99, *Stardust Marine;* and Case C-342/02, *Pearle. See, e.g.*, Commission Decision 82/73/EEC, *Gasunie* (OJ 1982 L 37/29); and the later Joined Cases 67, 68 and 70/85, *van der Kooy*, where the CJ did not find that it was necessary in order for Art. 107(1) to apply that there should be a requirement that aid from a private body should be financed via public resources, if the resources in question had been allocated as a consequence of an act of the state; *see* para. 37.

body and which could only be implemented with official approval, is covered by Article 107(1).[197]

3.2.4 Aid Provided on the Basis of the Legislation of a Member State

It is also possible that undertakings may receive an economic advantage on the basis of Member State legislation in circumstances other than those referred to in the preceding section. However, Article 107(1) does not apply if undertakings receive such an advantage without state resources being directly or indirectly involved.[198] However, in certain circumstances, the national provisions will involve a transfer of state resources from a body which falls within the definition of a state body, with the consequence that the measure may be brought within the scope of application of Article 107(1). Examples are given below of situations which have been referred to the CJ on whether the legislation in a Member State involves State aid subject to Article 107(1).

3.2.4.1 Taxes

The revenues which a state obtains on the basis of obligatory taxes which are imposed on undertakings and private individuals are considered to be state resources for the purposes of Article 107(1). This also applies where tax is paid directly to a publicly controlled fund, where the resources cannot be said to come directly from the state treasury.[199] Such resources could, therefore, be used to provide State aid in breach of Article 107(1) TFEU.[200]

An aid measure does not lose the character of a gratuitous advantage by the fact that it is wholly or partially financed by contributions imposed by the public authority and levied on the undertakings which receive the aid so that the contributions made correspond to the advantages which the undertakings receive from the aid.[201]

If a public or private body provides aid which is exclusively financed by voluntary contributions from private undertakings or persons, this aid will not be

---

197. Case 290/83, *CNCA*, para. 15. *See also* Case T-358/94, *Air France*, where the GC regarded aid which was financed by voluntary contributions by private investors who could, at any time, demand payment, as State aid.
198. Case C-379/98, *PreussenElektra*, para. 58.
199. Case 173/73, *Italy v. Commission*, para. 16, concerning a partial reduction of the social burdens of the textile industry. In this cases the CJ stated: 'As the funds in question are financed through compulsory contributions imposed by state legislation and as, as this case shows, they are managed and apportioned in accordance with the provisions of that legislation, they must be regarded as state resources within the meaning of Article 92 [now Art. 107], even if they are administered by institutions distinct from the public authorities.' *See also* Case 259/85, *France v. Commission*, which concerned aid to the French textile industry financed via tax-like duties collected on every delivery of domestically produced textile goods and Case C-333/07, *Regie Networks*.
200. Case C-126/01, *GEMO*; Case 259/85, *France v. Commission*; Joined Cases 67, 68 and 70/85, *van der Kooy*; and Joined Cases C-78–83/90, *Compagnie commerciale de l'Ouest*, para. 35.
201. Case 78/76, *Steinike & Weinlig*, para. 22.

covered by Article 107(1).[202] Where the Commission has required an aid measure to be terminated, and the measure has been continued by national employers' organisations using means which undertakings have provided 'voluntarily' through a national insurance scheme, the Commission found that this was indirect aid.[203]

> In Case 290/83, *CNCA*, voluntary payments to a state-controlled fund, which were thereafter given to undertakings, were also regarded as State aid covered by Article 107(1). However, in this case it was decisive to the assessment of the aid that the state controlled the use of the resources so the resources could be considered as state resources for the purpose of Article 107(1).

3.2.4.2 Social Regulation

In several cases, the CJ has had occasion to assess the compatibility of national social provisions with the rules on State aid, and on these occasions, it has shown itself reluctant to characterise the easing of social burdens as State aid.

> In Joined Cases C-72 and 83/91, *Sloman Neptun*, the CJ considered a German arrangement for merchant vessels which were entered in the German international shipping register. The arrangement allowed seafarers who were citizens of a third country and who had neither permanent abode nor residence in Germany not to be covered by German collective employment agreements, and to be subject to working conditions and rates of pay which were considerably less favourable than those applicable to German seafarers. In this way the arrangement made it possible for German shipping companies to reduce their costs for wages and social contributions, while the German state lost tax revenue.
>
> The CJ examined whether this arrangement involved giving advantages which could be considered to be aid given through state resources.[204] The CJ ruled that the arrangement did not constitute State aid within the meaning of Article 107(1), as neither by its purpose nor its general scheme was the arrangement intended to create an advantage for the shipping companies which could be an additional burden for the state. The arrangement only involved a change, to the advantage of the ship owners, of the framework which applied to contracts between the undertakings and their employees. The CJ found that the consequences of the arrangement in relation to the calculation of social contributions, and the loss of tax revenue because of the lower wages, were inseparable from the arrangement and

---

202. *See* Marco M. Slotboom: State Aid in Community Law: A Broad or Narrow Definition?, European Law Review 1995 pp. 289-301, at p. 296, note 57, which refers to the Commission's decision in the Milchföderungsfonds case (OJ 1985 L 35/35). However, such measures can be covered by Art. 101 TFEU.
203. Xth Report on competition policy, 1981 paras 163 and 220.
204. Joined Cases C-72 and 73/91, *Sloman Neptun*, para. 20.

were therefore not a means for providing the undertakings concerned with a particular advantage.[205] On this basis the CJ concluded that the arrangement did not constitute State aid within the meaning of Article 107(1).[206]

3.2.4.3   Protection of Employees

In Case C-189/91, *Kirsammer-Hack*, the CJ considered whether the prohibition of State aid applied to a law excluding small businesses from a national system of protection of workers against unfair dismissal. In the event of socially unjustified dismissals, small businesses were not obliged to pay compensation or to bear the legal expenses incurred in proceedings concerning the dismissal of workers.

The CJ held that the exclusion of small businesses from the protection system in question did not entail any direct or indirect transfer of state resources to those businesses.[207] The arrangement only established a special legal framework for working relationships between employers and employees in small businesses and avoided imposing financial burdens on those businesses which might hinder their development. The CJ therefore ruled that the arrangement did not constitute aid within the meaning of Article 107(1) TFEU.[208]

3.2.4.4   Minimum Price Harmonisation

Sometimes Member States impose price controls by laying down special maximum or minimum prices for certain products. Despite their general character, such price controls will often have a selective effect so that some undertakings, products or business sectors will be favoured. Minimum prices laid down by law can favour the seller, as sellers will be guaranteed minimum prices for their products, while maximum price harmonisation can favour buyers by giving them lower costs. On the face of it, there does not seem to be any reason to exclude such price controls from the Treaty prohibition of State aid.

The Commission has found that State aid exists within the meaning of Article 107(1) TFEU in cases where, in a particular business sector, a Member State lays down minimum prices which are higher than the market prices. Among other things, this has been the case in connection with a German draft law on the setting of a minimum price

---

205. Joined Cases C-72 and 73/91, *Sloman Neptun*, para. 21.
206. Joined Cases C-72 and 73/91, *Sloman Neptun*, para. 22. *See also* Joined Cases C-52–54/97, *Viscido*, paras 14 and 15.
207. Case C-189/91, *Kirsammer-Hack*, para. 17.
208. Case C-189/91, *Kirsammer-Hack*, para. 18.

for electricity supplies from renewable energy sources, where the Commission found that this was State aid covered by Article 107(1).[209]

However, the CJ has adopted a different approach. The key point for deciding whether a maximum or minimum price established by law is covered by the prohibition of State aid or not has been whether the benefit has been financed from state resources.

> In Case 82/77, *van Tiggele*, the CJ was asked whether a Dutch provision on minimum prices, for the domestic sale of spirits, should be regarded as a State aid which was incompatible with the internal market. The CJ stated that Article 107(1) does not cover measures which, with a view to favouring distributors of a product, lay down fixed minimum prices for sales at the retail level which only impose a burden on consumers.[210] The CJ justified this on the grounds that the advantages which the minimum prices gave to distributors were neither directly nor indirectly provided by state resources within the meaning of Article 107(1).[211]
>
> Case C-379/98, *PreussenElektra*, concerned a German law on the input of electricity from renewable energy resources to the public grid. This law contained provisions requiring private electricity supply companies to buy electricity produced in their supply areas from renewable energy, and to pay a minimum tariff for this laid down by law, which was higher than the true economic value of this kind of electricity. The law also contained a provision on the allocation of the consequent financial burden between the electricity supply companies and upstream private electricity network operators, so that in some circumstances the private electricity network operators, in this case *PreussenElektra*, would have to pay compensation to secondary electricity supply companies for the additional costs which were a consequence of the obligation to buy the electricity at the minimum price determined by law. The question was whether this arrangement amounted to State aid within the meaning of Article 107(1).[212]
>
> In its decision the CJ again emphasised that only advantages granted directly or indirectly through State resources are to be considered aid within the meaning of Article 107(1).[213] In relation to the case before it, the CJ commented that the obligation imposed on private electricity supply undertakings to purchase electricity produced from renewable energy sources at fixed minimum prices did not involve any direct or indirect transfer of State resources to undertakings which produce electricity from renewable energy

---

209. However, the arrangement was approved by the Commission; XXth Report on competition policy, 1991, para. 291.
210. Case 82/77, *van Tiggele*, para. 24.
211. Case 82/77, *van Tiggele*, para. 25. However, the measure did constitute a measure with an equivalent effect to a quantitative restriction, and was therefore contrary to Art. 28 (then Art. 30).
212. Case C-379/98, *PreussenElektra*, para. 56.
213. Case C-379/98, *PreussenElektra*, para. 58.

sources.²¹⁴ Nor could the allocation of the financial burden constitute a direct or indirect transfer of State resources.²¹⁵

In these circumstances the CJ found that the fact that the purchase obligation was laid down by law and led to an unquestioned advantage for certain undertakings did not mean that it could be characterised as State aid for the purposes of Article 107(1).²¹⁶

In the context of the law on State aid, there thus seems to be a decisive difference between whether the aid is financed through obligatory taxes imposed by public authority or even the potential recipients of the aid or whether the aid is financed by the state laying down minimum prices which are only a burden on the consumer. In the latter case, according to the practice of the CJ, this is not State aid within the meaning of Article 107(1).²¹⁷

3.3 Selectivity

In order for a State aid measure to be characterised as incompatible with the internal market, as laid down in Article 107(1), the measure must favour *certain undertakings* or the *production of certain goods*. The purpose of this criterion is, first and foremost, to exclude the application of the State aid provisions to the general economic measures of the Member States and thus limit such general measures to those measures which selectively favour certain undertakings. If an aid measure is general, it can be adopted and implemented as part of the powers of a Member State to implement the economic policy which it considers appropriate. However, if the measure is selective, it may fall within the scope of the prohibition of State aid.

The application of the selectivity criterion, therefore, requires first, that there is a definition of what is meant by *undertakings* and *production of certain goods* for the purposes of Article 107(1), and second, that it is established under what circumstances a measure is deemed to favour *certain* undertakings or the production of *certain* goods, and is therefore regarded as selective.

3.3.1 Undertakings and Productions of Goods

3.3.1.1 The Concept of Undertakings

The CJ has defined the concept of an *undertaking* as covering any entity engaged in an economic activity, regardless of its legal status and the way in which it is financed.²¹⁸

---

214. Case C-379/98, *PreussenElektra*, para. 59.
215. Case C-379/98, *PreussenElektra*, para. 60.
216. Case C-379/98, *PreussenElektra*, para. 61. *See also* para. 66.
217. *See* Case C-262/12, *Vent de Colère*, Case T-251/11, *Austria v. Commission*, and Case T-217/17, *FVE Holýšov I s. r. o.*, para. 118f.
218. Case C-244/94, *FFSA*, para. 14 and Joined Cases C-622/16 P and C-624/16 P, *Scuola Elementare Maria Montessori Srl*, para. 103.

In accordance with this definition, which applies to competition law in general, Article 107 thus covers undertakings in a broad sense.[219]

In this context, any activity which consists of offering goods or services in the market constitutes an economic activity.[220] It is not necessary to separate the activity that consists of the purchase of goods and the activity that consists of their subsequent use in order to determine whether an activity is an economic activity. It is thus the economic or non-economic use of the goods that necessarily determines the nature of the activity.[221]

All undertakings that carry on an economic activity covered by the Treaty can potentially receive State aid in breach of Article 107(1), regardless of whether the commercial activity is of an economic, cultural or other character and regardless of whether the undertaking operates in the retail, manufacturing or service sector.

Article 107(1) covers aid to both private and public undertakings. This follows from the practice of the CJ, as well as from the Transparency Directive[222] and Article 106 TFEU which states that public undertakings are subject to the Treaty competition rules.[223]

An undertaking need not be carried on for profit in order to be covered by the rules on State aid.[224] It is thus sufficient that the undertaking in fact carries on some economic activity.[225] This means that non-profit organisations will also be covered by the concept of an undertaking.[226]

There are no particular requirements as to the legal form of an undertaking. Public limited companies, private limited companies, trusts, mutual institutions, one-man businesses, etc., are all covered by the concept of an undertaking. Also, for public bodies it is irrelevant to the definition of an undertaking whether the body is an independent legal entity or part of the central government administration.[227]

However, the concept of an undertaking in competition law does not include the exercise of public authority or the carrying out of tasks of a societal nature. Where there is a transfer of resources between state bodies in connection with their exercise of authority, this will not be affected by the prohibition of State aid in Article 107(1).[228]

---

219. Case C-41/90, *Höfner & Elser,* para. 21; and Joined Cases C-159 and 160/91, *Poucet,* para. 17.
220. Case T-155/04, *Eurocontrol,* para. 50; and Case T-81–83/07, *Jan Rudolf Maas,* para. 178.
221. Case C-113/07 P, *Selex,* para. 102; and Case C-205/03, *FENIN,* para. 26.
222. Directive 2006/111/EC on the transparency of financial relations between Member States and public undertakings as well as on financial transparency within certain undertakings (OJ 2006 L 318/17).
223. Though with the reservation for the undertakings referred to in Art. 106(2).
224. Case C-41/90, *Höfner & Elsner,* paras 19–23, concerning a public employment agency; and Case C-244/94, *FFSA,* concerning a public organ which administered an old age pension arrangement.
225. Case C-437/09, *AG2R,* para. 65.
226. Case C-288/11 P, *Leipzig-Halle,* para. 50, which confirmed that the economic nature of an undertaking does not depend on the profitability of its activities.
227. Case 118/85, *Commission v. Italy,* para. 13; Case C-69/91, *Decoster,* para. 15; and Case C-92/91, *Taillandier,* para. 14.
228. Case C-364/92, *Eurocontrol,* which concerned Art. 102 (then Art. 86), where the CJ found that the provision of navigation services by Eurocontrol in order to ensure the safety of air traffic was the exercise of authority and thus Eurocontrol as not an undertaking within the meaning of Art. 102; *see* Art. 106. In its decision, among other things the CJ emphasised Eurocontrol's

The distinction between tasks of a societal nature and economic activities is not entirely clear,[229] and it is being developed in case law.[230] While the construction and development of infrastructure projects has previously been considered a societal task, now, according to the case law, the construction of infrastructure projects is considered to be an economic activity if the project will be of a commercial character, as the construction and development of infrastructure cannot be seen in isolation from its subsequent use.[231]

3.3.1.2   Production of Certain Goods

The provisions on State aid apply to aid that is provided for the *production of certain goods*, including aid to certain sectors, for example, the motor car or textile industries. The provision covers all production carried out by the entities which are covered by the concept of an undertaking defined immediately above.[232]

3.3.1.3   Private Households

Aid to private households or social benefits paid to individuals are not covered by the Treaty provisions on State aid. However, there could be State aid within the scope of Article 107(1) if certain undertakings were to derive an ultimate economic advantage from the aid so as to constitute indirect aid to the undertaking, regardless of whether an individual consumer or person is the direct recipient.

---

powers of enforcement, and the fact that Eurocontrol had a duty to provide its services to all airlines, whether or not they had paid a fee for the service.

229. For example, when determining whether social security arrangements and health services constitute economic activities, the emphasis is on whether the arrangements are administered on the basis of the principle of capitalisation or the principle of solidarity; *see, e.g.*, Case C-67/96, *Albany International*. There are similar problems of definition in areas such as education, research, culture, utility supplies and infrastructure investments; *see, e.g.*, Commission Decision in Case C(2013) 2740 of 15 May 2013 (SA.33728), *Finansiering af Multiarena i København*.
230. *See, e.g.*, the Commission Decisions in SA.36558, *Øresundsforbindelsen* and SA.39078, *Femernforbindelsen*, of which the latter is partially subject to an action for annulment – *see* Case T-364/20, *Denmark v. Commission*.
231. Case C-288/11 P, *Leipzig-Halle*, paras 43–44, confirming the decision of the GC in Case T-443/08, *Leipzig-Halle*. *See also* Commission Decision of 2 Jul. 2013 in Case SA.35118, paras 23–26. The delimitation of the notion of economic activity is however challenged in a pending case in regard to State aid awarded to Femern Bælt A/S, *see* Case T-364/20, *Denmark v. Commission. See also* Rass Holdgaard, Grith Skovgaard Ølykke and Rasmus Grønved Nielsen: Public Authority or Economic Activity in the Context of Public Infrastructures, European State Aid Law Quarterly (3) 2019, pp. 274–292.
232. Commission Decision 80/932/EEC (OJ 1980 L 264/28); and Case 203/82, *Commission v. Italy*, where a greater reduction in employers' health insurance contributions for female employees than for male employees could favour certain productions of goods in Italy in which there was a preponderance of female workers, such as the textile, clothing, footwear and leather sectors.

3.3.2 General and Selective Measures

The economic measures of the Member States will often lead to a direct or indirect reallocation of resources which will benefit some undertakings rather than others and thereby distort the competitive situation. However, this fact does not necessarily mean that the measure is covered by the prohibition of State aid in Article 107(1). The application of the State aid rules requires that the measure should be selective in the sense that the measure favours *certain* undertakings or the production of *certain* goods.

This requirement for selectivity means that, in indicating those who may be entitled to aid, the measure should contain an element of specificity or discrimination. Within the context of a given legal arrangement the measure must favour certain undertakings in comparison with other undertakings which, given the purpose of the measure in question, are in a comparable legal and factual situation.[233] Measures which benefit all the undertakings of a Member State, without distinction or measures which make a distinction but on an objective basis, will not be covered by the State aid prohibition.[234]

This definition is important, as distortions of competition which are the result of selective measures are covered by Article 107(1), while distortions of competition which are the result of general measures are covered by the harmonisation provisions in Articles 116 and 117 TFEU.[235] The application of the correct Treaty provision is important, as the different Treaty provisions apply different legal remedies.

3.3.2.1 General Measures

In order for a measure to be regarded as general, it must be open to all economic agents operating within the legal order which constitutes the reference framework for the assessment of selectivity, without regard to the size, nature, regional location or sector, and give the undertakings equal access to the measure.[236]

Such measures, for example, a Member State's reduction of interest rates, the structure of the tax system (e.g., the rules for depreciation or the remission of tax debts), the system for social security contributions (e.g., employers' and employees' financing of social benefits), or the decisions of the authorities concerning infrastructure, are usually considered to be part of a Member State's general economic and social policy.

---

233. Joined Cases C-106/09 P & 107/09 P, *Gibraltar*, para. 75; sag Case C-88/03, *The Azores*, paras 54 and 56, Case C-143/99, *Adria-Wien Pipeline*, para. 41 and Joined Cases C-885/19 P and C-898/19 P, *Fiat*, paras 67 and 69.
234. Case C-143/99, *Adria-Wien Pipeline*, para. 36.
235. According to the Commission, the economic argument for distinguishing between general and selective measures is based on the economic point of view that selective aid measures have a more direct and immediate effect on competition between Member States than general measures; *see* the Second Survey on State aid in the European Union in the Manufacturing and Certain Other Sectors, 1991 pp. 4 et seq.
236. *See* further Commission Notice on the notion of State aid, point 5 (OJ 2016 C 262/1).

In special cases, the general measures of a Member State can mean that certain undertakings or sectors derive a greater benefit from the measures than other undertakings in the Member State. For example, where a Member State introduces general reductions in payroll taxes or gives a subsidy for the employment of the long-term unemployed, on the face of it, this will benefit labour-intensive undertakings or sectors, while all things being equal more favourable tax rules for depreciation will benefit capital-intensive undertakings with substantial assets which qualify for depreciation. In the same way, tax incentives to promote investments in environmental protection, research and development, or training can benefit undertakings which undertake such investments. Where such advantages are merely a consequence of an arrangement which has been put together on the basis of proper objective criteria, it will not be considered to be selective in the context of State aid.[237]

The situation is different where the extent of a measure is reduced de facto by, for example, discretionary allocation by the state. The measure thereby acquires a selective element so that certain undertakings, sectors or regions can be given an advantage. If there is such a selective element, a measure which is expressed in general terms can be covered by the prohibition of incompatible State aid.[238]

On the basis of the above, it must be assumed that an aid measure must be considered general in relation to the State aid rules if it is phrased as being generally applicable and the allocation of aid is based on objective criteria, without the authorities being given discretionary powers in relation to it.

3.3.2.2 Selective Measures

Selective measures are characterised by the fact that they do not apply to all the undertakings or industrial sectors which ought, in principle, to benefit from the measure if the character of the Member State's economic system is taken into account. A measure will be characterised as a selective measure if it favours a specific sector, region, undertaking or group of undertakings.

The selectivity criterion is interpreted very broadly. For example, an aid measure that favours small- and medium-sized enterprises will be characterised as selective, even though the measure is general in terms of not being limited in respect of sectors or regions.[239] This will apply even if, for example, small- and medium-sized enterprises represent up to 95% of all undertakings in the Member State concerned. Aid for exports is also regarded as being selective within the meaning of Article 107(1), even if all

---

237. For example, this argument was tried in Joined Cases T-92 & 103/00, *Territorio Histórico de Álava*, para. 50.
238. Case C-241/94, *France v. Commission*, para. 23. This was the case in Joined Cases T-92 & 103/00, *Territorio Histórico de Álava*, para. 58. *See also* Joined Cases C-649/20 P, C-658/20 P and C-662/20 P, *Spain and Others v. Commission*, para. 57.
239. Commission Regulation (EC) No 70/2001 on the application of Arts 87 and 88 of the EC Treaty to State aid to small and medium-sized enterprises. *See also* Joined Cases T-92 and 103/00, *Territorio Histórico de Álava*, para. 40.

exporting undertakings in the Member State can in principle benefit from the measure.[240] According to the practice of the CJ, the same applies to aid measures which are targeted at sectors which are exposed to international competition.[241]

An aid measure can selectively favour a specific sector, such as the shipbuilding sector or the transport sector.[242] In this context, the term 'sector' is interpreted broadly. Thus, the Commission has found that the especially favourable treatment of the manufacturing sector, compared with the service sector, stated in the Irish corporation tax law, meant that the measure was characterised as selective within the meaning of Article 107(1).[243]

Aid measures with a limited geographic extent of a local or regional nature can also be characterised as selective.[244] However, such measures will often have a purely local competitive effect and will, therefore, not actually or potentially affect trade between Member States, as referred to in Article 107(1).[245]

However, the fact that a measure only grants benefits in one part of a Member State's territory is not in itself enough for the measure to be regarded as selective.[246] The definition of the reference framework for selectivity need not necessarily consist of the whole of the territory of the Member State in question, but in certain cases, it can be a limited part of the territory. Thus, in Case C-88/03, *The Azores*, the CJ established that it is possible that an infra-State body enjoys a legal or factual status which makes it sufficiently autonomous in relation to the central government of the Member State, with the result that by the measures it adopts, it is that body and not the central government which plays a fundamental role in the definition of the political and economic environment in which undertakings operate.[247]

For a measure to be regarded as having been adopted in the exercise of sufficiently autonomous powers, the CJ requires:

(1) That the aid decision must have been taken by a regional or local authority which has, from a constitutional point of view, a political and administrative status separate from that of the central government.
(2) The aid decision must have been adopted without the central government being able to directly intervene as regards its content.

---

240. Joined Cases 6 and 11/69, *Commission v. France*, paras 20 and 21; and Case 57/86, *Greece v. Commission*, para. 8.
241. Case C-75/97, *Maribel bis/ter*.
242. Case 248/84, *Germany v. Commission*, para. 18; and Case C-75/97, *Maribel bis/ter*, para. 33. See also Case 173/73, *Italy v. Commission*, concerning aid which benefited the textile industry; and Case C-143/99, *Adria-Wien Pipeline*, where undertakings which produced goods were favoured in relation to undertakings which provided services.
243. Commission Decision E/2/98, *Ireland* (OJ 1998 C 395/19). The Decision was discussed in the XXVIIIth Report on competition policy, 1999, para. 210.
244. Case 248/84, *Germany v. Commission*, concerning regional aid programmes that benefited undertakings that invested in Nord-Rhein-Westfalen.
245. *See* the Commission's assessment of tax deductions for reserves which Sparekassen Nordjylland was allowed to make in connection with the takeover of Himmerlandsbanken, Skat Udland, 1995 p. 68.
246. Case C-88/03, *The Azores*, para. 57.
247. Case C-88/03, *The Azores*, para. 58.

(3) The financial consequences of a reduction of the national tax rate for undertakings in the region must not be offset by aid or subsidies from other regions or the central government.[248]

If these criteria are met, the regional environment is then taken as the point of reference for whether the aid measure constitutes a benefit for some undertakings in relation to other undertakings which are in a corresponding legal and factual situation.

3.3.2.3 The Assessment of Selectivity

When assessing the general or selective character of an aid measure, the Commission first examines how the measure is framed and then it looks at its actual effect. It will often be clear from the aid measure whether it is intended to favour certain undertakings or sectors where, for example, it is directed at small- and medium-sized enterprises or at a specific undertaking.

Where the selective element of a measure is not immediately apparent, it is necessary to make a more detailed assessment of whether the measure, as part of a particular legal arrangement, can favour certain undertakings or the production of certain goods in relation to other undertakings which are in a corresponding legal and factual situation.[249]

According to case-law established on the basis of assessing selectivity in relation to tax measures,[250] the analysis consists of a three-step test in which: (1) the reference framework and general rule is determined;[251] (2) there is an assessment of whether the measure justifies an exception being made to the general rule by differentiating between operators who, according to the objective pursued,[252] are in a comparable

---

248. Case C-88/03, *The Azores*, para. 67. In the case in question only the first of these conditions was fulfilled and the arrangement was therefore regarded as selective; see paras 69–85. See also Joined Cases C-106/09 P & 107/09 P, *Gibraltar*.
249. Case C-88/03, *The Azores*, paras 54 and 56; Joined Cases C-106/09 P & 107/09 P, *Gibraltar*, para. 75; Case C-143/99, *Adria-Wien Pipeline*, para. 41; and similarly Case C-75/97, *Maribel bis/ter*, paras 28–31. See also C-518/13, *Eventech* (London Black Cabs), where London Black Cabs and private hire vehicles ('minicabs') were found to be in sufficiently distinct factual and legal situations to be considered not comparable, so the bus lane policy did not confer a selective economic advantage on Black Cabs; see paras 60 and 61.
250. This test is generally applicable. For case-law in the tax area see, e.g., Joined Cases C 20/15 P and C-21/15 P, *Banco Santander*, paras 53–60, T-20/17, *Hungary v. Commission*, C-51/19 P and C-64/19 P, *World Duty Free Group*, T-461/12, *Hansestadt Lübeck*, C-131/15 P, *Greek casinos*, and Case C-5/14, *Kernkraftwerke Lippe-Ems GmbH*, C-15/14 P, *MOL* and Case C-105/14, *Taricco*. Regarding selectivity in relation to the tax authorities' tax rulings in the Member States, see: https://ec.europa.eu/competition-policy/state-aid/tax-rulings_en, and, e.g., Joined Cases T-760/15 and T-636/16, *Starbucks*, Cases T-778/16 and T-892/16, *Apple*, (under appeal in Case C-465/20 P), and Cases T-816/17 and T-318/18, *Amazon*, (under appeal in Case C-457/21 P).
251. See Case C-562/19, *Commission v. Hungary*, see paras 38–39. The reference framework for the assessment of State aid is established in the light of the concrete tax systems in the individual Member States, see also Joined Cases C-885/19 P and C-898/19 P, *Fiat*, paras 65–74.
252. See more in Case T-20/17, *Hungary v. Commission*, para. 77. See also Case C-362/19, *Fútbol Club Barcelona*.

legal and factual situation[253] and, if so: (3) whether the exception is justified by the nature and administration of the system.[254]

Thus, it is possible that, after a more detailed analysis, measures which appear to be general are shown to involve differences in treatment which means that the measure will be considered selective for the purposes of Article 107(1).[255] This will be the case both where the measure allows certain discretionary powers to the authorities which administer the aid scheme in question[256] and where the effect of the measure is to favour certain undertakings unless such difference in treatment is justified by reasons relating to the nature and general scheme of the system of which it is part.[257]

> In Case C-241/94, *France v. Commission*, the CJ assessed a general aid measure which allowed special discretionary powers to the authority which was to administer the aid scheme. In this case, a fund was empowered to co-finance measures for following up social programmes that had been drawn up by undertakings with employment problems. The interventions of the fund were not restricted to certain sectors, regions or categories of undertaking, but the fund had certain powers of discretion over, among other things, the choice of who should benefit, the amount of the aid and the conditions under which aid was provided.[258] The aid scheme was therefore considered to be selective within the meaning of Article 107(1).[259]

> In Commission Decision 80/932/EEC, the Commission considered an Italian arrangement for the partial takeover by the State of the contributions to health insurance schemes of manufacturing undertakings and certain undertakings in the service sector; the Commission considered that this arrangement was selective. The arrangement provided for a greater reduction of employers' contributions for the health insurance of female employees than the contributions paid in respect of male employees. The measure thus supported those parts of the Italian manufacturing sector in which female employment was preponderant, such as the textile, clothing, footwear and leather sectors.[260] Despite the general nature of its wording, the actual effect of the measure thus favoured some sectors over others, and it was therefore regarded as selective for the purposes of Article 107(1).

> Corresponding considerations applied in connection with a proposed amendment to the Danish Law on electricity supply. This amendment gave electricity companies the possibility of taking account of their losses in the

---

253. *See* more in, e.g., Case T-696/17, *Hafenbedrijf Antwerpen NV*, paras 109–215.
254. *See*, *e.g.*, Case T-287/11, *Heitkamp Bauholding*, and Case T-60/16, *Groningen Seaports*.
255. This was the case in Joined Cases T-92 & 103/00, *Territorio Histórico de Álava*, para. 58.
256. It is not necessary to use the three-step test in such cases, *see* Joined Cases C-649/20 P, C-658/20 P and C-662/20 P, *Spain and others v. Commission*, paras 49, 57 and 68.
257. Case C-53/00, *Ferring SA*, para. 17; and Case C-143/99, *Adria-Wien Pipeline*, para. 42.
258. Case C-241/94, *France v. Commission*, paras 22 and 23.
259. Case C-241/94, *France v. Commission*, para. 24. Case C-295/97, *Piaggio*, para. 39; and Joined Cases T-92 and 103/00, *Territorio Histórico de Álava*, paras 33 and 35.
260. Commission Decision 80/932/EEC (OJ 1980 L 264/26); and Case 203/82, *Commission v. Italy*. *See also* Joined Cases T-92 and 103/00, *Territorio Histórico de Álava*, para. 39.

electricity prices, and was in principle applicable to the whole electricity supply sector. In practice it was only the SEAS company which was able to fulfil the conditions of the law for including losses in their electricity prices. The amendment to the Law on electricity supply was therefore regarded as selective.[261]

The Member States' legal orders may sometimes include provisions which selectively favour certain undertakings other than in connection with taxation or the payment of social benefits.

> For example, this was so in Case C-295/97, *Piaggio*, which concerned an arrangement whereby large industrial undertakings in difficulties which owed particularly large debts to certain, mainly public, classes of creditors could depart from the normal law of insolvency.[262] Subject to the discretion of the relevant government minister, such undertakings could obtain permission to continue trading in circumstances which would not have been allowed under the generally applicable insolvency law. In these circumstances the arrangement was regarded as selective within the meaning of Article 107(1).[263]

According to the CJ, selectivity will not exist if an aid arrangement, that may well constitute an advantage for the recipient, can be justified by the nature or general scheme of the arrangement.[264] In assessing whether an aid arrangement is selective, the Commission must thus establish how the general rules are framed and investigate how far an exception or differentiation within this system for the benefit of certain undertakings or the production of certain goods can be justified by the nature of the system.

Under special circumstances, it will be justifiable to treat certain sectors, regions or undertakings differently on the basis of an aid measure.

> The possibility for this was made clear in Case 173/73, *Italy v. Commission*, which concerned an Italian measure whereby there was a partial reduction of employers' social payments for family allowances to the advantage of all employers in the textile sector which, for a three year period, eased the social burdens of the exempt undertakings. The contributions of these undertakings were reduced from 15% to 10%. In respect of this the CJ

---

261. *See Henrik Mørch:* Summary of the Most Important Recent Developments, Competition Policy Newsletter (4) 1995 pp. 47-51, at p. 49; and *see* Commission Decision 2001/605/EC (OJ 2001 L 212/34), concerning a Spanish aid arrangement for the acquisition of commercial vehicles which was found to be selective, as the potential recipients of the aid had in fact to be natural persons and undertakings engaged in transport operations, either on their own account or for hire or reward; *see* para. 23 of the Decision.
262. Case C-295/97, *Piaggio*, para. 37.
263. Case C-295/97, *Piaggio*, para. 39.
264. Case C-143/99, *Adria-Wien Pipeline*, para. 42; Joined Cases C-106/09 P & 107/09 P, *Gibraltar*, para. 145; and Case C-88/03, *The Azores*, para. 52. *See also* Case 173/73, *Italy v. Commission*, para. 33; Case C-53/00, *Ferring SA*, para. 17, and Cases T-20/17 and C-596/19 P, *Hungary*, and Joined Cases T-826/16 and T-624/17, and C-562/19 P, *Poland*.

stated: 'It must be concluded that the partial reduction of social charges pertaining to family allowances devolving upon employers in the textile sector is a measure intended partially to exempt undertakings of a particular industrial sector from the financial charges arising from the normal application of the general social security system, without there being any justification for this exemption on the basis of the nature or general scheme of this system.'[265]

In Joined Cases T-92 and 103/00, *Territorio Histórico de Álava*, in respect of a tax measure, the GC stated that the measure could be justified on the basis of the nature or overall structure of the tax system, and that the measure concerned reflected consistency with the internal logic of the tax system in general.[266] As an example of this, the GC stated that the progressiveness of the tax which was justified by the system's aim of redistribution would not constitute State aid under Article 107(1).[267]

If the elective element of a measure can be justified in accordance with the above, the measure will not constitute an advantage amounting to a State aid within the meaning of Article 107(1). There is no such advantage where the difference in treatment is justified by reasons relating to the logic of the system.[268]

3.4 Aid Which Distorts or Threatens to Distort Competition and Which Affects Trade Between Member States

The prohibition of State aid in Article 107(1) only applies to aid measures to the extent that the aid distorts or threatens to distort competition and affects trade between Member States. These two criteria are closely linked to each other.[269] Thus, if an undertaking receives aid, with the effect that the undertaking's position is strengthened in relation to other undertakings with which the recipient undertaking competes in trade within the internal market, the CJ presumes that the criteria for the existence of incompatible State aid are fulfilled.[270]

Both the criteria of distortion of competition and the element of effect on trade are broadly interpreted by the CJ and the Commission, and in practice it does not require much for these criteria to be met. Article 107(1) does not require that the distortion of trade or the effect on trade should be appreciable. However, in the experience of the Commission, aid below a certain level does not affect trade or distort competition sufficiently for the criteria to be regarded as having been met. For this reason, the

---

265. Case 173/73, *Italy v. Commission*, para. 15 *See also* Case C-143/99, *Adria-Wien Pipeline*.
266. Joined Cases T-92 and 103/00, *Territorio Histórico de Álava*, para. 60. In this connection *see also* Case C-75/97, *Maribel bis/ter*, para. 39.
267. Joined Cases T-92 and 103/00, *Territorio Histórico de Álava*, para. 60. *See also* Cases T-20/17 and C-596/19 P, *Hungary*, and T-826/16, T-624/17 and C-562/19 P, *Poland*.
268. Case C-53/00, *Ferring SA*, para. 17.
269. The condition relating to distortion of competition and the effect on trade is also closely connected with the selectivity criterion. The distorting effect of a measure on competition will thus depend on whether the aid is given selectively.
270. Case 730/79, *Philip Morris*, para. 11.

Commission adopted Regulation (EU) No 2023/2831 on the application of Articles 107 and 108 of the Treaty to *de minimis* aid, according to which aid below a certain threshold is not considered fulfilling the criteria in Article 107(1), and does not, therefore, fall within the scope of the provision.[271]

3.4.1 Aid Which Distorts or Threatens to Distort Competition

The prohibition of State aid in Article 107(1) only applies to aid measures which distort or threaten to distort competition within the internal market. Aid which gives a selective advantage will, by its very nature, mean that competition will be distorted, as the aid will improve the financial position of those who receive it in relation to their competitors, which will normally result in an improvement in the recipients' competitiveness and market position.[272] The Commission interprets the term *competitiveness* as meaning an undertaking's ability to compete on a global level. This means that an undertaking must constantly adjust to the economic changes and new conditions which apply to a market. In the longer term, it means that the undertaking's revenues must cover its production costs and give a sufficient margin for investment and return on capital so as to secure the continued existence of the undertaking.[273] Therefore, if it can be shown that an undertaking's competitiveness and market position are strengthened on the basis of an aid measure which selectively benefits the undertaking in question, and this undertaking competes with other undertakings within the internal market, it can justifiably be assumed that competition is distorted.[274]

3.4.1.1 Competitive Effect

The State aid provisions prohibit both State aid which actually distorts competition and State aid that threatens to distort competition within the internal market.[275] In addition to this, State aid can distort actual and potential competition, for example, by reducing actual or potential competitors' possibilities for maintaining or increasing market shares or preventing the entry of new competitors to the market. It is, therefore, sufficient for the criteria to be met that there is potential competition and that the aid

---

271. Commission Regulation (EU) No 2023/2831 on the application of Arts 107 and 108 of the Treaty on the Functioning of the European Union to *de minimis* aid (OJ L, 2023/2831, 15.12.2023).
272. Case 730/79, *Philip Morris*, where the State aid was to contribute to an increase in the undertaking's production capacity by restructuring the production units. The undertaking's ability to supply the trade would thus be increased, which would improve its market position in relation to its competitors, and thus distort competition.
273. *See* Written Question No 562/80 by Mr Fernandez to the Commission: The concept of competitiveness as understood by the Commission (OJ 1980 C 283/7).
274. Case 173/73, *Italy v. Commission*; Case C-142/87, *Tubemeuse*. See also, e.g., *Tourisme social en Belgique* which granted associations organising leisure activities aimed at giving underprivileged persons access to tourism infrastructure, which could distort competition in the hotel trade as apart from their social role of promoting low-budget tourism and holidays for workers, the centres also operated traditional hotels which were in direct competition with others in the same category; see XXVIth Report on Competition Policy 1996, 1997 para. 173.
275. Case T-214/95, *VLM*, para. 44.

can potentially distort this competition,[276] and it is thus not a requirement that the aid should in fact have affected competition.[277]

Competition can exist between national competitors or between competitors from different Member States. In assessing whether an aid measure distorts competition, the starting point must be the competitive situation which existed in the internal market before the adoption of the measure in question.[278]

In addition to the effect on competition for the aid recipient's actual and potential competitors, State aid can have a competitive effect on the aid recipient's suppliers and customers. Aid measure can thus have a downstream effect on competition for undertakings that buy the products of the aid recipient.[279] This applies in particular where an undertaking buys the aid recipient's products and may obtain an indirect advantage in the form of lower prices. Correspondingly, an aid measure can have an upstream effect, as it can give the aid recipient's suppliers an indirect economic advantage in the form of increased supplies to the aid recipient.[280]

The fact that the competitors of an undertaking which receives aid have themselves received – possibly unlawful – aid cannot alter the assessment of whether the aid in question is compatible with the Treaty. In other words, a Member State cannot justify an infringement of the State aid provisions on the grounds that other Member States have likewise infringed the State aid provisions.[281] This also applies where a Member State provides compensation for legal differences between the Member States.[282] Such measures do not result in the smoothing out of distortions of competition but rather in the accumulation of distortions.

3.4.1.2 Evidence of Distortions of Competition

The presumption that State aid distorts competition seems to mean, on the face of it, that the Commission need not make a detailed assessment of the potential effect of the aid on competition in the sectors where there is trade between Member States.[283] However, according to the practice of the CJ, the Commission must make a certain analysis of the criteria and give a statement of reasons which show the distorting effect on competition of aid measures, also in cases where it appears from the circumstances in which aid is given, that it can distort competition.[284] The requirements to be satisfied by the statement of reasons depend on the circumstances of each case.[285] However, the Commission's decision must at least state which circumstances distort competition in

---

276. Joined Cases C-62/87 and C-72/87, *Walloon Regional Executive v. Commission*, para. 15.
277. Case T-214/95, *VLM*, para. 67.
278. Case 173/73, *Italy v. Commission*, para. 36.
279. Commission Decision 72/253/EEC (OJ 1972 L 164/22); and Commission Decision 84/508/EEC (OJ 1984 L 283/42).
280. Commission Decision 97/542/EC, *Biofuels* (OJ 1997 L 222/26).
281. Case T-214/95, *VLM*, para. 54; and Case 78/76, *Steinike & Weinlig*, para. 24.
282. Case C-6/97, *Italy v. Commission*, para. 19.
283. This is because, as noted initially, trade between Member States may be assumed to be affected where an undertaking which receives aid participates in trade between Member States.
284. Joined Cases 296 and 318/82, *Leeuwarder Papierwarenfabriek*, para. 24.
285. Joined Cases 296 and 318/82, *Leeuwarder Papierwarenfabriek*, para. 19.

the actual case,[286] as well as contain information which enables the CJ to exercise control of legitimacy. It must also be possible for the addressee of a Commission decision to confirm that the decision has a proper basis.[287] The Commission must, therefore, define the relevant geographic market and the relevant product market within which the distortion of competition may occur, as well as the period within which the distortion of competition takes place, though without making an analysis of the same thoroughness as is required in connection with Articles 101 and 102, or the Merger Control Regulation.[288] In addition to this, depending on the circumstances, the Commission may assess the market position of the aid recipient, including the size of the undertaking's market share, the volume of trade in the product which the undertaking produces, and the general circumstances, structure and situation of the relevant market.[289] It is sufficient that the Commission demonstrates the probability that the aid will have a distorting effect by showing that in the actual circumstances the aid can lead to a distortion of competition,[290] while it is not necessary to give evidence about what distortion of competition the aid will in fact cause.[291] If the Commission were obliged to give evidence about the actual effect of aid which has already been given, this would benefit the Member States that have provided aid in breach of notification and standstill obligations at the expense of those Member States that give notification of proposed aid.[292]

If there is a need to further determine the relevant market, the starting point will normally be the demand substitution between products.[293] This starting position is modified where a market capable of being distorted has not yet been established. However, Article 107 is also applicable where a market is only of a potential nature, as the aid may prevent new competitors from entering the market, regardless of the fact that there may not yet be competition there.[294]

The relevant product market covers both goods and services that are delivered to or demanded from the recipient undertaking, as well as goods which are produced on the basis of these goods and services and goods which are substitutable for them due

---

286. Joined Cases T-92 and 103/00, *Territorio Histórico de Álava*, para. 69; and Joined Cases C-15/98 and C-105/99, *Italy and Saedegna Lines v. Commission*, para. 66.
287. Joined Cases 296 and 318/82, *Leewarder Papierwarenfabriek*, paras 19 and 24.
288. Case 730/79, *Philip Morris*, paras 8–13, where the CJ rejected Philip Morris' claim that the Commission should have undertaken the same assessment as in cases under Arts 101 and 102.
289. Joined Cases 296 and 318/82, *Leewarder Papierwarenfabriek*, para. 24.
290. Joined Cases T-92 and 103/00, *Territorio Histórico de Álava*, para. 70.
291. Joined Cases T-92 and 103/00, *Territorio Histórico de Álava*, para. 77; and Case T-55/99, *CETM v. Commission*, para. 103.
292. Joined Cases T-92 and 103/00, *Territorio Histórico de Álava*, para. 77; and Case C-301/87, *Boussac*, para. 33.
293. See the Commission Notice on the definition of relevant market for the purposes of Community competition law, paras 15 et seq. (OJ 1997 C 372/5). The procedure for determining the relevant market set out in the Notice can in part be used as the basis for assessment in State aid cases; see note (1) of the Notice. (Please be aware that the Notice is currently under revision).
294. Joined Cases C-62/87 and C-72/87, *Walloon Regional Executive v. Commission*, para. 15. If aid is awarded to an undertaking engaged in activities in a non-liberalised market, the requirement of distortion of competition may be met, if the aid can be used for the benefit of activities in other markets subject to competition, see Case C-140/09, *Fallimento Traghetti del Mediterraneo*, paras 47–51.

to their characteristics, price or intended use.[295] Thus, the scope of the prohibition of State aid is not limited to measures that affect competition between two products that are in direct competition with each other, as is the case, for example, with different makes of cars. In this context, it is sufficient to establish that competition between two products that are substitutable is affected, as might be the case with car transport and railway transport.

The relevant geographic market is defined as 'the area in which the undertakings concerned are involved in the supply and demand of products or services, in which the conditions of competition are sufficiently homogeneous and which can be distinguished from neighbouring areas because the conditions of competition are appreciably different in those area.'[296] The relevant geographic market need not necessarily consist of a significant part of the internal market in order for Article 107(1) to apply. However, where aid to local or regional undertakings can only be assumed to affect competition in the local or regional area of the recipient undertakings, it is unlikely to affect trade between Member States.[297]

Competition within the internal market can be distorted even if the undertaking receiving the aid exports nearly all its production to third countries.[298] This can be the case where undertakings from the EU compete outside the internal market as well as inside it.

> In Case 142/87, *Tubemeuse*, the CJ stated that, 'having regard to the interdependence between the markets on which Community undertakings operate, it is possible that aid might distort competition within the Community, even if the undertaking receiving it exports almost all its production outside the Community. The exportation of part of the undertaking's production to non-member countries is only one of a number of circumstances which must be considered.'[299]

In the same way, the Member States' aid to undertakings in third countries could affect competition within the internal market, and such aid could, therefore, depending on the circumstances, also be assessed under the provisions on State aid.[300] In cases where third countries are granting aid to undertakings inside or outside the EU, the Regulation on foreign subsidies distorting the internal market may be applicable.[301]

---

295. Commission Notice on the definition of relevant market for the purposes of Community competition law, para. 7 (OJ 1997 C 372/5). *See also* Commission Decision 72/253/EEC (OJ 1972 L 164/22).
296. Commission Notice on the definition of relevant market for the purposes of Community competition law, para. 8 (OJ 1997 C 372/5).
297. Commission Decision 2001/605/EC, para. 29 (OJ 2001 L 212/34).
298. Case C-142/87, *Tubemeuse*, para. 35.
299. Case C-142/87, *Tubemeuse*, para. 32.
300. It is, however, doubtful whether the requirement for distortion of competition is met. *See* Case T-34/02, *EURL Le Levant 001*, paras 123–124.
301. *See* Regulation (EU) 2022/2560 on foreign subsidies distorting the internal market, OJ 2022 L 330/1. The Regulation became effective from 12 Jan. 2023.

3.4.2 Aid That Affects Trade Between Member States

Even though an aid measure distorts competition, it will only be covered by the State aid prohibition in Article 107(1) if it affects trade between Member States. Where the aid only affects trade internally within a Member State or a Member State's trade with a third country, the Treaty provisions on State aid are not applicable. In such cases, it is the Member State's own competition law and international trade agreements which govern the issue of State aid. The criterion of affecting trade thus contributes to the allocation of competences between the EU and the Member States.

Just as in relation to Articles 101 and 102, the term *trade* is interpreted broadly and covers all economic transactions between Member States, such as the exchange of goods, services and capital. An effect on trade will normally be revealed by an artificial fall or an artificial increase in the imports or exports of the Member States.

As earlier stated, the condition on the effect on trade between Member States is interpreted broadly. Thus, in Case 730/79, *Philip Morris*, the CJ held that when State aid strengthens the position of an undertaking compared with other undertakings competing in trade within the EU, that trade must be regarded as affected by that aid.[302]

The presumption previously referred to, that State aid distorts competition, thus leads to the presumption that such distortion of competition also affects trade between Member States, where it can be shown that the undertaking receiving the aid participates in trade within the EU.

However, it is not enough for the Commission merely to show that the undertaking in question participates in trade within the EU. The Commission has to show that it is probable that the aid actually or potentially involves an effect on trade between Member States.[303] However, this does not mean that the Commission has to show empirical evidence of the effect of the aid on trade within the EU, but in its decision, the Commission must clearly state the facts which means that the aid can affect trade between Member States.

The effect of State aid on trade between Member States will particularly depend on the exports of the undertaking in question to the other Member States.[304] However, trade within the EU is not only considered to be affected when the undertaking receiving the aid itself directly participates in trade between Member States. If the products which are produced by the undertaking receiving the aid are the subject of cross-border trade, it does not matter whether it is the undertaking receiving the aid itself which is involved in the trade. A Member State's aid to an undertaking can thus mean that its domestic production is maintained or even increased so that the opportunities for undertakings established in the other Member States to export their products or services to that Member State will be reduced.[305] Such aid can reduce the

---

302. Case 730/79, *Philip Morris*, para. 11. *See also* Case C-42/93, *Spain v. Commission*, para. 21.
303. Case C-142/87, *Tubemeuse*. See, *e.g.*, Case 730/79, *Philip Morris*, para. 11.
304. Joined Cases 296 and 318/82, *Leewarder Papierwarenfabriek*.
305. Case C-518/13, *Eventech* (London Black Cabs), where the CJ stated: 'it is conceivable that the effect of the bus lanes policy is to render less attractive the provision of minicab services in London, with the result that the opportunities for undertakings established in other Member

potential market for imports of products from other Member States and can, therefore, affect trade between Member States and distort competition.[306]

Trade between Member States will also be affected within the meaning of Article 107(1), where the undertaking receiving aid exports (nearly) all its production to countries outside the EU.[307]

State aid for direct investments in third countries can likewise affect trade between Member States within the meaning of Article 107(1).[308]

Member States sometimes give financial incentives to influence undertakings as to where they locate their activities. This occurs particularly at regional level where, for example, a local government authority may seek to attract or retain commercial undertakings. If an undertaking moves from one Member State to another, this will in itself affect trade between Member States, both because of the change in manufacturing location and because of the changes to the supply network to the undertaking.[309]

Trade between the Member States will not be affected, within the meaning of Article 107(1), if the aid only has a local effect.

> For this reason the Commission assessed that the unlawful tax deduction which Sparekassen Nordjylland was allowed to make in connection with the takeover of Himmerlandsbanken was not covered by the provisions of the Treaty. The aid measure could be considered State aid, but because of the local character of the undertaking, with its activities geographically limited to North Jutland, where there were no foreign banks active, it did not affect trade within the meaning of Article 107(1).[310]

In two press releases, the Commission has listed a number of decisions in which the effect on trade criterion is not fulfilled.[311] It appears from the decisions that the Commission, in its conclusion, puts emphasis on: 1) whether the aid recipient supplies goods or services to a limited area of a Member State; 2) whether it is unlikely that the aid recipient will be able to attract customers from other Member States; and 3)

States to penetrate that market'; *see* para. 70, as well as para. 71. *See also* Case T-301/02, *AEM*, paras 103–105 regarding State aid which adversely affected foreign undertakings' bidding for local public service concessions.

306. Case 102/87, *France v. Commission*, para. 19. See correspondingly Case C-303/88, *ENI-Lanerossi*, para. 27; and Joined Cases T-298/97 and others, *Alzetta*, para. 91.
307. See Case C-142/87, *Tubemeuse*, where the Tubemeuse company exported 90% of its production to third countries, para. 32.
308. XXIXth Report on competition policy, 2001 para. 260.
309. *See* Commission Decision 87/573/EEC (OJ 1987 L 347/64).
310. Skat Udland 1995 p. 68. *See also* Case C-280/00, *Altmark*, paras 78–82.
311. *See* the Commission press release of 29 Apr. 2015: State aid: Commission gives guidance on local public support measures that can be granted without prior Commission approval, (IP 15/4889). The press release referred to seven decisions in which aid was not found to have affected trade: SA.37432, *Hradec Králové public hospitals*, SA.37904, *Medical centre in Durmersheim*, SA.33149, *Wirtschaftbüro Gaarden – Kiel*, SA.38035, Landgrafen-Klinik, SA.39403, *Investment aid for Lauwersoog port*, SA.37963, *Glenmore Lodge*, and SA.38208, *Member-owned golf clubs. See also* Commission press release of 21 Sep. 2016: State aid: Commission gives guidance on local public support measures that do not constitute state aid, (IP 16/3141), which lists another five additional decisions.

whether it cannot be expected that the measures will have more than a marginal effect on cross-border investments and establishments.

However, aid measures which do not affect cross-border trade can be covered by national rules on State aid.

Trade between Member States can also be affected if, in connection with internal infrastructure projects, the market conditions for domestic undertakings are improved, giving them a dominant position to make it difficult for foreign undertakings to penetrate the market.

In several cases, the CJ has rejected arguments that the fact that aid is of a modest extent or that the undertaking receiving the aid is of a modest size automatically means that trade between the Member States will not be affected in one of the ways described above.[312] The CJ's practice thus does not leave room for the requirement that the effect on trade must be appreciable before Article 107(1) is applicable.[313]

3.4.3 The De Minimis *Rule*

As stated above, the application of the provision in Article 107(1) does not necessarily require that an aid measure affects competition and trade appreciably.[314] The CJ has not formulated an appreciability requirement as in the case of Article 101, but on the contrary, in several cases, it has held that even very small amounts of aid are incompatible with the internal market within the meaning of Article 107(1).[315]

The fact that the criterion for the effect on competition and trade between Member States is interpreted relatively broadly means that the Member States have an obligation to notify numerous small aid measures. In order to reduce the administrative burden of this mass of notifications and recognising that the Commission does not consider that aid measures without appreciable effect are covered by the State aid prohibition, in 1992, the Commission introduced a *de minimis* rule. This rule was originally adopted as a part of the framework provisions on State aid to small- and medium-sized enterprises before, in 1996, being separated out into a special *de minimis* notice.[316] The *de minimis* rules, previously laid down administratively, are now codified in Commission Regulation (EU) No 2023/2831 on the application of

---

312. Case C-142/87, *Tubemeuse*, paras 42 and 43; and Case C-113/00, *Spain v. Commission*, para. 33. *See also* Case C-280/00, *Altmark*, para. 81.
313. Case C-303/88, *ENI-Lanerossi*, para. 27, where the CJ stated that even relatively modest aid can affect trade between Member States when there is intense competition in the sector concerned. *See also* Case 259/85, *France v. Commission*, para. 24; Case C-173/03, *Heiser*, paras 32–35; Case C-42/93, *Spain v. Commission*, para. 21; and Case 234/84, *Meura*, para. 22.
314. Joined Cases T-92 and 103/00, *Territorio Histórico de Álava*, para. 78; Case C-142/87, *Tubemeuse*, paras 42 and 43; and Case T-55/99, *CETM v. Commission, para. 23*.
315. Case C-303/88, *ENI-Lanerossi*, para. 27; Case C-42/93, *Spain v. Commission*, para. 21; and Case 234/84, *Meura*, para. 22.
316. Community guidelines on State aid for small- and medium-sized enterprises (SMEs), para. 3.2 (OJ 1992 C 213/2); and Commission notice on the *de minimis* rule for State aid (OJ 1996 C 68/9).

Articles 107 and 108 of the Treaty to *de minimis* aid.[317] Aid covered by the *de minimis* notice is excluded from the obligation to notify the aid to the Commission.[318]

As a starting point, the *De minimis* Regulation covers horizontal aid to undertakings in all the sectors that are covered by the Treaty. However, certain forms of aid are excluded from the scope of the Regulation. This includes among others aid to undertakings in the fisheries and aquaculture sectors; aid to undertakings involved in the primary production of certain agricultural products; certain forms of aid for undertakings involved in the processing and marketing of agricultural products; aid for export-related activities; and aid contingent upon the use of domestic products over imported products.[319]

The *de minimis* provision is based on the assumption that State aid of below a certain amount does not affect trade between Member States and/or distort or threaten to distort competition and does not, therefore, fulfil the criteria for the prohibition in Article 107(1); see Article 3(1) of the *De minimis* Regulation.

In principle, the total *de minimis* aid to an individual undertaking may not exceed a value corresponding to a cash payment of EUR 300,000 over any period of three year.[320] This means that an undertaking may receive aid corresponding to EUR 300,000 without the aid having to be notified to the Commission.[321] If an aid measure leads to the threshold being exceeded, the aid measure as a whole must be notified to the Commission with a view to getting the Commission's approval.[322]

As a starting point, the *de minimis* rules are used in the assessment of whether awarding of future aid should be notified to the Commission. In cases where the Commission decides to recover unlawful and incompatible State aid, the Member States have, however, under certain circumstances, the possibility to use the *de minimis* rule in relation to an aid recipient retrospectively,[323] with the result that the de minimis aid should not be recovered.

4   APPROVAL OF STATE AID

An aid measure that fulfils all the criteria in Article 107(1) and which is therefore covered by the prohibition of State aid is in principle considered to be incompatible with the internal market. However, in Article 107(2) and (3), there are lists of situations

---

317. Commission Regulation (EU) No 2023/2831 on the application of Arts 107 and 108 of the Treaty on the Functioning of the European Union to *de minimis* aid (OJ L, 2023/2831, 15.12.2023).
318. Article 3 of Commission Regulation (EU) No 2023/2831 (OJ L, 2023/2831, 15.12.2023). In order to rely on the *de minimis* rules, certain conditions must however be fulfilled in connection with the award of aid.
319. Article 1 of Commission Regulation (EU) No 2023/2831 (OJ L, 2023/2831, 15.12.2023).
320. Commission Regulation (EU) No 2023/2831 (OJ L, 2023/2831, 15.12.2023), Art. 3(2). If aid is given in some other form than as cash, the aid must be calculated as the gross grant equivalent of the aid, Art. 3(5).
321. Commission Regulation (EU) No 2023/2831 (OJ L, 2023/2831, 15.12.2023), Art. 3(1). In relation to groups of companies, it will be the accumulated aid paid to the group as a whole which is relevant for the application of the *de minimis* provision, see Art. 2(2).
322. Commission Regulation (EU) No 2023/2831 (OJ L, 2023/2831, 15.12.2023), Art. 3(7).
323. *See* more in Commission Notice on the recovery of unlawful and incompatible State aid, (OJ 2019 C 247/1), para. 101, and the case-law mentioned herein.

which exhaustively state in what special circumstances the Commission *can* (Article 107(3)) or *must* (Article 107(2)) approve an aid measure as being compatible with the internal market. There is a similar provision in Article 108(2), third paragraph, whereby the Council may approve an aid measure as being compatible with the internal market.[324] In accordance with the practice of the CJ, these exemptions are interpreted restrictively.[325]

The overall aim of the Commission in the area of State aid is to confirm and strengthen the application of the provisions on State aid both by effective control of the Member States' aid measures and by the effective enforcement of the Treaty provisions on State aid, with a view to reducing the extent of aid provided by the Member States and thereby limiting distortions of competition in the internal market.

On the basis of the European Council's encouragement, in March 2005, for State aid to be reduced and to be better targeted with a view to achieving the goals of growth and employment under the Lisbon Strategy,[326] in 2005 the Commission presented its 'State aid action plan – Less and better-targeted State aid: a roadmap for State aid reform 2005–2009'.[327] The guidelines laid down for the reform include: less and better-targeted State aid; a more refined economic approach; more effective procedures and better enforcement, predictability and transparency; and shared responsibility between the Commission and the Member States.

This reform has most recently been followed up by the Commission Communication on EU State Aid Modernisation.[328] The Modernisation Plan has three main aims: (1) to foster sustainable, smart and inclusive growth in a competitive internal market; (2) to focus Commission *ex ante* scrutiny on cases with the biggest impact on the internal market while strengthening the Member States' cooperation in State aid enforcement; and (3) to streamline the rules and provide for faster decisions.[329] Most recently, the *Green Deal Industrial Plan (2023)*, which should contribute to the reinforcement of the competitiveness of the European net-zero industry and support a quick transition to climate neutrality, helps to shape the Commission's State aid policy.[330]

---

324. Under Art. 107(3)(e) the Council may also, on a proposal from the Commission, approve other categories of aid than those listed in the Article.
325. Case T-106/95, FFSA, para. 172.
326. The Lisbon Strategy, adopted at the Extraordinary Meeting of the European Council in Lisbon on 23–24 Mar. 2000, Council/00/900, is a strategy aimed at making the EU the most competitive and dynamic knowledge-based economy in the world by 2010. The Lisbon Strategy has now been replaced by the Europe 2020 Strategy, adopted by the Council on 17 Jun. 2010, which seeks to ensure that the EU is a knowledge-based, sustainable and inclusive economy which is capable of providing high levels of productivity and employment and characterised by social cohesion. *See* the Communication from the Commission: EUROPE 2020 A strategy for smart, sustainable and inclusive growth (COM(2010) 2020 final).
327. COM(2005) 107 final of 7 Jun. 2005.
328. Commission Communication of 8 May 2012 on EU State Aid Modernisation, COM(2012) 209 final. Since then the State aid modernisation package has been subject to a *Fitness Check* (launched by the Commission on 7 Jan. 2019), resulting in the evaluation and update of several of the State aid regulatory instruments.
329. Commission Communication on EU State Aid Modernisation, point 8.
330. Commission Notice: *A Green Deal Industrial Plan for the Net-Zero Age*, 1 Feb. 2023, COM(2023) 62 final. Thus, for example, the Commission's General Block *Exemption* Regulation, 651/2014

Since then, the Member States have targeted most of their State aid to horizontal goals of general interest rather than to supporting individual undertakings or sectors. In 2021, the total amount of State aid provided by the Member States is estimated to be EUR 334.5 billion (including COVID-19 aid).[331]

The high level of total State aid within the EU reflects the fact that, despite its policy aims, the Commission largely approves the Member States' provision of State aid. This approval practice is based on the fact that it is to a certain extent regarded as legitimate to use aid in support of purposes which have a high priority in the EU.[332] For example, this is the case in relation to aid for small- and medium-sized enterprises, environmental protection, research and development and innovation, employment, regions and culture, and COVID-19 aid which alone in 2021 totalled EUR 190.65 billion and thus approx. 57% of the total aid. In practice, however, more than 97% of the Member States' aid measures are implemented by the Member States themselves, within the framework of the Commission's General Block Exemption Regulation,[333] and thus without a concrete, individual assessment and decision-making by the Commission on the compatibility of the aid.

The Commission's approach to approving the State aid measures of the Member States is based on two significant requirements. First, the aid must promote the aims and interests of the *EU*.[334] This means that the interests of the Member State in giving the aid and the interests of the recipient in receiving it are irrelevant. Second, the aid must be *necessary* for promoting the aims and interests in question.[335] This requirement means that if, without the intervention of the Member State, market forces can promote the aims and interests to a sufficient degree, aid for the promotion of these aims cannot, as a starting, be approved.[336] The aid must thus attempt both to make good an identified market failure and encourage the undertaking that receives the aid to change its conduct in such a way that it initiates an activity which it would not otherwise have done without the aid or which it would only have carried out in a more limited or to a different extent. At the same time, the aid must be proportionate to its aim.

The Commission's approach to the application of the State aid rules in relation to the various industrial, environmental and social policy aims which can, under certain circumstances, be legitimately promoted via State aid are to some extent expressed in

---

L 2014 187/1 (GBER), is most recently amended by Commission Regulation (EU) 2023/1315 (OJ 2023 L 167/1) (Green Deal GBER Amendment).

331. See the State aid Scoreboard – *see*: https://competition-policy.ec.europa.eu/state-aid/scoreboard_en.
332. Article 107(2) and (3) lists a number of overriding purposes which mean or which can mean that a State aid measure is compatible with the internal market.
333. Commission Regulation (EU) 651/2014 (OJ 2014 L 187/1) (as amended).
334. Case 730/79, *Philip Morris*, paras 16 and 17.
335. Case 730/79, *Philip Morris*, para. 17. *See also* Commission Decision 98/251/EC (OJ 1998 L 103/28), on a proposal by Austria to give aid to Hoffmann-La Roche for the development of a medicine. At the time when it was proposed to give Hoffmann-La Roche research and development aid, the development project had already been brought to a successful conclusion, so the Member State was unable to show that the aid was necessary.
336. In relation to Art. 107(3)(c), however, it appears from Case C-594/18 P, *Austria (Hinkley Point)*, that the absence of a market failure does not necessarily mean that the conditions in the exemption regulation will not be satisfied, cf. para. 67.

the adoption of the block exemption regulations,[337] and to some extent in the publication of a number of soft law instruments in the form of guidelines, notices and framework provisions,[338] which the Commission has adopted in order to give some predictability about what State aid measures are likely to be approved. Thus, the Commission has adopted guidelines on the application of the State aid rules in relation to aid for rescuing and restructuring undertakings which are in financial difficulties, aid for measures for environmental protection, and aid for research and development and innovation.[339] In connection with the financial crisis and the COVID-19 crisis the Commission has used a number of temporary guidelines, which is also currently the case in relation to the crisis following the aggression against Ukraine by Russia.[340]

Just as the Commission has a positive view of certain purposes of State aid, there are also some purposes for State aid which are automatically considered incompatible with the internal market. This applies in particular to aid which is aimed at promoting an undertaking's exports. Measures which are aimed at supporting the operation of an undertaking are also considered, in principle, to be incompatible with the internal market.

4.1 Aid for Exports

The kinds of aid which are considered to be aid to export-related activities include 'aid directly linked to the quantities exported, to the establishment and operation of a distribution network or to other current expenditure linked to the export activity.'[341] The aim of such aid is to directly influence competition between the undertaking receiving the aid and its actual and potential competitors. The harmful effects of State aid for exports are, therefore, clear. For this reason, the Commission regards export aid for trade between the Member States as incompatible with the internal market, as the export aid is clearly contrary to the goals of the EU. For this reason, export aid is not

---

337. Commission Regulation (EU) No 2023/2831 on the application of Arts 107 and 108 of the Treaty on the Functioning of the European Union to *de minimis* aid (OJ L, 2023/2831, 15.12.2023); and Commission Regulation (EU) No 651/2014 declaring certain categories of aid compatible with the internal market in application of Arts 107 and 108 of the Treaty (the 'General block exemption Regulation') (OJ 2014 L 187/1).
338. For a more detailed discussion of soft law and the legal significance of its measures, *see* Case C-69/05, *Commission v. Luxembourg;* and Case T-198/01, *Technische Glaswerke.*
339. Communication from the Commission – Guidelines on State aid for rescuing and restructuring non-financial undertakings in difficulty (OJ 2014 C 249/1); Communication from the Commission – Guidelines on State aid for environmental protection and energy 2022 (OJ 2022 C 80/1); and Communication from the Commission – Framework for State aid for research and development and innovation (OJ 2022 C 414/1). When the Commission assesses whether State aid is compatible with the internal market, it uses the substantive rules which applied at the time when the aid was given; *see* Commission notice on the determination of the applicable rules for the assessment of unlawful State aid (OJ 2002 C 119/22). This approach is in line with the established practice of the courts; *see, e.g.*, Case T-357/02, *Freistaat Sachsen*, para. 94.
340. Temporary Crisis and Transition Framework for State Aid measures to support the economy following the aggression against Ukraine by Russia (OJ 2023/C 101/03).
341. Article 1(e) of Commission Regulation (EU) No 2023/2831 on the application of Arts 107 and 108 of the Treaty on the Functioning of the European Union to *de minimis* aid (OJ L, 2023/2831, 15.12.2023).

covered by the *De minimis* Regulation.[342] For the same reason, the Commission considers export aid as not suitable for exemption from the prohibition of State aid, regardless of the intensity or form of the aid or what other aims or reasons there may be for the aid.[343]

4.2 Operating Aid

An undertaking which receives operating aid is relieved of the expenses which it would normally have to bear in its day-to-day management and its usual activities.[344] The Commission interprets operating aid broadly, and in this respect, for example, aid for advertising campaigns and aid for market research are considered to be operating aid.[345] Aid of this kind has a direct effect on production costs and sales prices, and therefore in principle it distorts competition within the business sector where it is granted.[346] For this reason, operating aid will, in principle, not be exempted under Article 107(3), as such aid will not promote the purposes referred to in the provision.[347] When such aid comes to an end, the undertaking is back where it was before, without the aid having contributed to the promotion of the EU's aims or interests.

However, in special circumstances, operating aid could be covered by Article 107(3) as long as the aid is used for the promotion of one of the legitimate purposes of aid referred to above. The Commission has, therefore, exceptionally approved operating aid on condition that the aid is necessary, temporary and in principle regressive and that the aid only compensates for the additional costs incurred by the undertaking from the pursuit of the purpose in question. Such approvals have primarily concerned operating aid in the area of energy saving, among other things, in the form of tax advantages, as well as operating aid for the treatment of waste.

4.3 Investment Aid

In contrast to aid for exports and operating aid, investment aid will often contribute to the promotion of the EU's aims and interests. Aid for investment gives undertakings a financial incentive to make investments which are necessary to bring them into line with the applicable laws, such as investing in environmental protection measures which go beyond the applicable laws. For this reason, investment aid will, to a large extent, be approved by the Commission.

---

342. Article 1(e) of Commission Regulation (EU) No 2023/2831 on the application of Arts 107 and 108 of the Treaty on the Functioning of the European Union to *de minimis* aid (OJ L, 2023/2831, 15.12.2023).
343. VIIth Report on competition policy, 1978, para. 242. This view was acknowledged by the CJ in Joined Cases 6 and 11/69, *Commission v. France*. The case concerned a French preferential rate for rediscounting on the export of goods, with the aim that the exported goods could compete with the domestically produced goods in the other Member States.
344. *See* the definition of operating aid in Case T-459/93, *Siemens*, para. 48.
345. Case T-459/93, *Siemens*.
346. Commission Decision 92/398 (OJ 1992 L 207/47).
347. Case T-459/93, *Siemens*, para. 48. *See also* Case C-86/89, *Italy v. Commission*, para. 8.

The assessment of whether an aid measure is investment aid or operating aid is made in an EU context. It is thus irrelevant how national tax or accounting rules classify the aid.

4.4 Possibilities for Approval

4.4.1 Article 107(2)

Article 107(2) states that certain forms of aid *are* compatible with the internal market. According to this provision, this includes certain forms of aid of a social character, certain forms of aid to make good damage caused by natural disasters,[348] and certain forms of aid for areas of Germany affected by the division of Germany. What these forms of aid have in common is that they all aim to re-establish the financial and competitive situation of aid recipients prior to their being affected by the relevant event. The aid must, therefore, not go beyond what is necessary to re-establish the aid recipient's financial position.[349]

When applying Article 107(2), the Commission's powers are limited to establishing whether the aid measure satisfies the conditions for being covered by the exemption. If this is confirmed, the Commission must approve the measure unless the Commission finds that the measure is not proportionate to the aim pursued or is not compatible with the general principles of Union law or with the other provisions of the Treaty. This means that the Commission does not have any discretion to refuse approval.[350]

4.4.2 Article 107(3)

Article 107(3) gives the Commission the possibility of approving State aid for promoting development in certain regions[351] or areas of the economy,[352] as well as for realising important projects of common European interest[353] and for promoting and conserving culture.[354]

---

348. *See, e.g.*, XXIVth Report on competition policy, 1995, para. 354, concerning aid given because of flood damage caused by the Meuse going over its banks.
349. More details on the State aid framework can be found in the Commission's General block exemption Regulation, Commission Regulation 651/2014 (OJ 2014 L 187/1) (as amended), as well as in the Guidelines on State aid for climate, environmental protection and energy 2022 (OJ 2022 C 80/1). *See also* Commission Decisions in Case SA.33083 and Case SA.35083 on tax advantages granted by Italy to undertakings in areas affected by natural disasters.
350. Case 730/79, *Philip Morris*, para. 17.
351. Regional aid may be exempted, if the conditions in Art. 107(3)(a) are fulfilled.
352. *See* Art. 107(3)(c).
353. Article 107(3)(b). *See* further Commission Communication on Criteria for the analysis of the compatibility with the internal market of State aid to promote the execution of important projects of common European interest, (OJ 2021 C528/10).
354. In relation to the provision on aid for culture in Art. 107(3)(d), *see, e.g.*, Commission Decision 1999/133/EC, *CELF* (OJ 1999 L 44/37).

The Commission has wide discretion in deciding whether an aid measure can be approved in accordance with Article 107(3). The assessment of an aid measure's compatibility or lack of compatibility with the internal market raises a number of problems which involve considerations of a technical and a political nature, as well as consideration for the overall economic situation.[355] In this connection, the Commission has to take as its starting point an assessment of the need for aid in an EU context. This assessment covers not only the need to achieve the economic goals of the EU but also the need to achieve other goals which are important to the EU.[356] In this connection, the Commission carries out a balancing test, i.e. weighs the negative effects of the aid on trade and competition against the positive effect on the achievement of the EU's goals.

The Commission cannot approve an aid measure which conflicts with one of the other provisions of the Treaty. Regardless of whether an aid measure could be exempted from the prohibition of State aid, it cannot be approved if, for example, it conflicts with freedom of establishment or the right of free movement of goods.[357]

4.4.3 Article 108(2), Third Paragraph

According to Article 108(2), third paragraph, when exceptional circumstances justify it, the Council may decide, unanimously, that an aid measure should be considered compatible with the internal market. This applies regardless of the State aid assessment which may be made under the provisions in Article 107 or the regulations adopted in accordance with Article 109.

A Member State can submit a request to the Council for the application of Article 108(2), third paragraph, before the Commission decides that the aid in question is not compatible with the internal market. If the Commission has made such a decision on the incompatibility of the aid measure, the Council no longer has powers to apply Article 108(2), third paragraph, as a basis for declaring the State aid measure concerned to be incompatible with the internal market.[358]

The provision in Article 108(2), third paragraph, is not often used, but it has been used in a few cases to approve aid measures in the agricultural sector and the transport sector, among others.

Bibliography

Alexandra Miladinovic: *Selectivity and the Arm's Length Principle in EU State aid Law*, 2022.

---

355. Case T-149/95, *Ducros*, para. 63.
356. *See* the Opinion of Advocate General Capotorti in Case 730/79, *Philip Morris*.
357. *See also* Case C-594/18 P, *Austria (Hinkley Point)*, stating that State aid, which turns out to contravene rules of EU law on the environment, cannot be declared compatible with the internal market pursuant to Art. 107(3)(c), but still – in connection with TFEU Art. 194, and the freedom of the Member States to choose their energy sources – cannot be regarded as precluding, in all circumstances, the award of State aid for the construction and operation of a nuclear power plant, cf. paras 45–49.
358. Case C-110/02, *Commission v. Council*, para. 33; and Case C-399/03, *Commission v. Council*.

Caroline Buts & José Buendía Sierra (eds.): *Milestones in State Aid Case Law*, 2022.
Conor Quigley: *European State Aid Law and Policy*, 2009.
Franz Jürgen Saöcker & Frank Montag: *European State aid Law*, 2016.
Herwig C.H. Hofmann & Claire Micheau (eds.): *State Aid Law of the European Union*, 2016.
Juan Jorge Piernas López: *The Concept of State Aid under EU Law*, 2015.
Keylin Bacon: *European Union Law of State Aid*, 2017.
Leigh Hancher & Juan Jorge Perinas Ló;pez: *Research handbook on European State Aid Law*, 2021.
Leigh Hancher, Tom Ottervanger & Piet Jan Slot: *EU State Aids*, 2021.
Lisa Lovdahl Gormsen: *European State Aid and Tax Rulings*, 2019.
Philipp Werner & Vincent Verouden (eds.): *EU State Aid Control*, 2017.
Pier Luigi Parcu, Giorgi Monti & Marco Botta: *EU State aid Law, Emerging Trends at the National and EU Level*, 2020.

CHAPTER 10
Public Undertakings

1   INTRODUCTION

Over the last three decades, public undertakings have attracted considerable political attention. The number of cases which have been brought before the Court of Justice of the European Union (CJ) concerning the provisions on public undertakings has increased in line with this.

In principle, public undertakings are covered by the same provisions as private undertakings, in other words, primarily Articles 101 and 102. This applies to public undertakings which operate independently of public authorities and on an equal footing with other undertakings in the market. However, it is only a minority of public undertakings that are independent of public authorities. Most public undertakings have a connection to a public authority in the way in which they benefit from special rights, for example, concessions, legal monopolies. This means that the majority of public undertakings do not operate on an equal footing with private undertakings but have special advantages over competing undertakings. In the Treaty on the Functioning of the European Union (TFEU), Articles 106 and 37 contain provisions which are intended to ensure that competition is not distorted under the special conditions of competition which apply when one undertaking has been granted an exclusive right. While the subject of this chapter is public undertakings, Articles 106 and 37 apply equally to privately owned undertakings where they have been granted special or exclusive rights by a public authority. The granting of such rights makes these undertakings 'public' in the sense that by granting such rights, the granting authority establishes and maintains some form of influence over such undertakings. This means that the public authority has the possibility of influencing the market, so Articles 106 (and Article 37) are primarily aimed at the decisions of public authorities or the Member States.

To the extent that these privileged undertakings conduct themselves in a way which distorts competition independently and without reference to the exclusive or special right they have been granted, their conduct will not be governed by Article 106 (or Article 37) TFEU but by the ordinary competition rules in Articles 101 and 102.

In this chapter, the focus is primarily on one Treaty provision, namely Article 106. This provision governs the special situations where public entities do not act as administrative authorities but rather as market participants. The aim of this provision is to ensure that the Treaty provisions for securing the conditions of competition (i.e., the competition rules and the rules on freedom of movement) are also complied with in cases where there is a public undertaking, rather than the exercise of administrative authority.

2 PRESENTATION OF THE PROVISIONS

Article 106(1) TFEU provides that a Member State may not enact or maintain any measure contrary to the rules in the Treaty in respect of such undertakings as the Member State grants special or exclusive rights or in relation to their conduct towards public undertakings. The provision refers in particular to infringements of the Treaty competition rules and of the prohibition on discrimination in Article 18 TFEU.

According to Article 106(2), undertakings which have been entrusted with the operation of services of general economic interest or which have the character of a revenue-producing monopoly are subject to the Treaty rules, in particular to the rules on competition, in so far as the application of such rules does not obstruct the performance, in law or in fact, of the particular tasks assigned to them. It concludes by stating that the development of trade must not be affected to such an extent as would be contrary to the interests of the Union.

Finally, in Article 106(3), the Commission is given powers to address appropriate directives or decisions to Member States to ensure that the provisions of the Article are applied.

Article 37(1) TFEU, on State monopolies, states:

> Member States shall adjust any State monopolies of a commercial character so as to ensure that no discrimination regarding the conditions under which goods are procured and marketed exists between nationals of Member States.
>
> The provisions of this Article shall apply to any body through which a Member State, in law or in fact, either directly or indirectly supervises, determines or appreciably influences imports or exports between Member States. These provisions shall likewise apply to monopolies delegated by the State to others.

Under Article 37(2), Member States must refrain from introducing any new measure which is contrary to the principles laid down in Article 37(1).

In the following, the focus will be on the application of Article 106 (TFEU), as this provision is part of the overall picture of competition law in the EU. By contrast, there will be no further examination of Article 37 (TFEU). This provision regulates undertakings with special and statutory rights but is part of the rule on the free movement of goods and is thus without the scope of this book. As there are certain interfaces between the two provisions, Article 37 is included in certain places where it is relevant, see especially Section 3.1 below.

2.1 Terminology

The terminology used in the above provisions, as well as in a number of secondary acts of Union law, is very varied. For example, in relation to the exclusive right which is granted to undertakings, the terms used are 'exclusive right', 'legal monopoly', 'concession', etc. For the purposes of this presentation, it has been decided to use uniform terms when referring to general circumstances. Thus, the terms used are: *privileged undertaking*, in relation to entities that have been granted rights; *privileged activity*, for the activity which benefits from protection; and *exclusive or special rights*, in respect of the right which is granted to privileged undertakings. In respect of specific rights, the terms used are those used in the particular provisions concerned.

3 THE AIMS AND STRUCTURE OF THE PROVISIONS

Articles 106 and 37 differ in their formulation and in the contexts in which they apply, but they nevertheless have a sufficient degree of similarity in their content to enable them to be treated together here.

3.1 The Application of Article 106 and Article 37

The application of Article 106 TFEU requires knowledge of the provision but also knowledge of the distinction between Article 106 and Article 107, as there is a certain overlap (at least conceptually) between the two articles.

In essence, Article 345 TFEU states that the Member States have the right to organise themselves as they wish. This means that the Member States can organise their undertakings as they find best. At the same time, the organisation of undertakings in the individual Member States must naturally comply with the other Treaty rules on market conduct, i.e., in particular, the prohibition on discrimination on the grounds of nationality (Article 18); the freedoms of movement (in particular Articles 34, 45, 49 and 56); the competition rules (Articles 101 and 102); and the rules on State aid (Articles 107 and 108).

Article 106 should be read in conjunction with Article 345 which states that the Treaty in no way affects the rules of Member States governing the system of property ownership. Thus, the Treaty does not affect the right of Member States to organise an undertaking according to the legal form that each Member State may choose. Thus, in principle, it is primarily the *activities* of the undertaking in question more than the *existence of a monopoly* which the Treaty regulates[1]. There is nothing in the wording of Article 106 to prevent Member States from organising their activities as they find most

---

1. This can also be seen from the wording of Art. 37 in particular, which requires adaptation of the state trade monopolies and not liquidation.

appropriate. With reference to Articles 345 and 106, the Court, however, has also established that the state aid rules also apply to situations where the *recipient* of the state aid is public, as Article 106 precisely allows public undertakings to be covered by the compensation rules[2].

In its earlier practice, the CJ established that the only thing that could be disputed in connection with a public authority's allocation of rights to undertakings was not the rights themselves or their form (the existence of sole rights) but only the illegal exercise of the sole right; *see* Case 155/73, *Sacchi*.

At the start of the 1990s, this practice was modified so that even the right itself can now be found to be in breach of Article 106 (or Article 37).[3]

As is clear from the wording of the provisions, the basic difference between Articles 37 and 106 is that the rules on State monopolies of a commercial character contain an independent prohibition, while Article 106 refers to the other Treaty provisions.

Both Articles 37 and 106 cover measures adopted at the State level and regional and local measures.[4] Where references are made to the Member States, they must be interpreted broadly so as to cover all levels of public authorities in the Member States.

While Article 37 imposes obligations on Member States in relation to monopoly undertakings, the provision does not contain any specific obligations for the undertakings themselves. Article 106(1) contains an obligation for the Member States, while Article 106(2) contains both an obligation and an exception for undertakings.

Article 37 is concerned exclusively with imports (and exports) of goods, whereas Article 106 refers to all the Treaty provisions, and in particular, the competition rules and the prohibition of discrimination on the grounds of nationality.

For both articles it is the case that all undertakings and bodies which have been granted a State concession are covered, regardless of their legal status.[5]

It is clear from Article 37 and Article 106 that the two provisions overlap each other to a considerable degree. The distinction between Article 37 and Article 106 is that Article 37 has a *lex specialis* function in relation to Article 106(1), but it is subordinate to Article 106(2).

3.2 Those to Whom the Provisions Are Addressed

Article 106(1) is addressed in particular to the Member States. However, it does not only refer to central government authorities but also covers local and regional government bodies.[6] In addition, Article 106(2) also applies to the measures which the undertakings themselves adopt.

---

2. *See* C-385/18. Arriva Italia Srl, premis 67.
3. Thus, *see* Case C-320/91, *Corbeau*.
4. Case 30/87, *Bodson*, para. 13.
5. Case 30/87, *Bodson*, para. 13.
6. Case 30/87, *Bodson*.

3.3 The Application of Article 106

As is clear from the wording of Article 106 TFEU, the provision contains no direct independent prohibition, but refers to other Treaty provisions, some of which are emphasised.[7] These emphasised provisions are the prohibition on discrimination in Article 18 and the competition rules. The practice has shown that the primary application of Article 106 (at least in the early years) has been in connection with problems involving abuses of dominant positions, i.e., in connection with Article 102.

Article 106 has also been applied in connection with other Treaty provisions, in particular Article 56 on the freedom to provide services. In particular, Article 56 has been used in connection with Article 106(2) which provides for the application of the Treaty provisions to undertakings which have been entrusted with the provision of services of general economic interest.

Recent years have shown that Article 106 is now mainly applied in combination with the rules on state aid. At the same time, it can be seen that it is mostly Article 106(2), which is applied together with Article 107, partly because in some of the state aid rules, it must be examined whether an undertaking is entrusted with the operation of a public service (a service of general economic interest) and partly because Article 106(2) includes an exception from the Treaty's rules on prohibition, including Article 107(1)[8]

4 ARTICLE 106(1)

4.1 Concepts

4.1.1 *Special or Exclusive Rights*

Some of the decisive concepts in Article 106 are *special or exclusive rights*. The CJ has not given a clear definition of these terms, but there are a number of indications for how they should be understood.

The CJ has not explicitly decided on the question of when an exclusive right exists. However, in the legal literature, there is agreement that such a right exists when there is an exclusive right to carry on some specific activity, i.e., a legal monopoly.[9]

---

7. This indirect construction has been criticised several times; see, e.g., Gareth Davies who directly states that 'The Treaty, and society, would be better if it was gone', p. 67 in *Kajewski, Neergaard & Van de Gronden* (eds): *The Changing Legal Framework for Services of General Interest in Europe*, 2009.
8. See, e.g., the cases C-796/17, AB '*Achema*' and C-660/15, *Viasat Broadcasting UK v. Commission*.
9. Inspiration can be drawn from Art. 2(f) of Directive 2006/111, on the transparency of financial relations between Member States and public undertakings as well as on financial transparency within certain undertakings (as amended), in which exclusive rights are regarded as 'rights that are granted by a Member State to one undertaking through any legislative, regulatory or administrative instrument, reserving it the right to provide a service or undertake an activity within a given geographical area'.

The right of exclusivity means that it is (only) the owner of the right who may carry on the activity in question. In principle, it is irrelevant how the owner of the right in fact exercises this right. Thus, the owner of the right can make agreements with other undertakings for them to take on certain of the activities, as long as there is provision for this in the agreement with the entity granting the right.

It is more difficult to determine when a special right exists. The term *special right* has not been more precisely defined by the CJ.[10]

For a possible definition, reference can be made to the definition of the same term in Directive 2006/111 on the transparency of financial relations between Member States and public undertakings as well as on financial transparency within certain undertakings (as amended). 'Special rights' are defined there as: 'rights that are granted by a Member State to a limited number of undertakings, through any legislative, regulatory or administrative instrument, which, within a given geographical area:

- limits to two or more the number of such undertakings authorised to provide a service or undertake an activity, otherwise than according to objective, proportional and non-discriminatory criteria; or
- designates, otherwise than according to such criteria, several competing undertakings as being authorised to provide a service or undertake an activity; or
- confers on any undertaking or undertakings, otherwise than according to such criteria, any legal or regulatory advantages which substantially affect the ability of any other undertaking to provide the same service or to operate the same activity in the same geographical area under substantially equivalent conditions.'[11]

To the extent that authority can be found in secondary legislation, there can be special rights when more than one undertaking has been granted a right to carry on an activity in a given area or where one or more undertakings have been granted advantages in relation to other undertakings, but where the right to carry on the activity in question is open to all undertakings.

The question could be asked whether there are certain limits as to the kinds of advantages that will result in the application of Article 106. For example, to what extent will Article 106 be applicable to a situation where the competitors of an undertaking are subject to certain administrative burdens to which the privileged undertaking is not subject? It must be assumed that the competitive advantage must be given to the privileged undertaking rather than to its competitors. Where the competitors are subject to burdens, it is possible that the Treaty provisions on freedom of movement will apply instead. Furthermore, it must be considered how significant an advantage must be in order for Article 106 to be applicable. It is apparent from the definition in Directive 2006/111 on the transparency of financial relations between Member States and public undertakings that a special right will exist where the competitive advantage which a privileged undertaking obtains means that competition is not on 'substantially equivalent conditions'. On this basis, the granting of minor advantages, which only

---

10. However, in point 50 of his Opinion in Joined Cases 271, 281 and 289/90, *Spain, Belgium and Italy v. Commission* (on telecommunications services), Advocate General Jacobs argued there must be special rights when a right is given to a limited number of undertakings.
11. Directive 2006/111 Art. 2(g).

have a limited significance for the competitive situation, would presumably not be enough for it to be found that a special right exists.

Within the meaning of Article 106, the terms *special or exclusive rights* do not include intellectual property rights[12] or rights to practise a profession subject to authorisation.

4.1.2 The Grant of a Right

The grant of a special or exclusive right can be by means of traditional public law methods, such as by legislation or by an administrative decision, as well as by private law methods, such as by a contract. The assessment, which is used for determining whether a right has been granted, is thus functional and not formal. Where a grant is made in the form of a public law act, for example, by legislation, there will clearly be a grant, in the sense of the wording of Article 106. Where a grant is made in the form of an agreement, it is decisive whether the grant is made on the basis of legislation or some other administrative act and whether the measure making the grant is drawn up by a public authority or public undertaking. Where the grant is made by a public undertaking, this will probably not constitute a grant within the meaning of Article 106 since such a body will lack the powers of a public administrative body.

In Case 30/87, *Bodson*, the CJ considered whether the grant by local authorities of exclusive rights to provide funeral services was covered by Article 106. The CJ stated: 'As the Commission has rightly pointed out, Article 85 [now Article 101] of the Treaty applies, according to its actual wording, to agreements "between undertakings". It does not apply to contracts for concessions concluded between communes acting in their capacity as public authorities and undertakings entrusted with the operation of a public service'; *see* the eighteenth paragraph of the judgment. In Case C-393/92, *Almelo*, the CJ had to consider whether an agreement entered into between a regional energy supplier and a local energy supplier for the exclusive supply of energy was covered by Article 106. The CJ stated: 'IJM has not been granted an exclusive concession giving it a monopoly in the supply of electricity within the territory covered by the concession. Second, the contracts giving rise to the dispute before the national court were concluded not between the public authorities and IJM but between a regional distributor and local distributors. Moreover, those contracts determine the conditions under which IJM supplies electric power to the local distributors, and do not have the effect of transferring to those distributors the public service concession granted to the regional undertaking. The conditions of supply, in particular the exclusive purchasing clause, stem from the agreement between the parties and are not inherent in the territorial concession granted to IJM by the public authorities.'[13]

---

12. There are several reasons why the term 'exclusive rights' does not cover the exclusive rights granted under intellectual property law. First, the rights referred to in Art. 106 have a wider area of protection than intellectual property rights. Intellectual property rights protect individual trademarks or products, whereas Art. 106 is directed at certain activities. Furthermore, the basic consideration of intellectual property law is consideration for undertakings and their possibilities of commercially exploiting the products they develop and their trade reputation, whereas the concern behind Art. 106 is for the protection of the internal market as well as certain general interests of society; *see* Art. 106(2).
13. Paragraph 31 of the judgment.

4.1.3 Undertaking

The concept of an undertaking is important for both Article 106(1) and (2). An 'undertaking' is defined in Union competition law as an entity which is engaged in some economic activity. The difficult point in this context is *economic activity*.

Activities which are carried out in the private market will often naturally be characterised as economic activities. However, there are a number of activities which, to a certain extent, *can* be undertaken by the private market, but the private market may not give the same results as are obtained when the performance of the tasks is under public control.

According to the case law, for example, the business of an employment agency is covered by the term 'economic activity', while air traffic control and environmental monitoring and control of harbours are not considered economic activities. The CJ has also stated that the services of providing insurance and pensions *can* be economic activities, depending on the way in which the individual arrangements are set up. The CJ has also stated that the fact that an entity makes purchases and thereby acts on the market using economic means does not in itself mean that the public body in question qualifies as an undertaking. What is decisive for whether a purchase is regarded as part of the running of an undertaking is the subsequent use of the purchased product or service. If the product is to be part of a commercial arrangement and subsequently sold, the activity is regarded as an economic activity. If the product purchased is used in the ordinary running of the entity and is thus not resold, the purchase will not in itself be regarded as an economic activity; *see* Case C-205/03 P, *FENIN*.

It is possible to classify the situations where the CJ has had to consider to what extent they were an economic activity and, thus, an undertaking. First, there are individual services, which are characterised by being aimed at a specific person or a defined group of persons. Second, there are collective services which are characterised by the fact that the recipient of the service is society as a whole and not an individual or group of individuals.

Most of the cases which the CJ has considered in the category of individual services have concerned various forms of insurance, though primarily pension policies. *See*, for example, Case C-67/96, *Albany International*; Case C-244/94, *Fédération Francaise Societes d'Assurances*; Joined Cases C-159 and 160/91, *Poucet*; Case C-218/00, *Cisal*; and Case C-437/09, *AG2R*. In these cases, the CJ found that the most important factor in judging whether there was an economic activity was the element of solidarity, i.e., whether the insurance scheme was arranged so that there was no direct link between the premiums paid and the benefits obtained. When assessing other activities, it can be expected that the degree of solidarity which characterises the activity will be decisive – in other words, whether the activity is carried on for the benefit of society or whether there are exclusively individual arrangements between the service provider and the individual citizen.

The case law relating to collective service provision is dealt with primarily in two leading cases: Case C-364/92, *Eurocontrol*; and C-343/95, *Calì*. In the *Eurocontrol* case, the CJ considered whether the activity of air traffic control was covered by the term 'economic activity'. The CJ found that it was not, and emphasised the nature of the activity, the aim of the activity, and the rules to which the activity was subject. The CJ stated that: 'Taken as a whole, Eurocontrol's activities, by their nature, their aim and the rules to which they are subject, are connected with the exercise of powers relating to the control and supervision of air space which are typically those of a public authority. They are not of an economic nature justifying the application of the Treaty rules of competition.'[14]

4.1.4 Public Undertaking

The term 'public undertaking' is not defined in Article 106 or elsewhere in the Treaty. It can be said that a public undertaking will exist if the undertaking is in public or state ownership. It will not matter whether the undertaking is separated from the public authority as an independent legal person. Questions can arise where an undertaking is only partially in public ownership. The CJ has found it decisive whether there is a level of public control over the undertaking corresponding to the level of control which is required under Article 2 of Directive 2006/111 on the transparency of financial relations between Member States and public undertakings as well as on financial transparency within certain undertakings.[15] This means that an undertaking is public where a public authority can exercise direct or indirect control over the undertaking. There is an assumption that this is the case where a public authority: (1) directly or indirectly controls more than half of the undertaking's share capital; (2) controls more than half of the voting rights; or (3) can appoint more than half of the members of the undertaking's administration, management or supervisory bodies.

The decision whether an undertaking is a public undertaking should not be made on the basis of a formal interpretation, as this could lead to a risk of attempts at avoidance. Such attempts take one of two forms. First, the public authority could try to camouflage the economic activity as being the exercise of administrative authority or seek to integrate the economic activity with the exercise of administrative authority; second, the public authority could outsource the activity to a private company without maintaining any of the formal controls referred to above. However, regardless of the form of avoidance used, it will be caught by one of the Treaty's other provisions. As stated in Chapter 1, the exercise of public authority is covered by the Treaty provisions on freedom of movement, while the activities of private undertakings are directly covered by Articles 101 and 102.

4.2 The Application of Article 106

Infringements of Article 106(1) can occur in many different circumstances. There follows a systematic presentation of groups of arrangements that are assumed to be in breach of Article 106, in combination with the other provisions of the Treaty.

4.2.1 The Demand Doctrine

There can be an infringement of Article 106 (in connection with Article 102) if the exclusive right covers an activity which is not effectively taken care of by the privileged undertaking. The doctrine was laid down in Case C-41/90, *Höfner*. In this case, it was

---

14. Case C-364/92, *Eurocontrol*, para. 30.
15. Joined Cases 188 to 190/80, *France, Italy and United Kingdom v. Commission*.

claimed by Höfner that the State employment exchange could not meet the market demand for managers – a service that was provided by Höfner. The CJ held that it was contrary to Article 106, in conjunction with Article 102, to exclude private undertakings from providing this particular form of employment agency service, which places managers in vacant senior positions.

A similar, but not identical, problem is that of *special services*. The CJ has held that an exclusive right may not be expanded so as to cover special services which have not previously been offered; see Case C-320/91, *Corbeau*.

> In Case C-320/91, *Corbeau*, the CJ found that it was an abuse of a dominant position, and thus an infringement of Article 102 and Article 106, that an undertaking was prevented from providing a special service, so that an exclusive right was expanded to cover this service. The case concerned the Belgian postal monopoly. A businessman, Pierre Corbeau, offered a new postal service which consisted of collecting mail from the sender and delivering it before 12.00 on the following day. The Belgian postal authority argued that Corbeau's activity was covered by the postal monopoly and it was therefore not a lawful activity for Corbeau. In paragraph 19 of its judgment the CJ stated: 'the exclusion of competition is not justified as regards specific services dissociable from the service of general interest which meet special needs of economic operators and which call for certain additional services not offered by the traditional postal service, such as collection from the senders' address, greater speed or reliability of distribution or the possibility of changing the destination in the course of transit, in so far as such specific services, by their nature and the conditions in which they are offered, such as the geographical area in which they are provided, do not compromise the economic equilibrium of the service of general economic interest performed by the holder of the exclusive right.'

According to the practice of the CJ there are a number of conditions which must be fulfilled for a private undertaking to be able to claim that an exclusive right does not cover special services. *First*, the special service must not be connected with services of general economic interest; *second*, the special services in question must meet a particular need of business; *third*, the special service must be a supplementary service which the privileged undertaking does not offer; and *fourth*, the special service may not, according to its nature or the terms under which it is provided, disturb the economic stability of the exclusive right.

4.2.2 Cross-Subsidising

The activities which privileged undertakings have been granted the exclusive right to carry out will often be difficult to perform satisfactorily on market terms. Therefore, the performance of these activities will often be at a loss. As will be clear from the discussion below concerning Article 106(2), public undertakings are permitted to make some form of financial equalisation in order to cover for the loss-making privileged activity. This financial equalisation can be made by means of carrying out profitable activities alongside privileged activities.

The CJ has held that it is an infringement of Article 106, in conjunction with Article 102, to transfer financial resources from a protected activity to an activity which is exposed to competition. Thus, for example, it is not permitted to transfer public funds paid to support a privileged activity to an activity which is carried out in a competitive market. If this happens, there will be distortion of the competition in the free market.

Cross-subsidising also takes place within undertakings which have not been granted special rights, and in this case the cross-subsidisation only has to be assessed in relation to Article 102. In contrast to cross-subsidising by a privileged undertaking, cross-subsidising by a private undertaking is only contrary to Article 102 if the transferred funds are used for *predatory pricing*.

The General Court has accepted the use of means set aside for privileged activities for the acquisition of undertakings on other markets which are exposed to competition; *see* Case T-175/99, *UPS*.

4.2.3 *Expansion of the Exclusive Right*

In Case 18/88, *RTT*, the CJ had to decide on a referral for a judicial ruling under Article 267 TFEU. The case concerned the Belgian telecommunications monopoly RTT. The Belgian supermarket chain, GB-Inno-BM, had sold telephones which were not approved by RTT. RTT wanted GB-Inno-BM to stop selling the non-approved telephones. GB-Inno-BM argued that Union law prevented RTT from maintaining its powers of approval, as this meant that RTT should approve the products of its competitors and could therefore determine which products could be marketed. The CJ stated that:

> The Court has also held that an abuse within the meaning of Article 86 [now Article 106] is committed where, without any objective necessity, an undertaking holding a dominant position on a particular market reserves to itself an ancillary activity which might be carried out by another undertaking as part of its activities on a neighbouring but separate market, with the possibility of eliminating all competition from such undertaking.
>
> Therefore the fact that an undertaking holding a monopoly in the market for the establishment and operation of the network, without any objective necessity, reserves to itself a neighbouring but separate market, in this case the market for the importation, marketing, connection, commissioning and maintenance of equipment for connection to the said network.[16]

The CJ has held that there can be cases where, as part of its exclusive right, a privileged undertaking carries out activities which can give rise to problems concerning its legal capacity. An example of this is where the privileged undertaking must approve products before they can be put on the market but where the products in question compete with the privileged undertaking's own products.

---

16. Case 18/88, *RTT*, paras 18–19.

The first of these cases was Case C-260/89, *ERT*. In Greece, Elliniki Radiophonia Tiléorassi (ERT) had a monopoly on television broadcasting. The Greek authorities had given ERT an exclusive right to broadcast programmes produced by ERT itself and programmes produced by others. The CJ hinted, though without expressly stating, that the situation means that ERT had the possibility, and probably also the incentive, to prefer programmes it had produced itself rather than programmes produced by others. The CJ thus said: 'Article 90(1) [now: Article 106(1)] of the Treaty prohibits the granting of an exclusive right to transmit and an exclusive right to retransmit television broadcasts to a single undertaking, where those rights are liable to create a situation in which that undertaking is led to infringe Article 86 [now: Article 102] by virtue of a discriminatory broadcasting policy which favours its own programmes.'[17]

4.2.4 Essential Facilities

Under Article 106 TFEU, abuse can take the form of denying other undertakings access to the facilities of the privileged undertaking. The problem is well known in American antitrust law[18] and is called the 'essential facilities doctrine'.

The essential facilities problem is often found in connection with undertakings that have a natural monopoly. Such a situation will exist where an undertaking owns a network (electricity grid, railway network, etc.) or equivalent infrastructure (e.g., port facilities). The sectors in which such essential facilities are most important are the sectors that have traditionally been based on special and exclusive rights.

Certain sectors are characterised by the fact that participation in the market in question depends on access to such facilities. This refers in particular to the transport, telecommunications, and energy sectors, as well as television broadcasting. In addition, *there* are a number of other sectors where essential facilities may not play such a decisive role but where certain facilities are nevertheless significant. These include the postal sector and a number of other sectors where knowledge and products can constitute an essential part of the possibility of gaining access to the market.

The essential facility problem is not expressly regulated in EU law, but it arises as one of the relevant topics for the application of Article 106 and Article 102. The guidelines presented below are derived from the case law.

The starting point for competition law is that there should be freedom of contract for actors on the market. This means that undertakings have the right to choose with whom, when, how and with what content they wish to enter into agreements. On this basis, the essential facilities doctrine represents a departure from this principle. This necessarily means that it is only in exceptional circumstances that an undertaking can claim access to a competing undertaking's facilities. The reason why the principle of freedom of contract is departed from in special circumstances is that if competitors can be refused access to a facility which is essential for the performance of a service, then competition for the provision of the service is essentially excluded. It might be argued that freedom of contract should be so far-reaching that a duty to enter into a contract should never be imposed. However, the principle of proportionality and certain interests of society mean that this approach is not appropriate. This is because the alternative to accessing the essential facility is effectively either that an undertaking which wishes to operate on the market must establish its own network or infrastructure or that such

---

17. Case C-260/89, *ERT*, para. 37.
18. The doctrine was established in the case of *United States of America v. Terminal Railroad Association*, 224 U.S. 383 (1912).

undertakings cannot gain access to the market. The principle of proportionality means that such a solution would impose a disproportionately large burden on a potential competitor, compared with the disadvantages and restriction on freedom of contract which a third party's access to the network would cause for the owner of the network. From the point of view of society, it would be clearly undesirable to require the establishment of several networks since this would not be a sensible use of resources. One of the considerations which lies behind the European regulation of competition is that there should be an effective use of resources in the Member States. Where more networks are established than is necessary from the point of view of capacity, there will be a waste of resources. In addition to this, the establishment of several such networks would make it difficult for consumers to switch from one supplier to another if the consumer so wishes.

To the extent that a privileged undertaking is required to give access to an essential facility, it is possible to lay down a number of conditions for such access. Thus, it will be required that access be given on reasonable terms. An important condition will be that access should be given on equal and non-discriminatory terms. This means that if access is granted to one undertaking, access must be granted to other undertakings on the same terms, so that the price for access will be the same for all third parties which wish to use the facilities. It must also be assumed that this non-discrimination also covers the undertaking which owns the essential facility.

In determining what can be considered an essential facility, various circumstances must be taken into consideration. Consideration must be given to the importance of the facility for access to the market. As there is an obligation to enter into a contract, the obligation should only be imposed exceptionally. This means that the mere fact that access to the market is made *difficult* will not be sufficient to impose an obligation to enter into a contract. There must be an actual prevention of access to the market.

The conditions for imposing an obligation to enter into a contract in connection with access to an essential facility are:

(1) The undertaking must be *dominant* in the downstream market in question.
(2) For access to be granted, refusal of access must be connected with a high degree of probability that this will *eliminate competition* from the undertaking which seeks access.
(3) Access must be necessary, meaning that *there is only this possibility for gaining access to the market*, and thus, there is no alternative.
(4) It is not possible to give an *objective justification* for refusal.

4.2.5   Other Infringements

Article 106(1) TFEU is usually applied in conjunction with Article 102, and the CJ has considered the extent to which there is a requirement for specific abusive conduct on the part of a privileged undertaking. In Case C-553/12 P, *Commission v. DEI*, the CJ concluded that what is decisive is whether the State measures have actual or potential anti-competitive consequences.

However, Article 106 is sometimes applied together with other provisions, including the rules on freedom of movement, in particular Article 56 on the freedom to provide services.

When applying Article 106(1) in conjunction with Article 56, the former often does not play such a major role as it does when used in conjunction with Article 102. There are examples of this in connection with the granting of public procurement contracts (see Chapter 12). Here, Article 106 will often be applicable, but it will typically act to emphasise that Article 56 can apply; see Case C-410/04, *ANAV*, paragraph 23, and Case C-458/03, *Parking Brixen*, paragraph 52. The tendency for there to be limited application of Article 106 together with other provisions, other than Article 102, is also seen in connection with, among other things, national gambling rules which have been referred to the CJ. In a number of these cases, legislation has established legal monopolies or special rights for specific undertakings, in other words, potential Article 106 situations. Nevertheless, only the rules on freedom of movement have been used in these cases.

5   ARTICLE 106(2)

Article 106(2) TFEU covers undertakings that have been entrusted with the provision of services of general economic interest. Article 106(2) thus supports the prohibition in Article 106(1), but it covers a slightly different situation. At the same time, Article 106(2) is distinguished by containing an exception from the Treaty rules.

Practice shows that the development within Article 106 mainly has taken place in relation to Article 106(2), particularly in connection with the state aid rules[19].

5.1   Services of General Economic Interest

The scope of Article 106(2) covers undertakings which have been entrusted with the provision of services of general economic interest. The conditions for this are fulfilled by entrusting the provision of the service in question by a legal act of a public authority.[20] Services of general economic interest are general services which are of interest to society at large. The CJ has established that services such as telecommunications services, air traffic control, employment exchanges, television broadcasting, postal services and electricity supply are considered to be activities of general economic interest. The Member States have wide discretion to determine what they consider to be a service of economic interest. In this connection, the Commission only has the right to question a Member State's designation in cases where it is clearly wrong; see Case T-17/02, *Fred Olsen*, paragraph 216.

The importance of services of general economic interest has been increased by the inclusion of Article 14 in the Treaty. This provision states: 'Without prejudice to Article 4 of the Treaty on European Union or to Articles 93, 106 and 107 of this Treaty, and given the place occupied by

---

19. *See* among others C-114/17 P. *Spain v. Commission* and C-81/16P, *Spain & Commission.*
20. Case 127/73, *SABAM*, para. 20.

services of general economic interest in the shared values of the Union as well as their role in promoting social and territorial cohesion, the Union and the Member States, each within their respective powers and within the scope of application of the Treaties, shall take care that such services operate on the basis of principles and conditions, particularly economic and financial conditions, which enable them to fulfil their missions.' The provision is included in Part 1 of the Treaty under the heading of 'Principles', and this thereby emphasises that such services are important for the functioning of the Union. At the same time, it must be assumed that the most important role of Article 14 is as a statement of policy and that the provision is not intended to lead to any change in the actual practice concerning services of general economic interest.[21] The term 'services of general economic interest' is one that has attracted much attention over the last ten years.[22] In the most recent Procurement Directive (Directive 2014/24/EU), Article 1(4) states that the Directive 'does not affect the freedom of Member States to define, in conformity with Union law, what they consider to be services of general economic interest, how those services should be organised and financed'. The same provision goes on to state that the Directive 'does not affect the decision of public authorities whether, how and to what extent they wish to perform public functions themselves pursuant to Article 14 TFEU and Protocol No 26'.

5.2   Entrusted with the Operation of Services

The provision in Article 106(2) applies if a *right and a duty* is entrusted to an undertaking for the provision of a service of general economic interest. This can be entrusted by a central or local government entity. It is a condition that the right and duty should be entrusted by a *public authority*, but there is no requirement that it should be entrusted by means of legislation.[23] A right/duty can also be entrusted by an administrative agreement or by some other form of administrative measure. The entrusting of a right or duty on the basis of a purely private law agreement between a public authority and an undertaking does not constitute the entrusting of a right or duty for the purposes of Article 106(2).[24] However, there is nothing to stop a commercial undertaking which has been entrusted with the provision of a service of general economic interest from being involved in the process by which the task has been entrusted; *see* Case T-17/02, *Fred Olsen*, paragraph 189.

It is assumed that participation in the ownership of a public company is also not regarded as having been entrusted, if the owner of shares does not have special influence on the running of the company (the traditional company law instruments are thus insufficient). Nor can EU legislative acts or general public licences be regarded as entrusting a right/duty for the purposes of Article 106(2).[25]

---

21. However, in the Lisbon Treaty it was made clear that it must be possible for such services to be provided on economic and financial terms which make it possible for them to achieve their purposes.
22. *See, e.g.*, *Kajewski, Neergaard & Van de Gronden* (eds): The Changing Legal Framework for Services of General Interest in Europe, 2009.
23. Case 127/73, *SABAM*, para. 20.
24. Case C-393/92, *Almelo*, which concerned an agreement between a public body in its capacity as a supplier and a supplying undertaking; *see* especially para. 31.
25. *See Andreas Bala:* Art. 90 Abs. 2 im System unverfälschten Wettbewerbs, p. 62 and at p. 57. The background to this is that licences usually do not include an obligation to provide social services.

The granting of special or exclusive rights is not identical with entrusting an entity with the provision of services of general economic interest. These will often go together so that a grant under Article 106(1) will be covered by the concept of entrusting the provision of a service under Article 106(2). However, in principle, it is quite possible to grant an exclusive right which does not concern the provision of services of general economic interest, while it is also possible that entrusting to an undertaking the provision of services of general economic interest under Article 106(2) may not necessarily fulfil the conditions for being a grant of special or exclusive rights.

In order for an entity to be entrusted with the provision of services of general economic interest, the activity must be clearly defined. However, this does not exclude the possibility of subsequently changing the content of the obligation, at least as long as the changes are made between the parties, i.e., the public authority responsible and the privileged undertaking.[26] There is no obligation for the public authority to entrust the provision of services of general economic interest to an undertaking by using the public procurement rules. Such an obligation can be derived neither from the wording of Article 106(2) nor from the practice of the CJ; see Case T-17/02, *Fred Olsen*, paragraph 239.

5.3   The Exception in Article 106(2)

Article 106(2) provides that undertakings which have been entrusted with the provision of services of general economic interest must comply with the Treaty rules. At the same time, the provision enables the use of an exception to this to the extent that the service cannot be provided while complying with the Treaty rules.

5.3.1   Conditions for Exceptions

The practice shows that it is possible to exempt restrictions on competition from the Treaty provisions, as long as the restrictions on competition are necessary: (1) for it to be possible to provide services of general economic interest; (2) so that the services can be provided on acceptable financial terms; (3) so that in this connection the undertaking can have the possibility for equalising differences between profitable and non-profitable areas; (4) to prevent 'cherry-picking' (i.e., where private undertakings cream off profitable areas of the market); or (5) if the restrictions on competition are necessary for complying with national law/special obligations. The most probable defences will involve the financial circumstances for the performance of the sole right and the question of compliance with existing national laws.

5.3.2   Special Financial Circumstances

The financial circumstances of a privileged undertaking are of particular significance in connection with the exemption provision in Article 106(2). It is established that where

---

26. Case T-17/02, *Fred Olsen*, para. 202.

it is impossible for a privileged undertaking to provide services of general economic interest on acceptable financial terms, this is sufficient to justify an exemption from the Treaty rules; *see* Article 106(2). The CJ has not defined more precisely what is meant by acceptable terms, but it is clear that it is not required that the privileged activity should merely break even. A privileged undertaking is thus entitled to obtain a certain profit from its activities.

The financial equalisation which is permitted in order to give undertakings acceptable financial conditions can be achieved in many ways. One possibility is for a public authority to compensate the privileged undertaking for the losses arising from the provision of services of general economic interest. Another possibility is to reserve some other profitable activity for the privileged undertaking, so that the undertaking can make an internal financial equalisation – a form of cross-subsidy which is legitimate. A third possibility is for undertakings which carry on activities within the sector in which the privileged undertaking has an exclusive right to be required to pay a fee for financing the privileged activity.

If a public authority provides a subsidy to a privileged undertaking, in certain situations, this can be considered a State aid.[27] In this context, State aid is understood as the support provided on unilateral terms to the privileged undertaking. When financial aid is provided in connection with the equalisation of the loss which a privileged undertaking incurs through the provision of unprofitable services of general economic interest, the CJ has held that this is in accordance with the rules on State aid.[28]

> In the *Altmark* case, the CJ concluded that: 'public subsidies intended to enable the operation of urban, suburban or regional scheduled transport services are not caught by that provision (Article 107(1)) where such subsidies are to be regarded as compensation for the services provided by the recipient undertakings in order to discharge public service obligations. For the purpose of applying that criterion, it is for the national court to ascertain that the following conditions are satisfied:
>
> – first, the recipient undertaking is actually required to discharge public service obligations and those obligations have been clearly defined;
> – second, the parameters on the basis of which the compensation is calculated have been established beforehand in an objective and transparent manner;
> – third, the compensation does not exceed what is necessary to cover all or part of the costs incurred in discharging the public service obligations, taking into account the relevant receipts and a reasonable profit for discharging those obligations;
> – fourth, where the undertaking which is to discharge public service obligations is not chosen in a public procurement procedure, the level of compensation needed has been determined on the basis of an analysis of the costs which a

---

27. For more on State aid, *see* Ch. 9.
28. Case C-280/00, *Altmark*.

typical undertaking, well run and adequately provided with means of transport so as to be able to meet the necessary public service requirements, would have incurred in discharging those obligations, taking into account the relevant receipts and a reasonable profit for discharging the obligations.'[29]

With the *Altmark* case, the relationship between Article 107 and Article 106(2) was made more complex. The background for this is that the test in *Altmark* uses criteria which are highly reminiscent of those found in the case law concerning Article 106(2). The Commission has been quite energetic in distinguishing between these two provisions; *see* the latest regulatory package of 20 December 2011, consisting of a Commission Decision, two Communications from the Commission, and a proposal for a *de minimis* Regulation.

In practice, the Court has stated that the application of Article 106(2) does not require the inclusion of the conditions in Altmark (specifically conditions 2 and 4). The Court has more precisely defined that the application of the exception in Article 106(2) in terms of the test *follows* the application of the Altmark test (which is aimed at whether there is the presence of state aid) and thus does not require the fulfilment of certain Altmark conditions, but on the contrary, implies a separate test focusing on the requirements in Article 106(2).[30]

A final condition for exemption from the Treaty rules is that the exemption must not be *contrary to the interests of the Union*. The 'interests of the Union' is not a well-defined term, but the CJ has expressed a view on it in certain cases, and in can be said in general to concern the functioning of the internal market.

6 ARTICLE 106(3)

In Article 106(3), it is provided that the Commission has powers to initiate certain measures addressed to the Member States. The provision supports the general and exclusive powers of the Commission on questions of competition in the EU.

The provision gives the Commission powers to ensure compliance with Article 106(1) and (2). The Commission can ensure this by addressing appropriate directives or decisions to the Member States. With reference to this provision, the Commission has adopted several directives for the regulation of public undertakings and undertakings based on special or exclusive rights.

Thus, Directive 2006/111/EC, on the transparency of financial relations between Member States and public undertakings, as well as on financial transparency within certain undertakings, and several directives on telecommunications (e.g., Directive 2008/63/EC and Directive 2002/77/EC) have been adopted under the authority of Article 106(3).

---

29. *See also* Case C-53/00, *Ferring;* and the Opinion of Advocate General Jacobs in Case C-126/01, *GEMO.*
30. *See* C-706/17, *AB 'Achema',* premis 102 and C-660/15, *Viasat Broadcasting UK v. Commission,* premis 34.

6.1 The Adoption of Directives and Decisions

One of the most important questions in connection with the application of the powers in Article 106(3) concerns the limits to the Commission's powers under this provision on the one hand and on the other hand the other powers of the Commission and of other institutions.

In practice, it has been established that the Commission's powers under Article 106(3) (the adoption of directives and decisions) can be applied appropriately in different situations. Decisions can be used in the event of actual infringements of Article 106, whereas directives are of a more general character and are therefore addressed to the Member States in general and not in relation to specific infringements.[31]

In addition to its powers under Article 106(3), the Commission can also bring proceedings for breach of the Treaty under Article 258, and it can also use its powers under Article 108 on State aid and Article 103 concerning infringements of the general competition rules in Articles 101 and 102.

The Commission is allowed a broad scope in relation to the use of the powers given to it. According to the case law of the CJ, the Commission is not required to choose the procedure for breach of the Treaty under Article 258 rather than using any of its other powers. On the contrary, the Commission can initiate proceedings for infringements by making informal approaches to one or more of the Member States in question.

As for the Commission's powers to issue directives, directives issued under the authority of Article 106(3) are identical in form and effect to directives issued under other authority. At the same time, the procedures for adopting such directives are not the same under the different sources of authority. Thus, Article 114 lays down procedural requirements, while Article 106(3) contains no formal conditions for the procedure for adoption. This can give rise to questions of legal certainty. It is perhaps questionable that the Commission can avoid the normal procedure by using Article 106(3).

This is why the Commission is reluctant about adopting legal acts under the authority of Article 106(3). Far fewer decisions and directives have been adopted under this provision than under the other provisions concerning the internal market. At the same time, when applying Article 106(3), the Commission often follows a procedure that gives a measure of legal certainty.

The Commission can start proceedings on its own initiative, but it can also start proceedings on the basis of a complaint or a reference from a third party. However, the Commission is not obliged to bring proceedings, and where a complaint is rejected by the Commission, the complainant does not have the possibility of having the rejection tried either under Article 263 or Article 265 TFEU.

---

31. According to Art. 288 TFEU, decisions are binding in their entirety upon those to whom they are addressed. A directive is binding, as to the result to be achieved, upon each Member State to which it is addressed, but it leaves to the national authorities the choice of form and methods for implementation.

Regardless of which methods the Commission uses for carrying out its tasks, under Article 296, a statement of reasons is required for acts adopted within the EU. The statement of reasons must be adapted to the nature of the act in question and must clearly state the reasons for which the institution in question has issued the legal act so that the parties affected can know the basis for the act and so that a competent court can exercise its right of review.

There can be situations in which an infringement or a proposed regulatory initiative falls within the scope of two different authorising provisions, for example, an infringement of both the general competition rules and Article 106 or the regulation of the internal market in general and public undertakings in particular. In the first case, both Article 103 and Regulation (EC) No 1/2003 can be used, and in the second case, both Article 114 and Article 106(3) can be used as authority. In these cases, the Commission can use Article 106(3), but it may be expected to use the other provisions for the purposes of legal certainty.

To the extent that legal acts are adopted on the wrong legal basis, these will be annulled in connection with a suit for annulment. It has been argued that the relationship between the different authorising provisions should be determined by a *lex specialis* assessment.[32] According to this view, the source of authority will often be Article 106(3) since this provision will be special in relation to the more general rules on competition or the internal market. Regardless of whether the use of the *lex specialis* leads to the correct allocation, the Commission is still expected to be reluctant to use the authority of Article 106(3).

Where a decision is made concerning an actual infringement, the undertaking[33] which has committed an action which is contrary to competition law and the Member State in question have certain rights of appeal. These consist primarily of the use of different kinds of legal proceedings within the EU legal system.

6.2 The Directive on the Transparency of Relations Between Member States and Public Undertakings

Directive 2006/111/EC, on the transparency of financial relations between Member States and public undertakings as well as on financial transparency within certain undertakings (with subsequent amendments), is intended to ensure that there is transparency about, among other things, financial support paid by the Member States to public undertakings.

Under the Directive, the primary obligation is for Member States to ensure that financial relations between public authorities and public undertakings are transparent, as provided in the Directive so that the following are made clear:

(a) what public funds are made available directly by public authorities to the public undertakings concerned;

---

32. *See Rudolf Benesch:* Die Kompetenzen der EG-Kommission aus Art. 90 Abs. 3 EWG-V, pp. 63–64.
33. In this context the party entitled to appeal is not a trade organisation, but only the undertakings that have committed the infringement.

(b) what public funds made available by public authorities through the intermediary of public undertakings or financial institutions; and

(c) the use to which these public funds are actually put.[34]

In the Directive, a 'public undertaking' is defined as any undertaking, whether at the State, regional or local level, 'over which the public authorities may exercise directly or indirectly a dominant influence by virtue of their ownership of it, their financial participation therein, or the rules which govern it'; *see* Article 2(1) of the Directive.

The definition of special or exclusive rights as set out in this Directive is presented in section 4.1.1 above.

7 OTHER REGULATION

7.1 International Regulation

In addition to the EU rules, there are also rules at the international level on public undertakings and undertakings with special rights in the European Economic Area (EEA) and in the WTO agreements. In the EEA Agreement, Article 16 and Article 59 contain provisions corresponding to Article 37 and Article 106. The provisions are practically identical.[35]

In international trade cooperation under the WTO regime, the General Agreement on Tariffs and Trade 1994 contains a provision which is intended to cover the same circumstances as Article 37 and Article 106. This is in General Agreement on Tariffs and Trade (GATT) 1994, Article XVII on State trading enterprises. Article XVII.1(a) provides that where a WTO member establishes a State enterprise or grants to any enterprise exclusive or special privileges, the member must act in a manner consistent with the general principles of non-discriminatory treatment in GATT 1994. This is expanded in Article XVII.1(b) which provides that enterprises must make any purchases or sales solely in accordance with commercial considerations. Furthermore, WTO members must give enterprises of the other WTO members adequate opportunity to compete for participation in such purchases or sales. In Article XVII.1(c), it is provided that WTO members may not prevent any enterprise which is a public undertaking or has been granted privileges from acting in accordance with these principles. Article XVII.2 to 4 contains rules, for example, on exemption from the provisions in paragraph 1 in respect of imports of products for immediate or ultimate consumption in governmental use, an obligation to negotiate with a view to removing serious obstacles to trade in connection with such undertakings, as well as a number of formal obligations on the exchange of information between WTO members.

---

34. Article 1 of Directive 2006/111/EC.
35. Under the EEA regime the Commission's powers of enforcement are given to the corresponding body – the EFTA Surveillance Authority. In the EEA regime the equivalent to the CJ is the EFTA Court.

Bibliography

Blum & Logue: *State Monopolies under EC Law*, 1998.
Caroline Wehlander: *Who Is Afraid of SGEI?*, 2015.
David Edwards & Mark Hoskins: *Article 90: Deregulation and EC Law, Reflections Arising from the XVI FIDE Conference*, Common Market Law Review 1995.
Jonathan Faull & Ali Nikpay: *The EU Law of Competition*, 2014.
Jose Luis Buendia Sierra: *Exclusive Rights and State Monopolies under EC Law*, 1999.

Chapter 11
The Liberalised Sectors

This chapter is concerned with a number of commercial sectors which, in recent years, have been through a liberalisation process, among other things, because of a number of measures adopted by the Union. The title of the chapter has been chosen in order to reflect this. The first section includes a general introduction to those elements of Union law that are dealt with in this chapter. This is followed by a number of sector-specific sections which look at the most important elements of concrete EU regulation. The sectors chosen for this review of specific sectors include energy (electricity and natural gas supplies), transport (air transport and railways) and communications (telecommunications and postal services). This is not an exhaustive listing of the sectors which can be categorised as liberalised sectors. Only those aspects which are concerned with Union law are dealt with. **For** further information about the implementation of the Union law for these sectors by the Member States, **the** reader is referred to the specialist works on the specific topics.

1 GENERAL CROSS-SECTORAL CONSIDERATIONS

In post-war Europe, there was a widespread assumption that market failure in certain sectors was such as to make it necessary to use the involvement of public authorities, vertical integration and regulation of monopolies.

'Market failure' means that the market was unable to function as an efficient allocator of welfare. This is based on the first principle of a welfare economy that market equilibrium is an effective method of allocation (Pareto optimality, i.e., that no participant in the market can be better off without at least one other participant being worse off).[1]

Furthermore, pricing based primarily on marginal costs did not manage to cover the total costs in industries with large investments and overhead costs.[2]

---

1. Michael C. Blad & Hans Keiding: *Microeconomics* (1990).
2. Ronan Bolton, *Making Energy Markets*, p. 2 (2021).

This has been the case for a number of undertakings in the sectors concerned with energy supply, communications and public transport. At the same time, these sectors have been seen as being of vital importance for society and for its economic development, so society has had a strategic interest in these sectors. Public involvement in the running of these undertakings was assumed to be able to solve conflicts which could arise between private enterprise and the interests of society. This often resulted in the existence of a public monopoly, whether de facto or de jure, so that society was able to maintain a direct influence on these sectors.

The most direct way to obtain influence was through ownership. Full public ownership is not necessarily essential for obtaining influence equivalent to that of ownership.[3] The direct or indirect influence of the authorities can be achieved in many other ways, including ownership of a majority of the capital of a company, control of a majority of the voting rights, or the right to appoint a majority of the members of the board. This can be characterised as giving a dominant influence which is decisive in relation to the application of Article 106 of the Treaty on the Functioning of the European Union (TFEU or 'Treaty'). For a detailed discussion of Article 106, see Chapter 10 on public undertakings.

The conditions or regulations connected with the public grant of exclusive rights can be concerned with the same considerations. Accordingly, Article 2(1)(b) of Directive 2006/111/EC defines a public undertaking as 'any undertaking over which the public authorities may exercise directly or indirectly a dominant influence by virtue of their ownership of it, their financial participation therein, or the rules which govern it.' Also, contractual terms can involve control over the performance of some particular task, for example, through the tendering out of certain functions, while the responsibility for carrying out the functions remains with the public entity.

The liberalised sectors have been and often still are characterised by involving major investments. Historically, vertical integration (the gathering together of functions that represent different links in the value chain[4]) and the status of a monopoly have been used to allow individual undertakings to secure their investments while consumers bear the risk. The use of a monopoly can also afford protection against destructive competition. National monopolies have often been maintained by giving exclusive rights under public law to carry on a certain kind of undertaking. The term used in this connection is a de jure or legal monopoly. These often find expression in a concession legislation. The same monopoly situation can exist without the granting of such exclusive rights if an undertaking is in fact the only provider of a specific service in a specific geographic area; this is a de facto or an effective monopoly.

In the 1980s, there was a certain amount of pressure to liberalise some of these industries. Monopolies (exclusive rights) came to be regarded as being inappropriate. This was a feeling felt across large parts of the world. In Europe, the United Kingdom set the ball rolling with a number of privatisations.[5] In other European countries, the liberalisation process tended to take the form of doing away with exclusive rights and

---

3. Public ownership can exist both at national and at regional/local level.
4. The 'value chain' is the chain of activities which together create value for an undertaking and its owners.
5. Dieter Helm & Tim Jenkinson: *Introducing Competition into Regulated Industries*, in Dieter Helm & Tim Jenkinson (eds): *Competition in Regulated Industries*, p. 1 (1998).

introducing the right of third parties to have access to a network.[6] Thus, the liberalisation of these sectors refers to many different phenomena. In itself, the expression *liberalisation* is not very precise. Basically, it is an expression for the economic policy of freeing business life from restrictions. Among other things, it can be understood as the complete or partial repeal of the exclusive rights of public authorities or special organisations to be engaged in a particular area – it is the opening up of markets. This can also be referred to as de-monopolising. The term liberalisation is widely used together with other terms which relate to the increased use of market forces.

The term *tendering* is often used when private entities are involved in undertaking tasks such as production, supply and responsibility for personnel, while the public authorities retain responsibility for administrative tasks, management responsibility (defining quality and quantity), and any exclusive rights. Tendering typically involves *inviting offers*. This can be combined with a *control offer* from the public undertaking that has previously been responsible for carrying out the task. With *deregulation,* there is usually the removal or reduction of parts of the public law regulation of a sector, for example, by opening up a market to competition. This does not necessarily mean an end to public ownership of undertakings. Even though the expression is a negation of regulation, opening up for competition on the market will often be followed by an increased amount of legislation, etc., in the sector and is thus more in the nature of re-regulation. *Privatisation* consists of selling off public undertakings, publicly owned facilities and/or other assets or merely giving up public engagement in a sector which is thus left to private participants. However, the term 'privatisation' sometimes has a broader meaning, where public authorities and undertakings allow private operators to perform individual elements of the value chain as an alternative to carrying out such tasks themselves. Finally, the management of public undertakings can be reorganised along the lines of *undertakings under private law*. Thus, a number of State-owned limited companies, particularly public undertakings and mutually owned institutions, have been set up, and local government authorities have, for example, organised rubbish collection in jointly owned partnerships, and supply companies have been organised by the establishment of holding companies. This process can be referred to as *corporatisation* or *demutualisation.*[7]

At the Union level, true liberalisation can be said to have been introduced by the Single European Act of 1987 and the programme for the completion of the single market by 1 January 1993. In the EC Treaty then in force, there was a declaration on the establishment of the internal market in Article 3(1)(c). The Union's involvement in the liberalisation of sectors which have traditionally been public has, to a large extent, been driven by the desire to make these sectors part of the internal market. The establishment of the internal market had both the aim of furthering the policy of integration and a desire to open a given market to competition.

The liberalisation measures have had the aim of reducing the prices which European households and businesses (end users)[8] have had to pay for the goods and

---

6. *See* s. 1.4.4 on third party access to networks.
7. Ian Duncan & Alan Bollard: *Corporatization & Privatization* (1992).
8. Consumers and undertakings which buy a service or product with a view to using it themselves can be classified as 'end users'. The use of the terminology varies somewhat in relation to different categories of users of a network and of the goods or services supplied thereby. In the area of telecommunications, Directive EU 2018/1972 on a common regulatory framework for electronic communications networks and services) use the term 'end users' and uses 'consumers' to refer to non-commercial end users. Directive 97/67/EC on common rules for the development of the internal market of Community postal services and the improvement of quality of service uses

services which have traditionally been supplied by public undertakings. It can be said that this has had the aim of improving the efficient allocation of resources.[9] The increased competition expected through liberalisation is the means for promoting improved economic efficiency. This can be seen both from the point of view of the welfare of society (better use of resources, improved competitiveness) and from the point of view of the end user (lower prices, better quality and service). Further, it can be seen from the point of view of the producer (lower costs, higher profit). These three points of view represent the three welfare standards – consumer, producer and total (society as a whole) surplus.[10]

The political goals behind the liberalisation of traditional public sector undertakings can be other than pure considerations for improved efficiency. For example, there can be a desire to give consumers greater choice and a desire to reduce the involvement of the public authorities in the supply of goods and services. Liberalisation in the form of increasing the freedom of the participants in a market can thus be both an end and a means.[11]

In this way, due to its exposure to competition, the market must be capable of generating cheaper services for consumers. However, the market as such is not a perfect size, always creating the desired results. For one thing, the market may be hampered by too few or too dominant players, for another, the players of the market may be acting contrary to the general rules of competition, for final, the market may struggle to handle more extreme situations, which has been apparent lately in the markets for gas and electricity regarding supply failures with Russian gas.[12]

Today, the systems of ownership in the liberalised sectors vary widely from country to country and from sector to sector. In several cases, there will be a large, well-established national operator which is publicly owned in whole or in part.[13] In other sectors, there are local government-owned, consumer-owned and commercial participants. Finally, international undertakings are participating to an increasing extent in undertakings which were previously national monopolies (e.g., in the telecommunications and electricity supply sectors), which can still be under complete or partial public ownership. However, many national markets are still characterised by having one dominant participant in the shape of the previously public provider.

---

the term 'users'. In the Natural Gas Directive the terms 'system user' and 'final customer' are used. In the latest version the latter term has been supplemented by the terms 'household customer' and 'commercial customer' where the latter can also cover producers and wholesalers. The Electricity Directive only uses the term 'customer' and 'final customer'. The Regulation (EU) on risk-preparedness in the electricity sector uses the term 'customer' with reference to the Electricity Directive. Art. 2, no. 3, of Regulation (EU) No 2017/1938 concerning measures to safeguard security of gas supply uses the term 'household customers'. In the area of railway infrastructure, Directive 2012/34/EU establishing a single European railway area uses the terms 'applicant' and 'railway undertaking'.

9. Normally economics distinguish between allocative, productive and dynamic efficiencies. See Damian Chalmers, Gareth Davies and Giorgio Monti: *European Union Law*, p. 945 (2014).
10. Christopher Townsley: *Article 81 EC and Public Policy*, p. 15 (2009).
11. See also P.J. Slot & A.M. Skudder: *Common Features of Community Law Regulation in the Network-Bound Sectors*, Common Market Law Review, p. 120 (2001).
12. The handling of this has caused some problems. Price ceilings have been highlighted as a possible way forward. They have previously been introduced in the area of telecommunication.
13. Such an undertaking is regarded as the *incumbent*.

Even though the sectors covered by this chapter have traditionally been characterised by the existence of national or local monopolies, this has not necessarily meant that there has been a lack of cross-border exchange of services or goods. The participants in the market for the international exchange of goods or services have merely been restricted to national or local monopolies. Cooperation has been carried out on a private law basis. Thus, there have been both bilateral and multilateral cooperation agreements, often in connection with some trade organisations (e.g., the Universal Postal Union).

1.1   Which Sectors Are Dealt With?

The sectors which have been selected for study in this chapter have been referred to as (half) public sectors. The terms *regulated undertakings* or *utility undertakings* are also often used in these sectors.[14]

What characterises the sectors dealt with here is that, at one or more steps in the value chain, they have facilities or systems that have the characteristics of a network.

Networks are often distinguished between *distribution networks* (local networks which serve individual customers) and *transmission networks* (trunk networks which link the distribution networks).

In the Commission's Green Paper of 21 May 2003 on services of general interest (COM(2003) 270 final), such sectors have been described as 'Services of general economic interest provided by large network industries'. The existence of a network is obvious in connection with electricity supply, natural gas supply, the railways and parts of the telecommunications sector. These sectors have contiguous physical networks. These can be referred to as *physical networks*. Other systems, such as harbours and airports, and transmission masts, can also constitute networks, on which the supply of the services in question depend, even though the systems may not be physically linked. The same considerations apply to the delivery points for the postal service (post-boxes), sorting offices, and the distribution network (postal delivery workers). These have the character of a *non-physical network*.

In terms of cost, networks are characterised by having economies of scale, with cost regression as well as economies of scope. Furthermore, networks often have high sunk costs. Other parts of the value chain, i.e., those parts that have been exposed to competition as a result of liberalisation, can be seen to suffer from 'stranded costs'.

A sunk cost can be defined as a cost which has already been paid and which cannot be varied.[15] They are, in any event, irrecoverable. Stranded costs, especially in relation to the utilities sectors, can be defined as 'those costs that the utilities are currently permitted to recover through their rates but whose recovery may be impeded or prevented by the advent of competition'.[16] For example, in the electricity supply sector, stranded costs are found in the

---

14. The term *public utility* is often used. However, the use of this term is usually limited to the supply of telecommunications, electricity, gas and water.
15. Robert S. Pindyck & Daniel L. Rubinfeld: *Microeconomics*, p. 205 (2001).
16. William J. Baumol & J. Gregory Sidak: *Transmission Pricing and Stranded Costs in the Electric Power Industry*, p. 98 (1995).

form of power stations that have been built during the period of monopoly, when all the costs could be passed on to the end users. Because of their choice of technology and overcapacity, some power stations can be unable to give a return on their investment in an open electricity market. Stranded costs can also arise in the form of contractual obligations for the purchase of electricity for which there is no longer certainty of there being sales.[17] Article 24 of Directive 96/92/EC concerning common rules for the internal market in electricity ('the first Electricity Directive') contained some transitional provisions relating to stranded costs.[18]

The existence of a network with sunk and stranded costs means that new participants will not necessarily be attracted to the market, even if there is a profitable market or ineffective competitors. The investments required for entering a market which is characterised by the existence of a network are often considerable, especially if it is not possible to gain access to the networks of the established participants.

In addition to having a network, the provision of goods and services by the sectors dealt with in this chapter often cannot be stored or can only be stored at great expense. A train or an aircraft which departs with unused capacity loses the capacity. Currently, large quantities of electricity can only be stored at great expense, and its production must be adjusted to consumption.[19] There are typically wide variations of loading in the course of the day (rush hour, peak loading), the week and the year. If demand is always to be met, there must be a capacity which will be under-used at certain times of the day, week or year.

Finally, it is common to all the sectors that it is assumed that competition can be introduced in whole or in part in these sectors. This can be described as the competitive capacity of the market. The introduction of competition to a sector is often referred to as the initiation of competition or simply liberalisation. The Union has sought and still seeks to introduce competition-based market regulation, in whole or in part, to the sectors which have been selected for discussion in this chapter. The network structure and the special interests in the sectors have meant that segments which are exposed to competition and segments that are not exposed to competition exist side by side in the individual sectors. Consideration for the existing participants and their investments (stranded costs) has meant that in many cases the opening of the market to competition has been done in stages.

In the electricity supply sector, it was directly stated in the first Electricity Directive that a certain percentage of the market should be opened to competition. The percentage level was raised in steps. From the start, some end users (large commercial customers) were given the right to choose their suppliers. An end user who could choose their supplier was referred to as a *privileged customer*. The electricity market is now fully liberalised, and the distinction between privileged and non-privileged customers is only relevant where some customers are free to choose their supplier while others are not.

---

17. On stranded costs, *see* Peter Cameron: *Competition in Energy Markets*, p. 432-446 (2007).
18. The possibility of transitional arrangements has not been carried forward in the later editions of the Electricity Directive.
19. Consumption can also be adjusted to production, for example by paying large industrial users to reduce their consumption.

Despite the complete or partial opening of markets, many liberalised sectors are still characterised by the presence of one or more national participants (previous monopolists), which still have a dominant position on the market which is at least linked to those segments of the market which are not open to competition.

It should also be noted that the content and purpose of the varying degrees of liberalisation can vary considerably from sector to sector.[20] It is also stated in the Commission's Green Paper on services of general interest that the Union has adopted different regulatory strategies for different network industries and services of general interest. This is because of the differences between the different sectors (notably in their profitability, production structure, capital intensity, methods of service delivery, and demand structure) and because these industries are at different stages of the liberalisation process.[21]

1.2 Facilities of Special Significance

Networks of the kind described above are called *essential facilities*. This term has its roots in US antitrust law and was introduced in a judgment of the Supreme Court.[22] The term characterises facilities that are controlled by an individual supplier to the market, which cannot be substituted by some other solution, and which are of general importance to society. The importance of the facility (or infrastructure) consists in the fact that customers cannot be reached without using it. There will be no possibility of finding an alternative solution if the facility cannot be duplicated at a reasonable cost.[23]

The competition law interest in essential facilities concerns the right of access of market participants to facilities owned by another participant, even a competitor, as long as the facility in question is of particular importance for being able to operate on a given market. A right to such access has been developed in competition law in the *essential facilities doctrine*.

The doctrine can be stated as follows: 'Where facilities cannot practically be duplicated by would-be competitors, those in possession of them must allow them to be shared on fair terms.'[24] This obligation to make facilities available to others only concerns facilities which in practice cannot be duplicated. This is a description which, to a large extent, will only be applicable to the networks in the liberalised sectors.

---

20. For statements on this, see Klaus J. Hopt: *Transsectoral Issues of Regulation*, in Jürgen Basedow et al. (eds): *Economic Regulation and Competition*, p. 306 (2002).
21. COM(2003) 270 final, s. 3.2, para. 71. These comments are made in relation to network access and interconnectivity, but they have wider applicability.
22. *United States v. Terminal Railroad Association*, 224 U.S. 383 (1912).
23. See Daniel Glasl: *Draft Council Directive concerning Licences to Railway Undertakings: A Contribution to the Current Debate*, p. 307 (European Competition Law Review 1994). For a short review of the term in relation to third party access and the rejection of its direct applicability at Community level, see Friedrich von Burchard & Lutz Eckert: *Natural Gas and EU Energy Law*, p. 102-108 (1995).
24. A.D. Neale & D.G. Goyder: *Antitrust Laws of the United States of America*, p. 62 (1980).

'Essential facilities' is a concept which is not directly found in the TFEU.[25] The General Court (GC) (formerly the Court of First Instance)[26] has applied the principle of a right of access to such facilities several times in relation to individual sectors.[27] The same applies to the Commission.

The Commission has dealt with this question in two cases concerning a right of access to the harbour at Holyhead in Wales (the *B&I* case and the *Sea Containers* case from 1992 and 1993) as well as a case concerning *Rødby Harbour* in Denmark in 1994.[28] For a short commentary on essential facilities, *see* Antonio Capobianco, E.L. Rev. 2001 pp. 548–564. It is in particular in connection with access to infrastructure facilities that most cases arise. *See* also Chapter 6.

The principle has also been applied by the Court of Justice of the European Union (CJ)[29] in connection with the prohibition of abuse of dominant position under Article 102 TFEU. There is thus a presumption that possession of an essential facility is an expression of the existence of a dominant position. On the basis of the presumption, the CJ has considered a number of cases on the refusal to enter into trading relations. According to the cases, a product or service can only be regarded as essential if there is no actual or potential alternative.[30] In a case concerning a joint venture involving railways under Article 101 TFEU (then Article 85), it was further explained:[31]

> Consequently, with regard to an agreement such as that in the present case, setting up a joint venture, which falls within Article 85(1) of the Treaty [now Article 105(1) TFEU], the Court considers that neither the parent undertakings nor the joint venture thus set up may be regarded as being in possession of infrastructure, products or services which are 'necessary' or 'essential' for entry to the relevant market unless such infrastructure, products or services are not 'interchangeable' and unless, by reason of their special characteristics – in particular the prohibitive cost of and/or time reasonably required for reproducing them – there are no viable alternatives available to potential competitors of the joint venture, which are thereby excluded from the market.

These conditions are illustrated further in the *Bronner* case.[32] A publisher had a distribution network for its newspapers. The question was to what extent this publisher was required to give other publishers access to its network. The CJ accepted

---

25. For a review of the rules in an EU context *see* John Temple Lang: *Defining Legitimate Competition: Companies' Duties to Supply Competitors and Access to Essential Facilities*, p. 437 (Fordham International Law Journal).
26. Hereinafter referred to as the GC.
27. A non-exhaustive list of the cases includes Case T-504/93, *Tiercé Ladbroke v. Commission;* and Joined Cases T-374/94, T-375/94, T-384/94 and T-388/94, *European Night Services v. Commission.*
28. *See* the Commission's Decisions in Case 94/19/EC and Case 94/119/EC.
29. Hereinafter referred to as the CJ.
30. Joined Cases C-241/91 P and C-242/91 P, *Magill,* paras 53–54 (originally Case T-69/89 *RTE v. Commission* and Case T-76/89 *ITP v. Commission;* and Case T-504/93, *Tiercé Ladbroke v. Commission,* para. 131.
31. Joined Cases T-374/94, T-375/94, T-384/94 and T-388/94, *European Night Services and others v. Commission,* para. 209.
32. Case C-7/97, Bronner. For commentary on the case *see* Leo Flynn: *Access to the Postal Network: the Situation after Bronner,* in Damien Geradin (ed.): *The Liberalization of Postal Services in the European Union,* p. 190-192 (2002) and Ekaterina Rousseva: *Rethinking Exclusionary Abuses in EU Competition Law,* p. 95 (2010).

that there could be refusal of access to the network. The grounds for this were the existence of alternative means of distribution, both actual (via the postal service, sales via shops and kiosks – paragraph 43) and potential (the possibility of building up its own network – paragraph 44). The CJ thus restricted the application of the essential facilities doctrine to situations where there are no other actual or potential distribution possibilities.

The competition rules of the TFEU thus contain provisions that can give a right of access to a competitor's network, as long as exclusion from the network would effectively exclude a participant from entering or remaining in the market.

Certain networks have the character of a natural monopoly. This means that the costs for the essential facilities for the distribution of, for example, energy are so great that, because of the economies of scale, it is only cost-effective to have one set of facilities through which the service or product can be supplied.[33] Networks often face relatively high fixed-cost structures.[34] The monopoly situation will normally concern the provision of a specific good or service. On the demand side, there will usually be possibilities for substitution; for example, different forms of transport can be substituted for each other.[35]

In *Wiliam. J. Baumol* et al.: Weak Invisible Hand Theorems on the Sustainability of Multi-product Natural Monopoly, American Economic Review 1977 pp. 350–365, there is an alternative cost-related definition: 'By a natural monopoly we mean an industry whose cost function over some given set of products is such that no combination of several firms can produce an industry out-put vector as cheaply as it can be provided by a single supplier.'

The concept is linked to economic theory and as such is not a principle of competition law. The concept implies cost considerations in relation to the technology existing at the time. What is (economically) impossible or decidedly inappropriate seems to lie at the core of this. The way in which this fits with the concept of *essential facilities* is notable.

Not all infrastructures in the liberalised sectors have the character of networks which can be categorised as natural monopolies. This often depends on the specific market and the available technology. Until recently, local fixed-line telephone traffic (subscriber networks)[36] would perhaps have been considered a natural monopoly since a nationwide duplication of such a network would normally be impossible.[37] The increased use of mobile telephony and the spread of broadband networks make it

---

33. Economies of scale mean that the average costs per unit supplied will fall as the capacity usage rises. The marginal costs are thus lower than the average costs.
34. Ben W.F. Depoorter. *Regulation of Natural Monopoly*, in Bouckaert, Boudewijn and De Geest, Gerrit (eds), Encyclopedia of Law and Economics, Volume I. *The History and Methodology of Law and Economics*, p. 498 (2000). He is referring to telephone industry, electricity and water supply ass examples.
35. There are not always substitution possibilities, and sometimes they are of such a different quality (e.g., with respect to the time required) that the possibility is not realistic.
36. Subscriber links are the paired twisted wires constituting physical metallic leads which connect the terminal node of the subscriber to the main distributor of the local exchange or to an equivalent point on a fixed public telephone network.
37. The Commission's XXXI Report on Competition Policy, p. 34. However, this may change with the roll-out of fibre optic cables under the regime of the electricity supply undertakings.

questionable whether the subscriber network is still a natural monopoly. For connections between two large urban areas or exchanges, the existence of a natural monopoly has long been in doubt. Long-distance telephony is no longer regarded as a natural monopoly. There can also be local differences to some extent. While natural gas transmission has been regarded as a natural monopoly in most of Europe, in Germany parallel or alternative connections have been established in some places.[38]

There can be other hindrances to the duplication of a set of installations other than the purely economic. In some cases, individual undertakings may have been granted exclusive rights, or authorisation may be required. In other cases, there are legislative barriers which may involve long-lasting procedures for the establishment of certain installations. For example, this will typically be the case for the building of a railway network or an electricity supply network carried by pylons. Among other things, planning and environmental requirements for consultation and environmental impact assessment will complicate the establishment of such a network. These types of entry barriers pertain to public law.

The terms *essential facilities* and *natural monopolies* are linked to infrastructures or networks in the liberalised sectors. In connection with the liberalisation of these sectors, a distinction is often made between the infrastructure and the goods or services whose provision is dependent on the infrastructure in question.

There can be a distinction between goods and services. In the energy sector, electricity and gas are regarded as being goods, while the transport or transmission of these is considered to be a service.[39] In the transport and communications sectors, all the relevant provisions constitute services.

1.3 The Regulatory Background

The powers of the Union in this area are derived in part from the general provisions of the TFEU (including Articles 14, 37, 101, 102 and 106),[40] in part from the articles dealing with transport (Articles 90–100), and in part from the articles dealing with trans-European networks (Articles 170–172).

In the Commission's Notice on the application of the competition rules to access agreements in the telecommunications sector – framework, relevant markets and principles (OJ 1998 C 265/2), some views are expressed which seem to have wider validity.[41] Thus, it is assumed that the Union's competition rules and the sector-specific regulation constitute different sets of rules which apply independently of each other and have different purposes and different means of enforcement. However, the

---

38. Christopher W. Jones & William-James Kettlewell: *EU Energy Law*, p. 29 (Vol. I, 2010).
39. Case 6/64, *Costa v. ENEL*, in which electricity was presumed to be a good. In relation to Art. 34 TFEU [then Art. 28], this was confirmed by the CJ in Case C-393/92, *Almelo and others v. Energiebedrijf Ijsselmij*, para. 28 which refers to the Union's tariff nomenclature (code CN 27.16).
40. *See* Chs 2, 5 and 9 for discussions on Arts 101, 102 and 106 respectively.
41. *See* Pierre Larouche: *Telecommunications*, in Damien Geradin (ed.): *The Liberalization of State Monopolies in the European Union and Beyond*, pp. 284–316 (2000); and Laurent Garzaniti: *Telecommunications, Broadcasting and Internet: EU Competition Law and Regulation*, ss. 10–01 to 10–15 (2000).

competition rules are directly applicable,⁴² and it is not possible to introduce provisions via sectoral regulation that conflict with the competition rules laid down in the Treaty. Also, in other cases where EU law is observed, the competition rules must be complied with.⁴³ For example, as a consequence of this, the rules in the telecommunications sector must be interpreted so as to be in accordance with the general competition rules.⁴⁴

Whether a case involves public or private ownership is, in principle, not relevant to the application of the competition rules. This can be deduced from the principle of equal treatment expressed in Article 106 TFEU and the principle of neutrality expressed in Article 345 TFEU (the state aid rules must apply equally to both private and public undertakings).⁴⁵

Conversely, there is nothing to prevent sector-specific provisions from going further than the provisions that apply under the competition rules. However, the authority for this must be sought elsewhere.

The use of sector-specific regulation is characteristic of the liberalised sectors. Two main reasons can be given for this. First, there can be imperfect competition in a market so that for a period,⁴⁶ or perhaps permanently, it will not be possible to create a truly competitive market. This can be due to natural monopolies, for example, or the historical strength of the dominant participant in the market (depreciated investments, etc.). Second, the choice of sector-specific regulation can be based on considerations other than effective competition, such as security of supply, environmental protection and, to some extent, consumer protection. Such considerations cannot necessarily be taken care of through general competition rules.

Article 103 TFEU contains a provision whereby the Council, acting by a qualified majority on a proposal from the Commission and after consulting the European Parliament, can issue appropriate regulations or directives to give effect to the principles set out in Articles 101 and 102 TFEU. This provision has been used in the air transport and railways sectors. Moreover, the Commission publishes notices giving its understanding of the competition rules and the related administrative procedures. Such notices have been issued for the telecommunications and postal services sectors. Neither the Council nor the Commission has issued such guidelines or legislation in the area of energy supply.⁴⁷

A number of the most important provisions connected with liberalisation measures have been introduced via directives. These can be divided into two main groups:

---

42. Case 127/73, *BRT I*.
43. Case 66/86, *Ahmed Saeed v. Silver Line Reisebüro*.
44. The Commission's Notice on the application of the competition rules to access agreements in the telecommunications sector – framework, relevant markets and principles, para. 58 (OJ 1998 C 265/2).
45. *See* Leigh Hancher et al: *EU State Aids*, p. 249 (2012).
46. If the imperfect competition is only temporary, one can imagine that the sectoral regulation – at least in respect of its competition law provisions – will later be repealed, and the sector will be subject to the general competition rules.
47. In the following sector-specific section there is an emphasis on sector-specific provisions. The application of the TFEU's general competition law provisions is only dealt with to a limited extent. For more detailed treatment of these, the reader is referred to the other chapters in this book.

- *Liberalising directives*: These have been issued under the authority of Article 106 TFEU and are discussed in more detail in Chapter 9. In Article 106(1) it is stated: 'In the case of public undertakings and undertakings to which Member States grant special or exclusive rights, Member States shall neither enact nor maintain in force any measure contrary to the rules contained in the Treaties, in particular to those rules provided for in Article 18 and Articles 101 to 109.' The authority to issue directives or decisions is given in Article 106(3). For example, Directive 2002/77/EC on competition in the markets for electronic communications networks and services was issued under this authority. This authority has particularly been used in the telecommunications sector.
- *Harmonising directives*: These are issued under the authority of Article 114 TFEU, according to which: 'The European Parliament and the Council shall, acting in accordance with the ordinary legislative procedure and after consulting the Economic and Social Committee, adopt the measures for the approximation of the provisions laid down by law, regulation or administrative action in Member States which have as their object the establishment and functioning of the internal market'; see Article 114(1).[48] Directive (EU) 2019/944 concerning common rules for the internal market in electricity ('the Electricity Directive'), Directive 2009/73/EC concerning common rules for the internal market in natural gas ('the Natural Gas Directive'),[49] Regulation (EU) 2019/941 on risk-preparedness in the electricity sector, Directive 2005/89/EC concerning measures to safeguard the security of electricity supply and infrastructure investment, and Directive 97/67/EC on common rules for the development of the internal market of Community postal services and the improvement of quality of service are examples of this. In the telecommunications sector, where liberalising directives have also been issued, there are harmonizing directives in the form of Directive (EU) 2018/1972. In addition to these, examples of measures adopted under the authority of Article 114 include: Regulation (EC) No 715/2009 on conditions for access to the natural gas transmission networks; Decision No 676/2002/EC on a regulatory framework for radio spectrum policy in the European Community (Radio Spectrum Decision); and Decision No 128/1999/EC on the coordinated introduction of a third-generation mobile and wireless communications system (Universal Mobile Telecommunications System (UMTS)) in the Community.

The liberalising directives primarily identify and flesh out the rules of the TFEU. In particular, the provisions in Article 102 and Article 106(1) TFEU are relevant. In contrast, the harmonising directives provide, to a greater degree, for the issuing of new obligations.[50]

---

48. A distinction is often made between total harmonisation and minimum harmonisation, as the two main variations. Other less used variations can be used.
49. The Natural Gas Directive has been amended by Regulation (EU) 2018/1999, Directive (EU) 2019/692, and Regulation (EU) 2022/869.
50. Cf. *Bronner Leo Flynn: Access to the Postal Network:* The Situation after Bronner, in Damien Geradin (ed.): *The Liberalization of Postal Services in the European Union*, p. 204 (2002).

Furthermore, a number of secondary legal acts have been issued under the authority of Article 91 in the transport section of the Treaty. These relate in particular to the railway sector. Article 100(2) has been used in the air transport sector.[51] Some secondary legal acts have also been issued under the authority of Article 352 TFEU, according to which, if action by the Union should prove necessary to attain one of the objectives of the Union and the Treaty has not provided the necessary powers, the Council, acting unanimously on a proposal from the Commission and after obtaining the consent of the European Parliament, shall adopt the appropriate measures.

Article 122(1) TFEU (formerly Article 100(1) of the EC Treaty), under which the Council, acting by a qualified majority on a proposal from the Commission, may decide upon the measures appropriate to the economic situation, in particular if severe difficulties arise in the supply of certain products (especially in the energy sector), has been used as authority for the issue of the previous Regulation (EU) No 994/2010 concerning measures to safeguard security of gas supply.[52]

1.4 Regulating the Liberalised Sectors

The liberalising process which is in progress is based to a high degree on the idea that the introduction of partial competition can lead to greater efficiency in otherwise imperfect markets.[53] The background to this has also been the pressure within the EU to include traditional utility sectors in the internal market.

There are considerations other than purely competition interests that are associated with the liberalised sectors. Thus, regulation of the energy and transport sectors is of significant importance to environmental policy. The networks and production facilities associated with these sectors also affect the landscape and thus have a planning dimension. Moreover, there are significant security aspects associated with carrying out undertakings in these two areas. These affect employees, consumers and the surrounding society. Security of supply in the energy sector also affects the electricity and natural gas sectors. Both the EU and the Member States are involved in regulating these areas. Such regulation affects the market situation by acting as a barrier to entry into the market or by opening up the market. In some situations, environmental and planning applications can take years. However, these areas of policy will not be discussed in this chapter.

In order to include the liberalised sectors in the internal market, it is possible, in part, to use the general competition rules of the TFEU. The application of these is reviewed briefly in the individual sector sections below. However, the Union has primarily made use of framework regulation. This has mostly been expressed in

---

51. Under Art. 100(2) TFEU, The European Parliament and the Council, acting in accordance with the ordinary legislative procedure, may lay down appropriate provisions for sea and air transport.
52. In the current Regulation (EU) 2017/1938, art. 194(2) of the FEU-Treaty is now used as authority.
53. There is disagreement between economists as to whether a competitive market necessarily gives rise to greater efficiency than a monopoly market. *See* the experiences referred to in John J. Siegfried & Edwin H. Wheeler: *Cost Efficiency and Monopoly Power, Quarterly Review of Economics and Business* (1981); and Roger S. Frantz: *X-Efficiency: Theory, Evidence and Applications* (1997).

sector-specific directives and regulations. These address various important and often overlapping problems and solutions for opening up public utilities to competition. Many of these problems will be discussed below.

Many directives and regulations have been amended several times. When, in the following, a reference is made to a directive or a regulation, this includes the subsequent amendments unless it is made clear from the context that the reference is to the original version.

1.4.1 Exclusivity

Undertakings whose possible monopoly status or dominant position on a given market is due to a public grant of a right can be said to have exclusive rights. In relation to Article 106 TFEU, undertakings which enjoy such exclusive rights are referred to as *privileged undertakings*.

Exclusivity will have both a geographic limit (perhaps the territory of a Member State or part thereof) and a limit to one or more special business areas – in the terminology of competition law, geographic markets and product markets, respectively.

Exclusivity does not always occur as an exclusive right.[54] In certain areas, a few undertakings in the same product market or the same geographic market can have a joint exclusive right. Article 106 TFEU has thus been used for the grant of rights to more than one undertaking. See Case 173/83 *Commission v. France* (Waste oil), Case 66/86, *Ahmed Saeed Flugreisen*, and Case C-209/98 *Entreprenørforeningens Affalds/Miljøsektion v. Copenhagen*. However, in relation to the liberalised sectors, exclusivity will usually be in the form of an *exclusive right*.

There is no uniformly used terminology in this area in the context of Union law. Privileged undertakings are sometimes referred to as licensed undertakings or public undertakings. The exclusivity which is granted is sometimes referred to as an exclusive right, a sole right or a licence.

Exclusivity for network energy industries has been referred to as area licences, for example, the exclusive right to manage a distribution network in a given area. In contrast to this is a trading licence, which is more in the nature of an authorisation, for example, to trade in electricity, but it does not imply any exclusivity. The concept of a licence also applies to rights to exploit natural resources, such as the mining of raw materials.

Exclusivity is not a situation which is prohibited in principle by the Union. At the same time, the Community does seek to regulate the exploitation of exclusivity. For the liberalised sectors, the most important provision on this is Article 106(1) TFEU, according to which, in respect of public undertakings and undertakings to which they grant special or exclusive rights, the Member States must neither enact nor maintain in force any measure contrary to the rules contained in the Treaty. The term 'exclusive rights' is not defined in more detail in the Treaty.[55]

---

54. In José Luis Buendia Sierra: *Exclusive Rights and State Monopolies under EC Law*, p. 6 (1999), exclusivity seems to be linked to a 'single undertaking'.
55. The provision in Art. 106(2) TFEU on undertakings entrusted with the operation of services of general economic interest, is dealt with below in s. 1.4.6. The use of the term 'exclusive rights'

In secondary Union legislation, the exploitation of exclusivity is regulated in relation to the liberalised sectors. Here, there are also definitions of the concept of exclusivity. In the relation between a Member State and a privileged undertaking, there are thus special provisions in Article 2(1)(f) of Directive 2006/11/EC on the transparency of financial relations between Member States and public undertakings, as amended by Directive 2000/52/EC, whereby 'exclusive rights' are defined as 'rights that are granted by a Member State to one undertaking through any legislative, regulatory or administrative instrument, reserving it the right to provide a service or undertake an activity within a given geographical area'. There is a similar definition in Article 1(5) of Directive 2002/77/EC on competition in the markets for electronic communications networks and services.

Exclusivity can also be based on a grant under private law, for example, on the basis of intellectual property rights. By virtue of their ownership rights, public authorities can grant exclusive user rights to undertakings (licensees). In several Member States, this has been used in connection with the placing of networks alongside and over public roads.[56]

Exclusivity can be granted as part of planning, where a public authority lays down that there shall be a certain service on a certain route or area. Here, planning is used as an instrument to ensure a provision which might not otherwise be established to a sufficient extent or perhaps to serve the general economic interest by excluding a competing network. An example could be a licence to serve a particular air transport route or railway line or a licence to establish a natural gas distribution network in a limited area.

Article 4(4) of the Natural Gas Directive allows Member States to refrain from granting further authorisations to build and operate distribution pipeline systems in any particular area once such pipeline systems have been or are proposed to be built in that area and if existing or proposed capacity is not saturated. It is explicitly stated that this is for the purpose of the development of newly supplied areas and efficient operation generally.

---

in Art. 106(1) is not the subject of a separate discussion. The expression is predominantly used in respect of rights granted under public law that are given to a few undertakings. In Directive 2008/63/EC of 20 Jun. 2008 on competition in the markets in telecommunications terminal equipment, *special rights* are defined as 'rights that are granted by a Member State to a limited number of undertakings, through any legislative, regulatory or administrative instrument, which, within a given geographical area,

a) limits to two or more the number of such undertakings, otherwise than according to objective, proportional and non-discriminatory criteria; or
b) designates, otherwise than according to the criteria referred to in point (a), several competing undertakings; or
c) confers on any undertaking or undertakings, otherwise than according to the criteria referred to in points (a) and (b), any legal or regulatory advantages which substantially affect the ability of any other undertaking to import, market, connect, bring into service and/or maintain telecommunication terminal equipment in the same geographical area under substantially equivalent conditions.'

There is a similar definition in Art. 2(1)(g) of Directive 2006/111/EC.
56. In Germany licence fees are still collected for this. This has also been the case in certain areas in Denmark in connection with electricity supply, but is no longer so.

A company which is granted such a licence will often be under an obligation to supply in the licensed area or provide some other stated minimum service of a route or extent.[57]

Exclusivity can be combined with various other instruments which secure a special market position for the undertaking with exclusive rights. For example, this can concern an obligation to connect to a distribution network, with or without an obligation to accept supply of the service in question. End users can also be prohibited from securing the service for themselves by prohibiting or limiting the possibility of self-supply.

1.4.2 *Cross-Subsidisation*

In liberalised sectors, it is not unusual for finances from profitable areas of business to be transferred to other perhaps less profitable areas of business, or maybe one area of a business carries a smaller share of the shared costs than another area. In terms of competition law, this is cross-subsidisation.

'Cross-subsidisation means that an undertaking bears or allocates all or part of the costs of its activity in one geographical or product market to its activity in another geographical or product market.'[58] Geographic markets exist when the same product or service is priced differently, depending on where it is sold. In relation to product markets, the possibility of cross-subsidisation arises when there is a complete or partial overlap of the production of two products or services. Examples of this are travel by both economy and business class on the same aircraft or the joint production of electricity and heating.

This definition is based on a cost-based understanding of cross-subsidies.[59] As appears from the quotation above, such cross-subsidisation can occur internally within an undertaking. It can also take place between legal persons (companies) and within a corporate group. Cross-subsidisation can take place either through the incorrect allocation of costs or by transferring surpluses or other resources. It is not always easy to determine with certainty whether there is cross-subsidisation.[60]

Cross-subsidisation is not prohibited in principle in Union law.[61] In fact, it can be an expression of perfectly normal practice. Thus, it is not unusual for one market to contribute more to the shared costs than other markets. In business terms, this can be rational in order to remain in or to break into a less profitable market, as long as the

---

57. On obligations to supply, *see* s. 1.4.6.1 of this chapter.
58. The definition comes from the Commission Notice on the application of the competition rules to the postal sector and on the assessment of certain State measures relating to postal services (OJ 1998 C 39/2).
59. The alternative to this is an *efficient pricing approach*. In relation to this, prices depend on customers' willingness to pay (price elasticity) in order to obtain optimal pricing (Ramsey pricing) and thereby maximise welfare. See Giuseppe B. Abbamonte: *Cross-Subsidisation and Community Competition Rules: Efficient Pricing versus Equity, European Law Review*, p. 418 (1998).
60. *See* Leigh Hancher & José Luis Buendia Sierra: *Cross-Subsidization and EC Law, Common Market Law Review*, p. 906 (1998).
61. Giuseppe B. Abbamonte: *Cross-Subsidisation and Community Competition Rules: Efficient Pricing versus Equity, European Law Review*, p. 423 (1998).

marginal costs are covered. However, where a participant in a market has a dominant position, cross-subsidisation can be an expression of abuse of the dominant position. Likewise, it can be an expression of discrimination and State aid contrary to the Treaty.

When there is public involvement in a sector, there will be a risk of confusion about the roles of administrative authority and owner. This makes it desirable for there to be a certain degree of transparency in the relationship between an authority and its undertakings.

1.4.2.1 From Monopoly to Market

When a sector is split into one or more parts which are open to competition and a part which is subject to a monopoly, there is a risk that funds obtained from the area of a de jure monopoly will be used to subsidise activities which are subject to competition in the same undertaking or same group of undertakings. The opposite, cross-subsidisation from an activity that is subject to competition of a monopoly activity is not normally regarded as a problem under competition law. Nor is cross-subsidisation between monopoly activities seen as a problem. There is no risk of distortion of competition in monopoly markets.[62]

The term *cross subsidisation* is directly used in Article 56(3) of the Electricity Directive. In their internal accounting, integrated electricity companies have to keep separate accounts for each of their transmission and distribution activities, 'with a view to avoiding discrimination, cross subsidisation and distortion of competition'. There is a corresponding provision in Article 56(3) of the Natural Gas Directive in relation to transmission, distribution, liquefied natural gas (LNG) and storage activities. The requirement can be described as *unbundling of accounts* and is discussed in more detail below.

Cross-subsidisation from a monopoly activity to an activity which is subject to competition can constitute abuse of a dominant position. For example, it can be used to support dumping prices (predatory pricing)[63] in the business area which is subject to competition or to prevent market entry by new participants (competition concerns). Equally, the possibility for such a (abnormally large) cross-subsidy can be an indication that the monopoly is being exploited in order to take too high prices for the monopoly goods or services (consumer protection concerns). Such circumstances may not only be an expression of infringement of sector-specific provisions in secondary legislation, but they could also mean that there is a breach of the prohibition of abuse of dominant position. Article 102 TFEU does not have regard for whether the dominant position has arisen de jure or de facto.

In the area of postal services, the question of cross-subsidisation has been before the courts in connection with a merger in Case T-175/99, *UPS*. A

---

62. To a certain extent this form of cross-subsidising can be used to finance the obligation to supply. On this, *see* s. 1.4.6.1.
63. For a more detailed discussion of the link between cross subsidisation and predatory pricing, *see* Leigh Hancher & José Luis Buendia Sierra: *Cross-Subsidization and EC Law, Common Market Law Review*, p. 912 (1998).

postal undertaking (Deutsche Post) had possibly used funds obtained from an area where it had been granted exclusive rights to acquire a shareholding of 22.498% in an undertaking (DHL), which operated in a part of the postal sector which was subject to competition.

Two arguments were put forward for why this was contrary to Union law (paragraph 53):

a. the financing by Deutsche Post of the acquisition of its holding in DHL implies that it financed that acquisition from income obtained from its activities in the reserved letter market, thereby abusing its dominant position in that market; and
b. the future relationship between Deutsche Post and DHL will necessarily lead to cross-subsidisation of DHL's activities in the liberalised parcel market by income obtained by Deutsche Post from the reserved market.

Since the GC could not establish that the means which had been derived from the monopoly market had been obtained by an abuse of the monopoly, there was no problem under competition law. The GC's central considerations in relation to argument a) were stated in paragraph 61: 'In the absence of any evidence to show that the funds used by Deutsche Post for the acquisition in question derived from abusive practices on its part in the reserved letter market, the mere fact that it used those funds to acquire joint control of an undertaking active in a neighbouring market open to competition does not in itself, even if the source of those funds was the reserved market, raise any problem from the standpoint of the competition rules and cannot therefore constitute an infringement of Article 82 EC or give rise to an obligation on the Commission to examine the source of those funds in the light of that article.'

The key question seems to be whether there has been an abuse of the monopoly market (the privileged activity). If this is not the case, funds obtained from activities on the monopoly market can be used to make acquisitions in the sector which is subject to competition. A different result could have given rise to a number of problems in relation to other and earlier acquisitions in the liberalised sectors.

As for distortion of competition in the market itself, this was not accepted by the GC, but again, this is a question of evidence; *see* paragraph 64: 'As regards the applicant's second contention, to the effect that the future relationship between Deutsche Post and DHL would necessarily involve cross-subsidisation of DHL's business in the parcels market, it need merely be observed that it is clear from the undertaking given by Deutsche Post to the Commission, in response to the requirement to that effect imposed by the decision of 26 June 1998, that Deutsche Post is prohibited from engaging in any such cross-subsidisation, with the result that, for the purposes of this case, that question is academic. Consequently, if, in the future, the applicant were able to prove such cross-subsidisation on the part of Deutsche Post, it would be entitled to apply to the Commission or, by virtue of the direct effect of Article 82 EC, to the competent national court for appropriate penalties to be imposed.' In this case, the GC did not consider the legality of the exclusive right itself under Article 106 TFEU or in relation to the provisions on State aid. Subsequently, in amending Directive 2002/39/EC, an amendment was made to Article 12 of Directive 97/67/EC on postal services to the effect that 'cross-subsidisation of universal services outside the reserved sector out of revenues from services in the reserved sector shall be prohibited except to the extent to which it is shown to be strictly necessary to fulfil specific universal service obligations imposed in the competitive area'. The granting of exclusive or special rights for financing the provision of postal services was prohibited by Directive 2008/6/EC amending Directive 97/67/EC.

In a French case on postal services, it was established that even covering all the costs would not necessarily exclude cross-subsidisation and State aid.

In this case, the French public postal undertaking, La Poste, provided logistical support (including collection, sorting, distribution and delivery of letters, etc.) as well as business support for Chronopost.[64] Chronopost was 66% owned by La Poste. In this case, the CJ stated that, even if it was accepted that Chronopost had paid all La Poste's costs for logistical and business support, this would not in itself be sufficient to show that there had not been some form of State aid. The CJ emphasised that 'La Poste might, by virtue of its position as the sole public undertaking in a reserved sector, have been able to provide some of the logistical and commercial assistance at lower cost than a private undertaking not enjoying the same rights'. The CJ went on to say that, on the contrary, 'it is precisely a relationship in which the parent company operates in a reserved market and its subsidiary carries out its activities in a market open to competition that creates a situation in which State aid is likely to exist.'

There are sector-specific provisions on cross-subsidies in, for example, Article 3(1) of Regulation (EC) No 1775/2005 on conditions for access to the natural gas transmission networks, and Article 7(3) specifically states that undertakings must avoid cross-subsidisation between network users.

1.4.2.2 Joint Production

Cross-subsidisation occurs not only as a result of the exploitation of a dominant position in a market. There is often joint production (joint management or shared traffic) of several goods or services.

The decision as to whether cross-subsidisation exists is usually based on questions of the allocation of costs. It can be understood as a requirement for there to be true cost allocation for the individual good or service. If there is not such a true allocation,

---

64. Joined Cases C-83/01 P, C-93/01 P and C-94/01 P, *Chronopost and others v. Ufex and others*, which overturned the judgment of the GC in Case T-613/97, *Ufex*.

this will prompt a suspicion of cross-subsidisation. However, there is not one undisputed method for deciding the true cost allocation when there is joint production.

With joint production, some costs are specifically linked to a specific good or service (specific costs), while other costs are common for two or more goods or services (shared costs).[65] Two concepts have been developed with a view to using them to identify any cross-subsidisation: incremental costs and the stand-alone cost test. *Incremental cost* refers to the increase in costs caused by the production of a secondary good or service. *Stand-alone costs* refer to the hypothetical costs which each good or service would have incurred if it had been produced on its own. If the price for a good or service is equal to or greater than the incremental cost (the floor) and less than the stand-alone cost (the ceiling), the price is in the core area where cross-subsidisation will not be found to exist; *see* the *Faulhaber* rule. However, this theory does not include any particular requirements as to the allocation of costs.[66]

Under another cost-based method, the *fully distributed cost* method (FDC), also known as *fully allocated costs*, the costs are allocated systematically according to a key. If such an allocation system is not used, or if some specific good or service bears a significant part of the shared costs, there can be cross-subsidisation. This method seems to be preferred by the Commission.[67] For the liberalised sectors, the share of costs which an individual good or service (i) must bear under the FDC method can be described by the following model:

$$FDC_i = AC_i + f_iCC.$$

AC_i represents the specific costs for i, and f_iCC is the part of the shared costs (CC) attributable to i. The shared costs can thus be allocated according to different principles, including i's share of the total production costs of the undertaking (e.g., calculated on the basis of the distance travelled or the time taken), i's share of the total income of the undertaking, or i's share of the total specific costs. Such pricing models are practical in the sense that they are, to a certain extent, based on objective accounting data from the individual undertaking. However, these objective data are historical, and it has been argued that the method does not give any incentive for efficiency improvements.[68]

In the absence of such a key, it will often be a highly complex task to establish whether there has been cross-subsidisation.

---

65. In accounting terminology a distinction is often made between *joint costs*, which refers to the shared costs for two goods or services which are necessarily produced together, and *common costs* where the same input is used is used for the production of two goods or services. *See* David Heald: *Contrasting Approaches to the 'Problem' of Cross Subsidy, Management Accounting Research*, p. 54 (1996). In this chapter the term *shared costs* is used for both concepts.
66. For more on cost-based methods and the terms referred to above *see*: Giuseppe B. Abbamonte: *Cross-Subsidisation and Community Competition Rules: Efficient Pricing versus Equity, European Law Review*, p. 416 (1998); Leigh Hancher & José Luis Buendia Sierra: *Cross-Subsidization and EC Law, Common Market Law Review*, p. 906 (1998); and in particular David Heald: *Contrasting Approaches to the 'Problem' of Cross Subsidy, Management Accounting Research*, p. 56 (1996).
67. Giuseppe B. Abbamonte: *Cross-Subsidisation and Community Competition Rules: Efficient Pricing versus Equity, European Law Review*, p. 423 (1998).
68. Christian Bergqvist: *Mellem regulering og deregulering*, p. 348 (2007).

The questions of costs connected with joint production are closely related to questions on the payment for access to a network. In the now repealed Directive 97/33/EC on interconnection in Telecommunications with regard to ensuring universal service and interoperability through the application of the principles of Open Network Provision, in Annex V, a number of examples are given of costing standards which could be used in connection with interconnection (network access) in the telecommunications area: 'fully distributed costs, long-run average incremental costs, marginal costs, stand-alone costs, embedded direct costs, etc., including the cost base(s) used, i.e., historic costs (based on actual expenditure incurred for equipment and systems) or forward-looking costs (based on estimated replacement costs of equipment or systems).'[69] In respect of interconnection, in recital 10 of the Directive it is stated that 'whereas flexibility in the methods of charging for interconnection traffic should be possible, including capacity-based charging; whereas the level of charges should promote productivity and encourage efficient and sustainable market entry, and should not be below a limit calculated by the use of long-run incremental cost and cost allocation and attribution methods based on actual cost causation, nor above a limit set by the stand-alone cost of providing the interconnection in question; whereas charges for interconnection based on a price level closely linked to the long-run incremental cost for providing access to interconnection are appropriate for encouraging the rapid development of an open and competitive market.' Here it seems that the forward-looking long-run average incremental costs (FL-LRAIC) should be the floor, while the direct costs (stand-alone costs) should be the ceiling for the price calculation for the interconnection service in question.[70]

The aim of cross-subsidisation can be related to the undertaking, for example, the desire to strengthen competitiveness in certain areas of the market or to penetrate these areas. These instances will often fall under the prohibition of agreements which restrict competition or abuse of a dominant position. However, the aim can also be politically based, and can be determined by the authority which regulates or maybe owns the participant in question. For example, the aim can be to maintain uniform pricing for the same goods or services for different groups of customers or in different geographic areas where the costs for the provision of the goods or services differ (geographical equalisation).

In connection with the liberalised sectors, cross-subsidies could be used as sources of finance for maintaining the provision of services that are not, in themselves, profitable or for keeping prices low to ensure supplies to groups of the population which would not otherwise be able to afford to buy the services. This can be done by introducing price ceilings. Similarly, cross-subsidies can be used to reduce prices in geographical areas in which the provision of a given service would have higher costs than in other areas. This can result, for example, in there being different prices in different areas, according to their population densities.

Financing is generally via an exclusive right, reserving certain profitable activities to an undertaking which has an obligation to perform some unprofitable provision of goods or services.[71] To a certain extent, political motivations for such transfers have been the reasons why certain sectors have been granted exclusive rights or access to

---

69. 'Marginal costs' refers to the costs of producing a single additional unit.
70. *See also* COM(99) 539 final.
71. On cross subsidisation and EU law *see* Leigh Hancher & José Luis Sierra: *Cross-Subsidization and EC Law, Common Market Law Review* (1998); and Giuseppe B. Abbamonte: *Cross-Subsidisation and Community Competition Rules: Efficient Pricing versus Equity, European Law Review* (1998).

the market has been otherwise restricted.[72] Cross-subsidisation is thus a source of financing in connection with providing services of general economic interest, as discussed below.

There is a particular variant in the electricity supply sector where, under Article 31(4) of the Directive on the internal market in electricity, the Member States must require systems operators to give priority to production facilities which use renewable energy when allocating loading between production facilities. Member States can also give priority to the combined production of heat and electricity. This has particular regard for environmental considerations.

1.4.3 Division Between Undertakings Subject to Competition and Monopoly Undertakings, Etc.

The fact that not all parts of traditionally vertically integrated sectors are regarded as being capable of being subject to competition, or if it is merely that it is not wished to subject them to competition, makes it necessary to introduce a separation between what is to be subject to competition and what is not to be subject to competition. For example, control of a network is often put into a separate network undertaking or organisation.

Control of access to a network can perhaps be given to a system operator or infrastructure manager. This task can be given to a network undertaking as an independent undertaking. The Directive on the internal market in electricity and the Directive on the internal market in natural gas contained requirements for *system operator*, while Directive 2012/34/EU establishing a single European railway area refers to an *infrastructure manager*.

This form of separation of activities is often referred to as 'unbundling'. The separation can often be between different links in the value chain[73] and will, therefore, be vertical.[74] In the terminology of competition law, one can say that the value chain represents different product markets. In the liberalised sectors, there will be one or more markets for the good or service which is actually demanded by the end user (energy, transport, communications), and correspondingly, one or more product markets for the facilities that are necessary for the provision of that good or service (e.g., access to a network).

The provisions on unbundling have the same aims as the general competition rules which prohibit the abuse of a dominant position. However, the provisions on unbundling are more far-reaching since, on the one hand, they involve structural

---

72. Alberto Heimler & Paolo Saba: *Role and Enforcement of Competition Policy in Regulated Sectors*, in Proceedings of the OECD/World Bank Conference on Competition and Regulation in Network Industries, OECD, pp. 75 and 78(1995).
73. This splitting up of the tasks will not necessarily be noticed by the individual consumer, who often buys a single package of services that in fact consists of several different services.
74. There are also examples of horizontal separation, e.g., the separation between goods and passenger traffic on the railways. The two business areas are very different, apart from the fact that they use shared facilities, including the railway network. This horizontal division is thus not necessarily dependent on a division between an undertaking which is subject to competition and a monopoly undertaking.

requirements, and, on the other hand, they are imposed regardless of whether there has been abuse. The thinking behind the unbundling provisions is to limit the effects on competition of some of the less desirable incentives which exist in vertically integrated corporate structures. First, there is the incentive to favour companies which are part of the same corporate group. Such incentives are usually linked to the control of a network. A vertically integrated company that controls a network can favour giving associated companies access to the network. In addition, network companies automatically acquire information about other market participants' turnover and customers. Network companies can pass this information on to associated companies which thereby obtain a competitive advantage by acquiring insight into the commercially confidential information of their competitors. Furthermore, vertically integrated companies can exploit the monopoly advantages of control of the network by cross-subsidising the activities of associated companies which are exposed to competition.

A requirement for vertical unbundling is often introduced in connection with the liberalisation of public sectors. There can be unbundling at various levels. For example, there can be unbundling at the following levels:

- Accounting (separating different operating divisions)
- Management (functional)
- Organisational (legal personality, incorporation)
- Ownership.

These four levels are often perceived as expressing some form of progression. However, this is not necessarily the case. Requirements for management unbundling are not necessarily met by organisational or ownership unbundling.

Accounting unbundling consists of a requirement for keeping separate accounts for the different links of the value chain. It is primarily a method for obtaining greater transparency. It should not be possible to hide any abuse of a dominant position or cross-subsidising in accounts which separate out the individual areas of the business. See, for example, Article 31(3) of the Natural Gas Directive and Article 56(3) of the Electricity Directive.

Management unbundling refers to the situation where the management of one undertaking may not be subject to the instructions of another undertaking. This will typically be the case where a link in the value chain which is not subject to competition may not be managed by an undertaking which is subject to competition. This can be significant for example in relation to undertakings that administer access to networks or have responsibility for systems. There was an example of management unbundling in Article 7(6) of the first Electricity Directive 96/92/EC.

Organisational unbundling refers to separation into independent legal entities. There are examples of this in Article 8 of Directive 2002/77/EC on competition in the markets for electronic communications, and Article 44 of Directive (EU) 2018/1972 establishing the European Electronic Communications Code Organisational unbundling does not prevent the existence of corporate groups, where a parent company owns subsidiary companies which together represent a vertical structure. One of the key issues about the corporate group model is the possibility of an undertaking which is subject to competition and is in the same corporate group as a monopoly undertaking having access to better and quicker information than its competitors (asymmetric information). This is normally assumed to give rise to market failure. This can arise, for example, in connection with customer databases shared between an electricity supplier which is subject to competition and an undertaking which is responsible for a distribution network.

Ownership unbundling means a prohibition of overlapping ownership interests, and thus, it is a hindrance to the corporate group model.[75] However, neither organisational nor ownership unbundling prevents an overlap between the decision-makers of the individual participants. The property laws of the Member States are not affected by various Treaties; *see* Article 345 TFEU. There is debate as to the extent to which requirements for ownership unbundling can be included in secondary legislation.[76]

The provision in Article 345 TFEU established the Member States' freedom to determine the rules governing the system of property ownership in their territories. Among other things, a Member State can determine that certain undertakings must be operated and owned by public authorities. However, this freedom is not total. Where public ownership leads to a distortion of competition, it must be possible for the Union to regulate the scope of public ownership. Among other things, the CJ has established a requirement for the separation of commercial activities from the exercise of administrative authority so that a public authority has only a limited scope for operating and undertaking that is subject to competition while being responsible for administrative tasks in the same area. *See* the discussion of Case C-18/88, *RTT*; and Joined Cases C-46/90 and C-93/91, *Lagauche*, in section 1.4.5.2.

It is now the prevailing view that Article 345 TFEU cannot be relied on in support of an absolute prohibition of Union intervention in property rights and that Article 345 does not prevent some reorganisation of an industrial sector, even if the reorganisation makes changes to the ownership of assets and capital.[77] Article 345 does not exclude the Member States' rules governing their systems of property ownership from the scope of Union law,[78] but it presumably means that the Union cannot force a Member State to privatise publicly owned undertakings. However, ownership unbundling does not amount to a direction to privatise. According to the third liberalisation package, ownership unbundling means that the same legal person may not control both the infrastructure and an undertaking that is subject to competition.[79]

Nevertheless, there are examples of ownership unbundling in national regulation of the liberalised sectors.[80]

---

75. *See* in general the Commission staff working document, SWD(2013) 177 final: Ownership unbundling: assessing conflicts of interests.
76. In the case law of the CJ, property rights are regarded as a fundamental principle. *See* Case C-491/01, *British American Tobacco*, para. 149; Joined Cases C-20/00 and C-64/00, *Booker Aquaculture*, para. 69; Case C-368/96, *Generics*, para. 79; and Case 44/79, *Liselotte Hauer*, para. 15.
77. Case C-491/01, *British American Tobacco*, para. 147; and Joined Cases 56/64 and 58/64, *Consten and Grundig*.
78. *See* Case 182/83, *Fearon*, para. 7; and Case C-302/97, *Konle*, para. 38.
79. 'Control' is defined in accordance with its definition in Art. 3(2) of Regulation (EC) No 139/2004 on the control of concentrations between undertakings (the EC Merger Regulation).
80. This is the case with regard to the transmission system operator (TSO) in the area of electricity and natural gas.

In the Commission Decision of 20 March 2001 relating to a proceeding under Article 82 of the EC Treaty (Case COMP/35.141 – *Deutsche Post*) (OJ 2001 L 125/27), Deutsche Post accepted the obligation to separate its mail order parcels business in an independent company. The risk of cross-subsidisation was therefore limited. In this connection, the unbundling requirement was not directly derived from public regulation but was the result of conditional obligations in connection with a concrete case. The case is also discussed in the section on postal services (section 4.2.1.1).

In the case of publicly owned undertakings, it can also be desirable to separate the operator which carries on the business from the regulatory authority. This form of unbundling can reduce the risk of the abuse of power in favour of the authority's own operators. There is an example of this in Article 22 of Directive 97/67/EC on postal services, which requires the regulatory authorities for the postal sector to be legally separate from and operationally independent of the postal operators.

1.4.4   Access to Networks

In connection with network industries, where a network constitutes an essential facility or a natural monopoly, the exposure to competition of part of the value chain will usually involve all participants having access to the network, regardless of whether it is owned by a participant on the market exposed to competition. This is referred to as *third-party access*.[81] Without access to the network and other technical installations, a potential market participant is effectively denied access to the market. On markets characterised by the existence of networks, there will thus often be at least two kinds of market:

- A market for the provision of goods or services to end users.
- A market for access to the network.

The general competition rules of the Treaty apply to access to the network. In particular, the prohibition of abuse of a dominant position will be relevant because of the nature of the network as a natural monopoly. Usually, the sector-specific provisions will to some extent address the question of access to the network. However, these must not be contrary to the Treaty competition rules, and the Treaty provisions apply in parallel.

Provisions on third-party access are often associated with an obligation to give equal treatment in connection with access to a network. In such cases, the owner of the network cannot have better or cheaper access to the network than those who do not own the network. In this connection, the term *common carrier* is often used.[82]

---

81. For a general presentation of this, *see* Marcel Haag: *Der Netzzugang Dritter aus der Sicht des Europäischen Wettbewerbsrecht*, in Jürgen Schwarze (ed.): *Der Netzzugang für Dritte im Wirtscarftsrecht*, p. 57 (1999) and Christopher Jones & William-James Kettlewell (ed.): *EU Energy Law – The internal Energy Market*, Vol. I, p. 19-112 (2021).
82. The term is derived from the transport sector. There is an example of this in Art. 320(1) of the Electricity Directive, which requires third party access to the transmission and distribution systems based on published tariffs, applicable to all eligible customers and applied objectively and without discrimination between system users.

According to the common carrier concept in its classical form, if there is a lack of capacity, new suppliers must be allowed access on an equal footing with existing suppliers, leading to a form of rationing. However, this solution is not always used. *See* below in the discussion on regulated access.

The requirement for equal treatment does not prohibit giving special priority on proper grounds. For example, this may involve giving priority in an electricity supply network (load distribution) for renewable sources or highly efficient combined heat and power (CHP) production (*see* Article 31(4) of the Electricity Directive) or giving priority between passenger and goods traffic on the railways (*see* Article 45 of Directive 2012/34/EU).[83]

Imposing an obligation on a common carrier can be seen as a counterpart to any exclusive right which an undertaking may have been granted (e.g., in the form of permission to carry on a natural monopoly), or it may just be imposed as a step in the liberalisation process.

The requirements for equal treatment are supplemented by the prohibitions in the Treaty on discrimination on the grounds of nationality and the provisions on abuse of a dominant position. What is special about such requirements which are found in sector-specific legislation is that they also apply to participants whose networks are essentially intended for their own use as well as, where this is only partly the case, to their own use in relation to access for third parties.

Conditions are often imposed to the effect that the terms for access to a network must be equitable.

The regulation of third-party access in the EU sometimes takes the form of negotiated access and sometimes regulated access. Negotiated access respects the principle of individual agreements, which may need to be renewed with each new use of the network. There is an example of this in Article 33(3) of the Natural Gas Directive in relation to the storage of natural gas. The requirement for negotiated access will often be a minimum requirement so that a Member State can instead choose to give users the greater protection which lies in regulated access.[84] Conversely, *regulated access* means that the price is determined in advance by the undertaking providing the service. This latter recalls the common carrier. There are provisions in Article 6 of the Electricity Directive and Article 32 of the Natural Gas Directive (LNG facilities, transmission and distribution systems). Correspondingly, in the area of telecommunications Regulation (EC) No 2887/2000 on unbundled access to the local loop and Article 6 in Directive (EU) 2018/1972 on standard terms for access to networks.

In principle, the provisions on regulated access will be accompanied by provisions whereby lack of capacity will be a proper reason for refusing access. *See*, for example, Article 21 of the Natural Gas Directive and Article 6 of the Electricity Directive. When there is a lack of capacity, the existing capacity must be shared out. A pro rata system, first-come-first-served, and auctions are different ways of allocating

---

83. For a decision on this, *see* C-671/21, *Gargždų geležinkelis*.
84. For example, in Art. 19(4) of the Natural Gas Directive there is also the possibility of choosing regulated access.

capacity. Likewise, network rights can be linked to supply contracts (merit order).[85] In the area of energy supply, where the provision of energy using the network is more or less homogeneous, there can be a certain amount of equalisation on either side of a bottleneck.[86] For example, a system operator can implement upward or downward adjustments of production, or there can be a set-off in the case of natural gas so that only the net amount can be transmitted through the bottleneck.[87] There is great uncertainty as to whether the various methods in their different variations can be in breach of Article 102 TFEU.[88]

Agreements for the establishment and use of networks should be interpreted in the light of Articles 101 and 102 TFEU. There can very well be conduct which restricts competition in breach of the competition rules. There is especially a need for care in connection with the allocation of capacity when there are bottlenecks. These often occur in physical networks in connection with cross-border connections and often with divided ownership. When establishing new capacity, long-term contracts are often entered into on the use of the capacity. The Commission will not necessarily intervene against such agreements if they can be considered to improve the overall competitive situation, for example, by increasing capacity.

> An example of this is the *Viking Cable* case. A Norwegian electricity supply company and a German electricity supply company agreed to establish and operate a new undersea cable between Norway and Germany for the transmission of high-voltage electricity. The establishment of such a cable required a major capital investment, and the parties wanted to secure their investment by a twenty-five year agreement which included exclusive use of the cable. However, unused capacity could be disposed of on the spot market (Nord Pool) for twenty-four hours at a time. In an interim statement, the Commission found that the notified agreement was not contrary to Article 101 TFEU (then Article 81 of the EC Treaty), and it emphasised in particular the increase in capacity and the significant investment required.[89]
>
> In a corresponding case concerning a gas pipeline,[90] established as a joint venture. In its approval the Commission emphasised the furthering of competition in the linking of otherwise technically isolated markets and on the freedom of the participants to transfer their transmission rights. A

---

85. This is the case in connection with an electricity trader on the Nordic electricity exchange (Nord Pool). Transmission capacity is bought together with the current.
86. Those parts of the network where the capacity is less than the demand.
87. In the nature of things, the same cannot occur in the areas of transport and telecommunications.
88. Michael Albers: *Competition Law Issues Arising from the Liberalization Process*, in Damien Geradin (ed.): *The Liberalization of Electricity and Natural Gas in the European Union*, p. 7-10 (2001).
89. Notice on Case COMP/E-3/37.921 *Viking Cable* (OJ 2001 C 247/11). The Commission also stated, though without giving any grounds, that there was not a breach of the prohibition of abuse of dominant position. However, the cable was not laid as the parties later cancelled their agreement.
90. The gas pipeline between the United Kingdom and Belgium is referred to in the Commission's XXV Report on Competition Policy, 1995 p. 125.

provision on joint marketing of the transmission capacity which restricted competition was of less importance in the overall picture.

When there is limited capacity, there is a question of whether priority should be given to prior users of the facility. Regulation (EEC) No 95/93 on common rules for the allocation of slots at Union airports authorises giving such priority to owners of existing slots, provided they have been used; *see* Article 8(1). In contrast, Regulation (EC) No 714/2009 on conditions for access to the network for cross-border exchanges in electricity contains a principle whereby problems of capacity restrictions in a network must be resolved by means of transaction-based methods, i.e., methods which do not involve a choice between the contracts of the individual market operators; *see* Article 16(1). This could involve compensation.[91]

In some cases, the owners of rights to allocated capacity are prohibited from re-selling their capacity. In the area of railways, there is such a prohibition in Article 38(1) of Directive 2012/34/EU establishing a single European railway area. On the contrary, there can be a certain amount of exchange or transfer of capacity (landing and take-off slots) in the area of air transport; *see* Article 8 of Regulation (EEC) No 95/93.

There are variations as to whether the EU lays down a specific form for dealing with third-party access or leaves it to the Member States to decide. Third-party access is often accompanied by a requirement for the Member States to set up or appoint some kind of out-of-court dispute settlement authority to deal with disagreements about third-party access or the conditions for such access. There are examples of this in Article 6(2) of the Electricity Directive and Article 46(6) of Directive 2012/34/EU establishing a single European railway area. Such dispute settlement bodies are normally required to be impartial; *see* the examples referred to in the energy sector, where it is a requirement of Article 26 of the Electricity Directive.

Commission Recommendation 98/257/EC on the principles applicable to the bodies responsible for out-of-court settlement of consumer disputes lays down four principles which ought to apply to the settlement of disputes by consumer bodies; these are: independence, transparency, the adversarial principle, and effectiveness. In relation to the principle of independence, it is important that a person appointed to settle disputes cannot be dismissed during their period of office (if a single individual) and that a body of several persons should include an equal number of representatives from the commercial sector and consumers.

In some cases, the Union has also regulated the Member States' scope for introducing *price regulation*. Price regulation and the possibilities for third-party access are closely linked. An unrealistically high price for third-party access will have the same effect of restricting competition as a refusal of third-party access.

Among other things, price regulation has been introduced in the area of telecommunications in Article 74 of Directive (EU) 2018/1972 on establishing the European Electronic Communications Code (European Electronic Communications Code), which allows for cost-based pricing in connection with interconnection.[92] There is another example in Article 3 of Regulation (EC) No 1775/2005 on conditions for access to the

---

91. Proceedings has been brought against ACER in T-342/23.
92. *See* s. 4.1.3.3 for a more detailed discussion.

natural gas transmission networks, which states that tariffs for access to networks must 'reflect actual costs incurred, insofar as such costs correspond to those of an efficient and structurally comparable network operator and are transparent, whilst including appropriate return on investments, and where appropriate taking account of the benchmarking of tariffs by the regulatory authorities.'

Benchmarking is a term which is increasingly used to refer to a form of comparison whereby supervisory authorities use a comparison of undertakings that are not subject to competition, or where it is assumed that competition is not optimal. Used in connection with a special price regulation, benchmarking can identify the least cost-effective undertakings and can apply special incentive regulation to them, for example, by setting price or income ceilings to prevent them from covering their cost levels or profits hitherto.

1.4.4.1 Direct Lines

The establishment of direct lines between a provider and end users outside the normal network (network bypass) can be used as an alternative to third-party access. This means that the natural monopoly is not absolute. For example, both the Electricity Directive and the Natural Gas Directive provide for the establishment of direct lines.[93] In Germany, connections have been established to some extent by others than network and transmission undertakings so that end users can be supplied outside the distribution or transmission network. In connection with the possibility of establishing direct lines, Member States are required to lay down criteria for the issue of authorisations for setting up or managing such direct lines that must be objective, transparent and non-discriminatory.

1.4.4.2 Transit

Transit is understood as the carrying of a good or service for the fulfilment of transactions where none of the parties to the agreement buy or produce the good or service in an area through which the good or service is carried. In the EU, the regulation of transit is relevant where one Member State is the country of origin or the country where the good or service is received, while the good or service crosses the territory of a Member State which is neither the country of origin nor the country where the good or service is received.[94] The provisions on access to networks in connection with transit are relevant where two participants would not be able to trade together without using network facilities in a third Member State. It is thus relevant to electricity supply, natural gas supply, telecommunications and railways.

---

93. Article 38 of the Natural Gas Directive and Art. 7 of the Electricity Directive. 'Direct line' means a connection between a seller of a good or service and a customer for such good or service which is outside or complementary to the interconnected system. 'Direct line' is defined in Art. 2 of each of these directives.
94. *See, e.g.*, the definition in Art. 2(1) of the Electricity Directive and Art. 2(1) of the Natural Gas Directive.

The concepts of transit and rights of transit have been discussed for centuries. Thus, Grotius (Hugo de Groot) argued in the seventeenth century that there was a general right of transit over the territory of another country.[95] The right of transit has also been dealt with in international agreements; *see* the Barcelona Convention on Freedom of Transit (1921) and Article V in the General Agreement on Tariffs and Trade (GATT). In the area of energy, *see* also Article 7 in the Energy Charter Treaty.[96]

Transit can take place via an interconnected network. However, in a physical network, transit will usually be carried through some trunk lines in the network, referred to as the transmission lines.[97] In addition to this, there will often be special transnational connections which link national networks. Access to these will also be necessary for transit.

In Union law, access to transit is regulated by a number of sector-specific directives. In the area of the railways, the transit provisions are built into Directive 2012/34/EU, establishing a single European railway area, which deals with the ordinary provisions on third-party access. The same is the case with the Directive on establishing the European Electronic Communications Code. In the areas of electricity and natural gas, transit was dealt with in Directive 90/547/EEC on the transit of electricity through transmission grids and Directive 91/296/EEC on the transit of natural gas through grids. In these two sectors, the transit markets were opened to competition before the national markets, which was presumably why the transit provisions were included in separate directives. *See* now the two market directives as well as the Regulation on access to the natural gas transmission networks.[98]

Access to transit can be limited to special networks or special participants. In the railways sector, the right of transit is limited to the special groups of participants who have general third-party access rights in the Member State where they are established, the destination Member State or the transit Member State, in accordance with Directive 2012/34/EU.

1.4.4.3 *Expansion of Capacity*

From the financial point of view, the owners of a network ought to scale their network with a view to maximising their own profit. For a private network owner, the most appropriate capacity will not necessarily coincide with what is the most appropriate capacity for society as a whole. For example, a lack of capacity in a given network can be an expression of an inappropriate situation for the general economic interest.

If a network is owned by a commercial undertaking, there can be a need to ensure the appropriate capacity for society by other means. For example, payment can be given for the maintenance of a certain capacity on a given network. This is seen in the air transport and railways sectors.

---

95. *Hugo Grotius:* De Jure Belli ac Pacis II, 2, 13 (1625), as translated in Classics of International Law, 1925 pp. 196–197.
96. *Martha M. Roggenkamp:* Transit of Network-Bound Energy: The European Experience, in *Thomas Wälde* (ed.): The Energy Charter Treaty, 1996.
97. This is the terminology used, e.g., in the areas of electricity and natural gas.
98. Regulation (EC) No Regulation (EC) No 715/2009 on conditions for access to the natural gas transmission networks and repealing Regulation (EC) No 1775/2005.

If an expansion of capacity requires the expansion of a physical network or other structural changes, it can be necessary to make a full analysis. In connection with overloaded railway capacity, according to Articles 47, 50 and 51 of Directive 2012/34/EU, the infrastructure manager has to make a capacity analysis and prepare a capacity enhancement plan.

Another possibility is for Member States to require capacity to be increased. Article 35(2) of the Natural Gas Directive contains authority for Member States to take measures to ensure that a network owner who refuses third-party access to the network on the grounds of lack of capacity or a lack of connection makes the necessary enhancements to capacity. However, this presumes that it is economical to do so or that a potential customer is willing to pay for the enhancements.

1.4.5 Management of Networks

In connection with the management of a network, there are a number of tasks which must be taken care of in relation to the use of the network, cooperation with foreign network managers, decisions relating to disturbances of supply, and planning future network capacity. Such tasks are usually the responsibility of the owner of the network, a public authority or an independent undertaking. To a certain extent, the EU has regulated the performance of these tasks separately for the liberalised sectors.

An example of this is the regulation of infrastructure management in the railway sector. According to Directive 2012/34/EU, infrastructure managers have powers and responsibilities with regard to cooperation with other infrastructure managers (Article 40), with regard to lack of capacity (Articles 46–47), with regard to disturbances of service (Article 54), and with regard to planning capacity enhancement (Articles 50–51).

There is another example in the Electricity Directive and the Natural Gas Directive which contain requirements for the establishment of, among other things, transmission systems operators whose tasks include allocation of loading and access to networks, as well as interconnection, expansion and security of supply.

1.4.5.1 *Unbundling*

In some cases, the requirement for the establishment of such network managers is combined with a requirement for unbundling.

An alternative to having a private undertaking as the network manager is to allocate these tasks to a public authority. In the electricity supply sector, the organisation of the system operator function varies. There are cases where the function is the responsibility of undertakings with predominantly private ownership, of public undertakings, and of public authorities.

1.4.5.2 Authorities

The boundaries between the tasks of a public supervisory authority and the carrying on of an undertaking are often unclear. Where an actual undertaking has been carried on by an administrative authority, it has been natural for certain sector-specific administrative decisions to be taken by the same administrative authority as that which carries on the undertaking. Where the carrying on of the business has been separated out to be carried on by an independent private law entity but is in fact carried on by a state-owned monopoly, certain supervisory tasks and powers have a tendency to go with the new legal entity. But at the moment when parts of the business of the state-owned undertaking become subject to competition, it is highly questionable for the state-owned participant to exercise administrative authority which can have an influence on the conditions of competition.[99]

In a number of areas, the CJ has found that this combining of tasks is a breach of Article 102 TFEU.[100] In Case C-67/96, *Albany International v. Stichting Bedrijfspensioenfonds Textielindustrie*, which concerned the possibility for the public authorities to give a pension fund the exclusive right to administer a supplementary pension scheme in a particular industrial sector, the CJ accepted, on the basis of a number of specific reasons (*see* in particular paragraphs 116–122 of the judgment), that the pension fund in question could exercise administrative authority, without this being contrary to Articles 102 and 106 TFEU (then Articles 82 and 86 of the EC Treaty).

There is thus a requirement to separate commercial activities and the exercise of authority (where a public authority operates on a market that is subject to competition). According to the CJ's decision in Case C-18/88, *RTT*, it is contrary to Articles 102 and 106 TFEU (then Articles 82 and 86 of the EC Treaty) for a public undertaking to operate on a market while it has powers to supervise and grant licences to other operators on that market. According to the CJ's decision in Joined Cases C-46/90 and C-93/91, *Lagauche*, this is not contrary to Article 106 TFEU (then Article 86 of the EC Treaty) as long as the decision does not involve the exercise of any discretion.

Regardless of whether network management is delegated to a special organisation or authority, secondary EU legislation can impose requirements regarding the confidential treatment of commercial information both by the manager and by the undertaking which owns the essential facilities. *See*, for example, Article 41(1), no. 14 and 16 of the Natural Gas Directive.

1.4.6 Public Obligations

The aims of the Union include more than just consideration for the internal market and the promotion of competition. A number of the Treaty articles contain provisions

---

99. From the point of view of administrative law it is altogether questionable to give administrative authority to undertakings which are organised in the form of private law entities.
100. Case C-18/88, *Régie des télégraphes et des téléphones (RTT) v. GB-Inno-BM*; Case C-202/88, *France v. Commission*; Case C-260/89, *ERT*; Case C-91/94, *Tranchant and another*. Case C-18/88 and Case C-260/89 are discussed in Ch. 10 on Public Undertakings, s. 4.2.3.

concerning other and possibly even conflicting interests. The term 'services of general economic interest' has a special position in the EC Treaty, as appears from Article 14 TFEU (originally inserted as Article 16 in the EC Treaty by the Treaty of Amsterdam: 'Without prejudice to Article 4 of the Treaty on European Union or to Articles 93, 106 and 107 of this Treaty, and given the place occupied by services of general economic interest in the shared values of the Union as well as their role in promoting social and territorial cohesion, the Union and the Member States, each within their respective powers and within the scope of application of the Treaties, shall take care that such services operate on the basis of principles and conditions, particularly economic and financial conditions, which enable them to fulfil their missions.'

A corresponding term is used in Article 106(2) TFEU: 'Undertakings entrusted with the operation of services of general economic interest or having the character of a revenue-producing monopoly shall be subject to the rules contained in this Treaty, in particular to the rules on competition, in so far as the application of such rules does not obstruct the performance, in law or in fact, of the particular tasks assigned to them. The development of trade must not be affected to such an extent as would be contrary to the interests of the Community.'

These services of general economic interest differ from other ordinary services by the fact that they are considered by the public authorities to be necessary, regardless of whether the ordinary market incentives will be sufficient to ensure their supply.[101] Services of general economic interest have been defined as services of a commercial character which serve general public purposes.[102] In a case concerning the electricity supply sector,[103] the CJ stated that the aim of Article 106(2) TFEU (then Article 90(2) of the EC Treaty) is 'to reconcile the Member States' interest in using certain undertakings, in particular in the public sector, as an instrument of economic or fiscal policy with the Community's interest in ensuring compliance with the rules on competition and the preservation of the unity of the common market.'[104]

The terminology can differ. The term 'universal service obligation' is used in the Communication from the Commission – Services of general interest in Europe of 19.1.2001. Regulation (EEC) No 95/93 on common rules for the allocation of slots at Community airports uses the term 'public service obligations'. Article 3.9 of the Electricity Directive refers to 'universal service and public service obligations'. According to Article 3(2) in the Electricity Directive and in the Natural Gas Directive, 'public service obligations' may relate to 'security of supply, regularity, quality and price of supplies and environmental protection, including energy efficiency, energy from renewable sources and climate protection.' The concept of public service obligation is

---

101. Communication from the Commission – Services of general interest in Europe of 19.1.2001 (OJ 2001 C 17/4).
102. European Economic and Social Committee statement of 17.7.2002 on 'Services of general economic interest', and Communication from the Commission – Services of general interest in Europe of 19.1.2001 (OJ 2001 C 17/4).
103. Case C-159/94, *France v. Commission*, para. 55.
104. On public undertakings in general, *see* Ch. 10.

derived from French administrative law.[105] In relation to electricity supply, the content of the term has been described as:[106]

> 'Le principe de service public a à la fois des fondements juridiques (continuité de service, égalité d'accès et neutralité), économiques (planification, économies publiques) et sociales (pressions syndicales, problèmes d'emploi et le développement de 'l'Etat-providence').'[107]
>
> The expression 'special service obligations' has also been used in this context.[108]

The same term is used in the railway sector in Article 2(e) of Regulation (EC) No 1370/2007 on public passenger transport services by rail and by road. Here, it is stated that public service obligations include requirements to provide transport services that an operator would not provide if it were considering its own commercial interests.

The concept of a public service obligation can naturally be abused by Member States to promote the interests of their national participants in markets which are subject to competition. If so, this would be a breach of the general provisions of the Treaty. Individual liberalising directives can include provisions on notification in order to make the Commission's control of this easier. There are examples of this in Article 3(15) of the Electricity Directive and Article 3(11) of the Natural Gas Directive, according to which the Member States must inform the Commission of all measures adopted to fulfil universal service and public service obligations. Notification must be given whether or not such measures require a derogation under the Directive. The Member States must inform the Commission subsequently every two years of any changes to such measures.

1.4.6.1 *Obligations to Supply*

One of the general economic interests is the obligation to provide a particular good or service to a particular area at an affordable price and of uniform quality, regardless of the profitability of the particular activity – an obligation to supply. Regardless of whether the goods or services are provided by a public undertaking or on a commercial basis, there is a need to ensure their availability to all citizens. In this context, citizens are protected in their role as consumers, and the obligation to supply thus takes on the character of consumer protection, even if the obligation to supply extends to end users who use the goods or services as part of their commercial undertaking.

The obligation to supply has been accepted in Article 36 of the Charter of fundamental rights of the European Union: 'The Union recognises and respects access

---

105. Rosa Greaves: *EC Transport Law*, p. 20 (2000).
106. Jacques Asscher & Guy-Martial Weijer: *Energie et protection de l'environment dans la perspective européenne, Report to the FIDE Congress*, p. 238 (1996). The concept can be interpreted very broadly, and has been so by the CJ.
107. *See also* Heike Schweitzer: *Service of General Economic Interest: European Law's Impact on the Role of Markets and of Member States*, in Marise Cremona (ed.): *Market Integration and Public Service in the European Union*, pp. 13 f. (2011).
108. William J. Baumol & J. Gregory Sidak: *The Pricing of Inputs Sold to Competitors*, Yale Journal on Regulation, pp. 171–202 (1994).

to services of general economic interest as provided for in national laws and practices, in accordance with the Treaties, in order to promote the social and territorial cohesion of the Union.'[109] However, the expression is not enshrined in the EC Treaty. Instead, the obligation is derived from the expression 'services of general economic interest'. According to the White Paper on services of general interest, the term 'services of general interest' is broader than the term 'services of general economic interest' and covers 'both market and non-market services which the public authorities class as being of general interest and subject to specific public service obligations.'[110]

In other contexts, the expression 'universal services' is used. This concept can be understood as a requirement to supply goods or services at affordable prices to all customers who demand them (the principle of universality), without discrimination as to geographic location (the principle of equality) and on a permanent basis (the principle of continuity).[111] Barry M Mitnik calls this the 'Public Interest Concept'.[112] He quotes Charles Phillips[113] on the special obligations developed under the Common Law for regulated sectors of industry: 'Obligations were to serve all who request service; to give safe and adequate service; to serve all on an equal basis, forbidding unjust discrimination; and to require only a "just and reasonable" price for services.' The concept can be seen as a subset of the public service obligation. Some directives, for example, in the telecommunications sector, often lay down minimum requirements for universal service/the public service obligation.

There is an example of this in Article 3(1) of Directive 97/67/EC on common rules for Community postal services, which states that 'Member States shall ensure that users enjoy the right to a universal service involving the permanent provision of a postal service of specified quality at all points in their territory at affordable prices for all users.'

The concept of *affordability* has been developed in connection with the regulation of telecommunications. It has also subsequently been introduced in the postal services sector. It involves a requirement that a good or service of general economic

---

109. As published in OJ 2007 C 303/1.
110. Communication from the Commission – White Paper on services of general interest, COM(2004) 374 final, which merely repeats para. 16 from the Commission's Green paper on services of general interest, COM(2003) 270 final.
111. Damien Geradin & Christophe Humpe: *The Liberalization of Postal Services in the European Union: An Analysis of Directive 97/67*, Damien Geradin (ed.): *The Liberalization of Postal Services in the European Union*, p. 93 (2002). The extent of the principle of equality is limited In Art. 12 of Directive 97/67/EC on common rules for Community postal services, there is only a requirement for tariffs to be 'transparent and non-discriminatory'. There is not a requirement for there to be uniform tariffs, regardless of the geographic location of the user. On the other hand Member States can impose a requirement for the use of the same tariff for the whole of their national territory. Other possibilities for Member States to impose universal services are found in Art. 9 of the Natural Gas Directive.
112. Barry M. Mitnick: *The Political Economy of Regulation*, p. 243-279 (1980). *See also* Heike Schweitzer: *Service of General Economic Interest: European Law's Impact on the Role of Markets and of Member States*, in Marise Cremona (ed.): *Market Integration and Public Service in the European Union*, p. 43 ff. (2011).
113. Charles Franklin Phillips: *The Economics of Regulation: Theory and Practice in the Transportation and Public Utility Industries*, pp. 80–83 (1965). *See* in particular the section on 'Obligations', p. 81.

interest must be offered at an affordable price so that it is available to all.[114] This is supplemented by a requirement for price transparency.

In other contexts, there is a requirement for cost-sharing. In Article 6 of Directive 2002/77/EC on competition in the markets for electronic communications networks and services, it is required that any 'national scheme pursuant to Directive 2002/22/EC[115], serving to share the net cost of the provision of universal service obligations shall be based on objective, transparent and non-discriminatory criteria and shall be consistent with the principle of proportionality and of least market distortion'.

In other situations, it is up to the Member States themselves to define what the terms mean. For example, that is the case in the natural gas sector,[116] where, according to Article 3(3) of the Natural Gas Directive, the Member States must 'take appropriate measures to protect final customers, and shall, in particular, ensure that there are adequate safeguards to protect vulnerable customers.'[117] The Member States are subject to a number of minimum requirements for national protection, including requirements for transparency, notice of changes to conditions of supply, and prohibitions on the charging of fees for change of supplier; see Annex 1 to the Directive.

In certain situations, the obligation to supply can be given to a supplier which has special obligations.

According to Article 3(3) of the Electricity Directive, Member States may appoint a supplier of last resort. In particular, in the area of electricity supply, the CJ has made decisions which could indicate that the Member States have considerable freedom to define the content of the public service obligation.[118]

Requirements can be laid down for uniform charging rates (geographical equalisation) as part of an obligation to supply. Article 12 of the Postal Services Directive implies that Member States may lay down requirements for uniform postal rates. However, there is no obligation to do so. Here, the question arises as to whether a requirement for uniform rates excludes the possibility of making individual agreements, primarily for discounts for large customers. This must be assumed to be allowed, unless specifically stated otherwise. Article 12 of the Postal Services Directive explicitly states that the application of a uniform tariff does not exclude the right of universal service providers to conclude individual agreements on prices with customers. This opens up the possibility of granting discounts to large customers.

---

114. See the Commission's Green paper on services of general interest, COM(2003) 270 final.
115. Amended by Directive (EU) 2018/1972 on establishing the European Electronic Communications Code.
116. P. J. Slot & A. M. Skudder: *Common Features of Community Law Regulation in the Network-Bound Sectors, Common Market Law Review*, p. 123 (2001).
117. Article 3(8) of the Electricity Directive also contains a provision on addressing energy poverty, including in the broader context of poverty. This must be seen as an expression that electricity supply is a basic welfare service.
118. P.J. Slot & A.M. Skudder: *Common Features of Community Law Regulation in the Network-Bound Sectors, Common Market Law Review*, p. 124 (2001), which refers to the four judgments of the CJ in: Case C-159/94, *France v. Commission;* Case C-158/99, *Thermenhotel Stoiser Franz and others v. Commission;* Case C-159/99, *Commission v. Italy;* and Case C-160/99, *Commission v. France*.

1.4.6.2 *Exclusivity and the Obligation to Supply*

The obligation to supply has often been linked to the allocation of exclusive rights (de jure monopoly) or the existence of a natural or institutional monopoly. If a monopoly undertaking is made subject to an obligation to supply, this can be seen as an expression of taking care of services of general economic interest. In this connection, an exclusive right can be granted with a view to ensuring the provision (financing) of the obligation. This implies that parts of the area covered by the exclusive right are profitable or can be made so and that by means of cross-subsidisation, that can be (part) financing of the area where there is an obligation to supply. Without there being an exclusive right, other suppliers could establish competing undertakings in the profitable areas (skimming) and thereby deprive the undertaking with an obligation to supply of the possibility of obtaining a surplus which can be used to cover the deficit arising from supplying the unprofitable areas.

In parts of sector-specific legislation, special provisions have been introduced to finance the extra costs of obligations to supply. In the telecommunications sector, the Member States are required to revoke all special or exclusive rights. Instead, a sharing mechanism can be set up to cover the supplementary expenses for the provision of obligatory services on the basis of contributions from all providers of services; *see* Articles 7 and 9 of the Postal Services Directive. In the air transport sector, Member States can issue temporary exclusive licences on the basis of open offers to ensure regular services on certain routes so as to ensure sufficient service of the market.

However, an obligation to supply is not necessarily linked to exclusive rights. In Union law, there is nothing in principle to prevent a Member State from imposing on individual undertakings or groups of undertakings such obligations to supply, without them at the same time being granted an exclusive right. However, the obligation to supply must not be contrary to the general principles of Union law, for example, the discrimination principle.

1.4.6.3 *Financial Compensation*

An alternative to granting exclusive rights as a source for financing an obligation to supply is financial compensation from public funds (State aid or aid from other public bodies). Aid can be given from the state treasury (e.g., by subsidies or other financial advantages such as tax reliefs), contributions from market participants (e.g., a fund for the supply obligation), averaging of tariffs (e.g., nationwide uniform tariffs, despite significant variances in the cost of providing the service), and financing on the basis of social solidarity (e.g., national insurance contributions).

According to Article 90 of Directive (EU) 2018/1972 (European Electronic Communications Code Directive), it is possible to provide public aid in the telecommunications sector if the responsibility for the obligation to supply imposes an unreasonable burden. This Directive uses a part arrangement where the participants who do not have an obligation to supply help to bear the costs of the obligation to supply. This method is also found in Articles 7 and 9 of the Postal Services Directive.

In the postal services sector, compensation using public means is also a possibility; see Article 7(1) of the Postal Services Directive.

In other areas, there can be an obligation to submit such service provisions to a tender. This is the case with air transport; see Article 174 of Regulation (EC) No 1008/2008 of the European Parliament and of the Council of 24 September 2008 on common rules for the operation of air services in the Community.

It has been questioned whether aid for carrying out an obligation to supply constitutes State aid. The answer is: Yes. Over-compensation will clearly be State aid.

In the *Altmark* case,[119] the CJ held that State aid which had the aim of enabling the fulfilment of obligations to supply (in the case in question, urban, suburban or regional transport services) did not fall within the prohibition of State aid under Article 107(1) TFEU (the Article 87(1) of the EC Treaty), in so far as such aid should be seen as being compensation for discharging public service obligations. However, for such compensation to escape classification as State aid, a number of conditions must be satisfied:

- first, the recipient undertaking must actually have public service obligations to discharge, and the obligations must be clearly defined;
- second, the parameters on the basis of which the compensation is calculated must be established in advance in an objective and transparent manner;
- third, the compensation cannot exceed what is necessary to cover all or part of the costs incurred in the discharge of public service obligations, taking into account the relevant receipts and a reasonable profit for discharging those obligations;
- fourth, where the undertaking which is to discharge public service obligations, in a specific case, is not chosen pursuant to a public procurement procedure which would allow for the selection of the tenderer capable of providing those services at the least cost to the community, the level of compensation needed must be determined on the basis of an analysis of the costs which a typical undertaking, well run and adequately provided with means of transport so as to be able to meet the necessary public service requirements, would have incurred in discharging those obligations, taking into account the relevant receipts and a reasonable profit for discharging the obligations.

However, it can be relevant where the aid comes from.

The *PreussenElektra* case[120] concerned the German law, *Stromeinspeisungsgesetz*, on the purchase by electricity supply undertakings of electricity generated from hydraulic energy, wind energy, solar energy, gas from waste dumps and sewage treatment plants, or products or residues and biological waste from agriculture and forestry work, which was paid for by consumers. The law also laid down minimum prices for the electricity produced by such methods. The minimum prices were higher than the real economic value of the electricity. The CJ found that in the case in question the prohibition on State aid in Article 107(1) TFEU was not applicable, since there was not a transfer of State funds.

---

119. Case C-280/00, *Altmark Trans and another v. Nahverkehrsgesellschaft Altmark and another*.
120. Case C-379/98, *PreussenElektra v. Schhleswag*.

The referring national court had asked whether Article 107 TFEU (then Article 92 of the EC Treaty) should be interpreted so that the concept of State aid should also include national arrangements that only regulated the allocation of costs between undertakings at different levels of production involving purchase obligations and minimum payments, when this in fact led to an allocation of costs, without the undertaking which had to make payments receiving a return.

The disputed provision in paragraph 2 of the *Stromeinspeisungsgesetz* provided that electricity supply undertakings were obliged to purchase the electricity produced in their area of supply from renewable energy sources and to pay for it in accordance with the provisions of paragraph 3. According to this provision, a minimum price was laid down for electricity from certain forms of renewable energy. The price was based on a percentage of the average income per kilowatt from the electricity supply company's supply of electricity to the end user. After receiving many complaints from electricity supply companies, the Commission had informed the German Federal Finance Minister of its concern with regard to the question of whether, after a number of amendments which extended the scope of its application, the *Stromeinspeisungsgesetz* was still compatible with the provisions on State aid in the EC Treaty. However, the Commission's approach did not lead to any amendment of the German law.

In relation to the prohibition on State aid, the CJ argued that the obligation to purchase at fixed minimum prices, and the sharing out of the financial burden which the purchase obligation meant for the private electricity supply companies, between these and other private undertakings, did not constitute a direct or indirect transfer of State resources within the meaning of Article 87(1). It was thus somewhat surprisingly established that the German purchase obligation did not fall foul of the prohibition on State aid.

It was not disputed before the CJ that the obligation to buy electricity made from renewable energy at fixed minimum prices would give producers of this form of electricity a financial advantage, as it gave them risk-free higher earnings than they would otherwise have been able to obtain.

In paragraph 58 of its judgment the CJ noted that the distinction in Article 107(1) TFEU (then Article 92(1) of the EC Treaty) between 'aid granted by a Member State and aid granted through State resources' did not mean that all the benefits which were granted by a State constituted aid, regardless of whether they were financed by State resources or not. The distinction was merely intended to bring within that definition both advantages which are granted directly by the State and those granted by a public or private body designated or established by the State. In this particular case the CJ commented in paragraph 59 of its judgment that the obligation imposed on private electricity supply undertakings to purchase electricity produced from renewable energy sources at fixed minimum prices did not involve any direct or indirect transfer of State resources to undertakings which produced that type of electricity. Furthermore, the CJ found that the allocation of the financial burden arising from that obligation for those private electricity supply undertakings as between them and other private undertakings could not constitute a direct or indirect transfer of State resources (paragraph 60). Under these circumstances the CJ did not find that the fact that the purchase obligation was laid down in law, nor that it meant that there was an undoubted benefit for certain undertakings, gave the measure the character of a State aid within the meaning of Article 107(1) TFEU.

In C-391/23, a preliminary question has been brought on whether a Romanian scheme, which only imposes a tax on certain producers of electricity, constitutes notifiable state aid to the producents who are exempt from the tax.

1.4.6.4 Price Regulation

The pricing of such obligatory service provision will often be subject to regulation, whether or not there is an associated exclusive right. Technically, such obligation to provide a service can be imposed under public law (by a regulation), or it can be provided under private law (through a publicly owned undertaking or contractually, by an undertaking that is granted permission to exploit public rights).

As a rule, it is up to the Member State to decide whether to introduce price regulation. However, in certain cases, such a duty can be implicit. Thus, Article 12 of Directive 97/67/EC on postal services requires that prices must be affordable and must be such that all users have access to the services provided, that prices must be proportionate to costs, and must be transparent and non-discriminatory. This must be presumed to require some form of national regulation.

Article 12 of the Postal Services Directive implies that individual Member States may lay down requirements for uniform postal rates. However, it is explicitly stated that such a requirement does not prevent an undertaking from entering into individual agreements with users on postal rates. This allows for special discount agreements with large customers.

1.4.7 Authorisations

In a number of secondary legal acts, there is a requirement that the Member States should establish procedures for granting authorisations.

Authorisation refers to public regulation of access to the market. There are often specific requirements as to persons or undertakings which carry on a given profession. Such procedures can be called authorisation, approval, consent, grant, registration, permission, licence, concession, certification and so on. The word used is often determined by tradition. The word used does not indicate any special categorisation. Authorisations can reflect some special qualification, as in many of the liberal professions and in skilled trades, or there can be special organisational requirements, or authorisation can relate to special requirements as to the participant's financial standing. A requirement for authorisation can also be used as a means for ensuring that the norms of public law are complied with. The loss of authorisation can be a supplement to punishment by fine.

Authorisation normally only involves a right to carry on some particular business. It is not the same as giving a right, for example, to use essential facilities. Article 17(4) of Directive 2012/34/EU establishing a single European railway area specifically states that a licence does not in itself entitle the holder to have access to the railway infrastructure.

Authorisations which involve an exclusive right in a certain geographic area are often, though far from always, called a concession.[121] Territorial concessions are thus normal in connection with the establishment of a distribution network or, for example, the exploitation of sea areas for (wind) energy purposes. In addition to these procedures for authorisations, there are a number of conditions for licences connected with planning and environmental law. These will not be discussed in this chapter.

The requirement for the establishment of authorisation procedures is found in, among others, the Electricity Directive, Regulation (EC) No 1008/2008 on common rules for the operation of air services in the Community, and Directive 2012/34/EU establishing a single European railway area. In other sectors, it is up to Member States themselves to decide whether to introduce authorisation procedures. *See* Article 4 of the Natural Gas Directive which refers to this explicitly.[122] The regulation can be function-specific so that the requirements can differ at different stages of the value chain. Thus, it is quite normal for there to be requirements for authorisation for carrying on an undertaking which involves public obligations, while authorisation is not always necessary for those parts of the liberalised sectors which are subject to competition.

In connection with liberalisation, an authorisation procedure without an exclusive right (an authorisation procedure) has been established as an alternative to a tendering procedure. The authorisation procedure means that all can seek authorisation to carry on the relevant kind of undertaking. The capacity in the sector in question is thus determined by the market participants and the incentives that influence them. In a tendering procedure, it is up to the Member State, through its offering for tender the establishment of new capacity, which will at least in part determine the size of the overall capacity in a given area. It will be normal for a sector which is subject to market conditions to use an authorisation procedure. However, a tendering procedure could be used in a transitional phase or as a supplement, for example, to ensure the security of supply.

There is an example of the use of a tendering procedure as a transitional arrangement in Article 4 of the first Electricity Directive, Directive 96/92/EC, concerning common rules for the internal market in electricity, which provided for a tendering procedure as an alternative to an authorisation procedure. In Article 6 of the second Electricity Directive, the tendering procedure was done away with

---

121. In para. 2.4 of the Commission Interpretative Communication on Concessions under Community Law (OJ 2000 C 121/2), concessions are defined as 'acts attributable to the State whereby a public authority entrusts to a third party – by means of a contractual act or a unilateral act with the prior consent of the third party – the total or partial management of services for which that authority would normally be responsible and for which the third party assumes the risk.'
122. If the matter is not explicitly dealt with, the assumption is that national law can be used to determine whether an authorisation procedure is used, as long as it does not otherwise conflict with Community law.

In the telecommunications sector, it is acknowledged that the Member States can use tendering in the allocation of frequencies, telephone numbers, etc. Among other things, this has been used in connection with the UMTS network.

Provisions on authorisation procedures often contain administrative law provisions intended to prevent unequal treatment or other improper conduct in general. There is a requirement that the Member States' criteria for the grant of authorisations must be objective and non-discriminatory. Such provisions can be combined with a requirement that the procedures for the grant of authorisations should be made public, that reasons should be given for refusals and that the possibility of an appeal should be included. *See* Article 4 of the Natural Gas Directive, for example.

1.4.8 Transparency

There is a requirement for transparency in a number of secondary acts. The aim is to act as a support for the other goals that are built into the rules. Transparency is a tool which is intended to reveal or make it more difficult for there to be unlawful restrictions of competition or merely in appropriate measures which can be advantageously dealt with by legislation. Transparency thereby has a preventive effect. For example, provisions on transparency can be directed at unlawful State aid, abuse of dominant position, cross-subsidisation or against measures which reduce the effectiveness of competition in general. Transparency provisions can aim to give the authorities, customers and/or the general public insight into procedures.

Within the liberalised sectors, the requirement for transparency is found in connection with the Member States' scope for imposing public service obligations on undertakings. There are examples of this in Article 3(2) of the Natural Gas Directive and Article 9(2) of the Electricity Directive. There can also be requirements relating to quality controls and their publication; *see* Article 16 of Directive 97/67/EC on postal services. The requirement can also be found in connection with the presentation of accounts. This can be seen in the unbundling of accounts, special requirements for making information public, independent auditing and supervision by public authorities, or by a requirement for compliance with some set of accounting rules. There is an example of this in Article 31(2) of the Natural Gas Directive, which refers to Directive 78/660/EEC. There is a requirement for the independent auditing of certain kinds of undertakings in Article 15 of the Postal Services Directive.

There are often transparency requirements for provisions on access to networks. One example is Article 23 of the Natural Gas Directive which requires the publication of tariffs. Similarly, there are such requirements in connection with the establishment of the criteria for granting and administering authorisations. There is an example of this in Article 4 of the Natural Gas Directive which requires the criteria and procedures for the granting of authorisations to be made public.

The prices for services in the liberalised sectors are also subject to the requirement for transparency. For example, this is the case with the prices for gas and electricity to industrial end users. In fact, the transparency requirements are set out separately in special legislation – Regulation (EU) 2016/1952 of 26 October 2016 on

European statistics on natural gas and electricity prices, which seeks to ensure that Eurostat can produce statistics on the prices.

In EU legislation, transparency is not always expressed as a requirement. In certain cases, the possibility of transparency requirements is left to the Member States. Thus, the Directive of the European Electronic Communications Code does not impose a requirement for transparency, but the Member States are given the possibility of introducing such provisions for special kinds of undertakings, cf. the preamble, consideration, and enclosure I A9 of the Directive on European Electronic Communications Code.

At a more general level, in Article 1 of Directive 2006/111/EC on the transparency of financial relations between Member States and public undertakings as well as on financial transparency within certain undertakings ('the Transparency Directive'),[123] which was adopted under the authority of Article 106(3) TFEU, the Commission lays down the general obligations of the Member States:

1. The Member States shall ensure that financial relations between public authorities and public undertakings are transparent as provided in this Directive, so that the following emerge clearly:
    a. public funds made available directly by public authorities to the public undertakings concerned;
    b. public funds made available by public authorities through the intermediary of public undertakings or financial institutions;
    c. the use to which these public funds are actually put.
2. Without prejudice to specific provisions laid down by the Community the Member States shall ensure that the financial and organisational structure of any undertaking required to maintain separate accounts is correctly reflected in the separate accounts, so that the following emerge clearly:
    a. the costs and revenues associated with different activities;
    b. full details of the methods by which costs and revenues are assigned or allocated to different activities.

Originally, the Transparency Directive did not cover the energy, transport, postal or telecommunications sectors. However, this was changed by the introduction of a new Article 4 amending Directive 85/413/EEC. However, following the latest amendments by Directive 2005/81/EEC, the transparency requirements in Article 1(2) do not apply to undertakings whose annual net earnings are less than EUR 40 million in the two accounting years prior to a given year in which a special or exclusive right is granted by a Member State pursuant to Article 106(1) TFEU or is entrusted with the operation of a service of general economic interest pursuant to Article 106(2). Similarly, an undertaking is not covered if the public service compensation it receives in any form whatsoever, including subsidies, aid or compensation, is fixed for an appropriate period and according to an open, transparent and non-discriminatory procedure.

In relation to the individual end user, certain transparency requirements can be seen as an expression of consumer protection. This will be in accordance with Article 169 TFEU, under which consumers have a right to information.

---

123. Originally Directive 80/723/EEC.

Special provisions which require the reporting of statistical information are used as control instruments. Also, there are requirements for the Member States to publish special arrangements in the Official Journal of the European Union. There are such requirements, for example, in connection with issuing or revoking authorisations and the imposition of an obligation to supply (e.g., in the area of air transport).

1.4.9 The Cross-Border Provision of Services

Under Article 170(1) TFEU, the Union is required to contribute to the establishment and development of trans-European networks in the areas of transport, telecommunications and energy infrastructures. Also, under Article 170(2), the Union has the aim – within the framework of a system of open and competitive markets – of promoting the interconnection and interoperability of national networks as well as access to such networks. Consideration for the realisation of the internal market for, among other things, networked services was one of the main motivations for the inclusion of this wording.[124] However, the planning, establishment and management of such networks do not appear to fall under the provisions of Article 154 and must, therefore, fall within the scope of the powers of the Member States.

Trans-European networks are one of the Union's policy areas; *see* Title XVI TFEU. According to Article 170, 'the Union shall contribute to the establishment and development of trans-European networks in the areas of transport, telecommunications and energy infrastructures.' The actions of the Union are to be aimed at promoting the interconnection and interoperability of national networks as well as access to such networks. The Treaty provisions are to be supplemented by guidelines to identify projects of common interest, the implementation of any measures that may prove necessary to ensure the interoperability of the networks, in particular in the field of harmonisation of technical standardisation, and support for projects of common interest; *see* Article 171 TFEU.[125] Guidelines have been issued for the telecommunications sector, among others. In the area of network, the EU's policy is now expressed through Regulation (EU) 2021/1153 of 7 July 2021 on Connecting Europe Facility by the European Parliament and the Council and repeal of Regulation (EU) no. 1316/2013 and (EU) 283/2014.

Access to a network often requires a certain compatibility or technical harmonisation between the systems used in the Member States. If such do not exist, there will be technical barriers to trade. There is an example of a standardisation measure to remove such barriers in Regulation (EEC) No 3922/91 on the harmonisation of technical requirements and administrative procedures in the field of civil aviation, as

---

124. This part was included in connection with the signing of the Treaty on European Union, signed at Maastricht on 7 Feb. 1992.
125. Rules for support are laid down in Regulation (EC) No 2236/95 laying down general rules for the granting of Community financial aid in the field of trans-European networks. An overview of supported energy projects (1995–2006) can be found at: http://ec.europa.eu/ten/energy/studies/doc/ten_e_financed_projects_95_06.pdf and correspondingly for transport (1983–2004) at: http://ec.europa.eu/ten/transport/actions/doc/1983_2004_supported_actions_en.pdf.

well as in the Directive on European Electronic Communications Code (Directive (EU) 2018/1972).

In other cases, with regard to enabling systems to be interoperable, the Member States are required to ensure the drawing up of technical rules containing minimum requirements for their construction and operation which must be fulfilled in order to be linked to a network and to make these available. These technical rules must be objective and non-discriminatory. They must also be notified to the Commission in accordance with Article 8 of Directive 98/34/EC, laying down a procedure for the provision of information in the field of technical standards and regulations, as well as the rules for services in Europe's Information Society. *See*, for example, Article 8 of the Natural Gas Directive.

1.4.10 Public Authorities

In several sectors, there is a requirement that the Member States must establish a supervisory authority. This is often referred to as a *regulator*.

The requirement for the appointment of a regulator is often combined with a requirement for the regulator's independence from market participants, for example, in the form of a separation between the management of undertakings and the exercise of authority. This is particularly relevant when some public authority is still a market participant. In general, in terms of administrative law, it is appropriate for the supervisory authority, in its composition, to be independent at the political level. In particular, in the liberalised sectors, there often appears to be some political interest in individual cases.

In the telecommunications sector, Article 6 of the Directive on European Electronic Communications Code ((EU) 2018/1972) established that 'Member States shall guarantee the independence of national regulatory authorities by ensuring that they are legally distinct from and functionally independent of all organisations providing electronic communications networks, equipment or services.' Article 22, first paragraph, of the Postal Services Directive requires Member States to 'designate one or more national regulatory authorities for the postal sector that are legally separate from and operationally independent of the postal operators'. Article 57 of the Electricity Directive contains detailed requirements for the independence of regulatory authorities:

> 4. Member States shall guarantee the independence of the regulatory authority and shall ensure that it exercises its powers impartially and transparently. For this purpose, Member State shall ensure that, when carrying out the regulatory tasks conferred upon it by this Directive and related legislation, the regulatory authority:
>
>   a. is legally distinct and functionally independent from any other public or private entity;
>   b. ensures that its staff and the persons responsible for its management:
>   i. act independently from any market interest; and
>   ii. do not seek or take direct instructions from any government or other public or private entity when carrying out the regulatory tasks. This requirement is without prejudice to close cooperation, as appropriate,

with other relevant national authorities or to general policy guidelines issued by the government not related to the regulatory powers and duties under Article 37.

5. In order to protect the independence of the regulatory authority, Member States shall in particular ensure that:

a. the regulatory authority can take autonomous decisions, independently from any political body, and has separate annual budget allocations, with autonomy in the implementation of the allocated budget, and adequate human and financial resources to carry out its duties; and
b. the members of the board of the regulatory authority or, in the absence of a board, the regulatory authority's top management are appointed for a fixed term of five up to seven years, renewable once.

In regard to point (b) of the first subparagraph, Member States shall ensure an appropriate rotation scheme for the board or the top management. The members of the board or, in the absence of a board, members of the top management may be relieved from office during their term only if they no longer fulfil the conditions set out in this Article or have been guilty of misconduct under national law.

There is a corresponding provision in Article 39 of the Natural Gas Directive.

The fact that a distinction is made between operations and the exercise of authority does not necessarily exclude the possibility of the authorities supervising the interests of the regulated undertakings on the grounds of *regulatory capture*.[126] It can be difficult to prove the existence of such circumstances, and a general legal protection normally merely consists of a requirement for proper conduct.

The requirement for the appointment of a regulator is often accompanied by an obligation for the Member States to inform the Commission about which authorities have been given responsibility for which tasks under the respective directives.[127]

A supervisory authority can exercise control both *ex ante* (e.g., by requirements for prior authorisation) and *ex post* (e.g., control after the event). In the electricity and natural gas sectors, there is a minimum of *ex ante* approval of the methods used for the calculation of tariffs.

With the administration of a network and access to it, in certain sectors there is a requirement for a special entity to administrate this (system administrator/ infrastructure manager). Such an entity can be a public authority. This is discussed in the section on the administration of networks above.

There can also be a requirement for the establishment of an *appeals procedure*. The provisions on this can be combined with rules on whether the appeal tribunal must be a court or an administrative tribunal. Article 26 of the Directive on European Electronic Communications Code allows the use of a court. In some cases, there will be a requirement for a dispute resolution authority for access to a network. *See* the section

---

126. For further on this, *see* Rauf Gönenc et al.: *The Implementation and the Effects of Regulatory Reform: Past Experience and Current Issues*, OECD, p. 41(2000).
127. *See* Art. 22 of Directive 97/67/EC on postal services and Art. 5(4) of the Directive on European Electronic Communications Code (Directive (EU) 2018/1972).

on access to networks above. It is possible for the appeal tribunal and the supervisory authority to be one and the same. Under Article 60(11) of the Electricity Directive, the regulator is also a dispute resolution authority. It is possible for the Member States to introduce other mechanisms, including mediation of disputes. Such provisions can be combined with a deadline for the appeal tribunal to decide on a dispute if the parties have not reached an agreement beforehand, whereupon the case can be brought before a court by the complainant, i.e., the party seeking access to the network. The right of appeal can also cover other factors, such as the right of authorisation. *See*, for example, Article 4 of the Natural Gas Directive.

Secondary Community legal acts can include requirements for the application of administrative law rules. For example, in relation to the telecommunications sector, Article 31 of the Directive on European Electronic Communications Code provides that an appeal does not have a suspensive effect on the decisions of a supervisory authority which are appealed against unless the appeal body decides otherwise. There are also provisions on the duty of regulated undertakings to give such information to the supervising authority as is necessary for the authority to carry out its tasks. These are often linked to provisions on confidentiality. *See*, for example, Article 60(2) of the Directive on European Electronic Communications Code. Procedural deadlines can also be laid down for dealing with appeals. For example, there is a two-month deadline in Article 60(2) of the Electricity Directive, though with the possibility of extending it.

1.4.11 Authority at the EU Level

The Commission has a special role in the application of the general competition rules. As for sector-specific supervision, currently, European supervisory authorities have not been set up for some of the liberalised sectors. However, discussions on this have particularly related to the telecommunications sector. In the air transport sector, the European Aviation Safety Agency (EASA) was set up on 28 September 2003. The Agency was set up to help the Commission with the introduction of common standards for civil aviation safety and environmental protection, using the *comitology procedure*.

For most of the liberalised sectors, Union legislation contains special provisions on the use of the comitology procedure when laying down details for the implementation of the Union's basic legislation. In general, the Commission will first decide, after consulting either an advisory committee or a regulatory committee composed of representatives from the Member States. The topics which are dealt with are often those which are relevant to cross-border transactions, such as quality standards. A comitology committee has been appointed in the telecommunications, postal services, railways, air transport and electricity supply sectors.[128]

---

128. *See* the Commission's Green paper on services of general interest, COM(2003) 270 final. *See also* Commission Decision 2001/546/EC setting up a consultative committee, to be known as the 'European Energy and Transport Forum'; and Art. 11 of Regulation (EEC) No 2408/92 on access for Community air carriers to intra-Community air routes (now Art. 25 in Regulation (EC) No 1008/2008. For a more detailed discussion of the concept of comitology, *see* Helle Tegner Anker: *Comitology*, in Birgitte Egelund Olsen & Karsten Engsig Sørensen (ed.): *Regulation in the EU*, p. 429 (2006).

1.4.12 Reciprocity

Different levels of market openness in the Member States have given rise to fears of the creation of unequal conditions for competition. The problem is that an undertaking in one Member State should not benefit from legal protection in its home market but while being able to act freely on more open neighbouring markets. In some liberalised sectors, provisions on *reciprocity* have been introduced to limit this problem. This means that undertakings from one Member State can be refused access to a market in another Member State to the extent that the undertaking's national market is not open to participants from other Member States.[129]

The reciprocity clause has provoked much debate, as it seems to be contrary to the general Union law prohibiting discrimination. The aim of such a provision has been to avoid imbalances between the undertakings of the different Member States due to Member States liberalising their electricity sectors at different speeds.[130]

Such provisions have primarily been used in the energy sector; *see* Article 37 of the Natural Gas Directive, but they do not seem to be very relevant following a full opening up of a market.

Under Article 37(2) of the Natural Gas Directive, third-party access cannot be refused if the customer is considered to be privileged in both systems. The provision is not very clearly expressed and has been much criticised. Nevertheless, it seems that some Member States have made use of the opportunity.

Apart from this, there are only corresponding provisions in the air transport sector. In Article 12 of Regulation (EEC) No 95/93 on common rules for the allocation of slots at Community airports, there is a similar possibility of refusing to allocate slots where, in connection with the allocation of slots at airports, a third country does not grant Community air carriers treatment comparable to that granted by Member States to air carriers from that country. There is also a similar provision concerning computer reservation systems in Article 8 of Regulation (EC) No 80/2009 on a Code of Conduct for computerised reservation systems. According to this, the Commission may require all system vendors operating in the Union to treat air carriers of that third country in a manner that is equivalent to the treatment of Union air carriers in that third country.

1.4.13 *A Sustainable Future*

Security of supply and climate policy are two current considerations which will shape the liberalised sectors in the future. The European Green Deal and Fit for 55 are cases in point. Sustainable energy will play an even more important role in the energy sector.

---

129. A.K. Klom: *Liberalisation of Regulated Markets and its Consequences for Trade: The Internal Market for Electricity as a Case Study*, Journal of Energy & Natural Resources Law, p. 2 (1996), where examples are given of a lack of reciprocity. Such provisions must presumably be interpreted restrictively, and thus cannot be used, e.g., in the absence of unbundling.
130. *See* A. Johnston: *Maintaining the Balance of Power: Liberalization, Reciprocity and Electricity in the European Community*, Journal of Energy and Natural Resources Law, pp. 121–150 (1999).

The electrification of industry and transport is already well underway.[131] Hydrogen may be the energy carrier and might possibly require the development of a separate hydrogen network. Natural gas is unlikely to have the role that was intended just a few years ago. Not only because natural gas is a fossil fuel but also in the interest of the security of supply.

In 2018, a law on national plans for energy and climate (NEPs) was passed.[132] By the European law of climate,[133] objectives are set, and this will affect the energy markets, e.g., by a politically determined significant expansion of renewable energy. Correspondingly, the market itself will seek sustainable energy from solar and wind. Moreover, it must be expected that the number of prosumers[134] will continue to increase.[135]

In the area of communication, a decrease in the use of traditional mail is to be expected, whereas electronic communication will soar. The energy requirement for the internet, etc., is gradually quite significant.

2 ENERGY

From the start, energy policy has been a key policy area for the Union. Two of the three founding treaties – the Treaty of the European Coal and Steel Community (ECSC Treaty)[136] and the Treaty establishing the European Atomic Energy Community (Euratom Treaty) – were specifically related to energy policy. Later, the importance of coal as a source of energy was diminished by the availability of cheaper coal and natural gas.

Following the oil crises of the 1970s, security of supply played an important role in the Union's energy policy. Since then, environmental protection has also become a key issue. In respect of competition, the efforts have been concentrated on including electricity and natural gas supply in the internal market, and at the same time these

---

131. In more developed economies, switching to electric cars will constitute the largest single energy source for increased power consumption, whereas population growth and the need for comfort cooling elsewhere will increase the consumption. See IEA: World Energy Outlook, p. 227.
132. Regulation (EU) 2018/1999 of the European Parliament and of the Council of 11 Dec. 2018 on the Governance of the Energy Union and Climate Action, amending Regulations (EC) No 663/2009 and (EC) No 715/2009 of the European Parliament and of the Council, Directives 94/22/EC, 98/70/EC, 2009/31/EC, 2009/73/EC, 2010/31/EU, 2012/27/EU and 2013/30/EU of the European Parliament and of the Council, Council Directives 2009/119/EC and (EU) 2015/652 and repealing Regulation (EU) No 525/2013 of the European Parliament and of the Council.
133. Regulation (EU) 2021/1119 of the European Parliament and of the Council of 30 Jun. 2021 establishing the framework for achieving climate neutrality and amending Regulations (EC) No 401/2009 and (EU) 2018/1999 ('European Climate Law').
134. The definition can cover quite a wide range. In an energy supply context, a 'prosumer' refers to one or more end user(s) of electricity who (partially) covers their own consumption through own production and use the collective grid to cover the part of the consumption, which does not come from own production. See EEA Report No. 01/2022: Energy prosumers in Europe Citizen participation in the energy transition.
135. Often referred to as 'distributed electricity'.
136. The ECSC Treaty expired on 24 Jul. 2002. However, coal remains an important source of energy both in certain EU Member States and worldwide.

sectors have been important areas for environmental regulation and regulation of security of supply. Most recently, a supply crisis has arisen due to the conflict in Ukraine and the European independence on the import of Russian natural gas. This has led to special measures to increase the security of supply and combat energy poverty.[137]

The Treaty contains no special exceptions for energy, including electricity and natural gas supply.[138] Thus, the establishment of the internal market is also an important goal in the energy sector. This is clear from Articles 194 and 26 TFEU. According to the original version of the latter provision (Article 14 of the EC Treaty), in the period up to 31 December 1992, the Community (as it then was) should have adopted measures with a view to the gradual establishment of the internal market. The areas of energy ought thus by now to have been covered by the internal market. In principle, under the authority of Article 106(1) and (3) TFEU the Commission could have taken steps to prohibit existing monopolies. However, the Commission has never made use of Article 106(3) in the energy sectors, which has possibly delayed the liberalisation process.[139] Instead, the Commission has published a number of proposals for market directives.[140] In 1996, these proposals resulted in the adoption of the first Electricity Directive and in 1998 in the adoption of the first Natural Gas Directive.[141] Both of these were issued as harmonising directives. Previously, in its Green paper – for a European Union energy policy (COM(94) 659 final), paragraph 70, the Commission had laid out its strategy for the development of the market and listed the considerations which should be given priority:

> The integration of the market can be encouraged by regulation or liberalization of the market. It is in the Community's interest to limit Community regulation to the absolute minimum necessary to reconcile freedom of movement with the legitimate objectives of the Member States. In the field of energy, the essential and legitimate elements are:
>
> – protection of public service missions;
> – security of supply;
> – environmental protection
> – energy efficiency.

According to the Commission, the method by which at least some of these goals were to be achieved was by exposing parts of the sectors concerned to competition.

---

137. Arts 5, 28 and 29 on Regulation (EU) on the internal market for electricity, allow Member States to intervene to protect vulnerable customers or against energy poverty.
138. A.K. Klom: *Liberalisation of Regulated Markets and its Consequences for Trade: The Internal Market for Electricity as a Case Study*, Journal of Energy & Natural Resources Law, p. 8 (1996).
139. P.J. Slot & A.M. Skudder: *Common Features of Community Law Regulation in the Network-Bound Sectors*, Common Market Law Review, p. 92 (2001).
140. COM(91) 548 final; and COM(93) 643 final.
141. Directive 96/92/EC concerning common rules for the internal market in electricity ('the first Electricity Directive'); and Directive 98/30/EC concerning common rules for the internal market in natural gas.

The Union does not have exclusive regulatory powers in the area of energy. It shares these powers with the Member States; *see* Article 5 TFEU. On the contrary, the activities of the Member States include 'the adoption of an economic policy which is based on the close coordination of Member States' economic policies, on the internal market and on the definition of common objectives, and conducted in accordance with the principle of an open market economy with free competition'; *see* Article 119(1) TFEU. The authority in Article 103(3)(c) TFEU, 'to define, if need be, in the various branches of the economy, the scope of the provisions of Articles 101 and 102' has been applied in the energy sector.

Under Article 194 TFEU, energy is now a special policy area. The policy areas included are: the functioning of the energy market; security of energy supply in the Union; energy efficiency; and the interconnection of energy networks.

A special element of Article 194 is the statement 'in a spirit of solidarity between Member States'. It has been particularly relevant in regard to the problems with gas supply due to the war in Ukraine, where some Member States have been more dependent on Russian gas than others. In this connection, a special solidarity pact has been created to ensure the sharing of natural gas among the Member States should a shortage of gas arise. *See* also Article 122 TFEU, which gives authority to 'in a spirit of solidarity between Member States' adopt measures, 'in particular if severe difficulties arise in the supply of certain products, notably in the area of energy'.

From an overall perspective, the two energy market directives are relatively broad minimum framework directives. This has allowed for somewhat different implementation measures in the Member States. Among other things, these differences are reflected in a number of country reports.[142] In 2003, new directives were issued for both the electricity and natural gas sectors. These have led to increased liberalisation. Previously, it had been clear that the first market directives did not sufficiently create an internal market for energy. The main problem was the uneven implementation of the market directives between the Member States, discriminatory methods applied to access to networks, especially in relation to cross-border links, and the continued market strength of the previous monopoly undertakings.[143]

In 2009, the Union adopted the third energy package, with a number of further measures, including:[144]

- Stricter requirements for unbundling of transmission system operators (TSOs) and activities that are open to competition. The requirements are the same for transmission companies in the electricity and natural gas sectors. The starting point is a requirement for ownership unbundling so as to prevent corporate group structures, but two other kinds of structure are allowed. First, the establishment of an independent transmission operator (ITO) structure is allowed. This arrangement involves management independence, including

---

142. Damien Geradin: *The Liberalization of Electricity and Natural Gas in the European Union*, (2001).
143. Peter Cameron: *Legal Aspects of EU Energy Regulation*, p. 9 (2005). This book contains a general review of the market directives for the electricity and natural gas sectors, as well as their implementation in a number of Member States.
144. For a review of the third energy package, *see* Peter Cameron: *Legal Aspects of EU Energy Regulation*, p. 9 (2016) Christopher W. Jones (ed.): *EU Energy Law*, Vol. I (2020) and Ivo Van Bael & Jean-Francois Bellis: *Competition Law of the European Community*, p. 1410 ff. (2010).

operational and network development decisions being taken independently of group interests. This arrangement involves stricter supervision. Second, it became possible to use an independent system operator (ISO) structure, where there is merely a requirement for not very well-defined independence from group interests. This arrangement should merely be more effective than the ITO structure. Furthermore, Article 9(9) of the Natural Gas Directive contains a fourth possibility, the so-called ITO + or 'unbundling à la carte' option. The requirements for this option are very vague, merely requiring arrangements that guarantee more effective independence than the ITO structure. However, it can be difficult to comply with this fourth option. It requires both that the arrangements should have been in place by 3 September 2009 and that the TSOs should have belonged to a vertically integrated undertaking. Distribution system operators (DSOs) that are part of a vertically integrated undertaking must be independent in legal form, organisation and decision-making from activities not relating to distribution; see Article 26 of the Natural Gas Directive. It is possible to combine TSOs and DSOs; see Article 29 of the Natural Gas Directives[145]

- Stricter supervision, among other things, through the establishment of ACER – the EU Agency for the Cooperation of Energy Regulators, which builds further on previous cooperation.
- The establishment of European Networks of Transmission System Operators (ENTSOs). One has been established for electricity (pursuant to Article 5 of Regulation (EU) on the internal market for electricity), and one for natural gas (pursuant to Article 5 of Regulation (EC) No 715/2009 on conditions for access to the natural gas transmission networks). The role of ENTSOs is to work on network development plans and to draw up detailed rules for networks and cross-border links.

In 2015, the EU-Commission launched a strategy for the Energy Union based on elements of security of supply, the internal market of energy, energy efficiency, reduction of greenhouse gas emissions, and research. In 2018, the Regulation (EU) on governance[146] was passed as a special administrative system for the Energy Union.

As a follow-up on the Energy Union from 2015, the EU Winter Package[147] came in 2016, e.g., containing suggestions for a new electrical market design as well as

---

145. *See* in general: Commission staff working paper of 22 January 2010: Implementation note on unbundling in the Electricity Directive and the Natural Gas Directive.
146. Regulation (EU) 2018/1999 of the European Parliament and of the Council of 11 Dec. 2018 on the Governance of the Energy Union and Climate Action, amending Regulations (EC) No 663/2009 and (EC) No 715/2009 of the European Parliament and of the Council, Directives 94/22/EC, 98/70/EC, 2009/31/EC, 2009/73/EC, 2010/31/EU, 2012/27/EU and 2013/30/EU of the European Parliament and of the Council, Council Directives 2009/119/EC and (EU) 2015/652 and repealing Regulation (EU) No 525/2013 of the European Parliament and of the Council.
147. Also known as 'Clean Energy for all Europeans Package'.

suggestions for the readjustment of Directives on the promotion of the use of energy from renewable sources, energy efficiency, and the energy performance of buildings.[148]

In the following section, the electricity and natural gas sectors will be reviewed primarily in light of the present market directives.

The two market directives for the electricity and natural gas sectors have been supplemented by: Regulation (EU) No 2019/943 on the internal market for electricity; Regulation (EU) 2019/941 on risk-preparedness in the electricity sector; Regulation (EC) No 715/2009 on conditions for access to the natural gas transmission networks; Regulation (EC) No 714/2009 on conditions for access to the network for cross-border exchanges in electricity; Regulation (EC) No 713/2009 establishing an Agency for the Cooperation of Energy Regulators; and Regulation (EU) No 2017/1938 concerning measures to safeguard security of gas supply.

In addition, in the borderland between energy policy and environmental policy there are three directives which are important for electricity and natural gas supplies: Directive (EU) 2018/2001 on the promotion of electricity produced from renewable energy sources in the internal electricity market;[149] Directive (EU) 2023/1791 on energy efficiency and amending Regulation (repeals Directive 2012/27/EU on energy efficiency); and Directive 2003/87/EC establishing a scheme for greenhouse gas emission allowance trading within the Union. These will not be considered in detail in this chapter.[150]

2.1   Electricity Supply

Electricity supply is traditionally divided into four parts: production, supplying, transmission and distribution. Participants in these stages in the value chain are referred to in the Electricity Directive[151] as *electricity undertakings*.

The term 'electricity undertaking' is not defined in the Electricity Directive. However, the term is defined indirectly in connection with the definition, in Article 2(2), of an 'integrated electricity undertaking' which is defined as a 'vertically or horizontally integrated undertaking'. And both 'vertically integrated undertaking' and 'horizontally integrated undertaking' are defined.

Transmission and distribution are network functions by means of which the electricity is physically distributed. These two functions are normally regarded as natural monopolies.[152]

Transmission means the transport of electricity on extra high-voltage and high-voltage interconnected systems with a view to its delivery to final customers (end users) or to distributors. *Distribution* means the transport of electricity on high-voltage, medium voltage

---

148. Regarding the unbundling options under the Clean Energy Package, see Christopher Jones & William James Kettlewell (ed.): *EU Energy Law – The internal Energy Market*, Vol I, p 127-142 (2021)
149. Amended by Directive (EU) 2023/2413.
150. For a discussion of these, *see* Luc Werring (ed.): *EU Energy Law*, Vol. III, (2006).
151. Directive (EU) 2019/944 of the European Parliament and of the Council of 5 Jun. 2019 on common rules for the internal market for electricity and amending Directive 2012/27/EU. A special area is charging stations for electric vehicles. This special infrastructure is now supported by Directive (EU) 2023/1804 on the deployment of alternative fuels infrastructure).
152. On natural monopolies in relation to electricity supply *see*, among others: Michael Albers: *Competition Law Issues Arising from the Liberalization Process*, in Damien Geradin (ed.): *The Liberalization of Electricity and Natural Gas in the European Union*, p. 4 (2001).

and low-voltage distribution systems with a view to its delivery to customers (end users). These terms are defined in Article 2 of the Electricity Directive.

In contrast to the network functions, both electricity generation and supply are regarded as being subject to competition. The EU's regulation bears the marks of this distinction. Article 5 of the Electric Directive thus emphasises that the suppliers must be able to set the electricity prise freely.

2.1.1 EU Regulation

The electricity supply sector has been subject to several EU secondary legal acts. The primary set of rules is in the Electricity Directive, the current version of which dates from 2019. The provisions of this Directive were to be implemented by 3 March 2011 (opdateres), *see* Article 49 of the directive.

The Electricity Directive has now been supplemented by the Regulation (EU) on the internal market for electricity, e.g., containing the general principles for electricity markets, grid access, and handling of capacity limitations, provisions on ensuring resource sufficiency (security of supply), involvement of ENTSO-E and ACER[153] as well as regional coordination centres and the EU DSO Entity.[154]

The electricity supply sector has also been subject to liberalisation in stages on the route to establishing the internal market for electricity.[155] The process dates back to the energy working paper from 1988.[156] The first stage was the implementation of Directive 90/547/EEC on the transit of electricity through transmission grids, and the first Directive (90/377/EEC) to improve the transparency of gas and electricity prices charged to industrial end-users. The second stage was the adoption of the first Electricity Directive. The third stage was the adoption of the second Electricity Directive which stated that all end users should have free access to markets by 1 July 2007.

The second Electricity Directive was not necessarily to be the last. Even though one could be tempted to regard the liberalisation process as having been completed with the formal full opening of the market, in practice, the internal market for electricity does not function as a liberalised market. In its initiative with regard to the energy markets – an energy policy for

---

153. Regarding ACER, see Christopher Jones & William-James Kettlewell (ed.): *EU Energy Law – The internal Energy Market*, Vol. I, p. 321-466 (2021)
154. This is meant to, amongst other things, promote the operation and planning of distributional networks in coordination with the operation and planning of the transmission networks.
155. See COM(91) 548 final. See also Herbert von Bose: *Die Richtlinienvorschläge der Kommission betreffend gemeinsame Vorschriften für den Erdgas-Binnenmarkt bzw. für Elektrizitäts-Binnenmarkt*, in Jürgen F. Baur (ed.): *Die Europäische Gemeinschaft und das Recht der leitungsgebundenen Energie*, p. 144 (1993); and Wolfgang Hoffmann-Riem & Jens-Peter Schneider: *Wettbewerbs- und umweltorientierte Re-Regulierung im Großhandels-Strommarkt*, in Wolfgang Hoffmann-Riem & Jens-Peter Schneider (eds.): *Umwelt-politische Steuerung in einem liberalisierten Strommarkt*, p. 45 (1995).
156. The internal energy market, COM(88) 238. For a description of the development of the EU regulation, *see* Christian Berqvist: *Between Regulation and Deregulation*, pp. 235 ff (2016).

Europe[157] – the Commission suggested that there would be further measures, including unbundling. The unbundling requirements were strengthened with the adoption of the third Electricity Directive (2009/72/EC). The fourth Electricity Directive ((EU) 2019/944) focused on further developing the electricity market model and creating a consumer-driven green transaction through, amongst other things, provisions on citizen energy communities and aggregators.

With a view to monitoring and evaluating the effect of the Electricity Directive, its Article 69 provides that the Commission must submit an overall progress report.

2.1.1.1 The Electricity Directive and the Regulation on the Internal Market of Electricity

The purpose of the Electricity Directive has, since its first edition, been to contribute to the establishment of a fully operational internal electricity market. The Directive now regulates the generation, transmission, distribution, energy storage and supply of electricity; *see* Article 1. However, the choice of fuel is not governed by the Directive; that is up to the Member States.[158]

The electricity market has been completely liberalised since 1 July 2007 so that customers have been free to choose which producer or supplier they wish to buy electricity from. Since 1 July 2007, all non-household customers have been able to trade freely.[159]

Article 19(1) of the first Electricity Directive contained a provision on a minimum percentage of the electricity market which each Member State was required to open. The share of the national market was calculated on the basis of the Community share of electricity consumed by final customers consuming more than 40 GWh per year (on a consumption site basis and including autoproduction), corresponding to 22% of market opening. The first Electricity Directive did not distinguish between market opening at the wholesale level (purchases by distribution undertakings) and the final customer level. The Member States could, therefore, choose to fulfil their obligations under this part of the requirement for market opening either by including part of the purchases by distribution undertakings, part of the purchase by final purchasers, or a combination of both, corresponding to at least 22% of the electricity market in a system with access. According to Article 19(3) of the first Electricity Directive, the only requirement for the Member States' regulation of market opening at the wholesaler level was that distribution companies should have to be considered eligible customers at least for the volume of electricity being consumed by their customers designated as eligible within their distribution system, in order to supply those customers. The market share calculated above the 40 GWh threshold (corresponding to an average of 25.37% market opening) was subject in the first Electricity Directive to an ongoing adjustment, as three years after the entry into force of the Directive, the basis for calculation was to be reduced to 20 GWh (corresponding to about 28% market share), and after another three years to 9 GWh (corresponding to 33% market opening).[160] However, the provisions on the sizes of market shares could not prevent

---

157. Communication from the Commission to the European Council and the European Parliament – an energy policy for Europe (COM(2007) 1 final).
158. Among others, the EU's regulation of the electricity supply sector is discussed in *Christopher W. Jones:* EU Energy Law. The Internal Energy Market, Vol. I, 2010.
159. The term 'non-household customer' includes electricity producers and wholesalers.
160. *See* COM(1998) 212 final, p. 6. The Union's average market share was calculated at 34.53% for 2003; *see* the Commission's Report of 29 Oct. 2002 on the calculation of average market shares

participants who were not covered by national provisions on market opening from claiming that there was abuse of a dominant position under Article 82 of the EC Treaty (now Article 102 TFEU). This applied whether or not the national provisions were in accordance with the Directive.

In line with the Union's competition rules, the Electricity Directive does not contain any principles on pricing. However, Article 3, litra a) and b) states that the price of electricity should be market-based without further specifying what it entails. Article 10 contains a prohibition against an upper or a lower limit for the price of electricity in the wholesale market.

In general, the sector is regulated in accordance with the Treaty prohibition of abuse of a dominant position in Article 102 TFEU, including 'directly or indirectly imposing unfair purchase or selling prices or other unfair trading conditions'.[161] However, there are provisions in Articles 31 and 40 of the Electricity Directive which prohibit discrimination between system users. This also includes price discrimination. However, the Member States are free to include such provisions as part of public service obligations; *see* Article 9 of the Electricity Directive.

2.1.1.2 The Application of the General Competition Rules

As early as in Case 6/64, *Costa v. ENEL*, the assumption that electricity is good was something which was disputed because of its special physical nature. In relation to Article 36 TFEU (then Article 28 of the EC Treaty), this was confirmed in Case C-393/92, *Almelo and others v. Energiebedrijf Ijsselmij*, paragraph 28, which refers to the Union's tariff nomenclature (code CN 27.16).[162] The competition rules must, therefore, be assumed to apply in principle to the electricity sector. In accordance with this, the Commission applies the competition rules to the energy sector.[163]

A general cartel case as late as 2014 can be found in the Power Exchange case.[164] The EPEX Spot Nord Pool Spot AS (Norway) had infringed Article 101 of the TFEU and Article 53 of the European Economic Area (EEA) Agreement by participating in an agreement concerning, among others, an allocation of territories. In a settlement, EPEX Spot was fined EUR 3,651,000 and Nord Pool Spot EUR 2,328,000.

There has been a tendency for the security of supply aspect to be emphasised when applying the competition rules to the electricity supply sector. In the *Scottish*

---

after the opening of the electricity market as laid down in Directive 96/92/EC concerning common rules for the internal market in electricity.
161. Michael Albers: *Competition Law Issues Arising from the Liberalization Process*, in Damien Geradin (ed.): *The Liberalization of Electricity and Natural Gas in the European Union*, p. 5 (2001).
162. The CJ has more recently repeated this in Case C-158/94, *Commission v. Italy*, para. 17.
163. See the Commission's intervention in a dispute between an independent French producer and the two French and Italian electricity monopolists, discussed in the Commission's XXII Report on competition policy, para. 145. For a thorough review of the application of the Union's competition rules in the electricity supply sector, see Christopher W. Jones (ed.): *EU Energy Law*, Vol. II (2011).
164. Case AT 39.952. IP/14/215 available at https://ec.europa.eu/commission/presscorner/detail/en/IP_14_215

Nuclear Decision,[165] the Commission emphasised that a long-term contract with a take-or-pay clause[166] allowed the possibility of reliable production which could guarantee security of supply and energy independence.

> In connection with the prospective liberalisation of the British energy market, two independent vertically integrated electricity supply companies were set up in Scotland (Scottish Power and Scottish Hydro Electric), which were to compete with each other. At the same time, the Scottish nuclear power stations were put into a separate company (Scottish Nuclear Limited) which only had a generating licence. An agreement was entered into between the three companies under which Scottish Power and Scottish Hydro Electric bound themselves to take the whole of the production from Scottish Nuclear's two nuclear power stations on the basis of a fixed purchase contract. On its side, Scottish Nuclear bound itself to maximise its production and not to supply to others than Scottish Power and Scottish Hydro Electric. The Commission considered that the agreement restricted competition. The Commission gave the agreement an individual exemption under Article 85(3) (now Article 101(3)) provided that the duration of the agreement was reduced from thirty years to fifteen years. Thirty years corresponds to the normal life of a nuclear power station.

Security of supply was also a weighty consideration in the Commission's Decision on an agreement for the supply of German coal in the *Jahrhundertvertrag* case:[167]

> The case concerned an agreement between a group of German coal producers (*Gesamtverband des deutschen Steinkohlenbergbaus*) and a group of German electricity generating stations (*Vereinigung Deutscher Elektrizitätswerke*) on the supply of German coal for the period 1991–1995. The German State was not a party to the agreement, but it had encouraged the agreement by, among other things, providing full cover for the extra costs of using German coal. This cover was provided in the form of direct compensatory payments and the restriction of imports of third-country coal and the issuing of import licences. In Germany there was an import limit on coal from third countries. Regardless of the role of the State, the agreement was regarded by the Commission as being an agreement under Article 101(1) TFEU (then Article 85(1) of the EC Treaty). Since the agreement aimed at

---

165. Commission Decision 91/329/EEC of 30 Apr. 1991 in Case IV/33.473 – *Scottish Nuclear, Nuclear Energy Agreement*.
166. A take-or-pay clause means that the buyer is obliged to pay the full contractual amount, or a significant proportion of it, for the quantity contracted for, regardless of whether at the time of delivery the buyer is able to take the full quantity. The aim is to protect the investment linked to nuclear and natural gas power stations. These kinds of contracts are normal on the natural gas market, for example.
167. Notice of 29 Jun. 1990 pursuant to Art. 19(3) of Regulation No 17, concerning Case IV/33.151 – *Jahrhundertvertrag*. *See also* Commission Decision 93/126/EEC of 22 Dec. 1992 in Case IV/33.151 – *Jahrhundertvertrag*.

dividing up the market, it was in breach of this provision. However, the Commission accepted an exemption under Article 81(3), since it increased the security of supply and thereby contributed to improve electricity production and distribution. With regard to the establishment of the internal market for energy, the permission was granted for a limited period and a limited quantity.

In the *Pego* case,[168] in connection with the acceptance of fifteen-year exclusivity, the Commission especially took into account the liberalisation of the electricity sector which was about to take place in Portugal. There was thus an assessment under competition law of the effect on the market of the actual agreement. However, it also seems that the assessment indirectly took account of the fact that the capacity of the generating station was important to the fulfilment of the public supply obligation to which Electricidade de Portugal was subject. In other words, weight was attached to security of supply.

The case concerned an agreement between four large electricity supply companies from four different Member States: Electricidade de Portugal, National Power (UK), Electricité de France and Empresa National de Electricidad (Spain). The agreement concerned the construction and running of a power station in Portugal. The agreement contained a provision according to which the capacity of all the power station's capacity and production should be made available to Electricidade de Portugal for a twenty-eight year period. After negotiations with the Commission the period of exclusivity was reduced to fifteen years, after which Electricidade de Portugal could have first call on the electricity from the power station.

However, concern for security of supply cannot be extended so as to favour domestic end users, for example, by cutting off foreign demand through export restrictions.

This was the situation in a case concerning the interruption of exports to neighbouring countries by the Swedish State undertaking and electricity TSO, Svenske Kraftnët.[169] In periods of high domestic demand for electricity, the Swedish TSO interrupted exports of electricity to neighbouring countries with a view to being able to maintain Sweden as a unitary pricing zone.[170] This meant that electricity prices in Sweden were lower in periods

---

168. Notice 93/C 265/03 of 30 Sep. 1993, pursuant to Art. 19(3) of Council Regulation No 17 concerning a request for negative clearance or exemption pursuant to Art. 85(3) of the EEC Treaty [now Art. 101(3) TFEU] – Case No IV/34.598 – *Electricidade de Portugal/Pego* project. The decision is referred to briefly in Cross: Electric Utility Regulation in the European Union, 1996 p. 199.
169. Commission Decision of 14 Apr. 2010 – Case 39351 – *Swedish Interconnectors*.
170. Countries such as Denmark and Norway, which are part of the Nord Pool area together with Sweden, are divided into several pricing zones in order to be able to deal with the domestic physical limits to transmission capacity (bottlenecks). Sweden did not want to do the same, even though there are substantial bottlenecks in Sweden. Sweden has a large part of its

when exports were cut off, while the prices were correspondingly higher in the neighbouring countries.

The Commission made it clear that there were come overriding principles involved, such as non-discrimination and the prohibition of export restrictions and, with reference to the case law of the CJ, it stated that the rules on abuse of dominant position also applied in such a case: 'It is useful to recall the general principle enshrined in Article 18 TFEU according to which any discrimination on the basis of nationality is prohibited. Moreover, Article 35 TFEU expressly prohibits quantitative restrictions on exports and all measures having equivalent effect. It is thus clear that a Member State would not be entitled to restrict exports of electricity so as to reserve such electricity for domestic consumption. Similarly, a dominant undertaking cannot seek to achieve the same objective through its conduct on the market without falling foul of Union competition rules.[171] Practices that do so are generally considered to have as their object the restriction of competition'.[172]

Thereafter the Commission stated that the general conditions existed for the application of Article 102 TFEU, on abuse of dominant position.

The Commission accepted a Swedish proposal to refrain from using export restrictions for an interim period of ten years from 1 November 2011, and to start using pricing zones instead.

In a case in 2008, the Commission suspected that the German electricity supplier, E.ON, was abusing its dominant position by, among other things, adopting a special discounting strategy on the short-term market (the power exchange EEX) and abusing the balancing market.[173]

> The Commission suspected that E.ON was limiting the supply of electricity from certain plants on the short term market EEX, in order to increase the spot price for electricity. On the German electricity balancing market, the concern was that E.ON was abusing its dominant position by increasing its costs with a view to favouring its production affiliate and passing the costs on to the end user, and preventing power producers from other Member States from exporting balancing energy into E.ON's balancing market. The case resulted in undertakings being given by E.ON.

---

generating capacity in the north, while a large part of electricity demand is in the south (Stockholm, Gothenburg, Malmö).
171. Joined Cases 56 and 58-64, *Établissements Consten* and *Grundig v. Commission* [1966] ECR 299, p. 340.
172. Case 41-69, ACF *Chemiefarma v. Commission*, para. 128; and Joined Cases 56 and 58-64, *Établissements Consten* and *Grundig v. Commission*, paras 342 and 343.
173. Summary of Commission Decision of 26 Nov. 2008 relating to a proceeding under Art. 82 of the EC Treaty and Art. 54 of the EEA Agreement (Cases COMP/39.388 – *German Electricity Wholesale Market* and COMP/39.389 – *German Electricity Balancing Market*) (notified under document number C(2008) 7367 final).

In the Romanian Power Exchange/OPCOM, the Commission found that the Power Exchange hat abused its dominant position by requiring all participants in the Day-Ahead and Intraday Markets of the power exchange to have a Romanian VAT registration and consequently to establish business premises in Romania, even though foreign traders already have a VAT registration in their home country.[174]

It is especially in connection with the Member States' measures to promote renewable energy that there have been problems concerning State aid. The sector is specifically regulated by the guidelines on State aid for environmental protection. In relation to renewable energy, State aid can be provided in the following ways:

- compensation for the difference between the production costs for renewable energy and the market price on any given day;
- use of market mechanisms such as green certificates or a tendering procedure;
- support for operating costs on the basis of the external environmental costs which society saves by virtue of the establishment of electricity generating capacity based on renewable energy;
- use of general support arrangements for environmental protection.

These provide for regressive support over a maximum of five years.

Case C-379/98, *PreussenElektra v. Schhleswag*, concerned an obligation to buy electricity generated using renewable energy, where it was held that a specific arrangement involving consumer-financed support for renewable energy did not constitute State aid contrary to Article 107(1) TFEU (then Article 87(1) of the EC Treaty), even though it was a public law measure which provided for this support.[175] The decision raised the question of whether a corresponding obligation to purchase green certificates would also not be considered State aid. In connection with the *PreussenElektra* case, the Commission argued that the German arrangement was covered by the State aid provisions. It must now be considered extremely doubtful whether an obligation to purchase renewable energy will in future be considered to be State aid.[176]

2.1.2 Authorisation Procedures

The Electricity Directive lays down special requirements for authorisation procedures for new capacity (Article 8).[177] DSOs must be designated either by the Member State (by an administrative law measure, which is therefore like an authorisation) or by the Member State allowing those who are responsible for the relevant facilities to appoint the system operator (Articles 3). The latter procedure cannot be characterised as a true

---

174. Case AT 39984.
175. The case is discussed in s. 1.4.6.3.
176. For other examples, *see* COMP/B-1/38.700, Greek Lignite, C-17/03, VEMW and COMP/AT. 39727, CEZ.
177. In special cases there is a possibility of a tendering procedure in Art. 8.

grant of authorisation. It is up to the Member States to determine whether other parts of the national electricity supply sector should be subject to authorisation requirements. This is discussed in the section dealing with access to networks. In addition to this, there can be special requirements for the establishment of a network supervisor and the unbundling of the network in relation to the other participants. As far as the transmission operator is concerned, a certification requirement has been introduced according to Article 52.

2.1.2.1   Electricity Generation

The Electricity Directive contains a special chapter on electricity generation. According to Article 8, the Member States must adopt an authorisation procedure for the construction of new generating capacity. The system is based on the criteria of objectivity, transparency and non-discrimination; *see* Article 8(1).

An authorisation procedure means that any undertaking can seek permission to build a new generating capacity at any time. Article 8(2) lists the criteria which such a procedure can take account of. These *can* include: a) the safety and security of the electricity system, installations and associated equipment; b) protection of public health and safety; c) protection of the environment; d) land use and siting; e) use of public ground; f) energy efficiency; g) the nature of the primary sources; h) characteristics particular to the applicant, such as technical, economic and financial capabilities; i) compliance with measures adopted pursuant to Article 3, referring to public service obligations; j) contribution of the production capacity to the Union's general target that the share of energy from sustainable energy in the Union's final energy consumption amounts to at least 42.5 % by 2030 at the latest, cf. Article 3(1) of Directive (EU) 2018/2001 as amended by Directive (EU) 2023/2413; k) the contribution of the production capacity to reducing emissions; as well as l) alternatives for building new production capacity such as solutions regarding flexible energy consumption and energy storage. Both consideration for the environment and security of supply are constant themes in the list.

As indicated by the use of the word *can*, this list is not exhaustive. There are thus plentiful opportunities for Member States to supplement the criteria for authorisation.

A requirement in the first Electricity Directive, to send a notification to the Commission in the event of a refusal of a request to build new generating capacity, was not carried over into the second Electricity Directive. According to Recital 30 of that Directive, this proved to be an unnecessary administrative burden. However, the administrative law requirement to give reasons for a refusal has been carried over; *see* Article 7(4) of the third Electricity Directive. Thus, Article 7(4) also states that the authorisation procedures and criteria must be made public.

Under a tendering procedure, the Member States must designate an authority, public body or private body independent from the electricity industry to be responsible for the tendering procedure. This can be a regulator. The tendering conditions must be transparent, in the form of a detailed description of the contract specifications and of the procedure to be followed, and invitations to tender must be published in the Official

Journal of the European Union at least six months prior to the closing date for tenders, and an estimate of the expected need must be prepared and published every two years.

Under the first Electricity Directive, the Member States were free to choose between an authorisation procedure and a tendering procedure. The basic difference between an authorisation procedure and a tendering procedure is that an authorisation procedure leaves the initiative for installing new generating capacity to the market participants, while a tendering procedure leaves the initiative to the responsible public authorities. With authorisation, the initiative lies with the market participants who will only have financial incentives to expand or renew generating capacity as the expansion or renewal of capacity becomes profitable. Authorisation procedures should only be used if there is a demand-driven need for new or expanded capacity. All applications for the establishment of generating capacity which fulfils the pre-established criteria must be approved. In a liberalised market, the regulation of the amount of capacity is subject to market forces. If a participant thinks it is worth building new capacity, either to export electricity or to compete with existing participants in the market, an application for authorisation to build new capacity should not be refused on the grounds that there is a lack of domestic demand.[178] With a tendering procedure, the public authority will be more inclined to look at the need for new capacity. This means that the authorisation procedure leads to competition both in relation to new and existing generating capacity, while the tendering procedure will have a tendency, at least in the short term, to protect the existing generating facilities from domestic competition.[179]

2.1.2.2 Network Supervisor

Articles 43 and 30 of the Electricity Directive require the Member States to ensure that there are system operators for transmission networks (TSO) and for distribution networks (DSO). According to the Directive, there is nothing to prevent a transmission network system operator and a distribution network system operator from being part of the same corporate group. However, there is an unbundling requirement in Articles 35, 36 and 43. The systems operators are responsible for the operation, maintenance and management of energy flows and development of the network. Traditionally, these functions have been dealt with in vertically integrated electricity companies, often by a network owner who was also engaged in electricity production.

In contrast to a natural gas network, an electricity network is characterised by the fact that electricity cannot be stored in the network. Input (production) and output (consumption) must always correspond largely to each other in order to maintain the frequency at 50 Hz. Systems operators seek, by means of dispatching and balancing, to compensate for lack of inputs or excess inputs. Interruption of supply to end users can also be used for this purpose.[180] A network can be described as being like connected tanks. As long as the transmission capacity between two tanks is sufficient, it does not matter to the balance of the system where the inputs and outputs take place. If the transmission capacity is insufficient, there will be bottlenecks.

---

178. Environmental concerns are subject to national rules on the choice of fuel, emissions standards, quotas, etc.
179. Working Paper of the Commission on the Organisation of the Internal Electricity Market, SEC(95) 464 final, 22 Mar. 1995.
180. Interruptions of supply can be necessary to avoid a system falling out of balance if there is an acute lack of current, or on the basis of agreements on interruptions, whereby a consumer is compensated for agreeing to interruption of supply if there is lack of current.

With Regulation (EU) 2017/2195, the Commission has established guidelines for balancing electricity.

According to Articles 31(2) and 40(1), litra f, transmission and distribution system network operators can be independent participants or be owned by participants in the market since 'related undertakings' must not be favoured.

The first Electricity Directive did not contain requirements for unbundling at the distribution level. However, Article 35 of the present Electricity Directive introduced unbundling requirements for DSOs, corresponding to legal, organisational, and management unbundling. However, in particular, for distribution companies, there is scope for Member States to introduce a *de minimis* provision in the form of a threshold of 100,000 customers or serving small isolated systems; *see* Article 35(4). Below this limit, a Member State can refrain from imposing requirements for unbundling. This thus avoids splitting up smaller electricity distributors between supply companies and network companies.

As part of the requirement for unbundling, system operators at both transmission and distribution levels are subject to a duty of confidentiality with regard to commercially sensitive information which they receive in the course carrying out their tasks; *see* Article 41 on transmission and Article 37 on distribution. Confidentiality is not just intended as a security against general publication but includes a prohibition on passing on information about competitors' circumstances to market participants in the system operator's own corporate group.[181] Identical provisions in the two articles explicitly state that a system operator must 'prevent information about its own activities which may be commercially advantageous being disclosed in a discriminatory manner.' The fact a system operator can belong to the same corporate group as an electricity generating or supply company could give an incentive for discriminatory treatment of system users. The provisions make an exception for passing on information to the authorities; *see* Article 55(1). However, such authorities are themselves subject to a duty of confidentiality; *see* Article 55(2).

There is also a requirement for accounting unbundling for all electricity undertakings which are either vertically integrated or carry on some non-electricity-related activity alongside their electricity supply undertaking. Article 56 provides that the undertakings in question shall keep separate accounts for transmission and distribution activities and, where relevant, for non-electricity activities. Furthermore, there is a requirement for all electricity supply undertakings to keep accounts in accordance with the relevant national implemented provisions for the Directive (EU) 2013/34.

2.1.3 Access to Networks

In its Articles 16–20, the first Electricity Directive introduced a limited right to use others' electricity networks for certain electricity supply undertakings and end users in

---

181. COM(91) 548 final – Proposal for a Council Directive concerning common rules for the internal market in electricity, and Proposal for a Council Directive concerning common rules for the internal market in natural gas.

connection with entering into electricity supply agreements. The customers who thereby got access to networks and trading rights were designated eligible customers.[182]

Access to networks was not absolute. Access covered those participants which, in connection with their compliance with the degree of market opening referred to, the Member States had categorised as eligible customers. Both distributors and final customers could be included in the calculation of the degree of market openness. According to the then Article 19(3) of the first Electricity Directive, all final customers consuming more than 100 GWh per year, on a consumption site basis and including autoproduction, must be covered by access to networks.[183] The first Electricity Directive included an automatic adjustment of this threshold value.

Commercial customers have been 'eligible customers' since 1 July 2004, and household customers have been 'eligible customers' since 1 July 2007. Thereby, all final customers are now entitled to choose their suppliers.

Under Articles 40(1), 12(f) and 31(2), system operators must not discriminate between system users or classes of system users. This means that the Member States must also not require system operators to discriminate, for example, by giving individual users or classes of users prior rights to network access over others, unless there is an exceptional situation which can justify such discrimination and which is expressly provided for in the Electricity Directive. Such exceptions are provided for in Article 31(3) and (4) as well as Article 25(4) (priority for certain forms of generation); *see* below.

Article 12(1) of the Regulation (EU) on the internal market for electricity states that market conditions such as the primary principle for load distribution. In paragraph 2, however, supremacy is given to, amongst others, smaller VE-plants.

2.1.3.1 Procedures for System Access

Under Article 32 of the Electricity Directive, regulated third-party access to networks is made obligatory. This right of access is based on published tariffs. The Member States must ensure that the tariffs for third-party access, or the methods for their calculation, are approved prior to their entry into force. It is still possible to deny access by reference to lack of capacity. Substantiated reasons must be given for refusal of access. However, there is nothing to prevent the grant of access rights. In this case, it is up to the system operator to ensure that production and consumption are balanced on both sides of a bottleneck where capacity is too low.

The first Electricity Directive distinguished between two possibilities for access to the network: *negotiated access* and *single buyer access*. Negotiated access meant that the more detailed

---

182. See Art. 33 of Directive 2009/72/EC concerning common rules for the internal market in electricity. According to Art. 2(12) of the Directive, an 'eligible customer' means a customer who is free to purchase electricity from the supplier of his choice.
183. It could thus be decisive for an undertaking's possibility of access to a network whether its undertaking was geographically concentrated or spread out over a number of production units.

conditions for access to a network were subject to a normal negotiating procedure. However, there was a requirement for the publication of recommended tariffs. Single buyer access meant that it was possible for a Member State to appoint an undertaking as the sole undertaking for the territory covered by the system operator. The Member State could thereafter require the single buyer to buy the electricity for which an eligible customer had entered into a purchase agreement. A single buyer would thus retain control over the network, securing its status as a monopolist.

2.1.3.2 Direct Lines

In order to supply final customers, a supplier is dependent either on being able to use an existing network or establish a direct line. Article 7 of the Electricity Directive ensures that every electricity producer can establish a direct line to supply their own premises, subsidiaries and eligible customers on the basis of objective and non-discriminatory criteria. However, Member States may refuse to authorise a direct line if granting such authorisation would be contrary to the provisions of Article 9. Article 9 deals with the possibility of imposing a public service obligation[184] on an electricity undertaking and of departing from the provisions of the Directive if they hinder the fulfilment of the obligations imposed. Article 9 of the Electricity Directive refers to Article 106 TFEU. Only if the conditions in this provision are fulfilled can authorisation to establish direct lines be refused. Similarly, under Article 7(4) of the Directive, Member States may authorise the construction of a direct line subject either to the refusal of system access on the basis of lack of capacity or the initiation of a dispute resolution procedure. This provision may be seen as an expression of concern for environmental protection. Because they can disfigure the landscape, new installations can be prevented if they do not meet an actual need for capacity. If there is sufficient capacity, competition law measures will be sufficient to take care of competition concerns.

Article 7(3) of the Electricity Directive explicitly states that the possibility of supplying electricity through a direct line does not affect the possibility of supplying electricity in accordance with the right of third-party access.

2.1.3.3 Cross-Border Connections

Access to cross-border connections (interconnections) is important for the establishment of the internal market for electricity. Such interconnections link the transmission networks of different Member States.

The Electricity Directive does not provide for specific methods for arranging the allocation of access to these interconnections. In most cases, there will be times in the day or in the year when capacity is insufficient to meet demand. There will be a bottleneck and there will be a need to allocate a limited resource. According to Article 16(1) of the Regulation (EU) 2019/943, network 'congestion problems shall be solved

---

184. Regarding public service obligations, see Christopher Jones & William-James Kettlewell (ed.): *EU Energy Law – The internal Energy Market*, Vol. I, p. 539- 552 (2021).

by means of non-transaction-based methods' which give efficient economic signals to the market participants and TSOs involved. Network congestion problems shall be solved by means of non-transaction-based methods, namely methods that do not involve a selection between the contracts of individual market participants. The usual methods for making allocations are pro rata rationing and auctions. Other methods are first-come-first-served or linking network rights to contracts for supply (merit order). A special arrangement consists in giving free access to interconnections. The TSOs in question can be given the task of regulating both consumption and production on both sides of the bottleneck. This can be done by requiring producers to regulate production, possibly for compensation. It is also possible that consumers will be offered payment for agreeing to an interruption of supply, in whole or in part. This will only be relevant to industrial undertakings which are heavy users of energy.

Problems arise concerning exclusive rights, especially in connection with the establishment of new interconnecting lines. Such agreements are often necessary in order to secure investment and, thus, the financing of such new lines. Article 63 in Regulation (EU) on the internal market for electricity contains a possibility of exception for new direct current interconnection lines. However, there is a problem in relation to Article 101 TFEU about how long such exclusivity may last. It must be assumed that the duration must be sufficient to secure the investment. *See* the cases referred to above on the application of the Treaty's general competition rules.

2.1.4   Public Service Obligations

The Electricity Directive contains a number of special public service obligations. The provisions cover in part those concerns which *must* be the responsibility of the Member States and in part those that *can* be their responsibility.

Regulation (EU) on risk-preparedness in the electricity sector lays down special requirements for assessing risks of the security of electricity supply, drawing up regional and national electricity crisis scenarios, preparation of emergency preparedness plans, surveillance and evaluation.

2.1.5   Transparency

Together with Directive 90/547/EEC on the transit of electricity through transmission grids, the first Directive on price transparency[185] was implemented as part of the first phase of the liberalisation of the electricity sector. The Directive has been amended several times and was most recently adopted in partially amended form in 2008.[186] Subsequently, the directive has been superseded by Regulation (EU) 2016/1962 of 26

---

185. Directive 90/377/EEC concerning a Community procedure to improve the transparency of gas and electricity prices charged to industrial end-users.
186. Directive 2008/92/EC concerning a Community procedure to improve the transparency of gas and electricity prices charged to industrial end-users. The Directive is discussed generally in s. 1.4.8.

November 2016 concerning the classification of certain goods in the Combined Nomenclature.

Article 56(2) and (3) of the current Electricity Directive states that, whatever their system of ownership or legal form, electricity undertakings must draw up, submit to audit[187] and publish their annual accounts in accordance with the rules of national law on the annual accounts of limited liability companies adopted pursuant to national legislation on the annual accounts of capital companies adopted pursuant to Directive (EU) 2012/34. In Article 19(3), there is a requirement for accounting unbundling. Thus, in their internal accounting, electricity undertakings must 'keep separate accounts for each of their transmission and distribution activities as they would be required to do if the activities in question were carried out by separate undertakings, with a view to avoiding discrimination, cross subsidisation and distortion of competition. They shall also keep accounts, which may be consolidated, for other electricity activities not relating to transmission or distribution.' Moreover, the internal accounts must include a balance sheet and a profit and loss account for each activity.

2.1.6   *Public Authorities*

Under Article 57 of the Electricity Directive, each Member State is required to appoint a single national regulatory authority (a regulator). In most Member States, this has led to the appointment of an independent regulator. Until 2004, Germany was an exception to this. Here, the supervisory tasks were the responsibility of the ordinary competition authorities, as *ex post* control combined with a widespread special regulation. This was much criticised by the other Member States. It is up to the Member States to ensure the independence of regulators. Article 35(4) and (5) of the Electricity Directive sets explicit requirements:

- legally distinct and functionally independent from any other public or private entity;
- that personnel and management act independently of market interest;
- that personnel and management do not seek or take direct instructions from any government or other public or private entity when carrying out the regulatory tasks;
- that the regulator can take autonomous decisions, independently from any political body, and has the necessary human and financial resources for carrying out its tasks and exercise its powers in an efficient and effective manner; and
- and that the members of the board or top management can only be appointed and dismissed according to, among others, transparent criteria.

Pursuant to Article 59 of the Electricity Directive, regulators have the following powers and duties, among others:

---

187. According to Art. 31(4), the audit must verify that the obligation to avoid discrimination and cross-subsidies is respected.

- fixing or approving, in accordance with transparent criteria, transmission or distribution tariffs or their methodologies, or both;
- ensuring the compliance of TSOs and DSOs and, where relevant, system owners, as well as the compliance of any electricity undertakings and other market participants, with their obligations under this Directive, Regulation (EU) 2019/943, the network codes and the guidelines adopted pursuant to Articles 59, 60 and 61 of Regulation (EU) 2019/943, and other relevant Union law, including as regards cross-border issues, as well as with ACER's decisions;
- in close coordination with the other regulatory authorities, ensuring the compliance of the ENTSO for Electricity and the EU DSO entity with their obligations under this Directive, Regulation (EU) 2019/943, the network codes and guidelines adopted pursuant to Articles 59, 60 and 61 of Regulation (EU) 2019/943, and other relevant Union law, including as regards cross-border issues, as well as with ACER's decisions, and jointly identifying noncompliance of the ENTSO for Electricity and the EU DSO entity with their respective obligations; where the regulatory authorities have not been able to reach an agreement within a period of four months after the start of consultations for the purpose of jointly identifying non-compliance, the matter shall be referred to the ACER for a decision, pursuant to Article 6(10) of Regulation (EU) 2019/942;
- approving products and procurement processes for non-frequency ancillary services;
- implementing the network codes and guidelines adopted pursuant to Articles 59, 60 and 61 of Regulation (EU) 2019/943 through national measures or, where so required, coordinated regional or Union-wide measures;
- cooperating in regard to cross-border issues with the regulatory authority or authorities of the Member States concerned and with ACER, in particular through participation in the work of ACER's Board of Regulators pursuant to Article 21 of Regulation (EU) 2019/942;
- complying with and implementing any relevant legally binding decisions of the Commission and of ACER;
- ensuring that TSOs make available interconnector capacities to the utmost extent pursuant to Article 16 of Regulation (EU) 2019/943;
- reporting annually on its activity and the fulfilment of its duties to the relevant authorities of the Member States, the Commission and ACER, including on the steps taken and the results obtained as regards each of the tasks listed in this article;
- ensuring that there is no cross-subsidisation between transmission, distribution and supply activities or other electricity or non-electricity activities;
- monitoring investment plans of the TSOs and providing in its annual report an assessment of the investment plans of the TSOs as regards their consistency with the Union-wide network development plan; such assessment may include recommendations to amend those investment plans;

- monitoring and assessing the performance of TSOs and DSOs in relation to the development of a smart grid that promotes energy efficiency and the integration of energy from renewable sources based on a limited set of indicators, and publish a national report every two years, including recommendations;
- setting or approving standards and requirements for quality of service and quality of supply or contributing thereto together with other competent authorities and monitoring compliance with and reviewing the past performance of network security and reliability rules;
- monitoring the level of transparency, including wholesale prices, and ensuring compliance of electricity undertakings with transparency obligations;
- monitoring the level and effectiveness of market opening and competition at wholesale and retail levels, including on electricity exchanges, prices for household customers including prepayment systems, the impact of dynamic electricity price contracts and the use of smart metering systems, switching rates, disconnection rates, charges for maintenance services, the execution of maintenance services, the relationship between household and wholesale prices, the evolution of grid tariffs and levies, and complaints by household customers, as well as any distortion or restriction of competition, including by providing any relevant information, and bringing any relevant cases to the relevant competition authorities;
- monitoring the occurrence of restrictive contractual practices, including exclusivity clauses which may prevent customers from contracting simultaneously with more than one supplier or restrict their choice to do so, and, where appropriate, informing the national competition authorities of such practices;
- monitoring the time taken by TSOs and DSOs to make connections and repairs.

2.1.7 'Income Ceiling'

With the Council's Regulation (EU) 2022/1854 of 6 October 2022 on an emergency intervention to address high energy prices, measures have been introduced to mitigate the effects of high energy prices by capping the market revenues which certain producers receive from the production of electricity and by redistributing them to the electricity end costumers. The Member States are given the opportunity to apply measures in the form of public intervention in the pricing of electricity supply to households and SMVs. Moreover, the rules are laid down for a mandatory solidarity contribution from EU companies and permanent establishments working in the sectors of crude oil, natural gas, coal, and refinery so that these can contribute to affordable energy prices for households and companies.

Article 3 of the regulation holds a request, but not a direct obligation, for the Member States to reduce the gross electricity consumption by 10 %. Article 5 holds provisions stating that the measures must be clearly defined, transparent, proportional, targeted, non-discriminating, and controllable, and, in particular, meet the following conditions:

(a) where financial compensation is paid in addition to market revenues, the amount of that compensation shall be established through an open competitive process;
(b) only involve financial compensation when such compensation is paid for additional electricity not consumed compared to the expected consumption in the hour concerned without the tender;
(c) not unduly distort competition or the proper functioning of the internal market in electricity;
(d) not be unduly limited to specific customers or customer groups, including independent aggregators, in accordance with Article 17 of Directive (EU) 2019/944; and
(e) not unduly prevent the process of replacing fossil fuel technologies with technologies using electricity

Furthermore, a mandatory ceiling has been laid down on market revenues so that electrical producers using wind power, solar energy (solar heating and solar cells), geothermal energy, hydropower without a reservoir, biomass fuel (solid or gaseous) except biomethane, waste, nuclear power, lignite, crude oil products, and peat, is allowed a maximum of market revenue from production of electricity at 180 EUR per MWh electricity produces, cf. Articles 6 and 7. Article 10(1) states that Member States must insure that all extraordinary income from above the ceiling of market revenue is used for targeted financing of measures in support of electrical end costumers that mitigate the effect of the high electricity prices for these costumers.

Finally, a mandatory solidarity contribution will include extraordinary proceeds from EU companies and permanent establishments with activities in sectors of crude oil, natural gas, coal, and refinery unless the Member States have adopted corresponding measures. Article 17 states that Member States must use the proceeds from the temporary solidarity contribution with sufficiently timely impact for any of the following purposes:

(a) financial support measures for final energy customers, and in particular vulnerable households, to mitigate the effects of high energy prices in a targeted manner;
(b) financial support measures to help reduce energy consumption, such as through demand reduction auctions or tender schemes, lowering the energy purchase costs of final energy customers for certain volumes of consumption, promoting investments by final energy customers into renewables, structural energy efficiency investments or other decarbonisation technologies;
(c) financial support measures to support companies in energy-intensive industries provided that they are made conditional upon investments into renewable energies, energy efficiency or other decarbonisation technologies;
(d) financial support measures to develop energy autonomy, in particular, investments in line with the REPowerEU objectives set in the REPowerEU Plan and in the REPowerEU Joint European Action, such as projects with a cross-border dimension;

(e) in a spirit of solidarity between Member States, Member States may assign a share of the proceeds of the temporary solidarity contribution to the common financing of measures to reduce the harmful effects of the energy crisis, including support for protecting employment and the reskilling and upskilling of the workforce, or to promote investments in energy efficiency and renewable energy, including in cross-border projects, and in the Union renewable energy financing mechanism provided for in Article 33 of Regulation (EU) 2018/1999 of the European Parliament and of the Council.

The regulation has its authority in TFEU Article 122(1). Whether this authority holds up in the current situation – the provision requires serious supply difficulties – is not to be made a subject of discussion here.

Article 22(2) of the regulation holds an expiration date (sunset clause) for many of the provisions.

In the preliminary case C-423/23, the Court of Justice of the European Union has been asked to rule on whether Italian legislation, which puts a cap on producers' income from the sale of electricity, in particular regarding the renewable energy sector, is compatible with the EU regulation in the field.

2.1.8 'Prosumers and communities'

Article 2, no. 8, of the Electric Directive defines an 'active costumer' as a 'final customer, or a group of jointly acting final customers, who consumes or stores electricity generated within its premises located within confined boundaries or, where permitted by a Member State, within other premises, or who sells self-generated electricity or participates in flexibility or energy efficiency schemes, provided that those activities do not constitute its primary commercial or professional activity'. The article talks of prosumers that are taken into account by the latest Electricity Directive through, amongst other things, citizen energy communities,[188] for which the Member States, according to Article 16, are required to arrange a 'favourable' body of rules.

The Article is further supplemented by the provisions of the Renewable Energy (RE) Directive on RE self-consumers, community of RE consumers, and RE community, as defined in Article 2, nos 14–16 of the RE Directive.

---

188. Art. 2, no. 11 of the Electric Directive defines ' 'citizen energy community' as 'a legal entity that: (a) is based on voluntary and open participation and is effectively controlled by members or shareholders that are natural persons, local authorities, including municipalities, or small enterprises; (b) has for its primary purpose to provide environmental, economic or social community benefits to its members or shareholders or to the local areas where it operates rather than to generate financial profits; and (c) may engage in generation, including from renewable sources, distribution, supply, consumption, aggregation, energy storage, energy efficiency services or charging services for electric vehicles or provide other energy services to its members or shareholders'.

2.2 Natural Gas

In contrast to electricity, natural gas (primarily methane) is a primary form of energy, even though there is often some form of refining prior to the gas being used. Natural gas is not necessarily as homogeneous a product as electricity. The calorific value can vary according to where it comes from. However, inputs to a network can be made on the basis of a measurement of the calorific value of the gas input, or it can be refined to a specific calorific value.[189]

The recovery and supply of natural gas are regulated by different sets of rules. This section only deals with the supply of natural gas, often referred to as *downstream*, as opposed to *upstream* which refers to natural gas from the gas well to the refinery.[190]

As for the downstream market, this is defined in Article 2 of the third and most recent Natural Gas Directive,[191] which lists a number of different functions. These represent different stages of the value chain and are to some extent subject to different frameworks.

In Article 2(1) of the Natural Gas Directive, *natural gas undertaking* is defined as 'a natural or legal person carrying out at least one of the following functions: production, transmission, distribution, supply, purchase or storage of natural gas, including LNG, which is responsible for the commercial, technical and/or maintenance tasks related to those functions, but shall not include final customers.'[192]

Transmission is defined as 'the transport of natural gas through a network, which mainly contains high-pressure pipelines, other than an upstream pipeline network and other than the part of high-pressure pipelines primarily used in the context of local distribution of natural gas, with a view to its delivery to customers, but not including supply.'[193] *Distribution* means 'the transport of natural gas through local or regional pipeline networks with a view to its delivery to customers,[194] but not including supply.' Both transmission and distribution are considered to be natural monopolies. The legal entities which are responsible for the transmission and distribution functions are referred to as *TSOs* and *DSOs*, respectively.

---

189. If the calorific value varies too widely, this can give problems for gas installations which are optimised for a specific calorific value.
190. For a description of the Union's rules on the upstream sectors for hydrocarbons, *see* Piet Jan Cross et al.: *EC Energy Law*, in Martha Roggenkamp et al.: *Energy Law in Europe*, p. 336 (2007).
191. Directive 2009/73/EC concerning common rules for the internal market in natural gas. This was required to be implemented by 3 Mar. 2011, from which date the old Directive 2003/55/EC was repealed. For general comments on the first Directive 98/30/EC, *see* Eugene D. Cross et al.: *EC Energy Law*, in Martha Roggenkamp et al.: *Energy Law in Europe*, p. 308 (2001). The second Natural Gas Directive is described in Christopher W. Jones: *EU Energy Law*, Vol. I (2006); Martha Roggenkamp et al.: *Energy Law in Europe*, p. 364 (2007); and Peter Cameron: *Competition in Energy Markets* (2007). *See also* Ivo Van Bael & Jean-Francois Bellis: *Competition Law of the European Community*, p. 1417 ff. (2010).
192. LNG is the abbreviation for 'liquefied natural gas'.
193. *Customers* means wholesale and final customers of natural gas and natural gas undertakings which purchase natural gas.
194. This primarily refers to end users, designated as 'final customers' in the Natural Gas Directive.

A storage function will often be associated with a natural gas system, and this is the responsibility of *storage system operators*. This function is an essential part of a gas network and, thus, part of a natural monopoly. Most of these functions are performed by an integrated natural gas undertaking. These can be categorised as vertically integrated natural gas undertakings, which refers to a natural gas undertaking which performs two or more of the following functions: production, transmission, distribution, supply or storage of natural gas, and horizontally integrated natural gas undertakings which perform at least one of the following functions: production, transmission, distribution, supply or storage of natural gas, together with an activity not related to natural gas.

2.2.1   Regulation under EU Law

The primary regulation of competition in the natural gas sector is found in the Natural Gas Directive. The first Natural Gas Directive dates from 1998. In 2004, this was replaced by the second Natural Gas Directive, which was in turn replaced by the third Natural Gas Directive in 2009, which has been changed again in 2018, 2019 and 2022. The sector is also covered by Regulation (EU) 2016/1952 on European statistics on natural gas and electricity prices. The earlier Directive 91/296/EEC on the transit of natural gas through grids was repealed as from 1 July 2004, and this area is now covered by the Natural Gas Directive and by Regulation (EC) No 715/2009 on conditions for access to the natural gas transmission networks. Regulation (EU) 2017/1938 concerning measures to safeguard the security of gas supply is also applicable.[195]

2.2.1.1   The Natural Gas Directive

The primary purpose of the Natural Gas Directive is to open the market for natural gas to competition. Thus, Article 18 of the first Natural Gas Directive provided that, after the entry into force of the Directive, the national gas markets should have a degree of openness corresponding to at least 20% of the total annual gas consumption on the national gas market. This percentage was increased to 28% five years after the entry into force of the Directive, and 33% after ten years.

The Member States' abilities to reach these levels of market openness consisted mainly in regulating who could have free choice of their supplier, referred to as *eligible customers*. The Directive included minimum rules as to which customers should be *eligible*. If these minimum rules led to a greater degree of openness than the levels stated above, Article 18 gave the possibility of changing the minimum definition of eligible customers so that the level of market openness would be reduced to less than 30% of the total annual gas consumption of the national market. This percentage was increased to 38% five years after the entry into force of the Directive, and 43% after ten years.

---

195. *See* Christopher W. Jones & William-James Kettlewell (ed.): *EU Energy Law*, Vol I (2020). The Internal Energy Market, Vol. I, 2010, for a commentary on the EU regulation of the natural gas market following the adoption of the third energy package.

The second Natural Gas Directive moved this process on. Instead of regulating the degree of market openness, the starting point was the classification of customers. As from 1 July 2004, all non-household customers have had a free market. As from 1 July 2007, all customers have had a free market.

In common with the EU's competition rules, the third and current Natural Gas Directive does not contain any special principles for pricing. In general, the sector is regulated in line with the other Treaty prohibitions of abuse of a dominant position under Article 102 TFEU, including the prohibition of 'directly or indirectly imposing unfair purchase or selling prices or other unfair trading conditions.' However, the Natural Gas Directive contains provisions prohibiting discrimination between system users in Article 13(1) and Article 25(2). This also concerns pricing discrimination.

In addition, the general competition rules apply to the natural gas sector. These are relevant in particular in relation to network access.[196]

Similarly to the Electricity Directive, the Natural Gas Directive contains a provision on reciprocity. Article 37(2) states that contracts for the supply of an eligible customer in the system of another Member State may not be prohibited if the customer is eligible in both systems.[197] The relevance of this provision has lapsed in connection with the implementation of full market opening.

2.2.1.2 Application of the General Competition Rules

Like the electricity sector, the natural gas sector is subject to the Union's general competition rules. However, over the years, there have not been as many cases on natural gas as on electricity. In 2009, *E.ON Ruhrgas* and *GDF Suez* were each fined EUR 553 million in connection with an anti-competitive horizontal agreement on market sharing.[198]

In connection with the construction of a shared gas pipeline (the MEGAL pipeline), in 1975, the two parties (originally Ruhrgas and GDF) entered into an agreement not to sell gas transported over this pipeline in each other's home markets (Germany and France respectively). At that time, the market had not been liberalised. Until 2000, GDF had a legal monopoly on the import of natural gas to France, and until 1998, Ruhrgas had a de facto monopoly in its supply area via a set of agreements with other German supply undertakings. However, the parties maintained the market-sharing agreement after the market had been opened in 2000 by the first Natural Gas Directive (98/30/EC).

In relation to the German market, the Commission brought proceedings against RWE AG for abuse of its dominant position by denying third-party access and by using a margin squeeze.[199]

---

196. For a comprehensive review of the application of the Union's competition rules to the natural gas sector, *see* Christopher W. Jones (ed.): *EU Energy Markets*, p. 105 (2019).
197. Reciprocity is discussed in more detail in s. 1.4.12.
198. Decision IP/09/1099 of 8 Jul. 2009.
199. Commission Decision of 18 Mar. 2009 relating to a proceeding under Art. 82 of the EC Treaty and Art. 53 of the EEA Agreement (Case COMP/B-1/39.402 – *RWE Gas Foreclosure*) (OJ 2009/C 133/10).

In relation to third-party access, the Commission suspected that RWE may not have implemented an effective congestion management system to manage the scarce capacities on its network with a view to systematically excluding competitors from their network. Moreover, there were indications that RWE may have intentionally set its transmission tariffs at an artificially high level in order to squeeze RWE's competitors' margins (margin squeeze strategy). The case was settled after RWE had committed itself to selling its entire current German high-pressure gas transmission network.[200]

2.2.2 Authorisation Procedures

Under Article 4 of the Natural Gas Directive, the Member States may decide whether to use an authorisation procedure. Where a Member State does have a system of authorisation, it must lay down objective and non-discriminatory criteria which are to be met by an undertaking applying for authorisation to build and/or operate natural gas facilities or for authorisation to supply natural gas. These criteria and procedures for granting authorisations must be made public. The reasons for any refusal to grant an authorisation must be given to the applicant, and there must be procedures enabling the applicant to appeal against such refusal. There are similar requirements in respect of direct lines. The Member States can introduce authorisation procedures for this. Under Article 24(2), the Member States or a designated competent authority must lay down the criteria for the grant of authorisations for the construction or operation of direct lines in their territory.

In the interests of the development of newly supplied areas and efficient operation generally, Article 4(4) provides a special possibility for Member States to refuse to grant further authorisation to build and operate distribution pipeline systems in any particular area once such pipeline systems have been proposed to be built in that area and if the existing or proposed capacity is not fully used.

However, as discussed below, a system operator is to be appointed for transmission, storage and/or LNG facilities. This can be under an administrative act of the Member State or by the owners of the facilities in question appointing a system operator. In the latter case, this can hardly be considered an authorisation procedure.

2.2.2.1 Network Management

In contrast to the first Electricity Directive, the first Natural Gas Directive did not contain any requirement for the appointment of a system operator. However, in the second and third Natural Gas Directives, there is a requirement for the establishment of a system operator function at both the transmission and the distribution levels.

Thus, Article 9 of the third Natural Gas Directive lays down that the owner of a transmission system must act as a TSO and is thus subject to the rules that apply to TSOs.[201] According to Article 13(1) and (2), the primary tasks of such system operators

---

200. For other cases, see COMP/37.966, Distrigaz. COMP/39.316, GDF and COMP/39.317, E.On gas. See also T-136/19, *Bulgaria* and case 67, 68 and 70/85, *Van der Kooy*.
201. The deadline for implementing this specific requirement is 3 Mar. 2012.

are to operate, maintain and develop reliable and efficient facilities to secure an open market, with due regard to the environment, and ensure adequate means to meet service obligations. A system operator may not discriminate between system users or classes of system users and, in particular, not favour its related undertakings. Corresponding rules apply to DSOs. A system operator must also provide other system operators with sufficient information to ensure effective access to the system. There are special rules on network development (Article 22), ensuring compliance (Article 21), and supervision (Article 20). There are similar, if less strict, rules for DSOs (Articles 24–27) and storage and LNG system operators (Articles 12–13).

2.2.2.2 Unbundling

Under Article 31 of the Natural Gas Directive, whatever their system of ownership or legal form, natural gas undertakings must draw up, submit to audit and publish their annual accounts in accordance with the rules of national law concerning the annual accounts of limited liability companies adopted pursuant to the Fourth Council Directive 78/660/EEC on the annual accounts of certain types of companies (unbundling of accounts). Undertakings which are not legally obliged to publish their annual accounts must keep a copy of these at the disposal of the public at their head office. In their internal accounting, integrated natural gas undertakings must keep separate accounts for each of their transmission, distribution, LNG and storage activities and, where relevant, consolidated accounts for other activities not relating to transmission, distribution, LNG and storage of natural gas, as they would be required to do if the activities in question were carried out by separate undertakings. The internal accounts must include a balance sheet and a profit and loss account for each activity. The aim of these provisions on the unbundling of accounts is to avoid discrimination, cross-subsidisation and distortion of competition.

The unbundling requirements at the transmission level are either separation of ownership, ISO, ITO, or ITO+. At the distribution level, there are requirements for management and company unbundling.

2.2.3   Access to Networks

The main provisions on network access were found in Chapter VI of the first Natural Gas Directive. According to Article 18, the Member States should state which customers were eligible, with a view to achieving the required minimum level of market openness. Regardless of their annual consumption, gas-fired power stations and other final customers with a consumption of more than 25 million cubic metres of gas per year per consumption location were eligible, whether or not they were otherwise covered by the market opening.

Under the second Natural Gas Directive, all customers have been eligible since 1 July 2007. Article 32 of the third and current Natural Gas Directive regulates third-party access. However, lack of capacity, the fulfilment of public service obligations or economic and financial difficulties with take-or-pay contracts are valid grounds for refusing access; *see* below. In this connection, it is important to bear in mind that the Directive does not exclude long-term contracts as long as they comply with Union competition rules; *see* Article 32(3).

Article 35(2) of the Natural Gas Directive allows Member States to take measures to ensure that a natural gas undertaking which refuses access to a system on the basis of lack of capacity or a lack of connection makes the necessary enhancements as far as it is economical to do so or when a potential customer is willing to pay for them. The entitlement to do so becomes an obligation to do so if the Member State has made use of the possibility in Article 4(4) of the Directive to decline to grant further authorisation to build and operate distribution pipeline systems in a particular area if pipeline systems are already proposed to be built in that area.

2.2.3.1   Network Access Procedures

Under Articles 14–16 of the first Natural Gas Directive, Member States could generally choose between negotiated access and regulated access. Under Article 32 of the current Natural Gas Directive, Member States must use regulated network access. Only in relation to access to storage facilities and line pack[202] can Member States still choose between negotiated and regulated access; *see* Article 33 of the Directive. Both procedures must be administered in accordance with objective, transparent and non-discriminatory criteria.

Article 48 allows for the possibility of derogating from the provisions on network access. Thus, a natural gas undertaking that has or expects to have serious economic and financial difficulties because of its take-or-pay commitments in connection with one or more gas-purchase contracts can apply to the Member State in question or the designated competent authority for a temporary derogation from the provisions on network access. When deciding whether to grant such a derogation, the Member State or the designated competent authority must take into account a number of criteria including: the objective of achieving a competitive gas market; the need to fulfil public service obligations and ensure security of supply; and the extent to which, when accepting the take-or-pay commitments in question, the undertaking could reasonably have foreseen that serious difficulties were likely to arise. In any case, it must be assumed that the natural gas undertaking will not have serious difficulties if the sales of natural gas do not fall below the level of minimum offtake guarantees in take-or-pay contracts for the purchase of gas or if the take-or-pay contract for the purchase of gas can be adapted or the natural gas undertaking is able to find alternative outlets. Reasons for a refusal must be given.

Under Article 36, major new gas infrastructures (i.e., interconnectors between Member States, LNG and storage facilities) may, upon request, be exempted from the provisions of Article 32. The conditions for the application of this provision are, among other things, that the investment must enhance competition in gas supply and enhance

---

202. *Linepack* means the storage of gas by compression in gas transmission and distribution systems.

security of supply and that the level of risk attached to the investment is such that the investment would not take place unless an exemption was granted.

If an exemption is granted, the Member State or the designated competent authority must inform the Commission of its decision as soon as possible and send all information relevant to the exemption. Within eight weeks (for a take-or-pay contractor) or two months (for new infrastructure) after receiving such notification, the Commission can require the Member State or the designated competent authority to change or revoke its decision. Likewise, the reasons for any exception allowed for take-or-pay contracts must be published in the Official Journal of the European Union.

Finally, Article 49(2) of the Natural Gas Directive provides that where a Member State qualifies as an emergent market and where the implementation of this Directive would cause substantial problems, among other things, the provisions on network access in Article 32 of the Directive may be derogated from. Such exemptions expire at the same time as the Member State is no longer considered to be an emergent market.

In accordance with Article 13(1) of the Natural Gas Directive, system operators for transmission, storage and/or LNG may not discriminate between system users or classes of system users and, in particular, may not favour its related undertakings. There is a similar provision relating to DSOs in Article 25(2).

Under Article 16 of the Natural Gas Directive, each TSO and transmission system owner must preserve the confidentiality of commercially sensitive information obtained in the course of carrying out its activities, subject to any legal obligation to disclose information. This includes information received from third parties in connection with allocating or negotiating access to the system. For TSOs who are part of vertically integrated undertakings, it is explicitly stated that they must not disclose any commercially sensitive information to the remaining parts of the undertaking unless this is necessary for carrying out a business transaction. In this connection, Member States must ensure that the transmission system owner and the remaining part of the undertaking do not use joint services, such as joint legal services, apart from purely administrative or IT functions. There is a similar, though less strict, duty of confidentiality for DSOs in Article 27.

A Regulation on conditions for access to the natural gas transmission networks was introduced in 2006 with the aim of harmonising the setting of harmonised principles for tariffs, or the methodologies underlying their calculation, for access to the network, the establishment of third-party access services and harmonised principles for capacity allocation and congestion management, the determination of transparency requirements, balancing rules and imbalance charges and facilitating capacity trading. The current, and second, Regulation (Regulation (EC) No 715/2009) applies to 'the transport of natural gas through a network, which mainly contains high pressure pipelines, other than an upstream pipeline network and other than the part of high pressure pipelines primarily used in the context of local distribution of natural gas, with a view to its delivery to customers, but not including supply'; *see* the definition of *transmission* in the Regulation. The Regulation also applies to high-pressure pipelines linking local distributors to the gas network which are not primarily used for local distribution; *see* recital 6. The aim of the Regulation is to lay down non-discriminatory rules for access conditions to natural gas transmission systems, taking into account the specificities of national and regional markets with a view to ensuring the proper functioning of the internal gas market.

The Annex to the Regulation contains comprehensive guidelines to the Regulation in order to contribute to harmonisation. The Commission may adopt Guidelines on certain issues; *see* Article 23(2) of the Regulation.

Member States that have been granted a derogation under Article 49 of the Natural Gas Directive, as an emergent market, can apply to the Commission for a temporary exemption from the application of this Regulation; *see* Article 30. Nor does the Regulation apply to interconnections between Member States and other substantial increases in capacity to the existing infrastructure or changes to such infrastructure which enable the development of new sources of supply of gas, to the extent that these are exempt under Article 36 of the Natural Gas Directive. Furthermore, those gas transmission networks that are exempt as a result of take-or-pay obligations are exempted from the provisions of the Regulation; *see* Article 48 of the Natural Gas Directive.

Article 13(1) of the Regulation lays down that tariffs must be transparent, take into account the need for system integrity and improvement, and reflect actual costs incurred, corresponding to those of an efficient and structurally comparable network operator while giving an appropriate return on investment. There is a possibility for regulating authorities to approve other market-based tariff arrangements, such as auctions. According to Article 13, the tariffs applied must contribute to efficient gas trade and competition while avoiding cross-subsidisation between network users, providing incentives for investment and maintaining or creating interoperability for transmission networks. Equally, tariffs for network access must not restrict market liquidity nor distort cross-border trade between different transmission systems. If a system operator offers the same service to different customers, it must be on the same terms and conditions.

System operators are subject to a number of requirements with regard to non-discrimination. Also, as part of the fulfilment of the aim of transparency, system operators must make public detailed information regarding the services they offer and the relevant conditions applied, together with the technical information necessary for network users to gain effective network access; *see* Article 18(1).

The Regulation also imposes special requirements for balancing rules and imbalance charges and trading of capacity rights.

Pursuant to Article 41(6) of the Natural Gas Directive, the regulatory authorities are responsible for fixing transmission tariffs or the methodologies used to calculate tariffs.

2.2.3.2 *Direct Lines*

Article 38 of the Natural Gas Directive contains provisions on the establishment of direct lines. According to this, Member States must take measures to enable natural gas undertakings established within their territory to supply their customers through a direct line so that any customer within their territory can be supplied through a direct line by natural gas undertakings.[203]

Where a Member State requires authorisation to establish or operate direct lines, the criteria for the grant of authorisation must be objective, transparent and non-discriminatory.

Member States can grant permission to establish a direct line if network access has been refused on the basis of Article 35 or if a dispute resolution procedure has been initiated under Article 41.

In contrast to the Electricity Directive (Article 34(3)), the Natural Gas Directive does not explicitly provide that the possibility of supplying natural gas via a direct line should not affect the possibility of using a third-party arrangement. It has been argued by *Friedrich von Burchard* [204] that this means that the Member States could introduce a rule that the possibility of establishing a direct line should exclude the possibility of third-party access. This argument is rejected by *Moen & Dyrland*,[205] among other things, on the grounds that third-party access is the primary rule in the Natural Gas Directive, whereas the establishment of direct lines is secondary and can be made conditional on refusal of access to the existing network.

2.2.3.3 Transit

Up until 1 July 2004, Directive 91/296/EEC on the transit of natural gas through grids governed access to the overall high-pressure network for natural gas transmission. Since then, access to transmission networks has been governed by the general provisions of the Natural Gas Directive and, since 1 July 2006, by the Regulation on conditions for access to the natural gas transmission networks, as discussed above (originally Regulation (EC) No 1775/2005).

2.2.4 Public Service Obligations

Under Article 3 of the Natural Gas Directive, with regard to the general economic interest, Member States may impose public service obligations on undertakings operating in the gas sector which may relate to security, including security of supply, regularity, quality and price of supplies, and environmental protection, including energy efficiency and climate protection. Such obligations must be clearly defined, transparent, non-discriminatory, and verifiable. Furthermore, any subsequent changes to them must be notified every two years to the Commission.

This makes it possible for Member States to use long-term planning as a means for ensuring the fulfilment of public service obligations in relation to security of supply.

---

203. According to its wording, the provision only covers 'privileged' customers. However, since 1 Jul. 2007, all customers have been 'privileged'; *see* Art. 37 of the Natural Gas Directive.
204. *Friedrich von Burchard:* Netzzugang im Bereich der Gasversorgung, in *Jürgen Schwarze* (ed.): Der Netzzugang für Dritte im Wirtschaftsrecht, 1999 p. 201.
205. *Ketil Bøe Moen & Sondre Dyrland:* EU's gassmarkedsdirektiv, 2001 pp. 130–131.

However, accounts should also be taken of the possibility that third parties may seek access to the system.

In relation to distribution, Member States can derogate from the provisions in Article 4 (on objective and non-discriminatory criteria for authorisation procedures) if the application of these provisions would, in law or in fact, hinder the performance of the obligations imposed on natural gas undertakings in the general economic interest, and where the development of trade is not affected to such an extent as to be contrary to the interests of the Union; *see* Article 3(10).

Article 3(3) of the Natural Gas Directive contains a provision on *universal services*. According to this provision, Member States must take appropriate measures to protect final customers and to ensure high levels of consumer protection. In particular, they must ensure that there are adequate safeguards to protect vulnerable customers. In this context, the Member States can take appropriate measures to protect customers (end users) in remote areas who are connected to the gas system.[206] For this purpose, Member States can appoint a supplier of last resort for customers connected to the gas network. The Member States can thus impose on distribution undertakings or suppliers an obligation to supply to customers in a given area and/or of a particular category. Tariffs for such supplies can also be regulated, for example, by ensuring equal treatment of the customers concerned. Compared with the equivalent provision in the Electricity Directive, consumer protection seems weak. Clearly, natural gas is not considered to be as essential a service as electricity.

The provisions are supplemented by Regulation (EU) concerning measures to safeguard security of natural gas supply which, in Articles 7–8(1), requires Member States to comply with *security of gas supply standards* for ensuring protection for customers' supply to an appropriate extent, at least in the event of a partial disruption of national gas supplies during a nationally determined peak periods and periods of exceptionally high gas demand during the coldest weather periods.

2.2.5 *Technical Harmonisation*

Under Article 8 of the Natural Gas Directive, Member States must ensure that technical safety criteria are defined and that technical rules establishing the minimum technical design and operational requirements for connection to the system of LNG facilities, storage facilities, other transmission or distribution systems, and direct lines, are developed and made public. These technical rules must ensure the interoperability of systems and shall be objective and non-discriminatory. They must be notified to the Commission in accordance with Article 8 of Directive 98/34/EC, laying down a procedure for the provision of information in the field of technical standards and regulations and of rules on Information Society Services.

---

206. Article 3(4) of the Natural Gas Directive includes an obligation to take measures to address energy poverty. This must be seen as an expression that electricity supply is a basic welfare service.

2.2.6 Transparency

The first Directive on price transparency[207] was introduced together with Directive 91/296/EEC on the transit of natural gas through grids as part of the first phase of the liberalisation of the electricity sector. The current Regulation. According to its whereas-clause, the purpose of the Regulation is to enable the development of the Union's energy policy and monitor the energy markets of the Member States. Article 3 requires Member States to collect data on prices of natural gas and electricity and their components and sub-components regarding network costs, taxes, charges, duties, and consumption quantity.

2.2.7 Public Authorities

Under Article 21(1) of the first Natural Gas Directive, Member States had to ensure that parties negotiated for network access in good faith and that no party abused its negotiating position to prevent a positive outcome of the negotiations. The Directive did not include a specific requirement for the appointment of a regulatory authority. However, such a provision was introduced in the second Natural Gas Directive and is now in Article 39 of the third and current Natural Gas Directive.

Pursuant to Article 39 of the Directive, the regulatory authority must exercise its powers impartially and transparently. Member States must ensure that regulatory authorities are legally distinct and functionally independent from any other public or private entity; that their staff and management act independently from any market interest, and do not seek or take direct instructions from any government or other public or private entity when carrying out their regulatory tasks. Moreover, Member States must ensure that regulatory authorities can take autonomous decisions independently from any political body, with separate annual budget allocations, autonomy in the implementation of the allocated budget, and adequate human and financial resources to carry out their duties.

Regulatory authorities also have general responsibility for ensuring non-discrimination, effective competition and the efficient functioning of the market.

Pursuant to Article 41 of the Directive, the duties of regulatory authorities include:

- fixing or approving, in accordance with transparent criteria, transmission or distribution tariffs or their methodologies;
- ensuring compliance of transmission and DSOs, and where relevant, system owners, as well as of any natural gas undertakings, with their obligations under the Directive;

---

207. Directive 90/377/EEC concerning a Community procedure to improve the transparency of gas and electricity prices charged to industrial end-users. This Directive has now been replaced by Regulation (EU) 2016/1952 on European statistics on natural gas and electricity prices, which is discussed in s. 1.4.8.

- cooperating in regard to cross-border issues with the regulatory authorities of the Member States concerned and with the Agency;
- submitting annual reports;
- ensuring that there are no cross-subsidies between transmission, distribution, storage, LNG and supply activities;
- monitoring and evaluating the investment plans of the TSOs;
- monitoring compliance with network security and reliability rules;
- monitoring the level of transparency, including of wholesale prices;
- monitoring the occurrence of restrictive contractual practices, including exclusivity clauses;
- monitoring and reviewing the access conditions to storage, line pack and other ancillary services; and
- ensuring access to customer consumption data.

The regulatory authority also acts as a dispute resolution authority. In particular, this task covers disputes concerning the conditions for and denial of network access within the scope of the application of the Directive. The regulatory authority must decide within two months of receiving a complaint. This period can be extended by up to two months if the regulatory authority needs further information. This period can be extended further with the agreement of the complainant. Such a decision has a binding effect unless and until it is reversed on appeal. Bringing a complaint before the regulatory authority does not exclude the application of other legal remedies in accordance with Union law.

Article 30 of the Natural Gas Directive provides that, to the extent necessary for carrying out their functions, the Member States and the competent authorities designated by them have a right of access to the accounts of natural gas undertakings. These authorities must treat commercially sensitive information as confidential. However, the Member States can provide for the disclosure of such information where this is necessary for the competent authorities to carry out their functions.

2.2.8 *Price Cap*

Gas is traded wholesale in the EU, often on the basis of the pricing of the Dutch TTF (Title Transfer Facility), which is a virtual trading platform for both futures and physical trading of natural gas. It is precisely on futures that the price peaked in the late summer of 2022, although the season did not invite such a demand. The high prices of the time can be explained by the risk of future scarcity of natural gas and the circumstance that trading of futures invites precisely market speculation.

While this manuscript is being prepared, it is being discussed whether price caps or similar measures on natural gas should be introduced. The reason has been the very large price increases of natural gas and its consequences for consumers. However, how long and how large the price increases will be in the long term is highly uncertain. It is debatable whether a market intervention is needed or if there is a need for financial aid for energy consumers. Furthermore, joint EU purchases of gas should be in respect of the rules of competition. This discussion will not be part of this chapter.

A price cap is not unproblematic. It can lead to a decrease in gas deliveries if the suppliers have the opportunity to sell elsewhere. This is particularly relevant in relation to LNG, but piped gas can also be diverted if there are or can be created alternative pipe connections or access to LNG facilities.[208]

3 TRANSPORT

Transport is one of the original policy areas of the Union. Article 90 TFEU, in Title VI – Transport, states: 'The objectives of the Treaties shall, in matters governed by this Title, be pursued within the framework of a common transport policy'. At a general level, transport can be divided between land, sea and air transport. The EU has issued legislation in all three areas. The sectors chosen for study in this chapter, air transport and railways, thus represent only part of the total body of EU regulation on transport.

Article 58(1) TFEU states that 'Freedom to provide services in the field of transport shall be governed by the provisions of the Title relating to transport.' This refers to Articles 90–100 TFEU. This provision does not prevent the Treaty provisions on the other freedoms applying to the area of transport.[209] This primarily means that restrictions on domestic traffic are not covered by the provisions on the free movement of services. As long as it has not otherwise been provided for in secondary legislation, Member States are thus free to regulate the right to offer services in this area, including granting exclusive rights. However, the grant of exclusive rights to a company which is clearly not able to meet the demand could constitute an abuse of a dominant position.[210]

Article 91 TFEU gives authority to lay down special provisions in this area:

1. For the purpose of implementing Article 90, and taking into account the distinctive features of transport, the European Parliament and the Council shall, acting in accordance with the ordinary legislative procedure and after consulting the Economic and Social Committee and the Committee of the Regions, lay down:
   a. common rules applicable to international transport to or from the territory of a Member State or passing across the territory of one or more Member States;
   b. the conditions under which non-resident carriers may operate transport services within a Member State;
   c. measures to improve transport safety;
   d. any other appropriate provisions.
2. When the measures referred to in paragraph 1 are adopted, account shall be taken of cases where their application might seriously affect the standard of living and level of employment in certain regions, and the operation of transport facilities.

---

208. For further information on the development, *see*, for example, EUI Florence School of Regulation - https://fsr.eui.eu/a-price-cap-on-eu-gas-markets/.
209. *See* the judgment of the CJ of 23 Apr. 1991 in Case C-466/98, *Commission v. United Kingdom*, para. 40; Case C-467/98, *Commission v. Denmark*, para. 123; Case C-468/98, *Commission v. Sweden*, para. 114; Case C-469/98, *Commission v. Finland*, para. 119; Case C-471/98, *Commission v. Belgium*, para. 132; Case C-472/98, *Commission v. Luxembourg*, para. 123; Case C-475/98, *Commission v. Austria*, para. 131; and Case C-476/98, *Commission v. Germany*, para. 145.
210. Case C-41/90, *Höfner*, para. 31; and *see Hans Petter Graver* in Lov og Rett, 2006 p. 593.

Article 91 TFEU has been used as authority for issuing a number of directives for the railway sector.

Also, under Article 100(2) TFEU, the European Parliament and the Council may 'lay down appropriate provisions for sea and air transport. They shall act after consulting the Economic and Social Committee and the Committee of the Regions'. This division of the area of transport can be seen as a recognition that sea and air transport are already regulated by a large number of international agreements. This provision has been particularly applicable to air transport.

The Union's competition rules now apply to the whole area of transport, including air transport.[211]

The procedural rules are in Regulation (EC) No 1/2003 on the implementation of the rules on competition laid down in Articles 81 and 82 of the Treaty (now Articles 101 and 102 TFEU).

Previously, the transport sector differed in that the general Regulation No 17/62 did not apply to it. Thus, Article 1 of Regulation No 141/62 stated that the transport sector was not covered by Regulation No 17/62.

3.1 Air Transport

In the years following the Second World War, European air transport developed through cooperation between the authorities and the air transport companies. There was a need for public involvement in civil airports, which would sometimes share their facilities with military air bases. The public authorities often favoured one particular airline which may have been wholly or partly owned by the state – the so-called *flag carrier*. Among other things, this gave rise to a number of bilateral agreements between states, under which a particular international route would be served by one airline from each of the parties to the agreement – a duopoly. Such agreements often included market-sharing and pricing agreements.[212]

Since 1944, international air transport has been covered by the Chicago Convention (Convention on International Civil Aviation). This Convention secured sovereignty over its own airspace for each state. However, the Convention did not succeed in establishing multilateral agreements on the exchange of air transport rights.[213]

Many European airlines still have something of the character of a national flag carrier. These airlines often use one or more of the airports in their home country as a 'hub'. Passengers are flown to these hubs with a view to transiting to other destinations. This is the 'hub and spoke' system.[214]

---

211. Joined Cases 209 to 213/84, *Lucas Asjes and others* (the *Nouvelles Frontières* case).
212. *See* Ben van Houtte: *Air Transport*, in Damien Geradin (ed.): *The Liberalization of State Monopolies in the European Union and Beyond*, p. 67-97 (2000).
213. The Chicago Convention entered into force in 1947, replacing the Paris Convention of 1919 and the Havana Convention of 1928.
214. The Nordic Competition Authorities: *Competitive Airlines. Towards a More Vigorous Competition Policy in Relation to the Air Travel Market*, pp. 5, 13 and 46 (2002).

The Treaty has included transport policy ever since the Treaty of Rome. However, originally, air transport was not included. Liberalisation measures have appeared in several waves. Since 1997, the market within the EU has been totally deregulated.[215] However, in relation to third countries, the market is still characterised by the existence of bilateral agreements, even though attempts have been made to replace these with common EU-wide agreements.

Modern air transport is dependent on the existence of airports which have the necessary facilities for handling aircraft, cargo, passengers and their baggage. Transport will often be between two towns. Where a town can only realistically be served by one airport, that airport can be characterised as an essential facility.[216] At the same time, the hub and spoke system creates a structure like a network with considerable market strength for the company that operates the hub.[217]

Airport capacity is also, to some extent, a limited resource. Modern scheduled traffic arrivals and departures should preferably be scheduled so as to limit the waiting time of transit passengers. However, this leads to peak loading of airports. Airspace is also a limited resource. For safety reasons, aircraft must follow fixed routes. These routes constitute a network whose limited capacity is used by allocating slots. Airspace is under the control of the Member States. The lack of harmonisation and cooperation (e.g., in the form of one or more cross-border network administrators) has meant that, even on short flights between European airports, civil aircraft have to change altitude, change radio wavelength to a new controlling authority, and make major detours. In an attempt to do away with these problems, the Union introduced the Single European Sky initiative.

3.1.1 EU Regulation

The liberalisation of the air transport sector has taken place in stages. There have been three 'packages' with regulation for the sector in 1987, 1990 and 1992. In the first package, the Commission was given the power to act against conduct that restricted competition in the air transport sector in the same way as in other markets. This was the adoption of Regulation (EEC) No 3975/87, laying down the procedure for the application of the rules on competition to undertakings in the air transport sector.[218] The market for international flights within the Union was opened in January 1993. The market was further opened by the second package. The third package, from 1992 with a deadline for implementation in April 2007, introduced, among others, Regulation (EEC) No 2407/92 on licensing of air carriers. With the implementation of the third

---

215. Regarding the development of the EU air transportation regulation, *see* Ivo Van Bael & Jean-Francois Bellis: *Competition Law of the European Community*, p. 1342 ff. (2010).
216. Only the largest urban centres can support two or even three commercial airports. Bailey & Williams, p. 184 (1988).
217. *The Nordic Competition Authorities:* Competitive Airlines. Towards a More Vigorous Competition Policy in Relation to the Air Travel Market, 2002 p. 6, and for a general discussion of the character of networks in the air transport sector, *see* p. 41.
218. This is now regulated in Regulation (EC) No 1/2003.

package, the sector is considered to be liberalised within the EU. The regulation has been amended several times in 2018 and 2020.[219]

Regulation (EEC) No 2407/92, together with Regulation (EEC) No 2408/92 on access for Community air carriers to intra-Community air routes and Regulation (EEC) No 2409/92 on fares and rates for air services, have been gathered together in Regulation (EC) No 1008/2008 on common rules for the operation of air services in the Community.

It is characteristic of the air transport sector that only regulations are used. There is no consolidating or overall market directive. Instead, the sector has been liberalised by using measures which regulate specific elements, primarily concerned with market access, consumer protection and safety. The almost exclusive use of regulations to implement liberalisation has made national implementation by the Member States unnecessary. An overview of the regulation can be found on the website of the EASA.[220]

In particular, in connection with access to airspace, a number of regulations have been issued with the aim of improving the use of airspace and relations between civil and military flights.

See Regulation (EC) No 549/2004 laying down the framework for the creation of the single European sky (the Framework Regulation), Regulation (EC) No 551/2004 on the organisation and use of the airspace in the single European sky (the Airspace Regulation), and Regulation (EC) No 2150/2005 laying down common rules for the flexible use of airspace.

As for market access, among other things, there are rules on computer reservation systems, the issue of licences to air carriers and access to routes within the Union. These issues are discussed below. Safety is regulated by rules on the investigation of civil aviation air accidents and incidents and on the establishment of the EASA. These are also discussed below.

Consumer protection is regulated in particular by:

- Regulation (EC) No 261/2004 establishing common rules on compensation and assistance to passengers in the event of denied boarding and of cancellation or long delay of flights.[221]
- Regulation (EC) No 2027/97 on air carrier liability in the event of accidents, as amended by Regulation (EC) No 889/2002.[222]

There are also special rules on consumer protection in Directive (EU) 2015/2302 on package travel and linked travel arrangements. These will not be subject to detailed study in this chapter.

Regulation (EC) No 261/2004 lays down minimum rules for compensation for passengers with valid tickets and reservations[223] who are turned away because of

---

219. Amended by the Regulations (EU) 2018/1139, 2019/2, 2020/696, 2020/2114, and 2020/2115.
220. https://www.easa.europa.eu/en/regulations/basic-regulation
221. For preliminary cases brought, *see* C-516/23, C-411/23, and C-405/23.
222. *See* the judgment in C-510/21, *Austrian Airlines*.
223. Article 3(3) contains an exception for especially cheap or free tickets that cannot be obtained by the general public.

overbooking, cancellation or extended delays. The provisions apply to passengers for a flight departing from an airport in the EU or passengers flying with an airline based in the EU and flying to an airport situated in the EU.

Overbooking means that the number of passengers with confirmed reservations who have properly checked in by the deadline before departure exceeds the number of places available on the flight in question. This is a normal practice for airlines. This is because there are usually a number of passengers with valid tickets and reservations who do not show up.

Cancellation refers to a flight which is planned but not carried out and for which there is at least one reservation.

Delays are divided into different categories, depending on the length of delay, the duration of the flight, and whether it is within the EU or not. There are consequences when there are delays of more than two to four hours.

The principle with overbooking is that the airline must first try to find volunteers to change their reservation for payment of compensation. Where this is not possible, a passenger who is turned away must be able to choose between a refund for the unused portion of a ticket, transport as soon as possible, and the rerouting of their journey. In addition to this, such passengers are entitled to meals and hotel accommodation, as well as to make two free telephone calls, telefaxes or e-mails. In addition, compensation must be paid for passengers turned away in accordance with the following:

- EUR 250 for flights up to 1,500 km.
- EUR 400 for all flights within the Union of more than 1,500 km and for all other flights between 1,500 and 3,500 km.
- EUR 600 for all other flights.

Such compensation does not exclude claims for other kinds of compensation, such as under Regulation (EC) No 2027/97, as discussed below.

In Case C-344/04, *The Queen on the application of IATA and another v. Department for Transport*, the CJ held that the standard measures prescribed in Article 6 of Regulation No 261/2004 do not prevent the passengers concerned – should a delay also cause them damage giving entitlement to compensation – from being able to bring actions for compensation under the conditions laid down by the Montreal Convention.

In the event of a cancellation, there is a fixed right to a refund, meals and hotel accommodation. However, any compensation depends on whether due notice has been given to passengers and whether any event of force majeure has occurred. There are corresponding rights to meals and hotel accommodation in the event of a delay, and for delays of at least five hours, there is a right to a refund for the unused portion of the ticket. On the contrary, there is no right to compensation for delays.

Airlines have an obligation to inform their passengers of their rights.[224]

---

224. Regulation (EC) No 261/2004 has not been an unqualified success. The Commission has itself stated that, in certain areas, the Regulation is not clearly formulated and enforcement by the Member States has not been all that might be wished. *See* COM(2007) 168 final.

By virtue of an amendment in Regulation (EC) No 889/2002, Regulation (EC) No 2027/97 implements certain uniform rules for international air transport which were agreed in the Montreal Convention in 1999.[225] These provisions relate to liability for death or injury, for goods, delays for passengers or baggage, or loss of or damage to baggage. In principle, national procedures apply to the satisfaction of claims for compensation.

The Regulation and the Convention do not provide any upper limit for liability for compensation in the event of a passenger's death or injury. However, there is a lower limit of 100,000 SDR (special drawing rights), where there is strict liability. Above this level, there is a presumption of liability. There is also a deadline for the payment of an advance on compensation of fifteen days after it is established who is entitled to compensation. In the event of death, the advance must be at least 16,000 SDR.

When passengers are delayed, there is a fixed duty for airlines to pay compensation. The liability is limited to 4,150 SDR. There is also a duty to pay compensation for delays to baggage. However, an airline is not required to pay if it has adopted the necessary measures or if it is impossible to take the necessary measures. Liability for delays to baggage is limited to 1,000 SDR. There is the same limit to liability for destroyed, lost or damaged baggage. For baggage that has been checked-in, there is strict liability unless there are defects in the baggage. For non-checked baggage, there is liability equivalent to the standard for negligence. For damage to checked baggage, passengers must make their claims in writing within seven days and for delays, within twenty-one days from the date on which the baggage was made available to the passenger. There is a deadline of two years from the date on which the flight landed or ought to have landed for bringing a claim for compensation.

At the international level, there are also rules on the payment of compensation in the event of an accident in the Convention for the Unification of Certain Rules Relating to International Carriage by Air, Signed at Warsaw on 12 October 1929, and the amendment to it signed at the Hague on 28 September 1955, as well as the convention entered into on 18 September 1961 in Guadalajara (together called the 'Warsaw Convention'). This applies throughout the world. The introduction of the Montreal Convention's provisions for EU airlines was because the Warsaw Convention's compensation rules were considered too low, given modern economic and social norms.

3.1.1.1 *The Application of the General Competition Rules*

The CJ's decision in Joined Cases 209 to 213/84, *Lucas Asjes and others* (the *Nouvelles Frontières* case) established that Articles 81 and 82 of the EC Treaty also apply to air transport. Air transport now falls under Regulation (EC) No 1/2003.[226]

The general competition rules have been applied in a number of cases. Some of them are discussed in the following.

---

225. OJ 2001 L 194/39.
226. Regulation (EC) No 1/2003 is discussed in detail in Ch. 7. Air transport was previously covered by Regulation (EEC) No 3975/87 laying down the procedure for the application of the rules on competition to undertakings in the air transport sector.

In 2001, SAS and Maersk Air were fined EUR 39,375,000 and EUR 13,125,000, respectively, by the Commission for entering into a secret agreement on market-sharing. This came to light in connection with dealing with the notification of a cooperation agreement between the two companies on code sharing and frequent flyer programmes. In connection with the entry into force of the cooperation agreement, Maersk Air had withdrawn from the Copenhagen-Stockholm route, leaving SAS with a monopoly. Correspondingly, SAS had withdrawn from the Billund-Frankfurt route, leaving Maersk Air with a monopoly. SAS also stopped flying on the Copenhagen-Venice route which Maersk Air had started serving. These measures were an expression of a more comprehensive market-sharing agreement which covered the future flying of both domestic and international routes to and from Denmark. SAS appealed to the GC against the amount of the fine in Case T-241/01.

In Commission Decision 2000/74/EC of 14 July 1999 (IV/D-2/34.780 – *Virgin/British Airways*), where Virgin had brought a claim against British Airways (BA), BA had been fined EUR 6,800,000 for abuse of a dominant position by using loyalty based commission arrangements in trade with travel agents. The commission paid was based on the increase in the travel agents' sales of BA tickets compared with the previous year.

Commission Decision 92/213/EEC of 26 February 1992 (IV/33.544 – *British Midland v. Aer Lingus*) concerned the situation where Aer Lingus had excluded British Midland from interlining cooperation[227] on the Heathrow-Dublin route. This was regarded as an abuse of a dominant position, and Aer Lingus was fined EUR 750,000.[228]

The definition of the relevant market for passenger traffic can give rise to problems. In general, business passengers are more focused on short travelling times and avoiding transit arrangements than tourist passengers. However, the distinction between the two groups of passengers is not clear-cut. Many business travellers are increasingly focusing on price. In this connection, in defining the relevant market for air transport, the Commission has discussed dividing passenger groups on the basis of their focus on time. *See*, for example, the Commission Decision of 11 August 1999 in case M/JV-19 – *KLM-Alitalia*, paragraph 21, and the Commission Decision of 12 January 2001 in case M.2041 – *United Airlines/US Airways*, paragraph 18. However, in neither of these cases did the Commission find that such a definition was decisive. As for transit (one-stop) as an alternative to direct connections (non-stop), this distinction is most relevant on shorter routes. *See* Commission Decision of 12.1.2001 in case M.2041 – *United Airlines/US Airways*, paragraphs 13–17, and Commission Decision 2002/746/EC of 5 July 2002 (COMP/37.730 – *Austrian Airlines/Lufthansa*), paragraph 53.

Regulation (EC) No 487/2009 3976/87 of 25 May 2009 on the application of Article 81(3) of the Treaty to certain categories of agreements and concerted practices in the air transport sector has given the Commission authority to issue block exemptions regulations in accordance with Article 101(3) TFEU. According to Article 2(1), the Commission may adopt such regulations in respect of agreements, decisions or concerted practices concerning any of the following:

(a) joint planning and coordination of airline schedules;
(b) consultations on tariffs for the carriage of passengers and baggage and of freight on scheduled air services;

---

227. This means the possibility of one airline issuing tickets for the flights of another airline. This enables passengers to travel with a single set of documents between two destinations which are not served by a single airline, either directly or by changing flights, enabling the passenger to travel more quickly by taking the first flight, regardless of which airline is flying.
228. OJ 1992 L 96/34.

(c) joint operations on new, less busy scheduled air services;
(d) slot allocation at airports and airport scheduling; the Commission shall take care to ensure consistency with Council Regulation (EEC) No 95/93 of 18 January 1993 on common rules for the allocation of slots at Community airports;
(e) common purchase, development and operation of computer reservation systems relating to timetabling, reservations and ticketing by air transport undertakings; the Commission shall take care to ensure consistency with Council Regulation (EEC) No 2299/89 of 24 July 1989 on a code of conduct for computerised reservation systems.

The most important of these block exemption regulations was Regulation (EEC) No 1617/93 on the application of Article 85(3) of the Treaty to certain categories of agreements and concerted practices concerning joint planning and coordination of schedules, joint operations, consultations on passenger and cargo tariffs on scheduled air services and slot allocation at airports.[229] Following its latest amendment (by Regulation (EC) No 1105/2002), the Regulation expired on 30 June 2005. It was replaced by Regulation (EC) No 1459/2006 on the application of Article 81(3) of the EC Treaty (now Article 101(3) TFEU) to certain categories of agreements and concerted practices concerning consultations on passenger tariffs on scheduled air services and slot allocation at airports. This was a transitional regulation, various parts of it expiring at the end of 2006 and other parts expiring in the course of 2007.

There have been other block exemption regulations. Regulation (EEC) No 2671/88 on certain categories of agreements between undertakings, decisions of associations of undertakings and concerted practices concerning joint planning and coordination of capacity, sharing of revenue and consultations on tariffs on scheduled air services and slot allocation at airports, Regulation (EEC) No 2672/88 on certain categories of agreements between undertakings relating to computer reservation systems for air transport services, and Regulation (EEC) No 2673/88 on certain categories of agreements between undertakings, decisions of associations of undertakings and concerted practices concerning ground handling services all expired on 31 January 1991.

The Treaty rules on State aid are also generally applicable to the air transport sector. The Commission has issued Community guidelines on the financing of airports and start-up aid to airlines serving regional airports.[230]

In Commission Decision 2003/637/EC of 30 April 2003 on State aid from Austria to Austrian air carriers, certain forms of State aid were considered to be covered by Article 107(2)(b) TFEU (then Article 87(2)(b) of the EC Treaty), to make good the damage caused by natural disasters or exceptional circumstances, following the closing of airspace for some time after the terrorist attacks of 11 September 2001. However, a number of losses in the following period, which were only indirectly related to the closure of the airspace, could not be compensated for.

In Commission Decision 2003/196/EC of 11 December 2002 concerning a State aid scheme which France proposed to implement to assist French airlines, the Commission referred to its own Communication of 10 October 2001[231] on the repercussions of the terrorist attacks in the USA on the air transport industry, stating that the terrorist events of 11 September 2001 could qualify as exceptional circumstances in accordance with Article

---

229. This included *interlining* – *see* the definition above.
230. OJ 2005 C 312/1.
231. COM(2001) 574 final.

87(2)(b) of the EC Treaty (now Article 107(2)(b) TFEU). In this case, it was clear that the security measures made it more difficult for airlines to operate. However, the extra costs involved in this did not fall within the terms of the Treaty provision. Since the Commission found that the State aid in question was too much, the arrangement in question was found to be incompatible with the Treaty.

In its judgment of 13 May 2015 in Case T-511/09, *Austrian Airlines Group*, the GC upheld Commission Decision 2010/137/EC of 28 August 2009 on State aid C 6/09 (ex N 6663/08) on a restructuring plan under which the Austrian state granted restructuring aid to the Austrian Airlines Group in the context of a takeover by the Lufthansa Group. The sale had been made at a negative price corresponding to the State aid. However, this was compatible with Article 87(3)(c) EC (now Article 107(3)(c) TFEU), on aid to facilitate the development of certain economic activities or of certain economic areas, where such aid does not adversely affect trading conditions to an extent contrary to the common interest. See also C-164/15, Aer Lingus, and T-500/12, Ryanair, on recovery and T-358/94, Air France, on aid financed by voluntary contributions.

3.1.1.2 Bilateral Agreements

Air traffic between the Union and third countries is, to a certain extent, regulated by bilateral agreements between the two countries between which the flights are made. It is not contrary to EU law for individual Member States to enter into such agreements, but they cannot enter into agreements which breach the competition rules of the EC Treaty.[232] This was the case in a number of decisions which the CJ decided on 5 November 2002 concerning the infringement of the right of establishment when entering into a bilateral 'open skies' agreement between a number of Member States and the USA.[233]

Towards the end of and after the Second World War, a number of countries which subsequently became Member States of the EU entered into bilateral agreements with the USA on air traffic; these were referred to as the Bermuda Agreements. In 1992, the USA took the initiative to enter into new bilateral agreements with as many of the EU's Member States as possible. These agreements included free access to all air routes, unlimited route and traffic rights, and the possibility of agreeing to common codes. Moreover, the agreements contained a provision whereby the USA could refuse to issue licences or technical approval to airlines which may have been designated by a Member State but where a significant part of the ownership of the airline was not held by, and effective control was not exercised by the citizens of that Member State. Previously granted licences or technical approval could be revoked, suspended or restricted. Such measures could not be taken against airlines whose control rested with the Member State in question or its citizens.

In these cases, it was argued that the provisions in Article 351 TFEU (then Article 234 of the EC Treaty) applied, under which the rights and obligations arising from agreements concluded before 1 January 1958 or, for acceding States, before the date of their accession, between one or more Member States on the one hand, and one or more third countries on the other, are not affected by the provisions of the then EC Treaty. The CJ rejected this argument

---

232. Case C-66/86, *Ahmed Saeed;* and The Nordic Competition Authorities: *Competitive Airlines. Towards a More Vigorous Competition Policy in Relation to the Air Travel Market*, p. 29 (2002).
233. Case C-467/98, *Commission v. Denmark;* Case C-468/98, *Commission v. Sweden;* Case C-469/98, *Commission v. Finland;* Case C-471/98, *Commission v. Belgium;* Case C-472/98, *Commission v. Luxembourg;* Case C-475/98, *Commission v. Austria;* and Case C-476/98, *Commission v. Germany.*

on the basis that in all cases there had been later amendments which 'replaced' the agreements previously entered into, even though these previous agreements contained similar clauses.

As for freedom of establishment in Article 49 TFEU (previously Article 52 of the EC Treaty), the CJ found that the clause in the bilateral agreements which gave the USA the right to exclude EU airlines that were not controlled by the Member State in question or its citizens was contrary to Article 49 TFEU.[234]

Regulation (EC) No 847/2004 on the negotiation and implementation of air service agreements between Member States and third countries sets out the conditions under which Member States can enter into negotiations with third countries on new air transport agreements or amendments to existing agreements. Among other things, there is a requirement to notify the Commission and a prohibition on the introduction of more restrictive agreements than those existing. It is a general wish of the Commission that common EU agreements should be made in this area.

The possibility of taking action against State aid from third countries is governed by Regulation (EU) 2019/712 on safeguarding competition in air transport.

3.1.1.3 Pricing Regulation

Regulation (EC) No 1008/2008 on common rules for the operation of air services in the Community provides that airlines can freely set their own prices; *see* Article 22(1).

However, under public service obligations referred to in Article 16, it is still possible for a Member State to lay down requirements with regard to pricing.

3.1.2 Authorisation Procedures

Regulation (EC) No 1008/2008 on common rules for the operation of air services in the Community requires airlines established in the Union to be licensed. Thus, an undertaking that is established in the Union may only carry air passengers, mail and/or cargo for remuneration and/or hire if the undertaking has been granted the appropriate operating license; *see* Article 3(3). The Regulation does not cover carriage by air of passengers, mail and/or cargo, performed by non-power-driven aircraft and/or ultra-light power-driven aircraft, or local flights not involving carriage between different airports (round trips). In respect of these, Member States are free to introduce national authorisation requirements or not. The possession of a licence is important for access to a network; *see* below.

The authority to issue a licence lies with the Member States. The Regulation provides that, as a condition for issuing or renewing a licence, an undertaking's principal place of business and its registered office, if any, must be located in the licensing Member State, and its main occupation must be air transport, in isolation or combined with any other commercial operation of aircraft or repair and maintenance of aircraft; *see* Article 4. It is also a requirement under Article 4(f) that a majority of the

---

234. The Commission has described the consequences of the decisions in these cases in COM(2002) 649 final.

undertaking is owned and continues to be owned by Member States and/or nationals of Member States, subject to agreements and conventions to which the Union is a contracting party. There is an exemption for existing airlines which have been given special dispensation under previous legislation. Decisions to grant or revoke operating licences must be published in the Official Journal of the European Communities; *see* Article 10(3) of the Directive.

In Article 5, there are special provisions to ensure that licensed airlines have sufficient financial solidity for their operations to be carried out properly. This includes submitting audited annual accounts and informing the licensing authority of new routes. Accident insurance cover is also required in order to obtain a licence; *see* Article 11.

Article 12 of the Regulation prevents a Member State from making ownership of aircraft a condition for granting or maintaining an operating licence, but a Member State may require that a licensed air carrier has one or more aircraft at its disposal.

Under the Regulation on air navigation services in the single European sky,[235] all forms of air services in the Union are subject to certification by the Member States. *See* also Regulation (EC) No 1794/2006, laying down a common charging scheme for air navigation services, and Directive 91/670/EEC on mutual acceptance of personnel licences for the exercise of functions in civil aviation.

3.1.3 Network Access

The main provisions on network access are in Regulation (EC) No 1008/2008 on common rules for the operation of air services in the Community. The Regulation deals with both scheduled flights and charter flights, but only scheduled flights within the Union. The Regulation distinguishes between Community air carriers[236] and others. According to Article 15 of the Regulation, only Community air carriers can have traffic rights on routes within the Union.

> In Case C-92/01, *Stylianakis v. Elliniko Dimosio*, the CJ held that Article 3(1) of Regulation (EEC) No 2408/92 (now Article 15(1) in Regulation (EC) No 1008/2008) prevents measures being taken by a Member State whereby flights to other Member States are generally subject to higher airport taxes than those which are imposed on domestic flights in the Member State in question, unless it can be shown that the taxes relate to services provided at the airports which are necessary for passengers, and the costs of services for passengers travelling to other Member States are higher than the costs of the services which are necessary for passengers on domestic routes.

---

235. Regulation (EC) No 550/2004 on the provision of air navigation services in the single European sky.
236. A 'Community air carrier' is defined as an air carrier with a valid operating licence granted by a competent licensing authority in accordance with Chapter II of Regulation (EC) No 1008/2008; *see* Art. 2(11) of the Regulation.

When there is serious congestion or environmental problems, the Member State concerned can restrict traffic; *see* Article 20. This may not lead to discrimination or unreasonable distortion of competition.

Access to routes between the EU and third countries is regulated bilaterally. The conditions for being able to open a route are linked to a nationality criterion. There are no reciprocity conditions at the EU level.[237]

Fees for overflying, etc., are harmonised through Regulation (EC) No 1794/2006, laying down a common charging scheme for air navigation services. This lays down the guiding principles for the calculation of fees for overflying and entry into airspace.

Airspace constitutes an overall 'network' for air traffic. Without access to airspace, services cannot be provided. Regulation (EC) No 549/2004, laying down the framework for the creation of the single European sky (the framework Regulation), was adopted in accordance with the Union's goal of establishing an internal market. This Regulation starts from the position that airspace is a limited resource which must be regulated in order to achieve its effective exploitation. Article 6 of Regulation (EC) No 551/2004 on the organisation and use of the airspace in the single European sky (the airspace Regulation) provides for an air traffic management (ATM) network in the form of an authority responsible for ATM. This function is the responsibility of Eurocontrol (www.eurocontrol.int/). More detailed provisions are laid down in Regulation (EU) No 677/2011, laying down detailed rules for the implementation of ATM network functions and amending Regulation (EU) No 691/2010.

There is a special network problem related to the allocation of slots. Flag carriers have traditionally been allocated the most sought-after slots (an equally limited resource) in their home airport(s). They are allowed to renew these from year to year, provided that their use of them has been above 80%; *see* Articles 8 and 10 of Regulation (EEC) No 95/93 on common rules for the allocation of slots at Community airports.[238] These are referred to as 'grandfathered rights'. Since in most of the major airports there are only a limited number of slots available, it can be difficult for other operators to obtain attractive landing and take-off rights, which makes it difficult for new operators to penetrate the market. This is why terms which deal with the allocation of slots are so important in merger decisions. The provision can give airlines incentives to keep flying on otherwise unprofitable routes in order to prevent competitors from taking over desirable slots.

Regulation (EEC) No 95/93 contains rules for the allocation of slots at Community airports. Certain airports are designated as coordinated airports or fully coordinated airports. This involves the appointment of airport coordinators. To some extent, it is possible for individual

---

237. *P.J.G. Kapteyn & P. VerLoren van Themaat:* Introduction to the Law of the European Communities, 1998 pp. 1202–1203.
238. A special Art. 10a was previously inserted in Regulation (EC) No 894/2002 amending Council Regulation (EEC) No 95/93 on common rules for the allocation of slots at Community airports, under which air carriers were entitled to the same slots during for the summer of 2002 and winter of 2002/2003 as had been allocated to them as of 11 Sep. 2001 for summer 2001 and winter 2001/2002.

airlines to exchange slots, to transfer them within the same corporate group in connection with a merger, or to use them for other routes or other kinds of flights; see Article 8 of the Regulation. This possibility can give the allocated slots the character of a valuable asset.

Computerised reservation systems used in the airline industry can also be characterised as essential facilities. In this area, Regulation (EC) No 80/2009 on a Code of Conduct for computerised reservation systems applies.

A computerised reservation system is a system which contains information about, among other things, airline timetables, spare capacity, ticket prices and associated services. There can be associated services for making reservations or issuing tickets; see Article 2. In the Nordic countries, the Amadeus system is widely used.

According to Article 3 of Regulation (EC) No 80/2009, there is a prohibition on unreasonable conditions, on requiring customers to take other services (tied sales), on requirements for exclusive arrangements and on the payment of commission for promoting the sales of tickets of a particular airline. There are equivalent rules for parent carriers in Article 10. Under Article 8, it is possible to exclude non-EU airlines from such systems if the company or the third country from which it comes does not allow corresponding access to their computerised reservation system. There is, thus, a level of reciprocity.

Another essential facility is *ground handling*.[239] Major airlines often have their own ground-handling services. When there is only one ground handling company at a given airport, it will both have a dominant position and it will also often represent vertical integration. The independent airlines will thus become the customers of their competitors, with the risk of abuse of a dominant position. Directive 96/67/EC lays down the framework for the restrictions which the Member States can introduce on the right to provide these services, including the airlines' own provision of these services.

Bonus flying arrangements constitute a special problem in competition law. This refers to the giving of special points in connection with the purchase of flights. These points can later be redeemed for other flights, hotel accommodation, etc. Their existence can act as a barrier to the entry of new market participants.[240] In some cases, access to a programme has been used to reduce the effect of these programmes on restricting competition.[241] See the Commission's Decision of 16 January 1996 on the cooperation between SAS and Lufthansa.

---

239. The term covers a long list of activities that are carried out in airports in connection with the arrival and departure of aircraft, including dealing with passengers, goods and mail, as well as a number of tasks related to aircraft. The term is defined in more detail in Directive 96/67/EC on access to the ground handling market at Community airports.
240. An example of this is Eurobonus, which is a programme run by SAS. In Norway there is a prohibition on the earning of any form of bonus points, and in Sweden there is a prohibition on giving bonus points on domestic routes which are served by more than one airline.
241. *See* Commission Decision of 16 January 1996 on Case IV/35.545 – *Lufthansa/SAS*. For a review of the problem *see Susanne Storm:* Air Transport Policies and Frequent Flyer Programmes in the European Community – a Scandinavian Perspective, Unit of Tourism Research at Research Center Bornholm, Report No 14/1999.

3.1.4 Public Obligations

According to Article 16(1) of Regulation (EC) No 1008/2008 on common rules for the operation of air services in the Community, a Member State may impose a public service obligation for the provision of scheduled air services serving a peripheral or development region in its territory or on a thin route. It is a requirement that the route must be vital for the economic development of the region in question. The provision has the character of a universal service. The obligation can relate to matters such as continuity, regularity, capacity and pricing. The imposition of the obligation is subject to prior consultations with the other Member States concerned and after having informed the Commission and the airports and air carriers already operating on the route. The Commission will publish the existence of the public service obligation in the Official Journal of the European Communities. There is a requirement to use a tendering process and a possibility of making compensation for the provision of the public service.

The Community guidelines on financing of airports and start-up aid to airlines departing from regional airports (OJ 2005 C 312/1) apply when assessing the compatibility of State aid with the EU's State aid rules.

3.1.5 Technical Standards

Regulation (EEC) No 3922/91 on the harmonisation of technical requirements and administrative procedures in the field of civil aviation implemented the Union's joint aviation requirements (JARs) for technical safety standards. The JARs are prepared by the Joint Aviation Authorities (JAA), which is a group of European civil aviation authorities. The JARs have led to the harmonisation of standards for, among other things, the approval and certification of airline personnel, aircraft and airlines. In 2004 and 2007, the JAA stopped being responsible for tasks relating to aviation skills and tasks on operational questions and certification of personnel, as these tasks were taken over by the EASA, which is an EU agency.[242]

Further standards have been adopted by the European Parliament and the Council under the authority of Article 100(2) TFEU.

According to Articles 6 and 7 of Regulation (EEC) No 3922/91, an aircraft that is operated under a licence from one Member State in accordance with the common technical standards and administrative procedures can be operated under the same conditions in the other Member States, without further technical requirements or evaluations by another Member State. The Member States must recognise the certification granted under the Regulation by another Member State or by a body acting on its behalf, to bodies or persons under its jurisdiction and under its authority, who are concerned with the design, manufacture and maintenance of products and the operation of aircraft.

---

242. Regulation (EU) 2018/1139 of the European Parliament and of the Council of 4 Jul. 2018 on common rules in the field of civil aviation and establishing a EASA. The JAA is now responsible for a training office and for contacts with JAA members in non-EU countries. For a more detailed review of the rules of the two organisations *see* https://jaato.com/ and http://www.easa.europa.eu/.

The European Organisation for the Safety of Air Navigation (Eurocontrol)[243] is the body which, in accordance with the International Convention Relating to Co-operation for the Safety of Air Navigation, is appointed to adopt the necessary measures to solve safety problems in relation to European air traffic. It draws up the Eurocontrol standards which constitute the obligatory elements concerning the physical properties, form, materials, performance, personnel and procedural issues whose uniform application is recognised as being of significant importance for the implementation of an integrated system of air traffic services.

> There has been a CJ decision on whether Eurocontrol should be considered as a public authority or a private undertaking. This was in Case 364/92, *Eurocontrol*, where the CJ found that the tasks of the organisation concerning control and safety were typically the tasks of public bodies. The case arose over a complaint of abuse of a dominant position in connection with Eurocontrol's pricing of route charges.[244]

In Article 3 of the now repealed Directive 93/65/EEC on the definition and use of compatible technical specifications for the procurement of equipment and systems for air traffic management, the Commission was authorised to use special procedures to adopt the Eurocontrol standards and subsequent Eurocontrol amendments to those Eurocontrol standards, compliance with which was mandatory under Community law. However, Directive 93/65/EEC only dealt with the obligations of procurement authorities, and for this reason, it has been replaced by the Interoperability Regulation,[245] which also concerns the obligations of air navigation service providers, airspace users, industry and airports. In its Annex II, the Regulation lists requirements for a number of essential systems and procedures which must be complied with in the European air traffic system. It is also possible to lay down Community specifications, possibly in the form of obligatory standards or by the new method. There is also a requirement for the use of an EC declaration of conformity or suitability for the use of constituents linked to the Regulation.

3.1.6 Safety

Regulation (EU) No 996/2010 lays down requirements for the investigation of every accident or serious incident. The Member States are responsible for this.

Regulation (EU) No 376/2014 on the reporting, analysis and follow-up of occurrences in civil aviation established a framework for reporting occurrences such as operational interruptions, defects, faults or other irregular circumstances that have or

---

243. http://www.eurocontrol.int.
244. The case is commented on in Niels van Antwerpen: *The Single European Sky, Air & Space Law*, Vol. 27/2 (2002).
245. Regulation (EC) No 552/2004 on the interoperability of the European Air Traffic Management network.

may have influenced flight safety without resulting in an accident or serious incident covered by Directive 94/56/EC. The Directive requires the Member States to introduce an obligatory reporting system. Databases must be established for recording the information assembled. All bodies that are responsible for making rules for civil aviation safety or for investigating air accidents or serious incidents in the Union have access to these databases.

The European rules are, to some extent, the implementation of common European rules established by the Cyprus Agreement of 1990 on joint European aviation requirements. This set up the JAA which has laid down safety requirements. The Chicago Convention also contains provisions on safety requirements. For a more detailed discussion of safety requirements, see *Manuhutu* 2000.

The Commission has special powers to ban air carriers from operating in European airspace. *See* Regulation (EC) No 2111/2005 on the establishment of a Community list of air carriers subject to an operating ban within the Community and on informing air transport passengers of the identity of the operating air carrier, and repealing Article 9 of Directive 2004/36/EC; and Regulation (EC) No 474/2006 establishing the Community list of air carriers which are subject to an operating ban within the Community referred to in Chapter II of Regulation (EC) No 2111/2005 of the European Parliament and of the Council. Finally, Regulation (EC) No 300/2008 on common rules in the field of civil aviation security establishes common rules in the field of civil aviation security, the main objective of which is to establish and implement appropriate Union measures to prevent acts of unlawful interference (e.g., terrorism) against civil aviation. The common basic standards for air security are based on the current recommendations of the European Civil Aviation Conference (ECAC) and are laid down in detail in an Annex to the Regulation. Each Member State is responsible for preparing and implementing a national security training programme for civil aviation and must ensure that the airports and airlines that provide services from that State prepare, implement and maintain appropriate security programmes for such airports and airlines in order to fulfil the national security programme for civil aviation. These programmes must be laid before the supervisory authority for approval and are monitored by that authority.

Pursuant to Regulation (EC) No 300/2008 (or its predecessors), the Commission has issued Regulation (EU) No 2015/1998 of 5 November 2015, laying down detailed measures for the implementation of the common basic standards on aviation security.

Special insurance requirements are laid down in Regulation (EC) No 785/2004 for air carriers and aircraft operators. Several so-called PNR Agreements have been concluded between the EU and a number of countries[246] on the exchange of passenger behaviour. Directive (EU) 2016/681 of 27 April 2016 on the use of passenger name record (PNR) data for the prevention, detection, investigation and prosecution of terrorist offences and serious crime has also been issued.

---

246. Currently Australia, Canada and the USA.

3.1.7 Transparency

In the civil aviation sector, Regulation (EC) No 437/2003 on statistical returns in respect of the carriage of passengers, freight and mail by air lays down that the Member States must transmit to the Statistical Office of the European Communities a large amount of information about developments of passenger, freight and mail traffic. The aim is to support the implementation of the common air traffic policy.

The Regulation is supplemented by Regulation (EC) No 1358/2003, implementing Regulation (EC) No 437/2003 on statistical returns in respect of the carriage of passengers, freight and mail by air and amending Annexes I and II thereto.

3.1.8 Public Authorities

Europe's airspace is characterised by being subject to regulations and controls by national authorities. Apart from Luxembourg, all Member States have their own civil aviation authorities which control their own airspace. This has been seen as one of the most important reasons for why there is such an unsatisfactory use of airspace capacity in parts of Europe. These bottlenecks regularly lead to major delays in air traffic and an increased risk of collisions. With a view to increasing capacity, the EU has launched an initiative under the heading 'The Single European Sky'.[247]

In particular, in the field of safety, the EASA has been set up;[248] *see* Regulation (EU) 2018/1139. Its tasks are particularly concentrated on certification of airworthiness and environmental certification.[249]

In connection with accidents, according to Article 4 of Regulation (EU) No 996/2010 on the investigation and prevention of accidents and incidents in civil aviation, each Member State must have a permanent civil aviation body capable of acting as an investigation commission, functionally independent of the national aviation authorities responsible for airworthiness, certification, air traffic control, etc.

3.2 Railways

Since the end of the 1980s, Europe's railways have been subject to regulatory liberalisation. This has by no means been the most comprehensive liberalisation of a regulated sector. Nevertheless, it is remarkable how little competition has developed in this market. To some extent, new participants may have been deterred because of the high costs of rolling stock and personnel required to get established. At the same time, it seems that the traditional national undertakings prefer to cooperate rather than compete.[250]

---

247. For a description of this *see* Niels van Antwerpen: *The Single European Sky*, Air & Space Law, Vol. 27/2 (2002).
248. https://www.easa.europa.eu/.
249. *See also* Regulation (EC) No 488/2005 on the fees and charges levied by the EASA.
250. Andre Meyer: *Rail Transport*, in Damien Geradin (ed.): *The Liberalization of State Monopolies in the European Union and Beyond*, p. 113 (2000).

The market in the railways sector differs between passenger and goods services. On the passenger side, the authorities are often contractors for a certain (politically determined) provision of passenger transport. Competition between train operators is often for public contracts (tendering). There is significant competition in relation to private cars and buses. In the area of goods traffic, there is direct competition for the transport of freight with other train operators and other forms of transport. The businesses of the two areas have little in common. However, passenger traffic and goods traffic compete with each other for access to the networks which they both use. The same applies to some other related facilities (e.g., shunting yards), and certain traction power, including engine drivers, can cover both areas.

Even though the existence of railway lines is a common requirement for both categories of railway traffic, they do not have the same network requirements. The convenience of passengers makes different demands than the needs of goods traffic. If these differences are not reflected in the pricing, there can be cross-subsidisation between the two business areas.

There has been a considerable need for liberalisation. In particular, in the area of goods traffic in Europe, the railways have had difficulty competing with road haulage. From 1970 to 1998, the railways' share of the freight market fell from 21.1% to 8.4%; this reflects a fall in the total volume of freight carried at a time when the total market for freight had strong growth.[251]

In addition to the transport policy interests, the railways have been the subject of growing interest from the point of view of environmental and climate change policy because of the growth in emissions from European traffic. The preamble to Directive 2008/57/EC on the interoperability of the rail system within the Community refers to the Kyoto Protocol and the European Union's undertaking to reduce its gas emissions. This goal requires a change in the balance between different forms of transport and, therefore, an improvement in the competitiveness of the railways.

3.2.1   EU Regulation

The regulation of the different competition law aspects of the railways has been made in several steps. In 1969, the Council issued Regulation (EEC) No 1191/69 on action by Member States concerning the obligations inherent in the concept of a public service in transport by rail, road and inland waterway, as well as Regulation (EEC) No 1192/69 on common rules for the normalisation of the accounts of railway undertakings.[252]

At the end of the 1970s and the beginning of the 1980s, a number of regulations and decisions were issued on the accounting systems and annual accounts, costing principles, and commercial independence of railway undertakings.[253]

---

251. Commission White Paper – European transport policy for 2010: time to decide, COM(2001) 370 final, p. 27.
252. The regulation has now been repealed.
253. Regulation (EEC) No 2830/77 on the measures necessary to achieve comparability between the accounting systems and annual accounts of railway undertakings; Regulation (EEC) No 2183/78 laying down uniform costing principles for railway undertakings; Decision 82/529/EEC on the fixing of rates for the international carriage of goods by rail; and Decision

The most important legislation for the liberalisation of the railways was first adopted at the beginning of the 1990s, and today, these measures are Directive 2012/34/EU, establishing a single European railway area and the Railway Safety Directive.[254] The aim of the latter is to harmonise different safety rules. Among other things, the intention is to create equal conditions for all railway undertakings; *see* recital 120.

The previous sector-specific EU regulation was a very limited minimum liberalisation which gave only poor opportunities for enforcing competition in the Member States that choose minimum implementation. However, this has not prevented some Member States from creating some competition by putting out to tender some routes which can be considered public services.

Directive 2012/24/EU defines two fundamental types of undertakings:

- *Railway undertaking* means 'any public or private undertaking licensed according to applicable Community legislation, the principal business of which is to provide services for the transport of goods and/or passengers by rail with a requirement that the undertaking must ensure traction; this also includes undertakings which provide traction only'. Such an undertaking can also be referred to as an operator. In principle, such an undertaking is subject to competition.
- *Infrastructure manager* means 'any body or firm responsible in particular for establishing, managing and maintaining railway infrastructure, including traffic management and control-command and signalling; the functions of the infrastructure manager on a network or part of a network may be allocated to different bodies or firms'. This is a network undertaking or network owner, which in reality administers a natural monopoly.

In its white paper 'European transport policy for 2010: time to decide', the Commission announced further opening of the internal market for passenger transport by rail while ensuring that public service obligations are carried out. Furthermore, in its Communication on the Consumer Policy Strategy 2002–2006, the Commission set the goal of ensuring a high level of consumer protection in the area of transport. Subsequently, on 26 September 2007, the European Parliament adopted the EC's third railway package.

On 8 October 2015, the Council agreed on the general approach to the proposals on governance and market opening – the Forth Railway Package. With this, competition in the European railway sector has increased and the creation of a 'Single European Railway Area' is being supported.

There are now new legal acts on both the market and the technical part of the Fourth Railway Package.

The technical part consists of Regulation (EU) 2016/796 of the European Parliament and of the Council of 11 May 2016 on the European Union Agency for Railways,

---

83/418/EEC on the commercial independence of the railways in the management of their international passenger and luggage traffic. These have now been replaced.

254. *See* Directive (EU) 2016/798 on railway safety.

Directive (EU) 2016/797 of the European Parliament and of the Council of 11 May 2016 on the interoperability of the rail system within the European Union and Directive (EU) 2016/798 of the European Parliament and of the Council of 11 May 2016 on railway safety.

The market part consists of Regulation (EU) 2016/2338 of the European Parliament and of the Council of 14 December 2016 amending Regulation (EC) No 1370/2007 concerning the opening of the market for domestic passenger transport services by rail, Directive (EU) 2016/2370 of the European Parliament and of the Council of 14 December 2016 amending Directive 2012/34/EU as regards the opening of the market for domestic passenger transport services by rail and the governance of the railway infrastructure and Regulation (EU) 2016/2337 of the European Parliament and of the Council of 14 December 2016 repealing Regulation (EEC) No 1192/69 of the Council on common rules for the normalisation of the accounts of railway undertakings.

3.2.1.1 The Application of the General Competition Rules

As stated above, the Treaty competition rules apply to the railways sector. However, there is an exception in Regulation (EC) No 169/2009 which applies rules of competition to transport by rail, road and inland waterways.

The Regulation applies to 'agreements, decisions and concerted practices which have as their object or effect the fixing of transport rates and conditions, the limitation or control of the supply of transport, the sharing of transport markets, the application of technical improvements or technical co-operation, or the joint financing or acquisition of transport equipment or supplies where such operations are directly related to the provision of transport services and are necessary for the joint operation of services by a grouping within the meaning of Article 3 of road or inland waterway transport undertakings, and to the abuse of a dominant position on the transport market'. The Regulation also applies to undertakings carried on by recipients of aid in the transport sector when such undertakings have the aims or effects referred to.

Articles 2 and 3 of the Regulation make special exceptions in relation to the prohibition of agreements that restrict competition in Article 101(1) TFEU for defined technical agreements and groups of small and medium-sized undertakings.

> In the case of *Commission v. Union internationale des chemins de fer*, the Commission applied Regulation (EEC) No 17/62 to a leaflet concerning railway tickets, on the assumption that Regulation (EEC) No 1017/68 (now Regulation (EC) No 169/2009) did not apply. This view was rejected by the GC (Case T-14/93) and later by the CJ (Case C-264/95 P). Exemptions have also been given under Regulation (EEC) No 1017/68 (now Regulation (EC) in Commission Decision 93/174/EEC concerning tariff structures in the combined transport of goods, and Commission Decision 94/594/EC concerning a joint venture. Likewise the Commission has applied the Regulation in a case on the abuse of a dominant position in connection with different tariff treatment of containers, depending on whether they were unloaded in German ports or ports in other Member States (Commission

Decision 94/210/EC). This case resulted in a fine on Deutsche Bahn of EUR 11 million. This decision was upheld by the GC in Case T-229/94, and an appeal dismissed by the CJ in Case C-436/97.

3.2.1.2   Pricing

Article 95(1) TFEU contains an overall prohibition against price discrimination so that, in the case of transport within the Union, there is a prohibition of 'carriers charging different rates and imposing different conditions for the carriage of the same goods over the same transport links on grounds of the country of origin or of destination of the goods in question.' This provision is supplemented by Article 96(1) TFEU, under which the 'imposition by a Member State, in respect of transport operations carried out within the Union, of rates and conditions involving any element of support or protection in the interest of one or more particular undertakings or industries shall be prohibited, unless authorised by the Commission.' These provisions are expressed in more detail in EEC Council Regulation No 11 (of 1960) concerning the abolition of discrimination in transport rates and conditions in the implementation of Article 79(3) of the Treaty establishing the European Economic Community. Article 4(1) of Regulation 11/1960 repeats the prohibition in Article 75(1) of the Treaty, and in Article 4(2) it is more specifically stated that the fixing, by tariff or otherwise, of transport rates and conditions which, when applied, would constitute discrimination within the meaning of paragraph 1 is also prohibited.

In addition, Article 18 of Regulation 11/1960 contains provisions for intervention and the imposition of sanctions. There are also provisions on the Member States' supervisory responsibilities, the obligation of freight companies and the providers of transport services to make notifications, rules on the burden of evidence, requirements concerning the use of transport documentation, and the Member States' obligations to notify.

There is no specific price regulation regime under EU law. However, Article 5 of Directive 2012/34/EU establishing a single European railway area does require Member States to take measures to ensure that the goal of railway undertakings is to provide efficient and appropriate services at the lowest possible cost for the quality of service required. At the same time, it states that railway undertakings must be managed according to the principles that apply to commercial companies.

3.2.2   Authorisation Procedures

The general rules on the licensing of railway undertakings are in Directive 2012/34/EU which establishes a single European railway area. This Directive requires the Member States to introduce a licensing system. Under Article 2(2) of the Directive, Member States can exempt a number of undertakings from the scope of the Directive, as follows:

- undertakings which only operate rail passenger services on local and regional stand-alone railway infrastructure;
- undertakings which only operate urban or suburban rail passenger services;

- undertakings whose activity is limited to the provision of regional rail freight services; and
- undertakings which only carry out freight operations on privately owned railway infrastructure that exist solely for use by the infrastructure owner for its own freight operations.

Railway undertakings which fulfil the requirements laid down have a right to a licence; *see* Article 17 of Directive 2012/34/EU. Conversely, there is a prohibition on the issue or extension of validity of a licence for undertakings which do not fulfil the requirements; *see* Article 17(2). A licence is valid throughout the territory of the Union; *see* Article 23(1).

The requirements necessary to fulfil in order to obtain a licence as a railway undertaking are laid down in Articles 6–9 of the Directive. These include good repute, financial fitness, professional competence and insurance cover for civil liability. Among other things, the requirement for good repute includes that the undertaking must not have been declared bankrupt, or have been convicted of serious offences of a commercial nature or against specific legislation applicable to transport, or have been convicted of serious or repeated failure to fulfil social, labour or tax law obligations. As for financial fitness, an applicant's railway undertaking must show that it will be able to meet its actual and potential obligations for a period of twelve months. The requirements for professional competence relate to management, personnel, organisation and physical assets.

The Member States otherwise lay down regulations on technical standards and operations, safety, health, social insurance, workers' rights and consumer protection.

3.2.2.1   Unbundling

Article 4 of Directive 2012/34/EU requires the unbundling of accounts for businesses relating to the provision of transport services and accounts for businesses relating to the management of railway infrastructure. The provision also allows for organisational unbundling. Article 6 includes further requirements for the publication of profit and loss accounts and either balance sheets or annual statements of assets and liabilities by railway undertakings; funds paid for activities relating to the provision of passenger transport services as public service remits must be shown separately.

Under Article 6 (as amended by Directive 2001/12/EC), there is a prohibition on public funds paid for the provision of transport services being transferred to the management of railway infrastructure and vice versa. However, there is no specific prohibition of cross-subsidisation if it does not involve public funds.

3.2.2.2   Independence Between the State and Railway Undertakings

Article 4 of Directive 2012/34/EU requires there to be a separation between the State and railway undertakings with regard to management, administration and internal control over administrative, economic and accounting matters. Railway undertakings must hold independent assets, budgets and accounts which are separate from those of the State. This requirement can be satisfied by incorporation.

3.2.3 Access to Networks

The rules on third-party access to railway networks do not give an unconditional right of access. There are several forms of restriction. Thus, the regulation is primarily aimed at transport provided over longer distances. Railway undertakings whose activities only cover towns, suburbs and regional transport are not covered by Directive 2012/34/EU; see Article 2.[255] Only railway undertakings which are established or wish to become established in a Member State are covered by the Directive.

The railway undertakings covered by Directive 2012/34/EU have had access on reasonable terms to all the Member States' infrastructure, with a view to the provision of all forms of railway freight services.

Access to a network is given by the allocation of a *train path*, meaning the infrastructure capacity needed to run a train between two places over a given period. In principle, network access is given in the form of annual timetables. The transition to as new timetable takes place at midnight on the second Saturday in December.[256] Annex VII to Directive 2012/34/EU sets out the schedule for the allocation process. In principle, a train path is only allocated for a period corresponding to the timetable period; *see* Article 38(2). However, framework agreements can be made for the allocation of capacity to an applicant for five years or more if special commercial contracts, investments or risks justify this; *see* Article 42 of the Directive. This possibility should be seen against the background of the major investment which is often needed in equipment and personnel to penetrate a new market. Framework agreements may not exclude other applicants or services from using the relevant infrastructure. Finally, infrastructure managers can grant ad hoc requests; *see* Article 48. These relate to applications for individual train paths (e.g., for freight trains). Infrastructure managers must respond to ad hoc requests within five working days.

If a railway network does not have sufficient capacity to meet all the requests received, the infrastructure manager must attempt, through consultation with the applicants, to achieve a resolution; *see* Article 46 of Directive 2012/34/EU. In this situation, the infrastructure manager may, within reasonable limits, offer capacity which differs from that which has been applied for. The applicants must be consulted. A dispute resolution system must be made available to resolve disputes within ten working days.

If attempts to coordinate do not make it possible to satisfy all applications for capacity to a sufficient extent, the infrastructure manager must declare that that element of the infrastructure is congested; *see* Article 47 of Directive 2012/34/EU. In this situation, the infrastructure manager must carry out a capacity analysis. This

---

255. Railway undertakings whose operations are limited to providing shuttle services for road vehicles through the Channel Tunnel are excluded from the scope of the Directive.
256. Commission Decision 2002/844/EC of 23 Oc. 2002 amending Directive 2001/14/EC in respect of the date for changing the working timetable for rail transport.

situation can be resolved either through the imposition of infrastructure charges, *see* Article 31(4) or, if this cannot solve the problem, by using priority criteria. The priority criteria must take account of the importance of a service to society and the effects of prioritising on other Member States; *see* Article 47. Finally, it is possible that capacity use can be improved by re-routing services, re-scheduling services, speed alterations and infrastructure improvements; *see* Article 50.

There are similarities between infrastructure managers and system operators in the energy supply sector. This is apparent from the powers and tasks which are given to infrastructure managers by Directive 2012/34/EU. These include cooperation with other infrastructure managers (Article 40), tasks related to lack of capacity (Articles 46–47), tasks related to disruptions to services (Article 54), and planning tasks relating to capacity enhancement plans (Articles 50–51).

Train paths may not be assigned; *see* Article 38 of Directive 2012/34/EU which prohibits any trading in infrastructure capacity.

Annex II to Directive 2012/34/EU lists the services which must be provided to railway undertakings in connection with third-party access to a network. This also indicates what are considered to be the essential facilities in this sector:

Services to be supplied to the railway undertakings
1. The minimum access package must comprise:
    a) handling of requests for infrastructure capacity;
    b) the right to utilise capacity which is granted;
    c) use of the railway infrastructure, including track points and junctions;
    d) train control, including signalling, regulation, dispatching and the communication and provision of information on train movement;
    e) use of electrical supply equipment for traction current, where available; and
    f) all other information required to implement or operate the service for which capacity has been granted.
2. Access, including track access, shall be given to the following services facilities, when they exist, and to the services supplied in these facilities:
    a) passenger stations, their buildings and other facilities, including travel information display and suitable location for ticketing services;
    b) freight terminals;
    c) marshalling yards and train formation facilities, including shunting facilities;
    d) storage sidings;
    e) maintenance facilities, with the exception of heavy maintenance facilities dedicated to high-speed trains or to other types of rolling stock requiring specific facilities;
    f) other technical facilities, including cleaning and washing facilities;
    g) maritime and inland port facilities which are linked to rail activities;
    h) relief facilities; and
    i) refuelling facilities and supply of fuel in these facilities, charges for which shall be shown on the invoices separately.

With COM(2023) 443 final of 11.07.2023, amended rules are expected for the management of rail infrastructure capacity and traffic management, for monitoring the results of rail transport, for coordination of stakeholders and for the allocation of capacity for rail traffic as part of an intermodal transport chain. The proposal deals with the planning and allocation of railway infrastructure capacity, which is currently covered by two legal acts, Directive 2012/34/EU and Regulation (EU) No. 913/2010. It also provides for better coordination of rail services across the EU and for appropriate regulatory oversight.

With regulation (EU) 2021/782 of 29.4.2021 on the rights and obligations of rail passengers, regulation 1371/2007 has been revised. The regulation applies to international and domestic rail journeys throughout the EU. It includes, among other things:

- An obligation to offer pass-through tickets for operators that can be considered a 'single railway undertaking'.
- Infrastructure managers must make real-time traffic data available to railway undertakings, ticket issuers, travel agencies or station managers. Likewise, railway undertakings must make real-time dynamic travel information available to other railway undertakings selling their tickets as well as to ticket issuers and travel agencies.
- If passengers are not offered a rerouting within a reasonable time (100 minutes) when their journey is interrupted, they have the right to arrange for themselves an alternative public transport solution by train or bus and the operator must reimburse "necessary, appropriate and reasonable" costs incurred for such an additional ticket.
- On new trains and trains being upgraded, there will be a requirement for an appropriate number of bicycle spaces (total bicycles, not just folding bicycles).

3.2.3.1 Access to Other than the Track

In connection with access to the rail network, there has been a debate about whether anything other than access to the track and the facilities connected with it could constitute essential facilities in the eyes of the law. In the *European Night Services* case,[257] concerning a joint venture under Article 101 TFEU (then Article 81 of the EC Treaty), in connection with the setting of a condition, the Commission assumed that the provision of the locomotive, train crew and train path constituted essential facilities. The case was brought before the GC which rejected the idea that locomotives and personnel could be essential facilities. However, the GC did note that in this case, competitors without locomotives would be unable to penetrate the relevant market or continue operating on it. In particular, in relation to locomotives, the GC emphasised that in the case in question, the Commission had not shown that the necessary locomotives could not be bought or leased on the market. Moreover, the GC argued that the fact that the notifying undertakings had been the first to acquire the locomotives in question did not mean that they were alone in being able to do so.[258] In the case in

---

257. Commission Decision 94/663/EC of 21 Sep. 1994 on Case IV/34.600 *European Night Services*, para. 81.
258. Joined Cases T-374/94, T-375/94, T-384/94 and T-388/94, *European Night Services and others v. Commission*, paras 212 and 215–216.

question, the Commission's original decision was annulled by reference to the insufficiency of investigations. From this, it must be assumed that, in connection with the interpretation of Directive 2012/34/EU,[259] there must be overwhelming obstacles to acquiring locomotives for these to be regarded as essential facilities.

In particular, in respect of computer reservation systems, Regulation (EC) No 80/2009 on a Code of Conduct for computerised reservation systems has laid down special rules, among other things, for railway products. The Regulation is discussed above in connection with air transport in section 3.1.3.

3.2.3.2 Pricing

Article 8 of Directive 2012/34/EU provides that the fee for use of the railway infrastructure (user fee) must be laid down by the Member States after consulting the infrastructure manager.

According to Article 7 of Directive 2012/34/EU, provided an infrastructure manager is independent of any railway undertaking with regard to legal form, organisation or decision-making functions, the Member State may delegate price-setting powers to the infrastructure manager.[260] Otherwise, except for the collection of fees, such powers can be given to an independent charging body. In this connection, there is a requirement for the use of uniform and non-discriminatory charges for the same mode of transport in the same markets. Competing railway undertakings must compete on equal terms.

The principles for charging set out in Article 31 of Directive 2012/34/EU are that charges for the minimum access package and track access to service facilities must be set at the cost that is directly incurred in operating the train service. Among other things, charges may reflect the scarcity of capacity, environmental costs, performance incentives, reservations and discounts; *see* Articles 31, 33, 35 and 36.

3.2.3.3 Transit

In the railways sector, transit rights are restricted to special international groupings which have access and transit rights in the Member States where their constituent railway undertakings are established, as referred to in Article 10 of Directive 2012/34/EU.

---

259. Horn Normand: *Comments*, in Damien Geradin (ed.): *The Liberalization of State Monopolies in the European Union and Beyond*, p. 134 (2000) states that it was precisely the fear of creating a precedent of a right to locomotive facilities which was the reason for bringing the Commission's Decision before the GC. For a further comment on the case, *see* Andre Meyer: *Rail Transport*, in Damien Geradin (ed.): *The Liberalization of State Monopolies in the European Union and Beyond*, p. 122-125 (2000).
260. Thus, the minimum requirement on accounting unbundling in Art. 6 of Directive 2012/34/EU does not extend to the delegation of pricing competence.

3.2.4 Public Service Obligations

Regulation (EC) No 1370/2007 on public passenger transport services by rail and by road[261] contains special provisions on public service obligations in the railway sector.

Article 2 of the Regulation defines the concept of a public service obligation for the purposes of the railway sector as:

> a requirement defined or determined by a competent authority in order to ensure public passenger transport services in the general interest that an operator, if it were considering its own commercial interests, would not assume or would not assume to the same extent or under the same conditions without reward.

The provision of such public service is to be compensated, but the compensation 'may not exceed an amount corresponding to the net financial effect equivalent to the total of the effects, positive or negative, of compliance with the public service obligation on the costs and revenue of the public service operator'; *see* Article 2 in the Annex to Regulation (EC) No 1370/2007. However, these rules do not cover 'general rules on financial compensation for public service obligations which establish maximum tariffs for pupils, students, apprentices and persons with reduced mobility'; *see* Article 3(3). Such general rules must be notified in accordance with Article 108 TFEU.

According to Article 5 of Directive 2012/34/EU, the requirement that railway undertakings must be managed according to the principles that apply to commercial companies also applies to their public services and to public services contracts which they conclude with the competent authorities of the Member State.

3.2.5 Technical Harmonisation

The commercial operation of railway traffic on the trans-European network requires, among other things, coordination between the specifications of the infrastructure and the rolling stock, and it also requires the effective coordination of the information and communication systems of the various infrastructure managers and train operators. Technical harmonisation is, therefore, an important area for the creation of an internal market for railway traffic. The existence of many separate technical systems acts as a barrier. Thus, it is not unusual that when a train crosses a national border, it must change its locomotive. The areas in which there is a need for technical harmonisation include:

- Track gauges (Portugal, Spain and Finland differ from the rest of the EU).[262]
- Electric current, etc. (there are major national differences).
- Signals.
- Safety systems.
- Seat reservation systems.

---

261. Amended by Regulation (EU) 2016/2338. In C-186/22 *Sad Traspoto Locale*, the question of the regulation's application to mixed transport has been addressed.
262. The different track gauges were, among other things, a deliberate military strategic choice. New high-speed lines are being built in Spain using gauge the normally used in the EU.

– Licensing of locomotive drivers (licences often only cover one country, and training is the responsibility of individual train operators).

The need for harmonisation resulted in Directive (EU) 2016/797 of the European Parliament and of the Council of 11 May 2016 on the interoperability of the rail system within the European Union, which provides for technical specifications for interoperability (TSIs). These specifications are drawn up under a mandate from the Commission by The ERA.[263]

Under the authority of Article 6(1) of Directive 2008/57/EC (formerly Directive 96/48/EC), the Commission has laid down specifications for interoperability.[264]

In Article 7, the Member States are given the possibility of derogating from the TSIs, as follows:

(a) for a proposed new subsystem or part of it, for the renewal or upgrading of an existing subsystem or part of it, or for any element referred to in Article 1(1) which is at an advanced stage of development or which is the subject of a contract in the course of performance on the date of application of the TSI(s) concerned;
(b) where, following an accident or a natural disaster, the conditions for the rapid restoration of the network do not economically or technically allow for partial or total application of the relevant TSIs, in which case the nonapplication of the TSIs shall be limited to the period before the restoration of the network;
(c) for any proposed renewal, extension or upgrading of an existing subsystem or part of it when the application of the TSI(s) concerned would compromise the economic viability of the project and/or the compatibility of the rail system in the Member State concerned, for example, in relation to the loading gauge, track gauge, space between tracks or electrification voltage;
(d) for vehicles arriving from or going to third countries, the track gauge of which is different from that of the main rail network within the Union;
(e) for a proposed new subsystem or for the proposed renewal or upgrading of an existing subsystem in the territory of the Member State concerned when its rail network is separated or isolated by the sea or separated as a result of special geographical conditions from the rail network of the rest of the Union.

In all cases, the Member State concerned must serve prior notice of its intended derogation to the Commission and must forward to it a file setting out the TSIs or the parts of TSIs that it does not wish to be applied, as well as the corresponding specifications that it does wish to apply.

---

263. The European Railway Agency was set up under Regulation (EC) No 881/2004 establishing a European Railway Agency (Agency Regulation), which has been replaced by Regulation (EU) 2016/76.
264. Commission Decision 2002/735/EC concerning the technical specification for interoperability relating to the rolling stock subsystem of the trans-European high-speed rail system referred to in Art. 6(1) of Directive 96/48/EC; Commission Decision 2008/231/EC – operation subsystem; Commission Decision 2008/284/EC – energy subsystem; Commission Decision 2008/217/EC – infrastructure subsystem; Commission Decision 2006/860/EC – control-command and signalling subsystem; and Commission Decision 2002/730/EC – maintenance subsystem.

3.2.6 Transparency

Regulation (EU) 2018/643 of the European Parliament and of the Council of 18 April 2018 on rail transport statistics lays down reporting obligations in relation to data on passenger and goods transport by railway. The data are to be used by the Commission in order to monitor the development of the common transport policy, including transport safety.

The provisions are supplemented by Regulation (EC) No 332/2007 on the technical arrangements for the transmission of railway transport statistics.

3.2.7 Public Authorities

With Regulation (EU) 2016/796, the ERA was established. Among the tasks of the ERA is a One-Stop-Shop system, which will make it possible to get material, etc., approved in one place in Europe. According to Article 12, the Agency shall establish and manage an information and communication system with at least the following one-stop-shop functions:

(a) a single entry point through which the applicant shall submit its application files for type authorisation, vehicle authorisations for placing on the market and single safety certificates. Where the area of use or operation is limited to a network or networks within one Member State only, the single entry point shall be developed so as to ensure that the applicant selects the authority it wishes to process the application for issuing authorisations or single safety certificates for the whole procedure;
(b) a common information-exchange platform, providing the Agency and national safety authorities with information about all applications for authorisations and single safety certificates, the stages of these procedures and their outcome, and, where applicable, the requests and decisions of the Board of Appeal;
(c) a common information-exchange platform, providing the Agency and national safety authorities with information about requests for approvals by the Agency in accordance with Article 19 of Directive (EU) 2016/797 and applications for authorisations of trackside control-command and signalling subsystems involving European Train Control System (ETCS) and/or Global System for Mobile Communications – Railway (GSM-R) equipment, the stages of these procedures and their outcome, and, where applicable, the requests and decisions of the Board of Appeal;
(d) an early-warning system able to identify at an early stage the need for coordination between decisions to be taken by national safety authorities and the Agency in the case of different applications requesting similar authorisations or single safety certificates.

It is the Agency that handles issuing, etc., of EU single safety certificates (Article 14). The agency issues authorisations for the placing of the market railway vehicles

(Article 20). Before tendering for ERTMS equipment (European Railway Traffic Management System), the Agency checks that the technical solutions are in complete agreement with the relevant TSIs, thus being fully interoperable.

On a national level, Article 55 of Directive 2012/34/EU lays down requirements for the establishment of a regulatory body to act as an appeal body (dispute resolution authority) in relation to the infrastructure manager. This body must be independent of the infrastructure manager and operationally independent of the authorities that award contracts for public services. The regulatory body has the power to request relevant information from the infrastructure manager, applicants and any third party involved. The regulatory body is required to decide on any complaints within two months from receipt of all information. A decision of the regulatory body is binding on all parties. However, decisions of the regulatory body are subject to judicial review.

Responsibilities for establishing safety standards and rules, as well as for monitoring and enforcing such standards and rules, are matters for public authorities which must be dealt with by the Member States or by independent bodies; *see* Article 8 of Directive 2012/34/EU. The aim is to prevent the use of such rules for discrimination with regard to network access.

The infrastructure manager and any charging body are subject to a duty of confidentiality with regard to commercially confidential information; *see* Articles 29 of Directive 2012/34/EU.

4 COMMUNICATION

Both postal and telecommunications services have previously primarily been national monopolies. These have often been owned by the State and have been organised as administrative entities. To some extent, the traditional market actors are still dominant in the national markets, among other things, because of their control over existing networks.

Both sectors are characterised by the fact that those parts of the networks that are still in the nature of a monopoly service have become very limited.

4.1 Telecommunications

Telecommunication has traditionally been characterised by great investments, which only States or large companies could perform. In historical terms, national telecommunications monopolies were the main actors in the EU's telecommunications market up until the 1980s.[265] They cooperated bilaterally. The alternative to these monopolies was to provide telecommunications services for one's own use, and this was only a

---

265. Kjell A. Eliassen & Marit Sjøvaag: *European Telecommunications Liberalisation*, p. 9 (1999) and Ivo Van Bael & Jean-Francois Bellis: *Competition Law of the European Community*, p. 1259 ff (2010). *See* generally about EU legislation in the field of telecommunication in Adrej Savin: *EU Telecommunications Law* (2018).

realistic possibility for the largest entities. Where the national telecommunications undertakings had an exclusive right to establish (and own) telecommunications infrastructure, those entities that wanted to provide their own telecommunications services had to lease network capacity from the relevant monopolist. The costs of this were often very high compared to equivalent prices in the USA, especially for cross-border connections. This has been one of the major motivations behind the Union's liberalisation measures in this area.[266] Relatively early on, the Commission succeeded in establishing its right to use its authority under Article 106(3) TFEU in the telecommunications sector.[267] In contrast to the other liberalised sectors, the telecommunications sector is still characterised by being regulated in part by liberalising directives.

The telecommunications sector has been subject to a number of changes in recent years. Telecommunications undertakings that were previously organised as national monopolies have increasingly been organised as limited companies under private law and are now often parts of multinational telecommunications giants. In this connection, the EU has been active in promoting liberalisation and in setting the framework for competition. In 1984, the Council published its Recommendation 84/549/EEC concerning the implementation of harmonisation in the field of telecommunications (OJ 1984 L298/49).[268] This was followed up by the Commission's Green Paper COM(87) 290 final. Regulation has developed at different speeds.[269] 1 January 1998 was the deadline for Member States to remove the last obstacles to consumers being able to be offered telecommunications services on competitive markets.[270] In 2002, there was a whole package of new telecommunications directives dealing with both the technical and market aspects of development. These impose strict limits on the scope for Member States to restrict competition, for example, by favouring a national operator.

As part of the Lisbon strategy, the Commission published a Communication 'i2010 – A European Information Society for growth and employment' (COM(2005) 229 final), and a Communication on the review of the EU Regulatory Framework for

---

266. Pierre Larouche: *Telecommunications*, in Damien Geradin (ed.): *The Liberalization of State Monopolies in the European Union and Beyond*, p. 16 (2000).
267. Commission Decision 82/861/EEC Case IV/29.877 – *British Telecommunications*. The Decision was subsequently referred to the CJ, with a claim for annulment. In Case 41/83, *Italy v. Commission*, the CJ found in favour of the Commission, and the Commission's powers in this area were therefore confirmed. *See also* the later Case C-202/88, *France v. Commission. See* P.J. Slot & A.M. Skudder: *Common Features of Community Law Regulation in the Network-Bound Sectors*, Common Market Law Review, p. 92 (2001).
268. There was also liberalisation of a specific segment of the market via Directive 88/301/EEC on competition in the markets in telecommunications terminal equipment. *See also* Council Recommendation concerning the implementation of harmonisation in the field of telecommunications (COM(80) 422 final).
269. The development of Union regulation of the telecommunications sector is described in Pierre Larouche: *Competition Law and Regulation in European Telecommunications*, pp. 1–36 (2000) and Christian Berqvist: *Between Regulation and Deregulation*, pp. 169 ff. (2016).
270. Some Member States were allowed limited extensions to the deadlines in Directive 96/19/EC and Directive 96/2/EC. Extensions were granted to Ireland (Decision 97/114/EC), Portugal (Decision 97/310/EC), Luxembourg (Decision 97/568/EC), Spain (Decision 97/603/EC) and Greece (Decision 97/607/EC).

electronic communications networks and services (COM(2006) 334 final). Among other things, changes were made in 2009.

4.1.1   EU Regulation

At the international level, the Union is bound by its obligations under the WTO Telecommunications Agreement.[271] This is made clear in Council Decision 97/838/EC concerning the conclusion on behalf of the European Community, as regards matters within its competence, of the results of the WTO negotiations on basic telecommunications services.

The framework for the EU's telecommunications sector now consists of a liberalisation directive – Directive 2002/77/EC on competition in the markets for electronic communications networks and services. In addition to this, Directive (EU) 2018/1972 of the European Parliament and of the Council of 11 December 2018 establishing the European Electronic Communications Code provides a common regulatory framework for electronic communications networks and services (Framework Directive).[272] This is supplemented by three specific directives. There are also Directive 2002/58/EC[273] concerning the processing of personal data and the protection of privacy in the electronic communications sector (Directive on privacy and electronic communications) and especially Decision No 676/2002/676/2002/EC.

Together with the classic telecommunications services, Directive 2002/77/EC includes the dissemination and broadcasting of radio and television programmes under the general heading of electronic communications services and electronic communications networks.

The present rules primarily cover the circumstances concerning transmission, while content is regulated under other sets of rules. These cover, for example, electronic commerce and television broadcasting.[274] However, this chapter does not include a discussion of these special rules.

4.1.1.1   The Application of the General Competition Rules

The general Treaty competition rules apply to the telecommunications sector. The Commission has issued both guidelines for the application of the general competition

---

271. Agreement on Telecommunications Services (Fourth Protocol to General Agreement on Trade in Services, Geneva 15 Feb. 1997). The WTO Agreement is discussed in more detail in Raj Bhala & Kevin Kennedy. *World Trade Law*, p. 1209 (1990).
272. This Directive replaces four directives – the Access Directive 2002/19/EC, the Authorisation Directive 2002/20/EC, the Framework Directive 2002/21/EC, and the Universal Service Directive 2002/22/EC.
273. Directive on privacy and electronic communications, which supplements the GDPR-provisions.
274. *See* Directive 2010/13/EU on the coordination of certain provisions laid down by law, regulation or administrative action in Member States concerning the provision of audiovisual media services (Audiovisual Media Services Directive), and Directive 2000/31/EC on certain legal aspects of information society services, in particular electronic commerce, in the Internal Market (Directive on electronic commerce).

rules to the telecommunications sector in 1991 and a more specific Notice on the application of the competition rules to access agreements in the telecommunications sector in 1998.

The nature of guidelines means that the first set of guidelines referred to does not actually create rights which can be enforced through the courts, nor do they bind the GC and the CJ. Among other things, they contain guidelines for the calculation of the relevant market and give examples of the application of Articles 101 and 102 TFEU to the telecommunications sector.

The second Notice from 1998 is discussed in more detail below in the section on access to networks.

For an example of the application of the general competition rules, *see* Case C-52/09, *Konkurrensverket v. TeliaSonera Sverige*, on the application of the general provisions on abuse of a dominant position in connection with the fixing of resale prices for Asymmetric Digital Subscriber Line (ADSL) connections in the wholesale market in relation to retail prices; and Case C-280/08, *Deutsche Telekom v. Commission* on largely the same topic. *See* also Case T-135/12, *France v. Commission* and Case T-385/12, *Orange v. Commission* on State aid in connection with the financing of retirement pensions for civil servants working for France Télécom and cases T-208/13 and T-216/13 on an anti-competitive agreement between Telefónica and Portugal Telecom.[275] See also Case C-81/10 P, France Télécom, paragraph 80, on the timing of the granting of aid and C-39/94, SFEI/La Poste, on financial advantage.

4.1.2 Authorisation Procedures

Article 2 of Directive 2002/77/EC on competition in the markets for electronic communications networks and services prohibits Member States from granting or maintaining in force exclusive or special rights for the establishment and/or the provision of electronic communications networks or for the provision of publicly available electronic communications services.

The Member States are primarily required to make use of general authorisations[276] rather than individual authorisations; *see* Article 2(4) of Directive 2002/77/. More detailed provisions on this obligation are given in the Directive on European Electronic Communications Code. According to Article 12, there should thus be freedom to offer electronic communications networks and services. However, Article 12 of the Authorisation Directive does refer to the possibility of restricting this in accordance with TFEU Article 52(1) on grounds of public policy, public security or public health.

---

275. On EU competition law and telecommunication, *see* Andrej Savin: *EU Telecommunications Law*, p. 97-130 (2018).
276. A 'general authorisation' is defined in Art. 2(no. 22) of the Directive on European Electronic Communications Code (2018/1972) as 'a legal framework established by the Member State ensuring rights for the provision of electronic communications networks or services and laying down sector specific obligations that may apply to all or to specific types of electronic communications networks and services.'

Annex I of the Directive on European Electronic Communication Code sets out the conditions which may be attached to a general authorisation. This list is exhaustive; *see* Article 13 of the Directive.[277]

Among other things, the list covers conditions similar to the requirements of public service obligations, including financial contributions to the funding of universal service, interoperability of services and interconnection of networks, accessibility of numbers from the national numbering plan to end-users, environmental and town and country planning requirements, 'must carry' obligations, and general requirements for administrative charges and financial and technical guarantees which are necessary to ensure that the infrastructures function correctly. Article 10 contains a consultation procedure in connection with failures to comply with conditions. This includes a deadline for obligatory consultation.

An undertaking that requests access to a network or interconnection need not be authorised to operate in the Member State where access or interconnection is requested if it is not providing services and does not operate a network in that Member State; *see* Article 59(1) of the Directive on European Electronic Communications Code.

In connection with granting authorisations and user rights, Article 120(3) of the Directive on European Electronic Communications Code lays down requirements for transparency, according to which Member States must ensure that all relevant information on rights, conditions, procedures, charges, fees and decisions concerning general authorisations and rights of use is published and kept up to date in an appropriate manner so as to provide easy access to that information for all interested parties.

4.1.2.1 Telephone Numbers and Radio Frequencies

In the area of telecommunications, special user rights are associated with telephone numbers, etc., and radio frequencies. Their use is necessarily based on a certain measure of exclusivity. Decision No 676/2002/EC on a regulatory framework for radio spectrum policy in the European Community contains rules for the Union's radio frequency policy. At the European level, the European Conference of Postal and Telecommunications Administrations (CEPT)[278] prepares measures for the technical harmonisation of the use of radio frequencies across the Union's borders. This can be based on a mandate from the Commission; *see* Article 4(2) of the Decision No 676/2002/EC.

In addition to administration fees, charges can be made for the use of radio frequencies and numbers as a means of ensuring the optimal use of such resources. Such fees should not prevent the establishment of innovative services and competition on the market. Certain telephone numbers and radio frequencies have a special economic value. It is recognised that the Member States can use tendering procedures or similar procedures for their allocation. In connection with Decision No 128/1999/EC

---

277. However, special rules apply to providers of public service obligations.
278. CEPT covers 48 European countries (www.cept.org).

on the coordinated introduction of a third-generation mobile and wireless communications system (UMTS) in the Community, some Member States raised considerable licence fees via auctions, while others did not require payment for such licences. These differences have been criticised as it is possible that they can distort competition.[279]

Regarding radio frequencies, Article 28 of the Directive on European Electronic Communications Code requires that Member States and their competent authorities ensure that the use of radio frequencies is organised in a way in which no other Member State is prevented from allowing the use of harmonised radio frequencies in accordance with EU legislation, in particular as a result of cross-border, harmful interference between Member States. The Member States are neither obliged to allocate nor prevented from allocating the right to use numbers in the national numbering plan[280] or allocating licences to install facilities to other undertakings than providers of electronic communications networks and services. However, according to Article 9 of the Directive on European Electronic Communications Code (EU 2018/1972), Member States must issue a number of resources for availability on the basis of transparent, objective and non-discrimination criteria. Member States must also ensure that adequate numbers and numbering ranges are provided for all publicly available electronic communications services.

It is permitted to recover administration fees from providers of electronic communications services in order to finance the activities of the national regulatory authorities in administering the licensing system and the allocation of user rights. Such fees should only cover the actual administration costs of these activities.

4.1.2.2 Unbundling

Article 8 of Directive 2002/77/EC lays down a requirement for the organisational unbundling of an undertaking that provides public electronic communications networks and cable television networks. However, this is based on the assumption that such an undertaking is controlled by a Member State or benefits from special rights, is dominant in a substantial part of the internal market for the provision of public electronic communications networks and/or publicly available telephone services and operates a cable television network which has been established under special or exclusive right in the same geographic area.

Article 17 of the Directive on European Electronic Communications Code requires accounting or organisational unbundling for undertakings providing public electronic communications networks or publicly available electronic communications services which have special or exclusive rights for the provision of services in other sectors in the same or another Member State.

---

279. *P.J. Slot & A.M. Skudder:* Common Features of Community Law Regulation in the Network-Bound Sectors, Common Market Law Review 2001 p. 105.
280. A national plan for the numbering and addressing of telephones, ISDN and mobile communications can, e.g., be based on recommendations from the ITU.

4.1.3 Access to Networks

There can be a debate about the extent to which there is still a natural monopoly in the telecommunications sector. These days, communications can be transmitted by many means (cable, satellite, radio masts). In recent years, many new service providers have entered the market. In the area of transmission, undertakings in the electricity and railways sectors have begun to offer services on networks which they have established for their own use. Mobile telephone companies have established parallel networks of radio masts. At a technical level, technologies in the IT, media and telecommunications sectors have converged so that their signals can be sent using the same networks, whether these consist of cable connections, radio waves, fibre optic technology or other electromagnetic networks. The continued existence of natural monopolies depends to a great extent on the costs of duplicating networks or on competition between different kinds of networks (fixed as against mobile networks).

For a period, it will often be the previous national monopoly undertakings that control parts of the network, including the local loop, which in places still seems to have the character of a natural monopoly. Among other things, the rules on network access in the early phases of liberalisation ensured that entrants to the market could have access to the established network so as to ensure the rapid development of a competitive market.

In assessing whether third-party access to a network should be granted, Article 61 of the Directive on European Electronic Communications Code uses the term *undertakings with significant market power*. According to Article 63(2), this is a position equivalent to dominance, whether held individually or jointly with others.[281] At the latest on the date of entry into force of the Directive (24 April 2002), the Commission had to publish guidelines for market analysis and the assessment of significant market power. In relation to undertakings with significant market power, Member States had the possibility, but not the obligation, of introducing provisions on network access, whether access or interconnection. It would only be possible for a Member State to impose on an undertaking which does not have significant market power an obligation to give other undertakings access to its network.

Access means making facilities and/or services available to another undertaking, under defined conditions, on either an exclusive or non-exclusive basis, for the purpose of providing electronic communications services. *Interconnection* means the physical and logical linking of public communications networks used by the same or a different undertaking in order to allow the users of one undertaking to communicate with users of the same or another undertaking or to access services provided by another undertaking.

4.1.3.1 Access and Interconnection

The Directive on European Electronic Communications Code (EU 2018/1972) lays down harmonised rules for how the Member States can regulate access to and

---

281. *See also* Commission guidelines on market analysis and the assessment of significant market power under the Community regulatory framework for electronic communications networks and services (OJ 2002 C 165/6).

interconnection with electronic communications networks and associated facilities between public networks. The main provision is in Article 59, which states that Member States shall ensure that there are no restrictions which prevent undertakings in the same Member State or in different Member States from negotiating between themselves agreements on technical and commercial arrangements for access or interconnection in accordance with Union law.

Under Article 61, the national regulatory authorities must ensure adequate access, interconnection and interoperability of services. The aim is to promote efficiency, sustainable competition, and give maximum benefit to end-users.

4.1.3.2 The General Competition Rules

The provisions in Articles 101 and 102 TFEU apply in parallel with these rules. An undertaking might thereby be able to obtain third-party access to a network and other essential facilities, regardless of whether the Member State in question has made use of the provisions in Article 44 of the Directive on European Electronic Communications Code. In this connection, the 1998 Notice on the application of the competition rules to access agreements in the telecommunications sector – framework, relevant markets and principles applies.[282] This was issued under the old provisions for the telecommunications sector. Among other things, the Notice addresses questions concerning essential facilities. According to paragraph 149 of the Notice, the Commission considers that competition rules and sector-specific regulation form a coherent set of measures to ensure a liberalised and competitive market environment for telecommunications markets in the Community.

In particular, the Treaty prohibition of the abuse of a dominant position is probably applicable in connection with access to networks and other essential facilities. Paragraph 52 of the 1998 Notice states that some 'incumbent [telecommunications operators] may be tempted to resist providing access to third party service providers or other network operators, particularly in areas where the proposed service will be in competition with a service provided by the [telecommunications operator] itself. This resistance will often manifest itself as unjustified delay in giving access, a reluctance to allow access or a willingness to allow it only under disadvantageous conditions.'

This is expanded on in paragraph 95, where it is stated that '[d]ominant [telecommunications operators] have a duty to deal with requests for access efficiently: undue and inexplicable or unjustified delays in responding to a request for access may constitute an abuse. In particular, however, the Commission will seek to compare the response to a request for access with:

    a. the usual time frame and conditions applicable when the responding party grants access to its facilities to its own subsidiary or operating branch;
    b. responses to requests for access to similar facilities in other Member States;
    c. the explanations given for any delay in dealing with requests for access.'

---

282. OJ 1998 C 265/2. *See also* the Commission's Guidelines on the application of EEC competition rules in the telecommunications sector (OJ 1991 C 233/2).

4.1.3.3   Price Controls

In relation to public undertakings which are vertically integrated, the Member States must ensure that those that provide electronic communications networks and have a dominant position do not discriminate in favour of their own activities. This requirement indicates that they must act as a common carrier.

Article 74 of the Directive on European Electronic Communications Code provides that national regulatory authorities may impose obligations relating to the cost-orientation of prices and cost accounting systems for the provision of specific types of interconnection and/or access, where a market analysis indicates that a lack of effective competition means that the operator concerned can sustain prices at an excessively high level, or apply a price squeeze, to the detriment of end-users.

In connection with obligations concerning cost recovery and pricing controls under Article 74 of the Directive on European Electronic Communications Code, national regulatory authorities must have regard both for consumers and for service providers. Primarily, it must be ensured that the mechanisms used 'promote efficiency and sustainable competition and maximise consumer benefits'. The authorities may take account of prices available in comparable competitive markets. For calculating the cost of efficient provision of services, the national regulatory authorities are explicitly authorised to use cost accounting methods which are independent of those used by an undertaking. This allows for the use of benchmarking. Where the implementation of a cost accounting system is mandated in order to support price controls, a description of the cost accounting system must be made publicly available. It is the operator who has the burden of proving that charges are derived from costs, including a reasonable rate of return on investment, and the regulatory authorities may require an operator to adjust its prices. At the same time, the national regulatory authorities must take into account the investment made by operators and allow them a reasonable rate of return on the capital employed, taking into account the risks involved.

With Regulation (EC) No 717/2007 on roaming on public mobile telephone networks within the Community and amending Directive 2002/21/EC (the Roaming Regulation), a limit was introduced to the amount which the owner of a mobile network can charge the customers of a third party network in connection with mobile calls (wholesale charges), and a limit to how much the owner of a network (home provider) can take for its own customers' use of visited networks.[283]

4.1.4   Public Service Obligations

The Directive on European Electronic Communications Code lays down the rights of end-users and the corresponding obligations of undertakings that provide publicly available electronic communications networks and services. The Directive also lays down an obligation for universal services in the form of minimum services of a given

---

283. The regulation was a response to the high level of the charges payable by users of public mobile telephone networks when travelling abroad. The excessive retail charges resulted from both high wholesale charges levied by the foreign host network operators and, in many cases, from high retail mark-ups charged by the customers' own network operators; see Recital 1 of the Regulation.

quality, to which all end-users have a right of access at reasonable prices and without regard to national circumstances.

According to Articles 12 and 13, it is up to the individual regulatory authority to decide whether compensation is paid for the provision of the obligations imposed. If such compensation is paid, it can either be paid out of public funds or the costs can be allocated between the providers of electronic communications networks and services. In principle, only the net additional costs can be compensated for. Any commercial advantage of the obligation to supply must be set off.[284]

Member States may designate one or more undertakings to guarantee the provision of one or more of the universal services referred to in Articles 4-7. However, Article 8 does not allow a Member State to impose additional obligations on a service provider over and above those referred to.[285]

Article 6 of Directive 2002/77/EC provides that any national scheme to share the net cost of the provision of universal service obligations must be based on objective, transparent and non-discriminatory criteria and be consistent with the principle of proportionality and of least market distortion. Where universal service obligations are imposed on undertakings providing electronic communications services, this must be taken into consideration in calculating any contribution to the net cost of universal service obligations.

4.1.5 Technical Harmonisation

The establishment of the internal market for telecommunications requires technical standardisation. Thus, the harmonisation of interfaces between terminal equipment and networks is a means for promoting competitive markets both for terminal equipment and network services. This has been implemented by a number of harmonising directives. The first was Directive 86/361/EEC on the initial stage of the mutual recognition of type approval for telecommunications terminal equipment, followed by Directive 91/263/EEC on the approximation of the laws of the Member States concerning telecommunications terminal equipment, including the mutual recognition of their conformity. On the basis of these and following up on them, a large number of standards have been established, primarily in conjunction with the new method for regulating standards.

These have concerned the integrated services digital network (ISDN),[286] cellular digital land-based mobile communications (GMS),[287] land-based public radio paging (ERMES –

---

284. Case C-222/08, *Commission v. Belgium*.
285. Case C-16/10, *The Number (UK) v. British Telecommunications*.
286. Council Recommendation 86/659/EEC on the coordinated introduction of the integrated services digital network (ISDN) in the European Community; Council Resolution of 18 Jul. 1989 on the strengthening of the coordination for the introduction of the Integrated Services Digital Network (ISDN) in the European Community up to 1992; and Council Resolution of 5 Jun. 1992 on the development of the integrated services digital network (ISDN) in the Community as a European-wide telecommunications infrastructure for 1993 and beyond (OJ 1992 C 158/1).
287. Council Recommendation 87/371/EEC on the coordinated introduction of public pan-European cellular digital land-based mobile communications in the Community; Directive

European Radio Messaging System),[288] digital European cordless telecommunications (DECT),[289] and mobile and wireless communications system (UMTS).[290]

Furthermore, the use of the emergency call number (112) and the prefix for making international calls (00) were harmonised.[291] Article 39 of the Directive on European Electronic Communications Code now contains provisions on standardisation. The Commission shall draw up and publish in the Official Journal of the European Union a list of non-compulsory standards or specifications to serve as a basis for encouraging the harmonised provision of electronic communications networks, electronic communications services and associated facilities and associated services. Where necessary, the Commission may, following consultation of the Committee established by Directive (EU) 2015/1535, request that standards be drawn up by the European standardisation organisations (European Committee for Standardisation (CEN), European Committee for Electrotechnical Standardisation (Cenelec), and European Telecommunications Standards Institute (ETSI)). When the Commission intends to make the implementation of certain standards or specifications mandatory, the Official Journal of the European Union shall publish an invitation to all concerned parties to make their explanatory notes in public. By means of implementing acts, the Commission shall make the implementation of the relevant standards mandatory by designating them as mandatory standards in the list of standards and specifications that will be published in the Official Journal of the European Union.

At the international level, the International Telecommunication Union (ITU) has been a forum for technical harmonisation.

4.1.6 Public Authorities

The overall provisions are in Article 5 of the Directive on European Electronic Communications Code, according to which the Member States must ensure that each of the tasks assigned to national regulatory authorities in the Directive is undertaken by a competent authority, a regulatory authority. According to Article 6, Member States must guarantee the independence of national regulatory authorities by ensuring that

---

87/372/EEC on the frequency bands to be reserved for the coordinated introduction of public pan-European cellular digital land-based mobile communications in the Community; and Council Resolution of 14 Dec. 1990 on the final stage of the coordinated introduction of pan-European land-based public digital mobile cellular communications in the Community (GSM) (OJ 1990 C 329/25).

288. Council Directive 90/544/EEC on the frequency bands designated for the coordinated introduction of pan-European land-based public radio paging in the Community; and Council Recommendation 90/543/EEC on the coordinated introduction of pan-European land-based public radio paging in the Community.

289. Council Recommendation 91/288/EEC on the coordinated introduction of digital European cordless telecommunications (DECT) into the Community; and Directive 91/287/EEC on the frequency band to be designated for the coordinated introduction of DECT into the Community.

290. Decision No 128/1999/EC of the European Parliament and of the Council on the coordinated introduction of a third-generation mobile and wireless communications system (UMTS) in the Community.

291. Council Decision 91/396/EEC on the introduction of a single European emergency call number.

they are legally distinct from and functionally independent of all organisations providing electronic communications networks, equipment or services. If a Member State retains ownership or control of undertakings providing electronic communications networks and/or services, it must ensure effective structural separation of the regulatory function from activities associated with ownership or control. This must be understood as a requirement for both management and organisational unbundling.

The regulatory authority also acts as a dispute resolution body in relation to network access; *see* Article 25 of the Directive on European Electronic Communications Code. The Member States can choose to make use of other mechanisms, including mediation. If the dispute has not been settled after four months, and if it has not yet been brought before a court by the complaining party, the national authority shall, at the request of one of the parties, make a binding decision to settle a dispute as soon as possible, and in any case within four months. According to the wording of the provision, the bringing of a case before the courts by others other than the party seeking redress cannot exempt the regulatory authority from taking a decision. The decision of the national regulatory authority must be made available to the public, subject to the requirements of business confidentiality.

Article 31 of the Directive on European Electronic Communications Code requires the Member States to ensure that effective mechanisms exist at the national level under which any user or undertaking providing electronic communications networks and/or services who is affected by a decision of a national regulatory authority has the right of appeal against the decision to an appeal body that is independent of the parties involved. This body can be a court or an administrative tribunal. An appeal against a decision of a regulatory authority does not have a suspensive effect unless the appeal body decides otherwise.

Article 20 of the Directive on European Electronic Communications Code also contains administrative law provisions on the obligation of regulated undertakings to provide the information necessary for the regulatory authorities to carry out their tasks. The Member States shall ensure that undertakings providing electronic communications networks and services, associated facilities, or associated services provide all the needed information, including financial information, necessary for national regulatory authorities, other competent authorities, and Body of European Regulators for Electronic Communications (BEREC).[292] BEREC acts as a forum for cooperation between national regulatory authorities and between said authorities and the Commission in the performance of all their tasks pursuant to the Union Framework.

4.2 Postal Services

The postal sector has traditionally been characterised by the existence of national state participants who have been protected in whole or in part by a legal monopoly. These

---

292. Regulation (EU) 2018/1971 of the European Parliament and of the Council of 11 Dec. 2018 establishing the Body of European Regulators for Electronic Communications (BEREC) and the Agency for Support for BEREC (BEREC Office), amending Regulation (EU) 2015/2120 and repealing Regulation (EC) No 1211/2009

state undertakings did not compete with each other. To the extent that their monopolies were not absolute, there could be limited competition from private undertakings. It was first in the 1990s that individual European countries independently began to open their postal sectors to competition. This occurred in Sweden and Finland, among others.

Postal deliveries can be divided into three stages:[293]

- Collection (clearance) and rough sorting of post.
- Transport of the rough-sorted post from one area to another.
- Detailed sorting and delivery.

It is normal for a postal service to be involved in all three stages. Thus, this is a vertically integrated sector. However, the transport of the rough-sorted post from one area to another is, to a large extent, done by sub-contractors (common carriers), including railway companies, airlines and road haulage companies. To the extent that there are essential facilities in the postal sector, this is mainly at the delivery stage, where duplication of the non-physical distribution network (postmen/women) can be economically non-viable, especially in thinly populated areas.

These parts of the postal services have typically been monopolised, among other things, on the grounds that this is necessary to maintain a reasonable postal service at a reasonable and often uniform price. As certain parts of the business have been more profitable than others, there has traditionally been cross-subsidisation between the more profitable and less profitable business segments. The digitalisation of written communication has, in particular, challenged the economy of letter post.

At the Union level, the general rules of the Treaty have been applied to the sector.[294] On 11 November 1992, the Commission published a Green Paper on the Development of the Single Market for Postal Services, and this was followed on 2 June 1993 by the Commission's Guidelines for the Development of Community Postal Services. In 1997, there was the Postal Services Directive.[295] This Directive was issued under the authority of Article 114 TFEU and introduced a minimum framework for the liberalisation of the postal sector; *see* Article 26 of the Directive.

The Postal Services Directive has been amended three times.[296]

4.2.1 Regulation under EU Law

For many years, the national state monopolies have cooperated. Special sets of rules (The Universal Postal Convention, since 1874) have been developed by the Universal

---

293. James I. Campbell Jr.: *Evolution of Terminal Dues and Remail Provision in European and International Postal Law*, in Damien Geradin (ed.): *The Liberalisation of Postal Services in the European Union*, p. 3 (2002).
294. *See* Case C-320/91, *Corbeau*; and Joined Cases C-147/97 and C-148/97, *Deutsche Post*.
295. Directive 97/67/EC on common rules for the development of the internal market of Community postal services and the improvement of quality of service. Later amended by Directive 2002/39/EC.
296. By Directive 2002/39/EC; Regulation (EC) No 1882/2003; and Directive 2008/6/EC.

Postal Union, and the WTO rules are also relevant.[297] International cooperation in the form of cost-sharing between the collection of post in one country and its delivery in another is regulated by the Universal Postal Convention.[298]

The regulation in the Union has the character of a minimum requirement for liberalisation and service levels. The most important directive is Directive 97/67/EC on common rules for the development of the internal market of Community postal services and the improvement of quality of service (the Postal Services Directive).

According to the definition in Article 2 of the Postal Services Directive, *postal services* involve 'the clearance, sorting, transport and delivery of postal items', which means items addressed in their final form in which they are to be carried by the universal service provider. In addition to items of correspondence, *postal items* include books, catalogues, newspapers, periodicals and postal packages containing merchandise with or without commercial value. The Member States are entitled to organise the siting of letterboxes on public highways, the issue of postage stamps and the registered mail service used in the course of judicial or administrative procedures in accordance with their national legislation; *see* Article 8 of the Directive.

The European Parliament and the Council have most recently adopted Directive 2008/6/EC, amending Directive 97/67/EC with regard to the full accomplishment of the internal market of Community postal services. The main purpose of the amendment was to do away with exclusive rights in the area of postal services, thereby making postal services part of the internal market. It includes a special scope for financing to guarantee the provision of a universal service, where necessary. The provisions of the Directive had to be implemented by 31 December 2010. However, a number of Member States have been given extensions until 31 December 2012.[299]

4.2.1.1 The Application of the General Competition Rules

The sector-specific rules are supplemented by the Notice from the Commission of 6 February 1998 on the application of the competition rules to the postal sector and on the assessment of certain State measures relating to postal services (OJ 1998 C 39/2), which contains the Commission's interpretation of the relevant Treaty provisions and guiding principles which the Commission uses when applying the Treaty competition rules to cases in the postal sector.

Among other things, this concerns topics such as the granting of exclusive rights, abuse of dominant position in connection with a granted exclusive right, and cross-subsidisation.

---

297. These rules are not dealt with in this chapter. For further information the reader is referred to David Luff: *International Regulation of Postal Services: UPU v. WTO Rules*, in Damien Geradin (ed.): *The Liberalisation of Postal Services in the European Union* p. 39-88 (2002).
298. *See* James I. Campbell Jr.: *Evolution of Terminal Dues and Remail Provision in European and International Postal Law*, in Damien Geradin (ed.): *The Liberalisation of Postal Services in the European Union* p. 3-38 (2002), for a description of the development of cost allocation for international mail.
299. These are Cyprus, Czech Republic, Greece, Hungary, Latvia, Lithuania, Luxembourg, Malta, Poland, Romania and Slovakia.

In the area of postal services, the general competition rules have given rise to a number of cases:

> In its Decision of 20 March 2001 (*Deutsche Post AG I*) the Commission gave its first formal decision on abuse of dominant position in the postal sector. Deutsche Post was fined EUR 24 million for having protected the market for commercial parcel services by using a long-term arrangement with loyalty rebates. The complainant (United Parcel Service) also claimed that Deutsche Post had undertaken cross-subsidisation to finance its activities on the market for commercial parcel services, which was subject to competition, enabling Deutsche Post to undercut prices by using revenues from its monopoly on the market for letters. The Commission did not impose any fine in connection with this, as it found that the cost calculations which were intended to show that there had been under-pricing were insufficiently developed. In connection with this case, Deutsche Post undertook to separate its commercial parcel services in an independent company (unbundling). This company could buy services from Deutsche Post at market prices, and Deutsche Post undertook to provide the same services to other providers of commercial parcel services at the same prices (non-discrimination).
>
> In Commission Decision of 25 July 2001 *(Deutsche Post AG II)*, it was claimed that Deutsche Post had abused is dominant position on the German market. In connection with received international mail, Deutsche Post had discriminated between different customers, refused to provide delivery services/carriage, charged excessive prices and restricted the development of the German market for international mail and the British market for mail to Germany. The fine on Deutsche Post was set at a symbolic EUR 1,000, because of the legal uncertainty which existed at the time of the offences.
>
> In the Commission's Decision of 5 December 2001 the Belgian postal service *(De Post/La Poste)* was fined EUR 2.5 million for abuse of its dominant position. The Belgian postal service had exploited its monopoly on letter postal services to make a reduction in rates conditional on customers also entering into contracts on the market which was open to competition, where a private Belgian undertaking operated a special document exchange system between undertakings.
>
> *See* also Case C-23/14, *Post Danmark v. Konkurrencerådet*, on a preliminary ruling on Post Danmark's discount system for direct advertising mail and a possible abuse of a dominant position.

State aid in the postal services sector has also been dealt with by the CJ in Joined Cases C-83/01, C-93/01 and C-94/01, *Chronopost and others*, which concerned cross-subsidisation. This case is discussed above in section 1.4.2.1. *See* also the case on state aid SA.57991 (2021) regarding Post Danmark processed according to the European Union's framework regulations on state aid in the form of compensation for public service. In March 2021, Denmark notified the Commission of its plan to compensate Post Danmark with DKK 225 million to fulfil the universal service obligation in 2020. The measure was appealed, and the Commission opened an investigation. However, the Commission found that the model used for the calculation was robust and conservative, that the compensation for Post Danmark did not exceed the public service costs, and that Post Danmark was, therefore, not overly compensated. *See* also T-525/20, *PostNord Logistics*.

4.2.1.2 Unbundling

Article 14 of the Postal Services Directive contains a requirement for the unbundling of accounts. Thus, a distinction must be made between the services covered by the reserved sector and the non-reserved services. Separate accounts must be kept for the services within the reserved sector and for the non-reserved services. The provision should be seen from the perspective of competition law. The aim is to prevent cross-subsidisation from an activity which is covered by an exclusive right to an activity carried on in a market which is open to competition. The Commission considers it essential to avoid cross-subsidisation, which leads to unfair competition if the postal sector is to develop.[300]

Paragraph 3.1 of the Notice of 6 February 1998 from the Commission on the application of the competition rules to the postal sector and on the assessment of certain State measures relating to postal services defines cross-subsidisation:

> Cross-subsidisation means that an undertaking bears or allocates all or part of the costs of its activity in one geographical or product market to its activity in another geographical or product market.

According to paragraph 3.4 of the Notice, postal operators which have been granted special or exclusive rights may not 'use the income from the reserved area to cross-subsidise activities in areas open to competition'.

One of the problem areas is the allocation of the direct costs and the common and overhead costs of the operator. In paragraph 3.4 of the Notice, it is stated that the prices of competitive services must, in principle, be at least equal to the average total costs connected with the provision of the service. This includes 'the direct costs plus an appropriate proportion of the common and overhead costs of the operator'. It has been argued that in a later decision, the Commission has adopted a less strict approach to the allocation of common costs.[301] The Postal Services Directive (Article 14) also uses the distinction between costs which can be directly assigned to a particular service and common costs which cannot be directly assigned to a particular service. Common costs must be allocated on the basis of an analysis of the origin of the costs themselves, on the basis of an indirect linkage to another cost category, or, in the absence of anything better, on the basis of a general allocation key.

In connection with a merger, the question of cross-subsidisation from a monopoly business to a business which was subject to competition was tried in Case T-175/99, *UPS*. A postal services undertaking had possibly used means obtained in an area where it had been granted exclusive rights in order to acquire a shareholding in an undertaking that operated in a sector of the postal market that was open to competition.

---

300. Notice of 6 Feb. 1998 from the Commission on the application of the competition rules to the postal sector and on the assessment of certain State measures relating to postal services, para. 3.1. On financing on the state budget, *see* C-226/22, *Nexive*.
301. Commission Decision 2001/354/EC of 20 Mar. 2001 relating to a proceeding under Art. 82 of the EC Treaty [now Art. 102 TFEU] (Case COMP/35.141 – Deutsche Post AG) (OJ 2001 L 125/27). *See* the discussion in Damien Geradin & Christophe Humpe: *The Liberalisation of Postal Services in the European Union: An Analysis of Directive 97/67*, in Damien Geradin (ed.): *The Liberalisation of Postal Services in the European Union*, p. 113 (2002). Decision 2001/354/EC is discussed above and in the Commission's XXXI Report on Competition Policy, p. 32.

As the GC could not establish that these means had been acquired by an abuse of the monopoly, there was no issue under competition law. This case is discussed in more detail above in the general discussion of cross-subsidisation.

4.2.2 Authorisation Procedures

For postal services that are not covered by an exclusive right (*see* below), Article 9 of the Postal Services Directive allows Member States to introduce national requirements for authorisation. This applies where it is necessary in order to guarantee compliance with a number of essential requirements. These include a number of non-economic considerations listed in Article 2 (as amended by Directive 2008/6/EC):

> Essential requirements: general non-economic reasons which can induce a Member State to impose conditions on the supply of postal services. These reasons are the confidentiality of correspondence, security of the network as regards the transport of dangerous goods, respect for the terms and conditions of employment, social security schemes, laid down by law, regulation or administrative provision and/or by collective agreement negotiated between national social partners, in accordance with Community and national law and, where justified, data protection, environmental protection and regional planning. Data protection may include personal data protection, the confidentiality of information transmitted or stored and protection of privacy.

The list must be assumed to be exhaustive. Such requirements for authorisation can also cover postal services which are not covered by a universal service obligation.

4.2.3 Access to Networks

According to Article 11 of the Postal Services Directive, the European Parliament and the Council, acting on a proposal from the Commission, must adopt such harmonisation measures as are necessary to ensure that users and the universal service providers have access to the public postal network under conditions which are transparent and non-discriminatory.

In the postal sector, access to a network is joined together with the universal service obligation referred to below, which benefits both end users and other market participants. The universal service obligation, as an instrument for network access, is particularly relevant for overseas mail.

There is some uncertainty about how this right of network access is to be interpreted. From the perspective of consumer protection, network access can be understood as a legal right to use the postal network, both as a sender and a receiver. However, such rights are, to a large extent, already protected by the universal service obligation. From a competition point of view, network access can be understood as the right of one undertaking to have access to the network of another undertaking. In this connection, one can envisage that a postal services undertaking will use the traditional postal service to provide for delivery in more thinly populated areas, where the duplication of the distribution network is associated with relatively high costs.[302] That part of the network could perhaps be considered an essential facility. The lack of access to it could constitute an abuse of a dominant position under Article 82 of the EC Treaty. The Commission will use this provision against competitors, provided the necessary conditions are fulfilled.[303] These conditions are illustrated by the *Bronner* case, which is dealt with above in section 1.2.

4.2.4 Public Service Obligations

Article 3 of the Postal Services Directive defines the public service obligation of the Member States. In their respective territories, the Member States must ensure that users enjoy the right to a universal service involving the permanent provision of a postal service of specified quality at affordable prices for all users.[304] They must establish collections and deliveries in accordance with the needs of users, with at least one collection and one delivery each weekday (five days a week), with deliveries to the residences of all natural and legal persons. This obligation must at least cover the collection and distribution of postal items up to 2 kilograms, and postal packages up to 10 kg. For postal packages from other Member States, the delivery obligation is for packages up to 20 kg. In this connection, it is a requirement that one or more national universal service providers be appointed.

The quality of the service is sought to be ensured by establishing standards. These quality standards include routing times and the regularity and reliability of services. For domestic services, these standards are set by each Member State, and for cross-border services within the Union, they are set by the European Parliament (published as an annex to the Directive; *see* Article 16). For these standards, independent performance monitoring must be carried out and reports published at least once a year. More technical standards are left to the CEN to prepare on the basis of mandates given in accordance with the Information Procedure Directive.[305]

4.2.4.1 Pricing Regulations

Article 12 of the Postal Services Directives provides that a number of conditions must be applied to the pricing of services covered by the universal service obligation:

---

302. Damien Geradin & Christophe Humpe: *The Liberalisation of Postal Services in the European Union: An Analysis of Directive 97/67*, in Damien Geradin (ed.): *The Liberalisation of Postal Services in the European Union*, p. 103-105 (2002).
303. Notice of 6 Feb. 1998 from the Commission on the application of the competition rules to the postal sector and on the assessment of certain State measures relating to postal services, para. 2.8.
304. This principle is similar to the public service obligation in the telecommunications sector.
305. Directive 83/189/EEC laying down a procedure for the provision of information in the field of technical standards and regulations. Directive 83/189/EEC has now been replaced by Directive 98/34/EC.

- prices must be affordable and must be such that all users have access to the services provided;
- prices must be geared to costs; Member States may decide that a uniform tariff should be applied throughout their national territory;[306]
- the application of a uniform tariff does not exclude the right of universal service providers to conclude individual agreements on prices with customers;[307]
- tariffs must be transparent and non-discriminatory.

The Directive does not contain any provisions on the pricing of services which fall outside the scope of the universal service obligation. Subject to respect for the general provisions of Union law, the Member States can either let pricing be unregulated or lay down national provisions.

The pricing provisions in Article 12 of the Postal Services Directive leave a number of points unclear. Thus, the term 'affordable' is not defined. In the Preface to the Notice of 6 February 1998 from the Commission on the application of the competition rules to the postal sector and on the assessment of certain State measures relating to postal services, there is a reference to 'prices everyone can afford'. This is also not very precise. It must be up to the Member States to interpret this requirement in the first instance.

For terminal dues (the remuneration of universal service providers for the distribution of incoming cross-border mail comprising postal items from another Member State or from a third country), the Member States are required to encourage their universal service providers to set terminal dues in relation to the costs of processing and delivering incoming cross-border mail in the receiving Member State, having regard for the quality of the service, and the terminal dues must be transparent and non-discriminatory. These requirements seem to have been satisfied to some extent by the Reims II Agreement.[308]

The general competition provisions of the Treaty apply in parallel with these special provisions. Among other things, these have been applied to pricing agreements on cost allocation in connection with cross-border postal services.

A number of the traditional postal services of EU and EEA Member States have entered into the Reims II Agreement, which lays down the price which the postal service in the country of origin pays to the postal service in the destination country to deliver the post to the recipient (terminal dues). The Reims II Agreement linked terminal dues to the domestic postal charges in the receiving country and the quality of service provided by the postal service which delivers the post. According to the Agreement, the terminal dues were to be increased each year for four years until

---

306. It is quite normal for the same postal charges to be payable regardless of the distance the postal item is transported, and regardless of the costs differences related to population density.
307. It must be assumed that such individually set charging rates (primarily for large customers) will not be an expression of discriminatory charges.
308. Renewed Notification of an Agreement on Terminal Dues (REIMS II) between Postal Operators (Case No IV/36.748 – *REIMS II*) (OJ 1998 C 53/3).

(unless they were reduced as a sanction for failure to live up to the required service level) they reached 80% of the domestic charges in 2001. On a couple of points, the Agreement was granted exemptions under Article 81(3) of the EC Treaty.[309]

Abuse of a dominant position is also a possibility in a sector which usually has a national operator with certain exclusive rights. On this topic, *see* this book's chapter on Article 102 TFEU.[310]

4.2.4.2 Exclusive Rights

Until its amendment by Directive 2008/6/EC, Article 7 of the Postal Services Directive (1997/67/EC) gave the Member States the possibility of giving universal service providers exclusive rights to handle certain categories of letter post if it was necessary for the maintenance of the universal service. After 2006, the possibility of awarding exclusive rights was restricted to a very limited part of the area served.

The idea of the exclusive right was that surpluses obtained from the area of the exclusive right could be used to cross-subsidise other commercially unprofitable parts of the universal service. An example of cross-subsidisation in the postal sector is the transfer of means from profitable distribution activities in urban areas to unprofitable post distribution in rural areas.[311]

The possibility of awarding exclusive rights has now been replaced by the possibility of paying compensation; *see* below.

The exercise of exclusive rights in relation to Article 86 of the EC Treaty was tried in Case C-320/91, *Corbeau*[312] and Joined Cases C-147/97 and C-148/97, *Deutsche Post*. These have given extended application to exclusive rights. For a criticism of this, *see* Damien Geradin & Christophe Humpe: *The Liberalisation of Postal Services in the European Union: An Analysis of Directive 97/67*, in Damien Geradin (ed.): *The Liberalisation of Postal Services in the European Union*, p. 97 (2002).

---

309. See the Commission's Decision of 15 Sep. 1999 in Case IV/36.748. *Reims II* is discussed in Damien Geradin & Christophe Humpe: *The Liberalisation of Postal Services in the European Union: An Analysis of Directive 97/67*, in Damien Geradin (ed.): *The Liberalisation of Postal Services in the European Union*, p. 109-111 (2002). For a description of terminal dues and their development, see James I. Campbell Jr.: *Evolution of Terminal Dues and Remail Provision in European and International Postal Law*, in Damien Geradin (ed.): *The Liberalisation of Postal Services in the European Union*, p. 26-29 (2002).
310. For a specialised presentation of this topic, in relation to the postal sector, *see* J. Derenne & C. Stockford: *Abuse of Market Power in Postal Services: Lessons from the Commission's Decisional Practice and Court of Justice*, in Damien Geradin (ed.): *The Liberalisation of Postal Services in the European Union* p. 139-184 (2002); and S. Baker & J. Dodgson: *Market Definition in Postal Services*, in Damien Geradin (ed.): *The Liberalisation of Postal Services in the European Union* p. 121.137 (2002).
311. This example is given in Notice of 6 Feb. 1998 from the Commission on the application of the competition rules to the postal sector and on the assessment of certain State measures relating to postal services, para. 3.2.
312. In contrast to the GC's decision in Case T-175/99, *UPS*, in the *Corbeau* case the court did not decide on the possibility of the privileged undertaking acting on markets which were open to competition.

4.2.4.3 Financial Compensation

An alternative to or supplement to allowing the holder of an exclusive right to cross-subsidise is the payment of financial compensation. Articles 7 and 9 of the Postal Services Directive allow for the possibility of paying support from public means by establishing a compensation fund financed by all postal service providers or users. The condition for the use of such a compensation fund is that the universal service obligations represent an unfair financial burden for the universal service provider. The compensation fund can be used to finance the services covered by the universal service obligations in Article 3.

The fund is financed by making the grant of authorisations conditional on making contributions to the fund. The costs are thereby shared with undertakings which do not have universal service obligations. The compensation fund must be administered by a body independent of the beneficiary or beneficiaries. Likewise, the Member States must ensure that the principles of transparency, non-discrimination and proportionality are respected. However, there do not seem to be any special control mechanisms established in this area.[313]

4.2.5 Public Authorities

Article 22 of the Postal Services Directive contains a requirement for each Member State to designate one or more national regulatory authorities for the postal sector. The regulatory authorities must be legally separate from and operationally independent of the postal operators – an unbundling requirement.

The Member States must also ensure the existence of a competent body to supervise the accounting requirements set out in Article 14 of the Directive. The body must be independent of any universal service provider. There does not appear to be anything to prevent this body from being the same as the national regulatory authority.

The Directive provides for a complaints procedure to be set up in connection with refusals to grant authorisation under Article 9 and in connection with users' complaints, particularly in cases involving loss, theft, damage or non-compliance with service quality standards; *see* Article 19.

Under Article 15 of the Postal Services Directive, the financial accounts of all universal service providers must be drawn up, submitted to audit by an independent auditor and published in accordance with the relevant Union and national legislation relating to commercial undertakings. The publication requirement also applies to the quality standards; *see* Article 18.

Finally, under Article 9 of the Postal Services Directive, a Member State must give reasons for refusing authorisation under Article 9.

---

313. *See* Damien Geradin & Christophe Humpe: *The Liberalisation of Postal Services in the European Union: An Analysis of Directive 97/67*, in Damien Geradin (ed.): *The Liberalisation of Postal Services in the European Union*, p. 102 (2002), which is critical of this in relation to an earlier formulation.

Bibliography

Christian Berqvist: *Between Regulation and Deregulation*, forthcoming (2016).
Peter Cameron: *Legal Aspects of EU Energy Regulation* (2005).
Peter Cameron: *Competition in Energy Markets* (2007).
Damian Chalmers, Gareth Davies & Giorgio Monti: *European Union Law* (2014).
Marise Cremona (ed.): *Market Integration and Public Service in the European Union* (2011).
Eugene D. Cross: *Electric Utility Regulation in the European Union* (1996).
I.H.Ph. Diederiks Verschoor: *An Introduction to Air Law* (2012).
Kjell A. Eliassen & Marit Sjøvaag (eds): *European Telecommunications Liberalisation* (1999).
Peter Forsyth, Kenneth Button & Peter Nijkamp (eds): *Air Transport* (2002).
Damien Geradin (ed.): *The Liberalization of State Monopolies in the European Union and Beyond* (2000).
Damien Geradin (ed.): *The Liberalization of Electricity and Natural Gas in the European Union* (2001).
Damien Geradin (ed.): *The Liberalization of Postal Services in the European Union* (2002).
Leigh Hancher, Tom Ottervanger & Piet Jan Slot: *EU State Aids* (2012).
Dieter Helm & Tim Jenkinson: *Competition in Regulated Industries* (1998).
Christopher W. Jones (ed.): *EU Energy Law*, Vol. I-II (2010–11).
Christopher Jones & William-James Kettlewell (ed.): *EU Energy Law – The internal Energy Market*, Vol. I, (2021).
Frank Manuhutu 2000: *Aviation Safety Regulation in Europe*. Air and Space Law, Volume 25 (2000) Issue 6.
Martha M. Roggenkamp, Anita Rønne, Catherine Redgwell & Iñigo del Guayo: *Energy Law in Europe* (2007).
Ekaterina Rousseva: *Rethinking Exclusionary Abuses in EU Competition Law* (2010).
Christopher Townsley: *Article 81 EC and Public Policy* (2009).
Ivo Van Bael & Jean-Francois Bellis: *Competition Law of the European Community* (2010).
Luc Werring (ed.): *EU Energy Law*, Vol. III (2006).

CHAPTER 12
Public Procurement

1 INTRODUCTION

1.1 History and Background

Public procurement in the EU is regulated at two levels. First, the private law contracts of public authorities are subject to the general rules of the Treaty on the Functioning of the European Union (TFEU), primarily the rules on freedom of movement. In a number of cases, the Court of Justice of the European Union (CJ) has ruled on the compatibility of measures which national authorities have laid down in connection with public procurement. In this context, it has been established that it is not compatible with the rules on freedom of movement for discriminatory conditions to be applied to the granting of public contracts. Thus, it is not permitted to require that the goods in question must be from some specific source or that the workers employed in the provision of a service must be of a specific nationality.[1] The rules on freedom of movement apply regardless of whether the secondary rules on public procurement (i.e., the public procurement directives – *see* below) apply.[2]

Depending on the circumstances, the competition rules (in Articles 101 and 102 TFEU) can be applicable to public procurement.[3] However, these provisions do not apply to the conduct of public bodies which place orders (contracting authorities), as the rules are only binding on undertakings, and public authorities are not considered to be undertakings merely because they make purchases on the market; *see* Case C-205/03 P, *FENIN*. However, in connection with public procurement, the competition rules are applicable to relations between suppliers. This means that the rules cover the

---

1. Some of the leading cases on freedom of movement and public procurement are: Case C-243/89, *Commission v. Denmark* (the bridge over the Great Belt – *Storebælt*), Case 45/87, *Commission v. Ireland* (Dundalk), and Case C-113/89, *Rush Portuguesa and others*.
2. This is seen in Case C-324/98, *Telaustria*, and Case C-59/00, *Vestergaard*.
3. *See* s. 10 in this chapter.

situation where an agreement is made between tenderers that one particular tenderer will win the contract (collusive tendering). Under such an agreement, the other tenderers will often push up the prices for their tenders, so the favoured tenderer will give the lowest bid, and this will often be enough to win the contract. The competition rules are also applicable to consortium agreements, i.e., agreements between more undertakings to work together on a joint offer.

Already by the end of the 1960s, it was clear that the Treaty rules on public procurement were not sufficient to ensure the removal of all the obstacles to a free market for such contracts. On this basis, from the beginning of the 1970s, the regulation of public procurement by means of directives was initiated. The first directives took effect from 1970, but the first of the directives as we know them today (Directive 71/305/EEC concerning the coordination of procedures for the award of public works contracts) took effect from 1971. The next directive to see the light of day was Directive 77/62/EEC coordinating procedures for the award of public supply contracts, which was adopted in 1977. After that, there was a gap of more than ten years before the regulation of public procurement was addressed again. This occurred at the end of the 1980s when there was a focus both on the adoption of the first of two control directives and on the first directive for entering into public procurement contracts for the provision of services.[4] At the beginning of the 1990s, there was a considerable increase in regulatory activity. This was against the background of the White Paper on the Internal Market of 1985, which led to the adoption of the Single European Act. This White Paper identified a number of areas which needed to be strengthened if the internal market was to function optimally – areas that included public procurement. This process culminated in 1992 and 1993 when most of the present regulation was laid down with the adoption of four substantive directives: the three classic directives (Directives 92/50/EEC, 93/36/EEC and 93/37/EEC on the coordination of procedures for the award of public service contracts, public supply contracts and public works contracts, respectively) and Directive 93/38/EEC on the procurement procedures of entities operating in the water, energy, transport and telecommunications sectors – the Utilities Procurement Directive. Towards the end of the 1990s, minor amendments were made to these four directives by Directive 97/52/EC (amending the classic directives) and Directive 98/4/EC (amending the Utilities Procurement Directive).

In 1996, the Commission published a Green Paper – Public Procurement in the European Union: Exploring the way forward,[5] which addressed a number of problems related to public procurement. The Green Paper was followed by further Communication from the Commission.[6] This follow-up document presented a number of initiatives for changing the existing regulation. These initiatives were in part prompted by the responses to the Green Paper.

---

4. Directive 89/665/EEC 989 on the coordination of the laws, regulations and administrative provisions relating to the application of review procedures to the award of public supply and public works contracts supplemented by Directive 92/13/EEC. These have been amended by Directive 2007/66/EC.
5. COM(96) 583 final.
6. COM(98) 143 final.

The first proposals for new directives governing public procurement were presented in the Proposal for a Directive on the coordination of procedures for the award of public supply contracts, public service contracts and public works contracts (COM(2000) 275 final) and the Proposal for a Directive coordinating the procurement procedures of entities operating in the water, energy and transport sectors (COM(2000) 276 final); these were adopted as Directive 2004/17/EC coordinating the procurement procedures of entities operating in the water, energy, transport and postal services sectors, and Directive 2004/18/EC on the coordination of procedures for the award of public works contracts, public supply contracts and public service contracts respectively. To a large extent, the core of the procurement rules remains the same. However, some changes have occurred. The biggest changes included a greater focus on electronic communication, the introduction of new forms of tendering, the introduction of better possibilities for taking account of non-economic factors, the introduction of rules on framework agreements, and the consolidation of the three classic directives as one directive, the structuring of the directive to match the chronology of the procedure.

The development of Union procurement law took a further step forward with the Green Paper on the modernisation of EU public procurement policy – towards a more efficient European Procurement Market (COM(2011) 15 final). Here, the focus was on improving the framework for innovation, improving the business environment, encouraging wider use of green public procurement and generally improving the existing procurement rules. In December 2011, the work on the Green Paper resulted in a draft for a new Public Sector Directive (COM(2011) 896 final) and a new Utilities Directive (COM(2011) 895 final). In February 2014, the process culminated in the adoption of three new directives: at the same time as the new Procurement Directive (Directive 2014/24/EU),[7] a new Utilities Directive (Directive 2014/25/EU)[8] was adopted and for the first time a Concession Contracts Directive (Directive 2014/23/EU) was adopted.[9] The current status is that there are four substantive directives as well as directives regulating enforcement. The following section focuses on the Procurement Directive, and the other directives are discussed briefly in section 1.4.

1.2 The Aim

The aim of the public procurement directives is to ensure that undertakings in the internal market have the possibility of participating in competition for the award of public contracts and have the opportunity of having public contracts awarded to them. This is shown in, among other things, Case C-243/89, *Commission v. Denmark* (the bridge over the Great Belt – *Storebælt*), in which regard for competition was seen as being the basis for the principle of equal treatment which, according to the CJ, exists in public procurement law and is the fundamental principle in this field of law. It must be

---

7. Directive 2014/24/EU on public procurement.
8. Directive 2014/25/EU on procurement by entities operating in the water, energy, transport and postal services sectors.
9. Directive 2014/23/EU on the award of concession contracts.

assumed that the public procurement directives were and are intended to give the contracting authority the possibility of making advantageous agreements. The competitive situation which arises from inviting offers should lead to lower-priced bids, which is naturally to the advantage of purchasers. However, the benefit which the purchasers are expected to obtain is only secondary to the primary purpose of the directives, which is to open the market for public procurement to interested undertakings within the EU.

The means by which this goal is achieved is a set of rules which are intended to remove the protectionism which it is assumed characterised the making of public procurement contracts prior to the establishment of the internal market. In the view of the European institutions, contracting authorities can potentially be assumed to have a tendency to choose tenderers from their own area/Member State when allocating public contracts. The risk of such behaviour has made it difficult for undertakings from other Member States to gain access to the markets for public supplies. On this basis, the EU legislator has adopted a set of rules to ensure, on the one hand, that there is no discrimination between undertakings and, on the other hand, to achieve a certain measure of transparency in connection with the making of public contracts.

1.3 Description of the Tendering Procedure

Public procurement can take many different forms, depending on which type of procurement procedure is chosen, how the selection of undertakings is arranged, the criteria chosen for the award of a contract, etc. Regardless of these differences, it is possible to give a basic description of what generally characterises public procurement procedures.

The process starts with the publication of a contract notice, which has the aim of informing the market about the task for which offers of supply are sought. The contract notice must give the necessary information to enable potential tenderers to get an impression of the task. In order to ensure the content of the contract notice, standard forms for the publication of notices have been established in connection with the procurement directives.[10] Following this contract notice, interested undertakings must be given further information about the tendering procedure and the contract for which tenders are sought. This information can be given at different points in the procedure. The most important source of this information is the tender documentation which is given to the undertakings or made fully available to them on a website. The actual tendering process consists of assessing the suitability of undertakings for taking on the task in question, an assessment of the offers made, and ends with the award of the contract to the undertaking which has submitted the best offer.

In the following, there is a more detailed description of the individual elements of the tendering procedure.

---

10. *See* Regulation (EU) 2015/1986 and Regulation (EU) 2019/1780.

Chapter 12

1.4 The Other Procurement Directives

Of the four directives, the Procurement Directive has the broadest scope as it covers the whole of the public sector in all the Member States. Thus, the major focus here is on the Procurement Directive. The provisions discussed here are largely the same in all four directives, so the review of most of the rules of the Procurement Directive will also apply to the other directives. However, there are some differences, and the main differences are discussed in the following.

1.4.1 Particular Features of the Utilities Directive

The major difference between the Procurement Directive and the Utilities Directive is that if a contracting authority operates a utility undertaking and has to purchase goods and/or services for these activities, the Utilities Directive applies. For public entities (and certain private entities which have been granted special or exclusive rights) in the areas of water, energy, transport and postal services, the Utilities Directive constitutes the primary basis for purchasing. In the main, the Utilities Directive differs from the Procurement Directive by being more flexible in its approach to the procurement process. Among other things, this means that within the scope of the Utilities Directive, a procurement procedure which gives access to negotiations during the process can always be chosen - this opportunity does not exist in the Procurement Directive. The process also provides for some more flexible methods; for example, under the Utilities Directive, it is possible to use a qualification system which gives the procuring entity the possibility of having a number of qualified economic entities registered on a list from which the procuring entity can initiate a (faster and less burdensome) procurement process.

Finally, the Utilities Directive is characterised by the fact that to a certain extent its application depends on whether the purchase relates to an activity that is connected with the utilities activities covered by the Directive. If an entity covered by the Directive is to make a procurement for part of its organisation that does not work directly in the utility area concerned, this purchase should be made pursuant to the Procurement Directive. Correspondingly, if a contracting authority within the area covered by the Utilities Directive chooses to enter into a concession contract instead of a purchase contract, then the Concession Contracts Directive will apply. *See* more about concession contracts below in section 1.4.3.

1.4.2 Particular Features of the Defence Procurement Directive

A Defence Procurement Directive was adopted for the first time in 2009.[11] The particular feature of this sector is that defence and security procurement can be

---

11. Directive 2009/81/EC on the coordination of procedures for the award of certain works contracts, supply contracts and service contracts by contracting authorities or entities in the fields of defence and security.

sensitive. When purchasing advanced technology weapons, etc., there can be a need for a high level of confidentiality compared to traditional purchasing. This is reflected in the Treaty exceptions to its general provisions for certain procurements in the defence sector (*see* Article 346 TFEU) and in the fact that in several aspects, the Defence Procurement Directive is formulated differently from the Procurement Directive.

Among the primary differences between the Defence Procurement Directive and the Procurement Directive are that open procurement procedures cannot be used, that there are special requirements for confidentiality in connection with procurement, and that there can be special requirements on the use of subcontractors. All these factors reflect the desire for confidentiality associated with procurement in this sector, while the Procurement Directive puts considerable emphasis on transparency.

1.4.3 *Particular Features of the Concession Contracts Directive*

The starting points for the Procurement Directive, the Utilities Directive and the Defence Procurement Directive are that they apply to public procurement contracts, i.e., contracts under which a public body pays for the provision of the goods, services, etc., which it purchases. A concession contract is an alternative to a purchase contract. Typically, under a concession contract, 'one or more contracting authorities or contracting entities entrust the provision and the management of services ... to one or more economic operators, the consideration of which consists either solely in the right to exploit the services that are the subject of the contract or in that right together with payment' (Article 5(1)(b) of the Concession Contracts Directive). Basically, this definition means that the concessionaire takes on a considerable part of the operating risk associated with the building and construction project or service concerned. The EU found that special rules were required for concession contracts, and, as part of the procurement package, a Concession Contracts Directive was adopted for the first time in February 2014. Concession contracts had previously been excluded from the Procurement Directive, though there had been some light regulation of building and construction concessions contracts which were primarily governed by the general principles of Union law (equal treatment and transparency) and the provisions of the TFEU. Thus, the framework for entering into concession contracts has been very flexible, with considerable freedom for contracting authorities to arrange and carry out procurements. The framework established by such practice constitutes the basis for the provisions in the Concession Contracts Directive. In general, most of the Directive's provisions on the criteria and framework for selecting undertakings and assessing tenders are recognisable from the Procurement Directive, and the Concession Contracts Directive does not have rules on the procurement procedure itself, which is a marked difference. The fact that the Concession Contracts Directive does not lay down procurement procedures means that contracting authorities have broad scope to choose the procedure they consider appropriate for entering into a concession contract.

2 THE OBLIGATION TO INVITE OFFERS

There is no general obligation of public authorities to offer their procurements to public competition. Public authorities decide for themselves whether to invite tenders to carry out a task or whether to carry it out themselves. However, under certain conditions, public bodies have an obligation to put a task out to tender.

2.1 Ex-house Contracting

The obligation to submit procurements to public competition depends first of all on whether there is a mutual contract. The public procurement directives only regulate agreements between two separate entities, as it is not possible to enter into an agreement with oneself. From this comes the in-house rule, whereby only purchases which are entrusted to entities outside the contracting authority are subject to the rules of public procurement. Thus, purchases which are made within the same legal entity are not subject to the rules of public procurement. However, there can be situations where an entity is of such a size, with a number of divisions that are sufficiently separate from each other so as to be considered different entities for the purposes of the public procurement directives so that one division's purchases from another division can be considered to be third party purchases. However, exceptions to the principle that purchases made outside the legal entity are subject to the rules of public procurement also exist. Based on the requirement that contracts should be for pecuniary interest, the CJ has held that cooperation between public bodies can be such that the procurement rules do not apply. This case law covers both institutional cooperation (between one public authority and another entity which is controlled by the first authority) and contractual cooperation between autonomous public authorities.[12]

New provisions were included in Article 12 of the Procurement Directive, based on the CJ's case law. These provisions did not merely codify the case law but referred to further situations in which the procurement procedure can be omitted where there is cooperation between purchasing authorities.

According to these provisions, a procurement contract can be assigned from one contracting authority to another contracting authority without having to carry out a new procurement procedure as long as the first authority exercises control over the second authority and as long as at least 80% of the activities of the second authority are carried out for the first authority; see Article 12(1) of the Procurement Directive. Likewise, as a rule, an in-house situation only exists if there is no private sector participation in a controlling entity. As something new in relation to the case law, it is also possible to assign contracts from the controlled to the controlling authority and between two purchasing entities that are controlled by the same purchasing entity. In both these situations, the exception only applies as long as there is no private entity

---

12. The *Teckal* practice on institutional cooperation is followed; *see* Case C-107/98 *Teckal* and subsequent cases. The framework for contractual cooperation was first introduced by the CJ in Case C-480/06, *Commission v. Germany*.

involvement.[13] In relation to horizontal agreements, there can be assignment of contractual rights between two contracting authorities without carrying out procurement procedures, as long as: (a) the contract establishes or implements a cooperation between the participating contracting authorities with the aim of ensuring that public services they have to perform are provided so as to achieve objectives they have in common; (b) the implementation of this cooperation is governed solely by consideration for the public interest; and (c) the participating contracting authorities perform on the open market less than 20% of the activities concerned by the cooperation (*see* Article 12(4)).

2.2 Threshold Values

In addition to the condition that there must be a third-party purchase, there is also no obligation to comply with the public procurement rules unless the expected value of the contract exceeds the financial limits laid down in connection with the directives – the threshold values. These values are laid down for the different kinds of purchase (i.e., services, goods and public works contracts) and are laid down by the Commission for two years at a time and can be found on the website of the European Commission. The threshold values relate to the expected value of the contract, exclusive of VAT. For public works contracts, the threshold is around EUR 5,538 million, while it is somewhat lower for purchases of goods and services at EUR 221,000. These are the thresholds for local government authorities. For state purchases, the thresholds are lower.

On the basis of these thresholds, it could be advantageous for a contracting authority to have a contract categorised as a public works contract rather than a contract for goods or services. The contracting authority must make a genuine valuation of the expected value of the proposed purchase. It is naturally contrary to the rules for the contracting authority to deliberately make an incorrect valuation (setting the value of the contract below the threshold) with a view to avoiding the use of the public procurement procedure. Nor can the contracting authority satisfy the requirements by making a rough estimate of the value of the contract; it is required to demonstrate sufficient thoroughness in assessing the expected value of the contract.

One popular method for keeping the value of a purchase below the threshold values is to split up the contract so as to produce several contracts, each of a lower value. With a view to preventing such avoidance of the procurement obligations, a rule in the directives provides that, if there is such a splitting up of the contract, the contract values must be added together so as to determine whether the purchase is subject to the procurement rules.[14] Even though the aim of the provision is in accordance with the idea behind the procurement directives, it can be difficult to determine which contacts should be added together. Where several identical contracts are entered into at the

---

13. However, *see* Art. 12(1)(1) of Directive 2014/24/EU which allows the exception to apply even if there is involvement by a private entity as long as such involvement is not of a controlling or blocking nature and is required under national law.
14. *See* Art. 5(3) of Directive 2014/24/EU.

same time, there will be an assumption that this is to avoid the procurement rules. However, there can be other situations where the connection between the contracts is not so obvious. In assessing whether contracts have been artificially divided, an account must be taken of the content of the contracts, their timing, and other relevant circumstances.

After the entry into force of the WTO's procurement rules[15] (Agreement on Government Procurement (GPA)),[16] the threshold values are expressed in Special Drawing Rights (SDRs) in addition to the euro and national currencies. This is because of the harmonisation of the European threshold values with the international values in the GPA. Thus, the threshold values relate both to purchases under the EU regime and under the WTO regime.

3 CONTRACTING AUTHORITIES

The entities covered by the Procurement Directive ('contracting authorities') are defined in its Article 2(1)(1). The Directive is binding on public authorities, including state, regional or local authorities, as well as on bodies governed by public law and associations of such authorities.[17]

The term *public authorities* naturally covers state and regional/local administrative bodies. In addition to true administrative authorities, other entities which are linked to the public sector are covered. The assessment of this is based on a functional interpretation; *see* Case 31/87, *Beentjes*.

Bodies governed by public law are entities that: (1) meet a need of the general public in a non-commercial capacity; (2) are independent legal persons; and (3) are controlled in some form or other by a public authority or some other legal person governed by public law. These conditions are cumulative, i.e., they must all be fulfilled in order for an entity to be categorised as a body governed by public law. The concept is one that has frequently been considered by the CJ.[18]

For example, the condition of meeting the needs of the general public has been found to be fulfilled where the authority in question is responsible for forestry management, refuse collection, running a university, printing services, environmental management, running a housing association, conducting the business of an undertaker, as well as certain forms of trading in real property and property management. Furthermore, the CJ has stressed that it is not a requirement that the entity undertakes the service itself in order to meet the needs of the general public, but that the condition also is met if the entity undertakes a support function (e.g., manufactures or maintains locomotives and rolling stock for the railway sector, in cases where the railway service

---

15. From 1 January 1996.
16. On the GPA, *see* s. 12 below.
17. Under the Utilities Directive and the Concession Contracts Directive 'contracting authorities' includes purchasing entities that are not public bodies.
18. *See, e.g.*, Case C-360/96, *Arnhem*, Case C-44/96, *Mannesmann Anlagebau*, Case C-306/97, *Connemara Machine Turf*, Case C-380/98, *Cambridge University*, Joined Cases C-223/99 and C-260/99, *Agorà*, Case C-237/99, *Commission v. France*, Case C-373/00, *Adolf Truly*, and Case C-393/06, *Ing. Aigner*.

is meeting the needs of the general public).[19] Furthermore, arranging trade fairs has been accepted as meeting the needs of the general public; *see* Joined Cases C-223/99 and C-260/99, *Agorá*. In this case, the activity was, however, carried on in such a way that it was found to meet the needs of the general public but in a commercial area, so the undertaking fell outside the definition of a public law body. Among other things, the CJ emphasised that the undertaking was administered according to the criteria of performance, efficiency and cost-effectiveness. It also found that the undertaking operated in a competitive environment. However, this was not decisive in itself, but together with the way in which the activities were carried on, the CJ found that there was an undertaking of a commercial character.

It will often not be difficult to determine whether an entity is a legal person. An undertaking will often be organised as one of the known forms of corporation. However, there can be cases where it is not obvious whether an entity is a legal person. In these cases, the CJ must use a concrete evaluation to establish whether the undertaking is a legal person, presumably by seeing whether the entity has legal capacity, etc. To determine whether there is a dominant influence over the body in question, and in particular, over its purchasing, the procurement directives lay down three different criteria, of which one must be fulfilled. First, there can be a dominant influence by a contracting authority if the authority, directly or indirectly, holds the majority of the undertaking's subscribed capital, or controls the majority of the votes attached to shares issued by the undertaking, or can appoint more than half of the undertaking's administrative, management or supervisory body.

4   PREPARATION OF THE CONTRACT NOTICE

4.1   General

A number of steps must be taken before a contract notice is issued, including making a description of what is to be purchased so that undertakings which may be interested in tendering can participate in the competition for the order, and so the competing undertakings have a clear idea about the procurement procedures chosen and thus understand the basic principles of the competition.

As part of the preparations, it is often necessary to use the services of a technical adviser, as typically, the contracting authority does not always have the necessary specialist knowledge to prepare the contract notice on their own. Such cooperation can create a problem if the technical adviser then wants to take part in the competition for the order. This is a problem, as the adviser may have obtained a competitive advantage and be in a stronger competitive situation than other tenderers. The possibility of using technical advisers is dealt with in more detail below in the section on the principle of equal treatment.

---

19. *See* Case C-567/15, *LitSpecMet*.

4.2 Specification of the Object of the Contract

The specification of the object of the contract is made, on the one hand, by categorising the nature of the product required and, on the other hand, by giving a detailed description of what is wanted.

The first specification is made with reference to various standard nomenclatures, primarily the Common Procurement Vocabulary (CPV).[20]

The second specification is a detailed description of what goods or services are required. The object of a contract can be described in two different ways: either by the contracting authority's function-based description of the goods or services required or by reference to technical specifications, including standards. The first possibility was introduced in the former Procurement Directive 2004/18/EC on the basis that there had been a lack of a possibility to draw up a specification other than by reference to standards, etc. As for the second possibility (reference to technical specifications), the Directive establishes a hierarchy for which technical specifications are to be used and when. This hierarchy means that, where possible, European or international technical specifications are to be used. If no European specifications exist, then national technical specifications can be used as long as these give a better description. If it is not possible to find national standards, then other national specifications can be used.

In recent years, the possibility of focusing on function when describing a task has led to increased attention to the concept of functional requirements. These are not defined in the procurement rules, but in such procurements (functional procurements), the contracting authority does not give a detailed description in advance of how the task is to be performed but lays down a number of functional requirements (goals) instead. Thus, it is not the activities to be carried out during the contractual period that are described but the desired outcome. This is naturally reflected in the way in which the task is specified, and the functional, goal-oriented elements will predominate in the contract.

In principle, it is not permitted to describe the object of a contract by reference to a trademark or the specific manufacturer of a product. This is because reference to a specific trademark or manufacturer will give an advantage to the undertaking that produces the product in question, as the reference product can easily be understood as being the product required. Other products will thus start with a competitive handicap in relation to the reference product. On the contrary, it can be an obvious and convenient way for a purchaser to describe a task by referring to a product which is well known on the market and has a number of the characteristics which the purchaser wants. On this ground, it is possible in exceptional cases to use specific products or trademarks as a reference point. This is possible where a sufficiently precise and intelligible description of the subject matter of the contract is not otherwise possible. A condition for the use of a trademark as a reference point is that it must be accompanied by the words 'or equivalent'. This is to indicate that the product named merely represents the desired characteristics of the subject matter of the contract and that it is

---

20. *See* Art. 23 of the Directive 2014/24/EU.

not necessarily the reference product itself that is required but merely a product which has the same characteristics.

The CJ has considered this provision in a few cases. In Case 45/87, *Commission v. Ireland (Dundalk)*, an Irish local government authority had made a purchase in connection with the improvement of the water supply installations. In describing the installations, and specifying certain pipes, a reference had been made to a special Irish standard. In its judgment, the CJ held that the public procurement directives did not apply, but that Article 34 TFEU did.[21] The CJ held, with general applicability to all provisions on technical specifications, that a contracting authority may not reject an offer merely because it does not formally comply with the stated specification, but it is obliged to examine whether the product offered can in fact comply with the specifications. Case C-353/93, *Commission v. Netherlands (UNIX)*, concerned the purchase of a meteorological station, where the contracting authority had described the operating system by reference to the trademark UNIX. The contracting authority had not added 'or equivalent' after the reference, which in itself meant that the reference was in breach of the procurement rules. The CJ did not consider in more detail whether the requirements of necessity or adequacy were fulfilled in the case in question, but as there was apparently a possibility of describing the operating system objectively, the conditions for using the 'or equivalent' provision would not have been fulfilled. It is not enough that an objective description would have led to greater costs for the contracting authority than a reference to a product that was well known on the market. This decision was followed in Case C-328/96, *Commission v. Austria (UNIX II)* and in Case C-59/00, *Vestergaard*.

The use of standards has a clearly positive aspect in that it is possible to find objective references that are known by the whole market. However, there are also disadvantages connected with the use of technical specifications. For instance, the whole process of drawing up standards requires detailed work and takes a long time. This means that when a standard is finally adopted, it may not represent the latest technological developments in the area in question.

Furthermore, by referring in particular to trademarks and suchlike, it is not clear to the interested undertakings precisely which characteristics are decisive for the subject matter of the contract. Standards are often formulated as a description of the characteristics of the products in question. In such a case, it is primarily the most important qualities of the product which characterise the standard. With references to trademarks and suchlike, there is a reference not only to the product's characteristics but also to its design, composition, etc. This means that where there is merely a reference to a trademark, it is not always clear which specific characteristics of the reference product are required for the subject matter of the contract. It will often be assumed that the functional characteristics must be decisive for the reference and must be equally decisive for whether a product offered is regarded as having the desired characteristics.

---

21. The procurement took place before the current public procurement directives were adopted, and as water supply was excluded from the directive on public works procurement, the purchase fell outside the scope of the public procurement directives.

4.3 Publication

A requirement for establishing a competitive bidding procedure is that undertakings on the market should have the possibility, in one way or another, of being made aware that tenders are being invited. This is done by publishing a contract notice in the Official Journal of the European Union, S series. There are different kinds of notices, of which the notice at the commencement of the procurement procedure is one. There are special requirements for the framing of all forms of notices in the Official Journal.

Publication in the Official Journal is only a requirement if the threshold values for the different kinds of contracts are exceeded.

Publication in the Official Journal, series S, only takes place electronically, and the contract notices are available in Tenders Electronic Daily (TED)[22] which is an electronic medium which contains the same information and has the same function as series S of the Official Journal. Contracting authorities are permitted to publish contract notices in other national and international media. However, such advertising must first be made after the notice required by the directives has been sent to the Publications Office for the Official Journal, and the national advertisement may not contain information which is not given in the notice published in the Official Journal.

4.3.1 *Requirements for Publication*

The public procurement directives contain a number of specific requirements for the publication of contract notices which must be communicated as part of the procurement process. Thus, for each type of procurement, there are different requirements as to the content of the contract notice in the Official Journal.[23] In addition to the publication of contract notices, the contracting authority must also publish a *prior information notice*. A prior information notice is a notice about proposed purchases for the forthcoming year.

In addition to these requirements at the start of the procurement procedure, there are also requirements for publication when the procurement procedure is completed. The form of publication for this is also determined by the forms in annexes to the directives.

4.4 Determination of the Type of Task

Which type of task is involved is decisive for the application of the public procurement directives. Public contracts are divided into three categories: public supply contracts, public service contracts (two types exist)[24] and public works contracts. This division is

---

22. *See* the website: simap.ted.europa.eu.
23. Forms have been created for publication of each of the different contract notices, *see* Regulation (EU) 2015/1986 and Regulation (EU) 2019/1780. The latter Regulation repeals the first mentioned Regulation with effect from 25 October 2023.
24. *See* for instance the category 'general services' and the category 'social and other specific services'.

relevant in two respects. First, there are different threshold values for the different types of tasks; *see* above. Second, to some extent, different rules apply to the different tasks.

The assessment of whether a contract concerns a public service or a public construction work is based on the nature of the task in question. Thus, it must be considered whether what is being bought is a service, or building, or construction work. The distinction is usually not difficult, as most services are not confusable with building or construction work. For example, the collection of rubbish for a local government authority or providing public transport for a local government authority has no points of similarity with construction work. However, in a few cases, there can be doubt about whether a task constitutes building renovation (a service) or building and construction work. Article 2(1)(6) of the Procurement Directive will be the starting point here, and its three definitions of building and construction work. It is building and construction work if: (1) a reference is made to Annex II to the Procurement Directive where a list of five main groups of building and construction tasks is included; (2) a reference is made to the definition of building and construction work in Article 2(1)(7), according to which '"a work" means the outcome of building or civil engineering works taken as a whole which is sufficient in itself to fulfil an economic or technical function'; or (3) the execution of building and construction works corresponding to the requirements specified by the contracting authority (even though it is not the contracting authority's site or building. Where there is a conflict between a building and construction task and a service, the categorisation will be made in favour of a task being a building and construction task. This is on the basis of the provision in Article 2(1)(9) of the Procurement Directive, according to which a task will be considered to be a service if it is not regarded as a public works contract.

The distinction between public supply contracts, public service contracts and public works contracts seldom causes problems. There is an example in Case C-331/92, *Casino*. The contract involved the installation of a casino and certain building and construction services. However, the greater part of the value of the contract concerned the management of the casino, so the contract was not considered a public works contract. Another example is the distinction between goods and services. Buying standard software for computers is considered to be a purchase of goods, whereas buying specially tailor-made software is considered to be a purchase of services. Another problem which often arises is the question of how mixed contracts should be treated. A mixed contract can, for example, be a contract which concerns both the provision of goods and services. A concrete example of a mixed contract is an overall agreement for the purchase of computers and computer training. For such contracts, it is clearly important to determine how the contract is to be classified, as this is relevant for which rules will apply to the contract notice. The main rule is that such a contract should be awarded in accordance with the provisions applicable to the type of procurement that characterises the main subject of the contract in question; *see* Article 3(2) of the Procurement Directive. An important aid to determining the main subject of the contract can be to look at the financial value of each task covered by the contract.

In a couple of cases, the CJ has had to rule on a related question. In these cases, the situation was not whether a contract was for goods or services but whether an agreement concerned participation in a company or a purchase agreement since the agreements included elements of both aspects. If an agreement is a purchase agreement, then the procurement directives should apply. The CJ ruled that in such cases, the starting point must be the same considerations as those that apply to contracts for purchases of both goods and services. The CJ stated that if an agreement (dealing both with the formation of a company and purchases of goods) constitutes an indivisible whole, the nature of the contract is to be determined by looking at the central subject matter of the agreement. In Joined Cases C-145 and 149/08, *Hotel Club Loutraki*, the CJ found that there was effectively an agreement for participation in a company, whereas in Case C-215/09, *Mehiläinen Oy*, the contract was not an indivisible whole, and the part of the contract which concerned purchases whose value exceeded the threshold should be put out to tender in accordance with the requirements of the procurement directives.[25]

4.5 Documentation for Contract Notices

There are certain requirements for the contents of the documents which form the basis of the contract notice. There is a requirement that the documentation (i.e., the materials which give a more detailed description of the subject matter of the contract) must be sufficiently detailed to enable interested parties to prepare an offer that can satisfy the conditions of the contracting authority. Second, the offer must also be clear and comprehensible, and it must be in accordance with the contract notice.

Pursuant to Article 53 of the Procurement Directive, contracting authorities must offer unrestricted, full direct electronic access free of charge to the procurement documents from the date of publication of a procurement notice.

The liability for any lack of clarity in the contract notice or in offers naturally rests with the party which has prepared the material in question. If the contracting authority's framing of the contract notice is inadequate on one or more points, it will not be to the disadvantage of the tenderer if, as a result of this, the tenderer has to establish its own assumptions or correct the wrong information given by the contracting authority. However, this approach is not unproblematic as there is a risk that tenderers will have differing assumptions, so the procurement contest will have different conditions for different participants. In such a case, there would potentially be a breach of the principle of equal treatment.

The possibility of providing supplementary information or correcting the documentation is reviewed below in the section on making the award of the contract and the section on the prohibition of negotiation.

---

25. In Case C-332/20 *Roma Multiservizi*, the Court ruled that the two parts of the contract constituted an indivisible whole, and thus the contract should be categorised according to its objective. The Court found that the objective of the contract was provision of services, and not formation of a company, which constituted the other part of the contract.

4.6 Electronic Contract Notices

According to Article 22(1) of the Procurement Directive, all communication about a tender must take place in electronic form.[26] The Procurement Directive leaves it to the Member States to ensure that all communication and information exchanges are made using electronic communication in accordance with the requirement in Article 22 of the Directive. Among other things, the tools and devices used for electronic communication, as well as their technical characteristics, must be non-discriminatory, generally available and interoperable with information and communications technology products in general use and must not restrict economic operators' access to the procurement procedure.

In addition to the general rules for electronic communication, the Procurement Directive contains rules on public procurement procedures that can be conducted entirely electronically. First, Article 34 of the Directive describes a procedure for dynamic purchasing systems. Briefly, this procedure involves establishing a list of undertakings with a standing indicative tendering procedure, and when the contracting authority makes a specific purchase, it initiates a mini-tender among the participants on the list. Second, contracting authorities can conclude a tendering competition by means of a fully electronic reverse auction where the tenderers can compete with each other on price and other elements; *see* Article 35. Finally, Article 36 allows for the possibility of using electronic catalogues. Contracting authorities can thus require that tenders be submitted in the form of an electronic catalogue or that tenders should include such a catalogue.

4.7 Deadlines

The procurement directives lay down deadlines for the submission of tenders, applications for prequalification, etc. The deadline for requests to participate in restricted procedures, negotiated procedures, competitive dialogue and innovation partnerships is thirty days. There is a further deadline of thirty days for the submission of tenders under restricted procedures. For the other procedures referred to, the contracting authority must set an appropriate deadline for the receipt of tenders following the end of negotiations. For open procedures, the deadline for submitting tenders is thirty-five days. Where there is an urgent need, the deadline for submitting a tender under open procedures can be reduced to fifteen days, and for restricted procedures, depending on the circumstances, the deadline can be reduced to ten days, and the deadline for requests to participate in restricted procedures can be reduced to fifteen days; *see* further in Articles 28 and 29 of the Procurement Directive.

---

26. According to Art. 90(2) of the Procurement Directive, the transition to a full electronic tendering could be postponed until not later than 18 October 2018 (i.e., the ordinary time limit for implementation).

5 TYPES OF CONTRACT

It is possible to enter into different types of contracts. The traditional contracts are sales contracts in which the product in question, the quantity and the price are determined in advance. However, it is also possible to enter into contracts in which the final quantity is not predetermined – framework contracts. In addition to this, it is also possible to make concession contracts. A concession contract is an agreement which has the same characteristics as traditional contracts but where the payment consists of the right to carry on a particular activity, possibly in conjunction with paying for the right; *see* further in section 1.4.3 above.

In addition to contracts for outright sales, the Directive also covers contracts for the leasing of goods.

5.1 Framework Agreements

The procurement directives allow for the possibility of entering into framework agreements; *see* Article 33 of the Procurement Directive. A framework agreement is an agreement between one or more contracting authorities and one or more economic actors with the purpose of laying down the terms of the contracts, which should be awarded in a given period of time, especially with regard to price and, if relevant, to the intended quantities.[27] Even though it had been possible to use framework agreements for several decades, express rules on this were first introduced in Directive 2004/18/EC. A framework agreement is a contract like an ordinary sales contract, except that the quantity to be sold is not fixed. Thus, in the same way as with ordinary contracts, a framework agreement lays down all (or at least most of) the terms which are considered necessary for the purchase, except for the quantity that should be purchased. Framework agreements are entered into in situations where, over a given period (for up to four years), a contracting authority *may* need to make purchases or where it is certain that purchases will be made but where the quantity cannot be determined in advance. To the extent that the contracting authority wishes to make purchases of the product in question during the lifetime of the agreement, this purchase will be made in accordance with the conditions of the framework agreement, just as in the case of a traditional sales contract. If the contracting authority does not wish to make a purchase, for example, if it happens that there is no need which the contracting authority expected, the contracting authority can merely refrain from using the agreement. The contracting authority cannot decide to make a purchase from another supplier during the lifetime of the agreement, but if the need arises, it must make purchases from the designated undertaking. There are two types of framework agreement; *see* Article 33 of the Procurement Directive. First, there are agreements with a single economic operator. The use of such agreements is relatively unproblematic and follows the rules described above. Second, it is possible to enter into framework agreements with two or more economic operators. Where this model is used, the

---

27. Art. 33(1)(2) of the Procurement Directive.

criteria for awarding the specific contract must be established in the framework agreement. There are two possible ways of awarding specific contracts: either by application of the terms laid down in the framework agreement without reopening competition or after having established a competition between the suppliers who are parties to the framework agreement. The new Procurement Directive specifically provides for both possibilities to be included in the same framework agreement; however, it must be made clear which method must be used and when. The CJ has established that the contract notice must include a maximum amount for purchases under the framework contract. When this amount has been reached, the contract will no longer have effect.[28]

In addition to standing agreements in the form of framework agreements, there are also option agreements. Option agreements differ from framework agreements by the fact that option agreements are linked to a traditional main agreement for supply or provision, where the option gives the contracting authority a right to increase the purchased quantity. Framework agreements usually stand alone.

6   FORMS OF PUBLIC PROCUREMENT PROCEDURES

Contracting authorities have the possibility of using different kinds of public procurement procedures. *Open procedures* and *restricted procedures* are available to all contracting authorities under the Procurement Directive. In contrast, it is only exceptionally possible to use *negotiated procedures* (of which there are two versions) and *competitive dialogue* under the Procurement Directive. There is also a possibility of using innovation partnerships if the contracting authority wishes to enter into cooperation on innovation. Finally, there is also scope for holding design contests; these can be used if a contracting authority wishes to obtain proposals for solutions, for example, for architectural or ICT projects.[29]

The *open procedure* is characterised as being a procedure whereby any interested economic operator may submit a tender, while the restricted procedure is defined as a procedure in which only those economic operators invited by the contracting authority may submit a tender.[30]

Negotiated procedures are procedures whereby the contracting authorities consult the economic operators of their choice and negotiate the terms of the contract with one or more of these.[31] This procedure has two variants. First, there is the negotiated procedure *with* prior publication, and second, there is the negotiated procedure *without* prior publication. The negotiated procedure with prior publication can be freely used for purchases made under the Procurement Directive.

The same applies to procurement by *competitive* dialogue. Competitive dialogue can also only be used in exceptional cases. Competitive dialogue is a procedure where,

---

28. *See* Case C-216/17, *Autorita* and Case C-23/20, *Simonsen & Weel*.
29. A design contest does not necessarily result in award of a contract, and therefore it is considered to be more a contest than an actual public procurement procedure.
30. Articles 27 and 28 of Directive 2014/24/EU.
31. Articles 29 and 32 of Directive 2014/24/EU.

on the basis of an initial tender, there can be negotiations between contracting authorities and tenderers. The conditions in the Procurement Directive in regard to when to use negotiated procedures (with prior publication) and competitive dialogue are the same: (1) when the need of the contracting authority cannot be met without making adjustments to already available solutions; (2) when the contract involves design or innovative solutions; (3) where, because of specific circumstances related to the nature, complexity or legal and financial make-up or because of the risks attaching to them, a contract cannot be awarded without prior negotiation; or (4) where the technical specifications cannot be stipulated by the contracting authority with sufficient precision. These two procedures can also be used when only non-compliant or unacceptable tenders are submitted in connection with an open procedure or a restricted procedure.

Innovation partnerships are a new tendering procedure introduced by the new Procurement Directive. The purpose of an innovation partnership is to create an innovative development of new goods, services or construction works and to subsequently provide such innovative products, services or works; *see* Article 31(23) of the Procurement Directive. The award procedure for innovation partnerships is not unlike that known for other types of procurement; Article 31 provides that the best tender should be selected in the same way as for competitive dialogue. However, the procedure for innovation partnerships differs significantly from the other procedures as Article 31 also governs the contract period, i.e., the period after the contract has been entered into. The provision requires the contracting authority to establish a framework for the progress of the innovation, with regular reviews of the progress to be made, rules on payment and on who is to own the rights to the results and whether the partnership is to end before the product has been fully developed. If the partnership is terminated before the product has been fully developed, the contracting authority can appoint a new partner by a new procurement procedure.

Procurement by a *negotiated procedure without prior publication* can be used in situations where, for one reason or another, there is very little or no competition for the task. The procedure entails that the contracting authorities can enter into direct negotiations with a tenderer without prior publication of a tender notice. Thus, the procedure can be completed relatively quickly and be organised entirely according to the contracting authorities' wishes. As there is no publication of the tender notice, the procedure can only be used in extremely exceptional cases, for example, where no tenders have been submitted in open or restricted procedures or where, for various reasons, an award can only be made to one particular economic operator, such as where the operator has protected exclusive rights or where there is lack of competition for technical reasons; *see* Article 32 of the Procurement Directive. During the COVID-19 pandemic, the provision proved its worth, as Article 32(2)(c) allows procurement without a tender in situations where it to the extent strictly necessary and due to compelling reasons as a result of circumstances which the contracting authority could not have foreseen is not possible to meet the deadlines for public procurement, restricted procedures or negotiated procedures with publication. The pandemic was unpredictable, and as a result of the gravity of the situation, the conditions for using procurement without a tender were legitimate in this situation. The pandemic was special, however, as the societies remained in its grip for almost two years. Subsequently, it has been discussed how long the acute phase of the pandemic could justify procurement without a tender. At the end of 2020, the contracting authorities could foresee that there would be a need for face masks for some time, and thus, the procurement procedure could more easily be organised in accordance with the general procurement procedures with tender. There is probably no doubt that Article 32(2)(c) was only applicable during the first part of the pandemic, but it can be associated with some uncertainty in establishing when the contracting authority is expected to be able to plan its pandemic-related purchases, and thus no longer can fulfil the condition in Article 32.[32]

According to the directives, a *design contest* is a procedure which is only used in special situations.[33] Design contests are defined as procedures which enable a contracting authority to acquire, mainly in the fields of town and country planning, architecture and engineering, or data processing, a plan or design selected by a jury after being put out to competition.[34] Design contests are often used in connection with architectural designs. Several of the characteristics of other procurement procedures do not apply to design contests. For example, design contests are not determined by the traditional award criteria, which concern the most advantageous tender in regard to the best ratio between price and quality, cost efficiency or the lowest price (on these, *see* the next section). In principle, there is no restriction on the reasons for choosing a winning design in such a contest. However, the criteria for judgment must be made clear in the published invitation to take part in the contest. One of the special characteristics of design contests is that there are rules governing the composition of the jury. A jury must be composed of natural persons who are independent of the participants in the contest. If a particular professional qualification is required for participants in a contest (e.g., qualifications as an engineer), then at least a third of the members of the jury must have that qualification or an equivalent qualification.

7   SELECTION AND AWARD

Two evaluations must be made in connection with every procurement procedure. First, it is necessary to assess the qualifications of the undertakings which wish to participate in the tendering process. This part of the process is referred to as the selection of the candidates (selection phase). Second, an assessment is made of the tenders in order to choose the offer which best fulfils the requirements of the contracting authority. This part of the process is referred to as the award of the contract (award phase).

---

32. On 1 April 2020, the Commission published a communication with a guidance on how to handle the pandemic from a procurement law perspective, *see* Guidance from the European Commission on using the public procurement framework in the emergency situation related to the COVID-19 crisis (2020/C 108I/01).
33. *See* Arts 78-82 of Directive 2014/24/EU.
34. *See* Art. 2(1)(21) of Directive 2014/24/EU.

7.1 Selection of Candidates: Procedures and Criteria

The rules for the selection of candidates are set out in Articles 57-66 of the Procurement Directive. The various procurement procedures thus contain the same elements (selection and award), but these elements may be applied at different points in the process and in different ways, depending on the procedure used.

In the case of open procedures, the selection often takes place immediately prior to the award; in other words, the award process is a continuation of the selection process. Pursuant to Article 56(2) of the Procurement Directive, contracting authorities may examine tenders before making a selection. The contracting authorities can thereby gain the practical advantage that they first examine the tenders and then focus their time on the tender material from the undertakings from, for instance, the five economic operators which have made the best tenders. In this way, the contracting authority saves resources, as not all the material and tenders should be examined.

The selection is made on the basis of a number of selection criteria published in the contract notice. These criteria must relate to the qualifications and capacities of undertakings and must concern an undertaking's financial, economic, technical or professional qualifications. This list is exhaustive, so it is not possible to take other circumstances than those named into account. The directives list a number of examples of evidence of these circumstances. According to the frameworks for both the technical and financial capacities, there is a non-exhaustive list of matters which a contracting authority can ask about. Thus, depending on the type of task involved, the contracting authority may impose requirements to ensure that economic operators possess the necessary human and technical resources and experience to perform the contract to an appropriate quality standard; *see* Article 58(4) of the Procurement Directive. Financial and economic standing can be ensured by requiring evidence of a minimum annual turnover, annual accounts and professional risk indemnity insurance. Thus, contracting authorities can demand other evidence to substantiate an undertaking's financial and economic standing.

An undertaking can forward documentation for another undertaking's capacity and can invoke this capacity if the first undertaking has the capacity in question at its disposal, for example, via a group relationship. Other relations between the tenderers and third-party undertakings besides from corporate relations may also be sufficient as long as the tenderer can prove that the sufficient resources are at his disposal in order to fulfil the contract in question. A declaration from the supporting undertaking that documents that the supporting economic operator actually has either the technical competences or the economic capacity at his disposal is thus sufficient. Exploitation of other entities' capacities is regulated in Article 63 of the Public Procurement Directive.

If the contracting authority does not find the submitted material for examination of an undertaking sufficient, it is possible to request supplementary material from the undertaking in question.

In addition to the rules on selection criteria, there are also a number of other rules which make it possible to eliminate undertakings which it may be assumed do not, have the qualifications to undertake the task for which tenders are invited.[35] In the requirements, there is a distinction between situations in which the contracting authority *must* exclude an economic operator and situations in which the contracting authority *may* exclude an economic operator.[36] For this reason, an undertaking which is subject to bankruptcy or insolvency proceedings can be excluded from tendering. Furthermore, any candidate which has been found guilty of criminal acts which can give rise to doubts about the professional conduct of the candidate or which is guilty of grave professional misconduct (though not necessarily in court proceedings) can be excluded.[37] Where a contracting authority has sufficiently plausible reasons to believe that an economic operator has entered into an agreement with another economic operator to distort competition, that operator can be excluded from a procedure. The same applies where an undertaking has either gained a competitive advantage by having previously had an advisory function or on the basis of personal relations with a person who is to take part in the decision-making process (a conflict of interests); Article 57(4)(e) and (f) of the Procurement Directive provides that the contracting authority can exclude such undertakings.[38] In reality, contracting authorities will be obliged to exclude tenderers in such situations as there would otherwise be unequal treatment. Finally, it is possible to exclude candidates which have not fulfilled obligations to pay taxes or social security contributions or which have given incorrect information in connection with the procurement procedure. While a contracting authority *may* exclude undertakings in the situations referred to, there are also situations where a contracting authority *must* exclude undertakings. This applies where an undertaking has been found guilty of money laundering, corruption, fraud or organised crime; *see* Article 57(1) of the Directive.

The exclusion of an applicant or tenderer from participating in a competitive tendering procedure on the basis of an old conviction, or otherwise because of historical circumstances that no longer apply, can be regarded as contrary to the proportionality principle. Article 57(6) of the Procurement Directive provides that an economic operator may provide evidence that it has adopted measures sufficient to demonstrate its reliability despite the existence of a relevant ground for its exclusion. These measures fall within three categories: (1) the undertaking must prove that it has paid or undertaken to pay compensation in respect of any damage caused by its misconduct; (2) the undertaking must have clarified the facts and circumstances in a comprehensive manner by actively collaborating with the investigating authorities; and (3) the undertaking must have taken concrete technical, organisational and personnel measures appropriate to prevent further misconduct.

An undertaking can submit evidence of the capacity of another undertaking and rely on this as long as the first undertaking can make use of the capacity in question, for example, by being part of the same corporate group. Other connections between

---

35. *See* Art. 57 of the Public Procurement Directive.
36. *See* Art. 57(1) (mandatory exclusion), and Art. 57(4) (voluntary exclusion).
37. In the Danish procurement Act, this voluntary exclusion ground is made mandatory – *see* § 136(1-2) of the Danish Procurement Act.
38. These two voluntary exclusion reasons are also made mandatory in §136(1-2) of the Danish Procurement Act.

candidates and third-party undertakings can also satisfy the requirements as long as the candidate can show that he/she has access to sufficient resources to fulfil the contract for which a tender is sought. Reliance on the capacity of other entities is governed by Article 63 of the Procurement Directive.

If a contracting authority does not find that the documentation submitted for the assessment of a candidate undertaking is sufficient, it can ask the undertaking to submit supplementary information.

A situation can arise where too many qualified candidates seek to tender for a contract. A contracting authority can limit the number of participants in a tendering procedure to a given number, though not fewer than five tenderers for a restricted procedure and three tenderers for a negotiated procedure or competitive dialogue. If a contracting authority wishes to have a limited group of tenderers, this must be made clear in the contract notice, including the maximum number of applicants who will pre-qualify.

The two selection situations can be referred to as *qualitative* (the initial assessment of the candidates' qualifications) and *quantitative* (the subsequent restriction of the number of qualified candidates) selection.

Where a quantitative selection is to be made on the basis of a contracting authority's restriction of the number of participants in the tendering, this can be done in several ways. There is nothing in the public procurement directives which directly states how this selection must or may be made.[39] However, there is a requirement that the criteria used must be objective and non-discriminatory. A number of suggestions have been made in the legal literature as to which methods should be used. For example, there can be a *proportionate* application of the selection criteria which are the basis of the ordinary selection. Furthermore, selection can (possibly) be made, so that the undertakings which can give the *best competition* are selected. An example of a less likely method is quantitative selection, where the selection can possibly be made by the *drawing of lots*.[40]

The practical aspects of selection have been changed by the latest Procurement Directive. Prior to the new Procurement Directive (2014/24/EU), each applicant/tenderer had to submit the full selection material using various documents that had to be obtained. This meant it was necessary to obtain a number of documents from different places for use in the selection procedure. The Procurement Directive changed this so that applicants can submit a self-declaration based on EU specifications laid down in Article 59 – referred to as a European Single Procurement Document (ESPD). In this declaration, the applicant must show that they fulfil the criteria laid down by the contracting authority in the procurement notice. The idea is that when the procurement process is over and the winner of the tendering process has been selected, the winning tenderer should submit the full documentation, as described in the ESPD.

---

39. The framework for such a quantitative selection is available in Art. 65 of the Public Procurement Directive.
40. For further examples of how this quantitative selection can be made, *see Michael Steinicke & Lise Groesmeyer*, EU's udbudsdirektiver med kommentarer, comments on the (former) Art. 44(3).

7.2 Award of the Contract: Procedures and Criteria

The criteria for the award of a contract are aimed at establishing the framework for assessing tenders and for choosing the tender which is regarded as best and should, therefore, be awarded the contract. There were previously two different award criteria. First, there was the criterion of the *lowest bid*, and second, there was the criterion of the *most economically advantageous bid*. Under the new Procurement Directive, the situation is roughly the same as before, though the formal starting point differs. Thus, Article 67 of the Procurement Directive provides that the most economically advantageous tender shall be identified on the basis of (1) the price, or (2) the cost, using a cost-effectiveness approach, such as life-cycle costing in accordance with Article 68, or (3) the best price-quality ratio, which shall be assessed on the basis of criteria, including qualitative, environmental and/or social aspects, linked to the subject matter of the public contract in question.

Thus, there is formally only a single award criterion – the *most economically advantageous bid* – but this is divided into three sub-criteria that almost match the previous rules (provided two criteria). The Directive does not name the three variants of the most economically advantageous bid, but they are typically referred to as the 'lowest price' (or 'lowest cost') bid, the 'cost-efficiency', and the 'best relation between price and quality' bid.

In principle, the first criterion is both easy to define and to apply. According to this criterion, it is simply the offer that has the lowest overall price which wins the competition and is awarded the contract. This model has been fundamental not only for public procurement directives but also for a number of other procurement and tendering rules around the world.

The second criterion is also straightforward: the offer that represents the highest cost-efficiency will be awarded the contract. Costs may cover life-cycle costs which are any costs related to every phase of the life cycle of the product.

The third criterion is more complex. Here, the competition will be decided in favour of the tenderer that has given the most economically advantageous offer overall. The criterion takes account of other circumstances, and elements other than price can be relevant to the award of the contract. In buying a product, a contracting authority can attach importance to, e.g., the quality of the product and the delivery schedule, as well as the price. Thus, the tender which best fulfils these three criteria will win the contract. It is clear that the assessment of the best relation between price and quality is more difficult to make. This criterion gives the contracting authority wide discretion in its choice of supplier. The fact that a tenderer has given the best price does not necessarily mean it must be awarded the contract. If the tenderer has submitted an offer based on low quality and long delivery deadlines, the contract can be awarded to another tenderer who has offered a better *overall* solution.

The CJ has laid down conditions which must be fulfilled before a specific criterion can be used when awarding a contract on the basis of the best price-quality ratio. While this case law relates to the earlier rules, it is still the applicable law, and to some extent, the case law has been codified in the new Directive. These conditions are: (1) the criterion must be linked to the subject matter of the contract (*see* Article 67(3)); (2) the criterion must not confer an unrestricted freedom of choice on the contracting authority (*see* Article 67(4)); (3) the criterion must be expressly mentioned in the contract documents or the tender notice; and (4) the criterion must comply with all the fundamental principles of Union law, in particular the principle of non-discrimination.[41]

As the contracting authority has increased discretion in awarding a contract on the basis of the best price-quality ratio, the award phase becomes less transparent. This is because it is more difficult for the participating undertakings (and anyone other than the contracting authority) to predict which offer should be awarded the contract since, as can be seen above, the assessment can be complex. In order to counter this uncertainty about the result of the procedure, there is a rule in the directives that the contracting authority must, as far as possible, give weightings to the different sub-criteria. This weighting can be expressed in percentages or otherwise. For a tender where the sub-criteria are price, quality and delivery time, the weighting could be expressed as follows: price 40%, quality 35% and delivery time 25%. It is also possible to express the weightings within a range, for example, price 40%-45%.

If it is not possible to give weightings to the sub-criteria, the contracting authority must at least give a ranking of the sub-criteria, for example: (1) price; (2) quality; and (3) delivery time. Such prioritising does not give the same high degree of transparency for tenderers since in the above ranking there can be wide differences in the weightings which lie behind the rankings. The ranking given in the example could apply to a weighting of price 40%, quality 35% and delivery time 25%; but it could equally apply to a weighting of price 85%, quality 10% and delivery time 5%. An offer that is primarily based on a low price may not do well in the first situation, whereas it would have a markedly better chance of being awarded the contract in the second situation.

The criteria for the award of the contract must be published in the initial contract notice. If the contracting authority wishes to award on the basis of the best relation between price and quality, this must be stated in the contract notice.[42] It is not directly stated in the Procurement Directive that the sub-criteria must be made public in the contract notice, but the contract notice form also leaves a place for the sub-criteria. In Article 67(5) of the Procurement Directive, it is stated that the relative weighting must be stated in the procurement documents. Those elements of the award criteria which are not published in the contract notice, for example, certain details in regard to the sub-criteria and information on the sub-sub-criteria (criteria which describe the sub-criteria in more detail), must be stated in the tender documents. The 2014-directives lay down requirements for a simultaneous publication of the contract notice and the tender documents which entails that conditions in regard to the selection criteria by publication in the tender documents are also available for the economic operators already at the start of the tender. Thus, the economic operators can include information on the selection criteria in their assessment of whether they want to take part in the tender or not.

---

41. Case C-513/99, *Concordia*, para. 64.
42. *See* s. II.2.5 of the present standard form for public procurement.

7.2.1 Abnormally Low Tenders

Contracting authorities may reject tenders if they appear to have an abnormally low price compared to the actual elements in the contract notice.[43] However, a contracting authority must follow certain formal rules before making a final rejection. If a contracting authority believes that a tender is abnormally low, the tenderer must be given an opportunity to give details of the constituent elements of the tender before it is rejected. The provision has been included in order to give contracting authorities the possibility of rejecting abnormally low tenders, but it is possible that in certain situations there can be an obligation to reject abnormally low tenders in certain situations, as there could otherwise be a possibility of an evasion of the procurement rules by a contracting authority.[44]

The CJ has laid down a more detailed procedure for the rejection of abnormally low tenders.[45] The four steps of the procedure are as follows: first, the contracting authority must identify suspect tenders; second, the contracting authority must allow the undertakings concerned to demonstrate the genuineness of their tenders by asking them to provide the details which it considers appropriate; third, the contracting authority must assess the merits of the explanations provided by the persons concerned; and fourth, the contracting authority must take a decision as to whether to admit or reject the tenders.[46]

Under the provisions of Article 69(4) of the Procurement Directive, a contracting authority may reject a tender that is abnormally low because the tenderer has obtained unlawful State aid.

7.3 Selection or Award

In a number of cases, the CJ has held that a distinction must be drawn between the selection of candidates for tendering and the award of the contract. This has the practical (and obvious) significance that the selection criteria must be used in connection with the selection phase, and the award criteria must be used in connection with the award. In addition to this, the distinction means that the same criterion cannot be used twice in connection with the same procurement procedure. In other words, if in connection with the selection of candidates a contracting authority has required evidence of an undertaking's experience related to a specific kind of task in connection with a contract, the contracting authority cannot use this same criterion (experience) when awarding the contract.

---

43. Article 69 of Directive 2014/24/EU.
44. The contracting authority's favoured supplier could thus submit a tender with an abnormally low price and be certain of being awarded the contract. Once the contract has been awarded, the tenderer and the contracting authority can adjust the price to a more realistic level.
45. Joined Cases C-285/99 and C-286/99, *Impresa Lombardini*, para. 55.
46. The CJ has even stated that this procedure also must be applied in situations where a tender of EUR 0 is made, *see* C-367/19, *Tax-Fin-Lex*.

In Case C-532/06, *Lianakis*, the CJ emphasised as a general point that the two parts of the procurement procedure (selection and award) have different purposes, and the criteria and the conditions that apply to the two parts of the procedure are, in principle, different. On the basis of this, criteria used in the selection process cannot also be used in the awarding process. In Case C-315/01, *GAT*, the CJ stated that a simple list of references to the tasks carried out by a supplier, which only contains the names and number of the suppliers' previous customers without other details relating to the deliveries made to those customers, cannot provide any information to identify the offer which is the most economically advantageous, and therefore cannot constitute an award criterion (paragraph 66). In the same case the CJ held that a criterion according to which a tenderer's offer may be favourably assessed only if the product which is the subject of the offer is available for inspection by the contracting authority within a radius of 300 km of the authority cannot constitute an award criterion (paragraph 72). The CJ referred to the decision in the *Beentjes* case concerning the distinction between selection criteria and award criteria, but did not go further in relation to the actual provisions. It could have been natural for the CJ to have made a categorical rejection of lists of references for use as allocation criteria, since these have already been named as potential selection criteria; *see* Article 48(2)(a) of Directive 2004/18/EC. However, the CJ chose not to use such an approach, which may indicate that one cannot totally exclude the possibility of the use of such lists of references. In any case, it must be assumed that it will only be seldom that lists of references will be such that they will be able to identify the most economically advantageous contract.

In a later Case, C-601/13 *Ambisig*, the CJ clarified the relation between the two types of criteria. The CJ recognised the unclear approach in the area and stated that 'due to a contradiction between, on the one hand, the Court of Justice's case-law on verification of the ability of economic operators for the performance of a contract and criteria for awarding contracts, as resulting from the judgment in *Lianakis and Others* (C-532-/06, EU:C:2008: 40) and, on the other, the Commission's proposal aimed at reforming the legislation on public procurement procedures, and the fact that quality is one of the award criteria provided for by Article 53(1)(a) of Directive 2004/18, a criterion which may be linked to the composition, experience and academic and professional background of the team entrusted with performance of the contract', *see* paragraph 23. Subsequently, the CJ pointed out that the circumstances in Lianakis and Ambisig were different in that Lianakis concerned 'the staff and experience of the tenderers in general and not, as in present case, the staff and experience of the persons making up a particular team which must actually perform the contract'.[47]

---

47. Case C-601/13, *Ambisig*, para. 26.

By this, the CJ accepted that circumstances which as a rule relate to selection according to the circumstances can be used as award criteria.

See furthermore the newest decision in C-601/13, *Ambisig*, that seems to open a door to modifying the strict approach from *Lianakis*.

In contrast to the use of criteria where there is a clear distinction between selection and award, in the new Directive, there has been a merging of the two processes. In principle, the selection is made first, and then an award is made between the selected undertakings found to be qualified. Under Article 56(2) of the new Procurement Directive, with open procedures, a contracting authority may examine tenders before making the selection. In practice, this can mean that the contracting authority identifies the tenderer with the best tender before making the selection. Moreover, a tenderer can be excluded at any time, even after the award process has been carried out, on the grounds set out in Article 57.

7.4 Non-financial Criteria

It has previously been unclear to what extent it is possible to use non-economic criteria in connection with the selection of candidates or the award of contracts. The so-called non-economic criteria are those which do not concern economic or commercial factors, such as regard for the environment, social concerns or consumer concerns. The CJ has not yet given a clear ruling on this question, but more recent decisions, as well as the Commission's interpretative communications on social and environmental considerations,[48] suggest that there is now some clarity on the question.

The reason for being careful about allowing non-economic and non-commercial considerations to play a role in connection with public procurement is that the aim of the public procurement directives is to prompt contracting authorities to use a *commercial* approach and considerations in connection with public procurement and abstain from using non-commercial considerations which are the basis of their work as public authorities.

Social and environmental concerns can be protected in many other ways. In relation to the formulation of public procurement contracts, such concerns can be included in various ways. *First,* such considerations can be included as requirements for the contract; in other words, the goods or services to be bought can be described so as to fulfil

---

48. In 2001, the Commission published Interpretative communication COM(2001) 566 final, on the Community law applicable to public procurement and the possibilities for integrating social considerations into public procurement (OJ 2001 C 333/27) and Interpretative communication COM(2001) 274 final, on the Community law applicable to public procurement and the possibilities for integrating environmental considerations into public procurement (OJ 2001 C 333/12). Later communications include the Commission's Buying green? A handbook on green public procurement, 2016, and communication Public procurement for a better environment COM(2008) 400 final.

a number of different environmental requirements.[49] *Second*, such considerations can be taken care of, for example, by including social requirements in connection with the selection of undertakings accepted as candidates for tendering (selection criteria) or in the criteria which should decide the tender (award criteria). It has been pointed out, both by the CJ and the Commission, that in order to apply non-economic criteria for the selection of candidates or the award of contracts, it must be possible to use these criteria to assess the suitability of an undertaking to carry out a specific task or to assess the economic advantages of a tender. If the social requirements of a contracting authority cannot do this, such considerations cannot be used as criteria for selection or award.[50]

A third way of implementing these considerations is by making the fulfilment of these requirements a contractual obligation for being considered for the award of the contract. In other words, to win the contract, evidence must be given that certain contractual requirements (e.g., social requirements) will be fulfilled.

There has been discussion about the extent to which it is possible to include non-economic considerations as contractual requirements and, in extension of this, the extent to which it is possible to exclude offers which do not fulfil such requirements. In Case 31/87, *Beentjes*, and later in Case C-225/98, *Commission v. France*, the CJ has allowed that it was possible to lay down such requirements in public procurement contracts as long as these have been stated in advance in the contract notice and the requirements are non-discriminatory.[51]

There is a question as to whether such requirements can be the only requirements that can be made in connection with laying down non-economic contractual requirements. It has been argued that not all non-economic requirements should be allowed to form the basis of exclusion from the public procurement business. The argument behind this is that the public procurement directives are intended to direct contracting authorities towards a more commercial purchasing policy, so it would be contrary to this purpose to allow contracting authorities to attach decisive weight to non-commercial factors. It could be argued that, in extension of the two requirements referred to above, the consideration which is to be taken account of should have a *certain relevance* to the subject matter of the contract in question. Thus, extreme requirements which have no connection with the task should be excluded, while requirements that are intended to protect concerns which have a natural connection to the task or contract could be maintained. However, prior to the adoption of the new Procurement Directive, there was no support for this view in the case law. Under the new provision in Article 70, contracting authorities may lay down special conditions relating to the performance of a contract.

---

49. *See, e.g.,* Case C-513/99, *Concordia,* where a number of environmental requirements had been made with regard to the buses that were to be procured.
50. On the possibility of including environmental concerns for awarding a contract, *see* Case C-513/99, *Concordia.*
51. The CJ uses the terms 'special' or 'additional' criteria, which can be misunderstood as referring to selection of award criteria. This is not the case; *see* above.

8 EXCEPTIONS

8.1 General

There are a number of exceptions to the main rules laid down in the public procurement directives. These exceptions give contracting authorities the opportunity to use less strict procedures in certain cases. As is generally the case with exceptions under Union law, these exceptions must be interpreted restrictively, and the contracting authority has the burden of proof for showing that the conditions for granting the exceptions have been fulfilled.

There are two kinds of exceptions in relation to the public procurement directives. First, there are the exceptions which lead to total exclusion from the scope of the public procurement directives. Second, there are exceptions which affect the procedure for entering into contracts.

8.2 The Defence Exception

Directive 2004/18/EC made it clear that its provisions applied to public contracts awarded by contracting authorities in the field of defence, except for contracts subject to Article 346 TFEU. This is in Article 15 of the new Public Sector Directive.

Article 346 TFEU states that the provisions of the Treaty do not preclude any Member State taking 'such measures as it considers necessary for the protection of the essential interests of its security which are connected with the production of or trade in arms, munitions and war material; such measures shall not adversely affect the conditions of competition in the common market regarding products which are not intended for specifically military purposes'. Article 346 also states that no Member State is obliged to supply information, the disclosure of which it considers contrary to the essential interests of its security.

In connection with Article 346, there is a category of products which are referred to as *dual use products*. These are products the use of which can be both military (and are thus covered by the provision) and civil (and thus fall outside the scope of the provision). Examples of dual use products can be explosives which can be used both for military purposes and, for example, for the demolition of buildings, etc. It is not clear whether these products are covered by Article 346 TFEU. The scope of application of the provision in relation to dual use products can be delimited in two ways. One possibility is that dual use products fall within the scope of Article 346 to the extent that the proposed procurement is intended for military use. The other possibility is that only products which have military use are covered by Article 346. When considered in relation to the CJ's established practice on exceptions (that they should be interpreted restrictively), it must be assumed that the CJ will choose the latter possibility, whereby only products which have a military use are covered by Article 346 and are therefore outside the scope of the public procurement directives.

Directive 2009/81/EC was adopted to govern public procurement in the fields of defence and security. The provisions of this Directive are very similar to the corresponding provisions and procedures laid down in Directive 2004/18/EC. However, there are a few differences, for example, the stricter rules on the use of subcontractors in Article 21.

8.3 Special Provisions on the Provision of Services

8.3.1 Social and Other Specific Services

Formerly, services were divided between A services and B services, and only A services were subject to full procurement procedures. B services were only subject to very limited obligations under the Directive, though they could be subject to the Treaty provisions and the general principles of Union law. This model has been dropped in the 2014-directives, and instead, it provides exceptions for a smaller group of services – social services and other specific services (*see* Articles 74-77). In contrast to the former B services, for social and other specific services, there is a requirement for publication of a notice; in other words, a less intensive procurement procedure must be carried out (a 'light regime'). The services covered by this light regime are listed in Annex XIV to the Procurement Directive and include certain health and social services, welfare services, religious services, hotel and restaurant services, investigation and security services, prison services and legal services.

8.3.2 Other Exceptions for Services

The Procurement Directive contains a provision which, under special circumstances, exempts a contract from the full tendering obligation; *see* Article 11.

According to this provision, the Directive does not apply to public service contracts awarded by a contracting authority to another contracting authority on the basis of an exclusive right which they enjoy pursuant to a published law, regulation or administrative provision which is compatible with the Treaty.

The award must thus be made to the undertaking that has the exclusive right to perform the task in question. It must be assumed that the public entity itself decides which tasks are suitable for being performed pursuant to an exclusive right. This is supported by Article 345 TFEU, which provides that the Treaty 'shall in no way prejudice the rules in Member States governing the system of property ownership'; i.e., the Treaty does not determine the form in which public undertakings are carried on.[52]

Some kinds of services are wholly outside the scope of the Directive. Article 10 of the Procurement Directive provides that there is no need to use a procurement procedure in accordance with the Directive when entering into certain kinds of service

---

52. However, this rule is not entirely without exception; *see* the case law on Art. 106 TFEU, on undertakings that are allowed special or exclusive rights; *see* Michael Steinicke: Privilegerede virksomheder og EU-retten.

contracts. These include the acquisition or rental of land and existing buildings, the production of programme material intended for audio-visual or radio media services, arbitration and mediation services, certain legal services, financial services connected with the purchase and sale of securities, for taking a loan, for employment contracts and for services for political campaigns.

9 GENERAL PRINCIPLES

All the public procurement directives provide that some focal general principles must be complied with in the different processes. It appears from Article 18(1) of the Procurement Directive that compliance with the principles of equality, transparency and proportionality must take place. The equality principle and the principle of transparency are both created on the basis of the practice of the CJ and later included in the procurement directives. The principle of proportionality has always been part of the rules, which had to be complied with in connection with a tender, but has not been explicitly included until the 2014-directives. Aside from the principles mentioned above, other directives also play a role in connection with the procurement rules. At the EU level, the general principle of reciprocity may be especially relevant (for example, when foreign tenderers forward documentation for their capacity). Furthermore, at the national level, the Danish Complaints board for Public Procurement attach some importance to the principle of impartiality in certain contexts.

9.1 The Principle of Equal Treatment

The principle of equal treatment is the most important and the most often relied upon principle in public procurement law. The content of the principle is not described in more detail in the public procurement directives, but there have been many cases on the subject. As with the other principles, the principle of equal treatment must be complied with in all phases and situations involving public purchasing. It would be going too far, in this context, to list all the situations in which the principle of equal treatment is relevant. For this reason, the following is structured so as to focus on a number of areas in which the application of the principle of equal treatment is the primary legal basis. Where the principle of equal treatment most often comes into play is in connection with the prohibition of negotiation, reserved contracts, rules on technical dialogue and cancelled procedures.

9.1.1 *The Prohibition of Negotiation*

As a consequence of the principle of equal treatment, there is a prohibition of contracting authorities *negotiating* with tenderers in connection with open procedures and restricted procedures. The prohibition was originally derived from the principle of equal treatment (*see* Case C-243/89, *Commission v. Denmark*) and is now reflected in Article 18 of the Procurement Directive. As the prohibition is derived from a general principle, there are no specific guidelines for the application of the prohibition. In order to actualise the prohibition, the Commission and the Council have issued a joint statement which, to some extent, clarifies the content of the prohibition:

> The Council and the Commission state that in open and restricted procedures all negotiations with candidates or tenderers on fundamental aspects of contracts, variations in which are likely to distort competition, and in particular on prices, shall be ruled out; however, discussions with candidates or tenderers may be held but only for the purpose of clarifying or supplementing the content of their tenders or the requirements of the contracting entities and provided this does not involve discrimination.[53]

By and large, the joint statement has been relied upon by the authorities who apply the law without questioning its legal value. For example, several Advocates General have referred directly to the joint statement, while the CJ has merely used terminology corresponding to that used in the statement. Against this background, it is natural that analyses in the legal literature of the prohibition of negotiation have largely been based on the joint statement and its terminology.

The CJ has dealt with the prohibition of negotiation in a few cases. In Case C-243/89, *Commission v. Denmark*, the CJ held that it was not permitted to negotiate with a tenderer on the basis of a tender which did not comply with the tender conditions; *see* below. In Case C-87/94, *Commission v. Belgium (Walloon buses)*, the CJ held that the Belgian contracting authority had breached the public procurement rules by allowing certain amendments to be made to a tender.

9.1.1.1 Fundamental Aspects

It is clear from the joint statement that it is not permitted to negotiate about the *fundamental aspects* of a contract. Neither the directives nor practice offer any definition of the term *fundamental aspects*, but they must be assumed to be aspects that are relevant either to the award of the contract or to the tender procedure in general. The term 'fundamental aspects' should not be interpreted as referring only to aspects which concern decisive elements of the contract. It must be assumed that less important elements which nevertheless have some weight in the tendering procedure are also covered.

The CJ has not expressly ruled on the question of fundamental aspects, but it did make an implicit evaluation of this in Case C-87/94, *Commission v. Belgium*. The case concerned a contract for the supply of a number of buses. One of the tenderers sent some corrections to its tender to the contracting authority. These corrections are related to fuel consumption, the frequency of engine replacement and some comments on technical quality. The tenderer had given figures for fuel consumption of 54 litres per 100 km and had stated that there was a possibility of obtaining a reduction in fuel consumption of 5%-8%. In a later submission, the

---

53. OJ 1994 L 111/114. The statement is in the nature of soft law, and it is therefore difficult to be certain of its legal weight. It must be assumed that there is not an obligation to follow it word for word, but there may be an obligation to take account of the statement when interpreting the prohibition.

tenderer corrected the consumption figure to a reduction of 16.7%. There was clearly an amendment to the tender, and it was relevant whether this amounted to a fundamental change. As stated, the CJ did not expressly address this question, but since, on the one hand, the fuel consumption influenced the ranking between tenders, and on the other hand, it had a significant financial effect on the cost of running the buses, it must have been a fundamental aspect.

9.1.1.2 Price

It is clear from the joint statement that price plays a special role in connection with tenders. This is because price is the most important competitive parameter, and regardless of which criteria are chosen for the award of a contract, price will always have a high priority in public procurement procedures (*see* the award criteria: lowest price or most economically advantageous tender). On this basis, there is particular sensitivity to negotiations on price. In principle, negotiation on price is not permitted.[54] This means that if, in certain circumstances, negotiation is permitted, this may be on condition that there is no negotiation on price.

9.1.1.3 Clarification or Negotiation

In the joint statement, it is stated that there may be discussions with candidates or tenderers, but only for the purpose of *clarifying* or *supplementing* tenders and not for negotiation. The basic difference is that clarifying or supplementing does not result in changes being made to the tender documentation or to the offer, but is merely a confirmation of matters which are stated in the tender documentation or offer. In contrast, negotiation leads to or is intended to lead to changes in the existing documentation.

Thus, where there is confirmation, either in the form of clarification or supplementation or otherwise, discussions are permitted as long as they do not result in unequal treatment.

The CJ confirmed this in Case C-599/10, *Slovenko* and Case C-336/12, *Manova*. In these cases, the CJ stated that there was a requirement that undertakings should have the possibility of clarifying their bids, that the contracting authority's request for clarification should first be made after it has looked at all the tenders, that the request must relate to all sections of the tender which require clarification, and that a request may not lead to the submission of what would appear in reality to be a new tender (*Manova*, paragraphs 34-36). Moreover, when asking a tenderer to clarify its tender, the contracting authority must treat tenderers equally and fairly and in such a way that a request for clarification does not appear unduly to favour or disadvantage the tenderer or tenderers to which the request is addressed (*Manova*, paragraphs 37).

---

54. In the joint statement it is said that negotiation 'in particular on prices, shall be ruled out'.

9.1.1.4   Permitted Negotiations

The wording of the joint statement leaves the impression that negotiations can be permitted in certain circumstances. The possibility for this is naturally greatest in the case of negotiations on non-fundamental aspects; *see* above. However, if it is possible to negotiate lawfully, certain formal requirements must be laid down concerning the communication of information in connection with the negotiations. First, all information must be given in writing. This is to ensure the greatest possible transparency in connection with negotiations which are otherwise not particularly transparent. Second, all tenderers must have the same possibilities of amending their tenders. This is based on the principle of equal treatment.

9.1.1.5   The Scope for Making Corrections

Apart from the possibility of making clarifications and conducting lawful negotiations, there is also a limited possibility of making corrections to the tender documentation or to tenders. The right to make such corrections is shown by, among other things, the decision of the General Court (GC) in Case T-19/95, *Adia Interim*. The GC stated that there is no obligation on the contracting authority to make corrections but merely a right to do so if some fault is sufficiently apparent. The GC stated that 'even though the selection committee detected the presence of a systematic calculation error, it was unable to ascertain its exact nature or cause'.[55] Thus, the contracting authority has a right to make a correction as long as it is not only clearly apparent but also apparent how the fault has occurred.[56]

9.1.2   *Reservations*

Reservations (or provisos) are yet another area of public procurement law where there are no express rules and where the principle of equal treatment, therefore, plays an important role. *Reservations* refer to situations in which a tender contains conditions which differ from the conditions which the contracting authority has laid down in the contract notice. In other words, the tender differs from the basis for competition which the contracting authority has laid down in the conditions in the contract notice. The basic position in the law is that if a tenderer has included reservations in its tender, then the tender cannot be included in the competition for the award of the contract. The reason for this is that a tenderer should not be able to obtain a competitive advantage by breaching the rules for the competition which have been laid down by the contracting authority. There are differences about what can be accepted as a reservation, and not

---

55. Case T-19/95, *Adia Interim*, para. 47.
56. *See also* the Opinion of the Advocate General in Case 87/94, *Commission v. Belgium*.

least differences as to the strength and effect on a tender which various reservations can have. Therefore, in practice, not all reservations necessarily lead to the exclusion of a tender. The inclusion of reservations in a tender, and the strength which any reservation may be thought to have, is at the risk of the tenderer.

The factors which may lead to the rejection of a tender are as follows: (1) reservations concerning fundamental aspects; (2) unclear reservations; and (3) reservations in cases where the contracting authority has given prior notice of refusal to accept reservations. As a starting point, a tender that contains reservations is considered to be *unconditional*.

The first of these situations is related to the concept of fundamental aspects, as this is known from the joint statement and in the practice of the prohibition of negotiation. It is thus undisputed that where a reservation concerns fundamental aspects of the contract, the contracting authority cannot take the tender into account. Unclear reservations cannot be accepted because of the lack of clarity about the consequences of the reservation in the tender, so it is not immediately possible to make the necessary adjustments in order for the tender to be compared with the other tenders and be included in the competition for the contract. If a contracting authority has given prior notice that it will refuse to accept reservations, this must be considered one of the rules of the tendering process so that tenders with reservations must be rejected.

It appears from the above that in certain situations, it is possible to consider a tender even if it contains a reservation. However, a condition for admission to the competition of a tender with a reservation is that the reservation must be priced; in other words, an evaluation must be made of the price effect of the reservation, and this effect must be calculated against the price tendered.

Where there is no obligation on a contracting authority to exclude a tender from the procurement procedure on the basis of a minor reservation, the contracting authority may nevertheless choose to exclude such tender. In other words, the contracting authority has *a right but not a duty* to exclude tenders with 'minor' reservations.[57]

The CJ has ruled that it is not possible to negotiate away reservations in a tender, with a view to making the tender conditional.[58]

The question of fundamental aspects has not had such great importance in connection with negotiations, as the main rule is that all negotiations, regardless of whether they concern fundamental aspects or non-fundamental aspects, are prohibited; *see* the prohibition of negotiations. However, the distinction between fundamental aspects and non-fundamental aspects has greater significance in connection with reservations, as the distinction determines whether a contracting authority *can* or *must* reject a tender with a reservation.

---

57. In decision of 26 November 2004, E. Pihl & Søn A/S, the Danish Complaints board for Public Procurement stated that the contracting party cannot, however, reject a tender on the basis of trivial requirements.
58. Case C-243/89, *Commission v. Denmark*.

9.1.2.1 Variant Tenders

A number of public procurement procedures allow variant tenders to be taken into consideration; *see* Article 45 of the Procurement Directive. The contracting authority must state in the contract notice whether variant tenders will be considered; *see* Article 45 of the Directive. The condition for taking variant tenders into consideration is that they should fulfil the minimum requirements laid down by the contracting authority.

The contracting authority must state in the contract notice the minimum requirements which any variant tenders must satisfy, whether there are any *specific* requirements for such tenders, and if so what these requirements are.

It can be debated whether the minimum requirements must be expressly stated as being minimum requirements or whether a less expressed presentation is sufficient. It must be assumed that the minimum requirements must at least be presented in such a way that tenderers should be able to understand that they are minimum requirements and be able to establish the content of such requirements.

> In Case C-421/01, *Traunfellner*,[59] the contracting authority had referred in the contract notice to a provision of national legislation requiring an alternative tender 'to ensure the performance of work which is qualitatively equivalent to that for which tenders are invited'. There was not otherwise any minimum requirement laid down for variant tenders. In other words, there were no concrete minimum requirements the fulfilment of which was necessary for a variant tender to be considered. In this connection the CJ stated:[60] 'This being so, it is clear from the very wording of the second paragraph of Article 19 of the Directive that, where the contracting authority has not excluded the submission of variants, it is under an obligation to set out in the contract documents the minimum specifications with which those variants must comply. Consequently, the reference made in the contract documents to a provision of national legislation cannot satisfy the requirement laid down in the second paragraph of Article 19 of the Directive'. The CJ expanded on this by pointing out that: 'Tenderers may be deemed to be informed in the same way of the minimum specifications with which their variants must comply in order to be considered by the contracting authority only where those specifications are set out in the contract documents. This involves an obligation of transparency designed to ensure compliance with the principle of equal treatment of tenderers, which must be complied with in any procurement procedure governed by the Directive'.[61]

Neither the provisions in Article 45 of the Procurement Directive nor any other provision in the Directive contains a definition of a variant tender. Nor has the CJ

---

59. On this case, *see Martin Dischendorfer:* The Assessment of variants under the EC Public Procurement Rules: The Traunfellner Case, Public Procurement Law Review 2004 NA 67.
60. Case C-421/01, *Traunfellner,* paras 27-28.
61. Case C-421/01, *Traunfellner,* para. 29.

defined the term. As the term suggests, a variant tender will differ in one or more points from other tenders. However, there are both qualitative and quantitative limitations in the rules on variant tenders. The quantitative limitation means that, unless variant tenders are accepted, a tenderer cannot submit more than one tender. The qualitative limitation means that a variant tender contains a proposal for a different solution to the kind of solution which is suggested in the contract notice. The only requirement stated in the provision is that variants must be connected with the subject matter of the contract. This supports the assumption that a variant tender must relate to the method by which a task is performed, the function of a product or suchlike. And it suggests that a variant tender must not relate to the legal or financial circumstances of the contract, for example.

The CJ has pointed out that a distinction must be made between two different types of variant tenders. First, there is an *obligatory* variant tender. Such a tender is a necessity for a tender to be conditional. It is thus a requirement from the contracting authority that tenderers should find alternative solutions to a specific point in the contracted task in order for a tender to be conditional (Article 45(1) of the Procurement Directive). Second, there can be *optional* variant tenders, and it is typically these that are referred to when the term 'variant tender' is used. This kind of variant tender means that the tenderer submits a tender with an alternative solution to the 'ordinary solutions' which are suggested by the contract notice.

As stated, a variant tender is a tender which differs from the conditions of the contract notice. As can be seen, there are major similarities in the descriptions of reservations and variant tenders. It is also clear from the legal literature that it is not easy to draw the boundary between these two types of departures from the conditions of the contract notice and the other tender material. Below is a review of a possible procedure for distinguishing between reservations and variant tenders. The reason why it is necessary to make the distinction is that there are different consequences connected with the use of reservations and variant tenders.

To distinguish between reservations and variant tenders, the following assessment can be used. First, an assessment can be made as to whether minimum requirements and other conditions for variant tenders are laid down in the tendering documentation. If such conditions are not laid down, the tenderer does not have the possibility of submitting a variant tender, and any departures in the tender from the conditions in the tendering documentation must be treated as reservations. Second, the next assessment (where there is a possibility of submitting a variant tender) is based on whether the difference between the tender and the requirements in the tendering documentation concerns the content of the task or merely a number of less important provisions and elements of the contract. One way to assess this can be the extent to which it is possible to put a price on the stated changes. Where there is a greater or more fundamental difference between the requirements in the tendering documentation and the tender and where these are difficult to put a price on, this suggests that the case concerns a variant tender.

9.1.3 Technical Dialogue

The situation with contracting authorities will often be such that the personnel who are employed by the public authority will not have sufficient expertise to lay down the technical specifications and the needs which the subject matter of the procurement is to satisfy or the professional expertise to draft the tendering documentation. For this reason, a contracting authority will often engage a technical adviser to undertake professional evaluations. Obviously, this technical advice will precede the publishing of the contract notice. The use of a technical adviser is not in itself a problem, but it can be a problem if technical advisers themselves decide to tender for the contract they have been associated with as advisers. The problem is that the advisory function often gives the adviser important insight into the needs of the contracting authority in relation to the contract in question, and the adviser will often have a major influence on how the goods or services to be bought are to be specified. This gives rise to a potential risk that, via their roles in the initial phases of the tendering process, advisers acquire a number of competitive advantages. Such advantages can conflict with the contracting authority's obligation to ensure equal treatment of all tenderers. This means that in some situations, it can be necessary to exclude an adviser from participation in a tendering procedure, as competition would otherwise be distorted.

> In Joined Cases C-21/03 and C-34/03, *Fabricom*, the CJ stated that a contracting authority may not automatically exclude from tendering an undertaking that has acted as an adviser in the preparation of a public procurement. There must at least be a possibility for the undertaking to provide evidence that its participation in the tendering process will not influence the competition.

The new Procurement Directive has introduced provisions on the ineligibility of consultants; *see* Articles 40 and 41. These provisions express acceptance of the need for preliminary advice but that a contracting authority must ensure that the provision of advice does not result in discrimination or distortion of competition. Where it is not possible to avoid or make good potential competitive advantages based on the role of an adviser, the contracting authority must exclude the adviser from the procurement procedure.[62]

However, there is also another form of ineligibility which is of major importance in public procurement. This is general ineligibility or conflict of interest. The term 'general ineligibility' refers to the fact that, in addition to the principle of equal treatment, there is also a requirement for professional competence. This form of incapacity is referred to neither in the enacting terms nor in the preambles of the public procurement directives.

---

62. Article 57(4)(f) of Directive 2014/24/EU provides that contracting authorities may be required to exclude from participation in a procurement procedure any economic operator where a distortion of competition may arise from their prior involvement in the preparation of the procurement procedure. This cannot be assumed to be correct. The contracting authority must have a *clear obligation* to exclude such an economic operator.

Article 24, first paragraph, of the Procurement Directive provides that: 'Member States shall ensure that contracting authorities take appropriate measures to effectively prevent, identify and remedy conflicts of interest arising in the conduct of procurement procedures so as to avoid any distortion of competition and to ensure equal treatment of all economic operators.' The purpose of the provision is to ensure that no inappropriate financial, economic or other personal interests intrude in the procurement process. If such a conflict of interest arises and it is not possible to ensure equal treatment, then the contracting authority must exclude the applicant/tenderer involved in the conflict of interest.

9.1.4   Cancellation

A practice has developed whereby it is not in all circumstances that a contracting authority can cancel a procurement procedure that has been initiated. A contracting authority can have many good grounds for cancelling a procurement procedure; for example, the authority's needs may have changed, or budget cuts can mean that it does not have the financial resources to make the planned purchase. However, there are circumstances which argue against an unconditional right to cancel a procurement procedure. The primary argument is consideration for tenderers. The preparation of a tender can be costly, both with regard to personnel resources and time. It has thus been considered necessary to protect tenderers against arbitrary cancellations of procurement procedures. The CJ has adopted an interpretation which gives contracting authorities a broad right to cancel.

> According to the practice of the CJ, it is not contrary to the rules on public procurement to cancel a procedure if there is only one tender judged to be suitable; see Case C-27/98, *Metalmeccanica Fracasso*. In Case C-92/00, *Hospital Ingenieure Krankenhaustechnik Planungs-Gesellschaft*, the CJ held that there are limits to a contracting authority's possibilities for cancelling (withdrawing) a public procurement procedure. What was decisive for the possibility of cancellation was the general principles of Union law and the provisions of the Treaty on freedom of movement, particularly the principles of equal treatment, the principle of transparency and the prohibition of discrimination on the grounds of nationality. With these principles as the only restriction, the CJ may be said to have accepted that there is a broad right to cancel. Danish practice from the Complaints Board for Public Procurement has traditionally been based on a rule implying that cancellation could only take place on the basis of objective reasons. This approach is to be found in previous tendering practice and has been adopted by the Complaints Board and been applied in general also in connection with EU procurement rules. However, it seems as if the Complaints Board in recent years has combined the two approaches and made cancellation legitimate, if the cancellation was made on the basis of objective reasons, and no principles were violated.

9.2 The Transparency Principle

The principle of transparency is an important part of the legal basis for public procurement, and it is expressly referred to in Article 18 of the Procurement Directive. In recent years, the transparency principle has been of growing importance to the law on public procurement. In contrast to the principle of equal treatment, the transparency principle is expressed in a large number of the provisions in the public procurement directives, even where these do not expressly refer to the principle. For this reason, the transparency principle, as the default principle, will not have quite the same significance as the principle of equal treatment – the transparency principle is, to a great extent, already provided for in the provisions of the directives.

The transparency principle also seems to be of growing importance in relation to public purchases made outside the scope of the public procurement directives. This is because the CJ has established that the transparency principle must also be complied with for purchases that are undertaken below the threshold values or otherwise outside the scope of the directives. The CJ has not expressly defined what this principle consists of, but it is possible to obtain interpretative guidance from the cases in which the CJ has laid down the existence of the transparency principle. It has done so in, among others, Case C-275/98, *Unitron*; Case C-324/98, *Telaustria*; Case C-231/03, *Coname*; and Case C-458/03, *Parking Brixen*. In these cases, the CJ held that the transparency principle means that a contracting authority is bound to inform the market (or parts thereof) about proposed purchases so that potential suppliers have the opportunity to be considered for the contract. It must be assumed that there is an obligation to publish notice of the proposed procurement before carrying it out. The Commission has published an interpretative communication on the Union law applicable to contract awards which are not or are not fully subject to the provisions of the public procurement directives (OJ 2006 C 179/2). In addition to this, contracting authorities are required to ensure that the procedure is implemented transparently so that it is easier to monitor.[63]

9.3 Other Principles

Contracting authorities must respect a number of other principles, in addition to the principle of equal treatment and the transparency principle. These principles are generally applicable in Union law, even though they can take a particular form when applied in connection with public procurement because of the special character of this area of law.

It must be assumed that the *principle of non-discrimination* does not play a major independent role in connection with public procurement. This is because this principle

---

63. The question of contracting authorities' obligations outside the scope of the procurement directives has attracted a lot of attention; *see, e.g.*, Carina Risvig Hansen: Contracts not covered or not fully covered by the Public Sector Directive; Andrea Sundstrand: Offentlig upphandling – primärrättens reglering av offentliga kontrakter; and Dacian Dragos & Roberto Caranta (eds.): Outside the EU Procurement Directives – Inside the Treaty?

and the principle of equal treatment overlap to a large extent. Since the principle of equal treatment is well-embedded in public procurement law, and the case law has been built on the basis of this principle, it will presumably be applied more frequently than the principle of non-discrimination.

Specifically in relation to public procurement, the *proportionality principle* means that contracting authorities may not adopt measures which go further than necessary in order to achieve the intended aims of the measure. The principle is made clear in Article 18 of the new Procurement Directive, on general rules, where it is stated that contracting authorities must act in a 'proportionate manner'. More specifically, the proportionality principle means that every time a contracting authority makes a choice in connection with a purchase, it must choose the solution which helps the achievement of the aim, without restricting competition, and without making it difficult for suppliers to take part in the competition for the award of the contract.

The *principle of mutual recognition* is relevant in connection with public procurement in that a contracting authority may not reject candidates or tenders merely because these cannot deliver some particular form of (national) documentation. Thus, there is a requirement that contracting authorities must make a concrete evaluation of the qualifications, candidates, documentation, etc.

In addition to these principles, there are a number of other principles that are relevant to public procurement to a greater or lesser extent. For example, this includes the *principle of conformity* and the *principle of objectivity*. The principle of conformity is not referred to by the CJ, but it is the basis of the whole concept of public procurement: a procurement procedure is initiated where a tender is to be submitted on the basis of tender documentation and where neither the documentation nor the tenders may be altered in the course of the procurement procedure. The principle of objectivity primarily plays a role at the national level in certain Member States, for example, in Denmark. As stated above, the evaluation of objectivity plays a central role in the practice of the Danish Complaints Board in regard to the contracting parties' right to cancel tender procedures. According to established practice, cancellations can only be made on the basis of objective reasons.

10 PROCUREMENT AND THE COMPETITION RULES

As previously stated, the procurement rules are not formally linked to the Treaty rules on competition but are based on the rules on freedom of movement. However, it is beyond doubt that the procurement rules have some close resemblances to the competition rules. For example, there is some overlap between the aims of traditional competition law and the aims of the procurement rules.[64] There are many issues where procurement law and competition law touch or overlap, but it lies outside the scope of this chapter to deal with all of these.[65] However, the aim of the following is to identify

---

64. *See, e.g., Grith Ølykke:* Abnormally Low Tenders, Ch. 2, and *Albert Sanchez Graells:* Public Procurement and EU Competition Law, p. 80.
65. For a more detailed review of the relationship of the procurement rules and the competition rules, *see Albert Sanchez Graells:* Public Procurement and EU Competition Law.

some of the most important points of conflict between the traditional competition rules, including the State aid rules, on the one hand, and the procurement rules, on the other hand.

10.1 Procurement and the Competition Rules

In recent years, there has been considerable focus on the relationship between the procurement rules and the competition rules (in particular, Articles 101 and 102 of the Treaty). This relationship is particularly complex, and the complexity is only increased by the fact that there has not been any uniform approach in the way in which the case law has developed in these two areas of the law.

The basic approach is that the competition rules can be applied alongside the procurement directives. It is essential for the application of the competition rules that the general conditions for applying them are fulfilled. This means, to start with, that there must be an assessment of whether the contracting authority should be regarded as an undertaking for the purposes of the competition rules. According to the established case law, this must be determined according to whether the activities in question are to be regarded as economic activities. The CJ has established that what is decisive for whether a specific public procurement is to be regarded as an economic activity is whether the subsequent use of the product is associated with a commercial activity. Specifically, this means that the great majority of purchases made by State, regional or municipal authorities will not be subject to the competition rules, as the subsequent use of purchases will not be commercial. It can potentially be different in relation to public law entities that are characterised by the fact that they potentially undertake commercial activities and thus can potentially be regarded as undertakings in the eyes of competition law and thus subject to Articles 101 and 102.

Articles 37-39 of the Procurement Directive allow certain kinds of contracting authorities (e.g., central purchasing bodies) to carry out procurements on behalf of other contracting authorities. Depending on the circumstances, this activity – acting on behalf of other contracting authorities – can be regarded as an economic activity so that such entities will be subject to the competition rules.

If a contracting authority is in fact regarded as an undertaking subject to the competition rules, the prohibitions in Articles 101 and 102 can be applicable. However, a further challenge to the application of these prohibitions is that procurement procedures themselves are of a peculiar nature and unlike traditional agreements, so there can be some doubt about the application of the rules. The legislator has framed the procurement rules so as to focus largely on ensuring equal treatment and the transparency of the process, so there will seldom be any aspect of the award of a contract that will be covered by the provisions of competition law. There can potentially be competition law problems related to the provisions of the contracts entered into or to abnormal pricing in connection with predatory pricing by a tenderer.

One of the greatest challenges in the relationship between the procurement rules and the competition rules is the interaction between them during a procurement procedure. Situations can arise in which the two sets of rules lead to differing results or where the conditions for what is acceptable differ.

The following examples of this can be given. First, Article 19 of the Procurement Directive allows tenderers to organise themselves as a consortium with a view to submitting a tender. At the same time, competition law sets some clear restrictions on the possibility of forming a consortium. Thus, there appears to be a lack of cohesion or balance between the procurement rules and the competition rules. Second, it can be argued that the possibility of conducting an electronic auction pursuant to Article 35 of the Procurement Directive to some extent makes it easier for undertakings to coordinate a concerted practice. This is because the provision on electronic auctions makes strict demands for transparency with regard to tenderers. In this situation, the core principle of procurement law (on transparency) can make it easier to coordinate tendering, contrary to Article 101 of the Treaty.

The above describes some of the challenges that can arise from the conflicting aims of procurement law and competition law, and it can be seen from this that the most important issue in this area is the possibility of concerted practices between tenderers. This problem is not substantially different from the traditional scope of Article 101, so the reader is referred to the general chapters on this provision, and in particular, the chapters on Article 101 in general and on horizontal agreements. A central provision in this connection is Article 57(4)(d) of the Procurement Directive which states that a contracting authority can exclude economic operators if there are sufficient plausible indications that an agreement was made in order to distort competition. This is a provision which offers the contracting authority an express opportunity to react in regard to (a substantiated suspicion of) agreements made between the tenderers, but at the same time, the provision establishes that complex evaluations must be made.[66] In a single case, the CJ has commented on the provision and has established that even though the provision clearly covers violation of the competition rules, also other agreements on distortion of competition will be covered by the provision and may result in exclusion.[67] The central theme of the provision – when sufficient plausible indications are present – has not been tried by the CJ but rather dealt with several times in cases decided on by the Danish Complaints Board for Public Procurement. Here, it appears that different types of indications have been included, anything from structural indications (relations between undertakings), behavioural indications (tender behaviour in previous and present tendering processes, including whether the tenderers have borrowed tenders from each other), to indications of enforcement (e.g., whether the competition authorities have received any new cases). Practice shows that indications which are exclusively based on structural conditions (for example, that two tenderers are part of the same group/have

---

66. *See also* Commission notice on the use of this provision, *see* notice on tools to fight collusion in public procurement and on guidance on how to apply the related exclusion ground (Official Journal of the European Union 2021/C91/01). The provision is the only rule in the Procurement Directive which has been subject to such a guidance, which clearly shows the complexity of this area.
67. *See* Case C-416/21, *Landkreis Aichach-Friedberg*.

the same parent company) do not in themselves constitute a sufficient plausible indication, whereas it could be the case within the two other categories.

10.2 Procurement and the State Aid Rules

There are several facets to the relationship between the procurement rules and the State aid rules. First, there is the question of what role the State aid rules play in connection with procurements subject to the procurement directives, and second, there is the question of what role procurement plays under the State aid regime.

As discussed in section 7.2.1, the State aid rules are directly referred to in Article 69 of the Procurement Directive in connection with abnormally low tenders.

Other than in Article 69, the State aid rules are to some extent applicable to the conduct of a procurement procedure. The problems associated with the State aid rules that arise in connection with procurement procedures are often very limited. This is because of the requirement in State aid law that there must be an economic advantage for an undertaking that receives payment for a contract. It is the established assumption in State aid law that if a contract is entered into after a competitive tendering procedure, there will not be an advantage within the meaning of Article 107. This is because the market mechanism (the competitive situation) will mean that any overpayment that would constitute State aid will not be relevant under the procurement procedures: A tendered price that is too high will not be competitive against the other tenders submitted in the procurement procedure, and thus a bid based on market price will probably not win the contract. The winning bid will often contain the lowest price which is (by definition) at the market level and, therefore, not an expression of an illegitimate economic advantage.

One of the biggest challenges in the overlap between the State aid rules and the procurement rules is the lack of coordination or convergence between the two sets of rules. The clearest expression of this is the problem that can potentially arise in connection with an attempt to apply the provisions simultaneously; when awarding a contract, a contracting authority must simultaneously comply with the procurement rules and the State aid rules. The means for avoiding State aid are, in principle, the same as are required under the procurement rules, namely that there must be competitive tendering. The problem in this connection is that the kinds of procurement procedures that are acceptable under the State aid rules are not always in line with what is allowable under the procurement rules. This is a problem in practice since a contracting authority can naturally only hold one procurement procedure for one contract and should preferably be able to use a procedure that is acceptable under both sets of rules.[68]

---

68. For more on these problems *see Phedon Nicolaidis:* State Aid, Advantage and Competitive Selection: What Is a Normal Market Transaction?, European State Aid Law Quarterly 2010 p. 65 and *Michael Steinicke:* Public Contracts through Procurement – Can There still be State Aid?, in Konkurrensverket: Pros and Cons of Competition in/by the Public Sector, 2009 p. 139.

11 ENFORCEMENT

11.1 General

The public procurement directives are a set of EU rules, and the final interpretation of these rules is a matter for the CJ. In accordance with practice, EU law is initially enforced by national courts and with a view to ensuring that the Member States establish a suitable system for enforcing violations of the procurement directives, the EU institutions have adopted two directives to ensure the enforcement of the rules at the national level. These two directives are referred to as the Remedies Directives.[69] The Remedies Directives were amended by Directive 2007/66/EC. This Directive has introduced striking new perspectives to the possibilities for enforcement. In particular, it has introduced the possibility of declaring a contract to be 'ineffective'; *see* Article 2d of the Directive (and Act no. 593 of 2 June 2016 on enforcement of the competition rules, etc., §§ 16 and 17). What this means is that it is now possible to have a contract made invalid in practice, which is a very powerful sanction.

These directives require the introduction of measures by the Member States to ensure minimum review procedures for undertakings that feel a need to complain on the basis of a contracting authority's conduct of a procurement procedure. Such measures may include the setting up of special review bodies. However, the requirement can also be satisfied by providing the same guarantees via the ordinary court system if the Member State so wishes.

It is a general requirement of the enforcement system that the Member States' enforcement measures must ensure that decisions taken by bodies responsible for review procedures can be effectively enforced.[70] Behind this provision lies the effectiveness principle, which means that the sanctions and enforcement measures of the Member States must be effective and must have a deterrent effect.

One of the requirements that must be satisfied in national law is that it must be possible to cancel unlawful decisions taken in connection with public procurement, including the removal of discriminatory technical, economic or financial specifications in the invitation to tender, the contract documents or any other document relating to the contract award procedure; *see* Article 2(1)(b) of Directive 89/665/EEC.

It is also laid down that it must be possible under national law to take interim measures with the aim of correcting an alleged infringement or preventing further damage to the interests concerned.

Finally, it must be possible to obtain an award of damages for persons harmed by an infringement. This is discussed further below. The question of what consequences interim measures or cancellation will have is a matter of national law.

---

69. Directive 89/665/EEC on the coordination of the laws, regulations and administrative provisions relating to the application of review procedures to the award of public supply and public works contracts, and Directive 92/13/EEC coordinating the laws, regulations and administrative provisions relating to the application of Community rules on the procurement procedures of entities operating in the water, energy, transport and telecommunications sectors.
70. Article 2(7) of Directive 89/665/EEC.

11.2 Damages

The powers to grant damages and the conditions which must be fulfilled in order to obtain damages are determined under national law. In spite of this, the CJ does have certain requirements for national rules on damages in order to ensure that enforcement and the possibility of obtaining damages are applied in such a way as to ensure effective and non-discriminatory sanctions.

Detailed requirements with regard to damages are laid down in Article 2(7) of Directive 92/13/EC,[71] where it is stated that: 'Where a claim is made for damages representing the costs of preparing a bid or of participating in an award procedure, the person making the claim shall be required only to prove an infringement of Union law in the field of procurement or national rules implementing that law and that he would have had a real chance of winning the contract and that, as a consequence of that infringement, that chance was adversely affected.' It must be assumed that the provision does not lay down any conditions as to what form of infringement leads to liability for damages. In the same way that national rules on liability for damages are applied, it must be assumed that the establishment of the basis for damages is also a matter of national law.

As for the type of damages that can be awarded, the provision must be understood so that it is not only when it is possible to show positively that damage has been suffered that damages may be obtainable. There can also be liability for damages where the contracting authority has infringed the rules so that any real chance of winning the award of a contract ceases to exist.

It is required of national rules on the award of damages that they must not make it more difficult for undertakings from other Member States to obtain damages than undertakings from the same Member State as the contracting authority. And in general, it must not be unreasonably complicated to obtain damages.

12 OTHER RULES ON PUBLIC PROCUREMENT

12.1 General

The EU's rules on public procurement are the most important rules on public procurement within the EU. However, there are also other rules which supplement the directives in the different national legal systems as well as rules relating to the obligations which the Member States have accepted with regard to third countries, in particular agreements entered into via the EU.

---

71. The provision concerns the requirements for obtaining damages in relation to the procurement procedures of entities operating in the water, energy, transport and telecommunications sectors, but it must be assumed to apply equally to the award of public supply and public works contracts.

12.2 WTO Rules: The Government Procurement Agreement

There are many organisations which regulate trade between countries, both regionally and globally. The regulation which is most relevant to the EU and to the individual Member States is the World Trade Organization's GPA. The GPA is a bilateral agreement, which means that only Members of the WTO which are party to the GPA are governed by its provisions.[72]

Public procurement became part of the General Agreement on Tariffs and Trade (GATT) system[73] in connection with the Tokyo Round. The negotiations resulted in the Government Procurement Code at the end of the 1970s, which was the first attempt at an agreement on public procurement, and during the Uruguay Round, this was replaced by the GPA. Prior to the adoption of this explicit regulation of public procurement, public procurement was exempted from the general obligations laid down in the GATT Agreement. The obligations of the Members under this Agreement (e.g., non-discrimination) expressly exclude public procurement situations. Instead, corresponding provisions have been introduced in the GPA.

The GPA contains a long list of provisions which essentially correspond to the provisions in the public procurement directives. These include rules on the selection of candidates and award of contracts, as well as rules on the use of technical specifications, etc.[74]

Bibliography

Lichere, Caranta & Treumer (eds): *Modernising Public Procurement: The New Directive*, 2014.
Sue Arrowsmith: *The Law of Public and Utilities Procurement*, 2014.
Trybus, Caranta & Edelstam (eds): *EU Public Contract Law*, 2014.
Albert Sanchez Graells: *Public Procurement and EU Competition Law*, 2015.
Steinicke & Vesterdorf (eds.): *Brussels Commentary on EU Public Procurement Law*, 2018.

---

72. In contrast to bilateral agreements, most agreements under the WTO regime are, in principle, multilateral agreements, which means that as soon as a country becomes a Member of the WTO it automatically signs up to the multilateral agreements.
73. GATT stands for the General Agreement on Tariffs and Trade. Together with a number of individual agreements, including the GPA, the GATT Agreement constitutes the legal basis for the WTO.
74. For more on the GPA see *Sue Arrowsmith*: Government Procurement in the WTO, and *Birgitte Egelund Olsen* et al.: WTO Law from a European Perspective, Ch. 12.

Table of Cases

European Court of Justice

Case 30/59, *Steenkolenmijnen*, [1961] ECR-1, 360
Case C-25/62, *Plaumann*, [1963] ECR-95, 356
Case 26/62, *van Gend en Loos*, [1963] ECR-1, 6
Case 6/64 *Costa v. ENEL*, [1964] ECR-585, 344, 357, 434, 480
Joined Cases 56 and 58/64, *Consten and Grundig*, [1966] ECR-299, 12, 27, 49, 51, 158, 187, 232, 448
Case 32/65, *Italy v. Council and Commission*, [1966] ECR-389, 51
Case 56/65, *Société technique v. Maschinenbau Ulm*, [1966] ECR-235, 27, 49, 51, 53, 65, 67, 81, 91
Case 23/67, *Brasserie de Haecht v. Consorts Wilkin-Janssen*, [1967] ECR-407, 65
Case 24/67, *Parke Davis*, [1968] ECR-55, 160, 218, 219
Case 5/69, *Völk v. Vervaecke*, [1969] ECR-295, 33, 60
Joined Cases 6 and 11/69, *Commission v. France*, [1969] ECR-523, 382, 398
Case 41/69, *ACF Chemiefarma*, [1970] ECR-661, 13
Case 47/69, *France v. Commission*, [1970] ECR-487, 369
Case 40/70, *Sirena*, [1971] ECR-69, 218
Case 78/70, *Deutsche Grammophon*, [1971] ECR-487, 218
Case 22/71, *Béguelin*, [1971] ECR-949, 233
Case 6/72, *Continental Can*, [1973] ECR-215, 202, 217, 257
Case 8/72, *Cementhandelaren*, [1972] ECR-977, 114, 117
Case 70/72, *Kohlengesetz*, [1973] ECR-813, 348, 349
Case 77/72, *Capolongo*, [1973] ECR 611, 357
Joined Cases 6-7/73, *Commercial Solvents*, [1974] ECR-223, 223, 224, 232, 233
Joined Cases 40/73 and others, *Suiker Unie*, [1975] ECR-1663, 18, 75, 203, 212, 214, 222, 228
Case 120/73, *Lorenz*, [1973] ECR-1471, 342, 344, 357
Case 127/73, *BRT*, [1974] ECR-51, 44, 205, 219, 220, 416, 417, 435
Case 155/73, *Sacchi*, ECLI:EU:C:1974:40, 406
Case 173/73, *Italy v. Commission*, [1974] ECR-709, 359–361, 369, 373, 382, 385–388

Case 8/74, *Dassonville*, [1974] ECR-837, 27
Case 15/74, *Centrafarm BV and Adriaan Peijper v. Sterling Drug*, [1974] ECR-1147, 159, 161, 162, 172
Case 36/74, *Walrave*, [1974] ECR-1405, 5
Case 26/75, *General Motors*, [1975] ECR-1367, 213, 218
Case 51/75, *EMI*, [1976] ECR-811, 28
Case 13/76, *Doná*, [1776] ECR-1333, 5
Case 25/76, *Segoura*, [1976] ECR-1851, 14
Case 26/76, *Metro SB-Großmärkte (Metro I)*, [1977] ECR-1875, 31, 65, 83, 89
Case 27/76, *United Brands*, [1978] ECR-207, 199, 206, 208, 209, 212, 213, 216, 218, 223, 226, 286
Case 47/76, *De Norre v. Concordia*, [1997] ECR-65, 70
Case 78/76, *Steinicke & Weinlig*, [1977] ECR-595, 340, 340, 361, 369, 372, 373, 388
Case 85/76, *Hoffmann-La Roche*, [1979] ECR-461, 201, 202, 205-208, 211, 214, 215, 228, 233
Case 19/77, *Miller International Schallplatten*, [1978] ECR-131, 27, 59
Case 77/77, *BP*, [1978] ECR-1513, 213
Case 82/77, *van Tiggele*, [1978] ECR-25, 369, 376
Case 22/78, *Hugin*, [1979] ECR-1869, 214, 232
Case 30/78, *Distillers*, [1980] ECR-2229, 64
Case 120/78, *Cassis de Dijon*, [1979] ECR-649, 35
Joined Cases 209-215/78 and 218/78, *Van Landewyck*, [1980] ECR-3125, 115, 117, 128
Case 258/78, *Nungesser and Eisele*, [1982] ECR-2015, 66, 67, 81, 91, 187
Case 22/79, *SACEM*, [1979] ECR-3275, 232
Case 44/79, *Liselotte Hauer*, [1979] ECR-3727, 448
Case 61/79, *Denkavit*, [1980] ECR-1205, 359, 363, 364
Case 68/79, *Just*, [1980] ECR-501, 364, 365
Case 99/79, *Lancôme v. Etos*, [1980] ECR-2511, 60, 65
Case 730/79, *Philip Morris*, [1980] ECR-2671, 386, 387, 389, 391, 396, 399, 400
Case 31/80, *L'Oréal v. De Nieuwe AMCK*, [1980] ECR-3775, 33, 65, 84
Case 58/80, *Dansk Supermarked*, [1981] ECR-181, 2
Joined Cases 100-103/80, *Pioneer*, [1983] ECR-1825, 60
Case 172/80, *Züchner*, [1981] ECR-2021, 18, 19
Case 187/80, *Merck v. Stephar*, [1981] ECR-2063, 159, 162
Joined Cases 188-190/80, *France, Italy and United Kingdom v. Commission*, [1982] ECR-2545, 411
Joined cases 213-215/81, *BALM*, ECLI:EU:C:1982:351, 371
Case 322/81, *Michelin*, [1983] ECR-3461, 206, 208, 211, 214, 215, 228, 232
Joined Cases 28 and 30/82, *CRAM*, [1982] ECR-3927, 28
Case 84/82, *Germany v. Commission*, [1984] ECR-1451, 346
Case 86/82, *Hasselblad (GB) Limited*, [1984] ECR-883, 59
Joined Cases 96-102, 104, 105, 108 and 110/82, *IAZ International Belgium*, [1983] ECR-3369, 124
Case 107/82, *AEG*, [1983] ECR-3151, 14, 86
Case 203/82, *Commission v. Italy*, [1983] ECR-2525, 379, 384

Joined Cases 205-215/82, *Deutsche Milchkontor*, [1983] ECR-2633, 352
Case 260/82, *NSO*, ECLI:EU:C:1985:489, 115
Joined Cases 296 and 318/82, *Leewarder Papierwarenfabriek*, [1985] ECR-809, 388, 389, 391
Case 323/82, *Intermills*, [1984] ECR-3809, 356, 360, 363
Case 41/83, *Italy v. Commission*, [1985] ECR-873, 538
Case 123/83, *BNIC*, [1985] ECR-2195, 114
Case 170/83, *Hydrotherm*, [1984] ECR-2999, 22
Case 173/83, *Wasre Oil*, [1983] ECR-555, 438
Case 182/83, *Fearon*, [1984] ECR-3677, 448
Case 193/83, *Windsurfing International*, [1986] ECR-611, 182
Case 243/83, *SA Binon*, [1985]-2015, 13, 89
Case 290/83, *CNCA*, [1985] ECR-439, 220
Case 298/83, *CICCE*, [1985] ECR-1105, 220
Case 19/84, *Pharmon BV against Hoecgst AG*, [1985] ECR-2281, 159, 161
Joined Cases 25-26/84, *Ford*, [1985] ECR-2725, 14, 86,
Case 42/84, *Remia BV and others*, [1985] ECR-2545, 37, 38
Case 52/84, *Commission v. Belgium*, [1986] ECR-89, 351
Case 75/84, *Metro SB-Großmärkte (Metro II)*, [1986] ECR-3021, 85, 87, 206
Joined Cases 142 and 156/84, *British-American Tobacco & R.J. Reynolds*, [1987] ECR-4487, 154, 257
Case 161/84, *Pronuptia de Paris*, [1986] ECR-353, 38, 65, 67, 80, 92
Joined Cases 209-213/84, *Lucas Asjes and others (the Nouvelles Frontières Case)*, [1986] ECR-1425, 509, 513
Case 226/84, *British Leyland*, [1986] ECR-3263, 213, 218
Case 234/84, *Meura*, [1986] ECR-2263, 393
Case 248/84, *Germany v. Commission*, [1987] ECR-4013, 368, 382
Case 311/84, *CBEM*, [1985] ECR-3261, 208, 215, 223
Case 31/85, *ETA Fabriques d'Ébauches v. DK Investment and others*, [1985] ECR-3933, 85
Joined Cases 67, 68 and 70/85, *van der Kooy v. Commission*, [1988] ECR-219, 369, 370, 372, 373, 499
Joined Cases 89/85 and others, *Ahlström (Cellulose II)*, [1993] ECR I-1307, 18, 28, 29
Case 118/85, *Commission v. Italy*, [1987] ECR-2599, 200, 378
Case 223/85, *RSV*, [1987] ECR-4617, 353, 354
Case 259/85, *France v. Commission*, [1987] ECR-4393, 369, 373, 393
Case 310/85, *Deufil*, [1987] ECR-901, 353
Case 311/85, *van Vlaamse*, [1987] ECR-3801, 2, 77
Case 57/86, *Greece v. Commission*, [1988] ECR-2855, 362, 369, 383
Case C-62/86, *Akzo*, [1991] ECR I-3359, 206, 211, 220, 229
Case 65/86, *Bayer AG*, [1988] ECR-5249, 13, 192
Case 66/86, *Ahmed Saeed Flugreisen*, [1989] ECR-803, 22, 435, 438, 516
Case 246/86, *Belasco*, [1989] ECR-2117, 16, 27, 115, 124, 129
Case 247/86, *Alsatel*, [1988] ECR-5987, 220
Case 267/86, *Van Eycke*, [1988] ECR-4769, 26

Table of Cases

Case 27/87, *Erauw-Jacquéry v. la Hesbignonne SC*, [1988] ECR-1919, 66, 91, 181, 189
Case 30/87, *Bodson*, [1988] ECR-2479, 22, 203, 218, 406, 409
Case 31/87, *Beentjes*, [1988] ECR-4635, 567, 587
Case 35/87, *Thetford Corp. v. Fiamma SpA*, [1988] ECR-3585, 162
Case 45/87, *Commission v. Ireland (Dundalk)*, [1988] ECR-4929, 559, 570
Case 53/87, *Maxicar v. Renault*, [1988] ECR-6039, 165, 18, 219
Joined Cases 62/87 and 72/87, *Walloon Regional Executive*, [1988] ECR-1573, 388, 389
Case 94/87, *Commission v. Germany*, [1989] ECR-175, 353
Case 102/87, *France v. Commission*, [1988] ECR-4067, 392
Joined Cases 106-120/87, *Asteris*, [1988] ECR-5515, 354, 360, 365
Case C-142/87, *Tubemeuse*, [1990] ECR I-959, 352, 387, 390–393
Case 238/87, *Volvo v. Veng*, [1988] ECR-6211, 165
Joined Cases 266 and 267/87, *Royal Pharmaceutical Society*, [1989] ECR-1295, 5
Case C-277/87, *Sandoz*, [1990] ECR I-45, 14
Case C-279/87, *Tipp-Ex v. Kommissionen*, [1990] ECR I-261, 59
Case C-301/87, *Boussac*, [1990] ECR I-307, 389
Case 374/87, *Orkem*, [1989] ECR-3283, 247
Case C-395/87, Jean-Louis Tournier ECLI:EU:C:1989:319,Case C-286/13 P, *Dole Food Company Inc.*, ECLI:EU:C:2015:184, 218
Case 395/87, *Tournier*, [1989] ECR-2521, 218
Case C-18/88, *RTT*, [1991] ECR I-5941, 223, 413, 448, 456
Joined Cases 110, 241 and 242/88, *Lucazeau*, [1989] ECR-2811, 218
Case C-202/88, *France v. Commission*, [1991] ECR I-1223, 456, 538
Case C-303/88, *ENI-Lanerossi*, [1991] ECR I-1433, 364, 392, 393
Case C-322/88, *Grimaldi*, [1989] ECR-4407, 7
Case C-5/89, *Commission v. Germany*, [1990] ECR I-3437, 351–353
Case C-86/89, *Italy v. Commission*, [1990] ECR I-3891, 398
Case C-113/89, *Rush Portuguesa and others*, [1990] ECR I-1417, 559
Case C-234/89, *Stergios Delimitis v. Henninger Bräu*, [1991] ECR I-935, 44, 65, 67, 106
Case C-243/89, *Commission v. Denmark*, [1993] ECR I-3353, 559, 561, 590, 594
Case C-260/89, *ERT*, [1991] ECR I-2925, 205, 208, 414, 456
Case C-305/89, *Alfa Romeo*, [1991] ECR I-1603, 364, 369, 371
Case C-41/90, *Höfner & Elser*, [1991] ECR I-1979, 21, 200, 233, 378, 411, 508
Joined Cases C-46/90 and C-93/91, *Lagauche*, [1993] ECR I-5267, 448, 456
Joined Cases C-78-83/90, *Compagnie commerciale de l'Ouest*, [1992] ECR I-1847,
Case C-179/90, *Porto di Genova*, [1991] ECR I-5889, 212, 214, 222
Joined Cases C-271, 281 and 289/90, *Spain, Belgium and Italy v. Commission (on tele-communications services)*, [1992] ECR I-05833, 408
Case C-312/90, *Spain v. Commission*, [1992] ECR I-4117, 342
Case C-354/90, *FNCE*, [1991] ECR I-5505, 340, 357
Case C-2/91, *Meng*, [1993] ECR I-5751, 26
Case C-47/91, *Italy v. Commission*, [1994] ECR I-4635, 344
Case C-69/91, *Decoster*, [1993] ECR I-5335, 200, 378
Joined Cases C-72-73/91, *Sloman Neptun*, [1993] ECR I-887, 374, 375
Case C-92/91, *Taillandier*, [1993] ECR I-5383, 200, 378

Table of Cases

Joined Cases C-159-160/91, *Poucet*, [1993] ECR I-637, 25, 378, 410
Case C-185/91, *Reiff*, [1993] ECR I-5801, 25, 26
Case C-189/91, *Kirsammer-Hack*, [1993] ECR I-6185, 375
Case C-198/91, *Cook*, [1993] ECR I-2487, 356
Case C-225/91, *Matra*, [1993] ECR I-3203, 356
Joined Cases C-241-242/91 P, *Magill*, [1995] ECR I-743, 208, 213, 222, 224, 233, 432
Case C-320/91, *Corbeau*, [1993] ECR I-2533, 406, 412, 549, 556
Case C-49/92 P, *Anic*, [1999] ECR I-4125, 19, 20, 180
Case C-199/92 P, *Hüls*, [1999] ECR I-4287, 19
Case C-250/92, *Gøtrup-Klim*, [1994] ECR I-5641, 38, 152, 153, 205, 220
Case C-292/92, *Hünermund*, [1993] ECR I-6787, 5
Case C-331/92, *Casino*, [1994] ECR I-1329, 572
Case C-364/92, *Eurocontrol*, [1994] ECR I-43, 25, 200, 378, 410, 411, 522
Case C-376/92, *Metro SB-Großmärkte v. Cartier*, [1994] ECR I-15, 85, 88
Case C-387/92, *Banco Exterior*, [1994] ECR I-877, 359, 360
Case C-393/92 *Almelo*, [1994] ECR I-1477, 203, 204, 409, 417, 434, 480
Case C-42/93, *Spain v. Commission*, [1994] ECR I-4175, 391, 393
Case C-44/93, *Namur*, [1994] ECR I-3829, 370
Case C-70/93, *Bayerische Motorenwerke v. ALD Auto-Leasing*, [1995] ECR I-3439, 59
C-266/93, *Bundeskartellamt v. Volkswagen and VAG Leasing*, [1995] ECR I-3477, 75
Case C-353/93, *Commision v. Netherlands* (UNIX) [1995] ECR I-85, 570
Case C-399/93, *H. G. Oude Luttikhus*, [1995] ECR I-4515, 67, 151-153
Case C-415/93, *Bosman*, [1995] ECR I-4921, 5
Joined Cases C-430-431/93, *Van Schijndel*, [1995] ECR I-4705, 45
Case C-39/94, *SFEI v. La Poste*, [1996] ECR I-3547, 357, 359, 362, 363, 364, 371, 540
Joined Cases C-68/94 and C-30/95, *France and others v. Commission (Kali & Salz)*, [1998] ECR I-1375, 259, 283, 286, 287, 305, 313, 315, 336
Case C-87/94, *Commission v. Belgium*, [1994] ECR I-1395, 591, 593
Case C-91/94, *Tranchant*, ECLI:EU:C:1995:374, 456
Case C-96/94, *Centro Servizi Spediporto*, [1995] ECR I-2883, 202
Case C-158/94, *Commission v. Italy*, [1997] ECR I-5789, 480
Case C-159/94, *Commission v. France*, [1997] ECR I-5815, 457, 460
Case C-194/94, *CIA Securities*, [1996] ECR I-2201, 6
Case C-241/94, *France v. Commission*, [1996] ECR I-4551, 361, 381, 384
Case C-244/94, *FFSA*, [1995] ECR I-4013, 25, 377, 378, 410
Case C-333/94, *Tetra Pak II*, [1996] ECR I-5951, 211, 231
Case C-7/95 P, *John Deere*, [1998] ECR I-3111, 118
Case C-24/95, *Alcan*, [1997] ECR I-1591, 349, 351, 353, 354
Case C-73/95 P, *Viho Europe BV*, [1996] ECR I-5457, 22
Case C-169/95, *Spain v. Commission*, [1997] ECR I-135, 352, 354
Case C-185/95 P, *Baustahlgewebe v. Commission*, [1998] ECR I-8417, 241
Case C-219/95 P, *Ferriere Nord*, [1997] ECR I-4411, 31, 253
Case C-242/95, *GT-Link*, [1997] ECR I-4449, 212, 214, 217
Case C-261/95, *Palmisani v. INPS*, [1997] ECR I-4025, 71
Case C-264/95 P, *Commission v. UIC*, [1997] ECR I-1287, 527

611

Table of Cases

Joined Cases C-267-268/95, *Merck v. Primecrown*, [1996] ECR I-6285, 163
Case C-280/95, *Commission v. Italy*, [1998] ECR I-259, 351
Case C-343/95, *Diego Cali*, [1997] ECR I-1547, 25
Case C-353/95 P, *Ladbroke SA*, [1997] ECR I-7007, 363
Case C-355/95 P, *TWD*, [1997] ECR I-2549, 350
Joined Cases C-359/95 P and C-379/95 P, *Ladbroke Racing Ltd.*, [1997] ECR I-6265, 16
Case C-367/95 P, *Sytraval*, [1998] ECR I-1719, 356
Case C-44/96, *Mannesmann Anlagebau*, [1998] ECR I-73, 567
Case C-55/96, *Job Centre coop*, [1997] ECR I-7119, 24
Case C-67/96, *Albany International*, [1999] ECR I-5751, 22, 379, 410, 456
Case C-306/96, *Javico International v. Yves Saint Laurent Parfums*, [1998] ECR I-1983, 28, 59, 98, 171
Case C-328/96, *Commission v. Austria (UNIX II)*, [1999] ECR I-7479, 570
Case C-355/96, *Silhouette*, [1998] ECR I-4799, 161
Case C-360/96, *Arnhem*, [1998] ECR I-6821, 567
Case C-368/96, *Generics*, [1998] ECR I-7967, 448
Joined C-395-396/96 P, *CMB*, [2000] ECR I-1365, 202, 203, 226
Case C-6/97, *Italy v. Commission*, ECLI:EU:C:1999:251, 388
Case C-7/97, *Bronner*, [1998] ECR I-7791, 214, 225, 432
Case C-38/97, *Autotrasporti Librandi Snc di Librandi F & C*, [1998] ECR I-5955, 115
Joined Cases C-52-54/97, *Viscido*, [1998] ECR I-2629, 375
Case C-75/97, *Maribel bis/ter*, [1999] ECR I-3671, 359, 382, 383, 386
Joined Cases C-115-117/97, *Brentjens*, [1999] ECR I-6025, 22
Case C-126/97, *Eco Swiss China Time Ltd v. Benetton International BV*, [1999] ECR I-3055, 45
Joined Cases C-147 and 148/97, *Deutsche Post*, [2001] ECR I-825, 549, 556
Case C-174/97 P, *FFSA*, [1998] ECR I-1303, 367
Case C-219/97, *Maatschappij Drijvende Bokken BV*, [1999] ECR I-6121, 22
Case C-295/97, *Piaggio*, [1999] ECR I-3795, 384, 385
Case C-302/97, *Konle*, [1999] ECR I-3099, 448
Case C-306/97, *Connemara Machine Turf*, [1998] ECR I-8761, 567
Case C-436/97, *Deutsche Bahn AG*, [1999] ECR I -2387, 528
Joined Cases C-15/98 and C-105/99, *Italy and Saedegna Lines v. Commission*, [2000] ECR I-8855, 389
Case C-22/98, *Bécu*, [1999] ECR I-5665, 21
Case C-27/98, *Metalmeccanica Fracasso*, [1999] ECR I-5697, 598
Case C-107/98, *Teckal*, [1999] ECR I-8121, 565
Case C-209/98, *Sydhavnens Sten og Grus*, [2000] ECR I-3743, 438
Case C-225/98, *Commission v. France*, [2000] ECR I-7445, 587
Case C-275/98, *Unitron*, [1999] ECR I-8291, 599
Case C-281/98, *Angonese*, [2000] ECR I-4139, 5
Case C-286/98 P, *Stora Kopparbergs Bergslags*, [2000] ECR I-9925, 23
Case C-324/98, *Telaustria*, [2000] ECR I-10745, 559, 599
Case C-379/98, *PreussenElektra*, [2001] ECR I-2099, 368, 372, 373, 376, 462, 484
Case C-380/98, *Cambridge University*, [2000] ECR I-8035, 567

612

Case C-466/98, *Commission v. United Kingdom*, [2002] ECR I-9427, 508
Case C-467/98, *Commission v. Denmark*, [2002] ECR I-9519, 508, 516
Case C-468/98, *Commission v. Sweden*, [2002] ECR I-9575, 508, 516
Case C-469/98, *Commission v. Finland*, [2002] ECR I-9627, 508, 516
Case C-471/98, *Commission v. Belgium*, [2002] ECR I-9681, 508, 516
Case C-472/98, *Commission v. Luxembourg*, [2002] ECR I-9741, 508, 516
Case C-475/98, *Commission v. Austria*, [2002] ECR I-9797, 508, 516
Case C-476/98, *Commission v. Germany*, [2002] ECR I-4 9855, 508, 516
Case C-23/99, *Commission v. France*, [2000] ECR I-7653, 160
Case C-35/99, *Manuele Arduino*, [2002] ECR I-1529, 115
Case C-143/99, *Adria-Wien Pipeline*, [2001] ECR I-8365, 357, 362, 363, 380, 382–386
Case C-159/99, *Commission v. Italy*, [2001] ECR I-4007, 460
Case C-160/99, *Commission v. France*, [2000] ECR I-6137, 460
Case C-163/99, *Portugal v. Commission*, [2001] ECR I-2613, 199
Joined Cases C-223 and 260/99, *Agora*, [2001] ECR I-3605, 567, 568
Case C-237/99, *Commission v. France*, [2001] ECR I-939, 567
Case C-261/99, *Commission v. France*, [2001] ECR I-2537, 351
Joined Cases C-285 and 286/99, *Impresa Lombardini*, [2001] ECR I-9233, 584
Case C-309/99, *Wouters*, [2002] ECR I-1577, 17, 25, 38, 67, 73
Case C-340/99, *TNT Traco*, [2001] ECR I-4109, 214
Case C-453/99, *Courage*, [2001] ECR I-6297, 46, 71, 239, 254
Case C-482/99, *Stardust Marine*, [2002] ECR I-4397, 368, 370, 372
Case C-497/99, *Irish Sugar*, [2001] ECR I-5333, 204
Case C-513/99, *Concordia*, [2002] ECR I-7213, 583, 587
Joined Cases C-20 and 64/00, *Booker Aquaculture*, [2003] ECR I-7411, 448
Case C-23/00, *Ojala Yhtymä Oy*, [2002] ECR I-7411, 345
Case C-53/00, *Ferring SA*, [2001] ECR I-9067, 366, 367, 384, 384, 386, 420
Case C-59/00, *Vestergaard*, [2001] ECR I-9505, 559, 570
Case C-92/00, *Hospital Ingenieure*, [2002] ECR I-5553, 598
Case C-113/00, *Spain v. Commission*, [2002] ECR I-7601, 393
Case C-218/00, *Cisal*, [2002] ECR I-691, 410
Case C-277/00, *SMI*, [2004] ECR I-3925, 351, 352
Case C-280/00, *Altmark Trans*, [2003] ECR I-7747, 366, 367, 393, 419, 462
Case C-298/00 P, *Alzetta*, [2004] ECR I-4087, 353
Case C-373/00, *Adolf Truley*, [2003] ECR I-1931, 567
Joined Cases C-2 and 3/01 P, *Bunderverband der Arzneimittel-Importeure eV*, [2004] ECR I-23, 15
Case C-82/01 P, *Aéroports de Paris*, [2002] ECR I-9297, 25
Case C-83, 93 and 94/01, P, *Chronopost*, [2003] ECR I-6993, 363, 443, 551
Case C-92/01, *Stylianakis v. Elliniko Dimosio*, ECLI:EU:C:2003:72, 518
Case C-126/01, *GEMO*, [2003] ECR I-13769, 369, 373, 420
Joined Cases C-261 and 262/01, *van Calster*, [2003] ECR I-12249, 356
Joined Cases C-264, 306, 354 and 355/01, *AOK*, [2004] ECR I-2493, 201
Case C-297/01, *Sicilcassa*, [2003] ECR I-7849, 354
Case C-315/01, *GAT*, [2003] ECR I-6351, 585

Table of Cases

Case C-418/01, *IMS Health/NDC Health*, [2004] ECR I-5039, 223
Case C-421/01, *Traunfellner*, [2003] ECR I-11941, 595
Case C-491/01, *British American Tobacco*, [2002] ECR I-11453, 448
Case C-110/02, *Commission v. Council*, [2004] ECR I-6333, 400
Case C-345/02, *Pearle*, [2004] ECR I-7139, 358, 368-370
Case C-12/03 P, *Tetra Laval*, [2005] ECR I-987, 259, 318
Case C-17/03, *VEMW and Others*, [2005] ECR I-4983, 484
Joined Cases C-21 and 34/03, *Fabricom*, [2005] ECR I-1559, 597
Case C-53/03, *Syfait*, [2005] ECR I-4609, 199, 244
Case C-78/03 P, *ARE*, [2005] ECR I-10737, 356
Case C-88/03, *The Azores*, [2006] ECR I-7115, 363, 380, 382, 383, 385
Case C-173/03, *Heiser*, [2006] ECR I-5177, 393
Case C-205/03 P, *FENIN*, [2006] ECR I-6295, 200, 378, 410, 559
Case C-231/03, *Coname*, [2005] ECR I-7287, 599
Case C-250/03, *Mauri*, [2005] ECR I-1267, 26
Case C-399/03, *Commision v. Counsil*, [2006] ECR I-5629, 400
Case C-458/03, *Parking Brixen*, [2005] ECR I-8585, 416, 599
Joined Cases C-485 and 490/03, *Commission v. Spain*, [2006] ECR I-11887, 351
Case C-74/04 P, *Volkswagen AG*, [2006] ECR I-6585, 15
Joined Cases C-94/04 and C-202/04, *Cipolla*, [2006] ECR I-11421, 26
Case C-95/04 P, *British Airways*, [2007] ECR I-2331, 216
Joined Cases C-295-298/04, *Manfredi*, [2006] ECR I-6619, 27, 46
Case 120/73, *Lorenz*, [1973] ECR-1471, 342, 344, 357
Case C-301/04 P, *Commission v. SGL*, [2006] ECR I-5915, 247
Case C-344/04, *International Air Transport Association*, [2006] ECR I-403, 512
Case C-368/04, *Transapline Ölleitung*, [2006] ECR I-9957, 357
Case C-407/04 P, *Dalmine*, [2007] ECR I-829, 232, 233
Case C-410/04, *ANAV*, [2006] ECR I-3303, 416
Case C-519/04 P, *Meca-Medina*, [2006] ECR I-6991, 17, 38
Case C-69/05, *Commission v. Luxembourg*, [2006] ECR I-7, 397
Case C-119/05, *Lucchini*, [2007] ECR I-6199, 356
Case C-217/05, *CEPSA*, [2006] ECR I-11987, 77
Case C-232/05, *Commission v. France*, [2006] ECR I-10071, 351
Case C-238/05, *Asnef-Equifax*, [2006] ECR I-11125, 12, 120
Case C-446/05, *Doulamis*, [2008] ECR I-1377, 26
Case C-76/06 P *Britannia Alloys & Chemicals*, [2007] ECR I-4405, 252
Case C-199/06, *CELF*, [2008] ECR I-469, 358
Case C-279/06, *CEPSA*, [2008] ECR I-6681, 61
Case C-280/06, *ETI and others*, [2007] ECR I-893, 200
Case C-393/06, *Ing. Aigner*, [2008] ECR I-2339, 567
Case C-413/06 P, *Bertelsmann & Sony*, [2008] ECR I-4951, 203, 310
Joined Cases C-468-478/06, *GlaxoSmithKline*, [2008] ECR I-7139, 224
Case C-480/06, *Commission v. Germany*, [2009] ECR I-4747, 565
Joined Cases C-501, 513, 515, 519/06, *GlaxoSmith Kline Services v. Commission*, [2009] ECR I-9291, 64

Case C-532/06, *Lianakis*, [2008] ECR I-251, 585
Case C-113/07 P, *Selex*, [2009] ECR I-2207, 4, 25, 200, 378
Case C-202/07 P, *France Télécom*, [2009] ECR I-2369, 221, 229
Case C-209/07, *Competition Authority v. Beef Industry Development Society Ltd.*, [2008] ECR I-8637, 32
Case C-214/07, *Commission v. France*, [2008] ECR I-8357, 351, 352
Case C-260/07, *Pedro IV Servicios*, [2009] ECR I-2437, 61, 68, 104
Case C-333/07, *Regie Networks*, [2008] ECR I-10807, 373
Case C-350/07, *Kattner Stahlbau*, [2009] ECR I-1513, 25
Case C-385/07 P, *Der Grüne Punkt*, [2009] ECR I-6155, 217
Case C-8/08, *T-Mobile Netherlands BV*, [2009] ECR I-4529, 19, 32
Case C-97/08 P, *Akzo Nobel v. Commission*, [2009] ECR I-8237, 23, 24
Joined Cases C-145 and 149/08, *Hotel Club Loutraki*, [2010] ECR I-4165, 573
Case C-222/08, *Commission v. Belgium*, [2010] ECR I-9017, 546
Case C-279/08 P, *NOx*, [2011] ECR I-7671, 369
Case C-280/08, *Deutsche Telekom AG v. Commission*, [2010] ECR I-9555, 540
Case C-393/08, *Sbarigia*, [2010] ECR I-6337, 26
Case C-507/08, *Commission v. Slovak Republic*, [2010] ECR I-13489, 351
Case C-52/09, *Konkurrensverket v. TeliaSonera Sverige AB*, [2011] ECR I-527, 540
Joined Cases C-106 and 107/09 P, *Gibraltar*, [2011] ECR I-0, 363, 380, 383, 385
Case C-140/09, *Fallimento Traghetti*, [2010] ECR I-5243, 360, 362, 389
Case C-215/09, *Mehiläinen Oy*, [2010] ECR I-13749, 573
Case C-375/09 *Tele2 Polska*, [2011] ECR I-3055, 244
Case C-437/09, *AG2R*, [2011] ECR I-973, 200, 378, 410
Case C-439/09, *Pierre Fabre*, [2011] ECR I-9419, 83
Case C-480/09 P, *AceaElectrabel Produzione SpA*, [2010] ECR I-13355, Case C-521/09 P, *Elf Aquitaine*, [2010] ECR I-8947, 24, 137
Case C-521/09, *ELF Aquitaine*, ECLI:EU:C:2011:620, 23, 252
Case C-16/10, *The Number (UK) Ltd v. British Telecommunications plc*, [2011] ECR I-691, 546
Case C-81/10 P, *France Télécom*, ECLI:EU:C:2011:811, 350, 359, 361, 362, 540
Case C-209/10, *Post Danmark*, ECLI:EU:C:2012:172, 199, 215, 216, 221, 226, 229
Case C-288/11 P, *Leipzig-Halle*, ECLI:EU:C:2012:821, 378, 379
Case C-549/10 P, *Tomra*, ECLI:EU:C:2012:221, 227–229
Case C-599/10, *Slovensko*, ECLI:EU:C:2012:191, 592
Case C-32/11, *Allianz Hungária Biztosító Zrt. and others*, ECLI:EU:C:2013:160, 65
Case C-138/11, *Compass-Datenbank*, ECLI:EU:C:2012:449, 201
Case C-288/11 P, *Leipzig-Halle*, ECLI:EU:C:2012:821, 378, 379
Case C-444/11 P, *Team Relocations*, ECLI:EU:C:2013:464, 20
Case C-501/11 P, *Schindler Holding*, ECLI:EU:C:2013:522, 23, 24
Case C-536/11, *Donau Chemie AG*, ECLI:EU:C:2013:366, 47
Case C-630/11 P, *HGA*, ECLI:EU:C:2013:387, 354
Case C-1/12, *OTOC* ECLI:EU:C:2013:127, 17
Case C-68/12, *Slovenská sporitel'na a.s.* ECLI:EU:C:2013:71, 13
Case C-117/12, *La Retoucherie de Manuela*, ECLI:EU:C:2013:72, 104

Case C-179/12 P, *Dow Chemical*, ECLI:EU:C:2013:605, 137
Case C-262/12, *Vent de Colère*, ECLI:EU:C:2013:851, 377
Case C-336/12, *Manova*, ECLI:EU:C:2013:647, 592
Case C-327/12, *SOA*.
Case C-382/12 P, *Mastercard Inc*, ECLI:EU:C:2014:2201, 17, 38
Cases C-533/12 and C-536/12 P, *SNCM and France v. Corsica Ferries France*, [2014] ECLI:EU:C:2014:2142, 364
Case C-557/12, *Kone AG*, ECLI:EU:C:2014:1317, 47
Case C-67/13 P, *Groupement des cartes bancaires (CB)*, ECLI:EU:C:2014:2204, 40, 116
Case C-90/13 P, *1. garantovaná a.s.*, ECLI:EU:C:2014:326, 252
Case C-170/13, *Huawei Technologies*, ECLI:EU:C:2015:477, 208
Joined Cases C-184/13 and others, *API*, ECLI:EU:C:2014:2147, 26
Joint Cases C-293/13 P og C-294/13 P, *Fresh Del Monte Produce Inc*, ECLI:EU:C:2015:416, 137, 138
Case C-413/13, *FNV Kunsten Informatie en Media*, ECLI:EU:C:2014:2411, 21, 22
Case C-518/13, *Eventech (London Black cabs)*, ECLI:EU:C:2015:9, 360, 368, 383, 391
Case C-601/13, *Ambisig*, ECLI:EU:C:2015:204, 585, 586
Case C-5/14, *Kernkraftwerke Lippe-Ems GmbH*, ECLI:EU:C:2015:354, 383
Case C-15/14 P, *MOL*, ECLI:EU:C:2015:362, 383
Case C-23/14, *Post Danmark II*, ECLI:EU:C:2015:651, 202, 205, 216, 221, 228, 229, 551
Case C-74/14, *Eturas and Others*, ECLI:EU:C:2016:42, 114
Case C-105/14, *Taricco*, ECLI:EU:C:2015:555, 383
Case C-172/14, *ING Pensii*, ECLI:EU:C:2015:484, 27
Case C-345/14, *Maxima Latvija*, ECLI:EU:C:2015:784, 32
Case C-373/14 P, *Toshiba Corp*, ECLI:EU:C:2016:26, 32, 128
Case C-413/14 P, *Intel*, ECLI:EU:C:2017:632, 29, 221, 283
Case C-542/14, *SIA VM Remonts*, ECLI:EU:C:2016:578, 24
Joined Cases C-164/15 P, *Commission v. Aer Lingus* and C-165/15 P, *Commission v. Ryanair Designated Activity Company*, ECLI:EU:C:2016:990, 351, 362, 365
Case C-221/15, *Establissements Fr. Colrupt*, ECLI:EU:C:2016:704, 16
Case C-329/15, *ENEA*, ECLI:EU:C:2017:671, 368
Case C-567/15, *LitSpecMet*, ECLI:EU:C:2017:736, 568
Case C-588/15 P and C-622/15 P, *LG Electronics*, ECLI:EU:C:2017:679, 139
Case C-623/15 P, *Toshiba Corp*, ECLI:EU:C:2017:21, 137, 138
Case C-660/15, *Viasat Broadcasting UK*, ECLI:EU:C:2017:178, 367, 407, 420
Case C-74/16, *Congregación de Escuelas Pias Provincia Betania*, ECLI:EU:C:2017:496, 200, 201
Case C-81/16 P, *Spain v. commission*, ECLI:EU:C:2017:1003, 416
Case C-177/16, *Autortiesību un komunicēšanās konsultāciju aģentūra/Latvijas Autoru apvienība*, ECLI:EU:C:2017:68, 218, 219, 232, 233
Case C-233/16, *ANGED*, ECLI:EU:C:2018:280, 350
Case C-248/16, *Austria Asphalt GmbH & Co.*, ECLI:EU:C:2017:643, 274
Case C-230/16, *Coty*, ECLI:EU:C:2017:941, 83, 102
Case C-405/16 P, *Germany*, ECLI:EU:C:2019:268, 368
Case C-579/16 P, *FIH Holding A/S and FIH Erhvervsbank*, ECLI:EU:C:2018:159, 364

Case C-591/16 P, *Lundbeck A/S*, ECLI:EU:C:2021:243, 32, 131
Case C-611/16 P, *Xellia Pharmaceuticals*, ECLI:EU:C:2021:245, 131
Joined cases C-622/16 P and 624/16 P, *Scuola Elementare Maria Montessori Srl*, ECLI:EU:C:2018:873, 377
Case C-633/16, *Ernst & Young P/S*, ECLI:EU:C:2018:371, 331
Case C-114/17 P, *Spain*, ECLI:EU:C:2018:753, 416
Case C-216/17, *Autorita*, ECLI:EU:C:2018:1034, 576
Case C-265/17 P, *United Parcel Service Inc.*, ECLI:EU:C:2019:23, 260
Case C-349/17, *Eesti Pagar*, ECLI:EU:C:2019:172, 349
Case C-387/17, *Fallimento Traghetti*, ECLI:EU:C:2019:51, 343
Case C-598/17, *A-Fonds*, ECLI:EU:C:2019:352, 356, 357
Case C-706/17, *AB Achema*, ECLI:EU:C:2019:407, 420
Case C-10/18 P, *Mowi ASA*, ECLI:EU:C:2020:149, 330
Case C-75/18, *Vodafone*, ECLI:EU:C:2020:139, 340, 344
Case C-228/18, *Budapest Bank Nyrt.*, ECLI:EU:C:2020:265, 31, 32, 116
Case C-244/18 P, *Larko*, ECLI:EU:C:2020:238, 364
Case C-307/18, *Generics*, ECLI:EU:C:2020:52, 13, 32, 33, 131, 199, 208, 215
Case C-385/18, *Arriva Italia Srl*, ECLI:EU:C:2019:1121, 406
Case C-586/18 P, *Buonotourist Srl*, ECLI:EU:C:2020:152, 367
Case C-594/18 P, *Austria (Hinkley Point)*, ECLI:EU:C:2020:742, 396, 400
Case C-595/18 P, *Goldman Sachs Group*, ECLI:EU:C:2021:73, 24
Case C-51/19 P and C-64/19 P, *World Duty Free Group*, ECLI:EU:C:2021:793, 383
Case C-132/19 P, *Groupe Canal*, ECLI:EU:C:2020:1007, 46
Case C-362/19, *Fútbol Club Barcelona*, ECLI:EU:C:2021:169, 383
Case C-337/19 P, *Magnetrol International*, ECLI:EU:C:2021:741, 342
Case C-367/19, *Tax-Fin-Lex*, ECLI:EU:C:2020:685, 584
Case C-450/19, *Kilpailu- ja kuluttajavirasto*, ECLI:EU:C:2021:10, 13, 253
Case C-562/19 P, *Commission v. Poland*, ECLI:EU:C:2021:201, 383, 385, 386
Case C-596/19 P, *Commission v. Hungary*, ECLI:EU:C:2021:202, 385, 386
Case C-700/19 P, *Toshiba Samsung Storage Technology Corp.*, ECLI:EU:C:2022:484, 20
Case C-883/19 P, *HSBC Holdings plc*, ECLI:EU:C:2023:11, 35
Joined Cases C-885/19 P and C-898/19 P, *Fiat*, ECLI:EU:C:2022:859, 361, 363, 380, 383
Joined Cases C-915/19-917/19, *Eco Fox*, ECLI:EU:C:2021:887, 343
Case C-23/20, *Simonsen & Weel*, ECLI:EU:C:2021:490, 576
Case C-238/20, *Sātiņi-S*, ECLI:EU:C:2022:57, 360
Case C-306/20, *Visma Enterprise SIA*, ECLI:EU:C:2021:935, 31, 32, 58, 59
Case C-332/20, *Roma Multiservizi*, ECLI:EU:C:2022:610, 536, 573
Case C-376/20 P, *CK Telecoms UK Investments*, ECLI:EU:C:2023:561, 259, 303, 304, 305, 312
Case C-377/20, *Servizio Elettrico Nazionale*, ECLI:EU:C:2022:379, 198, 199, 215
Case C-470/20, *AS Veejaam and OÜ Espo*, ECLI:EU:C:2022:981, 343, 358
Joint Cases C-649/20 P, C-658/20 P and C-662/20 P, *Spain*, ECLI:EU:C:2023:60, 381, 384
Case C-680/20, *Unilever*, ECLI:EU:C:2023:33, 202, 221
Joined Case C-702/20 and C-17/21, *DOBELES HES*, ECLI:EU:C:2023:1, 350

Table of Cases

Case C-42/21 P, *Lietuvos*, ECLI:EU:C:2023:12, 223
Joint Cases C-102/21 and C-103/21, *Autonome Provinz Bozen*, ECLI:EU:C:2022:272, 349
Case C-251/21, *Piltenes Mezi SA*, ECLI:EU:C:2022:311, 360
Case C-416/21, *Landkreis Aichach-Friedberg v. J. Sch. Omnibusunternehmen and K. Reisen GmbH.*, ECLI:EU:C:2022:689, 602
Case C-449/21, *Towercast*, ECLI:EU:C:2023:207, 198, 217, 280
Joint Cases C-508/21 P og C-509/21 P, *Danske Erhverv*, ECLI:EU:C:2023:669, 368
Case C-510/21, *Austrian Airlines*, ECLI:EU:C:2023:550, 511
Case C-671/21, *Gargždų geležinkelis*, ECLI:EU:C:2023:709, 450
Case C-186/22, *Sad Traspoto Locale*, ECLI:EU:C:2023:795, 534
Case C-226/22, *Nexive*, ECLI:EU:C:2023:637, 552
Case C-746/21 P, *Altice Group Lux*, ECLI:EU:C:2023:836, 332
Case C-391/23, *2 Braila Winds*, 023 OJ C 321/28, 464
Case C-405/23, *Touristic Aviation Services*, 2023 OJ C 329/13, 511
Case C-411/23, *Sąd Okręgowy w Warszawie*, 2023 OJ C 43/0, 511
Case C-423/23, *Secab*, 2023 OJ C 321/30, 495
Case C-516/23, *Qatar Airways*, 2023 OJ C 126/0, 511

General Court

Case T-11/89, *Shell International Chemical Company*, [1992] ECR II-757, 21
Case T-30/89, *Hilti*, [1991] ECR II- 1439, 206, 226, 231
Case T-51/89, *Tetra Pak*, [1990] ECR II-309, 195, 222
Case T-61/89, *Dansk Pelsavlerforening*, [1992] ECR II-1931, 152
Case T-65/89, *BPB Industries*, [1993] ECR II-389, 215, 228
Joined Cases T-68, 77 and 78/89, *Italien Flat Glass*, [1992] ECR II-1403, 202, 203
Case T-69/89, *Magill*, [1991] ECR II-485, 432
Case T-19/91, *Vichy*, [1992] ECR II-415, 85, 88
Case T-83/91, *Tetra Pak II*, [1994] ECR II-755, 199, 205, 207, 208, 215, 220, 221, 226, 231
Case T-19/92, *Groupement d'achat Edouard Leclerc (Yves Saint Laurent)*, [1993] ECR I-1663, 84, 85
Case T-29/92, *Vereniging van Samenwerkende Prijsregelende Organisaties in de Bouwnijverheid*, [1995] ECR II-289, 116
Case T-35/92, *John Deere*, [1994] ECR II-957, 118
Case T-88/92, *Groupement d'achat Edouard Leclerc (Givenchy)*, ECLI:EU:T:1996:192, 85
Case T-96/92, *Comité Central d'Entreprise de la Société Générale des Grandes Sources and others v. Commission*, [1995] ECR II-1213, 312
Case T-2/93, *Air France*, [1994] ECR II-323, 265, 267, 283
Case T-3/93, *Air France*, [1994] ECR II-121, 265, 267, 290
Case T-7/93, *Langnese Iglo*, [1995] ECR II-1533, 73
Case T-12/93, *Vittel*, [1995] ECR II-1247,
Case T-14/93, *Union Internationale de Chemins de Fer*, [1995] ECR II-1503, 527
Case T-17/93, *Matra Hachette v. Commission*, [1994] ECR II-595, 41, 74

Table of Cases

Joined Cases T-24-26 and 28/93, *CMB*, [1996] ECR II–1201, 216
Joined Cases T-244 and 486/93, *Deggendorf*, [1995] ECR II–2265, 350
Case T-459/93, *Siemens*, [1995] ECR II–1675, 398
Case T-504/93, *Tiercé Ladbroke*, [1997] ECR II–923, 213, 432
Case T-513/93, *CNSD*, [2000] ECR II–1807, 16, 17, 25, 26
Case T-95/94, *Sytravel*, [1995] ECR II–2651, 355
Case T-229/94, *Deutsche Bahn AG*, [1997] ECR II–1689, 528
Case T-290/94, *Keysersberg*, [1997] ECR II–2137, 336
Joined Cases T-305-307, 313-316, 318, 325, 328, 329 and 335/94, *Limbrugse Vinyl Maat-schappij*, [1999] ECR II–931, 20
Case T-358/94, *Air France*, [1996] ECR II–2109, 368, 373, 516
Joined Cases T-374/94, T-375/94, T-384/94 and T-388/94, *European Night Services and others v. Commission*, [1998] ECR II–3141, 432, 532
Case T-395/94, *Atlantic Container v. Commissione (TAA Agreement)*, [2002] ECR II–875, 29
Case T-19/95, *Adia Interim*, [1996] ECR II–321, 593
Joined Cases T-25, 26, 30-32, 34-39, 42-46, 48, 50-65, 68-71, 87-88, 103 and 104/95, *Cimenteries CBR*, [2000] ECR II–491, 17, 20, 128
Case T-49/95, *Van Megen*, [1996] ECR II–1799, 57
Case T-106/95, *FFSA*, [1997] ECR II–229, 366, 367, 395
Case T-149/95, *Ducros*, [1997] ECR II–2031, 400
Case T-176/95, *Accinauto*, [1999] ECR II–1635, 58, 73, 98
Case T-214/95, *VLM*, [1998] ECR II–717, 387, 388
Case T-221/95, *Endemol Entertainment*, [1999] ECR II–1299, 259, 267, 268, 270
Case T-41/96, *Bayer AG*, [2000] ECR II–3383, 14, 15, 63
Case T-87/96, *Assicurazioni Generali and Unicredito*, [1999] ECR II–203, 270, 273
Joined Case T-102/96, *Gencor*, [1999] ECR II–753, 29, 259, 267, 268, 282, 296, 307, 308, 317
Case T-22/97, *Kesko v. Commission*, [1999] ECR II–3775, 259, 280, 294
Case T-46/97, *SIC*, [2000] ECR II–2125, 366
Joined Cases T-125 and 127/97, *Coca-Cola Company v. Commission*, [2000] ECR II–1733, 210, 315
Joined Cases T-204 and 270/97, *EPAC*, [2000] ECR II–2267, 360, 362
Case T-228/97, *Irish Sugar*, [1999] ECR II–2969, 204, 216, 226
Case T-288/97, *Friuli Venezia*, [2001] ECR II–1169, 343
Joined Cases T-298/97 and others, *Alzetta*, [2000] ECR II–2319, 352, 354, 392
Case T-613/97, *Ufex*, [2006] ECR II–1531, 364, 371, 443
Case T-65/98, *van den Bergh Foods*, [1996] ECR II–4653, 67
Case T-73/98, *Prayon-Rupel*, [2001] ECR II–867, 356
Joined Cases T-191/98 and T-212-214/98, *Atlantic Container Line and others v. Commission*, [2003] ECR II–3275, 198, 207
Case T-191/98, *Atlantic Container Line*, [2003] ECR II–3275, 207
Case T-25/99, *Roberts & Roberts v. Commission (the Greene King Case)*, [2001] ECR II–1881, 97
Case T-55/99, *CETM*, [2000] ECR II–3207, 353, 389, 393

Case T-112/99, *Métropole télévision (M6)*, [2001] ECR II-2459, 35, 50, 57, 67
Case T-175/99, *UPS*, [2002] ECR II-1915, 413, 441, 552, 556
Case T-219/99, *British Airways*, [2003] ECR II-5917, 201, 206
Case T-319/99, *FENIN*, [2003] ECR II-357, 201
Case T-342/99, *Airtours plc*, [2002] ECR II-2585, 204, 290, 305, 306, 310
Joined Cases T-92 and 103/00, *Territorio Histórico de Álava*, [2002] ECR II-1385, 381, 384, 386, 389, 393
Joined Cases T-185/00 and others, *Métropole Télévision SA (M6)*, ECLI:EU:T:2002:242, 40
Case T-212/00, *Nuove Industrie Molisane*, ECLI:EU:T:2002:21, 356
Case T-251/00, *Legardére SCA and Canal + SA v. Commission*, [2002] ECR II-4825, 320
Case T-374/00, *Verband der freien Rohrwerke*, [2003] ECR II-2275, 204
Case T-168/01, *GlaxoSmithKline Services*, [2006] ECR II-2969, 40
Case T-198/01, *Technische Glaswerke*, [2004] ECR II-2717, 397
Case T-208/01, *Volkswagen AG*, [2003] ECR II-5141, 15
Case T-210/01, *General Electric*, [2005] ECR II-5575, 259
Joined Cases T-236/01, T-239/01, T-244-246/01, T-251-252/01, *Tokai and others v. Commission*, [2004] ECR II-1181, 247
Case T-241/01, *Scandinavian Airlines System v. Commission*, [2005] ECR II-2917, 514
Case T-314/01, *Avebe*, [2006] ECR II-3085, 23, 137
Case T-5/02, *Tetra Laval/Sidel*, [2002] ECR II-4381, 290
Case T-80/02, *Tetra Laval*, ECLI:EU:T:2002:265, 336
Case T-17/02, *Fred Olsen*, [2005] ECR II-2031, 416–418
Case T-193/02, *Piau*, [2005] ECR II-209, 17, 201, 203–205
Case T-351/02, *Deutsche Bahn*, [2006] ECR II-1047, 355
Case T-357/02, *Freistaat Sachsen*, [2007] ECR II-1261, 397
Case T-212/03, *MyTravel Group*, [2008] ECR II-1967, 319
Case T-328/03, *O2*, [2006] ECR II-1231, 30, 35
Case T-340/03, *France Télécom*, [2007] ECR II-107, 202, 206, 207, 216, 220, 221
Case T-155/04, *SELEX*, [2006] ECR II-4797, 25
Case T-167/04, *Asklepios*, [2007] ECR II- 2379, 356
Case T-201/04, *Microsoft*, [2007] ECR II-3601, 222, 223, 231
Case T-395/04, *Air One SpA v. Commission*, [2006] ECR II-1343, 356
Case T-151/05, *NVV*, [2009] ECR II-1219, 286
Case T-432/05, *EMC Development*, [2010] ECR II-1629, 124
Case T-145/06, *Omya AG*, [2009] ECR II-145, 246
Case T-291/06, *Operator ARP*, [2009] ECR II-2275, 352
Joined Cases T-81-83/07, *Jan Rudolf Maas*, [2009] ECR II-2411, 200, 378
Case T-132/07, *Fuji Electronic System*, [2011] ECR II-4091, 24, 137
Case T-336/07, *Telefónica*, ECLI:EU:T:2012:172, 206–208
Case T-342/07, *Ryanair*, [2010] ECR II-3457, 296, 311, 319
Case T-53/08, *Italy v. Commission*, [2010] ECR II-3187, 365
Case T-62/08, *Terni v. Commission*, [2010] ECR II-3229, 365
Case T-77/08, *Dow Chemical*, ECLI:EU:T:2012:47, 137

Case T-111/08, *MasterCard*, ECLI:EU:T:2012:260, 68
Case T-141/08, *E.ON Energie AG*, [2010] ECR II-5761, 251
Joint Cases T-204/08 and T-212/08, *Team Relocations*, ECLI:EU:T:2011:286, 20
Case T-443/08, *Leipzig-Halle*, [2010] ECR II-1311, 379
Case T-587/08, *Fresh Del Monte Produce* ECLI:EU:T:2013:129, 252
Case T-286/09, *Intel Corp.*, ECLI:EU:T:2014:547, 29, 228
Case T-511/09, *Austrian Airlines Group*, ECLI:EU:T:2015:284, 516
Case T-519/09, *Toshiba*, ECLI:EU:T:2014:263, 128
Case T-162/10, *Niki Luftfahrt*, ECLI:EU:T:2015:283, 259, 319
Case T-251/11, *Austria v. Commission*, ECLI:EU:T:2014:1060, 377
Case T-342/11, *CEEES II*, ECLI:EU:T:2014:60, 243
Case T-471/11, *Édition Odile Jacob SAS*, ECLI:EU:T:2014:739, 315
Case T-674/11, *TV2*, ECLI:EU:T:2015:684, 372
Case T-135/12, *French Republic v. European Commission*, ECLI:EU:T:2015:116, 540
Case T-175/12, *Deutsche Börse AG*, ECLI:EU:T:2015:148, 312
Case T-385/12, *Orange v. European Commission*, ECLI:EU:T:2015:117, 540
Case T-461/12, *Hansestadt Lübeck*, ECLI:EU:T:2014:758, 383
Case T-473/12, *Irish Travel Tax* ECLI:EU:T:2015:78, 351
Case T-500/12, *Ryanair v. Commission*, ECLI:EU:T:2015:73, 365, 516
Case T-104/13, *Toshiba Corp.*, ECLI:EU:T:2015:610, 138
Case T-208/13, *Portugal Telecom v. commission*, ECLI:EU:T:2016:368, 540
Case T-216/13, *Telefónica v. Commission*, ECLI:EU:T:2016:369, 540
Case T-355/13, *easyJet Airline Co. Ltd*, ECLI:EU:T:2015:36, 244
Case T-684/14, *Krka*, ECLI:EU:T:2018:918, 33
Case T-704/14, *Marine Harvest ASA*, ECLI:EU:T:2017:753, 330
Case T-818/14, *BSCA*, ECLI:EU:T:2018:33, 350
Joint Cases T-37/15 and T-38/15, *Abertis Telecom Terrestre and Telecom Castilla-La Mancha*, ECLI:EU:T:2016:743, 367
Case T-47/15, *Germany*, ECLI:EU:T:2016:281, 368
Case T-747/15, *EDF*, ECLI:EU:T:2018:6, 364
Case T-116/16, *Port autonome du Centre et de Lóuest SCRL*, 346
Case T-399/16, *CK Telecoms*, ECLI:EU:T:2020:217, 303–305
Case T-105/17, *HSBC Holdings*, ECLI:EU:T:2019:675, 38, 119
Case T-217/17, *FVE Holýšov I s. r. o.*, ECLI:EU:T:2019:633, 377
Case T-324/17, *SAS Cargo Group*, ECLI:EU:T:2022:175, 29
Case T-380/17, *HeidelbergCement AG*, ECLI:EU:T:2020:471, 277
Case T-834/17, *United Parcel Service Inc.*, ECLI:EU:T:2022:84, 260
Case T-93/18, *International Skating Union*, ECLI:EU:T:2020:610, 38
Case T-235/18, *Qualcomm*, ECLI:EU:T:2022:358, 215
Case T-240/18, *LOT S.A.*, ECLI:EU:T:2021:723, 296
Case T-363/18, *Nippon Chemi-Con Corporation*, ECLI:EU:T:2021:638, 29
Case T-425/18, *Altice Europe NV*, ECLI:EU:T:2021:607, 332
Case T-604/18, *Google and Alphabet (Google Android)*, ECLI:EU:T:2022:541, 8, 208, 209, 221
Case T-136/19, *Bulgaria*, ECLI:EU:T:2023:669, 499

Table of Cases

Case T-609/19, *Canon Inc.*, ECLI:EU:T:2022:299, 333
Case T-212/00, *Nuove Industrie Molisane*, ECLI:EU:T:2002:21, 356
Case T-130/21, *CCPL*, ECLI:EU:T:2022:778, 23
Case T-227/21, *Illumina*, ECLI:EU:T:2022:447, 280
Joint Cases T-73/22 P and T-77/22 P, *Grupa Azoty*, ECLI:EU:C:2023:570, 356
Case T-342/23, *ACER*, 2023 OJ C 278/26, 452

Table of Commission Decisions

Merger Decisions

M.10, *Conagra/Idea*, decision of 30.5.1991, OJ 1991 C 175/18, 268
M.12, *Varta/Bosch*, decision of 31.7.1991, OJ 1991 L 320/26, 297, 298
M.23, *ICI/Tioxide*, decision of 28.11.1990, OJ 1990 C 304/27, 262
M.58, *Baxter/Nestle/Salvia*, decision of 6.2.1991, OJ 1991 C 37/11, 273, 274
M.102, *TNT/Canada Post and others*, decision of 13.12.1991, OJ 1991 C 322/19, 324
M.141, *UAP/Transatlantic/Sun Life*, decision of 11.11.1991, OJ 1991 C 296/12, 269
M.157, *Air France/Sabena*, decision of 5.10.1992, OJ 1992 C 272/5, 263
M.168, *Flachglas/Vegla*, decision of 13.4.1992, OJ 1992 C 120/30, 273
M.179, *Spar/Dansk Supermarket*, decision of 3.2.1992, OJ 1992 C 29, 273
M.190, *Nestlé/Perrier*, decision of 22.7.1992, OJ 1992 L 356/1, 284, 285, 295, 299, 300, 302, 307, 308, 316
M.221, *ABB/Brel*, decision of 26.5.1992, OJ 1992 C 142/18, 289
M.222, *Mannesmann/Hoesch*, decision of 12.11.1992, OJ 1993 L 114/34, 271, 274, 289, 296, 297, 301
M.249, *Northern Telecom/Matra Telecommunication*, decision of 10.8.1992, OJ 1992 C 240/15, 274
M.258, *CCIE/GTE*, decision of 25.9.1992, OJ 1992 C 265/0, 266
M.259, *British Airways/TAT*, decision of 27.11.1992, OJ 1992 C 326/16, 274, 318
M.269, *Shell/Montecatini*, decision of 8.6.1994, OJ 1994 L 332/48, 269, 289, 301, 317
M.289, *Pepsico/KAS*, decision of 21.12.1992, OJ 1993 C 8/2, 285, 295
M.308, *Kali + Salz/MDK/Treuhand*, decision of 14.12.1993, OJ 1994 L 186/38, 268, 287, 308, 313
M.310, *Harrisons & Crosfield / Akzo*, decision of 29.4.1993, OJ 1993 C 128/5, 271, 322
M.315, *Mannesmann/Vallourec/Ilva*, decision of 31.1.1994, OJ 1994 L 102/15, 287, 289, 295, 299, 305, 307, 310
M.330, *McCormick/CPC/Rabobank/Ostmann*, decision of 29.11.1993, OJ 1993 C 256/3, 266
M.346, *JCSAT/SAJAC*, decision of 30.6.1993, OJ 1993 C 219/14, 281
M.353, *British Telecom/MCI*, decision of 13.9.1993, OJ 1993 C 253/0, 273

M.358, *Pilkington-Techint/SIV*, decision of 21.12.1993, OJ 1994 L 158/24, 288, 298, 300, 301, 306
M.368, *Snecma/TI*, decision of 17.1.1994, OJ 1993 C 42/12, 287
M.376, *Synthomer/Yule Catto*, decision of 21.9.1993, OJ 1993 C 303/5, 262
M.382, *Philips/Grundig*, decision of 3.12.1993, OJ 1993 C 336/11, 270
M.397, *Ford/Hertz*, decision of 7.3.1994 OJ 1994 C 121/4, 265
M.409, *ABB/Renault Automation*, decision of 9.3.1993, OJ 1994 C 80/11, 324
M.425, *BS/BT*, decision of 28.3.1993, OJ 1994 C 134/4, 270
M.430, *Procter & Gamble/VP Schickedanz*, decision of 21.6.1994, OJ 1994 L 354/32, 295, 299, 300, 302
M.441, *Daimler Benz AG/RWE AG*, decision of 20.6.1994, OJ 1994 C 178/15, 273
M.469, *MSG Media Service*, decision of 9.11.1994, OJ 1994 L 364/1, 297, 301
M.477, *Mercedes-Benz/Kässbohrer*, decision of 14.2.1995, OJ 1995 L 211/1, 289, 295, 300
M.523, *Akzo Nobel/Monsanto*, decision of 19.1.1995, OJ 1995 C 37/3, 322
M.527, *Thomson/Deutsche Aerospace*, decision of 2.12.1995, OJ 1995 C 65/4, 271
M.550, *Union Carbide/Enichem*, decision of 13.3.1995, OJ 1995 C 123/3, 323
M.551, *ATR/BAe*, decision of 25.7.1995, OJ 1995 C 264/8, 272, 273
M.553, *RTL/Veronica/Endemol*, decision of 17.7.1996, OJ 1996 L 294/14, 288, 295
M.580, *ABB/Daimler-Benz*, decision of 18.10.1995, OJ 1997 L 11/1, 285, 289, 297, 302, 307
M.582, *Orkla/Volvo*, decision of 20.9.1995, OJ 1996 L 66/35, 285, 286, 288, 298, 299, 302
M.604, *Albacom*, decisions of 15.9.1995, OJ 1995 C 219/3, 259, 270
M.619, *Gencor/Lonrho*, decision of 24.4.1996, OJ 1997 L 11/30, 307, 308, 317
M.662, *Leisure Plan*, decision of 21.12.1995, OJ 1996 C 63/5, 270
M.683, *GTS- Hermes Inc./HIT Rail BV*, decision of 5.3.1996, OJ 1996 C 157/13, 270
M.697, *Lockheed Martine/Loral Corporation*, decision of 27.3.1996, OJ C 314/9, 266
M.722, *Teneo/Merrill Lynch/Bankers Trust*, decision of 15.4.1996, OJ 1996 C 159/4, 271, 274
M.737, *Ciba-Geigy/Sandoz*, decision of 17.7.1996, OJ 1997 L 201/1, 300, 318
M.754, *Anglo American Corporation/Lonrho*, decision of 23.4.1997, OJ 1998 L 149/21, 263, 264, 287, 301, 317
M.774, *Saint-Gobain/Wacker Chemie/NOM*, decision of 4.12.1996, OJ 1997 L 247/1, 294, 300, 301
M.784, *Kesko/Tuko*, decision of 19.2.1997, OJ 1997 L 174/47, 288
M.794, *Coca-Cola/Amalgamated Beverages GB*, decision of 22.1.1997, OJ 1997 L 218/15, 285, 286, 288, 295
M.833, *The Coca-Cola Company/Carlsberg A/S*, decision of 11.9.1997, OJ 1998 L 145/41, 285, 288, 297, 300, 302, 315, 316
M.877, *Boeing/McDonnell Douglas*, decision of 30.7.1997, OJ 1997 L 336/16, 281, 287, 297, 299, 300, 318, 319
M.890, *Blokker/Toys 'R' Us*, decision of 26.6.1997, OJ 1998 L 316/1, 266, 288, 296
M.902, *Warner Bros/Lusomundo/Sogecable*, decision of 12.5.1997, OJ 1997 C 202/4, 262

Table of Commission Decisions

M.904, *RSB/Tenex/Fuel Logistic*, decision of 2.4.1997, OJ 1997 C 168/5, 273
M.938, *Guinness/Grand Metropolitan*, decision of 15.10.1997, OJ 1998 L 288/24, 285, 288, 297
M.942, *VEBA/Degussa*, decision of 3.12.1997, OJ 1998 L 201/102, 308, 317
M.951, *Cable and wireless/Maersk Data – Nautec*, decision of 10.7.1997, OJ 1997 C 235/4, 324
M.967, *KLM/Air UK*, decision of 22.9.1997, OJ 1997 C 372/20, 265
M.969, *A.P. Møller*, decision of 10.2.1999, OJ 1999 L 183/29, 330
M.986, *Agfa-Gevaert/DuPoint*, decision of 11.2.1998, OJ 1998 L 211/22, 318
M.994, *Dupont/Hitachi*, decision of 24.10.1997, OJ 1998 C 6/2, 272, 281
M.998, *Danmark*, decision of 10.11.1997, OJ 1998 C 38/4, 268
M.1014, *British Steel/Europipe*, decision of 26.2.1998, OJ 1998 C 181/3, 262
M.1016, *Price Waterhouse/Coopers & Lybrand*, decision of 20.5.1998, OJ 1999 L 50/27, 288, 295, 306, 307
M.1046, *Ameritech/Tele Danmark*, decision of 5.12.1997, OJ 1998 C 25/18, 264
M.1049, *AKZO/PLV – EPL*, decision of 4.12.1997, OJ 1998 C 39/19, 271, 272
M.1080, *Thyssen/Krupp*, decision of 2.6.1998, OJ 1998 C 252/7, 317
M.1082, *Allianz/AGF*, decision of 8.5.1998, OJ 1998 C 246/4, 317
M.1113, *Nortel/Norweb*, decision of 18.3.1998, OJ 1998 C 123/3, 322
M.1132, *BT/ESB*, decision of 19.5.1998, OJ 1998 C 307/5, 322
M.1167, *ICI/Williams*, decision of 29.4.1998, OJ 1998 C 218/5, 322
M.1168, *DHL/Deutsche Post*, decision of 26.6.1998, OJ 1998 C 307/3, 318, 319
M.1188, *Kingfisher/Wegert/Promarkt*, decision of 18.6.1998, OJ 1998 C 342/3, 323
M.1229, *American Home Products/Monsanto*, decision of 28.9.1998, OJ 1999 C 109/4, 296, 317
M.1298, *Kodak/Imation*, decision of 23.10.1998, OJ 1999 C 17/2, 320, 324
M.1313, *Danish Crown/Vestjyske Slagterier*, decision of 9.3.1999, OJ 2000 L 20/1, 298, 300, 302, 308, 318
M.1327, *NC/Canal+/CDPQ/Bank America*, decision of 3.12.1998, OJ 1999 C 233/21, 326
M.1383, *Exxon/Mobil*, decision of 29.9.1999, OJ 2004 L 103/1, 306
M.1467, *Rohm and Haas/Morton*, decision of 19.4.1999, OJ 1999 C 157/7, 317
M.1524, *Airtours/First Choice*, decision of 22.9.1999, OJ 2000 L 93/1, 306–308
M.1845, *AOL/Time Warner*, decision of 11.10.2000, OJ 2001 L 268/28, 289
M.2041, *United Airlines/US Airways*, decision of 12.1.2001, 514
M.2268, *Pernod Richard/Diageo/Seagram Spirits*, decision of 8.5.2001, OJ 2002 C 16/13, 319
M.2314, *BASF/Eurodiol/Pantochim*, decision of 11.7.2001, OJ 2002 L 132/45, 314
M.2838, *P & O STENA LINE*, decision of 7.8.2002, OJ 2002 C 206/5, 262
M.2840, *Danapak/Teich/JV*, decision of 20.8.2002, OJ EFT 2002 C 226/20, 262
M.3333, *Sony/BMG*, decision of 19.7.2004, OJ 2005 L 62/30, 309, 310
M.3436, *Continental/Phoenix*, decision of 26.10.2004, OJ 2006 L 353/7, 317
M.3440, *EDP/ENI/GDP*, decision of 9.12.2004, OJ 2005 L 302/69, 317, 319
M.3465, *Syngenta CP/Advanta*, decision of 17.8.2004, OJ 2004 C 263/7, 303
M.3576, *ECT/PONL/EUROMAX*, decision of 22.12.2004, OJ 2004 C 288/2, 272

Table of Commission Decisions

M.3858, *Lehman Brothers/SCG/Starwood/Le Meridien*, decision of 20.7.2005, 274
M.4000, *Inco/Falconbridge*, decision of 4.7.2006, OJ 2007 L 72/18, 312
M.4980, *ABF/GBI Business*, decision of 23.9.2008, OJ 2009, C 145/12, 310
M.4994, *Electrabel/Compagnie Nationale du Rhône*, decision of 10.6.2009, OJ 2009 C 279/9, 330
M.5046, *Friesland Foods/Campina*, decision of 17.12.2008, OJ 2009 C 75/21, 318
M.5440, *Lufthansa/Austrian Airlines*, decision of 28.8.2009, OJ 2010 C 16/11, 318
M.5469, *RENOVA INDUSTRIES/SULZER*, decision of 17.6.2009, OJ 2009 C 173/5, 264
M.6360, *Nynas/Shell Harburg*, decision of 2.09.2013, OJ 2014 C 368/5, 314
M.6570, *UPS/TNT Express*, decision of 30.1.2013, OJ 2014 C 137/8, 311
M.6796, *Aegean/Olympic II*, decision of 9.10.2013, OJ 2015 C 25/7, 314
M.7184, *Marine Harvest/Morpol*, decision of 23.7.2014, OJ 2014 C 455/5, 330
M.7228, *Centrica/Bord Gais Energy*, decision of 5.5.2014, *OJ 2014 C 145/14, 289*
M.7612, *Hutchison 3G UK/Telefónica UK*, decision of 11.5.2016, *OJ 2016 C 357/15, 304*
M.7932, *Dow/DuPont*, decision of 27.3.2017, OJ 2017 C 353/9, 292
M.7993, *Altice/PT Portugal*, decision of 24.4.2018, OJ 2018 C 315/11, 332
M.8179, *Canon/Toshiba Medical Systems Corporations*, decision of 27.6.2019, OJ 2019 C 362/8, 333
M.8228, *Facebook/Whatsapp*, decision of 18.5.2017, OJ 2017 C 286/6, 329
M.8436, *General Electric/LM Wind Power*, decision of 8.4.2019, OJ 2020 C 24/12, 329
M.8792, *T-Mobile NL/Tele2 NL*, decision of 27.11.2018, OJ 2019 C 150/5, 307
M.8864, *Vodafone/Certain Liberty Global Cases*, decision of 18.7.2019, 318
M.9660, *Google/Fitbit*, decision of 17.12.2020, OJ 2021 C 194/7, 319
M.9730, *Fiat Chrysler/Peugeot*, decision of 21.12.2020, OJ 2021 C 423/14, 318
M.10493, *Illumina/GRAIL*, judgement general court of 13.7.2022, T-227/21, 334
JV.1, *Telia/Telenor/Schibsted*, decision of 27.5.1998, OJ 1999 C 220/28, 325–327
JV.2, *ENEL/FT/DT*, decision of 22.6.1998, OJ 1999 C 178/15, 269, 327
JV.3, *BT/Airetel*, decision of 8.7.1998, OJ 1999 C 369/24, 274
JV.4, *VIAG/Orange UK*, decision of 11.8.1998, OJ 1999 C 178/16, 269
JV.5, *Cegetel/Canal+/AOL/Bertelsmann*, decision of 4.8.1998, OJ 2000 C 24/4, 327
JV.6, *Ericsson/Nokia/Psion*, decision of 11.8.1998, OJ 1999 C 365/2, 327
JV.7, *Telia/Sonera/Lithuanian Telecommunications*, decision of 14.8.1998, OJ 1999 C 178/16, 326, 327
JV.8, *Deutsche Telekom/Springer/Holtzbrink/infoseek*, decision of 28.9.1998, OJ 1998 C 220/28, 327
JV.12, *Ericsson/Nokia/Psion/Motorola*, decision of 22.12.1998, OJ 1999 C 178/18, 259
JV.14, *Panagora/DG Bank*, decision of 26.11.1998, OJ 1999 C 68/10, 272
JV.15, *BT/AT&T*, decision of 30.3.1999, OJ 1998 C 342/4, 323
JV.19, *KLM/Alitalia*, decision of 11.8.1999, OJ 2000 C 96/5, 275
JV.21, *Skandia/Storebrand/Pohjola*, decision of 17.8.1999, OJ 1999 L 357/6, 326
JV.22, *Fujitsu/Siemens*, decision of 30.9.1999, OJ 1999 C 318/15, 272, 324, 326
JV.23, *Telefonica/Portugal Telecom/MEDI Telecom*, decision of 17.12.1999, OJ 2000 C 22/11, 272, 327
JV.24, *Bertelsmann/Planeta/Bol Spain*, decision of 3.12.1999, OJ 2000 C 67/9, 274

JV.28, *Sydkraft/HEW/Hansa Energy Trading*, decision of 30.9.1999 para. 17, 272
JV.29, *Lafarge/Readymix*, decision of 20.12.1999, OJ 2000 C 21/27, 288, 327
JV.32, *Granaria/Ültje/Interschnack/May Holding*, decision of 28.2.2000, OJ 1999 C 342, 302
JV.35, *Beiselen/Bay WA/ MG Chemag*, deicision of 1.2.2000, OJ 2000 C 56/09, 326, 327
JV.36, *TXU Europe/EDF-London Investmenst*, decision of 3.2.2000, OJ 2000 C 49/4, 271, 322
JV.37, *B Sky B/Kirch Pay TV*, decision of 21.3.2000, OJ 2000 C 110/45, 274, 318
JV.44, *Hitachi/NEC – Dream/JV*, decision of 3.5.2000, OJ 2000 C 153/8, 141, 272
JV.46, *Blackstone/CDPQ/Kabel Nordrhein – Westfalen*, decision of 19.6.2000, OJ 2000 C 262/5, 268
JV.50, *Blackstone/CDPQ/Kabel Baden-Württemberg*, decision of 1.8.2000, OJ 2000 C 323/4, 268
JV.56, *Hutchinson/ECT*, decision of 29.11.2001, OJ 2002 C 113/7, 317

Other Commission Decisions

70/488/EEC, *Omega*, OJ 1970 L 242/22, 83
72/253/EEC, *Farms in the Netherlands*, OJ 1972 L 164/22, 388, 390
72/474/EEC, *Re Cimbel*, OJ 1972 L 303/24, 120
73/109/EEC, *European sugar industry*, OJ 1973 L 140/17, 116
73/322/EEC, *Deutsche Philips GmbH*, OJ 1973 L 293/40, 63
74/431/EEC, *Papiers peints de Belgique*, OJ 1974 L 237/3, 117
74/634/EEC, 1974, *Franco-Japanese ball-bearings agreement*, OJ 1974 L 343/19, 15, 114
76/743/EEC, *Reuter/BASF*, OJ 1976 L 254/40, 36, 37
77/66/EEC, *Gerofabriek*, OJ 1977 L 16/8, 63
77/781/EEC, *GEC-Weir Sodium Circulators*, OJ 1977 L 327/26, 149
78/68/EEC, *Hugin/Liptons*, OJ 1978 L 22/23, 224
78/156/EEC, *Video cassette recorders*, OJ 1978 L 47/42, 125
78/163/EEC, *Distillers Company*, OJ 1978 L 50/16, 63
78/253/EEC, *Campari*, OJ 1978 L 70/69, 79
79/86/EEC, *Vaessen/Moris*, OJ 1979 L 19/32, 177
80/182/EEC, *FLORAL*, OJ 1980 L 39/51, 116
80/256/EEC, *Pioneer*, OJ 1980 L 60/21, 20
80/932/EEC, *Sickness insurance schemes*, OJ 1980 L 264/28, 379, 384
82/529/EEC, *Fixing of rates*, OJ 1982 L 234/5, 525
82/861/EEC, *British Telecommunications*, OJ 1982 L 360/36, 538
83/418/EEC, *Railways*, OJ 1983 L 237/32, 526
84/380/EEC, *Synthetic fibre*, OJ 1984 L 207/17, 123
84/387/EEC, *BPCL/ICI*, OJ 1984 L 212/1, 123
84/405/EEC, *Zinc Producer Group*, OJ 1984 L 220/27, 116
84/508/EEC, *Polypropylen fibers*, OJ 1984 L 283/42, 388
85/45/EEC, *Ideal Standard*, OJ 1985 L 20/38, 84
85/76/EEC, *Milchförderungsfonds*, OJ 1985 L 35/35, 129, 374
85/77/EEC, *Uniform Eurocheques*, OJ 1985 L 35/43, 117

Table of Commission Decisions

85/206/EEC, *Aluminium imports from Eastern Europe*, OJ 1985 L 92/1, 116
85/404/EEC, *Grundig*, OJ 1985 L 233/1, 90
85/410/EEC, *Velcro/Aplix*, OJ 1985 L 233/22, 192
85/616/EEC, *Villeroy & Boch*, OJ 1985 L 376/15, 85
86/399/EEC, *Roofing felt*, OJ 1986 L 232/15, 115, 120
86/405/EEC, *Optical fibres*, OJ 1986 L 236/30, 141, 146, 149
86/507/EEC, *Irish Banks' Standing Committee*, OJ 1986 L 295/28, 117
86/596/EEC, *MELDOC*, OJ 1986 L 348/50, 120
87/14/EEC, *Yves Rocher*, OJ 1987 L 8/49, 80
87/17/EEC, *Pronuptia*, OJ 1987 L 13/39, 80
87/69/EEC, *X/Open Group*, OJ 1987 L 35/36, 126
87/100/EEC, *Mitchell Cotts/Sofiltra*, OJ 1987 L 41/31, 141, 148
87/407/EEC, *Computerland*, OJ 1987 L 222/12, 80
87/500/EEC, *BBI/Boosey & Hawkes: Interim measures*, OJ 1987 L 286/36, 208, 223
87/573/EEC, *Redesignation of assisted areas in Denmark*, OJ 1987 L 347/64, 392
88/88/EEC, *Olivetti/Canon*, OJ 1988 L 52/51, 141, 144
88/143/EEC, *Rich Products*, OJ 1988 L 69/21, 191
88/172/EEC, *Konica*, OJ 1988 L 78/34, 63
88/477/EEC, *British Dental Trade Association*, OJ 1988 L 233/1, 130
88/491/EEC, *Bloemenveilingen Aalsmeer*, OJ 1988 L 262/27, 130
88/589/EEC, *London European – Sabena*, OJ 1988 L 317/47, 222, 224, 225
88/518/EEC, *British Sugar*, OJ L 284/41, 211, 222, 223, 227
88/604/EEC, *ServiceMaster*, OJ L 332/38, 79, 80
89/113/EEC, *Decca Navigator System*, OJ 1989 L 43/27, 208, 223
89/22/EEC, *BPB Industries PLC*, OJ 1989 L 10/50, 222
89/94/EEC, *Charles Jourdan*, OJ 1989 L 35/31, 80
89/467/EEC, *UIP*, OJ 1989 L 226/35, 129
90/186/EEC, *Moosehead/Whitbread*, OJ 1990 L 100/32, 79, 175
90/410/EEC, *Elopak/Metal Box-Odin*, OJ 1990 L 209/15, 37, 135, 148
91/130/EEC, *Screensport/EBU Members*, OJ 1991 L 63/32, 145
91/153/EEC, *Vichy*, OJ 1991 L 75/57, 85, 87
91/299/EEC, *Soda – Solvay*, OJ 1990 L 152/21, 228
91/301/EEC, *Ansac*, OJ 1991 L 152/54, 41, 116
91/329/EEC, *Scottish Nuclear*, OJ 1991 L 178/31, 481
91/335/EEC, *Gosme/Martell-DMP*, OJ 1991 L 185/23, 22, 63, 136, 137
91/396/EEC, *Emergency call number*, OJ 1991 L 217/31, 547
91/562/EEC, *Eirpage*, OJ 1991 L 306/22, 137, 145, 149
92/11/EEC, *Toyota*, OJ 1992 L 6/36, 362, 363
92/33/EEC, *Yves Saint Laurent*, OJ 1992 L 12/24, 60, 90
92/157/EEC, *UK Agricultural Tractor Registration Exchange*, OJ 1992 L 68/19, 118
92/163/EEC, *Tetra Pak II*, OJ 1992 L 72/1, 219
92/204/EEC, *Building and construction industry in the Netherlands*, OJ 1992 L 92/1, 130
92/213/EEC, *British Midland v Aer Lingus*, OJ 1992 L 96/34, 223, 514
92/389/EEC, *State aid*, OJ 1992 L 207/47, 398

Table of Commission Decisions

92/411/EEC, *State aid*, OJ 1992 L 223/28, 362
92/428/EEC, *Parfums Givenchy*, OJ 1992 L 236/11, 86
92/521/EEC, *Distribution of package tours*, OJ 1992 L 326/31, 21
93/46/EEC, *Ford Agricultural*, OJ 1993 L 20/1, 57
93/48/EEC, *Fiat/Hitachi*, OJ 1993 L 20/10, 147, 149
93/49/EEC, *Ford/Volkswagen*, OJ 1993 L 20/14, 140, 142, 149
93/59/EEC, *Astra*, OJ 1993 L 20/23, 145
93/126/EEC, *Jahrhundertvertrag*, OJ 1993 L 50/14, 481
93/174/EEC, *Tariff structures in the combined transport of goods*, OJ 1993 L 73/38, 527
93/252/EEC, *Warner-Lambert/Gillette*, OJ 1993 L 116/21, 153
93/403/EEC, *EBU/Eurovision*, OJ 1993 L 179/23, 144
93/405/EEC, *Schöller Lebensmittel*, OJ 1975 L 138/1, 65
93/406/EEC, *Langnese-Iglo GmbH*, OJ 1993 L 183/19, 65
94/19/EC, *Sea Containers v Stena Sealink*, OJ 1994 L 15/8, 223, 432
94/119/EC, *Rødby Havn*, OJ 1994 L 55/52, 432
94/210/EC, *HOV SVZ/MCN*, OJ 1994 L 104/34, 528
94/296/EC, *Stichting Baksteen*, OJ 1994 L 131/15, 123, 124
94/322/EC, *Exxon/Shell*, OJ 1994 L 144/20, 149
94/579/EC, *BT-MCI*, OJ 1994 L 223/36, 147
94/594/EC, *ACI*, OJ 1994 L 224/28, 527
94/599/EC, *PVC*, OJ 1994 L 239/14, 13
94/601/EC, *Cartonboard*, OJ 1994 L 243/1, 120
94/663/EC, *Night Services*, OJ L 259/20, 532
94/770/EC, *Pasteur Mérieux-Merck*, OJ 1994 L 309/1, 141, 144, 149
94/815/EC, *Cement*, OJ 1994 L 343/1, 128
94/823/EC, *Fujitsu AMD Semiconductor*, OJ 1994 L 341/66, 147
94/895/EC, *International Private Satellite Partners*, OJ 1994 L 354/75, 141, 148
94/896/EC, *Asahi/Saint-Gobain*, OJ 1994 L 354/87, 140
94/986/EC, *Philips-Osram*, OJ 1994 L 378/37, 140, 143, 144, 147–149
95/477/EC, *BASF Lacke, Farben AG and SA Accinauto*, OJ 1995 L 272/16, 99
96/180/EC, *Lufthansa/SAS*, OJ 1996 L 54/28, 520
96/434/EC, *Aid to enterprises in a state of insolvency in Italy*, OJ 1996 L 180/31, 354, 365, 366
96/438/EC, *Fenex*, OJ 1996 L 181/28, 61, 186
96/546/EC, *Atlas*, OJ 1996 L 239/23, 145, 147, 148
96/547/EC, *Phoenix/GlobalOne*, OJ 1996 L 239/57, 147, 148
97/39/EC, *Iridium*, OJ 1997 L 16/87, 141, 148
97/114/EC, *Additional implementation periods requested by Ireland*, OJ 1997 L 41/8, 538
97/123/EC, *Novalliance/Systemform*, OJ 1997 L 47/11, 62, 186
97/310/EC, *Additional implementation periods requested by Portugal*, OJ 1997 L 133/19, 538
97/542/EC, *Biofuels*, OJ 1997 L 222/26, 360, 361, 388
97/568/EC, *Additional implementation periods requested by Luxembourg*, OJ 1997 L 234/7, 538

Table of Commission Decisions

97/603/EC, *Additional implementation periods requested by Spain*, OJ 1997 L 243/48, 538
97/607/EC, *Additional implementation periods requested by Greece*, OJ 1997 L 245/6, 538
97/781/EC, *Uniworld*, OJ 1997 L 318/24, 149
98/190/EC, *Flughafen Frankfurt/Main AG*, OJ 1998 L 72/30, 225
98/251/EC, *Hoffmann-La Roche*, OJ 1998 L 103/28, 396
1999/60/EC, *Pre-Insulated Pipe Cartel*, OJ 1999 L 24/1, 18, 116, 128
1999/133/EC, *CELF*, OJ 1999 L 44/37, 399
1999/230/EC, *F3 –Whitbread*, OJ 1999 L 88/26, 65
1999/242/EC, *TPS*, OJ 1999 L 90/6, 147
1999/267/EC, *EPI*, OJ 1999 L 106/14, 129
1999/421/EC, *P & O Stena Line*, OJ 1999 L 163/61, 140
1999/573/EC, *Cégétel + 4*, OJ 1999 L 218/14, 148
1999/781/EC, *British Interactive Broadcastin/Open*, OJ 1999 L 312/1, 147, 148
2000/74/EC, *Virgin/British Airways*, OJ 2000 L 30/01, 514
2000/182/EC, *GEAE/P & W*, OJ 2000 L 58/16, 149
2001/135/EC, *Nathan-Bricolux*, OJ 2001 L 54/1, 57
2001/354/EC, *Deutsche Post AG*, OJ 2001 L 125/27, 552
2001/546/EC, *European Energy and Transport Forum*, OJ 2001 L 195/58, 471
2001/605/EC, *Aid Scheme*, OJ 2001 L 212/34, 385, 390
2001/696/EC, *Identrus*, OJ 2001 L 249/12, 145
2001/711/EC, *Volkswagen*, OJ 2001 L 262/14, 62, 186
2002/730/EC, *The trans-European high-speed rail system*, OJ 2002 L 245/1, 535
2002/735/EC, *The trans-European high-speed rail system*, OJ 2002 L 245/402, 535
2002/746/EC, *Lufthansa and Austrian Airlines*, OJ 2002 L 242/25, 514
2002/758/EC, *Mercedes-Benz*, OJ 2002 L 257/1, 77
2002/914/EC, *Visa International*, OJ 2002 L 318/17, 117
2003/196/EC, *Stata aid*, OJ 2003 L 77/61, 515
2006/860/EC, *The trans-European high-speed rail system*, OJ 2006 L 342/1, 535
2008/217/EC, *The Alpine biogeographical region*, OJ 2008 L 77/106, 535
2008/231/EC, *The trans-European high-speed rail system*, OJ 2008 L 84/1, 535
2008/284/EC, *The trans-European high-speed rail system*, OJ 2008 L 104/1, 535
2010/137/EC, *Austria Austrian Airlines – Restructuring Plan*, OJ 2010 L 59/1, 516
N 157/06, *UK Broadband*, decision of 22.11.2006, OJ 2007 C 80/01, 371
COMP/37.966, *Distrigaz*, decision of 11.10.2007, OJ 2008 C 9/8, 499
COMP/B-1/38.700, *Greek Lignite*, decision of 4.8.2009, OJ 2009 C 243/5, 484
COMP/39.316, *GDF*, decision of 3.12.2009, OJ 2010 C 57/13, 499
COMP/39.317, *E. ON Gas*, decision of 4.5.2010, OJ 2010 C 278/9, 499
COMP/39.351, *Swedish Interconnectors*, decision of 14.4.2010, OJ 2020 C 142/28, 482
COMP/39.388, *German electricity wholesale market*, decision of 26.11.2008, OJ 2009 C 36/8, 483
COMP/39.389, *German electricity balancing market*, decision of 26.11.2008, OJ 2009 C 36/8, 483
COMP/39.402, *RWE gas foreclosure*, decision of 18.3.2009, OJ 2009, C 133/10, 498

COMP/39.406, *Marine Hoses*, decision of 28.1.2009, OJ 2009 C168/6, 116, 117
COMP/39.579, *Consumer Detergents*, decision of 13.4.2011, OJ 2011 C 193/14, 130
COMP/AT.39727, *CEZ*, decision of 10.4.2013, OJ 2013 C 251/4, 484
SA.33083, *Aid measures in Italy*, decision of 14.8.2015, OJ 2016, L 43/1, 399
SA.33149, *Wirtschaftsbüro Gaarden – Kiel*, decision of 29.4.2015, OJ 2015 C 188/01, 392
SA.33728, *Financing of a new Multiarena in Copenhagen*, decision of 15.5.2013, OJ 2013 L 152/32, 379
SA.35083, *Reduced taxes/contributions in Italy*, decision of 14.8.2015, OJ 2016, L 43/1, 399
SA.35418, *Piraeus Port*, decision of 2.7.2013, OJ 2013 C 256/03, 379
SA.36558, *Øresundsbro Konsortiet*, decision of 15.10.2014, OJ 2014 C 437/01, 379
SA.37432, *Hradec Králové public hospitals*, decision of 29.4.2015, OJ 2015 C 203/01, 392
SA.37904, *Medical centre in Durmersheim*, decision of 29.4.2015, OJ 2015 C 188/01, 392
SA.37963, *Glenmore Lodge*, decision of 29.4.2015, OJ 2015 C 277/01, 392
SA.38035, *Landgrafen-Klinik*, decision of 29.4.2015, OJ 2015 C 188/01, 392
SA.38208, *Member-owned golf clubs*, decision of 29.4.2015, OJ 2015 C 277/01, 392
SA.39078, *Fehmarn Belt*, decision of 23.7.2015, OJ 2015 C 325/01, 379
SA.39403, *Investment aid for Lauwersoog port*, decision of 29.4.2015, OJ 2015 C 259/01, 392
SA.57991, *State Aid – Denmark*, decision of 10.8.2022, OJ 2023 L 2388, 551

Index

A

Abnormally low tenders, 584, 603
Abuse of a dominant position, 1, 55, 82, 159, 165, 197–233, 236, 239, 240, 412, 441, 445–447, 449, 450, 480, 498, 508, 514, 520, 522, 527, 540, 544, 551, 554, 556
Access to infrastructure, 432
Active sales, 82, 99, 100, 187
Actual competitors, 110, 140, 178, 209, 213, 295
Administrative activities, 4
Administrative authority, 2, 404, 411, 441, 448, 456, 567
Affordability, 459
Agency agreements, 74–79
Agreement on Government Procurement (GPA), 567, 606
Agricultural products, 151
Aid, concept of, 359–367
Air transport, 25, 225, 508–524
Allocation of competence, 240–245
Ancillary restraints, 35–38, 69, 73, 74, 81, 146, 148, 259, 320–324, 332, 335
Arbitration clause, 45
Area licences, 438
Article 234 of the EC Treaty, 516
Article 28 of the EC Treaty, 480
Article 86 of the EC Treaty, 456, 556
Article 90 of the EC Treaty, 457

A-services, 589
Association of undertakings, 11, 16, 62, 95, 204, 244, 248, 354
Authorisation Directive (2002/20/EC), 540
Authorisations, 464–466, 484–487, 499–500, 517–518, 528–530, 540–542, 553
Award of the contract, 562, 573, 578, 582–584, 587, 591, 593, 600

B

Barriers to entry, 112, 124, 131, 145, 208, 209, 293, 300, 301, 307
Benchmarking, 453, 545
Bid-rigging, 130
Block exemptions, 43, 51–72, 92–106, 169–180, 191–195
Bodies governed by public law, 567
B-services, 589
Bundling, 177, 178, 230, 231
Burden of proof, 19, 106, 194, 241, 304, 305, 588
By effect restriction, 117
By object restriction, 31–33, 109, 113, 116, 117, 120, 132

C

Cherry-picking, 418
Chicago Convention, 509, 523
Collective dominance, 202–205, 207, 290, 291, 303, 305–310, 326

633

Index

Comfort letters, 39, 238
Comitology procedure, 471
Commercial activity, 2, 4, 21, 77, 136, 262, 448, 456, 601
Commercialisation agreements, 112, 129-130
Commission decisions, 36, 37, 57, 62, 63, 65, 77, 83-87, 90, 99, 125, 128, 136, 145, 146, 170, 237, 244, 318, 420
Common sales company, 116
Communication, postal and tele, 537-557
Competition authorities243-245
Competition network, 241
Competitive dialogue, 574, 576, 577, 581
Concerted practice, 18-20
Concession contracts, 563, 564, 575
Concessions, 53, 403, 405, 406, 409, 561, 563-564, 575
Conditional approval, 314-319
Confidential information, 142, 250, 316, 322, 332, 447, 537
Consumer concerns, 586
Consumers, 11, 31, 39-41, 43, 53, 57, 64, 66, 68, 70, 88, 90, 93-95, 97, 99, 100, 107, 118, 120, 123, 125, 126, 129, 130, 133, 175, 178, 284-288, 293, 294, 304, 305, 308, 311, 415, 458, 495, 505, 507, 511, 586
Contract notice, 562, 568-574, 576, 579, 581, 583, 584, 587, 593, 595-597
Contracting authority, 567-568
Contractual obligation, 104, 192, 587
Control inspections, 242
Control of an undertaking, 263, 442
Control offer, 427
Cooperative company, 13, 150-153
Coordinated effect, 290, 298, 305-310
Corporate groups, 22, 23, 162, 252, 279, 440, 447-449, 580
Corporatisation, 427

Corruption, 580
Covid-19, 8, 396, 397, 577
Cross border connections, 451, 489-490, 538
Cross subsidisation, 371, 413, 440-446, 461, 556
Cross-supplies, 80, 102
Culpability based on intention, 251

D

De minimis, 28, 33-34, 73, 93, 109, 112, 238, 279, 341, 344, 387, 393-394, 398, 420, 487
De minimis notice, 28, 33-34, 93, 109, 112, 279
Deadlines, 86, 253, 314, 316, 328, 335, 346-348, 471, 510, 512, 513, 538, 541, 574, 577, 582
Decisions by associations, 11, 12, 17-18, 85
Defence exception, 588-589
Delays, 131, 210, 350, 474
Delays of flight, 511
Demand doctrine, 411-412
De-monopolising, 427
Deregulation, 427
Design contests, 576, 578
Digital economic, 278
Direct applicability, 6-7, 239, 241
Direct lines, 453, 489, 499, 503-505
Directive 2002/20/EC, 519, 539
Directive 2004/18/EC, 561, 569, 575, 585, 588
Directive 80/723/EEC, 467
Directorate General for Competition, 7, 8
Discount and bonus arrangements, 226-230
Discrimination on the grounds of nationality, 405, 406, 450, 598
Discriminatory pricing, 226
Distortion of competition, 11, 46, 55, 119, 215, 386-390, 441-443, 448, 597, 598, 602

634

Distribution agreements, 54–57, 59, 60, 64, 69, 72, 74, 88, 92, 96, 105–107, 169, 170, 172, 190, 191
Divestiture trustee, 316
Dominance test, 289–293
Dominant position, 197–233, 293–302
Dynamic purchasing systems, 574

E

Economic activity, 4, 17, 20, 21, 200, 260, 282, 377–379, 410, 411, 516, 601
Effect on trade, 27–29, 41, 231–233, 240, 280, 386, 391–393
Effect doctrine, 28, 29
Efficiency gains, 40, 43, 118, 130, 150, 216, 291, 293, 311, 312
Efficient pricing approach, 440
Electricity Directive, 479–480
Electronic auction, 602
Electronic means of communication, 561, 574
Element of solidarity, 410
Enforcement, 235–255, 604–605
Enforcement system, 235–238, 604
Equal treatment, 561, 564, 568, 573, 590–601
Essential facilities, 224–225, 318, 414–415, 431–434, 449, 520, 531–533
Eurocontrol, 25, 410, 519, 522
European Coal and Steel Community, 473
European Community, 1, 5, 160
European Economic Area (EEA), 62, 71, 171, 287, 329, 337, 423
Exchange of information, 15, 38, 96, 118–120, 241, 423
Exclusionary abuse, 216
Exclusive licence, 148, 182–183, 188, 189, 191, 192
Exclusive distribution, 54–56, 60, 64, 72, 88, 92, 95, 100–103, 105

Exercise of public authority, 18, 24–27, 200, 378, 411
Existing aid, 342–343
Export aid, 397–398
Export prohibition, 54, 57, 59, 60, 64, 161, 189

F

Failing firm defence, 313–314
Financial equalisation, 412, 413, 419
Fines, 8, 23, 34, 44, 46–47, 71, 137, 138, 236, 238, 243, 245, 251–253, 315, 330, 333, 336
Flag carrier, 509, 519
Framework agreements, 530, 561, 575–576
FRAND, 124, 125
Fraud, 580
Free rider, 63, 107
Freedom of contract, 166, 168, 223, 224, 414, 415
Freedom of movement, 1–3, 404, 408, 411, 416, 559, 598, 600
Freedom to provide services, 407, 416, 508
Full-function joint ventures, 258, 270–275, 277, 278, 281, 330, 335
Fully distributed cost method (FDC), 444

G

General Agreement on Tariffs and Trade (GATT), 423, 606
General principles, 40, 167, 192, 254, 352, 423, 564, 589, 590–600
Geographic market, 96, 97, 106, 212–213, 283, 284, 286–289, 299, 389, 390, 438
Green Paper–Public Procurement in the European Union, 560
Green Paper on Vertical Restraints in EC Competition Policy, 93
Group of companies, *see* Corporate group

Index

Gun jumping, 330

H

Hardcore restrictions, 34, 61, 68, 82, 91, 97–103, 105, 172, 178, 180–191, 193, 194
Hold-separate trustee, 316
Horizontal agreements, 12, 32, 34, 43, 50, 51, 55, 73, 109–155, 176, 178, 181, 566, 602
Horizontal effect, 6

I

Implementation doctrine, 29
Imports, 28, 53, 56, 58–60, 62, 63, 64, 80, 98, 99, 113, 137, 158, 160–163, 187–189, 212, 233, 287, 289, 404, 406, 423
Incapacity, 597
Income ceiling, 452–453, 493–495
Independent undertaking, 61, 79, 134–136, 139, 172, 173, 257, 262, 274
Individual exemptions, 39–43, 107, 238, 481
Informal procedures, 39, 238
Information, exchange of, 15, 38, 96, 118–120, 241, 423
Infrastructure manager, 446, 455, 470, 526, 530–534
In-house rule, 565
Inquiries into a particular sector of the economy, 246
Intellectual property rights, 95, 98, 122, 157–163, 166, 167, 173, 175, 179, 180, 191–193, 208, 219, 271, 315, 322, 323, 409
Interested parties, 93, 347, 354–358, 573
Invalidity, 44–45, 191, 250, 251

J

Joint bidding, 130, 141

Joint control, 137, 153, 261–270, 274–277, 279, 321, 336
Joint marketing, 129
Joint production, 121–123, 127, 134, 443–446
Joint ventures, 134–150, 270–275, 324–328

K

Killer acquisitions, 198, 278

L

Leasing, 76, 575
Legal monopolies, 403, 405, 407, 416, 426, 498
Legal person, 21, 199, 239, 246, 247, 254, 335, 411, 567, 568
Legitimate expectations, 352–354
Liberalising directives, 436, 458, 538
Licence agreements, 163–169, 172, 173, 175, 177, 178, 181, 188, 191, 192, 194, 322, 323

M

Margin squeeze, 226
Market economy operator principle, 364
Market sharing, 20, 32, 49, 62, 71, 91, 98, 99, 109, 110, 112, 127–130, 183–185, 187, 498, 509, 514
Maximum prices, 61, 115, 181, 186, 375
Merger control, 257–337
Merger control procedure, 324, 328–337
Minimum prices, 16, 26, 61, 63, 114, 181, 186, 375–377, 462
Minority shareholdings, 24, 153–155, 264, 317, 333
Mixed contracts, 572
Money laundering, 580
Monopoly, 441–443
Most economically advantageous bid, 582
Mutual contract, 565

N

National competition authorities, 105, 164, 199, 235, 236, 239, 240, 242, 243-245, 250, 281
National competition law, 239-240, 280
National courts, 356-358
Natural gas, 496-508
Natural Gas Directive, 497-498
Natural monopoly, 414, 433-435
Negative clearance, 482
Negligence, 251, 513
Negotiated procedures, 574, 576, 577, 581
Networks of joint ventures, 145-146
New aid, 343-345
Non-competition clause, 36, 37, 138, 141, 147, 148, 152, 321, 322
Non-coordinated oligopolies, 290-292, 303-305
Non-physical network, 429
Notice on immunity from fines in cartel cases, 252
Notification system, 39, 93, 238, 241, 245
NAAT-rule, 240

O

Objective justification, 216, 222, 224, 225, 415
Objective necessity, 413
Obligation to accept supply, 440
Obligation to connect, 440
Obligation to enter into a contract, 415
Obligation to invite offers, 565-567
Obligation to supply, 151, 152, 223, 458-462, 505, 515-516
Official Journal of the European Union, 258, 468, 502, 547, 571
Open exclusive licence, 188, 189
Open procedure, 574, 576-577, 579, 586, 590
Opening up of markets, 427, 437, 472

Organised crime, 580
Overbooking, 512

P

Parallel conduct, 18, 306
Parallel import, 14, 15, 53, 56, 59, 60, 63, 64, 80, 98, 99, 113, 137, 143, 161, 162, 187-189
Partial implementation (of merger), 333
Passive sales, 57, 58, 76, 99, 100, 103, 183, 184, 186, 187, 190
Patent, 95, 99, 125, 157, 159-164, 167-170, 174, 175, 187, 192, 263, 297, 301
Penalties, 186, 236, 237, 243, 248, 251-253, 336
Per se test, 35, 36, 57, 168
Perfect competition, 30, 435
Periodic penalty payments, 243, 251-253, 336
Postal services, 548-557
Potential competitors, 110-111, 297-301
Powers of investigation, 235, 237, 245-250
Predatory pricing, 116, 220-222, 229, 413, 441, 601
Price cap, 507-508
Price increases, 17, 18, 114-115, 128, 284
Price reduction, 220, 221, 226
Pricing agreements, 181, 307, 509, 555
Principle of equivalence, 71, 254
Principle of mutual recognition, 600
Prior information notice, 571
Private bodies, 2, 4, 369-370,
Privatisation, 426, 427
Privileged customer, 430
Privileged undertakings, 403, 405, 408, 411-415, 418, 419, 438-440
Procurement directives, 563-564
Production joint venture, 134, 149
Prohibition on discrimination on grounds of nationality, 405

Index

Proportionality principle, 84, 87-88, 321, 352, 580, 600
Public authority, 24-27, 368-369, 469-471, 491-493, 506-507, 524, 536-537, 547-548, 557
Public company, 417
Public contracts, 525, 559, 561, 562, 571, 582, 588
Public interest, 25, 243, 459, 566
Public procurement, 559-606
Public service obligations, 366-367, 419, 456-460, 490, 504-505, 521, 526, 534, 541, 545-546, 554-557
Prosumers, 473, 495
Public undertakings, 24-27, 403-423
Purchase and supply obligation, 148
Purchase and/or exclusive supply obligation, 122
Purchasing cooperation, 144, 150, 151
Purchasing joint venture, 150

Q

Quantitative restrictions, 87, 88-91, 98, 101, 107, 158, 187, 324, 483

R

Railways, 524-537
Reciprocity, 472, 590
Recommended prices, 61, 114, 181, 185, 186
Reference product, 569, 570
Refusal to supply, 14, 15, 222-224
Regard for the environment, 586
Regulation 1/2003, 106, 235-255
Regulation 17/62, 36, 43, 54, 71, 92, 236-238, 244
Regulator of electricity, 491
Regulatory activity, 2, 560
Relevant market, 176-178, 209-213, 283-289
Restricted procedures, 574, 576, 577, 581, 590, 591

Restriction on production, 120
Restructuring of a trade sector, 123-124
Revenue-producing monopoly, 404
Rule of reason, 35-36, 57, 66, 67, 74

S

Sales company, 116, 129
Sales contracts, 575
Sales joint venture, 150
Selection, 578-587
Selection criteria, 83, 579, 581, 583-585, 587
Selective distribution, 82-91, 101-102
Selective prices, 99-100, 221
Selectivity, 377-386
Services of general economic interest, 366-367, 404, 407, 412, 416-419, 431-434, 456-458
Single and continuous infringement, 20
Single economic entity, 22-24
Single European Act, 427, 560
Skimming, 461
Social concerns, 586
Soft law, 7, 34
Sole control, 260-267, 270, 275-277
Special or exclusive rights, 1, 366, 403, 404, 407-409, 418, 420, 423, 438-440, 461, 563
Special services, 412
Specialisation agreements, 111, 113, 121-123, 149
Spill-over effects, 135, 140, 141-143, 151
Standard conditions, 117-118
Standards, 124-126, 521, 522
Standstill obligation, 330-334, 341, 343, 346, 357, 389
State aid, 339-400
State control, 25, 369-371
State controlled undertaking, 263, 371
State monopolies, 288, 404, 406
State resources, 368-377
State-action doctrine, 5
Stranded costs, 429-430
Structural abuse, 216, 217

Structure of the Treaty, 2–5
Subsidies, 319, 390, 419
Suit for annulment, 422
Sunk costs, 63, 77, 208, 210, 300, 307, 429
Supplementary information, 573, 581
Supplier, 24, 34, 58, 60, 61, 69, 72, 78, 79, 80, 82, 94-98, 100–107, 113, 116, 120, 121, 132, 136, 144, 178, 209, 210, 217, 223, 228, 230, 231, 266, 273, 284, 286, 287, 293, 302, 303, 306-308, 318, 323, 388, 409, 415, 430, 431, 433, 448, 450, 460, 461, 468, 479, 483, 488, 489, 493, 497, 505, 508, 559, 575, 576, 582, 585, 599, 600
Sustainability agreements, 42, 112, 132–133
Sustainability objectives, 42, 43, 132, 312
Sustainability standardisation agreement, 132–133
Sustainable development, 1, 42

T

Taxes, 278, 360, 373–374, 580
Technical harmonisation, 124, 288, 468, 305, 534–535, 546–547
Technical specifications, 569, 570, 577, 597, 606
Technology transfer agreements, 12, 43, 96, 157–195
Telecommunications, 537–548
Tendering, 562, 584, 595–596
Tendering procedure, 562, 574, 577, 580, 581, 591, 597, 603
Tenders Electronic Daily (TED), 571
The Access Directive, 539

Third countries, 28, 29, 59–61, 71, 88, 98, 171, 238, 282, 374, 390–392, 605
Third party access, 449–453, 488–489, 500, 502–503, 530–533, 543–545
Threshold values, 34, 258, 275, 276, 566–567, 571, 572, 599
Trade between the Member States, 1, 55, 163, 231–233, 391–393, 397
Trade in goods, 27
Trading conditions, 61, 109, 113–118, 181, 219–220
Transit, 453–454, 504, 533
Transparency, 422, 466–468, 490–491, 506, 524, 536, 599
Transport, 508–537

U

Unbundling, 446–449, 455, 500, 529, 542
Unfair trading conditions, 219–220
Unreasonably high selling prices, 217–219
Up-front-buyer, 316

V

Variant offers, 595–596
Vertical agreements, 12, 32, 34, 42, 43, 49–107, 171, 175, 176, 178
Viking Cable case, 451

W

White Paper on the Internal Market, 560
Workable competition, 30–31, 172
World Trade Organisation (WTO), 423, 539, 550, 567, 606